D0164240

Century 21

# SOUTH-WESTERN
# Accounting 8E

**CLAUDIA BIENIAS GILBERTSON, CPA**
Teaching Professor
North Hennepin Community College
Brooklyn Park, Minnesota

**MARK W. LEHMAN, CPA**
Associate Professor
School of Accountancy
Mississippi State University
Starkville, Mississippi

**DAN PASSALACQUA, MA**
Oak Grove High School
San Jose, California

**KENTON E. ROSS, CPA**
Professor Emeritus of Accounting
Texas A&M University—Commerce
Commerce, Texas

SOUTH-WESTERN
CENGAGE Learning

Australia • Brazil • Japan • Korea • Mexico • Singapore • Spain • United Kingdom • United States

SOUTH-WESTERN
CENGAGE Learning

Advanced, Century 21 Accounting 8E
Claudia Bienias Gilbertson, CPA; Mark W. Lehman, CPA; Dan Passalacqua, MA; Kenton E. Ross, CPA

**VP/Editorial Director:**
Jack W. Calhoun

**VP/Editor-in-Chief:**
Karen Schmohe

**Acquisitions Editor:**
Marilyn Hornsby

**Project Manager:**
Carol Sturzenberger

**Consulting Editor:**
Bill Lee

**Verification Editors:**
Howard Rankin; Sara Wilson

**VP/Director of Marketing:**
Carol Volz

**Marketing Manager:**
Courtney Schulz

**Marketing Coordinator:**
Angela Russo

**Senior Promotions Manager:**
Terron Sanders

**Production Editor:**
Kim Kusnerak

**Production Manager:**
Patricia Matthews Boies

**Manufacturing Buyer:**
Kevin Kluck

**Manager of Technology-Editorial:**
Liz Prigge

**Senior Technology Project Editor:**
Mike Jackson

**Web Coordinator:**
Ed Stubenrauch

**Art Director:**
Tippy McIntosh

**Photography/Permissions Editor:**
Darren Wright

**Production House:**
Lachina Publishing Services

**Cover/Internal Design:**
Ann Small, a small design studio

**Cover Illustration:**
Philip Brooker

**Internal Illustration:**
Mark Shaver, The Wiley Group

**Printer:**
Quebecor World
Dubuque, IA

COPYRIGHT © 2006
by South-Western, a part of
Cengage Learning.

Printed in the United States
of America
1 2 3 4 5 6 7 8 9 10
09 08 07 06 05

Text
ISBN-13: 978-0-538-97420-2
ISBN-10: 0-538-97420-6
Data CD
ISBN-13: 978-0-538-97416-5
ISBN-10: 0-538-97416-8
Package
ISBN-13: 978-0-538-97229-1
ISBN-10: 0-538-97229-7

ALL RIGHTS RESERVED.

No part of this work covered by the
copyright hereon may be reproduced or used in any form or by
any means—graphic, electronic,
or mechanical, including photo-
copying, recording, taping, Web
distribution or information storage
and retrieval systems, or in any
other manner—without the written
permission of the publisher.

For permission to use material
from this text or product,
submit a request online at
www.cengage.com/permissions.
Any additional questions about
permissions can be submitted
by email to
permissionrequest@cengage.com.

For more information
contact South-Western Cengage
Learning
5191 Natorp Boulevard
Mason, Ohio 45040
USA
Or you can visit our Internet site
at: academic.cengage.com

Microsoft is a registered trademark of Microsoft Corporation in the U.S. and/or other countries.

The names of all products mentioned herein are used for identification purposes only and may be trademarks or
registered trademarks of their respective owners. South-Western Cengage Learning disclaims any affiliation,
association, connection with, sponsorship, or endorsement by such owners.

# Century 21 SOUTH-WESTERN Accounting 8E

## The Choice for Real-World Technology!

### Integrate technology into your advanced accounting course with solutions only available from South-Western Cengage Learning!

➡ **Automated Accounting**

The functionality of commercial software incorporated with educational features makes teaching and learning computerized accounting easy. *Automated Accounting 8.0* is fully integrated into every chapter of *Century 21 Accounting*.

| | |
|---|---|
| **Automated Accounting 8.0 Individual User CD (Windows)** | 0-538-97294-7 |
| **Automated Accounting 8.0 Site License (Windows)** | 0-538-44228-X |

➡ **Creating the Band**

An accounting simulation for Peachtree, QuickBooks, and Microsoft Excel. This text is designed to give realistic experience in keeping accounting records for a small business. Students will work as an accountant for CTB, which is a band whose members have formed a business partnership.

| | |
|---|---|
| **Student Text and Data CD** | 0-538-44150-X |

➡ **South-Western Accounting with Peachtree Complete 2005**

South-Western *Accounting with Peachtree Complete* is the ideal supplement for teachers who want to introduce Peachtree software. The text teaches students to work step-by-step through Century 21 problems using Peachtree. Interactive tutorials are also included on South-Western's Peachtree individual user disk and the site license.

| | |
|---|---|
| **Text/CD Package (softcover, 118 pages)** | 0-538-44209-3 |

➡ **South-Western Accounting for QuickBooks Pro**

This supplement is perfect for incorporating QuickBooks software into your *Century 21 Accounting* class. The text with data CD teaches students to journalize accounting transactions, post to ledger accounts, and prepare financial statements using QuickBooks Pro software.

| | |
|---|---|
| **Text Data/CD package (softcover, 272 pages)** | 0-538-44205-0 |

# How to Use This Book

**PART OPENERS** focus on a particular business that you'll learn about:

- **A listing of the chapters** covered in each Part helps you focus on what you'll be learning.

- The **Chart of Accounts** used in the entire Part is provided for easy reference as you work through the chapters.

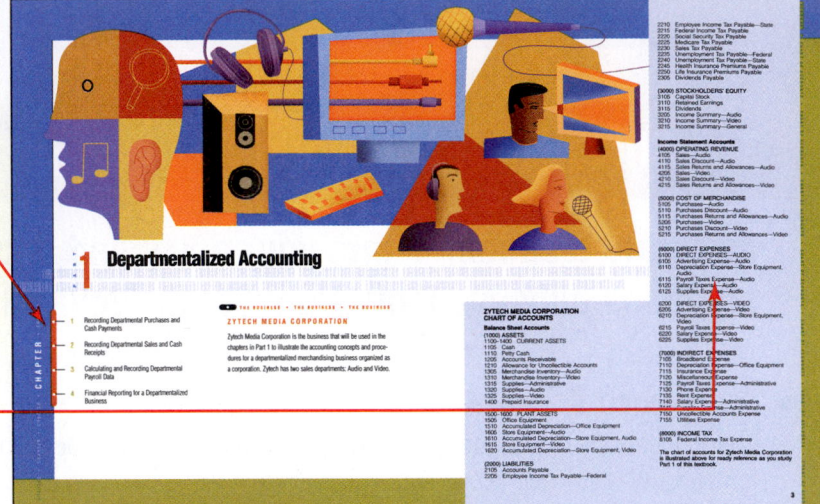

**CHAPTER OPENERS** introduce the subject matter you'll investigate:

- **Objectives** listed at the beginning of each chapter highlight lesson concepts and preview what you will learn.

- The **Terms Preview** displays all the key words introduced in the chapter. You can also find these terms and their definitions in the Glossary at the back of the text.

- **Accounting in the Real World** features a photo and description of a real company with questions linked to the chapter's content.

- **Internet Research Activity** sends you to the Internet to locate information to answer questions related to the chapter's subject matter.

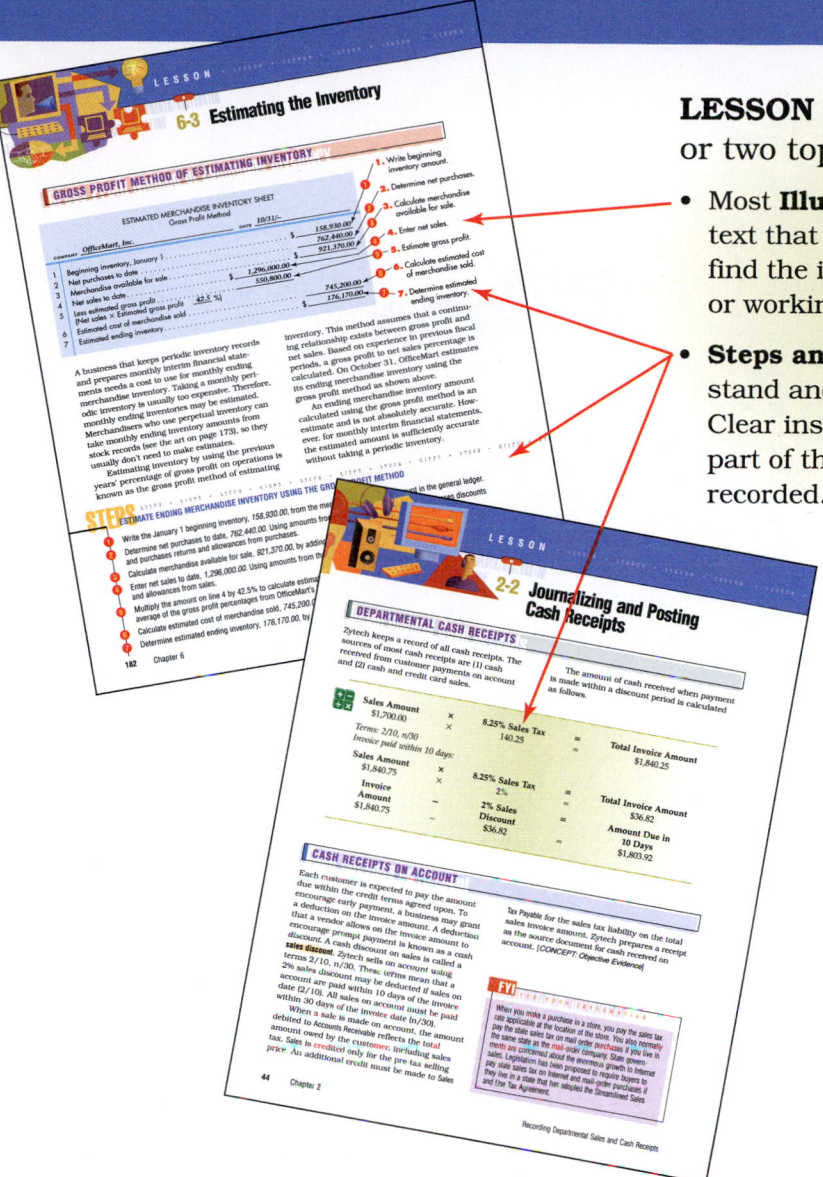

**LESSON OPENERS** focus on one or two topics:

- Most **Illustrations** are placed above the text that discusses them. You can quickly find the illustrations when you're reviewing or working problems.

- **Steps and callouts** make it easy to understand and apply the procedures you learn. Clear instructions are directly linked to the part of the illustration where the work is recorded.

**END-OF-LESSON PAGES** help you fully understand all concepts and procedures before moving on to the next lesson:

- **Terms Review** lists all the new words learned in the lesson.

- **Audit Your Understanding** asks two or more questions about the lesson material. You can check your answers in the Appendix.

- **Work Together** gives you guided practice through hands-on application of the lesson's procedures and concepts.

- **On Your Own** challenges you to complete problems by yourself.

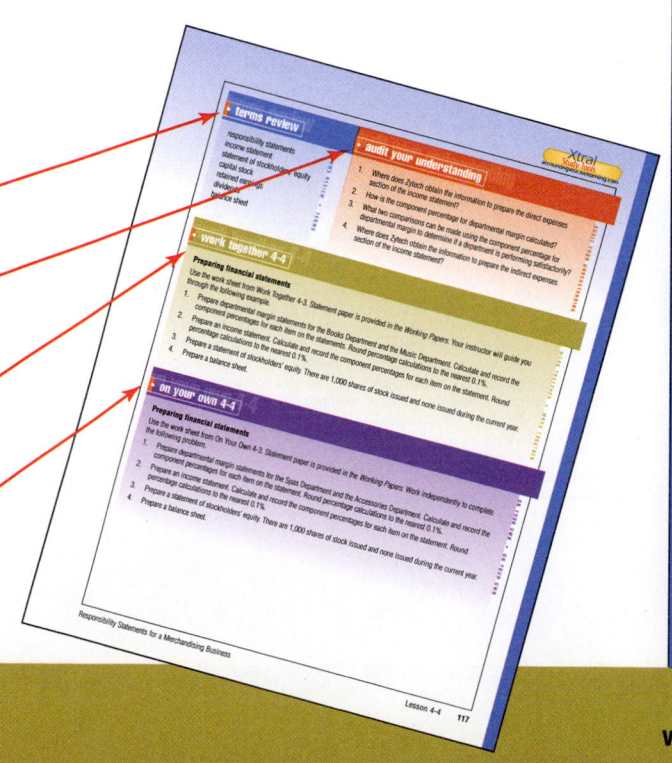

## careers in accounting

### Dianne Villanueva Conry, Part-Time Senior Accountant and Accounting Instructor

Employment in the accounting profession is sometimes associated with working long, intense hours. In many instances, this association may be true but certainly not in all. For Dianne Villanueva Conry, a career in accounting has allowed her to keep her primary focus on her family. Presently, Dianne works as a part-time senior accountant at Clinimetrics Research Associates, Inc., and teaches an evening accounting class at the University of California Santa Cruz Extension Program in Cupertino, California.

To reach her current positions, Dianne earned a Bachelor of Science degree in Business Administration with the Accountancy Option from California State University, Fresno. Following graduation, she remained at CSUF for another year and earned a Master of Science degree in Financial Accounting. Because of her strong academic background and part-time work experience with a local CPA, she was hired by PriceWaterhouseCoopers, one of the four largest accounting firms in the world. During her tenure at PWC, she acquired public accounting auditing experience and passed the certified public accountancy exam for the state of California. After three years of employment as a public accountant, she accepted a job offer from Sony Electronics. Dianne's new position helped satisfy her expanding interest in corporate accounting and allowed her to gain a more complete understanding of private industry practices.

After starting her family, Dianne had an opportunity to work part-time for Horn Murdock Cole. Working as the internal controller, start-up services instructor, and information technology troubleshooter, Dianne gained invaluable experience regarding all levels of consulting.

Presently, Dianne teaches an evening accounting class and works 24 to 28 hours per week at Clinimetrics Research Associates, Inc., a privately held firm that performs clinical research and drug trials related to the pharmaceutical, biotechnology, and medical device industries. At Clinimetrics, she handles accounting and payroll responsibilities, she finds special projects to be Although Dianne has recurring accounting and payroll responsibilities, she finds special projects to be the most rewarding.

**Salary Range:** A senior accountant could expect to earn $70,000–$150,000, depending on the industry, company, part of the country, and level of experience.

**Qualifications:** To qualify for entry-level employment in the accounting industry, Dianne recommends that students develop the ability to multi-task, acquire strong written and oral communication skills, build a solid knowledge of accounting basics, and obtain proficient spreadsheet and word processing skills. Dianne also encourages students to view accounting as a flexible profession that offers individuals a variety of career options and alternatives that can assist them with the attainment of personal goals.

**Occupational Outlook:** For the future, Dianne envisions more analyses of variances and expenses activities. Accountants will be needed to assist managers in determining why revenues and expenses are fluctuating from original budget projections. This critical information will be used by managers to make sound financial decisions.

## making ethical decisions

### Sharing Your Knowledge

John Oglesby is a certified public accountant who works as a computer consultant. He has just completed helping a local movie theater install a new ticketing system that tracks when and how often individuals come to the theater. The system will enable the theater to analyze its customers and select movies that target customers having specific movie preferences.

John has just received a phone call from another theater in the same city. The theater owner asks John to evaluate its existing computer systems and suggest any recommendations. After allowing the theater owner to present his request, John politely declines to accept the engagement.

**Instructions**

Use the AICPA *Code of Professional Conduct* to determine if John's actions violate the confidentiality rule. When researching the AICPA *Code of Professional Conduct*, begin by selecting the section title that most closely relates to the issue. Read the Rule and any related Interpretations. Then scan the titles of the Ethics Rulings for any case that may be similar to the issue.

**SPECIAL FEATURES** provide information about real-life issues:

- **Careers in Accounting** introduces you to actual people working in accounting or in positions where accounting knowledge is useful. This feature includes entry-level job requirements, career tracks, and projected trends for the future.

- **Making Ethical Decisions** helps you understand complicated issues in the business world, such as confidentiality and integrity.

- **Business Structures** provides information on characteristics of proprietorships, corporations, and partnerships.

## business structures

### Differentiating Between Personal and Business Taxes

When running a business, owners must differentiate between the *personal taxes* collected from employees and customers and the *business taxes* incurred by a company as a consequence of daily operations. Each category is handled differently. For example, businesses similar to Zytech are required to withhold payroll taxes from their employees, such as federal income tax and Medicare tax, and forward the tax amounts to the appropriate government agency. Consequently, these personal payroll taxes represent a liability for Zytech until they are paid.

The sales tax collected on the sale of merchandise or services is also classified as a personal tax. Like personal payroll taxes, it is paid by individuals, collected by businesses, and later remitted to the required government agency. Until the sales tax is paid, it too represents a liability.

Like individuals, businesses also pay taxes. For example, successful businesses like Zytech must pay income tax on business profits. Zytech is also required by law to pay taxes on the earnings of its employees. Based on its payroll, Zytech must pay social security tax, Medicare tax, and unemployment taxes. Companies classify the taxes paid by a business as expenses, although they are temporarily recorded in liability accounts until they are paid.

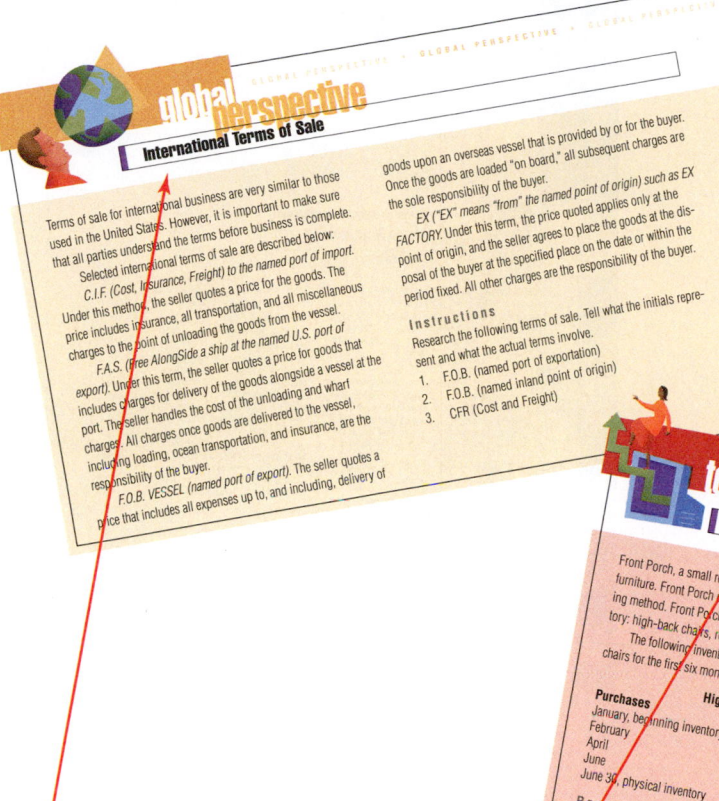

## global perspective
### International Terms of Sale

GLOBAL PERSPECTIVE • GLOBAL PERSPECTIVE • GLOBAL PERSPECTIVE

Terms of sale for international business are very similar to those used in the United States. However, it is important to make sure that all parties understand the terms before business is complete.

Selected international terms of sale are described below:

C.I.F. (Cost, Insurance, Freight) to the named port of import. Under this method, the seller quotes a price for the goods. The price includes insurance, all transportation, and all miscellaneous charges to the point of unloading the goods from the vessel.

F.A.S. (Free AlongSide a ship at the named U.S. port of export). Under this term, the seller quotes a price for goods that includes charges for delivery of the goods alongside a vessel at the port. The seller handles the cost of the unloading and wharf charges. All charges once goods are delivered to the vessel, including loading, ocean transportation, and insurance, are the responsibility of the buyer.

F.O.B. VESSEL (named port of export). The seller quotes a price that includes all expenses up to, and including, delivery of goods upon an overseas vessel that is provided by or for the buyer. Once the goods are loaded "on board," all subsequent charges are the sole responsibility of the buyer.

EX ("EX" means "from" the named point of origin) such as EX FACTORY. Under this term, the price quoted applies only at the point of origin, and the seller agrees to place the goods at the disposal of the buyer at the specified place on the date or within the period fixed. All other charges are the responsibility of the buyer.

**Instructions**

Research the following terms of sale. Tell what the initials represent and what the actual terms involve.
1. F.O.B. (named port of exportation)
2. F.O.B. (named inland point of origin)
3. CFR (Cost and Freight)

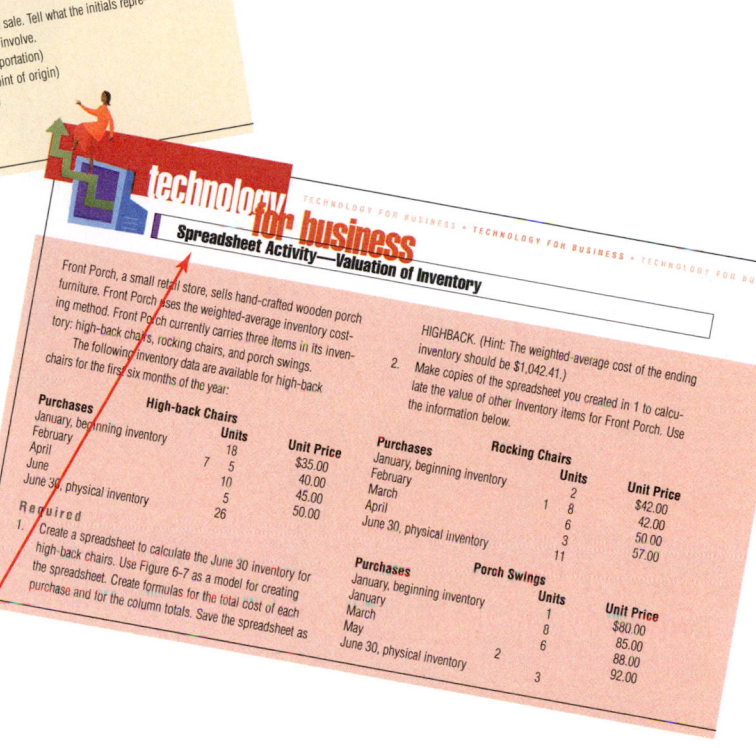

## technology for business
### Spreadsheet Activity—Valuation of Inventory

TECHNOLOGY FOR BUSINESS • TECHNOLOGY FOR BUSINESS • TECHNOLOGY FOR BUSINESS

Front Porch, a small retail store, sells hand-crafted wooden porch furniture. Front Porch uses the weighted-average inventory costing method. Front Porch currently carries three items in its inventory: high-back chairs, rocking chairs, and porch swings.

The following inventory data are available for high-back chairs for the first six months of the year:

**High-back Chairs**

| Purchases | Units | Unit Price |
|---|---|---|
| January, beginning inventory | 18 | $35.00 |
| February | | |
| April | 7 5 | 40.00 |
| June | 10 | 45.00 |
| June 30, physical inventory | 5 | 50.00 |
| | 26 | |

**Required**
1. Create a spreadsheet to calculate the June 30 inventory for high-back chairs. Use Figure 6-7 as a model for creating the spreadsheet. Create formulas for the total cost of each purchase and for the column totals. Save the spreadsheet as

HIGHBACK. (Hint: The weighted-average cost of the ending inventory should be $1,042.41.)
2. Make copies of the spreadsheet you created in 1 to calculate the value of other inventory items for Front Porch. Use the information below.

**Rocking Chairs**

| Purchases | Units | Unit Price |
|---|---|---|
| January, beginning inventory | 2 | $42.00 |
| February | | |
| March | 1 8 | 42.00 |
| April | 6 | 50.00 |
| June 30, physical inventory | 3 | 57.00 |
| | 11 | |

**Porch Swings**

| Purchases | Units | Unit Price |
|---|---|---|
| January, beginning inventory | 1 | $80.00 |
| January | 8 | 85.00 |
| March | 6 | 88.00 |
| May | 2 | 92.00 |
| June 30, physical inventory | 3 | |

* **Global Perspective** will expose you to some of the ways in which accounting and business differ in other countries.

* **Technology for Business** focuses on common business applications of technology.

* **Cultural Diversity** explains how different cultures have contributed to the field of accounting.

## cultural diversity
### African American Businesses

CULTURAL DIVERSITY • CULTURAL DIVERSITY • CULTURAL DIVERSITY

The Census Bureau's Survey of Minority-Owned Business Enterprises indicates that minority-owned enterprises are increasing in number and size. Firms owned by African Americans increased from 620,912 in 1992 to 823,000 in 1997. This represents a 32.5% increase. In 1997, these firms employed 718,300 people and generated $71.2 billion in revenue.

Six states—New York, California, Texas, Florida, Georgia, and Maryland—accounted for 47% of the nation's African American-owned businesses. The metropolitan areas of New York City, Washington, D.C., Los Angeles-Long Branch, Chicago, and Atlanta accounted for 28% of African American-owned firms.

Slightly more than half of businesses owned by African Americans operate in the service industries, such as health services, business services, and personal services. The retail trade accounted for the next largest concentration of African American-owned firms.

*Black Enterprise* magazine lists the nation's 100 largest black businesses in its "B.E. 100." The list is comprised of industrial and service businesses that are at least 51% African American-owned. It maintains separate listings for the "Auto Dealer 100," which lists the largest auto dealerships that are at least 51% African American-owned. It also has lists for companies such as advertising agencies, banks, and insurance companies. From the 2004 "B.E. 100," World Wide Technology, Inc., of Maryland Heights, Missouri, was ranked in first place.

Source: U.S. Census and "Black Enterprise 100."

**END-OF-CHAPTER PAGES** give you opportunities to check your knowledge of the chapter content:

- **Chapter Summary** restates the chapter objectives for your reference.

- **Explore Accounting** includes opportunities for higher-level learning.

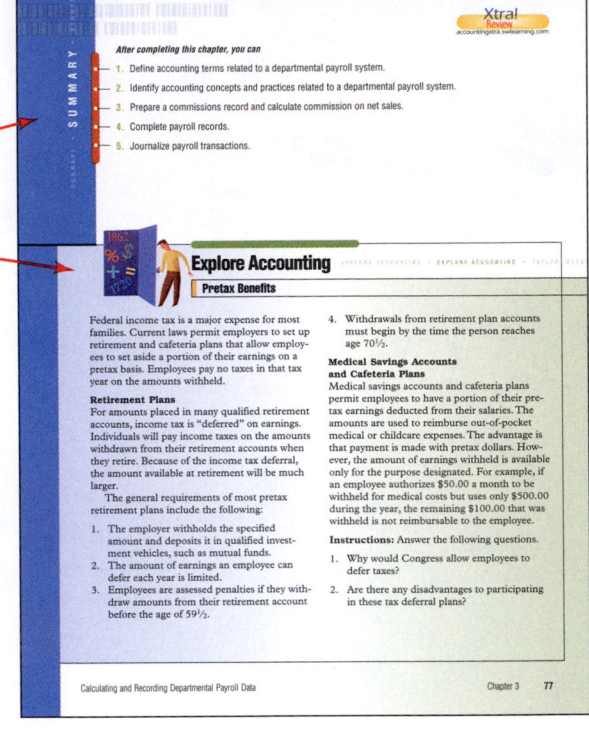

- Exercises contain at least one **Application Problem** for each lesson, plus one **Mastery Problem** and one **Challenge Problem** to test your understanding of the entire chapter. Many of these problems can also be worked using accounting software: **Automated Accounting, Peachtree®, and QuickBooks®!**

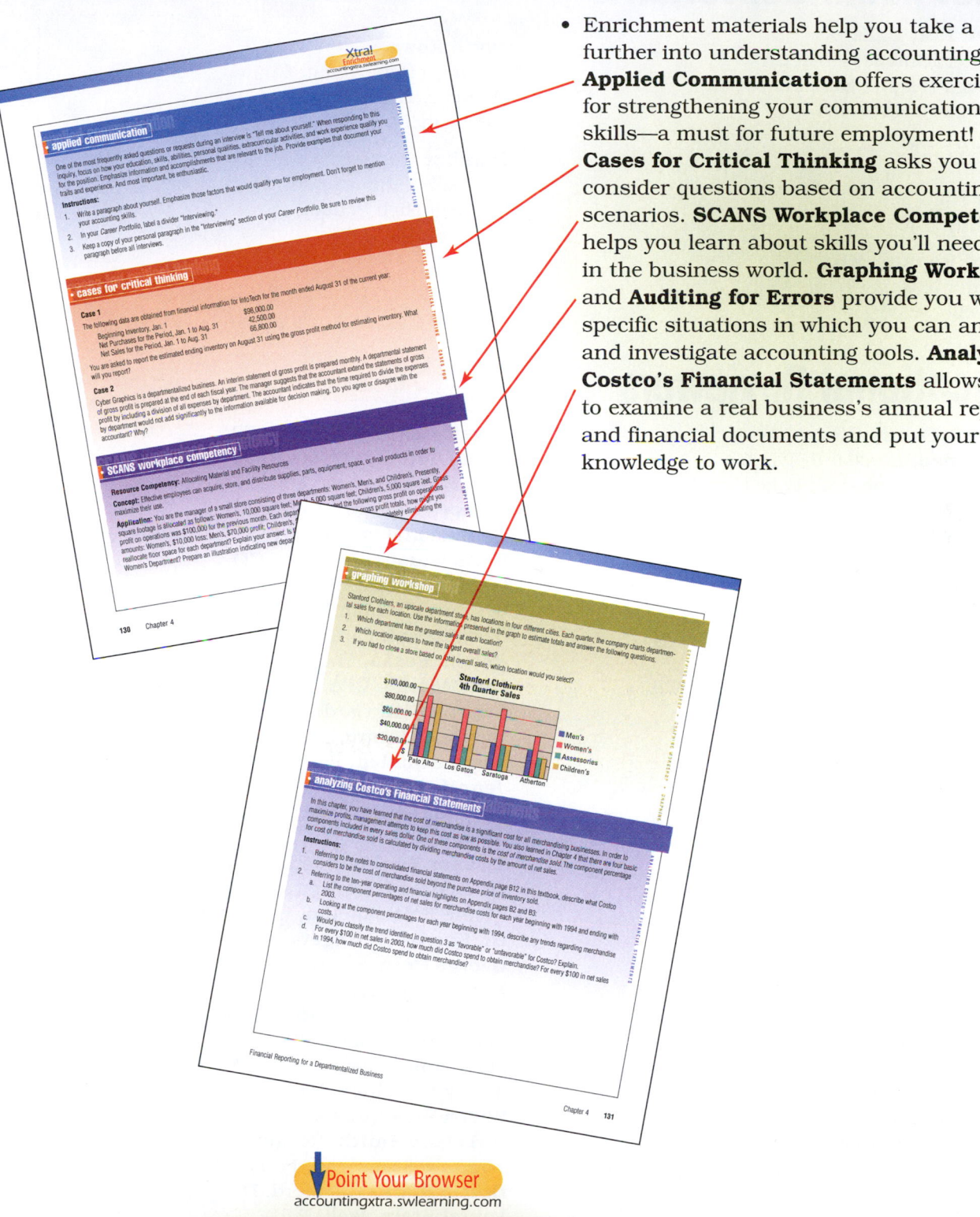

- Enrichment materials help you take a step further into understanding accounting. **Applied Communication** offers exercises for strengthening your communication skills—a must for future employment! **Cases for Critical Thinking** asks you to consider questions based on accounting scenarios. **SCANS Workplace Competency** helps you learn about skills you'll need in the business world. **Graphing Workshop** and **Auditing for Errors** provide you with specific situations in which you can analyze and investigate accounting tools. **Analyzing Costco's Financial Statements** allows you to examine a real business's annual report and financial documents and put your knowledge to work.

**Point Your Browser**
accountingxtra.swlearning.com

**THE ACCOUNTING XTRA! WEB SITE offers a variety of resources and activities for you to explore. As you use this textbook, watch for the Xtra! Web Site icons that will lead you to your online accounting connection!**

# Educational Consultants

**Carolyn Holt Balis**
Computer/Business Teacher
Cuyahoga Heights High School
Cuyahoga Heights, OH

**Madge Gregg**
Accounting Teacher
Hoover High School
Hoover, AL

**Howard Rankin, MBA**
Educational Consultant
Monticello, KY

**Joyce Rowe**
Business Department Chair
Monterey High School
Lubbock, TX

**Jennifer Wegner**
Business & Information Technology
Mishicot High School
Mishicot, WI

# Educational Reviewers

**Jon Abel,** Salem, OR
**Abe Aleman,** Levelland, TX
**Kathy Andreason,** Salt Lake City, UT
**Cynthia S. Aycock,** Eagle Lake, FL
**Carolyn Holt Balis,** Cuyahoga Heights, OH
**Anne Berten,** Portland, OR
**Chad E. Bobb,** Indianapolis, IN
**Ellen Clizbe,** Moreno Valley, CA
**Tony Composto,** Brooklyn, NY
**Becky Cornacchia,** Naples, FL
**Alicia E. Censi Corso,** Los Angeles, CA
**Donna Davis,** Charlotte, NC
**Paula Davis,** Atlanta, GA
**Sylvia Davis,** Lakewood, CA
**Dana Dingell,** Vienna, VA
**Kathy Dixon,** Richmond, VA
**Keith Downs,** Dallastown, PA
**Dr. Judith A. Drager-McCoy,** Lititz, PA
**Ann Droptini,** Gladewater, TX
**Jean Eckert,** Wexford, PA
**Julie Eckhart,** Salem, WI
**Carrie English,** Woodbridge, VA
**Barbara Erwin,** Orlando, FL
**K. Skip Fabritius,** Olympia, WA
**Debbie Fischer,** St. Petersburg, FL
**Kathleen Ford,** Rochester, MI
**Lance B. Garvin,** Indianapolis, IN
**Debbie Gentene,** Mason, OH
**Wendy Gentry,** Garden Grove, CA
**Andy Gilley,** Hendersonville, TN
**Kathy Goos,** Moreno Valley, CA
**Madge Gregg,** Hoover, AL
**Tracy Gutierrez,** Garden Grove, CA
**Craig Halberstadt,** Racine, WI
**Jean Harms,** Port Orange, FL
**Cindy Hiester,** Astoria, OR
**Beth Hubbard,** Virginia Beach, VA
**Lisa Huddlestun,** Kansas, IL
**Steve Ingmire,** Indianapolis, IN
**Gladys Jackson,** Woodbridge, NJ

**Beverly Kaesar,** Neenah, WI
**Fran Loos,** Salt Lake City, UT
**Ann M. Ludlow,** St. Louis, MO
**Frances Mallard,** Brentwood, TN
**H. Jean Malonson,** Hayward, CA
**Chris Marshall,** Denver, CO
**Libby Martin,** Chattanooga, TN
**Sally M. Graham Martin,** Nokesville, VA
**Barb Mason,** Paris, MO
**Kelvin Meeks,** Memphis, TN
**Lori Meseke, CPA,** Vandalia, IL
**Sonia Miller,** Garden Grove, CA
**Heather Moraru,** Suwanee, GA
**Joanne Mullen,** Pontiac, IL
**Jennifer Mundy,** O'Fallon, IL
**Barb Nichols,** Evansville, IN
**Katherine Prange,** Breese, IL
**Eleanor Rankin,** Rio Rico, AZ
**Dr. Andrea B. Reiter,** Dingman's Falls, PA
**Nicole Reitz-Larson,** Salt Lake City, UT
**Dr. Harriet D. Rogers,** Whitewater, WI
**George Roth,** Prairie du Sac, WI
**Peggy J. Scott,** Chesapeke, VA
**Christopher G. Shaffer,** Cincinnati, OH
**Janet Shaw,** Bailey, NC
**Mary Ann Shea,** Amherst, MA
**Jenny V. Shippy,** Naples, FL
**Sherri Small,** Las Vegas, NV
**H. Leland Smith,** Racine, WI
**Tommie Stanaland,** Perry, FL
**Dottie Starkey,** Milford, DE
**Laurel Stein,** Wall, NJ
**Claire Thoke,** Glendale, CA
**Donnie Thompson,** Pittsburgh, PA
**John Tingley,** Bradley, IL
**Linda Underwood,** Gilcrest, CO
**Jennifer Wegner,** Mishicot, WI
**Linda White,** Fayetteville, PA
**Parnell Wiggins,** Memphis, TN
**Lonnie Wilson,** Evansville, IN

# CONTENTS

CONTENTS • CONTENTS • CONTENTS • CONTENTS • CONTENTS • CONTENTS • CONTENTS • CONTENTS • CON

## PART 1
### Departmentalized Accounting

©GETTY IMAGES/PHOTODISC

©GETTY IMAGES/PHOTODISC

©GETTY IMAGES/PHOTODISC

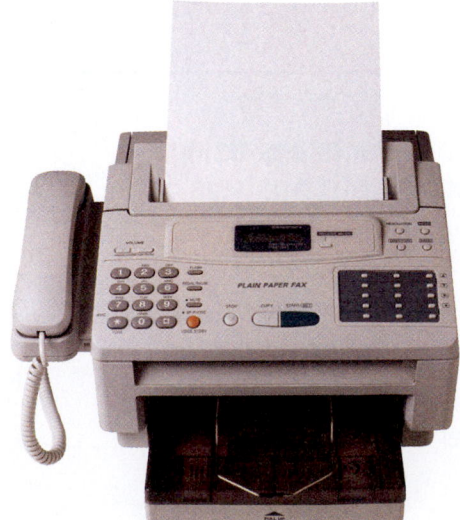

©GETTY IMAGES/PHOTODISC

# PART 7
## Other Accounting Systems ......................... 618

©GETTY IMAGES/PHOTODISC

## Additional Features in This Book

Additional Features in This Book

Contents

## Chapter Review and Practice

### Chapter Summary

### Application Problems

### Mastery Problems

### Challenge Problems

### Applied Communication

### Cases for Critical Thinking

### SCANS Workplace Competency

### Graphing Workshop

### Auditing for Errors

### Analyzing Costco's Financial Statements

# 1

# Departmentalized Accounting

THE BUSINESS • THE BUSINESS • THE BUSINESS

## ZYTECH MEDIA CORPORATION

Zytech Media Corporation is the business that will be used in the chapters in Part 1 to illustrate the accounting concepts and procedures for a departmentalized merchandising business organized as a corporation. Zytech has two sales departments: Audio and Video.

2210 Employee Income Tax Payable—State
2215 Federal Income Tax Payable
2220 Social Security Tax Payable
2225 Medicare Tax Payable
2230 Sales Tax Payable
2235 Unemployment Tax Payable—Federal
2240 Unemployment Tax Payable—State
2245 Health Insurance Premiums Payable
2250 Life Insurance Premiums Payable
2305 Dividends Payable

**(3000) STOCKHOLDERS' EQUITY**
3105 Capital Stock
3110 Retained Earnings
3115 Dividends
3205 Income Summary—Audio
3210 Income Summary—Video
3215 Income Summary—General

**Income Statement Accounts**
**(4000) OPERATING REVENUE**
4105 Sales—Audio
4110 Sales Discount—Audio
4115 Sales Returns and Allowances—Audio
4205 Sales—Video
4210 Sales Discount—Video
4215 Sales Returns and Allowances—Video

**(5000) COST OF MERCHANDISE**
5105 Purchases—Audio
5110 Purchases Discount—Audio
5115 Purchases Returns and Allowances—Audio
5205 Purchases—Video
5210 Purchases Discount—Video
5215 Purchases Returns and Allowances—Video

**(6000) DIRECT EXPENSES**
6100 DIRECT EXPENSES—AUDIO
6105 Advertising Expense—Audio
6110 Depreciation Expense—Store Equipment, Audio
6115 Payroll Taxes Expense—Audio
6120 Salary Expense—Audio
6125 Supplies Expense—Audio

6200 DIRECT EXPENSES—VIDEO
6205 Advertising Expense—Video
6210 Depreciation Expense—Store Equipment, Video
6215 Payroll Taxes Expense—Video
6220 Salary Expense—Video
6225 Supplies Expense—Video

**(7000) INDIRECT EXPENSES**
7105 Broadband Expense
7110 Depreciation Expense—Office Equipment
7115 Insurance Expense
7120 Miscellaneous Expense
7125 Payroll Taxes Expense—Administrative
7130 Phone Expense
7135 Rent Expense
7140 Salary Expense—Administrative
7145 Supplies Expense—Administrative
7150 Uncollectible Accounts Expense
7155 Utilities Expense

**(8000) INCOME TAX**
8105 Federal Income Tax Expense

The chart of accounts for Zytech Media Corporation is illustrated above for ready reference as you study Part 1 of this textbook.

**ZYTECH MEDIA CORPORATION**
**CHART OF ACCOUNTS**
**Balance Sheet Accounts**
**(1000) ASSETS**
1100–1400   CURRENT ASSETS
1105 Cash
1110 Petty Cash
1205 Accounts Receivable
1210 Allowance for Uncollectible Accounts
1305 Merchandise Inventory—Audio
1310 Merchandise Inventory—Video
1315 Supplies—Administrative
1320 Supplies—Audio
1325 Supplies—Video
1400 Prepaid Insurance

1500–1600   PLANT ASSETS
1505 Office Equipment
1510 Accumulated Depreciation—Office Equipment
1605 Store Equipment—Audio
1610 Accumulated Depreciation—Store Equipment, Audio
1615 Store Equipment—Video
1620 Accumulated Depreciation—Store Equipment, Video

**(2000) LIABILITIES**
2105 Accounts Payable
2205 Employee Income Tax Payable—Federal

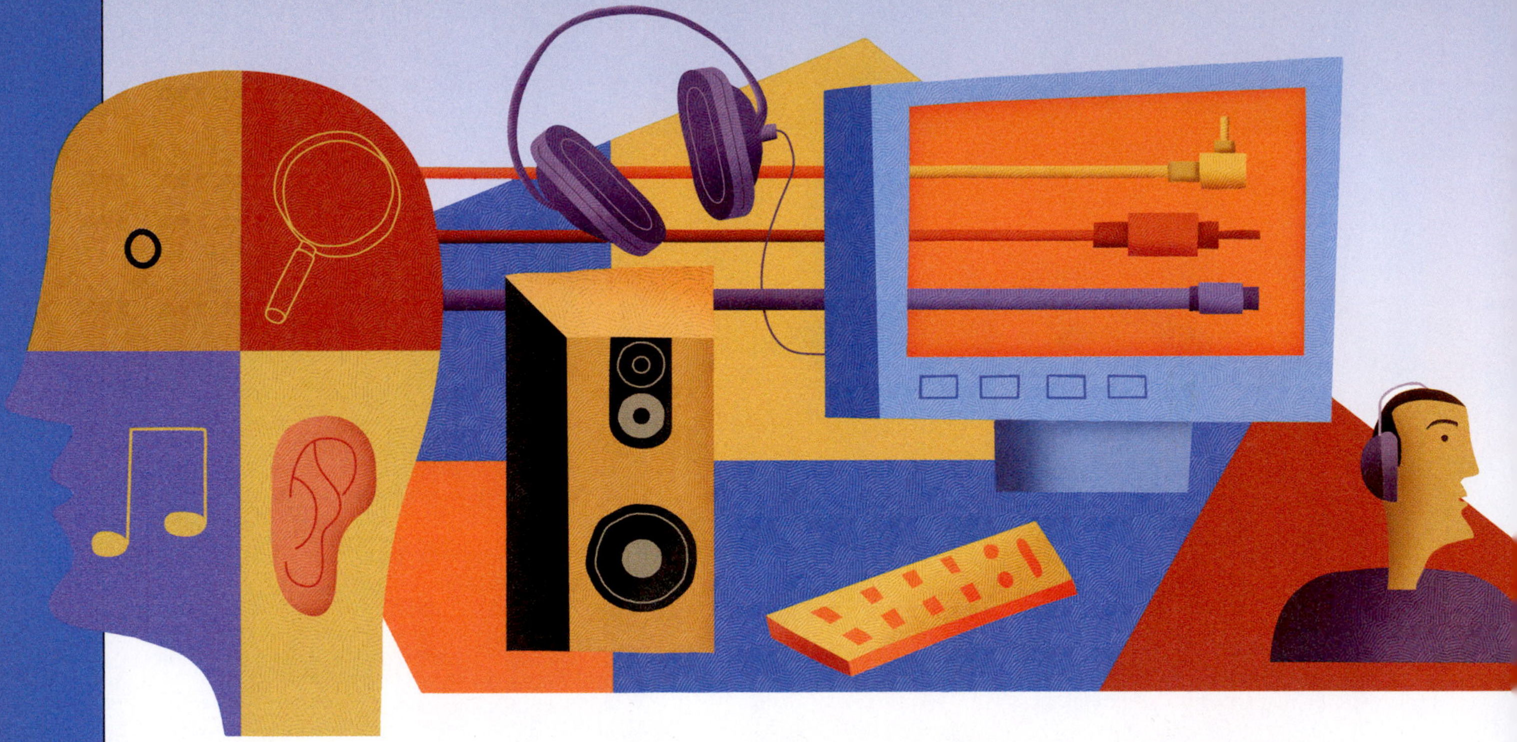

CHAPTER 1

# Recording Departmental Purchases and Cash Payments

OBJECTIVES & TERMS

***After studying Chapter 1, you will be able to:***

1. Define accounting terms related to departmental purchases and cash payments.
2. Identify accounting concepts and practices related to departmental purchases and cash payments.
3. Journalize and post departmental purchases and purchases returns.
4. Journalize and post departmental cash payments.

- asset
- liability
- equities
- owners' equity
- stockholders' equity
- accounting equation
- source documents
- double-entry accounting
- journal
- special journal
- account
- ledger
- general ledger
- subsidiary ledger
- controlling account
- file maintenance
- departmental accounting system
- merchandising business
- posting
- debit memorandum
- contra account
- cash discount
- purchases discount
- petty cash

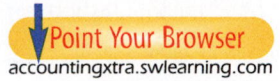

Point Your Browser
accountingxtra.swlearning.com

# • New Balance

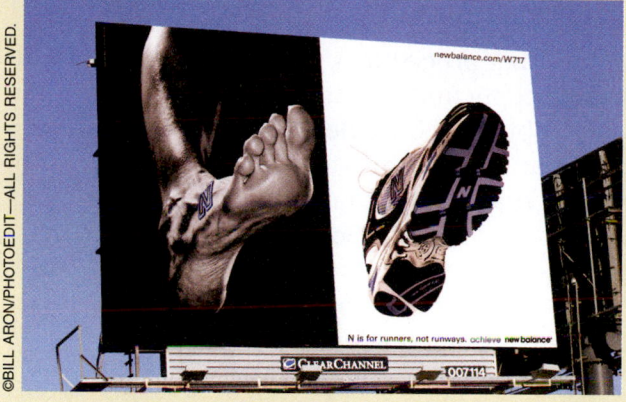

©BILL ARON/PHOTOEDIT—ALL RIGHTS RESERVED.

## FUNCTION OVER FASHION

Since its inception in 1906, New Balance has focused on producing quality footwear to ensure proper fit and performance. The company believes that no two athletes are alike and that each foot is structurally unique. Consequently, New Balance manufactures a wide variety of running and sport shoes in assorted lengths, widths, and materials to meet individual requirements for shock absorption, arch, motion control, cushioning, and function. Throughout its existence, New Balance has always adhered to the philosophy "better fit and technology mean better performance."

In recent years, New Balance has expanded into athletic apparel using innovative fabrics and features. Each product is engineered for fit, durability, moisture management, and water resistance in order to ensure maximum performance and comfort.

Over the past decade, sales have increased substantially, from $221 million in 1992 to $1.1 billion in 2000. The company also refrains from paying famous athletes to endorse its products. New Balance strongly believes that product quality and performance speak for themselves. Rather than allocate large sums of money for endorsements, New Balance prefers to invest those same dollars in research, design, and manufacturing techniques.

### Critical Thinking

1.  What are some of the possible reasons for New Balance's success during the last decade?
2.  Would you recommend that New Balance record apparel sales and expenses separately from shoe sales and expenses? Explain.

Source: www.newbalance.com

Xtra!
Today
accountingxtra.swlearning.com

## STUDENT CREDIT CARDS

Search the Internet for companies that offer a student credit card. Go to at least two different sites that offer such a card.

### Instructions

1.  Make a chart comparing the two companies' student credit cards, using the following criteria:
    a.  Introductory interest rate (if any)
    b.  Interest rate after the introductory period
    c.  Annual fee
    d.  Minimum finance charge (if any)
2.  Comment on which card offers the better terms.

# 1-1 Using Accounting Principles and Records

Financial information for a business can be recorded, summarized, and reported in a variety of ways. Accountants design accounting systems to meet the specific needs of the business. The way in which information is kept and reported in the accounting system is determined by the size, type, and complexity of the business. When designing financial records, the business should also consider the types of decisions that will be made, based on the financial statements.

If managers of individual departments want to use financial statements to assist in making decisions, information for each department must be recorded separately. The types of information

to be gathered by department include purchases, sales, and expenses. Payroll data may also be identified by department. Gathering information by department requires a somewhat different set of accounting procedures. Regardless of the accounting procedures used, the same accounting concepts and practices are followed.

If a business decides to record information by department, it must establish procedures to ensure that transactions are assigned to the correct department. Some businesses employ an accounting clerk for each department. The clerk's primary responsibility is to record day-to-day transactions for the department.

## making ethical decisions

### Researching Codes of Conduct

The Sarbanes-Oxley Act of 2002 requires publicly traded companies to have a code of conduct. Most companies make their codes available on the Internet. However, companies title and link their codes differently. Thus, accessing these codes on the Internet requires knowledge of common search terms and methods.

Begin your search by visually scanning the available links on the company's home page. "Code of Conduct," "Code of Ethics," and "Corporate Governance" are common links. A company whose web site is designed primarily to sell its product is unlikely to have an ethics-related link on its home page. In this case, look at the top or bottom of the web page and find a link such as "Investor Relations."

Most companies provide a search tool. Use the search tool to search for any of these terms: "ethics," "code of conduct," "code of ethics," and "corporate governance."

#### Instructions
Access the code of conduct for three publicly traded companies. Prepare a summary of the links and searches you used to access the code for each company.

---

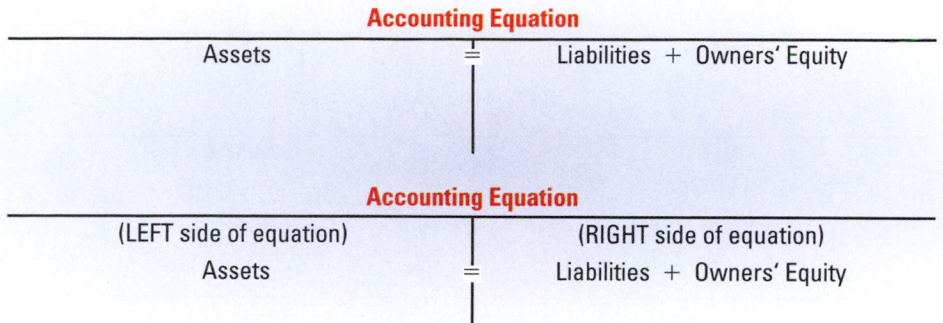

Anything of value that is owned is called an **asset**. An amount owed by a business is called a **liability**. Financial rights to the assets of a business are called **equities**. The amount remaining after the value of all liabilities is subtracted from the value of all assets is called **owners' equity**. The owners' equity in a corporation is called **stockholders' equity**.

An equation showing the relationship among assets, liabilities, and owners' equity is called the **accounting equation**. The accounting equation may be stated as assets = equities. More commonly, the equation is stated as assets = liabilities + owners' equity.

The equation is often viewed as forming a "T." In the figure above, assets are listed on the left side of the T account and equities (liabilities and owners' equity) on the right side of the T account. Total assets must always equal total liabilities plus owners' equity.

### Accounting Records

Accounting records show changes and the current account balance of each asset, liability, and owners' equity (or stockholders' equity) account. In the United States, the amounts are stated in dollars and cents. [CONCEPT: Unit of Measurement]

The unit of measurement concept states that business transactions are reported in numbers that have common values—that is, using a common unit of measurement. If part of the information in the accounting records is financial and part is nonfinancial, the financial statements will not be clear. For example, if Zytech Media Corporation states its sales in number of units sold (nonfinancial) and its expenses in dollars (financial), net profit cannot be calculated.

The preceding concept reference indicates the application of a specific accounting concept. For a complete statement and explanation of the concepts, refer to Appendix A in this text.

Information about business transactions is obtained from original business papers called **source documents**. Each journal entry must be supported by a source document proving that a transaction occurred. [CONCEPT: Objective Evidence]

The source document is the original business paper indicating that the transaction did occur and that the amounts recorded in the accounting records are accurate and true. When accounting information reported on the financial statements needs to be verified, an accountant will first check the accounting record. If the details of an entry need further checking, an accountant will then check the source documents as objective evidence that the transaction did occur.

**FYI** FOR YOUR INFORMATION

The government's first regulation of accounting information occurred in 1917 with the Federal Reserve Board's publication of "Uniform Accounts."

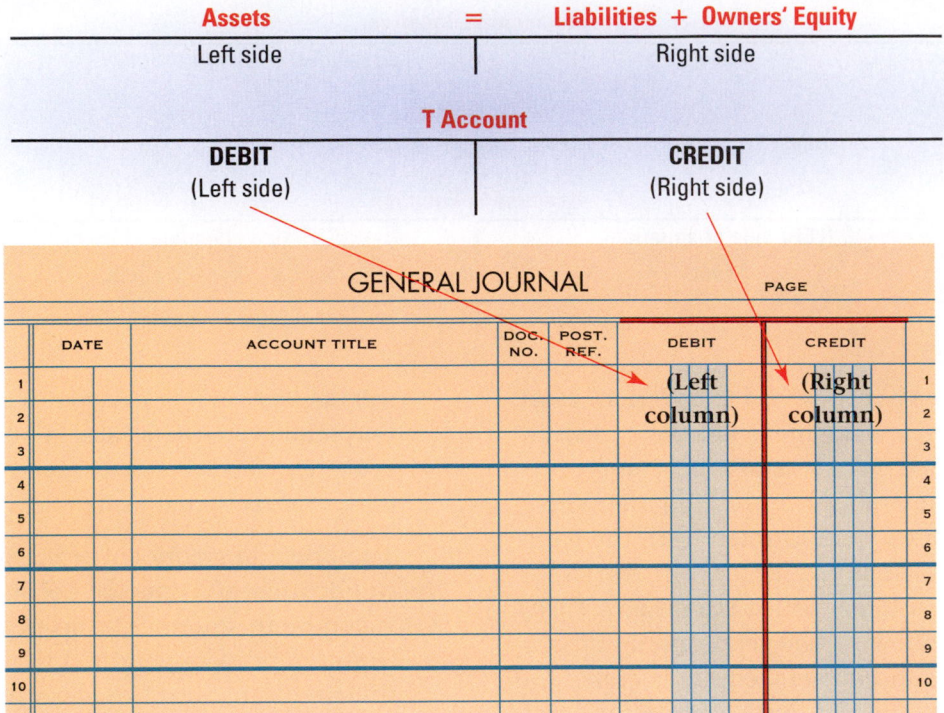

| | Assets | | = | Liabilities + Owners' Equity | |
|---|---|---|---|---|---|
| | Left side | | | Right side | |

**T Account**

| DEBIT (Left side) | CREDIT (Right side) |
|---|---|

**GENERAL JOURNAL**   PAGE

| | DATE | ACCOUNT TITLE | DOC. NO. | POST. REF. | DEBIT | CREDIT | |
|---|---|---|---|---|---|---|---|
| 1 | | | | | (Left column) | (Right column) | 1 |
| 2 | | | | | | | 2 |
| 3 | | | | | | | 3 |
| 4 | | | | | | | 4 |
| 5 | | | | | | | 5 |
| 6 | | | | | | | 6 |
| 7 | | | | | | | 7 |
| 8 | | | | | | | 8 |
| 9 | | | | | | | 9 |
| 10 | | | | | | | 10 |

The recording of debit and credit parts of a transaction is called **double-entry accounting**. With every transaction, at least two accounts will change. Two accounting principles are common to double-entry accounting: (1) The total value of things owned by a business (assets) equals the total value of claims of outsiders (liabilities) and claims of owners (owners' equity). (2) Debits equal credits for each business transaction recorded.

A form for recording transactions in chronological order is called a **journal**. A general journal may be used to record all business transactions. A general journal includes amount columns for recording the dollars and cents of a transaction. [*CONCEPT: Unit of Measurement*] The general journal has two amount columns. The left amount column is labeled *Debit*. The right amount column is labeled *Credit*. An entry recorded in the debit column is known as a *debit*. Likewise, an entry recorded in the credit column is known as a *credit*.

The "T" previously described in the accounting equation is also present in a general journal's debit and credit amount columns.

A journal used to record only one kind of transaction is called a **special journal**. A business with many daily transactions may use special journals. Special journals include amount columns used to record debits or credits to specific accounts. For example, a cash payments journal includes a Cash Credit amount column. Zytech uses four special journals along with a general journal to record its transactions:

1. Purchases journal—for all purchases of merchandise on account
2. Cash payments journal—for all cash payments
3. Sales journal—for all sales of merchandise on account
4. Cash receipts journal—for all cash receipts

Zytech uses a general journal to record all other transactions.

**REMEMBER**   Total assets must always equal total liabilities plus total owners' equity.

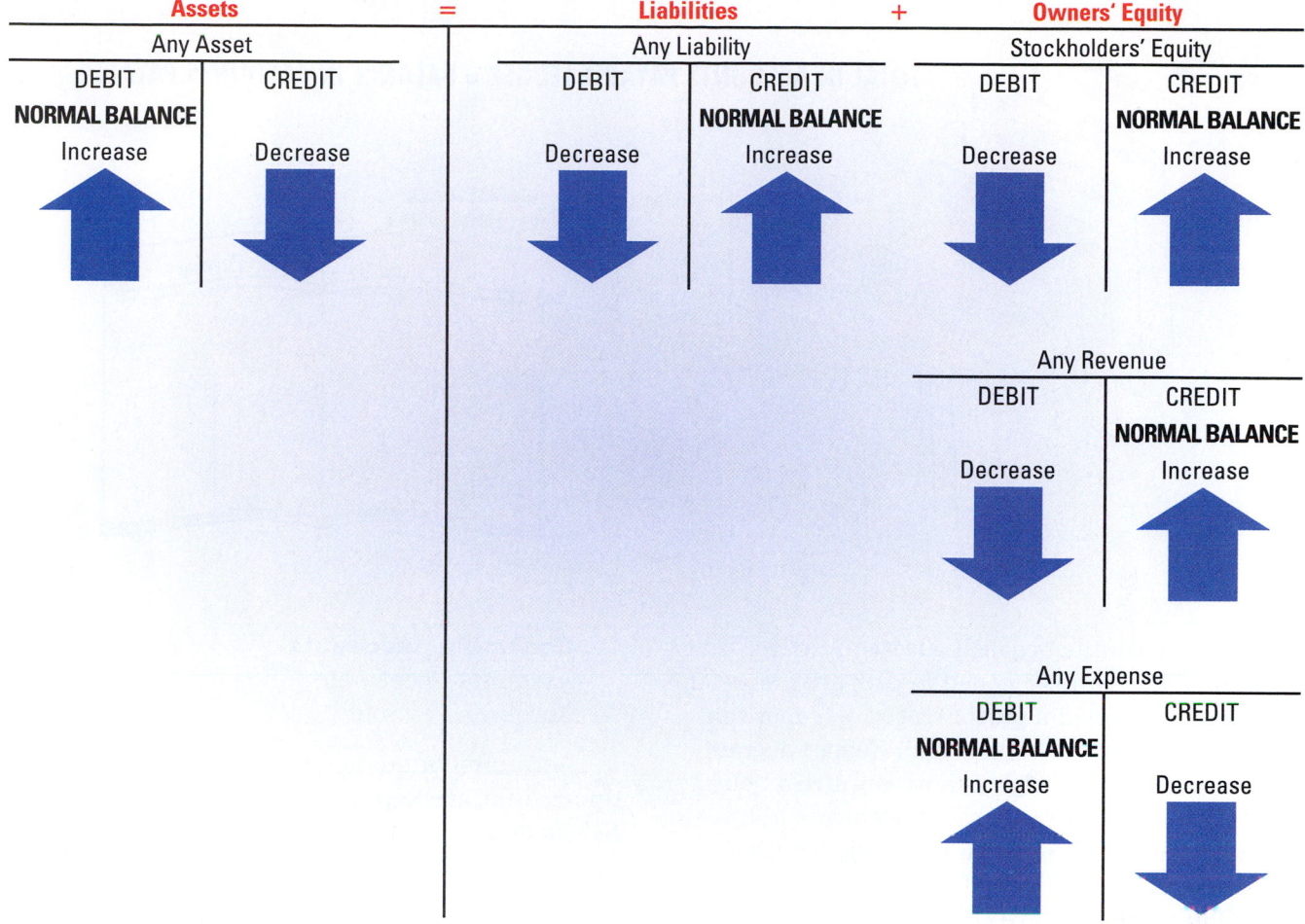

Transactions are journalized in chronological order. Periodically, information is sorted to summarize like kinds of information. A record summarizing all the information pertaining to a single item in the accounting equation is called an **account**.

The amount in an account is known as an *account balance.* Each business transaction causes a change in two or more account balances. Increases in an account balance are recorded in the same column as its normal balance. Decreases in an account balance are recorded in the column opposite its normal balance. The normal balances of different classifications of accounts are shown in the figure above.

Asset account balances are increased by debits and decreased by credits. Liability and owners' equity account balances as well as revenue account balances are increased by credits and decreased by debits. Expense account balances are increased by debits and decreased by credits.

{ **REMEMBER** Increases in revenue accounts increase owners' equity. Therefore, the normal credit balance of revenue accounts is the same as the normal balance of owners' equity. Increases in expense accounts decrease owners' equity. Therefore the normal debit balance of expense accounts is opposite the normal balance of owners' equity. }

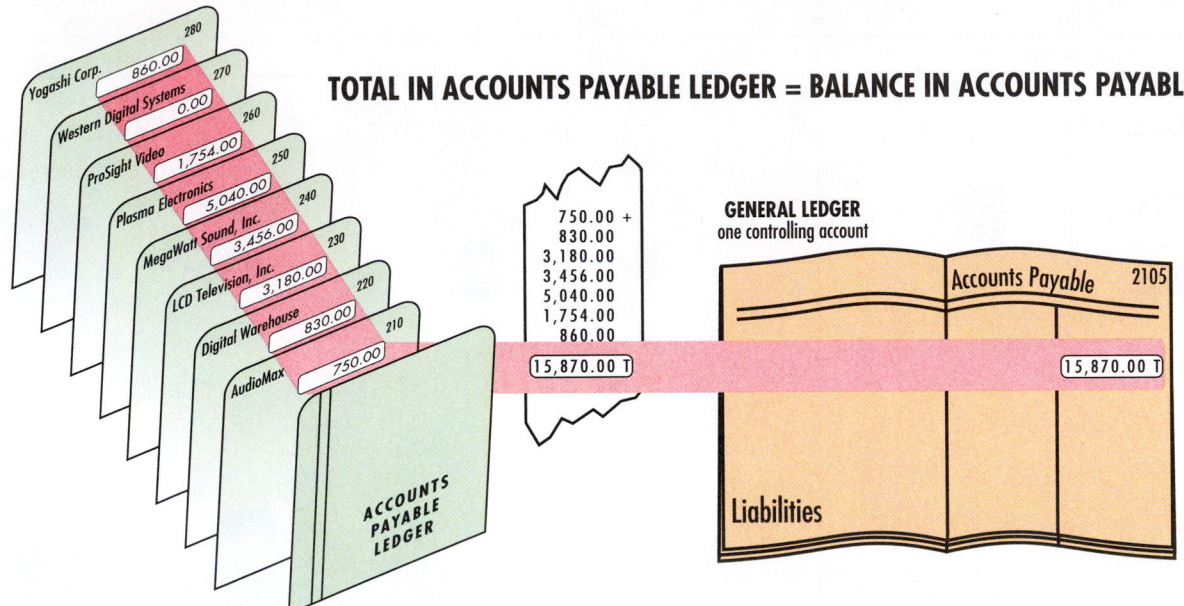

**TOTAL IN ACCOUNTS PAYABLE LEDGER = BALANCE IN ACCOUNTS PAYABLE**

A group of accounts is called a **ledger**. A ledger that contains all accounts needed to prepare financial statements is called a **general ledger**. A ledger that is summarized in a single general ledger account is called a **subsidiary ledger**. An account in a general ledger that summarizes all accounts in a subsidiary ledger is called a **controlling account**. Two subsidiary ledgers and two general ledger controlling accounts are commonly used:

### Subsidiary Ledgers
Accounts Receivable Ledger
Accounts Payable Ledger

### Controlling Accounts
Accounts Receivable
Accounts Payable

Accounts for customers who buy merchandise on account are kept in an accounts receivable ledger. The corresponding controlling account is Accounts Receivable. Separate accounts are kept in an accounts payable ledger for vendors to whom money is owed. The corresponding controlling account is Accounts Payable. The total of the subsidiary ledger account balances should equal the balance of the controlling account.

## GENERAL AND SUBSIDIARY LEDGER FILE MAINTENANCE

Zytech uses a general ledger account numbering system that meets three needs: (1) A separate numeric listing is provided for each ledger division. (2) A predesigned arrangement of numbers is provided within each ledger division. (3) Account number digits are spaced to allow the addition of new accounts. The procedure for arranging accounts in a general ledger, assigning account numbers, and keeping records current is called **file maintenance**.

Zytech's general ledger chart of accounts has eight divisions. The first digit of each four-digit account number shows the general ledger division in which the account is located. The accounts in some divisions, such as Assets, are divided into categories. The second digit of the account number shows the category in which the account is located. The last two digits show the location of a specific account with respect to other accounts in that division and category.

## terms review

asset
liability
equities
owners' equity
stockholders' equity
accounting equation
source documents
double-entry accounting
journal
special journal
account
ledger
general ledger
subsidiary ledger
controlling account
file maintenance

TERMS REVIEW • TERMS REVIEW • TERMS REVIEW • TERMS

## audit your understanding

1. How is the accounting equation most commonly stated?
2. What is the normal balance of an asset account? A revenue account?
3. What are the three needs met by Zytech's account numbering system?

## work together 1-1

WORK TOGETHER • WORK TOGETHER • WORK TOGETHER •

**Determining the normal balance, increase, and decrease sides for accounts**

Write the answers to the following problems in the *Working Papers.* Your instructor will guide you through the following examples.

Prepaid Insurance
Advertising Expense
Lee Enterprises (an account payable)
Capital Stock

Merchandise Inventory
Nguyen Entertainment (an account receivable)
Sales
Cash

For each of the accounts above, complete the following.
1. Prepare a T account for each account. Enter the title of the account.
2. In parentheses to the right of the account title, identify the account as asset, liability, owners' equity, revenue, or expense.
3. Label the *debit* and *credit* sides.
4. Label each side of the T account using the labels *Normal Balance, Increase Side,* or *Decrease Side.*

## on your own 1-1

ON YOUR OWN • ON YOUR OWN • ON

**Determining the normal balance, increase, and decrease sides for accounts**

Write the answers to the following problems in the *Working Papers.* Work this problem independently.

Rent Expense
Sales
Pacifico Studio (an account receivable)
Supplies

Gardena A/V Supply (an account payable)
Capital Stock
Petty Cash
Prepaid Insurance

For each of the accounts above, complete the following.
1. Prepare a T account for each account. Enter the title of the account.
2. In parentheses to the right of the account title, identify the account as asset, liability, owners' equity, revenue, or expense.
3. Label the *debit* and *credit* sides.
4. Label each side of the T account using the labels *Normal Balance, Increase Side,* or *Decrease Side.*

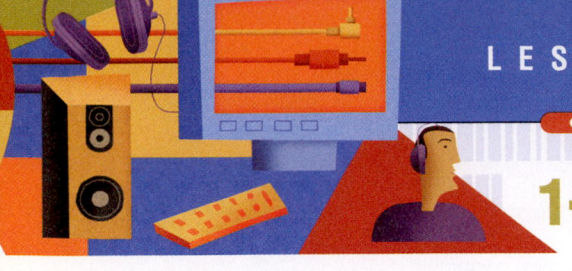

# 1-2 Journalizing and Posting Purchases and Purchases Returns

## DEPARTMENTAL ACCOUNTING SYSTEM

Management decisions depend on accounting information about each phase of a business. When a business has two or more departments, accounting information can help management decide whether a department's performance is acceptable or unacceptable. Accounting information can also determine the kinds of merchandise that produce the greatest or the least profit.

An accounting system showing accounting information for two or more departments is called a **departmental accounting system**. In a departmental accounting system, gross profit is calculated for each department. The general ledger, therefore, must include a number of separate departmental accounts. Shoe stores, furniture stores, computer stores, department stores, and sporting goods stores are examples of firms that commonly organize on a departmental basis.

A business that purchases and sells goods is called a **merchandising business**. Zytech Media Corporation sells audio equipment and video equipment. The business is a corporation organized on a departmental basis.

Merchandising businesses may have two types of equipment: (1) equipment purchased for sale to customers and (2) equipment used in the operation of the business. Zytech purchases and sells audio and video equipment. Zytech uses office equipment and store equipment to operate the business.

Zytech uses a departmental accounting system. Accounting information is recorded and reported for two departments: (1) Audio and (2) Video. The separate departmental accounts for Zytech are in the chart of accounts at the beginning of Part 1. All accounts for the audio department include "audio" in the account title. All accounts for the video department include "video" in the account title. For example, the audio department's inventory account is titled

Merchandise Inventory—Audio and is assigned number 1305. The first digit, *1*, indicates that the account is an asset. The second digit, *3*, shows the account is in the third category (inventory accounts) of the asset division. The last two digits, *05*, show the location of the account with respect to the other accounts in the inventory account category.

Purchase invoices are used as the source documents for all purchases on account. [*CONCEPT: Objective Evidence*]

All departmental purchases of merchandise on account are recorded in a purchases journal. A business with more than one department records a purchase on account in the same way as a business with a single department, except for two differences: (1) Each purchase invoice has a notation placed on it showing to which department the purchase applies. (2) Each department has a separate Purchases Debit column in the purchases journal. Zytech's purchases journal, shown on the next page, has special Purchases Debit columns for each department—Audio and Video.

©GETTY IMAGES/PHOTODISC

*Recording Departmental Purchases and Cash Payments*

## JOURNALIZING PURCHASES ON ACCOUNT

**WESTERN DIGITAL SYSTEMS**
976 CENTURY BLVD.
DUBLIN, CA 94565-1101

SOLD TO Zytech Media Corporation
4750 Appian Way
San Jose, CA 95125-0210

DATE May 29, 20--
OUR ORDER NO. 98-117
CUSTOMER'S ORDER NO. 336
SHIP VIA TRUCK

TERMS 2/10, n/30

| QUANTITY | STOCK NO. | DESCRIPTION | UNIT PRICE | TOTAL AMOUNT |
|---|---|---|---|---|
| 2 ea. | 36HDFSM | 36″ HD Flat Screen Monitor | 375.00 | 750.00 |
| 2 ea. | 36WMU | 36″ Wall Mount Unit | 47.50 | 95.00 |
| | Approved D.P. 6/1/20- | Total Invoice Video DEPT. | | 845.00 |

1. Write approval date.
2. Write vendor name.
3. Record invoice number.
4. Write invoice amount.
5. Write invoice amount.

PURCHASES JOURNAL PAGE 6

| | DATE | | ACCOUNT CREDITED | PURCH. NO. | POST. REF. | 1 ACCOUNTS PAYABLE CREDIT | 2 PURCHASES DEBIT AUDIO | 3 PURCHASES DEBIT VIDEO | |
|---|---|---|---|---|---|---|---|---|---|
| 1 | 20-- June | 1 | Western Digital Systems | 336 | | 845 00 | | 845 00 | 1 |
| 2 | | | | | | | | | 2 |

***June 1. Purchased video equipment on account from Western Digital Systems, $845.00. Purchase Invoice No. 336.***

In the general ledger, Purchases—Video increases by an $845.00 debit. Accounts Payable increases by an $845.00 credit. In the accounts payable ledger, Western Digital Systems increases by an $845.00 credit.

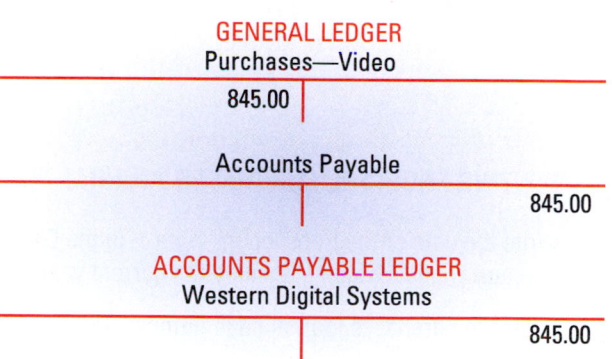

GENERAL LEDGER

| Purchases—Video | |
|---|---|
| 845.00 | |

| Accounts Payable | |
|---|---|
| | 845.00 |

ACCOUNTS PAYABLE LEDGER

| Western Digital Systems | |
|---|---|
| | 845.00 |

STEPS • STEPS • STEPS • STEPS • STEPS • STEPS • STEPS • STEPS • STEPS • STEPS

### JOURNALIZING A PURCHASE ON ACCOUNT

1. Write the date the invoice was received and approved, *June 1,* in the Date column of the purchases journal. Since this is the first entry on page 6, include the current year, *20--.*
2. Enter the vendor name, *Western Digital Systems,* in the Account Credited column.
3. Record the invoice number, *336,* in the Purch. No. column. Since only purchase invoice numbers are recorded in the column, no identifying letter is necessary.
4. Write the credit amount, *$845.00,* in the Accounts Payable Credit column. (Dollar signs are not written on ruled accounting forms.)
5. Record the debit amount, *$845.00,* in the Purchases Debit Video column.

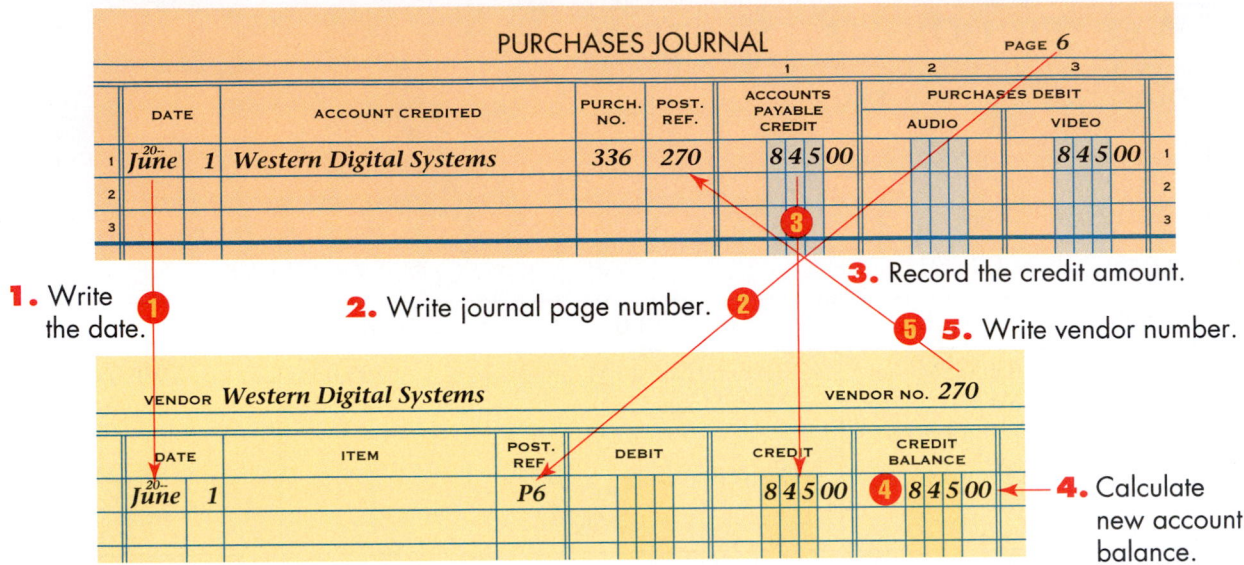

**1.** Write the date.

**2.** Write journal page number.

**3.** Record the credit amount.

**5.** Write vendor number.

**4.** Calculate new account balance.

Transferring transaction information from a journal entry to a ledger account is called **posting**. Zytech keeps vendor accounts in an accounts payable ledger. Individual amounts in the Accounts Payable Credit column of the purchases journal are posted often to the appropriate vendor accounts. The purchases journal is abbreviated as *P* in the Post. Ref. column of the ledger accounts. Posting from the Accounts Payable Credit column of the purchases journal to a ledger account is shown above.

**FYI** FOR YOUR INFORMATION

CPAs help small businesses avoid many of the pitfalls of doing business. Business owners rely on CPAs for advice in such areas as taxation, payroll requirements, banking policies, and business planning.

## STEPS

STEPS • STEPS • STEPS • STEPS • STEPS • STEPS • STEPS • STEPS • STEPS • STEPS

### POSTING FROM THE PURCHASES JOURNAL TO THE ACCOUNTS PAYABLE LEDGER

**1.** Write the date of the transaction, *June 1*, in the Date column of the ledger account. Since this is the first ledger entry for Western Digital Systems, include the current year, *20--*, in the Date column.

**2.** Enter the purchases journal page number, *P6*, in the Post. Ref. column of the ledger account.

**3.** Record the credit amount, *$845.00*, in the Credit column of the account for Western Digital Systems. All postings from the purchases journal to the ledger accounts will be to the Credit amount column of the ledger.

**4.** Add the amount in the Credit amount column to the previous balance in the Credit Balance column. Write the new account balance in the Credit Balance column. Since Western Digital Systems has no balance, simply enter the amount, *$845.00*, in the Credit amount column in the Credit Balance column.

**5.** Record the vendor number in the Post. Ref. column of the journal. The vendor number shows that the posting for this entry is complete.

{ **REMEMBER** Only purchases of merchandise on account are recorded in the purchases journal. }

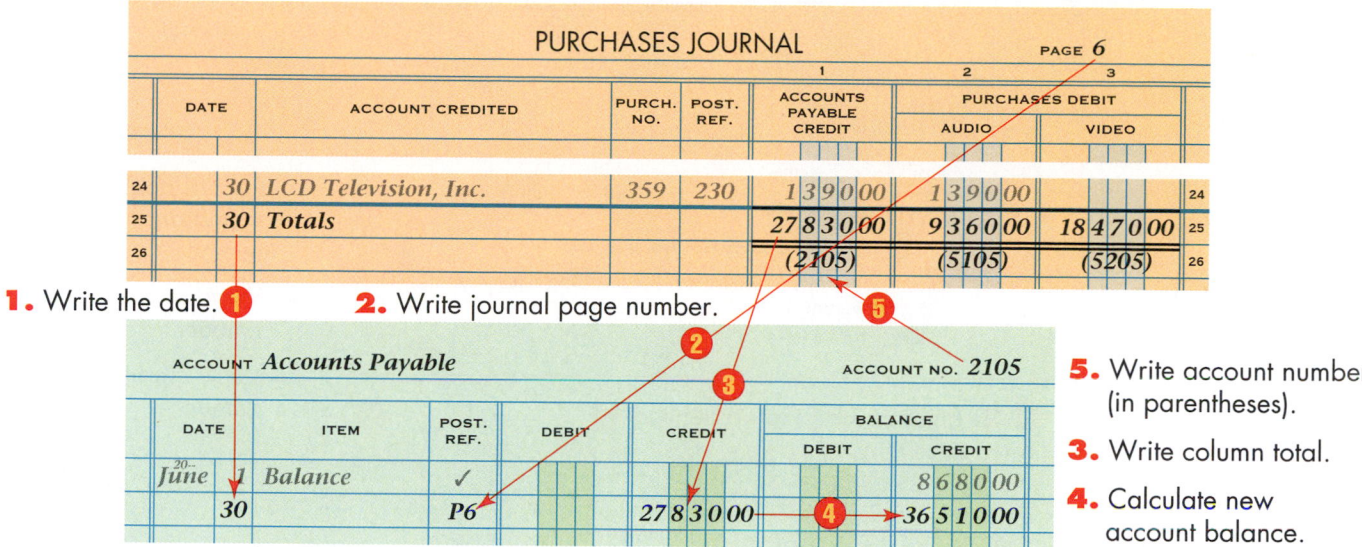

**PURCHASES JOURNAL** PAGE 6

| | DATE | ACCOUNT CREDITED | PURCH. NO. | POST. REF. | ACCOUNTS PAYABLE CREDIT (1) | PURCHASES DEBIT AUDIO (2) | PURCHASES DEBIT VIDEO (3) | |
|---|---|---|---|---|---|---|---|---|
| 24 | 30 | LCD Television, Inc. | 359 | 230 | 1 3 9 0 00 | 1 3 9 0 00 | | 24 |
| 25 | 30 | Totals | | | 27 8 3 0 00 | 9 3 6 0 00 | 18 4 7 0 00 | 25 |
| 26 | | | | | (2105) | (5105) | (5205) | 26 |

**1.** Write the date. ①     **2.** Write journal page number.

ACCOUNT **Accounts Payable**     ACCOUNT NO. **2105**

| DATE | ITEM | POST. REF. | DEBIT | CREDIT | BALANCE DEBIT | BALANCE CREDIT |
|---|---|---|---|---|---|---|
| June 1 | Balance | ✓ | | | | 8 6 8 0 00 |
| 30 | | P6 | | 27 8 3 0 00 | | 36 5 1 0 00 |

**5.** Write account number (in parentheses).

**3.** Write column total.

**4.** Calculate new account balance.

The purchases journal is proved and ruled at the end of each month. A purchases journal is proved by adding each column and then proving that the sum of the debit column totals equals the credit column total. Double lines are then ruled across the amount columns to show that the totals have been verified as correct. Each amount column total is posted to the general ledger account named in the column heading. The posting of the purchases journal's Accounts Payable Credit column total to the Accounts Payable account in the general ledger is shown above. The same procedure is used to post the totals of the Purchases Debit—Audio and the Purchases Debit—Video columns.

**STEPS**   STEPS • STEPS • STEPS • STEPS

### POSTING THE TOTAL OF THE ACCOUNTS PAYABLE COLUMN TO THE GENERAL LEDGER

① Write the date, *30*, in the Date column of the account.

② Write the purchases journal page number, *P6*, in the Post. Ref. column of the account.

③ Write the Accounts Payable Credit column total, *$27,830.00*, in the Credit amount column of the *Accounts Payable* account.

④ Calculate and record the new account balance, *$36,510.00*, in the Balance Credit column.

⑤ Write the general ledger account number in parentheses, *(2105)*, below the column total in the purchases journal.

©GETTY IMAGES/PHOTODISC

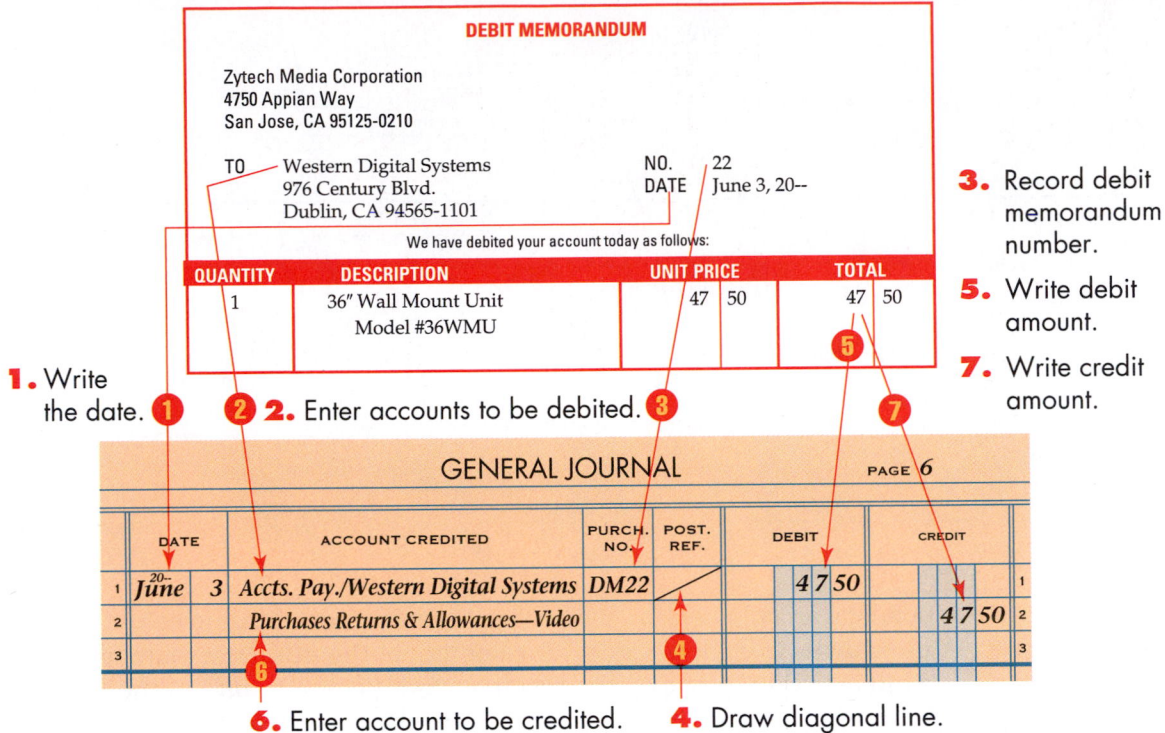

**3.** Record debit memorandum number.

**5.** Write debit amount.

**7.** Write credit amount.

**1.** Write the date.

**2.** Enter accounts to be debited.

**6.** Enter account to be credited.

**4.** Draw diagonal line.

When merchandise is returned to a vendor, the vendor's account and Accounts Payable are reduced by a debit. An allowance may also be given for merchandise that is not returned. A form prepared by the customer showing the price deduction for purchase returns and allowances is called a **debit memorandum**.

Zytech documents all purchases returns and allowances with a debit memorandum and records the transaction in a general journal. Zytech's general journal is shown above.

*June 3. Returned video equipment (one damaged wall mount unit) to Western Digital Systems, $47.50, from Purchase Invoice No. 336. Debit Memorandum No. 22.*

In the general ledger, Accounts Payable decreases by a $47.50 debit. An account that reduces a related account on a financial statement is known as a **contra account**. The purchases returns and allowances accounts are contra cost accounts. Purchases Returns and Allowances—Video increases by a $47.50 credit. In the accounts payable ledger, the vendor account, Western Digital Systems, decreases by a $47.50 debit.

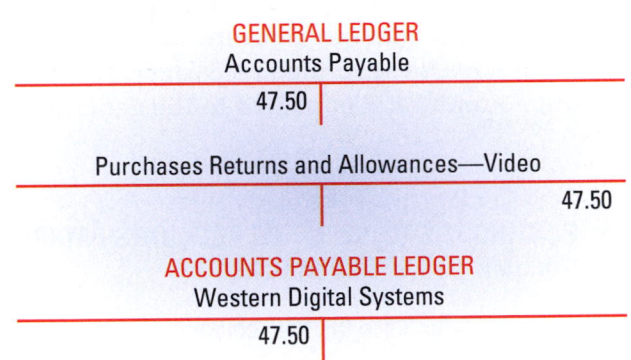

**GENERAL LEDGER**
Accounts Payable

| 47.50 | |

Purchases Returns and Allowances—Video

| | 47.50 |

**ACCOUNTS PAYABLE LEDGER**
Western Digital Systems

| 47.50 | |

## STEPS • STEPS • STEPS • STEPS
### JOURNALIZING A PURCHASES RETURN

**1** Write the date, *June 3*, in the Date column of the general journal. Since this is the first entry on page 6 of the general journal, include the current year, *20--*.

**2** Write the titles of the accounts to be debited, *Accts. Pay./ Western Digital Systems*, in the Account Title column.

**3** Record the debit memorandum number, *DM22*, in the Doc. No. column.

**4** Draw a diagonal line in the Post. Ref. Column to indicate that the single debit amount is posted to two accounts.

**5** Write the debit amount, *$47.50*, in the Debit column.

**6** Indent and write the title of the account to be credited, *Purchases Returns and Allowances—Video*, in the Account Title column.

**7** Record the credit amount, *$47.50*, in the Credit column.

## terms review

departmental accounting system
merchandising business
posting
debit memorandum
contra account

## audit your understanding

1. When Zytech's video department purchases merchandise on account, what general ledger accounts are affected, and how?

2. What general ledger accounts are affected, and how, by a purchases return of video equipment?

## work together 1-2

**Journalizing and posting purchases on account and purchases returns and allowances**

City Music has two departments: Discs and Tapes. A purchases journal, general journal, partial general ledger, and accounts payable ledger are provided in the *Working Papers*. The balances are recorded as of March 1 of the current year. Your instructor will guide you through the following examples.

**Transactions:**

Mar.  1. Purchased tapes on account from Raymond Wholesalers, $1,350.00. P283.
2. Purchased discs on account from Artex Music, $965.00. P284.
5. Returned discs to Dade, Inc., $165.00, from P280. DM36.
6. Received an allowance on tapes from Raymond Wholesalers, $100.00, from P283. DM37.
18. Purchased tapes on account from Quality Tapes, $268.00. P285.
23. Purchased tapes on account from Castle Records and Tapes, $993.00. P286.

1. Journalize each transaction. Source documents are abbreviated as follows: debit memorandum, DM; purchase invoice, P.

2. Post the items that are to be posted individually from the purchases journal.

3. Post from the general journal.

4. Prove and rule the purchases journal. Post the totals.

The ledgers used in this problem are needed to complete On Your Own 1-2.

## on your own 1-2

**Journalizing and posting purchases on account and purchases returns and allowances**

Use the ledger accounts from Work Together 1-2 and the purchases journal in the *Working Papers*. Work this problem independently.

**Transactions:**

Apr.  4. Purchased tapes on account from Quality Tapes, $425.00. P287.
12. Purchased tapes on account from Castle Records and Tapes, $2,100.00. P288.
18. Purchased discs on account from Park Recording Company, $1,624.00. P289.
20. Returned discs to Artex Music, $120.00, from P284. DM38.
22. Purchased discs on account from Artex Music, $850.00. P290.
30. Received an allowance on tapes from Castle Records and Tapes, $150.00, from P289. DM39.

1. Journalize each transaction.

2. Post the items that are to be posted individually from the purchases journal.

3. Post from the general journal.

4. Prove and rule the purchases journal. Post the totals.

# 1-3 Journalizing and Posting Cash Payments

## DEPARTMENTAL CASH PAYMENTS

Most of Zytech's cash payments are made by check. Therefore, checks are the source documents for most cash payments. [CONCEPT: Objective Evidence] All cash payments are recorded in the cash payments journal.

### Cash Payment on Account

Purchases on account are expected to be paid within the stated credit period. A seller may encourage early payment by allowing a deduction from the invoice amount. A deduction that a vendor allows on the invoice amount to encourage prompt payment is called a **cash discount**. A cash discount on purchases taken by a customer is called a **purchases discount**.

A purchases discount is usually stated as a percentage. For example, the terms of an invoice may be written as *2/10, n/30.* The expression *2/10* means that 2% of the invoice amount may

be deducted from the amount due if payment is made within 10 days of the invoice date. The expression *n/30* means that payment of the total invoice amount must be made within 30 days of the invoice date. No discount can be deducted, however, if payment is made after 10 days from the invoice date. Zytech takes advantage of all discounts allowed by vendors.

A purchases discount reduces the net amount of cash paid for a purchase. The account Purchases Discount—Video is in the cost of merchandise division of Zytech's general ledger. Purchases discounts are kept in separate accounts and not deducted directly from the purchases accounts. This procedure helps the business see what proportion of purchases on account were allowed purchases discounts.

CULTURAL DIVERSITY   •   CULTURAL DIVERSITY   •   CULTURAL DIVERSITY

## cultural diversity
### Professional Organizations

How do you meet other people in your profession? Join a professional organization. Several professional accounting organizations exist to serve the needs of various ethnic groups. Among these organizations are The Association of Latino Professionals in Finance and Accounting (www.alpfa.org); The National Association of Black Accountants, Inc. (www.nabainc.org); and The Association of Asian American Attorneys and Certified Public Accountants.

These associations maintain an informal network among members. Such networks allow people in the profession to meet, to

use services of other association members, and to share ideas and career opportunities. They also promote career opportunities for their members, work to expand representation of their ethnic groups in the workforce, and offer various forms of continuing education.

In addition to their national organizations, each has various chapters around the country. All three offer student memberships to college students who are studying accounting.

## JOURNALIZING A PURCHASES DISCOUNT

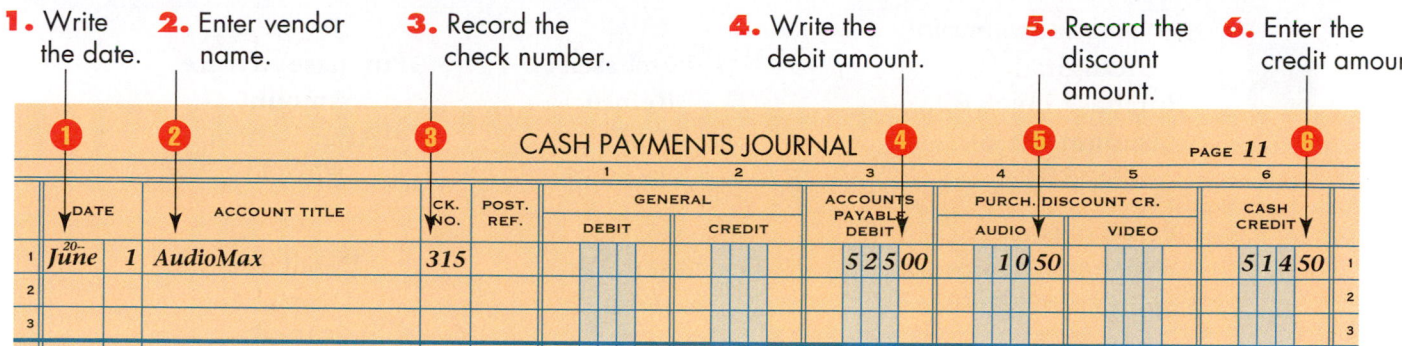

**1.** Write the date.  **2.** Enter vendor name.  **3.** Record the check number.  **4.** Write the debit amount.  **5.** Record the discount amount.  **6.** Enter the credit amount.

Zytech's cash payments journal has two debit columns—General Debit and Accounts Payable Debit. The journal also has four credit columns—General Credit, a Purchases Discount Credit column for each of the two departments, and Cash Credit.

---

*June 1. Paid cash on account to AudioMax, $514.50, covering Purchase Invoice No. 331 for surround sound audio equipment for $525.00, less 2% discount, $10.50. Check No. 315.*

---

The source document for this transaction is a check. [CONCEPT: Objective Evidence]

In the general ledger, Accounts Payable decreases by a $525.00 debit. Cash decreases by a $514.50 credit. Purchases Discount—Audio increases by a $10.50 credit. In the accounts payable ledger, AudioMax decreases by a $525.00 debit.

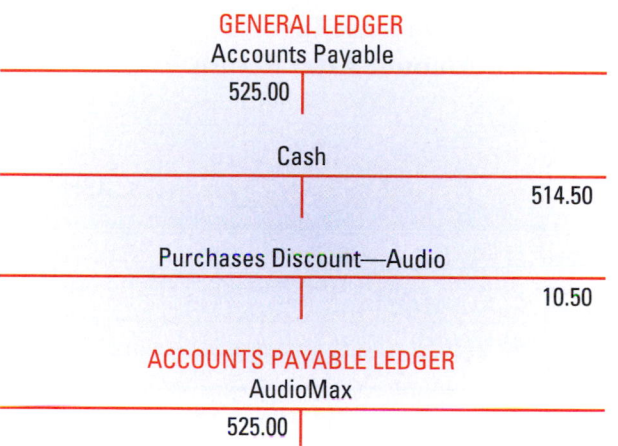

## STEPS

STEPS • STEPS • STEPS • STEPS • STEPS • STEPS • STEPS • STEPS • STEPS • STEPS

### JOURNALIZING A CASH PAYMENT THAT INCLUDES A PURCHASES DISCOUNT

**1** Write the date, *June 1,* in the Date column of the cash payments journal. Since this is the first entry on page 11 of the cash payments journal, include the current year, *20--*.

**2** Enter the vendor name, *AudioMax,* in the Account Title column.

**3** Record the check number, *315,* in the Ck. No. column.

**4** Write the debit amount, *$525.00,* in the Accounts Payable Debit column.

**5** Record the discount credit amount, *$10.50,* in the Purchases Discount Credit Audio column.

**6** Enter the cash credit amount, *$514.50,* in the Cash Credit column.

*Amount owed on invoice:*

| Original Purchase Invoice Amount (P336) | − | Purchases Return (DM22) | = | Purchase Invoice Amount After Return | |
|---|---|---|---|---|---|
| $845.00 | − | 47.50 | = | $797.50 | **1** |

*Purchases discount:*

| Purchase Invoice Amount After Return | × | Purchases Discount Rate | = | Purchases Discount | |
|---|---|---|---|---|---|
| $797.50 | × | 2% | = | $15.95 | **2** |

*Amount due after purchases discount:*

| Purchase Invoice Amount After Return | − | Purchases Discount | = | Total Amount Due | |
|---|---|---|---|---|---|
| $797.50 | − | $15.95 | = | $781.55 | **3** |

### CASH PAYMENTS JOURNAL

PAGE *11*

| | DATE | ACCOUNT TITLE | CK. NO. | POST. REF. | GENERAL DEBIT | GENERAL CREDIT | ACCOUNTS PAYABLE DEBIT | PURCH. DISCOUNT CR. AUDIO | PURCH. DISCOUNT CR. VIDEO | CASH CREDIT | |
|---|---|---|---|---|---|---|---|---|---|---|---|
| 1 | June 1 | AudioMax | 315 | | | | 525 00 | 10 50 | | 514 50 | 1 |
| 2 | 2 | Western Digital Systems | 316 | | | | 797 50 | | 15 95 | 781 55 | 2 |
| 3 | | | | | | | | | | | 3 |

**4**

An additional calculation is necessary when a discount is taken after a purchase return or allowance has been granted. The discount is calculated on the amount owed at the time the invoice is paid. Therefore, the amount of the return or allowance must be deducted from the amount of the original purchase before the discount can be calculated.

> **June 2.** Paid cash on account to Western Digital Systems, $781.55, covering Purchase Invoice No. 336 for video equipment for $845.00, less Debit Memorandum No. 22 for $47.50, and less 2% discount, $15.95. Check No. 316.

The source document for this transaction is a check. [*CONCEPT: Objective Evidence*]

The total amount due for this purchase after the return and the discount is calculated as shown above.

This transaction is journalized in the same way as a payment of cash when there is no purchases return or allowance. The only difference is the way in which the amounts are calculated.

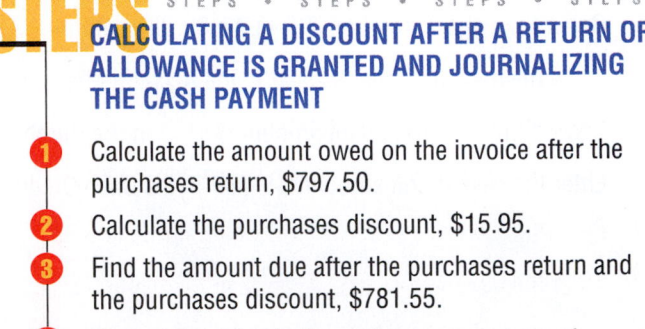

**GENERAL LEDGER**

Accounts Payable

797.50 |

Cash

| 781.55

Purchases Discount—Video

| 15.95

**ACCOUNTS PAYABLE LEDGER**

Western Digital Systems

797.50 |

## STEPS

STEPS • STEPS • STEPS • STEPS

### CALCULATING A DISCOUNT AFTER A RETURN OR ALLOWANCE IS GRANTED AND JOURNALIZING THE CASH PAYMENT

**1** Calculate the amount owed on the invoice after the purchases return, $797.50.

**2** Calculate the purchases discount, $15.95.

**3** Find the amount due after the purchases return and the purchases discount, $781.55.

**4** Record the entry in the cash payments journal.

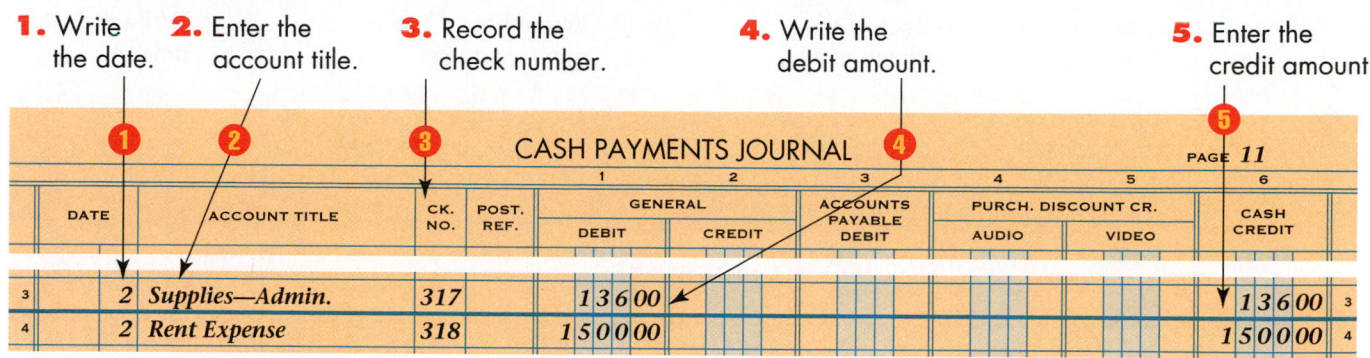

1. Write the date.
2. Enter the account title.
3. Record the check number.
4. Write the debit amount.
5. Enter the credit amount.

**CASH PAYMENTS JOURNAL**    PAGE 11

| | DATE | ACCOUNT TITLE | CK. NO. | POST. REF. | GENERAL DEBIT | GENERAL CREDIT | ACCOUNTS PAYABLE DEBIT | PURCH. DISCOUNT CR. AUDIO | PURCH. DISCOUNT CR. VIDEO | CASH CREDIT | |
|---|---|---|---|---|---|---|---|---|---|---|---|
| 3 | 2 | Supplies—Admin. | 317 | | 1 3 6 00 | | | | | 1 3 6 00 | 3 |
| 4 | 2 | Rent Expense | 318 | | 1 5 0 0 00 | | | | | 1 5 0 0 00 | 4 |

*June 2. Paid cash for administrative supplies, $136.00. Check No. 317.*

Supplies—Administrative increases by a $136.00 debit. Cash decreases by a $136.00 credit.

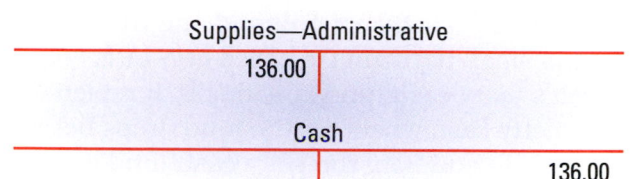

### STEPS   JOURNALIZING BUYING OFFICE SUPPLIES FOR CASH

1. Write the date, *2,* in the Date column.

2. Enter the account title, *Supplies—Administrative,* in the Account Title column. It is acceptable to abbreviate account titles to fit the space in the journal.

3. Record the check number, *317,* in the Ck. No. column.

4. Write the debit amount, *$136.00,* in the General Debit column.

5. Record the credit amount, *$136.00,* in the Cash Credit column.

*June 2. Paid cash for rent, $1,500.00. Check No. 318.*

Rent Expense increases by a $1,500.00 debit. Cash decreases by a $1,500.00 credit.

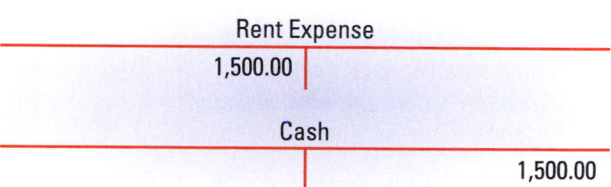

### STEPS   JOURNALIZING THE CASH PAYMENT OF AN EXPENSE

1. Write the date, *2,* in the Date column.

2. Enter the account title, *Rent Expense,* in the Account Title column.

3. Record the check number, *318,* in the Ck. No. column.

4. Write the debit amount, *$1,500.00,* in the General Debit column.

5. Record the credit amount, *$1,500.00,* in the Cash Credit column.

## CASH PAYMENT TO REPLENISH PETTY CASH

**1.** Write the date.  **2.** Enter account titles.  **3.** Record the check number.  **4.** Write the debit amounts.  **5.** Write the credit amount.

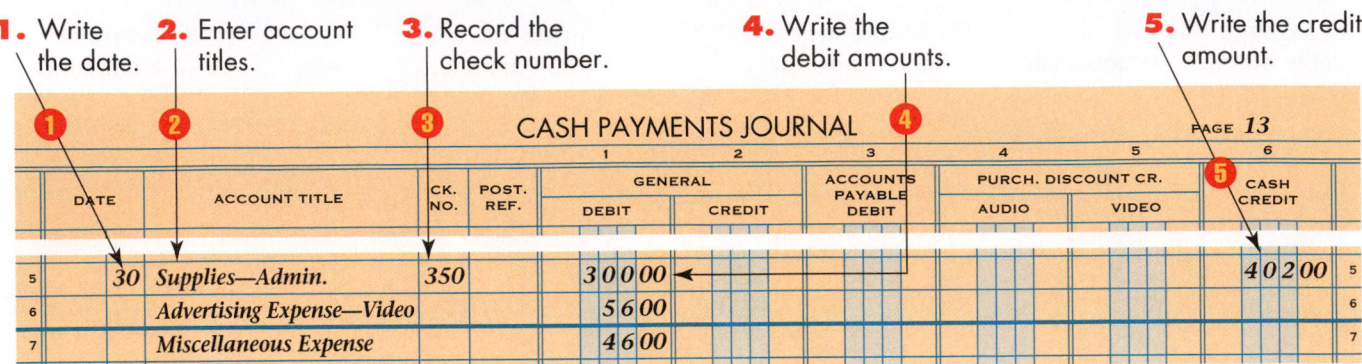

### CASH PAYMENTS JOURNAL — PAGE 13

| | DATE | ACCOUNT TITLE | CK. NO. | POST. REF. | GENERAL DEBIT | GENERAL CREDIT | ACCOUNTS PAYABLE DEBIT | PURCH. DISCOUNT CR. AUDIO | PURCH. DISCOUNT CR. VIDEO | CASH CREDIT | |
|---|---|---|---|---|---|---|---|---|---|---|---|
| 5 | 30 | Supplies—Admin. | 350 | | 3 0 0 00 | | | | | 4 0 2 00 | 5 |
| 6 | | Advertising Expense—Video | | | 5 6 00 | | | | | | 6 |
| 7 | | Miscellaneous Expense | | | 4 6 00 | | | | | | 7 |

An amount of cash kept on hand and used for making small payments is called **petty cash**. Zytech's petty cash fund is $500.00. It replenishes petty cash whenever the fund drops below $100.00. In addition, the petty cash fund is replenished on the last business day of each fiscal period, to assure that all expenses are recorded during the fiscal period in which they occurred. [*CONCEPT: Matching Expenses with Revenue*]

Business activities for an accounting period are summarized in financial statements. To adequately report how a business performed during an accounting period, all revenue earned as a result of business operations must be reported.

Likewise, all expenses incurred in producing the revenue during the same accounting period must be reported. Matching expenses with revenue gives a true picture of business operations for an accounting period.

To replenish petty cash, a check is written for the amount spent from the fund. The check is cashed and the money placed back in the fund.

> *June 30. Paid cash to replenish the petty cash fund, $402.00: administrative supplies, $300.00; advertising expense—video, $56.00; miscellaneous expense, $46.00. Check No. 350.*

## STEPS
STEPS • STEPS • STEPS • STEPS • STEPS • STEPS • STEPS • STEPS • STEPS • STEPS

### JOURNALIZING THE CASH PAYMENT TO REPLENISH PETTY CASH

**1** Write the date, *30*, in the Date column.

**2** Enter the account titles, *Supplies—Administrative, Advertising Expense—Video*, and *Miscellaneous Expense*, in the Account Title column.

**3** Record the check number, *350*, in the Ck. No. column on the first line of the entry.

**4** Write the debit amounts for the appropriate accounts, *$300.00, $56.00*, and *$46.00*, in the General Debit column.

**5** Record the credit amount, *$402.00*, in the Cash Credit column on the first line of the entry.

©GETTY IMAGES/PHOTODISC

Recording Departmental Purchases and Cash Payments

**CASH PAYMENTS JOURNAL**  PAGE 13

|  | DATE | ACCOUNT TITLE | CK. NO. | POST. REF. | GENERAL DEBIT | GENERAL CREDIT | ACCOUNTS PAYABLE DEBIT | PURCH. DISCOUNT CR. AUDIO | PURCH. DISCOUNT CR. VIDEO | CASH CREDIT |  |
|---|---|---|---|---|---|---|---|---|---|---|---|
|  |  |  |  |  | 1 | 2 | 3 | 4 | 5 | 6 |  |
| 12 | 30 | Miscellaneous Expense | 353 | 7120 | 4 1 80 |  |  |  |  | 4 1 80 | 12 |
| 13 | 30 | Utilities Expense | 354 | 7155 | 2 4 0 15 |  |  |  |  | 2 4 0 15 | 13 |
| 14 | 30 | MegaWatt Sound, Inc. | 355 | 240 |  |  | 4 3 0 00 | 8 60 |  | 4 2 1 40 | 14 |
| 15 | 30 | Plasma Electronics | 356 | 250 |  |  | 6 5 0 00 |  | 13 00 | 6 3 7 00 | 15 |
| 16 | 30 | Totals |  |  | 19 5 2 0 00 | 1 7 3 0 00 | 43 9 3 0 00 | 1 4 1 30 | 3 3 1 50 | 61 2 4 7 20 | 16 |
| 17 |  |  |  |  | (√) | (√) | (2105) | (5110) | (5210) | (1105) | 17 |
| 18 |  |  |  |  |  |  |  |  |  |  | 18 |

The accounting procedures for posting from a cash payments journal are the same as those followed for posting from the purchases journal. During the month, Zytech posts often from the General Debit and General Credit columns to the general ledger. Zytech also posts frequently from the Accounts Payable Debit column to the accounts payable ledger. Frequent posting permits Zytech to keep each vendor account balance in the accounts payable ledger up to date.

At the end of each month, the cash payments journal is proved and ruled. Totals of the special amount columns are posted to their respective accounts in the general ledger. The general ledger account number is written in parentheses immediately below the total. A check mark is recorded in parentheses below the totals of the General Debit and Credit columns to show that these totals are not posted. Zytech's departmental cash payments journal is shown after all posting has been completed.

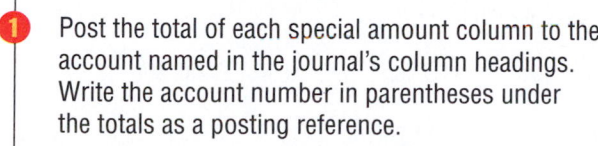

## STEPS
STEPS • STEPS • STEPS • STEPS • STEPS • STEPS • STEPS • STEPS • STEPS • STEPS

### POSTING FROM A CASH PAYMENTS JOURNAL

**During the month:**

**1** Post individual amounts from the General Debit and General Credit columns to the appropriate accounts in the general ledger. Do this often during the month.

**2** Post individual vendor amounts from the Accounts Payable Debit column to the appropriate accounts in the accounts payable ledger. Do this frequently during the month.

**At the end of the month:**

**1** Post the total of each special amount column to the account named in the journal's column headings. Write the account number in parentheses under the totals as a posting reference.

**2** Do *not* post the totals of the General Debit and Credit columns. (Place a check mark in parentheses under these columns to show that these totals are not posted.)

©GETTY IMAGES/PHOTODISC

## terms review

cash discount
purchases discount
petty cash

TERMS REVIEW •

## audit your understanding

1. What general ledger accounts are affected, and how, by a cash payment on account for video equipment that includes a purchases discount?

2. Where are cash payments affecting accounts that are not listed in the column headings recorded?

3. Why is a petty cash fund always replenished on the last day of a fiscal period?

AUDIT YOUR

## work together 1-3

### Journalizing and posting departmental cash payments

Village Music Center has two departments: Guitars and Keyboards. Page 17 of a cash payments journal, a partial general ledger, and an accounts payable ledger are provided in the *Working Papers*. Source documents are abbreviated as follows: check, C; debit memorandum, DM; and purchase invoice, P. Your instructor will guide you through the following examples.

### Transactions:

Sept. 5. Paid cash on account for guitars from Peninsula Guitar covering P358 for $1,150.00; no discount. C241.
    7. Paid cash for administrative supplies, $120.00. C242.
    9. Paid cash on account for keyboards from Magic Keyboards covering P360 for $2,210.00, less DM53 for $210.00, and less 2% discount. C243.
  16. Paid cash on account for keyboards from Magic Keyboard covering P361 for $1,800.00, less 2% discount. C244.
  19. Paid cash on account for guitars to Peninsula Guitar covering P359 for $1,680.00; no discount. C245.
  30. Paid cash to replenish the petty cash fund, $64.00: administrative supplies, $15.00; advertising expense, $22.00; miscellaneous expense, $27.00. C246.

1. Journalize the transactions.
2. Post items that are to be posted individually.
3. Prove and rule the cash payments journal. Post the totals.

WORK TOGETHER • WORK TOGETHER • WORK TOGETHER • WORK TOGETHER

## on your own 1-3

### Journalizing and posting departmental cash payments

Design, Inc., has two departments: Carpet and Furniture. Use page 18 of a cash payments journal in the *Working Papers*. Work this problem independently.

### Transactions:

Oct. 5. Paid cash on account for furniture from Sophos Furniture Co. covering P408 for $2,160.00. C218.
    7. Paid cash for carpet department supplies, $160.00. C219.
    8. Paid cash on account for furniture from Sophos Furniture Co. covering P412 for $3,210.00, less DM53 for $270.00, and less 2% discount. C220.
  12. Paid cash on account for carpet from Luxor Carpet, Inc. covering P413 for $1,200.00, less 2% discount. C221.
  17. Paid cash on account for carpet from Duro Weave, Inc. covering P414 for $2,600.00, less 2% discount. C222.
  19. Paid cash on account for carpet to Luxor Carpet, Inc. covering P411 for $1,775.00. C223.
  30. Paid cash to replenish the petty cash fund, $98.00: carpet department supplies, $52.00; advertising expense, $31.00; miscellaneous expense, $15.00. C224.

1. Journalize the transactions.
2. Post items that are to be posted individually.
3. Prove and rule the cash payments journal. Post the totals.

ON YOUR OWN • ON YOUR OWN • ON YOUR OWN • ON YOUR OWN

## SUMMARY

**After completing this chapter, you can**

1. Define accounting terms related to departmental purchases and cash payments.
2. Identify accounting concepts and practices related to departmental purchases and cash payments.
3. Journalize and post departmental purchases and purchases returns.
4. Journalize and post departmental cash payments.

# Explore Accounting

EXPLORE ACCOUNTING   •   EXPLORE ACCOUNTING   •   EXPLORE ACCO

## Accounting Professionals

As a company grows, it can adopt two strategies to satisfy its need for accounting expertise. The company can add to its full-time accounting staff. As an alternative, the company could hire independent consultants. Regardless of which strategy is adopted, the search for accounting professionals should include examining their professional certification.

The *Certified Public Accountant (CPA)* is the most widely recognized certification. To become a CPA, an individual must pass a certifying examination and meet the educational and experience requirements of the board of accountancy in the individual's state. A CPA is qualified to perform a variety of accounting functions, including processing accounting information, auditing financial statements, preparing tax returns, and providing tax planning.

A partial list of additional certifications available in accounting and related areas follows:

*Certified Management Accountant:* Responsible for the accounting information system; assists managers in using accounting information in decision making; works to provide the company with adequate financial resources to conduct business.

*Certified Internal Auditor:* Audits the accounting information system and other operational reporting systems.

*Certified Information Systems Analyst:* Designs computer information systems that provide timely accounting information while assuring that the information is accessible only to authorized personnel.

*Certified Fraud Examiner:* Investigates alleged fraudulent activities by examining accounting records and interviewing personnel; prepares evidence for admission into court.

*Certified Financial Planner:* Manages the company's employee benefits and assists employees to develop investment strategies to meet future needs.

*Certified Contingency Planner:* Develops plans that enable the company and its accounting information system to continue operations in the event of a natural disaster.

**Instructions:** Identify an individual who has one of the certifications listed above. Ask the individual to describe how the certification has played a role in his or her professional career.

# 1-1 APPLICATION PROBLEM

## Determining the normal balance, increase, and decrease sides for accounts

Write the answers for the following problem in the *Working Papers*.

Sales—Video
Prepaid Insurance
Cash
Miscellaneous Expense

Supplies—Audio
Sanford Studios (an account receivable)
Capital Stock
TechCorp (an account payable)

| 1 | 2 | 3 | 4 | 5 | 6 | 7 | 8 |
|---|---|---|---|---|---|---|---|
| Account Title | Account Classification | Account's Normal Balance | | Increase Side | | Decrease Side | |
| | | Debit | Credit | Debit | Credit | Debit | Credit |
| Sales—Video | Revenue | | ✓ | | ✓ | ✓ | |

### Instructions:

Do the following for each account. The Sales—Video account is given above as an example.
1. Write the account title in Column 1.
2. Write the account classification in Column 2.
3. Place a check mark in either Column 3 or 4 to indicate the normal balance of the account.
4. Place a check mark in either Column 5 or 6 to indicate the increase side of the account.
5. Place a check mark in either Column 7 or 8 to indicate the decrease side of the account.

# 1-2 APPLICATION PROBLEM  PEACHTREE  QUICKBOOKS

## Journalizing and posting departmental purchases on account and purchases returns and allowances

Zenix Communications has two departments: Cellular Phones and Pagers. A purchases journal, general journal, partial general ledger, and accounts payable ledger are provided in the *Working Papers*. The balances are recorded as of October 1 of the current year. Source documents are abbreviated as follows: debit memorandum, DM; purchase invoice, P.

### Transactions:

Oct.  1.  Purchased phones on account from CarPhone Wholesalers, $1,270.00. P183.
      2.  Purchased pagers on account from PageMax, Inc., $970.00. P184.
      5.  Purchased phones on account from ExecuPhone, $2,100.00. P185.
      6.  The order from Western Distributors contained 5 defective pagers. Returned pagers, $205.00, from P180. DM40.
      9.  Purchased pagers on account from Cell Advantage, Inc., $945.00. P186.
      13. Purchased pagers on account from ComSystems, $2,240.00. P187.
      17. Returned phones to CarPhone Wholesalers, $120.00, from P183. DM41.
          **Posting.** Post the items that are to be posted individually from the purchases journal. Post from the general journal. Post from the journals in this order: purchases journal and general journal.
      19. Purchased phones on account from Telecom Corporation, $450.00. P188.
      20. Returned pagers to PageMax, Inc., $90.00, from P184. DM42.
      23. Issued P189 to purchase phones on account from ExecuPhone, $1,003.00.
      30. Returned $75.00 of phones to Phone Solution, from P181. DM43.
          **Posting.** Post the items that are to be posted individually from the purchases journal. Post from the general journal.

### Instructions:

1. Journalize the transactions completed during October of the current year. Use page 11 of a purchases journal and page 3 of a general journal.
2. Prove and rule the purchases journal. Post the totals.

## 1-3 APPLICATION PROBLEM AUTOMATED ACCOUNTING
### Journalizing and posting departmental cash payments

CraftMart has two departments: Crafts and Plants. A partial general ledger and accounts payable ledger are given in the *Working Papers.* The balances are recorded as of November 1 of the current year. Source documents are abbreviated as follows: check, C; memorandum, M.

**Transactions:**

Nov.  1.  Paid cash for miscellaneous expense, $150.00. C303.
     2.  Paid cash for rent, $1,300.00. C304.
     4.  Paid cash on account to Wholesale Crafts, Inc. covering P287 for crafts for $885.00, less 2% discount. C305.
     5.  Paid cash for advertising, $83.50. C306.
     8.  Paid cash for administrative supplies, $95.50. C307.
   10.  Paid cash on account to Northtown Plants covering P288 for plants for $1,550.00, less DM107 for $300.00, less 2% discount. C308.
   13.  Paid cash on account to Century Crafts, Inc., covering P289 for crafts for $963.00, less 2% discount. C309.
   15.  Paid cash for miscellaneous, $33.50. C310.
      **Posting.** Post the items that are to be posted individually.
   21.  Paid cash for administrative supplies, $52.00. C311.
   23.  Paid cash on account to Evergreen Trees & Shrubs covering P290 for plants for $1,840.00, less 2% discount. C312.
   27.  Paid cash on account to Evergreen Trees & Shrubs covering P292 for plants for $1,460.00, less 2% discount. C313.
   30.  Paid cash to replenish the petty cash fund, $212.00: administrative supplies, $89.00; advertising, $83.40; miscellaneous, $39.60. C314.
      **Posting.** Post the items that are to be posted individually.

**Instructions:**

1. Journalize the transactions completed during November of the current year. Use page 21 of a cash payments journal. All of the vendors from which merchandise is purchased on account offer terms of 2/10, n/30.
2. Prove and rule the cash payments journal. Post the totals.

## 1-4 MASTERY PROBLEM AUTOMATED ACCOUNTING
### Journalizing departmental purchases and cash payments

Outdoor Sport has two departments: Backpacks and Accessories. Source documents are abbreviated as follows: check, C; debit memorandum, DM; purchase invoice, P.

**Transactions:**

Apr.  1.  Paid cash for advertising, $95.00. C273.
    1.  Paid cash for rent, $1,250.00. C274.
    2.  Purchased accessories on account from CampWorld Supplies, $800.00. P262.
    3.  Paid cash on account to PackGear covering P259 for backpacks for $500.00, less 2% discount. C275.
    3.  Purchased backpacks on account from SierraPack, $840.00. P263.
    5.  Paid cash on account to CampWorld Supplies covering P261 for accessories for $645.00, less 2% discount. C276.
    7.  Returned backpacks to SierraPack, $88.00, from P263. DM28.
   10.  Purchased backpacks on account from TahoeDesigns, $388.00. P264.
   11.  Paid cash for administrative supplies, $82.50. C277.
   14.  Paid cash on account to CampWorld Supplies covering P262 for accessories; no discount. C278.
      **Posting.** Post the individual items from the purchases journal, then the cash payments journal. Post from the general journal.

| Apr. | 16. | Returned accessories to Sequoia Sporting Goods, $132.50, from P260. DM29. |
|---|---|---|
| | 17. | Purchased accessories on account from CampAll, Inc., $550.00. P265. |
| | 17. | Paid cash on account to TahoeDesigns covering P264 for backpacks for $388.00, less 2% discount. C279. |
| | 18. | Paid cash on account to SierraPack covering P263 for backpacks for $840.00, less DM28 for $88.00; no discount. C280. |
| | 18. | Returned accessories to CampAll, Inc., $75.00, from P265. DM30. |
| | 19. | Purchased backpacks on account from SierraPack, $1,120.00. P266. |
| | 21. | Paid cash for administrative supplies, $62.30. C281. |
| | 23. | Purchased accessories on account from Sequoia Sporting Goods, $336.00. P267. |
| | 24. | Paid cash on account to CampAll, Inc. covering P265 for accessories for $550.00, less DM30 for $75.00, and less 2% discount. C282. |
| | 24. | Purchased backpacks on account from PackGear, $626.40. P268. |
| | 26. | Paid cash on account to SierraPack covering P266 for backpacks for $1,120.00, less 2% discount. C283. |
| | 28. | Paid cash for administrative supplies, $53.00. C284 |
| | 30. | Paid cash to replenish the petty cash fund, $221.00: administrative supplies, $57.10; advertising, $62.50; miscellaneous, $101.40. C285. |

**Posting.** Post the individual items from the purchases journal, then the cash payments journal. Post from the general journal.

**Instructions:**

1. Journalize the transactions completed during April of the current year. Use page 11 of a purchases journal, page 8 of a general journal, and page 21 of a cash payments journal. All of the vendors from which merchandise is purchased on account offer terms of 2/10, n/30.
2. Prove and rule the special journals.
3. Post the totals of the special journals.

# 1-5  CHALLENGE PROBLEM

## Journalizing purchases at net amount and using the account Discounts Lost

*Introductory remarks:* Some businesses record purchases at the net amount to be paid when the cash discount is taken. For example, merchandise is purchased for $1,000.00 with a 2% discount allowed if the account is paid within 10 days. The discount will reduce the price from $1,000.00 to $980.00. To record this purchase on account transaction, Purchases is debited for $980.00 and Accounts Payable is credited for $980.00. When the account is paid, Accounts Payable is debited for $980.00 and Cash is credited for $980.00. Purchases returns and allowances are also recorded at the discounted amount. For example, a purchase return of $100.00 would be a debit to Accounts Payable of $98.00 and a credit to Purchases Returns and Allowances of $98.00.

If the discount period expires before payment is made, the entry in the cash payments journal for the example above would be as follows: debit Accounts Payable for $980.00, debit Discounts Lost for $20.00, and credit Cash for $1,000.00. Because most cash discounts are taken, there are few entries involving the discounts lost account. For this reason, no special amount column is provided for the account in the cash payments journal. Instead, the amounts debited to this account are recorded in the General Debit column.

**Instructions:**

1. Journalize the transactions for Mastery Problem 1-4 following the method described above. Use page 11 of a purchases journal, page 8 of a general journal, and page 21 of a cash payments journal. All of the vendors from which merchandise is purchased on account offer terms of 2/10, n/30.
2. Prove and rule the special journals.

## • applied communication

APPLIED COMMUNICATION

The preparation of a *Career Portfolio* can be an extremely useful tool in helping you make the transition from school to work. The purpose of the portfolio is to assist you in collecting, organizing, and documenting data, information, work samples, achievements, and skills related to a specific career area. A *Career Portfolio* can be created very simply by purchasing a 1½- to 2-inch binder and inserting dividers.

One divider in your *Career Portfolio* should be labeled "Resume." A resume states your education, work experience, and qualifications. Your resume should be accurate, honest, and perfect in every respect. It is preferable to limit the resume to one typed page.

**Instructions:**

1. Research how to prepare an appropriate resume.

2. Prepare a personal resume that you could send to a prospective employer.

3. Keep several copies of your resume in your *Career Portfolio*.

## • case for critical thinking

CASE FOR CRITICAL

Maria Hector manages a card and gift shop. The shop's general ledger includes a single sales account and a single purchases account. Periodically, Ms. Hector has an accountant review her accounting records and procedures. The accountant recommends that Ms. Hector change to a departmental accounting system. The accountant recommends that separate revenue and cost accounts be kept for the two types of merchandise sold—cards and gifts. Ms. Hector objects to the accountant's recommendation. She sees no advantage in complicating the accounting system by having separate departmental revenue and cost accounts. With whom do you agree? Why?

## • SCANS workplace competency

SCANS WORKPLACE

**Interpersonal Competency:** Participating as a Member of a Team

**Concept:** Effective employees work cooperatively with others and contribute to groups with ideas, suggestions, and effort. Good team members share tasks, encourage others, recognize individual strengths, resolve differences, and accept personal responsibility for accomplishing goals.

**Application:** Form a team of 3-4 students. Identify some departmentalized businesses in your community. List the name of each business, the merchandise sold, and possible departments within each company. Share your findings with the class.

An office clerk at FastCom just prepared the chart below, which lists all the account titles from the firm's chart of accounts. For each account, a "+" or "−" was recorded in the appropriate debit and credit column to show the impact of a debit or credit to each account's balance. The last column indicates the normal balance for each account. The intent of creating the chart is to provide an easy reference tool to help new accounting clerks accurately record journal entries and calculate general ledger balances.

Review the office clerk's chart below. Make a new chart so that the reference tool is accurate.

| Account Title | Debit | Credit | Normal Balance |
|---|---|---|---|
| Cash | + | − | Dr. |
| Accts. Receivable | − | + | Dr. |
| All. For Uncoll. Accts. | + | − | Dr. |
| Mdse. Inventory | + | − | Dr. |
| Office Equipment | + | − | Dr. |
| Acc. Depr.—Off. Equip. | − | + | Dr. |
| Accounts Payable | − | + | Cr. |
| Dividends Payable | − | + | Cr. |
| Capital Stock | − | + | Cr. |
| Retained Earnings | + | − | Cr. |
| Dividends | + | − | Cr. |
| Income Summary | − | + | Cr.=Net Inc. Dr.=Net Loss |
| Sales | − | + | Cr. |
| Sales Ret. & Allow. | − | + | Cr. |
| Purchases | + | − | Dr. |
| Purchases Discount | + | − | Dr. |
| Advertising Expense | + | − | Dr. |
| Rent Expense | + | − | Dr. |
| Federal Inc. Tax Exp. | + | − | Dr. |

## • analyzing Costco's financial statements

Selected published financial information for Costco Wholesale Corporation is reproduced in Appendix B of this textbook. Like many companies, Costco rounds off dollar amounts when reporting financial data on various financial statements. It is very important when reviewing data in Costco's annual report to determine if the amounts presented have been rounded off to the nearest million, nearest thousand, or not rounded at all. Look at page B-2 in Appendix B. Under the heading at the top of the page, notice the phrase "dollars in millions, except per share data." This means that all dollar amounts, except the dollar amounts reported under **Per Share Data-Diluted,** are rounded to the nearest million. For example, the reported 2003 Net Sales amount of $41,693 actually represents $41,693,000,000. Actual dollar amounts on this page are calculated by multiplying the amount reported by 1,000,000 ($41,693 × 1,000,000 = $41,693,000,000).

**Instructions:** Refer to the ten-year operating and financial highlights on page B-2.

1. List the actual dollar amount of Merchandise Costs and Operating Income for 2003.
2. List the number of Gold Star members at the end of 2003.
3. List Costco's net income per diluted share for 2003.

# Automated Accounting

## Automated Entries for Purchases and Cash Payments

In the Automated Accounting software, transactions are recorded in journals similar to the purchases, general, and cash payments journals described in Chapter 1. The cash payments journal window is shown below. Journals are accessed by clicking the Journal Entries option from the Data menu or clicking the Journal toolbar button. Click the tab for the journal you wish to use.

The cash payments journal above shows three kinds of transactions: (1) two cash payments on account with purchase discounts; (2) cash payment for an asset (supplies); and (3) cash payment of an expense (Rent Expense).

Entries in the automated cash payments journal are similar to entries in a manual cash payments journal. The software automatically calculates the amount in the Cash Credit column; notice that these amounts are grey in the illustration. The Cash credit amount should be inspected and any errors corrected before an entry is posted. Entering an amount in the A.P. Debit column (Accounts Payable) automatically opens the Vendor column where an accounts payable ledger account must be selected.

The general ledger account number is entered in the Account No. column when amounts will be entered in the General Debit or General Credit column. No account number is entered for entries that are recorded entirely in special amount columns.

A journal entries report may be displayed or printed by clicking the Reports toolbar button, then clicking Journals and then the name of the journal.

**AUTOMATING APPLICATION PROBLEM 1-3: Journalizing and posting departmental cash payments**

**AUTOMATING MASTERY PROBLEM 1-4: Journalizing departmental purchases and cash payments**

**Instructions:**

1. Load the *Automated Accounting 8.0* or higher software.

2. Select data file A01-3 or A01-4 from the appropriate directory/folder ("A" indicates Advanced Course).

3. Select File from the menu bar and choose Save As. Key the path to the drive and directory that contains your data files. Save the data file with a filename of A01-3 or A01-4 XXX XXX (where the X's are your first and last name).

4. Access Problem Instructions through the Browser tool. Read the Problem Instruction screen.

5. Key the data listed in the problem on page 27.

6. Save your file and exit the Automated Accounting software.

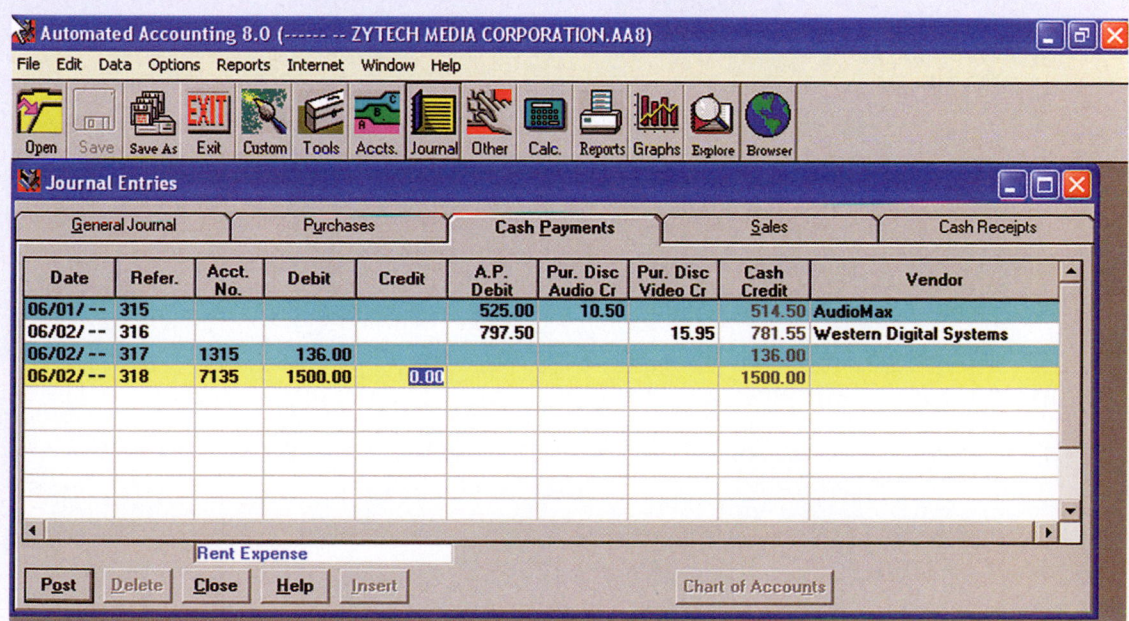

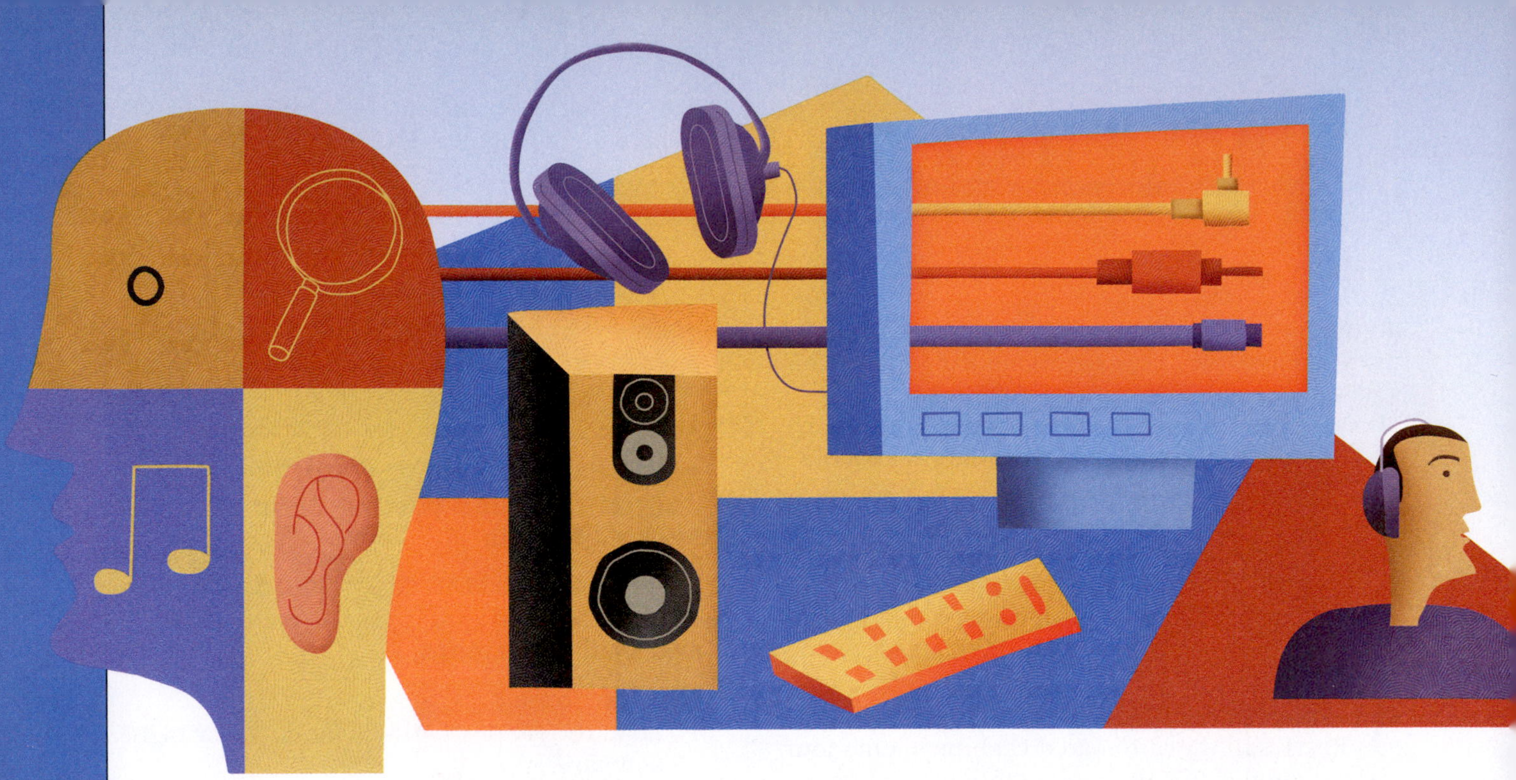

# CHAPTER 2 Recording Departmental Sales and Cash Receipts

OBJECTIVES & TERMS

***After studying Chapter 2, you will be able to:***

1. Define terms related to departmental sales and cash receipts.
2. Identify concepts and practices related to departmental sales and cash receipts.
3. Journalize and post departmental sales on account and sales returns and allowances.
4. Journalize and post departmental cash receipts.

- credit memorandum
- sales discount
- point-of-sale (POS) terminal
- terminal summary

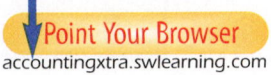

Point Your Browser
accountingxtra.swlearning.com

# • Blockbuster, Inc.

©RICK MAIMAN/BLOOMBERG NEWS/LANDOV

## BLOCKBUSTER ADAPTS TO CHANGES IN MEDIA FORMATS

Blockbuster opened its first video rental store in 1985 in Dallas, Texas. During the last two decades, the company has expanded from that single facility to approximately 8,900 company-owned and franchised stores throughout the world. Today, Blockbuster is recognized as one of the strongest entertainment brands in the world and is the leading renter of videos, DVDs, and video games. On an average day, over three million customers visit their neighborhood stores. In recent years, worldwide revenues have exceeded $5.9 billion.

Over the last 20 years, Blockbuster has wisely adapted its business model to keep pace with the changing formats in media reproduction. In 1985, movies were originally available only on videocassette tapes. Advancements in technology have prompted the company to now offer DVD and video game rentals. Other innovative management changes include opportunities for rental subscriptions, a store-within-a-store concept, movie and game trading, unlimited rentals without due dates, and the retail sale of movies and games.

In the upcoming years, Blockbuster will continue to be challenged by changing technologies and new competitors. As it has in the past, Blockbuster's managerial staff will have to remain diligent, adapt to the current business environment, and update its corporate strategies to remain competitive.

## Critical Thinking

1. List several strategies that a company like Blockbuster might use to dramatically expand sales.
2. What types of challenges might Blockbuster face in the future?

Source: www.blockbuster.com

Xtra!
Today
accountingxtra.swlearning.com

## FEDERAL DEPOSIT INSURANCE CORPORATION (FDIC)

Go to the homepage for the Federal Deposit Insurance Corporation (FDIC) (www.fdic.gov). Search for information about the FDIC.

### Instructions

1. Briefly describe the FDIC and its purpose.
2. Up to what amount are checking accounts, savings accounts, money market deposit accounts, and certificates of deposit insured by the FDIC?

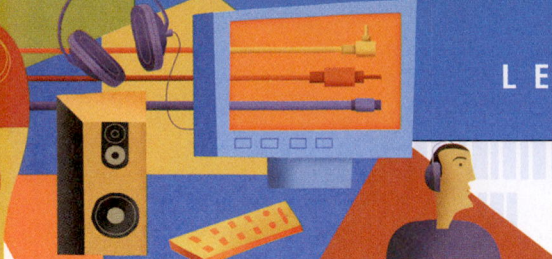

# 2-1 Departmental Sales on Account and Sales Returns and Allowances

Managers use departmental data to make decisions relating to business operations. Companies such as Zytech Media Corporation are often organized into departments, based on the different types of products or services they sell. In order to maximize business operations, Zytech Media Corporation identified two departments based on the two categories of equipment it sells—audio and video. Zytech's management team uses departmental information to analyze the profitability of each department, set annual goals, evaluate managers, and determine company bonuses.

In order to have comprehensive departmental data, however, a business should record sales and cash receipts data separately for each department. For example, gross profit from operations for each department is one type of valuable information for management decision making. Departmental gross profit from operations helps business managers decide if each department is earning an appropriate profit. If not, departmental information can help managers determine which items are causing the problem. To determine departmental gross profit from operations, the business must keep records of sales and cost of merchandise sold by department.

©GETTY IMAGES/PHOTODISC

Recording Departmental Sales and Cash Receipts

# making ethical decisions

## At What Price Safety?

Willcutt Industries assembles a safety system for passenger automobiles. This system substantially reduces severe injuries to drivers involved in accidents. In an effort to increase profits, Willcutt recently took steps to cut costs and increase production. Willcutt began using some less expensive components, reducing the production costs by $50.00 per unit. The new components increase the system's estimated failure rate from 12 to 15 failures per 10,000 accidents. Despite this increased failure rate, the company continues to exceed the government's safety standard of 20 failures per 10,000 accidents. Willcutt has reduced the unit sales price by $40.00, which has substantially increased unit sales.

The ethical decision-making model has four steps:

1. Recognize you are facing an ethical dilemma.
2. Identify the action taken or the proposed action.
3. Analyze the action.
   a. Is the action illegal?
   b. Does the action violate company or professional standards?
   c. Who is affected, and how, by the action?
4. Determine if the action is ethical.

First analyze the first two steps. Then analyze the action. If the action is either illegal or violates company or professional standards, the action should not be taken. However, it is often necessary to analyze the action further to determine whether it is ethical by determining the parties that would be affected and whether they are affected in a negative or positive way. A sample solution follows.

### Instructions

Access the *Ford Motor Company Standards of Corporate Conduct*. Using this code as a guide, use the ethical model to help determine whether the action by Willcutt Industries demonstrates ethical behavior.

### Suggested Solution for Willcutt Industries' Ethical Dilemma:

1. *Recognize you are facing an ethical dilemma.* Willcutt Industries is intentionally increasing the failure rate of its safety system. Willcutt's managers should recognize that this decision requires ethical analysis.
2. *Identify the action taken or the proposed action.* Willcutt increased the failure rate of its safety system to reduce its production costs and increase profits.
3. *Analyze the action.*
   a. *Is the action illegal?* No. The new system still exceeds government quality standards.
   b. *Does the action violate company or professional standards?* Possibly. In the Product Safety and Quality section of the *Ford Motor Company Standards of Corporate Conduct*, the code states that "the issue of cost should not preclude consideration of possible alternatives, and priorities should be based on achieving the greatest anticipated practical safety benefit." The word "practical" implies that consumers may be willing or able to pay for only a certain level of safety. Further analysis using the ethics model is necessary.
   c. *Who is affected, and how, by the action?*
4. *Determine if the action is ethical.* Answers may vary.

| Stakeholders | Negative | Positive |
| --- | --- | --- |
| Willcutt Industries | Increases the risk of litigation. | Reduces production costs and increases profits by $10.00 per unit. Increases sales, further increasing profits. |
| Stockholders | | Increases return on investment. |
| Car manufacturers | | Lower costs promote higher car sales and profits. |
| Car owners who would have been willing to pay for a car with the original safety system. | Increases slightly the chance of incurring a serious injury if involved in an accident. | Reduces the cost of a car by $40.00. |
| Car owners who can now afford a car with a safety system (although a less reliable one). | | Substantially reduces the chance of incurring a serious injury if involved in an accident. |

## DEPARTMENTAL SALES ON ACCOUNT

In Chapter 1, you learned to record purchases transactions for a departmental merchandising business. To have complete departmental data, Zytech also records all sales transactions by department. Zytech makes sales on account to individuals, business firms, and schools. It sells merchandise in two departments. The audio department sells audio equipment such as surround sound systems, speakers for home theaters, 3-way tower speakers for small stadiums and large gymnasiums, and other sound-related equipment. The video department sells video equipment including high definition televisions, plasma monitors, flat screens, and jumbo video panels.

Zytech records all departmental sales on account in a sales journal. The sales journal has one debit column—Accounts Receivable Debit. The journal also has three credit columns—Sales Tax Payable Credit and special Sales Credit columns for Audio and Video.

The Sales Tax Payable Credit column is used to record all sales tax amounts that Zytech collects. Most states require vendors to collect sales tax from their customers. The city and state in which Zytech is located have a combined sales tax rate of 8.25%. In most states, some customers are not required to pay a sales tax. Many agencies supported by local and state government and nonprofit educational institutions are exempt from paying a sales tax. For example, the Wawona School District is a tax-exempt customer of Zytech.

Zytech prepares sales invoices in duplicate for each sale on account. [CONCEPT: Objective Evidence] Each sales invoice shows the amount of merchandise sold by department. The customer receives the original copy of the sales invoice. The duplicate copy is the source document for journalizing the transaction. Zytech records all departmental sales at the time of sale, regardless of when payment is made. [CONCEPT: Realization of Revenue]

The realization-of-revenue concept states that revenue is recorded at the time goods or services are sold. A business may sell either goods or services. Cash may be received at the time of sale, or an agreement may be made to receive payment at a later date. Regardless of when the business actually receives cash, the business records the sale amount in the accounting records at the time of sale. For example, a business sells office furniture for $2,000.00. The business agrees to an initial payment of $400.00 with the remaining balance to be divided in four monthly payments of $400.00 each. The business records the full $2,000.00 of revenue at the time of sale, even though $1,600.00 will be paid later.

### SMALL BUSINESS SPOTLIGHT

Most small businesses have the same kind of training needs as huge corporations. New employees, seasoned professionals, and executives all benefit from training throughout their careers. This includes everything from job-specific training to professional enrichment. While the needs may be the same, the budget and staffing might be quite different. Small businesses are finding solutions for their training needs within their own company and through outside sources. Small businesses frequently look to community colleges, trade groups, and professional associations for high-quality instruction. In many cases, small businesses are partnering with vendors for some of their training needs.

©GETTY IMAGES/PHOTODISC

**1.** Write the date.  **2.** Write the customer name.  **3.** Write the sales invoice number.

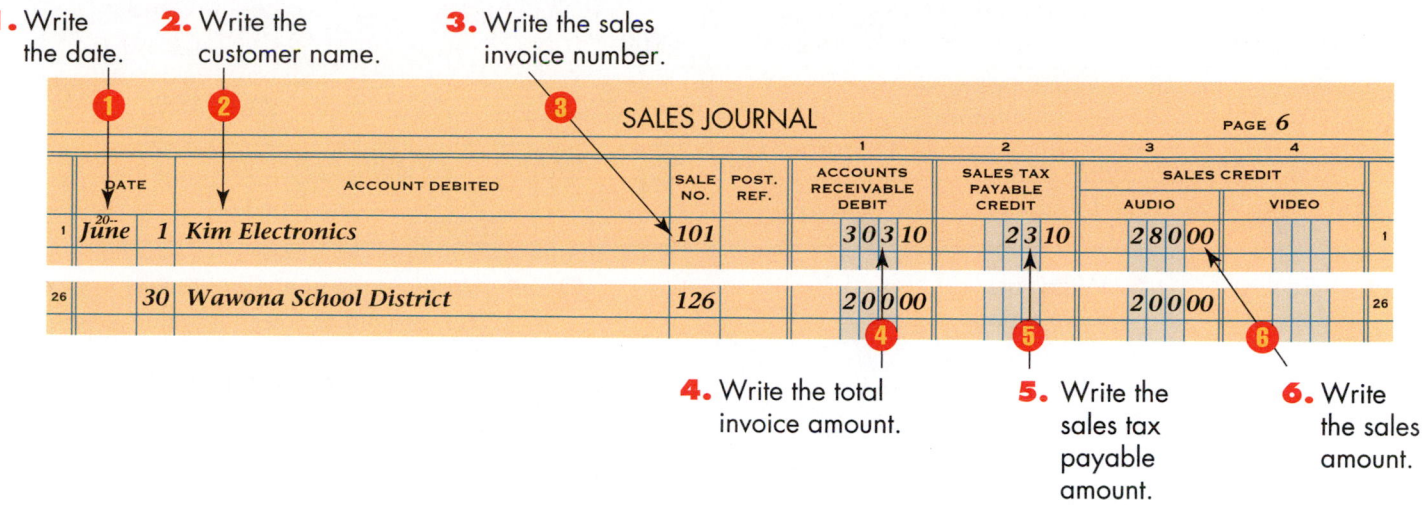

| | DATE | ACCOUNT DEBITED | SALE NO. | POST. REF. | ACCOUNTS RECEIVABLE DEBIT | SALES TAX PAYABLE CREDIT | SALES CREDIT AUDIO | VIDEO | |
|---|---|---|---|---|---|---|---|---|---|
| 1 | 20-- June 1 | Kim Electronics | 101 | | 303 10 | 23 10 | 280 00 | | 1 |
| 26 | 30 | Wawona School District | 126 | | 200 00 | | 200 00 | | 26 |

SALES JOURNAL  PAGE 6

**4.** Write the total invoice amount.  **5.** Write the sales tax payable amount.  **6.** Write the sales amount.

---

**June 1. Sold audio equipment on account to Kim Electronics, $280.00, plus sales tax, $23.10; total, $303.10. Sales Invoice No. 101.**

This transaction is recorded in the departmental sales journal. The source document for this transaction is a sales invoice. [CONCEPT: Objective Evidence]

In the general ledger, Accounts Receivable is increased by a $303.10 debit. The amount that the customer owes represents the price of the merchandise plus the sales tax. All sales tax received is later remitted to the state in which Zytech is located. Therefore, the liability account Sales Tax Payable is increased by a $23.10 credit. Sales—Audio is increased by a $280.00 credit. In the accounts receivable ledger, Kim Electronics is increased by a $303.10 debit.

The transaction on line 26 of the sales journal shows a transaction for a tax-exempt customer.

Since the Wawona School District is an educational institution, it is not required by the state to pay sales tax.

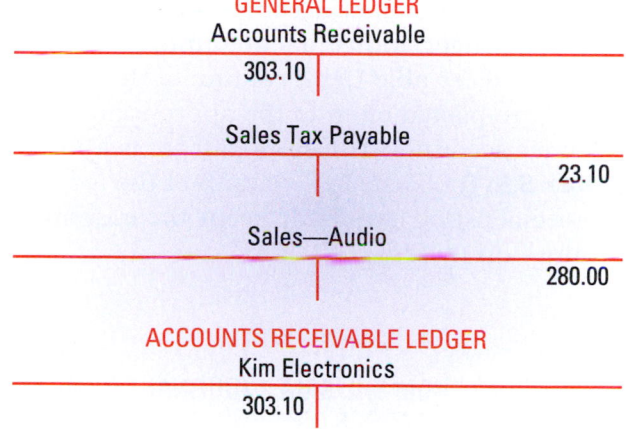

GENERAL LEDGER

Accounts Receivable

| 303.10 | |

Sales Tax Payable

| | 23.10 |

Sales—Audio

| | 280.00 |

ACCOUNTS RECEIVABLE LEDGER

Kim Electronics

| 303.10 | |

**FYI** FOR YOUR INFORMATION

All businesses and nonprofit entities that have employees must have a federal tax identification number. This number is used in much the same way that individuals use their social security numbers. The Internal Revenue Service identifies entities that are exempt from federal income tax by their federal identification numbers. States may require vendors to keep a written record of the federal tax identification numbers of their tax-exempt customers.

**STEPS** STEPS • STEPS • STEPS • STEPS • STEPS

### RECORDING THE SALE IN THE SALES JOURNAL

1. Write the date, *20--, June 1,* in the Date column.

2. Write the customer name, *Kim Electronics,* in the Account Debited column.

3. Write the sales invoice number, *101,* in the Sale No. column.

4. Write the total invoice amount, *$303.10,* in the Accounts Receivable Debit column.

5. Write the credit amount, *$23.10,* in the Sales Tax Payable Credit column.

6. Write the credit amount, *$280.00,* in the Sales Credit Audio column.

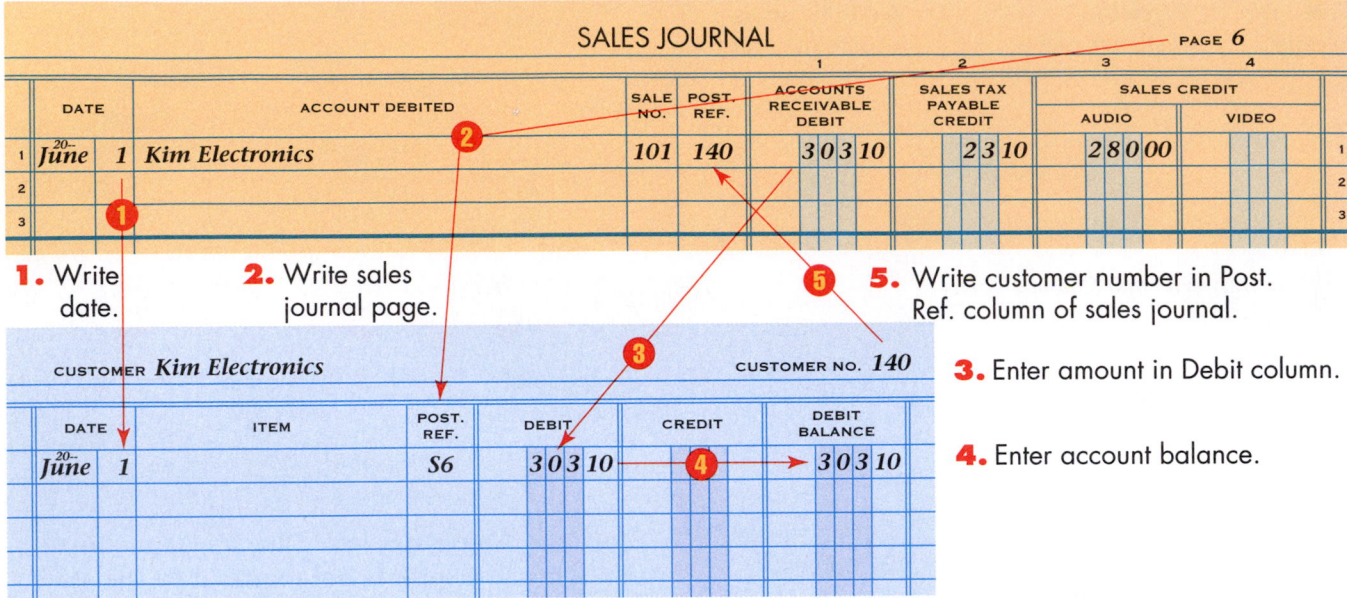

**SALES JOURNAL** — PAGE 6

| | DATE | ACCOUNT DEBITED | SALE NO. | POST. REF. | 1 ACCOUNTS RECEIVABLE DEBIT | 2 SALES TAX PAYABLE CREDIT | 3 SALES CREDIT AUDIO | 4 SALES CREDIT VIDEO | |
|---|---|---|---|---|---|---|---|---|---|
| 1 | 20-- June 1 | Kim Electronics | 101 | 140 | 303 10 | 23 10 | 280 00 | | 1 |
| 2 | | | | | | | | | 2 |
| 3 | | | | | | | | | 3 |

**1.** Write date.  **2.** Write sales journal page.  **5.** Write customer number in Post. Ref. column of sales journal.

CUSTOMER **Kim Electronics** — CUSTOMER NO. **140**

| DATE | ITEM | POST. REF. | DEBIT | CREDIT | DEBIT BALANCE |
|---|---|---|---|---|---|
| 20-- June 1 | | S6 | 303 10 | | 303 10 |

**3.** Enter amount in Debit column.

**4.** Enter account balance.

Zytech keeps customer accounts in an accounts receivable ledger. Individual amounts in the Accounts Receivable Debit column of the sales journal are posted often to the appropriate customer accounts. The sales journal is abbreviated as *S* in the Post. Ref. column of the ledger accounts. Posting frequently keeps the customers' accounts up to date.

**FYI** FOR YOUR INFORMATION

Sales taxes collected by businesses must be sent to the appropriate governmental agency. In many states, sales taxes are paid monthly. The payment is accompanied by a form that provides information such as total sales, sales tax collected, and sales exempt from sales tax.

**STEPS** • STEPS • STEPS • STEPS • STEPS • STEPS • STEPS • STEPS • STEPS • STEPS

### POSTING FROM THE SALES JOURNAL TO THE ACCOUNTS RECEIVABLE LEDGER

1. Write the date, *20--, June 1,* in the account's Date column.

2. Write *S6* in the Post. Ref. column of the subsidiary ledger account to indicate that the posting came from page 6 of the sales journal.

3. Write the debit amount, *$303.10,* in the account's Debit column. This is the total amount due from the customer. It includes the price of the audio equipment and the sales tax.

4. Write the new account balance in the Debit Balance column. When the customer has an existing balance, add the amount in the Debit column to the previous balance in the Debit Balance column. *Kim Electronics* had no account balance before this transaction.

5. Write the customer number, *140,* in the Post. Ref. column of the sales journal to show that posting is completed for this line.

©GETTY IMAGES/PHOTODISC

Recording Departmental Sales and Cash Receipts

## SALES JOURNAL                                                                PAGE 6

| | DATE | | ACCOUNT DEBITED | SALE NO. | POST. REF. | ACCOUNTS RECEIVABLE DEBIT 1 | SALES TAX PAYABLE CREDIT 2 | SALES CREDIT AUDIO 3 | SALES CREDIT VIDEO 4 | |
|---|---|---|---|---|---|---|---|---|---|---|
| 1 | June | 1 | Kim Electronics | 101 | 140 | 303 10 | 23 10 | 280 00 | | 1 |
| 2 | | 1 | Jason Campari | 102 | 110 | 2 424 80 | 184 80 | | 2 240 00 | 2 |
| 3 | | 1 | DTS Systems | 103 | 120 | 930 95 | 70 95 | | 860 00 | 3 |
| 25 | | 30 | DTS Systems | 125 | 120 | 270 63 | 20 63 | 250 00 | | 25 |
| 26 | | 30 | Wawona Schools | 126 | 170 | 200 00 | | | 200 00 | 26 |
| 27 | | 30 | Totals | | | 19 836 50 | 1 405 55 | 8 990 65 | 9 440 30 | 27 |
| 28 | | | | | | (1205) | (2230) | (4105) | (4205) | 28 |

**1.** Write date.

**2.** Write sales journal page.

**5.** Write general ledger account number in parentheses.

ACCOUNT *Accounts Receivable*                                          ACCOUNT NO. *1205*

| DATE | | ITEM | POST. REF. | DEBIT | CREDIT | BALANCE DEBIT | BALANCE CREDIT |
|---|---|---|---|---|---|---|---|
| June | 1 | Balance | ✓ | | | 18 182 20 | |
| | 30 | | S6 | 19 836 50 | | 38 018 70 | |

**3.** Enter debit amount.

**4.** Enter account balance.

The sales journal is proved and ruled at the end of each month. Each amount column total is posted to the general ledger account named in the column heading.

STEPS • STEPS • STEPS • STEPS • STEPS • STEPS • STEPS • STEPS • STEPS • STEPS

**STEPS**

### POSTING A COLUMN TOTAL FROM THE SALES JOURNAL TO THE GENERAL LEDGER

**1** Write the date, *30,* in the account's Date column.

**2** Write *S6* in the Post. Ref. column of the ledger account to indicate that the posting came from page 6 of the sales journal.

**3** Write the column total, *$19,836.50,* in the Debit column of the ledger account.

**4** Add the amount in the Debit column, $19,836.50, to the previous balance of $18,182.20 to arrive at a new accounts receivable balance of *$38,018.70.*

**5** Write the general ledger account number, *1205,* in parentheses immediately below the column total in the sales journal to show that the amount has been posted.

**REMEMBER**   Proving a journal means verifying that the total debits equal the total credits. To prove a journal:
1. Add each amount column and write the total.
2. Add the column totals for all debit columns.
3. Add the column totals for all credit columns.
4. Verify that total debits and total credits are equal. Once a journal is proved, it should be ruled.

# JOURNALIZING SALES RETURNS AND ALLOWANCES

1. Write date.  2. Enter accounts to be debited.  3. Record credit memorandum number.  4. Write debit amounts.

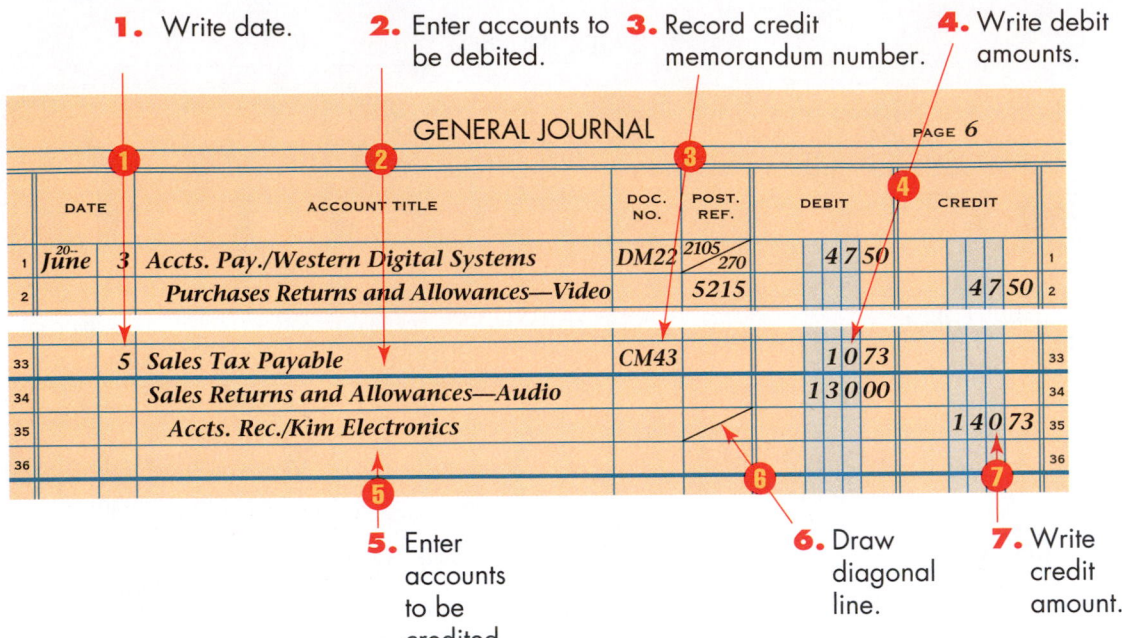

5. Enter accounts to be credited.  6. Draw diagonal line.  7. Write credit amount.

Zytech records all sales returns and allowances in a general journal. Zytech's general journal is shown above.

An account that reduces a related account on a financial statement is known as a *contra account*. An account showing deductions from a sales account is a contra revenue account. Sales Returns and Allowances—Audio is a contra revenue account. Sales returns and allowances are kept in a separate account and not deducted directly from the sales account. This procedure helps the business see what proportion of the merchandise sold was returned by customers. [*CONCEPT: Adequate Disclosure*]

> **June 5.** Granted credit to Kim Electronics for audio equipment returned, $130.00, plus sales tax, $10.73, from Sales Invoice No. 101; total, $140.73. Credit Memorandum No. 43.

The source document prepared by the vendor showing the amount deducted for returns and allowances is called a **credit memorandum**. [*CONCEPT: Objective Evidence*]

When a sales return is accepted or an allowance is granted, the sales tax amount is no longer due. In the general ledger, Sales Tax Payable is decreased by a $10.73 debit. Sales Returns and Allowances—Audio is increased by a $130.00 debit. Accounts Receivable is decreased by a $140.73 credit. In the accounts receivable ledger, Kim Electronics is decreased by a $140.73 credit.

Details of the transaction involving Credit Memorandum No. 43 are recorded on lines 33, 34, and 35 of the general journal shown above.

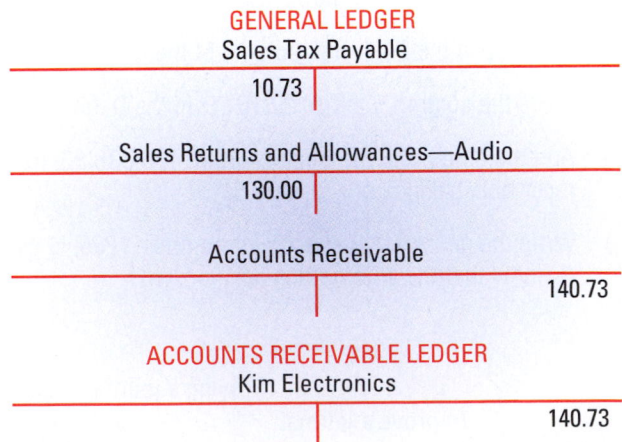

**REMEMBER** A contra account has a normal balance that is opposite its related account. For example, *Sales—Audio* has a normal credit balance. Therefore, *Sales Returns and Allowances—Audio* has a normal debit balance.

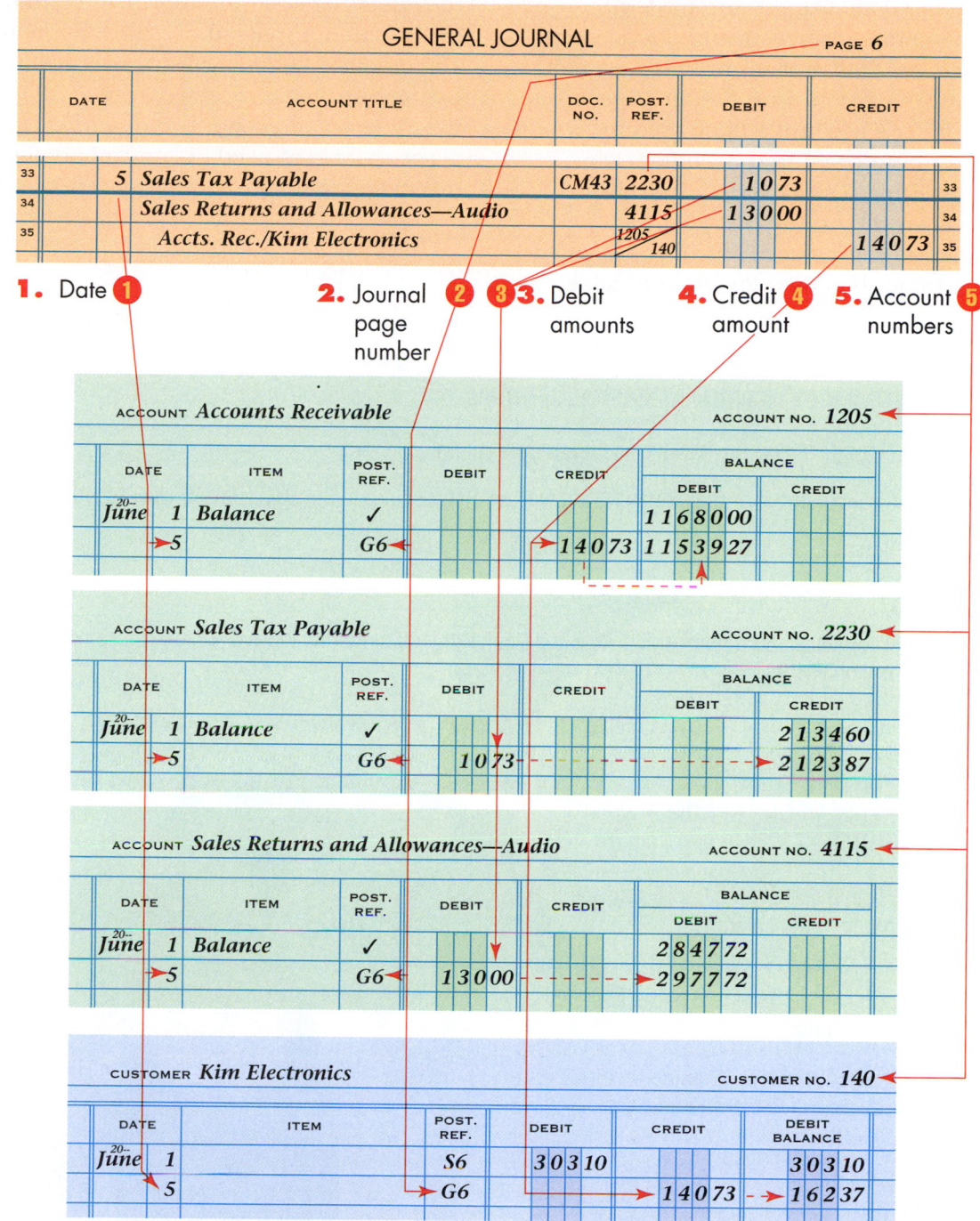

(Steps for posting from a general journal are shown on page 42.)

Sales returns and allowances are posted frequently to a customer's account in the accounts receivable ledger. This procedure keeps an individual customer's account up to date. Specifically, a customer's account will be credited to reduce the amount owed to the vendor. The posting of the June 5 sales return from Kim Electronics is shown on the previous page.

When a sales return or allowance is granted after the customer has paid for the purchase, the customer account after posting may have a credit balance instead of a normal debit balance. The credit balance, a contra balance, reduces the amount to be received from a customer for future sales on account. When a three-column account form is used, a contra balance is shown by enclosing the amount in parentheses.

STEPS • STEPS • STEPS • STEPS • STEPS • STEPS • STEPS • STEPS • STEPS • STEPS

### STEPS   POSTING DEBIT AMOUNTS FROM A GENERAL JOURNAL

1. Write the date, *5,* in the Sales Tax Payable account's Date column.

2. Write *G* and the page number of the journal, *6,* in the Post. Ref. column of the *Sales Tax Payable* account.

3. Write the debit amount, *$10.73,* in the Sales Tax Payable Debit column.

4. Calculate and write the new balance, *$2,123.87.*

5. Record the appropriate account number, *2230,* in the Post. Ref. column of the journal. Follow the same steps for the debit entry on line 34.

STEPS • STEPS • STEPS • STEPS

### STEPS   POSTING A CREDIT AMOUNT FROM A GENERAL JOURNAL

1. Write the date, *5,* in the Accounts Receivable and Kim Electronics accounts' Date columns.

2. Write *G* and the page number of the journal, *6,* in the Post. Ref. columns of the *Accounts Receivable* and *Kim Electronics* accounts.

3. Write the credit amount, *$140.73,* in the Credit columns of the *Accounts Receivable* and *Kim Electronics* accounts.

4. Calculate and write the new balances: *$11,539.27* in the *Accounts Receivable* account and *$162.37* in the *Kim Electronics* account.

5. Record the appropriate account numbers in the Post. Ref. column of the general journal. Write the account number for *Accounts Receivable, 1205,* to the left of the diagonal line in the Post Ref. column of the general journal. Write the customer number for *Kim Electronics, 140,* to the right of the diagonal line.

©GETTY IMAGES/PHOTODISC

## term review

credit memorandum

## audit your understanding

1. What is a tax-exempt customer? Give an example.
2. For what purpose is a credit memorandum issued?

## work together 2-1

**Journalizing and posting departmental sales on account and sales returns and allowances**

The sales journal, general journal, and partial accounts receivable and general ledgers for Manhattan Beach Swimwear are provided in the *Working Papers*. Manhattan Beach has two departments: Swimwear and Accessories. Your instructor will guide you through the following examples.

1. Journalize each of the following sales on account and sales returns and allowances. The sales tax rate is 6%. Source documents are abbreviated as follows: sales invoice, S; credit memorandum, CM.

**Transactions:**

Sept. 1. Sold a bathing suit to Emily Branford for $40.00, plus sales tax. S12.
10. Sold three beach mats to Roger Minkow for $75.00, plus sales tax. S13.
14. Sold bathing suits to Oak Grove High School Swim Team for $310.00. No sales tax. S14.
15. Granted credit to Roger Minkow for one beach mat returned, $25.00, plus sales tax from sales invoice S13. Issued CM23.
    **Posting.** Post the items that are to be posted individually from the sales journal and then from the general journal.
18. Sold beach towel to Sara Nunez for $15.00, plus sales tax. S15.
24. Sold a beach umbrella to Emily Branford for $70.00, plus sales tax. S16.
30. Granted credit to Sara Nunez as an allowance for a defective beach towel, $15.00, plus sales tax from sales invoice S15. Issued CM24.
    **Posting.** Post the items that are to be posted individually from the sales journal and then from the general journal.

2. Prove and rule the sales journal. Post the totals to the general ledger.

## on your own 2-1

**Journalizing and posting departmental sales on account and sales returns and allowances**

The sales journal, general journal, and partial accounts receivable and partial general ledgers for Office Outfitters are provided in the *Working Papers*. Office Outfitters has two departments: Equipment and Supplies. Work this problem independently.

1. Journalize each of the following sales on account and sales returns. The sales tax rate is 6%. Source documents are abbreviated as follows: sales invoice, S; credit memorandum, CM.

**Transactions:**

Oct. 2. Sold a laser printer to Libby Products Co. for $515.00, plus sales tax. S410.
6. Sold office supplies to United Charities (tax exempt) for $410.00. S411.
10. Sold office copiers to Dunford, Inc., for $3,200.00, plus sales tax. S412.
13. Granted credit to Dunford, Inc., for one copier returned, $800.00, plus sales tax from sales invoice S412. Issued CM127.
    **Posting.** Post the items that are to be posted individually from the sales journal and then from the general journal.
17. Sold office supplies to Professional Services Corporation for $602.00, plus sales tax. S413.
22. Sold laminating equipment to Libby Products Co. for $2,650.00, plus sales tax. S414.
28. Granted credit to Professional Services Corp. as an allowance for defective supplies, $55.00, plus sales tax from sales invoice S413. Issued CM128.
    **Posting.** Post the items that are to be posted individually from the sales journal and then from the general journal.

2. Prove and rule the sales journal. Post the totals to the general ledger.

# 2-2 Journalizing and Posting Cash Receipts

## DEPARTMENTAL CASH RECEIPTS

Zytech keeps a record of all cash receipts. The sources of most cash receipts are (1) cash received from customer payments on account and (2) cash and credit card sales.

The amount of cash received when payment is made within a discount period is calculated as follows.

| Sales Amount | + | 8.25% Sales Tax | = | Total Invoice Amount |
|---|---|---|---|---|
| $1,700.00 | + | $140.25 | = | $1,840.25 |

*Terms: 2/10, n/30*
*Invoice paid within 10 days:*

| Invoice Amount | × | Discount Rate | = | Sales Discount |
|---|---|---|---|---|
| $1,840.25 | × | 2% | = | $36.81 |

| Total Invoice Amount | − | 2% Sales Discount | = | Amount Due in 10 Days |
|---|---|---|---|---|
| $1,840.25 | − | $36.81 | = | $1,803.44 |

## CASH RECEIPTS ON ACCOUNT

Each customer is expected to pay the amount due within the credit terms agreed upon. To encourage early payment, a business may grant a deduction on the invoice amount. A deduction that a vendor allows on the invoice amount to encourage prompt payment is known as a *cash discount*. A cash discount on sales is called a **sales discount**. Zytech sells on account using terms 2/10, n/30. These terms mean that a 2% sales discount may be deducted if sales on account are paid within 10 days of the invoice date (2/10). All sales on account must be paid within 30 days of the invoice date (n/30).

When a sale is made on account, the amount debited to Accounts Receivable reflects the total amount owed by the customer, including sales tax. Sales is credited only for the pre-tax selling price. An additional credit must be made to Sales

Tax Payable for the sales tax liability on the total sales invoice amount. Zytech prepares a receipt as the source document for cash received on account. [CONCEPT: Objective Evidence]

**FYI** FOR YOUR INFORMATION

When you make a purchase in a store, you pay the sales tax rate applicable at the location of the store. You also normally pay the state sales tax on mail order purchases if you live in the same state as the mail-order company. State governments are concerned about the enormous growth in Internet sales. Legislation has been proposed to require buyers to pay state sales tax on Internet and mail-order purchases if they live in a state that has adopted the Streamlined Sales and Use Tax Agreement.

Recording Departmental Sales and Cash Receipts

## JOURNALIZING A CASH RECEIPT WITH A SALES DISCOUNT

**1.** Write the date.  **2.** Write the customer name.  **3.** Record the receipt number.  **4.** Write the accounts receivable credit amount.  **5.** Write the sales discount debit amount.

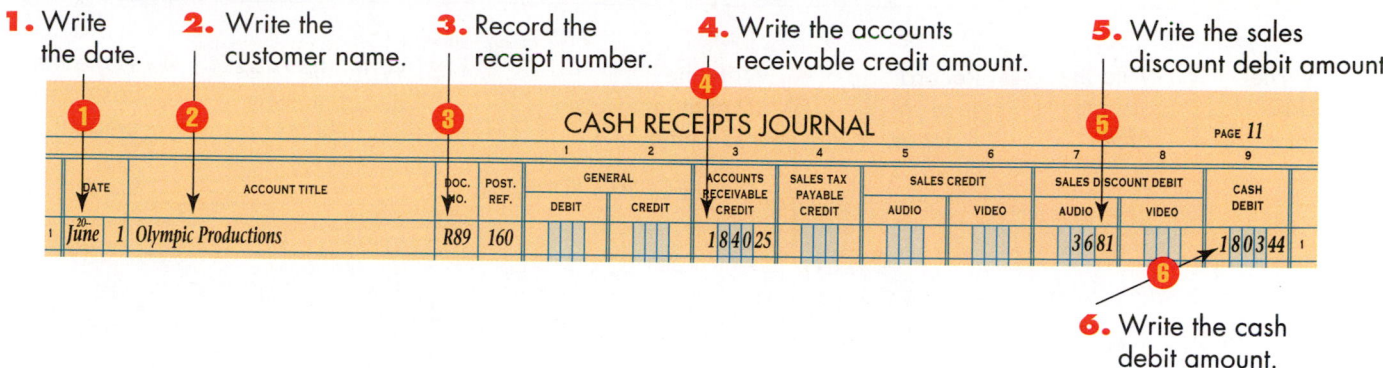

**6.** Write the cash debit amount.

Zytech records all cash receipts in a cash receipts journal. The journal has five credit columns—General Credit, Accounts Receivable Credit, Sales Tax Payable Credit, Sales Credit Audio, and Sales Credit Video. The journal also has four debit columns—General Debit, Sales Discount Debit—Audio, Sales Discount Debit—Video, and Cash Debit.

---

*June 1. Received cash on account from Olympic Productions, $1,803.44, covering Sales Invoice No. 96 for audio equipment for $1,840.25 ($1,700.00 plus sales tax, $140.25), less 2% discount, $36.81. Receipt No. 89.*

---

Cash is increased by a $1,803.44 debit. The contra revenue account, Sales Discount—Audio, is increased by a $36.81 debit. Using a separate account to record discounts allows the business to determine the proportion of available discounts that customers actually take. Accounts Receivable is decreased by a $1,840.25 credit. In the accounts receivable ledger, Olympic Productions is decreased by a $1,840.25 credit.

The customer's payment on account is shown above. Use the following steps to make the journal entry.

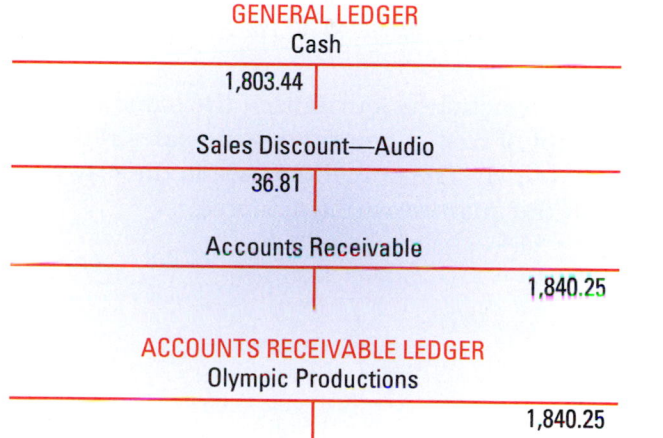

STEPS • STEPS • STEPS • STEPS • STEPS • STEPS • STEPS • STEPS • STEPS •

**RECORDING THE RECEIPT OF CASH WHEN THE SALES DISCOUNT IS TAKEN**

**1** Write the date, *20--, June 1,* in the Date column.

**2** Write the customer name, *Olympic Productions,* in the Account Title column.

**3** Record the document number, *R89,* in the Doc. No. column.

**4** Write the credit amount, *$1,840.25,* in the Accounts Receivable Credit column.

**5** Write the debit amount, *$36.81,* in the Sales Discount Debit Audio column.

**6** Write the debit amount, *$1,803.44,* in the Cash Debit column.

## JOURNALIZING A CASH RECEIPT WITH A SALES RETURN AND A SALES DISCOUNT

**1.** Write date.

**2.** Write the customer name.

**3.** Record receipt number.

**4.** Write the account receivable credit amount.

**5.** Write the sales discount debit amount.

**6.** Write the cash debit amount.

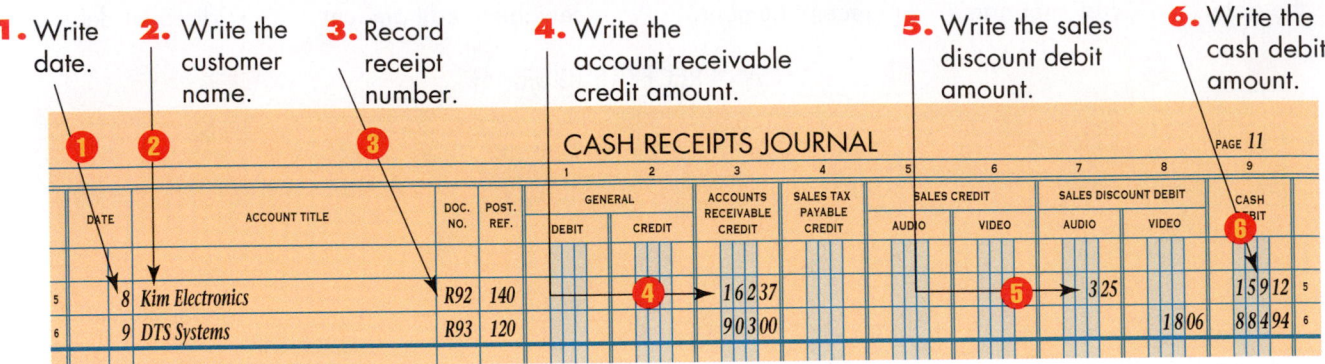

June 8. Received cash on account from Kim Electronics, $159.12, covering Sales Invoice No. 101 for $303.10 ($280.00 plus sales tax, $23.10), less Credit Memorandum No. 43 for $140.73 ($130.00 plus sales tax, $10.73), less 2% discount, $3.25. Receipt No. 92.

This transaction is journalized the same way as a receipt of cash when there is no sales return or allowance. The only difference is the way in which the amounts are calculated.

Sales discounts are calculated on the amount owed at the time the invoice is paid. When a customer takes a discount after being granted a return or an allowance, the amount of the return or allowance must be deducted from the amount of the original sale before the discount can be calculated. To calculate the amount of cash received, (1) find the sales discount amount and (2) determine the amount of cash to be received. The calculation for each of these items is shown below.

|  |  | Amount of Sale | + | Sales Tax | = | Total Receivable |
|---|---|---|---|---|---|---|
|  | Original Sales Invoice Amount (S101) | $280.00 | + | $23.10 | = | $303.10 |
| less | Sales Return (CM43) | 130.00 | + | 10.73 | = | 140.73 |
| equals | Sales Invoice Amount after Return | $150.00 | + | $12.37 | = | $162.37 |

| Sales Invoice Amount after Return | × | Sales Discount Rate | = | Sales Discount |
|---|---|---|---|---|
| $162.37 | × | 2% | = | $3.25 |

**1.** Write the date.

**3.** Record terminal summary number.

**7.** Enter cash debit amount.

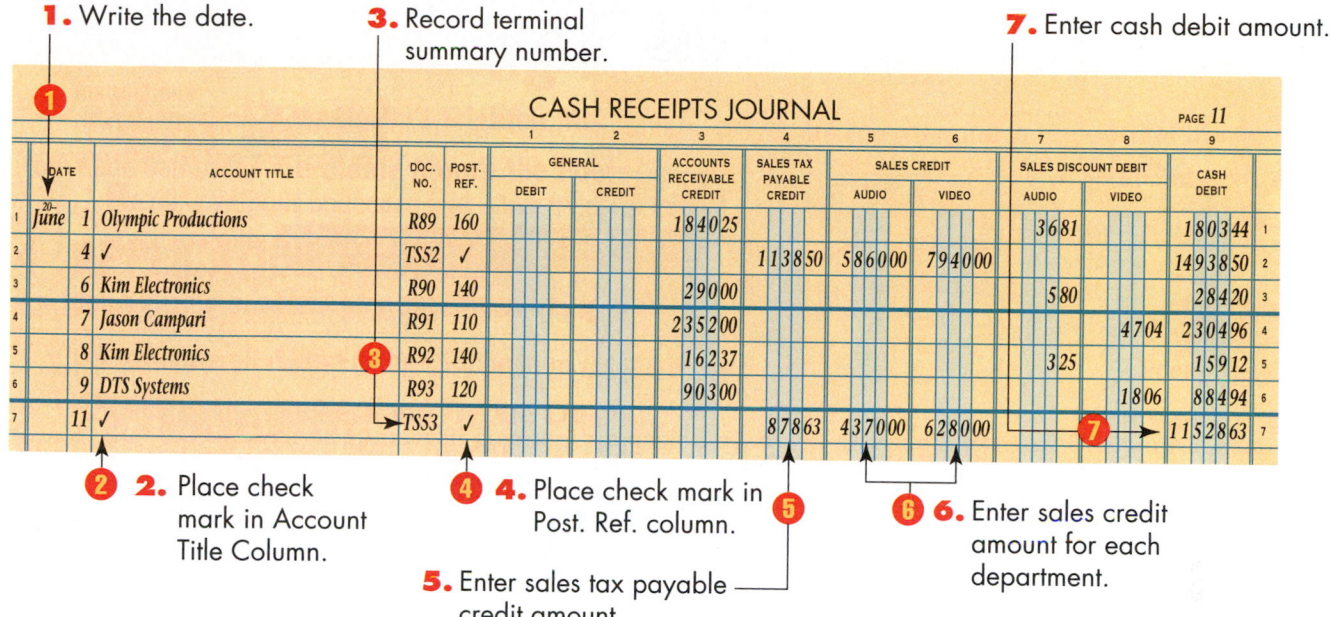

CASH RECEIPTS JOURNAL — PAGE 11

| DATE | ACCOUNT TITLE | DOC. NO. | POST. REF. | GENERAL DEBIT | GENERAL CREDIT | ACCOUNTS RECEIVABLE CREDIT | SALES TAX PAYABLE CREDIT | SALES CREDIT AUDIO | SALES CREDIT VIDEO | SALES DISCOUNT DEBIT AUDIO | SALES DISCOUNT DEBIT VIDEO | CASH DEBIT |
|---|---|---|---|---|---|---|---|---|---|---|---|---|
| June 1 | Olympic Productions | R89 | 160 | | | 1 840 25 | | | | 36 81 | | 1 803 44 |
| 4 | ✓ | TS52 | ✓ | | | | 1 138 50 | 5 860 00 | 7 940 00 | | | 14 938 50 |
| 6 | Kim Electronics | R90 | 140 | | | 290 00 | | | | | 5 80 | 284 20 |
| 7 | Jason Campari | R91 | 110 | | | 2 352 00 | | | | | 47 04 | 2 304 96 |
| 8 | Kim Electronics | R92 | 140 | | | 162 37 | | | | 3 25 | | 159 12 |
| 9 | DTS Systems | R93 | 120 | | | 903 00 | | | | | 18 06 | 884 94 |
| 11 | ✓ | TS53 | ✓ | | | | 878 63 | 4 370 00 | 6 280 00 | | | 11 528 63 |

**2.** Place check mark in Account Title Column.

**4.** Place check mark in Post. Ref. column.

**5.** Enter sales tax payable credit amount.

**6.** Enter sales credit amount for each department.

Zytech accepts cash or credit cards from its customers. An independent company or bank hired by Zytech to process credit card sales automatically deposits the daily total of credit card sales to Zytech's bank account. Because credit card sales result in an immediate increase in the bank account balance, credit card sales and cash sales are recorded together in the cash receipts journal.

Both cash and credit card sales are entered into a modern version of a cash register. A computer used to collect, store, and report all the information of a sales transaction is called a **point-of-sale (POS) terminal**. The POS terminal prints a receipt for the customer and internally accumulates data about total sales. At the end of each week, Zytech instructs the POS terminal to print a report of all cash and credit card sales. The report that summarizes the cash and credit card sales of a point-of-sale terminal is called a **terminal summary**. The terminal summary is identified with a *TS* and a sequential number. Zytech uses the terminal summary as the source document for cash and credit card sales. [*CONCEPT: Objective Evidence*]

*June 11. Recorded cash and credit card sales, audio equipment, $4,370.00; video equipment, $6,280.00; plus sales tax, $878.63; total, $11,528.63. Terminal Summary No. 53.*

Cash increases by a $11,528.63 debit. Sales Tax Payable increases by a $878.63 credit. Sales—Audio is increased by a $4,370.00 credit, and Sales—Video increases by a $6,280.00 credit.

The details of Terminal Summary No. 53 are recorded on line 7 of the cash receipts journal. The steps needed to record this transaction are similar to those required to record other cash receipts transactions.

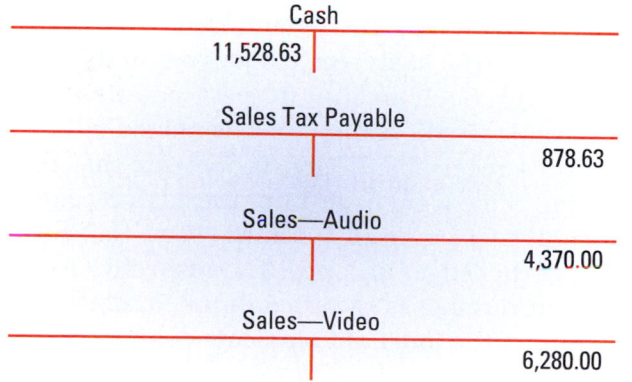

| Cash | |
|---|---|
| 11,528.63 | |

| Sales Tax Payable | |
|---|---|
| | 878.63 |

| Sales—Audio | |
|---|---|
| | 4,370.00 |

| Sales—Video | |
|---|---|
| | 6,280.00 |

**FYI** FOR YOUR INFORMATION

Even though a business may print a terminal summary and journalize cash and credit card sales weekly, it would normally deposit excess cash daily as a security measure.

## CASH RECEIPTS JOURNAL — PAGE 11

| | DATE | ACCOUNT TITLE | DOC. NO. | POST. REF. | GENERAL DEBIT | GENERAL CREDIT | ACCOUNTS RECEIVABLE CREDIT | SALES TAX PAYABLE CREDIT | SALES CREDIT AUDIO | SALES CREDIT VIDEO | SALES DISCOUNT DEBIT AUDIO | SALES DISCOUNT DEBIT VIDEO | CASH DEBIT | |
|---|---|---|---|---|---|---|---|---|---|---|---|---|---|---|
| 1 | 20-- June 1 | Olympic Productions | R89 | 160 | | | 1840 25 | | | | 36 81 | | 1803 44 | 1 |
| 2 | 4 | ✓ | TS52 | ✓ | | | | 1138 50 | 5860 00 | 7940 00 | | | 14938 50 | 2 |
| 3 | 6 | Kim Electronics | R90 | 140 | | | 290 00 | | | | 5 80 | | 284 20 | 3 |
| 4 | 7 | Jason Campari | R91 | 110 | | | 2352 00 | | | | | 47 04 | 2304 96 | 4 |
| 5 | 8 | Kim Electronics | R92 | 140 | | | 162 37 | | | | 3 25 | | 159 12 | 5 |
| 6 | 9 | DTS Systems | R93 | 120 | | | 903 00 | | | | | 18 06 | 884 94 | 6 |
| 7 | 11 | ✓ | TS53 | ✓ | | | | 878 63 | 4370 00 | 6280 00 | | | 11528 63 | 7 |

## CASH RECEIPTS JOURNAL — PAGE 12

| | DATE | ACCOUNT TITLE | DOC. NO. | POST. REF. | GENERAL DEBIT | GENERAL CREDIT | ACCOUNTS RECEIVABLE CREDIT | SALES TAX PAYABLE CREDIT | SALES CREDIT AUDIO | SALES CREDIT VIDEO | SALES DISCOUNT DEBIT AUDIO | SALES DISCOUNT DEBIT VIDEO | CASH DEBIT | |
|---|---|---|---|---|---|---|---|---|---|---|---|---|---|---|
| 2 | 30 | Wawona School District | R108 | 170 | | | 399 00 | | | | 7 98 | | 391 02 | 2 |
| 3 | 30 | ✓ | TS56 | ✓ | | | | 885 00 | 5620 00 | 6130 00 | | | 12635 00 | 3 |
| 4 | 30 | Totals | | | | | 19706 10 | 3821 50 | 24520 00 | 27910 00 | 147 00 | 169 00 | 75641 60 | 4 |
| 5 | | | | | (1205) | (2230) | (4105) | (4205) | (4110) | (4210) | (1105) | | | 5 |

**1.** Individual amounts are posted to the accounts receivable ledger.

**2.** Column totals are posted to the account named in the column heading.

Individual amounts are posted often from the cash receipts journal. Frequent postings are required to keep the customers' accounts up to date. During the month, Zytech posts each amount written in the General Debit and Credit columns of the cash receipts journal to the general ledger. Each amount in the Accounts Receivable Credit column is also posted to the accounts receivable ledger. To indicate that the posting came from page 11 of the cash receipts journal, *CR11* is recorded in the Post. Ref. column of the ledger account. The respective ledger account number is recorded in the Post. Ref. column of the journal to indicate completion of posting.

Transactions involving entries in the General Debit and Credit columns of a cash receipts journal are described in Chapter 10.

At the end of the month, the cash receipts journal is proved and ruled. Totals of the special amount columns are then posted to their respective accounts in the general ledger. The general ledger account number is written in parentheses immediately below the total. A check mark is placed in parentheses below the totals of the General Debit and Credit columns to show that the totals are not posted. Zytech's departmental cash receipts journal, page 12, after all posting has been completed, is shown above.

**FYI** FOR YOUR INFORMATION

Many businesses use automated equipment to verify credit card transactions. This verification process protects consumers and merchants and helps prevent fraud.

# ORDER OF POSTING FROM JOURNALS

Businesses post transactions affecting vendor and customer accounts often during the month so that balances of subsidiary ledger accounts are kept up to date. General ledger account balances are needed only when financial statements are prepared. Therefore, posting to general ledger accounts may be done less frequently than posting to subsidiary ledgers. However, all transactions, including special amount column totals, must be posted at the end of a fiscal period. The recommended order in which to post journals is listed as follows.

1. Sales journal
2. Purchases journal
3. General journal
4. Cash receipts journal
5. Cash payments journal

This posting order generally places the debits and credits in the accounts in the order that the transactions occurred.

©GETTY IMAGES/PHOTODISC

## global perspective

GLOBAL PERSPECTIVE • GLOBAL PERSPECTIVE • GLOBAL PERSPECTIV

### International Terms of Sale

Terms of sale for international business are very similar to those used in the United States. However, it is important to make sure that all parties understand the terms before business is complete.

Selected international terms of sale are described below:

*C.I.F. (Cost, Insurance, Freight) to the named port of import.* Under this method, the seller quotes a price for the goods. The price includes insurance, all transportation, and all miscellaneous charges to the point of unloading the goods from the vessel.

*F.A.S. (Free AlongSide a ship at the named U.S. port of export).* Under this term, the seller quotes a price for goods that includes charges for delivery of the goods alongside a vessel at the port. The seller handles the cost of the unloading and wharf charges. All charges once goods are delivered to the vessel, including loading, ocean transportation, and insurance, are the responsibility of the buyer.

*F.O.B. VESSEL (named port of export).* The seller quotes a price that includes all expenses up to, and including, delivery of goods upon an overseas vessel that is provided by or for the buyer. Once the goods are loaded "on board," all subsequent charges are the sole responsibility of the buyer.

*EX ("EX" means "from" the named point of origin) such as EX FACTORY.* Under this term, the price quoted applies only at the point of origin, and the seller agrees to place the goods at the disposal of the buyer at the specified place on the date or within the period fixed. All other charges are the responsibility of the buyer.

---

## terms review

sales discount
point-of-sale (POS) terminal
terminal summary

## audit your understanding

1. What does 2/10, n/30 mean?
2. Why are credit card sales and cash sales recorded together in the sales journal?

## work together 2-2

### Journalizing and posting departmental cash receipts

The cash receipts journal, partial accounts receivable ledger, and partial general ledger for Norwalk Interiors are provided in the *Working Papers*. Norwalk Interiors has two departments, Furniture and Carpeting, and offers credit terms of 2/10, n/30.

1. Journalize each of the following cash receipts transactions. The sales tax rate is 6%; assume sales tax was paid on all cash and credit card sales. Source documents are abbreviated as follows: credit memorandum, CM; receipt, R; sales invoice, S; terminal summary, TS. Your instructor will guide you through the following examples.

### Transactions:
Feb. 1. Received cash on account from Melinda Ashworth, $2,908.64 for five area carpets, purchased January 25 on S230 for $3,180.00, less CM29 ($200.00 plus sales tax), less discount. R343.
7. Recorded cash and credit card sales for the week: carpeting, $3,074.00; furniture, $3,286.00; plus sales tax. TS81.
12. Received a check from Filo Raines for furniture purchased February 3 on S231 for $1,272.00, less discount. R344.
14. Recorded cash and credit card sales for the week: carpeting, $2,112.00; furniture, $2,862.00; plus sales tax. TS82.
**Posting.** Post the items that are to be posted individually.
19. Received a check from Carlee Hanks for furniture purchased on February 12 on S232 for $848.00, less discount. R345.
21. Recorded cash and credit card sales for the week: carpeting, $2,851.00; furniture, $4,103.00; plus sales tax. TS83.
28. Recorded cash and credit card sales for the week: carpeting, $2,967.00; furniture, $2,803.00; plus sales tax. TS84.
**Posting.** Post the items that are to be posted individually.

2. Prove and rule the cash receipts journal. Post the totals to the general ledger.

## on your own 2-2

### Journalizing and posting departmental cash receipts

The cash receipts journal, partial accounts receivable ledger, and partial general ledger for Electronic Warehouse, Inc., are provided in the *Working Papers*. Electronic Warehouse has two departments, Hardware and Software, and offers credit terms of 2/10, n/30.

1. Journalize each of the following cash receipts transactions. The sales tax rate is 7%; assume sales tax was paid on all cash and credit card sales. Source documents are abbreviated as follows: credit memorandum, CM; receipt, R; sales invoice, S; terminal summary, TS. Work this problem independently.

### Transactions:
Feb. 1. Received cash on account from QuikPrint Co., for computers purchased on January 23 on S411 for $3,959.00, less CM29 ($300.00 plus sales tax), less discount. R343.
7. Recorded cash and credit card sales for the week: hardware, $3,264.00; software, $4,196.00; plus sales tax. TS81.
12. Received a check from Data Systems, Inc., for software purchased on February 3 on S413 for $1,230.50, less discount. R344.
14. Recorded cash and credit card sales for the week: hardware, $5,645.00; software, $2,098.00; plus sales tax. TS82.
**Posting.** Post the items that are to be posted individually.
19. Received a check from Gear Web Design Co. for scanners purchased on February 12 on S428 $1,203.75, less discount. R345.
21. Recorded cash and credit card sales for the week: hardware, $4,781.00; software, $2,876.00; plus sales tax. TS83.
28. Recorded cash and credit card sales for the week: hardware, $5,847.00; software, $1,955.00; plus sales tax. TS84.
**Posting.** Post the items that are to be posted individually.

2. Prove and rule the cash receipts journal. Post the totals to the general ledger.

## SUMMARY

**After completing this chapter, you can**

1. Define terms related to departmental sales and cash receipts.

2. Identify concepts and practices related to departmental sales and cash receipts.

3. Journalize and post departmental sales on account and sales returns and allowances.

4. Journalize and post departmental cash receipts.

# Explore Accounting

EXPLORE ACCOUNTING • EXPLORE ACCOUNTING • EXPLORE ACCOU

### Transfer Pricing

Departmental accounting allows managers to evaluate the performance of individual departments. Some companies use departmental income from operations as a basis for rewarding effective managers. A management incentive plan could base a manager's salary on the amount of departmental income from operations, the percentage of income to net sales, or some other measure of profitability.

This type of incentive program becomes difficult to administer when a manager is responsible for a department in which the product is transferred to another department. Consider the following example.

Cement Art has two departments: design and casting. The design department creates molds used by the casting department to make a variety of cement statues, bird baths, and planters. The casting department purchases its molds from the design department, pours cement in the molds, and sells the finished product to retail stores. The manager of each department receives a bonus equal to .05% of the department's profit on operations.

The incentive plan would seem to be a good idea. However, if the casting department is required to purchase molds from the design department at any price, the design department manager has no incentive to control production costs. Thus, management must establish policies to determine the prices of molds transferred between the departments. Setting prices for the transfer of products between the departments is known as *transfer pricing*. Several transfer pricing methods are available:

1. Set the price consistent with the prices charged by other suppliers of the same or similar products.
2. Set the price based on the price that the product could be sold to other companies.
3. If the product is unique, use a percentage markup. This method must include a provision for containing increases in production costs.

**Instructions:** With another student, assume the roles of the design and casting department managers. Assume that the current cost of producing a mold is $20.00, and the mold is sold to the casting department for $25.00. The casting department adds $10.00 of other materials and labor to the product and sells the finished product to customers for $60.00. Negotiate a transfer pricing policy that provides an incentive salary for each manager. The policy should include a provision for the design manager to increase the price of a mold for an increase in production costs.

Xtra!
Quizzing
accountingxtra.swlearning.com

## 2-1 APPLICATION PROBLEM  PEACHTREE

### Journalizing and posting departmental sales on account and sales returns and allowances

Sequoia Sport Apparel is a retail store with two departments: Clothing and Shoes. The general ledger and accounts receivable ledger are included in your *Working Papers.* The balances are recorded as of April 1 of the current year.

**Instructions:**

1. Journalize the transactions for April of the current year. Use page 4 of a sales journal and page 6 of a general journal. The sales tax rate is 5%. Source documents are abbreviated as follows: credit memorandum, CM; sales invoice, S.

**Transactions:**

April   1. Sold shoes on account to Sridhar Duggirala, $85.00, plus sales tax. S63.
        2. Sold clothing on account to Thuc Quan, $150.00, plus sales tax. S64.
        5. Granted credit to Sridhar Duggirala for shoes returned, $85.00, plus sales tax from S63. CM12.
        5. Sold shoes on account to Dean Fujiwara, $60.00, plus sales tax. S65.
        5. Sold shoes on account to Gail Mahr, $180.00, plus sales tax. S66.
        7. Sold clothing on account to Thuc Quan, $230.00, plus sales tax. S67.
       10. Granted credit to Gail Mahr for shoes returned, $100.00, plus sales tax from S66. CM13.
       12. Sold clothing on account to Jeffrey O'Connell, $350.00, plus sales tax. S68.
       15. Granted credit to Thuc Quan for clothing returned, $140.00, plus sales tax from S67. CM14.

       **Posting.** Sequoia Sport Apparel posts items individually to the accounts receivable and general ledgers at mid-month and at the end of the month. Post the items accounted for through April 15. Post from the sales journal first and then from the general journal.

       17. Sold shoes on account to Sridhar Duggirala, $46.00, plus sales tax. S69.
       19. Sold clothing on account to the Andersen Vocational Center, $242.00. No sales tax. S70.
       24. Granted credit to Jeffrey O'Connell for clothing returned, $120.00, plus sales tax from S68. CM15.
       27. Sold clothing on account to Elias Carrasco, $98.00, plus sales tax. S71.
       30. Sold shoes on account to Tianshu Jian, $124.00, plus sales tax. S72.

       **Posting.** Post the items individually to the accounts receivable and general ledgers.

2. Prove and rule the sales journal. Post the totals to the general ledger.

## 2-2 APPLICATION PROBLEM  AUTOMATED ACCOUNTING  PEACHTREE  QUICKBOOKS

### Journalizing and posting departmental cash receipts

Colonial Furnishings has two departments: Tables and Chairs. The general ledger and accounts receivable ledger are provided in the *Working Papers.* The balances are recorded as of June 1 of the current year.

**Instructions:**

1. Journalize the transactions for June of the current year. Use page 18 of a cash receipts journal. Colonial Furnishings offers credit terms of 2/10, n/30. The sales tax rate is 5%; assume sales tax was paid on all cash and credit card sales. Source documents are abbreviated as follows: receipt, R; sales invoice, S; terminal summary, TS.

**Transactions:**

June   1. Received cash on account from Wayne Miller for chairs purchased May 25 on S147 for $157.50, less discount. R110.
       2. Received cash on account from Amy Cannon for two tables purchased May 26 on S148 for $388.50, less discount. R111.

6. Received cash on account from Bob Witt for chairs purchased on account for $210.00, no discount. R112.

6. Recorded cash and credit card sales for the week: tables, $6,240.00; chairs, $5,060.00; plus sales tax. TS66.

11. Received cash on account from Dawn Sanzone for a table purchased June 1 on S149 for $525.00, less discount. R113

13. Recorded cash and credit card sales for the week: tables, $5,640.00; chairs, $3,570.00; plus sales tax. TS67.

    **Posting.** Post the items that are to be posted individually.

17. Received cash on account from Amy Cannon for a table purchased on June 9 on S150 for $336.00, less discount. R114.

18. Received cash on account from David Ring for a table purchased on June 9 on S151 for $451.50, less discount. R115.

20. Recorded cash and credit card sales for the week: tables, $7,110.00; chairs, $4,850.00; plus sales tax. TS68.

24. Received cash on account from Joe Ricardo for eight chairs and a table purchased June 15 on S152 for $892.50 ($420.00 for the chairs and $472.50 for the table), less CM42 for two chairs ($100.00 plus $5.00 sales tax), less discount. R116.

27. Recorded cash and credit card sales for the week: tables, $6,890.00; chairs, $5,150.00; plus sales tax. TS69.

30. Recorded cash and credit card sales for the period June 28–30: tables, $3,200.00; chairs, $2,980.00; plus sales tax. TS70.

    **Posting.** Post the items individually to the accounts receivable ledger.

2. Prove and rule the cash receipts journal. Post the totals to the general ledger.

# 2-3 MASTERY PROBLEM

## Journalizing departmental sales, sales returns and allowances, and cash receipts

EuroFashions has two departments: Jewelry and Watches.

**Instructions:**

1. Journalize the transactions completed during April of the current year. Use page 9 of a sales journal and a general journal and page 12 of a cash receipts journal. EuroFashions offers its customers terms of 2/10, n/30. The sales tax rate is 5%; assume sales tax was paid on all cash and credit card sales. Source documents are abbreviated as follows: credit memorandum, CM; receipt, R; sales invoice, S; terminal summary, TS.

**Transactions:**

April 1. Sold jewelry on account to Ronn Hughes, $810.00, plus sales tax. S134.

3. Sold jewelry on account to Dara San, $520.00, plus sales tax. S135.

4. Received cash on account from Bill Melendez for watches purchased on March 27 covering S132 for $441.00, less discount. R83.

4. Recorded cash and credit card sales: jewelry, $2,560.00; watches, $2,130.00; plus sales tax. TS74.

6. Received cash on account from Katie Minko for jewelry purchased on March 29 on S131 for $640.50, less discount. R84.

8. Granted credit to Dara San for jewelry returned, $110.00, plus sales tax, from S135. CM28.

9. Received cash on account from Dara San for a watch purchased on April 3 for $302.40, less discount. R85.

11. Received cash on account from Ronn Hughes for jewelry purchased on April 4 on S134 for $850.50, less discount. R86.

11. Sold jewelry on account to Dan Tran, $780.00, plus sales tax. S136.

11. Recorded cash and credit card sales for the week: jewelry, $5,340.00; watches, $3,910.00; plus sales tax. TS75.
13. Received cash on account from Dara San, for jewelry purchased on S135 for $546.00, less CM28 ($110.00 plus sales tax), less discount. R87.
15. Sold two watches on account to Alana Austin, $510.00, plus sales tax. S137.
17. Sold jewelry on account to Katie Minko, $320.00, plus sales tax. S138.
18. Recorded cash and credit card sales: jewelry, $4,730.00; watches, $5,260.00; plus sales tax. TS76.
21. Received cash on account from Dan Tran, for jewelry purchased on S136 for $819.00, less discount. R88.
21. Granted credit to Alana Austin for returned watch, $150.00, plus sales tax, from S137. CM29.
25. Recorded cash and credit card sales for the week: jewelry, $3,470.00; watches, $2,681.00; plus sales tax. TS77.
28. Sold watches on account to The Hamilton Foundation, $660.00; no sales tax. S139.
30. Recorded cash and credit card sales: jewelry, $1,860.00; watches, $965.00; plus sales tax. TS78.

2. Prove and rule the sales journal.
3. Prove and rule the cash receipts journal.

## 2-4 CHALLENGE PROBLEM

**Journalizing departmental sales, sales returns and allowances, and cash receipts**

Assume that EuroFashions, the business described in Mastery Problem 2-3, is located in a state that does not charge a retail sales tax. Also assume that EuroFashions offers customers terms of 1/10, n/30. The journals with the proper headings are provided in the *Working Papers.*

**Instructions:**

1. Journalize the transactions given in Mastery Problem 2-3 without sales tax but with 1% sales discounts. Use page 9 of a sales journal, page 15 of a general journal, and page 12 of a cash receipts journal.
2. Prove and rule the special journals.

©GETTY IMAGES/PHOTODISC

Recording Departmental Sales and Cash Receipts

## applied communication

The preparation of a *Career Portfolio* was discussed in the Applied Communication activity in Chapter 1. In addition to labeling one divider "Resume," label another divider "Personal Letters." One type of personal letter is a cover letter. When sending your resume, a cover letter is your opportunity to introduce yourself to an employer and highlight your strongest qualifications.

The cover letter, or letter of application, consists of at least three paragraphs. In the first paragraph, introduce yourself, state the job for which you are applying, and express an interest in the job. The second paragraph should contain a description of your qualifications and related work experience. In the third paragraph, include an action statement—request an interview, ask for a phone call, indicate how you will follow-up, and—most importantly—thank the reader for her or his time and consideration.

**Instructions:**

1.  Research how to write a strong cover letter.

2.  In a newspaper or online, locate a job advertisement for a position for which you are qualified. Prepare a cover letter for the position you have selected.

3.  Keep copies of all cover letters in the "Personal Letters" section of your *Career Portfolio*.

## cases for critical thinking

### Case 1

Pacific Patio specializes in tables, umbrellas, and barbeques. All accounting records are kept on a departmental basis. When a customer returns merchandise or receives an allowance, a journal entry is made debiting the appropriate sales account and crediting Accounts Receivable and the customer account. Do you agree or disagree with this accounting procedure? Why?

### Case 2

Ogden's, Inc., sells a complete line of hardware and lawn and garden products. To encourage early payment for sales on account, it offers a sales discount. The company has separate departmental accounts for purchases, sales, discounts, and returns and allowances. Thomas Gordon, who has been recording journal entries for sales and cash receipts, suggests that the Sales Tax Payable account also be split to have separate accounts for each of the two departments. The company's accountant disagrees with this suggestion. With whom do you agree? Why?

## SCANS workplace competency

**Basic Skill:** Speaking

**Concept:** Employers seek workers who possess the ability to organize their ideas and speak effectively. Employees spend much of their workday using oral communication skills to interact with other employees, managers, and customers.

**Application:** Prepare and give an oral report identifying the accounting and personal skills you possess that qualify you for entry-level employment.

APPLIED COMMUNICATION • APPLIED

CASES FOR CRITICAL THINKING

SCANS WORKPLACE COMPETENCY

## • graphing workshop

Stanford Clothiers, an upscale department store, has locations in four different cities. Each quarter, the company charts departmental sales for each location. Use the information presented in the graph to estimate totals and answer the following questions.

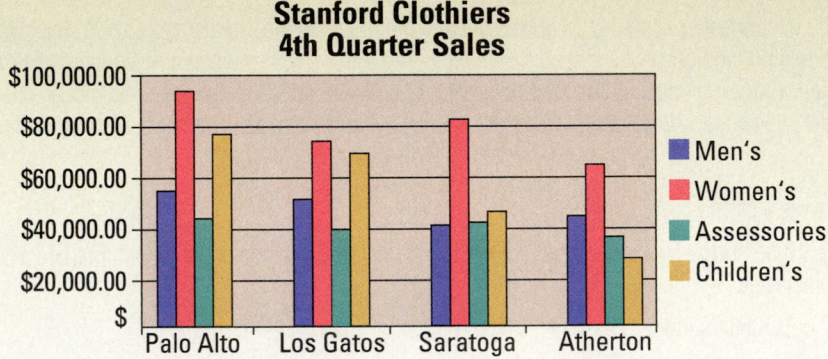

1. Which department has the greatest sales at each location?

2. Which location appears to have the largest overall sales?

3. If you had to close a store based on total overall sales, which location would you select?

## • analyzing Costco's financial statements

Published financial statements include notes that provide a better understanding of some of the amounts, terms, and accounting policies used in preparing the financial statements. On a financial statement, the term "Cash and Cash Equivalents" includes more than just cash on hand. Checking accounts, savings accounts, highly liquid investments, and proceeds due from credit and debit card transactions are also included in this total.

**Instructions:**

1. Using the Consolidated Balance Sheets in Appendix B of this textbook, identify the actual amount of Costco's Cash and Cash Equivalents as of August 31, 2003.

2. Referring to the Notes to Consolidated Financial Statements in Appendix B, list the items Costco considers to be "cash equivalents."

3. Referring to the Notes to Consolidated Financial Statements in Appendix B, identify the amount of credit and debit card receivables with settlement terms of less than five days as of August 31, 2003. Calculate the amount of cash remaining in checking, savings, and highly liquid investments.

# Automated Accounting

## Recording Entries for Sales and Cash Receipts Using Special Journals

In the Automated Accounting software, transactions are recorded in journals similar to the sales, general, and cash receipts journals described in Chapter 2. The cash receipts journal window is shown below. Journals are accessed by clicking the Journal Entries option from the Data menu or clicking the Journal toolbar button. Click the tab for the journal you wish to use.

The cash receipts journal below shows two kinds of transactions: (1) three cash receipts on account with sales discounts; and (2) cash and credit card sales.

Entries in the automated cash receipts journal are similar to entries in a manual cash receipts journal. The software automatically calculates the amount in the Cash Debit column; notice that these amounts are grey in the illustration. Entering an amount in the A.R. Debit column (Accounts Receivable) automatically opens the Customer column where an accounts receivable ledger account must be selected.

The general ledger account number is entered in the Account No. column only when amounts will be entered in the general Debit or general Credit columns. Note that in the illustration, the Account No. and general Debit and Credit columns are not shown. The cash receipts journal window is too wide to display on most monitors. Therefore, the portions of the journal that are displayed change as you tab across the columns.

A journal entries report may be displayed or printed by clicking the Reports toolbar button, then clicking Journals and then the name of the journal.

### AUTOMATING APPLICATION PROBLEM 2-2: Journalizing and posting departmental cash receipts

### AUTOMATING MASTERY PROBLEM 2-3: Journalizing departmental sales, sales returns and allowances, and cash receipts

### Instructions:

1. Load the *Automated Accounting 8.0* or higher software.

2. Select data file A02-2 or A02-3 from the appropriate directory/folder ("A" indicates Advanced Course).

3. Select File from the menu bar and choose Save As. Key the path to the drive and directory that contains your data files. Save the database with a filename of A02-2 or A02-3 XXX XXX (where the X's are your first and last name).

4. Access Problem Instructions through the Browser tool. Read the Problem Instruction screen.

5. Key the data listed in the problem on pages 52–54.

6. Save your file and exit the Automated Accounting software.

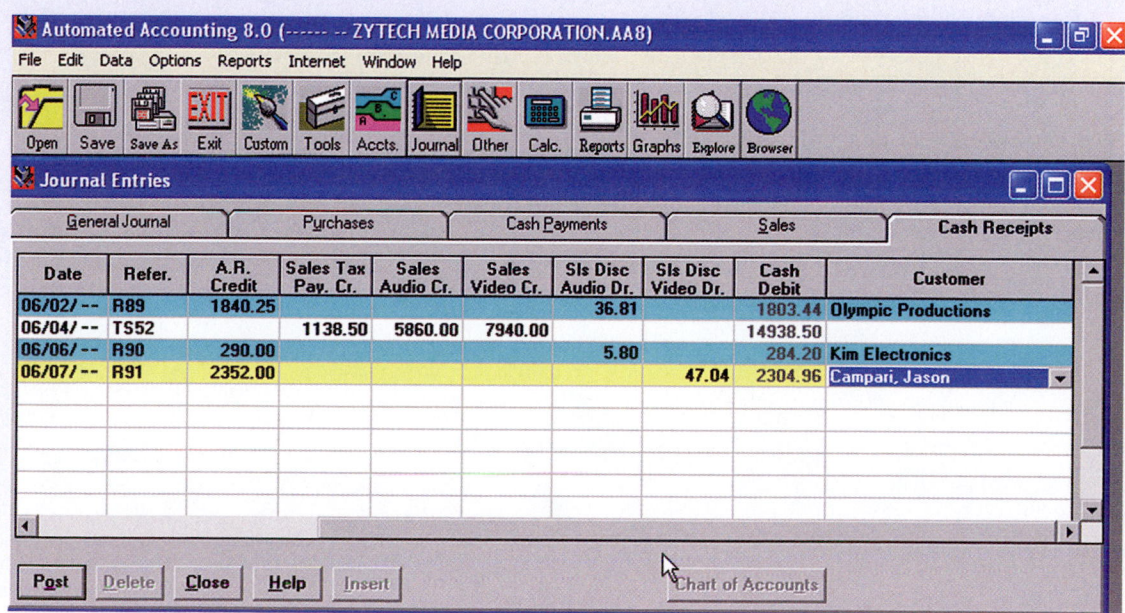

# Calculating and Recording Departmental Payroll Data

**OBJECTIVES & TERMS**

*After studying Chapter 3, you will be able to:*

1. Define accounting terms related to a departmental payroll system.

2. Identify accounting concepts and practices related to a departmental payroll system.

3. Prepare a commissions record and calculate commission on net sales.

4. Complete payroll records.

5. Journalize payroll transactions.

- salary
- pay period
- payroll
- payroll taxes

- withholding allowance
- tax base
- payroll register

- employee earnings record
- automatic check deposit
- electronic funds transfer (EFT)

Point Your Browser
accountingxtra.swlearning.com

# • Cisco Systems, Inc.

©NOAH BERGER/BLOOMBERG NEWS/LANDOV

## CISCO SYSTEMS, INC. DELIVERS INFORMATION ACROSS THE INTERNET

Founded in 1984, Cisco Systems, Inc., has become the worldwide leader in networking for the Internet. Actually, the Internet would not be possible without an organized system that connects computer devices and databases around the world at corporations, universities, governmental agencies, and other institutions. Cisco's hardware, software, and routing technology allow bundles of information to be transferred across the Internet and delivered to the appropriate computer networks and devices.

Chapter 3 discusses payroll data. One payroll measure that Cisco uses to analyze the productivity of its employees is the dollar amount of sales generated per employee each year. For the year 2004, for example, Cisco's chairman reported productivity per employee of $690,000 revenue per employee, an increase of 23% over the previous year.

### Critical Thinking

1. There are two ways businesses can improve their sales revenue per employee. What do you think they are?
2. Research two other companies and determine their sales revenues per employee for the past three years. What trends did you see for each company?

Xtra!
Today
accountingxtra.swlearning.com

Source: www.cisco.com

## internet activity

### PAYROLL TAX SUPPORT

Go to the homepage for the Internal Revenue Service (IRS) (www.irs.gov). Search the site for resources a small business owner can use to set up a system for deducting taxes and sending the taxes to the IRS.

### Instructions

1. List at least three resources available to the small business owner related to payroll deductions.
2. Pick one of these resources and explain why you think it would be helpful to the small business owner.

# 3-1 Completing Payroll Records for Employee Earnings and Deductions

Employees are an essential element of the business world. Businesses depend on competent employees in order to operate successfully. Employees provide services to a business in exchange for money. The money paid for employee services is called a **salary**. Federal, state, and local laws require employers to keep accurate records of the money paid to employees and of other payments related to employee services. Payroll records are maintained for the business and for each employee. The actual payroll system used differs among businesses. A business protects itself by keeping complete and accurate payroll records of all required information.

The period covered by a salary payment is called a **pay period**. The total amount earned by all employees for a pay period is called a **payroll**. In addition to salaries, a business must pay taxes based on the payroll. Taxes based on the

payroll of a business are called **payroll taxes**. Employers are also required by law to withhold certain payroll taxes from employee salaries each pay period.

Periodically, employers must pay government agencies all payroll taxes withheld from employee salaries as well as the employer payroll taxes. A business must also provide a yearly report to each employee showing the total salary earned and the total taxes withheld. The yearly report is provided to each employee on Form W-2. Businesses must distribute this form to their employees by January 31, reporting earnings and amounts withheld for the previous calendar year. Therefore, a business must keep records of each employee's earnings, amounts withheld, and net amount paid. Payroll records also must show the total amount of payroll taxes that a business must pay.

## making ethical decisions

### Insider Trading

Marcus Humphries, a loan officer for a regional bank, has just closed a loan agreement with Coastal Trucking Company. He was very impressed with the company's management and business plan. With the additional resources the loan will provide, Coastal Trucking Company should experience rapid growth during the next few years. The corporation's stock should also show a dramatic increase in market price.

Upon returning to the office, Marcus places an order to purchase 500 shares of the company's stock, currently trading

at $35.60 per share. This purchase is a substantial investment for Marcus.

**Instructions**

Access the *Code of Conduct* of Citigroup and insider trading information of the Securities and Exchange Commission (SEC). Using this information and the ethical decision-making model, determine whether Marcus's purchase of the stock of Coastal Trucking Company was ethical.

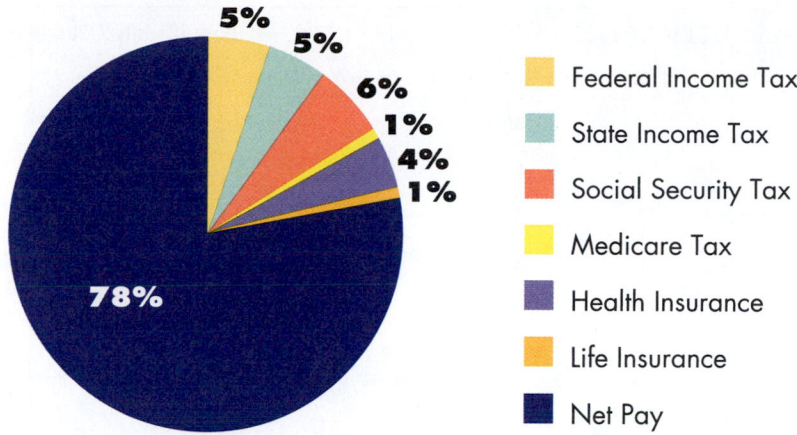

Federal Income Tax

State Income Tax

Social Security Tax

Medicare Tax

Health Insurance

Life Insurance

Net Pay

Zytech is required by law to withhold federal income tax and two FICA taxes (social security tax and Medicare tax) from each employee's pay. *FICA* is the abbreviation for the *Federal Insurance Contributions Act.*

The total earnings, marital status, and number of withholding allowances claimed by an employee determine the federal income tax amount to be withheld. For each person supported, including the employee, an employee is entitled to a reduction in the amount on which income tax is calculated. A deduction from total earnings for each person legally supported by a taxpayer is called a **withholding allowance**.

The Federal Insurance Contributions Act (FICA) provides for a federal system of old-age, survivors, disability, and hospital insurance. The old-age, survivors, and disability insurance portion is financed by the social security tax. The hospital insurance portion is financed by the Medicare tax. Each of these taxes is reported separately. Social security tax is calculated on employee earnings up to a maximum paid in a calendar year. The maximum amount of earnings on which a tax is calculated is called a **tax base**. Congress sets the tax base and the tax rates for social security tax. An act of Congress can change the tax base and tax rate at any time. The social security tax rate and base used in this textbook are 6.2% of earnings up to a maximum of $87,000.00 in each calendar year. Medicare does not have a tax base. Therefore, Medicare tax is calculated on total employee earnings. The Medicare tax rate used in this text is 1.45% of total employee earnings.

Some cities and states also require that employers deduct amounts for income and other taxes from employee earnings. Laws for handling state, city, and county taxes vary.

Some businesses also make deductions from employee earnings for health insurance, life insurance, pension plans, and savings deposits. Zytech makes deductions from its employee salaries for federal income tax, state income tax, social security tax, Medicare tax, health insurance, and life insurance. The payroll components for Mary Dennenberg are shown in the graph above.

©GETTY IMAGES/PHOTODISC

| Hours Worked: ALL EMPLOYEES | | | | June 18–July 2, 20-- | |
|---|---|---|---|---|---|
| Name | ID No. | Regular-1 | Overtime-1 | Regular-2 | Overtime-2 |
| Balero, Samantha R. | 7 | 40 | 2 | 40 | 3 |
| Dennenberg, Mary E. | 10 | ----- | | ----- | |
| Dunnston, Shawn T. | 16 | 40 | | 40 | 2 |
| Easthouse, Vern T. | 9 | 40 | | 40 | |
| Fabio, Dante R. | 15 | ----- | | ----- | |
| Famquez, Carlos M. | 11 | 40 | 2 | 40 | 1 |
| Yamaguchi, Sam F. | 8 | 40 | | 40 | 2 |

Zytech pays an hourly salary biweekly to sales-clerks and accounting department employees. Zytech's biweekly pay period is 80 hours, consisting of two regular 40-hour work weeks. The store is open six days a week. However, employees usually work only a five-day week of 40 hours. The pay rate for Zytech's salesclerks and accounting employees is stated as an hourly rate.

Zytech uses an employee identification card scanner to log employee hours. All employees have identification badges with a magnetic strip coded to include employee name and identification number. Employees slide the card through the card scanner when they begin and end each work period. At the end of a payroll period, a report listing employee hours worked is printed to provide the data for calculating employee earnings. The employee hours worked report for the biweekly period June 18 through July 2 is

shown above. The software that supports the card scanner can produce a variety of reports. For example, to monitor employee attendance, a report of the actual times an employee arrives and leaves work can also be generated.

All time worked in excess of 40 hours in any one week is considered overtime. Employees are paid 1½ times the regular rate for overtime hours. However, managers are paid a base salary plus commissions, so their hours worked are indicated by dashes.

Employee regular earnings are calculated by multiplying the hourly rate by the number of regular hours. Employee overtime earnings are calculated by multiplying the regular rate by 1.5 and multiplying the result by the number of overtime hours. The calculations are shown below for Samantha R. Balero.

| Regular Hours | × | Regular Rate | = | Regular Earnings | | |
|---|---|---|---|---|---|---|
| 80 | × | $7.00 per hour | = | $560.00 | | |
| Overtime Hours | × | Regular Rate | × | 1.5 | = | Overtime Earnings |
| 5 | × | $7.00 | × | 1.5 | = | $52.50 |
| Regular Earnings | + | Overtime Earnings | = | Total Earnings | | |
| $560.00 | + | $52.50 | = | $612.50 | | |

# COMMISSIONS RECORD

**1** Record heading information.

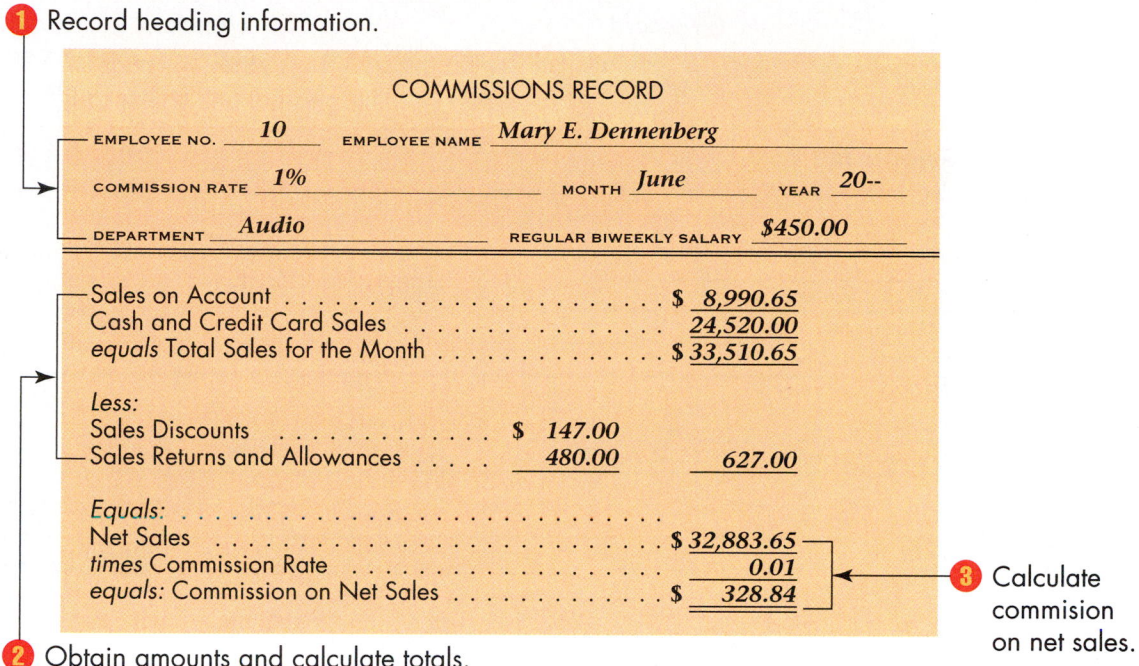

COMMISSIONS RECORD

EMPLOYEE NO. _10_    EMPLOYEE NAME _Mary E. Dennenberg_

COMMISSION RATE _1%_    MONTH _June_    YEAR _20--_

DEPARTMENT _Audio_    REGULAR BIWEEKLY SALARY _$450.00_

| | |
|---|---|
| Sales on Account . . . . . . . . . . . . . . . . . . . . | $ _8,990.65_ |
| Cash and Credit Card Sales . . . . . . . . . . . . | _24,520.00_ |
| *equals* Total Sales for the Month . . . . . . . . . . . . | $ _33,510.65_ |

*Less:*

| | | |
|---|---|---|
| Sales Discounts . . . . . . . . . . . | $ _147.00_ | |
| Sales Returns and Allowances . . . . . | _480.00_ | _627.00_ |

*Equals:* . . . . . . . . . . . . . . . . . . . . .
| | |
|---|---|
| Net Sales . . . . . . . . . . . . . . . . . . . . . | $ _32,883.65_ |
| *times* Commission Rate . . . . . . . . . . . . . . . | _0.01_ |
| *equals:* Commission on Net Sales . . . . . . . . . . | $ _328.84_ |

**3** Calculate commision on net sales.

**2** Obtain amounts and calculate totals.

An employee's basic salary may be supplemented by other types of earnings. For example, an employee may receive commissions, cost-of-living adjustments, a share of profits, or a bonus.

At Zytech, department supervisors are paid a regular biweekly salary. They are not paid for overtime hours. However, to encourage increased sales, the supervisors are paid a 1% commission on the department's monthly net sales.

The store manager is also paid a regular biweekly salary and receives no salary for overtime hours. The store manager also earns an annual bonus based on the sales record for both departments.

Commissions for the previous month's net sales are included with the first biweekly pay period of a month. A commissions record is used to calculate each department supervisor's commission.

# STEPS
STEPS • STEPS • STEPS • STEPS • STEPS • STEPS • STEPS • STEPS • STEPS • STEPS

## PREPARING A COMMISSIONS RECORD

**1** Record the employee number, employee name, commission rate, month, year, department, and regular biweekly salary at the top of the form.

**2** Calculate department net sales for the month:
- Write the amount of sales on account for the department, *$8,990.65,* from the sales journal.
- Write the amount of cash and credit card sales for the month, *$24,520.00,* from the cash receipts journal.
- Add the two sales amounts and write the total sales for the month, *$33,510.65.*
- Write the amount of sales discounts, *$147.00,* from the cash receipts journal.
- Write the amount of sales returns and allowances, *$480.00.* This amount can be obtained from the general journal entries or the month's postings to the general ledger account.
- Write the total of sales discounts and sales returns and allowances, *$627.00.*

**3** Calculate the commission on net sales for the month.
- Calculate the difference between total sales for the month, $33,510.65, less total sales discounts and returns and allowances, $627.00. Write the amount of net sales, *$32,883.65.*
- Write the commission rate of 1%, *0.01.*
- Multiply the commission rate times the net sales amount and write the commission on net sales, *$328.84.*

The June commission for Mary E. Dennenberg is calculated as shown in the illustration.

① Record heading information.

④ Write total hours, regular earnings, overtime earnings, and total earnings.

③ Enter employee no., name, marital status, no. of allow-ances.

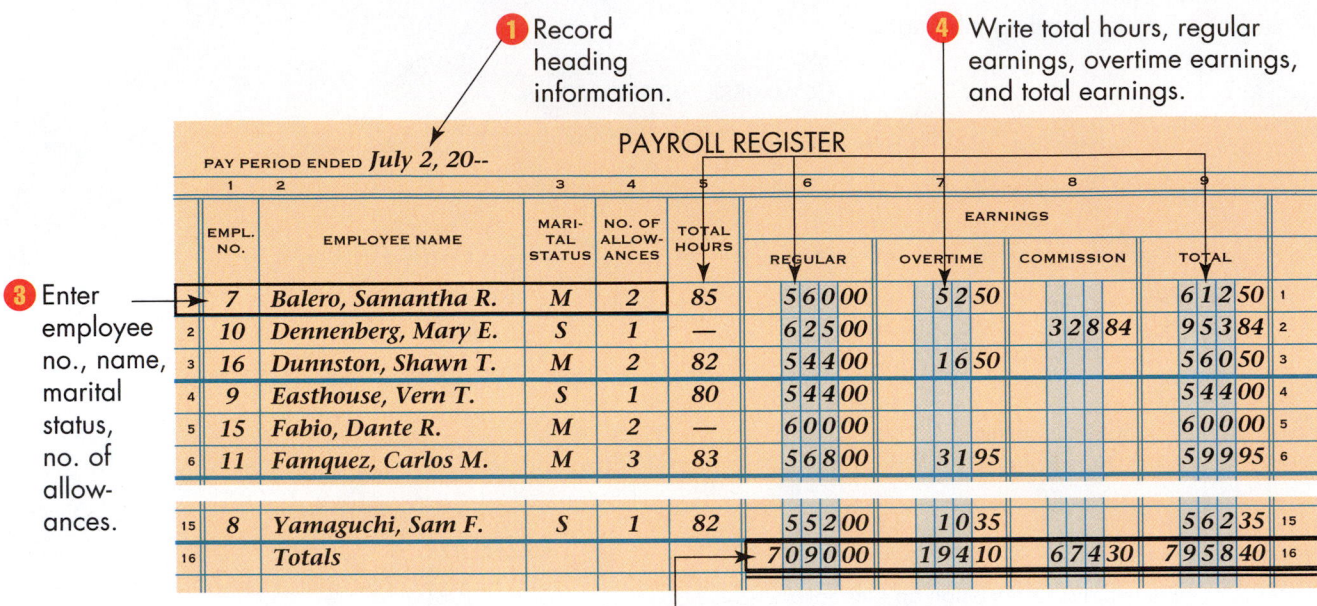

PAYROLL REGISTER

PAY PERIOD ENDED *July 2, 20--*

| | EMPL. NO. | EMPLOYEE NAME | MARI-TAL STATUS | NO. OF ALLOW-ANCES | TOTAL HOURS | EARNINGS | | | | |
|---|---|---|---|---|---|---|---|---|---|---|
| | 1 | 2 | 3 | 4 | 5 | REGULAR (6) | OVERTIME (7) | COMMISSION (8) | TOTAL (9) | |
| 1 | 7 | *Balero, Samantha R.* | M | 2 | 85 | 560 00 | 52 50 | | 612 50 | 1 |
| 2 | 10 | *Dennenberg, Mary E.* | S | 1 | — | 625 00 | | 328 84 | 953 84 | 2 |
| 3 | 16 | *Dunnston, Shawn T.* | M | 2 | 82 | 544 00 | 16 50 | | 560 50 | 3 |
| 4 | 9 | *Easthouse, Vern T.* | S | 1 | 80 | 544 00 | | | 544 00 | 4 |
| 5 | 15 | *Fabio, Dante R.* | M | 2 | — | 600 00 | | | 600 00 | 5 |
| 6 | 11 | *Famquez, Carlos M.* | M | 3 | 83 | 568 00 | 31 95 | | 599 95 | 6 |
| 15 | 8 | *Yamaguchi, Sam F.* | S | 1 | 82 | 552 00 | 10 35 | | 562 35 | 15 |
| 16 | | *Totals* | | | | 7090 00 | 194 10 | 674 30 | 7958 40 | 16 |

⑨ Total each amount column.

A business form used to record payroll informa-tion is called a **payroll register**. A payroll register summarizes the payroll for one pay period and shows total earnings, amounts withheld, and net pay for all employees. Zytech prepares a separate payroll register for each biweekly (every two weeks) payroll.

To provide better cost control, Zytech sepa-rates employee earnings into three classifications:

Audio Department, Video Department, and Administrative. The earnings of salesclerks and departmental managers are recorded in their respective departmental classification. The earn-ings of the store manager and accounting and office employees are recorded in the Administra-tive classification.

---

## STEPS ⋅ STEPS ⋅ STEPS ⋅ STEPS ⋅ STEPS ⋅ STEPS ⋅ STEPS ⋅ STEPS ⋅ STEPS ⋅ STEPS

### PREPARING A PAYROLL REGISTER

*For each pay period:*

① Enter the last day of the biweekly payroll period, *July 2, 20--*, at the top of the payroll register.

② Record the date of payment, *July 9, 20--*, also at the top of the payroll register. The time between the end of a pay period and the date of payment is needed in order to prepare the payroll records and payroll checks.

*For each employee:*

③ Enter employee number, *7*; name, *Balero, Samantha R.*; marital status, *M*; and number of allowances, *2*, in columns 1, 2, 3, and 4. This information is taken from personnel records kept for each employee.

④ Write total hours, *85*; regular earnings, *$560.00*; overtime earnings, *$52.50*; and total earnings, *$612.50*, in columns 5, 6, 7, and 9. The hours are from the employee hours worked report, and the earnings are calculated.

Department supervisors are not paid by the hour; therefore, a line is drawn through the Total Hours column, column 5, as shown on line 2 of the payroll register. The amount of a commission is entered in column 8. The salary amount is recorded in the Regular Earnings column, column 6. Regular earnings and commission earnings are added together to determine total earnings for the biweekly pay period.

The salaries of the store manager and non-sales employees, such as accounting department employees, are entered in the Admin. Salaries column, column 12 of the payroll register shown above.

⑤ Extend total earnings to the appropriate department column or Administrative Salaries.

**5** Record total earnings by department.

**2** Record date of payment.

**6** Enter payroll deductions.

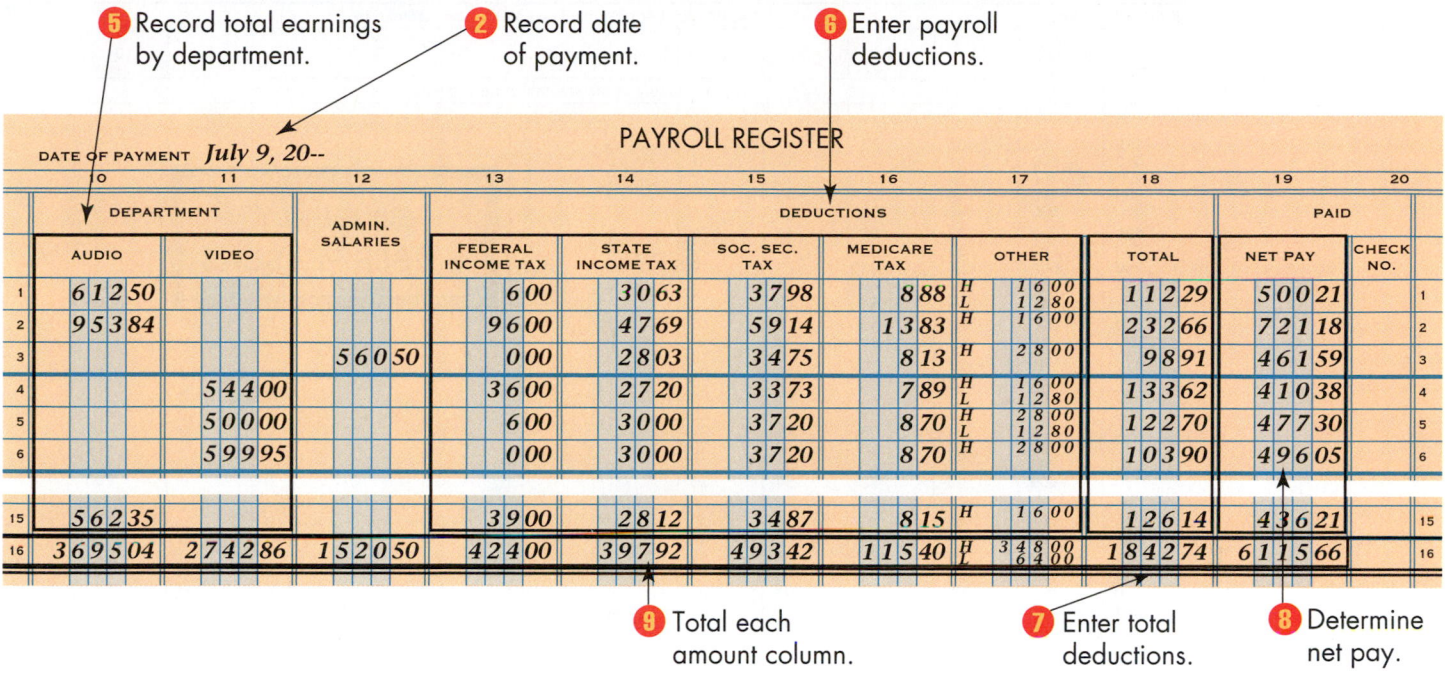

DATE OF PAYMENT  *July 9, 20--*

PAYROLL REGISTER

| | DEPARTMENT | | ADMIN. SALARIES | DEDUCTIONS | | | | | | PAID | | |
|---|---|---|---|---|---|---|---|---|---|---|---|---|
| | AUDIO | VIDEO | | FEDERAL INCOME TAX | STATE INCOME TAX | SOC. SEC. TAX | MEDICARE TAX | OTHER | | TOTAL | NET PAY | CHECK NO. |
| 1 | 612 50 | | | 6 00 | 30 63 | 37 98 | 8 88 | H L | 16 00 12 80 | 112 29 | 500 21 | 1 |
| 2 | 953 84 | | | 96 00 | 47 69 | 59 14 | 13 83 | H | 16 00 | 232 66 | 721 18 | 2 |
| 3 | | | 560 50 | 0 00 | 28 03 | 34 75 | 8 13 | H | 28 00 | 98 91 | 461 59 | 3 |
| 4 | | 544 00 | | 36 00 | 27 20 | 33 73 | 7 89 | H L | 16 00 12 80 | 133 62 | 410 38 | 4 |
| 5 | | 500 00 | | 6 00 | 30 00 | 37 20 | 8 70 | H L | 16 00 12 80 | 122 70 | 477 30 | 5 |
| 6 | | 599 95 | | 0 00 | 30 00 | 37 20 | 8 70 | H | 28 00 | 103 90 | 496 05 | 6 |
| 15 | 562 35 | | | 39 00 | 28 12 | 34 87 | 8 15 | H | 16 00 | 126 14 | 436 21 | 15 |
| 16 | 3695 04 | 2742 86 | 1520 50 | 424 00 | 397 92 | 493 42 | 115 40 | H L | 348 00 64 00 | 1842 74 | 6115 66 | 16 |

**9** Total each amount column.

**7** Enter total deductions.

**8** Determine net pay.

**6** Enter the payroll deductions: federal income tax, *$6.00;* state income tax, *$30.63;* social security tax, *$37.98;* Medicare tax, *$8.88;* health insurance, *$16.00;* and life insurance, *$12.80.* Federal income tax withholding is calculated using withholding tables, such as the ones shown on page 66. The state in which Zytech operates calculates state income tax at 5% of total earnings. Samantha Balero's social security tax deduction for the biweekly pay period ended July 2 is calculated as shown here.

| | **Total Earnings** | × | **Social Security Tax Rate** | × | **Social Security Tax Deduction** |
|---|---|---|---|---|---|
| | $612.50 | × | 6.2% | × | $37.98 |

Ms. Balero's Medicare tax deduction for the biweekly pay period ended July 2 is calculated as shown here.

| | **Total Earnings** | × | **Medicare Tax Rate** | = | **Medicare Tax Deduction** |
|---|---|---|---|---|---|
| | $612.50 | × | 1.45% | = | $8.88 |

The health insurance deduction is $16.00 per biweekly pay period for each insured single employee claiming one allowance and each married employee who chooses single coverage. The deduction is $28.00 for all other married employees and single employees who claim more than one dependent. The health insurance deduction is identified by writing the letter *H* in front of the amount. The life insurance deduction is $12.80 per biweekly pay period for employees desiring life insurance. The deduction is identified by writing the letter *L* in front of the amount.

**7** Add the amounts for deductions and enter the total, *$112.29,* in column 18.

**8** Subtract the total deductions from total earnings to determine net pay, *$500.21.* The net pay for Samantha Balero is calculated as shown here.

| | **Total Earnings** (column 9) | – | **Total Deductions** (column 18) | = | **Net Pay** (column 19) |
|---|---|---|---|---|---|
| | $612.50 | – | $112.29 | = | $500.21 |

*At the end of the payroll period:*

**9** When the net pay has been entered for all employees, total each payroll register amount column. Subtract the Total Deductions column, $1,842.74, from the Total Earnings column. The result should equal the total of the Net Pay column. If the totals do not agree, find and correct the errors. Rule the payroll register.

| If the wages are— | | And the number of withholding allowances claimed is— | | | | | | | | | | |
|---|---|---|---|---|---|---|---|---|---|---|---|---|
| At least | But less than | 0 | 1 | 2 | 3 | 4 | 5 | 6 | 7 | 8 | 9 | 10 |
| | | The amount of income tax to be withheld is— | | | | | | | | | | |
| 450 | 460 | 39 | 23 | 11 | 0 | 0 | 0 | 0 | 0 | 0 | 0 | 0 |
| 460 | 470 | 41 | 24 | 12 | 1 | 0 | 0 | 0 | 0 | 0 | 0 | 0 |
| 470 | 480 | 42 | 25 | 13 | 2 | 0 | 0 | 0 | 0 | 0 | 0 | 0 |
| 480 | 490 | 44 | 26 | 14 | 3 | 0 | 0 | 0 | 0 | 0 | 0 | 0 |
| 490 | 500 | 45 | 28 | 15 | 4 | 0 | 0 | 0 | 0 | 0 | 0 | 0 |
| 500 | 520 | 48 | 30 | 17 | 5 | 0 | 0 | 0 | 0 | 0 | 0 | 0 |
| 520 | 540 | 51 | 33 | 19 | 7 | 0 | 0 | 0 | 0 | 0 | 0 | 0 |
| 540 | 560 | 54 | 36 | 21 | 9 | 0 | 0 | 0 | 0 | 0 | 0 | 0 |
| 560 | 580 | 57 | 39 | 23 | 11 | 0 | 0 | 0 | 0 | 0 | 0 | 0 |
| 580 | 600 | 60 | 42 | 25 | 13 | 1 | 0 | 0 | 0 | 0 | 0 | 0 |
| 600 | 620 | 63 | 45 | 27 | 15 | 3 | 0 | 0 | 0 | 0 | 0 | 0 |
| 620 | 640 | 66 | 48 | 30 | 17 | 5 | 0 | 0 | 0 | 0 | 0 | 0 |
| 640 | 660 | 69 | 51 | 33 | 19 | 7 | 0 | 0 | 0 | 0 | 0 | 0 |
| 660 | 680 | 72 | 54 | 36 | 21 | 9 | 0 | 0 | 0 | 0 | 0 | 0 |
| 680 | 700 | 75 | 57 | 39 | 23 | 11 | 0 | 0 | 0 | 0 | 0 | 0 |
| 700 | 720 | 78 | 60 | 42 | 25 | 13 | 1 | 0 | 0 | 0 | 0 | 0 |
| 720 | 740 | 81 | 63 | 45 | 27 | 15 | 3 | 0 | 0 | 0 | 0 | 0 |
| 740 | 760 | 84 | 66 | 48 | 30 | 17 | 5 | 0 | 0 | 0 | 0 | 0 |
| 760 | 780 | 87 | 69 | 51 | 33 | 19 | 7 | 0 | 0 | 0 | 0 | 0 |
| 780 | 800 | 90 | 72 | 54 | 36 | 21 | 9 | 0 | 0 | 0 | 0 | 0 |
| 800 | 820 | 93 | 75 | 57 | 39 | 23 | 11 | 0 | 0 | 0 | 0 | 0 |
| 820 | 840 | 96 | 78 | 60 | 42 | 25 | 13 | 1 | 0 | 0 | 0 | 0 |
| 840 | 860 | 99 | 81 | 63 | 45 | 27 | 15 | 3 | 0 | 0 | 0 | 0 |
| 860 | 880 | 102 | 84 | 66 | 48 | 30 | 17 | 5 | 0 | 0 | 0 | 0 |
| 880 | 900 | 105 | 87 | 69 | 51 | 33 | 19 | 7 | 0 | 0 | 0 | 0 |
| 900 | 920 | 108 | 90 | 72 | 54 | 36 | 21 | 9 | 0 | 0 | 0 | 0 |
| 920 | 940 | 111 | 93 | 75 | 57 | 39 | 23 | 11 | 0 | 0 | 0 | 0 |
| 940 | 960 | 114 | 96 | 78 | 60 | 42 | 25 | 13 | 1 | 0 | 0 | 0 |
| 960 | 980 | 117 | 99 | 81 | 63 | 45 | 27 | 15 | 3 | 0 | 0 | 0 |
| 980 | 1,000 | 120 | 102 | 84 | 66 | 48 | 30 | 17 | 5 | 0 | 0 | 0 |

**BIWEEKLY SINGLE PERSONS**

## MARRIED Persons—BIWEEKLY Payroll Period

| If the wages are— | | And the number of withholding allowances claimed is— | | | | | | | | | | |
|---|---|---|---|---|---|---|---|---|---|---|---|---|
| At least | But less than | 0 | 1 | 2 | 3 | 4 | 5 | 6 | 7 | 8 | 9 | 10 |
| | | The amount of income tax to be withheld is— | | | | | | | | | | |
| 440 | 450 | 14 | 2 | 0 | 0 | 0 | 0 | 0 | 0 | 0 | 0 | 0 |
| 450 | 460 | 15 | 3 | 0 | 0 | 0 | 0 | 0 | 0 | 0 | 0 | 0 |
| 460 | 470 | 16 | 4 | 0 | 0 | 0 | 0 | 0 | 0 | 0 | 0 | 0 |
| 470 | 480 | 17 | 5 | 0 | 0 | 0 | 0 | 0 | 0 | 0 | 0 | 0 |
| 480 | 490 | 18 | 6 | 0 | 0 | 0 | 0 | 0 | 0 | 0 | 0 | 0 |
| 490 | 500 | 19 | 7 | 0 | 0 | 0 | 0 | 0 | 0 | 0 | 0 | 0 |
| 500 | 520 | 20 | 8 | 0 | 0 | 0 | 0 | 0 | 0 | 0 | 0 | 0 |
| 520 | 540 | 22 | 10 | 0 | 0 | 0 | 0 | 0 | 0 | 0 | 0 | 0 |
| 540 | 560 | 24 | 12 | 0 | 0 | 0 | 0 | 0 | 0 | 0 | 0 | 0 |
| 560 | 580 | 26 | 14 | 2 | 0 | 0 | 0 | 0 | 0 | 0 | 0 | 0 |
| 580 | 600 | 28 | 16 | 4 | 0 | 0 | 0 | 0 | 0 | 0 | 0 | 0 |
| 600 | 620 | 30 | 18 | 6 | 0 | 0 | 0 | 0 | 0 | 0 | 0 | 0 |
| 620 | 640 | 32 | 20 | 8 | 0 | 0 | 0 | 0 | 0 | 0 | 0 | 0 |
| 640 | 660 | 34 | 22 | 10 | 0 | 0 | 0 | 0 | 0 | 0 | 0 | 0 |
| 660 | 680 | 36 | 24 | 12 | 0 | 0 | 0 | 0 | 0 | 0 | 0 | 0 |
| 680 | 700 | 38 | 26 | 14 | 2 | 0 | 0 | 0 | 0 | 0 | 0 | 0 |
| 700 | 720 | 40 | 28 | 16 | 4 | 0 | 0 | 0 | 0 | 0 | 0 | 0 |
| 720 | 740 | 42 | 30 | 18 | 6 | 0 | 0 | 0 | 0 | 0 | 0 | 0 |
| 740 | 760 | 44 | 32 | 20 | 8 | 0 | 0 | 0 | 0 | 0 | 0 | 0 |
| 760 | 780 | 46 | 34 | 22 | 10 | 0 | 0 | 0 | 0 | 0 | 0 | 0 |
| 1,380 | 1,400 | 135 | 117 | 99 | 81 | 63 | 49 | 37 | 25 | 13 | 1 | 0 |
| 1,400 | 1,420 | 138 | 120 | 102 | 84 | 66 | 51 | 39 | 27 | 15 | 3 | 0 |
| 1,420 | 1,440 | 141 | 123 | 105 | 87 | 69 | 53 | 41 | 29 | 17 | 5 | 0 |
| 1,440 | 1,460 | 144 | 126 | 108 | 90 | 72 | 55 | 43 | 31 | 19 | 7 | 0 |
| 1,460 | 1,480 | 147 | 129 | 111 | 93 | 75 | 57 | 45 | 33 | 21 | 9 | 0 |
| 1,480 | 1,500 | 150 | 132 | 114 | 96 | 78 | 60 | 47 | 35 | 23 | 11 | 0 |
| 1,500 | 1,520 | 153 | 135 | 117 | 99 | 81 | 63 | 49 | 37 | 25 | 13 | 1 |

**BIWEEKLY MARRIED PERSONS**

**1.** Locate the range containing the total earnings.

**2.** Find the column with the correct number of withholding allowances.

**3.** Find the intersection of the row and column.

STEPS • STEPS • STEPS • STEPS • STEPS • STEPS • STEPS • STEPS • STEPS • STEPS • STEPS

**STEPS**

**EXAMPLE: SAMANTHA BALERO IS MARRIED AND CLAIMS 2 WITHHOLDING ALLOWANCES. HER TOTAL EARNINGS FOR THE PAY PERIOD ARE $612.50.**

1. Use the left two columns of the Biweekly Married Persons tax table shown here to locate the range containing the total earnings—*At least 600 but less than 620.*

2. Find the column with the correct number of withholding allowances, *2.*

3. Find the intersection of the row and column. The amount of income tax to be withheld is *$6.00.*

# PREPARING AN EMPLOYEE EARNINGS RECORD

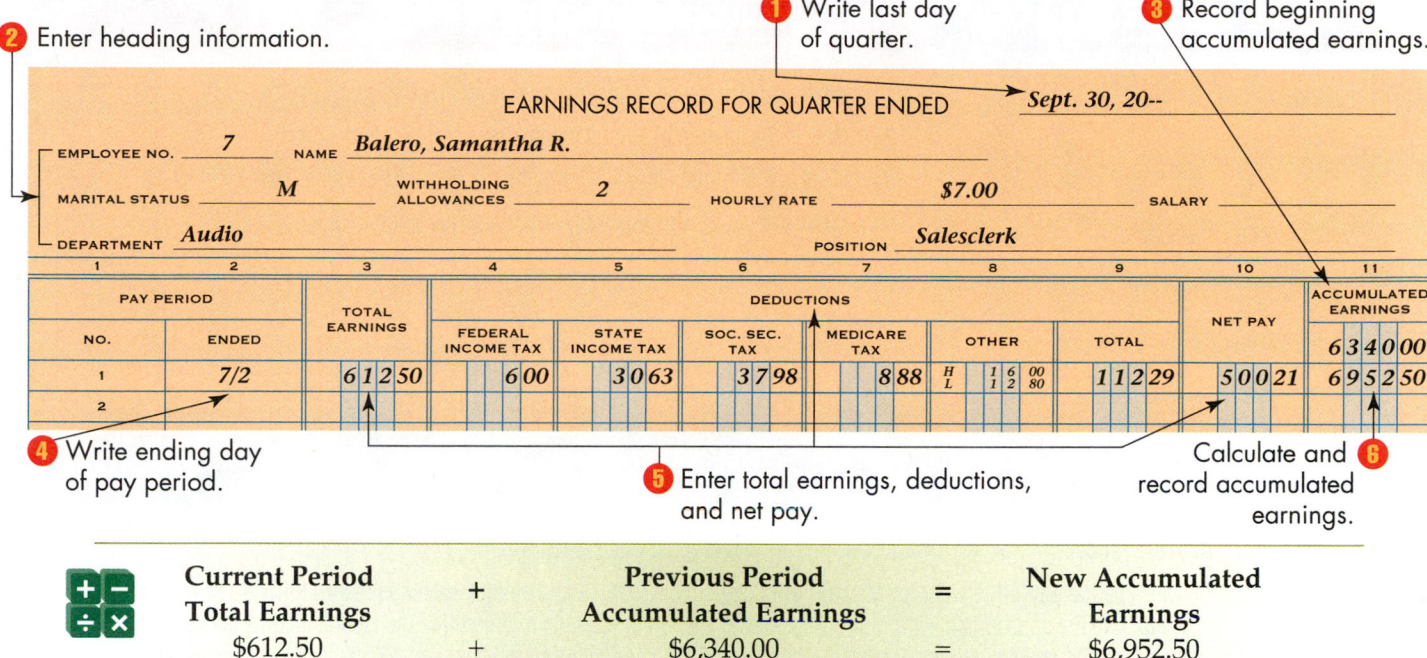

**2** Enter heading information.

**1** Write last day of quarter.

**3** Record beginning accumulated earnings.

EARNINGS RECORD FOR QUARTER ENDED    Sept. 30, 20--

| EMPLOYEE NO. | 7 | NAME | Balero, Samantha R. | | | |
| MARITAL STATUS | M | WITHHOLDING ALLOWANCES | 2 | HOURLY RATE | $7.00 | SALARY |
| DEPARTMENT | Audio | | | POSITION | Salesclerk | |

| | 1 | 2 | 3 | 4 | 5 | 6 | 7 | 8 | | 9 | 10 | 11 |
|---|---|---|---|---|---|---|---|---|---|---|---|---|
| | PAY PERIOD | | TOTAL EARNINGS | | | DEDUCTIONS | | | | | NET PAY | ACCUMULATED EARNINGS |
| | NO. | ENDED | | FEDERAL INCOME TAX | STATE INCOME TAX | SOC. SEC. TAX | MEDICARE TAX | OTHER | TOTAL | | | |
| | | | | | | | | | | | | 6 3 4 0 00 |
| | 1 | 7/2 | 6 1 2 50 | 6 00 | 3 0 63 | 3 7 98 | 8 88 | H L / 1 6 00 / 2 80 | 1 1 2 29 | | 5 0 0 21 | 6 9 5 2 50 |
| | 2 | | | | | | | | | | | |

**4** Write ending day of pay period.

**5** Enter total earnings, deductions, and net pay.

**6** Calculate and record accumulated earnings.

| Current Period Total Earnings | + | Previous Period Accumulated Earnings | = | New Accumulated Earnings |
|---|---|---|---|---|
| $612.50 | + | $6,340.00 | = | $6,952.50 |

A business must send a quarterly report to federal and state governments showing employee taxable earnings and taxes withheld from employee earnings. Detailed information about each employee's earnings is summarized in a single record for each employee. A business form used to record details affecting payments made to an employee is called an **employee earnings record**. An employee's total earnings and deductions for each pay period are summarized on one line of the employee earnings record.

Zytech prepares a new earnings record for each employee each quarter. Samantha Balero's earnings record for the third quarter is shown here.

Accumulated earnings are often referred to as *year-to-date earnings*. Accumulated earnings are needed for each employee because certain payroll taxes do not apply after an employee's earnings reach a certain tax base. For example, employers pay federal and state unemployment taxes only on the first $7,000.00 of each employee's earnings during a calendar year. Social security taxes also are paid only on a maximum amount determined by law. A tax base of $87,000.00 is used in this text. Medicare tax does not have a tax base. Therefore, Medicare tax is calculated on total employee earnings.

## STEPS

STEPS • STEPS • STEPS • STEPS • STEPS • STEPS • STEPS • STEPS • STEPS • STEPS

### PREPARING AN EMPLOYEE EARNINGS RECORD

**1** Write the last day of the yearly quarter, *Sept. 30, 20--,* at the top of the earnings record.

**2** Enter the employee's number, name, marital status, withholding allowances, hourly rate or salary, department, and position in the appropriate space. This information is taken from the employee's personnel records.

**3** Record the fiscal year's accumulated earnings, *$6,340.00,* for the beginning of the current quarter. This information is taken from the ending accumulated earnings for the previous quarter. The Accumulated Earnings column of the employee earnings record shows the accumulated earnings since the beginning of the fiscal year.

**4** Write the ending date of the current pay period, *7/2.*

**5** Enter the total earnings, deductions, and net pay in the assigned columns of the earnings record. This information is taken from the current pay period's payroll register.

**6** Calculate and record the new accumulated earnings, *$6,952.50,* on the same line as the other payroll information for the pay period ended July 2.

## terms review

salary
pay period
payroll
payroll taxes
withholding allowance
tax base
payroll register
employee earnings record

## audit your understanding

1. What three federal taxes are withheld from an employee's pay?
2. How is the amount of federal income tax withholding determined?
3. What is the formula for calculating net pay on the payroll register?
4. What amount is added to the accumulated earnings to get the new accumulated earnings to date?

## work together 3-1

### Completing payroll records

Santa Clara Hardware's partial payroll register for the pay period ended July 3, 20-- and a blank earnings record form are provided in the *Working Papers.* Use the appropriate withholding tax tables shown in this lesson to determine the federal income tax. Deductions for all employees are 5% of total earnings for state income tax, 6.2% for social security tax, and 1.45% for Medicare tax. Use *H* to indicate health insurance and *L* to indicate life insurance. Your instructor will guide you through the following examples. Save your work to complete Work Together 3-2.

1. Prepare a commissions record for Allison Cavero, Supervisor of the Hardware Department, for June of the current year. Ms. Cavero, Employee No. 2, is paid a biweekly salary of $1,200.00 and receives a monthly commission of 1% of net sales. Commissions for the previous month are paid in the first pay period of the current month. Accounting records for the Hardware Department for the month ended June 30 of the current year are as follows: sales on account, $17,895.00; cash and credit card sales, $15,523.00; sales discount, $179.00; sales returns and allowances, $2,039.00.

2. Prepare the payroll register entries for the following two employees:
   a. On line 1: Allison Cavero, Employee No. 2, Hardware Department supervisor, married, two allowances, regular salary of $1,200.00 per pay period plus 1% of net sales. Use the commission calculated in instruction 1. Health insurance premium is $56.00, and life insurance premium is $25.60.
   b. On line 4: James Lee, Employee No. 4, Hardware Department salesclerk, single, one allowance, regular salary of $10.00 per hour with overtime paid at 1½ times the regular rate. He worked 80 hours regular time and 8 hours overtime. Health insurance premium is $28.00.

3. Prepare James Lee's earnings record for the first pay period of the quarter ended September 30, 20--. Accumulated earnings for the quarter ended June 30, 20-- are $11,900.00.

Xtra!
Study Tools
accountingxtra.swlearning.com

## on your own 3-1

### Completing payroll records

Santa Clara Hardware's partial payroll register for the pay period ended October 2, 20-- and a blank earnings record form are provided in the *Working Papers*. Use the appropriate withholding tax tables to determine the federal income tax. Deductions for all employees are 5% of total earnings for state income tax, 6.2% for social security tax, and 1.45% for Medicare tax. Use *H* to indicate health insurance and *L* to indicate life insurance. Work this problem independently. Save your work to complete On Your Own 3-2.

1. Prepare a commissions record for Karla Ramirez, Supervisor of the Paint Department, for September of the current year. Ms. Ramirez, Employee No. 5, is paid a biweekly salary of $1,100.00 and receives a monthly commission of 1% of net sales. Commissions for the previous month are paid in the first pay period of the current month. Accounting records for the Paint Department for the month ended September 30 of the current year are as follows: sales on account, $18,561.20; cash and credit card sales, $13,970.80; sales discount, $196.90; sales returns and allowances, $1,835.10.

2. Prepare the payroll register entries for the following two employees:
   a. On line 11: Karla Ramirez, Employee No. 5, Paint Department supervisor, married, one allowance, regular salary of $1,100.00 per pay period plus 1% of net sales. Use the commission calculated in instruction 1. Health insurance premium is $28.00, and life insurance premium is $25.60.
   b. On line 12: Aaron Sutphin, Employee No. 12, Paint Department salesclerk, single, one allowance, regular salary of $9.50 per hour with overtime paid at 1½ times the regular rate. Sutphin worked 80 hours regular time and 10 hours overtime. Health insurance premium is $28.00.

3. Prepare Aaron Sutphin's earnings record for the first pay period of the quarter ended December 31, 20--. Accumulated earnings for the quarter ended September 30, 20-- are $19,000.00.

# 3-2 Recording a Payroll and Payroll Taxes

## PAYROLL BANK ACCOUNT

Zytech pays its employees biweekly by check. A special payroll checking account and special payroll checks are used. After a biweekly payroll register has been completed, a check is written on Zytech's general checking account payable to Payroll for the total net pay. This check is deposited in a special payroll checking account against which payroll checks are written for each employee's net pay.

The amount of the biweekly deposit to the payroll account equals the sum of the biweekly salary payments. The special payroll account balance, therefore, is reduced to zero as soon as all employees have cashed their payroll checks. Because the special payroll bank account has a balance only until all payroll checks are cashed, no special account is needed in the general ledger.

## AUTOMATIC CHECK DEPOSIT

Employees may authorize an employer to deposit payroll checks directly in their checking accounts at a specified bank. Depositing payroll checks directly to an employee's checking or savings account in a specific bank is called **automatic check deposit**. When automatic check deposit is used, the employer sends the check to the employee's bank for deposit.

Employers may also transfer payroll checks electronically from the employer's account directly to the employee's bank account. A computerized cash payments system that transfers funds without the use of checks, currency, or other paper documents is called **electronic funds transfer (EFT)**. Electronic funds transfer eliminates the need for preparing payroll checks. Under this system, each employee receives a statement of earnings and deductions similar to the detachable stub on a payroll check.

The use of automatic check deposit or electronic funds transfer for payroll does not change the accounting procedures for recording payroll. [CONCEPT: Consistent Reporting]

## EMPLOYER PAYROLL TAXES

Most employers have four separate payroll taxes:

1. Employer social security tax
2. Employer Medicare tax
3. Federal unemployment tax
4. State unemployment tax

Unemployment taxes are used to pay cash benefits to qualified workers for limited periods of unemployment.

 **FYI** FOR YOUR INFORMATION

Federal income tax, social security tax, and Medicare tax withheld from employee earnings are taxes paid by the employee. The employer does not pay federal income tax on a payroll. However, an employer does pay the employer's share of social security and Medicare taxes.

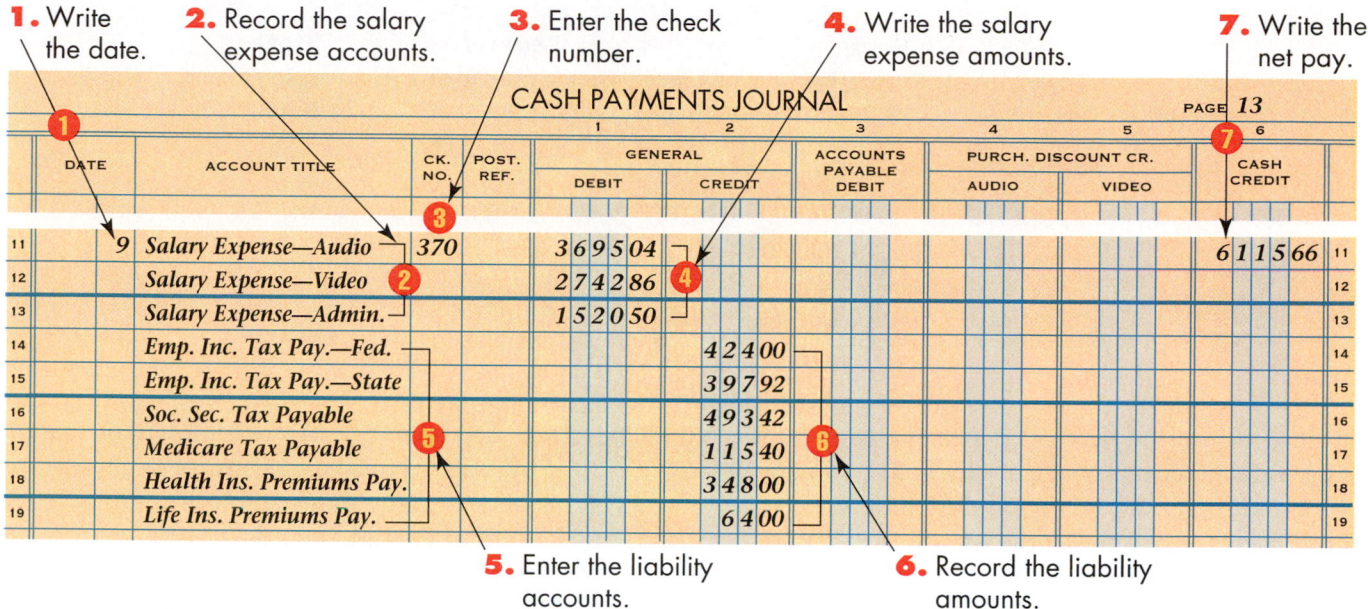

1. Write the date.
2. Record the salary expense accounts.
3. Enter the check number.
4. Write the salary expense amounts.
7. Write the net pay.
5. Enter the liability accounts.
6. Record the liability amounts.

Zytech's payroll register contains the information needed to journalize a payroll as shown in the cash payments journal. The source document for journalizing a payroll payment is the check written for the net payroll amount. [CONCEPT: *Objective Evidence*]

*July 9. Paid cash for biweekly payroll, $6,115.66 (total payroll: audio, $3,695.04; video, $2,742.86; administrative, $1,520.50; less deductions: employee income tax—federal, $424.00; employee income tax—state, $397.92; social security tax, $493.42; Medicare tax, $115.40; health insurance, $348.00; life insurance, $64.00). Check No. 370.*

The T accounts show the debits and credits to all affected accounts.

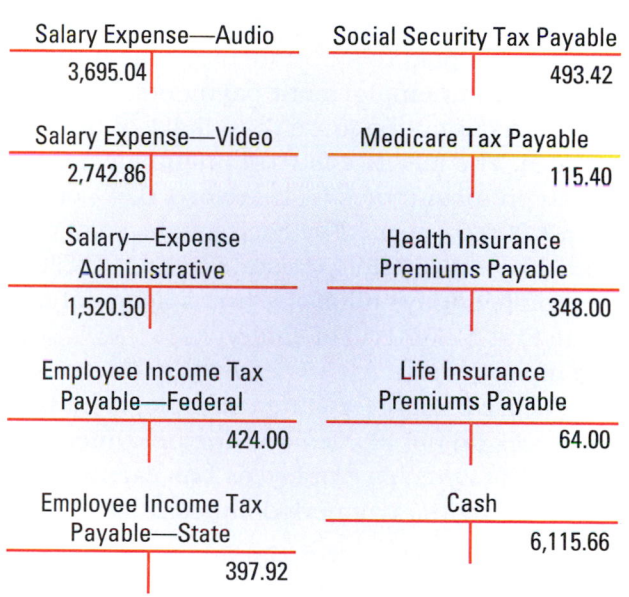

STEPS • STEPS • STEPS • STEPS • STEPS • STEPS • STEPS • STEPS • STEPS • STEPS •

### JOURNALIZING PAYMENT OF A PAYROLL

1. Write the date, *9*, in the Date column of the cash payments journal.

2. Record the salary expense accounts, *Salary Expense—Audio, Salary Expense—Video, Salary Expense—Admin.,* in the Account Title column.

3. Enter the check number, *370,* in the Ck. No. column.

4. Write the salary expense amounts, *$3,695.04, $2,742.86,* and *$1,520.50,* in the General Debit column.

5. Enter the liability accounts, *Emp. Inc. Tax Pay.—Fed., Emp. Inc. Tax Pay.—State, Soc. Sec. Tax Pay., Medicare Tax Pay., Health Ins. Premiums Pay.,* and *Life Ins. Premiums Pay.,* in the Account Title column.

6. Record the liability amounts, *$424.00, $397.92, $493.42, $115.40, $348.00,* and *$64.00,* in the General Credit column.

7. Write the net pay, *$6,115.66,* in the Cash Credit column.

| Department | Taxable Earnings | Social Security 6.2% | Medicare 1.45% | Federal Unemployment 0.8% | State Unemployment 5.4% | Total |
|---|---|---|---|---|---|---|
| Audio | $3,695.04 | $229.09 | $ 53.58 | $29.56 | $199.53 | $ 511.76 |
| Video | 2,742.86 | 170.06 | 39.77 | 21.94 | 148.11 | 379.88 |
| Administrative | 1,520.50 | 94.27 | 22.05 | 12.16 | 82.11 | 210.59 |
| Total | $7,958.40 | $493.42 | $115.40 | $63.66 | $429.75 | $1,102.23 |

Employer payroll taxes expense is based on a percentage of employee earnings. The employer social security tax (6.2%) and Medicare tax (1.45%) rates are the same as the rates used for employees. The federal unemployment tax is 6.2% of the first $7,000.00 earned by each employee. An employer generally can deduct the amounts paid to state unemployment funds from federal unemployment payments. This deduction cannot be more than 5.4% of taxable earnings. The effective federal unemployment tax rate in most states is, therefore, 0.8% on the first $7,000.00 earned by each employee. (Federal 6.2% − deductible for state 5.4% = 0.8%.) The employer pays all of the unemployment tax on the first $7,000.00 of salary.

Employees in a few states have deductions from their earnings for state unemployment tax. Employees do not pay federal unemployment tax.

None of Zytech's employees has earned $7,000.00 by the pay period ended July 2.

Therefore, Zytech's federal unemployment tax is 0.8% of $7,958.40 total earnings, or $63.67. Zytech's state unemployment tax is 5.4% of $7,958.40 total earnings, or $429.75.

Zytech reports employee earnings by department in order to be able to determine what expenses were incurred in earning a department's revenue. Likewise, some of Zytech's expenses are assigned to individual departments when they are directly related to the department. Payroll taxes are a direct result of the employees working in each department. Therefore, payroll taxes expenses are also reported by department.

The department salary column totals of the payroll register are used to calculate the employer's payroll taxes for each department. The calculations are summarized in the table at the top of the page. The calculations for the Audio Department are shown below as an example.

| | Total Taxable Earnings | | Tax Rate | | Audio Department Tax |
|---|---|---|---|---|---|
| Social Security | $3,695.04 | × | 6.2% | = | $229.09 |
| Medicare | $3,695.04 | × | 1.45% | = | 53.58 |
| Unemployment—Federal | $3,695.04 | × | 0.8% | = | 29.56 |
| Unemployment—State | $3,695.04 | × | 5.4% | = | 199.53 |
| Total Audio Department Payroll Taxes Expense | | | | | $511.76 |

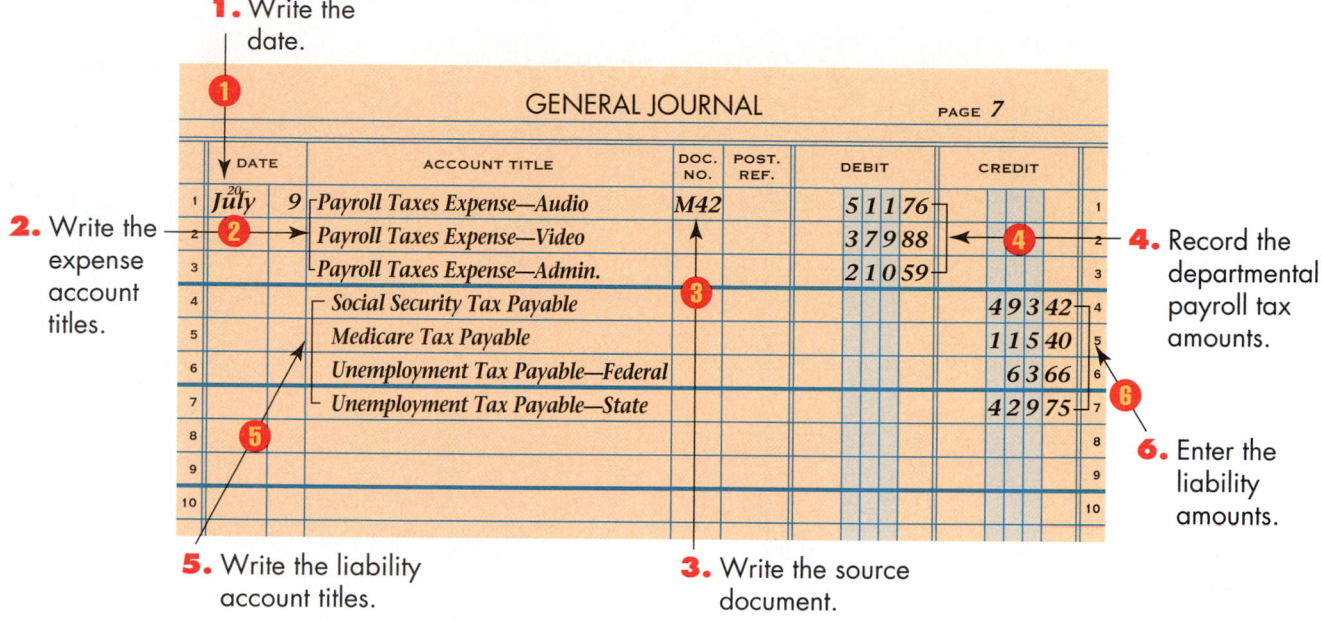

**1.** Write the date.

**2.** Write the expense account titles.

**3.** Write the source document.

**4.** Record the departmental payroll tax amounts.

**5.** Write the liability account titles.

**6.** Enter the liability amounts.

**July 9.** *Recorded employer payroll taxes for the biweekly pay period ended July 2. Taxes owed are social security tax, $493.42; Medicare tax, $115.40; federal unemployment tax, $63.66; state unemployment tax, $429.75; total payroll taxes by department are Audio, $511.76; Video, $379.88; and Administrative, $210.59. Memorandum No. 42.*

The journal entry to record the employer's payroll taxes is shown in the general journal above.

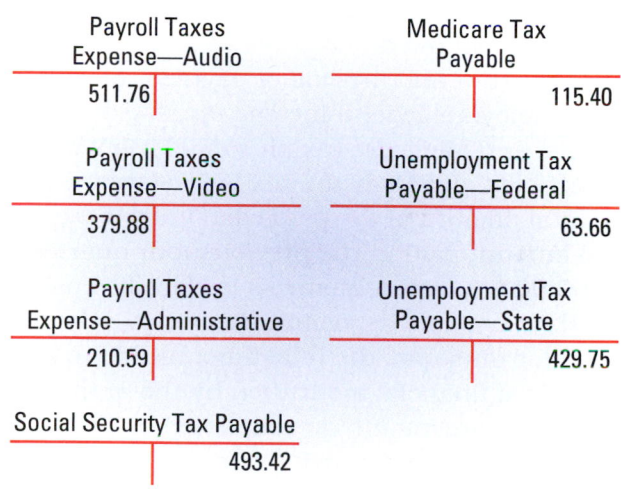

## STEPS

STEPS • STEPS • STEPS • STEPS • STEPS • STEPS • STEPS • STEPS • STEPS • STEPS

### JOURNALIZING EMPLOYER PAYROLL TAXES

**1** Write the date, *July 9,* in the Date column of the general journal.

**2** Write the expense account titles, *Payroll Taxes Expense—Audio, Payroll Taxes Expense—Video,* and *Payroll Taxes Expense—Admin.,* in the Account Title column.

**3** Enter the source document, *M42,* in the Doc. No. column.

**4** Record the amount of payroll taxes expense, *$511.76, $379.88,* and *$210.59,* in the debit column.

**5** Enter the liability account titles, *Social Security Tax Payable, Medicare Tax Payable, Unemploy. Tax Payable—Fed.,* and *Unemploy. Tax Payable—State,* in the Account Title column.

**6** Enter the liability amounts, *$493.42, $115.40, $63.66,* and *$429.75,* in the Credit column.

### FYI
FOR YOUR INFORMATION

Rounding differences can occur when percentage calculations are performed on parts of a total amount and then compared with the percentage of the total. For example, in the calculations on the previous page, federal unemployment tax calculations for the departments resulted in amounts of $29.56, $21.94, and $12.16, for a total of $63.66. However, if the federal unemployment tax rate of 0.8% is applied to the total payroll amount, $7,958.40, the result is $63.6672, which would be rounded to $63.67.

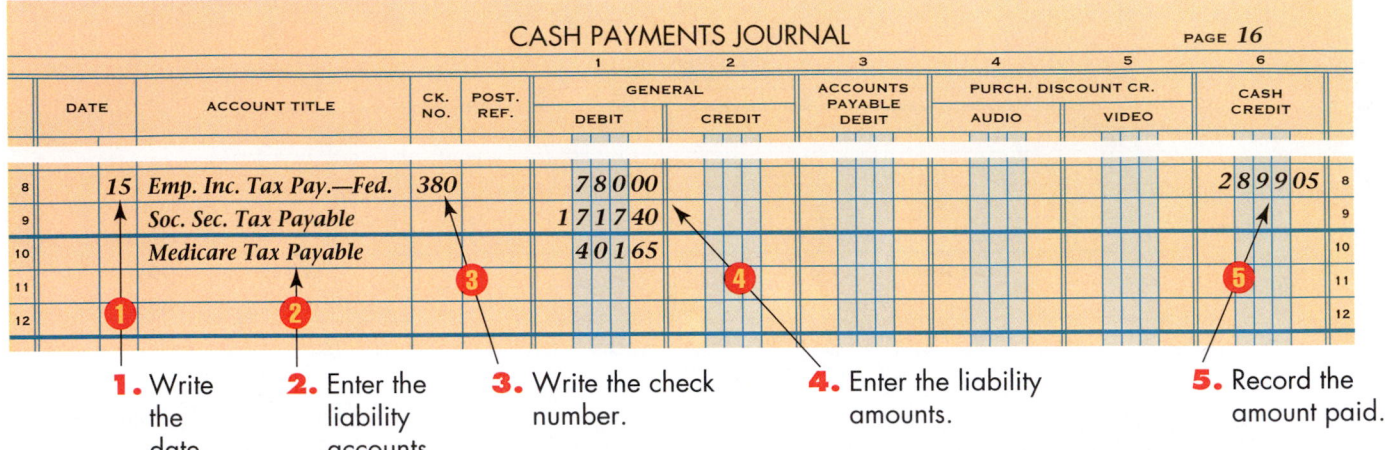

1. Write the date.
2. Enter the liability accounts.
3. Write the check number.
4. Enter the liability amounts.
5. Record the amount paid.

Employers must pay to federal, state, and local governments all payroll taxes withheld from employee earnings as well as the employer payroll taxes. The frequency of payments is determined by the amount owed.

Frequency and method of payment of withheld employees' federal income tax, social security tax, and Medicare tax plus employer's social security tax and Medicare tax are determined by the total amount of tax paid each year. If the total amount paid in the previous four quarters is $50,000 or less, a business is classified as a monthly schedule depositor. A monthly schedule depositor must pay the total amount due to an authorized financial institution by the 15th day of the following month accompanied by Form 8109, Federal Tax Deposit Coupon.

If the total amount paid in the previous four quarters is more than $50,000, a business is classified as a semiweekly schedule depositor. A semiweekly schedule depositor must deposit amounts accumulated on salary payments made on Saturday, Sunday, Monday, or Tuesday by the following Friday. For salary payments made on Wednesday, Thursday, or Friday, payment must be made by the following Wednesday. Companies depositing more than $200,000 in a calendar year must make payments directly to the Internal Revenue Service using the Electronic Federal Tax Payment System (EFTPS).

There are two exceptions to the standard tax payment schedules: (1) If less than $2,500 tax liability is accumulated during a three-month quarter, the deposit may be paid at the end of the month following the end of the quarter. (2) If a tax liability of $100,000 or more is accumulated on any day, the amount must be deposited on the next banking day.

Zytech is classified as a monthly schedule depositor. The biweekly pay days are July 9 and 23. Therefore, the payroll taxes are deposited by August 15.

*August 15. Paid cash for liability for employee federal income tax, $780.00, and for employees' and employer's social security tax, $1,717.40, and Medicare tax, $401.65; total, $2,899.05. Check No. 380.*

Zytech's federal income tax, social security tax, and Medicare tax liabilities for the biweekly pay period ended July 2 and paid on July 9 are deposited on Friday, July 15 as shown here. Zytech's liability for state income tax withholding is paid at the end of each quarter.

**FYI** FOR YOUR INFORMATION

Methods of paying payroll taxes described on this page were in effect when this textbook was written. Businesses with payroll tax liabilities of more than $200,000.00 in 2003 must pay electronically using the EFTPS System. At some future date, all businesses probably will be required to pay payroll taxes electronically. The Treasury Department prefers receiving electronic payroll tax payments.

## JOURNALIZING PAYMENT OF FEDERAL UNEMPLOYMENT TAX LIABILITY

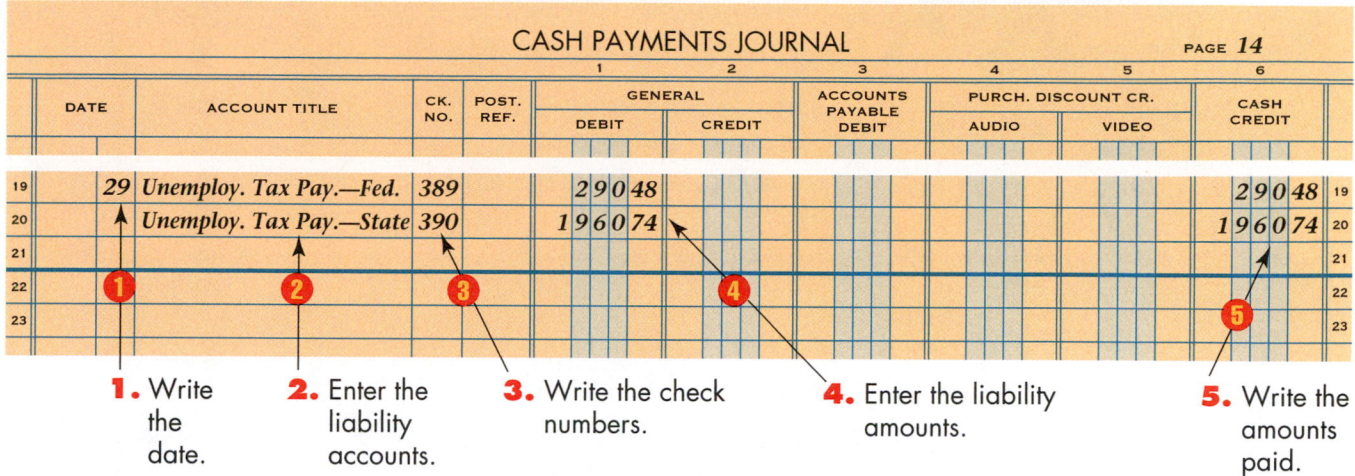

**CASH PAYMENTS JOURNAL**                                            PAGE 14

| | | | | 1 | 2 | 3 | 4 | 5 | 6 | |
|---|---|---|---|---|---|---|---|---|---|---|
| | DATE | ACCOUNT TITLE | CK. NO. | POST. REF. | GENERAL | | ACCOUNTS PAYABLE DEBIT | PURCH. DISCOUNT CR. | | CASH CREDIT |
| | | | | | DEBIT | CREDIT | | AUDIO | VIDEO | |
| 19 | 29 | Unemploy. Tax Pay.—Fed. | 389 | | 2 90 48 | | | | | 2 90 48 | 19 |
| 20 | | Unemploy. Tax Pay.—State | 390 | | 1 9 60 74 | | | | | 1 9 60 74 | 20 |
| 21 | | | | | | | | | | | 21 |
| 22 | | | | | | | | | | | 22 |
| 23 | | | | | | | | | | | 23 |

**1.** Write the date.

**2.** Enter the liability accounts.

**3.** Write the check numbers.

**4.** Enter the liability amounts.

**5.** Write the amounts paid.

If the annual federal unemployment tax for a business is $100.00 or less, it must pay the tax in one payment by January 31 of the following year. If its annual tax is more than $100.00, the business must make quarterly payments in the month following the end of the quarter.

Zytech's federal unemployment tax for the second quarter is $290.48. Therefore, it must make its payment during the first month of the following quarter, July.

> *July 29. Paid cash for federal unemployment tax liability for quarter ended June 30, $290.48. Check No. 389.*

The T accounts show the debits and credits to all affected accounts.

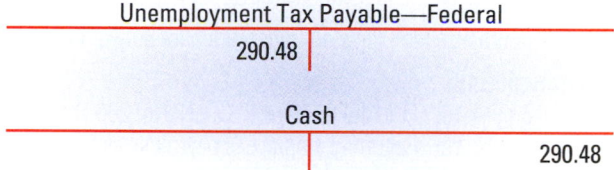

## JOURNALIZING PAYMENT OF STATE UNEMPLOYMENT TAX LIABILITY

Requirements for paying state unemployment taxes vary from state to state. Usually, employers are required to pay the state unemployment tax during the month following each calendar quarter.

Zytech's state unemployment tax for the second quarter is $1,960.74.

> *July 29. Paid cash for state unemployment tax liability for quarter ended June 30, $1,960.74. Check No. 390.*

The T accounts show the debits and credits to all affected accounts.

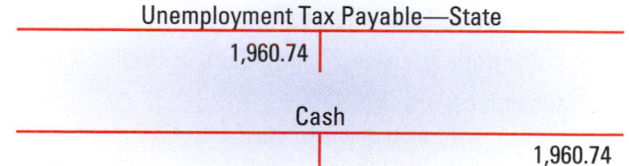

**REMEMBER** Employees do not pay federal unemployment tax.

Xtra!
Study Tools
accountingxtra.swlearning.com

terms review

## terms review

audit your understanding

## audit your understanding

automatic check deposit
electronic funds transfer (EFT)

1. When a payroll is journalized, which account is credited for the total net amount paid to all employees?

2. What four separate payroll taxes do most employers have to pay?

work together 3-2

## work together 3-2

### Journalizing and paying payroll and payroll taxes

Use the solution from Work Together 3-1. A cash payments journal, page 15, and general journal, page 7, are provided in the *Working Papers.* Your instructor will guide you through the following examples.

1. Use a grid similar to the one in this lesson to calculate departmental payroll taxes. You will need two taxable earnings columns, one for FICA Taxable Earnings and one for Unemployment Taxable Earnings, since the bases for these two classes of salaries are different for this period. Social security and Medicare taxes are due on total earnings for this period. Unemployment taxes are due on the following earnings for this period: Hardware, $2,132.00; Paint, $1,983.00; and Administrative, $985.00.

2. Journalize the following transactions for July of the current year.

**Transactions:**

July 10. Paid July 3 payroll. Check No. 260.
　　　10. Recorded employer's payroll taxes for the pay period ended July 3. Memo. No. 33.
　　　15. Paid employees' federal income tax withholding, social security tax, and Medicare tax liabilities for the pay period ended July 3. Check No. 265.
　　　29. Paid federal unemployment tax, $745.84, and state unemployment tax, $5,034.44, for the quarter ended June 30. Check No. 270.

on your own 3-2

## on your own 3-2

### Journalizing and paying payroll and payroll taxes

Use the solution from On Your Own 3-1. A cash payments journal, page 18, and general journal, page 10, are provided in the *Working Papers.* Work independently to complete the following problem.

1. Use a grid similar to the one in this lesson to calculate departmental payroll taxes. You will need two taxable earnings columns, one for FICA Taxable Earnings and one for Unemployment Taxable Earnings, since the bases for these two classes of salaries are different for this period. Social security and Medicare taxes are due on total earnings for this period. Unemployment taxes are due on the following earnings for this period: Hardware, $2,050.00; Paint, $1,850.00; and Administrative, $1,010.00.

2. Journalize the following transactions for October of the current year.

**Transactions:**

Oct. 9. Paid October 2 payroll. Check No. 335.
　　　9. Recorded employer's payroll taxes for the pay period ended October 2. Memo. No. 48.
　　 14. Paid employees' federal income tax withholding, social security tax, and Medicare tax liabilities for the pay period ended October 2. Check No. 339.
　　 28. Paid federal unemployment tax, $91.65, and state unemployment tax, $618.64, for the quarter ended September 30. Check No. 344.

## SUMMARY

*After completing this chapter, you can*

1. Define accounting terms related to a departmental payroll system.

2. Identify accounting concepts and practices related to a departmental payroll system.

3. Prepare a commissions record and calculate commission on net sales.

4. Complete payroll records.

5. Journalize payroll transactions.

# Explore Accounting

EXPLORE ACCOUNTING • EXPLORE ACCOUNTING • EXPLORE ACCOU

## Pretax Benefits

Federal income tax is a major expense for most families. Current laws permit employers to set up retirement and cafeteria plans that allow employees to set aside a portion of their earnings on a pretax basis. Employees pay no taxes in that tax year on the amounts withheld.

### Retirement Plans

For amounts placed in many qualified retirement accounts, income tax is "deferred" on earnings. Individuals will pay income taxes on the amounts withdrawn from their retirement accounts when they retire. Because of the income tax deferral, the amount available at retirement will be much larger.

The general requirements of most pretax retirement plans include the following:

1. The employer withholds the specified amount and deposits it in qualified investments, such as mutual funds.
2. The amount of earnings an employee can defer each year is limited.
3. Employees are assessed penalties if they withdraw amounts from their retirement account before the age of $59\frac{1}{2}$.

4. Withdrawals from retirement plan accounts must begin by the time the person reaches age $70\frac{1}{2}$.

### Medical Savings Accounts and Cafeteria Plans

Medical savings accounts and cafeteria plans permit employees to have a portion of their pretax earnings deducted from their salaries. The amounts are used to reimburse out-of-pocket medical or childcare expenses. The advantage is that payment is made with pretax dollars. However, the amount of earnings withheld is available only for the purpose designated. For example, if an employee authorizes $50.00 a month to be withheld for medical costs but uses only $500.00 during the year, the remaining $100.00 that was withheld is not reimbursable to the employee.

**Instructions:** Answer the following questions.

1. Why would Congress allow employees to defer taxes?

2. Are there any disadvantages to participating in these tax deferral plans?

Xtra!
Quizzing
accountingxtra.swlearning.com

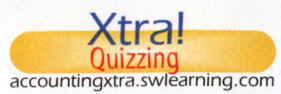

# 3-1 APPLICATION PROBLEM
### Preparing departmental commissions records

CarpetWorld employs a departmental supervisor for each of its two departments, Carpet and Drapery. Departmental supervisors receive a biweekly salary and monthly commissions of 1% of net sales. They receive their commissions for the previous month in the first pay period of the current month. The following data are from the accounting records for the month ended February 28 of the current year.

a.  Carpet Department: sales on account, $8,623.40; cash and credit card sales, $12,936.20; sales discount, $148.90; sales returns and allowances, $1,699.30.
b.  Drapery Department: sales on account, $7,223.89; cash and credit card sales, $13,987.11; sales discount, $337.17; sales returns and allowances, $654.33.

**Instructions:**
Prepare February's commissions record for each of the following departmental supervisors. Save your work to complete Application Problem 3-2.

a.  **Carpet Department**
   Employee name: Sarah Logan
   Employee number: 9
   Regular salary: $540.00

b.  **Drapery Department**
   Employee name: Ryan Paniaqua
   Employee number: 14
   Regular salary: $520.00

# 3-2 APPLICATION PROBLEM
### Completing a payroll register

CarpetWorld has two departments, Carpet and Drapery. It uses a biweekly payroll system. It pays its salesclerks and employees in the accounting department on an hourly basis, and they receive 1½ times the regular hourly pay rate for all hours worked in excess of 40 hours in one week. The employee hours worked and pay rates for selected employees are shown below.

| Name | Department | ID No. | Hours | Hourly Rate | Salary |
|---|---|---|---|---|---|
| Bodade, Nilesh | Carpet | 7 | 83 | $7.00 | |
| Logan, Sarah | Carpet | 10 | — | | $540.00 |
| Paniaqua, Ryan | Drapery | 16 | — | | $520.00 |
| Quinn, Benjamin | Administrative | 9 | 84 | $6.50 | |
| Ragasa, Corazan | Drapery | 15 | 85 | $8.00 | |

A partially completed payroll register for the biweekly pay period ended March 12 of the current year is provided in the *Working Papers*.

Use the commissions records from Application Problem 3-1 and the partially completed payroll register provided in the *Working Papers* to complete the payroll register. The following additional information is also needed:

a.  A deduction for federal income tax is to be made from each employee's total earnings. Use the appropriate income tax withholding tables shown in Lesson 3-1.
b.  A deduction of 2% for state income tax is to be made from each employee's total earnings.
c.  A deduction of 6.2% for social security and 1.45% for Medicare tax is to be made from each employee's total earnings.
d.  All employees have dental insurance, $9.40, and health insurance, $13.20, deducted from their pay each biweekly pay period. These deductions are to be recorded in the Other Deductions column of the payroll register. Use *D* to indicate the dental insurance deduction. Use *H* to indicate the health insurance deduction. Both of these deductions are written on one line of the payroll register for each employee.

**Instructions:**
Complete the payroll register for the pay period ended March 12 and paid on March 19 of the current year. Save your work to complete Application Problems 3-3 and 3-4.

# 3-3 APPLICATION PROBLEM
## Completing an employee earnings record

Use the payroll register from Application Problem 3-2. A partially completed employee earnings record for each of CarpetWorld's employees appears in the *Working Papers.*

**Instructions:**

Complete the employee earnings record for each employee. This pay period is the sixth of the first quarter of the current year.

# 3-4 APPLICATION PROBLEM
## Journalizing payment of a departmental payroll

Use the payroll register from Application Problem 3-2.

**Instructions:**

1. Record the March 19 payroll payment on page 6 of a cash payments journal. The source document is Check No. 463.
2. Use a grid similar to the one in Lesson 3-2 to calculate departmental payroll taxes. Because this payroll is early in the year, all employee earnings are subject to all payroll taxes.
3. Record the employer payroll taxes on page 6 of a general journal. Use March 19 of the current year as the date. The source document is Memorandum No. 41.

# 3-5 APPLICATION PROBLEM   PEACHTREE   QUICKBOOKS
## Calculating and journalizing payment of payroll tax liabilities

Use the following payroll data for John's Automotive for the first quarter of the current year. Employer tax rates are social security, 6.2%; Medicare, 1.45%; federal unemployment, 0.8%; and state unemployment, 5.4%.

| Period | Total Earnings | Social Security Tax Withheld | Medicare Tax Withheld | Federal Income Tax Withheld |
|---|---|---|---|---|
| Biweekly Period Ended March 28 | $ 7,742.00 | $480.00 | $112.26 | $911.00 |
| First Quarter | 46,452.00 | — | — | — |

**Instructions:**

1. Calculate the liability for employee federal income tax, social security tax, and Medicare tax for the biweekly pay period ended March 28. Include both the employees' tax withheld and the employer liability for social security and Medicare taxes. Record the payment of federal income tax withholding, social security tax, and Medicare tax on page 7 of a cash payments journal. The payment is made on April 3 using Check No. 492 as the source document.
2. Calculate the federal unemployment tax liability for the first quarter. Record the payment on page 8 of a cash payments journal. The payment is made on April 30 using Check No. 515 as the source document.
3. Calculate the state unemployment tax liability for the first quarter. Record the payment on page 8 of a cash payments journal. The payment is made on April 30 using Check No. 516 as the source document.

### Completing payroll records, journalizing payment of a payroll, and journalizing payroll taxes

ColdGuard has two departments, Windows and Doors. It uses a biweekly payroll system of 26 pay periods per year. ColdGuard pays salesclerks and employees in the accounting department on an hourly basis, and they receive 1½ times the regular hourly pay rate for all hours worked in excess of 40 hours in one week. The hours worked report shows the following information.

| Name | ID No. | Dept. | Reg-1 | OT-1 | Reg-2 | OT-2 |
|---|---|---|---|---|---|---|
| Bullock, Andrea E. | 2 | Windows | — | | — | |
| Demars, Scott R. | 3 | Doors | 40 | 2 | 40 | 1 |
| Kabic, Zora E. | 1 | Windows | 40 | 1 | 40 | 2 |
| Mondero, Teodora C. | 4 | Doors | — | | — | |
| Purdy, Julie M. | 5 | Windows | 40 | 2 | 40 | 1.5 |
| Trang, Phuong M. | 6 | Admin. | 40 | 4 | 40 | 3 |

Hourly rates and salaries are as follows:

| | |
|---|---|
| Bullock, Andrea E. | $600.00 |
| Demars, Scott R. | $7.50 per hour |
| Kabic, Zora E. | $7.40 per hour |
| Mondero, Teodora C. | $620.00 |
| Purdy, Julie M. | $6.60 per hour |
| Trang, Phuong M. | $6.50 per hour |

Department supervisors receive a biweekly salary and monthly commissions of 1% of net sales. Commissions for the previous month are paid in the first pay period of the next month.

ColdGuard's partially completed payroll records for selected employees for the pay period ended March 14 and paid on March 21 of the current year are provided in the *Working Papers*.

### Instructions:

1. Complete the commissions record for each departmental supervisor. The following data are from the accounting records for the month of February of the current year:
   a. Windows Department: sales on account, $5,543.89; cash and credit card sales, $8,047.02; sales discount, $92.01; sales returns and allowances, $285.40.
   b. Doors Department: sales on account, $5,312.32; cash and credit card sales, $9,409.85; sales discount, $148.63; sales returns and allowances, $1,478.21.
2. Use the time records and completed commissions records to complete the payroll register for the pay period ended March 14 and paid March 21 of the current year. Use the following additional data to complete the payroll register:
   a. A deduction for federal income tax is to be made from each employee's total earnings. Use the appropriate income tax withholding tables shown in Lesson 3-1 in this chapter.
   b. A deduction of 3% for state income tax is to be made from each employee's total earnings.
   c. Deduction of 6.2% for social security tax and 1.45% for Medicare tax are to be made from each employee's total earnings.
   d. All employees have medical insurance, $14.80, and dental insurance, $8.20, deducted from their pay each biweekly pay period. Use *M* to indicate the medical insurance deduction. Use *D* to indicate the dental insurance deduction.
3. Complete the employee earnings record for each employee. This pay period is the fifth of the first quarter of the current year.
4. Journalize the March 21 payroll payment on page 5 of a cash payments journal. The source document is Check No. 211.
5. Use a grid similar to the one in this chapter to calculate departmental payroll taxes. You will need only one taxable earnings column, since no employee's accumulated earnings are greater than the base for unemployment tax. Employer tax rates are social security, 6.2%; Medicare, 1.45%; federal unemployment, 0.8%; and state unemployment, 5.4%.
6. Journalize the employer payroll taxes on page 7 of a general journal. Use March 21 of the current year as the date. The source document is Memorandum No. 33.

# 3-7 CHALLENGE PROBLEM

### Completing a payroll register, journalizing payment of a payroll, and journalizing payroll taxes

Assume Congress recently past an Act raising all payroll taxes. The new rates are as follows:
- Social Security: 7.1% of earnings up to a maximum of $94,500 in each calendar year
- Medicare: 2.05% of all earnings in a calendar year
- Federal Unemployment: 6.8% of the first $10,000.00 earned by each employee during a calendar year. Employers are permitted to deduct up to a maximum of 5.9% paid to state unemployment funds. The effective unemployment rates for the state ColdGuard operates in are 0.9% for federal unemployment and 5.9% for state unemployment.

**Instructions:**

1. Use the earnings data from Mastery Problem 3-6. Complete a new payroll register for the pay period ended March 14. Use the new tax rates passed by Congress. Medical and dental insurance remains the same for each employee. (Compare the payroll registers completed in problems 3-6 and 3-7. Note the impact of higher taxes on each individual's net pay.)
2. Journalize the March 21 payroll payment on page 5 of a cash payments journal. The source document is Check No. 211.
3. Use a grid similar to the one in this chapter to calculate departmental payroll taxes.
4. Journalize the employer payroll taxes on page 7 of a general journal. Use March 21 of the current year as the date. The source document is Memorandum No. 33. (Compare the employer payroll taxes expense entries completed in problems 3-6 and 3-7. Note the impact of higher taxes on the employer.)

## applied communication

Write a letter to two local payroll processing companies. Request information about their services. When you receive the information, compare and contrast the services offered by the two companies. Keep a copy of your letters in the "Personal Letters" section of your *Career Portfolio*.

## case for critical thinking

Zytech deducts department sales returns and allowances and sales discounts from sales before calculating manager discounts. Mary Dennenberg, manager of the Audio Department, does not think this policy is fair. "I work hard to train my salesclerks to close their sales, and I work hard on closing my own sales. Why should I be penalized if a customer returns the merchandise?" As the company president, how would you respond to Ms. Dennenberg?

## SCANS workplace competency

**Information Competency:** Using Computers to Process Information

**Concept:** Employers need individuals who can use computers to acquire, organize, analyze, and communicate information. Competent employees are familiar with word processing, spreadsheet, database, multimedia, and Internet software.

**Application:** Use a spreadsheet program to complete the payroll register in Application Problem 3-2. Use formulas to calculate totals, net pay, state income tax, social security and Medicare taxes, and column totals.

## • auditing for errors

Tony Parducci, a new payroll clerk for PowerGlide, prepared the commissions record shown here for Dianne Connelly. PowerGlide pays all salespersons a biweekly salary of $1,300.00 plus a monthly commission of 1.5% of department net sales. Commissions for the previous month are paid in the first pay period of the current month. Accounting records for Ms. Connelly's department for the month ended November 30 of the current year indicate: sales on account, $55,170.32; cash and credit card sales, $12,371.40; sales discount, $1,452.22; sales returns and allowances, $954.65.

**Instructions:** As the senior accounting clerk, you have responsibility for reviewing the work prepared by new hires. Examine the commissions record prepared by Mr. Parducci. Calculate the new commission on net sales if errors are found.

### COMMISSIONS RECORD

EMPLOYEE NO. ___6___          EMPLOYEE NAME _Dianne Connelly_____

COMMISSION RATE __1%__                    MONTH _December_   YEAR _20--_

DEPARTMENT __Skates__                    REGULAR BIWEEKLY SALARY _$1,300.00_

| | | |
|---|---|---|
| Sales on Account . . . . . . . . . . . . . . . . . . . . . . . . . | | $ 55,710.32 |
| Cash and Credit Card Sales . . . . . . . . . . . . . | | 12,371.40 |
| *equals* Total Sales for the month . . . . . . . . . . . . . | | $ 68,081.72 |
| *Less:* | | |
| Sales Discounts . . . . . . . . . . . . . | $ 145.22 | |
| Sales Returns and Allowances . . . . . | 954.65 | 1,099.87 |
| *Equals:* . . . . . . . . . . . . . . . . . . . . . . . . . . . . . | | |
| Net Sales . . . . . . . . . . . . . . . . . . . . . . . . . . . . | | $ 66,981.85 |
| *times* Commission Rate . . . . . . . . . . . . . . . . . . . . | | 0.01 |
| *equals:* Commission on Net Sales . . . . . . . . . . . . . | | $ 6,698.19 |

## • analyzing Costco's financial statements

Expenses incurred in one fiscal period but not paid until a later date are called *accrued expenses.* During the last fiscal period of each year, Costco incurs salary and benefit expenses that are not paid until the following fiscal year. This occurs when a fiscal year ends in the middle of a payroll period. The accounting concept *Matching Revenue with Expenses* requires that financial statements must show all business expenses for a fiscal period. Consequently, Costco must report the unpaid salary and benefit amount even though it has not yet paid out cash. The unpaid amount owed for incurred employee salaries and benefits represents a liability. Use the material shown in Appendix B of this text to answer the questions below.

**Instructions:**

1. Referring to the consolidated balance sheets on page B-5, (a) list the title of the account that represents an amount owed for salaries and benefits and (b) list the amounts owed for this account on August 31, 2003, and September 1, 2002.

2. Referring to the ten-year operating and financial highlights on page B-2, identify one fact that would help explain the increase in this liability. List at least two other reasons that might explain the increase.

## Automating Payroll Accounting Data—Payroll Procedures

### Payroll Transactions

Every pay period, employee payroll information is entered into the payroll system. The information needed for each employee includes the date, pay information, and employee deductions. The employee taxes are entered or automatically calculated by the Automated Accounting program. Payroll transaction information is entered into the Payroll screen.

The payroll register can be accessed on the Payroll tab of the Other Activities window. The fields in the payroll register are shown in the two illustrations below. Use the horizontal scroll bar at the bottom of the work area to move to the right and left.

### Entering Payroll Transactions

For each employee, the information shown on the payroll window is entered for each pay period:

hours worked, regular and overtime, tax deductions, and employee deductions. Accuracy is very important when entering this data in order to eliminate under- or overpayments.

Employee transaction data is entered in the Payroll tab in the Other Activities window. Click on the Payroll tab to display the payroll screen. Use the following steps to enter payroll transactions.

1. Enter the date of the check.

2. Select the employee from the Employee drop-down list or key the first letter of the last name until the correct name appears.

3. Verify that the check number displayed in the Check No. cell is correct. If it is not correct, enter the correct check number.

4. Use the Tab key to enter salary information. If the employee is salaried, the salary amount

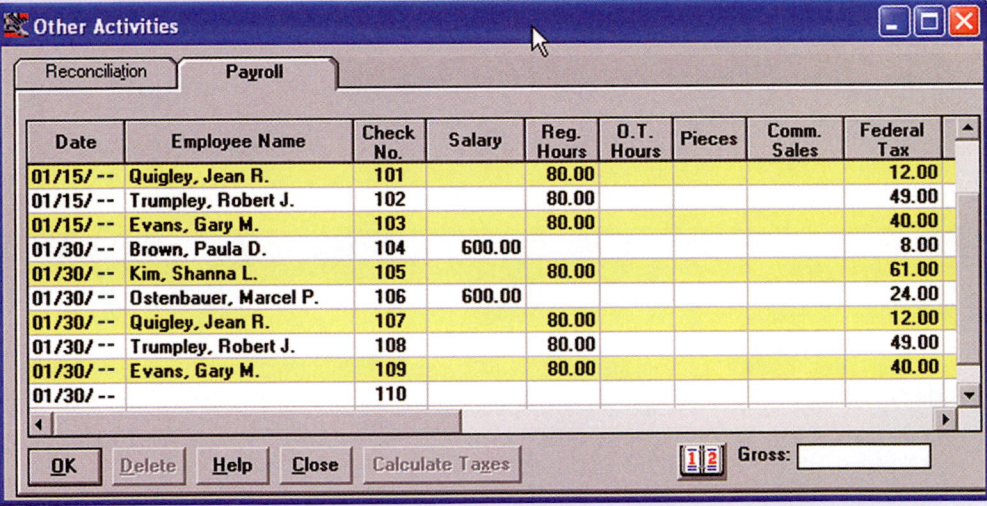

will be displayed. If it is necessary to key a different salary, the salary amount cell can be changed. Entering a new amount will override the salary amount in the cell.

5. If the employee is paid by the hour, enter the regular hours worked in the Reg. Hours cell.

6. If the employee is paid hourly and has worked overtime, enter the overtime hours worked in the O.T. Hours cell.

7. Click on the Calculate Taxes button to have the software automatically calculate the employee taxes. After the calculations are completed, the employee taxes are displayed in the various employee taxes cells. Visually check each cell to verify that an amount appears.

8. Enter all employee deductions.

9. Click OK. A display of the payroll check will be shown on the screen.

10. Click the Close button to continue or click Print to print the check.

## Generating Payroll Journal Entries for the Period

The payroll journal entries can be generated automatically without any calculations by selecting the Current Payroll Journal Entry menu item from the Options menu. When the confirmation box appears, click Yes after checking the entry for accuracy. The general journal window automatically appears, displaying the payroll journal entries that were created. Click the Post button. Posting is done after verifying that the journal entry appears to be correct.

## Generating the Journal Entry for Employer's Payroll Taxes

Generating the journal entry for the employer's payroll taxes can be done by using the menu item for employer's payroll taxes. Automated Accounting allows you to automatically generate the entry for the employer's portion of the payroll taxes. To automatically generate the journal entry, use the following steps.

1. Choose Employer's Payroll Taxes from the Options menu.

2. When the confirmation box appears, click Yes.

3. The entry is automatically generated. Click the Post button.

4. Click the Close button of the general journal.

## AUTOMATING MASTERY PROBLEM 3-6: Completing payroll records, journalizing payment of a payroll, and journalizing payroll taxes

### Instructions:

1. Load the *Automated Accounting 8.0* or higher software.

2. Select data file A03-6.

3. Select File from the menu bar and choose Save As. Key the path to the drive and directory that contains your data files. Save the database with a filename of A03-6 XXX XXX (where the X's are your first and last name).

4. Access Problem Instructions through the Browser tool. Read the Problem Instruction screen.

5. Key the data listed in the problem on page 80.

6. Save your file and exit the Automated Accounting software.

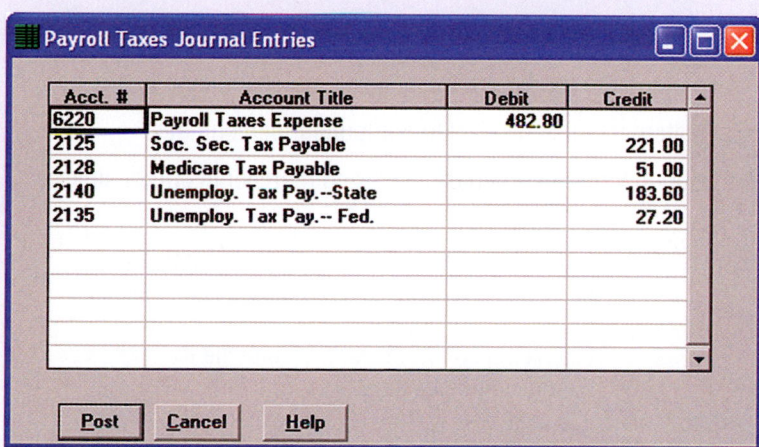

# CHAPTER 4

# Financial Reporting for a Departmentalized Business

**After studying Chapter 4, you will be able to:**

1. Define accounting terms related to cost accounting and financial reporting for a departmentalized merchandising business.

2. Identify accounting concepts and practices related to cost accounting and financial reporting for a departmentalized merchandising business.

3. Distinguish between direct and indirect expenses.

4. Prepare an interim departmental statement of gross profit.

5. Prepare a work sheet for a departmentalized merchandising business.

6. Prepare financial statements for a departmentalized merchandising business.

7. Analyze financial statements using selected component percentages.

8. Complete end-of-period work for a departmentalized merchandising business.

- fiscal period
- responsibility accounting
- direct expense
- indirect expense
- departmental margin
- departmental margin statement
- gross profit
- departmental statement of gross profit
- periodic inventory
- perpetual inventory
- gross profit method of estimating an inventory
- component percentage
- schedule of accounts receivable
- schedule of accounts payable
- work sheet
- trial balance
- plant assets
- depreciation expense
- responsibility statements
- income statement
- statement of stockholders' equity
- capital stock
- retained earnings
- dividends
- balance sheet
- adjusting entries
- closing entries
- post-closing trial balance
- accounting cycle

**Point Your Browser**
accountingxtra.swlearning.com

## • Trek Bicyles

COURTESY OF TREK BICYCLE CORPORATION

### TREK BICYCLES ADJUSTS PRODUCT LINE TO CONSUMER TRENDS AND TECHNOLOGICAL ADVANCEMENTS

Trek Bicycles started producing hand-built, steel bike frames in 1976 in an old barn located in Waterloo, Wisconsin. During the last 30 years, the company has grown into a global enterprise employing over 1,600 employees worldwide. Trek seized international recognition when Texan Lance Armstrong rode the first American bike frame to victory in the world's most prestigious bicycle race, the Tour de France.

Over the years, Trek has expanded its operation and now designs and produces a complete line of high-end bicycles, components, and accessories. The company manufacturers a variety of both road and mountain bicycles incorporating innovative designs and aerospace composites, as well as helmets, gloves, clothing, lights, tools, hydration packs, locks, pumps, and lubricants.

Initially, road bikes were 75% of Trek's business. Gradually, however, mountain bikes exceeded road bikes in popularity. By 1996, 80% of Trek's product offerings consisted of mountain bikes. Today, Trek continues to be a privately held corporation and has matured into the world's largest producer of bicycles sold through specialty retail stores.

### Critical Thinking

1. Why is it important that Trek maintain separate sales records for road and mountain bikes?
2. Trek no longer manufactures bicycles solely using steel. What is the advantage of using technologically advanced materials in building bicycle frames, and how might that affect sales?

Source: www.trekbikes.com

Xtra!
Today
accountingxtra.swlearning.com

### ACCOUNTING FIRMS

Go to the homepage for the following two international accounting firms:

PricewaterhouseCoopers: www.pwcglobal.com

Ernst & Young: www.ey.com/global/

### Instructions

Create a table listing the following data for each company:

1. Number of global employees.
2. Amount of global revenue.
3. Number of countries in which it operates.

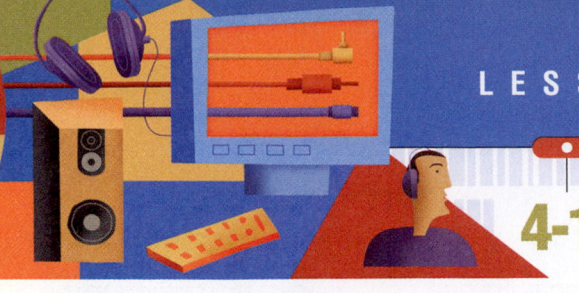

# 4-1 Responsibility Accounting for a Merchandising Business

Financial statements summarize the financial information that a business records. These statements are then analyzed to evaluate the financial position and progress of the business. The managers of a business use the statements to make financial decisions for future operations. The financial statements are also used in preparing tax reports and other reports, such as those required by the SEC, which must be completed at least once a year. Therefore, financial statements are prepared at least once a year. The length of time for which a business summarizes and reports financial information is called a **fiscal period**. [CONCEPT: Accounting Period Cycle]

The accounting period cycle concept states that changes in financial information are reported for a specific period of time in the form of financial statements. The time period for which financial statements are prepared depends on the needs of the business. An accounting period may be one month, three months, six months, or one year. For tax purposes, every business prepares financial statements at the end of each year.

Successful businesses generally prepare financial statements monthly to analyze results and take corrective action when needed. A fiscal period may be any length of time, but it is generally considered to refer to a year. Each business determines the length of the fiscal period it uses. Zytech uses a calendar-year fiscal period.

©GETTY IMAGES/PHOTODISC

## making ethical decisions

### Sharing Your Knowledge

John Oglesby is a certified public accountant who works as a computer consultant. He has just completed helping a local movie theater install a new ticketing system that tracks when and how often individuals come to the theater. The system will enable the theater to analyze its customers and select movies that target customers having specific movie preferences.

John has just received a phone call from another theater in the same city. The theater owner asks John to evaluate its existing computer systems and suggest any recommendations. After allowing the theater owner to present his request, John politely declines to accept the engagement.

**Instructions**

Use the AICPA *Code of Professional Conduct* to determine if John's actions violate the confidentiality rule. When researching the AICPA *Code of Professional Conduct,* begin by selecting the section title that most closely relates to the issue. Read the Rule and any related Interpretations. Then scan the titles of the Ethics Rulings for any case that may be similar to the issue.

1. Each manager is assigned responsibility for only those revenues, costs, and expenses for which the manager can make decisions and affect the outcome.
2. The revenues, costs, and expenses for which a manager is responsible must be readily identifiable with the manager's unit. For example, if a manager is responsible for advertising expense, that manager should make decisions about advertising. Also, a separate record should be kept for the manager's advertising expense. Thus, responsibility accounting traces revenues, costs, and expenses to the individual managers who are responsible for making decisions about those revenues, costs, and expenses.

Controlling costs is essential to a business's success. However, who should control a business's costs? Good management practices require that each manager be responsible for controlling all costs incurred by the manager's business unit. Assigning control of business revenues, costs, and expenses as a responsibility of a specific manager is called **responsibility accounting**. Merchandising businesses with effective cost controls generally use some kind of responsibility accounting. The two important features of a successful responsibility accounting system are described above.

A typical merchandising business income statement reports net income earned during a fiscal period. However, the statement usually does not report specific information that a department manager can use to control departmental costs. Therefore, merchandising businesses often prepare departmental statements to show each department's contribution to net income.

In responsibility accounting, operating expenses are classified as either direct or indirect expenses. An operating expense identifiable with and chargeable to the operation of a specific department is called a **direct expense**. The cost of supplies used by a specific department is an example of a direct expense. An operating expense chargeable to overall business operations and not identifiable with a specific department is called an **indirect expense**. Therefore, the cost of electricity used by a business's overall operation is an example of an indirect expense. A department manager has little or no control over the use of electricity in the department.

The revenue earned by a department less its cost of merchandise sold and less its direct expenses is called **departmental margin**. A statement that reports departmental margin for a specific department is called a **departmental margin statement**.

Zytech uses responsibility accounting to help control costs and expenses. Zytech has two merchandising departments: Audio and Video. Each department's revenue, cost of merchandise sold, and direct expenses are recorded in separate departmental general ledger accounts as shown in Zytech's chart of accounts.

Each business develops a chart of accounts to best meet its needs. Zytech groups its departmental accounts by type, such as operating revenue, cost of merchandise, direct expenses, and indirect expenses. For example, accounts under Direct Expenses—Audio are 6100 numbers. Accounts under Direct Expenses—Video are 6200 numbers.

©GETTY IMAGES/PHOTODISC

| | | | | CASH PAYMENTS JOURNAL | | | | | | PAGE 16 |
| | | | | 1 | 2 | 3 | 4 | 5 | 6 | |
| DATE | ACCOUNT TITLE | CK. NO. | POST. REF. | GENERAL | | ACCOUNTS PAYABLE DEBIT | PURCH. DISCOUNT CR. | | CASH CREDIT | |
| | | | | DEBIT | CREDIT | | AUDIO | VIDEO | | |
| 1 | Apr.²⁰⁻ 1 Advertising Exp.—Audio | 610 | | 40 00 00 | | | | | 40 00 00 | 1 |

Procedures for recording revenue, cost, and expense transactions are similar for most merchandising businesses. The journalizing procedures used by Zytech were discussed in Chapters 1 and 2. Zytech maintains separate accounts for each department's merchandise inventory, sales, purchases, and direct expenses. Departmental direct expenses include advertising, depreciation, payroll taxes, salaries, and supplies. Separate departmental accounts for sales, merchandise inventory, purchases, and direct expenses provide information needed to prepare departmental margin statements.

A journal entry prepared by Zytech to record a direct expense is shown above. Zytech's Audio Department manager decided to buy the advertising services. The advertising promotes the department's sale of audio equipment. Since the department manager controls the advertising expense and the department receives the benefits, the expense is classified as a direct expense. To ensure that such expenses are recorded as direct expenses, the account title also includes the department's name, Advertising Expense—Audio. Other direct expenses are shown in cash payments journal entries in Chapters 1 and 3. Debits to expense accounts that have a department name in the account title are entries for direct expenses.

| | | | | CASH PAYMENTS JOURNAL | | | | | | PAGE 16 |
| | | | | 1 | 2 | 3 | 4 | 5 | 6 | |
| DATE | ACCOUNT TITLE | CK. NO. | POST. REF. | GENERAL | | ACCOUNTS PAYABLE DEBIT | PURCH. DISCOUNT CR. | | CASH CREDIT | |
| | | | | DEBIT | CREDIT | | AUDIO | VIDEO | | |
| 8 | 1 Rent Expense | 611 | | 1 50 00 00 | | | | | 1 50 00 00 | 8 |

A journal entry prepared by Zytech to record an indirect expense is shown above. The Audio Department uses a portion of the space rented by Zytech. However, the decision to rent the specific facility was made by the company president, not the Audio Department manager. In addition, rent expense is not separated by departments but is one payment for the entire facility used by all departments. Since this expense is not separated by departments, the expense is recorded as an indirect expense. Indirect expenses are reported in the company's income statement but not in departmental margin statements. Direct and indirect expenses are reported in the same way each fiscal period. [CONCEPT: Consistent Reporting]

Other journal entries for indirect expenses are shown in Chapter 1. The same accounting procedures must be followed in the same way in each accounting period. Business decisions are based on the financial information reported on financial statements. Some decisions require a comparison of current financial statements with previous financial statements. If accounting information is recorded and reported differently each accounting period, comparisons from one accounting period to another may not be possible.

TERMS REVIEW • TERMS
AUDIT YOUR UNDERSTANDING
WORK TOGETHER • WORK TOGETHER • WORK TOGETHER • WORK TOGETHER • WORK TOGETHER

## • terms review

fiscal period
responsibility accounting
direct expense
indirect expense
departmental margin
departmental margin statement

## • audit your understanding

1. What two features are required if responsibility accounting is to be successful?

2. For what type of accounts does Zytech have separate departmental accounts in the general ledger?

3. In order to ensure the features of a responsibility accounting system, what should be done if a direct expense used by departments is documented by a single invoice?

## • work together 4-1

### Identifying direct and indirect expenses

Mulberry, Inc., has two departments: Crafts and Fabrics. Mulberry completed the transactions below.

Use a form similar to the one below. For each transaction, indicate:

   a.   Whether the expense is a direct expense (identifiable with a specific department) or an indirect expense.

   b.   The title of the expense account.

The first transaction is completed as an example.

| Trans. No. | Direct Expense or Indirect Expense | Expense Account Title |
|---|---|---|
| 1 | Indirect | Utilities Expense |

1. Paid cash for utilities bill.

2. Paid cash for advertising in a craft fair program. The ad was prepared by the Craft Department and includes craft products only.

3. Paid cash for rush delivery (delivery expense) on a special order of fabric for a regular customer.

4. Paid cash for bimonthly payroll for all administrative, fabric, and crafts employees. Salesclerks are hired by specific department managers.

5. Paid cash for maintenance on the company's web site.

6. Paid a consultant to train all salesclerks in effective selling techniques.

7. Paid a retainer fee to an attorney for legal advice.

8. Paid cash for monthly payroll taxes (consider the taxes on the accounting employees only).

9. Paid cash for a promotional mailing to past customers to announce a new line of craft supplies.

10. Paid cash for food and beverages for the annual employee party.

## on your own 4-1

**Identifying direct and indirect expenses**

Elegant Interiors, Inc., has two departments: Furniture and Accessories. Elegant Interiors completed the transactions below.

Use a form similar to the one used in Work Together 4-1 to summarize whether the following transactions are direct or indirect expenses.

1. Paid cash for rent of the company building.
2. Paid cash for newspaper advertising of a new furniture line.
3. Paid cash for overnight delivery of special accessories items.
4. Paid monthly bill for Internet service for all company computer stations.
5. Paid cash for refreshments for the opening of an art show in the Accessories Department.
6. Paid cash for company credit card fees charged on total monthly sales.
7. Reimbursed Furniture Department manager for travel costs to a seminar on furniture finishes.
8. Paid to have the carpeting in the store cleaned.
9. Paid cash for uniforms for the elementary school's girls' soccer team to promote the store.
10. Recorded the bank service charge on the store's checking account.

*ON YOUR OWN • ON YOUR OWN • ON YOUR OWN • ON YOUR OWN • ON*

# business structures

BUSINESS STRUCTURES • BUSINESS STRUCTURES • BUSINESS STRUCTURE

## Differentiating Between Personal and Business Taxes

When running a business, owners must differentiate between the *personal taxes* collected from employees and customers and the *business taxes* incurred by a company as a consequence of daily operations. Each category is handled differently. For example, businesses similar to Zytech are required to withhold payroll taxes from their employees, such as federal income tax and Medicare tax, and forward the tax amounts to the appropriate government agency. Consequently, these personal payroll taxes represent a liability for Zytech until they are paid.

The sales tax collected on the sale of merchandise or services is also classified as a personal tax. Like personal payroll taxes, it is paid by individuals, collected by businesses, and later remitted to the required government agency. Until the sales tax is paid, it too represents a liability.

Like individuals, businesses also pay taxes. For example, successful businesses like Zytech must pay income tax on business profits. Zytech is also required by law to pay taxes on the earnings of its employees. Based on its payroll, Zytech must pay social security tax, Medicare tax, and unemployment taxes. Companies classify the taxes paid by a business as expenses, although they are temporarily recorded in liability accounts until they are paid.

LESSON • LESSON • LESSON • LESSON • LESSON • LESSON

# 4-2 Interim Departmental Statement of Gross Profit

## INTERIM FINANCIAL STATEMENTS

A departmentalized business prepares the same financial statements in the same form as a nondepartmentalized business. In addition, a departmentalized business usually prepares reports about the performance of each department. In the last lesson, you learned that companies interested in controlling costs often prepare a departmental margin statement. This statement shows the revenue earned by a department less its cost of merchandise sold and less its direct expenses. You will learn how to prepare a departmental margin statement in Lesson 4-4.

The amount of revenue from sales less the cost of goods sold is called **gross profit**. Gross profit, therefore, shows the direct relationship between sales and sales price and merchandise inventory and the cost of merchandise inventory. By analyzing a department's gross profit data, managers can determine the amount of revenue remaining after the cost of merchandise has been deducted from net sales. A statement showing gross profit for each department is called a **departmental statement of gross profit**. A review of gross profit information may show a need to do the following:

1. Change merchandise selling prices.
2. Change suppliers of merchandise.
3. Add, delete, or change products.
4. Discontinue a department.

Gross profit information reflects changes between costs and selling prices. Departmental gross profit data also provide information that can be used to quickly determine potential profits. Businesses prepare annual financial statements at the end of each fiscal year. However, a successful business does not wait a full year to analyze its gross profit and take action to reverse negative trends. Therefore, businesses often pre-

pare an interim departmental statement of gross profit at the end of a month or quarter. The word *interim* means *between terms* or *in the meantime*.

### Determining Ending Merchandise Inventory

To prepare an interim departmental statement of gross profit, both beginning and ending inventory amounts are needed. The ending inventory for one month becomes the beginning inventory for the next month.

Two principal methods are used to determine actual amounts of merchandise on hand. A merchandise inventory determined by counting, weighing, or measuring items of merchandise on hand is called a **periodic inventory**. A periodic inventory is sometimes referred to as a *physical inventory*. A merchandise inventory determined by keeping a continuous record of increases, decreases, and balance on hand is called a **perpetual inventory**.

The cost of merchandise inventory is relatively easy to determine at any time when a perpetual inventory is kept. However, keeping a perpetual inventory for a merchandising business with many inventory items requires a good computer database system. The increased use of point-of-sale terminals or cash registers and barcodes on merchandise has made perpetual inventories increasingly common.

For a periodic inventory, the business takes a physical count of merchandise. However, a periodic inventory on a monthly basis may not be practical. When a perpetual inventory is not kept and a monthly periodic inventory is not practical, a business may estimate merchandise inventory. Estimating inventory by using the previous year's percentage of gross profit on operations is called the **gross profit method of estimating an inventory**.

# ESTIMATING ENDING MERCHANDISE INVENTORY

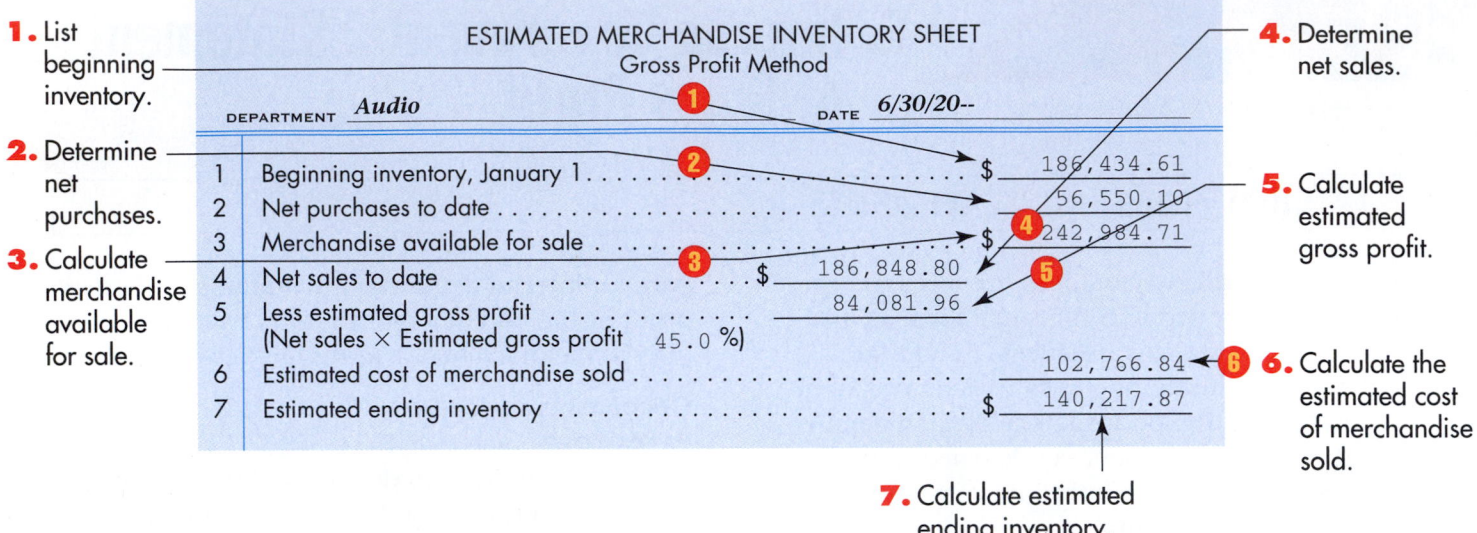

**1.** List beginning inventory.

**2.** Determine net purchases.

**3.** Calculate merchandise available for sale.

**4.** Determine net sales.

**5.** Calculate estimated gross profit.

**6.** Calculate the estimated cost of merchandise sold.

**7.** Calculate estimated ending inventory.

**ESTIMATED MERCHANDISE INVENTORY SHEET**
Gross Profit Method

DEPARTMENT *Audio*   DATE *6/30/20--*

| | | |
|---|---|---|
| 1 | Beginning inventory, January 1 | $ 186,434.61 |
| 2 | Net purchases to date | 56,550.10 |
| 3 | Merchandise available for sale | $ 242,984.71 |
| 4 | Net sales to date | $ 186,848.80 |
| 5 | Less estimated gross profit (Net sales × Estimated gross profit 45.0%) | 84,081.96 |
| 6 | Estimated cost of merchandise sold | 102,766.84 |
| 7 | Estimated ending inventory | $ 140,217.87 |

Zytech uses a periodic inventory system. It uses the gross profit method of estimating an inventory to determine monthly ending inventory. The Audio Department's estimated inventory sheet prepared on June 30 is shown above. Zytech used the following steps to prepare the estimated merchandise inventory sheet.

## STEPS · STEPS · STEPS · STEPS · STEPS · STEPS · STEPS · STEPS · STEPS · STEPS

### PREPARING AN ESTIMATED MERCHANDISE INVENTORY SHEET

**1** Obtain the beginning inventory, January 1, from the general ledger. The balance of *Merchandise Inventory—Audio*, *$186,434.61,* is the actual merchandise inventory on hand at the beginning of the fiscal year. The amount is the result of the periodic inventory count from December 31 of the previous year.

**2** Determine net purchases to date, *$56,550.10,* as follows:

| | | |
|---|---|---|
| | Purchases—Audio | $59,430.60 |
| − | Purchases Discount—Audio | − 1,090.20 |
| | | $58,340.40 |
| − | Purchases Returns and Allowances—Audio | − 1,790.30 |
| = | Net Purchases to Date (January 1–June 30) | $56,550.10 |

**3** Add lines 1 and 2 to determine the merchandise available for sale, *$242,984.71.*

**4** Determine net sales to date, *$186,848.80,* as follows:

| | | |
|---|---|---|
| | Sales—Audio | $190,540.20 |
| − | Sales Discount—Audio | − 680.60 |
| | | $189,859.60 |
| − | Sales Returns and Allowances—Audio | − 3,010.80 |
| = | Net Purchases to Date (January 1–June 30) | $186,848.80 |

**5** Calculate the estimated gross profit, *$84,081.96,* by multiplying line 4 by 45.0%. The percentage used is a gross profit estimate based on records of previous years' operations.

**6** Calculate the estimated cost of merchandise sold, *$102,766.84,* by subtracting line 5 from line 4.

**7** Calculate the estimated ending inventory, *$140,217.87,* by subtracting line 6 from line 3. This estimate is used on the interim departmental statement of gross profit.

Financial Reporting for a Departmentalized Business

**Zytech Media Corporation**
**Interim Departmental Statement of Gross Profit**
**For Month Ended June 30, 20--**

| | Audio | *% of Net Sales | Video | % of Net Sales | Total | % of Net Sales |
|---|---|---|---|---|---|---|
| Operating Revenue: | | | | | | |
| Net Sales . . . . . . . . . . . . . . . | $32,883.65 | 100.0 | $36,546.30 | 100.0 | $69,429.95 | 100.0 |
| Cost of Merchandise Sold: | | | | | | |
| Est. Mdse. Inv., June 1. . . . . . | $149,387.48 | | $145,799.62 | | $295,187.10 | |
| Net Purchases . . . . . . . . . . . . | 8,916.40 | | 17,073.50 | | 25,989.90 | |
| Mdse. Available for Sale. . . . . | $158,303.88 | | $162,873.12 | | $321,177.00 | |
| Less Est. End. Inv., June 30. . | 140,217.87 | | 138,772.66 | | 278,990.53 | |
| Cost of Merchandise Sold . . . | | 18,086.01 | 55.0 | 24,100.46 | 65.9 | 42,186.47 | 60.8 |
| Gross Profit on Operations . . . . | $14,797.64 | 45.0 | $12,445.84 | 34.1 | $27,243.48 | 39.2 |

*Rounded to nearest 0.1%

Zytech's interim departmental statement of gross profit for the month ended June 30 is shown above. The data are organized into three sections:

1. Operating revenue.
2. Cost of merchandise sold.
3. Gross profit on operations.

The beginning inventory for each department is the estimated ending inventory from the interim departmental statement of gross profit for the month ended May 31 of the current year.

An interim departmental statement of gross profit can be prepared whether perpetual or periodic inventory methods are used. When a perpetual method is used, the up-to-date inventory amount for the end of a month is readily available. When a periodic inventory method is used, the inventory value at the end of the month is estimated using the gross profit method.

# ANALYZING AN INTERIM DEPARTMENTAL STATEMENT OF GROSS PROFIT

To help a manager analyze financial information, relationships between items in a financial statement are calculated. The percentage relationship between one financial statement item and the total that includes that item is called a **component percentage**. Component percentages may be shown in a separate column on a financial statement. Four basic components are included in every sales dollar:

1. Cost of merchandise sold.
2. Gross profit on operations.
3. Total operating expenses.
4. Net income before federal income tax.

Zytech analyzes its interim departmental statement of gross profit monthly by calculating a component percentage for cost of merchandise sold and gross profit on operations. The component percentages for operating expenses and net income are calculated and analyzed at the end of each fiscal period.

{ **REMEMBER** Gross profit is the difference between net sales and cost of merchandise sold. Direct and indirect expenses are not considered when calculating gross profit. }

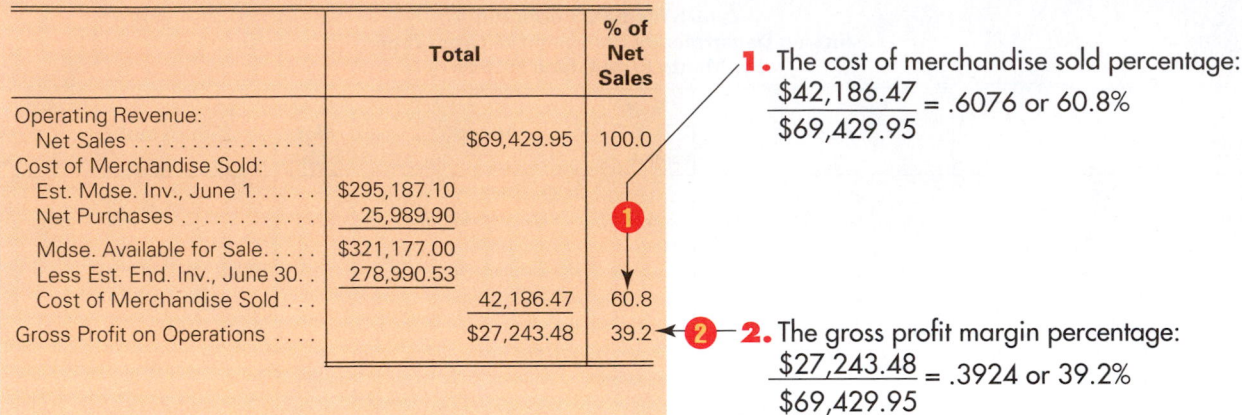

| | Total | % of Net Sales |
|---|---|---|
| Operating Revenue: | | |
| Net Sales . . . . . . . . . . . . . . . | $69,429.95 | 100.0 |
| Cost of Merchandise Sold: | | |
| Est. Mdse. Inv., June 1. . . . . . | $295,187.10 | |
| Net Purchases . . . . . . . . . . . | 25,989.90 | |
| Mdse. Available for Sale. . . . . | $321,177.00 | |
| Less Est. End. Inv., June 30. . | 278,990.53 | |
| Cost of Merchandise Sold . . . | 42,186.47 | 60.8 |
| Gross Profit on Operations . . . . | $27,243.48 | 39.2 |

**1.** The cost of merchandise sold percentage:
$$\frac{\$42,186.47}{\$69,429.95} = .6076 \text{ or } 60.8\%$$

**2.** The gross profit margin percentage:
$$\frac{\$27,243.48}{\$69,429.95} = .3924 \text{ or } 39.2\%$$

The cost of merchandise sold is a significant cost for all merchandising businesses. Management attempts to keep this cost as low as possible. The calculation of Zytech's component percentage for total cost of merchandise sold is shown above. Both the cost of merchandise sold percentage and the gross profit percentage use net sales in the denominator of the equation. From these percentages, we learn that for every $100 in sales, Zytech spent $60.80 to obtain the goods sold. The remainder, $39.20, represents the gross profit on operations. Gross profit on operations must be large enough to cover total operating expenses and produce a net income.

Since Zytech is a departmental business, similar calculations are made for each department. Zytech uses the departmental component percentages to analyze the results of each department.

# DETERMINING ACCEPTABLE LEVELS OF PERFORMANCE

For component percentages to be useful, a business must know acceptable levels of performance. Two sources are frequently used to determine acceptable performance. A business's historical records provide percentages that can be compared across time. The business should investigate significant changes in component percentages over time.

Industry performance standards are another source that businesses use for comparison. Industry trade organizations survey businesses and publish significant data such as component percentages. While these percentages represent industry averages, they allow useful comparisons to be made.

Based on these sources, Zytech determines that the total cost of merchandise sold percentage should be 60.0% or less. As a result, total gross profit on operations should be 40.0% or more. Zytech further determines that these percentages are also good targets for each of the departments.

An analysis of the interim departmental statement of gross profit for the month ended June 30 indicates some unacceptable levels of performance. The component percentage for total cost of merchandise sold, 60.8%, is slightly more than 60.0%. The component percentage for total gross profit on operations, 39.2%, is less than 40.0%. Further review shows that the component percentages for the Audio Department are at acceptable levels but those of the Video Department are not. The company must find ways to improve gross profit on operations. Possible action could be to form strategies for increasing net sales or decreasing the cost of purchases. It is important to understand that if Zytech did not prepare monthly departmental statements of gross profit, the need for improvement in the Video Department might not have been discovered until the end of the year.

accountingxtra.swlearning.com

## • terms review

TERMS REVIEW • TERMS

gross profit
departmental statement
   of gross profit
periodic inventory
perpetual inventory
gross profit method of estimating
   an inventory
component percentage

## • audit your understanding

AUDIT YOUR UNDERSTANDING

1. In addition to regular financial statements, what other reports does a departmentalized business prepare?

2. What are the two principal methods for determining amounts of merchandise on hand?

3. What are the three sections of a departmental statement of gross profit?

## • work together 4-2

WORK TOGETHER • WORK TOGETHER • WORK TOGETHER • WORK TOGETHER

### Preparing an interim departmental statement of gross profit

The following data are obtained from the accounting records of Willow Glen Interior Design on May 31 of the current year. Estimated merchandise inventory forms and statement paper are provided in the *Working Papers.* Your instructor will guide you through the following examples.

|  | Kitchen | Bath |
|---|---|---|
| Beginning Inventory, January 1 | $110,000.00 | $84,000.00 |
| Estimated Beginning Inventory, May 1 | 111,426.00 | 87,072.00 |
| Net Purchases, January 1 to April 30 | 42,500.00 | 30,100.00 |
| Net Sales, January 1 to April 30 | 78,600.00 | 52,300.00 |
| Net Purchases for May | 8,300.00 | 5,400.00 |
| Net Sales for May | 20,200.00 | 8,400.00 |
| Estimated Gross Profit Percentage | 48.0% | 45.0% |

1. Prepare an estimated merchandise inventory sheet for each department for the month ended May 31.

2. Prepare an interim departmental statement of gross profit for the month ended May 31. Calculate and record component percentages for cost of merchandise sold and gross profit on operations. Round percentage calculations to the nearest 0.1%.

## on your own 4-2

**Preparing an interim departmental statement of gross profit**

The following data are obtained from the accounting records of Lassen Heating and Air Conditioning, Inc., on April 30 of the current year. Estimated merchandise inventory forms and statement paper are provided in the *Working Papers.* Work this problem independently.

|  | Commercial | Residential |
|---|---|---|
| Beginning Inventory, January 1 | $280,000.00 | $108,000.00 |
| Estimated Beginning Inventory, April 1 | 287,894.00 | 124,884.00 |
| Net Purchases, January 1 to March 31 | 120,500.00 | 62,300.00 |
| Net Sales, January 1 to March 31 | 196,600.00 | 88,400.00 |
| Net Purchases for April | 66,200.00 | 13,400.00 |
| Net Sales for April | 71,100.00 | 14,400.00 |
| Estimated Gross Profit Percentage | 42.0% | 48.0% |

1.  Prepare an estimated merchandise inventory sheet for each department for the month ended April 30.

2.  Prepare an interim departmental statement of gross profit for the month ended April 30. Calculate and record component percentages for cost of merchandise sold and gross profit on operations. Round percentage calculations to the nearest 0.1%.

©GETTY IMAGES/PHOTODISC

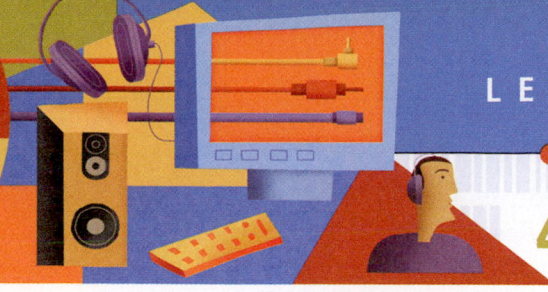

# 4-3 Preparing a Work Sheet for a Departmentalized Business

## PROVING THE ACCURACY OF POSTING TO SUBSIDIARY LEDGERS

**Zytech Media Corporation**
**Schedule of Accounts Receivable**
**December 31, 20--**

| | |
|---|---:|
| Jason Campari | $ 950.60 |
| DTS Systems | 644.70 |
| Kim Electronics | 1,785.00 |
| Links Golf Supply | 1,592.50 |
| Katie Matthews | 245.70 |
| Olympic Productions | 1,391.25 |
| Wawona School District | 775.25 |
| Bianca Velario | 3,675.00 |
| David Young | 2,695.00 |
| Total Accounts Receivable | $13,755.00 |

Zytech prepares a report showing the total of all accounts receivable ledger accounts. A list of customer accounts, account balances, and total amount due from all customers is called a **schedule of accounts receivable**. The total of a schedule of accounts receivable must equal the balance of the general ledger controlling account, Accounts Receivable. Zytech's schedule of accounts receivable is shown above.

Zytech also prepares a report showing the total of all accounts payable ledger accounts.

A list of vendor accounts, account balances, and total amount due all vendors is called a **schedule of accounts payable**. The total of a schedule of accounts payable must equal the balance of the controlling account, Accounts Payable. Zytech's schedule of accounts payable is shown below.

The balances of both controlling accounts, Accounts Receivable and Accounts Payable, agree with the totals shown on the two schedules. Therefore, posting to subsidiary ledgers is assumed to be correct.

**Zytech Media Corporation**
**Schedule of Accounts Payable**
**December 31, 20--**

| | |
|---|---:|
| AudioMax | $ 3,660.60 |
| Digital Warehouse | 9,420.00 |
| LED Television, Inc. | 1,590.00 |
| MegaWatt Sound, Inc. | 1,514.30 |
| Plasma Electronics | 10,840.00 |
| Western Digital Systems | 3,610.40 |
| Yogashi Corporation | 725.00 |
| Total Accounts Payable | $31,360.30 |

Zytech completes the end-of-fiscal-period work as of December 31 each year. A columnar accounting form used to summarize the general ledger information needed to prepare financial statements is called a **work sheet**. Zytech uses an expanded work sheet to sort information needed for departmental margin statements. The 12-column work sheet prepared by Zytech on December 31 is shown on pages 102–103. Besides the standard eight amount columns that normally appear on a work sheet, Zytech uses four additional columns: Departmental Margin Statement—Audio Debit and Credit and Departmental Margin Statement—Video Debit and Credit. Information in these four additional columns is used to prepare departmental margin statements.

## Trial Balance on a Departmental Work Sheet

If debits equal credits in journals and if posting is done correctly, debits will equal credits in a general ledger. A proof of the equality of debits and credits in a general ledger is called a **trial balance**. A trial balance can be prepared at any time to check the equality of debits and credits in the general ledger. A trial balance should always be prepared as part of the end-of-fiscal-period activities.

A trial balance is prepared in the Trial Balance columns of the work sheet. General ledger accounts are listed in the Account Title column in the same order in which they appear in the general ledger. All accounts are listed, regardless of whether there is a balance or not. Zytech's trial balance for the current year ended December 31 is shown on the work sheet. When Zytech prepares its departmental work sheet, notice that three income summary accounts are used. Two are used for adjusting inventory accounts related to separate departments, Income Summary—Audio and Income Summary—Video. They are also used to close the revenue, cost, and direct expense accounts of both departments. Income Summary—General is used for other closing entries.

Also notice that Zytech writes the account Federal Income Tax Expense on the work sheet two lines below Departmental Margin—Video. This location simplifies subtotaling the income statement columns and calculating additional income tax

expense. Procedures for calculating corporate income tax are described in Chapter 13.

After all general ledger accounts and balances have been entered, the Trial Balance columns are totaled, checked for equality, and ruled. The two column totals, $1,325,257.99, are the same.

## Adjustments on a Work Sheet with Departmental Margins

Some of the general ledger accounts are not up to date. For example, uncollectible accounts expense has not been recorded. The entries needed to bring accounts up to date are planned in the Adjustments columns of the work sheet.

The information needed for adjusting Zytech's general ledger accounts for the year ended December 31 of the current year begins on the page following the work sheet illustration.

Zytech's adjustments are in the work sheet's Adjustments columns. The departmental merchandise inventory adjustments are recorded in each department's appropriate income summary account. Adjustments are made for uncollectible accounts expense, changes in departmental merchandise inventory, supplies used, insurance expired, depreciation, and estimated federal income tax expense.

©GETTY IMAGES/PHOTODISC

# careers in accounting

## Dianne Villanueva Conry, Part-Time Senior Accountant and Accounting Instructor

COURTESY OF DIANNE VILLANUEVA CONRY

Employment in the accounting profession is sometimes associated with working long, intense hours. In many instances, this association may be true but certainly not in all. For Dianne Villanueva Conry, a career in accounting has allowed her to keep her primary focus on her family. Presently, Dianne works as a part-time senior accountant at Clinimetrics Research Associates, Inc., and teaches an evening accounting class at the University of California Santa Cruz Extension Program in Cupertino, California.

To reach her current positions, Dianne earned a Bachelor of Science degree in Business Administration with the Accountancy Option from California State University, Fresno. Following graduation, she remained at CSUF for another year and earned a Master of Science degree in Financial Accounting. Because of her strong academic background and part-time work experience with a local CPA, she was hired by PricewaterhouseCoopers, one of the four largest accounting firms in the world. During her tenure at PWC, she acquired public accounting auditing experience and passed the certified public accountancy exam for the state of California. After three years of employment as a public accountant, she accepted a job offer from Sony Electronics. Dianne's new position helped satisfy her expanding interest in corporate accounting and allowed her to gain a more complete understanding of private industry practices.

After starting her family, Dianne had an opportunity to work part-time for Horn Murdock Cole. Working as the internal controller, start-up services instructor, and information technology troubleshooter, Dianne gained invaluable experience regarding all levels of consulting.

Presently, Dianne teaches an evening accounting class and works 24 to 28 hours per week at Clinimetrics Research Associates, Inc., a privately held firm that performs clinical research and drug trials related to the pharmaceutical, biotechnology, and medical device industries. At Clinimetrics, she has successfully combined her experience and knowledge in auditing, private industry, and consulting. Although Dianne has recurring accounting and payroll responsibilities, she finds special projects to be the most rewarding.

**Salary Range:** A senior accountant could expect to earn $70,000–$150,000, depending on the industry, company, part of the country, and level of experience.

**Qualifications:** To qualify for entry-level employment in the accounting industry, Dianne recommends that students develop the ability to multi-task, acquire strong written and oral communication skills, build a solid knowledge of accounting basics, and obtain proficient spreadsheet and word processing skills. Dianne also encourages students to view accounting as a flexible profession that offers individuals a variety of career options and alternatives that can assist them with the attainment of personal goals.

**Occupational Outlook:** For the future, Dianne envisions more analyses of variances and business activities. Accountants will be needed to assist managers in determining why revenues and expenses are fluctuating from original budget projections. This critical information will be used by managers to make sound financial decisions.

**Zytech Media Corporation**
**Work Sheet**
**For Year Ended December 31, 20--**

| ACCOUNT TITLE | TRIAL BALANCE DEBIT | TRIAL BALANCE CREDIT | ADJUSTMENTS DEBIT | ADJUSTMENTS CREDIT | DEPT. MARGIN AUDIO DEBIT | DEPT. MARGIN AUDIO CREDIT | DEPT. MARGIN VIDEO DEBIT | DEPT. MARGIN VIDEO CREDIT | INCOME STATEMENT DEBIT | INCOME STATEMENT CREDIT | BALANCE SHEET DEBIT | BALANCE SHEET CREDIT |
|---|---|---|---|---|---|---|---|---|---|---|---|---|
| Cash | 3891000 | | | | | | | | | | 3891000 | |
| Petty Cash | 50000 | | | | | | | | | | 50000 | |
| Accounts Receivable | 1375500 | | | | | | | | | | 1375500 | |
| Allow. for Uncoll. Accts. | | 24060 | | (a) 210940 | | | | | | | | 235000 |
| Merchandise Inventory—Audio | 18643461 | | (b) 1842039 | | | | | | | | 20485500 | |
| Merchandise Inventory—Video | 19984460 | | | (c) 936000 | | | | | | | 19048460 | |
| Supplies—Administrative | 697300 | | | (d) 292200 | | | | | | | 405100 | |
| Supplies—Audio | 1021500 | | | (e) 429400 | | | | | | | 592100 | |
| Supplies—Video | 984200 | | | (f) 775300 | | | | | | | 208900 | |
| Prepaid Insurance | 985000 | | | (g) 565000 | | | | | | | 420000 | |
| Office Equipment | 1690000 | | | | | | | | | | 1690000 | |
| Acc. Depr.—Office Equipment | | 596000 | | (h) 149000 | | | | | | | | 745000 |
| Store Equipment—Audio | 3890000 | | | | | | | | | | 3890000 | |
| Acc. Depr.—Store Equipment, Audio | | 1800000 | | (i) 400000 | | | | | | | | 2200000 |
| Store Equipment—Video | 2665200 | | | | | | | | | | 2665200 | |
| Acc. Depr.—Store Equipment, Video | | 1550000 | | (j) 350000 | | | | | | | | 1900000 |
| Accounts Payable | | 3136030 | | | | | | | | | | 3136030 |
| Employee Income Tax Payable—Federal | | 268075 | | | | | | | | | | 268075 |
| Employee Income Tax Payable—State | | 111819 | | | | | | | | | | 111819 |
| Federal Income Tax Payable | | | | (k) 85207 | | | | | | | | 85207 |
| Social Security Tax Payable | | 273057 | | | | | | | | | | 273057 |
| Medicare Tax Payable | | 63013 | | | | | | | | | | 63013 |
| Sales Tax Payable | | 313964 | | | | | | | | | | 313964 |
| Unemployment Tax Payable—Federal | | 2360 | | | | | | | | | | 2360 |
| Unemployment Tax Payable—State | | 15930 | | | | | | | | | | 15930 |
| Health Insurance Premiums Payable | | 226116 | | | | | | | | | | 226116 |
| Life Insurance Premiums Payable | | 35019 | | | | | | | | | | 35019 |
| Dividends Payable | | 3000000 | | | | | | | | | | 3000000 |
| Capital Stock | | 34000000 | | | | | | | | | | 34000000 |
| Retained Earnings | | 5615550 | | | | | | | | | | 5615550 |
| Dividends | 3000000 | | | | | | | | | | 3000000 | |
| Income Summary—Audio | | | | (b) 1842039 | | 1842039 | | | | | | |
| Income Summary—Video | | | (c) 936000 | | | | 936000 | | | | | |
| Income Summary—General | | | | | | | | | | | | |
| Sales—Audio | | 35103281 | | | | 35103281 | | | | | | |
| Sales Discount—Audio | 160585 | | | | 160585 | | | | | | | |
| Sales Returns and Allowances—Audio | 495050 | | | | 495050 | | | | | | | |
| Sales—Video | | 43834175 | | | | | | 43834175 | | | | |
| Sales Discount—Video | 200525 | | | | | | 200525 | | | | | |
| Sales Returns and Allowances—Video | 618180 | | | | | | 618180 | | | | | |
| Purchases—Audio | 21574568 | | | | 21574568 | | | | | | | |
| Purchases Discount—Audio | | 405895 | | | | 405895 | | | | | | |
| Purch. Returns and Allowances—Audio | | 828248 | | | | 828248 | | | | | | |
| Purchases—Video | 23176662 | | | | | | 23176662 | | | | | |
| Purchases Discount—Video | | 433455 | | | | | | 433455 | | | | |

| | | | | | | | | | | | | | |
|---|---|---|---|---|---|---|---|---|---|---|---|---|---|
| 46 | Purch. Returns and Allowances—Video | | 8897 52 | | | | | | 8897 52 | | | | |
| 47 | Advertising Expense—Audio | 1650 00 | | | | 1650 00 | | | | | | | |
| 48 | Depr. Exp.—Store Equipment, Audio | | | (i) 4000 00 | | 4000 00 | | | | | | | |
| 49 | Payroll Taxes Expense—Audio | 9401 80 | | | | 9401 80 | | | | | | | |
| 50 | Salary Expense—Audio | 90924 19 | | | | 90924 19 | | | | | | | |
| 51 | Supplies Expense—Audio | | | (e) 4294 00 | | 4294 00 | | | | | | | |
| 52 | Advertising Expense—Video | 2140 00 | | | | | | 2140 00 | | | | | |
| 53 | Depr. Exp.—Store Equipment, Video | | | (j) 3500 00 | | | | 3500 00 | | | | | |
| 54 | Payroll Taxes Expense—Video | 7509 82 | | | | | | 7509 82 | | | | | |
| 55 | Salary Expense—Video | 72627 02 | | | | | | 72627 02 | | | | | |
| 56 | Supplies Expense—Video | | | (f) 7753 00 | | | | 7753 00 | | | | | |
| 57 | Broadband Expense | 1440 00 | | | | | | | | 1440 00 | | | |
| 58 | Depr. Exp.—Office Equipment | | | (h) 1490 00 | | | | | | 1490 00 | | | |
| 59 | Insurance Expense | | | (g) 5650 00 | | | | | | 5650 00 | | | |
| 60 | Miscellaneous Expense | 5958 48 | | | | | | | | 5958 48 | | | |
| 61 | Payroll Taxes Expense—Administrative | 4515 30 | | | | | | | | 4515 30 | | | |
| 62 | Phone Expense | 2390 00 | | | | | | | | 2390 00 | | | |
| 63 | Rent Expense | 18000 00 | | | | | | | | 18000 00 | | | |
| 64 | Salary Expense—Administrative | 43667 19 | | | | | | | | 43667 19 | | | |
| 65 | Supplies Expense—Administrative | | | (d) 2922 00 | | | | | | 2922 00 | | | |
| 66 | Uncollectible Accounts Expense | | | (a) 2109 40 | | | | | | 2109 40 | | | |
| 67 | Utilities Expense | 3202 28 | | | | | | | | 3202 28 | | | |
| 68 | | | | | | 332572 02 | 381794 63 | 342843 51 | 451573 82 | | | | |
| 69 | Department Margin—Audio | | | | | 49222 61 | | | | | 49222 61 | | |
| 70 | Department Margin—Video | | | | | | | 108730 31 | | | 108730 31 | | |
| 71 | | | | | | 381794 63 | 381794 63 | 451573 82 | 451573 82 | | | | |
| 72 | Federal Income Tax Expense | 10800 00 | | (k) 852 07 | | | | | | 11652 07 | | | |
| 73 | | 1325257 99 | 1325257 99 | 60350 86 | 60350 86 | | | | | 102996 72 | 157952 92 | 577217 60 | 522261 40 |
| 74 | Net Income after Federal Income Tax | | | | | | | | | 54956 20 | | | 54956 20 |
| 75 | | | | | | | | | | 157952 92 | 157952 92 | 577217 60 | 577217 60 |

### Adjustment Information, December 31

Uncollectible accounts expense—estimated as 1.0% of total sales on account.

| | |
|---|---:|
| Total sales on account for year | $210,940.00 |
| Merchandise Inventory—Audio | 204,855.00 |
| Merchandise Inventory—Video | 190,484.60 |
| Supplies Used—Administrative | 2,922.00 |
| Supplies Used—Audio | 4,294.00 |
| Supplies Used—Video | 7,753.00 |
| Value of Prepaid Insurance | 4,200.00 |
| Depreciation Expense—Office Equipment | 1,490.00 |
| Depreciation Expense—Store Equipment, Audio | 4,000.00 |
| Depreciation Expense—Store Equipment, Video | 3,500.00 |
| Federal Income Tax Expense for Year | 11,652.07 |

# ADJUSTMENTS SHOWN ON WORK SHEET

## Uncollectible Accounts Expense Adjustment

Merchandise is sometimes sold on account to customers who later are unable to pay the amounts owed. Amounts that cannot be collected from customers are business expenses. All expenses must be recorded in the fiscal period in which the expenses contribute to earning revenue. [CONCEPT: Matching Expenses with Revenue]

Zytech has found from past experience that approximately 1% of the total sales on account will be uncollectible. Total sales on account for the current year are $210,940.00. Zytech's uncollectible accounts expense is calculated as follows:

| Total Sales on Account | × | Percentage | = | Estimated Uncollectible Accounts Expense |
|---|---|---|---|---|
| $210,940.00 | × | 1% | = | $2,109.40 |

Zytech estimates that of the $210,940.00 sales on account during the year, $2,109.40 will eventually be uncollectible. Zytech considers the estimated uncollectible amount of $2,109.40 to be an administrative expense. Consequently, the amount is recorded in a separate account titled Allowance for Uncollectible Accounts and is listed in the indirect expense section of the income statement.

Uncollectible Accounts Expense increases by a $2,109.40 debit. Allowance for Uncollectible Accounts, a contra asset account, increases by a $2,109.40 credit. The Allowance for Uncollectible Accounts balance represents the total estimated amount that Zytech believes will not be collected from accounts receivable. This estimated amount is not deducted from the Accounts Receivable balance until Zytech knows for sure which customers will not pay.

**Uncollectible Accounts Expense**

| | |
|---|---|
| Adj. (a)  2,109.40 | |

**Allowance for Uncollectible Accounts**

| | |
|---|---|
| | Dec. 31 Bal.  240.60 |
| | Adj. (a)  2,109.40 |
| | (New Bal.  2,350.00) |

The Uncollectible Accounts Expense adjustment is recorded on the work sheet, lines 4 and 66. The adjustment is labeled (a) because it is the first adjustment recorded. Entries related to uncollectible accounts expense are described in Chapter 7.

## Merchandise Inventory Adjustments

The merchandise inventory account balances in the trial balance are the beginning inventory amounts for a fiscal period. The amount of the ending inventory is determined by taking a periodic inventory at the end of a fiscal period.

The beginning Audio merchandise inventory, $186,434.61, is shown on line 5 in the Trial Balance Debit column of the work sheet. The periodic inventory taken on December 31 shows that the cost of Audio merchandise inventory is $204,855.00. To bring the Audio merchandise inventory up to date, the balance of Merchandise Inventory—Audio needs to be increased by $18,420.39 ($204,855.00 ending inventory less $186,434.61 beginning inventory).

| Merchandise Inventory—Audio | |
|---|---|
| Dec. 31 Bal. | 186,434.61 |
| Adj. *(b)* | 18,420.39 |
| *(New Bal.* | *204,855.00)* |

| Income Summary—Audio | |
|---|---|
| | Adj. *(b)* 18,420.39 |

The account Merchandise Inventory—Audio is debited for $18,420.39. Income Summary—Audio is credited for $18,420.39. The balance of Merchandise Inventory—Audio after this adjustment, $204,855.00, is equal to the actual ending inventory.

A similar adjustment is made for Merchandise Inventory—Video. The beginning Video merchandise inventory, $199,844.60, is shown on line 6 in the Trial Balance Debit column of the work sheet. The periodic inventory taken on December 31 shows that the cost of Video merchandise inventory is $190,484.60. Therefore, the balance of Merchandise Inventory—Video needs to be decreased by $9,360.00 ($199,844.60 beginning inventory less $190,484.60 ending inventory).

| Income Summary—Video | |
|---|---|
| Adj. *(c)* 9,360.00 | |

| Merchandise Inventory—Video | |
|---|---|
| Dec. 31 Bal. 199,844.60 | Adj. *(c)* 9,360.00 |
| *(New Bal.* 190,484.60) | |

Income Summary—Video is debited for $9,360.00. Merchandise Inventory—Video is credited for $9,360.00. The balance of Merchandise Inventory—Video after this adjustment, $190,484.60, is equal to the actual ending inventory.

The two inventory adjustments are entered on the work sheet. The Merchandise Inventory—Audio adjustment is labeled *(b)*. The Merchandise Inventory—Video adjustment is labeled *(c)*.

## Supplies Adjustments

A supplies inventory account balance in a trial balance includes two items: (1) the account balance on January 1 and (2) the cost of supplies bought during the year. The account balance does not reflect the cost of any supplies used during the year, which is an operating expense. The amount of the ending inventory is determined by taking a periodic inventory at the end of a fiscal period.

©GETTY IMAGES/PHOTODISC

Zytech keeps a record of supplies used by each department so that supplies expense can be charged to the appropriate department. Zytech's records indicate that the following supplies amounts were used by each department: Audio, $4,294.00; Video, $7,753.00; and Administrative, $2,922.00.

Separate asset and expense accounts are maintained for each department and for administrative uses. The administrative account records the use of supplies by any person who does not work in one of the departments. For example, the use of supplies by the accounting staff would be recorded in the administrative account. The effect of the supplies adjustment for the year is shown in the T accounts.

Zytech's supplies account balances are shown on lines 7 to 9 in the Trial Balance Debit column of the work sheet. To bring Zytech's supplies inventories up to date, the balance of each supplies account needs to be decreased by the total amount used by each department and the administrative staff. Since supplies are an asset, the supplies accounts must be decreased with credits of $2,922.00, $4,294.00, and $7,753.00. The balances of the supplies accounts after these adjustments are equal to the actual ending inventories.

The supplies adjustments are entered on lines 7–9, 51, 56, and 65 on the work sheet and labeled (d), (e), and (f).

| Supplies Expense—Administrative | |
|---|---|
| Adj. (d) | 2,922.00 |

| Supplies Expense—Audio | |
|---|---|
| Adj. (e) | 4,294.00 |

| Supplies Expense—Video | |
|---|---|
| Adj. (f) | 7,753.00 |

| Supplies—Administrative | | | |
|---|---|---|---|
| Dec. 31 Bal. | 6,973.00 | Adj. (d) | 2,922.00 |
| (New Bal. | 4,051.00) | | |

| Supplies—Audio | | | |
|---|---|---|---|
| Dec. 31 Bal. | 10,215.00 | Adj. (e) | 4,294.00 |
| (New Bal. | 5,921.00) | | |

| Supplies—Audio | | | |
|---|---|---|---|
| Dec. 31 Bal. | 9,842.00 | Adj. (f) | 7,753.00 |
| (New Bal. | 2,089.00) | | |

## Prepaid Insurance Adjustment

The prepaid insurance account balance includes two items. (1) The account balance on January 1. (2) The amount of insurance premiums paid during the year. The account balance does not reflect the amount of any insurance used during the year, which is an operating expense. The amount of unexpired insurance is determined at the end of a fiscal period.

Zytech's prepaid insurance account balance, $9,850.00, is shown on line 10 in the Trial Balance Debit column of the work sheet. The actual unexpired prepaid insurance on December 31 is $4,200.00. To bring Zytech's prepaid insurance account up to date, the balance of Prepaid Insurance must be decreased by $5,650.00 (December 31 balance, $9,850.00, less unexpired insurance, $4,200.00).

| Insurance Expense | |
|---|---|
| Adj. (g) | 5,650.00 |

| Prepaid Insurance | | | |
|---|---|---|---|
| Dec. 31 Bal. | 9,850.00 | Adj. (g) | 5,650.00 |
| (New Bal. | 4,200.00) | | |

Insurance Expense increases by a $5,650.00 debit. Prepaid Insurance is decreased by a $5,650.00 credit. The balance of Prepaid Insurance after this adjustment, $4,200.00, is equal to the actual unexpired prepaid insurance.

The prepaid insurance adjustment is entered on the work sheet. The adjustment is labeled (g).

## Depreciation Expense Adjustments

Assets that will be used for a number of years in the operation of a business are called **plant assets**. Plant assets are not bought for resale to customers in the normal course of business. Plant assets decrease in value because of use, the passage of time, and the availability of new models. The portion of a plant asset's cost that is transferred to an expense account in each fiscal period during a plant asset's useful life is called **depreciation expense**. The decrease in the value of equipment because of use and passage of time is an operating expense. [CONCEPT: Matching Expenses with Revenue]

The amount of depreciation is an estimate. The actual decrease in equipment value is not known until equipment is disposed of or sold. For this reason, the estimated depreciation is recorded in a separate contra asset account for each type of equipment. Calculating the amount of depreciation is described more fully in Chapter 8.

Zytech estimates that the yearly depreciation on office equipment is $1,490.00. To adjust for the depreciation of office equipment, Depreciation Expense—Office Equipment increases by a $1,490.00 debit. The contra asset account, Accumulated Depreciation—Office Equipment, increases by a $1,490.00 credit. The depreciation expense adjustment is entered on the work sheet and labeled *(h)*.

| Depreciation Expense—Office Equipment | |
|---|---|
| Adj. *(h)* 1,490.00 | |

| Accumulated Depreciation—Office Equipment | |
|---|---|
| | Dec. 31 Bal. 5,960.00 |
| | Adj. *(h)* 1,490.00 |
| | (New Bal. 7,450.00) |

Similar adjustments are made for Depreciation Expense—Store Equipment, Audio and Depreciation Expense—Store Equipment, Video.

These two depreciation expense adjustments are entered on the work sheet. The Depreciation Expense—Store Equipment, Audio adjustment is labeled *(i)*. The Depreciation Expense—Store Equipment, Video adjustment is labeled *(j)*.

**Federal Income Tax Expense Adjustment**

Corporations anticipating federal income taxes of $500.00 or more are required to pay estimated taxes each quarter. The estimated tax is paid in quarterly installments in April, June, September, and December. Even though a corporation pays a quarterly estimated tax, the actual income tax must be calculated at the end of each fiscal year.

Zytech estimated $10,800.00 federal income tax for the current year. Each quarterly income tax payment is recorded in a cash payments journal as a debit to Federal Income Tax Expense and a credit to Cash. At the end of the fiscal year, Zytech determines that the federal income tax is $11,652.07. To bring its federal income tax expense account up to date, the balance of Federal Income Tax Expense must be increased by $852.07

(federal income tax amount, $11,652.07, less the December 31 balance in Federal Income Tax Expense, $10,800.00).

Federal Income Tax Expense increases by an $852.07 debit. Federal Income Tax Payable increases by an $852.07 credit. The balance of Federal Income Tax Expense after this adjustment, $11,652.07, is equal to the total federal income tax for the fiscal year.

The Federal Income Tax Expense adjustment, labeled *(k)*, is entered on the work sheet.

Calculating the actual federal income tax is described in more detail in Chapter 13.

After all adjustments have been entered on a work sheet, the Adjustments columns are totaled and checked for equality. The two column totals, $60,350.86, are the same. The work sheet's Adjustments columns are ruled as shown on line 73 of the work sheet.

| Federal Income Tax Expense | |
|---|---|
| Dec. 31 Bal. 10,800.00 | |
| Adj. *(k)* 852.07 | |
| (New Bal. 11,652.07) | |

| Federal Income Tax Payable | |
|---|---|
| | Adj. *(k)* 852.07 |

©GETTY IMAGES/PHOTODISC

Preparing a Work Sheet for a Departmentalized Business

## COMPLETING A WORK SHEET WITH DEPARTMENTAL MARGIN COLUMNS

Refer to the work sheet illustration to follow these steps:

**1** Extend the asset, liability, and stockholders' equity account balances to the Balance Sheet Debit and Credit columns (Lines 1–31). When an account is not affected by an adjustment, the amount in the Trial Balance Debit or Credit column is extended to either the Balance Sheet Debit or Credit column. For those accounts affected by adjustments, new balances are calculated and extended. For example, *Allowance for Uncollectible Accounts*, line 4 of the work sheet, has a Trial Balance Credit balance of $240.60. The Adjustments Credit column amount of $2,109.40 makes the new account balance $2,350.00 ($240.60 plus $2,109.40). The new credit balance, $2,350.00, is extended to the Balance Sheet Credit column (Line 4).

**2** Extend the up-to-date balances of the income summary, revenue, cost, and direct expense accounts for the Audio Department to the Departmental Margin—Audio Debit and Credit columns (Lines 32, 35–37, 41–43, and 47–51). When an account is affected by an adjustment, the new balance is calculated and extended. For example, the balance of *Supplies Expense—Audio* in the Trial Balance Debit column is zero. The zero balance is not up to date because this account is affected by an adjustment. The debit balance, $0.00, *plus* the debit adjustment, $4,294.00, *equals* the adjusted balance, $4,294.00. Extend the up-to-date adjusted debit balance, $4,294.00, to the Departmental Margin—Audio Debit column. Do not forget to extend the amount in the Adjustments columns for *Income Summary—Audio* to the Departmental Margin— Audio Debit or Credit columns (Line 32).

**3** Extend the up-to-date balances of the income summary, revenue, cost, and direct expense accounts for the Video Department to the Departmental Margin Statements—Video Debit and Credit columns (Lines 33, 38–40, 44–46, and 52–56). The procedure for extending these income statement amounts is the same as that for the Audio Department amounts described in step 2.

**4** Extend the indirect expense items to the Income Statement Debit column (Lines 57–67).

**5** Calculate the departmental margin for each department (Lines 69 and 70).
   a. Rule a single line across the Departmental Margin Statements—Audio Debit and Credit columns on the line with the last expense account, line 67. Add each column and write the totals under the ruled line. Subtract the smaller total from the larger total ($381,794.63 − $332,572.02 = $49,222.61). Write the difference, *$49,222.61,* in the Departmental Margin Statements—Audio Debit column on the next line, line 69. Write the same amount in the Income Statement Credit column on the same line. Write the words *Departmental Margin—Audio* on the same line in the Account Title column. The amount written on this line, *$49,222.61,* is the departmental margin for the Audio Department for the year ended December 31 of the current year.
   b. The same procedure is followed to calculate departmental margin for the Video Department. The totals for the Video Debit and Credit columns are written on the same line as the totals of the Audio columns. This departmental margin is recorded in the work sheet's Departmental Margin Statements—Video Debit column and in the Income Statement Credit column. The amounts are written on the line below the departmental margin for the Audio Department, line 70.
   c. The Departmental Margin Statements columns for the two departments are totaled and ruled as shown on line 71.

**6** Extend the adjusted balance of federal income tax expense amount ($10,800.00 + $852.07) and record it in the Income Statement Debit column (Line 72) on the work sheet. The procedure for calculating federal income tax expense is described in Chapter 13.

**7** Total the Income Statement and Balance Sheet columns. Calculate and record net income after federal income tax. The difference between the two Income Statement column totals on the work sheet is the net income or net loss for a fiscal period. If the Credit column total is larger than the Debit column total as shown in the work sheet, the difference is the net income. The net income, *$54,956.20,* is written under the work sheet's Income Statement Debit column total to make the two Income Statement columns balance. The words *Net Income after Federal Income Tax* are written in the Account Title column.

**8** The difference between the two Balance Sheet column totals on the work sheet also represents the net income or net loss for a fiscal period. A net income increases stockholders' equity. Since stockholders' equity is increased with a credit, Zytech's net income, *$54,956.20,* is written under the Balance Sheet Credit column total to make the two Balance Sheet columns balance.

**9** After the net income amount is written in the two work sheet columns, the last four columns are totaled again. The totals for each pair of columns must be the same. The two Income Statement totals are the same, $157,952.92. The two Balance Sheet totals are the same, $577,217.60. If columns do not balance, errors must be found and corrected before final ruling is done.

**10** Rule the work sheet as shown on lines 73–75.

**1.** Write department loss in Dept. Marg. Stmt. Credit column.

**2.** Write department loss in Income Statement Debit column.

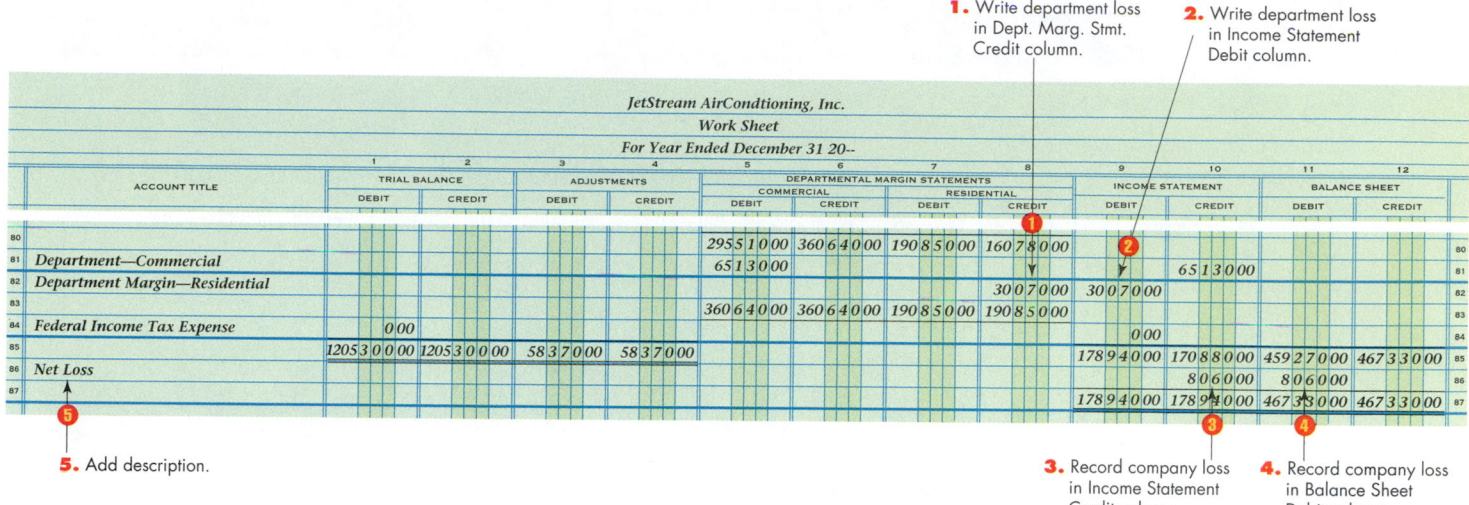

**JetStream AirCondtioning, Inc.**
**Work Sheet**
**For Year Ended December 31 20--**

| ACCOUNT TITLE | TRIAL BALANCE DEBIT | TRIAL BALANCE CREDIT | ADJUSTMENTS DEBIT | ADJUSTMENTS CREDIT | DEPARTMENTAL MARGIN STATEMENTS COMMERCIAL DEBIT | COMMERCIAL CREDIT | RESIDENTIAL DEBIT | RESIDENTIAL CREDIT | INCOME STATEMENT DEBIT | INCOME STATEMENT CREDIT | BALANCE SHEET DEBIT | BALANCE SHEET CREDIT | |
|---|---|---|---|---|---|---|---|---|---|---|---|---|---|
| 80 Department—Commercial | | | | | 295510 00 | 360640 00 | 190850 00 | 160780 00 | | | | | 80 |
| 81 | | | | | 65130 00 | | | | | 65130 00 | | | 81 |
| 82 Department Margin—Residential | | | | | | | | 30070 00 | 30070 00 | | | | 82 |
| 83 | | | | | 360640 00 | 360640 00 | 190850 00 | 190850 00 | | | | | 83 |
| 84 Federal Income Tax Expense | 0 00 | | | | | | | | 0 00 | | | | 84 |
| 85 | 1205300 00 | 1205300 00 | 58370 00 | 58370 00 | | | | | 178940 00 | 170880 00 | 459270 00 | 467330 00 | 85 |
| 86 Net Loss | | | | | | | | | | 8060 00 | 8060 00 | | 86 |
| 87 | | | | | | | | | 178940 00 | 178940 00 | 467330 00 | 467330 00 | 87 |

**5.** Add description.

**3.** Record company loss in Income Statement Credit column.

**4.** Record company loss in Balance Sheet Debit column

If a department's Departmental Margin Statements Debit column total is larger than the Credit column total, as shown above for the Residential Department, the difference represents a departmental operating loss. A departmental operating loss occurs when the total of a department's cost of merchandise sold plus direct expenses exceeds its net sales. To record the departmental net loss on a work sheet, the net loss amount is written in the appropriate Departmental Margin Statements Credit column and the Income Statement Debit column.

If the Income Statement Debit column total is larger than the Credit column total, as also shown above, the difference represents a company net loss. When a company net loss occurs, the net loss amount is written on a work sheet in the Income Statement Credit and Balance Sheet Debit columns. The difference represents a decrease in stockholders' equity resulting from a net loss.

## cultural diversity

CULTURAL DIVERSITY • CULTURAL DIVERSITY • CULTURAL DIVERSITY

### African American Businesses

The Census Bureau's Survey of Minority-Owned Business Enterprises indicates that minority-owned enterprises are increasing in number and size. Firms owned by African Americans increased from 620,912 in 1992 to 823,000 in 1997. This represents a 32.5% increase. In 1997, these firms employed 718,300 people and generated $71.2 billion in revenue.

Six states—New York, California, Texas, Florida, Georgia, and Maryland—accounted for 47% of the nation's African American-owned businesses. The metropolitan areas of New York City, Washington, D.C., Los Angeles-Long Branch, Chicago, and Atlanta accounted for 28% of African American-owned firms.

Slightly more than half of businesses owned by African Americans operate in the service industries, such as health services, business services, and personal services. The retail trade accounted for the next largest concentration of African American-owned firms.

*Black Enterprise* magazine lists the nation's 100 largest black businesses in its "B.E. 100." The list is composed of industrial and service businesses that are at least 51% African American-owned. It maintains separate listings for the "Auto Dealer 100," which lists the largest auto dealerships that are at least 51% African American-owned. It also has lists for companies such as advertising agencies, banks, and insurance companies. From the 2004 "B.E. 100," World Wide Technology, Inc., of Maryland Heights, Missouri, was ranked in first place.

Source: U.S. Census and "Black Enterprise 100."

TERMS REVIEW • TERMS
AUDIT YOUR
WORK TOGETHER • WORK
ON YOUR OWN • ON YOUR OWN

## terms review

schedule of accounts receivable
schedule of accounts payable
work sheet
trial balance
plant assets
depreciation expense

## audit your understanding

1. What two reports are prepared to prove the accuracy of posting to subsidiary ledgers?

2. Why are adjustments made to certain accounts at the end of the fiscal period?

3. What account balances are extended to the Balance Sheet columns of a work sheet?

## work together 4-3

**Preparing a work sheet with departmental margins**

Callostay Co. has two departments: Books and Music. The trial balance and adjustment information for Callostay are provided in the *Working Papers*. Your instructor will guide you through the following examples. Save your work to complete Work Together 4-4.

1. Record the adjustments on the work sheet and total the adjustments columns.

2. Extend amounts to the proper debit and credit columns for the Departmental Margin Statements columns. Accounts on trial balance lines 56–65 are classified as indirect expenses. Total and rule the work sheet.

## on your own 4-3

**Preparing a work sheet with departmental margins**

Saratoga Spas has two departments: Accessories and Spas. The trial balance and adjustment information for Saratoga Spas are provided in the *Working Papers*. Work this problem independently. Save your work to complete On Your Own 4-4.

1. Record the adjustments on the work sheet and total the adjustments columns.

2. Extend amounts to the proper debit and credit columns for the Departmental Margin Statements columns. Accounts on trial balance lines 56–65 are classified as indirect expenses. Total and rule the work sheet.

# 4-4 Responsibility Statements for a Merchandising Business

## DEPARTMENTAL MARGIN STATEMENT—AUDIO

**Zytech Media Corporation**
**Departmental Margin Statement—Audio**
**For Year Ended December 31, 20--**

|  |  |  |  | % of Net Sales* |
|---|---|---|---|---|
| Operating Revenue: |  |  |  |  |
| Sales | | | $ 351,032.81 | 101.9 |
| Less: Sales Discount | $ 1,605.85 | | | 0.5 |
| Sales Returns and Allowances | 4,950.50 | 6,556.35 | | 1.4 |
| Net Sales | | | $ 344,476.46 | 100.0 |
| Cost of Merchandise Sold: | | | | |
| Merchandise Inv., Jan. 1, 20-- | | | $ 186,434.61 | 54.1 |
| Purchases | | $ 215,745.68 | | 62.6 |
| Less: Purchases Discount | $4,058.95 | | | 1.2 |
| Purchases Returns and Allowances | 8,282.48 | 12,341.43 | | 2.4 |
| Net Purchases | | | 203,404.25 | 59.0 |
| Total Cost of Mdse. Avail. For Sale | | | $ 389,838.86 | 113.2 |
| Less Mdse. Inv., Dec. 31, 20-- | | | 204,855.00 | 59.5 |
| Cost of Merchandise Sold | | | 184,983.86 | 53.7 |
| Gross Profit on Operations: | | | $ 159,492.60 | 46.3 |
| Direct Expenses: | | | | |
| Advertising Expense | | $ 1,650.00 | | 0.5 |
| Deprec. Exp.—Store Equipment | | 4,000.00 | | 1.2 |
| Payroll Taxes Expense | | 9,401.80 | | 2.7 |
| Salary Expense | | 90,924.19 | | 26.4 |
| Supplies Expense | | 4,294.00 | | 1.2 |
| Total Direct Expenses | | | 110,269.99 | 32.0 |
| Departmental Margin | | | $ 49,222.61 | 14.3 |

*Rounded to the nearest 0.1%

**1.** Determine net sales for department. ❶

**2.** Determine cost of merchandise sold for department. ❷

**3.** Calculate gross profit. ❸

**4.** Record direct expenses of the department. ❹

**5.** Calculate the departmental margin. ❺

Financial statements reporting revenue, costs, and direct expenses under a specific department's control are called **responsibility statements**. Zytech prepares the usual end-of-fiscal-period financial statements: income statement, statement of stockholders' equity, and balance sheet. In addition, Zytech prepares two responsibility statements: (1) departmental margin statement—audio and (2) departmental margin statement—video. Since the departmental margin statements include information regarding each department's gross profit, Zytech does not prepare separate departmental statements of gross profit at the end of a fiscal period.

Zytech's departmental margin statement—audio for the year ended December 31 is shown above. Information for this statement is obtained from the Departmental Margin Statements—Audio columns of the work sheet, pages 102–103.

The departmental margin statement includes information about operating revenue, cost of merchandise sold, and the direct expenses that can be identified with Zytech's Audio Department. The format of the statement is similar to an income statement. However, only direct expenses for the Audio Department are included on the departmental margin statement.

The departmental margin statements help department managers determine how revenue, costs, and direct expenses affect department results. With this knowledge, managers can make informed decisions to improve department results.

| Departmental Margin | ÷ | Net Sales | = | Component Percentage for Departmental Margin |
|---|---|---|---|---|
| $49,222.61 | ÷ | $344,476.46 | = | 14.3% |

| | Component Percentages | | |
|---|---|---|---|
| | 20X3 | 20X2 | 20X1 |
| Departmental Margin | 14.3% | 13.4% | 13.1% |

Zytech calculates component percentages on departmental margin statements to help management interpret the information. The component percentages are calculated by dividing the amount on each line by the amount of departmental net sales. For the departmental margin statement—audio, the departmental margin component percentage is calculated as shown above.

A company may set departmental margin goals for each of its departments to encourage and determine acceptable performance by each department. Zytech has set a minimum departmental margin goal of 13.0% for the Audio Department. Departmental goals are determined by reviewing the department's previous achievements and evaluating changes in selling prices and department costs.

Component percentages for the current fiscal period also are compared to component percentages for previous fiscal periods. The audio department's departmental margin component percentages for the current (20X3) and two preceding fiscal years (20X2 and 20X1) are also shown above.

Since a department has control of and can affect its departmental margin by specific departmental action, this component percentage is an excellent measure of a department's performance. Zytech's Audio Department manager can determine whether the department is performing satisfactorily by making two comparisons: (1) current period's departmental margin component percentage compared with the company-assigned goal of at least 13.0% departmental margin and

(2) current period's departmental margin component percentage compared with previous periods' departmental margin component percentages. During the years 20X1 through 20X3, the department exceeded the company-assigned goal—a favorable result. The Audio Department increased its departmental margin component percentage from 13.1% to 14.3% in two years—a favorable trend.

When changes in component percentages occur for an item on the departmental margin statement, the department manager seeks the reasons for the changes. If changes are positive, the policies resulting in favorable changes are continued. If changes are negative, the manager seeks to change policies to prevent further declines.

Departmental revenue may increase because of special sales and advertising programs. The cost of merchandise may change because lower prices are obtained when merchandise is purchased. Other component percentages may change because of an increase or decrease in direct expenses. Without the information on the departmental margin statement, a department manager will not know which policies to continue and which to change.

Thus, departmental margin statements provide information to help managers identify unusual changes in revenue and cost amounts. The statements also provide information to assist company officers as well as department managers in evaluating departmental performance.

**Zytech Media Corporation**
**Departmental Margin Statement—Video**
**For Year Ended December 31, 20--**

| | | | % of Net Sales* |
|---|---|---|---|
| Operating Revenue: | | | |
| Sales . . . . . . . . . . . . . . . . . . . . . . . . . . | | $438,341.75 | 101.9 |
| Less: Sales Discount . . . . . . . . . . . . . | $ 2,005.25 | | 0.5 |
| Sales Returns and Allowances . . . . | 6,181.80 | 8,187.05 | 1.4 |
| Net Sales . . . . . . . . . . . . . . . . . . . . | | $430,154.70 | 100.0 |
| Cost of Merchandise Sold: . . . . . . . . . . . | | | |
| Merchandise Inv., Jan. 1, 20-- . . . . . . . | | $199,844.60 | 46.5 |
| Purchases . . . . . . . . . . . . . . . . . . . . . . | $231,766.62 | | 53.9 |
| Less: Purchases Discount . . . . . . . . . $4,334.55 | | | 1.0 |
| Purchases Returns and Allowances 8,897.52 | 13,232.07 | | 2.1 |
| Net Purchases . . . . . . . . . . . . . . . . . . . | | 218,534.55 | 50.8 |
| Total Cost of Mdse. Avail. For Sale . . . . | | $418,379.15 | 97.3 |
| Less Mdse. Inv., Dec. 31, 20-- . . . . . . . | | 190,484.60 | 44.3 |
| Cost of Merchandise Sold . . . . . . . . . | | 227,894.55 | 53.0 |
| Gross Profit on Operations: | | $202,260.15 | 47.0 |
| Direct Expenses: | | | |
| Advertising Expense . . . . . . . . . . . . . . | $ 2,140.00 | | 0.5 |
| Deprec. Exp.—Store Equipment . . . . . . | 3,500.00 | | 0.8 |
| Payroll Taxes Expense . . . . . . . . . . . . . | 7,509.82 | | 1.7 |
| Salary Expense . . . . . . . . . . . . . . . . . | 72,627.02 | | 16.9 |
| Supplies Expense . . . . . . . . . . . . . . . . | 7,753.00 | | 1.8 |
| Total Direct Expenses . . . . . . . . . . . . | | 93,529.84 | 21.7 |
| Departmental Margin . . . . . . . . . . . . . . . | | $108,730.31 | 25.3 |

*Rounded to the nearest 0.1%

**1.** Determine net sales for department. ➊

**2.** Determine cost of merchandise sold for department. ➋

**3.** Calculate gross profit. ➌

**4.** Record direct expenses of the department. ➍

**5.** Calculate the departmental margin. ➎

Zytech prepares a departmental margin statement for both the Video and Audio departments.

The departmental margin statement—video for the year ended December 31 is shown above.

CULTURAL DIVERSITY • CULTURAL DIVERSITY • CULTURAL DIVERSITY

## cultural diversity

### Hispanic-Owned Firms Growing Rapidly

U.S. Census Bureau data indicates continuing growth in the Hispanic population in the United States. From 2000 to 2004, the number of Hispanics grew 13%, nearly half of the population growth in the country. With the growing population comes a Hispanic market that Hispanic-owned firms, among others, are racing to serve.

The U.S. Economic Census Survey of Minority-Owned Business Enterprises found a 76% increase from 1987 to 1992. Growth slowed to 30% from 1992 to 1997. However, the number of Hispanic-owned businesses was over 1,000,000. At the time of this text's publication, projections were that Hispanic-owned businesses would top 2 million in 2004, with revenues of $273.81 billion.

Source: www.hispanicbusiness.com and www.census.gov.

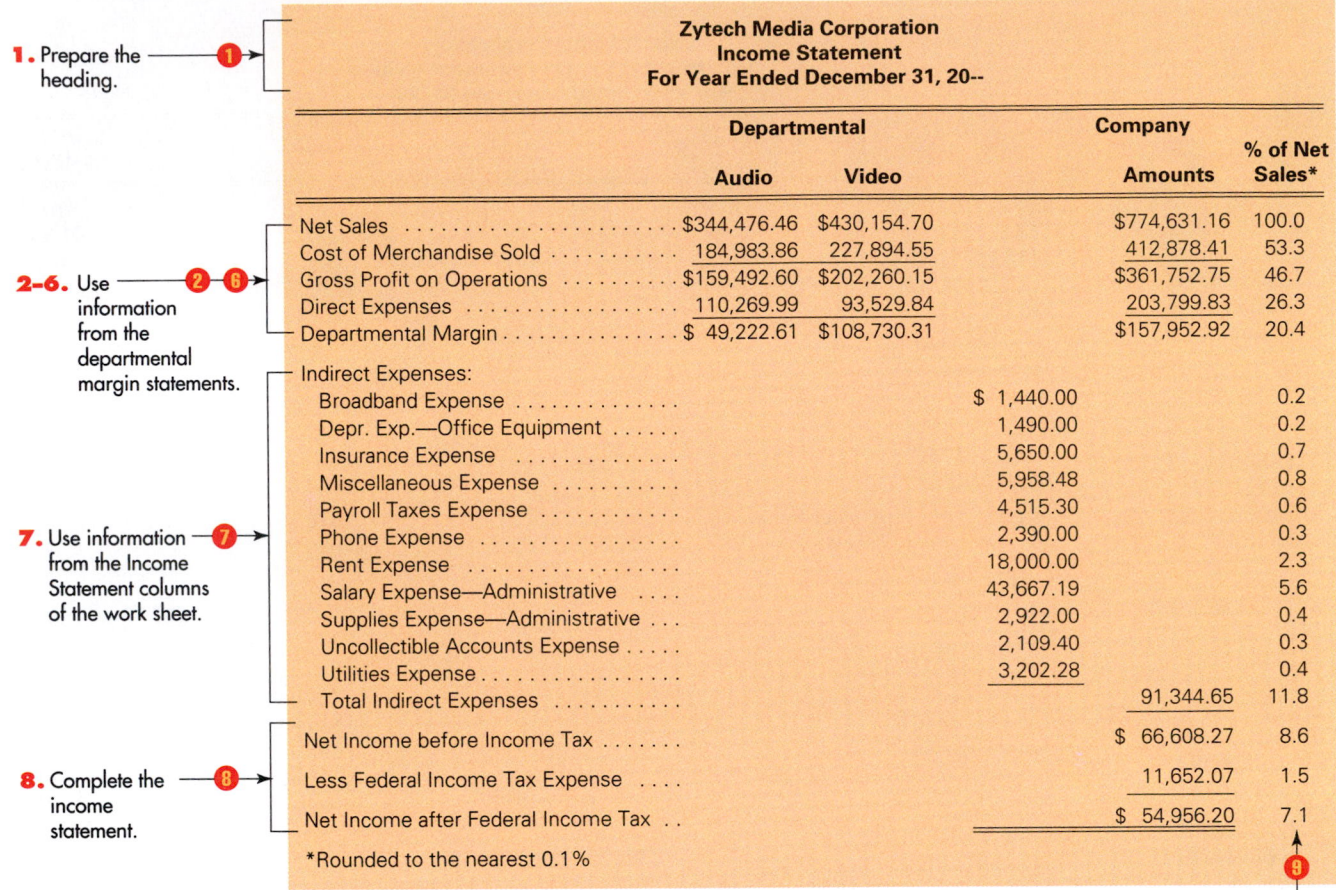

**1.** Prepare the heading.

**2-6.** Use information from the departmental margin statements.

**7.** Use information from the Income Statement columns of the work sheet.

**8.** Complete the income statement.

**9.** Calculate component percentages.

**Zytech Media Corporation**
**Income Statement**
**For Year Ended December 31, 20--**

| | Departmental | | Company | |
| --- | --- | --- | --- | --- |
| | Audio | Video | Amounts | % of Net Sales* |
| Net Sales | $344,476.46 | $430,154.70 | $774,631.16 | 100.0 |
| Cost of Merchandise Sold | 184,983.86 | 227,894.55 | 412,878.41 | 53.3 |
| Gross Profit on Operations | $159,492.60 | $202,260.15 | $361,752.75 | 46.7 |
| Direct Expenses | 110,269.99 | 93,529.84 | 203,799.83 | 26.3 |
| Departmental Margin | $ 49,222.61 | $108,730.31 | $157,952.92 | 20.4 |
| Indirect Expenses: | | | | |
| Broadband Expense | | | $ 1,440.00 | 0.2 |
| Depr. Exp.—Office Equipment | | | 1,490.00 | 0.2 |
| Insurance Expense | | | 5,650.00 | 0.7 |
| Miscellaneous Expense | | | 5,958.48 | 0.8 |
| Payroll Taxes Expense | | | 4,515.30 | 0.6 |
| Phone Expense | | | 2,390.00 | 0.3 |
| Rent Expense | | | 18,000.00 | 2.3 |
| Salary Expense—Administrative | | | 43,667.19 | 5.6 |
| Supplies Expense—Administrative | | | 2,922.00 | 0.4 |
| Uncollectible Accounts Expense | | | 2,109.40 | 0.3 |
| Utilities Expense | | | 3,202.28 | 0.4 |
| Total Indirect Expenses | | | 91,344.65 | 11.8 |
| Net Income before Income Tax | | | $ 66,608.27 | 8.6 |
| Less Federal Income Tax Expense | | | 11,652.07 | 1.5 |
| Net Income after Federal Income Tax | | | $ 54,956.20 | 7.1 |

*Rounded to the nearest 0.1%

A financial statement showing the revenue and expenses for a fiscal period is called an **income statement**. Zytech's income statement for the year ended December 31 is shown above. The income statement is prepared with five columns: two for departmental amounts and three for company amounts and component percentages.

STEPS • STEPS • STEPS • STEPS • STEPS • STEPS • STEPS • STEPS • STEPS • STEPS

## STEPS
### PREPARING AN INCOME STATEMENT

**1** Write the heading. Center the name of the company, name of the report, and date of the report on three separate lines at the top of the statement.

**2** Prepare the net sales section. Totals are obtained from the departmental margin statements.

**3** Prepare the cost of merchandise sold section. Totals are obtained from the departmental margin statements.

**4** Prepare the gross profit section. Totals are obtained from the departmental margin statements.

**5** Prepare the direct expenses section. Totals are obtained from the departmental margin statements. Details about direct expenses are not listed. Managers can refer to departmental margin statements for the details.

**6** Prepare the departmental margin section. Information is obtained from the departmental margin statements. Company amounts in steps 2–6 are totals of departmental amounts.

**7** Prepare the indirect expenses section. Account titles and balances are obtained from the Income Statement columns of the work sheet.

**8** Complete the income statement. Show the net income before and after Federal Income Tax.

**9** Calculate the component percentages. The procedure is the same as calculating the percentages of net sales on departmental margin statements. However, the percentages are based on company net sales.

**Zytech Media Corporation**
**Statement of Stockholders' Equity**
**For Year Ended December 31, 20--**

| | | | |
|---|---|---|---|
| Capital Stock: | | | |
| $170.00 Per Share | | | |
| January 1, 20--, 2,000 Shares Issued . . . . . . . . . . . . . . . . . . . . | | $340,000.00 | |
| Issued during Current Year, None . . . . . . . . . . . . . . . . . . . . | | 0.00 | |
| Balance, December 31, 20--, 2,000 Shares Issued. . . . . . . . . | | | $340,000.00 |
| Retained Earnings: | | | |
| Balance, January 1, 20-- . . . . . . . . . . . . . . . . . . . . . . . . . . . . | | $ 56,155.50 | |
| Net Income after Federal Income Tax for 20-- . . . . . . . . . . . . | $54,956.20 | | |
| Less Dividends Declared during 20-- . . . . . . . . . . . . . . . . . . . | 30,000.00 | | |
| Net Increase during 20--. . . . . . . . . . . . . . . . . . . . . . . . . . . | | 24,956.20 | |
| Balance, December 31, 20--. . . . . . . . . . . . . . . . . . . . . . . . . | | | 81,111.70 |
| Total Stockholders' Equity, December 31, 20-- . . . . . . . . . . . . . | | | $421,111.70 |

A financial statement that shows changes in a corporation's ownership for a fiscal period is called a **statement of stockholders' equity**. Zytech's statement of stockholders' equity for the fiscal year ended December 31 is shown above.

A statement of stockholders' equity contains two major sections:

1. *Capital stock.* Total shares of ownership in a corporation are called **capital stock**.
2. *Retained earnings.* An amount earned by a corporation and not yet distributed to stockholders is called **retained earnings**.

The first section shows that Zytech started the fiscal year with $340,000.00 in capital stock. This capital stock consisted of 2,000 shares of stock issued prior to January 1. During the year, Zytech did not issue any additional stock. Thus, at the end of the fiscal year, Zytech still had $340,000.00 in capital stock. This information is obtained from the previous year's statement of stockholders' equity and the capital stock account.

The second section of Zytech's statement of stockholders' equity shows that the business started the fiscal year with $56,155.50 in retained earnings. This amount represents previous years' earnings that have been kept in the business.

For the current fiscal year ended December 31, Zytech earned net income after federal income tax of $54,956.20. This amount is obtained from line 74 of the work sheet on page 103.

Net income increases the retained earnings of a corporation. Some income may be retained by a corporation for business expansion. Some income may be distributed to stockholders as a return on their investment. Earnings distributed to stockholders are called **dividends**.

Zytech's board of directors declared dividends of $30,000.00 during the year. The amount of dividends declared is obtained from line 31 of the Balance Sheet Debit column of the work sheet. The amount of dividends declared, $30,000.00, is subtracted from the amount of net income for the year, $54,956.20, to obtain the net increase in Retained Earnings for the year, $24,956.20. The net increase in Retained Earnings, $24,956.20, is added to the January 1 balance of Retained Earnings, $56,155.50, to obtain the December 31 balance, $81,111.70. Zytech's capital stock, $340,000.00, plus retained earnings, $81,111.70, equals total stockholders' equity on December 31, $421,111.70.

Declaration and payment of dividends are described in Chapter 11.

**Zytech Media Corporation**
**Balance Sheet**
**December 31, 20--**

## ASSETS

| | | | |
|---|---|---|---|
| **Current Assets:** | | | |
| Cash | | $ 38,910.00 | |
| Petty Cash | | 500.00 | |
| Accounts Receivable | $13,755.00 | | |
| Less Allowance for Uncollectible Accounts | 2,350.00 | 11,405.00 | |
| Merchandise Inventory—Audio | | 204,855.00 | |
| Merchandise Inventory—Video | | 190,484.60 | |
| Supplies—Administrative | | 4,051.00 | |
| Supplies—Audio | | 5,921.00 | |
| Supplies—Video | | 2,089.00 | |
| Prepaid Insurance | | 4,200.00 | |
| Total Current Assets | | | $462,415.60 |
| **Plant Assets:** | | | |
| Office Equipment | $16,900.00 | | |
| Less Accumulated Depreciation–Office Equipment | 7,450.00 | $ 9,450.00 | |
| Store Equipment—Audio | 38,900.00 | | |
| Less Accumulated Depreciation—Store Equipment, Audio | 22,000.00 | 16,900.00 | |
| Store Equipment—Video | 26,652.00 | | |
| Less Accumulated Depreciation—Store Equipment, Video | 19,000.00 | 7,652.00 | |
| Total Plant Assets | | | 34,002.00 |
| Total Assets | | | $496,417.60 |

## LIABILITIES

| | | |
|---|---|---|
| **Current Liabilities:** | | |
| Accounts Payable | $ 31,360.30 | |
| Employee Income Tax Payable—Federal | 2,680.75 | |
| Employee Income Tax Payable—State | 1,118.19 | |
| Federal Income Tax Payable | 852.07 | |
| Social Security Tax Payable | 2,730.57 | |
| Medicare Tax Payable | 630.13 | |
| Sales Tax Payable | 3,139.64 | |
| Unemployment Tax Payable—Federal | 23.60 | |
| Unemployment Tax Payable—State | 159.30 | |
| Health Insurance Premiums Payable | 2,261.16 | |
| Life Insurance Premiums Payable | 350.19 | |
| Dividends Payable | 30,000.00 | |
| Total Liabilities | | $75,305.90 |

## STOCKHOLDERS' EQUITY

| | | |
|---|---|---|
| Capital Stock | $340,000.00 | |
| Retained Earnings | 81,111.70 | |
| Total Stockholders' Equity | | 421,111.70 |
| Total Liabilities and Stockholders' Equity | | $496,417.60 |

A financial statement that reports assets, liabilities, and owners' equity on a specific date is called a **balance sheet**. A balance sheet reports the financial condition of a business on a specific date. Zytech's balance sheet for December 31 is shown above. Data used in preparing a balance sheet come from two sources: Balance Sheet columns of the work sheet and Statement of Stockholders' Equity.

On a balance sheet, the total assets must equal the total liabilities plus stockholders' equity. Zytech's balance sheet shows total assets of $496,417.60 and total liabilities and stockholders' equity of the same amount. Therefore, Zytech's balance sheet is in balance and is assumed to be correct.

Financial analysis of balance sheet items is described in Chapter 17.

## terms review

responsibility statements
income statement
statement of stockholders' equity
capital stock
retained earnings
dividends
balance sheet

## audit your understanding

1. Where does Zytech obtain the information to prepare the direct expenses section of the income statement?

2. How is the component percentage for departmental margin calculated?

3. What two comparisons can be made using the component percentage for departmental margin to determine if a department is performing satisfactorily?

4. Where does Zytech obtain the information to prepare the indirect expenses section of the income statement?

## work together 4-4

**Preparing financial statements**

Use the work sheet from Work Together 4-3. Statement paper is provided in the *Working Papers.* Your instructor will guide you through the following example.

1. Prepare departmental margin statements for the Books Department and the Music Department. Calculate and record the component percentages for each item on the statements. Round percentage calculations to the nearest 0.1%.

2. Prepare an income statement. Calculate and record the component percentages for each item on the statement. Round percentage calculations to the nearest 0.1%.

3. Prepare a statement of stockholders' equity. There are 2,000 shares of stock issued for $100.00 per share and none issued during the current year.

4. Prepare a balance sheet.

## on your own 4-4

**Preparing financial statements**

Use the work sheet from On Your Own 4-3. Statement paper is provided in the *Working Papers.* Work this problem independently.

1. Prepare departmental margin statements for the Spas Department and the Accessories Department. Calculate and record the component percentages for each item on the statement. Round percentage calculations to the nearest 0.1%.

2. Prepare an income statement. Calculate and record the component percentages for each item on the statement. Round percentage calculations to the nearest 0.1%.

3. Prepare a statement of stockholders' equity. There are 1,000 shares of stock issued for $159.00 per share and none issued during the current year.

4. Prepare a balance sheet.

# 4-5 End-of-Period Work for a Departmentalized Business

## JOURNALIZING ADJUSTING ENTRIES FOR A DEPARTMENTALIZED BUSINESS

**1.** Write *Adjusting Entries* in Account Title column.

**2.** Enter the adjusting entries without additional explanation.

| | DATE | | ACCOUNT TITLE | DOC. NO. | POST. REF. | DEBIT | CREDIT | |
|---|---|---|---|---|---|---|---|---|
| 1 | | | *Adjusting Entries* | | | | | 1 |
| 2 | Dec 20-- | 31 | *Uncollectible Accounts Expense* | | | 2 1 0 9 40 | | 2 |
| 3 | | | *Allowance for Uncoll. Accounts* | | | | 2 1 0 9 40 | 3 |
| 4 | | 31 | *Merchandise Inventory—Audio* | | | 18 4 2 0 39 | | 4 |
| 5 | | | *Income Summary—Audio* | | | | 18 4 2 0 39 | 5 |
| 6 | | 31 | *Income Summary—Video* | | | 9 3 6 0 00 | | 6 |
| 7 | | | *Merchandise Inventory—Video* | | | | 9 3 6 0 00 | 7 |
| 8 | | 31 | *Supplies Expense—Administrative* | | | 2 9 2 2 00 | | 8 |
| 9 | | | *Supplies—Administrative* | | | | 2 9 2 2 00 | 9 |
| 10 | | 31 | *Supplies Expense—Audio* | | | 4 2 9 4 00 | | 10 |
| 11 | | | *Supplies—Audio* | | | | 4 2 9 4 00 | 11 |
| 12 | | 31 | *Supplies Expense—Video* | | | 7 7 5 3 00 | | 12 |
| 13 | | | *Supplies—Video* | | | | 7 7 5 3 00 | 13 |
| 14 | | 31 | *Insurance Expense* | | | 5 6 5 0 00 | | 14 |
| 15 | | | *Prepaid Insurance* | | | | 5 6 5 0 00 | 15 |
| 16 | | 31 | *Depreciation Exp.—Office Equip.* | | | 1 4 9 0 00 | | 16 |
| 17 | | | *Accum. Depr.—Office Equip.* | | | | 1 4 9 0 00 | 17 |
| 18 | | 31 | *Depreciation Exp.—Store Equip., Audio* | | | 4 0 0 0 00 | | 18 |
| 19 | | | *Accum. Depr.—Store Equip., Audio* | | | | 4 0 0 0 00 | 19 |
| 20 | | 31 | *Depreciation Exp.—Store Equip., Video* | | | 3 5 0 0 00 | | 20 |
| 21 | | | *Accum. Depr.—Store Equip., Video* | | | | 3 5 0 0 00 | 21 |
| 22 | | 31 | *Federal Income Tax Expense* | | | 8 5 2 07 | | 22 |
| 23 | | | *Federal Income Tax Payable* | | | | 8 5 2 07 | 23 |

GENERAL JOURNAL — PAGE 13

Account balances are changed only by posting journal entries. Journal entries recorded to update general ledger accounts at the end of a fiscal period are called **adjusting entries**. At the end of a fiscal period, the temporary account balances are transferred to an income summary account. This procedure summarizes, in one account, the effect of operating the business.

Zytech's adjusting entries are shown above. After the adjusting entries are posted, general ledger accounts will be up-to-date as of December 31.

## STEPS · STEPS · STEPS · STEPS · STEPS · STEPS · STEPS · STEPS · STEPS · STEPS

### JOURNALIZING ADJUSTING ENTRIES

**1** Write the words *Adjusting Entries* in the Account Title column. This heading identifies the group of adjusting entries.

**2** Enter each adjusting entry using information from the Adjustments column of the work sheet. The letters used to identify the adjustments provide the order for these entries. For example, adjustment *(a)* is the first adjusting entry to be recorded. No source document or explanation is written for each adjusting entry.

**1.** Write *Closing Entries* in Account Title column.

**2.** Record entry to close income statment accounts with credit balances.

**3.** Write *(continued on general journal page 15)* to show that the closing entries are continued.

### GENERAL JOURNAL

PAGE **14**

| | DATE | | ACCOUNT TITLE | DOC. NO. | POST. REF. | DEBIT | CREDIT | |
|---|---|---|---|---|---|---|---|---|
| 1 | | | Closing Entries | | | | | 1 |
| 2 | Dec²⁰⁻⁻ | 31 | Income Summary—Audio | | | 18 420 39 | | 2 |
| 3 | | | Sales—Audio | | | 351 032 81 | | 3 |
| 4 | | | Sales—Video | | | 438 341 75 | | 4 |
| 5 | | | Purchases Discount—Audio | | | 4 058 95 | | 5 |
| 6 | | | Purchases Ret. and Allow.—Audio | | | 8 282 48 | | 6 |
| 7 | | | Purchases Discount—Video | | | 4 334 55 | | 7 |
| 8 | | | Purchases Ret. and Allow.—Video | | | 8 897 52 | | 8 |
| 9 | | | Income Summary—General | | | | 833 368 45 | 9 |
| 10 | | | (continued on general journal page 15) | | | | | 10 |

Journal entries used to prepare temporary accounts for a new fiscal period are called **closing entries**. Zytech's closing entries made on December 31 are shown above and on the next page.

The information to journalize closing entries is obtained from the Departmental Margin Statements and the Income Statement columns of the work sheet.

## EXPLANATION OF CLOSING ENTRIES

At the end of each fiscal period, Zytech records the following four closing entries:

1. Closing entry for income statement accounts with credit balances (revenue and contra cost accounts).
2. Closing entry for income statement accounts with debit balances (cost, contra revenue, and expense accounts).
3. Closing entry to record net income or net loss in the retained earnings account and to close the income summary account.
4. Closing entry for the dividends account.

### Recording Closing Entries on Two General Journal Pages

Zytech's closing entries require 44 lines of the general journal to record. However, each page of the general journal is only 36 lines long. If all lines of the first page were filled and then the closing entries continued on the next page, the closing entry for income statement accounts would be split between two journal pages. It is not a good practice to split a journal entry between two pages because the debit and credit parts of the entry cannot be seen together. Therefore, Zytech uses the following procedure to be sure there is no misunderstanding when two general journal pages are used to record closing entries:

1. Record the first closing entry, using lines 1–9.
2. Write the note *(continued on general journal page 15)* on the line after the last line of the first closing entry.
3. Write the heading *Closing Entries (continued)* on the first line of the next page of the general journal.
4. Record the rest of the closing entries.

**4.** Write *Closing Entries (continued)* in the Account Title Column.

**5.** Record entry to close income statement accounts with debit balances.

**6.** Record entry to close Income Summary to Retained Earnings.

**7.** Record entry for Dividends.

| | DATE | | ACCOUNT TITLE | DOC. NO. | POST. REF. | DEBIT | CREDIT | |
|---|---|---|---|---|---|---|---|---|
| 1 | | | *Closing Entries (continued)* | | | | | 1 |
| 2 | 20-- Dec | 31 | Income Summary—General | | | 778 41 2 25 | | 2 |
| 3 | | | Income Summary—Video | | | | 9 36 0 00 | 3 |
| 4 | | | Sales Discount—Audio | | | | 1 60 5 85 | 4 |
| 5 | | | Sales Returns and Allow.—Audio | | | | 4 95 0 50 | 5 |
| 6 | | | Sales Discount—Video | | | | 2 00 5 25 | 6 |
| 7 | | | Sales Returns and Allow.—Video | | | | 6 18 1 80 | 7 |
| 8 | | | Purchases—Audio | | | | 215 74 5 68 | 8 |
| 9 | | | Purchases—Video | | | | 231 76 6 62 | 9 |
| 10 | | | Advertising Expense—Audio | | | | 1 65 0 00 | 10 |
| 11 | | | Depr. Exp.—Store Equipment, Audio | | | | 4 00 0 00 | 11 |
| 12 | | | Payroll Taxes Expense—Audio | | | | 9 40 1 80 | 12 |
| 13 | | | Salary Expense—Audio | | | | 90 92 4 19 | 13 |
| 14 | | | Supplies Expense—Audio | | | | 4 29 4 00 | 14 |
| 15 | | | Advertising Expense—Video | | | | 2 14 0 00 | 15 |
| 16 | | | Depr. Exp.—Store Equipment, Video | | | | 3 50 0 00 | 16 |
| 17 | | | Payroll Taxes Expense—Video | | | | 7 50 9 82 | 17 |
| 18 | | | Salary Expense—Video | | | | 72 62 7 02 | 18 |
| 19 | | | Supplies Expense—Video | | | | 7 75 3 00 | 19 |
| 20 | | | Broadband Expense | | | | 1 44 0 00 | 20 |
| 21 | | | Depr. Exp.—Office Equipment | | | | 1 49 0 00 | 21 |
| 22 | | | Insurance Expense | | | | 5 65 0 00 | 22 |
| 23 | | | Miscellaneous Expense | | | | 5 95 8 48 | 23 |
| 24 | | | Payroll Taxes Expense—Admin. | | | | 4 51 5 30 | 24 |
| 25 | | | Phone Expense | | | | 2 39 0 00 | 25 |
| 26 | | | Rent Expense | | | | 18 00 0 00 | 26 |
| 27 | | | Salary Expense—Administrative | | | | 43 66 7 19 | 27 |
| 28 | | | Supplies Expense—Administrative | | | | 2 92 2 00 | 28 |
| 29 | | | Uncollectible Accounts Expense | | | | 2 10 9 40 | 29 |
| 30 | | | Utilities Expense | | | | 3 20 2 28 | 30 |
| 31 | | | Federal Income Tax Expense | | | | 11 65 2 07 | 31 |
| 32 | | 31 | Income Summary—General | | | 54 95 6 20 | | 32 |
| 33 | | | Retained Earnings | | | | 54 95 6 20 | 33 |
| 34 | | 31 | Retained Earnings | | | 30 00 0 00 | | 34 |
| 35 | | | Dividends | | | | 30 00 0 00 | 35 |
| 36 | | | | | | | | 36 |

## Closing Entry for Income Statement Accounts with Credit Balances

The closing entry for Zytech's income statement credit balance accounts on December 31 is shown on lines 2–9 on page 14 of the general journal. Income statement credit balance accounts are the departmental income summary accounts with a credit balance (Income Summary—Audio), the revenue accounts (Sales—Audio and Sales—Video), and the contra cost accounts (Purchases Discount—Audio, Purchases Returns and Allowances—Audio, Purchases Discount—Video, and Purchases Returns and Allowances—Video).

Information needed for closing income statement credit balance accounts is obtained from the Departmental Margin Statements Credit columns of the work sheet.

## Closing Entry for Income Statement Accounts with Debit Balances

The closing entry for Zytech's income statement debit balance accounts on December 31 is shown on lines 2–31 on page 15 of the general journal. Income statement debit balance accounts are the departmental income summary accounts with a debit balance (Income Summary—Video), the contra revenue accounts (Sales Discount—Audio, Sales Returns and Allowances—Audio, Sales Discount—Video, and Sales Returns and Allowances—Video), the cost accounts (Purchases—Audio and Purchases—Video), and the expense accounts.

Information needed for closing income statement debit balance accounts is obtained from the Departmental Margin Statements and Income Statement Debit columns of the work sheet.

©GETTY IMAGES/PHOTODISC

## Closing Entry to Record Net Income or Net Loss in the Retained Earnings Account and to Close the Income Summary Account

The closing entry to record Zytech's net income in the retained earnings account and close the income summary account on December 31 is shown on lines 32–33 on page 15 of the general journal.

The balance of Income Summary—General is equal to the net income (or net loss) for the fiscal period. A corporation's net income is recorded in Retained Earnings. Information needed for this entry is obtained from line 74 of Zytech's work sheet.

After the entry to record net income is posted, Income Summary has a zero balance. The net income, $54,956.20, has been recorded as a credit to Retained Earnings.

## Closing Entry for the Dividends Account

The closing entry for Zytech's dividends account on December 31 is shown on lines 34–35 on page 15 of the general journal. The debit balance of a dividends account is the total amount of dividends declared during a fiscal period. Since dividends decrease the earnings that a corporation retains, the dividends account is closed to Retained Earnings.

Information needed for closing Zytech's dividends account is obtained from line 31 of the Balance Sheet Debit column of the work sheet.

After the closing entry for the dividends account is posted, Dividends has a zero balance. The amount of the dividends, $30,000.00, has been recorded as a debit to Retained Earnings.

After closing entries are posted, all temporary accounts have zero balances and are prepared for a new fiscal period.

**FYI** FOR YOUR INFORMATION

In most commercial computerized accounting systems, year-end closing is performed by the computer. The accountant selects a menu item to close the accounting records for the year. The software automatically updates its database. In some systems, year-end closing cannot be undone.

## POST-CLOSING TRIAL BALANCE FOR A DEPARTMENTALIZED BUSINESS

**Zytech Media Corporation**
**Post-Closing Trial Balance**
**December 31, 20--**

| Account Title | Debit | Credit |
|---|---|---|
| Cash | $ 38,910.00 | |
| Petty Cash | 500.00 | |
| Accounts Receivable | 13,755.00 | |
| Allowance for Uncollectible Accounts | | $ 2,350.00 |
| Merchandise Inventory—Audio | 204,855.00 | |
| Merchandise Inventory—Video | 190,484.60 | |
| Supplies—Administrative | 4,051.00 | |
| Supplies—Audio | 5,921.00 | |
| Supplies—Video | 2,089.00 | |
| Prepaid Insurance | 4,200.00 | |
| Office Equipment | 16,900.00 | |
| Acc. Depr.—Office Equipment | | 7,450.00 |
| Store Equipment—Audio | 38,900.00 | |
| Acc. Depr.—Store Equipment, Audio | | 22,000.00 |
| Store Equipment—Video | 26,652.00 | |
| Acc. Depr.—Store Equipment, Video | | 19,000.00 |
| Accounts Payable | | 31,360.30 |
| Employee Income Tax Payable—Federal | | 2,680.75 |
| Employee Income Tax Payable—State | | 1,118.19 |
| Federal Income Tax Payable | | 852.07 |
| Social Security Tax Payable | | 2,730.57 |
| Medicare Tax Payable | | 630.13 |
| Sales Tax Payable | | 3,139.64 |
| Unemployment Tax Payable—Federal | | 23.60 |
| Unemployment Tax Payable—State | | 159.30 |
| Health Insurance Premiums Payable | | 2,261.16 |
| Life Insurance Premiums Payable | | 350.19 |
| Dividends Payable | | 30,000.00 |
| Capital Stock | | 340,000.00 |
| Retained Earnings | | 81,111.70 |
| Totals | $547,217.60 | $547,217.60 |

Debits must always equal credits in general ledger accounts. The trial balance recorded on the work sheet proves that debits do equal credits before adjusting and closing entries are posted. After adjusting and closing entries are posted, equality of general ledger debits and credits is proved again. This procedure ensures that the equality of debits and credits has been maintained in preparation for a new fiscal period.

A trial balance prepared after the closing entries are posted is called a **post-closing trial balance**. Zytech's post-closing trial balance prepared on December 31 is shown above. The total of debit balances, $547,217.60, is the same as the total of credit balances. The equality of general ledger debits and credits is proved. Zytech's general ledger is ready for the next fiscal period. [*CONCEPT: Accounting Period Cycle*]

**REMEMBER** Only temporary accounts are closed. Permanent account balances are needed to continue conducting business in the next accounting cycle.

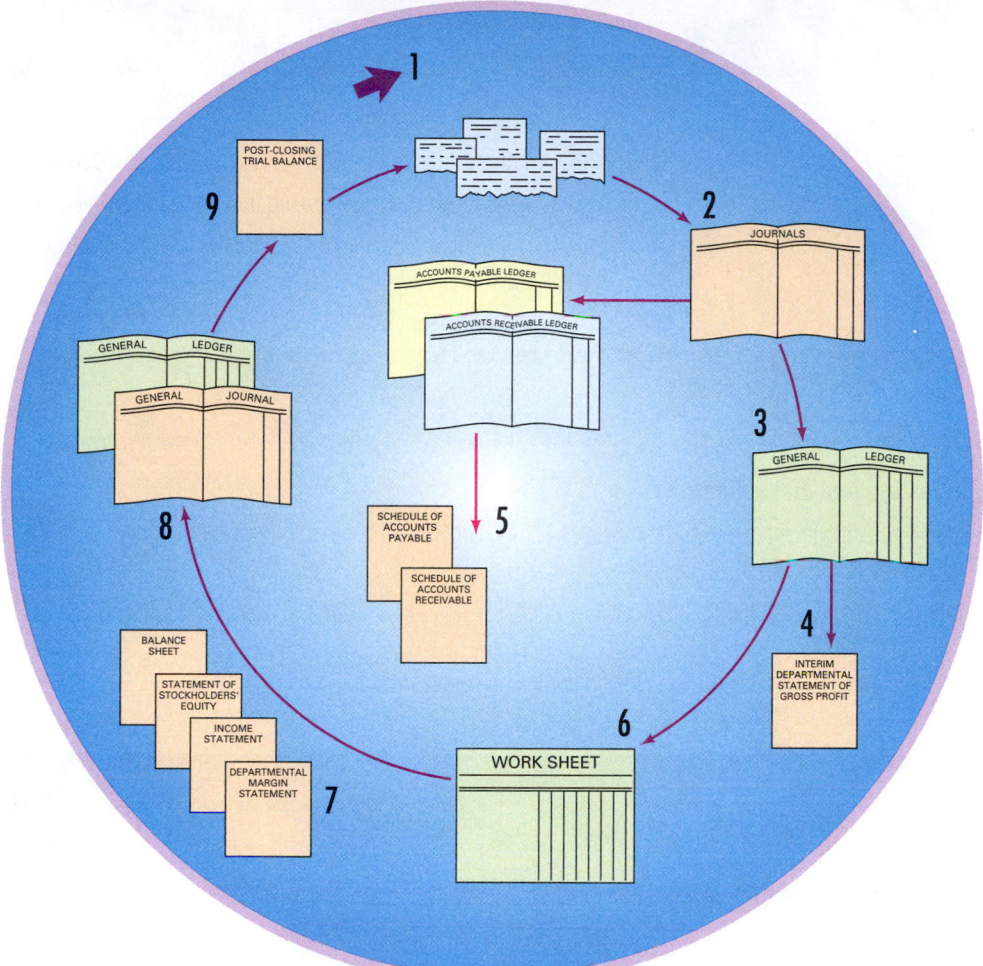

Accounting procedures used by Zytech, a departmentalized merchandising business, are described in Chapters 1 through 4. The same procedures are used from year to year. [CONCEPT: Consistent Reporting] The series of accounting activities included in recording financial information for a fiscal period is called an **accounting cycle**. Zytech's complete accounting cycle is shown above. Accounting cycle procedures provide information for preparing interim and end-of-fiscal-period financial statements. [CONCEPT: Accounting Period Cycle]

# STEPS

STEPS • STEPS • STEPS • STEPS • STEPS • STEPS • STEPS • STEPS • STEPS • STEPS •

## ACCOUNTING ACTIVITIES IN THE ACCOUNTING CYCLE FOR A DEPARTMENTALIZED BUSINESS

1. Verify source documents for accuracy. The source documents describe transactions and prove that the transactions did occur.

2. Record entries in journals using the information on the source documents.

3. Post journal entries to the ledgers.

4. Prepare an interim departmental statement of gross profit. Zytech prepares this statement monthly to assess the operating efficiency of each department.

5. Prepare schedules of accounts receivable and accounts payable from the subsidiary ledgers.

6. Prepare a trial balance on the work sheet. Complete the work sheet to summarize a business's financial condition.

7. Prepare financial statements using information on the work sheet and in the accounting records.

8. Journalize and post adjusting and closing entries using information from the work sheet.

9. Prepare a post-closing trial balance to check the equality of debits and credits in the general ledger. The accounting records for the fiscal period are complete and ready for the start of the next fiscal period.

## • terms review

*TERMS REVIEW •*

adjusting entries
closing entries
post-closing trial balance
accounting cycle

## • audit your understanding

*AUDIT YOUR*

1. What is the purpose of adjusting entries?
2. Which accounts are closed at the end of an accounting period?
3. What is the purpose of a post-closing trial balance?
4. Which accounting activities in the accounting cycle are performed at the end of a fiscal period?

## • work together 4-5

*WORK TOGETHER • WORK*

### Journalizing adjusting and closing entries

Use the work sheet from Work Together 4-3 and 4-4. Pages 13, 14, and 15 of a general journal are provided in the *Working Papers*. Your instructor will guide you through the following example.

1. Using the information presented in the Adjustments columns of Callostay's work sheet, journalize the adjusting entries on page 13 of a general journal.
2. Using Callostay's work sheet, journalize the closing entries on pages 14 and 15 of a general journal.

## • on your own 4-5

*ON YOUR OWN • ON YOUR OWN*

### Journalizing adjusting and closing entries

Use the work sheet from On Your Own 4-3 and 4-4. Pages 13, 14, and 15 of a general journal are provided in the *Working Papers*. Work this problem independently.

1. Using the information presented in the Adjustments columns of Saratoga Spa's work sheet, journalize the adjusting entries on page 13 of a general journal.
2. Using Saratoga Spa's work sheet, journalize the closing entries on pages 14 and 15 of a general journal.

SUMMARY · SUMMARY · SUMMARY

## *After completing this chapter, you can*

1. Define accounting terms related to cost accounting and financial reporting for a departmentalized merchandising business.
2. Identify accounting concepts and practices related to cost accounting and financial reporting for a departmentalized merchandising business.
3. Distinguish between direct and indirect expenses.
4. Prepare an interim departmental statement of gross profit.
5. Prepare a work sheet for a departmentalized merchandising business.
6. Prepare financial statements for a departmentalized merchandising business.
7. Analyze financial statements using selected component percentages.
8. Complete end-of-period work for a departmentalized merchandising business.

# Explore Accounting

EXPLORE ACCOUNTING · EXPLORE ACCOUNTING · EXPLORE ACCO

## Exception Reports

The amount of financial information available to managers can become immense. Responsibility accounting is one way that managers focus accounting information on one aspect of the business. A departmental margin statement, for example, focuses on the revenue and expenses controlled by the manager of a single department. Even departmental margin statements can be overwhelming for a large company with hundreds of departments. How does an upper-level manager examine all of these statements to identify problems?

Rather than reviewing every line of every departmental statement, a manager can instruct the computer system to prepare a report of only those accounts for which the actual results differ significantly from expected results. These reports, often called *exception reports*, should identify both positive and negative situations. For example, an exception report could identify those accounts that differ by more than 10% from departmental budgets. This shorter report would allow the manager to quickly focus on areas that deserve attention.

Managers must gather information and be objective when investigating the reasons for excessive expenses. Does salary expense exceed-

ing budget by 20% indicate that workers lack discipline? Although this explanation is possible, other reasons could cause even the best employees to be unproductive. For example, note these factors:

1. Workers have not received adequate training.
2. Equipment is obsolete and often broken.
3. Parts are frequently out of stock.

It is natural for managers to focus on negative situations. The manager can work with the department manager to correct the problem. Too often, managers neglect to investigate the reasons for positive performances. If a department has generated sales 20% more than its budget, the manager should investigate what strategies and methods can account for the successful results. This information can then be shared with other departments to improve sales throughout the company.

**Instructions:** A manager of Summertime Furniture receives an exception report showing that lumber costs of its picnic table department are 32% above the budget. List possible explanations for the apparent problem in the purchase and use of lumber.

## 4-1 APPLICATION PROBLEM
### Identifying direct and indirect expenses

Harbour House Interiors has two departments: Paint and Wallpaper. Harbor House completed the transactions below.

**Instructions:**

Use a form similar to the one below. For each transaction, indicate:
- a. Whether the expense is a direct expense (identifiable with a specific department) or an indirect expense.
- b. The title of the expense account.

The first transaction is completed as an example.

| Trans. No. | Direct Expense or Indirect Expense | Expense Account Title |
|---|---|---|
| 1 | *Indirect* | *Utilities Expense* |

1. Paid cash for utilities bill.
2. Paid cash for new accounting software for the company.
3. Paid cash for an instructor to conduct classes on wallpapering to encourage customers to enter the store.
4. Paid cash to a courier to deliver paint to a construction site.
5. Paid cash to rent a hall for the annual employee party.
6. Paid cash for bimonthly payroll for all administrative, paint, and wallpaper employees. Salesclerks are hired by specific department managers.
7. Donated paint and wallpaper to a group sponsoring a youth center.
8. Paid for advertising in the newspaper in a special home decorating supplement.
9. Paid monthly federal income tax expense.
10. Paid cash for monthly payroll taxes (consider the taxes on the Wallpaper Department employees only).

## 4-2 APPLICATION PROBLEM
### Preparing an interim departmental statement of gross profit; calculating component percentages

LightSource has two departments, Office and Residential. The following data are obtained from the accounting records on March 31 of the current year:

|  | Office | Residential |
|---|---|---|
| Beginning Inventory, January 1 | $124,640.00 | $166,500.00 |
| Estimated Beginning Inventory, March 1 | 101,344.00 | 135,660.00 |
| Net Purchases, January 1 to February 28 | 23,360.00 | 24,840.00 |
| Net Sales, January 1 to February 28 | 77,760.00 | 92,800.00 |
| Net Purchases for March | 13,497.00 | 9,978.00 |
| Net Sales for March | 29,200.00 | 33,600.00 |
| Estimated Gross Profit Percentage | 40.0% | 50.0% |

**Instructions:**

1. Prepare an estimated merchandise inventory sheet, similar to the one in this chapter, for each department for the month ended March 31 of the current year.
2. Prepare an interim departmental statement of gross profit. Calculate and record component percentages for departmental and total cost of merchandise sold and gross profit on operations. Round percentage calculations to the nearest 0.1%.

## 4-3 APPLICATION PROBLEM AUTOMATED ACCOUNTING QUICKBOOKS
### Preparing a work sheet with departmental margins

AllSports Center is a merchandising business that sells sports clothing and equipment. AllSports Center's December 31 trial balance is recorded on a 12-column work sheet in the *Working Papers.* The following adjustment information is available:

### Adjustment Information, December 31

Uncollectible accounts expense—estimated as 1.0% of sales on account.

| | |
|---|---:|
| Sales on account for the year | $145,700.00 |
| Merchandise Inventory—Clothing | 88,950.00 |
| Merchandise Inventory—Equipment | 93,678.80 |
| Supplies Used—Clothing | 1,925.00 |
| Supplies Used—Equipment | 1,287.00 |
| Supplies Used—Administrative | 834.00 |
| Insurance Expired | 7,200.00 |
| Depreciation Expense—Office Equipment | 1,100.00 |
| Depreciation Expense—Store Equipment, Clothing | 3,720.00 |
| Depreciation Expense—Store Equipment, Equipment | 1,850.00 |
| Federal Income Tax Expense for the Year | 16,421.38 |

**Instructions:**

1. Complete the work sheet for the month ended June 30 of the current year. Record the adjustments on the work sheet using the adjustment information for December 31.
2. Extend amounts to the proper debit and credit columns for Departmental Margin Statement— Clothing, Departmental Margin Statement—Equipment, Income Statement, and Balance Sheet. Accounts on trial balance lines 51–65 are classified as indirect expenses. Save your work to complete Application Problems 4-4 and 4-5.

## 4-4 APPLICATION PROBLEM AUTOMATED ACCOUNTING
### Preparing financial statements

**Instructions:**

The work sheet from Application Problem 4-3 is needed to complete this problem.

1. Prepare departmental margin statements for AllSports Center's Clothing Department and Equipment Department. Calculate and record the component percentages for each item on the statements. Round percentage calculations to the nearest 0.1%. Save your work to complete Application Problem 4-5.
2. Prepare an income statement for AllSports Center. Calculate and record the component percentages for each item on the statements. Round the percentage calculations to the nearest 0.1%.
3. Prepare a statement of stockholders' equity. Use the following additional information:

| | |
|---|---|
| January 1 balance of capital stock account | $100,000.00 |
|    (1,000 shares issued for $100.00 per share) | |
| No additional capital stock issued. | |
| January 1 balance of retained earnings account | 68,372.00 |
| Dividends declared during current quarter | 5,000.00 |

4. Prepare a balance sheet.

## 4-5 APPLICATION PROBLEM  AUTOMATED ACCOUNTING   PEACHTREE
### Journalizing adjusting and closing entries for a departmentalized business

**Instructions:**

The work sheet from Application Problem 4-3 is needed to complete this problem.

1. Journalize the adjusting entries for AllSports Center. Use page 13 of a general journal.
2. Journalize the closing entries for AllSports Center. Use pages 14 and 15 of a general journal. Dividends declared during the current quarter were $12,000.00.

## 4-6 MASTERY PROBLEM  AUTOMATED ACCOUNTING   QUICKBOOKS
### Completing end-of-fiscal-period work for a merchandising business using departmental margins

Klein Sporting Goods is a merchandising business that specializes in golf and tennis equipment. The company uses a yearly fiscal period. Klein's December 31 trial balance is recorded on a 12-column work sheet in the *Working Papers*. The adjustment information for December 31 follows.

### Adjustment Information, December 31

Uncollectible accounts expense—estimated as 1.5% of sales on account.

| | |
|---|---|
| Sales on account for year | $605,780.00 |
| Merchandise Inventory—Golf | 136,491.00 |
| Merchandise Inventory—Tennis | 154,040.00 |
| Supplies Used—Administrative | 2,013.00 |
| Supplies Used—Golf | 2,381.00 |
| Supplies Used—Tennis | 3,246.00 |
| Insurance Expired | 6,700.00 |
| Depreciation Expense—Office Equipment | 1,270.00 |
| Depreciation Expense—Store Equipment, Golf | 2,240.00 |
| Depreciation Expense—Store Equipment, Tennis | 1,850.00 |
| Federal Income Tax Expense for the Year | 21,173.44 |

**Instructions:**

1. Complete a work sheet for the year ended December 31 of the current year. Record the adjustments using the reported information for December 31.
2. Extend amounts to the proper debit and credit columns for Departmental Margin Statement—Golf, Departmental Margin Statement—Tennis, Income Statement, and Balance Sheet. Accounts on trial balance lines 57–65 are classified as indirect expenses.
3. Prepare departmental margin statements for each department. Calculate and record the percentages for each item on the statements. Round percentage calculations to the nearest 0.1%.
4. Prepare an income statement. Calculate and record the component percentages for each item on the statement. Round percentage calculations to the nearest 0.1%.
5. Prepare a statement of stockholders' equity. Use the following additional information:

| | |
|---|---|
| January 1 balance of capital stock account | $270,000.00 |
|    (5,400 shares issued for $50.00 per share) | |
| No additional capital stock issued. | |
| January 1 balance of retained earnings account | 66,851.25 |
| Dividends declared during current year | 10,000.00 |

6. Prepare a balance sheet.
7. Journalize the adjusting entries. Use page 13 of a general journal.
8. Journalize the closing entries. Use pages 14 and 15 of a general journal.

# 4-7 CHALLENGE PROBLEM

## Analyzing a departmental margin statement

The departmental margin statement for the Personal Digital Assistant (PDA) department of Digital-Help, Inc., for the years 20X8 and 20X9 is provided in the *Working Papers.* The company has set a goal for the PDA Department to contribute a minimum of 25.0% departmental margin. For the years 20X3 through 20X8, the departmental margin for the PDA Department has varied from 25.5% to 29.0% of net sales.

**Instructions:**

1. Calculate and record the component percentages for each item on the 20X9 departmental margin statement. Round percentage calculations to the nearest 0.1%.
2. Calculate the changes in percentage of Net Sales from 20X8 to 20X9 for the following items: (a) cost of merchandise sold, (b) gross profit, (c) total direct departmental expenses, and (d) departmental margin.
3. From an analysis of the departmental margin statement and the amounts obtained from instructions 1 and 2, answer the following questions:
   a. Is the departmental margin for the PDA Department at a satisfactory percentage of sales? Explain why it is or is not satisfactory.
   b. Is the trend of the cost of merchandise sold percentage favorable or unfavorable? Explain why it is or is not favorable. Suggest some possible reasons for the change in cost of merchandise sold from 20X8 to 20X9.
   c. Is the trend of the total direct departmental expenses percentage favorable or unfavorable? Explain why the trend is or is not favorable.

accountingxtra.swlearning.com

## applied communication

One of the most frequently asked questions or requests during an interview is "Tell me about yourself." When responding to this inquiry, focus on how your education, skills, abilities, personal qualities, extracurricular activities, and work experience qualify you for the position. Emphasize information and accomplishments that are relevant to the job. Provide examples that document your traits and experience. And most important, be enthusiastic.

**Instructions:**

1. Write a paragraph about yourself. Emphasize those factors that would qualify you for employment. Don't forget to mention your accounting skills.

2. In your *Career Portfolio,* label a divider "Interviewing."

3. Keep a copy of your personal paragraph in the "Interviewing" section of your *Career Portfolio.* Be sure to review this paragraph before all interviews.

## cases for critical thinking

### Case 1

The following data are obtained from financial information for InfoTech for the month ended August 31 of the current year:

| | |
|---|---|
| Beginning Inventory, Jan. 1 | $98,000.00 |
| Net Purchases for the Period, Jan. 1 to Aug. 31 | 42,500.00 |
| Net Sales for the Period, Jan. 1 to Aug. 31 | 66,800.00 |

You are asked to report the estimated ending inventory on August 31 using the gross profit method for estimating inventory. What will you report?

### Case 2

Cyber Graphics is a departmentalized business. An interim statement of gross profit is prepared monthly. A departmental statement of gross profit is prepared at the end of each fiscal year. The manager suggests that the accountant extend the statements of gross profit by including a division of all expenses by department. The accountant indicates that the time required to divide the expenses by department would not add significantly to the information available for decision making. Do you agree or disagree with the accountant? Why?

## SCANS workplace competency

**Resource Competency:** Allocating Material and Facility Resources

**Concept:** Effective employees can acquire, store, and distribute supplies, parts, equipment, space, or final products in order to maximize their use.

**Application:** You are the manager of a small store consisting of three departments: Women's, Men's, and Children's. Presently, square footage is allocated as follows: Women's, 10,000 square feet; Men's, 5,000 square feet; Children's, 5,000 square feet. Gross profit on operations was $100,000 for the previous month. Each department contributed the following gross profit on operations amounts: Women's, $10,000 loss; Men's, $70,000 profit; Children's, $40,000 profit. Based on gross profit totals, how might you reallocate floor space for each department? Explain your answer. Is there a negative consequence to completely eliminating the Women's Department? Prepare an illustration indicating new department boundaries.

APPLIED COMMUNICATION • APPLIED

CASES FOR CRITICAL THINKING • CASES FOR

SCANS WORKPLACE COMPETENCY

## • auditing for errors

A new accounting clerk for CalTech Corporation prepared the following trial balance using the general ledger account balances listed below.

1. Total the trial balance columns for the accounting clerk. If total debits do not equal credits, check your addition.

2. Review CalTech's trial balance for accuracy and make needed corrections. Re-total the trial balance columns. Continue checking until total debits = total credits.

3. Prepare a list identifying the general types of errors made.

| Gen. Ledger | Account Title | Trial Balance | |
|---|---|---|---|
| 42,370.00 | Cash | 4,237.00 | |
| 10,500.00 | Accts. Receivable | 10,500.00 | |
| 1,500.00 | All. For Uncoll. Accts. | 1,500.00 | |
| 30,510.00 | Mdse. Inventory | 30,510.00 | |
| 11,220.00 | Office Equipment | 11,220.00 | |
| 1,350.00 | Acc. Depr.—Off. Equip. | 1,350.00 | |
| 27,840.00 | Accounts Payable | | 274,800.00 |
| 10,000.00 | Dividends Payable | | 10,000.00 |
| 40,000.00 | Capital Stock | | 40,000.00 |
| 2,150.00 | Retained Earnings | | 2,150.00 |
| 10,000.00 | Dividends | | 10,000.00 |
| | Income Summary | | |
| 136,540.00 | Sales | | 163,540.00 |
| 1,120.00 | Sales Discount | 1,120.00 | |
| 780.00 | Sales Ret. & Allow. | | 780.00 |
| 48,230.00 | Purchases | 48,230.00 | |
| 1,850.00 | Purchases Discount | | 1,850.00 |
| 20,000.00 | Advertising Expense | | |
| 40,500.00 | Rent Expense | 40,500.00 | |
| 6,000.00 | Federal Inc. Tax Exp. | | 6,000.00 |
| | **Totals** | | |

## • analyzing Costco's Financial Statements

In this chapter, you have learned that the cost of merchandise is a significant cost for all merchandising businesses. In order to maximize profits, management attempts to keep this cost as low as possible. You also learned in Chapter 4 that there are four basic components included in every sales dollar. One of these components is the *cost of merchandise sold*. The component percentage for cost of merchandise sold is calculated by dividing merchandise costs by the amount of net sales.

### Instructions:

1. Referring to the notes to consolidated financial statements on Appendix page B-12 in this textbook, describe what Costco considers to be the cost of merchandise sold beyond the purchase price of inventory sold.

2. Referring to the ten-year operating and financial highlights on Appendix pages B-2 and B-3:
   a. List the component percentages of net sales for merchandise costs for each year beginning with 1994 and ending with 2003.
   b. Looking at the component percentages for each year beginning with 1994, describe any trends regarding merchandise costs.
   c. Would you classify the trend identified in question 3 as "favorable" or "unfavorable" for Costco? Explain.
   d. For every $100 in net sales in 2003, how much did Costco spend to obtain merchandise? For every $100 in net sales in 1994, how much did Costco spend to obtain merchandise?

## Completing End-of-Fiscal-Period Work for a Departmental Business

During the fiscal period, many transactions are analyzed, journalized, and posted. When a transaction affects more than one accounting period, an adjusting entry may be needed to match revenues and expenses. To complete the accounting cycle, a trial balance is prepared. Adjusting entries are recorded, entered into the computer, and verified for accuracy. Financial statements are generated, and finally closing entries are generated and posted by the software. No work sheet is prepared in an automated accounting system.

### Processing a Trial Balance

After all the usual transactions of the business are entered as journal entries, a preliminary trial balance is generated. A trial balance should be displayed and printed before adjusting entries are recorded. The trial balance indicates that debits equal credits. To display and print a trial balance:

1. Click the Reports button.
2. Select Ledger Reports from the Report Selection dialog box.
3. Choose Trial Balance from the Choose a Report to Display list.
4. Click the Print button to print a copy of the trial balance.

### Adjusting Entries

This trial balance and period-end adjustment data are used as the basis for the adjusting entries. The General Journal tab within the Journal Entries window is used to enter and post the adjusting entries. All of the adjusting entries are dated the last day of the fiscal period and use *Adj. Ent.* as the reference.

### Processing Financial Statements

The automated accounting system prepares financial statements from the information in the database. Financial statements can be displayed and printed at any time. They are always printed at the end of the fiscal period. These statements include:

- Departmental Gross Profit Statements
- Income statement
- Balance sheet
- Retained earnings statement

To display and print the statements:

1. Click the Reports button.
2. Select Financial Statements from the Report Selection dialog box.
3. Choose the statement you want to print from the Choose a Report to Display list.
4. Click the Print button to print a copy of the statement.

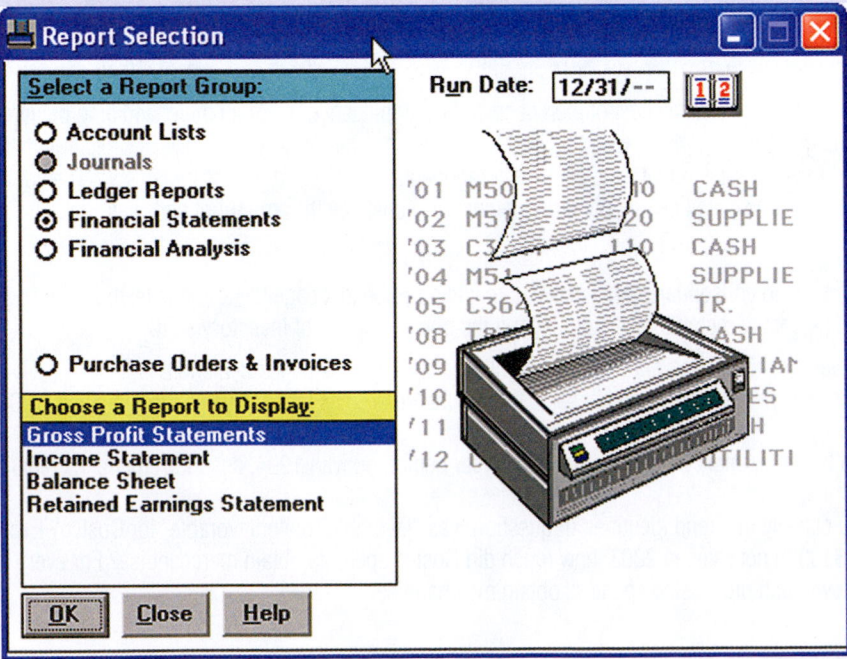

## Closing Entries for a Departmentalized Business

In an automated accounting system, closing entries are generated and posted by the software. The software automatically closes net income to the retained earnings account after closing the revenue and expense accounts. The dividends account is closed as well.

1. Choose Generate Closing Journal Entries from the Options menu.

2. Click Yes to generate the closing entries.

3. The general journal will appear, containing the journal entries.

4. Click the Post button.

5. Display a post-closing trial balance report.

   a. Click on the Reports toolbar button, or choose the Reports Selection menu item from the Reports menu.

   b. Select the Ledger Reports option button from the Report Selection dialog box.

   c. Choose Trial Balance report.

## AUTOMATING APPLICATION PROBLEMS 4-3, 4-4, and 4-5:
## Preparing a work sheet with departmental margins
## Preparing financial statements
## Journalizing adjusting and closing entries for a departmentalized business

### Instructions:

1. Load *Automated Accounting 8.0* or higher software.

2. Select data file A04-3 (Advanced Course Application Problem 4-3).

3. Select File from the menu bar and choose the Save As menu command. Key the path to the drive and directory that contains your data files. Save the database with a filename of A04-5 XXX XXX (where the Xs are your first and last names).

4. Access Problem Instructions through the Browser tool. Read the Problem Instruction screen.

5. Refer to pages 127 and 128 for data used in this problem.

6. Save your file and exit the Automated Accounting software.

## AUTOMATING MASTERY PROBLEM 4-6:
## Completing end-of-fiscal-period work for a merchandising business using departmental margins

### Instructions:

1. Load *Automated Accounting 8.0* or higher software.

2. Select data file A04-6.

3. Select File from the menu bar and choose the Save As menu command. Key the path to the drive and directory that contains your data files. Save the database with a filename of A04-6 XXX XXX (where Xs are your first and last names).

4. Access Problem Instructions by clicking the Browser tool. Read the Problem Instruction screen.

5. Refer to page 128 for data used in this problem.

6. Save your file and exit the Automated Accounting software.

# Processing and Reporting Departmentalized Accounting Data

AUTOMATED ACCOUNTING

EXCEL

AUTOMATED AC

This activity reinforces selected learning from Part 1, Chapters 1 through 4. The complete accounting cycle is for a departmentalized merchandising business organized as a corporation.

## BOOKSPLUS, INC.

BooksPlus, Inc., has two departments: Books and Magazines. BooksPlus, Inc., is open for business Monday through Saturday. A monthly rent is paid on the building. The business owns the office and store equipment.

BooksPlus sells books and magazines to individuals and schools. Cash sales and sales on account are made. The business uses a national credit card service in addition to its own company credit card.

BooksPlus's fiscal year is January 1 through December 31. During the fiscal year, a monthly interim departmental statement of gross profit is prepared.

BooksPlus uses the chart of accounts shown on the following page. The journals and ledgers used by BooksPlus are similar to those illustrated in Part 1. The journal and ledger forms are provided in the *Working Papers*. Beginning balances have been recorded in the ledgers.

## PREPARING AN INTERIM DEPARTMENTAL STATEMENT OF GROSS PROFIT

BooksPlus prepares an interim departmental statement of gross profit each month. The following data are obtained from the accounting records at the end of November of the current year.

|  | Books | Magazines |
|---|---|---|
| Beginning inventory, January 1 | $164,164.20 | $147,840.30 |
| Estimated beginning inventory, November 1 | 180,205.05 | 157,195.78 |
| Net purchases January 1 to October 31 | 120,332.40 | 118,395.82 |
| Net sales, January 1 to October 31 | 194,198.95 | 204,848.94 |
| Net purchases for November | 13,007.20 | 14,162.58 |
| Net sales for November | 19,480.60 | 20,240.30 |
| Gross profit on operation as a percent of sales | 45.0% | 47.0% |

**Instructions:**

1. Use the gross profit method of estimating an inventory to prepare an estimated merchandise inventory sheet for each department for the month ended November of the current year.
2. Prepare an interim departmental statement of gross profit for the month ended November 30 of the current year. Calculate and record component percentages for departmental and total cost of merchandise sold and gross profit on operations. Round percentage calculations to the nearest 0.1%.

# GENERAL LEDGER CHART OF ACCOUNTS

**Balance Sheet Accounts**

**(1000) ASSETS**

1100–1400 CURRENT ASSETS
| | |
|---|---|
| 1105 | Cash |
| 1110 | Petty Cash |
| 1205 | Accounts Receivable |
| 1210 | Allowance for Uncollectible Accounts |
| 1305 | Merchandise Inventory—Books |
| 1310 | Merchandise Inventory—Magazines |
| 1315 | Supplies—Administrative |
| 1320 | Supplies—Books |
| 1325 | Supplies—Magazines |
| 1405 | Prepaid Insurance |

1500–1600 PLANT ASSETS
| | |
|---|---|
| 1505 | Display Equipment—Books |
| 1510 | Accumulated Depreciation—Display Equipment, Books |
| 1515 | Display Equipment—Magazines |
| 1520 | Accumulated Depreciation—Display Equipment, Magazines |
| 1605 | Office Equipment |
| 1610 | Accumulated Depreciation—Office Equipment |

**(2000) LIABILITIES**
| | |
|---|---|
| 2105 | Accounts Payable |
| 2205 | Employee Income Tax Payable—Federal |
| 2210 | Employee Income Tax Payable—State |
| 2215 | Federal Income Tax Payable |
| 2220 | Social Security Tax Payable |
| 2225 | Medicare Tax Payable |
| 2230 | Sales Tax Payable |
| 2235 | Unemployment Tax Payable—Federal |
| 2240 | Unemployment Tax Payable—State |
| 2245 | Health Insurance Premiums Payable |
| 2305 | Dividends Payable |

**(3000) STOCKHOLDERS' EQUITY**
| | |
|---|---|
| 3105 | Capital Stock |
| 3110 | Retained Earnings |
| 3115 | Dividends |
| 3205 | Income Summary—Books |
| 3210 | Income Summary—Magazines |
| 3215 | Income Summary—General |

**Income Statement Accounts**

**(4000) OPERATING REVENUE**
| | |
|---|---|
| 4105 | Sales—Books |
| 4110 | Sales Discount—Books |
| 4115 | Sales Returns and Allowances—Books |
| 4205 | Sales—Magazines |
| 4210 | Sales Discount—Magazines |
| 4215 | Sales Returns and Allowances—Magazines |

**(5000) COST OF MERCHANDISE**
| | |
|---|---|
| 5105 | Purchases—Books |
| 5110 | Purchases Discount—Books |
| 5115 | Purchases Returns and Allowances—Books |
| 5205 | Purchases—Magazines |
| 5210 | Purchases Discount—Magazines |
| 5215 | Purchases Returns and Allowances—Magazines |

**(6000) DIRECT EXPENSES**
| | |
|---|---|
| 6100 | DIRECT EXPENSES—BOOKS |
| 6105 | Advertising Expense—Books |
| 6110 | Depreciation Expense—Display Equipment, Books |
| 6115 | Payroll Taxes Expense—Books |
| 6120 | Salary Expense—Books |
| 6125 | Supplies Expense—Books |

**(6200) DIRECT EXPENSES—MAGAZINES**
| | |
|---|---|
| 6205 | Advertising Expense—Magazines |
| 6210 | Depreciation Expense—Display Equipment, Magazines |
| 6215 | Payroll Taxes Expense—Magazines |
| 6220 | Salary Expense—Magazines |
| 6225 | Supplies Expense—Magazines |

**(7000) INDIRECT EXPENSES**
| | |
|---|---|
| 7105 | Credit Card Fee Expense |
| 7110 | Depreciation Expense—Office Equipment |
| 7115 | Insurance Expense |
| 7120 | Miscellaneous Expense |
| 7125 | Payroll Taxes Expense—Administrative |
| 7130 | Rent Expense |
| 7135 | Salary Expense—Administrative |
| 7140 | Supplies Expense—Administrative |
| 7145 | Uncollectible Accounts Expense |

**(8000) INCOME TAX**
| | |
|---|---|
| 8105 | Federal Income Tax Expense |

# SUBSIDIARY LEDGERS CHARTS OF ACCOUNTS

**Accounts Receivable Ledger**
| | |
|---|---|
| 110 | Marcella Amco |
| 120 | Matthew Barasso |
| 130 | Tanya Dockman |
| 140 | Brian Fadstad |
| 150 | Gilmore Public Schools |
| 160 | Belinda Judd |
| 170 | Janelle Kamschorr |
| 180 | Donald Lindgren |
| 190 | Renville Public Schools |

**Accounts Payable Ledger**
| | |
|---|---|
| 210 | A-1 Publishing |
| 220 | CBG Distributors |
| 230 | Grandway Products |
| 240 | H & B Books |
| 250 | Maryland Books & Magazines |
| 260 | Oliver Books, Inc. |
| 270 | Strup Publishers, Inc. |

**Instructions:**

3. Use the appropriate journal to record the following transactions completed during December of the current year. Calculate and record sales tax on all sales and sales returns and allowances as described in Chapter 2. The sales tax rate is 5.0%. No sales tax is charged on sales to schools. BooksPlus offers its customers terms of 2/10, n/30. All of the vendors from which merchandise is purchased on account offer terms of 2/10, n/30. Source documents are abbreviated as follows: check, C; credit memorandum, CM; debit memorandum, DM; memorandum, M; purchase invoice, P; receipt, R; sales invoice, S; terminal summary, TS.

Dec. 1. Paid cash for monthly payroll, $7,899.83 (total payroll: books, $4,522.20; magazines, $4,310.40; administrative, $2,630.25, less deductions: employee income tax-federal, $1,204.00; employee income tax—state, $538.11; Social Security tax, $710.70; Medicare tax, $166.21; health insurance, $944.00). C340.

　　1. Recorded employer payroll taxes, $924.26, for the monthly pay period ended November 30. Taxes owed are: Social Security tax, $710.70; Medicare tax, $166.21; federal unemployment tax, $6.11; state unemployment tax, $41.24. Payroll taxes are distributed among the departments as: books, $367.04; magazines, $356.00; and administrative, $201.22. M40.

　　1. Paid cash for rent, $1,200.00. C341.

　　2. Paid cash for Book Department supplies, $135.00. C342.

　　2. Purchased books on account from Oliver Books, Inc., $1,933.00. P115.

　　3. Recorded cash and credit card sales: books, $2,478.00; magazines, $2,588.50; plus sales tax. TS33.

**Posting.** Post the items that are to be posted individually. Post from the journals in this order: sales journal, purchases journal, general journal, cash receipts journal, cash payments journal.

　　5. Sold books on account to Matthew Barasso, $880.00, plus sales tax. S97.

　　5. Received cash on account from Tanya Dockman, $493.92, covering S92 for magazines for $504.00 ($480.00 plus sales tax), less discount. R139.

　　6. Paid cash on account to CBG Distributors, $2,185.50, covering P111 for books for $2,230.10, less discount. C343.

　　7. Paid cash on account to H & B Books, $5,321.55, covering P112 for books for $5,430.15, less discount. C344.

　　7. Returned books to Oliver Books, Inc., $300.00, from P115. DM59.

　　8. Received cash on account from Gilmore Public Schools, $6,115.40, covering S94 for magazines for $6,240.20, less discount. R140.

　　8. Received cash on account from Belinda Judd, $257.25, covering S95 for books for $262.50 ($250.00 plus sales tax), less discount. R141.

　　8. Received cash on account from Renville Public Schools, $9,389.87, covering S96 for books for $9,581.50, less discount. R142.

　　8. Paid cash on account to Maryland Books & Magazines, $554.09, covering P113 for magazines for $565.40, less discount. C345.

　　9. Paid cash on account to Oliver Books, Inc., $4,821.80, covering P114 for books for $4,920.20, less discount. C346.

　　9. Granted credit to Matthew Barasso for books returned, $100.00, plus sales tax, from S97. CM33.

10. Recorded cash and credit card sales: books, $4,946.50; magazines, $3,650.00; plus sales tax. TS34.

   **Posting.** Post the items that are to be posted individually.

12. Paid cash on account to Oliver Books, Inc., $1,600.34, covering P115 for books for $1,933.00, less DM59, and less discount. C347.

13. Sold magazines on account to Marcella Amco, $450.00, plus sales tax. S98.

15. Paid cash for liability for federal employee income tax, $1,240.00; social security tax, $1,286.11; Medicare tax, $300.78; total, $2,826.89. C348.

15. Paid cash for quarterly federal income tax estimate, $1,200.00. C349. (Debit Federal Income Tax Expense; credit Cash.)

15. Received cash on account from Matthew Barasso, $802.62, covering S97 for books for $924.00 ($880.00 plus sales tax), less CM33, less discount. R143.

17. Recorded cash and credit card sales: books, $3,820.60; magazines, $3,240.50; plus sales tax. TS35.

   **Posting.** Post the items that are to be posted individually.

22. Sold magazines on account to Renville Public Schools, $4,750.00; no sales tax. S99.

22. Purchased magazines on account from Strup Publishers, Inc., $1,647.00. P116.

22. Purchased magazines on account from A-1 Publishing, $1,278.50. P117.

23. Sold books on account to Brian Fadstad, $1,720.00, plus sales tax, S100.

23. Sold magazines on account to Janelle Kamschorr, $920.00, plus sales tax. S101.

23. Received cash on account from Marcella Amco, $463.05, covering S98 for magazines for $472.50 ($450.00 plus sales tax), less discount. R144.

24. Purchased books on account from CBG Distributors, $1,500.00. P118.

24. Paid cash for advertising for the magazine department, $500.00. C350.

24. Recorded cash and credit card sales: books, $4,160.10; magazines, $3,420.50; plus sales tax. TS36.

   **Posting.** Post the items that are to be posted individually.

26. Sold magazines on account to Donald Lindgren, $540.00, plus sales tax. S102.

26. Returned magazines to A-1 Publishing, $265.00, from P117. DM60.

27. Purchased books on account from Maryland Books & Magazines, $2,440.50. P119.

27. Purchased magazines on account from Grandway Products, $3,157.99. P120.

28. Sold books on account to Donald Lindgren, $650.00, plus sales tax. S103.

30. Received bank statement showing December bank service charge, $11.40 (debit Miscellaneous Expense). M41.

30. Recorded credit card fee expense for December, $354.20. M42.

31. Granted credit to Renville Public Schools for magazines returned, $1,500.00, from S99. CM34.

31. Sold books on account to Gilmore Public Schools, $6,200.00; no sales tax. S104.

31. Paid cash to replenish petty cash fund, $415.00: supplies for the books department, $145.00; advertising—books, $160.00; miscellaneous, $110.00. C351.

31. Recorded cash and credit card sales: books, $3,580.40; magazines, $2,480.00; plus sales tax. TS37.

   **Posting.** Post the items that are to be posted individually.

**Instructions:**

4.  Prove and rule the sales journal. Post the totals of the special columns.
5.  Prove and rule the purchases journal. Post the totals of the special columns.
6.  Prove the cash receipts journal and the cash payments journal.
7.  Prove cash. The balance on the next unused check stub is $59,773.67.
8.  Rule the cash receipts journal. Post the totals of the special columns.
9.  Rule the cash payments journal. Post the totals of the special columns.

## END-OF-FISCAL-PERIOD WORK

**Instructions:**

10. Prepare a schedule of accounts receivable and a schedule of accounts payable. Compare each schedule total with the balance of the controlling account in the general ledger. The total and the balance should be the same.
11. Prepare a trial balance on a work sheet.
12. Complete the work sheet. Record the adjustments on the work sheet using the following information.

### Adjustment Information, December 31

Uncollectible accounts expense estimated as 1.0% of sales on account.

Sales on account for year, $241,257.00.

| | |
|---|---:|
| Merchandise inventory—Books | $174,469.25 |
| Merchandise inventory—Magazines | 151,439.85 |
| Supplies used—Books | 940.00 |
| Supplies used—Magazines | 1,080.00 |
| Supplies used—Administrative | 706.00 |
| Insurance Expired | 880.00 |
| Annual depreciation expense—Display Equipment, Books | 870.00 |
| Annual depreciation expense—Display Equipment, Magazines | 940.00 |
| Annual depreciation expense—Office Equipment | 1,260.00 |
| Federal income tax expense for the year | 5,013.75 |

13. Prepare separate departmental margin statements for BooksPlus's Book Department and Magazine Department. Calculate and record component percentages for each item on the statements. Round percentage calculations to the nearest 0.1%.
14. Prepare an income statement. Calculate and record component percentages for each item on the statement. Round component percentage calculations to the nearest 0.1%.
15. Prepare a statement of stockholders' equity. Use the following additional information.

> January 1 balance of capital stock account . . . . . . $300,000.00
>    (3,000 shares issued for $100.00 per share)
> No additional capital stock issued.
> January 1 balance of retained earnings account . . . . 97,525.70

16. Prepare a balance sheet.
17. Use page 13 of a general journal. Journalize and post the adjusting entries.
18. Use pages 14 and 15 of a general journal. Journalize and post the closing entries.
19. Prepare a post-closing trial balance.

*Activities in Sounds, Inc.:*

1. Recording transactions in special journals and a general journal.

2. Calculating and recording departmental payroll data.

3. Posting items to be posted individually to a general ledger and subsidiary ledgers.

4. Proving and ruling journals.

5. Posting column totals to a general ledger.

6. Preparing schedules of accounts receivable and accounts payable.

7. Preparing a trial balance on a work sheet.

8. Planning adjustments and completing a work sheet.

9. Preparing financial statements.

10. Journalizing and posting adjusting entries.

11. Journalizing and posting closing entries.

12. Preparing a post-closing trial balance.

# A Business Simulation
# Sounds, Inc.

Sounds, Inc., is a departmentalized merchandising business organized as a corporation. This business simulation covers the realistic transactions completed by Sounds, Inc., which has two departments: Music and Accessories. The activities included in the accounting cycle for Sounds, Inc., are listed here.

This simulation is available from the publisher in either manual or automated versions.

# 2 Accounting Adjustments and Valuation

1200   Plant Assets
1205   Delivery Equipment
1210   Accumulated Depreciation—Delivery Equipment
1215   Office Equipment
1220   Accumulated Depreciation—Office Equipment
1225   Store Equipment
1230   Accumulated Depreciation—Store Equipment

### (2000) LIABILITIES
2100   Current Liabilities
2105   Vouchers Payable
2110   Employee Income Tax Payable—Federal
2115   Employee Income Tax Payable—State
2120   Federal Income Tax Payable
2125   Social Security Tax Payable
2128   Medicare Tax Payable
2130   Sales Tax Payable
2135   Unemployment Tax Payable—Federal
2140   Unemployment Tax Payable—State
2145   Dividends Payable

### (3000) STOCKHOLDERS' EQUITY
3105   Capital Stock
3110   Retained Earnings
3115   Dividends
3120   Income Summary

### Income Statement Accounts

### (4000) OPERATING REVENUE
4105   Sales
4110   Sales Discount
4115   Sales Returns and Allowances

### (5000) COST OF MERCHANDISE
5105   Purchases
5110   Purchases Discount
5115   Purchases Returns and Allowances

### (6000) OPERATING EXPENSES
6100   SELLING EXPENSES
6105   Advertising Expense
6110   Delivery Expense
6115   Depreciation Expense—Delivery Equipment
6120   Depreciation Expense—Store Equipment
6125   Miscellaneous Expense—Sales
6130   Salary Expense—Sales
6135   Supplies Expense—Sales

6200   ADMINISTRATIVE EXPENSES
6205   Depreciation Expense—Office Equipment
6210   Insurance Expense
6215   Miscellaneous Expense—Administrative
6220   Payroll Taxes Expense
6225   Rent Expense
6230   Salary Expense—Administrative
6235   Supplies Expense—Administrative
6240   Uncollectible Accounts Expense
6245   Utilities Expense

### (7000) INCOME TAX EXPENSE
7105   Federal Income Tax Expense

The chart of accounts for OfficeMart, Inc. is illustrated above for ready reference as you study Part 2 of this textbook.

## OFFICEMART, INC.
## CHART OF ACCOUNTS

### Balance Sheet Accounts

### (1000) ASSETS
1100   CURRENT ASSETS
1105   Cash
1110   Petty Cash
1115   Accounts Receivable
1120   Allowance for Uncollectible Accounts
1125   Merchandise Inventory
1130   Supplies—Sales
1135   Supplies—Administrative
1140   Prepaid Insurance

# CHAPTER 5

# A Voucher System

*After studying Chapter 5, you will be able to:*

1. Define accounting terms related to a voucher system.

2. Identify accounting concepts and practices related to a voucher system.

3. Prepare a voucher.

4. Journalize data from vouchers in a voucher register.

5. Journalize voucher payment transactions in a check register.

6. Journalize purchases returns and allowances and payroll transactions in a voucher system.

- voucher
- voucher system
- voucher register
- voucher check
- check register

Point Your Browser
accountingxtra.swlearning.com

## • Procter & Gamble

©DANIEL ACKER/BLOOMBERG NEWS/LANDOV

### PURCHASING AT PROCTER & GAMBLE

Crest, Folgers, Pampers, Tide, Pringles, Charmin, Downey, and Clairol—these are just a few of the nearly 300 products marketed by the Procter & Gamble Company (P&G). Established in 1837 as a family-operated soap and candle company, P&G markets its products in over 160 countries.

With annual sales exceeding $40 billion, just imagine the amount of products and services P&G buys from other companies! P&G purchases buildings, equipment, raw materials, supplies, and packaging to produce its products. The company must install computer systems to fulfill its information needs. Administrative employees need office equipment and supplies. P&G's active research unit requires scientific supplies. The list can stagger the imagination.

To fulfill its mission to its stockholders, P&G must ensure that it receives the best value possible for every purchase. Before any payment for goods and services is completed, internal controls require that those individuals involved ensure that four objectives are met: (1) P&G buys only goods and services that it needs, (2) goods and services are ordered at the most favorable terms, (3) goods and services are received and meet quality standards, and (4) payment is made for the agreed-upon amount.

### Critical Thinking

1. Two companies bid different amounts to supply P&G with a raw material. Why might P&G elect to purchase the materials from the company offering the higher price?
2. As a consumer, what do you do to ensure you receive the best price?

Source: www.pg.com/about_pg/sectionmain.jhtml, www.pg.com/annualreports/2002/pdf/pg_ar2002.pdf

Xtra!
Today
accountingxtra.swlearning.com

### ACCOUNTING FIRMS (PART 2)

Go to the homepage for the following two international accounting firms:

Deloitte & Touche: http://deloitte.com

KPMG: http://kpmg.com

### Instructions

Create a table listing the following items for each company:

1. Number of global employees
2. Amount of global revenue
3. Number of countries in which it operates

# 5-1 Vouchers and Voucher Registers

An accounting system includes procedures for recording and reporting accurate and up-to-date financial information. An accounting system should also include procedures to assist management in controlling a company's daily operations. Management is particularly concerned with procedures and records to control and protect assets. One asset that should be controlled and protected is cash. Cash is the asset most likely to be misused because its ownership is easily transferred. Also, transactions generally affect the cash account more often than other general ledger accounts. Many businesses, therefore, use specific cash control procedures.

Among the procedures used to control cash are storing it in a safe place, making bank deposits regularly, and approving all cash payments. Cash payments should be approved before being paid to ensure that the goods or services were ordered, have been received, and the amounts due are correct. In small businesses, the owner or manager usually approves cash payments. In large businesses, several persons may have authority to approve cash payments. A business form used to show an authorized person's approval for a cash payment is called a **voucher**. A set of procedures for controlling cash payments by preparing and approving vouchers before payments are made is called a **voucher system**. In a voucher system, NO check can be issued without a properly authorized voucher.

MAKING ETHICAL DECISIONS • MAKING ETHICAL DECISIONS • MAKING ETHICAL DECISIO

## making ethical decisions

### Integrity in Management Accounting

The Institute of Management Accountants (IMA) is an organization dedicated to providing its members with professional development opportunities in management accounting, financial management, and information management. The Institute supports lifelong learning by its members through self-study courses, seminars, conferences, and webcasts. Members are encouraged to demonstrate their knowledge by becoming a Certified Management Accountant (CMA) or Certified in Financial Management (CFM).

An important element of the IMA's mission is to encourage its members and their organizations to adopt ethical business practices. One section of the IMA's *Standards of Ethical Conduct* defines *integrity*. Individuals may attempt to influence management accountants to misrepresent facts to achieve short-term objectives that are contrary to the organization's long-term goals. Management accountants must be people of high integrity to resist these individuals and ensure that accounting information is accurate and reliable.

**Instructions**

Access the IMA's *Standards of Ethical Conduct*. How does the IMA define *integrity*?

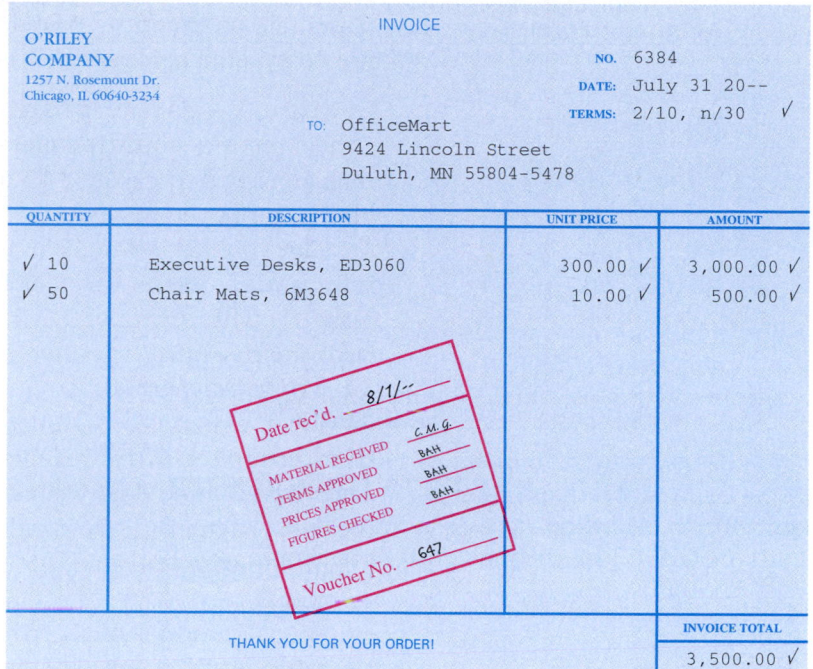

OfficeMart, a merchandising business, sells office furniture and supplies. When OfficeMart receives an invoice, a verification form is stamped on the invoice, as shown above.

OfficeMart's receiving clerk verifies that the items were received in the correct quantities. A clerk in OfficeMart's purchasing department verifies that the terms and prices are correct. The calculations on the invoice are also verified. Each person doing a part of the work places a check mark next to the items verified and initials the verification form to show responsibility for that part.

## A VOUCHER

After an invoice is checked for accuracy, a voucher is prepared for each invoice received from a vendor.

---

*August 1. Purchased merchandise on account from O'Riley Company, $3,500.00. Voucher No. 647.*

---

When a voucher system is used, the source document for an approved cash payment is the voucher. The source document for this transaction is Voucher No. 647. [*CONCEPT: Objective Evidence*]

In a voucher system, the general ledger liability account, Vouchers Payable, is used instead of Accounts Payable. Accounts Payable has been used to record only amounts of items bought on account.

In a voucher system, Vouchers Payable is used to record *ALL* amounts to be paid by check. Since Vouchers Payable is a liability account, the normal balance is on the credit side of the account. With a voucher system, an accounts payable ledger is not kept. Instead, vouchers needing to be paid are kept in an unpaid vouchers file. The unpaid vouchers file shows all amounts owed and to whom they are owed.

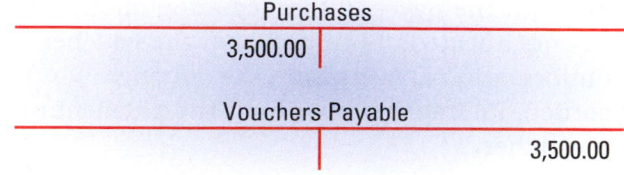

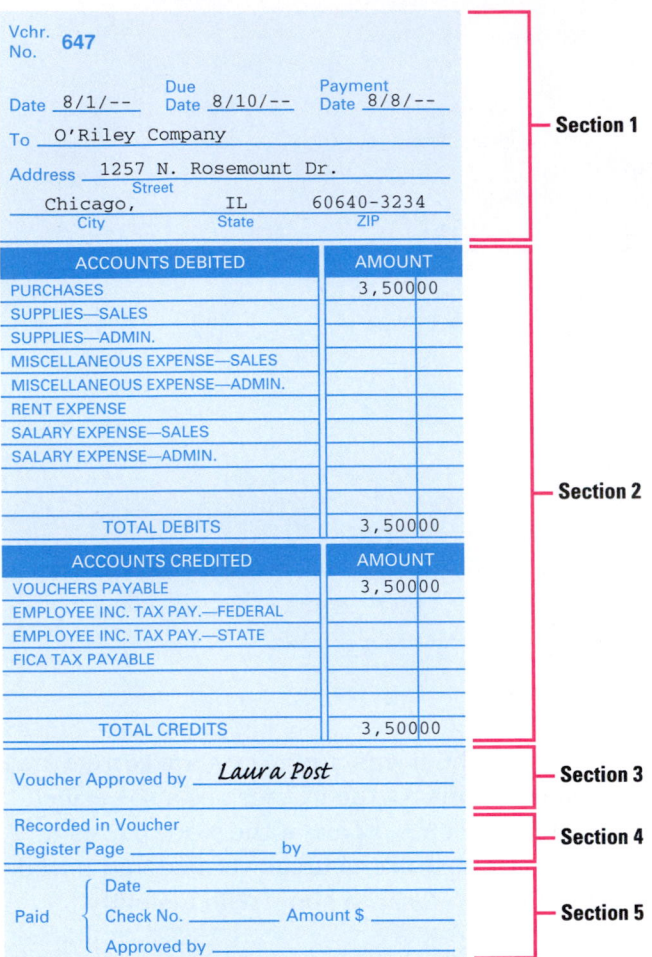

| Vchr. No. **647** | | |
|---|---|---|
| Date _8/1/--_ | Due Date _8/10/--_ | Payment Date _8/8/--_ |
| To  O'Riley Company | | |
| Address  1257 N. Rosemount Dr. | | |
|         Street | | |
| Chicago, | IL | 60640-3234 |
| City | State | ZIP |

← Section 1

| ACCOUNTS DEBITED | AMOUNT |
|---|---|
| PURCHASES | 3,500 00 |
| SUPPLIES—SALES | |
| SUPPLIES—ADMIN. | |
| MISCELLANEOUS EXPENSE—SALES | |
| MISCELLANEOUS EXPENSE—ADMIN. | |
| RENT EXPENSE | |
| SALARY EXPENSE—SALES | |
| SALARY EXPENSE—ADMIN. | |
| | |
| TOTAL DEBITS | 3,500 00 |
| ACCOUNTS CREDITED | AMOUNT |
| VOUCHERS PAYABLE | 3,500 00 |
| EMPLOYEE INC. TAX PAY.—FEDERAL | |
| EMPLOYEE INC. TAX PAY.—STATE | |
| FICA TAX PAYABLE | |
| | |
| TOTAL CREDITS | 3,500 00 |

← Section 2

Voucher Approved by _Laura Post_   ← Section 3

Recorded in Voucher
Register Page _____ by _____   ← Section 4

Paid { Date _____
Check No. _____ Amount $ _____
Approved by _____ }   ← Section 5

A form is printed on the outside of a voucher to summarize the contents and provide space for approving payments, as shown above. After the invoice is summarized on the voucher, the voucher is folded so that related documents can be placed inside. For this reason a voucher is sometimes known as a voucher jacket.

OfficeMart uses prenumbered voucher forms and must account for all voucher numbers. Therefore, the prenumbered vouchers serve as an additional control within OfficeMart's voucher system.

The outside of OfficeMart's voucher has five sections for recording information: (1) Information about the payee. (2) Information about the accounts affected. (3) Approval of the voucher. (4) Information about where the voucher is recorded. (5) Information about the payment of the voucher.

Sections 1, 2, and 3 of the voucher are completed at the time it is prepared. Sections 4 and 5 are completed as described later in this chapter.

## Section 1—Payee Information

OfficeMart's accounting clerk uses the verified invoice shown on page 145 to enter information about the payee in Section 1 of the voucher.

The voucher's due date is calculated using information on the invoice. The invoice is dated July 31, with terms of 2/10, n/30. Therefore, to take the discount, the invoice must be paid no later than August 10.

From experience, OfficeMart has learned that most checks are received within two days. Therefore, OfficeMart writes and mails checks for cash payments two days before the due date. Thus, the payment date for Voucher No. 647 is August 8.

After Section 1 of the voucher is completed, the voucher number, 647, is recorded on the invoice's verification stamp, as shown on page 145.

## Section 2—Accounts Affected

Two accounts are affected by this transaction: the cost account, Purchases, is debited, and the liability account, Vouchers Payable, is credited. Section 2 of the voucher lists preprinted account titles for accounts most often affected by cash payments. Purchases is preprinted under the heading Accounts Debited. Vouchers Payable is preprinted under the heading Accounts Credited. Therefore, only the amount of the invoice, *$3,500.00*, must be entered in Section 2. Total Debits and Total Credits are also calculated and entered. If additional account titles are needed, they are entered on the blank lines in Section 2.

## Section 3—Voucher Approval

As a double check, many businesses authorize one person, sometimes more, to approve vouchers before they are journalized. Laura Post, accountant, is authorized to approve vouchers for OfficeMart. When Laura verifies that the voucher is correct, she approves it by signing her name in Section 3.

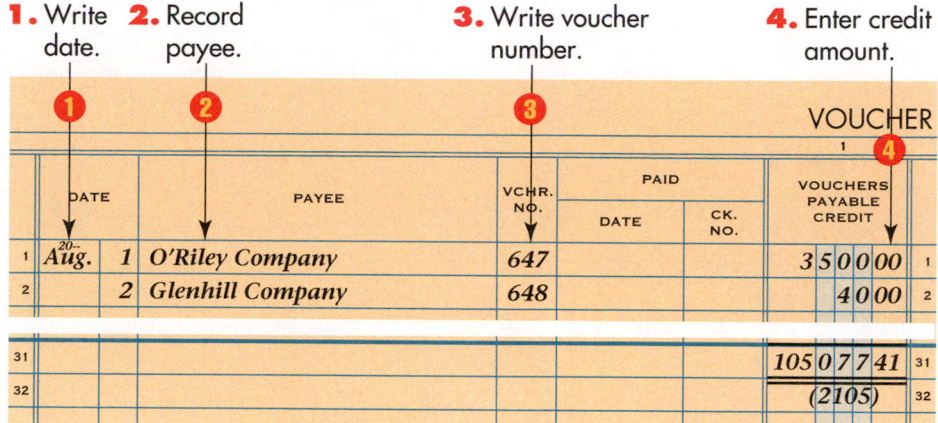

**1.** Write date.  **2.** Record payee.  **3.** Write voucher number.  **4.** Enter credit amount.

VOUCHER

| | DATE | PAYEE | VCHR. NO. | PAID | | VOUCHERS PAYABLE CREDIT | |
| --- | --- | --- | --- | --- | --- | --- | --- |
| | | | | DATE | CK. NO. | | |
| 1 | Aug. 1 | O'Riley Company | 647 | | | 3 5 0 0 00 | 1 |
| 2 | 2 | Glenhill Company | 648 | | | 4 0 00 | 2 |
| 31 | | | | | | 105 0 7 7 41 | 31 |
| 32 | | | | | | (2105) | 32 |

After it has been approved, a voucher is recorded, as shown above. A journal used to record vouchers is called a **voucher register**. A voucher register is similar to and replaces a purchases journal. Since OfficeMart's vouchers are prenumbered, all vouchers can be accounted for. A missing voucher number shows that a voucher has not been recorded.

### Journalizing a Voucher in a Voucher Register's Special Columns

OfficeMart's voucher register has special columns for Vouchers Payable Credit, Purchases Debit, Supplies—Sales Debit, and Supplies—Administrative Debit. For accounts with no special amount columns, information is recorded in the General columns. Voucher 647 is recorded on line 1 of the voucher register.

### Section 4 of a Voucher—Where the Voucher Is Recorded

The person who records the voucher in the voucher register also completes Section 4 of the voucher. The person makes a notation indicating the page on which the information is recorded in the voucher register. The person also initials the space provided on the voucher. Placing the voucher register page number on the voucher provides easy reference to the entry's location in the voucher register.

Recorded in Voucher Register Page _____ 21 _____ by _____ G. R. S. _____

After Voucher No. 647 is journalized and the notation is made in Section 4, the voucher is filed in an unpaid vouchers file. The vouchers are placed in this file according to the payment date. Filing the vouchers by payment date makes it easier to determine which vouchers need to be paid each day. This method helps ensure payment of invoices within the discount period. Thus, Voucher No. 647 is filed under the date on which it is to be paid, August 8.

Payment of a voucher is described later in this chapter.

**STEPS** · STEPS · STEPS · STEPS · STEPS · STEPS · STEPS · STEPS · STEPS · STEPS · STEPS ·

### JOURNALIZING A VOUCHER IN THE SPECIAL COLUMNS OF A VOUCHER REGISTER

**1** Write the date of the voucher, *Aug. 1, 20--,* in the Date column.

**2** Record the name of the payee, *O'Riley Company,* in the Payee column.

**3** Write the voucher number, *647,* in the Vchr. No. column.

**4** Enter the credit amount, *3,500.00,* in the Vouchers Payable Credit column.

**5** Record the debit amount, *3,500.00,* in the appropriate debit column. Since this is a purchase transaction, the debit is made to Purchases.

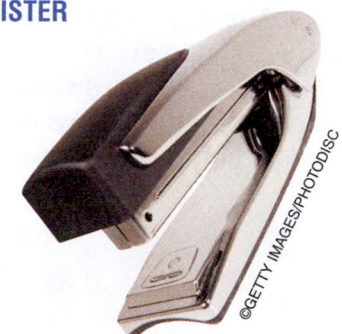

©GETTY IMAGES/PHOTODISC

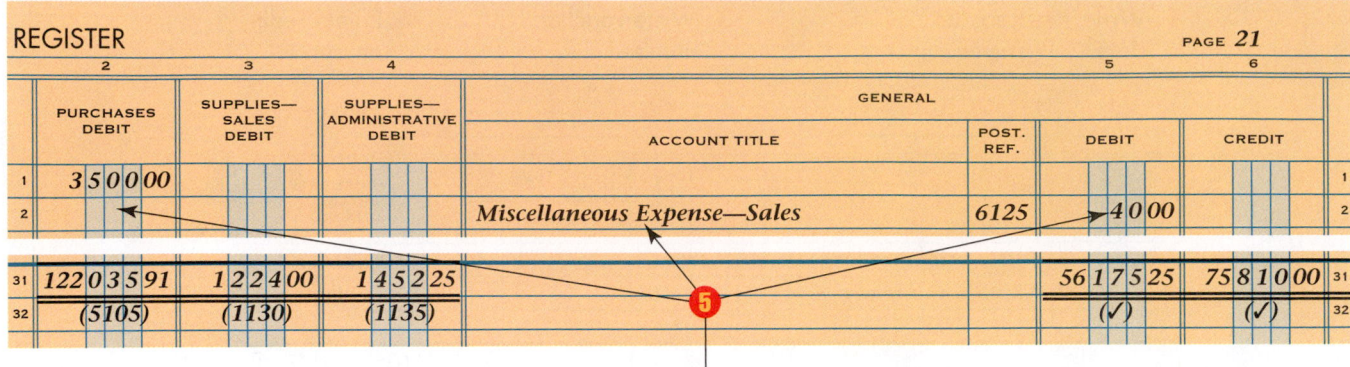

**5.** Record debit amount.

## Journalizing a Voucher in the General Columns of a Voucher Register

OfficeMart's voucher register has special debit amount columns for Purchases Debit, Supplies—Sales Debit, and Supplies—Administrative Debit. When an account other than these four is affected, the information is recorded in the General columns.

---

**August 2. Received invoice for sales miscellaneous expense from Glenhill Company, $40.00. Voucher No. 648.**

---

Voucher No. 648 is prepared in the same manner as Voucher No. 647. Voucher No. 648 is recorded on line 2 of the voucher register.

A notation is made on Voucher No. 648 in Section 4 to show where the voucher was recorded and by whom.

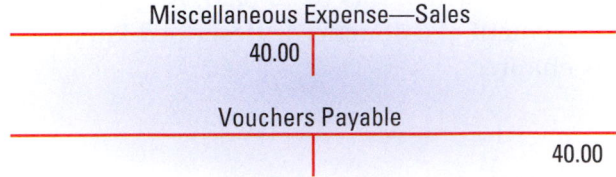

## Proving, Ruling, and Posting a Voucher Register

Separate amounts recorded in the General Debit and General Credit columns of a voucher register are posted individually during the month. As

each amount is posted, the account number is written in the Post. Ref. column of the voucher register.

At the end of each month, OfficeMart's voucher register is proved and ruled. The procedures for proving and ruling a voucher register are the same as those previously described for special journals.

As previously described for special journals, totals of special amount columns are posted to the general ledger accounts listed in the column headings. Totals of General Debit and General Credit amount columns are not posted.

## STEPS
STEPS • STEPS • STEPS • STEPS

### JOURNALIZING A VOUCHER IN THE GENERAL COLUMNS OF A VOUCHER REGISTER

**1** Write the date of the voucher, *Aug. 2,* in the Date column.

**2** Record the name of the payee, *Glenhill Company,* in the Payee column.

**3** Enter the voucher number, *648,* in the Vchr. No. column.

**4** Record the credit amount, *40.00,* in the Vouchers Payable Credit column.

**5** Record the debit amount, *40.00,* in the General Debit column. Write the title of the account to be debited, *Miscellaneous Expense—Sales,* in the General Account Title column.

## terms review

voucher
voucher system
voucher register

## audit your understanding

1. In a voucher system, what general ledger account is used to record all amounts to be paid by check?

2. What is the purpose of using prenumbered voucher forms?

3. A voucher register is similar to and replaces what journal?

## work together 5-1

**Preparing a voucher and journalizing vouchers in a voucher register**

A voucher and page 10 of a voucher register for Cloverleaf Crafts is provided in the *Working Papers*. Your instructor will guide you through the following examples. The abbreviation for voucher is *V.*

Oct.    1. Purchased merchandise on account from Dickens Company, 11200 Irving Street, Minneapolis, MN 55411, terms 2/10, n/30, $600.00. V152.
       2. Received invoice for October rent from Land Development Co., $1,300.00. V153.
       4. Bought sales supplies on account from University Supplies, $350.00. V154.
       8. Received invoice for delivery service from City Delivery Co., $25.00. V155.

1. Prepare Voucher 152 for the October 1 transaction.

2. Journalize the transactions completed during October of the current year.

3. Prove and rule the voucher register. Save your work to complete Work Together 5-2.

## on your own 5-1

**Preparing a voucher and journalizing vouchers in a voucher register**

A voucher and page 8 of a voucher register for Trails End are provided in the *Working Papers*. Work independently to complete the following problem. The abbreviation for voucher is *V.*

Aug.    1. Purchased merchandise on account from Darst Corporation, 7020 Niles Lane, Centuria, WI 54824, terms 2/10, n/30, $300.00. V89.
       3. Received invoice for miscellaneous expense from G & G Company, $75.00. V90.
       5. Bought administrative supplies on account from Heartland Supplies, $200.00. V91.
       8. Received invoice for advertising from City News, $225.00. V92.

1. Prepare Voucher 89 for the August 1 transaction.

2. Journalize the transactions completed during August of the current year.

3. Prove and rule the voucher register. Save your work to complete On Your Own 5-2.

# 5-2 Voucher Check and Check Registers

## PREPARING A VOUCHER CHECK

**1.** Enter voucher no.

**2.** Enter payee's invoice no.

**6.** Prepare check to payee for net amount of invoice.

**3.** Enter amount of invoice.

**4.** Enter amount of discount.

**5.** Enter net amount.

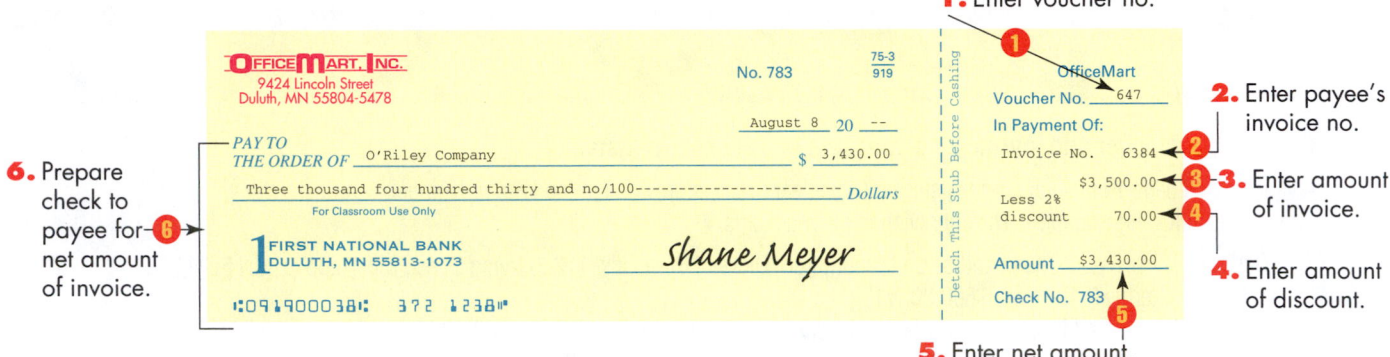

OfficeMart pays each voucher by check as shown above. It prepares a check for the amount of each voucher less any purchases discount. The check and voucher are presented to a person authorized to approve payment. A check with space for writing details about a cash payment is called a **voucher check**. OfficeMart prepares voucher checks in duplicate. The original is given to the payee and OfficeMart keeps the duplicate. The duplicate check is used as the source document for a cash payment transaction. [CONCEPT: Objective Evidence]

On August 8, vouchers to be paid on that day are removed from the unpaid vouchers file. Included in this group is Voucher No. 647. OfficeMart's cash payments clerk prepares the voucher checks.

OfficeMart uses the detachable section at the right of the voucher check to record details about the cash payment. On Check No. 783, the information includes the following items:

1. OfficeMart's voucher number, 647.
2. Payee's invoice number, 6384.
3. Amount of invoice, $3,500.00.
4. Amount of discount, $70.00.
5. Net amount for which check is written, $3,430.00.

Before a payee deposits or cashes a voucher check, the detachable section showing details of the transaction is removed. It is kept by the payee as a record of the check.

### Section 5 of a Voucher—Payment of a Voucher

The person who prepares the check also completes part of Section 5 of the voucher by noting the date paid, the check number, and the amount. The manager, Shane Meyer, verifies that the information on the check and on the voucher agrees and is accurate. After verification, he signs the check and initials Section 5 of the voucher.

| Paid | Date | Aug. 8, 20-- | | |
|------|------|--------------|--------------|-----------------|
| | Check No. | 783 | Amount $ | 3,430.00 |
| | Approved by | S.M. | | |

Information about this payment must also be recorded in the voucher register. The person who prepares the check usually makes this notation. The date on which this voucher is paid, Aug. 8, and the check number, 783, are written in the Paid columns of the voucher register. This information is written on the same line as the original entry for Voucher No. 647.

The check is given or sent to the payee, and the voucher is filed in the paid vouchers file according to the name of the vendor.

# JOURNALIZING CASH PAYMENTS

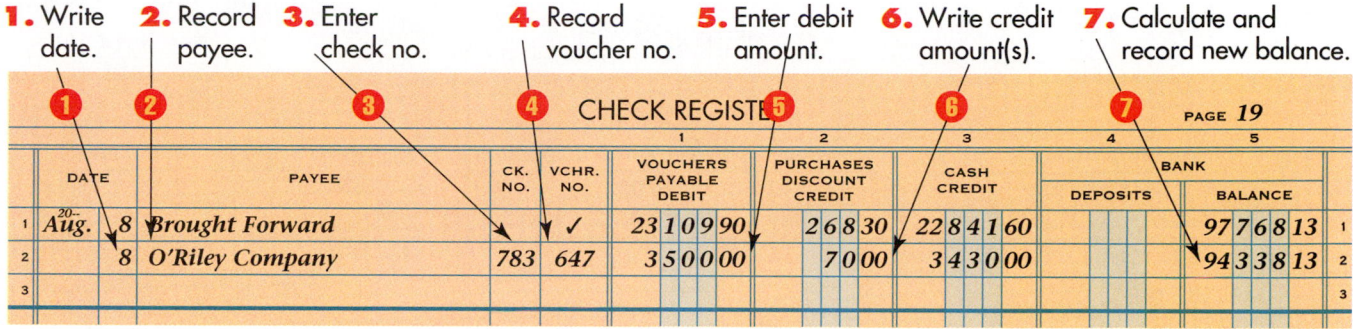

**1.** Write date.  **2.** Record payee.  **3.** Enter check no.  **4.** Record voucher no.  **5.** Enter debit amount.  **6.** Write credit amount(s).  **7.** Calculate and record new balance.

| | DATE | PAYEE | CK. NO. | VCHR. NO. | VOUCHERS PAYABLE DEBIT | PURCHASES DISCOUNT CREDIT | CASH CREDIT | BANK DEPOSITS | BANK BALANCE | |
|---|---|---|---|---|---|---|---|---|---|---|
| 1 | Aug. 8 | Brought Forward | | ✓ | 23 1 0 9 90 | 2 6 8 30 | 22 8 4 1 60 | | 97 7 6 8 13 | 1 |
| 2 | 8 | O'Riley Company | 783 | 647 | 3 5 0 0 00 | 7 0 00 | 3 4 3 0 00 | | 94 3 3 8 13 | 2 |
| 3 | | | | | | | | | | 3 |

CHECK REGISTER — PAGE 19

A journal used in a voucher system to record cash payments is called a **check register**. The check register is similar to and replaces a cash payments journal.

## Maintaining Bank Columns in a Check Register

OfficeMart uses a check register to maintain the checking account balance. OfficeMart's check register has two Bank columns, Deposits and Balance. Using these two Bank columns, Office-Mart keeps an up-to-date record of cash in the checking account. The Bank Deposits column is used to record the amounts deposited in the checking account. The Bank Balance column shows the checking account balance after each check and each deposit are recorded in the check register.

## Journalizing Checks in a Check Register

OfficeMart prepares a voucher for each approved cash payment. Therefore, each check is issued in payment of a voucher. Checks are recorded in the check register in the order they are written.

In OfficeMart's voucher system, only three general ledger accounts are affected by a cash payment: Vouchers Payable, Purchases Discount, and Cash. Therefore, OfficeMart's check register has only three special amount columns: Vouchers Payable Debit, Purchases Discount Credit, and Cash Credit. Each check is recorded in a check register as a debit to the liability account, Vouchers Payable, and a credit to the asset account, Cash. If a discount is taken for prompt payment, the discount amount is recorded as a credit to the contra cost account, Purchases Discount.

*August 8. Paid cash to O'Riley Company, $3,430.00, covering Voucher No. 647 for $3,500.00, less 2% discount, $70.00. Check No. 783.*

The liability account, Vouchers Payable, is debited for $3,500.00. The contra cost account, Purchases Discount, is credited for $70.00. Cash is credited for the net amount paid, $3,430.00.

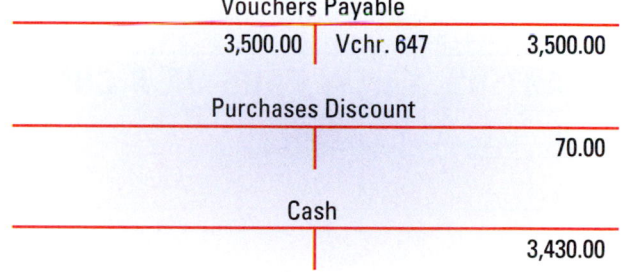

| Vouchers Payable | | |
|---|---|---|
| 3,500.00 | Vchr. 647 | 3,500.00 |

| Purchases Discount | |
|---|---|
| | 70.00 |

| Cash | |
|---|---|
| | 3,430.00 |

## STEPS

STEPS • STEPS • STEPS • STEPS • STEPS • STEPS • STEPS • STEPS • STEPS • STEPS

### JOURNALIZING CHECKS IN A CHECK REGISTER

**1.** Write the date of the payment, *8*, in the Date column.

**2.** Record the name of the payee, *O'Riley Company*, in the Payee column.

**3.** Enter the check number, *783*, in the Ck. No. column.

**4.** Record the number of the voucher being paid, *647*, in the Vchr. No. column.

**5.** Enter the debit amount, *3,500.00*, in the Vouchers Payable Debit column.

**6.** Write the credit amounts, *70.00* and *3,430.00*, in the Cash and the Purchases Discount Credit columns.

**7.** Calculate and record the new cash balance, *94,338.13*, in the Bank Balance column.

| | DATE | | PAYEE | CK. NO. | VCHR. NO. | VOUCHERS PAYABLE DEBIT (1) | PURCHASES DISCOUNT CREDIT (2) | CASH CREDIT (3) | BANK DEPOSITS (4) | BANK BALANCE (5) | |
|---|---|---|---|---|---|---|---|---|---|---|---|
| 1 | Aug. 8 | | Brought Forward | | ✓ | 23 109 90 | 268 30 | 22 841 60 | | 97 768 13 | 1 |
| 2 | | 8 | O'Riley Company | 783 | 647 | 3 500 00 | 70 00 | 3 430 00 | | 94 338 13 | 2 |
| 3 | | 11 | Jacobs Equipment | 784 | 649 | 973 91 | 19 48 | 954 43 | | 93 383 70 | 3 |
| 4 | | 14 | Petty Cash Cust., OfficeMart | 785 | 656 | 212 50 | | 212 50 | | 93 171 20 | 4 |
| 5 | | 14 | Deposit | | ✓ | | | | 18 767 15 | 111 938 35 | 5 |
| 22 | | 31 | Payroll | 800 | 694 | 4 331 96 | | 4 331 96 | | 95 373 21 | 22 |
| 23 | | 31 | Deposit | | ✓ | | | | 19 294 78 | 114 667 99 | 23 |
| 24 | | 31 | Totals | | | 103 452 22 | 566 88 | 102 885 34 | | | 24 |
| 25 | | | | | | (2105) | (5110) | (1105) | | | 25 |

CHECK REGISTER — PAGE 19

At the end of each month, the special amount columns of the check register are proved, ruled, and posted.

OfficeMart's procedures for posting from its check register are the same as those previously described for special journals. However, no separate amounts are posted individually because the check register does not have a General Debit or General Credit column. The three special amount column totals are posted to the general ledger accounts listed in the column headings. After each total is posted, the account number is written in parentheses below the column total.

The two Bank columns are used to summarize the status of the checking account balance. These two columns are neither ruled nor posted.

A deposit in the checking account is shown on line 5 above. The Deposits column does not need to be totaled and posted because each cash receipt is recorded in the cash receipts journal and posted from that journal. At the end of each month, cash is proved by comparing the last amount in the Balance column of the check register with the balance in the general ledger cash account. Cash is proved if the two amounts are the same.

## STARTING A NEW PAGE OF A CHECK REGISTER

| | DATE | | PAYEE | CK. NO. | VCHR. NO. | VOUCHERS PAYABLE DEBIT (1) | PURCHASES DISCOUNT CREDIT (2) | CASH CREDIT (3) | BANK DEPOSITS (4) | BANK BALANCE (5) | |
|---|---|---|---|---|---|---|---|---|---|---|---|
| 1 | Sept. | 1 | Brought Forward | | ✓ | | | | | 114 667 99 | 1 |
| 2 | | | | | | | | | | | 2 |

CHECK REGISTER — PAGE 20

A new page of a check register may be needed either during a month or at the start of a new month. When a new page is started during a month, the totals of the Vouchers Payable Debit, Purchases Discount Credit, and Cash Credit columns are brought forward from the previous page. The balance of the Bank Balance column is also brought forward. No amount is brought forward for the Bank Deposits column.

OfficeMart begins a new page of the check register at the beginning of each month. Only the balance of the Bank Balance column is brought forward. The totals of the special amount columns are not brought forward because they were posted at the end of the previous month.

TERMS REVIEW

## terms review

voucher check
check register

## audit your understanding

1. A check register is similar to and replaces what journal?
2. In what order are paid vouchers filed?
3. What account is debited for each check recorded in a check register?

AUDIT YOUR

## work together 5-2

**Journalizing cash payments and deposits in a check register**

Use the working papers from Work Together 5-1. Page 10 of a check register for Cloverleaf Crafts is provided in the *Working Papers*. Your instructor will guide you through the following examples. Source documents are abbreviated as follows: check, C; voucher, V.

Oct. 8. Paid cash to Dickens Company, $588.00, covering V152 for $600.00, less 2% discount, $12.00. C309.
9. Paid cash to University Supplies, $350.00, covering V154. C310.
11. Paid cash to Land Development Co., $1,300.00, covering V153. C311.
16. Made a deposit in the checking account, $3,775.09.

1. Record the bank balance brought forward on October 1 of the current year, $18,765.55.

2. Journalize the transactions completed during October of the current year. As each cash payment is journalized, make the appropriate notation in the voucher register.

3. Prove and rule the check register.

WORK TOGETHER • WORK TOGETHER • WORK

## on your own 5-2

**Journalizing cash payments and deposits in a check register**

Use the working papers from On Your Own 5-1. Page 8 of a check register for Trails End is provided in the *Working Papers*. Work this problem independently. Source documents are abbreviated as follows: check, C; voucher, V.

Aug.   8.   Paid cash to Darst Corp., $294.00, covering V89 for $300.00, less 2% discount, $6.00. C222.
      9.   Paid cash to Heartland Supplies, $200.00, covering V91. C223.
   11.   Paid cash to C & G Company, $75.00, covering V90. C224.
   15.   Made a deposit in the checking account, $1,388.12.

1.   Record the bank balance brought forward on August 1 of the current year, $5,422.67.

2.   Journalize the transactions completed during August of the current year. As each cash payment is journalized, make the appropriate notation in the voucher register.

3.   Prove and rule the check register.

©GETTY IMAGES/PHOTODISC

A Voucher System

# 5-3 Selected Transactions in a Voucher System

## PURCHASES RETURNS AND ALLOWANCES

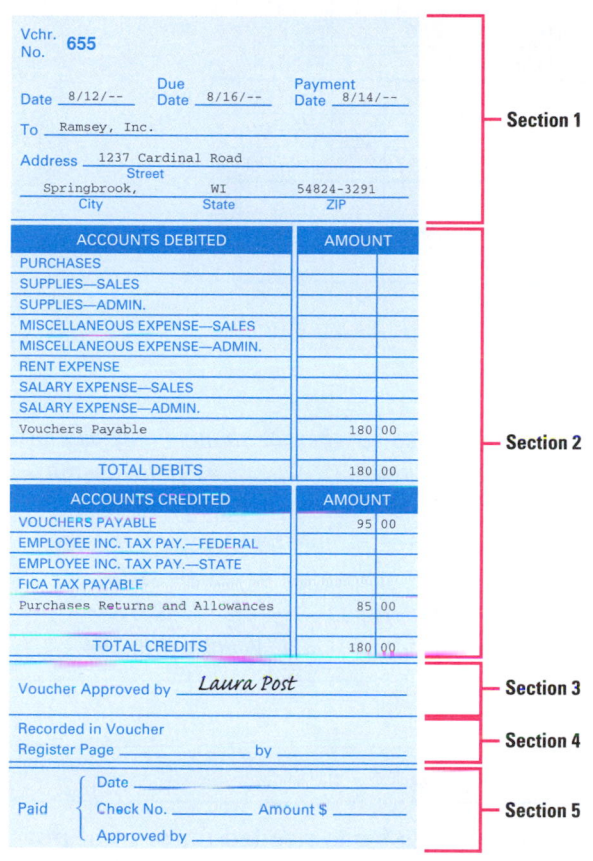

| | | |
|---|---|---|
| Vchr. No. | **655** | |

Date _8/12/--_   Due Date _8/16/--_   Payment Date _8/14/--_

To _Ramsey, Inc._

Address _1237 Cardinal Road_
        Street
   _Springbrook,_    _WI_    _54824-3291_
   City          State         ZIP

**— Section 1**

| ACCOUNTS DEBITED | AMOUNT |
|---|---|
| PURCHASES | |
| SUPPLIES—SALES | |
| SUPPLIES—ADMIN. | |
| MISCELLANEOUS EXPENSE—SALES | |
| MISCELLANEOUS EXPENSE—ADMIN. | |
| RENT EXPENSE | |
| SALARY EXPENSE—SALES | |
| SALARY EXPENSE—ADMIN. | |
| Vouchers Payable | 180 00 |
| TOTAL DEBITS | 180 00 |
| ACCOUNTS CREDITED | AMOUNT |
| VOUCHERS PAYABLE | 95 00 |
| EMPLOYEE INC. TAX PAY.—FEDERAL | |
| EMPLOYEE INC. TAX PAY.—STATE | |
| FICA TAX PAYABLE | |
| Purchases Returns and Allowances | 85 00 |
| TOTAL CREDITS | 180 00 |

**— Section 2**

Voucher Approved by _Laura Post_       **— Section 3**

Recorded in Voucher
Register Page _____ by _____       **— Section 4**

Paid { Date _____
       Check No. _____  Amount $ _____       **— Section 5**
       Approved by _____

Using a voucher system requires that some transactions follow different procedures. Two examples are purchases returns and allowances and payroll transactions.

A purchases returns and allowances transaction reduces the total amount owed for an invoice. Therefore, the voucher record for that invoice must be changed to show the reduction in the amount owed.

---

*August 12. Issued Debit Memorandum No. 98 to Ramsey, Inc. for return of merchandise purchased, $85.00. Cancel Voucher No. 652. Voucher No. 655.*

---

Voucher No. 655 is prepared for this transaction and is the source document for the entry. [CONCEPT: Objective Evidence]

The liability account, Vouchers Payable, is debited for $180.00 to cancel Voucher No. 652. Vouchers Payable is credited for $95.00, the difference between Voucher No. 652 ($180.00) and Debit Memorandum No. 98 ($85.00). The contra cost account, Purchases Returns and Allowances, is credited for $85.00, the amount of merchandise returned.

OfficeMart follows five steps in changing the original amount owed for Voucher No. 652 because of the purchases return. The entry recording this voucher is on lines 6 and 9 of the voucher register on the next page.

## STEPS

STEPS • STEPS • STEPS • STEPS

### CHANGING THE ORIGINAL AMOUNT OF A VOUCHER BECAUSE OF A PURCHASE RETURN

1. Remove the original voucher, No. 652, from the unpaid vouchers file. Write *Canceled* across Section 5.

2. Prepare a new voucher, No. 655. Place the canceled voucher and the debit memorandum inside.

3. In the voucher register, on the same line as the original voucher, write *See Vchr. 655* in the Paid columns. The number indicates the new voucher number.

4. Record the new voucher on the next available line of the voucher register. Enter the new credit amount, *95.00*, in the Vouchers Payable Credit column. Write the title of the account debited, *Vouchers Payable*, in the General Account Title column. Write the amount of the canceled voucher, *180.00*, in the General Debit column. On the next line of the register, write the other account title, *Purchases Returns and Allowances*, in the General Account Title column. Enter the amount of the return, *85.00*, in the General Credit column.

5. File the new voucher by its payment date in the unpaid vouchers file. The payment date is based on the terms of the original invoice. Therefore, the new voucher has the same payment date as the original voucher.

| | DATE | PAYEE | VCHR. NO. | PAID | | VOUCHERS PAYABLE CREDIT | |
|---|---|---|---|---|---|---|---|
| | | | | DATE | CK. NO. | | |
| 1 | Aug. 20-- 1 | O'Riley Company | 647 | Aug. 8 | 783 | 3 5 0 0 00 | 1 |
| 2 | 2 | Glenhill Company | 648 | | | 4 0 00 | 2 |
| 3 | 4 | Jacobs Equipment | 649 | Aug. 11 | 784 | 9 7 3 91 | 3 |
| 4 | 5 | Salem Wholesale Instruments | 650 | | | 4 5 1 00 | 4 |
| 5 | 7 | Bob's Delivery Service | 651 | Aug. 17 | 786 | 6 3 00 | 5 |
| 6 | 7 | Ramsey, Inc. | 652 | See Vchr. 655 | | 1 8 0 00 | 6 |
| 7 | 10 | Superior Office Supplies | 653 | | | 8 7 00 | 7 |
| 8 | 12 | Kuker Company | 654 | Aug. 19 | 788 | 2 7 6 00 | 8 |
| 9 | 12 | Ramsey, Inc. | 655 | | | 9 5 00 | 9 |
| 10 | | | | | | | 10 |
| 11 | 14 | Petty Cash Custodian, OfficeMart | 656 | Aug. 14 | 785 | 2 1 2 50 | 11 |
| 12 | | | | | | | 12 |
| 26 | 31 | Payroll | 694 | Aug. 31 | 800 | 4 3 3 1 96 | 26 |

OfficeMart pays its employees semimonthly. A payroll register showing details for each payroll is prepared. The payroll register is prepared in a way similar to the description in Chapter 3. Information from a payroll register is used in preparing a voucher for payroll.

*August 31. Recorded voucher for semimonthly payroll for period ended August 31, $4,331.96 (total payroll: sales, $3,000.00; administrative, $2,854.00; less deductions: employee income tax payable—federal, $878.10; employee income tax payable—state, $175.62; social security tax payable, $380.51; Medicare tax payable, $87.81). Voucher No. 694.*

## A PAYROLL VOUCHER

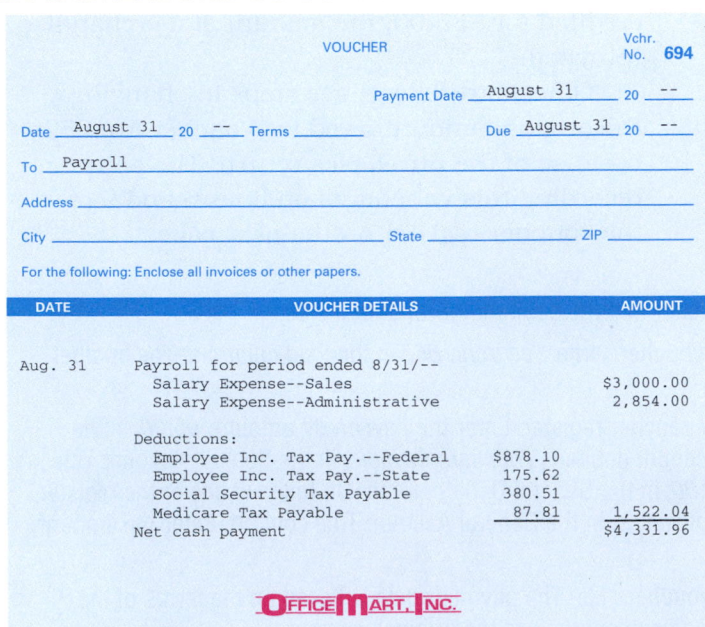

A payroll register is needed for several purposes, as described in Chapter 3. Therefore, the payroll register cannot be placed inside a voucher for payroll. For this reason, information from the payroll register is summarized on the inside of Voucher No. 694 as shown here.

The inside of the voucher allows additional space so that more detailed information about the transaction can be noted.

The outside of a payroll voucher is completed in a manner similar to the completion of other vouchers.

**REGISTER**                                                                                                    PAGE *21*

| | PURCHASES DEBIT | SUPPLIES—SALES DEBIT | SUPPLIES—ADMINISTRATIVE DEBIT | GENERAL | | | | |
| --- | --- | --- | --- | --- | --- | --- | --- | --- |
| | 2 | 3 | 4 | ACCOUNT TITLE | POST. REF. | DEBIT (5) | CREDIT (6) | |
| 1 | 3 5 0 0 00 | | | | | | | 1 |
| 2 | | | | Miscellaneous Expense—Sales | 6125 | 4 0 00 | | 2 |
| 3 | 9 7 3 91 | | | | | | | 3 |
| 4 | 4 5 1 00 | | | | | | | 4 |
| 5 | | 6 3 00 | | | | | | 5 |
| 6 | 1 8 0 00 | | | | | | | 6 |
| 7 | | | 8 7 00 | | | | | 7 |
| 8 | 2 7 6 00 | | | | | | | 8 |
| 9 | | | | Vouchers Payable | 2105 | 1 8 0 00 | | 9 |
| 10 | | | | Purchases Returns and Allowances | 5115 | | 8 5 00 | 10 |
| 11 | | 4 0 00 | 5 5 25 | Advertising Expense | 6105 | 4 7 00 | | 11 |
| 12 | | | | Miscellaneous Expense—Administrative | 6215 | 7 0 25 | | 12 |
| 26 | | | | Salary Expense—Sales | 6130 | 3 0 0 0 00 | | 26 |
| 27 | | | | Salary Expense—Administrative | 6230 | 2 8 5 4 00 | | 27 |
| 28 | | | | Employee Income Tax Payable—Federal | 2110 | | 8 7 8 10 | 28 |
| 29 | | | | Employee Income Tax Payable—State | 2115 | | 1 7 5 62 | 29 |
| 30 | | | | Social Security Tax Payable | 2125 | | 3 8 0 51 | 30 |
| 31 | | | | Medicare Tax Payable | 2128 | | 8 7 81 | 31 |

The voucher register entry to record Voucher No. 694 is shown on lines 26 to 31. An entry is made in OfficeMart's general journal for the employer's payroll taxes. This entry is the same as the one described in Chapter 3. Later, when payroll taxes are due, vouchers are prepared, approved, and paid. One voucher is prepared for total payroll taxes owed to the federal government. Another voucher is prepared for total payroll taxes owed to the state government.

©GETTY IMAGES/PHOTODISC

## ADVANTAGES OF A VOUCHER SYSTEM

A voucher system has the following advantages for businesses that make many cash payments.

1. Only a few people can authorize and approve all cash payments. This procedure helps protect and control cash.
2. A voucher jacket provides a convenient way to file invoices and related business papers for future reference. This is especially true when invoices received from vendors are of different sizes.
3. Unpaid vouchers are filed by their payment dates to help ensure payment of invoices within the discount periods.
4. An unpaid vouchers file and a paid vouchers file eliminate posting to an accounts payable ledger.

5. A paid vouchers file provides three different and easy ways to find information about a paid voucher:
   a. *If only the voucher number is known,* look in the voucher register for that number and find the payee's name on the same line. The voucher will be in the paid vouchers file under the name of the payee.
   b. *If only the check number used to pay the voucher is known,* look in the check register for the check number. The payee's name is on the same line. The voucher will be in the paid vouchers file under the name of the payee.
   c. *If only the name of the payee is known,* look in the paid vouchers file where vouchers are filed under the name of the payee.

©GETTY IMAGES/PHOTODISC

## • audit your understanding

1. What accounts are affected, and how, when a debit memorandum is issued for the return of merchandise purchased and the original voucher is canceled?

2. What is the first step in canceling a voucher?

3. Where is the information obtained for preparing a voucher for payroll?

## • work together 5-3

**Journalizing purchases returns and allowances and payroll in a voucher register**

A voucher register for Gille Company is provided in the *Working Papers*. Source documents are abbreviated as follows: debit memorandum, DM; voucher, V. Your instructor will guide you through the following examples.

May  1. Purchased merchandise on account from Casey Corporation, $1,500.00. V75.
      4. Issued DM4 to Casey Corporation for return of merchandise purchased, $300.00. Cancel V75. V76.
     15. Recorded voucher for semimonthly payroll for period ended May 15, $3,308.18 (total payroll: sales, $2,780.52; administrative, $1,690.00, less deductions: employee income tax payable—federal, $670.58; employee income tax payable—state, $134.12; social security tax payable, $290.58; Medicare tax payable, $67.06). V77.

1. Journalize the transactions completed during May of the current year. Use page 5 of a voucher register. When a voucher is canceled, make appropriate notations in the voucher register.

## • on your own 5-3

**Journalizing purchases returns and allowances and payroll in a voucher register**

A voucher register for Geist Company is provided in the *Working Papers*. Source documents are abbreviated as follows: debit memorandum, DM; voucher, V. Work independently to complete the following problem.

June  1. Purchased merchandise on account from Prickett Corporation, $900.00. V110.
      4. Issued DM56 to Prickett Corporation for return of merchandise purchased, $300.00. Cancel V110. V111.
     15. Recorded voucher for semimonthly payroll for period ended June 15, $4,778.63 (total payroll: sales, $3,957.61; administrative, $2,500.00, less deductions: employee income tax payable—federal, $968.64; employee income tax payable—state, $193.73; social security tax payable, $419.75; Medicare tax payable, $96.86). V112.

1. Journalize the transactions completed during June of the current year. Use page 6 of a voucher register. When a voucher is canceled, make appropriate notations in the voucher register.

accountingxtra.swlearning.com

**After completing this chapter, you can**

1. Define accounting terms related to a voucher system.

2. Identify accounting concepts and practices related to a voucher system.

3. Prepare a voucher.

4. Journalize data from vouchers in a voucher register.

5. Journalize voucher payment transactions in a check register.

6. Journalize purchases returns and allowances and payroll transactions in a voucher system.

# Explore Accounting

EXPLORE ACCOUNTING · EXPLORE ACCOUNTING · EXPLORE ACCO

## Internal Control Systems

A company should establish policies and procedures to protect the assets of the company and to insure the reliability of the company's accounting records. Such a set of policies and procedures is known as an internal control system. The American Institute of Certified Public Accountants defines an internal control structure as "the policies and procedures established to provide reasonable assurance that specific entity objectives will be achieved." A reliable internal control structure requires that *all* employees follow the policies and procedures established.

An accurate accounting system is an important part of a reliable internal control structure. Accounting controls must support internal controls. This chapter introduced one such accounting control, the voucher system.

A widely used internal control is "separation of duties." This means that no one employee is given authority to totally control an asset. For example, in this chapter's discussion, one employee prepared the voucher, another employee approved the voucher, and a third employee approved the check payment. Without this control mechanism, an employee has a better chance of stealing from the employer.

**Required:**
*In-Class Assignment:* In groups of 3 or 4, determine why internal controls are important. Who are they designed to protect?

*Research Assignment:* Contact at least one business in your community. Ask what internal controls have been established to protect the company's assets. Summarize and present your findings to your class.

# 5-1 APPLICATION PROBLEM

### Preparing a voucher and journalizing vouchers in a voucher register

TeleTronics uses a voucher register similar to the one described in this chapter.

**Transactions:**

Sept. 1. Purchased merchandise on account from Eastern Company, 9424 Denison Pkwy., Corning, NY, 14830, terms: 2/10, n/30, $3,100.00. V87.
2. Post Real Estate Developers sent an invoice for $1,150.00 for September's rent. V88.
5. Bought sales supplies on account from Supra Supply Company, $258.00. V89.
8. Received invoice for advertising from Newport News, $87.50. V90.
11. Purchased merchandise on account from Hoyer Company, $3,347.75. V91.
18. Received invoice for delivery service from Rapid Rabbit, $235.15. V92.
19. Purchased $1,973.00 of merchandise on account from Beggen Company. V93.
23. Bought office equipment on account from Syracuse Company, $1,315.00. V94.
25. Received invoice for utilities from Northside Electric Cooperative, $185.00. V95.
29. Bought administrative supplies on account from Northern Supply, $317.00. V96.
30. Manley Maintenance Company sent an invoice for $25.00. The amount was for a miscellaneous sales expense. V97.

**Instructions:**

1. Prepare Voucher 87 for the September 1 transaction.
2. Journalize the transactions completed during September of the current year. Use page 9 of a voucher register. The abbreviation for voucher is V.
3. Prove and rule the voucher register.

The voucher register prepared in Problem 5.1 is needed to complete Problem 5.2.

# 5-2 APPLICATION PROBLEM

### Journalizing cash payments and deposits in a check register

TeleTronics uses a check register similar to the one described in this chapter.

**Transactions:**

Sept. 2. Paid cash to Post Real Estate Developers, $1,150.00, covering V88. C83.
8. Paid cash to Newport News, $87.50, covering V90. C84.
9. Paid cash to Eastern Company, $3,038.00, covering V87 for $3,100.00, less 2% discount, $62.00. C85.
13. Paid cash to Supra Supply Company, $258.00, covering V89. C86.
18. Paid cash to Rapid Rabbit, $235.15, covering V92. C87.
19. Paid cash to Hoyer Company, $3,280.79, covering V91 for $3,347.75, less 2% discount, $66.96. C88.
24. Made a deposit in the checking account, $5,684.54.
25. Paid cash to Northside Electric Cooperative, $185.00, covering V95. C89.
30. Paid cash to Manley Maintenance Company, $25.00, covering V97. C90.

**Instructions:**

1. Use page 9 of a check register. Record the bank balance brought forward on September 1 of the current year, $19,443.13.
2. Continue using page 9 of the check register. Journalize the cash payments and deposits completed during September of the current year. As each cash payment is journalized, make the appropriate notation in the voucher register. Source documents are abbreviated as follows: check, C; voucher, V.
3. Prove and rule the check register.

## 5-3 APPLICATION PROBLEM
### Journalizing purchases returns and allowances in a voucher register

Nygren Supply Company uses a voucher register similar to the one described in this chapter.

**Transactions:**

Feb.    1.    Purchased merchandise on account from Hamline Corporation, $2,700.00. V10.

4.    Issued DM2 to Hamline Corporation for return of merchandise purchased, $200.00. Cancel V10. V11.

15.    Purchased merchandise on account from Moorhead, Inc., $1,778.00. V12.

17.    Issued DM3 to Moorhead, Inc., for return of merchandise purchased, $350.00. Cancel V12. V13.

**Instructions:**

Journalize the transactions completed during February of the current year. Use page 2 of a voucher register. When a voucher is canceled, make appropriate notations in the voucher register. Source documents are abbreviated as follows: debit memorandum, DM; voucher, V.

## 5-4 APPLICATION PROBLEM
### Preparing and journalizing a voucher for payroll

Bowman Service Center uses a voucher form and a voucher register similar to the ones described in this chapter. Bowman Service Center's payroll register for May 15 of the current year shows the following information. The abbreviation for voucher is V.

**Transactions:**

May    15.    Recorded voucher for semimonthly payroll for period ended May 15, $3,120.97 (total payroll: sales, $2,530.53; administrative, $1,687.00, less deductions: employee income tax payable—federal, $632.63; employee income tax payable—state, $126.53; social security tax payable, $274.14; Medicare tax payable, $63.26). V51.

**Instructions:**

1. Prepare a voucher for the payroll on May 15 of the current year.
2. Use page 5 of a voucher register. Journalize the voucher for the payroll. Assume that the voucher has been approved. After the voucher is journalized, complete Section 4 of the voucher.

## 5-5 MASTERY PROBLEM

### Journalizing transactions in a voucher system

Jameson Company uses a voucher register and a check register similar to the ones described in this chapter.

**Transactions:**

Nov.
1. Purchased merchandise on account from Georgia Company, $975.00. V68.
2. Bought $216.80 of administrative supplies on account from Supply World. V69.
4. Bought store equipment on account from Equipment Plus, $1,998.00. V70.
8. Purchased merchandise on account from North Heights Corporation, $1,695.15. V71.
8. Paid $955.50 to Georgia Company covering V68 for $975.00, less 2% discount, $19.50. C57.
10. Made a deposit in the checking account, $3,579.00.
14. Received invoice for delivery service from Quick Delivery, $24.10. V72.
14. Paid cash to Quick Delivery, $24.10, covering V72. C58.
14. Issued DM10 to North Heights Corporation for return of merchandise purchased, $225.00. Cancel V71. V73.
15. Paid cash to North Heights Corporation, $1,440.75, covering V73 for $1,470.15, less 2% discount, $29.40. C59.
16. Recorded voucher for semimonthly payroll for period ended November 15, $1,459.64 (total payroll: sales, $1,183.50; administrative, $789.00; less deductions: employee income tax payable—federal, $295.88; employee income tax payable—state, $59.18; social security tax payable, $128.21; Medicare tax payable, $29.59). V74.
16. Paid cash for semimonthly payroll, $1,459.64, covering V74. C60.
22. Paid cash to Supply World, $216.80, covering V69. C61.
25. Issued Voucher No. 75 to buy office equipment on account from Fischer Equipment, $2,350.00.
29. Deposited $1,170.15 in the checking account.
30. Purchased merchandise on account from Georgia Company, $2,258.50. V76.

**Instructions:**

1. Use page 20 of a check register. Record the bank balance brought forward on November 1 of the current year, $11,676.77.
2. Journalize the transactions completed during November of the current year. Use page 22 of a voucher register and page 20 of a check register. When a voucher is paid or canceled, make appropriate notations in the voucher register. Source documents are abbreviated as follows: check, C; debit memorandum, DM; voucher, V.
3. Prove and rule both the voucher register and the check register.

## 5-6 CHALLENGE PROBLEM

### Journalizing purchases invoices at the net amount in a voucher system

Cayman Company uses a voucher system. All of the vendors with whom Cayman Company does business offer terms of 2/10, n/30. Cayman has a policy of paying all invoices within the discount period. The business records invoice vouchers at the net amount (invoice total less a 2% discount). Thus, a $1,000.00 invoice, allowing a 2% discount of $20.00, is recorded at the net amount, $980.00. Purchases is debited and Vouchers Payable is credited for $980.00. A purchases discount account is not used.

If an invoice *is not* paid within the discount period, Cayman Company loses the discount. This loss is recorded in an account titled Discounts Lost. Thus, if the $1,000.00 invoice described above *is not* paid within the discount period, the business must pay the full $1,000.00. However, one of the controls in a voucher system is that no check can be written for more than the voucher amount. Therefore, for a check to be written for the full $1,000.00, the original voucher must be canceled. A new voucher for $1,000.00 must be prepared, approved, and recorded.

This new voucher would include a debit to Discounts Lost of $20.00, a debit to Vouchers Payable of $980.00 (the amount of the original voucher), and a credit to Vouchers Payable of $1,000.00. Once this voucher is approved, a check can be written for $1,000.00 to pay the full amount due.

If an invoice is recorded at its net amount, all purchases returns and allowances are recorded at net amounts. A $1,000.00 invoice recorded at net with a 2% discount has a $100.00 purchase return and allowance. Thus, the $100.00 return is discounted by 2% and recorded as $98.00. For the return, Vouchers Payable is debited $980.00 (the amount of original voucher), Purchases Returns and Allowances is credited for $98.00, and Vouchers Payable is credited for $882.00 (the amount of the new voucher).

Cayman's voucher register is similar to the one described for OfficeMart in this chapter. However, the third amount column is titled Discounts Lost. There is only one Supplies Debit column because there is only one supplies account. Cayman's check register has two special amount columns: Vouchers Payable Debit and Cash Credit.

## Transactions:

Dec. 11. Purchased merchandise on account from Knotts Company, $2,000.00.
15. Made a deposit in the checking account, $1,000.00.
15. Bought supplies on account from Fairgate Supply Company, $200.00.
18. Bought store equipment on account from Hightop Company, $1,000.00.
18. Paid cash to Knotts Company covering V109. C80.
19. Purchased merchandise on account from Neal Company, $500.00.
22. Made a deposit in the checking account, $2,000.00.
25. Paid cash to Hightop Company covering V111. C81.
26. Paid cash to Fairgate Supply Company covering V110. C82.
28. Bought supplies on account from Peerless Supply Company, $300.00.
28. Issued DM30 to Neal Company for return of merchandise purchased, $50.00. Cancel V112.
29. Made a deposit in the checking account, $1,000.00.
31. Paid cash to Neal Company covering V115. C83.

## Instructions:

1. Use page 20 of a check register. Record the amounts brought forward on December 11 of the current year.

| | |
|---|---|
| Vouchers Payable Debit | $1,395.00 |
| Cash Credit | 1,395.00 |
| Bank Balance | 8,500.00 |

2. Journalize the transactions completed during December of the current year. Use page 25 of a voucher register. Assume that for all purchases of merchandise, equipment, or supplies, the invoice terms are 2/10, n/30. When a voucher is paid or canceled, make appropriate notations in the voucher register. Number vouchers consecutively starting with Voucher No. 109. Source documents are abbreviated as follows: check, C; debit memorandum, DM; voucher, V.
3. Prove and rule both the voucher register and the check register.

accountingxtra.swlearning.com

## • applied communication

Information is the key to a successful business. The loss of information can inhibit the ability of accountants to prepare reports and managers to make business decisions. Computer viruses can cause the information in computer files to be destroyed and, therefore, are a serious problem for businesses of all sizes.

**Required:**

1.  Go to the library and research computer viruses.

2.  Write a short report about computer viruses. Include the following items:
    a.  A description of one particular computer virus.
    b.  The origin of the virus.
    c.  Ways to prevent your computer from getting a virus.
    d.  The action to take if you detect a virus.

## • cases for critical thinking

### Case 1

Kelly White, the bookkeeper for Greenfield, Inc., is setting up the company's voucher system. As she plans, she is trying to decide how many columns to use in the voucher register. She is also trying to decide what headings to use for the special columns in the voucher register. What should Ms. White consider in making her decision about these special columns?

### Case 2

Review the entries you made for the Challenge Problem. Compare these entries with the entries for purchases on account made in the Mastery Problem. What is your opinion of recording purchases invoices at the net amount?

## • SCANS workplace competency

**Systems Competency:** Understanding Systems

**Concept:** Competent employees know how social, organizational, and technological systems work and operate effectively within them. Capable individuals know which people to ask for information, how to respond to the demands of the organization, and how to function within a company's formal or informal codes.

**Application:** Design a flow chart, construct a bulletin board, or prepare a multimedia presentation that illustrates the complete accounting cycle for a departmental merchandising business. Include verifying source documents, journalizing, posting, preparing interim statements, preparing AR and AP schedules, completing a work sheet, preparing financial statements, journalizing and posting adjusting and closing entries, and preparing a post-closing trial balance.

## • auditing for errors

Harper Company uses a voucher system for cash payments. Jonathan Bartell, the bookkeeper, receives and verifies the invoices. He then prepares the voucher and enters the voucher in the voucher register. When the voucher is due, Mr. Bartell prepares and signs the check and enters the payment in the check register.

**Instructions:**

Auditing involves more than checking the accuracy of amounts and calculations. It also includes checking processes to see whether proper procedures are being used. In this example, is Harper Company following proper procedures for its voucher system? Explain.

## • analyzing Costco's financial statements

### What Is Included in Merchandise Costs?

The cost of an asset should include all the costs necessary for making the asset available for its intended use. Costco considers merchandise inventory available for its intended use when the items are available for sale to a member.

Read the section "Merchandise Costs" in Note 1 (B-9–B-17) of Costco's financial statements in Appendix B of this textbook. Use the following information to determine the unit cost of inventory purchased on a purchase invoice:

| | |
|---|---|
| 100 units of BE-45 electronic can opener | $1,200 |
| Shipping & handling | 100 |
| Wages and benefits of depot employees receiving items from vendor | 400 |
| Transportation costs from the depot to the warehouse | 300 |
| Wages and benefits of warehouse employees to stock the items on display shelves | 100 |
| Wages and benefits to warehouse employees to sell the items | 200 |

## Safety Tips to Maintain Your Computer and Disks

### Electrical Equipment

The following rules protect the operator of the equipment, other persons in the environment, and the equipment itself.

1. Do not unplug equipment by pulling on the electrical cord. Instead, grasp the plug at the outlet and remove it.

2. Do not stretch electrical cords across an aisle where someone might trip over them.

3. Avoid food and beverages near equipment where a spill might result in an electrical short.

4. Do not attempt to remove the cover of equipment for any reason while the power is turned on.

5. Do not attempt to repair equipment while it is plugged in. To avoid damage most repairs should be done by an authorized service technician.

6. Always turn the power off when finished using equipment.

7. Do not overload extension cords.

8. Follow manufacturer recommendations for safe use.

9. Replace frayed electrical cords immediately.

### Computers

1. To avoid damage to the drives, do not insert pencils or other implements in floppy disk or CD-ROM drives.

2. To prevent overheating, avoid blocking air vents.

3. Position keyboards to prevent bumping or dropping them off the work surface.

4. Take care not to spill food or liquid on or in any computer component. If you do, turn off the computer immediately; unplug it; and notify your instructor before cleaning up the spill or turning on the equipment.

5. Avoid jolting or jostling your computer if it becomes necessary to move it.

6. Do NOT attempt to open or repair any part of the computer or monitor unless directed to do so by your instructor.

### Monitors

1. Most manufacturers advise repair by authorized service technicians only.

2. Adjust brightness and focus for comfortable viewing.

3. Reposition computer or use glare visors to avoid glare on the monitor screen.

4. Do not leave fingerprints on the screen. Keep the screen clear of dust. Only use a soft cloth for cleaning the screen.

### Printers

1. Do not let jewelry, ties, scarves, loose sleeves, or other clothing get caught in the machinery. This could result in damage to the machinery and could cause personal injury.

2. Exercise caution when using toxic chemicals such as toner in order to avoid spills.

### Disks and Disk Drives

1. Do not bend disks.

2. Do not touch exposed surfaces of disks.

3. Be sure the disk drive is not running when you insert or remove a disk.

4. Keep disks away from extreme hot or cold temperatures. Do not leave disks in a car during very hot or cold weather.

5. Keep disks away from magnetic fields such as transformers and magnets.

6. Keep disks away from smoke, ashes, and dust, including chalk dust.

7. Be sure to make back-up copies.

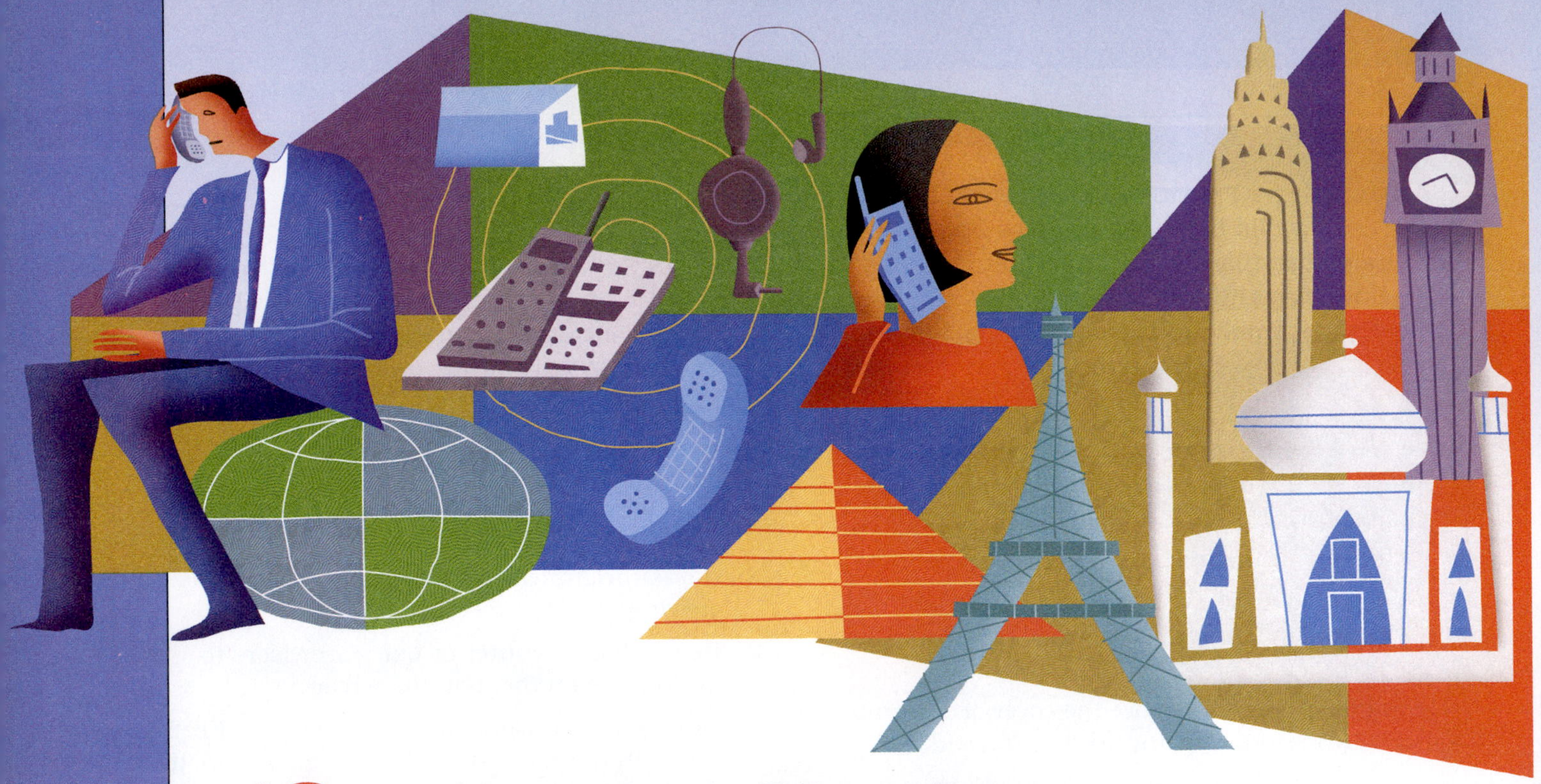

CHAPTER 6

# Inventory Planning and Valuation

OBJECTIVES & TERMS

***After studying Chapter 6, you will be able to:***

1. Define accounting terms related to planning and costing inventory.
2. Identify accounting concepts and practices related to planning, counting, and costing inventory.
3. Describe the nature of merchandise inventory.
4. Determine the cost of merchandise inventory using selected costing methods.
5. Estimate the cost of merchandise inventory using selected estimating methods.
6. Calculate merchandise inventory turnover ratio and average number of days' sales in merchandise inventory.

- consignment
- consignee
- consignor
- stock record
- stock ledger
- purchase order
- inventory record
- first-in, first-out inventory costing method
- last-in, first-out inventory costing method
- weighted-average inventory costing method
- lower of cost or market inventory costing method
- retail method of estimating inventory
- merchandise inventory turnover ratio
- average number of days' sales in merchandise inventory

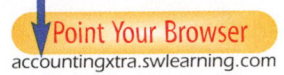

Point Your Browser
accountingxtra.swlearning.com

## • Toys"R"Us

©DANIEL ACKER/BLOOMBERG NEWS/LANDOV

### MANAGING INVENTORY AND EMPLOYEES AT TOYS"R"US

Say "Toys"R"Us" to most children, and their eyes light up with excitement. Their heads dance with a vision of rows of toys and games. With 1,600 stores worldwide and sales over $11 billion, Toys"R"Us buys and sells huge amounts of inventory each year.

Different stores within the Toys"R"Us family offer different merchandise. Toys"R"Us offers toys, children's apparel, and baby products. Kids"R"Us focuses on quality-name-brand children's wear at competitive prices. Babies"R"Us offers baby needs such as apparel, furniture, car seats, bedding, and strollers.

The Toys"R"Us employees who purchase this merchandise are expected to comply with a Professional Conduct code. Among other things, this code prohibits the employee from accepting gifts or gratuities from any supplier, prohibits the employee from buying merchandise from suppliers for personal use, and states that the selection of a supplier must be based on quality, need, performance, and cost and must promote the best interests of the company.

Exceptions to this policy have to be approved by someone in management—sometimes as high as the Chief Executive Officer of the company.

### Critical Thinking

1. Why would a company like Toys"R"Us establish and enforce an employee policy controlling gifts from suppliers?
2. Why is it beneficial to a company to have a few employees buying merchandise for all stores rather than having each store purchase its own merchandise?

Source: www2.toysrus.com

Xtra!
Today
accountingxtra.swlearning.com

## internet activity

### FASB MISSION STATEMENT

The Financial Accounting Standards Board (FASB) has the authority to make new accounting rules. FASB was given this authority by the Securities and Exchange Commission (SEC). Go to the homepage of the FASB (www.fasb.org). Click on "News Center" and then click on "Fact Sheet."

### Instructions

1. List the one-paragraph mission of the FASB.
2. List at least two ways in which the FASB acts in order to accomplish its mission.

# 6-1 The Nature of Merchandise Inventory

For most merchandising businesses, merchandise inventory is the largest asset. Merchandising businesses implement good control measures in managing their inventory. A successful business must maintain an adequate amount of merchandise inventory that customers are willing to buy. A business may fail if it keeps too much or too little merchandise inventory on hand.

Business managers frequently analyze sales and inventory transactions to assist them in planning future inventory purchases. From this analysis, managers can determine the items of inventory that are selling well and the items that are not selling well. Managers also examine sales and inventory transactions to identify any seasonal trends in sales. This information allows managers to order the right kinds of merchandise at the right time.

Many businesses now maintain their inventory records on computer. Computerized inventory systems can keep more accurate records of the amount of inventory on hand than other systems can. Computerized systems also provide more frequent inventory information to managers. Managers use this information to make effective business decisions.

©GETTY IMAGES/PHOTODISC

## making ethical decisions

### Is Someone Reading Your E-mail?

Janice Tillman had just been escorted from the plant by security guards. Twenty minutes earlier she lost her job for sending e-mail messages containing threatening statements directed toward Michael Ulman, her supervisor. When confronted with the messages, Janice tried to casually dismiss them as a joke. Then she accused Michael of invading her privacy, claiming that she selected the "private message" option when sending the e-mails to a friend.

The company's code of conduct states, "E-mail communication on the company computer systems is subject to electronic monitoring."

**Instructions**
Use the ethical model to evaluate Michael's decision to fire Janice.

## FLOW OF INVENTORY COSTS

Merchandise is continually being purchased and sold. A business's actual merchandise inventory changes from day to day. The flow of inventory costs through the records of a business is shown above. The cost of the merchandise available for sale consists of:

1. The cost of the beginning merchandise inventory.
2. The cost of the net purchases added to the inventory during the fiscal period.

At the end of each fiscal period, the cost of the merchandise available for sale is divided into:

1. The cost of the ending merchandise inventory. The ending merchandise inventory represents a *current* asset that will be charged as costs in *future* fiscal periods.
2. The cost of the merchandise sold during the *current* fiscal period. This cost materially affects the amount of net income reported for the fiscal period. [*CONCEPT: Adequate Disclosure*]

## EFFECTS OF ERRORS IN COSTING AN INVENTORY

| Reports and Items Affected | If Ending Inventory Is | |
| --- | --- | --- |
| | **Understated** | **Overstated** |
| Income Statement: | | |
| Cost of Merchandise Sold........... | Overstated | Understated |
| Gross Profit...................... | Understated | Overstated |
| Net Income...................... | Understated | Overstated |
| Statement of Stockholders' Equity: | | |
| Net Income...................... | Understated | Overstated |
| Retained Earnings................ | Understated | Overstated |
| Stockholders' Equity............. | Understated | Overstated |
| Balance Sheet: | | |
| Merchandise Inventory............ | Understated | Overstated |
| Total Assets..................... | Understated | Overstated |
| Stockholders' Equity............. | Understated | Overstated |

The cost of both beginning and ending merchandise inventory affects items on an income statement, a statement of stockholders' equity, and a balance sheet. The effects are shown above.

An accurate merchandise inventory cost must be determined to adequately report the financial progress and condition of a merchandising business. [*CONCEPT: Adequate Disclosure*] If the ending inventory is understated, the cost of merchandise sold will be overstated. Consequently, the net income will be understated. As a result, total assets and total stockholders' equity will be understated. If the ending inventory is overstated, the reverse will be true, and additional income tax must be paid on the overstated income. In neither situation will financial statements report accurate information. [*CONCEPT: Adequate Disclosure*]

Items in the merchandise inventory of a merchandising business are frequently referred to as *goods*. Typically, a business counts as part of its inventory all goods that it legally owns. The cost of these goods includes:

1. The price paid to vendors for the merchandise. This price includes the purchase invoice amount less discounts, returns, and allowances granted by the vendors.
2. The cost involved in getting the goods to the place of business and ready for sale. This cost includes transportation charges paid by the buyer.

Merchandising businesses must know both the cost of the goods and the number of goods in inventory. Businesses use two methods to determine the number of goods in inventory:

1. Taking a physical count of the individual items in inventory. All goods in inventory as of a given date are included in a physical inventory count.
2. Keeping a continuous record for each merchandise item showing the number purchased and the number sold. Using this method, a business can determine the number of goods in inventory at any point in time.

## Goods in Transit

Merchandising businesses purchase goods from suppliers. The suppliers ship the goods to the businesses. For goods in transit at the time of a physical count of inventory, the business must determine who holds title to the goods. When title to goods in transit passes from the supplier to the buyer, the goods become part of the buyer's inventory regardless of where they are physically located.

A vendor's terms of sale may include the provision *FOB shipping point*. FOB is an abbreviation for the phrase *Free On Board*. FOB shipping point means that the buyer pays the transportation charges. Under FOB shipping point terms, the title to the goods passes to the buyer as soon as the vendor delivers the goods to a transportation business. These goods in transit, but not yet received by the buyer, are part of the *buyer's* inventory.

If the terms of sale are *FOB destination*, the vendor pays the transportation charges. Title to the goods passes to the buyer when the buyer receives the goods. These goods in transit, but not yet received by the buyer, are part of the *vendor's* inventory. The buyer does not include these goods in the cost of inventory.

## Goods on Consignment

Goods that are given to a business to sell but for which title remains with the vendor, are called a **consignment**. The person or business that receives goods on consignment is called the **consignee**. The person or business that gives goods on consignment is called the **consignor**.

The consignee agrees to receive, care for, and attempt to sell the consigned goods. If the goods are sold, the consignee deducts a commission from the sale amount and sends the remainder to the consignor. In a consignment, title to the goods does not pass to the consignee. The goods on consignment are part of the consignor's inventory. The consignee does not include consigned goods in the cost of its inventory.

A consignee agrees to care for the goods on consignment and to make adequate attempts to sell them. Therefore, a consignee has implied liabilities if anything should happen to the goods before they are sold. A consignee often reports the cost of consigned goods as an attachment or footnote to its balance sheet.

**FYI** FOR YOUR INFORMATION

Inventory management consists of determining the quantity of goods on hand and developing procedures for ordering, receiving, and maintaining the inventory.

1. Record the description information.

2. Write the beginning quantity.

3. Record all sales transactions.

4. Enter all purchase transactions.

## STOCK RECORD

Description **3½" Computer Diskettes (boxes)**    Stock No. **F106**
Reorder **1,000**    Minimum **300**    Location **Bin 26**

| | INCREASES | | | DECREASES | | BALANCE |
|---|---|---|---|---|---|---|
| 1 | 2 | 3 | 4 | 5 | 6 | 7 |
| DATE | PURCHASE INVOICE NO. | QUANTITY | DATE | SALES INVOICE NO. | QUANTITY | QUANTITY |
| Jan. 1 20-- | | | | | | 700 |
| | | | Jan. 16 | 1761 | 120 | 580 |
| | | | Feb. 21 | 1923 | 310 | 270 |
| | | | Mar. 6 | 2071 | 230 | 40 |
| Mar. 7 | 669 | 1,000 | | | | 1,040 |
| | | | Oct. 31 | 2967 | 160 | 670 |

A continuous record of merchandise inventory increases, decreases, and balance on hand is known as a perpetual inventory. OfficeMart, Inc., sells office furniture, equipment, and supplies. It maintains a perpetual inventory.

A perpetual inventory provides day-to-day records about the quantity of merchandise on hand. Based on the records, management knows when an item of inventory is low and needs to be reordered. For each inventory item, the record shows the number on hand, the number purchased, and the number sold. A form used to show the type of merchandise, quantity received, quantity sold, and balance on hand is called a **stock record**. A file of stock records for all merchandise on hand is called a **stock ledger**.

OfficeMart's stock record for the diskettes is shown above. It includes a notation of the minimum balance at which a reorder is to be placed. For example, OfficeMart determines that two weeks are required to order and to receive a shipment of boxes of 3½" diskettes from a vendor. In a two-week period, OfficeMart will sell an average of 300 boxes of diskettes. Therefore, OfficeMart reorders diskettes when the inventory reaches 300 boxes, or units. Each reorder is for 1,000 units. On February 21, the inventory balance falls below the reorder point. An order is immediately placed for 1,000 boxes. The order is received on March 7.

A completed form authorizing a seller to deliver goods with payment to be made later is called a **purchase order**. OfficeMart prepares purchase orders for all purchases.

During the year, sales are recorded on the stock record when the sale is made. Purchases are recorded on the stock record when the goods are received. Unit prices are not recorded on the stock records. They are obtained from copies of the purchase invoices.

## STEPS    STEPS • STEPS • STEPS • STEPS • STEPS • STEPS • STEPS • STEPS • STEPS • STEPS •

### MAINTAINING A STOCK RECORD

1. Record the description of the inventory item, *3½" Computer Diskettes (boxes)*, the stock number, *F106*, the reorder quantity, *1,000*, the minimum number, *300*, and the warehouse location, *Bin 26*.

2. Write the beginning quantity. On *Jan. 1, 20--*, the quantity on hand was *700*.

3. Record all sales transactions in the Decreases columns of the stock record. After each sale, enter the new quantity in column 7. For the sale on January 16, write *Jan. 16* in column 4, the sales invoice number, *1761*, in column 5, and the quantity sold, *120*, in column 6. In column 7, record the new balance of inventory, *580*.

4. Enter all purchase transactions in the Increases columns of the stock record when the goods are received. Enter the date, purchase invoice number, quantity, and balance.

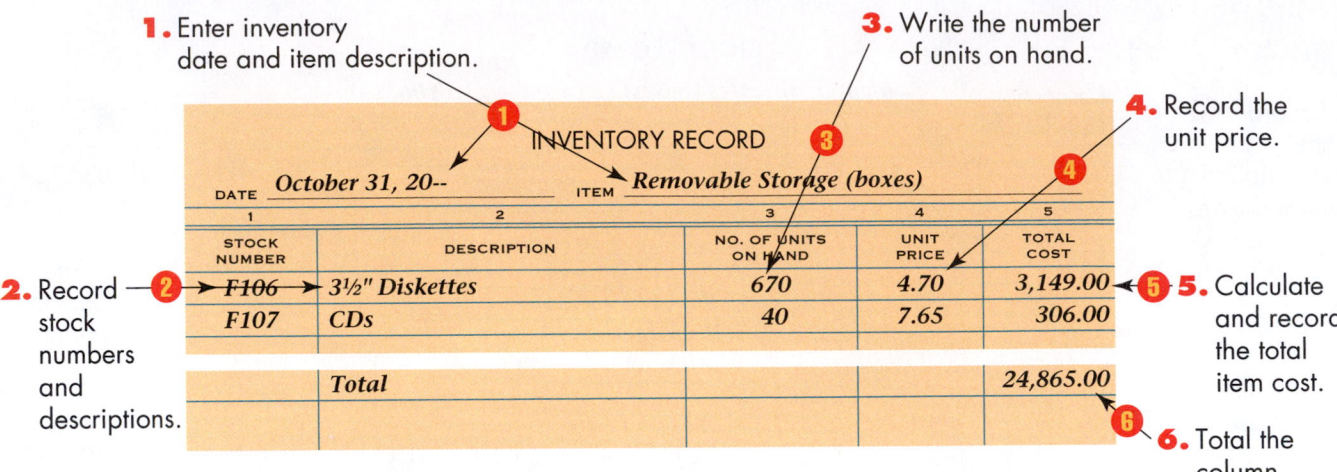

**1.** Enter inventory date and item description.

**2.** Record stock numbers and descriptions.

**3.** Write the number of units on hand.

**4.** Record the unit price.

**5.** Calculate and record the total item cost.

**6.** Total the column.

### INVENTORY RECORD

DATE *October 31, 20--*     ITEM *Removable Storage (boxes)*

| 1<br>STOCK NUMBER | 2<br>DESCRIPTION | 3<br>NO. OF UNITS ON HAND | 4<br>UNIT PRICE | 5<br>TOTAL COST |
|---|---|---|---|---|
| *F106* | *3½" Diskettes* | *670* | *4.70* | *3,149.00* |
| *F107* | *CDs* | *40* | *7.65* | *306.00* |
| | *Total* | | | *24,865.00* |

A merchandise inventory determined by counting, weighing, or measuring items of merchandise on hand is known as a periodic inventory. Counting, weighing, or measuring merchandise on hand for a periodic inventory is commonly referred to as "taking an inventory." For businesses with a large quantity of merchandise on hand, taking an inventory count is expensive. Therefore, businesses usually take a periodic inventory only once each fiscal period.

When only a periodic inventory is used, the low quantity of a merchandise item can be overlooked. When this happens, the business may not have the merchandise when customers want it. For this reason, OfficeMart uses the perpetual inventory method. Errors can occur, however, even when the perpetual inventory method is used. Therefore, OfficeMart takes a periodic inventory once each year to check the accuracy of the perpetual inventory.

A form used during a periodic inventory to record information about each item of merchandise on hand is called an **inventory record**. One inventory record is used for each item or category of items in inventory. When taking an inventory, OfficeMart uses an inventory record for categories of merchandise as shown above.

The periodic inventory count is compared to the perpetual inventory. Any differences are adjusted on the stock records. In the case of stock item F106, the physical count of boxes of the 3½" diskettes matched the quantity listed on the stock record. Therefore, no adjustment was needed. If large differences are found, the business should review its recording and control procedures to ensure that the inventory and the inventory records are being properly maintained.

## STEPS · STEPS · STEPS · STEPS · STEPS · STEPS · STEPS · STEPS · STEPS · STEPS

### COMPLETE THE INVENTORY RECORD

**1** Enter the date of the periodic inventory, *October 31, 20--*, and the item description, *Removable Computer Storage (boxes)*.

**2** Record the stock number, *F106*, and description, *3½" Diskettes*.

**3** Write the actual number of units on hand, *670*.

**4** Record the unit price, *4.70*. The unit price data are obtained from purchase invoices. In this case, all *3½"* diskettes in inventory were purchased at the same price. Additional lines of the record are used to record units purchased at a different unit price.

**5** Calculate and record the total cost, *3,149.00*. Total cost for each item is calculated by multiplying the unit price, column 4, by the number of items on hand, column 3.

**6** Determine the total cost for these inventory items, *24,865.00*. The total of all inventory records is the total cost of the ending merchandise inventory.

TERMS REVIEW • TERMS

AUDIT YOUR UNDERSTANDING

WORK TOGETHER • WORK TOGETHER • WORK

ON YOUR OWN • ON YOUR OWN

## terms review

consignment
consignee
consignor
stock record
stock ledger
purchase order
inventory record

## audit your understanding

1. What two elements are included in the cost of merchandise available for sale?
2. If ending merchandise inventory is understated, will the net income be overstated or understated?
3. Name two ways to determine the number of inventory items on hand.

## work together 6-1

**Completing a stock record for a perpetual inventory system**

A stock record form and an inventory record form for Tower Television are provided in the *Working Papers.* Your instructor will guide you through the following examples.

1. Fill in the top portion of the stock record form with the following information: Description, 19″ color television set; Stock No., K087; Reorder, 80; Minimum, 20; and Location, Bin 12.

2. Record the following information. Save your work to complete On Your Own 6-1.

| Date | Purchase Invoice No. | Sales Invoice No. | Quantity | Balance |
|------|---------------------|-------------------|----------|---------|
| Sept. 1 | | | | 62 |
| Sept. 12 | | 475 | 40 | |
| Sept. 16 | | 508 | 8 | |
| Sept. 17 | 183 | | 80 | |
| Sept. 20 | | 653 | 15 | |

## on your own 6-1

**Completing a stock record for a perpetual inventory system and comparing it to an inventory record**

Use the working papers from the Work Together above. Work independently to complete the following problem.

1. Record the remaining information for product number K087 on the stock record.

| Date | Purchase Invoice No. | Sales Invoice No. | Quantity | Balance |
|------|---------------------|-------------------|----------|---------|
| Sept. 23 | | 714 | 40 | |
| Sept. 25 | | 761 | 22 | |
| Sept. 26 | 255 | | 80 | |
| Sept. 30 | | 850 | 12 | |

2. Compare the ending balance in units from the stock record with the number of units on hand for product K087 in the inventory record. Make sure they are equal.

## 6-2 Inventory Costing

### FIRST-IN, FIRST-OUT INVENTORY COSTING METHOD

**FIFO Inventory Costing Method**

| Purchase | | | Ending Inventory | |
|---|---|---|---|---|
| Date | Units | Unit Price | Units | Total Cost |
| January, beginning inventory. . . . | 500 | $1.00 | 0 | 0.00 |
| June . . . . . . . . . . . . . . . . . . | 500 | 1.20 | 200 | $240.00 |
| November . . . . . . . . . . . . . . . | 500 | 1.25 | 500 | 625.00 |
| Totals. . . . . . . . . . . . . . . . . . | | | 700 | $865.00 |

**3.** Multiply ending inventory units by unit price.

**1.** Assign units from most recent purchase.

700 Units in ending inventory
– 500 From Nov. purchase
200 Units to be assigned
– 200 From June purchase
0 Units to be assigned

**4.** Total the ending inventory columns.

**2.** Assign units from the next most recent purchase.

Once OfficeMart takes a periodic inventory, it determines a dollar cost for each item. [CONCEPT: Unit of Measurement] The unit prices are obtained from purchase invoices. For example, as shown above, the 670 F106 boxes of diskettes have a unit price of $4.70 and a total cost of $3,149.00.

Various methods may be used to determine the cost of merchandise inventory. A business selects the method that best matches the revenue and costs for that business. [CONCEPT: Matching Expenses with Revenue]

Using the price of merchandise purchased first to calculate the cost of merchandise sold first is called the **first-in, first-out inventory costing method**. FIFO is an abbreviation for first in, first out. The FIFO method of determining the cost of

merchandise on hand assumes that the merchandise purchased first (first in) is the merchandise sold first (first out). Thus, the FIFO method uses the most recent purchase prices to determine the cost of merchandise inventory remaining. For example, OfficeMart has an inventory of 700 three-ring binders on November 30. If OfficeMart used the FIFO method, the binders would be costed as shown above.

Using the FIFO method, the remaining 300 units from the June purchase and the 500 units in beginning inventory are designated as the units that were sold. These binders are *first in*. Therefore, the business assumes that they are also the *first out*, or first sold.

**STEPS** • STEPS • STEPS • STEPS • STEPS • STEPS • STEPS • STEPS • STEPS • STEPS • STEPS

### CALCULATE INVENTORY COSTS USING THE FIFO METHOD

**1** Assign ending inventory units from the most recent purchase. The number of units in ending inventory is 700. All *500* units from the November purchase are assigned to ending inventory.

**2** If all units of ending inventory have not been assigned, assign units from the next most recent purchase. As shown above, 200 units have not been assigned. The next most recent purchase, June, includes 500 units. Therefore, all 200 units to be assigned will come from the June purchase. All 700 units in ending inventory have now been assigned.

**3** Multiply the units in the Ending Inventory Units column by the unit prices. Enter the results, *$240.00* and *625.00*, in the Total Cost column.

**4** Total the two Ending Inventory columns. The total number of units, *700*, is equal to the number of units on hand as determined by the periodic inventory. The total cost assigned to the ending inventory using the FIFO method is *$865.00*.

## LAST-IN, FIRST-OUT INVENTORY COSTING METHOD

**LIFO Inventory Costing Method**

| | Purchase | | Ending Inventory | |
|---|---|---|---|---|
| Date | Units | Unit Price | Units | Total Cost |
| January, beginning inventory.... | 500 | $1.00 | 500 | $500.00 |
| June ...................... | 500 | 1.20 | 200 | 240.00 |
| November ................. | 500 | 1.25 | 0 | 0.00 |
| Totals.................... | | | 700 | $740.00 |

**3.** Multiply ending inventory units by unit price.

**1.** Assign units from earliest purchase.

```
  700 Units in ending inventory
– 500 From beginning inventory
  200 Units to be assigned
– 200 From June purchase
    0 Units to be assigned
```

**2.** Assign units from next earliest purchase.

**4.** Total the ending inventory columns.

Using the price of merchandise purchased last to calculate the cost of merchandise sold first is called the **last-in, first-out inventory costing method.** LIFO is an abbreviation for last in, first out. The LIFO method assumes that the merchandise purchased last (last in) is the merchandise sold first (first out). Thus, the LIFO method uses the earliest purchase prices to determine the cost of merchandise inventory. If OfficeMart used the LIFO method, the 700 binders would be costed as shown above.

Of the 700 units on hand, 500 units are assumed to be the units in the beginning inventory at $1.00 per unit. The remaining 200 units are assumed to have been purchased on the next earliest date, June, at $1.20 each. None is considered to be part of the 500 units purchased on the most recent date, November. The total cost, using the LIFO method, is $740.00.

Using the LIFO method, the remaining 300 units from the June purchase and the 500 units from the November purchase are designated as the units that were sold. These binders are *last in.* Therefore, the business assumes that they are also the *first out,* or first sold.

## WEIGHTED-AVERAGE INVENTORY COSTING METHOD

**Weighted-Average Inventory Costing Method**
**Quantity on Hand, 700 units**

| | Purchase | | Total Cost |
|---|---|---|---|
| Date | Units | Unit Price | |
| January, beginning inventory.... | 500 | $1.00 | $ 500.00 |
| June ...................... | 500 | 1.20 | 600.00 |
| November ................. | 500 | 1.25 | 625.00 |
| Totals.................... | 1,500 | | $1,725.00 |

| Total of Beginning Inventory and Purchases | ÷ | Total Units | = | Weighted-Average Price per Unit |
|---|---|---|---|---|
| $1,725.00 | ÷ | 1,500 | = | $1.15 |

| Units in Ending Inventory | × | Weighted-Average Price per Unit | = | Cost of Ending Inventory |
|---|---|---|---|---|
| 700 | × | $1.15 | = | $805.00 |

**REMEMBER** FIFO uses the most recent purchase prices to determine the cost of merchandise inventory.

Using the average cost of beginning inventory plus merchandise purchased during a fiscal period to calculate the cost of merchandise sold is called the **weighted-average inventory costing method**. This method is based on the assumption that the cost is an average of the price paid for similar items purchased during the fiscal period. If OfficeMart used the weighted-average method, the 700 binders would be costed as shown at the bottom of page 177.

The total cost, $1,725.00, is divided by the total units purchased, 1,500, to calculate the weighted-average cost per unit, $1.15. The 700 units currently on hand are assumed to have been purchased at an average cost of $1.15 each. Therefore, the total cost of ending merchandise inventory using the weighted-average method is $805.00. If OfficeMart used the weighted-average method, it would use the same weighted-average cost per unit, $1.15, to determine the cost of merchandise sold.

©GETTY IMAGES/PHOTODISC

## COSTING INVENTORY DURING PERIODS OF INCREASING PRICES

### Summary of Three Methods of Costing Inventory of 700 units of Ring Binders during a Period of Increasing Prices

| Purchase | | FIFO Method | | LIFO Method | | Weighted-Average Method |
| Date | Unit Price | Units | Cost | Units | Cost | |
|---|---|---|---|---|---|---|
| Jan., begin. inv. | $1.00 | 0 | 0.00 | 500 | $500.00 | Average Cost $1.15 |
| June | 1.20 | 200 | $240.00 | 200 | 240.00 | |
| Nov. | 1.25 | 500 | 625.00 | 0 | 0.00 | |
| Totals | | 700 | $865.00 | 700 | $740.00 | $805.00 |

**If prices are rising:**

| | FIFO | LIFO | Weighted-Average |
|---|---|---|---|
| Ending inventory valuation | Highest | Lowest | Always falls |
| Cost of merchandise sold | Lowest | Highest | between |
| Reported net income | Highest | Lowest | FIFO and LIFO |

In the inventory costing situations described for the ring binders, prices increased from $1.00 to $1.25 per unit. Three ways of costing the inventory of 700 ring binders during a period of increasing prices are summarized above.

The cost of the ending inventory affects the cost of merchandise sold amount on the income statement. The higher the ending inventory, the lower the cost of merchandise sold amount, and vice versa. Therefore, during a period of *increasing prices*, the FIFO method usually results in the lowest cost of merchandise sold. The LIFO method usually results in the highest cost of merchandise sold.

The higher the cost of merchandise sold, the lower the net income reported on financial statements, and vice versa. Therefore, during a period of *increasing prices*, the FIFO method usually results in the highest reported net income. The LIFO method usually results in the lowest reported net income.

To reiterate: During a period of rising prices, the FIFO method shows a higher ending inventory than the other methods do. This results in a lower cost of merchandise sold, which in turn yields a higher reported net income. The opposite holds true for the LIFO method.

**Summary of Three Methods of Costing Inventory of 700 units
of Ring Binders during a Period of Decreasing Prices**

| Purchase | | FIFO Method | | LIFO Method | | Weighted-Average Method |
|---|---|---|---|---|---|---|
| Date | Unit Price | Units | Cost | Units | Cost | |
| Jan., begin. inv. | $1.25 | 0 | 0.00 | 500 | $625.00 | Average Cost $1.15 |
| June | 1.20 | 200 | $240.00 | 200 | 240.00 | |
| Nov. | 1.00 | 500 | 500.00 | 0 | 0.00 | |
| Totals | | 700 | $740.00 | 700 | $865.00 | $805.00 |

Prices for inventory items may also decrease. If OfficeMart determined the cost of inventory during a period of decreasing prices, the three inventory costing methods would be summarized as shown above.

During a period of *decreasing prices*, as shown in the figure above, the FIFO method usually results in the lowest merchandise inventory cost. This lower inventory cost results in a higher cost of merchandise sold and a lower net income. During a period of *decreasing prices*, the LIFO method usually results in the highest merchandise inventory cost. This higher inventory cost results in a lower cost of merchandise sold and a higher net income.

# RESULTS OF THE THREE INVENTORY COSTING METHODS COMPARED

**Comparison of Three Methods of Costing
Inventory during Periods of Increasing
or Decreasing Prices**

| Prices are | Total Inventory Cost Using | | |
|---|---|---|---|
| | FIFO Method | LIFO Method | Weighted-Average Method |
| Increasing | $865.00 | $740.00 | $805.00 |
| Decreasing | $740.00 | $865.00 | $805.00 |

A comparison of three methods of costing inventory during periods of increasing and decreasing prices is shown above.

The weighted-average method usually results in a total cost between the FIFO and LIFO total costs in both periods of increasing and decreasing prices. For businesses that purchase items with frequent fluctuations in price, the weighted-average method results in more consistent reporting of merchandise inventory costs.

Each business selects the method of costing merchandise inventory that best fits its policies and goals. A business selects one method of costing merchandise inventory and uses it for a number of years. In this way, the information on a series of financial statements can be compared easily. [CONCEPT: Consistent Reporting]

## FYI
### FOR YOUR INFORMATION

The goal of the Japanese concept, the just-in-time (JIT) system, is to minimize inventory. Materials should be received only when they are needed for production; they should not be kept in inventory. The JIT system works well when vendors and buyers work together as a team to plan inventory levels.

### Lower of Cost or Market Inventory Costing Method

| Costing Method | Cost | Market Price (700 units × 1.10 current market price) | Lower of Cost or Market |
|---|---|---|---|
| Weighted Average | $805.00 | $770.00 | $770.00 |
| FIFO | 865.00 | 770.00 | 770.00 |
| LIFO | 740.00 | 770.00 | 740.00 |

**1.** Calculate the cost.

**2.** Calculate the market price.

**3.** Determine the smaller number to use as the lower of cost or market amount.

Using the lower of cost or market price to calculate the cost of ending merchandise inventory is called the **lower of cost or market inventory costing method**. In this context, *market* refers to the current replacement cost of the merchandise item. For example, OfficeMart may currently have to pay a vendor $1.10 to purchase a ring binder. The market price, therefore, is $1.10. When merchandise is purchased, the unit price is used to record inventory costs. [*CONCEPT: Historical Cost*]

The historical cost concept states that the actual amount paid for merchandise or other items bought is recorded. OfficeMart purchased a delivery truck valued at $20,000.00 and advertised at a sale price of $18,000.00. OfficeMart negotiated to purchase the delivery truck for $17,000.00. The amount recorded in accounting records for the delivery truck is the historical cost, $17,000.00—the actual amount paid.

Six months later, OfficeMart sells the delivery truck to Flowers by Giverney for $15,000.00. For Flowers by Giverney, the historical cost of the delivery truck is $15,000.00.

If the unit price is higher than the market price at the end of a fiscal period, the inventory cost is reduced to the current market price. However, if the unit price is lower than the market price, the inventory cost is maintained at the unit price.

Two amounts are needed to apply the lower of cost or market method:

1. The cost of the inventory using the FIFO, LIFO, or weighted-average method.
2. The current market price of the inventory.

These two amounts are then compared, and the lower of the two is used to cost the inventory. For example, OfficeMart uses the weighted-average method of costing inventory. The weighted-average cost and the current market price for 700 ring binders are shown above. The weighted-average cost is $805.00, and the current market price is $770.00. Using the lower of cost or market method, the market price of the binders is lower than the weighted-average cost. Therefore, the market value of $770.00 is used as the cost of the binders.

If OfficeMart used the FIFO method, the FIFO cost would be $865.00. The $770.00 market price is lower than the FIFO cost, so the market price would be used instead of the FIFO cost. If OfficeMart used the LIFO method, the LIFO cost would be $740.00. The LIFO cost is lower than the market price, so the LIFO cost would be used to cost the inventory.

**FYI** FOR YOUR INFORMATION

New models of computers tend to drive down the market prices of existing models. In this case, the market prices of the existing models may be less than the cost of the computers. Good inventory management attempts to minimize inventory for which the market price is lower than the cost.

TERMS REVIEW • TERMS

## terms review

first-in, first-out inventory costing method

last-in, first-out inventory costing method

weighted-average inventory costing method

lower of cost or market inventory costing method

## audit your understanding

AUDIT YOUR UNDERSTANDING

1. What inventory costing method does a business usually use?

2. Which inventory costing method uses the earliest purchase prices to determine the cost of merchandise inventory?

3. During a period of increasing prices, what inventory costing method will result in the highest reported net income?

4. What two amounts are needed to apply the lower of cost or market inventory costing method?

## work together 6-2

WORK TOGETHER • WORK TOGETHER

**Costing ending inventory using FIFO, LIFO, and weighted average**

Forms for calculating inventory costs for Cassie's Kitchen are provided in the *Working Papers*. Your instructor will guide you through the following examples.

1. Cassie's Kitchen had the following beginning inventory and purchases for a salad maker, stock number T1150. At the end of the year, 140 units remained in ending inventory. Determine the cost of the ending inventory using the FIFO, LIFO, and weighted-average inventory costing methods.

| | Units | Unit Price |
|---|---|---|
| January, Beginning Inventory | 120 | $20.00 |
| July, Purchase | 100 | $22.00 |
| October, Purchase | 100 | $27.60 |

## on your own 6-2

ON YOUR OWN • ON YOUR OWN

**Costing ending inventory using FIFO, LIFO, and weighted average**

Forms for calculating inventory costs for Cassie's Kitchen are provided in the *Working Papers*. Work independently to complete the following problem.

1. Cassie's Kitchen had the following beginning inventory and purchases for a frying pan, stock number M1030. At the end of the year, 75 units remained in ending inventory. Determine the cost of the ending inventory using the FIFO, LIFO, and weighted-average inventory costing methods.

| | Units | Unit Price |
|---|---|---|
| January, Beginning Inventory | 50 | $4.20 |
| March, Purchase | 70 | $4.50 |
| November, Purchase | 60 | $5.05 |

# 6-3 Estimating the Inventory

## GROSS PROFIT METHOD OF ESTIMATING INVENTORY

**ESTIMATED MERCHANDISE INVENTORY SHEET**
Gross Profit Method

COMPANY *OfficeMart, Inc.*                                    DATE  *10/31/--*

| | | |
|---|---|---|
| 1 | Beginning inventory, January 1 . . . . . . . . . . . . . . . . . . . . . . $ | 158,930.00 |
| 2 | Net purchases to date . . . . . . . . . . . . . . . . . . . . . . | 762,440.00 |
| 3 | Merchandise available for sale . . . . . . . . . . . . . . . . . . . . $ | 921,370.00 |
| 4 | Net sales to date . . . . . . . . . . . . . . . . . $ | 1,296,000.00 |
| 5 | Less estimated gross profit . . . . . . . . . . . . . . (Net sales × Estimated gross profit *42.5* %) | 550,800.00 |
| 6 | Estimated cost of merchandise sold . . . . . . . . . . . . . . . . . | 745,200.00 |
| 7 | Estimated ending inventory . . . . . . . . . . . . . . . . . . . $ | 176,170.00 |

1. Write beginning inventory amount.
2. Determine net purchases.
3. Calculate merchandise available for sale.
4. Enter net sales.
5. Estimate gross profit.
6. Calculate estimated cost of merchandise sold.
7. Determine estimated ending inventory.

A business that keeps periodic inventory records and prepares monthly interim financial statements needs a cost to use for monthly ending merchandise inventory. Taking a monthly periodic inventory is usually too expensive. Therefore, monthly ending inventories may be estimated. Merchandisers who use perpetual inventory can take monthly ending inventory amounts from stock records (see the stock record on page 173), so they usually don't need to make estimates.

Estimating inventory by using the previous years' percentage of gross profit on operations is known as the gross profit method of estimating

inventory. This method assumes that a continuing relationship exists between gross profit and net sales. Based on experience in previous fiscal periods, a gross profit to net sales percentage is calculated. On October 31, OfficeMart estimates its ending merchandise inventory using the gross profit method as shown above.

An ending merchandise inventory amount calculated using the gross profit method is an estimate and is not absolutely accurate. However, for monthly interim financial statements, the estimated amount is sufficiently accurate without taking a periodic inventory.

## STEPS

STEPS • STEPS • STEPS • STEPS • STEPS • STEPS • STEPS • STEPS • STEPS • STEPS

### ESTIMATE ENDING MERCHANDISE INVENTORY USING THE GROSS PROFIT METHOD

1. Write the January 1 beginning inventory, *158,930.00*, from the merchandise inventory account in the general ledger.

2. Determine net purchases to date, *762,440.00*. Using amounts from the general ledger, subtract purchases discounts and purchases returns and allowances from purchases.

3. Calculate merchandise available for sale, *921,370.00*, by adding lines 1 and 2.

4. Enter net sales to date, *1,296,000.00*. Using amounts from the general ledger, subtract sales discount and sales returns and allowances from sales.

5. Multiply the amount on line 4 by 42.5% to calculate estimated gross profit, *550,800.00*. The percentage, 42.5%, is an average of the gross profit percentages from OfficeMart's income statements for the past three years.

6. Calculate estimated cost of merchandise sold, *745,200.00*, by subtracting line 5 from line 4.

7. Determine estimated ending inventory, *176,170.00*, by subtracting line 6 from line 3.

# RETAIL METHOD OF ESTIMATING INVENTORY

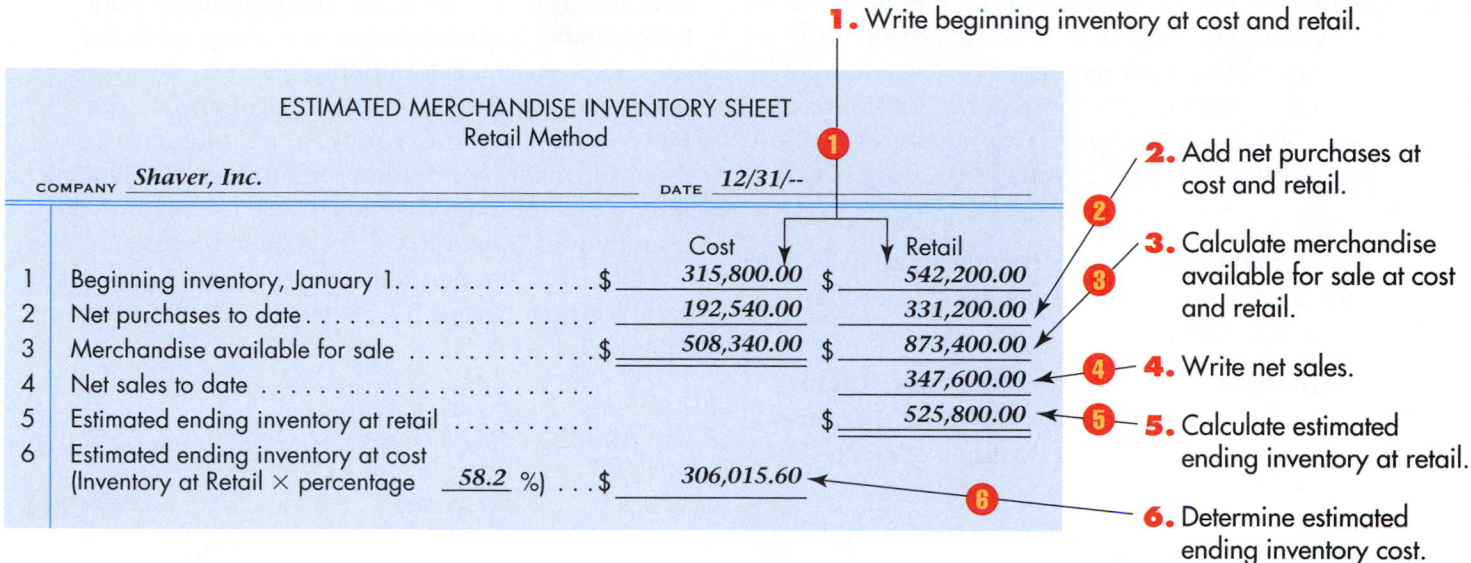

**1.** Write beginning inventory at cost and retail.

**2.** Add net purchases at cost and retail.

**3.** Calculate merchandise available for sale at cost and retail.

**4.** Write net sales.

**5.** Calculate estimated ending inventory at retail.

**6.** Determine estimated ending inventory cost.

**ESTIMATED MERCHANDISE INVENTORY SHEET**
Retail Method

COMPANY **Shaver, Inc.**                    DATE **12/31/--**

| | | Cost | Retail |
|---|---|---|---|
| 1 | Beginning inventory, January 1 . . . . . . . . . . . . . .$ | 315,800.00 $ | 542,200.00 |
| 2 | Net purchases to date . . . . . . . . . . . . . . . . | 192,540.00 | 331,200.00 |
| 3 | Merchandise available for sale  . . . . . . . . . . . .$ | 508,340.00 $ | 873,400.00 |
| 4 | Net sales to date . . . . . . . . . . . . . . . | | 347,600.00 |
| 5 | Estimated ending inventory at retail  . . . . . . . . . | $ | 525,800.00 |
| 6 | Estimated ending inventory at cost (Inventory at Retail × percentage  58.2 %) . . .$ | 306,015.60 | |

Estimating inventory by using a percentage based on both cost and retail prices is called the **retail method of estimating inventory**. The retail method may be used instead of the gross profit method. To use the retail method, a business must keep separate records of both cost and retail prices for net purchases, net sales, and beginning merchandise inventory. An estimated ending merchandise inventory, using the retail method, for Shaver, Inc., is shown above.

STEPS · STEPS · STEPS · STEPS · STEPS · STEPS · STEPS · STEPS · STEPS · STEPS

## STEPS ESTIMATE ENDING MERCHANDISE INVENTORY USING THE RETAIL METHOD

**1** Write the January 1 beginning inventory at cost, *315,800.00*, from the merchandise inventory account in the general ledger. Write the beginning inventory at retail, *542,200.00*, which is obtained from the separate record of retail prices that must be maintained to use the retail method.

**2** Add net purchases to date at cost, *192,540.00*. Using amounts from the general ledger, subtract purchases discounts and purchases returns and allowances from purchases to determine net purchases at cost. Add net purchases to date at retail, *331,200.00*, from the separate record of retail prices.

**3** Calculate merchandise available for sale at cost, *508,340.00*, and at retail, *873,400.00*, by adding lines 1 and 2.

**4** Write net sales to date at retail, *347,600.00*. Using amounts from the general ledger, subtract sales discount and sales returns and allowances from sales. Recall that a merchandising business always records sales at retail.

**5** Calculate estimated ending inventory at retail, *525,800.00*, by subtracting line 4 from line 3.

**6** Determine estimated ending inventory at cost, *306,015.60*, by multiplying line 5 by 58.2%. The percentage of merchandise available for sale at cost to merchandise available for sale at retail, 58.2%, is calculated from the amounts on line 3.

| Merchandise Available for Sale at Cost | ÷ | Merchandise Available for Sale at Retail | = | Percentage |
|---|---|---|---|---|
| $508,340.00 | ÷ | $873,400.00 | = | 58.2% |

Many businesses that need to estimate ending merchandise inventory use the gross profit method rather than the retail method. The gross profit method does not require separate records for cost and retail prices. Since OfficeMart uses a perpetual inventory, monthly ending inventories are available from the stock records without estimating or taking a monthly inventory.

# MERCHANDISE INVENTORY TURNOVER

The more rapidly a business sells merchandise, the more chance it has to make a satisfactory net income. For example, more revenue results from selling 100 ring binders per day than from selling 60 binders per day. Two measures of the speed with which merchandise inventory is sold are:

1. Merchandise inventory turnover ratio.
2. Average number of days' sales in merchandise inventory.

## Merchandise Inventory Turnover Ratio

The number of times the average amount of merchandise inventory is sold during a specific period of time is called the **merchandise inventory turnover ratio**. A merchandise inventory turnover ratio expresses a relationship between an average inventory and the cost of merchandise sold. Merchandise inventory represents a large investment for most merchandising businesses. Therefore, a low merchandise inventory turnover ratio usually indicates a low return on investment.

OfficeMart's merchandise inventory turnover ratio for the current fiscal year is calculated as follows.

| | January 1 Merchandise Inventory | + | December 31 Merchandise Inventory | ÷ | 2 | = | Average Merchandise Inventory |
|---|---|---|---|---|---|---|---|
| | ($168,365.00 | + | $173,325.00) | ÷ | 2 | = | $170,845.00 |

| | Cost of Merchandise Sold | ÷ | Average Merchandise Inventory | | = | | Merchandise Inventory Turnover Ratio |
|---|---|---|---|---|---|---|---|
| | $925,368.00 | ÷ | $170,845.00 | | = | | 5.4 times |

A 5.4 merchandise inventory turnover ratio means that the business sold the average merchandise inventory 5.4 times during the current year. National trade associations publish this ratio and others. OfficeMart can compare its ratio with the ratio for similar businesses which have an average merchandise inventory turnover ratio of 7.0 times. OfficeMart's turnover ratio of 5.4 is below the industry standard of 7.0. To correct this situation, OfficeMart's managers should consider taking action to better control the quantity of merchandise inventory on hand.

## Average Number of Days' Sales in Merchandise Inventory

The period of time needed to sell an average amount of merchandise inventory is called the **average number of days' sales in merchandise inventory**. The average number of days' sales in merchandise inventory based on a 5.4 merchandise inventory turnover ratio is calculated as shown below.

| | Days in Year | ÷ | Merchandise Inventory Turnover Ratio | = | Average Number of Days' Sales in Merchandise Inventory |
|---|---|---|---|---|---|
| | 365 | ÷ | 5.4 | = | 68 days |

The average number of days' sales in merchandise inventory is rounded to the nearest day. This level of accuracy provides managers with adequate information to make sound business decisions.

An average of 68 days means that, on average, each item in merchandise inventory is sold 68 days after it is purchased. Published averages from trade associations show that businesses similar to OfficeMart have an average number of days' sales in merchandise inventory of 53. OfficeMart's management should seek ways to increase its turnover of merchandise inventory.

The higher the number of days in merchandise inventory, the longer merchandise tends to remain unsold. A business can increase the merchandise inventory turnover ratio and reduce the number of days' sales in merchandise inventory by reducing the size of the inventory kept on hand. However, a lower inventory level may not allow a business to meet customers' demands. A business also can improve its turnover ratio and the number of days' sales in merchandise inventory by increasing the amount of merchandise sold during a month or a year.

©GETTY IMAGES/PHOTODISC

# technology for business

TECHNOLOGY FOR BUSINESS • TECHNOLOGY FOR BUSINESS • TECHNOLOGY FOR BUSIN

## Spreadsheet Activity—Valuation of Inventory

Front Porch, a small retail store, sells hand-crafted wooden porch furniture. Front Porch uses the weighted-average inventory costing method. Front Porch currently carries three items in its inventory: high-back chairs, rocking chairs, and porch swings.

The following inventory data are available for high-back chairs for the first six months of the year:

### High-back Chairs

| Purchases | Units | Unit Price |
|---|---|---|
| January, beginning inventory | 18 | $35.00 |
| February | 75 | 40.00 |
| April | 10 | 45.00 |
| June | 5 | 50.00 |
| June 30, physical inventory | 26 | |

### Required

1. Create a spreadsheet to calculate the June 30 inventory for high-back chairs. Use the weighted-average inventory costing method, shown on page 177, as a model for creating the spreadsheet. Create formulas for the total cost of each purchase and for the column totals. Save the spreadsheet as

HIGHBACK. (Hint: The weighted-average cost of the ending inventory should be $1,042.41.)

2. Make copies of the spreadsheet you created in 1 to calculate the value of other inventory items for Front Porch. Use the information below.

### Rocking Chairs

| Purchases | Units | Unit Price |
|---|---|---|
| January, beginning inventory | 2 | $42.00 |
| February | 18 | 42.00 |
| March | 6 | 50.00 |
| April | 3 | 57.00 |
| June 30, physical inventory | 11 | |

### Porch Swings

| Purchases | Units | Unit Price |
|---|---|---|
| January, beginning inventory | 1 | $80.00 |
| January | 8 | 85.00 |
| March | 6 | 88.00 |
| May | 2 | 92.00 |
| June 30, physical inventory | 3 | |

AUDIT YOUR

TERMS REVIEW • TERMS

## terms review

retail method of estimating
  inventory
merchandise inventory turnover
  ratio
average number of days' sales in
  merchandise inventory

## audit your understanding

1. On what assumptions is the gross profit method of estimating inventory based?

2. To use the retail method of estimating inventory, what records must be kept?

3. Explain a merchandise inventory turnover ratio of 5.0.

4. How is the average number of days' sales in merchandise inventory calculated?

## work together 6-3

### Estimating inventory using the gross profit and retail methods

The following information is available for Handy Hardware for the month of April. Estimated merchandise inventory sheets are provided in the *Working Papers*. Your instructor will guide you through the following examples.

|  | Cost | Retail |
|---|---|---|
| Beginning Inventory, April 1 | $124,850 | $193,400 |
| Net Purchases | 73,230 | 110,340 |
| Net Sales |  | 138,500 |

Gross Profit Percentage: 37%
Percentage of merchandise available for sale at cost to merchandise available at retail: 65.2%

1. Estimate the ending inventory using the gross profit method.

2. Estimate the ending inventory using the retail method.

WORK TOGETHER • WORK TOGETHER

## on your own 6-3

### Estimating inventory using the gross profit and retail methods

The following information is available for Handy Hardware for the month of October. Estimated merchandise inventory sheets are provided in the *Working Papers*. Work independently to complete the following problem.

|  | Cost | Retail |
|---|---|---|
| Beginning Inventory, October 1 | $182,570 | $276,380 |
| Net Purchases | 115,440 | 190,730 |
| Net Sales |  | 204,340 |

Gross Profit Percentage: 37%
Percentage of merchandise available for sale at cost to merchandise available at retail: 63.8%

1. Estimate the ending inventory using the gross profit method.

2. Estimate the ending inventory using the retail method.

ON YOUR OWN • ON YOUR OWN • ON YOUR OWN

**Xtra!**
Review
accountingxtra.swlearning.com

*After completing this chapter, you can*

1. Define accounting terms related to planning and costing inventory.

2. Identify accounting concepts and practices related to planning, counting, and costing inventory.

3. Describe the nature of merchandise inventory.

4. Determine the cost of merchandise inventory using selected costing methods.

5. Estimate the cost of merchandise inventory using selected estimating methods.

6. Calculate merchandise inventory turnover ratio and average number of days' sales in merchandise inventory.

# Explore Accounting

EXPLORE ACCOUNTING · EXPLORE ACCOUNTING · EXPLORE ACCO

## Computerized Purchasing Systems

The traditional method for purchasing inventory requires many documents and manual steps to complete. The process involves many employees, requires several days to place an order, and is subject to many clerical errors.

A modern, computerized purchasing system might work as follows: The company's computer continually monitors stock levels against minimum quantities established by management. When the quantity of any inventory item falls below its reorder point, the computer automatically sends a message to a vendor's computer with the order information. (Management frequently enters into long-term contracts with selected vendors that govern prices and delivery schedules.) The vendor's computer immediately informs its warehouse to ship the items. When the items are received, the company's computer sends a message to its bank's computer instructing the bank to transfer funds to the vendor's account.

The direct transfer of information between computers of two or more companies is called electronic data interchange (EDI). EDI reduces the cost of placing an order by reducing paperwork and labor costs. The most important advantage, however, results from improved delivery times. The traditional manual ordering system required several days or weeks to process an order. An EDI system can have the order in transit on the same day the order is placed. Improved delivery time allows companies to reduce inventory levels, which results in substantial cost savings.

**Required:**
Contact your local bank and inquire if its computer system uses EDI to support its customers' purchasing systems.

# 6-1 APPLICATION PROBLEM

**Keeping perpetual inventory records**

AUTOMATED ACCOUNTING   PEACHTREE   QUICKBOOKS    accountingxtra.swlearning.com

Bowman Lawn and Garden sells lawn and garden equipment to a variety of customers. For many years the business used a periodic inventory system. However, it switched to a perpetual merchandise inventory system two years ago. The perpetual system gives the company better control of its inventory.

**Instructions:**

1. Complete the heading of a stock record for each of the following two inventory items. Also record the balance on April 1 of the current year for each item.

    Lawn mower:
        Stock number R263
        Reorder, 60
        Minimum, 15
        Location, bin 41
        Number on hand April 1, 32
    Hedge trimmer:
        Stock number J184
        Reorder, 35
        Minimum, 8
        Location, bin 49
        Number on hand April 1, 17

2. Record on the stock records the merchandise items received and sold during April of the current year. Source documents are abbreviated as follows: sales invoice, S; purchase invoice, P.

**Transactions:**

April   2.   Sold 9 lawn mowers to Rogers Lawn and Garden, S211.
        3.   Sold 5 hedge trimmers to Besotral, Inc., S212.
        6.   Lawn Haven bought 6 lawn mowers and 6 hedge trimmers, S213.
     10.   Received 35 hedge trimmers from Hughes Manufacturing, P742.
     11.   Gilbert Co. bought 10 hedge trimmers, S214.
     15.   Five more lawn mowers were sold to Rogers Lawn and Garden, S215.
     16.   Lawn King Manufacturing shipped 60 lawn mowers, P743.
     19.   Sold 30 lawn mowers to Christie's Landscaping, S216.
     20.   Home Beautiful bought 20 lawn mowers and 15 hedge trimmers, S217.
     24.   Twelve more lawn mowers were sold to Lawn Haven, S218.
     25.   Received 60 lawn mowers from Lawn King Manufacturing, P744.
     28.   Sold 10 hedge trimmers to Greene, Inc., S219.
     29.   Hughes Manufacturing shipped 35 hedge trimmers, P745.
     30.   Sold 7 lawn mowers to Movin' Mowers, S220.

# 6-2 APPLICATION PROBLEM  AUTOMATED ACCOUNTING  QUICKBOOKS

## Determining inventory cost using FIFO, LIFO, weighted average, and lower of cost or market

Accounting records at Wayne, Inc., show the following purchases, periodic inventory counts, and market prices.

| Stock No. | January 1 Inventory | | First Purchase | | Second Purchase | | Third Purchase | | Fourth Purchase | | December 31 Inventory | December 31 Market Price |
|---|---|---|---|---|---|---|---|---|---|---|---|---|
| | No. | Unit Price | No. | Unit Price | No. | Unit Price | No. | Unit Price | No. | Unit Price | | |
| A30 | 15 | $8.00 | 15 | $10.00 | 15 | $12.00 | 20 | $14.00 | 20 | $10.00 | 35 | $12.00 |
| B18 | 10 | 9.00 | 10 | 9.00 | 12 | 9.00 | 12 | 8.00 | 12 | 8.00 | 30 | 7.50 |
| C45 | 22 | 5.00 | 30 | 6.00 | 30 | 6.00 | 30 | 7.00 | 30 | 8.00 | 64 | 8.00 |
| D12 | 12 | 7.00 | 5 | 7.00 | 5 | 9.00 | 10 | 8.00 | 5 | 7.00 | 20 | 7.50 |

**Instructions:**

1. Calculate the inventory costs using the FIFO, LIFO, and weighted average inventory costing methods. Assume that the lower of cost or market method is applied to each inventory item separately. Use a form similar to the following. The inventory cost for Stock No. A30 is given as an example.

| Stock No. | Dec. 31 Inventory | Market Price | Inventory Costing Method | | | | | | | | | |
|---|---|---|---|---|---|---|---|---|---|---|---|---|
| | | | FIFO | | | LIFO | | | Weighted Average | | | |
| | | | Unit Price | Total Cost | Lower of Cost or Market | Unit Price | Total Cost | Lower of Cost or Market | Unit Price | Total Cost | Lower of Cost or Market | |
| A30 | 35 | 35 @ $12.00 = $420.00 | 20 @ $10.00 15 @ 14.00 } | $410.00 | $410.00 | 15 @ $8.00 15 @ 10.00 5 @ 12.00 } | $330.00 | $330.00 | 35 @ $10.94 | $382.90 | $382.90 | |

2. Total the three Lower of Cost or Market columns.
3. Which of the three methods of costing inventory results in the highest inventory cost for Wayne, Inc.? Which results in the lowest inventory cost?

# 6-3 APPLICATION PROBLEM

## Estimating cost of merchandise inventory using estimating methods

The records of Walker, Inc., show the following on December 31 of the current year.

| Item | Cost | Retail |
|---|---|---|
| Beginning merchandise inventory......... | $ 42,400.00 | $ 70,000.00 |
| Net purchases to date.................. | 136,000.00 | 227,400.00 |
| Net sales to date..................... | — | 208,800.00 |
| Gross profit percentage............... | 40% | |

**Instructions:**

1. Calculate the corporation's estimated ending inventory using the gross profit method of estimating inventory. Round the percentages to the nearest 0.1%.
2. Calculate the corporation's estimated ending inventory using the retail method of estimating inventory. Round the percentages to the nearest 0.1%.

# 6-4 APPLICATION PROBLEM

**Calculating merchandise inventory turnover ratio and average number of days' sales in merchandise inventory**

Selected information for three corporations follows.

| | Corporation | | |
|---|---|---|---|
| Item | A | B | C |
| Beginning Merchandise Inventory | $ 15,800.00 | $ 80,500.00 | $ 64,300.00 |
| Ending Merchandise Inventory | 21,200.00 | 78,900.00 | 54,600.00 |
| Cost of Merchandise Sold | 167,700.00 | 848,000.00 | 567,400.00 |

**Instructions:**

1. For each corporation, calculate the merchandise inventory turnover ratio. Round the ratio to the nearest 0.1%.
2. For each corporation, calculate the average number of days' sales in merchandise inventory. Round the amount to the nearest day.
3. Which corporation has the best merchandise inventory turnover ratio?

# 6-5 MASTERY PROBLEM

**Determining cost of merchandise inventory; estimating cost of merchandise inventory using estimating methods; calculating merchandise inventory turnover ratio and average number of days' sales in merchandise inventory**

On December 31 of the current year, Sowell, Inc., took a periodic inventory. The following information is obtained from Sowell's records.

| Stock No. | January 1 Inventory | | First Purchase | | Second Purchase | | December 31 Inventory | Market Price |
|---|---|---|---|---|---|---|---|---|
| | No. | Unit Price | No. | Unit Price | No. | Unit Price | | |
| R46 | 14 | $ 7.00 | 15 | $ 8.00 | 15 | $ 9.00 | 18 | $ 9.50 |
| S10 | 16 | 5.00 | 10 | 5.00 | 10 | 8.00 | 26 | 4.75 |
| T76 | 8 | 12.00 | 15 | 11.00 | 15 | 11.00 | 25 | 10.00 |
| U92 | 7 | 8.00 | 7 | 8.00 | 7 | 8.00 | 10 | 8.00 |
| V17 | 5 | 4.00 | 10 | 6.00 | 10 | 7.00 | 5 | 6.00 |

**Instructions:**

1. Calculate the inventory costs using the FIFO, LIFO, and weighted-average inventory costing methods. Use the form in the *Working Papers*.
2. Total the three Total Cost columns.
3. Sowell uses the LIFO inventory costing method to determine the cost of inventory. Use the market price given in the form at the beginning of the problem to determine the cost of inventory using the lower of cost or market. Total the Lower of Cost or Market column. Use the form in the *Working Papers*.
4. Calculate the corporation's estimated ending inventory using the gross profit method of estimating inventory. The corporation's records show the following on December 31 of the current year.

| Item | Cost | Retail |
|---|---|---|
| Beginning merchandise inventory.......... | $21,200.00 | $ 35,000.00 |
| Net purchases to date................... | 68,000.00 | 113,700.00 |
| Net sales to date...................... | — | 103,700.00 |
| Gross profit percentage................ | 40% | |

5. Calculate the corporation's estimated ending inventory using the retail method of estimating inventory. Round the percentage to the nearest 0.1%.
6. Use the information and the estimated inventory calculated in Instruction 4. Calculate the corporation's merchandise inventory turnover ratio. Round the ratio to the nearest 0.1%.
7. Calculate the corporation's average number of days' sales in merchandise inventory. Round the amount to the nearest day.

# 6-6 CHALLENGE PROBLEM

**Determining the unit price of merchandise inventory purchases**

Minder, Inc., recently received a shipment of merchandise inventory. Minder maintains a perpetual inventory using unit prices including freight and cash discounts. The following information is from the purchase invoice for the shipment.

| Stock No. | Quantity | Unit Price | Total Cost |
|---|---|---|---|
| A69 | 50 | $2.00 | $100.00 |
| V56 | 15 | 6.00 | 90.00 |
| X28 | 30 | 4.00 | 120.00 |
| W12 | 20 | 3.00 | 60.00 |
| S92 | 5 | 8.00 | 40.00 |
| Subtotal | | | $410.00 |
| Freight | | | 20.50 |
| Cash Discount | | | (8.20) |
| Total Cost | | | $422.30 |

**Instructions:**
1. Divide the total cost by the subtotal. Round the percentage to the nearest 0.1%.
2. Calculate the adjusted unit price of each item by multiplying the percentage calculated in Instruction 1 by the unit price of the item.
3. Calculate the adjusted total cost for each item by multiplying the quantity by the adjusted unit price.

©GETTY IMAGES/PHOTODISC

## applied communication

Each year, retail businesses lose millions of dollars to theft and fraud. As consumers, we all pay for these illegal actions in the form of higher prices.

**Required:**

1.  Research the actions that retail businesses take to control theft and fraud. Write a short report about your findings.

2.  Explain why businesses must charge higher prices for their goods as a result of theft and fraud.

3.  Discuss in class what actions you would take if you were with a friend who was shoplifting.

## cases for critical thinking

### Case 1

Quitman, Inc., keeps a perpetual merchandise inventory. A new member of the board of directors notices that two employees work full time keeping the inventory records. The director suggests that the corporation stop using the perpetual inventory system and take a periodic inventory once a year when information is needed for financial statements. The director also suggests that the salaries saved by eliminating the positions of the two inventory employees will be more than the cost of an annual periodic inventory. What is your opinion of this suggestion? Explain your answer.

### Case 2

Hastings, Inc., sells many different items of sports equipment. The corporation takes a periodic inventory once every three months for use in preparing quarterly financial statements. A newly employed accountant suggests that the corporation change over to a perpetual inventory. What would you recommend? Explain your recommendation.

## SCANS workplace competency

**Resource Competency:** Allocating Time

**Concept:** Employers need workers who can identify job tasks, rank tasks in order of importance, estimate time to accomplish tasks, develop a schedule for completing tasks, and adjust task schedules as needed. Wasted time costs employers money.

**Application:** Prepare a daily schedule for yourself for one week. List all activities that you need to complete daily, including classes, extracurricular activities, homework, employment hours, social events, meals, hygiene, etc. Allocate time slots during each day to complete each task. As you progress through the week, make changes to your schedule as needed.

## • auditing for errors

The following information was taken from the records of Centuria Music Store for the month of September.

|  | Cost | Retail |
|---|---|---|
| Beginning Inventory, September 1 | $174,636 | $279,418 |
| Net Purchases | 60,842 | 97,347 |
| Net Sales |  | 225,300 |

The bookkeeper prepared the following estimated merchandise inventory sheet. Verify the numbers on the report. List any errors and the correct amounts.

### Estimated Merchandise Inventory Sheet
#### Retail Method

Company: Centuria Music Store                Date: September, 20--

|  | Cost | Retail |
|---|---|---|
| Beginning inventory, September 1 | 174,636 | 279,418 |
| Net purchases to date | 60,482 | 97,347 |
| Merchandise available for sale | 235,118 | 376,765 |
| Net sales to date |  | 225,300 |
| Estimated ending inventory at retail |  | 151,465 |
| Estimated ending inventory at cost | 94,514.16 |  |
| (Inventory at Retail × percentage 62.4%) |  |  |

## • analyzing Costco's financial statements

Most companies include information about inventory in the first note to the financial statement, "Summary of Significant Accounting Policies." This note usually tells the reader which method the company uses to value the cost of its ending inventory.

**Instructions:**

1.  Using Note 1, beginning on page B-9 of Appendix B in this textbook, locate the paragraph titled "Merchandise Inventories." List the method Costco primarily uses to value the cost of its U.S. merchandise inventory and the method Costco primarily uses to value the cost of its foreign merchandise inventory.

2.  Calculate Costco's merchandise inventory turnover ratio and average number of days' sales in merchandise inventory as of August 31, 2003. Use the information on the Ten Year Operating and Financial Highlights on pages B-2 and B-3 and the Consolidated Balance Sheets on page B-5.

3.  Go to Costco's web site (www.costco.com) and locate the financial statements for the most current year available. (Look for "Investor Relations" or a similar link.) Calculate Costco's merchandise inventory turnover ratio and average number of days' sales in merchandise inventory for the current year.

4.  Did these measures improve or worsen from 2003 to the current year?

## Inventory Planning and Valuation

Inventory planning and valuation is necessary to accurately account for inventory and report asset values in financial statements. Merchandise inventory is usually the largest current asset of a merchandising business. Therefore, it is important to select an inventory system that provides the most accurate and up-to-date inventory valuations. Inventory planning and valuation may be accomplished by using either a manual or an automated inventory system. Today, most businesses use automated inventory systems.

### Inventory Processing

Inventory processing includes recording items sold, ordered, and received in the inventory records. The inventory records are stored in a database that is separate from the general ledger database. To update the inventory records:

1. Click the Other Activities toolbar button.
2. Select the Inventory tab to display the data entry window.
3. Enter the data for items sold, ordered, and received.
4. Click OK.

   *Automated Accounting 8.0* has a more complete inventory system:

1. When inventory items are ordered, a purchase order is recorded in the Purch. Order tab of the Other Activities window.
2. When an order is received, a purchase invoice is issued and recorded in the Purch. Invoice tab of the Other Activities window.
3. When merchandise is sold, the sales invoice is entered in the Sales Invoice tab of the Other Activities window.

   After all inventory processing data have been keyed, an Inventory Transaction report should be displayed, verified for accuracy, and printed. To print the Inventory Transaction report:

1. Click the Reports toolbar button.
2. Choose Inventory Reports from Select a Report Group.
3. Select Inventory Transactions from the Choose a Report to Display list.

4. Click OK.
5. Enter the Start and End date for the report.
6. Click OK.

   The inventory transactions report is checked for accuracy by comparing the report totals with the totals on the inventory source documents or forms.

### Inventory Exceptions

Inventory exceptions are those inventory items that require close monitoring. When inventory levels are low or there are no stock items, management will need to reorder or take action. The software provides an option for generating an exception report. This report lists items that are out of stock and items that are at or below the reorder point. To generate the report, select Inventory Exceptions from the list of inventory reports.

### Inventory Valuation

*Automated Accounting 8.0* or higher allows users to determine inventory costs using the average cost, LIFO, or FIFO costing methods. Reports can be generated to see the valuations using each of the inventory cost methods mentioned.

1. Click the Reports toolbar button.
2. Choose the Inventory Reports option button from the Select a Report Group list.
3. Select a valuation option from the Choose a Report to Display list.

### Yearly Sales

The yearly sales report accumulates total sales throughout the year for each stock item. Therefore, a yearly sales report showing total sales for January, generated at month end, would include only sales for January. February's month-end report would show the accumulation of total sales for the months of January and February.

   The yearly sales report provides management with unit and dollar sales for each inventory item.

1. Click the Reports toolbar button.
2. Select the Inventory Reports option from the Select a Report Group.
3. Choose the Yearly Sales option.
4. Click OK.

## AUTOMATING ACCOUNTING PROBLEM 6-1

**Instructions:**

1. Load *Automated Accounting 8.0* or higher software.

2. Select database A06-1 (Advanced Course Application Problem 6-1) from the accounting template disk.

3. Select File from the menu bar and choose the Save As menu command. Key the path to the drive and directory that contains your data files. Save the database with a filename of XXX061 (where XXX are your initials).

4. Read the Problem Instruction screen by clicking the Browser toolbar button.

5. Refer to page 188 for data used in this problem.

6. Exit the Automated Accounting software.

## AUTOMATING ACCOUNTING PROBLEM 6-2

**Instructions:**

1. Load *Automated Accounting 8.0* or higher software.

2. Select database A06-2 (Advanced Course Application Problem 6-2) from the accounting template disk.

3. Select File from the menu bar and choose the Save As menu command. Key the path to the drive and directory that contains your data files. Save the database with a filename of XXX062 (where XXX are your initials).

4. Read the Problem Instruction screen by clicking the Browser toolbar button.

5. Refer to page 189 for data used in this problem.

6. Exit the Automated Accounting software.

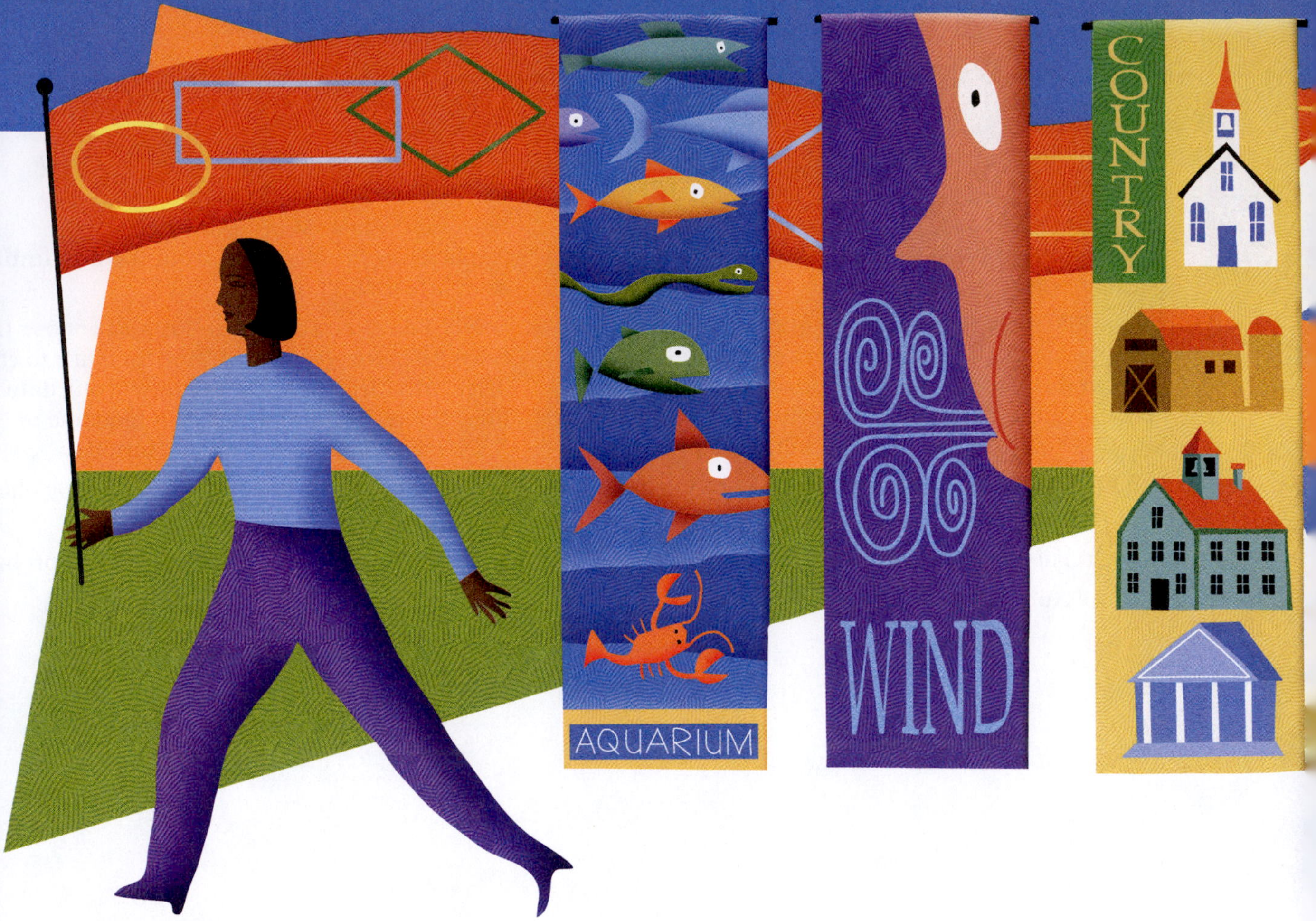


# PART 3 General Accounting Adjustments

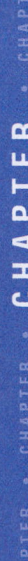

# CHART OF ACCOUNTS

**Balance Sheet Accounts**

| (1000) | ASSETS |
|---|---|
| 1100 | CURRENT ASSETS |
| 1105 | Cash |
| 1110 | Petty Cash |
| 1115 | Notes Receivable |
| 1120 | Interest Receivable |
| 1125 | Accounts Receivable |
| 1130 | Allowance for Uncollectible Accounts |
| 1135 | Merchandise Inventory |
| 1140 | Supplies—Administrative |
| 1145 | Supplies—Sales |
| 1150 | Supplies—Warehouse |
| 1155 | Prepaid Insurance |
| 1160 | Prepaid Interest |
| 1200 | PLANT ASSETS |
| 1205 | Land |
| 1215 | Building |
| 1220 | Accumulated Depreciation—Building |
| 1225 | Office Equipment |
| 1230 | Accumulated Depreciation—Office Equipment |
| 1235 | Store Equipment |
| 1240 | Accumulated Depreciation—Store Equipment |
| 1245 | Warehouse Equipment |
| 1250 | Accumulated Depreciation—Warehouse Equipment |
| (2000) | LIABILITIES |
| 2100 | CURRENT LIABILITIES |
| 2105 | Notes Payable |
| 2110 | Interest Payable |
| 2115 | Accounts Payable |
| 2120 | Employee Income Tax Payable |
| 2125 | Federal Income Tax Payable |
| 2130 | Social Security Tax Payable |
| 2133 | Medicare Tax Payable |
| 2135 | Salaries Payable |
| 2140 | Sales Tax Payable |
| 2145 | Unearned Rent |
| 2150 | Unemployment Tax Payable—Federal |
| 2155 | Unemployment Tax Payable—State |
| 2200 | LONG-TERM LIABILITY |
| 2205 | Mortgage Payable |
| (3000) | STOCKHOLDERS' EQUITY |
| 3105 | Capital Stock |
| 3110 | Retained Earnings |
| 3115 | Income Summary |

**Income Statement Accounts**

| (4000) | OPERATING REVENUE |
|---|---|
| 4105 | Sales |
| 4110 | Sales Discount |
| 4115 | Sales Returns and Allowances |
| (5000) | COST OF MERCHANDISE |
| 5105 | Purchases |
| 5110 | Purchases Discount |
| 5115 | Purchases Returns and Allowances |
| (6000) | OPERATING EXPENSE |
| 6100 | ADMINISTRATIVE EXPENSES |
| 6105 | Depreciation Expense—Building |
| 6110 | Depreciation Expense—Office Equipment |
| 6115 | Insurance Expense |
| 6120 | Miscellaneous Expense—Administrative |
| 6125 | Payroll Taxes Expense |
| 6130 | Property Tax Expense |
| 6135 | Salary Expense—Administrative |
| 6140 | Supplies Expense—Administrative |
| 6145 | Uncollectible Accounts Expense |
| 6200 | SELLING EXPENSES |
| 6205 | Advertising Expense |
| 6210 | Credit Card Fee Expense |
| 6215 | Depreciation Expense—Store Equipment |
| 6220 | Miscellaneous Expense—Sales |
| 6225 | Salary Expense—Sales |
| 6230 | Supplies Expense—Sales |
| 6300 | WAREHOUSE EXPENSES |
| 6305 | Depreciation Expense—Warehouse Equipment |
| 6310 | Miscellaneous Expense—Warehouse |
| 6315 | Salary Expense—Warehouse |
| 6320 | Supplies Expense—Warehouse |
| (7000) | OTHER REVENUE |
| 7105 | Gain on Plant Assets |
| 7110 | Interest Income |
| 7115 | Rent Income |
| 7120 | Collection of Uncollectible Accounts |
| (8000) | OTHER EXPENSES |
| 8105 | Interest Expense |
| 8110 | Loss on Plant Assets |
| (9000) | INCOME TAX |
| 9105 | Federal Income Tax Expense |

The chart of accounts for Appliance Center, Inc., is illustrated above for ready reference as you study Part 3 of this textbook.

# CHAPTER 7

# Accounting for Uncollectible Accounts

OBJECTIVES & TERMS · OBJECTIVES & TERMS · OBJECTIVES & TERMS · OBJECTIVES & TERMS

*After studying Chapter 7, you will be able to:*

1. Define accounting terms related to uncollectible accounts.

2. Identify accounting concepts and practices related to uncollectible accounts.

3. Calculate and record estimated uncollectible accounts expense using the direct write-off method.

4. Calculate and record estimated uncollectible accounts expense using the allowance method.

5. Calculate and analyze accounts receivable turnover ratios.

- uncollectible accounts
- writing off an account
- direct write-off method of recording losses from uncollectible accounts

- allowance method of recording losses from uncollectible accounts
- aging accounts receivable

- accounts receivable turnover ratio
- book value of accounts receivable

Point Your Browser
accountingxtra.swlearning.com

# · J.C. Penney

©NEAL HAMBERG/BLOOMBERG NEWS/LANDOV

## J.C. PENNEY AND THE GOLDEN RULE

The J.C. Penney Company is one of the oldest department stores in the country. However, it has not always been known as the J.C. Penney Company. When James Cash Penney opened his first store in 1902 in Kemmerer, Wyoming, it was called the Golden Rule Store. It wasn't until 1913 that the chain incorporated as J.C. Penney Company, Inc.

It was not a coincidence that Mr. Penney chose this name for his store. "Do unto others as you would have others do unto you" became the cornerstone for setting his store apart from his competition. Mr. Penney stated, "In setting up a business under the name and meaning of the Golden Rule, I was publicly binding myself, in my business relations, to a principle which had been a real and intimate part of my family upbringing. To me the sign on the store was much more than a trade name. . . . We took our slogan 'Golden Rule Store' with strict literalness. Our idea was to make money and build business through serving the community with fair dealing and honest value."

Today, the J.C. Penney Company operates stores in all 50 states, Puerto Rico, and Mexico.

### Critical Thinking

1. J.C. Penney Company allows customers to use bank credit cards (such as VISA) but also offers its own credit card. What is the cost to J.C. Penney Company of offering its own credit card? What are the benefits?
2. How could the Golden Rule philosophy apply to credit card customers?

accountingxtra.swlearning.com

Source: www.jcpenney.com

## RESUME WRITING

Go to the homepage for the American Institute of Certified Public Accountants (AICPA) (www.aicpa.org). Find the link for students. Search for information about how to prepare a resume and how to write appropriate letters.

### Instructions

1. List the six items, in order, that this site recommends to include in a resume.
2. What two types of letters are recommended by this site?

# 7-1 Direct Write-Off Method of Recording Uncollectible Accounts

Many business transactions are completed on account rather than for cash. Businesses offer credit terms to attract new customers, increase sales to current customers, and encourage customer loyalty. Before a business sells merchandise on account, it should investigate the customer's credit rating to ensure that the customer will pay promptly.

Regardless of the care taken in granting credit, some customers will not pay when payment is due. Accounts receivable that cannot be collected are called **uncollectible accounts**. Uncollectible accounts are sometimes referred to as bad debts.

When a business makes a sale on account to a customer, it records the amount in a general ledger account titled Accounts Receivable. The amount remains recorded in this asset account until it is paid or until it is specifically known to be uncollectible.

When a customer account is believed to be uncollectible, the account is no longer an asset. An uncollectible account should be canceled and removed from the assets of the business. Canceling the balance of a customer account because the customer is not expected to pay is called **writing off an account**.

Occasionally an account that has been written off is collected. The account balance is restored and the receipt of cash is recorded. A complete history of the transactions for each customer is maintained.

©GETTY IMAGES/PHOTODISC

## making ethical decisions

### Sharing the News

Phillip Walters left the meeting and went straight to the phone to call his wife. "Corporate headquarters just informed us they plan to close the plant. They're going to announce the closing next Monday. I'll be able to keep my job if we're willing to move."

**Instructions**

Access the *Code of Business Conduct* of Dow. Using this information and the ethical model, determine whether Phillip acted ethically by informing his wife of the impending plant closing.

| | DATE | | ACCOUNT TITLE | DOC. NO. | POST. REF. | DEBIT | CREDIT | |
|---|---|---|---|---|---|---|---|---|
| GENERAL JOURNAL | | | | | | | PAGE 11 | |
| 1 | Nov. 20-- | 15 | Uncollectible Accounts Expense | M21 | | 50 00 | | 1 |
| 2 | | | Accounts Rec./James Nordquist | | / | | 50 00 | 2 |

An amount owed by a specific customer is part of the accounts receivable account balance until it is paid or is written off as uncollectible. An uncollectible account is closed by transferring the balance to a general ledger account titled Uncollectible Accounts Expense.

Northwest Cleaners dry cleans clothing for its customers. Most of the business's sales are made for cash or are paid with a credit card. The business does make a few sales on account. The business has a small number of accounts receivable and very few of these accounts become uncollectible. Therefore, Northwest Cleaners records uncollectible accounts expense only when a specific account is actually known to be uncollectible. Recording uncollectible accounts expense only when an amount is actually known to be uncollectible is called the **direct write-off method of recording losses from uncollectible accounts**.

On November 15, Northwest Cleaners learned that James Nordquist is unable to pay his account. Northwest Cleaners decides that James Nordquist's account is uncollectible. The entry to record the write-off is made in the general journal as shown above.

*November 15. Wrote off James Nordquist's past due account as uncollectible, $50.00. Memorandum No. 21.*

After this entry is journalized and posted, the balance of Accounts Receivable no longer includes the $50.00 as part of the business's assets. Also, James Nordquist's account has a zero balance and is written off.

**GENERAL LEDGER**

Uncollectible Accounts Expense

| Write off | 50.00 | |
|---|---|---|

Accounts Receivable

| Bal. | 54,789.05 | Write off | 50.00 |
|---|---|---|---|
| (New Bal. | 54,739.05) | | |

**ACCOUNTS RECEIVABLE LEDGER**

James Nordquist

| Bal. | 50.00 | Write off | 50.00 |
|---|---|---|---|
| (New Bal. zero) | | | |

**FYI** FOR YOUR INFORMATION

A credit rating is an evaluation of the willingness and ability of an individual or business to pay debts on a timely basis. Credit ratings are maintained by a variety of organizations.

**REMEMBER** Uncollectible accounts are also referred to as bad debts. Thus, the accounts used could be titled Bad Debt Expense and Collection of Bad Debts.

**1.** Make an entry to reopen the account.

**2.** Make an entry to record the cash receipt.

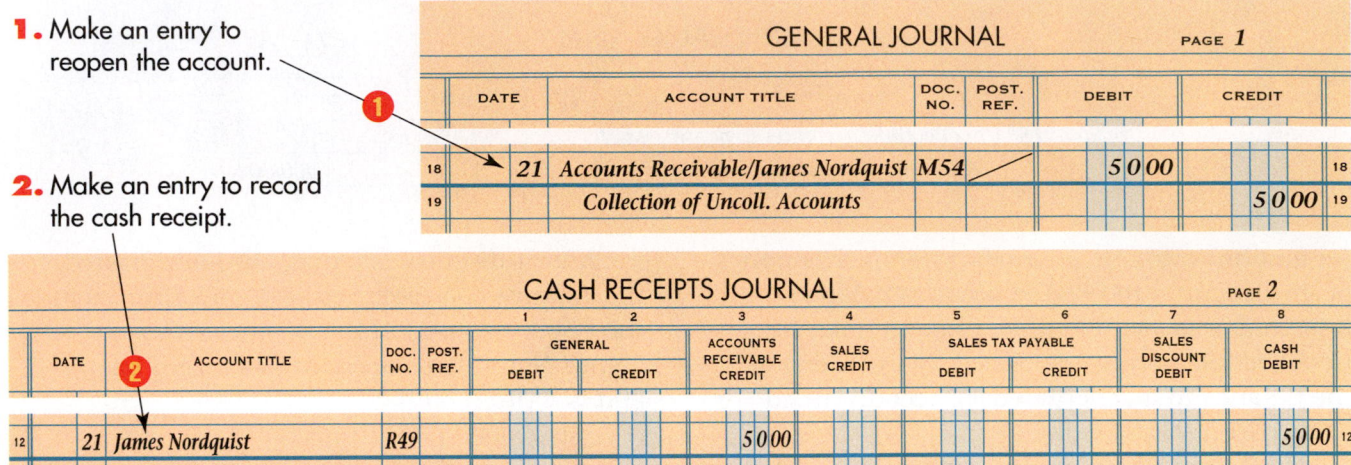

| DATE | ACCOUNT TITLE | DOC. NO. | POST. REF. | DEBIT | CREDIT |
|------|---------------|----------|------------|-------|--------|
| 21 | Accounts Receivable/James Nordquist | M54 | | 50 00 | |
| | Collection of Uncoll. Accounts | | | | 50 00 |

GENERAL JOURNAL — PAGE 1

CASH RECEIPTS JOURNAL — PAGE 2

| DATE | ACCOUNT TITLE | DOC. NO. | POST. REF. | GENERAL DEBIT | GENERAL CREDIT | ACCOUNTS RECEIVABLE CREDIT | SALES CREDIT | SALES TAX PAYABLE DEBIT | SALES TAX PAYABLE CREDIT | SALES DISCOUNT DEBIT | CASH DEBIT |
|------|---------------|----------|------------|---------------|----------------|----------------------------|--------------|-------------------------|--------------------------|----------------------|------------|
| 21 | James Nordquist | R49 | | | | 50 00 | | | | | 50 00 |

Sometimes a customer's written-off account is later collected. When the account is written off, the balance is recorded as an expense. When the account is later collected, the amount is recorded as other revenue.

> **January 21. Received cash in full payment of James Nordquist's account, previously written off as uncollectible, $50.00. Memorandum No. 54 and Receipt No. 49.**

Northwest Cleaners needs a complete history of each customer's credit activities. Therefore, two journal entries are recorded for the collection of a written-off account receivable as shown above.

1. A general journal entry to reopen the customer account.
2. A cash receipts journal entry to record the cash received on account.

The account Collection of Uncollectible Accounts is used for recording collection of previously written-off accounts. The account is closed to Income Summary at the end of a fiscal period and is reported on an income statement as part of Other Revenue.

### GENERAL LEDGER
**Cash**

| | | | |
|---|---|---|---|
| Received | 50.00 | | |

**Accounts Receivable**

| | | | |
|---|---|---|---|
| Bal. | 54,789.05 | Write off | 50.00 |
| Reopen | 50.00 | Received | 50.00 |

**Collection of Uncollectible Accounts**

| | | | |
|---|---|---|---|
| | | Reopen | 50.00 |

### ACCOUNTS RECEIVABLE LEDGER
**James Nordquist**

| | | | |
|---|---|---|---|
| Bal. | 50.00 | Write off | 50.00 |
| Reopen | 50.00 | Received | 50.00 |
| (New Bal. zero) | | | |

## STEPS
STEPS • STEPS • STEPS • STEPS

### COLLECTING A WRITTEN-OFF ACCOUNT USING THE DIRECT WRITE-OFF METHOD

**1** Record an entry in the general journal to debit *Accounts Receivable/James Nordquist* and credit *Collection of Uncollectible Accounts* for the amount of the receipt, *50.00.*

**2** Record an entry on the cash receipts journal to debit Cash and credit Accounts Receivable for the amount of the receipt, *50.00.*

## FYI
FOR YOUR INFORMATION

Uncollectible accounts are also referred to as bad debts. Thus, the accounts used could be titled Bad Debts Expense and Collection of Bad Debts.

## terms review

TERMS REVIEW

uncollectible accounts
writing off an account
direct write-off method of recording
  losses from uncollectible
  accounts

## audit your understanding

AUDIT YOUR

1. Why should the amount of an uncollectible account be removed from the assets of a business?
2. In the direct write-off method, how is an uncollectible account closed?
3. Why is the customer account reopened when cash is received for an account previously written off as uncollectible?

## work together 7-1

WORK TOGETHER • WORK TOGETHER

### Journalizing entries to write off uncollectible accounts—direct write-off method

Cracker, Inc., uses the direct write-off method of recording uncollectible accounts expense. A general journal and a cash receipts journal are provided in the *Working Papers*. Source documents are abbreviated as follows: memorandum, M; receipt, R. Your instructor will guide you through the following examples.

1. Journalize the following transactions completed during the current year.

   Jan. 10. Wrote off Melinda Sanford's past due account as uncollectible, $261.54. M13.
   Mar. 12. Wrote off Mark Polk's past due account as uncollectible, $45.00. M24.
   Apr. 13. Received cash in full payment of Andrew Leslie's account, previously written off as uncollectible, $67.42. M31 and R158.
   Nov. 15. Received cash in full payment of Melinda Sanford's account, previously written off as uncollectible, $261.54. M84 and R313.

## on your own 7-1

ON YOUR OWN • ON YOUR OWN • ON YOUR

### Journalizing entries to write off uncollectible accounts—direct write-off method

Kelley, Inc., uses the direct write-off method of recording uncollectible accounts expense. A general journal and a cash receipts journal are provided in the *Working Papers*. Source documents are abbreviated as follows: memorandum, M; receipt, R. Work this problem independently.

1. Journalize the following transactions completed during the current year.

   Jan. 20. Wrote off Belinda Rafferty's past due account as uncollectible, $265.48. M15.
   Feb. 15. Wrote off Ervin Bond's past due account as uncollectible, $52.00. M21.
   Apr. 10. Received cash in full payment of Stephanie Byrd's account, previously written off as uncollectible, $178.43. M34 and R89.
   Oct. 5. Received cash in full payment of Belinda Rafferty's account, previously written off as uncollectible, $265.48. M104 and R135.

# 7-2 Allowance Method of Recording Uncollectible Accounts Expense

## ESTIMATING UNCOLLECTIBLE ACCOUNTS EXPENSE

Some businesses use the direct write-off method and record uncollectible accounts expense only when a specific customer account is determined to be uncollectible. However, when the direct write-off method is used, the expense may be recorded in a fiscal period different from the fiscal period of the sale. Uncollectible accounts expense should be recorded in the same fiscal period in which the sales revenue is received. [CONCEPT: Matching Expenses with Revenue]

At the time sales on account are made, a business has no way to know for sure which customer will not pay an amount due. Therefore, the business makes an estimate based on its past history of uncollectible accounts. Crediting

the estimated value of uncollectible accounts to a contra account is called the **allowance method of recording losses from uncollectible accounts**. Two methods are commonly used to estimate uncollectible accounts expense:

1. Percentage of sales method.
2. Percentage of accounts receivable method.

The *percentage of sales method* assumes that a percentage of each sales dollar will become an uncollectible account. The *percentage of accounts receivable method* assumes that a percentage of accounts receivable at the fiscal year-end will become uncollectible. Regardless of the method used, the estimated amount is charged to Uncollectible Accounts Expense.

# Explore Accounting

## Representative Payees for Social Security Benefits

Retirees receive Social Security benefits. Supplemental Security Income (SSI) is received by disabled individuals and children of deceased workers. For those who need assistance managing their money, the Social Security Administration (SSA) allows a friend, relative, or other interested party to be appointed as a representative payee. The representative payee receives the Social Security or SSI payment on behalf of the beneficiary.

Before the SSA allows an individual to serve as a representative payee, it carefully investigates the individual's trustworthiness and ability to carefully manage the beneficiary's benefits. Among a representative payee's duties are:

• Regular contact with the beneficiary to determine how benefits can be used for his or her personal care or well-being.

• Good recordkeeping of how the funds were spent. Periodically, the SSA requires representative payees to complete a Representative Payee Report accounting for the funds received on behalf of the beneficiary.

All monies received from the SSA must be used for the personal care and well-being of the beneficiary. There is no specific list of approved expenditures; however, the SSA requires that the money first be used to ensure that the beneficiary's day-to-day needs for food and shelter are met.

### Instructions

Go to the Web site of the Social Security Administration (www.ssa.gov) and report on an aspect of Social Security relevant to someone you know.

Accounting for Uncollectible Accounts

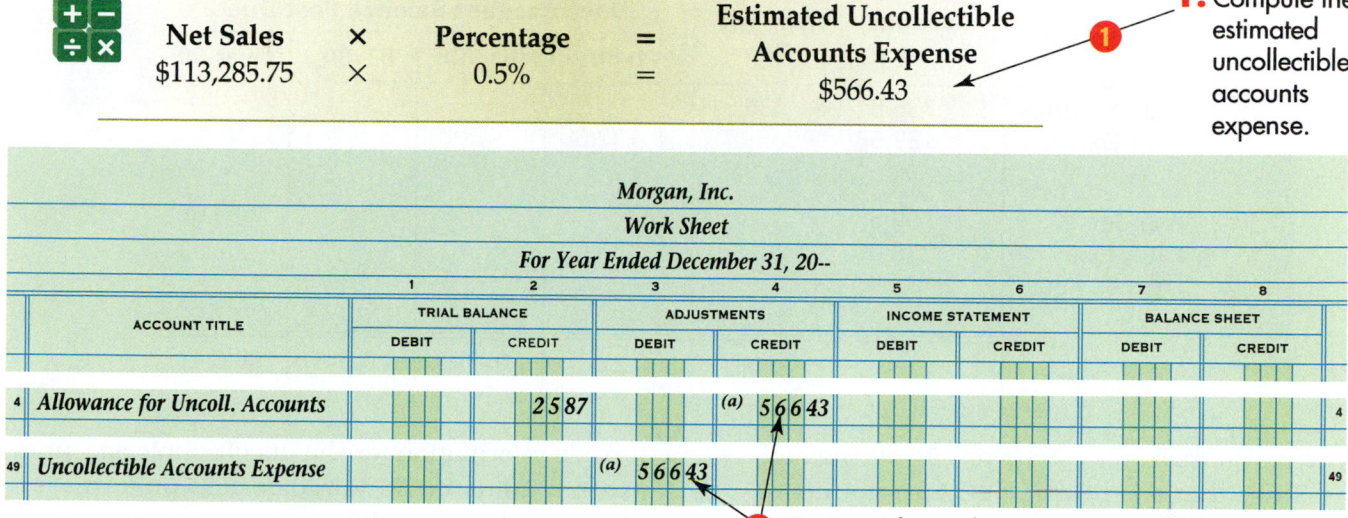

| Net Sales | × | Percentage | = | Estimated Uncollectible Accounts Expense |
|---|---|---|---|---|
| $113,285.75 | × | 0.5% | = | $566.43 |

**1.** Compute the estimated uncollectible accounts expense.

*Morgan, Inc.*

*Work Sheet*

*For Year Ended December 31, 20--*

| | | 1 | 2 | 3 | 4 | 5 | 6 | 7 | 8 | |
|---|---|---|---|---|---|---|---|---|---|---|
| | ACCOUNT TITLE | TRIAL BALANCE | | ADJUSTMENTS | | INCOME STATEMENT | | BALANCE SHEET | | |
| | | DEBIT | CREDIT | DEBIT | CREDIT | DEBIT | CREDIT | DEBIT | CREDIT | |
| 4 | Allowance for Uncoll. Accounts | | 25 87 | | (a) 566 43 | | | | | 4 |
| 49 | Uncollectible Accounts Expense | | | (a) 566 43 | | | | | | 49 |

**2.** Record an adjustment on a worksheet.

Past experience of Morgan, Inc., indicates that approximately 0.5% of its net sales will prove to be uncollectible. On December 31, Morgan estimated that 0.5% of its $113,285.75 net sales, $566.43, eventually will prove to be uncollectible. Morgan does not yet know which customer accounts in the accounts receivable ledger will become uncollectible. Therefore, the amount cannot be recorded directly in accounts receivable.

Before the adjustment is made, Morgan's general ledger shows Allowance for Uncollectible Accounts with a $25.87 credit balance. This balance is what remains of estimates made in previous fiscal periods but not yet specifically identified by customer. The new balance, $592.30, is an estimate of the accounts receivable that will become uncollectible.

At the end of a fiscal period, an adjustment for uncollectible accounts expense is planned on a work sheet as shown above.

The balance of Allowance for Uncollectible Accounts may increase from year to year. A large increase may indicate that an incorrect percentage is being used to calculate the uncollectible amount. When this occurs, a new percentage should be calculated based on actual experience for the past two or three years.

| Uncollectible Accounts Expense | | |
|---|---|---|
| Adj. | 566.43 | |

| Allowance for Uncollectible Accounts | | |
|---|---|---|
| | Bal. | 25.87 |
| | Adj. | 566.43 |
| | (New Bal. | 592.30) |

## STEPS

STEPS • STEPS • STEPS • STEPS

### ESTIMATING UNCOLLECTIBLE ACCOUNTS EXPENSE BY USING THE PERCENTAGE OF SALES METHOD

1. Compute the estimated uncollectible accounts expense by multiplying net sales, *113,285.75*, by the percentage estimate, 0.5%, which totals *566.43*.

2. Record an adjustment on the worksheet, recording a debit to Uncollectible Accounts Expense and a credit to Allowance for Uncollectible Accounts.

### FYI
FOR YOUR INFORMATION

A company can elect to base its estimate of uncollectible accounts expense on a percentage of total sales on account. The calculation of the allowance amount is the same as when total net sales is used.

| Customer | Account Balance | Not Yet Due | Days Account Balance Past Due | | | |
|---|---|---|---|---|---|---|
| | | | 1–30 | 31–60 | 61–90 | Over 90 |
| Louise Asmus | $ 735.51 | $ 735.51 | | | | |
| Mark Darby | 132.58 | | 132.58 | | | |
| ⋮ | ⋮ | ⋮ | ⋮ | ⋮ | ⋮ | ⋮ |
| Ann Gabriel | 99.55 | | | | | 99.55 |
| Kathy Quay | 238.00 | 200.00 | 38.00 | | | |
| Thomas Yost | 133.67 | | | | 133.67 | |
| Totals | $12,891.97 | $8,734.08 | $2,952.90 | $749.54 | $238.45 | $217.00 |
| Percentages | — | 0.1% | 0.2% | 0.4% | 10.0% | 80.0% |

The *percentage of accounts receivable method* assumes that a percentage of the accounts receivable account balance is uncollectible. Therefore, emphasis is placed on estimating a percentage of accounts receivable that will not be collected. An amount that will bring the balance of Allowance for Uncollectible Accounts up to the estimated amount is recorded in that account.

Analyzing accounts receivable according to when they are due is called **aging accounts receivable**. Rosedale, Inc., ages accounts receivable at the end of each fiscal period, as shown above, to provide information for the uncollectible accounts expense adjustment. Rosedale sells on terms of 2/10, n/30. Rosedale expects customers to pay in full within 30 days. If Rosedale has not received cash within 30 days, it mails reminders to the customers. If it has not received cash after 60 days, the company makes special attempts to collect the amount due. If the business has not collected an amount from a customer after 90 days, it may stop selling on account to that customer until collection has been made.

GLOBAL PERSPECTIVE • GLOBAL PERSPECTIVE • GLOBAL PERSPECTI

## global perspective

### Business Introductions

People from other countries may decide from your first meeting whether they want to do business with you. Therefore, it is very important that introductions be handled correctly.

Do not use first names with foreign business associates until invited to do so.

In Japan and India, address a person by adding Mr. or Mrs. to their last name. Use a title such as Dr. if appropriate. Address people from the Middle East as their name appears on their business card. Usually Mr. or Sheik will be used. If they are members of a royal family, use Your Excellency.

Chinese names appear in the reverse order of names in the United States. The family name or "last" name precedes the first name. For example, Mr. Wu Ho is called Mr. Wu because Ho is his given name.

In Latin America, address a person as Señor, Señora, or Señorita, followed by the last name. If they have a title such as doctor, be sure to use it.

**Required**

Research foreign business introductions. Find the appropriate introduction for meeting someone from Germany, South Africa, and England.

## ADJUSTMENT USING PERCENTAGE OF ACCOUNTS RECEIVABLE

| Age Group | Amount | Percentage | Uncollectible | | |
|---|---|---|---|---|---|
| Not Yet Due | $ 8,734.08 | 0.1% | $ 8.73 | | |
| 1–30 Days | 2,952.90 | 0.2% | 5.91 | | |
| 31–60 Days | 749.54 | 0.4% | 3.00 ← ① | **1.** | Compute an estimate for each age group. |
| 61–90 Days | 238.45 | 10.0% | 23.85 | | |
| Over 90 Days | 217.00 | 80.0% | 173.60 | | |
| Totals | $12,891.97 | — | $215.09 ← ② | **2.** | Compute the total estimate. |
| Current Balance of Allowance for Uncollectible Accounts | | | 40.78 | | |
| Estimated Addition to Allowance for Uncollectible Accounts | | | $174.31 ← ③ | **3.** | Compute the addition to the allowance account. |

Based on past records, Rosedale determines that a percentage of each accounts receivable age group will become uncollectible in the future. For example, 0.4% of the accounts receivable overdue 31–60 days will probably become uncollectible. Also, 80.0% of the accounts overdue more than 90 days probably will become uncollectible.

Using these percentages, Rosedale calculates the total amount of estimated uncollectible accounts receivable, as shown above. Of the total accounts receivable on December 31, $12,891.97, the business estimates that $215.09 will prove to be uncollectible in the future.

Rosedale's general ledger shows that Allowance for Uncollectible Accounts has a $40.78 credit balance. This balance is what remains of estimates made in previous fiscal periods but not yet specifically identified by customer. The allowance account is increased by a $174.31 credit. The new balance of the allowance account, $215.09 (previous

balance, $40.78, *plus* adjustment, $174.31), equals the estimate of uncollectible accounts.

**GENERAL LEDGER**

Uncollectible Accounts Expense

| | | | |
|---|---|---|---|
| Adj. | 174.31 | | |

Allowance for Uncollectible Accounts

| | | | |
|---|---|---|---|
| | | Bal. | 40.78 |
| | | Adj. | 174.31 |
| | | *(New Bal.* | *215.09)* |

**FYI** FOR YOUR INFORMATION

An estimate of the amount of uncollectible accounts expense can also be computed by using a single percentage of the total accounts receivable account balance. Although this method is easier to compute, a method using age group information typically yields a better estimate of the expense.

**STEPS** · STEPS · STEPS · STEPS · STEPS · STEPS · STEPS · STEPS · STEPS ·

**ESTIMATING THE BALANCE OF UNCOLLECTIBLE ACCOUNTS EXPENSE USING THE PERCENTAGE OF ACCOUNTS RECEIVABLE METHOD**

① Compute the estimate for each age group. Multiply the amount of each age group by the percentage estimate.

② Compute the total, *$215.09*, of the uncollectible estimates.

③ Subtract the current balance, *40.78*, from the total estimate to determine the addition to the allowance account, *$174.31*. (If the allowance account has a debit balance, add the current balance to the total estimate.)

| | DATE | ACCOUNT TITLE | DOC. NO. | POST. REF. | DEBIT | CREDIT | |
|---|---|---|---|---|---|---|---|
| GENERAL JOURNAL | | | | | | PAGE 1 | |
| 4 | 5 | *Allowance for Uncollectible Accts.* | M71 | | 42 80 | | 4 |
| 5 | | *Accounts Rec./Candace Rhode* | | | | 42 80 | 5 |
| 6 | | | | | | | 6 |

The procedures for writing off an account are the same regardless of the allowance method used to calculate the estimated uncollectible accounts expense. When a specific customer account is thought to be uncollectible, the account balance is written off as shown above. Appliance Center determined that Candace Rhode will probably not pay the amount she owes, $42.80. The balance is no longer *estimated* to be uncollectible; it is *actually determined* to be uncollectible.

**January 5. Wrote off Candace Rhode's past due account as uncollectible, $42.80. Memorandum No. 71.**

After this entry is journalized and posted, Candace Rhode's account has a zero balance, and the account is written off.

Appliance Center did not notify Candace Rhode that it wrote off her account. Although Appliance Center believes the account is probably uncollectible, it may continue its attempts to collect the account. In some cases, customers do subsequently pay accounts that have been written off.

In a previous fiscal period, an adjusting entry was recorded for estimated uncollectible accounts expense resulting in an Allowance for Uncollectible Accounts balance of $1,363.88. This balance is the estimated amount of uncollectible accounts. The $42.80 debit entry in this account removes an amount that is no longer estimated but is actual.

Uncollectible Accounts Expense is not affected when a business writes off an account using the allowance method. The expense is recorded in an adjusting entry at the end of a previous fiscal period.

**GENERAL LEDGER**
**Allowance for Uncollectible Accounts**

| Write off | 42.80 | Bal. | 1,363.88 |
|---|---|---|---|

**Accounts Receivable**

| Bal. | 45,462.79 | Write off | 42.80 |
|---|---|---|---|

**ACCOUNTS RECEIVABLE LEDGER**
**Candace Rhode**

| Bal. | 42.80 | Write off | 42.80 |
|---|---|---|---|
| (New Bal. zero) | | | |

**FYI** FOR YOUR INFORMATION

Businesses extend credit to encourage sales. Restricting customers' ability to purchase on account may have a negative impact on both sales and net income. Managers must carefully balance the goals of maximizing sales while limiting uncollectible accounts expense. Although every business can determine its own credit terms, managers must consider competitors' credit terms. Having more restrictive credit terms than competitors could have a negative impact on sales.

**FYI** FOR YOUR INFORMATION

Proper internal control requires that the custody, recording, and authority for a transaction be segregated. The employee responsible for writing off an account should not also have access to the cash received from customers paying their accounts.

# COLLECTING A WRITTEN-OFF ACCOUNT—ALLOWANCE METHOD

**1.** Reopen the account.

**2.** Record the cash receipt.

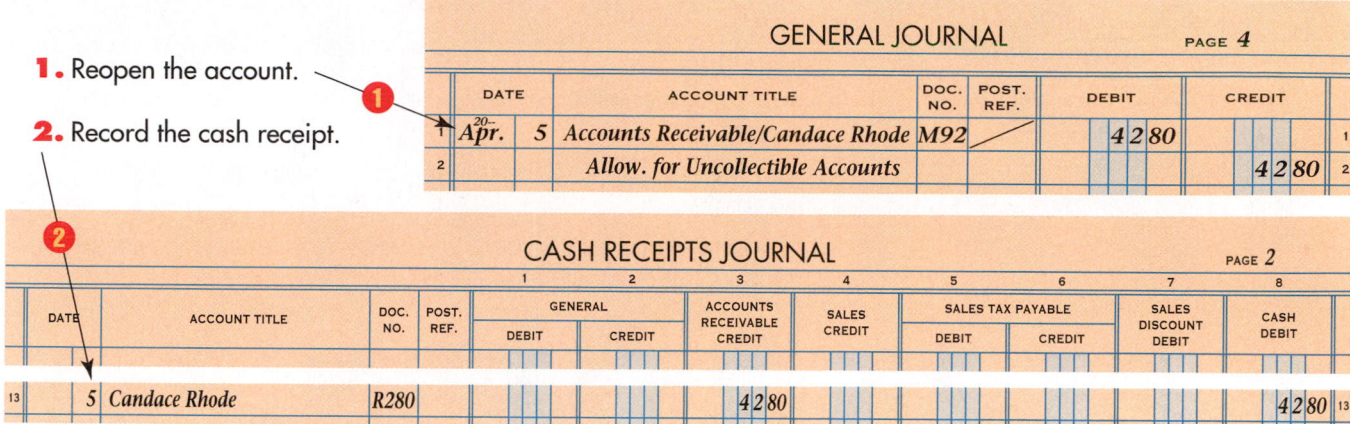

GENERAL JOURNAL — PAGE 4

| DATE | | ACCOUNT TITLE | DOC. NO. | POST. REF. | DEBIT | CREDIT | |
|---|---|---|---|---|---|---|---|
| 20-- Apr. | 5 | Accounts Receivable/Candace Rhode | M92 | | 4 2 80 | | 1 |
| | | Allow. for Uncollectible Accounts | | | | 4 2 80 | 2 |

CASH RECEIPTS JOURNAL — PAGE 2

| | DATE | ACCOUNT TITLE | DOC. NO. | POST. REF. | GENERAL DEBIT | GENERAL CREDIT | ACCOUNTS RECEIVABLE CREDIT | SALES CREDIT | SALES TAX PAYABLE DEBIT | SALES TAX PAYABLE CREDIT | SALES DISCOUNT DEBIT | CASH DEBIT | |
|---|---|---|---|---|---|---|---|---|---|---|---|---|---|
| 13 | 5 | Candace Rhode | R280 | | | | 4 2 80 | | | | | 4 2 80 | 13 |

Later in the year, Appliance Center received a check in full payment of the amount owed by Candace Rhode.

---

*April 5. Received cash in full payment of Candace Rhode's account, previously written off as uncollectible, $42.80. Memorandum No. 92 and Receipt No. 280.*

---

Appliance Center's records must show a complete history of Ms. Rhode's credit dealings. The collection of a written-off account receivable involves two journal entries as shown above.

A general journal entry is recorded to reopen the customer account. The $42.80 debit increases Accounts Receivable and Candace Rhode's account in the accounts receivable ledger. The account balances now appear as they were before Ms. Rhode's account was written off as uncollectible.

The cash received from Ms. Rhode is then recorded in the cash receipts journal. The $42.80 credit decreases Accounts Receivable and Ms. Rhode's account in the accounts receivable ledger.

### GENERAL LEDGER
#### Cash
| | | | |
|---|---|---|---|
| Received | 42.80 | | |

#### Accounts Receivable
| | | | |
|---|---|---|---|
| Bal. | 45,462.79 | Write off | 42.80 |
| Reopen | 42.80 | Recieved | 42.80 |

#### Allowance for Uncollectible Accounts
| | | | |
|---|---|---|---|
| Write off | 42.80 | Bal. | 1,363.88 |
| | | Reopen | 42.80 |

### ACCOUNTS RECEIVABLE LEDGER
#### Candace Rhode
| | | | |
|---|---|---|---|
| Bal. | 42.80 | Write off | 42.80 |
| Reopen | 42.80 | Received | 42.80 |
| (New Bal. zero) | | | |

## STEPS

STEPS • STEPS • STEPS • STEPS • STEPS • STEPS • STEPS • STEPS • STEPS • STEPS

### JOURNALIZING THE COLLECTION OF A WRITTEN-OFF ACCOUNT—ALLOWANCE METHOD

**1** Reopen the account by debiting Accounts Receivable and crediting Allowance for Doubtful Accounts for the amount of the receipt, *42.80*.

**2** Record an entry in the cash receipts journal to debit Cash and credit Accounts Receivable for the amount of the receipt, *42.80*.

{ **REMEMBER** Entries for the collection of a written-off account present evidence of the customer's credit history. Managers can use this information to make informed decisions about extending credit to the customer in the future. }

---

Allowance Method of Recording Uncollectible Accounts Expense

## terms review

TERMS REVIEW • TERMS

allowance method of recording
  losses from uncollectible
  accounts
aging accounts receivable

## audit your understanding

1. What are the two methods commonly used to estimate uncollectible accounts expense?
2. What is the formula for estimating uncollectible accounts expense based on net sales?
3. How is the addition to allowance for uncollectible accounts calculated using the percentage of accounts receivable method?

## work together 7-2

**Estimating amount of uncollectible accounts expense; journalizing the adjusting entry**

General journal pages are provided in the *Working Papers*. Your instructor will guide you through the following independent examples.

1. Lynum, Inc., had net sales of $245,321.09 during the current year. It estimates that the amount of uncollectible accounts expense is equal to 0.5% of net sales. Journalize the adjusting entry for uncollectible accounts expense on December 31 of the current year.

2. The aging of accounts receivable for Kersten, Inc., as of December 31 of the current year and estimated percentages of uncollectible accounts by age group are presented in the Working Papers. Calculate the estimated balance of Allowance for Uncollectible Accounts. Then journalize the adjusting entry for uncollectible accounts expense. The balance of Allowance for Uncollectible Accounts on December 31 before adjusting entries are recorded is $63.24.

## on your own 7-2

**Estimating amount of uncollectible accounts expense; journalizing the adjusting entry**

General journal pages are provided in the *Working Papers*. Work this problem independently.

1. Hillcrest, Inc., had net sales of $685,409.50 during the current year. It estimates that the amount of uncollectible accounts expense is equal to 0.8% of net sales. Journalize the adjusting entry for uncollectible accounts expense on December 31 of the current year.

2. The aging of accounts receivable for Malloy, Inc., as of December 31 of the current year and estimated percentages of uncollectible accounts by age group are presented in the *Working Papers*. Calculate the estimated balance of Allowance for Uncollectible Accounts. Then journalize the adjusting entry for uncollectible accounts expense. The balance of Allowance for Uncollectible Accounts on December 31 before adjusting entries are recorded is $391.75.

# 7-3 Accounts Receivable Turnover Ratio

## CALCULATING THE ACCOUNTS RECEIVABLE TURNOVER RATIO

|  | Total Accounts Receivable | − | Allowance for Uncollectible Accounts | = | Book Value of Accounts Receivable |  |  |
|---|---|---|---|---|---|---|---|
| Beginning | $50,329.14 | − | $1,416.83 | = | $48,912.31 |  |  |
| Ending | $45,462.79 | − | $1,363.88 | = | $44,098.91 | ◄ ❶ | **1.** Compute the beginning and ending book value. |

| (Beginning Book Value of Accounts Receivable | + | Ending Book Value of Accounts Receivable) | ÷ | 2 | = | Average Book Value of Accounts Receivable |  |  |
|---|---|---|---|---|---|---|---|---|
| ($48,912.31 | + | $44,098.91) | ÷ | 2 | = | $46,505.61 | ◄ ❷ | **2.** Compute the average book value. |

| Net Sales on Account | ÷ | Average Book Value of Accounts Receivable | = | Accounts Receivable Turnover Ratio |  |  |
|---|---|---|---|---|---|---|
| $330,312.85 | ÷ | $46,505.61 | = | 7.1 times | ◄ ❸ | **3.** Compute the accounts receivable turnover. |

| Days in Year | ÷ | Accounts Receivable Turnover Ratio | = | Average Number of Days for Payment |  |  |
|---|---|---|---|---|---|---|
| 365 | ÷ | 7.1 | = | 51 | ◄ ❹ | **4.** Compute the average number of days for payment. |

Appliance Center needs cash to purchase additional merchandise to sell to customers and to pay for operating expenses. If it does not collect amounts due from customers promptly, too large a share of the assets of the business will be in accounts receivable and not immediately usable. All businesses selling on account need prompt collection from credit customers.

Appliance Center analyzes how frequently customers make payments on account. If customers are not paying promptly, the business will adopt new procedures to speed collections. One way to analyze the collection efficiency of a business is to calculate the accounts receivable turnover ratio. The number of times the average amount of accounts receivable is collected during a specified period is called the **accounts receivable turnover ratio**. The accounts receivable turnover

ratio is calculated by dividing net sales on account by the average book value of accounts receivable. Businesses may calculate this ratio monthly, quarterly, or yearly.

The difference between the balance of Accounts Receivable and its contra account, Allowance for Uncollectible Accounts, is called the **book value of accounts receivable**.

An accounts receivable turnover ratio of 7.1 times means that Appliance Center turns over (or collects) its average accounts receivable about seven times a year. The number of days in a year, 365, divided by the accounts receivable turnover ratio, 7.1, yields the average number of days required to pay. Appliance Center's customers are taking an average of 51 days to pay their accounts in full.

## CALCULATING THE ACCOUNTS RECEIVABLE TURNOVER RATIO AND THE AVERAGE NUMBER OF DAYS FOR PAYMENT

**1** Compute the beginning and ending book value of accounts receivable. The book values are computed by subtracting the allowance for doubtful accounts from the total accounts receivable.

**2** Compute the average book value of accounts receivable, $46,505.61, by adding the beginning book value, $48,912.31, to the ending book value, $44,098.91, and dividing the total by 2.

**3** Compute the accounts receivable turnover ratio by dividing net sales on account, $330,312.85, by the average book value of accounts receivable, $46,505.61.

**4** Compute the average number of days for payment, 51, by dividing 365 days by the accounts receivable turnover ratio, 7.1.

## ANALYZING ACCOUNTS RECEIVABLE TURNOVER RATIOS

### Appliance Center, Inc.—Accounts Receivable Turnover Ratios

| Year | 20X1 | 20X2 | 20X3 | 20X4 | 20X5 | 20X6 | 20X7 |
|---|---|---|---|---|---|---|---|
| Ratio | 6.2 | 6.4 | 6.0 | 6.4 | 6.8 | 6.8 | 7.1 |
| Days for Payment | 59 | 57 | 61 | 57 | 54 | 54 | 51 |

Most of Appliance Center's customers do pay their accounts, but many customers take much longer than the expected 30 days.

From 20X1 through 20X7, the accounts receivable turnover ratio rose from 6.2 to 7.1 times as shown above. In 20X1, customers took an average of 59 days to pay their accounts in full. In 20X7, customers took an average of 51 days to pay their accounts in full, 8 fewer days than in 20X1.

With the exception of 20X3, the turnover ratio has been steadily increasing. On the average, customers have been paying their accounts in full in a fewer number of days each year. Appliance Center wants this favorable trend to continue.

Appliance Center needs to plan additional ways to encourage customers to pay their accounts in less time. With n/30 credit terms, the goal should be to have a turnover ratio of 12.0 times (365 days/12.0 accounts receivable turnover ratio = 30 average number of days for payment).

The business might take several steps to create a more favorable accounts receivable turnover ratio.

1. Send statements of account to customers more often, including a request for prompt payment.
2. Not sell on account to any customer who has an account for which payment is overdue more than 30 days.
3. Encourage more cash sales and fewer sales on account.
4. Conduct a more rigorous credit check on new customers before extending credit to them.

Sometimes the demand for quicker payment can result in a loss of business. Some customers might start buying from competitors. A business must weigh a change in credit policies against the effect the change will have on total sales.

**FYI** FOR YOUR INFORMATION

A business that does not record sales on account separately from cash sales uses total net sales to compute the accounts receivable turnover ratio.

Accounting for Uncollectible Accounts

TERMS REVIEW • TERMS

## • terms review

accounts receivable turnover ratio
book value of accounts receivable

AUDIT YOUR

## • audit your understanding

1. What is the formula for calculating the accounts receivable turnover ratio?

2. How would you interpret the situation of a business that desires an accounts receivable turnover ratio of 12.0 times but actually has a turnover ratio of 6.0 times?

3. How can extremely restrictive credit terms have a negative impact on a business?

WORK TOGETHER • WORK TOGETHER

## • work together 7-3

### Calculating accounts receivable turnover ratios

Millikin Industries offers its customers n/30 credit terms. The turnover ratio for the prior year was 8.7. The following account balances were obtained from Millikin Industries' records for the current year. Your instructor will guide you through the following examples.

| Account | January 1 | December 31 |
|---------|-----------|-------------|
| Accounts Receivable | $264,483.18 | $275,486.58 |
| Allowance for Uncollectible Accounts | $8,234.22 | $10,723.36 |
| Net Sales on Account | | $2,396,656.10 |

1. Calculate the accounts receivable turnover ratio for the current year.

2. Calculate the average number of days for payment.

3. Is Millikin Industries effective in collecting its accounts receivable?

ON YOUR OWN • ON YOUR OWN • ON YOUR OWN

## • on your own 7-3

### Calculating accounts receivable turnover ratios

Stokes Building Supply offers its customers n/45 credit terms. The turnover ratio for the prior year was 5.8. The following account balances were obtained from the records of Stokes Building Supply for the current year. Work independently to complete the following problem.

| Account | January 1 | December 31 |
|---------|-----------|-------------|
| Accounts Receivable | $163,874.05 | $186,383.48 |
| Allowance for Uncollectible Accounts | $6,544.83 | $7,745.86 |
| Net Sales on Account | | $872,895.94 |

1. Calculate the accounts receivable turnover ratio for the current year.

2. Calculate the average number of days for payment.

3. Is Stokes Building Supply effective in collecting its accounts receivable?

Xtra!
Review
accountingxtra.swlearning.com

**After completing this chapter, you can**

1. Define accounting terms related to uncollectible accounts.

2. Identify accounting concepts and practices related to uncollectible accounts.

3. Calculate and record estimated uncollectible accounts expense using the direct write-off method.

4. Calculate and record estimated uncollectible accounts expense using the allowance method.

5. Calculate and analyze accounts receivable turnover ratios.

# Explore Accounting

EXPLORE ACCOUNTING · EXPLORE ACCOUNTING · EXPLORE ACCO

## Credit Scoring Systems

To help reduce the amount of uncollectible accounts, a business should evaluate the creditworthiness of potential customers before granting credit. The traditional credit evaluation involves a credit analyst manually evaluating financial information to determine if the customer has the financial resources to pay the account.

The benefit of reducing bad debt expenses should exceed the costs of performing credit evaluations. A business must consider the cost, in both time and money, involved in credit evaluations. A business should not, for example, spend $70,000 in salaries and other expenses to evaluate credit if the business can only reduce its annual bad debt expense by $50,000. In addition, customers may be unwilling to wait for a business to perform a traditional credit evaluation, favoring to purchase goods from another business.

A more cost-effective method for evaluating creditworthiness is available. A statistical method used to predict a customer's willingness to pay its account on a timely basis is called a credit scoring system. In addition to considering financial information, a credit scoring system considers other factors that have been shown to be

predictors of creditworthiness, such as: frequency of delinquent accounts, length of credit history, types of credit, available credit, frequency of credit applications, number of credit inquiries, industry comparative data, number of employees, management problems, and prior bankruptcies.

A score is assigned to each factor. The higher the score, the more creditworthy the customer. An effective credit scoring system will utilize information obtained from a credit application or available from public sources. A company can maintain its own system or use systems maintained by independent credit rating companies.

Credit scoring systems are optimally used for routine credit decisions that must be made quickly on relatively low-dollar sales on account. For sales on account that are relatively large, the credit decisions should involve the human decision of the traditional credit evaluation.

Regardless of how credit is evaluated, a company must assure that its decisions are consistent. Federal laws exist to assure that individuals and businesses have equal access to credit.

**Required:**
Research the Fair Credit Reporting Act. How does this act protect the rights of the consumer?

# 7-1 APPLICATION PROBLEM  AUTOMATED ACCOUNTING

## Journalizing entries to write off uncollectible accounts—direct write-off method

Stallworth uses the direct write-off method of recording uncollectible accounts expense.

**Instructions:**

Journalize the following transactions completed during the current year. Use page 3 of a general journal and page 4 of a cash receipts journal. Source documents are abbreviated as follows: memorandum, M; receipt, R.

**Transactions:**

| | | |
|---|---|---|
| Feb. | 16. | Wrote off William Rose's past due account as uncollectible, $215.64. M18. |
| Mar. | 23. | Received cash in full payment of Emma Peden's account, previously written off as uncollectible, $175.00. M43 and R215. |
| May | 7. | Wrote off Tom Ming's past due account as uncollectible, $187.32. M61. |
| Aug. | 10. | Received cash in full payment of William Rose's account, previously written off as uncollectible, $215.64. M78 and R341. |

# 7-2 APPLICATION PROBLEM

## Estimating amount of uncollectible accounts expense by using a percentage of net sales—allowance method; journalizing the adjusting entry

Jacobs Market had net sales of $863,245.32 during the current year. The corporation estimates that the amount of uncollectible accounts expense is equal to 0.6% of net sales.

**Instructions:**

Journalize the adjusting entry for uncollectible accounts expense on December 31 of the current year. Use page 24 of a general journal.

# 7-3 APPLICATION PROBLEM

## Estimating the balance of Allowance for Uncollectible Accounts by aging accounts receivable—allowance method; journalizing the adjusting entry

The following information has been taken from the records of Rosetta Company as of December 31 of the current year.

| Customer | Account Balance | Not Yet Due | 1–30 | 31–60 | 61–90 | Over 90 |
|---|---|---|---|---|---|---|
| | | | | Days Account Balance Past Due | | |
| Acorn & Karr | $623.74 | | | $623.74 | | |
| Base Industries | 723.22 | $723.22 | | | | |
| . | . | . | . | . | . | . |
| . | . | . | . | . | . | . |
| . | . | . | . | . | . | . |
| Wright Stores | 612.67 | | | | | 612.67 |
| Yui Co. | 1,723.33 | 1,048.99 | $674.34 | | | |
| Totals | $89,363.45 | $44,434.51 | $25,623.64 | $10,535.20 | $5,235.40 | $3,534.70 |
| Percentages | — | 0.2% | 0.5% | 1.0% | 5.0% | 60.0% |

**Instructions:**

1. Calculate the estimated balance of Allowance for Uncollectible Accounts.
2. Journalize the adjusting entry for uncollectible accounts expense on December 31 of the current year. Use page 12 of a general journal. The balance of Allowance for Uncollectible Accounts on December 31 before adjusting entries are recorded is $589.63.

## 7-4 APPLICATION PROBLEM  AUTOMATED ACCOUNTING   PEACHTREE

**Journalizing entries to write off uncollectible accounts and collect written-off accounts—allowance method**

McCafferty, Inc., uses the allowance method of recording uncollectible accounts expense.

**Instructions:**
Journalize the following transactions completed during the current year. Use page 3 of a general journal and page 8 of a cash receipts journal. Source documents are abbreviated as follows: memorandum, M; receipt, R.

**Transactions:**
Feb. 14. Wrote off Peggy King's past due account as uncollectible, $357.00. M16.
Apr. 25. Wrote off Mel Kober's past due account as uncollectible, $84.98. M34.
May 12. Received cash in full payment of Carolyn Kelly's account, previously written off as uncollectible, $74.00. M43 and R264.
Aug. 2. Wrote off Lynn Hartman's past due account as uncollectible, $74.93. M71.
Oct. 6. Received cash in full payment of Peggy King's account, previously written off as uncollectible, $357.00. M92 and R484.

## 7-5 APPLICATION PROBLEM

**Calculating the accounts receivable turnover ratio**

Fleming Company offers its customers n/30 credit terms. The turnover ratio for the prior year was 4.5. The following account balances were obtained from the records of Fleming Company for the current year:

| Account | January 1 | December 31 |
| --- | --- | --- |
| Accounts Receivable | $584,348.48 | $604,285.25 |
| Allowance for Doubtful Accounts | $20,153.35 | $23,485.62 |
| Net Sales | | $3,848,348.27 |

**Instructions:**
1. Calculate the accounts receivable turnover ratio for the current year.
2. Calculate the average number of days for payment.
3. Is Fleming Company effective in collecting its accounts receivable?

## 7-6 APPLICATION PROBLEM

**Accounts receivable transactions using the allowance method**

Cofield Engineering uses the allowance method of recording uncollectible accounts expense.

**Instructions:**
Journalize the following transactions completed during the current year. Use page 4 of a general journal and page 10 of a cash receipts journal. Source documents are abbreviated as follows: memorandum, M; receipt, R.

**Transactions:**
Mar. 23. A phone call to Larry Wade, president of Wade Supply, confirmed that the company is intending to file bankruptcy. Mr. Wade stated that no money would likely be available to pay its creditors. The Wade account of $4,000.00 is over 180 days past due. M32.

Apr.   4.   Last year you wrote off the $3,200.00 balance of Creative Decor. The account was over 180 days past due and collection seemed doubtful. Today you received a $3,200.00 check from Creative Decor along with a letter stating that the company had just received a large contract and they wished to reestablish a credit account with your company. M45 and R156.

May   14.   Received a reply to a collection request letter sent to Raymond Fisher. Mr. Fisher refuses to pay the remaining $75.00 of his bill, stating that the original bill was larger than the agreed-upon price. Although your records clearly indicate the $75.00 was an appropriate charge, your manager believes that further efforts to collect this account are pointless. M54.

Oct.   10.   Today you received an $800.00 check from Wade Supply. In the enclosed letter, Mr. Wade stated that the bankruptcy court ordered the company to pay 20 cents for every dollar owed to its creditors. Thus, the $800.00 is the only amount that Wade Supply would ever be able to pay of its original account balance of $4,000.00. M72 and R348.

Nov.   21.   A letter sent to Mary Crawford was returned in the mail, with a U.S. Postal Service stamp stating that the party no longer lives at the address and has left no forwarding address. Ms. Crawford owed $600.00 from an invoice dated January 24. M89.

## 7-7  MASTERY PROBLEM  `AUTOMATED ACCOUNTING`

### Journalizing entries for uncollectible accounts—allowance method; calculating and journalizing the adjusting entry for uncollectible accounts expense

Northern, Inc., uses the allowance method of recording uncollectible accounts expense. The following information was obtained from Northern's records for the current year.

| Account | January 1 | December 31 |
|---|---|---|
| Accounts Receivable | $49,576.17 | $62,791.30 |
| Allowance for Doubtful Accounts | $1,463.89 | $3,813.98 |
| Net Sales on Account | | $349,562.10 |

**Transactions:**

Jan.   9.   Wrote off Jane Martinez's past due account as uncollectible, $634.65. M20.

Mar.   4.   Wrote off Jason Young's past due account as uncollectible, $782.50. M29.

Mar.   28.   Received cash in full payment of Jane Martinez's account, previously written off as uncollectible, $634.65. M40 and R24.

June   20.   Wrote off Allison Aanerud's past due account as uncollectible, $617.16. M58.

Oct.   7.   Wrote off Meredith Darst's past due account as uncollectible, $808.15. M74.

Dec.   11.   Received cash in full payment of Jason Young's account, previously written off as uncollectible, $782.50. M82 and R92.

**Instructions:**

1. Journalize the transactions above that were completed during the current year. Use page 1 of a general journal and page 1 of a cash receipts journal. Source documents are abbreviated as follows: memorandum, M; receipt, R.

2. Journalize the adjusting entry for uncollectible accounts expense on December 31 of the current year. Northern estimates that the amount of uncollectible accounts expense is equal to 1% of its net sales of $377,539.58.

3. Compute the accounts receivable turnover and average days for payment.

## 7-8 CHALLENGE PROBLEM

**Estimating and journalizing uncollectible accounts expense by aging accounts receivable—allowance method; calculating and journalizing the adjusting entry for uncollectible accounts expense**

A complete list of the accounts receivable of Wind Refrigeration follows:

| Account | Amount | Invoice Date |
|---|---|---|
| Atkins Co. | $2,523.64 | May 16 |
| Bankhead Supply | 2,435.75 | December 13 |
| Coffman Distributing | 943.74 | November 30 |
| Fleet Trucking | 2,643.23 | December 23 |
| Griffin Industries | 7,896.54 | October 16 |
| Miskelly & Sons | 2,754.48 | November 15 |
| Oswalt, Inc. | 8,723.54 | December 4 |
| Rice Shipping Co. | 4,363.27 | August 25 |
| Smith Stores | 1,324.76 | September 20 |

**Instructions:**

1. Age the accounts receivable by determining the age group for each invoice and totaling the invoice amounts in each age group category.
2. Calculate the estimated balance of Allowance for Uncollectible Accounts using the following percentages: not yet due, 0.3%; 1–30 days past due, 1.0%; 31–60 days, 4.0%; 61–90 days, 20%; and over 90 days, 60%.
3. Journalize the adjusting entry for uncollectible accounts expense on December 31 of the current year. Use page 12 of a general journal. The Allowance for Uncollectible Accounts has a debit balance of $692.16 on December 31 of the current year before adjusting entries are recorded.

©GETTY IMAGES/PHOTODISC

accountingxtra.swlearning.com

## applied communication

Stegall Company had experienced no growth in sales or net income for several years. At your suggestion, the company changed its credit terms on January 1, 20X4, from n/60 to 2/10, n/30. In addition, the company loosened its requirements to extend credit to new customers. All sales are on account. Selected information, in thousands of dollars, taken from the December 31 financial statements for the past four years follows.

| Item | 20X1 | 20X2 | 20X3 | 20X4 |
|---|---|---|---|---|
| Accts. Receivable | $496 | $492 | $514 | $384 |
| Allow. for Doubtful Accts. | 17 | 17 | 18 | 42 |
| Net Sales | 2,653 | 2,676 | 2,689 | 2,945 |
| Uncollectible Accts. Exp. | 26 | 26 | 27 | 58 |
| Net Income | 253 | 259 | 262 | 284 |

Alice Shirley, a member of the board of directors, has suggested that the company return to its previous credit policies, citing the significant rise in the uncollectible accounts expense.

**Required:**

Write a memorandum to Alice supporting the new credit policy.

## case for critical thinking

Westermen, Inc., sells merchandise for cash and on account. The business uses the direct write-off method of recording uncollectible accounts expense. For the past two years, the amount of uncollectible accounts written off each year has been about 1.0% of the net sales. Net sales last year totaled $416,228.00. An accountant recommends that the business change to the allowance method of recording uncollectible accounts expense. However, management is reluctant to accept the recommendation because the business has used the direct write-off method for a long time and personnel fully understand it. What do you recommend and why?

## SCANS workplace competency

**Systems Competency: Improving and Designing Systems**

**Concept:** Employers value workers who make suggestions to modify existing systems to improve products or services, as well as develop new or alternative systems in order to enhance company performance.

**Application:** As the manager of accounts receivable, you have been directed to prepare a chapter for the new training manual. Your chapter must describe and illustrate the procedures for recording an uncollectible account using the allowance method, as well as collecting a past due account. In addition to your written explanation, design a flowchart that illustrates your system of handling uncollectibles.

# • graphing workshop

The Accounts Receivable Turnover and the Days for Payment for Clifford Company are given below in both table and graph formats.

| Ratio | 1 | 2 | 3 | 4 | 5 | 6 | 7 |
| --- | --- | --- | --- | --- | --- | --- | --- |
| A/R Turnover | 5.0 | 5.4 | 5.9 | 6.8 | 6.7 | 7.2 | 7.5 |
| Days for payment | 73.0 | 67.6 | 61.9 | 53.7 | 54.5 | 50.7 | 48.7 |

**Instructions:** Analyze the charts to answer the following questions.

1. What general statement can you make about the relationship between the Accounts Receivable Turnover and the Days for Payment?

2. Is the trend for Clifford Company a good or a bad trend?

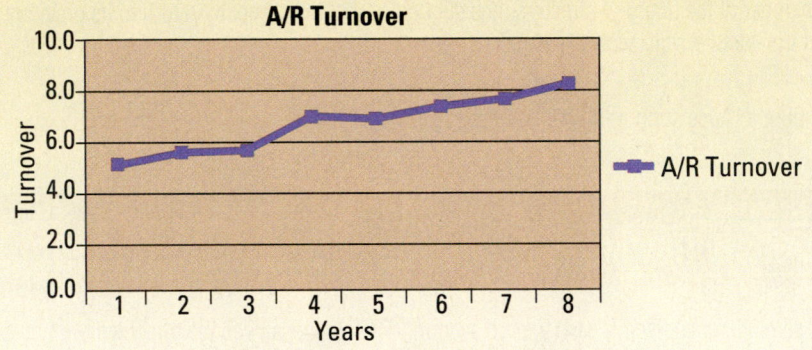

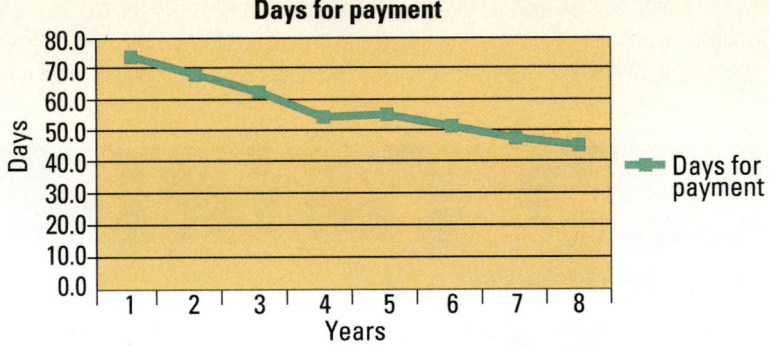

## • analyzing Costco's financial statements

As shown in the financial statements in Appendix B of this textbook, Costco's balance sheet lists "Receivables, net" under the heading "Current Assets." This amount represents Costco's receivables after the allowance for doubtful accounts estimate has been deducted. Gross accounts receivable must be calculated. Additional information necessary for the calculation is usually included in Note No. 1, "Summary of Significant Accounting Policies."

**Instructions:**

1. Using Note 1, beginning on page Appendix B-9, locate the paragraph titled "Receivables, net." This paragraph lists the allowance for doubtful account balances for August 31, 2003, and September 1, 2002. Use this information and Costco's Balance Sheet to calculate the gross accounts receivable for August 31, 2003, and September 1, 2002.

2. How have the gross receivables and the allowance for doubtful accounts changed from 2002 to 2003? What does this say about Costco's expectations for collecting its receivables?

# Automated Accounting

## Automated Entries for Uncollectible Accounts and Write-offs

### Recording Uncollectible Accounts

Using the direct write-off method, Uncollectible Accounts Expense and Accounts Receivable are used to write off an uncollectible account.

Using the allowance method, an allowance for uncollectible accounts is maintained. Manual calculations are required to determine the amount of the allowance to be recorded as an adjusting entry at the end of the accounting period. The process is described in Chapter 7.

When an account is determined to be uncollectible, it is written off using the general ledger accounts: Allowance for Uncollectible Accounts and Accounts Receivable. In *Automated Accounting 8.0*, the journal entries should be entered after the amounts have been calculated.

### Reinstating a Written-off Account

Occasionally a customer will make payment on an account that has been written off. When this occurs, the account receivable is reinstated and the payment is recorded as described in the chapter.

### Other Computerized Accounting Systems

The automated accounting systems used in many businesses today will calculate the amounts that should be posted and will also do the posting based on how the system is set up to handle uncollectible accounts expenses and write-offs. In these cases, it is important to verify that the amounts posted to the accounts are accurate.

### AUTOMATING APPLICATION PROBLEM 7-1

**Instructions:**

1. Load *Automated Accounting 8.0* or higher software.

2. Select database A07-1 (Advanced Course Application Problem 7-1) from the accounting template disk.

3. Select File from the menu bar and choose the Save As menu command. Key the path to the drive and directory that contain your data files. Save the database with a filename of XXX071 (where XXX are your initials).

4. Read the Problem Instruction screen by clicking the Browser toolbar button.

5. Key the data listed in the problem.

6. Exit the Automated Accounting software.

### AUTOMATING APPLICATION PROBLEM 7-4

**Instructions:**

1. Load *Automated Accounting 8.0* or higher software.

2. Select database A07-4 (Advanced Course Application Problem 7-4) from the accounting template disk.

3. Select File from the menu bar and choose the Save As menu command. Key the path to the drive and directory that contain your data files. Save the database with a filename of XXX074 (where XXX are your initials).

4. Read the Problem Instruction screen by clicking the Browser toolbar button.

5. Key the data listed in the problem.

6. Exit the Automated Accounting software.

### AUTOMATING MASTERY PROBLEM 7-7

**Instructions:**

1. Load *Automated Accounting 8.0* or higher software.

2. Select database A07-7 (Advanced Course Mastery Problem 7-7) from the accounting template disk.

3. Select File from the menu bar and choose the Save As menu command. Key the path to the drive and directory that contain your data files. Save the database with a filename of XXX077 (where XXX are your initials).

4. Read the Problem Instruction screen by clicking the Browser toolbar button.

5. Key the data listed in the problem.

6. Exit the Automated Accounting software

# CHAPTER 8

# Accounting for Plant Assets

*After studying Chapter 8, you will be able to:*

1. Define accounting terms related to plant assets and depreciation.

2. Identify accounting concepts and practices related to accounting for plant assets and depreciation.

3. Journalize entries for buying plant assets.

4. Calculate and record property tax expense.

5. Calculate and record depreciation expense for a plant asset using straight-line depreciation.

6. Journalize entries for disposing of plant assets.

7. Calculate depreciation expense using other methods.

- plant asset record
- real property
- personal property
- assessed value
- straight-line method of depreciation

- book value of a plant asset
- declining-balance method of depreciation
- sum-of-the-years' digits method of depreciation

- production-unit method of depreciation
- Modified Accelerated Cost Recovery System
- depletion

Point Your Browser
accountingxtra.swlearning.com

## • Sysco

COURTESY OF SYSCO CORPORATION

### SYSCO: TRANSPORTING GOODS ACROSS THE COUNTRY

Assume you just opened a restaurant. You have already purchased the equipment necessary to prepare meals and the dishes and silverware needed to serve meals and beverages. It's time to order supplies and food inventories. Where do you turn? Do you have to use a different supplier for each item you need? Isn't there a more efficient way?

Sysco Corporation strives to efficiently move food from "farm to fork." They do this by purchasing food and restaurant supplies from a variety of manufacturers and warehousing this inventory in over 145 locations across the country. They then distribute the food and supplies to restaurants, hospitals, schools, and other businesses involved in food service.

In order to accomplish this efficiently, Sysco has equipment to help move the inventory into and out of the warehouses. It also has trucks to deliver the goods to its customers. In a recent annual report, Sysco listed its cost of equipment at over $1.8 billion dollars and stated that the useful life of this equipment ranged from 3 to 20 years. This equipment is depreciated each year, which causes Depreciation Expense to lower net income on Sysco's income statement.

### Critical Thinking

1. What effect would increasing the estimated useful life of an asset have on net income for a company like Sysco?
2. What information would you need to help identify the useful life of a piece of equipment?

Xtra!
Today
accountingxtra.swlearning.com

Source: www.sysco.com

## internet activity

### OCCUPATIONAL OUTLOOK HANDBOOK

Go to the homepage of the U.S. Department of Labor's *Occupational Outlook Handbook* (www.stats.bls.gov/oco). Read the directions on how to search the *Handbook*. Pick an occupation connected to accounting or bookkeeping.

### Instructions

Summarize the following information for the occupation chosen:

1. Working conditions
2. Minimum training required
3. Job outlook
4. Range of earnings
5. Related occupations

## 8-1 Buying Plant Assets

A business owns a variety of assets, all of which are used to help it earn a profit. Some assets such as cash, accounts receivable, and supplies are exchanged for cash or consumed within a year. Cash and other assets expected to be exchanged for cash or consumed within a year are known as current assets. Other assets, such as land, buildings, and equipment, are expected to help the business earn a profit for more than one year. Assets that will be used for a number of years in the operation of a business are known as plant assets. Plant assets are sometimes referred to as fixed assets or long-term assets.

Since businesses expect to remain in business indefinitely, the accounting records must be kept up-to-date as plant assets are bought and used. [CONCEPT: Going Concern]

The going concern concept states that financial statements are prepared with the expectation that a business will remain in operation indefinitely. A business bought store equipment for $30,000.00. The store equipment is expected to last 10 years. Yearly depreciation, therefore, is recorded and

reported based on the expected life of the equipment. After six years of the expected 10-year life, the equipment's book value (cost less accumulated depreciation) is $13,200.00. If the business ended operations and the equipment had to be sold, the amount received may be less than the $13,200.00. However, accounting records are maintained with the expectation that the business will remain in operation indefinitely and that the cost will be allocated over the useful life of the equipment.

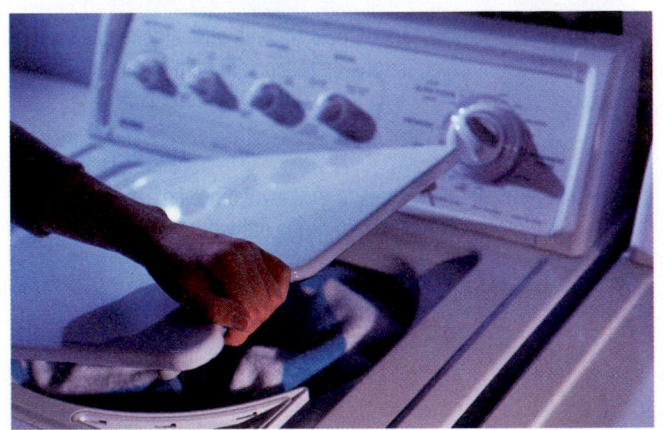

©GETTY IMAGES/PHOTODISC

## making ethical decisions

### The Land of Opportunity?

As the director of corporate development, Kelly Maben is finishing the final touches on a proposal to locate a resort in Destin, Florida. Confident the proposal will be approved, Kelly is considering the purchase of a family-owned restaurant across the street from the proposed building site.

**Instructions**

Obtain the *Code of Business Conduct and Ethics* of Hilton Hotels Corporation. Using this information and the ethical model, provide Kelly with guidance on her proposed restaurant purchase. Is Kelly violating her company's code of conduct or simply seizing an opportunity?

Accounting for Plant Assets

# PLANT ASSET RECORD

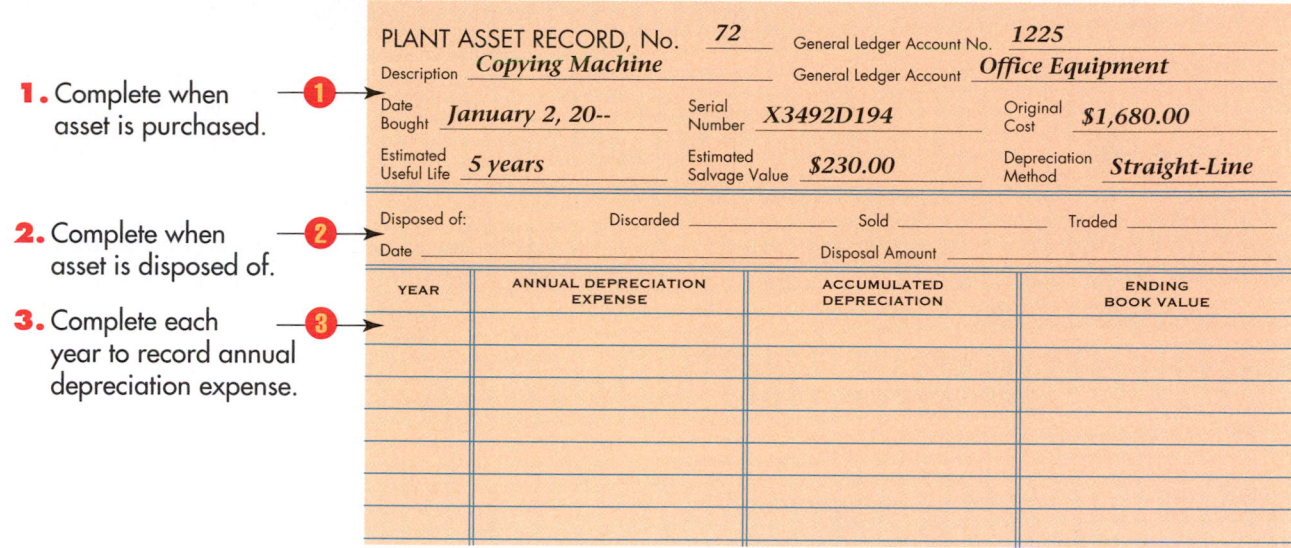

**1.** Complete when asset is purchased. ①

**2.** Complete when asset is disposed of. ②

**3.** Complete each year to record annual depreciation expense. ③

PLANT ASSET RECORD, No. _72_    General Ledger Account No. _1225_
Description _Copying Machine_    General Ledger Account _Office Equipment_
Date Bought _January 2, 20--_    Serial Number _X3492D194_    Original Cost _$1,680.00_
Estimated Useful Life _5 years_    Estimated Salvage Value _$230.00_    Depreciation Method _Straight-Line_

Disposed of:    Discarded _____    Sold _____    Traded _____
Date _____    Disposal Amount _____

| YEAR | ANNUAL DEPRECIATION EXPENSE | ACCUMULATED DEPRECIATION | ENDING BOOK VALUE |
|------|-----------------------------|--------------------------|-------------------|
|      |                             |                          |                   |

A business keeps a separate record of each plant asset it owns. An accounting form on which a business records information about each plant asset is called a **plant asset record**. Appliance Center uses a printed card as its plant asset record as shown above.

Appliance Center's plant asset record has three sections. Section 1 is prepared when the company buys a plant asset. Information in this section shows a description of the item, the general ledger account title and number, date bought, serial number, and information needed to calculate annual depreciation expense for the plant asset. Section 2 provides space for recording the disposition of the plant asset. Section 3 provides space for recording annual depreciation expense.

Calculating depreciation and disposing of plant assets are described later in this chapter.

## STEPS · STEPS · STEPS · STEPS · STEPS · STEPS · STEPS · STEPS · STEPS · STEPS · STEPS

### PREPARE A PLANT ASSET RECORD

① When an asset is bought, enter the general information about the asset in the top section of the plant asset record.

② The center section will be completed when the asset is discarded, sold, or traded.

③ At the end of each year, record the annual depreciation expense, the accumulated depreciation, and the ending book value.

©GETTY IMAGES/PHOTODISC

{ **REMEMBER** A building and the land it is located on are typically purchased together for a single price. Separate values must be assigned to each asset. If a sales contract does not specify separate amounts for the land and building, a professional appraisal may be used to determine separate amounts. }

## BUYING A PLANT ASSET FOR CASH

### CASH PAYMENTS JOURNAL

PAGE 1

| | DATE | ACCOUNT TITLE | CK. NO. | POST. REF. | GENERAL DEBIT | GENERAL CREDIT | ACCOUNTS PAYABLE DEBIT | PURCHASES DISCOUNT CREDIT | CASH CREDIT | |
|---|---|---|---|---|---|---|---|---|---|---|
| 1 | Jan. 2 | Office Equipment | 62 | | 1 6 8 0 00 | | | | 1 6 8 0 00 | 1 |

Appliance Center needs a new copying machine. Because this plant asset is to be used in the office, it is classified as office equipment.

---

*January 2. Paid cash for new copying machine, $1,680.00. Check No. 62.*

---

The entry is recorded in the cash payments journal as shown above. Appliance Center has three kinds of plant assets: office equipment,

store equipment, and warehouse equipment. A separate general ledger account is used for each of these plant assets.

```
        Office Equipment
    1,680.00   |
```

```
              Cash
               |   1,680.00
```

## BUYING A PLANT ASSET ON ACCOUNT

### GENERAL JOURNAL

PAGE 1

| | DATE | ACCOUNT TITLE | DOC. NO. | POST. REF. | DEBIT | CREDIT | |
|---|---|---|---|---|---|---|---|
| 1 | Jan. 2 | Office Equipment | M70 | | 3 3 0 0 00 | | 1 |
| 2 | | Accts. Pay./Discount Computers | | / | | 3 3 0 0 00 | 2 |

Not all plant assets are bought for cash. Appliance Center sometimes buys a plant asset on one date and pays for it on a later date.

---

*January 2. Bought an office computer on account from Discount Computers, $3,300.00. Memorandum No. 70.*

---

This transaction does not involve the purchase of merchandise. Therefore, the entry is not recorded in a purchases journal. It is recorded in the general journal as shown above. The entry is posted to both the general ledger and the accounts payable ledger.

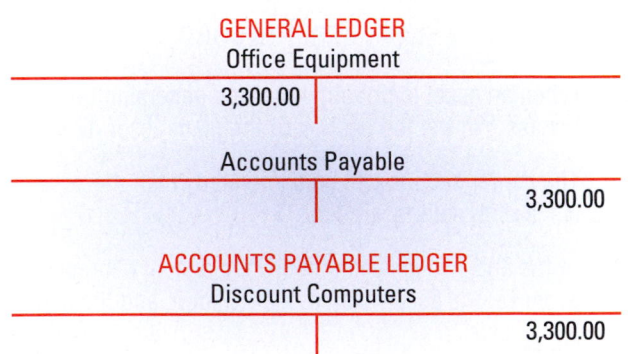

GENERAL LEDGER
Office Equipment

```
    3,300.00   |
```

Accounts Payable

```
               |   3,300.00
```

ACCOUNTS PAYABLE LEDGER
Discount Computers

```
               |   3,300.00
```

**FYI** FOR YOUR INFORMATION

An office equipment business may sell such things as desks, chairs, file cabinets, and typewriters. These items are for sale to customers and are not used in the operation of the office equipment business. Therefore, equipment purchased to sell to customers is classified as merchandise rather than as plant assets.

| CASH PAYMENTS JOURNAL | | | | | | | | | | PAGE 23 | |
|---|---|---|---|---|---|---|---|---|---|---|---|
| | | | | | 1 | 2 | 3 | 4 | 5 | | |
| | DATE | ACCOUNT TITLE | CK. NO. | POST. REF. | GENERAL | | ACCOUNTS PAYABLE DEBIT | PURCHASES DISCOUNT CREDIT | CASH CREDIT | | |
| | | | | | DEBIT | CREDIT | | | | | |
| 1 | Feb. 20-- 1 | Property Tax Expense | 122 | | 3 2 5 0 00 | | | | 3 2 5 0 00 | | 1 |
| 2 | | | | | | | | | | | 2 |

In most states, businesses have to pay taxes on plant assets. For tax purposes, state and federal governments define two kinds of property: real and personal. Land and anything attached to it is called **real property**. Real property is sometimes referred to as real estate. All property not classified as real property is called **personal property**.

## Assessed Value of Property

The value of an asset determined by tax authorities for the purpose of calculating taxes is called the **assessed value**. Assessed value is usually based on the judgment of persons referred to as assessors. Assessors are elected by citizens or are specially trained employees of a governmental unit.

An asset's assessed value may not be the same as the book value on the business's or individual's records. The assessed value is assigned to an asset for tax purposes only. Often the assessed value is only a part of the true value of the asset. However, many persons and businesses use the assessed value to estimate the market value of an asset.

## Calculating Property Tax on Plant Assets

Most governmental units with taxing power have a tax based on the value of real property. The real property tax is used on buildings and land. Some governmental units also tax personal property such as cars, boats, trailers, and airplanes.

A governmental taxing unit determines a tax rate to use in calculating taxes. The tax rate is multiplied by an asset's *assessed* value, not the book value recorded on a business's records.

Appliance Center's buildings and land have been assessed for a total of $65,000.00. The city tax rate is 5%.

| Assessed Value | × | Tax Rate | = | Annual Property Tax |
|---|---|---|---|---|
| $65,000.00 | × | 5% | = | $3,250.00 |

## Paying Property Tax on Plant Assets

On February 1, Appliance Center paid its property tax as shown above.

*Feb 1. Paid cash for property tax, $3,250.00. Check No. 122.*

Payment of property taxes is necessary if a firm is to continue in business. Therefore, Appliance Center classifies property tax as an operating expense.

```
          Property Tax Expense
          3,250.00    |

                Cash
                      |    3,250.00
```

©GETTY IMAGES/PHOTODISC

Xtra!
Study Tools
accountingxtra.swlearning.com

## terms review

plant asset record
real property
personal property
assessed value

## audit your understanding

1. What are the three sections of a plant asset record?
2. Why are asset purchases not recorded in a purchases journal?
3. What accounts are affected, and how, by an entry to pay property tax?

## work together 8-1

**Journalizing asset purchase and property tax transactions**

Depreciate all plant assets using the straight-line method. Plant asset records, a general journal, and a cash payments journal are provided in the *Working Papers*. Source documents are abbreviated as: check, C; memorandum, M. Your instructor will guide you through the following examples.

Jan. 3. Paid cash for scanner (plant asset no. 162), $600.00: no estimated salvage value; estimated useful life, three years; serial no. V2GR34. C310.

Jan. 5. Bought freight scale (plant asset no. 163) on account from Trent, Inc., $2,800.00: estimated salvage value, $400.00; estimated useful life, five years; serial no. GY52232B. M61.

Feb. 27. Paid property taxes on real property with an assessed value of $215,000.00. The tax rate in the city where the property is located is 3.5% of assessed value. C389.

1. Journalize the transactions completed during 20X1. General ledger accounts are: Office Equipment, 1225 and Warehouse Equipment, 1245.

2. Complete section 1 of a plant asset record for new asset purchases. Save your work to complete Work Together 8-2.

## on your own 8-1

**Journalizing asset purchase and property tax transactions**

Depreciate all plant assets using the straight-line method. Plant asset records, a general journal, and a cash payments journal are provided in the *Working Papers*. Source documents are abbreviated as: check, C; memorandum, M. Work independently to complete the following problem.

Jan. 2. Bought a cash register (plant asset no. 416) on account from JP Enterprises, $800.00: estimated salvage value, $200.00; estimated useful life, five years; serial no. G3HR644. M35.

Jan. 6. Paid cash for an office chair (plant asset no. 417), $500.00: estimated salvage value, $10.00; estimated useful life, seven years; serial no. FB1523. C415.

Feb. 26. Paid property taxes on real property with an assessed value of $280,000.00. The tax rate in the city where the property is located is 4.2% of assessed value. C489.

1. Journalize the transactions completed during 20X1. General ledger accounts are: Office Equipment, 1225 and Store Equipment, 1235.

2. Complete section 1 of a plant asset record for new asset purchases. Save your work to complete On Your Own 8-2.

# 8-2 Calculating and Journalizing Depreciation Expense

## FACTORS USED TO CALCULATE DEPRECIATION

Plant assets may wear out, may no longer be needed in the operation of a business, or may become outdated by new models. To match revenue with the expenses incurred to earn it, the cost of a plant asset should be allocated to an expense account over the useful life of the plant asset. [CONCEPT: Matching Expenses with Revenue] The portion of a plant asset's cost that is transferred to an expense account in each fiscal period during a plant asset's useful life is known as depreciation expense.

Because of its permanent nature, land is not subject to depreciation. Increases or decreases in land value are usually recorded only when land is sold or otherwise disposed of.

Three factors are used to calculate a plant asset's annual depreciation expense:

1. Original cost.
2. Estimated salvage value.
3. Estimated useful life.

### Original Cost
The original cost of a plant asset includes all costs paid to make the asset usable to a business. These costs include the purchase price, delivery costs, and any necessary installation costs. [CONCEPT: Historical Cost]

### Estimated Salvage Value
When a plant asset is disposed of, some part of its original value may remain. When a plant asset is bought, its final value can only be estimated. The estimated salvage value is the amount an owner expects to receive when a plant asset is removed from use. Salvage value is also referred to as residual value, scrap value, or trade-in value.

Until a plant asset is disposed of, most businesses have difficulty determining its *exact* salvage value. Thus, until actually disposed of, a plant asset's salvage value can only be *estimated*. Because salvage value is used to calculate a plant asset's annual depreciation, the most accurate estimate possible is made when a plant asset is bought.

### Estimated Useful Life
The estimated useful life of a plant asset is the number of years it is expected to be useful to a business. A plant asset's useful life differs from one situation to another. Most businesses use past experience as the basis for estimating a plant asset's useful life. If a calculator usually lasts five years for a specific business, then the business uses five years as the estimated useful life of a new calculator. Sometimes, however, a business has difficulty estimating a plant asset's useful life. In these cases, it may use the Internal Revenue Service's guidelines that give the estimated useful life for many plant assets.

### Depreciation Methods
Various depreciation methods are illustrated in this chapter. A business should select the depreciation method that provides the best financial information. A business typically uses the same depreciation method for all assets within a plant asset category.

> **REMEMBER** Two of the three values used to compute depreciation are estimates.

# STRAIGHT-LINE DEPRECIATION

Plant asset: Computer
Depreciation method: Straight-line

Original cost: $2,000.00
Estimated salvage value: $175.00
Estimated useful life: 5 years

| Year | Beginning Book Value | Annual Depreciation | Ending Book Value |
|------|---------------------|---------------------|-------------------|
| 1 | $2,000.00 | $ 365.00 | $1,635.00 |
| 2 | 1,635.00 | 365.00 | 1,270.00 |
| 3 | 1,270.00 | 365.00 | 905.00 |
| 4 | 905.00 | 365.00 | 540.00 |
| 5 | 540.00 | 365.00 | 175.00 |
| Total Depreciation | — | $1,825.00 | — |

Charging an equal amount of depreciation expense for a plant asset in each year of useful life is called the **straight-line method of depreciation**.

On January 2, 20X1, Appliance Center bought a computer for $2,000.00 with an estimated salvage value of $175.00 and an estimated useful life of five years. The details of the purchase and the depreciation amounts for each year of the asset's estimated useful life are shown above.

The estimated total depreciation expense is divided by the estimated useful life to compute the annual depreciation expense. The annual depreciation expense is the same for each year if the asset is used for the entire year.

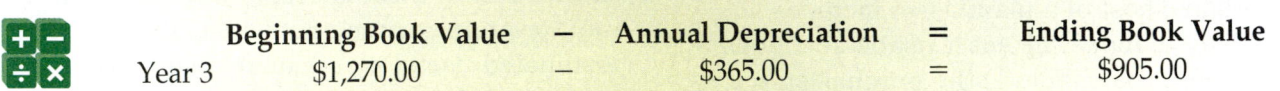

|   | | |
|---|---|---|
| − | Original Cost | $ 2,000.00 |
|   | Estimated Salvage Value | − 175.00 |
| = | Estimated Total Depreciation Expense | $ 1,825.00 |
| ÷ | Years of Estimated Useful Life | ÷ 5 |
| = | Annual Depreciation Expense | $ 365.00 |

The annual depreciation expense is subtracted from the beginning book value to compute the ending book value. The beginning book value for a year is the ending book value of the prior year.

| | **Beginning Book Value** | − | **Annual Depreciation** | = | **Ending Book Value** |
|---|---|---|---|---|---|
| Year 3 | $1,270.00 | − | $365.00 | = | $905.00 |

**FYI** FOR YOUR INFORMATION

Annual depreciation expense also may be calculated using an annual percentage rate. In the preceding example, the plant asset has an estimated useful life of five years. Therefore, the annual depreciation rate is 20% (100% divided by 5 equals .20, or 20%). Estimated total depreciation expense, $1,825.00, times depreciation rate, 20%, equals annual depreciation expense, $365.00.

©GETTY IMAGES/PHOTODISC

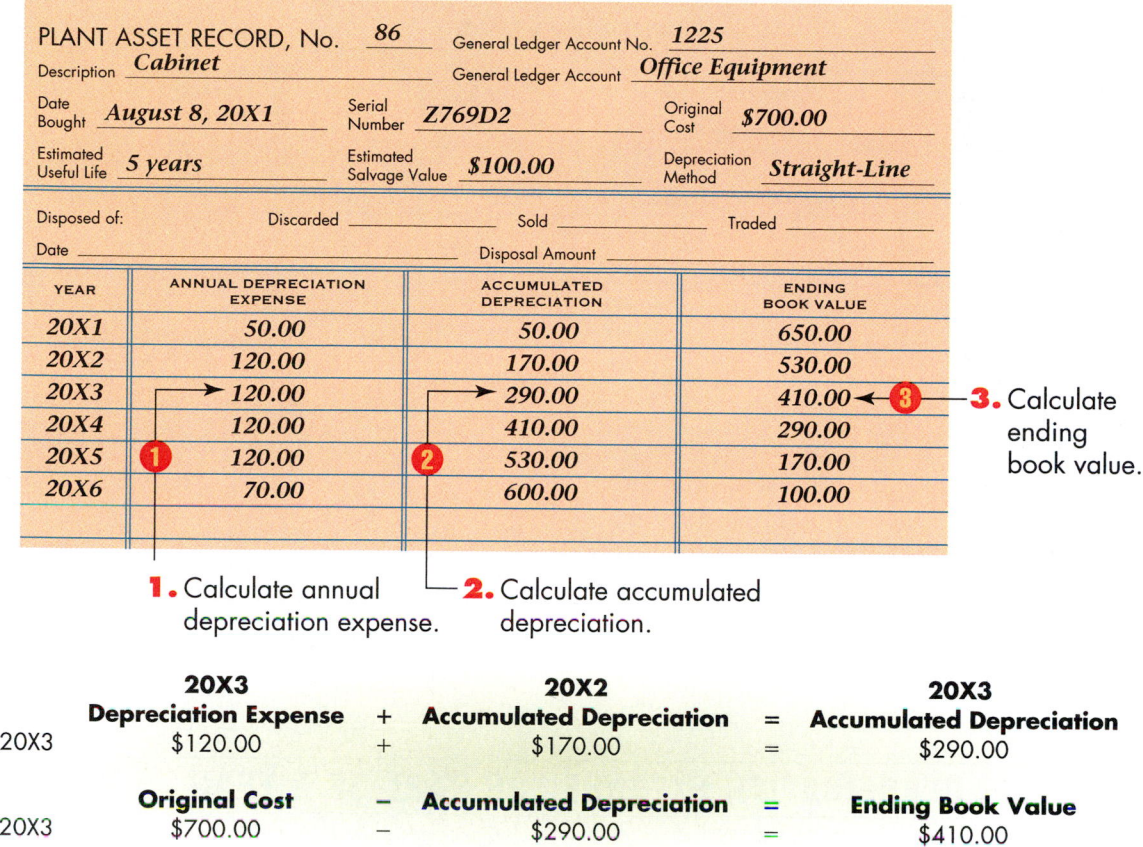

| PLANT ASSET RECORD, No. _86_ | General Ledger Account No. _1225_ |
| --- | --- |
| Description _Cabinet_ | General Ledger Account _Office Equipment_ |

| Date Bought _August 8, 20X1_ | Serial Number _Z769D2_ | Original Cost _$700.00_ |
| --- | --- | --- |

| Estimated Useful Life _5 years_ | Estimated Salvage Value _$100.00_ | Depreciation Method _Straight-Line_ |
| --- | --- | --- |

Disposed of:  Discarded _____  Sold _____  Traded _____

Date _____  Disposal Amount _____

| YEAR | ANNUAL DEPRECIATION EXPENSE | ACCUMULATED DEPRECIATION | ENDING BOOK VALUE |
| --- | --- | --- | --- |
| 20X1 | 50.00 | 50.00 | 650.00 |
| 20X2 | 120.00 | 170.00 | 530.00 |
| 20X3 | 120.00 | 290.00 | 410.00 |
| 20X4 | 120.00 | 410.00 | 290.00 |
| 20X5 | 120.00 | 530.00 | 170.00 |
| 20X6 | 70.00 | 600.00 | 100.00 |

**1.** Calculate annual depreciation expense.

**2.** Calculate accumulated depreciation.

**3.** Calculate ending book value.

|  | **20X3** Depreciation Expense | + | **20X2** Accumulated Depreciation | = | **20X3** Accumulated Depreciation |
| --- | --- | --- | --- | --- | --- |
| 20X3 | $120.00 | + | $170.00 | = | $290.00 |

|  | Original Cost | – | Accumulated Depreciation | = | Ending Book Value |
| --- | --- | --- | --- | --- | --- |
| 20X3 | $700.00 | – | $290.00 | = | $410.00 |

Appliance Center records annual depreciation expense in two places for each plant asset:

1. On the plant asset record.
2. As part of the adjusting entries that are posted to general ledger accounts.

On December 31, Appliance Center recorded the annual depreciation expense on each plant asset record. The plant asset record for a cabinet used as office equipment is shown above.

In section 3 of the plant asset record, the year is recorded in the Year column. The depreciation expense for the plant asset is recorded in the Annual Depreciation Expense column. The amount recorded in the Annual Depreciation Expense column is $50.00, the depreciation expense for the months that the cabinet was used in 20X1. For a full year, the annual depreciation expense is $120.00. The amount of accumulated depreciation is recorded in the Accumulated Depreciation column. The accumulated depreciation is the sum of the previous year's accumulated depreciation and the annual depreciation expense for the current year.

The original cost of a plant asset minus accumulated depreciation is called the **book value of a plant asset**. A new book value is calculated and recorded in the Ending Book Value column.

At the end of the estimated useful life, the cabinet should be depreciated down to its estimated salvage value. At the end of the sixth year, the ending book value is equal to the estimated salvage value, *$100.00*. The calculation for depreciation uses an *estimated* useful life. The cabinet's *actual* useful life may exceed the estimate made when the asset was put into use. If a plant asset is used longer than the estimated useful life, depreciation is *not* recorded once the book value equals the estimated salvage value.

| | DATE | ACCOUNT TITLE | DOC. NO. | POST. REF. | DEBIT | CREDIT | |
|---|---|---|---|---|---|---|---|
| | | GENERAL JOURNAL | | | | PAGE *13* | |
| 1 | | *Adjusting Entries* | | | | | 1 |
| 22 | 31 | *Depr. Exp.—Office Equipment* | | | 11 5 7 1 00 | | 22 |
| 23 | | *Accum. Depr.—Office Equipment* | | | | 11 5 7 1 00 | 23 |
| 24 | | | | | | | 24 |

After depreciation expense is recorded on the plant asset records, depreciation amounts for the year are totaled.

An adjusting entry is made to record the total depreciation expense for the fiscal year for each category of plant assets. Appliance Center records separate adjusting entries for office equipment, store equipment, warehouse equipment, and building. The adjusting entry for office equipment is shown above.

**Depreciation Expense—Office Equipment**

| Dec. 31 Adj. | 11,571.00 | |

**Accumulated Depreciation—Office Equipment**

| | Jan. 1 Bal. | 37,434.00 |
| | Dec. 31 Adj. | 11,571.00 |
| | *Dec. 31 Bal.* | *49,005.00* |

## CALCULATING DEPRECIATION EXPENSE FOR PART OF A YEAR

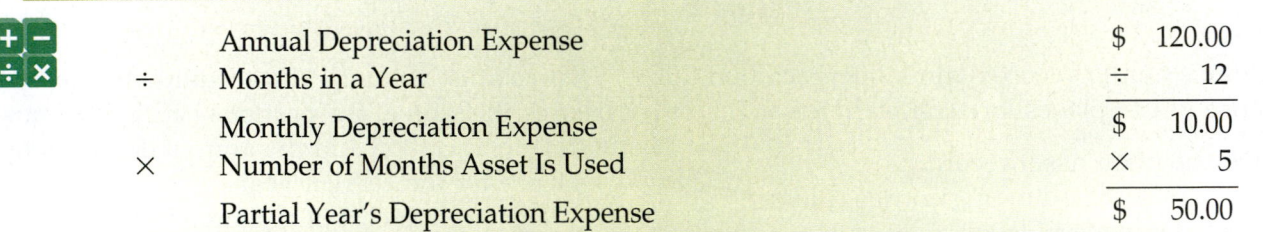

|  |  |  |
|---|---|---|
| | Annual Depreciation Expense | $ 120.00 |
| ÷ | Months in a Year | ÷ 12 |
| | Monthly Depreciation Expense | $ 10.00 |
| × | Number of Months Asset Is Used | × 5 |
| | Partial Year's Depreciation Expense | $ 50.00 |

A calendar month is the smallest unit of time used to calculate depreciation. A plant asset may be placed in service at a date other than the first day of a fiscal period. In such cases, depreciation expense is calculated to the nearest first of a month. To calculate depreciation expense for part of a year, the annual depreciation expense is divided by 12 to determine depreciation expense for a month. The monthly depreciation is then multiplied by the number of months the plant asset was used that year.

Appliance Center bought a cabinet on August 8, 20X1. The annual straight-line depreciation expense is $120.00. The depreciation expense for the part of the year that Appliance Center used the cabinet (August through December equals 5 months) is $50.00.

**FYI** FOR YOUR INFORMATION

Calculating depreciation expense for part of a year also is used when a plant asset is discarded or sold during a fiscal year. The partial year's depreciation expense is computed for the period from the start of the fiscal year to the date the asset is discarded or sold.

When a long-term asset is purchased, it is recorded at its *historic cost,* the actual amount paid for the asset. There are some circumstances when that historic cost could change over the life of the asset.

After an asset is put into service, money might have to be paid to maintain, repair, or replace a part of the asset. The accountant will have to decide if the payment qualifies as a repair or an improvement. The decision determines the accounts affected by the transaction.

If the expenditure merely maintains the asset in its normal operation, it should be treated as an expense in the period the payment is made. This category would include painting the inside or outside of a building, minor repairs on a delivery truck, regular maintenance on a piece of factory equipment, repairing gutters, and engine tune-ups. These costs typically bring the asset back to an original condition.

Therefore, the entry to record the payment of $500 for an engine tune-up would be as follows:

| | | |
|---|---|---|
| Repairs Expense | $500.00 | |
| Cash | | $500.00 |

If the expenditure adds to the value or extends the useful life of the asset, the cost must be added to the historic cost of the asset instead of treated as an immediate expense. This category would include adding a wing to a building, replacing the engine in a vehicle, and redoing the ventilation system of a building to include a state-of-the art air purification system.

The entry to record the payment of $10,000 to add an air purification system to a building would be:

| | | |
|---|---|---|
| Building | $10,000.00 | |
| Cash | | $10,000.00 |

By increasing the cost of the asset, the amount of depreciation to be recorded during the remaining useful life of the asset will also change.

Therefore, as odd as it may seem, the historic cost of an asset may not stay the same over the life of the asset.

**Instructions**

1. State whether each of the following expenditures would be treated as an expense or as an addition to the historic cost of the asset.
   a. Cost of plastering over a hole in a wall.
   b. Cost of replacing 20 shingles on the roof.
   c. Cost of lubricating a strapping machine.
   d. Cost of a major overhaul of the engine on the delivery truck, which will extend its useful life.
   e. Painting a machine to match other machines.

2. Suggest some other plant assets and the expenditures that might be made that would be considered as an addition to the historic cost of the asset.

Xtra!
Study Tools
accountingxtra.swlearning.com

## terms review

straight-line method of
  depreciation
book value of a plant asset

## audit your understanding

1. To match revenue with the expenses incurred to earn it, the cost of a plant asset should be allocated to an expense over what period of time?
2. Which accounting concept is being applied when depreciation expense is recorded for plant assets?
3. Why is annual depreciation for land not recorded?
4. What three factors are used to calculate a plant asset's annual depreciation expense?
5. What is the smallest unit of time used to calculate depreciation?

## work together 8-2

### Calculating and journalizing depreciation

Use the plant asset records from Work Together 8-1. Depreciation tables and a general journal are provided in the *Working Papers*. Your instructor will guide you through the following examples.

1. Complete the depreciation table for each asset using the straight-line depreciation method. If the asset was not purchased at the beginning of 20X1, compute the depreciation expense for the part of 20X1 that the company owned the asset.
2. Complete each plant asset record for 20X1 through 20X4.
3. Journalize the adjusting entries to record depreciation expense for 20X1. Save your work to complete Work Together 8-3.

## on your own 8-2

### Calculating and journalizing depreciation

Use the plant asset records from On Your Own 8-1. Depreciation tables and a general journal are provided in the *Working Papers*. Work this problem independently.

1. Complete the depreciation table for each asset using the straight-line depreciation method. If the asset was not purchased at the beginning of 20X1, compute the depreciation expense for the part of 20X1 that the company owned the asset.
2. Complete each plant asset record for 20X1 through 20X4.
3. Journalize the adjusting entries to record depreciation expense for 20X1. Save your work to complete On Your Own 8-3.

# LESSON · LESSON · LESSON · LESSON · LESSON · LESSON

## 8-3 Disposing of Plant Assets

## DISCARDING A PLANT ASSET WITH NO BOOK VALUE

### GENERAL JOURNAL                                                    PAGE 1

| | DATE | ACCOUNT TITLE | DOC. NO. | POST. REF. | DEBIT | CREDIT | |
|---|---|---|---|---|---|---|---|
| 7 | 5 | Accum. Depr.—Office Equipment | M72 | | 2 7 5 00 | | 7 |
| 8 | | Office Equipment | | | | 2 7 5 00 | 8 |

**1.** Record entry to remove plant asset from accounts. ①

---

**PLANT ASSET RECORD, No.** _74_    General Ledger Account No. _1225_

Description _Storage Cabinet_    General Ledger Account _Office Equipment_

Date Bought _January 3, 20X1_    Serial Number _AX5034_    Original Cost _$275.00_

Estimated Useful Life _5 years_    Estimated Salvage Value _zero_    Depreciation Method _Straight-Line_

Disposed of:    Discarded _✓_    Sold _____    Traded _____

Date _January 5, 20X6_    Disposal Amount _zero_

| YEAR | ANNUAL DEPRECIATION EXPENSE | ACCUMULATED DEPRECIATION | ENDING BOOK VALUE |
|---|---|---|---|
| 20X1 | 55.00 | 55.00 | 220.00 |
| 20X2 | 55.00 | 110.00 | 165.00 |
| 20X3 | 55.00 | 165.00 | 110.00 |
| 20X4 | 55.00 | 220.00 | 55.00 |
| 20X5 | 55.00 | 275.00 | — |

**2.** Write the date, amount, and type of disposal. ②

---

Appliance Center usually disposes of plant assets in one of three ways:

1. The plant asset is discarded because no useful life remains.
2. The plant asset is sold because it is no longer needed even though it might still be usable.
3. The plant asset is traded for another plant asset of the same kind.

If a plant asset has a salvage value of zero and its total accumulated depreciation is equal to the original cost value, the plant asset has no book value. When a plant asset with no book value is discarded, a journal entry is recorded that removes the original cost of the plant asset and its related accumulated depreciation as shown above.

*January 5, 20X6. Discarded storage cabinet: original cost, $275.00; total accumulated depreciation*

*through December 31, 20X5, $275.00. Memorandum No. 72.*

| Accumulated Depreciation—Office Equipment | |
|---|---|
| 275.00 | Bal. 275.00 |

| Office Equipment | |
|---|---|
| Bal. 275.00 | 275.00 |

## STEPS  STEPS · STEPS · STEPS · STEPS

### DISCARDING A PLANT ASSET WITH NO BOOK VALUE

① Record an entry on the general journal to remove the original cost, *275.00*, from Office Equipment and Accumulated Depreciation—Office Equipment. When this entry is posted, all amounts for the discarded cabinet are removed from the two accounts.

② Check the type of disposal, *Discarded*, and write the date, *Jan. 5, 20X6*, and disposal amount, *zero*, on the plant asset record. These notations complete the history of the plant asset.

| | DATE | ACCOUNT TITLE | DOC. NO. | POST. REF. | DEBIT | CREDIT | |
|---|---|---|---|---|---|---|---|
| | | | | | **GENERAL JOURNAL** | PAGE 6 | |
| 4 | 30 | Depr. Exp.—Office Equipment | M92 | | 20 00 | | 4 |
| 5 | | Accum. Depr.—Office Equipment | | | | 20 00 | 5 |
| 6 | 30 | Accum. Depr.—Office Equipment | M92 | | 160 00 | | 6 |
| 7 | | Loss on Plant Assets | | | 40 00 | | 7 |
| 8 | | Office Equipment | | | | 200 00 | 8 |
| 9 | | | | | | | 9 |

**1.** Record a partial year's depreciation expense.

**4.** Record entry to remove plant asset from accounts.

**3.** Write the date, amount, and type of disposal.

Disposed of: Discarded ✓   Sold _____   Traded _____
Date **June 30, 20X6**   Disposal Amount **zero**

| YEAR | ANNUAL DEPRECIATION EXPENSE | ACCUMULATED DEPRECIATION | ENDING BOOK VALUE |
|---|---|---|---|
| 20X2 | 20.00 | 20.00 | 180.00 |
| 20X3 | 40.00 | 60.00 | 140.00 |
| 20X4 | 40.00 | 100.00 | 100.00 |
| 20X5 | 40.00 | 140.00 | 60.00 |
| 20X6 | 20.00 | 160.00 | 40.00 |

**2.** Record the partial year's depreciation.

A plant asset may be disposed of at any time during its useful life. When a plant asset is disposed of, its depreciation expense from the beginning of the current fiscal year to the date of disposal is recorded as shown above.

When an asset with a book value is discarded, a journal entry is recorded to: (1) Remove the original cost of the plant asset and its related accumulated depreciation. (2) Recognize the loss on disposal of the asset.

*June 30, 20X6. Discarded office table: original cost, $200.00; total accumulated depreciation through December 31, 20X5, $140.00; additional depreciation to be recorded through June 30, 20X6, $20.00. Memorandum No. 92.*

The loss from discarding a plant asset with a book value is equal to the asset's book value. The loss is not an operating expense. Therefore, Loss on Plant Assets is classified as an Other Expense.

**Depreciation Expense—Office Equipment**

| | | |
|---|---|---|
| Add. Depr. | 20.00 | |

**Accumulated Depreciation—Office Equipment**

| | | Bal. | 140.00 |
|---|---|---|---|
| Disposal | 160.00 | Add. Depr. | 20.00 |

**Loss on Plant Assets**

| | | |
|---|---|---|
| Disposal | 40.00 | |

**Office Equipment**

| | | | |
|---|---|---|---|
| Bal. | 200.00 | Disposal | 200.00 |

## STEPS

STEPS • STEPS • STEPS • STEPS • STEPS • STEPS • STEPS • STEPS • STEPS • STEPS

### DISCARDING AN ASSET WITH A BOOK VALUE

**1.** Record a partial year's depreciation expense, *20.00*, by debiting Depreciation Expense—Office Equipment and crediting Accumulated Depreciation—Office Equipment.

**2.** Record the depreciation in section 3 of the plant asset record.

**3.** Check the type of disposal, *Discarded*, and write the date, *June 30, 20X6*, and the disposal amount, *zero*, on the plant asset record. These notations complete the history of the plant asset.

**4.** Record an entry to remove the original cost, *200.00*, from Office Equipment and *160.00* from Accumulated Depreciation—Office Equipment. Record the loss on disposal, *40.00*, as a debit to Loss on Plant Assets.

Accounting for Plant Assets

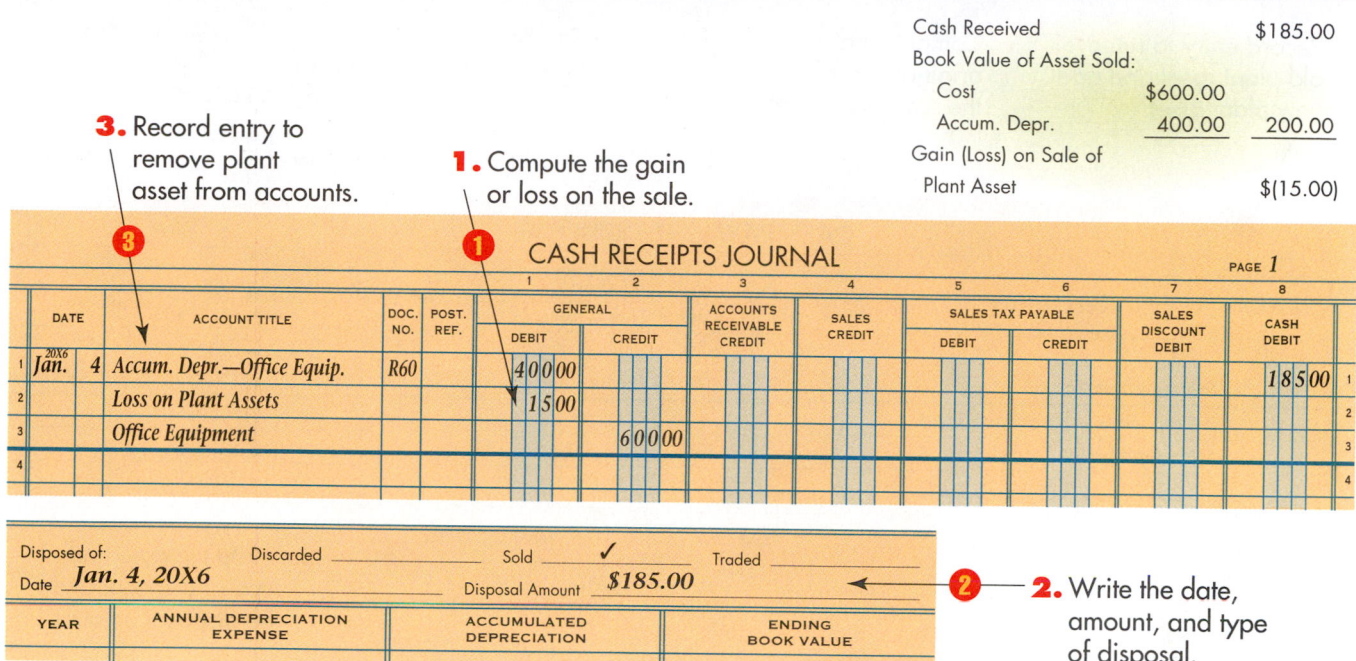

## SELLING A PLANT ASSET

**3.** Record entry to remove plant asset from accounts.

**1.** Compute the gain or loss on the sale.

| Cash Received | | $185.00 |
|---|---|---|
| Book Value of Asset Sold: | | |
| Cost | $600.00 | |
| Accum. Depr. | 400.00 | 200.00 |
| Gain (Loss) on Sale of Plant Asset | | $(15.00) |

**CASH RECEIPTS JOURNAL**

PAGE 1

| | | | | | GENERAL | | ACCOUNTS RECEIVABLE CREDIT | SALES CREDIT | SALES TAX PAYABLE | | SALES DISCOUNT DEBIT | CASH DEBIT | |
|---|---|---|---|---|---|---|---|---|---|---|---|---|---|
| | DATE | ACCOUNT TITLE | DOC. NO. | POST. REF. | DEBIT | CREDIT | | | DEBIT | CREDIT | | | |
| 1 | 20X6 Jan. 4 | Accum. Depr.—Office Equip. | R60 | | 400 00 | | | | | | | | 185 00 | 1 |
| 2 | | Loss on Plant Assets | | | 15 00 | | | | | | | | | 2 |
| 3 | | Office Equipment | | | | 600 00 | | | | | | | | 3 |
| 4 | | | | | | | | | | | | | | 4 |

| Disposed of: | Discarded _____ | Sold ✓ | Traded _____ |
|---|---|---|---|
| Date *Jan. 4, 20X6* | | Disposal Amount $185.00 | |

**2.** Write the date, amount, and type of disposal.

| YEAR | ANNUAL DEPRECIATION EXPENSE | ACCUMULATED DEPRECIATION | ENDING BOOK VALUE |
|---|---|---|---|

When a plant asset is sold, a journal entry is recorded to:

1. Remove the original cost of the plant asset and its related accumulated depreciation.
2. Recognize the cash received.
3. Recognize the gain or loss on disposal of the asset.

*January 4, 20X6. Received cash from sale of fax machine, $185.00: original cost, $600.00; total accumulated depreciation through December 31, 20X5, $400.00. Receipt No. 60.*

The amount of gain or loss is calculated by subtracting the book value from the cash received. The $15.00 loss on disposal is recorded as a debit to Loss on Plant Assets as shown above.

The sale of plant assets is not a normal operating activity of Appliance Center. A loss from the sale of plant assets is classified as Other Expense.

| Cash | |
|---|---|
| 185.00 | |

| Accumulated Depreciation—Office Equipment | |
|---|---|
| 400.00 | Bal. 400.00 |

| Loss on Plant Assets | |
|---|---|
| 15.00 | |

| Office Equipment | |
|---|---|
| Bal. 600.00 | 600.00 |

## STEPS

STEPS • STEPS • STEPS • STEPS • STEPS • STEPS • STEPS • STEPS • STEPS • STEPS

### SELLING A PLANT ASSET

1. Compute the gain or loss, *15.00 loss*, by subtracting the book value of the asset, 200.00, from the cash received, *185.00*.
2. Check the type of disposal, *Sold*, and write the date, *January 4, 20X6*, and the disposal amount, *$185.00*, on the plant asset record. These notations complete the history of the plant asset.
3. Record an entry on the cash receipts journal to remove the original cost, *600.00*, from Office Equipment and *400.00* from Accumulated Depreciation—Office Equipment. Record the loss on sale, *15.00*, as a debit to Loss on Plant Assets.

## TRADING A PLANT ASSET

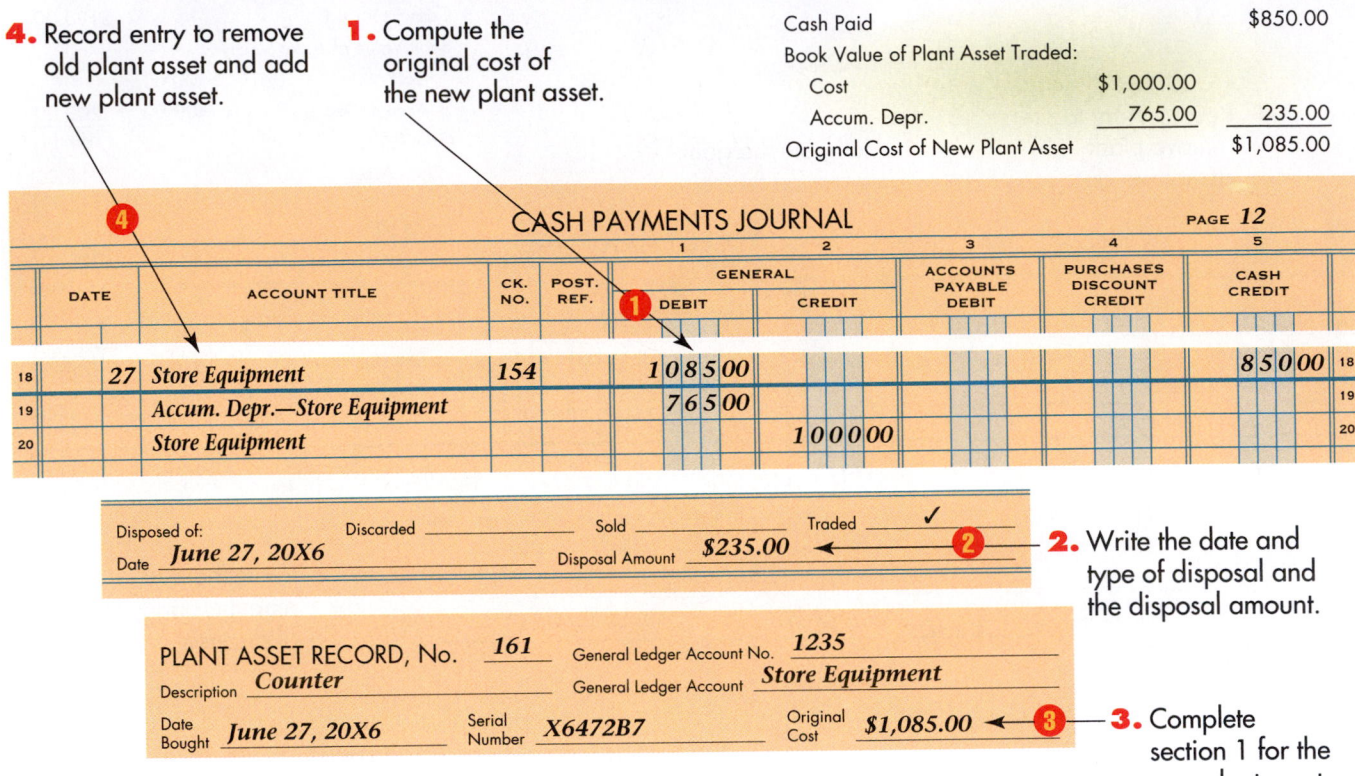

**4.** Record entry to remove old plant asset and add new plant asset.

**1.** Compute the original cost of the new plant asset.

| | |
|---|---:|
| Cash Paid | $850.00 |
| Book Value of Plant Asset Traded: | |
| Cost | $1,000.00 |
| Accum. Depr. | 765.00    235.00 |
| Original Cost of New Plant Asset | $1,085.00 |

**CASH PAYMENTS JOURNAL**                                            PAGE 12

|  |  | | | | | 1 | 2 | 3 | 4 | 5 |  |
|---|---|---|---|---|---|---|---|---|---|---|---|
|  |  | | CK. | POST. | | GENERAL | | ACCOUNTS PAYABLE DEBIT | PURCHASES DISCOUNT CREDIT | CASH CREDIT |  |
| DATE | ACCOUNT TITLE | | NO. | REF. | | DEBIT | CREDIT | | | |  |
| 18 | 27 | Store Equipment | 154 | | | 1 0 8 5 00 | | | | 8 5 0 00 | 18 |
| 19 |  | Accum. Depr.—Store Equipment | | | | 7 6 5 00 | | | | | 19 |
| 20 |  | Store Equipment | | | | | 1 0 0 0 00 | | | | 20 |

Disposed of:   Discarded _____   Sold _____   Traded ✓

Date **June 27, 20X6**   Disposal Amount **$235.00** ←

**2.** Write the date and type of disposal and the disposal amount.

PLANT ASSET RECORD, No. **161**   General Ledger Account No. **1235**

Description **Counter**   General Ledger Account **Store Equipment**

Date Bought **June 27, 20X6**   Serial Number **X6472B7**   Original Cost **$1,085.00** ←

**3.** Complete section 1 for the new plant asset.

---

Appliance Center needed a new store counter. The vendor agreed to take cash and an old store counter in trade. The new plant asset's original cost equals the cash *actually* paid plus the book value of the asset traded. [*CONCEPT: Historical Cost*]

When an old plant asset is traded for a new plant asset, the journal entry:

1. Removes the original cost of the old plant asset and its related accumulated depreciation.
2. Recognizes the cash paid.
3. Records the new plant asset at its original cost.

*June 27, 20X6. Paid cash, $850.00, plus old counter for new store counter: original cost of old counter, $1,000.00; total accumulated depreciation through June 27, 20X6, $765.00. Memorandum No. 130 and Check No. 154.*

| Store Equipment | | | |
|---|---:|---|---:|
| Bal. | 1,000.00 | Trade-in | 1,000.00 |
| New Equip. | 1,085.00 | | |

| Accumulated Depreciation—Store Equipment | | | |
|---|---:|---|---:|
| | 765.00 | Bal. | 765.00 |

| Cash | |
|---|---:|
| | 850.00 |

## STEPS

STEPS • STEPS • STEPS • STEPS

### TRADING A PLANT ASSET

**1** Compute the original cost of the new asset, *$1,085.00*, by adding the book value of the asset traded, *$235.00*, and the cash paid, *$850.00*.

**2** Check the type of disposal, *Traded*, and write the date, *June 27, 20X6*, and the disposal amount, *$235.00*, on the plant asset record of the traded asset.

**3** Complete section 1 of the plant asset record for the new asset.

**4** Record the journal entry to reflect the trade of plant assets.

# SELLING LAND AND BUILDINGS

**2.** Write the date, type, and amount of disposal.

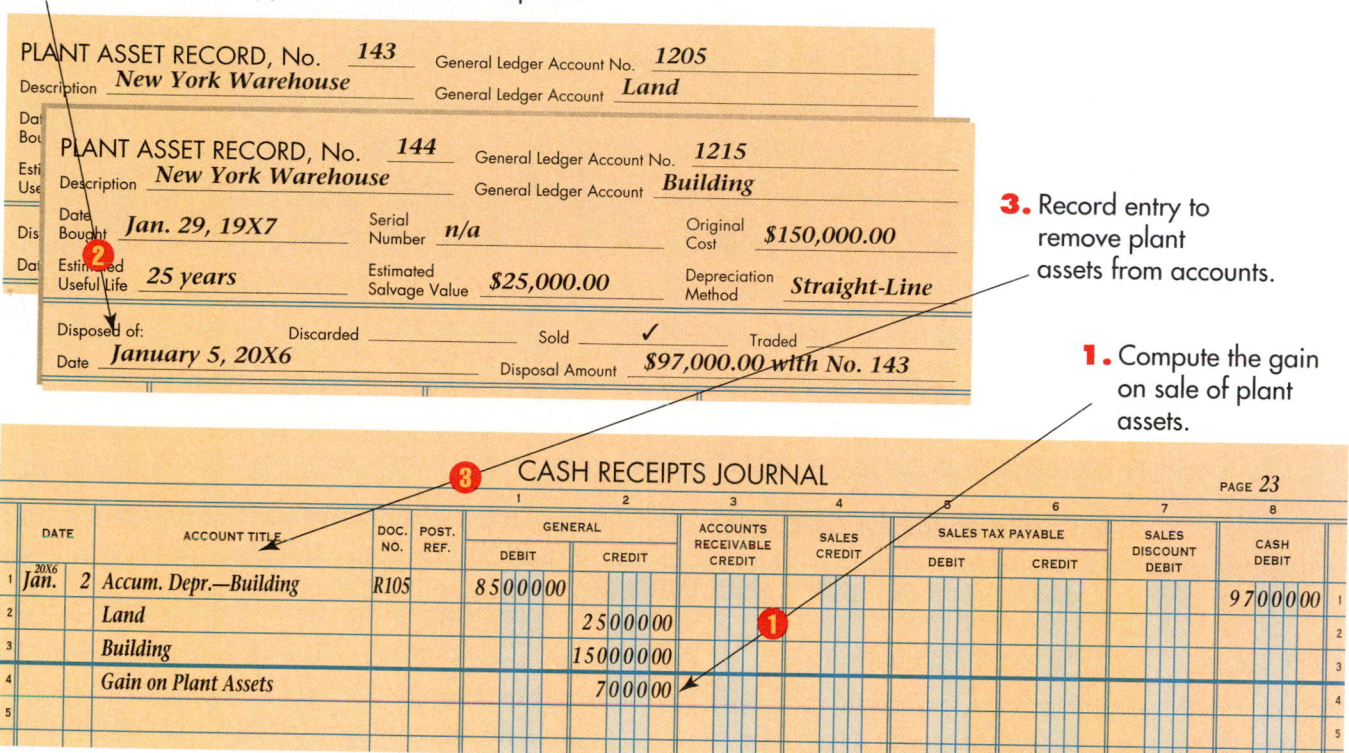

PLANT ASSET RECORD, No. **143**    General Ledger Account No. **1205**

Description   **New York Warehouse**    General Ledger Account **Land**

---

PLANT ASSET RECORD, No. **144**    General Ledger Account No. **1215**

Description **New York Warehouse**    General Ledger Account **Building**

| Date Bought | **Jan. 29, 19X7** | Serial Number | **n/a** | Original Cost | **$150,000.00** |
| Estimated Useful Life | **25 years** | Estimated Salvage Value | **$25,000.00** | Depreciation Method | **Straight-Line** |

Disposed of:   Discarded _____   Sold **✓**   Traded _____

Date **January 5, 20X6**   Disposal Amount **$97,000.00 with No. 143**

**3.** Record entry to remove plant assets from accounts.

**1.** Compute the gain on sale of plant assets.

## CASH RECEIPTS JOURNAL

PAGE **23**

| | DATE | ACCOUNT TITLE | DOC. NO. | POST. REF. | GENERAL DEBIT | GENERAL CREDIT | ACCOUNTS RECEIVABLE CREDIT | SALES CREDIT | SALES TAX PAYABLE DEBIT | SALES TAX PAYABLE CREDIT | SALES DISCOUNT DEBIT | CASH DEBIT | |
|---|---|---|---|---|---|---|---|---|---|---|---|---|---|
| 1 | 20X6 Jan. 2 | Accum. Depr.—Building | R105 | | 85000 00 | | | | | | | 97000 00 | 1 |
| 2 | | Land | | | | 25000 00 | | | | | | | 2 |
| 3 | | Building | | | | 150000 00 | | | | | | | 3 |
| 4 | | Gain on Plant Assets | | | | 7000 00 | | | | | | | 4 |
| 5 | | | | | | | | | | | | | 5 |

Land is considered to be a permanent plant asset. Therefore, its useful life is not estimated, and annual depreciation is not recorded for it. The book value of land is the original cost. [CONCEPT: Historical Cost]

Land is seldom discarded (abandoned). Usually land is sold at the same time that the buildings on it are sold. A separate plant record is maintained for the land and the building. Each record is updated when a sale is made.

> January 2, 20X6. Fidelity Company sold land with a building for $97,000.00 cash; original cost of land, $25,000.00; original cost of building, $150,000.00; total accumulated depreciation on building through December 31, 20X5, $85,000.00. Receipt No. 105.

The journal entry:

1. Removes the original cost of the land and building and the building's related accumulated depreciation.
2. Recognizes the cash received.
3. Recognizes the gain on disposal of the plant assets.

## STEPS   STEPS • STEPS • STEPS • STEPS

### SELLING LAND AND BUILDINGS

**1** Compute the gain on the sale of plant assets, *$7,000.00,* by subtracting the book value of the land and buildings, *$90,000.00,* from the cash received, *$97,000.00.*

**2** Check the type of disposal, *Sold,* and write the date, *Jan. 2, 20X6,* and the disposal amount, *$97,000.00,* on each plant asset record. Include a reference to the other plant asset included in the sale.

**3** Record an entry on the cash receipts journal to remove the original cost of land, *25,000.00,* and buildings, *150,000.00,* and to remove *85,000.00* from Accumulated Depreciation—Building. Record the gain on sale, *7,000.00,* as a credit to Gain on Plant Assets.

The amount of the gain is the cash received less the book value of the assets sold.

| | Land | Building | Total |
|---|---|---|---|
| Cash Received | | | $97,000.00 |
| Cost of Assets | $25,000.00 | $150,000.00 | |
| Accumulated Depreciation | | 85,000.00 | |
| Book Values of Assets Sold | 25,000.00 | 65,000.00 | 90,000.00 |
| Gain on Sale of Plant Assets | | | $ 7,000.00 |

# Explore Accounting

EXPLORE ACCOUNTING • EXPLORE ACCOUNTING • EXPLORE ACCOUNTING

## Limitations of Historic Cost Concept

Most assets are recorded at their historic cost, the actual cost paid for the asset. Over time, this historic cost can be quite different than the fair market value of the asset, which is the amount for which the asset could be sold at any time.

The difference between the historic cost and the fair market value of an asset can make a difference when performing financial statement analysis during a period of changing prices. Any calculation that includes total assets will be affected by the required use of historic cost instead of fair market value for assets.

One example of the limitations of using historic cost is if two businesses own identical buildings. Company A bought the building 10 years ago and paid $50,000. Company B bought the building yesterday and paid $150,000. Company A can show an asset of only $50,000, while Company B will show an asset of $150,000 for the identical building. A potential investor could be led to believe that Company B has a more valuable building than Company A. A banker may be willing to give a bigger loan to Company B.

Regardless of which amount is more accurate, GAAP requires the use of historic cost for most assets.

**Instructions**

The table below shows the historic cost and the current market value for the assets owned by the Smith Company.

| Account Title | Historic Cost | Market Value |
|---|---|---|
| Cash | $10,000 | $10,000 |
| Accounts Receivable | 3,000 | 3,000 |
| Equipment | 15,000 | 10,000 |
| Building | 25,000 | 45,000 |
| Land | 20,000 | 75,000 |

1. Calculate the total assets using historic cost.

2. Calculate the market value of the assets owned by the Smith Company.

3. Which amount do you feel is more relevant to a bank loan officer in determining if Smith Company qualifies for a loan?

4. Why does GAAP require that most assets be listed at historic cost?

## • audit your understanding

1. What is recorded on a plant asset record for a plant asset that has been discarded?

2. When an asset is disposed of after the beginning of the fiscal year, what entry may need to be recorded before an entry is made for a discarded plant asset?

3. What is the formula to compute the gain or loss on the sale of a plant asset?

4. When cash is paid and old store equipment is traded for new store equipment, what is the formula for calculating the new equipment's original cost?

## • work together 8-3

### Recording the disposal of plant assets

Use the plant asset records from Work Together 8-2. The following transactions occurred in 20X5. A general journal, cash receipts journal, and plant asset records are provided in the *Working Papers*. Source documents are abbreviated as follows: check, C; memorandum, M; receipt, R. Your instructor will guide you through the following examples.

Jan. 3. Discarded scanner, no. 162. M65.
Mar. 30. Received cash for sale of freight scale, no.163, $600.00. M125 and R145.
June 26. Received cash for sale of a desk, no. 127, $500.00. M151 and R273.
Dec. 28. Paid cash, $30,000.00, plus old truck, no. 116, for new truck, no. 172. M222 and C671.
Dec. 30. Sold land, no. 105, and a building, no.106, for $110,000.00. M224 and R663.

1. Journalize additional depreciation, if needed. Journalize the disposal of each plant asset.

2. Make appropriate notations in the plant asset records.

## • on your own 8-3

### Recording the disposal of plant assets

Use the plant asset records from On Your Own 8-2. The following transactions occurred in 20X5. A general journal, cash receipts journal, and plant asset records are provided in the *Working Papers*. Source documents are abbreviated as follows: check, C; memorandum, M; receipt, R. Work this problem independently.

Jan. 4. Discarded office chair, no. 417. M5.
May 28. Received cash for sale of cash register, no. 416, $100.00. M52 and R243.
June 30. Sold land, no. 390, and a building, no. 391, for $106,000.00. M63 and R283.
Oct. 2. Discarded office file cabinet, no. 369. M121.
Dec. 29. Paid cash, $1,200.00, plus old computer, no. 428, for new computer, no. 439. M153 and C775.

1. Journalize additional depreciation, if needed. Journalize the disposal of each plant asset.

2. Make appropriate notations in the plant asset records.

AUDIT YOUR UNDERSTANDING • WORK TOGETHER • WORK TOGETHER • ON YOUR OWN • ON YOUR OWN • ON YOUR OWN

Disposing of Plant Assets

Lesson 8-3   241

# 8-4 Other Methods of Depreciation

## DECLINING-BALANCE METHOD OF DEPRECIATION

|   | Total Depreciation Expense | 100% |
|---|---|---|
| ÷ | Estimated Useful Life | ÷ 5 years |
| = | Straight-Line Rate | 20% |
| × | Double the Rate | × 2 |
| = | Declining-Balance Rate | 40% |

**1.** Calculate the declining-balance rate.

Plant asset: Computer
Depreciation method: Declining balance

Original cost: $2,000.00
Estimated salvage value: $175.00
Estimated useful life: 5 years

| Year | Beginning Book Value | Declining-Balance Rate | Annual Depreciation | Ending Book Value |
|---|---|---|---|---|
| 1 | $2,000.00 | 40% | $ 800.00 | $1,200.00 |
| 2 | 1,200.00 | 40% | 480.00 | 720.00 |
| 3 | 720.00 | 40% | 288.00 | 432.00 |
| 4 | 432.00 | 40% | 172.80 | 259.20 |
| 5 | 259.20 | 40% | 84.20 | 175.00 |
| Total Depreciation | | — | $1,825.00 | — |

**2**

**2.** Calculate the annual depreciation.

| | Beginning Book Value | × | Depreciation Rate | = | Annual Depreciation Expense |
|---|---|---|---|---|---|
| Year 3 | $720.00 | × | 40% | = | $288.00 |

Many plant assets depreciate more in the early years of useful life than in the later years. Charging more depreciation expense in the early years of a plant asset may be more accurate than charging the same amount each year.

Multiplying the book value at the end of each fiscal period by a constant depreciation rate is called the **declining-balance method of depreciation**. Although the depreciation rate is the same each year, the annual depreciation expense declines from year to year.

The declining-balance depreciation rate is based on the straight-line rate. A declining-balance rate that is twice the straight-line rate is commonly used. This method of depreciation is referred to as the double declining-balance method. For example, a plant asset with an

estimated useful life of five years would have a depreciation rate of 40%.

When the declining-balance method is used, the annual depreciation expense is calculated using the beginning book value for each year. The beginning book value is the same as the ending book value from the previous year. In the asset's first year of service, the beginning book value equals its original cost.

A plant asset is never depreciated below its estimated salvage value. Therefore, in the last year, only enough depreciation expense is recorded to reduce the book value of the plant asset to its salvage value. Thus, the depreciation expense in the fifth year is limited to $84.20 ($259.20 − $175.00).

**REMEMBER** The declining-balance method does not use the estimated salvage value to compute annual depreciation. The estimated salvage value is used only to limit the last year's depreciation expense.

Accounting for Plant Assets

# SUM-OF-THE-YEARS'-DIGITS METHOD OF DEPRECIATION

| Years' Digits | Fraction |
|---|---|
| 1 | 5/15 |
| 2 | 4/15 |
| 3 | 3/15 |
| 4 | 2/15 |
| 5 | 1/15 |
| Total | 15 |

**① 1.** Calculate the fraction.

Plant asset: Computer
Depreciation method: Sum-of-the-years'-digits

Original cost: $2,000.00
Estimated salvage value: $175.00
Estimated useful life: 5 years

| Year | Beginning Book Value | Fraction | Total Depreciation | Annual Depreciation | Ending Book Value |
|---|---|---|---|---|---|
| 1 | $2,000.00 | 5/15 | $1,825.00 | $ 608.33 | $1,391.67 |
| 2 | 1,391.67 | 4/15 | $1,825.00 | 486.67 | 905.00 |
| 3 | 905.00 | 3/15 | $1,825.00 | 365.00 | 540.00 |
| 4 | 540.00 | 2/15 | $1,825.00 | 243.33 | 296.67 |
| 5 | 296.67 | 1/15 | $1,825.00 | 121.67 | 175.00 |
| Total Depreciation | | | | $1,825.00 | |

| | |
|---|---|
| Original Cost | $2,000.00 |
| Estimated Salvage Value | −175.00 |
| Estimated Total Depreciation Expense | $1,825.00 |
| Year's Fraction | × 5/15 |
| Annual Depreciation Expense | $608.33 |

**② 2.** Calculate the annual depreciation.

Another method of calculating depreciation is based on a fraction derived from the years' digits for the useful life of a plant asset. Using fractions based on the number of years of a plant asset's useful life is called the **sum-of-the-years'-digits method of depreciation**.

The fractions are determined as follows: The years' digits are added (1 + 2 + 3 + 4 + 5 = 15). Then, using the sum of the years' digits, a fraction is created for each year with the years' digits in reverse order. Year 1 has a fraction of 5/15. Year 5 has a fraction of 1/15.

The depreciation expense for each year is calculated by multiplying the total depreciation expense times the fraction for that year.

The sum-of-the-years'-digits method results in a last year ending book value equal to the plant asset's salvage value.

## FYI    FOR YOUR INFORMATION

A company can select any generally accepted depreciation method. Once it has selected a method, however, the company cannot change the method unless it can show that the new method would better report the company's financial activities.

**REMEMBER**   Like the straight-line method, the estimated salvage value is subtracted from the original cost to compute an estimated total depreciation expense. Thus, the estimated salvage value is used to compute each year's annual depreciation expense.

# COMPARISON OF THREE METHODS OF DEPRECIATION

Plant asset: Computer
Depreciation method: Comparison

Original cost: $2,000.00
Estimated salvage value: $175.00
Estimated useful life: 5 years

| Year | Straight-Line Method | Double Declining-Balance Method | Sum-of-the-Years'-Digits Method |
|---|---|---|---|
| 1 | $ 365.00 | $800.00 | $ 608.33 |
| 2 | 365.00 | 480.00 | 486.67 |
| 3 | 365.00 | 288.00 | 365.00 |
| 4 | 365.00 | 172.80 | 243.33 |
| 5 | 365.00 | 84.20 | 121.67 |
| Total Depreciation | $1,825.00 | $1,825.00 | $1,825.00 |

Regardless of the depreciation method used, the total depreciation expense over the useful life of an asset is the same as that shown above.

Each of these depreciation methods conforms to generally accepted accounting principles. The straight-line method is easy to calculate. The same amount of depreciation expense is recorded for each of the five years of estimated life.

The double declining-balance method is relatively easy to calculate. This method records a larger depreciation expense in the early years than the straight-line method does.

The sum-of-the-years'-digits method is not as easy to use as the straight-line or declining-balance methods. This method also records a higher depreciation expense in the early years than the straight-line method does. Both the declining-balance method and the sum-of-the-years'-digits method are known as accelerated depreciation methods.

# technology for business

## Spreadsheet Activity—Depreciation Schedule

Briarwood Center, an executive conference center, uses a spreadsheet to calculate depreciation. The following information is available for a high-volume photocopy machine:

| | |
|---|---|
| Original cost | $22,700 |
| Estimated salvage value | $4,500 |
| Estimated useful life, in years | 5 |

**Required**

1. Create a depreciation schedule spreadsheet. Use the schedule at the top of page 230 as a model. Write formulas to calculate annual depreciation, ending book value, and total depreciation.

2. Make copies of the spreadsheet you created in 1 to calculate the depreciation for the display equipment. Use the information below.

| | |
|---|---|
| Original cost | $6,800 |
| Estimated salvage value | $1,200 |
| Estimated useful life, in years | 3 |

|   | | |
|---|---|---|
| | Original cost | $ 18,200.00 |
| − | Estimated Salvage Value | − 2,000.00 |
| = | Estimated Total Depreciation Expense | $ 16,200.00 |
| ÷ | Estimated Useful Life | ÷ 90,000 miles |
| = | Depreciation Rate | $0.18/mile |

Plant asset: Truck
Depreciation method: Production-unit
Original cost: $18,200.00
Estimated salvage value: $2,000.00

**1.** Calculate the depreciation rate.

Estimated total depreciation: $16,200.00
Estimated useful life: 90,000 miles
Depreciation rate: $0.18 per mile driven

| Year | Beginning Book Value | Miles Driven | Annual Depreciation | Ending Book Value |
|------|---------------------|--------------|---------------------|-------------------|
| 1 | $18,200.00 | 9,000 | $ 1,620.00 | $16,580.00 |
| 2 | 16,580.00 | 23,000 | 4,140.00 | 12,440.00 |
| 3 | 12,440.00 | 25,000 | 4,500.00 | 7,940.00 |
| 4 | 7,940.00 | 22,000 | 3,960.00 | 3,980.00 |
| 5 | 3,980.00 | 8,000 | 1,440.00 | 2,540.00 |
| Totals | | 87,000 | $15,660.00 | |

| | Total Miles Driven | × | Depreciation Rate | = | Annual Depreciation Expense |
|--------|-------------------|---|------------------|---|----------------------------|
| Year 1 | 9,000 | × | $0.18 | = | $1,620.00 |

**2.** Calculate the annual depreciation.

Sometimes the useful life of a plant asset depends on how much the asset is used. For example, an automobile will wear out faster if it is driven 80,000 miles a year rather than 60,000 miles. Calculating estimated annual depreciation expense based on the amount of production expected from a plant asset is called the **production-unit method of depreciation**.

Mariah Delivery Service owns a small truck. The truck originally cost $18,200.00, and had an estimated salvage value of $2,000.00 and an estimated useful life of 90,000 miles. The depreciation rate for the truck is calculated by dividing the estimated total depreciation expense by the estimated useful life.

Depreciation expense for each year of the truck's estimated useful life is calculated at 18 cents per mile driven. The annual depreciation expense for the truck is calculated by multiplying the total number of miles driven by the depreciation rate. After five years, $15,660.00 of depreciation has been expensed, as shown above. Additional depreciation expense will be recorded in future years as the truck approaches its 90,000 miles of useful life.

## FYI
### FOR YOUR INFORMATION

Although relatively easy to compute, the production-units method of depreciation significantly increases the work required to compute depreciation. The company must collect the production units for each asset. For large companies with many locations, the collection of this information can be a difficult task.

**REMEMBER** The accounts used to record depreciation expense are the same regardless of the depreciation method used.

Plant asset: Printer
Depreciation method: MACRS

Original cost: $2,000.00
Property class: 5 year

| Year | Depreciation Rate | Annual Depreciation |
|---|---|---|
| 1 | 20.00% | $400.00 |
| 2 | 32.00% | 640.00 |
| 3 | 19.20% | 384.00 |
| 4 | 11.52% | 230.40 |
| 5 | 11.52% | 230.40 |
| 6 | 5.76% | 115.20 |
| Totals | 100.00% | $2,000.00 |

Most businesses use one of the generally accepted accounting methods to calculate depreciation for financial reporting purposes. A depreciation method required by the Internal Revenue Service to be used for income tax calculation purposes for most plant assets placed in service after 1986 is called the **Modified Accelerated Cost Recovery System**. This depreciation system is generally referred to as MACRS, the initials of its full name.

MACRS is a depreciation method with prescribed periods for nine classes of useful life for plant assets. A property is assigned to a specified class based on its characteristics and general life expectancy. The two most common classes, other than real estate, are the five-year and the seven-year property classes. The five-year property class includes cars, general-purpose trucks, computers, manufacturing equipment, and office machinery.

The seven-year property class includes office furniture and fixtures. The depreciation for these two property classes approximates the use of the double declining-balance method.

To calculate depreciation using MACRS, the Internal Revenue Service has prescribed methods that use annual percentage rates to determine depreciation for each class of plant asset. These rates are applied to the total cost of the plant asset without considering a salvage value. All plant assets are assumed to be placed in service in the middle of the year and taken out of service in the middle of the year. For example, the five-year property class depreciation is spread over six years, as shown above.

Annual depreciation is calculated by multiplying the plant asset's original cost times the depreciation rate for its specific class. A printer is classified as five-year property.

| | Original Cost | × | Depreciation Rate | = | Annual Depreciation Rate |
|---|---|---|---|---|---|
| Year 3 | $2,000.00 | × | 19.20% | = | $384.00 |

## FYI
FOR YOUR INFORMATION

Congress writes the depreciation rules used in filing federal income taxes. The Internal Revenue Service is given the responsibility to enforce the tax laws.

# DEPLETION

|   | | |
|---|---|---|
| | Original cost | $ 100,000.00 |
| − | Estimated Salvage Value | − $12,250.00 |
| = | Estimated Total Value of Coal | $ 87,750.00 |
| ÷ | Estimated Tons of Recoverable Coal | ÷ 50,000 |
| = | Depletion Rate per Ton of Coal | $ 1.755 |

Plant asset: Coal mine
Depletion method: Production-unit
Original cost: $100,000.00
Estimated salvage value: $12,250.00

**1.** Calculate the depletion rate.

❶ Estimated total depletion: $87,750.00
Estimated tons of recoverable coal: 50,000 tons
Depletion rate: $1.755 per ton

| Year | Beginning Book Value | Tons Recovered | Annual Depletion | Ending Book Value |
|---|---|---|---|---|
| 1 | $100,000.00 | 6,000 | $10,530.00 | $89,470.00 |
| 2 | 89,470.00 | 12,000 | 21,060.00 | 68,410.00 |
| 3 | 68,410.00 | 13,000 | 22,815.00 | 45,595.00 |
| 4 | 45,595.00 | 9,000 | 15,795.00 | 29,800.00 |
| 5 | 29,800.00 | 6,000 | 10,530.00 | 19,270.00 |
| Totals | | 46,000 | $80,730.00 | |

❷

| | Tons of Coal Removed | × | Depletion Rate | = | Annual Depletion Expense |
|---|---|---|---|---|---|
| Year 1 | 6,000 | × | $1.755 | = | $10,530.00 |

**2.** Calculate the annual depletion.

Some plant assets decrease in value because part of these plant assets is physically removed in the operation of a business. For example, a lumber business owns land on which many trees grow. The business removes the trees to use for lumber. The land with the trees still growing on it is more valuable than the land from which the trees have been removed. The decrease in the value of a plant asset because of the removal of a natural resource is called **depletion**.

McGladden Company owns land on which a coal mine is located. The land with the coal has an original cost of $100,000.00. The company's experts estimate that the land contains 50,000 tons of recoverable coal. The estimated value of the remaining land after the coal is removed is

$12,250.00. Therefore, each ton of coal taken from the land decreases the land's value by $1.755.

In the first year of operation, the business removed 6,000 tons of coal. The depletion expense for the first year is $10,530.00 as shown above. McGladden uses the general ledger accounts Mine, Accumulated Depletion—Mine, and Depletion Expense—Mine to record depletion.

**FYI** FOR YOUR INFORMATION

Depletion is used to charge the cost of a variety of natural resources, including oil, gas, coal, gravel, minerals, and timber.

**REMEMBER** The method used to compute depletion is the same as the production-unit method of depreciation. A rate per unit of production is multiplied by the amount of production to compute depletion.

## terms review

TERMS REVIEW • TERMS REVIEW

declining-balance method of
 depreciation
sum-of-the-years'-digits method
 of depreciation
production-unit method of
 depreciation
Modified Accelerated Cost
 Recovery System
depletion

## audit your understanding

AUDIT YOUR UNDERSTANDING

1. Which depreciation method does not use the estimated salvage value to compute annual depreciation?
2. What is the basis for the production-unit method of calculating depreciation?
3. How does a mining company calculate the amount of depletion for a year?

## work together 8-4

WORK TOGETHER • WORK TOGETHER • WORK TOGETHER

**Computing depreciation using various depreciation methods and calculating depletion**

The following information relates to a delivery truck purchased on January 2, 20X1. Depreciation tables are provided in the *Working Papers*. Your instructor will guide you through the following examples.

|  |  | Miles Driven |  |
|---|---|---|---|
| Original Cost | $90,000.00 | 20X1 | 34,600 |
| Estimated Salvage Value | $6,000.00 | 20X2 | 47,300 |
| Estimated Useful Life | 3 years or 200,000 miles | 20X3 | 52,800 |
| MACRS Property Class | 5-year | 20X4 | 36,900 |

1. Complete depreciation tables showing depreciation expense calculated using the double declining-balance, sum-of-the-years'-digits, production-unit, and MACRS methods of depreciation.

The following data relate to a mineral mine owned by Kellogg, Inc. A depletion table is provided in the *Working Papers*.

|  |  | Tons Mined |  |
|---|---|---|---|
| Original Cost | $260,000.00 | 20X1 | 3,500 |
| Estimated Salvage Value | $60,000.00 | 20X2 | 12,500 |
| Estimated Tons of Recoverable Minerals | 60,000 tons | 20X3 | 15,600 |

2. Complete a table showing depletion expense calculated using the production-unit method.

## • on your own 8-4

**Computing depreciation using various depreciation methods and calculating depletion**

The following information relates to a machine purchased on January 3, 20X1. Work independently to complete the following problem.

| | | Year | Hours |
|---|---|---|---|
| Original Cost | $13,500.00 | 20X1 | 600 |
| Estimated Salvage Value | $1,500.00 | 20X2 | 1,200 |
| Estimated Useful Life | 5 years or 5,000 hours | 20X3 | 900 |
| MACRS Property Class | 5 year | 20X4 | 1,000 |
| | | 20X5 | 800 |

1. Complete tables showing depreciation expense calculated using the double declining-balance, sum-of-the-years'-digits, production-unit, and MACRS methods of depreciation.

The following data relate to a gas well owned by JH Enterprises.

| | | Year | MCF Recovered |
|---|---|---|---|
| Original Cost | $920,000.00 | 20X1 | 30,000 |
| Estimated Salvage Value | $20,000.00 | 20X2 | 90,000 |
| Estimated MCF of Recoverable Gas | 600,000 MCF | 20X3 | 100,000 |
| | | 20X4 | 120,000 |

2. Complete a depletion table for this well; show depletion expense calculated using the production-unit method.

Xtra!
Review

## SUMMARY

*After completing this chapter, you can*

1. Define accounting terms related to plant assets and depreciation.

2. Identify accounting concepts and practices related to accounting for plant assets and decpreciation.

3. Journalize entries for buying plant assets.

4. Calculate and record property tax expense.

5. Calculate and record depreciation expense for a plant asset using straight-line depreciation.

6. Journalize entries for disposing of plant assets.

7. Calculate depreciation expense using other methods.

# Explore Accounting

EXPLORE ACCOUNTING • EXPLORE ACCOUNTING • EXPLORE ACCO

## Tax Laws Encourage Plant Assets Purchases

Tax law and generally accepted accounting principles (GAAP) often have conflicting objectives. Tax law is enacted to generate tax revenues. In contrast, GAAP are designed to report the results of operations.

The primary purpose of federal income tax laws is to guide the government's collection of tax revenue. However, Congress also uses income tax law to influence businesses. To promote economic development, Congress has periodically passed tax laws that provide businesses with financial incentives to purchase plant assets.

A business that purchases plant assets will likely hire more employees, purchase additional raw materials, and earn a higher net income—all resulting in increasing economic activity and income tax revenues. Congress has used the following three tax laws to enable businesses to recover a larger portion of their plant asset purchases in the first year than would be permitted by simply using straight-line depreciation.

*Accelerated Depreciation:* To spur the economy after World War II, Congress modified the tax laws in 1954 to permit the use of accelerated depreciation methods.

*Investment Tax Credit:* In 1962, President Kennedy proposed a tax credit for certain purchases of plant assets. Congress has periodically changed the percentage credits, purchase limitations, and qualifying assets. Unlike a tax deduction, a tax credit is a reduction in the tax paid. For example, a company purchasing an 8% qualifying asset for $50,000 could reduce its tax liability by $4,000.

*Section 179 Property:* In 1986, the rising federal debt motivated Congress to reduce the investment tax credit in favor of a tax law that enabled a business to expense up to $17,500 of plant asset purchases each year. For example, a company purchasing $50,000 of equipment could expense $17,500 of the equipment in the year of purchase and depreciate the remaining $32,500 using the current tax rates.

GAAP allow the use of accelerated depreciation methods. However, neither the investment tax credit nor Section 179 property rules can be used for financial reporting.

**Required:**
Obtain a copy of IRS Form 4562, Depreciation and Amortization. Identify the parts of the form used to report Section 179 property and MACRS depreciation. Prepare a list of amounts and other information that is required to prepare the form.

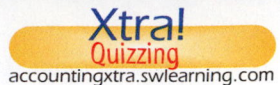

## 8-1 APPLICATION PROBLEM

### Journalizing entries to record buying plant assets

Mannings, Inc. uses three plant asset accounts: Office Equipment, Store Equipment, and Warehouse Equipment.

**Transactions:**

Jan.  2.  Paid cash for office file cabinet (plant asset no. 1), $500.00: estimated salvage value, $50.00; estimated useful life, five years; serial no. FC2467. C130.

Jan.  3.  Bought office word processor (plant asset no. 2) on account from Darst, Inc., $400.00: no estimated salvage value; estimated useful life, five years; serial no. X4672Y101. M11.

Apr.  4.  Bought hand truck (plant asset no. 3) for warehouse on account from Boeser, Inc., $100.00: estimated salvage value, $25.00; estimated useful life, five years; serial no. 23D4689. M24.

May  1.  Paid cash for used truck (plant asset no. 4) to be used between warehouses, $8,500.00: estimated salvage value, $1,000.00; estimated useful life, five years; serial no. 45J3257XF29. C210.

July  1.  Paid cash for store shelving (plant asset no. 5), $500.00: estimated salvage value, $25.00; estimated useful life, 10 years; no serial no. C250.

**Instructions:**

1. Journalize the transactions completed during the current year. Use page 1 of a general journal and page 1 of a cash payments journal. General ledger accounts are: Office Equipment, 1225; Store Equipment, 1235; and Warehouse Equipment, 1245. Source documents are abbreviated as follows: check, C; memorandum, M.
2. Complete Section 1 of a plant asset record for each plant asset. Save the plant asset records from Application Problem 8-1 to complete Application Problems 8-3, 8-4, and 8-5.

## 8-2 APPLICATION PROBLEM

### Calculating and journalizing property tax

Dependable Deliveries, Inc., has real property with an assessed value of $350,000.00. The annual tax rate in the city where the property is located is 4.5% of assessed value. Half of the annual tax is collected every six months.

**Instructions:**

1. Calculate Dependable Deliveries' total annual property tax.
2. Journalize the payment of the tax on February 26 with check No. 124. Use page 3 of a cash payments journal.

## 8-3 APPLICATION PROBLEM

### Calculating depreciation using the straight-line method

Use the plant asset record from Application Problem 8-1. Complete a depreciation table for each of the plant assets bought by Mannings, Inc. Save the depreciation tables from Application Problem 8-3 to complete Application Problem 8-4.

## 8-4 APPLICATION PROBLEM

### Journalizing annual depreciation expense

Use the plant asset records from Application Problem 8-1 and the depreciation tables from Application Problem 8-3.

**Instructions:**

1. Use the plant asset records prepared in Application Problem 8-1. For each plant asset, record depreciation for 20X1 in section 3 of the plant asset record.

2. Use page 12 of a general journal and the depreciation tables prepared in Application Problem 8-3. Journalize the three adjusting entries for office, store, and warehouse depreciation expense on December 31, 20X1.
3. For each plant asset, record depreciation for 20X2, 20X3, and 20X4 in section 3 of the plant asset record.
4. Journalize the three adjusting entries for December 31, 20X2. Save the plant asset records from Application Problem 8-4 to complete Application Problem 8-5.

## 8-5 APPLICATION PROBLEM
### Recording disposal of plant assets

Use the plant asset records from Application Problem 8-4. Mannings, Inc., completed the following transactions. Use the appropriate plant asset records from Application Problem 8-4 for additional information needed. Use page 1 of a general journal, page 6 of a cash receipts journal, and page 12 of a cash payments journal. Source documents are abbreviated as follows: check, C; memorandum, M; receipt, R.

**Transactions:**
Jan. 21, 20X5. An office word processor, plant asset no. 2, was no longer being used. It was discarded. M522.
Jan. 28, 20X5. Discarded office file cabinet, plant asset no. 1. M523.
Mar. 29, 20X6. Received cash for sale of hand truck, $10.00, plant asset no. 3. M575 and R645.
Dec. 31, 20X6. Received cash for sale of store shelving, $250.00, plant asset no. 5. M631 and R733.
Dec. 31, 20X6. Paid $8,000.00 in cash plus old truck, plant asset no. 4, for new truck, plant asset no. 29. M632 and C815.

**Instructions:**
1. For each transaction in 20X5, do the following.
   a. Journalize an entry for additional depreciation if needed.
   b. Journalize the disposal of the plant asset.
   c. Make appropriate notations in the plant asset record.
2. Complete each plant asset record for the year.
3. Repeat instructions 1 and 2 for 20X6.

## 8-6 APPLICATION PROBLEM
### Recording the sale of land and building

On January 2, 20X6, Jamestown, Inc., sold land and a company operations building it is no longer using. The following data relating to the land and building are obtained from the accounting records of Jamestown:

| | |
|---|---|
| Cash Received | $73,000.00 |
| Original Cost of Land | 20,000.00 |
| Original Cost of Building | 100,000.00 |
| Accumulated Depreciation on Building to 12/31/X5 | 61,200.00 |

**Instructions:**
1. Journalize the sale of the land and building. Use page 12 of a cash receipts journal. The source document is receipt no. 125.
2. Make appropriate notations in the plant asset records.

## 8-7 APPLICATION PROBLEM AUTOMATED ACCOUNTING

### Calculating depreciation expense using the straight-line, declining-balance, and sum-of-the-years'-digits methods

The following data relating to an office desk are obtained from the accounting records of Byrum, Inc.

| | |
|---|---|
| Original Cost | $2,400.00 |
| Estimated Salvage Value | 200.00 |
| Estimated Useful Life | 4 years |

**Instructions:**

Prepare a depreciation table showing depreciation expense calculated using the straight-line, declining-balance, and sum-of-the-years'-digits methods.

## 8-8 APPLICATION PROBLEM

### Calculating depreciation expense using the production-unit method

The following data relating to a truck are obtained from the accounting records of Marcotte, Inc.:

| | |
|---|---|
| Original Cost | $10,000.00 |
| Estimated Salvage Value | 1,000.00 |
| Estimated Useful Life | 120,000 miles |

**Instructions:**

1. Calculate the depreciation rate.
2. Prepare a depreciation table for this truck showing depreciation expense calculated using the production-unit method.

## 8-9 APPLICATION PROBLEM

### Calculating depreciation expense using MACRS

The following data relating to a computer are obtained from the accounting records of Caesar Company.

| | |
|---|---|
| Original Cost | $3,300.00 |
| Property Class | 5-year property |

**Instructions:**

Prepare a depreciation table showing depreciation expense calculated using MACRS.

## 8-10 APPLICATION PROBLEM

### Calculating depletion expense using production-unit method

The following data relating to a coal mine are obtained from the accounting records of Geist, Inc.

| | |
|---|---|
| Original Cost | $45,000.00 |
| Estimated Salvage Value | 1,000.00 |
| Estimated Tons of Recoverable Coal | 50,000 tons |

**Instructions:**

Prepare a depletion table for this mine showing depletion expense calculated using the production-unit method.

## 8-11 MASTERY PROBLEM    AUTOMATED ACCOUNTING    PEACHTREE    QUICKBOOKS
### Recording entries for plant assets

Western, Inc., uses the straight-line method of calculating depreciation expense. Western uses one plant asset account, Office Equipment, account no. 1230. The plant asset records for Western are given in the *Working Papers*.

**Transactions:**

Jan.    2.    Paid cash for new computer, plant asset no. 172, $1,900.00: estimated salvage value, $400.00; estimated useful life, five years; serial no. SD345J267. C122.

Jan.    2.    Discarded desk, serial no. D3481, plant asset no. 167. M47.

Mar.    29.    Discarded table, serial no. T3929, plant asset no. 168. M52.

Mar.    30.    Received cash from sale of word processor, $100.00: serial no. TM48194H32, plant asset no. 170. M54 and R191.

June    29.    Received cash from sale of filing cabinet, $150.00: serial no. FC125, plant asset no. 169. M62 and R224.

July    2.    Paid cash, $500.00, plus old copying machine, serial no. C56M203, plant asset no. 171, for new copying machine: estimated salvage value of new machine, $100.00; estimated useful life of new machine, five years; serial no., C35194, plant asset no. 173. M70 and C239.

**Instructions:**

1. Journalize the transactions completed during 20X9. Journalize an entry for additional depreciation expense if needed. Use page 1 of a general journal, page 6 of a cash receipts journal, and page 8 of a cash payments journal. Source documents are abbreviated as follows: check, C; memorandum, M; receipt, R.
2. Make needed notations on plant asset records or prepare new records.


## 8-12 CHALLENGE PROBLEM    AUTOMATED ACCOUNTING    PEACHTREE    QUICKBOOKS
### Recording entries for plant assets

McNeilley, Inc., uses the straight-line method to calculate depreciation expense. McNeilley uses two plant asset accounts, Office Equipment and Delivery Equipment.

**Transactions:**

Jan. 1, 20X1.    Paid cash for new office word processor, plant asset no. 1, $600.00: estimated salvage value, $100.00; estimated useful life, eight years; serial no. T45M3409. C130.

Mar. 1, 20X1.    Paid cash for office desk, plant asset no. 2, $700.00: estimated salvage value, $150.00; estimated useful life, five years; serial no. D345. C190.

June 30, 20X1.    Paid cash for office chair, plant asset no. 3, $125.00: estimated salvage value, $10.00; estimated useful life, five years; no serial no. C200.

July 1, 20X1.    Paid cash for delivery truck, plant asset no. 4, $10,000.00: estimated salvage value, $1,000.00; estimated useful life, five years; serial no. 345X32LD54. C220.

Jan. 2, 20X3.    Paid cash, $400.00, plus old word processor, serial no. T45M3409, for new word processor: estimated salvage value of new word processor, $100.00; estimated useful life of new word processor, plant asset no. 5, five years; new word processor serial no. T64M4391. M50 and C300.

July 1, 20X3.    Discarded office chair bought on June 30, 20X1. M66.

Sept. 1, 20X3.    Paid cash, $5,500.00, plus old delivery truck, serial no. 345X32LD54, for new delivery truck: estimated salvage value of new truck, $2,000.00; estimated useful life of new truck, plant asset no. 6, five years; new truck serial no. 432XY30LE25. M70 and C310.

**Instructions:**

Journalize the transactions. Use page 7 of a general journal and page 12 of a cash payments journal. Source documents are abbreviated as follows: check, C; memorandum, M; receipt, R.

## • applied communication

Examine the comparison of depreciation methods in the schedule at the top of page 244. Although the amount of depreciation recorded each year varies, the total depreciation over the asset's full life is the same.

**Required:**

Prepare a graph comparing the three depreciation methods. Make sure the graph is clearly labeled. The declining-balance method and the sum-of-the-years'-digits method are often referred to as accelerated depreciation methods. Use the graph to explain what is meant by accelerated depreciation.

## • cases for critical thinking

### Case 1

A corporation's plant assets include office equipment, a building, and the land on which the building is located. The corporation's general ledger includes a single account, Plant Assets, and a single account, Accumulated Depreciation—Plant Assets. The corporation's accountant suggests that the plant assets be divided into three accounts, Office Equipment, Building, and Land. The corporation's president does not think this is a good idea. With whom do you agree and why?

### Case 2

A corporation owns land on which there are both an active coal mine and timber. The corporation also owns an office building and the land on which it is located. The corporation uses three plant asset accounts: (1) Land and Buildings (depreciation calculated using the straight-line method). (2) Timber (depreciation calculated using the declining-balance method). (3) Coal Mine (depreciation calculated using the declining-balance method). Do you agree with the accounting procedures being used? Explain your answers.

### Case 3

A corporation currently uses straight-line depreciation for all plant assets. Its balance sheet reports accumulated depreciation and its income statement reports the depreciation expense for the current period. When the corporation's tax accountant prepares the corporate income tax return, all depreciation is reported using MACRS. Assume that all of the company's assets are one or two years old. Further assume that all the assets are in the 5-year property class. Will the net income reported on the tax return be greater than or less than the net income reported on the income statement? Explain your reasoning.

### Case 4

The city in which a corporation is located has a business property tax. This tax is 1% of all business property over $50,000. The corporation is a small service business. Its assets that are subject to the tax are only $10,000. The law states that all businesses must file a return even if they owe no tax. The penalty for not filing is $100. The corporation's accountant has attempted to complete the tax return. However, some parts of the return are very technical. The accountant gets an estimate from a tax specialist to prepare the return. The estimate is $125 for the first year and $75 for the second and third years. What should the accountant do?

## SCANS workplace competency (part I)

*(The information collected and organized in this activity is used to complete the SCANS Workplace Competency in Chapter 9.)*

**Information Competency:** Organizing and Maintaining Information

**Concept:** Competent employees possess the ability to organize, process, and maintain written or computerized records and other forms of information in a systematic fashion. The ability to sort, classify, and organize data from computerized databases, spreadsheets, videodisks, and paper files is critical.

**Application:** Visit the admissions pages of at least three college web sites. Select and organize information that compares a variety of admission data and requirements. Your comparison might include recommended high school subjects, cost of applying, required test scores, letters of recommendation, high school transcripts, entrance essays, deadlines, number of applicants, average GPAs and SAT scores of freshmen, ethnicity, average class size, and geographic origin of students. Save collected data for use in the next chapter's SCANS activity.

## auditing for errors

On June 5, 20X3, Fairborn, Inc., purchased a new cutting machine for use in its factory. The machine cost $15,000.00 and has an estimated salvage value of $1,000.00 and an estimated useful life of five years. Fairborn used the double-declining balance method of depreciation. The bookkeeper prepared the following plant asset record.

| PLANT ASSET RECORD, No. | 305 | General Ledger Account No. | 1150 |
|---|---|---|---|

Description: *Cutting Machine*   General Ledger Account: *Factory Equipment*

Date Bought: *June 5, 20X3*   Serial Number: *G77U3JK298*   Original Cost: *$15,000.00*

Estimated Useful Life: *5 years*   Estimated Salvage Value: *$1,000.00*   Depreciation Method: *Double-declining Balance*

Disposed of: Discarded ✓   Sold ____   Traded ____

Date: *January 5, 20X6*   Disposal Amount: *zero*

| YEAR | ANNUAL DEPRECIATION EXPENSE | ACCUMULATED DEPRECIATION | ENDING BOOK VALUE |
|---|---|---|---|
| 20X3 | 5,600.00 | 5,600.00 | 9,400.00 |

**Instructions:**

1. Find the error in the plant asset record.
2. Write a written explanation of the error to the bookkeeper. In your explanation, give the correct calculation.

## analyzing Costco's financial statements

An income statement is a financial statement prepared on an accrual basis. A statement of cash flows is a financial statement prepared on a cash basis. It shows how and where the company received cash and spent cash. On a statement of cash flows, outflows of cash are usually shown in parenthesis. Inflows of cash are shown as positive amounts. These inflows and outflows of cash are organized into three categories—operating activities, investing activities, and financing activities. Buying and selling plant assets are classified as investing activities.

**Instructions:**

1. Go to the statement of cash flows for Costco on Appendix B page B-8. Find the heading "Cash flows from investing activities." Find the largest outflow of cash from investing activities for 2003. List the item and the amount of the outflow.
2. Find the largest inflow of cash from investing activities for 2003. List the item and the amount of the inflow.
3. How much cash has been used to purchase property and equipment over the last three years?
4. How much cash has been received from the sale of property and equipment over the last three years?

## Automated Depreciation and Creating Depreciation Schedules

In *Automated Accounting 8.0*, depreciation schedules can be maintained using the following methods: straight-line (SL), double-declining-balance (DDB), and sum-of-the-years'-digits (SYD).

### Adding Plant Asset Data

Complete plant asset information is required for each plant asset. The information is entered in the Plant Assets tab of the Account Maintenance window. To add a new asset, enter all the requested information on a new line. Then click the Add Asset button.

Plant asset data can also be changed by clicking on the cell containing the data to be changed. The Add Asset button changes to the Change Asset button.

### Displaying or Printing Plant Asset Reports

A plant asset list and depreciation schedules can be displayed and printed by selecting the appropriate report. When selecting the depreciation schedules report, select the asset or range of assets for the depreciation schedules you want to generate.

### Generating Depreciation Adjusting Entries

Choose Depreciation Adjusting Entries from the Option menu. Click Yes to generate the depreciation adjusting entries. The software will analyze the plant asset records, calculate an amount based on the period, and generate the depreciation adjusting entries. The journal entries will display on the screen for your review and confirmation. Verify the accuracy of the entries, then click the Post button.

### AUTOMATING APPLICATION PROBLEM 8-7

**Instructions:**

1. Load *Automated Accounting 8.0* or higher software.
2. Select database A08-07 (Advanced Course Application Problem 8-7) from the accounting template disk.
3. Select File from the menu bar and choose the Save As menu command. Key the path to the drive and directory that contain your data files. Save the database with a filename of XXX087 (where XXX are your initials).
4. Read the Problem Instruction screen by clicking the Browser toolbar button.
5. Refer to page 253 for data used in this problem.
6. Exit the Automated Accounting software.

### AUTOMATING MASTERY PROBLEM 8-11

**Instructions:**

1. Load *Automated Accounting 8.0* or higher software.
2. Select database A08-11 (Advanced Course Mastery Problem 8-11) from the accounting template disk.
3. Select File from the menu bar and choose the Save As menu command. Key the path to the drive and directory that contain your data files. Save the database with a filename of XXX0811 (where XXX are your initials).
4. Read the Problem Instruction screen by clicking the Browser toolbar button.
5. Key the data listed in the problem.
6. Exit the Automated Accounting software.

### AUTOMATING CHALLENGE PROBLEM 8-12

**Instructions:**

1. Load *Automated Accounting 8.0* or higher software.
2. Select database A08-12 (Advanced Course Challenge Problem 8-12) from the accounting template disk.
3. Select File from the menu bar and choose the Save As menu command. Key the path to the drive and directory that contain your data files. Save the database with a filename of XXX0812 (where XXX are your initials).
4. Read the Problem Instruction screen by clicking the Browser toolbar button.
5. Key the data listed in the problem.
6. Exit the Automated Accounting software.

# CHAPTER 9

# Accounting for Notes Payable, Prepaid Expenses, and Accrued Expenses

*After studying Chapter 9, you will be able to:*

1. Define accounting terms related to notes payable, prepaid expenses, and accrued expenses.

2. Identify accounting concepts and practices related to notes payable, prepaid expenses, and accrued expenses.

3. Journalize transactions for notes payable.

4. Journalize adjusting and reversing entries for prepaid expenses initially recorded as expenses.

5. Journalize adjusting and reversing entries for accrued expenses.

- promissory note
- notes payable
- date of a note
- principal of a note
- maturity date of a note
- interest
- interest rate of a note
- interest expense
- maturity value
- prepaid expenses
- reversing entry
- accrued expenses

Point Your Browser
accountingxtra.swlearning.com

## • The Mall of America

©BILL ALKOFER/BLOOMBERG NEWS/LANDOV

### AN ENTIRE CITY UNDER ONE ROOF— THE MALL OF AMERICA

Around the world, the Mall of America is considered the premier place to shop. However, the Mall of America (MOA) is not just a shopping mall. It is the largest retail and entertainment complex in the United States.

Many people are aware of some of the entertainment options available at the MOA, including Camp Snoopy (the nation's largest indoor theme park), Underwater Adventures (a $1.2 million walk-through aquarium), a 14-screen movie theater, and nearly 60 sit-down or fast food restaurants and nightclubs.

What really makes the MOA a city under one roof, however, is some of the other opportunities it offers. You can attend classes at the first-ever college campus in a mall. You can get health care at the Sage Clinic. You can complete all your banking needs, including foreign currency exchanges, at a bank in the mall. You can use the services of the post office—the only full-service post office located in a mall in the U.S. You can join the Walksport Mall Stars, a walking club with over 4,000 members who use the MOA as a place to exercise and socialize. You can even get married in the Chapel of Love Wedding Chapel!

The Mall of America certainly is an entire city under one roof.

### Critical Thinking

1.  Assume you are a tenant at the Mall of America and must pay your rent one year in advance. Besides Cash, what other account would you use to record this transaction?
2.  The Mall of America calls itself a "retail and entertainment" complex. Why is the idea of combining retail stores and entertainment attractive to consumers?

Source: www.mallofamerica.com

Xtra!
Today
accountingxtra.swlearning.com

### SERVICE CORPS OF RETIRED EXECUTIVES (SCORE)

Go to the homepage of the Service Corps of Retired Executives (SCORE) (www.score.org).

#### Instructions

1.  Briefly describe SCORE.
2.  Find the location of the SCORE chapter nearest you. List the address of this chapter.
3.  Go to the web site for this SCORE chapter. List one requirement for becoming a SCORE consultant.

# 9-1 Notes Payable

Business transactions occur throughout a fiscal period. Some transactions begin in one accounting period and are completed in a different accounting period. Accounting records for each period, however, must show all information needed to prepare the financial statements of a business. [CONCEPT: *Adequate Disclosure*] Therefore, some financial activities require the use of special accounting procedures.

Most expenses occur in the same period in which a cash payment is made for the expense. Some expenses, such as insurance and advertising, require cash payment before the benefit is received. Thus, a cash payment for these expenses may occur in the fiscal period before the related expense should be recognized. In addition, a business may borrow money in one period and repay it in another period. Interest owed in the current period must be included in the financial statements of the current period. [CONCEPT: *Matching Expenses with Revenue*]

©GETTY IMAGES/PHOTODISC

## making ethical decisions

### Reporting Ethics Violations

What should employees do when they witness another employee possibly violating a law or the company's code of conduct? Many companies instruct their employees to report the possible violation to an ethics officer or compliance department. A phone number that allows an individual to provide confidential information regarding possible ethics violations is often referred to as a *hotline*.

For a hotline to be effective, employees must have confidence that their information is being treated seriously. One way Hewlett-Packard achieves this objective is to publish a report that describes the number and types of calls received by its Office of Business Practices.

**Instructions**

Access the global citizenship report of Hewlett-Packard. What are the five most common categories of issues reported to the Office of Business Practices? Identify the year of the report, total number of issues reported, and the percent of issues of the top five categories.

| | DATE | ACCOUNT TITLE | DOC. NO. | POST. REF. | GENERAL | | ACCOUNTS RECEIVABLE CREDIT | SALES CREDIT | SALES TAX PAYABLE | | SALES DISCOUNT DEBIT | CASH DEBIT | |
|---|---|---|---|---|---|---|---|---|---|---|---|---|---|
| | | | | | DEBIT | CREDIT | | | DEBIT | CREDIT | | | |
| 1 | Mar. 2 | Notes Payable | R143 | | | 1 5 0 0 00 | | | | | | 1 5 0 0 00 | 1 |
| 2 | | | | | | | | | | | | | 2 |
| 3 | | | | | | | | | | | | | 3 |

CASH RECEIPTS JOURNAL — PAGE 5

A written and signed promise to pay a sum of money at a specified time is called a **promissory note**. Promissory notes signed by a business and given to a creditor are called **notes payable**. The day a note is issued is called the **date of a note**. The original amount of a note is called the **principal of a note**. The date a note is due is called the **maturity date of a note**. An amount paid for the use of money for a period of time is called **interest**. The percentage of the principal that is paid for use of the money is called the **interest rate of a note**.

Appliance Center occasionally borrows money from a bank. It signs a note payable with the bank as evidence of the debt.

*March 2. Signed a 180-day, 10% note, $1,500.00. R143.*

Upon signing the note, Appliance Center receives the $1,500.00. It records the transaction in the cash receipts journal as shown above. Appliance Center issues a receipt that is used as the source document for the transaction. [*CONCEPT: Objective Evidence*]

| Cash | |
|---|---|
| 1,500.00 | |

| Notes Payable | |
|---|---|
| | 1,500.00 |

**FYI**
FOR YOUR INFORMATION

A note payable that will be repaid during the next fiscal year should be recorded in an account classified as a current liability. A note payable scheduled to mature in later fiscal periods should be classified as a long-term liability. When borrowing money for five or more years, many companies issue written promises referred to as bonds. The accounting for bonds is presented in Chapter 12.

**small business spotlight**
SMALL BUSINESS SPOTLIGHT

Finding new markets is a key to growing any business. For many small businesses, those new markets span the globe. It is not unusual to find new markets as close to home as Canada and Mexico and as far away as Africa and the Pacific Rim. With the number of small businesses on the increase, the U.S. Commerce Department has developed and expanded programs aimed at helping small businesses export their products.

# CALCULATING THE MATURITY DATE

| Time | Number of Days | | |
|---|---|---|---|
| March 2 through March 31 | 29 | (31 – 2 = 29) ◄ | ① 1. Compute the number of days in the first month. |
| April | 30 | | |
| May | 31 | | |
| June | 30 | | ② 2. Add the number of days in subsequent months until the total equals the number of days of the note. |
| July | 31 | | |
| August 1 through August 29 | 29 | (Maturity date: August 29) | |
| | 180 | days | |

The number of days in each month during the term of the note impacts the maturity date. The maturity date for Appliance Center's 180-day, March 2 note payable is August 29. The maturity date is determined as shown above.

## STEPS • STEPS • STEPS • STEPS

### CALCULATING THE MATURITY DATE

① Compute the number of days in the first month, *29*, by subtracting the date of the note, *2*, from the number of days in the month the note was signed, *31*.

② Continue adding the number of days in each of the following months until the total equals the number of days of the note, *180*.

## FYI — FOR YOUR INFORMATION

The term of a note can be stated in months or years. Thus, a six-month note dated March 2 matures on September 2. The number of days between March 2 and September 2 must be determined to use in interest calculations.

# CALCULATING INTEREST

| Principal | × | Interest Rate | × | Time as Fraction of Year | = | Interest for Fraction of Year |
|---|---|---|---|---|---|---|
| $1,500.00 | × | 10% | × | $\dfrac{180}{360}$ | = | $75.00 |

The interest rate of the note is stated as an annual rate. The interest paid on the note is calculated by applying the annual rate for the portion of the year that the note is outstanding as shown above. For ease of calculation, most banks use 360 rather than 365 as the number of days in a year.

## FYI — FOR YOUR INFORMATION

Agencies of the federal government generally use a 365-day year when calculating interest. Consumer interest also is generally calculated on a 365-day year. However, most banks use a 360-day year when calculating interest. Therefore, the interest calculations in this textbook use a 360-day year.

## PAYING A NOTE PAYABLE

**1.** Principal of note.

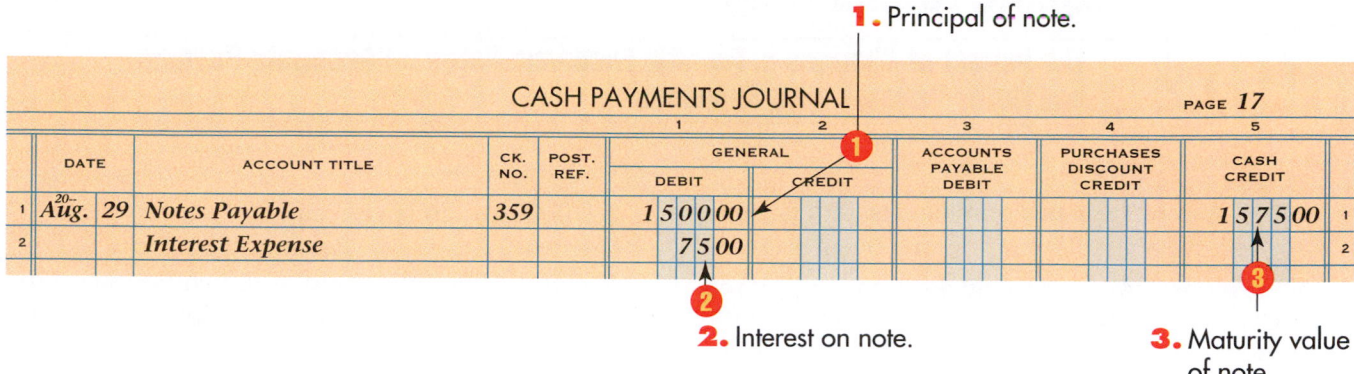

CASH PAYMENTS JOURNAL                                          PAGE 17

| | DATE | ACCOUNT TITLE | CK. NO. | POST. REF. | GENERAL DEBIT | GENERAL CREDIT | ACCOUNTS PAYABLE DEBIT | PURCHASES DISCOUNT CREDIT | CASH CREDIT | |
|---|---|---|---|---|---|---|---|---|---|---|
| 1 | Aug. 29 | Notes Payable | 359 | | 1500 00 | | | | 1575 00 | 1 |
| 2 | | Interest Expense | | | 75 00 | | | | | 2 |

**2.** Interest on note.

**3.** Maturity value of note.

The interest accrued on money borrowed is called **interest expense**. On the maturity date, the borrower pays both the principal of the note payable and the interest expense. The payment of the note is recorded in the cash payments journal as shown above. The amount that is due on the maturity date of a note is called the **maturity value**. Appliance Center pays the maturity value of its note on the maturity date.

> August 29. Paid cash for the maturity value of the Mar. 2 note: principal, $1,500.00, plus interest, $75.00; total, $1,575.00. Check No. 359.

Interest Expense is listed as an Other Expense on Appliance Center's chart of accounts. Expenses that are not a part of the normal operating expenses of a business are classified as other expenses.

| Notes Payable | |
|---|---|
| 1,500.00 | Bal.     1,500.00 |

| Interest Expense | |
|---|---|
| 75.00 | |

| Cash | |
|---|---|
| | 1,575.00 |

**FYI** FOR YOUR INFORMATION

The interest rate that banks charge their most creditworthy customers is known as the prime rate. The interest rate of a note payable to a bank is typically based on the prime rate. Depending on a company's credit history, banks charge a percentage amount over the prime rate. Thus, a bank may offer a company an interest rate of "prime plus 1½." If the prime rate is 8%, the note payable is written for 9½%.

A bank may require interest to be paid monthly during the period of the note. Monthly payments are recorded as a debit to Interest Expense and a credit to Cash. The final payment on the maturity date, therefore, includes the principal of the note payable plus the final month's interest.

©GETTY IMAGES/PHOTODISC

# Explore Accounting

## The Impact of Changes in Foreign Exchange Rates on Accounts Payable and Notes Payable with Suppliers

Often U.S. companies purchase products from foreign suppliers. Even though a business purchases a foreign product in a foreign country using foreign currency, that transaction will ultimately have to be presented in dollars by the U.S. firm. [*CONCEPT: Unit of Measurement*] Consequently, any changes in foreign exchange rates can have an impact on a firm's accounts payable and notes payable.

Suppose an American firm, PhoneCom, purchases semiconductors on account from ChinaSemi, a Chinese corporation, priced at 800,000 yuan (a denomination of Chinese currency). The terms of the purchase are for the American company to pay 800,000 yuan in 60 days. If the rate for exchanging a yuan to the dollar rises or declines during the 60-day credit period, there will be an impact on the value of the final payment amount. Assume on the date of the purchase that the exchange rate is one yuan equals .10 dollars. In other words, one yuan costs 10 cents to buy. At this exchange rate, 800,000 yuan is equal to $80,000 ($800,000 × .10). Suppose, however, that during the 60-day credit period the exchange rate changes. If the new rate is one yuan equals .12 dollars (12 cents), PhoneCom will now have to pay more for each yuan. It will now cost PhoneCom $96,000 (800,000 × .12) to buy 800,000 yuan. The rise of 2 cents in the exchange rate for the yuan means the American company will have to pay $16,000 more to settle its purchase on account agreement.

It is also possible that the exchange rate for yuan to dollars may decline. Assume an American company, CalTech, purchases equipment for 2,000,000 yuan from a Chinese firm, XianCorp. The Chinese company accepts a 12-month, 5% note in lieu of cash at the time of sale. In 12 months, CalTech will pay 2,100,000 yuan (principal + 5% interest) in payment of the note. Assuming an exchange rate at the beginning and at the end of the note of one yuan equals .10 dollars, CalTech would need $210,000 (2,100,000 × .10) to pay its note. Suppose, however, that during the 12-month credit period the exchange rate declines. If the new rate is one yuan equals .09 dollars (9 cents), the American company will now pay less for each yuan. Due to the decline in the exchange rate, CalTech will need only $189,000 (2,100,000 × .09) to buy 2,100,000 yuan. The decline of one cent in the exchange rate for the yuan means that CalTech will pay $21,000 less to settle its purchase on account agreement.

### Critical Thinking Activity

An American company, Fashion Clothiers, purchases men's clothing on account from a Canadian firm, Delmar, Inc., for 50,000 Canadian dollars. At the time of the sale, the exchange rate is one Canadian dollar equals .82 U.S. dollars. Thirty days later, when Fashion Clothiers pays the 50,000 Canadian dollars, the exchange rate has risen. One Canadian dollar can now be exchanged for .87 dollars. How much will it cost Fashion Clothiers to purchase Canadian dollars at the new rate? Will the American company realize a gain or a loss on the transaction? In your answer, state the amount of the gain or loss.

### Optional Critical Thinking Activity

Use the Internet or newspaper to track the exchange rate between the Canadian dollar and U.S. dollar for one week. Did the rate for exchanging one Canadian dollar for one U.S. dollar increase or decrease? State the amount of change.

## terms review

promissory note
notes payable
date of a note
principal of a note
maturity date of a note
interest
interest rate of a note
interest expense
maturity value

TERMS REVIEW • TERMS REVIEW

## audit your understanding

1. What formula does Appliance Center use to calculate interest on notes?
2. How is the interest rate on a note stated?
3. The borrower pays what two amounts at the note's maturity?

## work together 9-1

WORK TOGETHER • WORK TOGETHER • WORK

### Journalizing notes payable transactions

A cash receipts journal and a cash payments journal are provided in the *Working Papers*. Source documents are abbreviated as: check, C; receipt, R. Your instructor will guide you through the following examples.

1. Using the current year, journalize the following transactions in the cash receipts journal.

   May    14.  Signed a 90-day, 12% note with First National Bank, $5,000.00. R145.
   June    5.  Signed a 180-day, 10% note with American Bank, $8,000.00. R213.

2. Calculate the maturity date of each note and the total amount of interest due at maturity for each note.

3. Journalize the following transactions in the cash payments journal. Use the maturity dates and interest amounts calculated in the previous steps.

   Paid cash for the maturity value of the $5,000.00 note. C345.
   Paid cash for the maturity value of the $8,000.00 note. C652.

## on your own 9-1

ON YOUR OWN • ON YOUR OWN • ON YOUR OWN

### Journalizing notes payable transactions

A cash receipts journal and a cash payments journal are provided in the *Working Papers*. Source documents are abbreviated as: check, C; receipt, R. Work this problem independently.

1. Using the current year, journalize the following transactions in the cash receipts journal.

   Mar.    23.  Signed a 180-day, 10% note with Commerce Bank, $6,000.00. R84.
   July    12.  Signed a 60-day, 12% note with Farmers National Bank, $12,000.00. R151.

2. Calculate the maturity date for each note and the total amount of interest due at maturity for each note.

3. Journalize the following transactions on page 14 of a cash payments journal. Use the maturity dates and interest amounts calculated in the previous steps.

   Paid cash for the maturity value of the $12,000.00 note. C455.
   Paid cash for the maturity value of the $6,000.00 note. C464.

# 9-2 Prepaid Expenses

## DESCRIPTION OF PREPAID EXPENSES

Expenses paid in one fiscal period but not reported as expenses until a later fiscal period are called **prepaid expenses**. Prepaid expenses include items such as supplies, insurance, advertising, and income taxes. Only that portion of cash payment for expenses that have been used in the current fiscal period should be reported as an expense in that fiscal period. [*CONCEPT: Matching Expenses with Revenue*]

Prepaid expenses may be recorded initially as assets or as expenses. Zytech, described in Part 1, initially records cash payments for supplies and insurance as assets. Appliance Center, in contrast, initially records these payments as expenses. Both methods are acceptable provided that the company consistently applies its chosen method from year to year.

Prepaid expenses are assets until they are actually used. For example, Appliance Center has a quantity of sales supplies on hand on any given day during the year. The company will use these sales supplies in the current and future fiscal periods. The amount recorded in the account Supplies Expense—Sales prior to the fiscal year-end adjustments represents a mixture of an expense (supplies already used) and an asset (supplies not yet used).

Appliance Center records an adjusting entry to recognize as an expense only those sales supplies used during the fiscal year. An adjusting entry could be made each day to recognize the sales supplies used that day. However, as a practical accounting procedure, this adjusting entry is made only when financial statements need to be prepared. [*CONCEPT: Adequate Disclosure*] Appliance Center records adjustments on December 31, the end of its fiscal year.

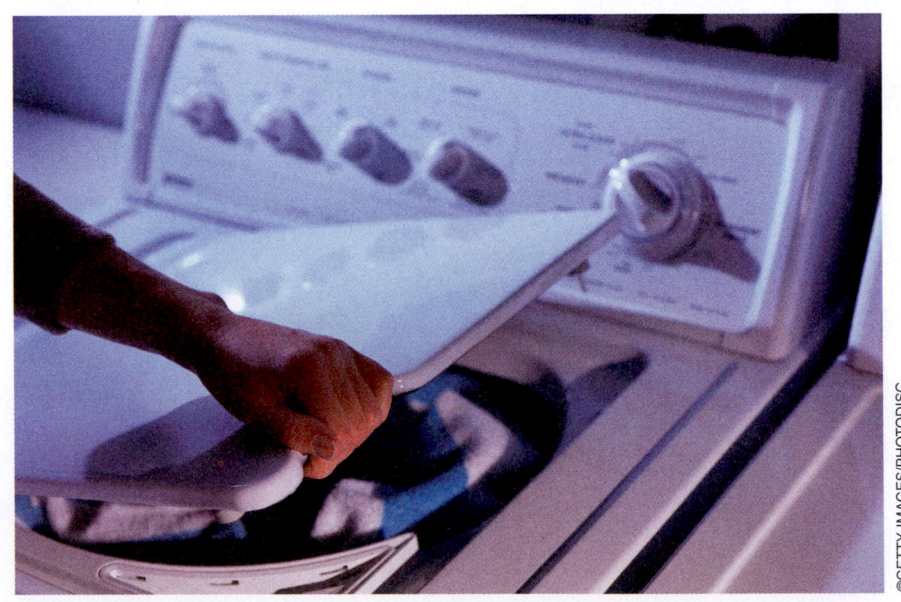

©GETTY IMAGES/PHOTODISC

**1.** Debit the expense account.

| | DATE | ACCOUNT TITLE | DOC. NO. | POST. REF. | DEBIT | CREDIT | |
|---|---|---|---|---|---|---|---|
| | | GENERAL JOURNAL | | | | PAGE *13* | |
| 1 | | *Adjusting Entries* | | | | | 1 |
| 2 | *Dec.* 20-- 31 | *Supplies Expense—Office* | | | 9 9 5 0 00 | | 2 |
| 3 | | *Supplies—Office* | | | | 9 9 5 0 00 | 3 |
| 4 | | | | | | | 4 |

**2.** Credit the asset account.

When Zytech, described in Part 1, buys office supplies, the asset Supplies—Office is debited and Cash is credited. Zytech recorded adjusting entries for supplies at the end of a fiscal period as shown above. Adjusting entries are recorded so that the supplies used during a fiscal period are reported as expenses and the supplies not used are reported as assets. [CONCEPT: Matching Expenses with Revenue]

Zytech initially recorded the prepaid supplies in the asset account Supplies—Office. The $12,700.00 debit balance represents the beginning inventory of supplies plus the total amount of all office supplies bought during the fiscal period. Nothing has been recorded in Zytech office supplies expense account during the fiscal period.

Zytech determined that the actual amount of office supplies inventory was $2,750.00. An adjusting entry of $9,950.00 ($12,700.00 – $2,750.00) is necessary.

After recording the adjustment, the new balance of Supplies—Office, *$2,750.00*, is the ending office supplies inventory on December 31. The new balance of Supplies Expense—Office, *$9,950.00*, represents supplies used during the current year.

| Supplies—Office | | |
|---|---|---|
| 12/31 Bal. 12,700.00 | 12/31 Adj. | 9,950.00 |
| (New Bal. 2,750.00) | | |

| Supplies Expense—Office | |
|---|---|
| 12/31 Adj. 9,950.00 | |

### Closing Entries

To prepare a general ledger for the next fiscal period, closing entries are journalized and posted.

After its closing entries have been posted, Zytech's general ledger accounts are ready for the next fiscal period. On December 31, the amount of the office supplies inventory, $2,750.00, is recorded in the account in which it can be added to the amount of supplies that will be bought in the next fiscal period.

| Income Summary | |
|---|---|
| 12/31 Clos. 9,950.00 | |

| Supplies Expense—Office | |
|---|---|
| 12/31 Adj. 9,950.00 | 12/31 Clos. 9,950.00 |
| (New Bal. zero) | |

---

**{ REMEMBER** Similar entries are made for each supply account, such as Supplies—Administrative and Supplies—Warehouse. **}**

---

**1.** Debit the asset account.

| | DATE | | ACCOUNT TITLE | DOC. NO. | POST. REF. | DEBIT | CREDIT | |
|---|---|---|---|---|---|---|---|---|
| 1 | | | *Adjusting Entries* | | | | | 1 |
| 11 | 31 | | *Supplies—Sales* | | | 8 0 0 00 | | 11 |
| 12 | | | *Supplies Expense—Sales* | | | | 8 0 0 00 | 12 |
| 13 | | | | | | | | 13 |

GENERAL JOURNAL   PAGE *13*

**2.** Credit the expense account.

When Appliance Center buys sales supplies, Supplies Expense—Sales is debited and Cash is credited. The $2,000.00 debit balance of Supplies Expense—Sales represents the amount of the beginning sales supplies inventory plus the total amount of all sales supplies bought during the fiscal period. Nothing has been recorded in Appliance Center's sales supplies account during the fiscal period.

On December 31, Appliance Center takes a physical count of the sales supplies on hand. It determines that the sales supplies ending inventory is $800.00 and records the necessary adjusting entry as shown above.

The new balance of Supplies—Sales, *$800.00*, represents the ending sales supplies inventory on December 31. The new balance of Supplies Expense—Sales, *$1,200.00*, recognizes the amount of sales supplies used during the current year.

Supplies—Sales

| 12/31 Adj. | 800.00 | |
|---|---|---|

Supplies Expense—Sales

| 12/31 Bal. | 2,000.00 | 12/31 Adj. | 800.00 |
|---|---|---|---|
| (New Bal. | 1,200.00) | | |

### Closing Entry for Supplies Expense

To prepare a general ledger for the next fiscal period, closing entries are journalized and posted. After the closing entry is recorded, the Supplies Expense—Sales account balance is zero. The debit balance of $800.00 in Supplies—Sales represents the amount of sales supplies on hand on December 31.

Income Summary

| 12/31 Clos. | 1,200.00 | |
|---|---|---|

Supplies Expense—Sales

| 12/31 Bal. | 2,000.00 | 12/31 Adj. | 800.00 |
|---|---|---|---|
| (New Bal. zero) | | 12/31 Clos. | 1,200.00 |

**REMEMBER** Although Zytech and Appliance Center use different procedures, both correctly separate and record the asset and expense portions of the cost of supplies. Both procedures meet the requirements of the *Matching Expenses with Revenue* concept.

**1.** Debit the expense account.

| | DATE | | ACCOUNT TITLE | DOC. NO. | POST. REF. | DEBIT | CREDIT | |
|---|---|---|---|---|---|---|---|---|
| 1 | | | *Reversing Entries* | | | | | 1 |
| 7 | | 1 | *Supplies Expense—Sales* | | | 8 0 0 00 | | 7 |
| 8 | | | *Supplies—Sales* | | | | 8 0 0 00 | 8 |
| 9 | | | | | | | | 9 |

GENERAL JOURNAL    PAGE *1*

**2.** Credit the asset account.

After the closing entries have been posted, Zytech's general ledger accounts are ready for the next fiscal period. However, Appliance Center's general ledger accounts are not ready for the next fiscal period.

Appliance Center initially records the amount of all supplies bought in an expense account. On December 31, the amount of Appliance Center's sales supplies inventory, *$800.00*, is the debit balance of Supplies—Sales. On January 1, the $800.00 should be returned as a debit in Supplies Expense—Sales. The $800.00 debit can then be added to the amount of sales supplies bought during the next year.

Some businesses that initially record prepaid items as expenses reverse the adjusting entries for prepaid expenses at the beginning of each fiscal period. An entry made at the beginning of one fiscal period to reverse an adjusting entry made in the previous fiscal period is called a **reversing entry**. Thus, a reversing entry is the exact opposite of the related adjusting entry.

Appliance Center initially records supplies as expenses and therefore needs to record reversing entries. Accountants use the following rule of thumb to determine whether a reversing entry is needed: If an adjusting entry *creates* a balance in an asset or a liability account, the adjusting entry is reversed.

Because Appliance Center's adjusting entry for sales supplies created a balance in Supplies—Sales, a reversing entry is needed. The reversing entry is shown above.

After the reversing entry is posted, the cost of the sales supplies inventory, *$800.00*, is recorded in the account where it can be added to the amount of supplies bought in the next fiscal period. The balance of Supplies—Sales is zero, as it was before the adjusting entry.

**Supplies Expense—Sales**

| 12/31 Bal. | 2,000.00 | 12/31 Adj. | 800.00 |
|---|---|---|---|
| 1/1 Rev. | 800.00 | 12/31 Clos. | 1,200.00 |
| (New Bal. | 800.00) | | |

**Supplies—Sales**

| 12/31 Adj. | 800.00 | 1/1 Rev. | 800.00 |
|---|---|---|---|
| (New Bal. zero) | | | |

**REMEMBER** Zytech initially records supplies as assets but *does not* record reversing entries. On December 31, the amount of the office supplies inventory, $2,750.00, is recorded in the account where it can be added to the amount of supplies bought in the next fiscal period.

**REMEMBER** Although Zytech and Appliance Center use different accounting procedures, both correctly separate and record the asset and expense portions of supply costs.

## PREPAID INSURANCE INITIALLY RECORDED AS AN EXPENSE

**1.** Debit the asset account.

**2.** Credit the expense account.

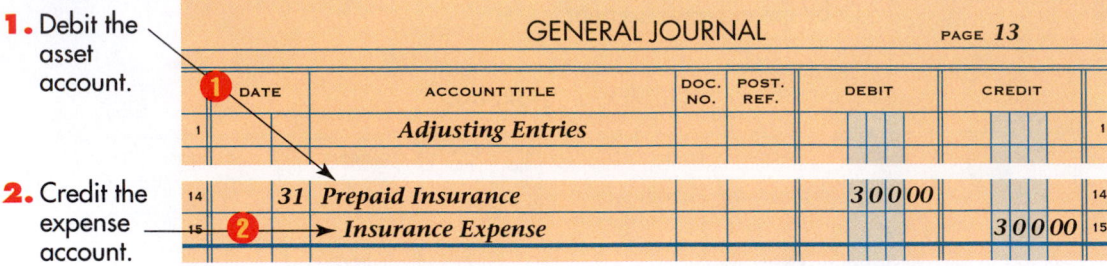

Appliance Center initially records insurance premiums as expenses. When Appliance Center pays insurance premiums, Insurance Expense is debited and Cash is credited.

On December 31, Appliance Center determines that the amount of the unexpired insurance premiums totals $300.00 and records the necessary adjusting entry as shown above.

The new balance of Prepaid Insurance, *$300.00*, represents the amount of unexpired insurance

premiums at the end of the fiscal period. The new balance of Insurance Expense *$600.00*, indicates the insurance expense for the fiscal period.

| Prepaid Insurance | | |
|---|---|---|
| 12/31 Adj. | 300.00 | |

| Insurance Expense | | |
|---|---|---|
| 12/31 Adj. | 900.00 | 12/31 Adj.    300.00 |
| (New Bal. | 600.00) | |

## REVERSING ENTRY FOR PREPAID INSURANCE

**1.** Debit the expense account.

**2.** Credit the asset account.

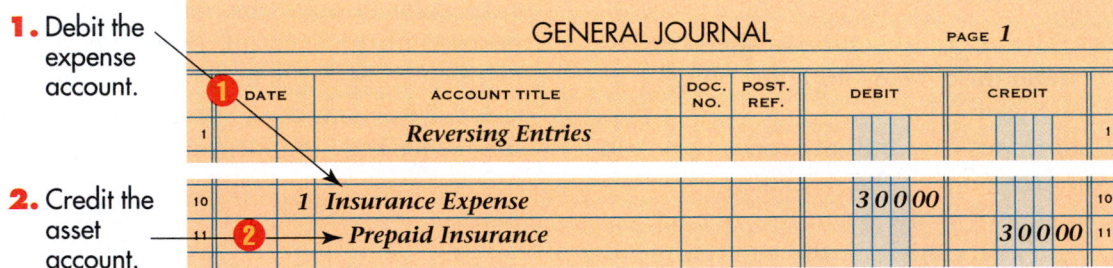

Insurance Expense is closed as part of Appliance Center's closing entries.

Appliance Center's adjusting entry for insurance expense created a balance in the asset account Prepaid Insurance. Therefore, on January 1, Appliance Center needs a reversing entry for insurance expense. The reversing entry is shown above.

The new balance of Insurance Expense, *$300.00*, can now be added to the amount of insurance premiums paid during the next fiscal period. The

new balance of Prepaid Insurance is zero, as it was before the adjusting entry.

| Insurance Expense | | |
|---|---|---|
| 12/31 Bal. | 900.00 | 12/31 Adj.    300.00 |
| (New Bal. zero) | | 12/31 Clos.    600.00 |
| 1/1 Rev. | 300.00 | |
| (New Bal. | 300.00) | |

| Prepaid Insurance | | |
|---|---|---|
| 12/31 Adj. | 300.00 | 1/1 Rev.    300.00 |
| (New Bal. zero) | | |

> **REMEMBER** No reversing entry is required when expenses are initially charged to a prepaid expense account.

## terms review

prepaid expenses
reversing entry

## audit your understanding

1. Which accounting concept is being applied when an adjusting entry is recorded for prepaid expenses?

2. Why is an adjusting entry made for supplies at the end of a fiscal period?

3. What rule of thumb can accountants follow to determine whether a reversing entry is needed?

## work together 9-2

**Journalizing adjusting and reversing entries for prepaid expenses initially recorded as expenses**

Janson, Inc., has the following general ledger balances on December 31 of the current year before it records adjusting entries. A general journal is provided in the *Working Papers*. Your instructor will guide you through the following examples.

| | | | |
|---|---|---|---|
| Supplies Expense—Administrative | $3,200.00 | Insurance Expense | $2,000.00 |
| Supplies Expense—Sales | 1,500.00 | | |

1. Using the following adjustment information, journalize the adjusting entries for supplies and insurance on December 31 of the current year.

| | | | |
|---|---|---|---|
| Administrative Supplies Inventory | $500.00 | Value of Prepaid Insurance | $600.00 |
| Sales Supplies Inventory | 400.00 | | |

2. Journalize the reversing entries on January 1 of the next year.

## on your own 9-2

**Journalizing adjusting and reversing entries for prepaid expenses initially recorded as expenses**

Wren Industries has the following general ledger balances on December 31 of the current year before it records adjusting entries. A general journal is provided in the *Working Papers*. Work this problem independently.

| | | | |
|---|---|---|---|
| Supplies Expense—Administrative | $4,600.00 | Insurance Expense | $6,000.00 |
| Supplies Expense—Sales | 4,800.00 | | |

1. Using the following adjustment information, journalize the adjusting entries for supplies and insurance on December 31 of the current year.

| | | | |
|---|---|---|---|
| Administrative Supplies Inventory | $800.00 | Value of Prepaid Insurance | $900.00 |
| Sales Supplies Inventory | 600.00 | | |

2. Journalize the reversing entries on January 1 of the next year.

# 9-3 Accrued Expenses

## JOURNALIZING ACCRUED INTEREST EXPENSE

| Principal | × | Interest Rate | × | Time as Fraction of Year | = | Interest for 15 Days |
|---|---|---|---|---|---|---|
| $7,500.00 | × | 10% | × | $\frac{15}{360}$ | = | $31.25 |

**1.** Determine the amount of accrued interest. ❶

**2.** Debit the expense account. ❷

**3.** Credit the liability account. ❸

**GENERAL JOURNAL**   PAGE 1

| | DATE | ACCOUNT TITLE | DOC. NO. | POST. REF. | DEBIT | CREDIT | |
|---|---|---|---|---|---|---|---|
| 1 | | *Adjusting Entries* | | | | | 1 |
| 25 | Dec. 31 | *Interest Expense* | | | 31 25 | | 25 |
| 26 | ❸ | *Interest Payable* | | | | 31 25 | 26 |
| 27 | | | | | | | 27 |

Expenses incurred in one fiscal period but not paid until a later fiscal period are called **accrued expenses**. In any fiscal period, Appliance Center may need to account for four types of accrued expenses.

1. Accrued interest expense.
2. Accrued salary expense.
3. Accrued employer payroll taxes expense.
4. Accrued federal income tax expense.

On December 31, Appliance Center has a 60-day, 10% note payable for $7,500.00, dated December 16, on which interest has accrued. On December 31, Appliance Center owes 15 days worth of accrued interest on the note, *$31.25*. The accrued interest expense for this note should be reported in the current fiscal period. [CONCEPT: Matching Expenses with Revenue] The adjusting entry shown above records the accrued interest adjustment.

**Interest Expense**

| | |
|---|---|
| 12/31 Bal. | 2,142.50 |
| 12/31 Adj. | 31.25 |
| *(New Bal.* | *2,173.75)* |

**Interest Payable**

| | |
|---|---|
| | 12/31 Adj.  31.25 |

**STEPS** • STEPS • STEPS • STEPS • STEPS

### RECORDING THE ADJUSTING ENTRY FOR ACCRUED INTEREST EXPENSE

❶ Determine the interest expense for the current period, *$31.25*.

❷ Record the debit to *Interest Expense*, *31.25*. The debit increases the expense in the current period.

❸ Record the credit to *Interest Payable*, *31.25*. The credit increases the liability in the current period.

**REMEMBER** Any adjustment that creates an asset or liability should be reversed.

# REVERSING ENTRY FOR ACCRUED INTEREST

**1.** Debit the liability account.

| | DATE | | ACCOUNT TITLE | DOC. NO. | POST. REF. | DEBIT | CREDIT | |
|---|---|---|---|---|---|---|---|---|
| 1 | | | *Reversing Entries* | | | | | 1 |
| 14 | Jan. | 1 | *Interest Payable* | | | 3 1 25 | | 14 |
| 15 | | | *Interest Expense* | | | | 3 1 25 | 15 |
| 16 | | | | | | | | 16 |
| 17 | | | | | | | | 17 |
| 18 | | | | | | | | 18 |

GENERAL JOURNAL    PAGE **1**

**2.** Credit the expense account.

Appliance Center's adjusting entry for accrued interest expense creates a balance in a liability account. After preparing its financial statements, Appliance Center journalizes and posts closing entries. To prepare the accounts for the next year, Appliance Center records a reversing entry for accrued interest expense, as shown above.

When Appliance Center pays the note on February 14 of the following year, the total interest expense payment is *$125.00*. The total interest expense should be divided between the two fiscal periods. Interest for the prior year, *$31.25*, is charged for the 15 days the note was outstanding in that year. Interest for the current period, *$93.75*, relates to the 45 days from the start of the fiscal year to the maturity date.

**Interest Payable**

| | | | |
|---|---|---|---|
| 1/1 Rev. | 31.25 | 12/31 Adj. | 31.25 |
| | | (New Bal. zero) | |

**Interest Expense**

| | | | |
|---|---|---|---|
| 12/31 Bal. | 2,142.50 | 12/31 Clos. | 2,173.75 |
| 12/31 Adj. | 31.25 | | |
| (New Bal. zero) | | | |
| | | 1/1 Rev. | 31.25 |

# PAYMENT OF NOTE AT MATURITY

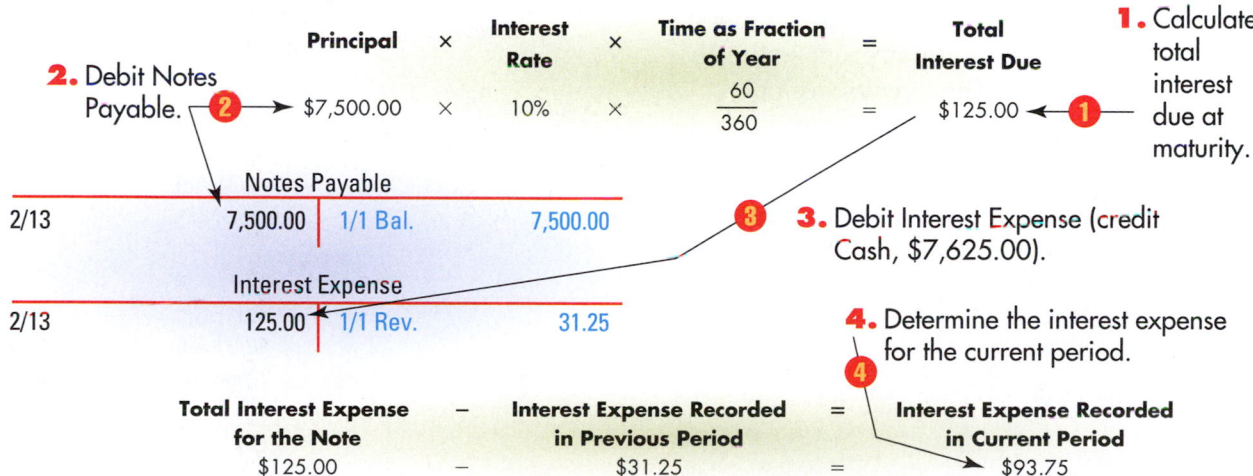

**2.** Debit Notes Payable.

| Principal | × | Interest Rate | × | Time as Fraction of Year | = | Total Interest Due |
|---|---|---|---|---|---|---|
| $7,500.00 | × | 10% | × | $\frac{60}{360}$ | = | $125.00 |

**1.** Calculate total interest due at maturity.

**Notes Payable**

| | | | |
|---|---|---|---|
| 2/13 | 7,500.00 | 1/1 Bal. | 7,500.00 |

**3.** Debit Interest Expense (credit Cash, $7,625.00).

**Interest Expense**

| | | | |
|---|---|---|---|
| 2/13 | 125.00 | 1/1 Rev. | 31.25 |

**4.** Determine the interest expense for the current period.

| Total Interest Expense for the Note | – | Interest Expense Recorded in Previous Period | = | Interest Expense Recorded in Current Period |
|---|---|---|---|---|
| $125.00 | – | $31.25 | = | $93.75 |

On the maturity date, Appliance Center writes a check for the maturity value of $7,625.00. This decreases Notes Payable by a $7,500.00 debit. The $125.00 debit to Interest Expense, less the $31.25 credit balance created by the reversing entry, equals the $93.75 interest expense for the current period.

| | DATE | ACCOUNT TITLE | DOC. NO. | POST. REF. | DEBIT | CREDIT | |
|---|---|---|---|---|---|---|---|
| 1 | | **Adjusting Entries** | | | | | 1 |
| 28 | 31 | Salary Expense—Administrative | | | 7 5 0 00 | | 28 |
| 29 | | Salary Expense—Sales | | | 8 5 0 00 | | 29 |
| 30 | | Salary Expense—Warehouse | | | 4 5 0 00 | | 30 |
| 31 | | Salaries Payable | | | | 1 5 6 0 00 | 31 |
| 32 | | Employee Income Tax Payable | | | | 3 2 6 00 | 32 |
| 33 | | Social Security Tax Payable | | | | 1 3 3 25 | 33 |
| 34 | | Medicare Tax Payable | | | | 3 0 75 | 34 |
| 35 | | | | | | | 35 |

**GENERAL JOURNAL**    PAGE 13

**1.** Debit the expense accounts.

**2.** Credit the liability accounts.

Appliance Center pays its employees each Friday for the time they worked during the previous week. On December 31, Appliance Center owes, but has not paid, the employees for Monday through Friday of the previous week. On Friday, January 5, the employees will receive a paycheck that includes five days' pay from the previous fiscal period.

On December 31, even though the employees have not been paid, salaries for five days are reported as an expense of the current fiscal period. [CONCEPT: Matching Expenses with Revenue] The financial statements must show all the business expenses for a fiscal period. [CONCEPT: Adequate Disclosure]

On December 31, Appliance Center owes $1,560.00 of salaries to employees who work in its three departments. To determine the adjusting entry, Appliance Center must prepare the payroll register. However, the checks are not prepared or distributed to employees until the normal payment date, January 5. The adjusting entry to record the accrued salary expense is shown above.

**Salary Expense—Administrative**

| | | |
|---|---|---|
| 12/31 Bal. | 37,062.50 | |
| 12/31 Adj. | 750.00 | |
| (New Bal. | 37,812.50) | |

**Salary Expense—Sales**

| | | |
|---|---|---|
| 12/31 Bal. | 45,075.00 | |
| 12/31 Adj. | 850.00 | |
| (New Bal. | 45,925.00) | |

**Salary Expense—Warehouse**

| | | |
|---|---|---|
| 12/31 Bal. | 22,037.50 | |
| 12/31 Adj. | 450.00 | |
| (New Bal. | 22,487.50) | |

**Salaries Payable**

| | | |
|---|---|---|
| | 12/31 Adj. | 1,560.00 |

**Employee Income Tax Payable**

| | | |
|---|---|---|
| | 12/31 Adj. | 326.00 |

**Social Security Tax Payable**

| | | |
|---|---|---|
| | 12/31 Bal. | 402.59 |
| | 12/31 Adj. | 133.25 |
| | (New Bal. | 535.84) |

**Medicare Tax Payable**

| | | |
|---|---|---|
| | 12/31 Bal. | 92.91 |
| | 12/31 Adj. | 30.75 |
| | (New Bal. | 123.66) |

{ **REMEMBER** When a company incurs a salary expense, it must recognize this expense as a liability in the period in which employees provide their services to the company. }

| | GENERAL JOURNAL | | | | | PAGE *14* | |
|---|---|---|---|---|---|---|---|
| | DATE | ACCOUNT TITLE | DOC. NO. | POST. REF. | DEBIT | CREDIT | |
| 1 | | *Reversing Entries* | | | | | 1 |
| 15 | *1* | *Salaries Payable* | | | 1 5 6 0 00 | | 15 |
| 16 | | *Employee Income Tax Payable* | | | 3 2 6 00 | | 16 |
| 17 | | *Social Security Tax Payable* | | | 1 3 3 25 | | 17 |
| 18 | | *Medicare Tax Payable* | | | 3 0 75 | | 18 |
| 19 | | *Salary Expense—Administrative* | | | | 7 5 0 00 | 19 |
| 20 | | *Salary Expense—Sales* | | | | 8 5 0 00 | 20 |
| 21 | | *Salary Expense—Warehouse* | | | | 4 5 0 00 | 21 |
| 22 | | | | | | | 22 |
| 23 | | | | | | | 23 |

**1.** Debit the liability accounts. ➊

**2.** Credit the expense accounts. ➋

After Appliance Center records closing entries for payroll, the three payroll expense accounts have zero balances. The salaries payable account reflects the $1,560.00 salaries to be paid on January 5.

The entry to reverse the payroll adjustment removes the adjusting entry amounts from the four payroll liability accounts, as shown above. The three salary expense accounts have contra (credit) balances after the reversing entry. When Appliance Center pays the payroll in January, the amount debited in each account is offset by the credit contra balance.

Fiscal years often end in the middle of payroll periods. Therefore, payroll expense must be accrued for the number of days of the payroll period in the current fiscal year. Estimates of the tax liabilities, based on previous payroll periods, are used to prepare the adjusting entry.

**Salaries Payable**

| 1/1 Rev. | 1,560.00 | 12/31 Adj. | 1,560.00 |
|---|---|---|---|
| | | (New Bal. zero) | |

**Employee Income Tax Payable**

| 1/1 Rev. | 326.00 | 12/31 Adj. | 326.00 |
|---|---|---|---|
| | | (New Bal. zero) | |

**Social Security Tax Payable**

| 1/1 Rev. | 133.25 | 12/31Bal. | 535.84 |
|---|---|---|---|
| | | 12/31 Adj. | 133.25 |
| | | (New Bal. | 535.84) |

**Medicare Tax Payable**

| 1/1 Rev. | 30.75 | 12/31 Bal. | 123.66 |
|---|---|---|---|
| | | 12/31 Adj. | 30.75 |
| | | (New Bal. | 123.66) |

**Salary Expense—Administrative**

| 12/31 Bal. | 37,062.50 | 12/31 Clos. | 37,812.50 |
|---|---|---|---|
| 12/31 Adj. | 750.00 | 1/1 Rev. | 750.00 |
| | | (New Bal. | 750.00) |

**Salary Expense—Sales**

| 12/31 Bal. | 45,075.00 | 12/31 Clos. | 45,925.00 |
|---|---|---|---|
| 12/31 Adj. | 850.00 | 1/1 Rev. | 850.00 |
| | | (New Bal. | 850.00) |

**Salary Expense—Warehouse**

| 12/31 Bal. | 22,037.50 | 12/31 Clos. | 22,487.50 |
|---|---|---|---|
| 12/31 Adj. | 450.00 | 1/1 Rev. | 450.00 |
| | | (New Bal. | 450.00) |

**FYI** FOR YOUR INFORMATION

Reversing entries eliminate the need to remember that the payroll liability accounts reflect an expense from the previous accounting period.

**GENERAL JOURNAL**　　　　PAGE *13*

| | DATE | ACCOUNT TITLE | DOC. NO. | POST. REF. | DEBIT | CREDIT | |
|---|---|---|---|---|---|---|---|
| 1 | | *Adjusting Entries* | | | | | 1 |
| 33 | 31 | *Payroll Taxes Expense* | | | 1 9 1 90 | | 33 |
| 34 | | *Social Security Tax Payable* | | | | 1 3 3 25 | 34 |
| 35 | | *Medicare Tax Payable* | | | | 3 0 75 | 35 |
| 36 | | *Unemployment Tax Payable—Federal* | | | | 3 60 | 36 |
| 37 | | *Unemployment Tax Payable—State* | | | | 2 4 30 | 37 |
| 38 | | | | | | | 38 |

**1.** Debit the expense account.

**2.** Credit the liability accounts.

Employer payroll taxes for accrued salaries must be recorded at the end of a fiscal period. Appliance Center has four employer payroll taxes:

1. Social security tax.
2. Medicare tax.
3. Federal unemployment tax
4. State unemployment tax.

The entry to record the accrued employer payroll taxes on December 31 of the current year is shown above.

**GENERAL JOURNAL**　　　　PAGE *16*

| | DATE | ACCOUNT TITLE | DOC. NO. | POST. REF. | DEBIT | CREDIT | |
|---|---|---|---|---|---|---|---|
| 1 | | *Reversing Entries* | | | | | 1 |
| 18 | 1 | Social Security Tax Payable | | | 1 3 3 25 | | 18 |
| 19 | | *Medicare Tax Payable* | | | 3 0 75 | | 19 |
| 20 | | *Unemployment Tax Payable—Federal* | | | 3 60 | | 20 |
| 21 | | *Unemployment Tax Payable—State* | | | 2 4 30 | | 21 |
| 22 | | *Payroll Taxes Expense* | | | | 1 9 1 90 | 22 |
| 23 | | | | | | | 23 |

**1.** Debit the liability accounts.

**2.** Credit the expense account.

After Appliance Center records closing entries for payroll taxes, the payroll taxes expense account has a zero balance. The four payroll tax liability accounts reflect the tax payments to be made during the next fiscal year.

The entry to reverse the payroll taxes adjustment removes the adjusting entry amounts from the four payroll tax liability accounts, as shown above. The payroll tax expense account has a contra (credit) balance after the reversing entry. When the payroll taxes are paid, the amount debited to Payroll Taxes Expense will be offset by the credit contra balance. Thus, the transaction recorded is the same as other payroll tax payments during the fiscal year.

# JOURNALIZING ACCRUED FEDERAL INCOME TAX EXPENSE

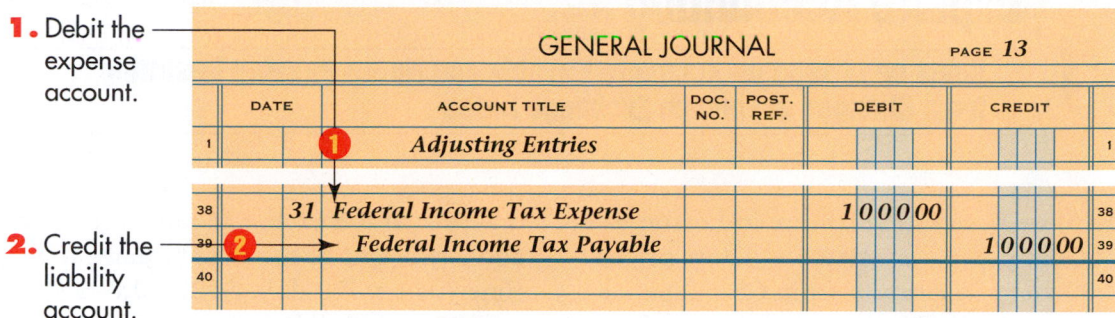

**1.** Debit the expense account.

**2.** Credit the liability account.

| | DATE | ACCOUNT TITLE | DOC. NO. | POST. REF. | DEBIT | CREDIT | |
|---|---|---|---|---|---|---|---|
| | | GENERAL JOURNAL | | | | PAGE *13* | |
| 1 | | *Adjusting Entries* | | | | | 1 |
| 38 | *31* | *Federal Income Tax Expense* | | | 1 0 0 0 00 | | 38 |
| 39 | | *Federal Income Tax Payable* | | | | 1 0 0 0 00 | 39 |
| 40 | | | | | | | 40 |

Corporations must pay federal income tax on net income. At the beginning of each year, Appliance Center makes an estimate of its federal income tax obligation. It pays the estimated amount in four quarterly payments. At the end of a year, Appliance Center revises its income tax estimate for the year. Any unpaid federal income tax is an accrued expense for which an adjusting entry must be made.

On December 31, Appliance Center's records show that quarterly income tax payments have been made for a total of $9,000.00. On December 31, Appliance Center estimates that its income tax will be $10,000.00. Thus, the accrued federal income tax remaining to be paid is $1,000.00 (total tax, $10,000.00, *minus* amount paid, $9,000.00). The adjusting entry for the accrual is shown above.

Federal Income Tax Payable is a current liability account. Federal Income Tax Expense is an expense account located in the general ledger division titled *Income Tax.*

During the year, cash will be paid for accrued income tax expense for the previous year plus periodic payments for the current year's income tax expense. To avoid confusing the amount of tax expense recorded for each of these years and to provide year-to-date income tax expense information for each year, Appliance Center does not reverse this adjusting entry.

## cultural diversity
### Hispanic American Businesses

CULTURAL DIVERSITY • CULTURAL DIVERSITY • CULTURAL DIVERSITY

The Census Bureau's Survey of Minority-Owned Business Enterprises indicates that minority-owned enterprises are increasing in number and size. One of the fastest growing segments of U.S. business population during the period from 1987 to 1992 was businesses owned by Hispanic Americans. During this period, the number of Hispanic-owned businesses increased from 422,373 to 771,708. In addition, their total receipts more than tripled, from $24.7 billion to $72.8 billion.

With the impressive growth in Hispanic-owned businesses, *Hispanic Business* magazine has created lists of successful

Hispanic-owned businesses, including the Hispanic Business 500, the Hispanic Business High Tech 50, and the Fast-Growing 100. The 1997 Hispanic Business 500 gives the honor of largest Hispanic-owned corporation to Burt Automotive Network of Englewood, Colorado. Its chief executive office (CEO) is Lloyd G. Chavez. This automotive sales and service company was started in 1939, employs over 800, and had total revenue in 1996 of about $813 million.

# Explore Accounting

## Gains or Losses on Accounts Payable and Notes Payable Resulting from Changes in Foreign Exchange Rates

In the Explore Accounting feature in Lesson 9-1, PhoneCom purchases semiconductors priced at 800,000 yuan on account from ChinaSemi, a Chinese corporation. The terms of the purchase are for PhoneCom, an American company, to pay 800,000 yuan in 60 days. At the time of the purchase, the exchange rate between the yuan and the dollar is one yuan equals .10 dollars, meaning that one yuan costs 10 cents to buy. On the date of the purchase, 800,000 yuan equals $80,000 dollars (800,000 × .10). During the 60-day period credit period, however, the exchange rate for the yuan rises to .12 dollars. This higher exchange rate means that a single yuan now costs $.12 dollars (12 cents) to purchase. When PhoneCom makes a payment of 800,000 yuan in 60 days, the 800,000 yuan will cost $96,000.00 U.S. dollars (800,000 yuan × $.12). Due to the 2-cent increase in the exchange rate, PhoneCom will spend an extra $16,000 through the currency exchange process. PhoneCom accounts for the loss on accounts payable with the entry below. The account *Gain or Loss on Foreign Currency Exchange* is classified as an other revenue account.

    Accounts Payable/ChinaSemi
        Corp. . . . . . . . . . . . . . . . . 80,000
    Gain or Loss on Foreign
        Currency Exchange . . . . . . 16,000
        Cash . . . . . . . . . . . . . . . . . . . . . . . . . 96,000

In the previous Explore Accounting feature, another example was provided in which Cal-Tech, an American firm, gives XianCorp, a Chinese corporation, a 12-month, 5% note payable for 2,000,000 yuan. Including the interest of 100,000 yuan (2,000,000 yuan × .05), CalTech will pay XianCorp 2,100,000 yuan in one year. If the exchange rate at the beginning and at the end of the note remains the same (one yuan = .10 dollar), 2,100,000 yuan will cost $210,000 dollars (2,100,000 yuan × $.10). Suppose, however, that during the 12-month period, the exchange rate between the yuan and the dollar declines from $.10 to $.09. Since a yuan costs less, CalTech can now purchase 2,100,000 yuan for $189,000 (2,100,000 yuan × $.09). Due to the one-cent decline in the exchange rate, CalTech realizes a gain of $21,000 ($210,000 − $189,000) through the currency exchange process. CalTech accounts for the gain on accounts payable using the entry below.

    Accounts Payable/
        XianCorp . . . . . . . . . . 200,000
    Interest Expense . . . . . . . . . . 10,000
        Cash . . . . . . . . . . . . . . . . . . . . . . . . 189,000
    Gain or Loss on Foreign
        Currency Exchange . . . . . . . . . . . . 21,000

### Critical Thinking Activity

An American company, Fashion Clothiers, purchases men's clothing on account from a Canadian firm, Delmar, Inc., for 50,000 Canadian dollars. At the time of the sale, the exchange rate is one Canadian dollar equals .82 U.S. dollars. Thirty days later, when Fashion Clothiers pays the 50,000 Canadian dollars, the exchange rate has risen. One Canadian dollar can now be exchanged for .87 dollars. How much will it cost Fashion Clothiers to purchase Canadian dollars at the new rate? Will the American company realize a gain or a loss on the transaction? Use T accounts to show the impact of the gain or loss on accounts payable.

# Explore Accounting

## Gains or Losses on Accounts Payable and Notes Payable Resulting from Changes in Foreign Exchange Rates

In the Explore Accounting feature in Lesson 9-1, PhoneCom purchases semiconductors priced at 800,000 yuan on account from ChinaSemi, a Chinese corporation. The terms of the purchase are for PhoneCom, an American company, to pay 800,000 yuan in 60 days. At the time of the purchase, the exchange rate between the yuan and the dollar is one yuan equals .10 dollars, meaning that one yuan costs 10 cents to buy. On the date of the purchase, 800,000 yuan equals $80,000 dollars (800,000 × .10). During the 60-day credit period, however, the exchange rate for the yuan rises to .12 dollars. This higher exchange rate means that a single yuan now costs $.12 dollars (12 cents) to purchase. When PhoneCom makes a payment of 800,000 yuan in 60 days, the 800,000 yuan will cost $96,000.00 U.S. dollars (800,000 yuan × $.12). Due to the 2-cent increase in the exchange rate, PhoneCom will spend an extra $16,000 through the currency exchange process. PhoneCom accounts for the loss on accounts payable with the entry below. The account *Gain or Loss on Foreign Currency Exchange* is classified as an other revenue account.

|  |  |  |
|---|---|---|
| Accounts Payable/ChinaSemi | | |
| Corp. . . . . . . . . . . . . . . . . | 80,000 | |
| Gain or Loss on Foreign | | |
| Currency Exchange . . . . . . | 16,000 | |
| Cash . . . . . . . . . . . . . . . . . . . . . . . . . | | 96,000 |

In the previous Explore Accounting feature, another example was provided in which Cal-Tech, an American firm, gives XianCorp, a Chinese corporation, a 12-month, 5% note payable for 2,000,000 yuan. Including the interest of 100,000 yuan (2,000,000 yuan × .05), CalTech will pay XianCorp 2,100,000 yuan in one year. If the exchange rate at the beginning and at the end of the note remains the same (one yuan = .10 dollar), 2,100,000 yuan will cost $210,000 dollars (2,100,000 yuan × $.10). Suppose, however, that during the 12-month period, the exchange rate between the yuan and the dollar declines from $.10 to $.09. Since a yuan costs less, CalTech can now purchase 2,100,000 yuan for $189,000 (2,100,000 yuan × $.09). Due to the one-cent decline in the exchange rate, CalTech realizes a gain of $21,000 ($210,000 − $189,000) through the currency exchange process. CalTech accounts for the gain on accounts payable using the entry below.

|  |  |  |
|---|---|---|
| Accounts Payable/ | | |
| XianCorp . . . . . . . . . | 200,000 | |
| Interest Expense . . . . . . . . . . | 10,000 | |
| Cash . . . . . . . . . . . . . . . . . . . . . . . | | 189,000 |
| Gain or Loss on Foreign | | |
| Currency Exchange . . . . . . . . . . . . | | 21,000 |

### Critical Thinking Activity

An American company, Fashion Clothiers, purchases men's clothing on account from a Canadian firm, Delmar, Inc., for 50,000 Canadian dollars. At the time of the sale, the exchange rate is one Canadian dollar equals .82 U.S. dollars. Thirty days later, when Fashion Clothiers pays the 50,000 Canadian dollars, the exchange rate has risen. One Canadian dollar can now be exchanged for .87 dollars. How much will it cost Fashion Clothiers to purchase Canadian dollars at the new rate? Will the American company realize a gain or a loss on the transaction? Use T accounts to show the impact of the gain or loss on accounts payable.

**SUMMARY · SUMMARY · SUMMARY**

### After completing this chapter, you can

1. Define accounting terms related to notes payable, prepaid expenses, and accrued expenses.

2. Identify accounting concepts and practices related to notes payable, prepaid expenses, and accrued expenses.

3. Journalize transactions for notes payable.

4. Journalize adjusting and reversing entries for prepaid expenses initially recorded as expenses.

5. Journalize adjusting and reversing entries for accrued expenses.

# Explore Accounting

EXPLORE ACCOUNTING · EXPLORE ACCOUNTING · EXPLORE ACCO

## Accounting for Warranty Expenses

Sunset Pools offers its customers a two-year warranty on its swimming pools. Sunset Pools makes all repairs resulting from defective parts free of charge to the customer.

When Sunset Pools sells a swimming pool, it does not know how much repair will be required during the warranty period. Some pools have no problems; other pools, called "lemons," require extensive repairs. Sunset Pools estimates that it spends an average of $150 on warranty repairs for each pool.

Applying the matching concept, expenses associated with earning revenue should be recorded in the same accounting period. Thus, the cost of repairing a pool during the warranty period should be recorded in the same period as the pool sale. For each pool sold, Sunset Pools records the following entry:

```
Warranty Exp. . . . . . . . . . . . . 150.00
    Accrued Warranty Exp. . . . . . . . . . . . 150.00
```

When costs are incurred to repair a pool under warranty, Sunset Pools records the following entry:

```
Accrued Warranty Exp. . . . . . . 45.00
    Cash . . . . . . . . . . . . . . . . . . . . . . . . . . 45.00
```

Accountants must periodically analyze the accrued warranty expense account. If the actual costs incurred are significantly more or less than the $150 per pool charge, a new warranty expense estimate is computed.

Warranty expenses demonstrate the impact of accounting estimates on financial statements. Companies must hire accountants with the proper training to ensure that these estimates are as accurate as possible.

**Required:**
Sunset Pools is starting to sell outdoor spas. It will maintain warranty expenses in a separate accrual account. Industry publications report that the average spa requires $50 of repairs during its one-year warranty period. After seven sales, Sunset Pools incurs a $500 repair. What is the balance in Accrued Spa Warranty Expense? Does the balance indicate that the $50 estimate is inaccurate? Explain.

## 9-1 APPLICATION PROBLEM   AUTOMATED ACCOUNTING   PEACHTREE   QUICKBOOKS

### Journalizing notes payable transactions

Raecker, Inc., completed the following transactions during the current year. Source documents are abbreviated as follows: check, C; receipt, R.

**Transactions:**

Aug. 1. Signed a 90-day, 11% note with City National Bank for $1,100.00. R143.
Sept. 12. Signed a 60-day, 12% note with First American Bank for $1,200.00. R176.
Oct. 21. Signed a 60-day, 10% note with Commercial State Bank for $800.00. R203.

**Instructions:**

1. Journalize the transactions on page 15 of a cash receipts journal.
2. Calculate the maturity dates for each note.
3. Calculate the total amount of interest due at maturity for each note.
4. Journalize the following transactions on page 21 of a cash payments journal. Use the maturity dates and the interest amounts calculated in the preceding steps.

   Paid cash for the maturity value of the City National Bank note. C245.
   Paid cash for the maturity value of the First American Bank note. C352.
   Paid cash for the maturity value of Commercial State Bank note. C459.

## 9-2 APPLICATION PROBLEM

### Journalizing adjusting and reversing entries for prepaid expenses initially recorded as expenses

Dupre, Inc., has the following general ledger balances on December 31 of the current year before adjusting entries are recorded.

| | |
|---|---|
| Supplies Expense—Administrative | $1,500.00 |
| Supplies Expense—Sales | 2,500.00 |
| Insurance Expense | 3,000.00 |

**Instructions:**

1. Use the following adjustment information. Journalize the adjusting entries for supplies and insurance on December 31 of the current year. Use page 13 of a general journal.

   | | |
   |---|---|
   | Administrative Supplies Inventory | $450.00 |
   | Sales Supplies Inventory | 800.00 |
   | Value of Prepaid Insurance | 720.00 |

2. Journalize the reversing entries on January 1 of the next year. Use page 1 of a general journal.

## 9-3 APPLICATION PROBLEM

### Journalizing adjusting and reversing entries for accrued expenses

Auxbury, Inc., has gathered the following information relating to accrued interest, accrued payroll, accrued employer payroll taxes, and accrued federal income tax on December 31 of the current year.

a. One note payable is outstanding on December 31: 180-day, 12% note with First National Bank, $15,000, dated October 22.

b. Payroll information from the December 31 payroll is as follows:

| Payroll and Employee Payroll Taxes | | Employer Payroll Taxes | |
|---|---|---|---|
| Salaries—Administrative | $600.00 | Social Security Tax | $71.50 |
| Salaries—Sales | 500.00 | Medicare Tax | 16.50 |
| Federal Income Tax Withheld | 240.00 | Federal Unemployment Tax | 8.80 |
| Social Security Tax Withheld | 71.50 | State Unemployment Tax | 59.40 |
| Medicare Tax Withheld | 16.50 | | |

c. Estimated federal income tax quarterly payment, $1,300.00.

**Instructions:**

1. Journalize the adjusting entries for accrued interest, accrued payroll, accrued employer payroll taxes, and accrued federal income tax on December 31 of the current year. Use page 13 of a general journal.

2. Journalize the appropriate reversing entries on January 1 of the next year. Use page 1 of a general journal.

## 9-4 MASTERY PROBLEM

### Journalizing adjusting and reversing entries for prepaid expenses initially recorded as expenses and for accrued expenses

Sass, Inc., completed the following transactions during the current year. Sass initially records prepaid expenses as expenses. Source documents are abbreviated as follows: check, C; receipt, R.

**Transactions:**

| | | |
|---|---|---|
| July | 1. | Signed a 60-day, 12% note with Southern Bank for $700.00. R123. |
| Oct. | 10. | Signed a 45-day, 10% note with American Bank for $1,500.00. R149. |
| Nov. | 1. | Signed a 90-day, 11% note with Commercial Bank for $1,000.00. R152. |

**Instructions:**

1. Journalize the transactions on page 15 of a cash receipts journal.
2. Calculate the maturity dates for each note.
3. Journalize the following transactions on page 21 of a cash payments journal. Use the maturity dates calculated in the prior step.

> Paid cash for the maturity value of the Southern Bank note. C105.
> Paid cash for the maturity value of the American Bank note. C195.

4. Sass, Inc., has the following general ledger balances on December 31 of the current year before adjusting entries are recorded.

| | |
|---|---|
| Supplies Expense—Administrative | $400.00 |
| Supplies Expense—Sales | 600.00 |
| Insurance Expense | 900.00 |

Use the following information to journalize adjusting entries for prepaid expenses and accrued expenses on December 31 of the current year. The estimated federal income tax is $800.00. Include the adjusting entry for the outstanding note payable. Use page 13 of a general journal.

| | |
|---|---|
| Administrative Supplies Inventory | $200.00 |
| Sales Supplies Inventory | 300.00 |
| Value of Prepaid Insurance | 350.00 |

| | **Payroll and Employee Payroll Taxes** | | **Employer Payroll Taxes** | |
|---|---|---|---|---|
| | Salaries—Administrative | $350.00 | Social Security Tax | $49.73 |
| | Salaries—Sales | 415.00 | Medicare Tax | 11.47 |
| | Federal Income Tax Withheld | 120.00 | Federal Unemployment Tax | 6.12 |
| | Social Security Tax Withheld | 49.73 | State Unemployment Tax | 41.31 |
| | Medicare Tax Withheld | 11.47 | | |

5. Journalize the appropriate reversing entries on January 1 of the next year. Use page 1 of a general journal.

# 9-5  CHALLENGE PROBLEM

## Journalizing entries for notes payable and when no reversing entries are recorded

Reversing entries eliminate the balance of an asset or liability created by an adjusting entry. Unlike the Appliance Center's accounting procedures illustrated in this chapter, Baird Company has elected not to record reversing entries. Instead, Baird's accounting personnel must assign different accounts and amounts to subsequent transactions to correctly eliminate the asset or liability account balances.

The following transactions occurred related to a note payable.

**Transactions:**
Nov.  1, 20X1. Signed a 180-day, 12% note payable with First National Bank for $10,000.00. R142
Dec. 31, 20X1. Accrued interest expense.
Dec. 31, 20X1. Closed the interest expense account.
Apr. 30, 20X2. Paid the maturity value of the First National Bank note. C154

**Instructions:**
1. Journalize the transactions and record them in T accounts. Record the first three transactions correctly. Record the April 30 transaction, assuming that an accounting clerk fails to recognize that the transaction relates to a December 31 adjusting entry. Describe the error resulting from the accounting clerk's failure.
2. Create another set of T accounts and journalize the transactions again. Determine the correct accounts and amounts for the April 30 transaction to ensure that the final account balances are correct.

## applied communication

As the financial vice president of Mason Co., you are responsible for ensuring that an adequate supply of cash exists to pay operating expenses. The marketing department has secured a huge order that will require funds for increased inventory and employee levels. A budget analysis reveals that a $100,000, 270-day note will be required to adequately fund the production of the order.

Over the past three years, Mason Co. has signed seven notes totaling $200,000 with First National Bank. Each note was for 90 days or less, was issued at prime plus 2-1/2, and was repaid on the due date.

Assume that the class is the bank loan committee of First National Bank. Make an oral presentation to persuade the loan committee to approve the $100,000, 270-day note at prime plus 2%. Recognize that the committee will be hesitant because of the amount of the note, the term of the note, and the lower interest rate. The following facts about Mason Co.'s five-year history may be used to support your request:

- 120% sales growth
- double number of items produced
- 20% annual increase in net income
- 100% increase in employment
- stable upper management

- 20% reduction in customer complaints
- increased market share from 25% to 33%
- 10% increase in dividends
- liabilities declined from 45% to 25% of assets

## cases for critical thinking

### Case 1

Roberta Wagner owns Wagner Books. At the end of each month, Wagner Books borrows money from a bank and uses the proceeds to pay all of its outstanding accounts payable. The business signs a 15-day, 12.5% note payable for each loan. Each month to date, Wagner Books has been able to pay the notes payable when due. Mrs. Wagner uses this procedure to maintain good credit ratings with vendors. Is her reasoning sound? Explain your answer.

### Case 2

Jennifer Pier, owner and manager of Pier, Inc., does not record adjusting or reversing entries for accrued payroll. Ms. Pier says that the matter is taken care of when the first payroll is recorded in the next month. The CPA who advises Ms. Pier suggests that the adjusting and reversing entries should be made. He states that omission of these entries affects the information reported on the business' financial statements. With whom do you agree? Explain your answer.

## SCANS workplace competency (part II)

*(The data collected and organized in the SCANS Workplace Competency in Chapter 8 is needed to complete this activity.)*

**Information Competency:** Interpreting and Communicating Information

**Concept:** Employers value employees who can select and analyze information and communicate the results to others, using oral, written, graphic, pictorial, or multimedia methods.

**Application:** Using the college admissions information you collected in the previous chapter's SCANS activity, prepare an oral report presenting your findings. A successful presentation will incorporate the use of handouts, charts, overhead transparencies, bar graphs, pie charts, line graphs, and other forms of organized visuals. Slideshow software may also make an effective presentation.

## graphing workshop

Target Corporation lists the following current liabilities in its 2003 Annual Report. The data for January 31, 2004 are plotted in the pie chart below.

|  | January 31, 2004 | February 1, 2003 |
|---|---|---|
| Accounts Payable | 5448 | 4684 |
| Accrued Liabilities | 1618 | 1545 |
| Income Taxes Payable | 382 | 319 |
| Current Portion of Long Term Debt | 866 | 975 |
| Total Current Liabilities | 8314 | 7523 |

**Instructions:** Create a pie chart using the data for February 1, 2003.

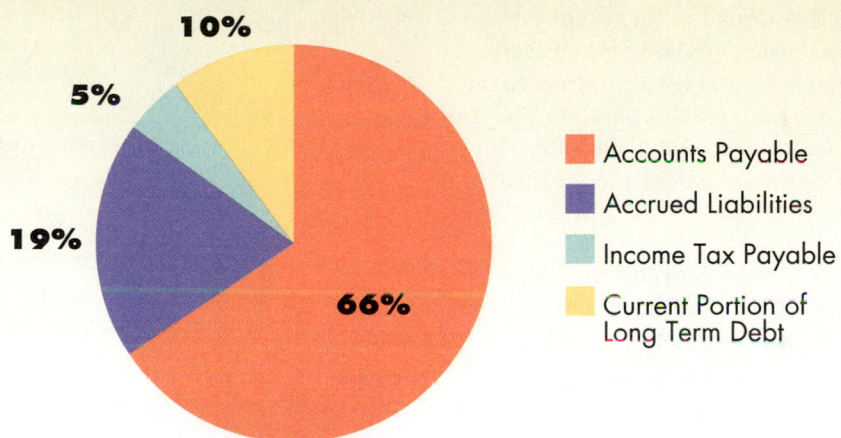

January 31, 2004

- Accounts Payable
- Accrued Liabilities
- Income Tax Payable
- Current Portion of Long Term Debt

## analyzing Costco's financial statements

Following the financial statements in an annual report is what is called the "Notes to Consolidated Financial Statements." These notes are an important part of the financial statements and can help clarify some of the amounts on the financial statements.

No. 1 is usually titled "Summary of Significant Accounting Policies."

**Instructions:**

1. In Appendix B of this textbook, read the last paragraph in Note No. 1, which is on page B-17. Summarize the note in one sentence.

2. Give at least one example of an estimate that is used in accounting.

3. Why is it necessary to use estimates in accounting?

## Calculating Notes and Interest Using Planning Tools

### Planning Tools

Planning tools are easy-to-use applications for producing results for different types of financial investments. There are five different tabs included on the Planning Tools screen:

- College Planner
- Savings Planner
- Loan Planner
- Retirement Plan
- Notes and Interest

### Notes and Interest

In this section, the Notes and Interest planning tool will be explored. As discussed in Chapter 9, a written and signed promise to pay a sum of money at a specified time is called a **promissory note**. Promissory notes signed by a business and given to a creditor are called **notes payable**. The day a note is issued is called the **date of the note**. The original amount of a note is called the **principal of a note**. The date a note is due is called the **maturity date of a note**.

The Notes and Interest planning tool is located on the Notes & Interest tab on the Planning Tools screen, as shown above. The tool is used to:

- Determine the maturity date of the note
- Calculate the amount of interest
- Calculate the maturity value of the note

### Entering Note Data in the Notes and Interest Planning Tool

To use the tool, you must know the date of the note, the principal amount of the note, the interest rate, and the number of days (months) for which the note will be outstanding. The following steps are used for any note.

1. Click on the Tools toolbar button.

2. Select the Notes & Interest tab.

3. Select the time basis by clicking on the appropriate radio button. There are three time basis options: number of days (based on 360 days); number of days (based on 365 days); and number of months.

4. Enter the date of the note, which is the date the note was issued.

5. Enter the principal amount of the note.

6. Enter the interest rate.

7. Enter the number of days (time period for which the note is outstanding). If you select Number of Months as the time basis, you enter the number of months, rather than the number of days.

Once all the data are entered, the results are displayed at the bottom on the planner's screen.

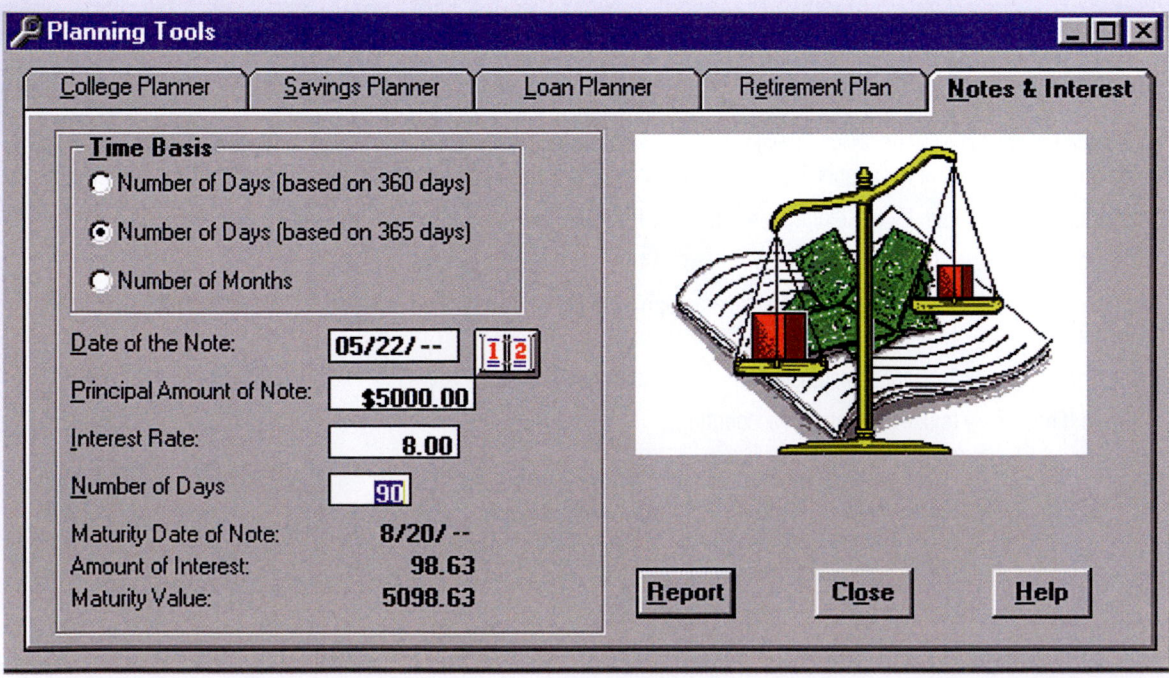

Accounting for Notes Payable, Prepaid Expenses, and Accrued Expenses

### Displaying or Printing the Note Analysis Report

A sample Notes Analysis report is shown on the next page. To display or print the report, use the following steps:

1. Click the Report button on the Notes & Interest screen.

2. Choose the Print button if you wish to print the report. (You may choose to view the report, instead of printing it.)

3. Click the Close button. You also have the option to copy the report to the clipboard so that you may include the note data in a separate document.

### AUTOMATING APPLICATION PROBLEM 9-1

**Instructions:**

1. Load *Automated Accounting 8.0* or higher software.

2. Select database A09-1 (Advanced Course Application Problem 9-1) from the accounting template disk.

3. Select File from the menu bar and choose the Save As menu command. Key the path to the drive and directory that contains your data files. Save the database with a filename of XXX091 (where XXX are your initials).

4. Read the Problem Instruction screen by clicking the Browser toolbar button.

5. Key the data listed in the problem.

6. Exit the Automated Accounting software.

### AUTOMATING MASTERY PROBLEM 9-4

**Instructions:**

1. Load *Automated Accounting 8.0* or higher software.

2. Select database A09-4 (Advanced Course Mastery Problem 9-4) from the accounting template disk.

3. Select File from the menu bar and choose the Save As menu command. Key the path to the drive and directory that contains your data files. Save the database with a filename of XXX094 (where XXX are your initials).

4. Read the Problem Instruction screen by clicking the Browser toolbar button.

5. Key the data listed in the problem.

6. Exit the Automated Accounting software.

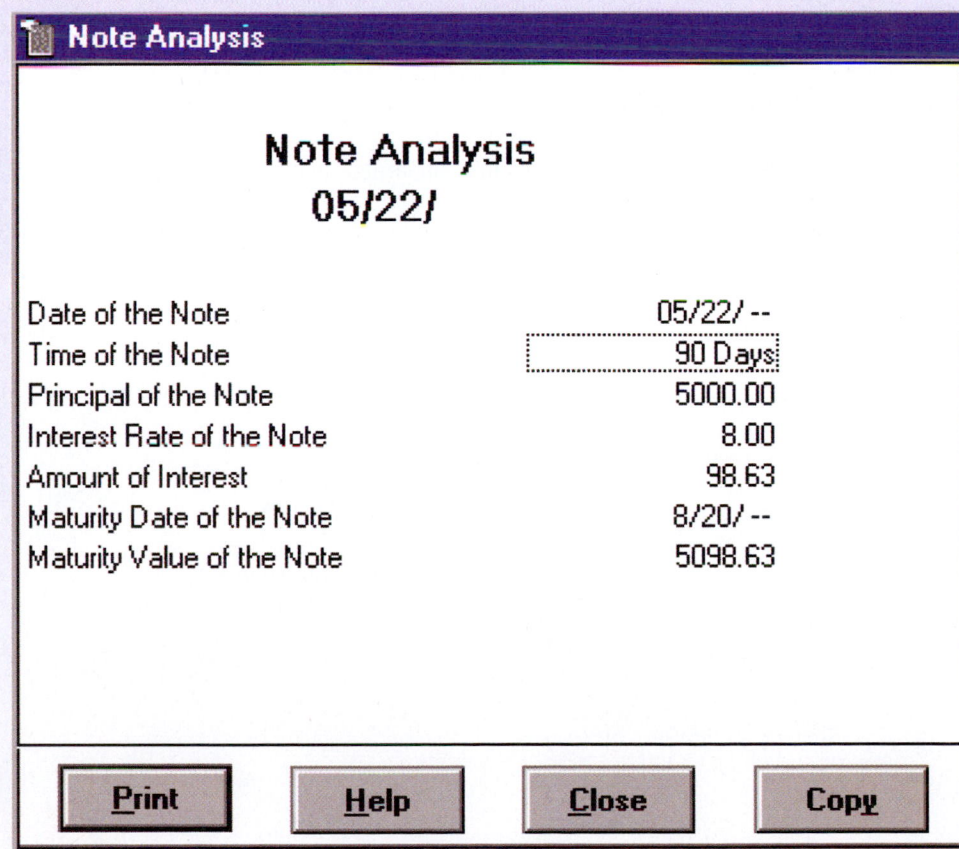

# 10 Accounting for Notes Receivable, Unearned Revenue, and Accrued Revenue

*After studying Chapter 10, you will be able to:*

1. Define accounting terms related to notes receivable, unearned revenue, and accrued revenue.

2. Identify accounting concepts and practices related to notes receivable, unearned revenue, and accrued revenue.

3. Journalize transactions for notes receivable.

4. Journalize adjusting and reversing entries for unearned revenue initially recorded as revenue.

5. Journalize adjusting and reversing entries for accrued revenue.

- notes receivable
- dishonored note

- unearned revenue
- accrued revenue

Point Your Browser
accountingxtra.swlearning.com

# • Northwest Airlines

ACCOUNTING IN THE REAL WORLD • ACCOUNTING IN THE REAL WORLD • ACCOUNTING IN THE REAL WORLD •

INTERNET RESEARCH ACTIVITY • INTERNET RESEARCH ACTIVITY • INTERNET RESEARCH ACTIVITY

## internet activity

©REBECCA COOK/REUTERS/LANDOV

### NORTHWEST AIRLINES GETS PAID IN ADVANCE

The "red tail" in the sky is famous worldwide as a trademark for Northwest Airlines. The first airplane tail was painted red in 1948. However, that wasn't the beginning of Northwest Airlines, Inc. The company began by flying mail between Minneapolis and Chicago in 1926. Passenger service started one year later. Today, Northwest and its global travel partners operate over 1,500 flights to more than 750 destinations in 120 countries on 6 continents, and have about 40,000 employees worldwide.

In many industries, the company provides the goods or services to a customer and either gets paid immediately or at a later date. However, the airline industry does not operate that way. In the airline industry, the company gets paid when the customer purchases a ticket, but it usually does not provide the service until sometime in the future. Another way in which the airline industry is unique is the frequent flyer program that many companies offer. This provides free transportation after the customer flies or accumulates a certain number of miles.

Both of these situations affect the financial statements of an airline company. Northwest Airlines records both of these events as a liability called "air traffic liability." This liability can make up a substantial portion of a company's current liabilities.

### Critical Thinking:

1. Assume an airline company records a liability when a customer purchases a ticket for a future flight. When will the company decrease the liability?
2. When the company reduces the liability, what other account will be affected?

Source: www.nwa.com

Xtra!
Today
accountingxtra.swlearning.com

### ACCOUNTING TERMS

Search the Internet for a site that lists the definition of accounting terms.

### Instructions

1. List the definitions of the following words:
   a. unearned revenue (or unearned income)
   b. accrued revenue
   c. prepaid expense
2. Compare these definitions with those given in the textbook. How are they similar? How are they different?

## 10-1 Notes Receivable

A business entity must report accurate and up-to-date information about notes receivable and accrued revenue on its financial statements at the end of a fiscal period. [*CONCEPT: Adequate Disclosure*] Because of the nature of notes receivable and some types of revenue, special accounting procedures may be required at the end of a fiscal period. For example, a note receivable issued in one fiscal period with a maturity date in the following fiscal period requires special accounting procedures. Special accounting procedures also are required for two types of revenue:

1. Revenue received in one fiscal period but not earned until the next fiscal period.
2. Revenue earned in one fiscal period but not received until the next fiscal period.

The special accounting procedures are designed so that the correct amount of revenue earned in the fiscal period is recognized in the financial statements. [*CONCEPT: Matching Expenses with Revenue*]

©GETTY IMAGES/PHOTODISC

## making ethical decisions

### Conflicts of Interest

Nicole Huckaby is a buyer for Extal Industries. An expert in raw metals, she is responsible for buying the company's copper requirements at the most favorable terms (price, delivery costs, metal purity, etc.). Nicole purchases from several suppliers to ensure a constant supply of copper at competitive prices.

Being an expert in metals, Nicole invests in the stock of metal companies. In fact, she just purchased 500 shares of Atlantic Metals, one of the companies that supplies Extal Industries with copper.

**Instructions**

Access the *Code of Ethics* of International Paper. Using this code as a guide, determine whether Nicole should own the stock of a vendor.

## ISSUING A NOTE RECEIVABLE FOR AN ACCOUNT RECEIVABLE

| | DATE | | ACCOUNT TITLE | DOC. NO. | POST. REF. | DEBIT | CREDIT | |
|---|---|---|---|---|---|---|---|---|
| | | | **GENERAL JOURNAL** | | | PAGE **4** | | |
| 1 | Apr. 20-- | 3 | Notes Receivable | NR11 | | 3 0 0 00 | | 1 |
| 2 | | | Accounts Rec./Duane Jansen | | | | 3 0 0 00 | 2 |

Promissory notes that a business accepts from customers are called **notes receivable**. Notes receivable are usually due within a year. Therefore, notes receivable are classified as current assets.

Notes receivable can be issued to customers who need an extension of time to pay on account.

---

**April 3. Accepts a 30-day, 12% note from Duane Jansen for an extension of time on his account, $300.00. Note Receivable No. 11.**

---

The amount to be received is changed from an account receivable to a note receivable, as shown above. In the accounts receivable ledger, the customer account, Duane Jansen, is decreased by a $300.00 credit. The balance of Mr. Jansen's accounts receivable account is zero.

**GENERAL LEDGER**

Notes Receivable

| 4/3 | 300.00 | |

Accounts Receivable

| | 4/3 | 300.00 |

**ACCOUNTS RECEIVABLE LEDGER**

Duane Jansen

| Bal. | 300.00 | 4/3 | 300.00 |
| | | (New Bal. zero) | |

## ISSUING A NOTE FOR A SALE

| | DATE | ACCOUNT TITLE | DOC. NO. | POST. REF. | DEBIT | CREDIT | |
|---|---|---|---|---|---|---|---|
| | | **GENERAL JOURNAL** | | | PAGE **4** | | |
| 3 | 4 | Notes Receivable | NR12 | | 4 5 0 00 | | 3 |
| 4 | | Sales | | | | 4 5 0 00 | 4 |

Most sales on account assume that the customer will pay within 30 days or less. To promote sales, a company may allow its customers to sign a note extending payment over a longer period of time. If no cash is received, the sale is recorded on a general journal, as shown above. If a cash down payment is received, the transaction could be recorded in a cash receipts journal.

---

**April 4. Accepts a 90-day, 12% note from Mark Carver for the sale of an appliance, $450.00. Note Receivable No. 12.**

---

Notes Receivable

| 4/4 | 450.00 | |

Sales

| | 4/4 | 450.00 |

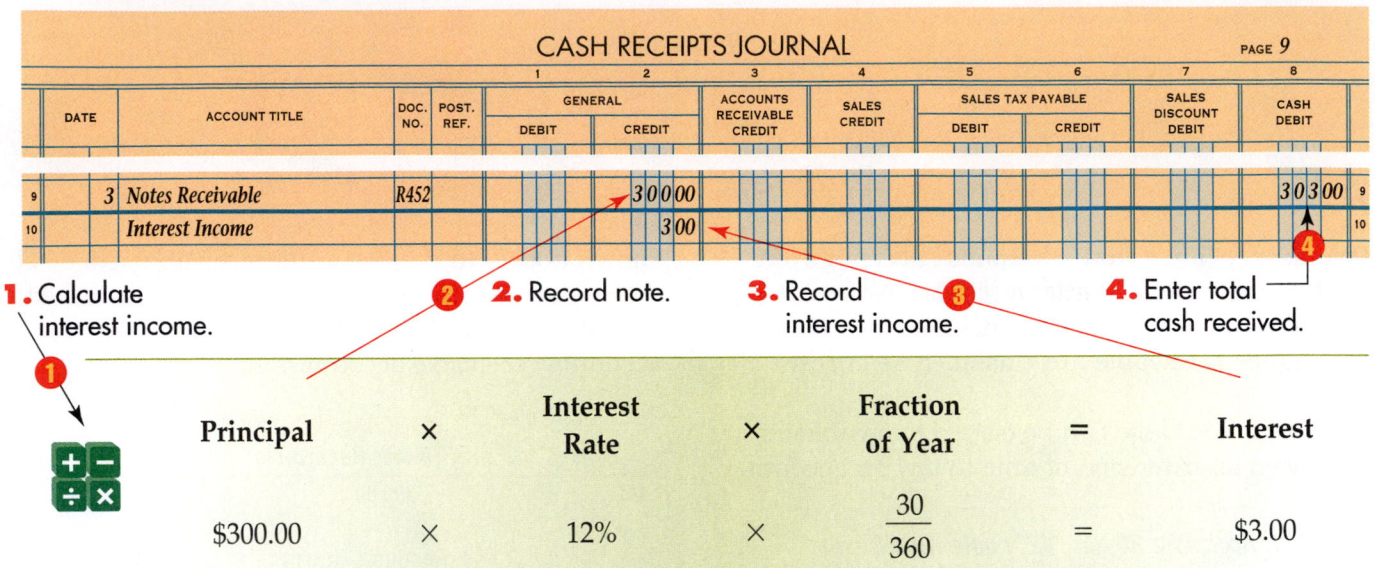

| | | | | | GENERAL | | ACCOUNTS RECEIVABLE CREDIT | SALES CREDIT | SALES TAX PAYABLE | | SALES DISCOUNT DEBIT | CASH DEBIT | |
|---|---|---|---|---|---|---|---|---|---|---|---|---|---|
| CASH RECEIPTS JOURNAL | | | | | | | | | | | | PAGE 9 | |
| | | | | | 1 | 2 | 3 | 4 | 5 | 6 | 7 | 8 | |
| | DATE | ACCOUNT TITLE | DOC. NO. | POST. REF. | DEBIT | CREDIT | | | DEBIT | CREDIT | | | |
| 9 | 3 | Notes Receivable | R452 | | | 3 0 0 00 | | | | | | 3 0 3 00 | 9 |
| 10 | | Interest Income | | | | 3 00 | | | | | | | 10 |

1. **Calculate interest income.**
2. **2.** Record note.
3. **3.** Record interest income.
4. **4.** Enter total cash received.

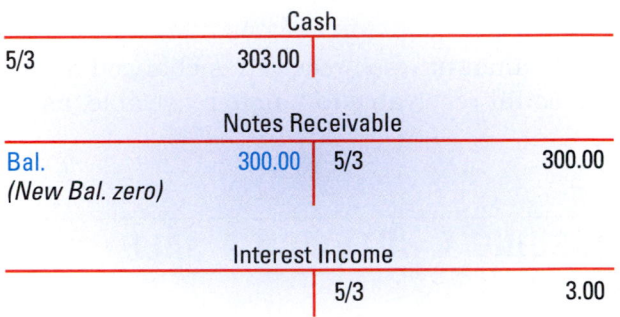

| Principal | × | Interest Rate | × | Fraction of Year | = | Interest |
|---|---|---|---|---|---|---|
| $300.00 | × | 12% | × | $\dfrac{30}{360}$ | = | $3.00 |

Interest is earned for the period of time a note is outstanding. Because the interest rate is stated as an annual rate, the actual interest earned must be computed as a fraction of a year. For ease of calculation, most companies use a 360-day year to calculate interest. The calculation of interest and the receipt of cash in payment of the note receivable are shown above.

Whether a note is accepted for the extension of time for an account receivable or for a sale, the transaction to record the receipt of cash on the maturity date is the same.

> **May 3.** Received cash for the maturity value of Note Receivable No. 11: principal, $300.00, plus interest, $3.00; total, $303.00. Receipt No. 452.

Interest Income is classified as Other Revenue, as shown on Appliance Center's chart of accounts.

| Cash | |
|---|---|
| 5/3    303.00 | |

| Notes Receivable | |
|---|---|
| Bal.    300.00 | 5/3    300.00 |
| (New Bal. zero) | |

| Interest Income | |
|---|---|
| | 5/3    3.00 |

## FYI  FOR YOUR INFORMATION

A company may issue notes receivable to employees for a variety of reasons. To recruit a talented individual, a company may offer the individual a temporary loan to pay off education loans, pay moving costs, or fund a home down payment. A current employee may have a severe financial need caused by a personal tragedy, such as flood damage to a home or excessive uninsured medical bills. A loan to an employee is included in a group of transactions known as related-party transactions. Business owners should establish the policies used to determine the extent, if any, that managers may issue notes receivable to employees.

**REMEMBER** The interest rate on a note is stated as an annual rate. To compute the interest for a period of time, the interest rate must be multiplied by the fraction of a year that the note was outstanding.

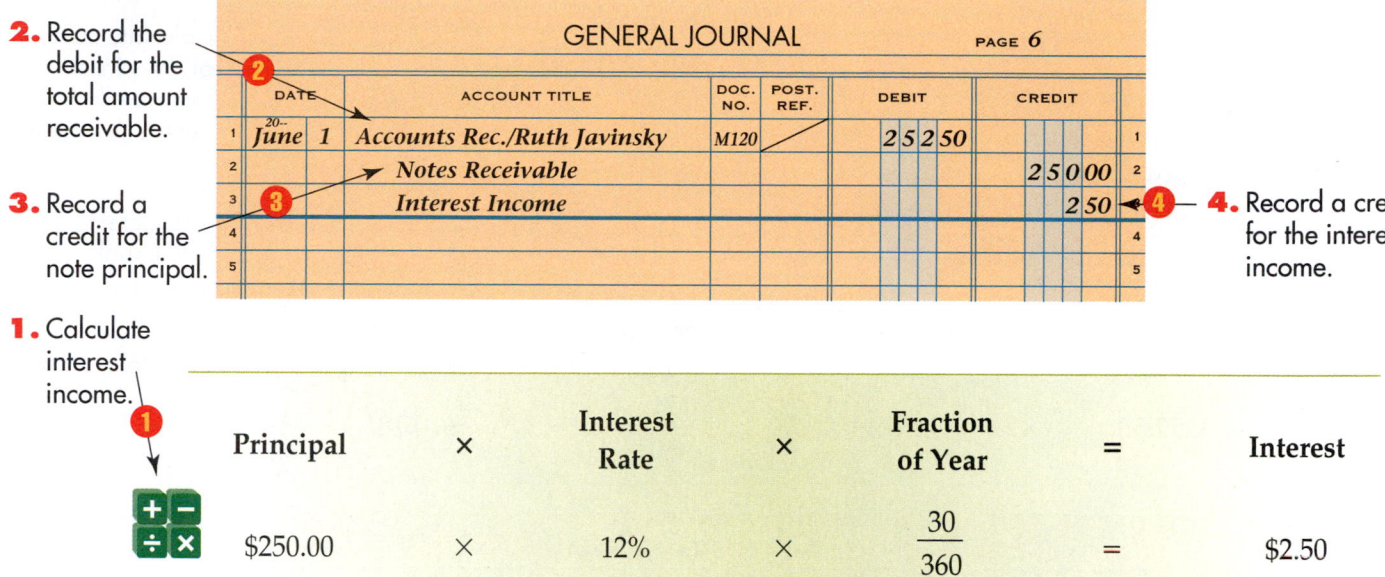

**2.** Record the debit for the total amount receivable.

**3.** Record a credit for the note principal.

**4.** Record a credit for the interest income.

**1.** Calculate interest income.

| Principal | × | Interest Rate | × | Fraction of Year | = | Interest |
|---|---|---|---|---|---|---|
| $250.00 | × | 12% | × | $\frac{30}{360}$ | = | $2.50 |

A note that is not paid when due is called a **dishonored note**. The notes receivable account balance should include only the amount of notes receivable that a business expects to collect. Otherwise, Notes Receivable will be reported incorrectly on a balance sheet. [CONCEPT: *Adequate Disclosure*]

On June 1, the maturity date of Note Receivable No. 8, Ruth Javinsky owes the principal, $250.00, plus accrued interest. Interest is accrued for the 30-day term of the note.

Although the note is dishonored, Ruth still owes the money to Appliance Center. A journal entry is recorded to transfer the maturity value of the note to accounts receivable, as shown above.

> June 1. Ruth Javinsky dishonored Note Receivable No. 8, a 30-day, 12% note, maturity value due today: principal, $250.00; interest, $2.50; total, $252.50. Memorandum No. 120.

The journal entry for a dishonored note receivable does not cancel the debt. Appliance Center does not inform Ruth Javinsky that the note's maturity value was transferred to Accounts Receivable. Appliance Center continues to try to collect the account. However, the debt is transferred to Accounts Receivable and carried on the records until Ruth pays the amount or her account is declared uncollectible.

**GENERAL LEDGER**

**Accounts Receivable**

| | |
|---|---|
| 6/1    252.50 | |

**Notes Receivable**

| | |
|---|---|
| 5/1    250.00 | 6/1    250.00 |

**Interest Income**

| | |
|---|---|
| | 6/1    2.50 |

**ACCOUNTS RECEIVABLE LEDGER**

**Ruth Javinsky**

| | |
|---|---|
| 6/1    252.50 | |

**REMEMBER** The accounting for uncollectible accounts was presented in Chapter 7. Dishonored notes receivable, when added to the balance of Accounts Receivable, are considered when computing adjustments to Allowance for Uncollectible Accounts. If the dishonored note, after being transferred to Accounts Receivable, is deemed uncollectible, the account is written off using the procedures discussed in Chapter 7.

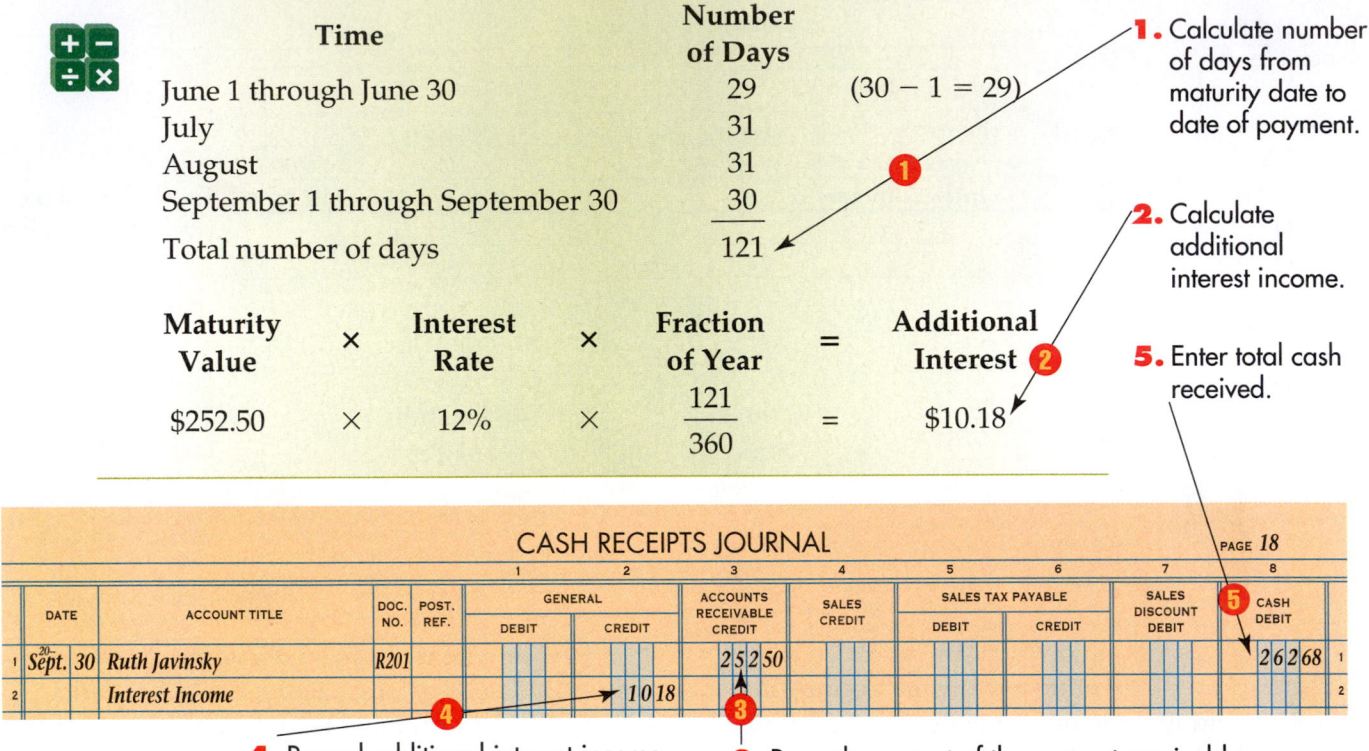

| Time | Number of Days | |
|---|---|---|
| June 1 through June 30 | 29 | (30 − 1 = 29) |
| July | 31 | |
| August | 31 | |
| September 1 through September 30 | 30 | |
| Total number of days | 121 | |

**1.** Calculate number of days from maturity date to date of payment.

| Maturity Value | × | Interest Rate | × | Fraction of Year | = | Additional Interest |
|---|---|---|---|---|---|---|
| $252.50 | × | 12% | × | $\frac{121}{360}$ | = | $10.18 |

**2.** Calculate additional interest income.

**5.** Enter total cash received.

**CASH RECEIPTS JOURNAL**    PAGE *18*

| | | | | | 1 | 2 | 3 | 4 | 5 | 6 | 7 | 8 |
|---|---|---|---|---|---|---|---|---|---|---|---|---|
| | DATE | ACCOUNT TITLE | DOC. NO. | POST. REF. | GENERAL DEBIT | GENERAL CREDIT | ACCOUNTS RECEIVABLE CREDIT | SALES CREDIT | SALES TAX PAYABLE DEBIT | SALES TAX PAYABLE CREDIT | SALES DISCOUNT DEBIT | CASH DEBIT |
| 1 | Sept. 30 | Ruth Javinsky | R201 | | | | 252 50 | | | | | 262 68 |
| 2 | | Interest Income | | | | 10 18 | | | | | | |

**4.** Record additional interest income.

**3.** Record payment of the account receivable.

Sometimes payment may be received on a previously dishonored note. Additional interest is charged from maturity date to payment date.

On September 30, Ruth Javinsky paid Appliance Center the maturity value of her note plus interest. The time for computing additional interest begins when the note is dishonored and ends on the day cash is received. The number of days for which interest is owed is calculated using the same method as determining the due date of a note. Instead of adjusting the date of the last month to equal a predetermined number of days, the payment date is used to determine the number of days in the final month, as shown above.

The interest rate is adjusted for the fraction of the year from the date the note was dishonored to the payment date. The additional interest is based on the maturity value of the note on the date the note was dishonored, *$252.50*.

*September 30. Received cash from Ruth Javinsky for dishonored Note Receivable No. 8: maturity value, $252.50, plus additional interest, $10.18; total, $262.68. Receipt No. 201.*

Ruth Javinsky's account in the accounts receivable ledger provides a complete history of the transactions. Management should use this information when making any future decisions to extend credit to this customer.

**GENERAL LEDGER**

Cash

| | | |
|---|---|---|
| 9/30 | 262.68 | |

Accounts Receivable

| | | | | |
|---|---|---|---|---|
| Bal. | 252.50 | 9/30 | 252.50 |

Interest Income

| | | | |
|---|---|---|---|
| | | 9/30 | 10.18 |

**ACCOUNTS RECEIVABLE LEDGER**

Ruth Javinsky

| | | | | |
|---|---|---|---|---|
| Bal. | 252.50 | 9/30 | 252.50 |
| (New Bal. zero) | | | |

# Explore Accounting

## The Impact of Changes in Foreign Exchange Rates on Accounts Receivable and Notes Receivable

In Chapter 1 you learned that the unit of measurement concept states that business transactions are reported in numbers that use a common unit of measurement. In the United States, that common unit of measurement is the dollar. So what happens if a U.S. business completes a transaction in Italy? Should that transaction be measured in dollars or in euros, the currency of Italy? The unit of measurement accounting concept states that the transaction occurring in Italy will ultimately need to be presented in dollars for a U.S. company. Imagine how difficult it would be to analyze a company's income statement if some sales were presented in dollars and others in euros.

To understand the impact of changes in foreign currency exchange rates on a U.S. company's accounts receivable, let's analyze the following example. A U.S. company, CyclePart, sells road bike components to companies in both the United States and Italy. Recently, CyclePart sold on account a variety of American-made bicycle components priced at 10,000 euros to the Bicicletta Company in Italy. The terms of the sale on account are that Bicicletta will pay CyclePart 10,000 euros in 60 days. During the 60-day time period, the exchange rate between the euro and the dollar remains exactly even. An even exchange rate of 1 to 1 means that 1 euro can be exchanged for 1 dollar. Sixty days later, if the exchange rate is still even, CyclePart's 10,000 euros will be worth exactly $10,000. But what happens if during the 60-day credit period, the exchange rate for the euro rises to $1.20? This higher exchange rate means that a single euro can now be exchanged for more dollars ($1.20). When CyclePart receives payment of 10,000 euros in 60 days, the 10,000 euros can be exchanged for $12,000.00 U.S. dollars (10,000 euros × $1.20). The 20-cent rise in the exchange rate means that CyclePart will gain an extra $2,000 through the exchange process.

It is also possible that the exchange rate for euros to dollars may decline. For example, assume the exchange rate for one euro declines from $1 to $.90. This means that if you exchange 10 euros for dollars, you will receive only $9.00 (10 euros × .90). A declining exchange rate for euros to dollars can have a significant impact on foreign transactions. Suppose on January 1 of the current year, Bicicletta gives CyclePart a 12-month, 6% note receivable for 100,000 euros. Including the interest of 6,000 euros (100,000 euros × .06), Bicicletta will pay CyclePart 106,000 euros in one year. If the exchange remains even (one euro = one dollar) during the entire 12 months, 106,000 euros will be worth $106,000. Suppose, however, that during the 12-month period, the exchange rate between the euro and the dollar declines from $1 to $.90. Since a euro now equals less than a dollar, CyclePart will exchange the 106,000 euros it receives on December 31 for only $95,400 (106,000 euros × .90).

### Critical Thinking Activity

An American company sells watch parts on account to a Swiss firm, SwissTime, for 20,000 Swiss francs. At the time of the sale, the exchange rate for francs to dollars is one franc equals .85 dollars. Thirty days later, when the American company collects the 2,000 Swiss francs, the exchange rate has risen. One franc can now be exchanged for .95 dollars. If the American company exchanges the francs for dollars at the new rate, will the company realize a gain or a loss on the transaction? In your answer, identify the amount of the gain or loss.

accountingxtra.swlearning.com

## • terms review

notes receivable
dishonored note

## • audit your understanding

1. Why might a business accept a note receivable from a customer?

2. What happens to the maturity value of a note when a note receivable is dishonored?

3. What is the time for computing interest when payment is received on a dishonored note?

## • work together 10-1

### Journalizing notes receivable transactions

Page 5 of a general journal and page 8 of a cash receipts journal are provided in the *Working Papers*. Source documents are abbreviated as follows: memorandum, M; note receivable, NR; receipt, R. Your instructor will guide you through the following example.

1. Journalize the following transactions made during the current year.

May   1. Accepted a 60-day, 15% note from Patrick Sampson for an extension of time on his account, $400.00. NR1.

June   1. Accepted a 180-day, 18% note from Sandy Adams for the sale of equipment, $700.00. NR2.

June  30. Patrick Sampson dishonored NR1; maturity value, $400.00 plus interest. M142.

Nov.  28. Received cash for the maturity value of NR2: principal, $700.00 plus interest. R310.

Dec.  12. Received cash from Patrick Sampson for dishonored NR1, $410.00 plus additional interest. R432.

## • on your own 10-1

### Journalizing notes receivable transactions

Page 6 of a general journal and page 9 of a cash receipts journal are provided in the *Working Papers*. Source documents are abbreviated as follows: memorandum, M; note receivable, NR; receipt, R. Work this problem independently.

1. Journalize the following transactions made during the current year.

May   14. Accepted a 90-day, 18% note from Pamula Yates for an extension of time on her account, $320.00. NR19.

June   1. Accepted a 120-day, 18% note from Walt Harrison for the sale of furniture, $1,500.00. NR20.

Aug.  12. Pamula Yates dishonored NR19; maturity value, $320.00 plus interest. M82.

Oct.  26. Received cash for the maturity value of NR20, $1,500.00 plus interest. R430.

Dec.  22. Received cash on account from Pamula Yates for dishonored NR19, $334.40 plus additional interest. R753.

## 10-2 Unearned and Accrued Revenue

### ADJUSTING ENTRY FOR UNEARNED REVENUE INITIALLY RECORDED AS A REVENUE

**1.** Debit the revenue account.

| | DATE | | ACCOUNT TITLE | DOC. NO. | POST. REF. | DEBIT | CREDIT | |
|---|---|---|---|---|---|---|---|---|
| 1 | | | *Adjusting Entries* | | | | | 1 |
| 36 | 31 | | *Rent Income* | | | 4 0 0 0 00 | | 36 |
| 37 | | | *Unearned Rent* | | | | 4 0 0 0 00 | 37 |

**GENERAL JOURNAL**      PAGE *13*

**2.** Credit the liability account.

Some revenue is received during a fiscal period but is not actually earned until the next fiscal period. Revenue received in one fiscal period but not earned until the next fiscal period is called **unearned revenue**. Unearned revenue is also known as deferred revenue.

Unearned revenue may be recorded initially as a liability or as revenue. Appliance Center rents part of its building to Pace Delivery and initially records rent receipts as revenue.

On December 1, Appliance Center received $6,000.00 from Pace Delivery, $2,000.00 per month for December, January, and February rent. The receipt was recorded as rent income and is included in the $28,000.00 balance of Rent Income.

Only that part of rent actually earned should be recorded as revenue in a fiscal period. An adjusting entry is recorded to separate the earned and unearned portions of the rent recorded in Rent Income, as shown above. The January and February rent is unearned and should be reported in Unearned Rent.

The $4,000.00 balance of Unearned Rent, a liability account, represents the value of two months of rent owed to Pace Delivery. The new

balance of Rent Income, $24,000.00, correctly reflects 12 months of rent at $2,000.00 per month.

Unearned Rent is classified as a Current Liability and Rent Income is classified as Other Revenue, as shown on Appliance Center's chart of accounts.

| Unearned Rent | |
|---|---|
| | Adj.     4,000.00 |

| Rent Income | |
|---|---|
| Adj.     4,000.00 | Dec. 31 Bal.    28,000.00 |
| | (New Bal.      24,000.00) |

**FYI** FOR YOUR INFORMATION

A company can elect to record rent payments as Unearned Rent during the year. At December 31, it records an adjusting entry to recognize the revenue earned during the year. Initially recording unearned revenue either as a liability or as revenue is acceptable accounting practice. Appliance Center prefers recording unearned revenue as revenue because the unearned revenue eventually will become revenue as the building space is used.

**1.** Debit the liability account.

| | DATE | ① | ACCOUNT TITLE | DOC. NO. | POST. REF. | DEBIT | CREDIT | |
|---|---|---|---|---|---|---|---|---|
| | | | *Reversing Entries* | | | | | 1 |
| 24 | | 1 | *Unearned Rent* | | | 4 0 0 0 00 | | 24 |
| 25 | | | *Rent Income* | | | | 4 0 0 0 00 | 25 |

GENERAL JOURNAL     PAGE **1**

②

**2.** Credit the revenue account.

On December 31, Rent Income is closed as part of Appliance Center's closing entries. After closing entries are posted, the balance in Rent Income is zero and ready to record transactions in the next fiscal period.

Reversing entries for prepaid and accrued expenses are described in Chapter 9. If an adjusting entry *creates* a balance in an asset or liability account, the adjusting entry is reversed. Reversing entries for unearned revenue are made for the same reason as for prepaid expenses. The amount of unearned revenue must be returned to the account in which it was initially recorded.

Appliance Center's adjusting entry created a balance in the liability account, Unearned Rent. Therefore, Appliance Center needs to make a reversing entry for unearned rent on January 1, as shown above.

On January 1, after the reversing entry is posted, the new balance of Unearned Rent is zero as it was before the adjusting entry. Rent Income has a $4,000.00 credit balance. The rent received in advance for January and February, $4,000.00, is part of the rent revenue earned in the new fiscal period.

**Unearned Rent**

| Rev. | 4,000.00 | Adj. | 4,000.00 |
|---|---|---|---|
| | | *(New Bal. zero)* | |

**Rent Income**

| Adj. | 4,000.00 | Dec. 31 Bal. | 28,000.00 |
|---|---|---|---|
| Clos. | 24,000.00 | *(New Bal. zero)* | |
| | | Rev. | 4,000.00 |
| | | *(New Bal.* | *4,000.00)* |

# technology for business

TECHNOLOGY FOR BUSINESS • TECHNOLOGY FOR BUSINESS • TECHNOLOGY FOR BUS

## The Federal Government Is Learning to Shop at Electronic Stores

The federal government purchases billions of dollars of goods and services every year. Various government agencies have developed Web-based electronic stores. The Government Services Administration (GSA) administers GSA Advantage, the largest of these electronic stores. GSA Advantage supplies more than 4 million items to other government agencies. Other departments and agencies, including NASA and the various branches of the Armed Services, operate smaller electronic stores.

Authorized federal employees can make purchases from these electronic stores. Currently, purchases are made by "credit cards" with various purchasing limits. Eventually, the credit cards will be replaced by smart cards.

The Web-based electronic stores reduce the purchasing cycle by more than 50 percent. Substantial cost savings result from lower inventory levels and reduced paperwork.

| Note | Principal | × | Interest Rate | × | Fraction of Year | = | Accrued Interest Income |
|------|-----------|---|---------------|---|------------------|---|--------------------------|
| 12 | $500.00 | × | 10% | × | $\frac{30}{360}$ | = | $4.17 |
| 13 | $700.00 | × | 10% | × | $\frac{15}{360}$ | = | 2.92 |

Total accrued interest income, December 31. . . . $7.09 ← **1**    **1.** Calculate interest earned on the notes.

**2.** Record entry to accrue interest income.

**GENERAL JOURNAL**    PAGE 13

| | DATE | ACCOUNT TITLE | DOC. NO. | POST. REF. | DEBIT | CREDIT | |
|---|------|---------------|----------|-----------|-------|--------|---|
| 1 | | Adjusting Entries | | | | | 1 |
| 2 | Dec. 31 | Interest Receivable | | | 7 09 | | 2 |
| 3 | | Interest Income | | | | 7 09 | 3 |

Revenue earned in one fiscal period but not received until a later fiscal period is called **accrued revenue**. For example, a business accepts a 30-day note on December 15. During December, the business earned interest for 16 days. However, the business will not receive any of the interest until the note's maturity in January. Interest for the first 16 days must be recorded in the current fiscal period. [CONCEPT: *Matching Expenses with Revenue*]

On December 31, Appliance Center has two notes receivable outstanding.

*Note Receivable No. 12,* a 60-day, 10% note dated December 1, $500.00.

*Note Receivable No. 13,* a 30-day, 10% note dated December 16, $700.00.

Accrued interest for each note is calculated from the date of the note through the end of the fiscal year, as shown above.

The accrued interest for all notes is totaled to compute the adjusting entry amount. The adjusting entry increases the balance of Interest Income to include interest that has been earned but not received in cash.

The amount of interest owed to the company is reported as Interest Receivable. Interest Receivable is classified as a Current Asset, as shown on Appliance Center's chart of accounts.

Interest Receivable

| Adj. | 7.09 | |
|------|------|---|

Interest Income

| | Dec. 31 Bal. | 65.70 |
|---|-------------|-------|
| | Adj. | 7.09 |
| | (New Bal. | 72.79) |

**FYI** FOR YOUR INFORMATION

A company that accepts a large number of notes might benefit from using a ledger system similar to an accounts receivable ledger. The ledger enables management to identify the total amount of notes outstanding with any single customer. Thus, management could make more informed decisions about extending additional credit to a particular customer.

| | DATE | | ACCOUNT TITLE | DOC. NO. | POST. REF. | DEBIT | CREDIT | |
|---|---|---|---|---|---|---|---|---|
| 1 | | | *Reversing Entries* | | | | | 1 |
| 2 | 20--<br>Jan. | 1 | *Interest Income* | | | 7 09 | | 2 |
| 3 | | | *Interest Receivable* | | | | 7 09 | 3 |

GENERAL JOURNAL PAGE 1

Interest Income is closed as part of Appliance Center's closing entries. After closing entries are posted, Interest Income has a zero balance. The $7.09 balance in Interest Receivable represents interest that Appliance Center has earned but has not yet received in cash.

The adjusting entry for accrued interest income created a balance in the asset account Interest Receivable. Therefore, on January 1, Appliance Center needs to reverse the adjusting entry that created the balance in Interest Receivable, as shown above.

The new balance of Interest Receivable is zero, as it was before the adjusting entry. The new debit balance, *$7.09*, in Interest Income is a contra balance. When cash is received on the maturity date of each note, a credit to Interest Income will offset the debit balance.

| Interest Income | | | |
|---|---|---|---|
| Clos. | 72.79 | Dec. 31 Bal. | 65.70 |
| | | Adj. | 7.09 |
| Rev. | 7.09 | | |
| *(New Bal.* | *7.09)* | | |

| Interest Receivable | | | |
|---|---|---|---|
| Adj. | 7.09 | Rev. | 7.09 |
| *(New Bal. zero)* | | | |

©GETTY IMAGES/PHOTODISC

**REMEMBER** Reversing entries eliminate the need for accounting personnel to remember to apply different account distributions to selected transactions. Without reversing entries, accounting personnel need to determine whether each interest payment was part of a prior year-end adjusting entry. If previously adjusted, the interest payment needs to be divided between Interest Receivable and Interest Income. With reversing entries, however, accounting personnel can simply record all interest payments to Interest Income.

# Explore Accounting

## Gains or Losses on Accounts Receivable and Notes Receivable Resulting from Changes in Foreign Exchange Rates

In the previous Explore Accounting feature, CyclePart sells on account a variety of American-made bicycle components priced at 10,000 euros to the Bicicletta Company in Italy. The transaction requires Bicicletta to pay CyclePart 10,000 euros in 60 days. At the time of the sale, the exchange rate between the euro and the dollar is exactly 1 to 1, meaning that 1 euro can be exchanged for 1 dollar. On the date of the sale, 10,000 euros equals $10,000 dollars. During the 60-day credit period, however, the exchange rate for the euro rises to $1.20. This higher exchange rate means that a single euro can now be exchanged for $1.20. When CyclePart receives payment of 10,000 euros in 60 days, the 10,000 euros are exchanged for $12,000.00 (10,000 euros × $1.20). Due to the 20-cent rise in the exchange rate, CyclePart gains an extra $2,000 through the currency exchange process. CyclePart accounts for the gain on accounts receivable with the entry below. The account Gain or Loss on Foreign Currency Exchange is classified as an other revenue account.

| | |
|---|---|
| Cash . . . . . . . . . . . . . . . . . . . . 12,000 | |
| Accounts Receivable/ | |
| Bicicletta Company . . . . . . . . . . . . . | 10,000 |
| Gain or Loss on Foreign | |
| Currency Exchange . . . . . . . . . . . . . | 2,000 |

In the previous Explore Accounting feature, another example was provided in which Bicicletta gives CyclePart a 12-month, 6% note receivable for 100,000 euros. Including the interest of 6,000 euros (100,000 euros × .06), Bicicletta will pay CyclePart 106,000 euros in one year. If the exchange rate remains even (1 euro = 1 dollar) during the entire 12 months,

106,000 euros will be worth $106,000. Suppose, however, that during the 12-month period, the exchange rate between the euro and the dollar declines from $1 to $.90. Since a euro now equals less than $1, CyclePart will exchange the 106,000 euros it receives on December 31 for only $95,400 dollars (106,000 euros × .90). CyclePart accounts for the loss on notes receivable using the entry below. Due to the 10-cent decline in the exchange rate, CyclePart suffers a loss of $10,600 through the currency exchange process.

| | |
|---|---|
| Cash . . . . . . . . . . . . . . . . . . . . 95,400 | |
| Gain or Loss on Foreign | |
| Currency Exchange . . . . 10,600 | |
| Notes Receivable/ | |
| Bicicletta Company . . . . . . . . . . . | 100,000 |
| Interest Income . . . . . . . . . . . . . . . . . | 6,000 |

### Critical Thinking Activity

An American company sells watch parts on account to a Swiss firm, SwissTime, for 30,000 Swiss francs. At the time of the sale, the exchange rate for francs to dollars is 1 franc equals .9 dollars. The American company accepts a 6-month note from SwissTime at 8% interest. Six months later, when the American company collects the 30,000 Swiss francs for the note receivable plus the interest, the exchange rate has risen. One franc can now be exchanged for .95 dollars. If the American company exchanges the francs for dollars at the new rate, will the company realize a gain or a loss on the transaction? Show the impact of the gain or loss on accounts receivable as a journal entry similar to the example.

Xtra!
Study Tools
accountingxtra.swlearning.com

TERMS REVIEW • TERMS REVIEW

## terms review

unearned revenue
accrued revenue

## audit your understanding

1. What accounts are affected, and how, when rent received in advance is initially recorded as a revenue?

2. What is the rule for determining whether an adjusting entry should be reversed?

3. What accounts are affected, and how, by a reversing entry for rent revenue when rent receipts are initially recorded as a revenue?

4. What accounts are affected, and how, by an adjusting entry for accrued interest income?

5. What accounts are affected, and how, by a reversing entry for accrued interest income?

AUDIT YOUR UNDERSTANDING

## work together 10-2

**Journalizing adjusting and reversing entries for unearned revenue initially recorded as revenue and for accrued revenue**

Valentine, Inc., is preparing its December 31 financial statements for the current year. On December 1, the company received a $2,100.00 rent payment from Owens & Nolen, LLP. The payment is the $700.00 per month rent for December of the current year through February of the next year. Valentine initially records rent receipts as revenue. General journal pages are provided in the *Working Papers*. Your instructor will guide you through the following examples.

1. Journalize the adjusting entry for unearned rent. Use page 13 of a general journal.

2. Journalize the reversing entry for unearned rent. Use page 14 of a general journal.

Valentine, Inc., has two notes receivable outstanding on December 31 of the current year.

| Note No. | Interest Rate | Term | Principal | Date |
|---|---|---|---|---|
| 14 | 15% | 60-days | $2,000.00 | November 14 |
| 15 | 16% | 60-days | $3,000.00 | December 6 |

3. Journalize the adjusting entry for accrued interest income. Use page 13 of a general journal.

4. Journalize the reversing entry for accrued interest income. Use page 14 of a general journal.

WORK TOGETHER • WORK TOGETHER • WORK TOGETHER

## on your own 10-2

**Journalizing adjusting and reversing entries for unearned revenue initially recorded as revenue and for accrued revenue**

K-98.1 Radio is preparing its December 31 financial statements for the current year. On October 30, Parker Discount Stores paid $1,500.00 to K-98.1 Radio for advertising. The advertising contract requires K-98.1 to provide Parker with $500.00 of advertising time per month for November of the current year through January of the next year. K-98.1 initially records advertising receipts as revenue. General journal pages are provided in the *Working Papers*. Work this problem independently.

1. Journalize the adjusting entry for unearned advertising revenue. Use page 19 of a general journal.

2. Journalize the reversing entry for unearned advertising revenue. Use page 20 of a general journal.

K-98.1 Radio has two notes receivable outstanding on December 31 of the current year.

| Note No. | Interest Rate | Term | Principal | Date |
|---|---|---|---|---|
| 26 | 18% | 90-days | $4,000.00 | November 8 |
| 29 | 16% | 60-days | $1,500.00 | December 12 |

3. Journalize the adjusting entry for accrued interest income. Use page 19 of a general journal.

4. Journalize the reversing entry for accrued interest income. Use page 20 of a general journal.

accountingxtra.swlearning.com

1. Define accounting terms related to notes receivable, unearned revenue, and accrued revenue.

2. Identify accounting concepts and practices related to notes receivable, unearned revenue, and accrued revenue.

3. Journalize transactions for notes receivable.

4. Journalize adjusting and reversing entries for unearned revenue initially recorded as revenue.

5. Journalize adjusting and reversing entries for accrued revenue.

# Explore Accounting

EXPLORE ACCOUNTING • EXPLORE ACCOUNTING • EXPLORE ACC

## Factoring Accounts Receivable

New businesses must have an adequate amount of working capital to purchase inventory, rent or buy fixed assets, and pay employees during the planning, construction, and opening periods. Access to independent sources of working capital, such as bank loans, is often limited until a business proves it can maintain profitability.

Accounts receivable can become a significant drain on working capital. Inventory sold on account does not immediately provide cash to purchase new inventory. Customers unable to purchase out-of-stock items shop elsewhere. The more successful a business is at selling inventory on account, the greater its need for working capital.

A solution to this problem is that a business can sell its accounts receivable to another company for cash. Assigning the rights to accounts receivable to an independent company in exchange for cash is known as factoring. The factoring company pays 85% to 95% of the value of the accounts receivable sold. The factoring company assumes the responsibility and cost of collecting the accounts.

Factoring costs the business 5% to 15% of sales on account. However, the immediate cash received allows the business to continue operations. In addition, management can focus

its attention on more important aspects of the business than on the collection of accounts receivable.

**Required:**
Accounting equations are provided in the *Working Papers.* Record transactions using the following assumptions for eight weeks, with and without factoring. Would you recommend that Chism Company factor accounts receivable at 90% of value?

1. All cash was used to purchase $10,000 of inventory.

2. Disregard other operating expenses.

3. With a complete inventory, sales are $2,000 per week ($1,000 cost). If the inventory levels drop below $10,000, however, sales for out-of-stock items are lost. Chism can still sell 20% of available inventory each week.

4. All sales are on account with n/30 terms. Cash collected is used to restock inventory up to $10,000.

5. Accounts receivable are factored at 90% of value.

Accounting for Notes Receivable, Unearned Revenue, and Accrued Revenue

# 10-1 APPLICATION PROBLEM

AUTOMATED ACCOUNTING    PEACHTREE    QUICKBOOKS

## Journalizing transactions for notes receivable

Bellingham, Inc., completed the following transactions during the current year.

**Transactions:**

Aug.  1.  Bellingham agreed to an extension of time on James Huber's account by accepting a 60-day, 10% note from him, $200.00. NR1.

Aug.  1.  Accepted a 60-day, 12% note from Frank Otto for a sale on account, $300.00. NR2.

Sept.  30.  The 60-day, 10% note from James Huber (NR1) was dishonored; $200.00 plus interest. M12.

Sept.  30.  Accepted a 60-day, 10% note from Melissa Carr for an extension of time on her account, $500.00. NR3.

Sept.  30.  Received cash for the maturity value of NR2, $300.00 plus interest. R10.

Nov.  30.  Principal, $500.00, plus interest was received for the maturity value of NR3. R32.

Dec.  1.  James Huber sent a check for dishonored NR1, $203.33 plus additional interest. R33.

**Instructions:**

Use page 8 of a general journal and page 15 of a cash receipts journal to journalize the transactions. Source documents are abbreviated as follows: memorandum, M; note receivable, NR; receipt, R.

# 10-2 APPLICATION PROBLEM

## Journalizing adjusting and reversing entries for unearned revenue initially recorded as revenue

On November 1 of the current year, Billies, Inc., received a $2,700.00 rent payment from Simms & Ulman. The payment covers rent of office space for November through April, $450.00 per month. Billies initially records rent payments as revenue.

**Instructions:**

1.  Journalize the adjusting entry for unearned rent on December 31 of the current year. Use page 13 of a general journal.
2.  Journalize the reversing entry for unearned rent on January 1 of the next year. Use page 1 of a general journal.

# 10-3 APPLICATION PROBLEM

## Journalizing adjusting and reversing entries for accrued revenue

On December 31 of the current year, McNeilson, Inc., has two notes receivable.

*Note Receivable No. 1,* a 90-day, 10% note dated November 1, $200.00.
*Note Receivable No. 2,* a 60-day, 10% note dated December 1, $300.00.

**Instructions:**

1.  Calculate the accrued interest on the notes as of December 31.
2.  Journalize the adjusting entry for accrued interest income on December 31 of the current year. Use page 13 of a general journal.
3.  Journalize the reversing entry for accrued interest income on January 1 of the next year. Use page 1 of a general journal.

## 10-4 MASTERY PROBLEM    AUTOMATED ACCOUNTING    PEACHTREE    QUICKBOOKS

### Journalizing notes receivable, unearned revenue, and accrued revenue initially recorded as revenue transactions

Marier, Inc., completed the following transactions during the current year. Marier initially records prepaid and unearned items as revenue.

**Transactions:**

| | | |
|---|---|---|
| July | 1. | Accepted a 90-day, 10% note from Timothy Johnson for a sale on account, $500.00. NR12. |
| July | 5. | Accepted a 90-day, 12% note from Gerald Kammer for an extension of time on his account, $600.00. NR13. |
| Sept. | 29. | Timothy Johnson dishonored NR12, a 90-day, 10% note, $500.00 plus interest. M32. |
| Oct. | 3. | Received cash for the maturity value of NR13, $600.00 plus interest. R65. |
| Nov. | 1. | Received cash for November through January rent, $500.00 per month, in advance from Centuria, Inc., $1,500.00. R70. |
| Dec. | 1. | Received cash from Timothy Johnson for dishonored NR12, $512.50 plus additional interest. R81. |
| Dec. | 4. | Accepted a 90-day, 12% note from Jackie Webb for sale on account, $900.00. NR14. |

**Instructions:**

1. Use page 7 of a general journal and page 19 of a cash receipts journal to journalize the transactions. Source documents are abbreviated as follows: memorandum, M; note receivable, NR; receipt, R.
2. Continue using page 7 of the general journal. Journalize the necessary adjusting entries.
3. Journalize the reversing entries on January 1 of the next year. Use page 1 of a general journal.

## 10-5 CHALLENGE PROBLEM

### Journalizing accounts and notes receivable

Hillsdale, Inc., sells on account with n/30 terms. If the account is not paid within 30 days, Hillsdale begins charging customers 18% interest on their outstanding balance. At 120 days past due, Hillsdale asks customers to sign a 60-day, 18% note for the original amount of the sale plus 90 days of accrued interest. During the year, Hillsdale accrues interest income when notes are issued or payments on account are made.

Unfortunately, customers are not always willing to pay all or any of the interest charges. Because the amounts are often small, Hillsdale must consider the negative impact that attempting to collect these amounts may have on its image. Thus, it writes off many interest charges as uncollectible.

**Transactions:**

| | | |
|---|---|---|
| July | 4. | Accepted a 60-day, 18% note from Steven Bozeman for an extension of time, $500.00 plus accrued interest. NR26. |
| July | 12. | Received $618.00 cash from Pierre Black on payment of NR18, a $627.00 note ($600.00 plus $27.00 accrued interest) issued 60 days ago. Mr. Black included a letter stating that he would pay interest only on the note and only for the original sale amount. R70. |
| July | 15. | Received $250.00 cash in payment of John Hamilton's account. The account balance resulted from a sale on account of $250.00 on May 16. R71. |
| July | 31. | Hillsdale's credit manager decided not to attempt to collect the interest charges on the accounts of Pierre Black and John Hamilton. M46. |

**Instructions:**

Journalize the transactions made during the current year. Calculate amounts as needed. Use page 7 of a general journal and page 7 of a cash receipts journal. Source documents are abbreviated as follows: memorandum, M; note receivable, NR; receipt, R.

## • applied communication

You have just been hired as the new credit manager for Harrell and Company, a chain of lumber stores. While evaluating the accounting system, you notice that many of the credit accounts are 120 to 180 days past due. Although these customers ultimately pay their accounts, they do not abide by the n/30 terms specified on the sales invoice.

At your suggestion, management has approved a plan to change the credit terms to 2/10, n/30, with 18% interest charged on overdue accounts. In addition, you will require a note receivable to be signed for accounts over 90 days past due as a condition for the customer to receive additional credit.

**Required:**

Prepare a letter to send to current credit customers informing them of the new credit terms.

## • cases for critical thinking

### Case 1

Farmland, Inc., issued a 60-day, 12%, $600.00 note receivable to a customer. The customer dishonored the note at maturity. The accounting clerk recorded the dishonored note receivable by debiting Accounts Receivable and crediting Notes Receivable for the maturity value, $612.00. Thirty days later, the customer paid $618.12 for the dishonored note. The accounting clerk recorded this amount by debiting Cash and crediting Notes Receivable. Farmland's bookkeeper checked the work and decided that the journal entries were both incorrect. Do you agree? Explain your answer.

### Case 2

At the beginning of December, Maxim Floral, Inc., received three months' rent in advance. Maxim initially records rent payment as a revenue. On December 31, Maxim does not make an adjusting entry for unearned rent. What effect will this have on the firm's financial statements?

## • SCANS workplace competency

**Thinking Skills:** Problem Solving

**Concept:** Business needs usually involve an underlying problem that must be first recognized and then solved. Solving a business problem involves devising a plan and then implementing the plan.

**Application:** Your construction company increasingly fails to win contracts for state and municipal construction jobs because of requirements for minority representation on your workforce. You know that many minority workers apply for jobs with your company but few are hired. Devise a plan for recruiting and hiring more minority workers for your company.

## • auditing for errors

The Stephens Company has the following notes receivable outstanding on December 31.

| No. | Date of Note | Term | Interest | Principal |
|-----|--------------|------|----------|-----------|
| 56 | September 12 | 120 days | 10% | $1,600.00 |
| 59 | October 3 | 90 days | 10% | $900.00 |
| 63 | November 30 | 60 days | 9% | $2,000.00 |

In preparation for adjusting entries, the accounting clerk has calculated accrued interest as follows:

Note 56: $120/360 \times 10\% \times 1,600.00 = 53.33$

Note 59: $89/360 \times 10\% \times 900.00 = 22.24$

Note 63: $31/360 \times 9\% \times 2,000.00 = 15.50$

**Instructions:**

1. Verify the calculations.

2. If you find any errors, recalculate to find the correct amount of accrued interest.

## • analyzing Costco's financial statements

Costco Wholesale Corporation is a membership company. Customers pay a yearly membership fee, which gives them the right to shop at Costco. When Costco receives the yearly fee from a customer, it cannot count all of it as revenue at that time. Revenue must be recognized as it is earned. Costco earns the revenue over the next year. Therefore, when Costco receives the cash for the fee, cash is debited, and a liability account is credited. This unearned revenue is a liability, because the company "owes" that customer the right of membership for the remainder of the membership period.

**Instructions:**

Using Appendix B in this textbook, find the paragraph in Note No. 1 titled "Revenue Recognition" on page B-12. Read the note related to membership fee revenue and answer the following questions.

1. When does Costco count the membership fee as revenue?

2. Look at Costco's balance sheet on page B5. What account title does Costco use for this liability account?

3. How much unearned revenue did Costco list as a liability for the fiscal period ending August 31, 2003?

4. How much unearned revenue did Costco list as a liability for the fiscal period ending September 1, 2002?

## Correction of Errors

When entering data into journals it is very easy to make errors unless you are careful. It is important to check your work as you enter transactions into the accounting system. People use different methods in order to lessen the likelihood of entering incorrect transactions and amounts, and entering transactions into the wrong journal.

Sometimes it may be necessary to locate and correct journal entries that have already been posted to the ledgers. The same procedure is used to locate and correct errors in all journals.

### Finding a Journal Entry

Use the following steps to find a journal entry:

1. Click on the special journal tab to which the journal entry was made (General, Purchases, Cash Payments, Sales, Cash Receipts).

2. Choose the Find menu item from the Edit menu.

3. Enter the date, reference, vendor name, or amount of the transaction you want to find in the Find What text box. Then click OK.

4. If a matching transaction is found, it will be displayed onscreen so that it may be changed or deleted.

### Changing Transactions

When changing or deleting journal transactions:

1. Click the journal tab in which you want to make a change.

2. Select the specific transaction that you wish to change.

3. Enter the correct journal entry and click the Post command button.

Accounting systems can be very efficient in processing data but it is the responsibility of the individual entering data to make accuracy a high priority. When producing a business's financial reports from an accounting system, if transactions were entered with errors, the reports will not represent the true financial position of the company.

An error can cause management to make business decisions based on inaccurate information, which could have serious consequences for a business.

### AUTOMATING APPLICATION PROBLEM 10-1

**Instructions:**

1. Load *Automated Accounting 8.0* or higher software.

2. Select database A10-1 (Advanced Course Application Problem 10-1) from the accounting template disk.

3. Select File from the menu bar and choose the Save As menu command. Key the path to the drive and directory that contain your data files. Save the database with a filename of XXX101 (where XXX are your initials).

4. Read the Problem Instruction screen by clicking the Browser toolbar button.

5. Key the data listed in the problem.

6. Exit the Automated Accounting software.

### AUTOMATING MASTERY PROBLEM 10-4

**Instructions:**

1. Load *Automated Accounting 8.0* or higher software.

2. Select database A10-4 (Advanced Course Mastery Problem 10-4) from the accounting template disk.

3. Select File from the menu bar and choose the Save As menu command. Key the path to the drive and directory that contain your data files. Save the database with a filename of XXX104 (where XXX are your initials).

4. Read the Problem Instruction screen by clicking the Browser toolbar button.

5. Key the data listed in the problem.

6. Exit the Automated Accounting software.

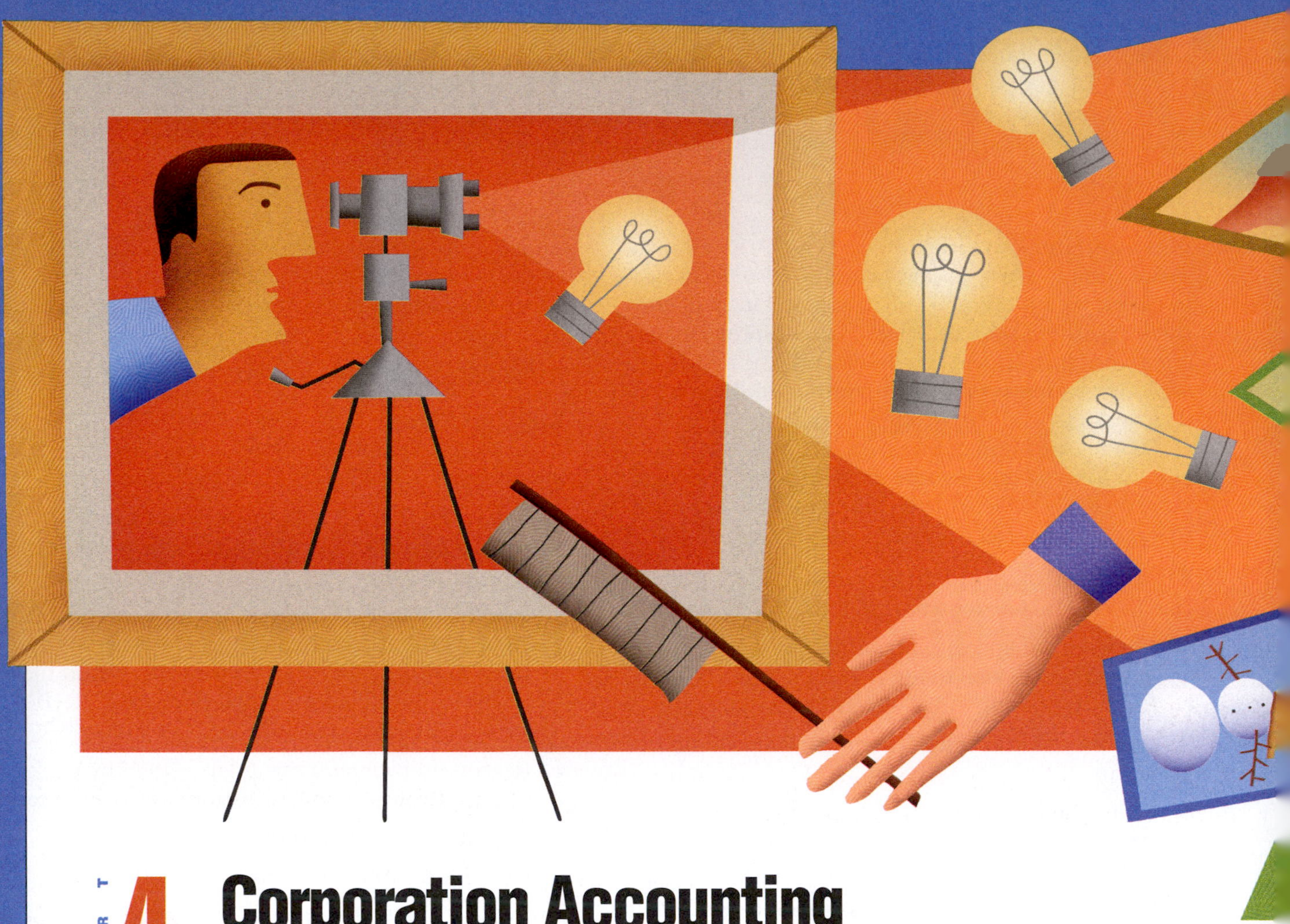

# PART 4 Corporation Accounting

CHAPTER • CHAPTER • CHAPTER • CHAPTER • CHAPTER

## LAMPLIGHT INC.
## CHART OF ACCOUNTS

### Balance Sheet Accounts

**(1000) ASSETS**

| | |
|---|---|
| 1100 | CURRENT ASSETS |
| 1105 | Cash |
| 1110 | Petty Cash |
| 1115 | Notes Receivable |
| 1120 | Interest Receivable |
| 1125 | Accounts Receivable |
| 1130 | Allowance for Uncollectible Accounts |
| 1135 | Subscriptions Receivable |
| 1140 | Merchandise Inventory |
| 1145 | Supplies—Store |
| 1150 | Supplies—Administrative |
| 1155 | Prepaid Insurance |
| 1160 | Prepaid Interest |
| 1200 | LONG-TERM INVESTMENT |
| 1205 | Bond Sinking Fund |
| 1300 | PLANT ASSETS |
| 1305 | Store Equipment |
| 1310 | Accumulated Depreciation—Store Equipment |
| 1315 | Building |
| 1320 | Accumulated Depreciation—Building |
| 1325 | Office Equipment |
| 1330 | Accumulated Depreciation—Office Equipment |
| 1335 | Land |

| | |
|---|---|
| 1400 | INTANGIBLE ASSET |
| 1405 | Organization Costs |

**(2000) LIABILITIES**

| | |
|---|---|
| 2100 | CURRENT LIABILITIES |
| 2105 | Interest Payable |
| 2110 | Accounts Payable |
| 2115 | Employee Income Tax Payable |
| 2120 | Federal Income Tax Payable |
| 2125 | Social Security Tax Payable |
| 2130 | Medicare Tax Payable |
| 2135 | Salaries Payable |
| 2140 | Sales Tax Payable |
| 2145 | Unemployment Tax Payable—Federal |
| 2150 | Unemployment Tax Payable—State |
| 2155 | Health Insurance Premiums Payable |
| 2160 | Dividends Payable |
| 2200 | LONG-TERM LIABILITY |
| 2205 | Bonds Payable |

**(3000) STOCKHOLDERS' EQUITY**

| | |
|---|---|
| 3105 | Capital Stock—Common |
| 3110 | Stock Subscribed—Common |
| 3115 | Paid-in Capital in Excess of Stated Value—Common |
| 3120 | Capital Stock—Preferred |
| 3125 | Stock Subscribed—Preferred |
| 3130 | Paid-in Capital in Excess of Par Value—Preferred |
| 3135 | Discount on Sale of Preferred Stock |
| 3140 | Treasury Stock |
| 3145 | Paid-in Capital from Sale of Treasury Stock |
| 3150 | Retained Earnings |
| 3155 | Dividends—Common |
| 3160 | Dividends—Preferred |
| 3165 | Income Summary |

### Income Statement Accounts

**(4000) OPERATING REVENUE**

| | |
|---|---|
| 4105 | Sales |
| 4110 | Sales Discount |
| 4115 | Sales Returns and Allowances |

**(5000) COST OF MERCHANDISE**

| | |
|---|---|
| 5105 | Purchases |
| 5110 | Purchases Discount |
| 5115 | Purchases Returns and Allowances |

**(6000) OPERATING EXPENSES**

| | |
|---|---|
| 6100 | SELLING EXPENSES |
| 6105 | Advertising Expense |
| 6110 | Credit Card Fee Expense |
| 6115 | Depreciation Expense—Store Equipment |
| 6120 | Miscellaneous Expense—Sales |
| 6125 | Salary Expense—Sales |
| 6130 | Supplies Expense—Sales |
| 6200 | ADMINISTRATIVE EXPENSES |
| 6205 | Depreciation Expense—Building |
| 6210 | Depreciation Expense—Office Equipment |
| 6215 | Insurance Expense |
| 6220 | Miscellaneous Expense—Administrative |
| 6225 | Payroll Taxes Expense |
| 6230 | Property Tax Expense |
| 6235 | Salary Expense—Administrative |
| 6240 | Supplies Expense—Administrative |
| 6245 | Uncollectible Accounts Expense |
| 6250 | Utilities Expense |

**(7000) OTHER REVENUE**

| | |
|---|---|
| 7105 | Gain on Plant Assets |
| 7110 | Interest Income |

**(8000) OTHER EXPENSES**

| | |
|---|---|
| 8105 | Interest Expense |
| 8110 | Loss on Plant Assets |
| 8115 | Organization Expense |

**(9000) INCOME TAX**

| | |
|---|---|
| 9105 | Federal Income Tax Expense |

The chart of accounts for LampLight, Inc. is illustrated above for ready reference as you study Part 4 of this textbook.

# 11 Organizing a Corporation and Paying Dividends

*After studying Chapter 11, you will be able to:*

1. Define accounting terms related to corporate accounting.

2. Identify accounting concepts and practices related to corporate accounting.

3. Journalize transactions related to starting a corporation.

4. Journalize transactions related to stock subscriptions.

5. Prepare a balance sheet for a newly formed corporation.

6. Calculate dividends for a corporation.

7. Journalize transactions of a corporation related to declaring and paying dividends.

- corporation
- board of directors
- articles of incorporation
- charter
- common stock
- preferred stock

- stock certificate
- par value
- par-value stock
- no-par-value stock
- stated-value stock
- organization costs

- subscribing for capital stock
- intangible assets
- declaring a dividend
- date of declaration
- date of record
- date of payment

Point Your Browser

accountingxtra.swlearning.com

## • General Mills

DANIEL ACKER/BLOOMBERG NEWS/LANDOV

### THE "BIG G" COULD MEAN DIVIDENDS FOR AN INVESTOR IN GENERAL MILLS

Long before "Wheaties, the breakfast of champions," was available, General Mills was in existence. In fact, its history can be traced back more than 130 years.

What helps some companies, like General Mills, survive so long? It may be because General Mills has continually added products, either by internal development or by buying already-established product lines.

At General Mills, research and development is focused on new product development, product improvement, process design and improvement, packaging, and exploratory research in new business areas. In 2003, General Mills acquired Pillsbury. Overnight it doubled its revenues, workforce, and ownership of leading brands.

Regardless of how new products are brought into the General Mills family, they are all added with the hope that they will increase the bottom-line profit for the company. A steady stream of profit can mean a steady stream of dividends to stockholders.

General Mills has quite a record when it comes to paying dividends. It has "paid shareholder dividends, uninterrupted and without reduction, for 105 consecutive years." That's a long time.

### Critical Thinking

1. Why would a company stress the fact that it has paid dividends for "105 consecutive years"?
2. Some companies have never paid a dividend and don't intend to pay a dividend in the near future. Why would an investor still be willing to invest in such a company?

Source: www.generalmills.com

Xtra!
Today
accountingxtra.swlearning.com

## internet activity

### NEW YORK STOCK EXCHANGE (NYSE)

Go to the homepage for the New York Stock Exchange (NYSE) (www.nyse.com). Search the site for information about a "seat" on the exchange.

### Instructions

1. Briefly summarize why a membership in the NYSE is called a "seat."
2. List how many seats are available on the NYSE.
3. What is the highest price ever paid for a seat on the NYSE?

# 11-1 Starting a Corporation

Selecting the form of business ownership is an important decision of new business owners. An organization with the legal rights of a person and that may be owned by many persons is called a **corporation**. [CONCEPT: Business Entity] A corporation is organized by law to exist separately and apart from its owners. Corporations differ from other forms of businesses principally in the nature of ownership and management.

A corporation's ownership is divided into units. Each unit of ownership is known as a share of stock. Total shares of ownership in a corporation are known as capital stock. An owner of one or more shares of a corporation is known as a stockholder.

Stockholders share a corporation's earnings. Earnings distributed to stockholders are known as dividends. Corporations may retain some or all of their earnings to finance future business expansion and improvement. However, most corporations distribute a portion of their earnings to stockholders.

©GETTY IMAGES/PHOTODISC

## making ethical decisions

### Just Following Orders

Step Productions is under contract with the federal government to produce training videos for the Environmental Protection Agency. The contract entitles Step Productions to charge its cost plus 15%. A government document outlines which expenditures qualify as "contract costs." The document specifically states that "expenses to entertain employees, suppliers, or other business partners do not qualify as contract costs."

After the annual company picnic, the company president told Jared Stern, who is a CPA, to record the picnic costs as a salary expense. "This picnic will raise worker morale. The workers will be more productive—for every dollar we spend, we'll save two dollars on our payroll," stated the president, justifying his request.

**Instructions**
Use the ethical model to analyze whether the accountant's recording of the picnic costs as salary expense would demonstrate ethical behavior.

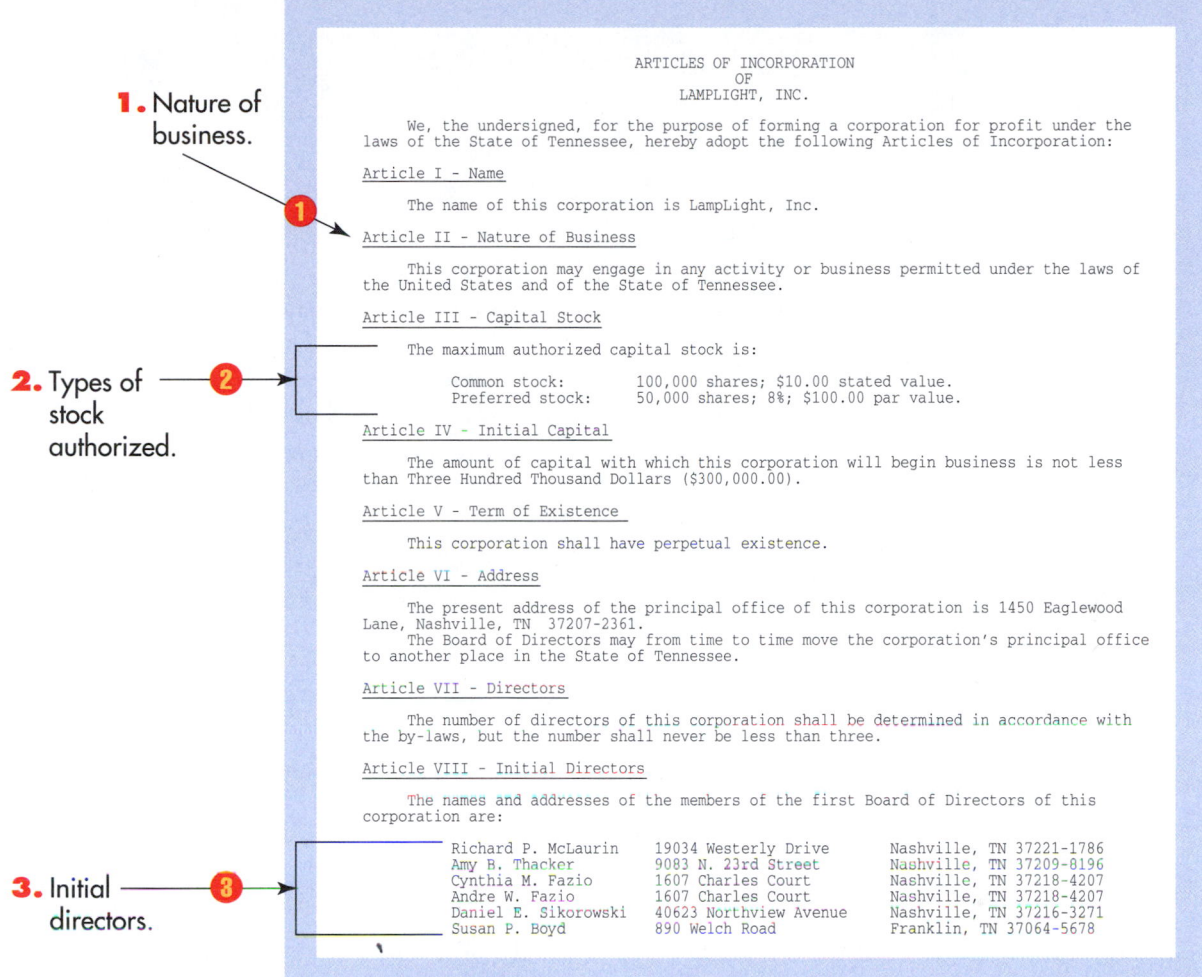

**1.** Nature of business.

**2.** Types of stock authorized.

**3.** Initial directors.

ARTICLES OF INCORPORATION
OF
LAMPLIGHT, INC.

We, the undersigned, for the purpose of forming a corporation for profit under the laws of the State of Tennessee, hereby adopt the following Articles of Incorporation:

Article I - Name

The name of this corporation is LampLight, Inc.

Article II - Nature of Business

This corporation may engage in any activity or business permitted under the laws of the United States and of the State of Tennessee.

Article III - Capital Stock

The maximum authorized capital stock is:

Common stock:     100,000 shares; $10.00 stated value.
Preferred stock:   50,000 shares; 8%; $100.00 par value.

Article IV - Initial Capital

The amount of capital with which this corporation will begin business is not less than Three Hundred Thousand Dollars ($300,000.00).

Article V - Term of Existence

This corporation shall have perpetual existence.

Article VI - Address

The present address of the principal office of this corporation is 1450 Eaglewood Lane, Nashville, TN 37207-2361.
The Board of Directors may from time to time move the corporation's principal office to another place in the State of Tennessee.

Article VII - Directors

The number of directors of this corporation shall be determined in accordance with the by-laws, but the number shall never be less than three.

Article VIII - Initial Directors

The names and addresses of the members of the first Board of Directors of this corporation are:

| | | |
|---|---|---|
| Richard P. McLaurin | 19034 Westerly Drive | Nashville, TN 37221-1786 |
| Amy B. Thacker | 9083 N. 23rd Street | Nashville, TN 37209-8196 |
| Cynthia M. Fazio | 1607 Charles Court | Nashville, TN 37218-4207 |
| Andre W. Fazio | 1607 Charles Court | Nashville, TN 37218-4207 |
| Daniel E. Sikorowski | 40623 Northview Avenue | Nashville, TN 37216-3271 |
| Susan P. Boyd | 890 Welch Road | Franklin, TN 37064-5678 |

A corporation may have many owners. Most owners do not participate in the management of the business. Instead, they elect a small group to represent their combined interests and to be responsible for management of the corporation. A group of persons elected by the stockholders to manage a corporation is called a **board of directors**. A board of directors determines corporate policies and selects corporate officers to supervise the day-to-day management of the corporation.

## Legal Requirements for Forming a Corporation

Persons seeking to form a corporation must submit an application to the state in which the company is to be incorporated. A written application requesting permission to form a corporation is called the **articles of incorporation**. Some articles of incorporation are submitted to the federal government, but most are submitted to a state government. When the articles of incorporation are approved, a corporation comes into existence. The approved articles of incorporation are called a **charter**. A charter is also referred to as a certificate of incorporation.

LampLight, Inc. is a corporation that sells lighting fixtures. The articles of incorporation submitted for LampLight, Inc. are shown above and on the next page.

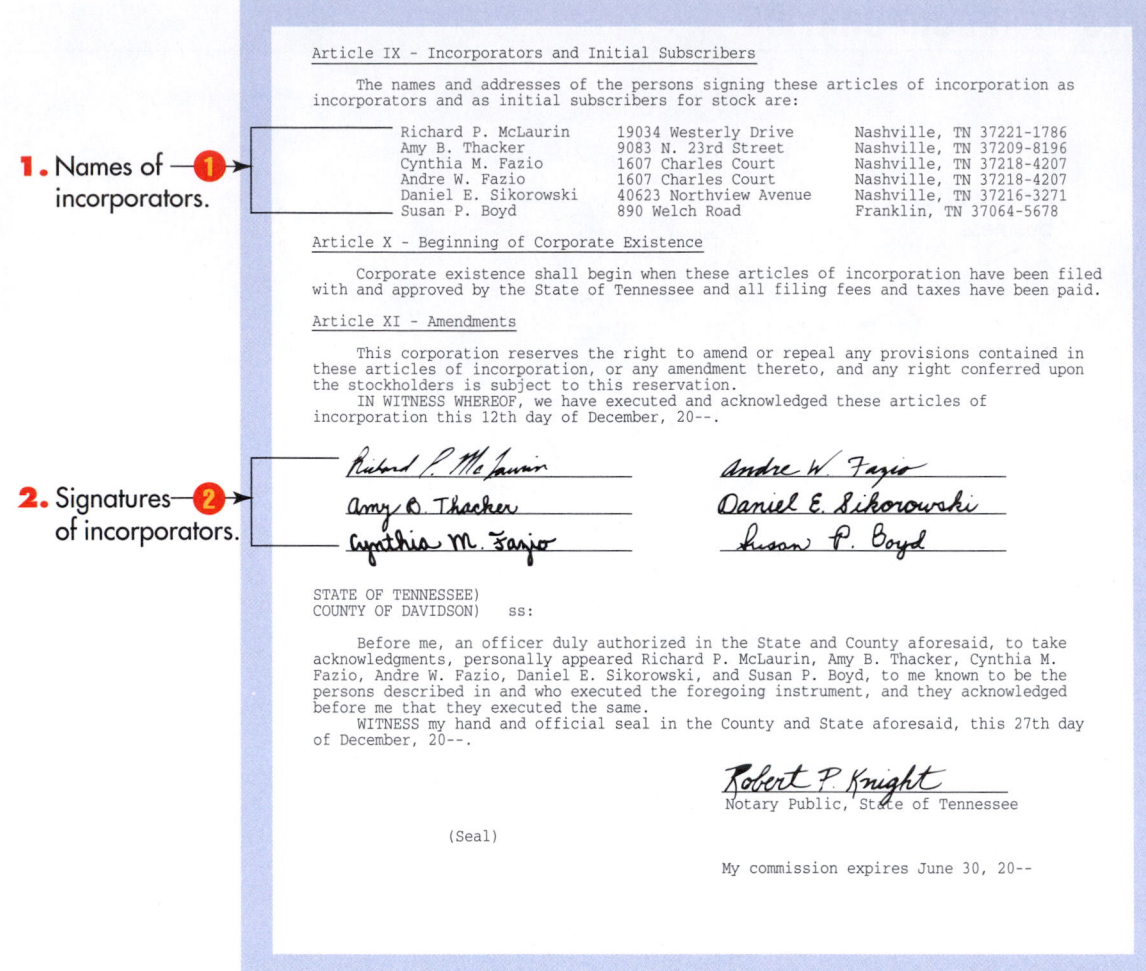

**1.** Names of incorporators.

**2.** Signatures of incorporators.

Article IX - Incorporators and Initial Subscribers

The names and addresses of the persons signing these articles of incorporation as incorporators and as initial subscribers for stock are:

| | | |
|---|---|---|
| Richard P. McLaurin | 19034 Westerly Drive | Nashville, TN 37221-1786 |
| Amy B. Thacker | 9083 N. 23rd Street | Nashville, TN 37209-8196 |
| Cynthia M. Fazio | 1607 Charles Court | Nashville, TN 37218-4207 |
| Andre W. Fazio | 1607 Charles Court | Nashville, TN 37218-4207 |
| Daniel E. Sikorowski | 40623 Northview Avenue | Nashville, TN 37216-3271 |
| Susan P. Boyd | 890 Welch Road | Franklin, TN 37064-5678 |

Article X - Beginning of Corporate Existence

Corporate existence shall begin when these articles of incorporation have been filed with and approved by the State of Tennessee and all filing fees and taxes have been paid.

Article XI - Amendments

This corporation reserves the right to amend or repeal any provisions contained in these articles of incorporation, or any amendment thereto, and any right conferred upon the stockholders is subject to this reservation.
IN WITNESS WHEREOF, we have executed and acknowledged these articles of incorporation this 12th day of December, 20--.

STATE OF TENNESSEE)
COUNTY OF DAVIDSON)    ss:

Before me, an officer duly authorized in the State and County aforesaid, to take acknowledgments, personally appeared Richard P. McLaurin, Amy B. Thacker, Cynthia M. Fazio, Andre W. Fazio, Daniel E. Sikorowski, and Susan P. Boyd, to me known to be the persons described in and who executed the foregoing instrument, and they acknowledged before me that they executed the same.
WITNESS my hand and official seal in the County and State aforesaid, this 27th day of December, 20--.

Notary Public, State of Tennessee

(Seal)

My commission expires June 30, 20--

As stated, LampLight is organized as a corporation to sell lighting fixtures and accessories. However, Article II of its articles of incorporation describes the nature of the business in broad, general terms. This broad purpose enables LampLight to expand into other kinds of business activities, if it desires, without applying for a new charter.

## Rights of Stockholders
Most stockholders have three basic rights.

1. To vote at stockholders' meetings unless an exception is made for holders of a particular kind of stock.

2. To share in a corporation's earnings.
3. To share in the distribution of the assets of the corporation if it ceases operations and sells all its assets.

## Capital Stock of a Corporation
Corporations may issue two basic kinds of stock: common and preferred. Stock that does not give stockholders any special preferences is called **common stock**. Stock that gives stockholders preference in earnings and other rights is called **preferred stock**. LampLight is authorized to issue both common and preferred stock as described in Article III of the illustration on the previous page.

**REMEMBER** Although the format of the articles of incorporation varies from one corporation to another, the articles usually address similar items.

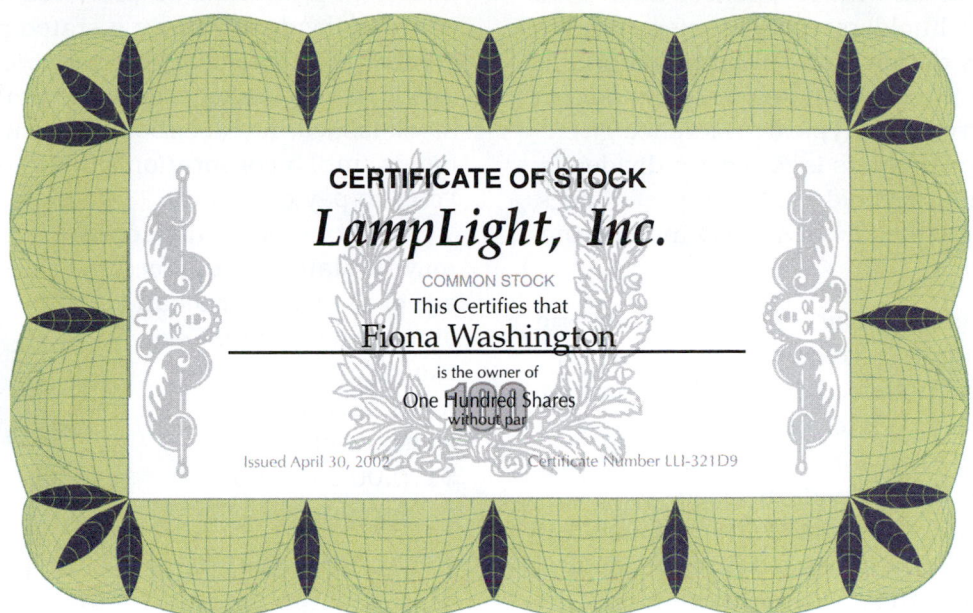

CERTIFICATE OF STOCK
*LampLight, Inc.*
COMMON STOCK
This Certifies that
Fiona Washington
is the owner of
One Hundred Shares
without par
Issued April 30, 2002          Certificate Number LLI-321D9

Written evidence of the number of shares that each stockholder owns in a corporation is called a stock certificate. A corporation issues a stock certificate when it receives full payment for the stock. A **stock certificate**, such as the one shown above, usually states the issue date, certificate number, number of shares, and name of the stockholder.

A corporation keeps a record of stock issued to each stockholder. A stockholder may later decide to sell some or all shares of stock owned. Changing ownership of stock is referred to as a stock transfer. Some corporations handle the issuing and transferring of stock certificates as well as the record of stock ownership. Most corporations, however, engage a transfer agent, such as a bank, to issue certificates and keep stock ownership records.

## Value of Stock

Shares of stock are frequently assigned a value. A value assigned to a share of stock and printed on the stock certificate is called **par value**. A share of stock that has an authorized value printed on the stock certificate is called **par-value stock**.

A share of stock that has no authorized value printed on the stock certificate is called **no-par-value stock**. Some states require that no-par-value stock be assigned a stated or specific value. No-par-value stock that is assigned a value by a corporation is called **stated-value stock**. Stated-value stock is similar to par-value stock except that the value is not printed on the stock certificates.

## Common Stock

If a corporation issues only one type of stock, that stock is common stock. If a corporation issues only common stock, the common stockholders are entitled to all of the dividends. In most corporations, only owners of common stock have a right to vote on matters brought before the stockholders. LampLight is authorized to issue no-par-value common stock with a stated value of $10.00.

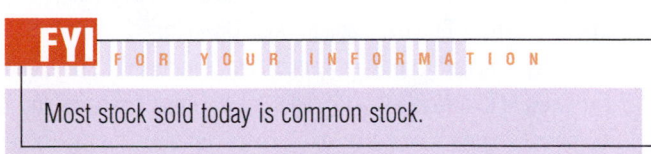

**FYI** FOR YOUR INFORMATION

Most stock sold today is common stock.

## Preferred Stock

To attract more investors, a corporation may offer preferred stock with preferences as to some of the basic stockholders' rights. Preferred stockholders usually do not have voting rights and cannot influence when and how much is paid in dividends. Therefore, a typical preference given to preferred stockholders is to receive dividends before common stockholders. Other preferences granted preferred stockholders may include the following:

1. Unpaid dividends may accumulate from one year to another. In years that dividends are not paid, the preferred dividends accumulate and are paid in a later year. Accumulated preferred dividends must be paid before any common stock dividends are paid.
2. Dividends may be shared with common stockholders above a stated percentage or amount. Once the dividend to common stockholders equals the stated percentage of the preferred stock, additional dividends may be shared between preferred and common stockholders.

Every preference granted to preferred stockholders comes at the expense of common stockholders. For example, if preferred stockholders share in dividends above a stated percentage, common stockholders give up a right to some dividends. However, regardless of the type of stock issued, no stockholder is entitled to dividends until a corporation's board of directors votes to pay dividends.

Preferred stock dividends may be stated as a percentage of par value or as an amount per share. For example, LampLight has authorized the issuance of 8%, $100.00 par-value preferred stock.

©GETTY IMAGES/PHOTODISC

## global perspective

GLOBAL PERSPECTIVE • GLOBAL PERSPECTIVE • GLOBAL PERSPECTIV

### International Packages and Customs Inspections

When sending a package overseas, appropriate documentation must accompany the package to verify its contents. Customs officials will read the documentation and may open the package to verify its contents.

All major trading nations use the Harmonized Commodity Description and Coding System (HS). HS establishes a single ten-digit code for each type of commodity. This code may be obtained from the Census Bureau's Foreign Trade Division.

Shipping restrictions apply to certain commodities. The Food and Drug Administration (FDA) regulates the import of items such as foods, pharmaceuticals, medical devices, and cosmetics. These restrictions protect American citizens from improperly tested items that could cause physical harm.

The U.S. Department of Agriculture (USDA) regulates the import of items such as meat and meat products, insects, plants, fruits, and vegetables. Restrictions on shipments protect domestic horticulture from infection by disease or insects.

The Federal Communications Commission (FCC) regulates the import of such items as cordless telephones, video games, microwave ovens, and radio transmitters to protect the quality of consumer products.

**Required**

Obtain a guide from a carrier that provides the guidelines for sending a package internationally. Select a foreign country and assume that you are sending a package that contains a ten-page legal document. The package weighs less than two pounds.
1. Which forms must be completed to send the document?
2. How should you package the document?
3. How much will it cost?
4. When will it be delivered?

**1.** Write the date.  **2.** Enter the account title.

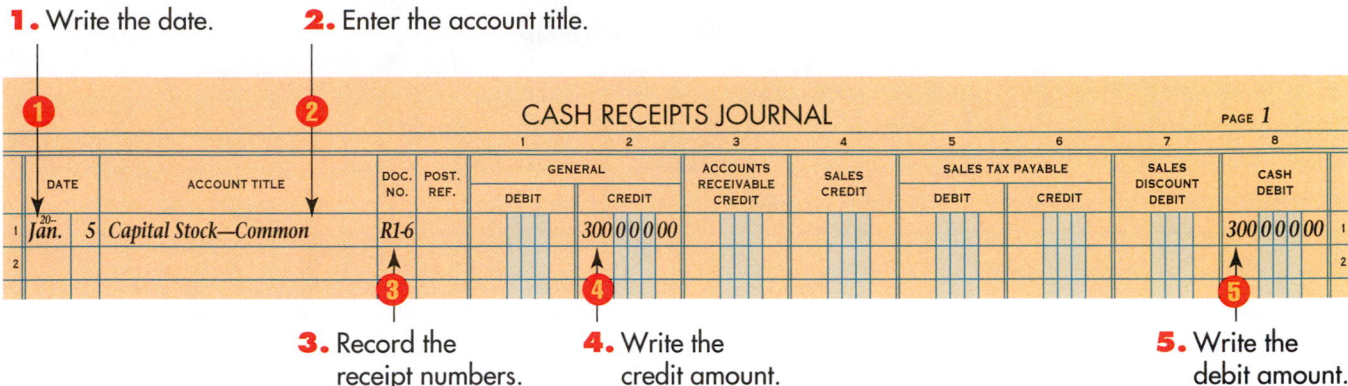

**3.** Record the receipt numbers.  **4.** Write the credit amount.  **5.** Write the debit amount.

LampLight's charter is its legal authorization to begin business in the name of the corporation. The corporation needs assets to operate. It obtains its initial capital by selling stock to the incorporators.

## Capital Accounts of a Corporation

Because of the number of owners, a corporation does not keep a separate capital account for each stockholder. Instead, it maintains a single summary general ledger capital account for each kind of stock issued. When a corporation issues only common stock, the value of all stock issued is recorded in a single capital stock account. When a corporation issues both common and preferred stock, separate capital stock accounts are used for common and preferred stock.

A corporation's net income is recorded in the capital account Retained Earnings. Using this account keeps the net income separate from the recorded values of issued capital stock. A net income is credited and a net loss is debited to Retained Earnings.

## Issuing Capital Stock When Forming a Corporation

When the corporation is formed, each of Lamp-Light's six incorporators agrees to buy 5,000 shares of common stock at the stated value. Thus, a total of 30,000 shares of common stock, stated value $10.00, is issued for a total of $300,000.00.

> **January 5. Received cash from six incorporators for 30,000 shares of $10.00 stated-value common stock, $300,000.00. Receipt Nos. 1–6.**

Cash is debited for $300,000.00. Capital Stock—Common is credited for $300,000.00, the value of the issued common stock. The journal entry to record this transaction is shown above.

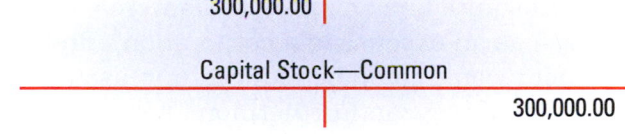

| Cash | |
|---|---|
| 300,000.00 | |

| Capital Stock—Common | |
|---|---|
| | 300,000.00 |

## STEPS • STEPS • STEPS • STEPS

### JOURNALIZE THE ENTRY TO RECORD CASH RECEIVED FOR COMMON STOCK

**1** Write the current year and the date in the Date column of the cash receipts journal.

**2** Enter *Capital Stock—Common* in the Account Title column.

**3** Record the receipt numbers, *R1–6*, in the Doc. No. column.

**4** Write the credit amount, *300,000.00*, in the General Credit column.

**5** Record the debit amount, *300,000.00*, in the Cash Debit column.

**FYI** FOR YOUR INFORMATION

A debit balance in Retained Earnings is often referred to as a deficit.

# ORGANIZATION COSTS OF A CORPORATION

| | | | | | GENERAL | | ACCOUNTS PAYABLE DEBIT | PURCHASES DISCOUNT CREDIT | CASH CREDIT | |
|---|---|---|---|---|---|---|---|---|---|---|
| | DATE | ACCOUNT TITLE | CK. NO. | POST. REF. | DEBIT | CREDIT | | | | |

**CASH PAYMENTS JOURNAL**      PAGE 1

| | DATE | | ACCOUNT TITLE | CK. NO. | POST. REF. | GENERAL DEBIT | GENERAL CREDIT | ACCOUNTS PAYABLE DEBIT | PURCHASES DISCOUNT CREDIT | CASH CREDIT | |
|---|---|---|---|---|---|---|---|---|---|---|---|
| 1 | Jan. | 5 | Organization Costs | 1 | | 2 400 00 | | | | 2 400 00 | 1 |
| 2 | | | | | | | | | | | 2 |
| 3 | | | | | | | | | | | 3 |

Fees and other expenses of organizing a corporation are called **organization costs**. Organization costs may include the following:

1. An incorporation fee paid to the state when the articles of incorporation are submitted.
2. Attorney fees for legal services during the process of incorporation.
3. Other incidental expenses incurred prior to receiving a charter.

A corporation cannot be formed without organization costs. Until it receives a charter, a corporation does not exist to pay the organization costs. The planning required to start a new corporation often takes months. Therefore, one of the incorporators usually agrees to pay these costs until the charter is granted. The incorporator or incorporators who agree to pay the organization cost should keep accurate and complete records of all amounts paid on behalf of the corporation. After it receives a charter, a corporation reimburses the incorporator for the organization costs.

If substantial organization costs were recorded as an expense in a corporation's first year, net income could be reduced unreasonably during that first year. Furthermore, benefits derived from these expenditures extend over many years. Therefore, these costs are recorded in an asset account, Organization Costs, until charged as an expense. [*CONCEPT: Matching Expenses with Revenue*]

Adjusting entries to record portions of the organization costs as an expense each year are described in Chapter 13.

Amy Thacker agreed to pay the organization costs for LampLight until the company receives its charter. On January 5, Amy submitted a statement of organization costs, $2,400.00, that she had incurred prior to the receipt of the charter.

---

*January 5. Paid cash to Amy Thacker as reimbursement for organization costs, $2,400.00. Check No. 1.*

---

Organization Costs is debited for $2,400.00. Cash is credited for $2,400.00. The journal entry to record this transaction is shown above.

| Organization Costs | |
|---|---|
| Jan. 5    2,400.00 | |

| Cash | |
|---|---|
| | Jan. 5    2,400.00 |

**FYI**   FOR YOUR INFORMATION

Some corporations provide stockholders with the right to maintain the same percentage of ownership in a corporation. If additional stock is issued, existing stockholders have first choice to buy additional shares to maintain their same percentage of ownership.

©GETTY IMAGES/PHOTODISC

# Explore Accounting

## Intangible Assets

Assets of a nonphysical nature that have value for a business are known as *intangible assets*. Patents, trademarks, organization costs, brand names, copyrights, and goodwill (to be discussed in Chapter 21) are all examples of intangible assets.

When an intangible asset is acquired, it is recorded at its historic cost. On January 1, 20X1, Lyons Company purchased a patent from another company for $200,000. Lyons would make the following entry on the purchase date:

    Patent. . . . . . . . . . . . . . . $200,000
        Cash . . . . . . . . . . . . . . . . . . . . . . . $200,000

The portion of a plant asset's cost that is transferred to an expense account in each fiscal period during a plant asset's useful life is known as *depreciation expense*. The portion of an intangible asset's cost that is transferred to an expense account in each fiscal period during the life of the intangible asset is referred to as *amortization expense*.

The amount of yearly amortization expense should be based on the intangible asset's useful or legal life, whichever is less. When Lyons purchased the patent, it had a remaining legal life of five years. Lyons believed that the patent would be useful for at least five years. Therefore, the cost of the patent should be spread out over five years, the remaining useful life of the patent.

On December 31, 20X1, Lyons would make the following entry:

    Amortization Expense  . . . . $40,000
        Patent . . . . . . . . . . . . . . . . . . . . . . $40,000

Under normal circumstances, Lyons would repeat this entry at the end of each of the next four years. At the end of the fifth year, when the patent expires, the balance of the Patent account would be zero. However, during 20X2 a competitor patents a device that makes Lyons's patent worthless. GAAP requires that a company must reevaluate the value of an intangible asset each year. If the asset value has been impaired, the asset must be written down immediately. Therefore, Lyons would make the following entry:

    Amortization Expense  . . . $160,000
        Patent . . . . . . . . . . . . . . . . . . . . . . $160,000

### Instructions

On January 1, 20X1, Hayner Company purchased a copyright for $50,000. The copyright will expire on December 31, 20X4. Answer the following questions:

1.  On January 1, 20X1, Hayner Company will debit Copyright for what amount?

2.  On December 31, 20X1, Hayner Company will debit Amortization Expense for what amount?

3.  On December 31, 20X2, Hayner Company determines that the copyright no longer has any value to the company. What must the company do?

## terms review

TERMS REVIEW • TERMS REVIEW • TERMS REVIEW • TERMS

corporation
board of directors
articles of incorporation
charter
common stock
preferred stock
stock certificate
par value
par-value stock
no-par-value stock
stated-value stock
organization costs

## audit your understanding

AUDIT YOUR UNDERSTANDING • AUDIT YOUR

1. What are the responsibilities of a corporation's board of directors?
2. What three basic rights do stockholders usually have?
3. What two basic kinds of stock may a corporation issue?
4. In place of a general ledger capital account for each owner, how does a corporation show stock ownership?
5. What accounts are affected, and how, when a corporation initially sells and issues common stock to incorporators?
6. What three items may be included in the organization costs of a corporation?

## work together 11-1

WORK TOGETHER • WORK TOGETHER • WORK TOGETHER

**Journalizing transactions for starting a corporation**

Presidential Limousine, Inc., received its corporate charter on April 2 of the current year. The corporation is authorized to issue 50,000 shares of $20.00 stated-value stock. A cash receipts journal and a cash payments journal are provided in the *Working Papers*. Source documents are abbreviated as follows: check, C; receipt, R. Your instructor will guide you through the following examples.

1. Journalize the following transactions. Save your work to complete Work Together 11-2 on page 327.

   Apr.  3. Received cash from four incorporators for 30,000 shares of $20.00 stated-value common stock, $600,000.00. R1–4.
         4. Paid cash to Julie Albrecht as reimbursement for organization costs, $10,000.00. C1.

## on your own 11-1

### Journalizing transactions for starting a corporation

Sierra Corporation received its corporate charter on June 3 of the current year. The corporation is authorized to issue 80,000 shares of $10.00 stated-value stock. A cash receipts journal and a cash payments journal are provided in the *Working Papers*. Source documents are abbreviated as follows: check, C; receipt, R. Work this problem independently.

1. Journalize the following transactions. Save your work to complete On Your Own 11-2 on page 327.

    June 3. Received cash from three incorporators for 40,000 shares of $10.00 stated-value common stock, $400,000.00. R1–3.

    5. Paid cash to Raul Mendoza as reimbursement for organization costs, $15,000.00. C1.

# cultural diversity

CULTURAL DIVERSITY • CULTURAL DIVERSITY • CULTURAL DIVERSITY

### Businesses Owned by Asian Americans and Other Related Groups

The Census Bureau's Survey of Minority-Owned Business Enterprises indicates that minority-owned enterprises are increasing in number and size. The Census Bureau groups together its statistics about businesses owned by Asian Americans, American Indians, Alaskan Natives, and Pacific Islanders. For this discussion, such businesses will be referred to as API/AIAN-owned businesses. Firms owned by this segment of the population increased from 376,711 in 1987 to 606,438 in 1992. This represents a 61 percent increase. During the same period, total receipts increased by 194 percent from $34 billion to $100 billion. These increases represent the fastest growing segment of the minority-enterprise business groups.

About 83 percent of API/AIAN-owned firms operated as proprietorships in 1992. These businesses accounted for 35.4 percent of the gross receipts of API/AIAN-owned businesses. During the period from 1987 to 1992, there was a large increase in both partnerships and Subchapter S corporations owned by Asian Americans, American Indians, Alaskan Natives, and Pacific Islanders.

Forty-five percent of API/AIAN-owned businesses operated in the service industries, primarily in business, personal, and health services. Another 22 percent of the API/AIAN-owned firms operated in the retail trades. Average receipts of API/AIAN-owned businesses were $165,000, compared with $193,000 for all U.S. firms. Average receipts of API/AIAN-owned companies exceeded those for all U.S. firms in the construction and service industries.

# LESSON · LESSON · LESSON · LESSON · LESSON · LESSO

## 11-2 Stock Subscriptions and the Balance Sheet

### JOURNALIZING A STOCK SUBSCRIPTION

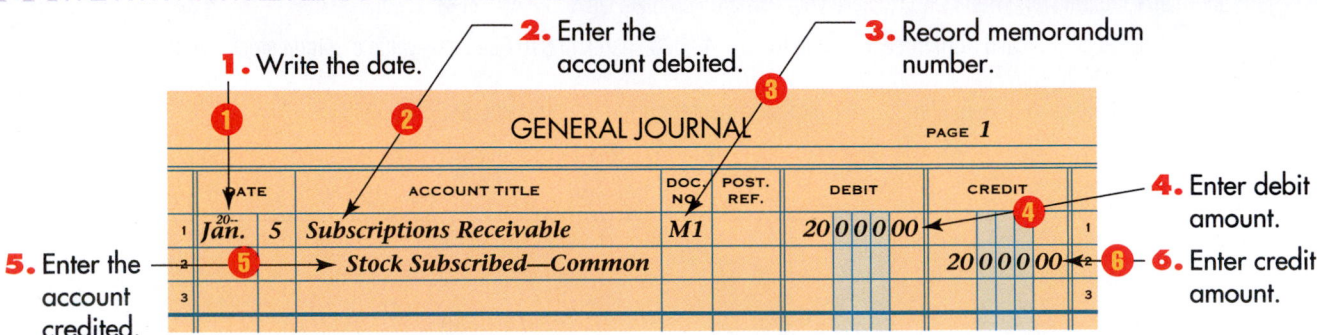

**1.** Write the date.

**2.** Enter the account debited.

**3.** Record memorandum number.

**4.** Enter debit amount.

**5.** Enter the account credited.

**6.** Enter credit amount.

| DATE | | ACCOUNT TITLE | DOC. NO. | POST. REF. | DEBIT | CREDIT | |
|---|---|---|---|---|---|---|---|
| 1 | Jan. 5 | Subscriptions Receivable | M1 | | 20 00 0 00 | | 1 |
| 2 | | Stock Subscribed—Common | | | | 20 00 0 00 | 2 |
| 3 | | | | | | | 3 |

GENERAL JOURNAL  PAGE 1

Corporations frequently contract with investors to sell capital stock with payment to be received at a later date. Future payment for the stock may be made all at one time or on an installment plan. Entering into an agreement with a corporation to buy capital stock and pay at a later date is called **subscribing for capital stock**.

On January 5, Daniel Herring subscribed for 2,000 shares of LampLight's common stock at $10.00 a share. He agreed to pay $10,000.00 on March 1 and $10,000.00 not later than July 1.

> *January 5. Received a subscription from Daniel Herring for 2,000 shares of $10.00 stated-value common stock, $20,000.00. Memorandum No. 1.*

The journal entry to record this transaction is shown above. Subscriptions Receivable is debited for $20,000.00. The asset account Subscriptions Receivable shows the unpaid amount of all subscriptions. Stock Subscribed—Common is credited for $20,000.00. The capital account Stock Subscribed—Common shows the total amount of stock subscribed but not issued. This capital account is used because stock certificates are issued only when the stock is fully paid for. The amounts are recorded in Capital Stock—Common only when stock is fully paid for and stock certificates are issued.

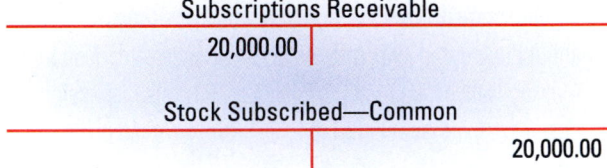

| Subscriptions Receivable | |
|---|---|
| 20,000.00 | |

| Stock Subscribed—Common | |
|---|---|
| | 20,000.00 |

---

## STEPS · STEPS · STEPS · STEPS · STEPS · STEPS · STEPS · STEPS · STEPS · STEPS

### JOURNALIZE THE ENTRY TO RECORD A STOCK SUBSCRIPTION

**1** Write the current year and the date in the Date column of the general journal.

**2** Enter the title of the account debited, *Subscriptions Receivable*, on line 1 in the Account Title column.

**3** Record memorandum number, *M1*, in the Doc. No. column.

**4** Write the debit amount, *20,000.00*, in the Debit column.

**5** Enter the title of the account credited, *Stock Subscribed—Common,* in the Account Title column.

**6** Write the credit amount, *20,000.00*, in the Credit column.

{ **REMEMBER** Holders of subscribed stock have no voting rights. }

# JOURNALIZING CASH RECEIVED FOR A STOCK SUBSCRIPTION

| | | | | | | GENERAL | | ACCOUNTS RECEIVABLE CREDIT | SALES CREDIT | SALES TAX PAYABLE | | SALES DISCOUNT DEBIT | CASH DEBIT | |
|---|---|---|---|---|---|---|---|---|---|---|---|---|---|---|
| | DATE | ACCOUNT TITLE | DOC. NO. | POST. REF. | | DEBIT | CREDIT | | | DEBIT | CREDIT | | | |
| 1 | 20-- Mar. 1 | Subscriptions Receivable | R45 | | | | 10 000 00 | | | | | | 10 000 00 | 1 |

*CASH RECEIPTS JOURNAL — PAGE 3*

On March 1, LampLight received cash from Daniel Herring in payment of half of his stock subscription. The journal entry to record this transaction is shown above.

> **March 1. Received cash from Daniel Herring in partial payment of stock subscription, $10,000.00. Receipt No. 45.**

Cash is debited for $10,000.00. Subscriptions Receivable is credited for $10,000.00. The new balance of this account, $10,000.00, is the amount

that Daniel still owes for his stock subscription. A similar journal entry is made on July 1 when Daniel pays the second installment of the stock subscription.

| Cash | |
|---|---|
| Mar. 1 | 10,000.00 |

| Subscriptions Receivable | | |
|---|---|---|
| Jan. 5 | 20,000.00 | Mar. 1 | 10,000.00 |
| (New Bal. | 10,000.00) | |

# JOURNALIZING ISSUANCE OF STOCK PREVIOUSLY SUBSCRIBED

| | DATE | ACCOUNT TITLE | DOC. NO. | POST. REF. | DEBIT | CREDIT | |
|---|---|---|---|---|---|---|---|
| 1 | 20-- July 1 | Stock Subscribed—Common | M67 | | 20 000 00 | | 1 |
| 2 | | Capital Stock—Common | | | | 20 000 00 | 2 |

*GENERAL JOURNAL — PAGE 7*

When a stock subscription is fully paid for, a stock certificate is issued to the stockholder. The journal entry to record the issuance of stock to Daniel is shown above.

> **July 1. Issued Stock Certificate No. 7 to Daniel Herring for 2,000 shares of $10.00 stated-value common stock. Memorandum No. 67.**

Stock Subscribed—Common is debited for $20,000.00. Capital Stock—Common is credited for $20,000.00. The new balance of this account, $320,000.00, is the value of all common stock issued by LampLight.

LampLight records the issuance of stock only to the original stockholder. A stockholder may later

decide to sell shares of stock. LampLight does not journalize such stock transfers because these transactions do not generate additional capital for the corporation. However, the name of the new stockholder must be entered in LampLight's stock ownership records so that future dividend payments will be made to the correct person.

| Stock Subscribed—Common | | |
|---|---|---|
| July 1 | 20,000.00 | Jan. 5 | 20,000.00 |
| | | (New Bal. zero) |

| Capital Stock—Common | | |
|---|---|---|
| | | Jan. 5 | 300,000.00 |
| | | July 1 | 20,000.00 |
| | | (New Bal. | 320,000.00) |

**LampLight, Inc.**
**Balance Sheet**
**January 5, 20--**

| | | | |
|---|---|---|---|
| **ASSETS** | | | |
| Current Assets: | | | |
| Cash......................................... | $297,600.00 | | |
| Subscriptions Receivable................... | 20,000.00 | | |
| Total Current Assets........................ | | $317,600.00 | |
| Intangible Asset: | | | |
| Organization Costs......................... | | 2,400.00 | |
| Total Assets .............................. | | | $320,000.00 |
| **STOCKHOLDERS' EQUITY** | | | |
| Paid-in Capital: | | | |
| Capital Stock—Common (30,000 shares, $10.00 stated value)..... | | $300,000.00 | |
| Stock Subscribed— Common (2,000 shares) ............... | | 20,000.00 | |
| Total Paid-in Capital................... | | | 320,000.00 |
| Total Stockholders' Equity.............. | | | $320,000.00 |

**1.** List intangible assets as the last category of assets. ➊ →

**2.** List sources of paid-in capital. ➋ →

LampLight's balance sheet at the end of business on January 5 is shown above.

LampLight's cash on hand, January 5, is the original $300,000.00 paid by the incorporators *minus* the $2,400.00 paid for organization costs. The subscriptions receivable on January 5 is the amount due from Daniel Herring.

Assets of a nonphysical nature that have value for a business are called **intangible assets**. The heading, Intangible Asset, is listed on the balance sheet as the last subdivision in the Assets section. The asset account Organization Costs is presented in the intangible assets section. A corporation with long-term investments and plant assets shows them on a balance sheet before intangible assets.

Paid-in capital is a subdivision of the stockholders' equity section of a balance sheet. Lamp-Light's paid-in capital on January 5 consists of $300,000.00 in issued common stock plus $20,000.00 in common stock subscribed. Lamp-Light has not yet issued any preferred stock. Therefore, no amount for preferred stock is shown on the balance sheet.

**FYI** FOR YOUR INFORMATION

The Securities and Exchange Commission (SEC), established in 1934, helps regulate the offering, buying, and selling of securities, including capital stock.

{ **REMEMBER** To publicly sell large issues of stock, a corporation must have the approval of the Securities and Exchange Commission (SEC) to certify that information about the business is not being concealed. }

## • terms review

subscribing for capital stock
intangible assets

## • audit your understanding

1. What accounts are affected, and how, when subscribed stock is issued?
2. How are assets of a nonphysical nature reported on the balance sheet?

## • work together 11-2

**Journalizing transactions for stock subscriptions and preparing a balance sheet**

Use the working papers from Work Together 11-1 on page 322. A general journal and statement paper are provided in the *Working Papers*. Source documents are abbreviated as follows: memorandum, M; receipt, R. Your instructor will guide you through the following examples.

1. Journalize the following transactions.

Apr. 7. Received a subscription from Robert Companari for 5,000 shares of $20.00 stated-value common stock, $100,000.00. M1.
24. Received cash from Robert Companari in payment of stock subscription, $100,000.00. R5.
25. Issued Stock Certificate No. 5 to Robert Companari for 5,000 shares of $20.00 stated-value common stock, $100,000.00. M2.

2. Prepare a balance sheet for Presidential Limousine as of April 30 of the current year.

## • on your own 11-2

**Journalizing transactions for stock subscriptions and preparing a balance sheet**

Use the working papers from On Your Own 11-1 on page 323. A general journal and statement paper are provided in the *Working Papers*. Source documents are abbreviated as follows: memorandum, M; receipt, R. Work this problem independently.

1. Journalize the following transactions.

June 11. Received a subscription from Jan Lee for 1,000 shares of $10.00 stated-value common stock, $10,000.00. M1.
19. Received a subscription from Bill Ackermann for 3,000 shares of $10.00 stated-value common stock, $30,000.00. M2.
24. Received cash from Jan Lee in payment of stock subscription, $10,000.00. R4.
25. Issued Stock Certificate No. 4 to Jan Lee for 1,000 shares of $10.00 stated-value common stock, $10,000.00. M3.

2. Prepare a balance sheet for Sierra Corporation as of June 30 of the current year.

# 11-3 Calculating and Journalizing Dividends for a Corporation

## DIVIDENDS

Once operations begin, a new corporation usually retains a portion of net income to finance future business expansion and improvement. However, most corporations distribute a portion of the earnings to stockholders.

Corporate earnings distributed to stockholders are known as dividends. Action by a board of directors to distribute corporate earnings to stockholders is called **declaring a dividend**. The board determines when and what amount of the retained earnings will be distributed. A corporation has no obligation to distribute money to stockholders until the board of directors has declared a dividend.

Three important dates are involved in distributing a dividend:

1. Date of declaration. The date on which a board of directors votes to distribute a dividend is called the **date of declaration**.
2. Date of record. The date that determines which stockholders are to receive dividends is called the **date of record**. Stockholders may buy and sell stock at any time. However, only persons listed as stockholders on the date of record will receive dividends.

3. Date of payment. The date on which dividends are actually to be paid to stockholders is called the **date of payment**. Ordinarily, the date of payment occurs several weeks after the date of record. Thus, a corporation has time to determine who is entitled to receive dividends and to prepare dividend checks to mail on the date of payment.

Transactions are recorded in a corporation's accounts on two of the three dates: (1) date of declaration and (2) date of payment.

### Calculating a Dividend

When a board of directors declares a dividend, the corporation is obligated to pay it. At the date of declaration, the corporation incurs a liability that must be recorded.

The board of directors of CompuForm, Inc. has decided to declare an annual dividend of $24,000.00. On the date of record, the corporation has issued 1,000 shares of 8%, $100.00 par-value preferred stock and 16,000 shares of $20.00 stated-value common stock. The value of the preferred and common stock is calculated as follows.

| Number of Preferred Shares | × | Par Value | = | Value of Preferred Stock |
|---|---|---|---|---|
| 1,000 | × | $100.00 | = | $100,000.00 |

| Number of Common Shares | × | Stated Value | = | Value of Common Stock |
|---|---|---|---|---|
| 16,000 | × | $20.00 | = | $320,000.00 |

**REMEMBER** No stockholder is guaranteed a dividend.

The value of preferred stock is used to calculate the dividend on preferred stock. The distribution of the $24,000.00 dividend between preferred and common stock is calculated as follows:

|  Value of Preferred Stock | × | Preferred Dividend Rate | = | Preferred Dividend Amount |
|---|---|---|---|---|
| $100,000.00 | × | 8% | = | $8,000.00 |

| Total Amount Available for Dividends | − | Preferred Dividend Amount | = | Amount Available for Common Dividends |
|---|---|---|---|---|
| $24,000.00 | − | $8,000.00 | = | $16,000.00 |

The dividend rate for common stock is calculated as follows:

| 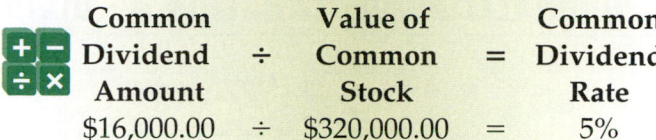 Common Dividend Amount | ÷ | Value of Common Stock | = | Common Dividend Rate |
|---|---|---|---|---|
| $16,000.00 | ÷ | $320,000.00 | = | 5% |

A summary of CompuForm's dividends follows.

|  | Amount | Rate |
|---|---|---|
| Preferred Stock Dividends | $ 8,000.00 | 8% |
| Common Stock Dividends | 16,000.00 | 5% |

In subsequent years, CompuForm may elect to increase its annual dividend. CompuForm's preferred stock dividend rate will never exceed 8%. Therefore, additional dividends will be distributed to common stock, increasing the common stock dividend rate. The common stock dividend rate may be less than, equal to, or more than the preferred stock dividend rate.

# business structures

BUSINESS STRUCTURES • BUSINESS STRUCTURES • BUSINESS STRUCTURE

## Advantages and Disadvantages of a Corporation

Organizing a corporation is as simple as filing an application with the appropriate state agency. The approved application establishes the corporation as a legal entity, giving the corporation many of the same legal rights and risks as individuals have, including owning assets, borrowing money, paying taxes, and being sued.

The corporate form of business organization has several advantages over a sole proprietorship:

- *Limited liability.* The liability of stockholders is limited to their investment in the corporation.
- *Supply of capital.* Individuals are more willing to invest in a corporation because their personal assets are protected by limited liability.

However, there are also some disadvantages to a corporation:

- *Shared decision making.* Significant business decisions must be approved by a vote of the stockholders.
- *Shared profits.* The earnings of the corporation are divided among the stockholders.
- *Taxation.* The earnings of a corporation may be subject to federal and state income taxes. When the earnings of the

corporation are distributed to the stockholders, individual stockholders may also have to pay income taxes on the dividends. Thus, the earnings of a corporation can be taxed twice, a concept known as *double taxation*.

Proper planning can offer stockholders the advantage of limited liability while avoiding the disadvantage of double taxation. Thus, although the application for incorporation can be prepared without the help of an attorney or accountant, consulting with these professionals is recommended.

### Critical Thinking

1. Think of two businesses you might be interested in starting. Describe whether the proprietorship or corporation form of organization would be better suited for this business.
2. Often a person who has started a proprietorship and run it successfully for many years sells the business to a corporation. Why would a corporation be interested in buying such a business?

| | DATE | | ACCOUNT TITLE | DOC. NO. | POST. REF. | DEBIT | CREDIT | |
|---|---|---|---|---|---|---|---|---|
| 1 | 20-- Dec. | 15 | Dividends—Common | M132 | | 16 0 0 0 00 | | 1 |
| 2 | | | Dividends—Preferred | | | 8 0 0 0 00 | | 2 |
| 3 | | | Dividends Payable | | | | 24 0 0 0 00 | 3 |

**GENERAL JOURNAL**     PAGE *12*

The journal entry to record the transaction needed when the dividends are declared is shown above.

*December 15. CompuForm's board of directors declared an annual dividend of $24,000.00. Preferred stock issued is $100,000.00 of 8%, $100.00 par-value preferred stock. Common stock issued is $320,000.00 of $20.00 stated-value common stock. Date of payment is January 15. Memorandum No. 132.*

Dividends—Common is debited for $16,000.00. Dividends—Preferred is debited for $8,000.00. Dividends Payable is credited for $24,000.00.

## JOURNALIZING PAYMENT OF A DIVIDEND

**CASH PAYMENTS JOURNAL**     PAGE *1*

| | DATE | ACCOUNT TITLE | CK. NO. | POST. REF. | 1 GENERAL DEBIT | 2 GENERAL CREDIT | 3 ACCOUNTS PAYABLE DEBIT | 4 PURCHASES DISCOUNT CREDIT | 5 CASH CREDIT | |
|---|---|---|---|---|---|---|---|---|---|---|
| 18 | 15 | Dividends Payable | 432 | | 24 0 0 0 00 | | | | 24 0 0 0 00 | 18 |

On January 15, CompuForm issued a single check for $24,000.00, the total amount of the dividends to be paid. The check is deposited in a special dividend checking account. A separate check to each eligible stockholder is written against the special checking account. This procedure avoids a large number of entries in CompuForm's cash payments journal. The special dividend checking account also reserves cash specifically for paying the dividends.

CompuForm's dividend check is given to an agent who handles the details of preparing and mailing stockholders' checks. CompuForm's agent is the bank with which the corporation has its checking account.

*January 15. Paid cash for annual dividend declared December 15, $24,000.00. Check No. 432.*

Dividends Payable is debited and Cash is credited for $24,000.00. The journal entry to record this transaction is shown above.

**REMEMBER**   Dividends may be paid in additional capital stock, known as a stock dividend, instead of cash. Dividends Payable is debited and Capital Stock is credited when the stock is issued on the date of payment.

# careers in accounting

## Steve Robertson, Diverse Accounting Background

COURTESY OF STEVE ROBERTSON

Silicon Valley in California is recognized throughout the world for its innovation, development, and creative uses of technology. Many of the high-tech applications developed there have had an impact on movie making, the Internet, portable music players, computer games, semiconductors, computer security, wireless applications, cellular phones, personal digital assistants, telecommunications, and biotechnology. With such a diverse business environment in the San Francisco Bay area, a wide variety of career possibilities exists.

From the beginning of his professional life, Steve Robertson was determined to accumulate a variety of business experiences. Before changing employers during his career, however, Steve decided he would follow two important criteria: (1) each new job had to be more challenging and (2) each new job had to increase significantly in terms of responsibility and scope.

After graduating from Santa Clara University with a major in accounting, Steve accepted a position with Ernst & Young, LLP, where he audited a variety of companies and reviewed financial statements for accuracy. Shortly after becoming a certified public accountant (CPA), he moved into corporate finance at Silicon Graphics, Inc., where he gained valuable experience as a financial analyst.

Steve's next employment was as an assistant controller at HMT Technology Corporation. At HMT, he became very proficient at month-end closings, cost accounting, and creating financial reports for stockholders and other interested parties in the public domain. Steve's next position was controller at RockShox, Inc., where he was responsible for the entire accounting department, banking, insurance issues, and financial reporting as required by the Securities and Exchange Commission.

At this point in his career, Steve decided he needed to experience life at a startup company. He became controller at Counterpane Internet Security, Inc., where he handled not only the accounting duties but also human resources, contract administration, purchasing, and all corporate budgeting and forecasting.

Recently, Steve began working at Echelon Corporation. There, he is involved in all aspects of accounting and finance functions for the entire global organization, as well as treasury components, insurance, investor relations, and other regulatory issues.

Steve is not finished with his career yet. With his experience, he expects that eventually he will become a vice-president of finance, a corporate treasurer, a chief financial officer, or perhaps a financial consultant. Steve's diverse accounting and financial background makes it all very possible.

**Salary Range:** $135,000–$175,000 for accountants in upper-management positions.

**Qualifications:** Steve recommends earning a bachelor's degree in business and enrolling in a solid core of accounting classes. He feels that one of the most critical components for success in the accounting field is an individual's ability to identify the accounts being affected by an actual or hypothetical transaction and understanding the transaction's impact on a balance sheet and income statement. Steve also advocates that students participate in job shadowing experiences to acquaint themselves with the many career possibilities within accounting.

**Occupational Outlook:** During the next decade, Steve foresees a renewed interest in hiring experienced and competent certified public accountants. He believes that recent accounting scandals and the financial disasters occurring during the dot-com craze emphasize the need for sound accounting practices.

## terms review

declaring a dividend
date of declaration
date of record
date of payment

## audit your understanding

1. Who determines when and what amount of retained earnings that a corporation will distribute as dividends?
2. Why does a corporation record a liability when a dividend is declared?
3. What are two reasons for using a special dividend checking account?

## work together 11-3

### Calculating and journalizing the dividends for a corporation

On January 10 of the current year, the board of directors of Eagle Express, Inc. declared an annual dividend of $60,000.00. On the date of record, the corporation had issued 2,000 shares of 6%, $100.00 par-value preferred stock and 30,000 shares of $22.00 stated-value common stock.

Page 4 of a general journal and page 11 of a cash payments journal are provided in the *Working Papers*. Source documents are abbreviated as follows: check, C; memorandum, M. Your instructor will guide you through the following examples.

1. Calculate the value of preferred stock.
2. Calculate the amount of dividends for the current year to be paid to preferred and common shareholders.
3. Journalize the entry to record the declaration of a dividend on January 10. M29.
4. Journalize the entry to record the payment of the dividend on January 30. C124.

## on your own 11-3

### Calculating and journalizing the dividends for a corporation

On July 2 of the current year, the board of directors of StarVideo Corporation declared an annual dividend of $90,000.00. On the date of record, the corporation had issued 3,500 shares of 8%, $80.00 par-value preferred stock and 60,000 shares of $12.00 stated-value common stock.

Page 7 of a general journal and page 14 of a cash payments journal are provided in the *Working Papers*. Source documents are abbreviated as follows: check, C; memorandum, M. Work this problem independently.

1. Calculate the value of preferred stock.
2. Calculate the amount of dividends for the current year to be paid to preferred and common shareholders.
3. Journalize the entry to record the declaration of a dividend on July 2. M87.
4. Journalize the entry to record the payment of the dividend on August 2. C326.

SUMMARY · SUMMARY · SUMMARY

*After completing this chapter, you can*

1. Define accounting terms related to corporate accounting.
2. Identify accounting concepts and practices related to corporate accounting.
3. Journalize transactions related to starting a corporation.
4. Journalize transactions related to stock subscriptions.
5. Prepare a balance sheet for a newly formed corporation.
6. Calculate dividends for a corporation.
7. Journalize transactions of a corporation related to declaring and paying dividends.

# Explore Accounting

EXPLORE ACCOUNTING • EXPLORE ACCOUNTING • EXPLORE ACCO

## Stock Splits

Most stock purchases are made in multiples of 100 shares. A stock trade of 100 shares is called a round lot. A stock trade in an amount other than a multiple of 100 shares is called an odd lot. Because brokerage firms typically charge additional fees for odd lot trades, investors have a financial incentive to trade stock only in round lots.

As the market price per share rises, the total cost of a round lot can exceed the financial resources of the average individual investor. For example, a round lot of a stock trading at $60 per share would cost $6,000 plus brokerage fees. The demand for the stock declines when individual investors become unable to purchase the stock. This decline in demand has a negative effect on the stock's market value.

One solution to this problem is to reduce the stock's market price to a reasonable amount. To reduce the market price, a corporation can increase the number of shares outstanding by dividing each outstanding share into two or more shares. Dividing a share of stock into a larger

number of shares is called a stock split. In a 2-for-1 stock split, the company doubles the number of shares and reduces each share's par value by half. Thus, an investor holding 100 shares of $10 par value stock then owns 200 shares of $5 par value stock. More important, the market price of the stock, once at $60 per share, immediately drops to $30 per share.

Some investors mistakenly think that a stock split increases their ownership in the company and the value of their investment. Before the stock split, the investor owned 100 shares of $60 stock valued at $6,000. After the stock split, the investor owns 200 shares of $30 stock, also valued at $6,000. Because all stockholders now own twice the number of shares, each investor's percentage ownership in the corporation remains the same.

**Required:**
Explain the concept of stock splits using a pizza as a symbol for the total value of the corporation.

# 11-1 APPLICATION PROBLEM

### Journalizing transactions for starting a corporation

Pacific Technologies Corporation received its charter on January 4 of the current year. The corporation is authorized to issue 200,000 shares of $10.00 stated-value common stock and 50,000 shares of 12%, $100.00 par-value preferred stock.

**Transactions:**

Jan.   4.   Received cash from three incorporators for 48,000 shares of $10.00 stated-value common stock, $480,000.00. R1–3.

   4.   Paid cash to Joseph Garza as reimbursement for organization costs, $2,000.00. C1.

**Instructions:**

Journalize the transactions. Use page 1 of a cash receipts journal, a cash payments journal, and a general journal. Source documents are abbreviated as follows: check, C; receipt, R. Save your work to complete Application Problem 11-2.

# 11-2 APPLICATION PROBLEM   QUICKBOOKS

### Journalizing transactions for stock subscriptions and preparing a balance sheet

Use the working papers for Application Problem 11-1.

**Transactions:**

Jan.   5.   Received a subscription from Karen Yoshihara for 2,000 shares of $10.00 stated-value common stock, $20,000.00. M1.

   16.   Received a subscription from Tyronne Carter for 10,000 shares of $10.00 stated-value common stock, $100,000.00. M2.

Feb.   1.   Received cash from Karen Yoshihara in payment of stock subscription, $20,000.00. R4.

   1.   Issued Stock Certificate No. 4 to Karen Yoshihara for 2,000 shares of $10.00 stated-value common stock, $20,000.00. M3.

   8.   Received cash from Tyronne Carter in partial payment of stock subscription, $50,000.00. R5.

   15.   Received a subscription from Cindy Coburn for 300 shares of $10.00 stated-value common stock, $3,000.00. M4.

Mar.   1.   Received cash from Tyronne Carter in final payment of stock subscription, $50,000.00. R6.

   1.   Issued Stock Certificate No. 5 to Tyronne Carter for 10,000 shares of $10.00 stated-value common stock, $100,000. M5.

**Instructions:**

1. Journalize the transactions. Source documents are abbreviated as follows: memorandum, M; receipt, R.

2. Prepare a balance sheet for Pacific Technologies Corporation as of March 2 of the current year.

# 11-3 APPLICATION PROBLEM

### Calculating dividends for a corporation

The information shown on page 335 is available from the accounting records of two different corporations.

**Instructions:**

1. Calculate the value of preferred stock.

2. Calculate the amount of dividends to be paid each year to preferred and common shareholders.

## Corporations

| | Edison | Carmac |
|---|---|---|
| **Preferred Stock:** | | |
| Description | $100.00 par-value | $50.00 par-value |
| Dividend Rate | 10% | 8% |
| Shares Issued | 2,000 | 10,000 |
| **Common Stock:** | | |
| Description | $2.00 stated-value | $1.00 stated-value |
| Shares Issued | 300,000 | 200,000 |
| **Annual Dividend:** | | |
| Year 1 | $25,000.00 | $50,000.00 |
| Year 2 | $30,000.00 | $60,000.00 |
| Year 3 | $35,000.00 | $75,000.00 |

## 11-4 APPLICATION PROBLEM   PEACHTREE   QUICKBOOKS

### Journalizing transactions for declaring and paying dividends

PlasticTech, Inc. completed the following transactions during the current year.

**Transactions:**

Aug. 12. PlasticTech's board of directors declared an annual dividend of $180,000.00. Preferred stock issued is $500,000.00 of 10%, $100.00 par-value preferred stock. Common stock issued is $1,000,000.00 of $1,000.00 stated-value common stock. Date of payment is November 15. M65.

Nov. 15. Paid $180,000.00 cash for annual dividend declared August 12. C139.

**Instructions:**

Journalize the transactions. Use page 8 of a general journal and page 21 of a cash payments journal. Source documents are abbreviated as follows: check, C; memorandum, M.

## 11-5 MASTERY PROBLEM   PEACHTREE

### Journalizing transactions for starting a corporation, declaring and paying dividends, and preparing a balance sheet

SkyPark, Inc. received its charter on August 1 of the current year. The corporation is authorized to issue 150,000 shares of $5.00 stated-value common stock and 50,000 shares of 10%, $100.00 par-value preferred stock.

**Transactions:**

20X2

Aug. 4. Ten incorporators pay cash for 50,000 shares of $5.00 stated-value common stock, $250,000.00. R1–10.

4. Dan O'Brien was reimbursed for organization costs, $6,500.00. C1.

6. Diane Scalacci subscribed to purchase 500 shares of $5.00 stated-value common stock, $2,500.00. M1.

21. McCabe Daniels subscribed to purchase 3,000 shares of $5.00 stated-value common stock, $15,000.00. M2.

Sept. 16. Diane Scalacci made full payment on stock subscription, $2,500.00. R11.

16. Issued Stock Certificate No. 11 to Diane Scalacci for 500 shares. M3.

Oct. 1. McCabe Daniels made a partial payment on stock subscription, $7,500.00. R12.

15. Kay Mehta subscribed to purchase 6,000 shares of $5.00 stated-value common stock, $30,000.00. M4.

Nov. 1. McCabe Daniels made final payment on stock subscription, $7,500.00. R13.

1. Issued Stock Certificate No. 12 to McCabe Daniels for 3,000 shares. M5.

**Instructions:**

1. Journalize the transactions. Use page 1 of a cash receipts journal, a cash payments journal, and a general journal. Source documents are abbreviated as follows: check, C; memorandum, M; receipt, R.
2. Prepare a balance sheet for SkyPark, Inc. as of November 2 of the current year.
3. Journalize the following additional transactions completed during the following two years to record the declaration and payment of the dividends. Continue using page 1 of the general journal and the cash payments journal.

**Additional Transactions:**

20X3

Nov. 15. SkyPark's board of directors declared an annual dividend of $40,000.00. Preferred stock issued is $100,000.00 of 10%, $100.00 par-value preferred stock. Common stock issued is $400,000.00 of $5.00 stated-value common stock. Date of payment is January 15. M206.

20X4

Jan. 15. Paid cash for annual dividend declared November 15, $40,000.00. C339.

# 11-6 CHALLENGE PROBLEM

## Journalizing transactions for a corporation

On January 1, 20X1, Atlantic Semiconductor Corporation had issued the following stock:

250,000 shares of $10.00 stated-value common stock.
20,000 shares of 12%, $100.00 par-value preferred stock.

**Transactions:**

20X1

June 7. A subscription was received from Grace Young for 2,000 shares of $10.00 stated-value common stock, $20,000.00. M234.

Oct. 15. Grace Young paid cash in partial payment of stock subscription, $10,000.00. R245.

Nov. 1. Atlantic Semiconductor's board of directors declared an annual dividend of $400,000.00. Date of payment is January 15, 20X2. M245.

20X2

Jan. 15. The annual dividend declared November 1, $400,000.00, was paid. C1489.

Feb. 21. Grace Young paid cash in final payment of stock subscription, $10,000.00. R296.

21. Issued Stock Certificate No. 132 to Grace Young for 2,000 shares of $10.00 stated-value common stock, $20,000.00. M262.

Oct. 12. A subscription was received from James Richards for 1,000 shares of $100.00 par-value preferred stock, $100,000.00. M289.

Nov. 1. Atlantic Semiconductor's board of directors declared an annual dividend of $450,000.00. Date of payment is January 15, 20X3. M292.

20X3

Jan. 15. Paid annual dividend declared November 1, $450,000.00. C1654.

May 12. Cash was received from James Richards in full payment for 1,000 shares of $100.00 par-value preferred stock, $100,000.00. R312.

May 12. Stock Certificate No. 87 was issued to James Richards for 1,000 shares. M324.

Nov. 1. Atlantic Semiconductor's board of directors declared an annual dividend of $450,000.00. Date of payment is January 15, 20X4. M364.

**Instructions:**

Journalize the transactions. Use page 12 of a cash receipts journal, page 14 of a cash payments journal, and page 6 of a general journal. Source documents are abbreviated as follows: check, C; memorandum, M; receipt, R.

## applied communication

Most accountants actively participate in professional organizations. The organizations have periodic dinner meetings at which guest speakers make presentations regarding current accounting topics. As a member of a professional organization, you may be asked to introduce a guest speaker.

**Required:**

Prepare an introduction for a business professional you know personally. Identify the individual's most significant professional qualifications that allow him or her to speak on the topic. Include information regarding the speaker's community service and personal information to highlight his or her personal qualities.

## cases for critical thinking

### Case 1

Jennifer Hester is considering whether she should buy stock as an investment. She asks you whether it would be better to buy common stock or preferred stock. How would you answer her? Explain your suggestions.

### Case 2

Salvatoro, 22 years old, recently inherited $5,000.00. He has decided to invest the money in the stock market. He wants his investment to grow quickly. A friend recommended mutual funds as a good way to invest in the stock market. Salvatoro has asked you to research the types of mutual funds available and recommend how he should proceed.

## SCANS workplace competency

**Basic Skill:** Writing

**Concept:** Employers seek workers who possess the ability to communicate thoughts, ideas, information, and messages in writing. During their workday, employees are often required to create documents such as letters, directions, manuals, reports, graphs, and flow charts.

**Application:** Prepare a memorandum to your staff announcing the addition of an accounts payable clerk position. Include a description of the job, skill and education requirements, desired personal traits, hours, salary, company benefits, and other relevant details.

APPLIED COMMUNICATION

CASES FOR CRITICAL THINKING

SCANS WORKPLACE COMPETENCY

## • graphing workshop

Northwest Floors, Inc., has paid dividends every year since it started business in 20X1.

The total dividend paid and the number of shares issued are given below for each year.

| Year | Total Dividend | Number of Shares Issued |
|------|----------------|-------------------------|
| 20X1 | $45,000 | $15,000 |
| 20X2 | $55,000 | $20,000 |
| 20X3 | $51,700 | $22,000 |
| 20X4 | $65,000 | $25,000 |

**Instructions:**

1. Calculate the dividend per share for each year.

2. Develop a bar chart of the dividend per share for all four years.

## • analyzing Costco's financial statements

As stated in this chapter, a corporation's board of directors decides the dividend policy for the corporation. As shown in Appendix B of this textbook, the 2003 Annual Report for Costco states, "Costco has never paid regular dividends and presently has no plans to declare a cash dividend." Changing tax laws have lowered the tax rate that a stockholder pays when receiving a dividend. This change has resulted in more companies paying dividends.

One ratio of interest to stockholders is the dividend yield. It is calculated as: dividend per share ÷ market price per share = dividend yield.

**Instructions:**

1. Look at Costco's Balance Sheet to determine the number of shares of common stock issued as of August 31, 2003.

2. Assume that Costco's board of directors declares a $.20 dividend per share. Calculate the total dividend Costco would pay.

3. The highest price for Costco's stock in 2003 was $37.43 per share. Calculate the dividend yield assuming Costco declared an $.80 dividend per share.

# Automated Accounting

## Using the Loan Planner

### Planning Tools

Planning tools are easy-to-use applications within an accounting system that provide fast and easy ways of making calculations that are commonly needed for journal entries and reports. Five planning tools have been included in *Automated Accounting 8.0* and higher.

The Automated Accounting section in Chapter 9, pages 286 and 287, introduced the notes and interest planning tool. When a business uses notes receivable or notes payable to finance transactions, information about interest amounts, payment amounts, and due dates may be calculated using the appropriate planner. Planning tools are also efficient and easy-to-use tools to use for what-if scenarios.

### Loan Planner

The Loan Planner is similar to the Notes and Interest tool. It is used to calculate the amount of a loan, the loan payment amount, and the number of payments. A common use of this tool is to compute the monthly payment when a loan is made using the stated interest rate. The loan planner may then be used to generate an amortization schedule that will show the amount of principal and interest associated with each payment. To use the Loan Planner:

1. Click on the *Tools* toolbar button or select Planning Tools from the Data menu.

2. Click the *Loan Planner* tab.

3. Select the Loan Amount, Loan Payment Amount, or the Number of Payments option button in the Calculate option group. The unknown amount to be calculated text box will be dimmed, based upon the option selected.

4. Enter the data in the text boxes and press the Tab key. The calculated results will appear at the bottom of the Planning dialog box.

5. Click on the *Report* command button to produce a Loan Amortization Schedule. Once displayed, the report may be printed or copied to the clipboard for entering into a spreadsheet or word processor.

6. Click on *Close* to exit the report and return to the planner. Steps 3–5 may then be repeated for different calculation options, or for different data sets.

7. Click on Close, or press ESC, to exit the planner.

### Displaying or Printing the Loan Amortization Schedule

The Loan Amortization Schedule can be generated by following these steps:

1. Click on the Reports button on the Loan Planner screen after entering the data.

2. Choose the Print button if you wish to print the report or you may choose to view only.

3. Click the Close button. You also have the option to copy the report to the clipboard so that you may include the loan data on a separate document.

### Using Special Tools: The Loan Planner

**Instructions:**

1. Load *Automated Accounting 8.0* or higher software.

2. Select New from the File menu. Enter your User name.

3. Click on the Tools toolbar button.

4. Click on the Loan Planner tab. Select Loan Payment Amount from the Calculate box. Enter a loan amount of $14,000.00, an interest rate of 8.00%, and 36 payments. The payment amount will be automatically calculated.

5. Click on the Report command button from within the Loan Planner tab. Print the report, or copy it to the clipboard for entering into a word processor or spreadsheet application.

6. Click Close to return to the planner. Steps 4 and 5 may then be repeated for different calculation options, or for different data sets.

7. Click Close to exit the planner. When you exit a planning tool, your data will not be saved. Be sure to print a report, or copy it to a word processor or spreadsheet and save it in that application.

8. Exit the Automated Accounting software.

# 12 Acquiring Additional Capital for a Corporation

*After studying Chapter 12, you will be able to:*

1. Define accounting terms related to acquiring capital for a corporation.

2. Identify accounting concepts and practices related to acquiring capital for a corporation.

3. Journalize entries for issuing additional capital stock.

4. Journalize entries for buying and selling treasury stock.

5. Journalize entries for bonds payable.

- discount on capital stock
- treasury stock
- bond

- bond issue
- trustee
- bond sinking fund

- retiring a bond issue
- term bonds
- serial bonds

Point Your Browser
accountingxtra.swlearning.com

## • Famous Dave's

©FAMOUS DAVE'S, INC.

### MEETING THE CHALLENGES OF GROWTH AT FAMOUS DAVE'S

Are you hungry for some authentic hickory-smoked, flame-grilled barbecue ribs or chicken? Famous Dave's Barbecue offers these and many more choices, all served in a distinctive and comfortable environment. "Famous Dave" Anderson opened his first restaurant in 1995. Since then, his idea has expanded to 38 company-owned and 68 franchise-operated locations, with another 150 franchise restaurant commitments.

Famous Dave's features hickory-smoked St. Louis-style ribs, Texas beef brisket, and their award-winning Rich & Sassy® BBQ sauce. Additionally, the menu offers barbeque and country-roasted chicken, BBQ sandwiches, burgers, and salads.

While rapid growth is good, it also has its challenges. It takes a great deal of capital to expand a business, both in terms of opening new restaurants and in growing the administrative side of the business. More restaurants mean more employees to train. Information systems must grow with the company. More people are required to keep the company operating. All of this takes money.

Where can a company turn for this money? One option is to sell stock in the company. In 1996, Famous Dave's stock was first offered to the general public. This is called an "initial public offering," or IPO. Famous Dave's IPO of 2,645,000 shares of stock netted over $15 million dollars to help support the growth of the company.

### Critical Thinking

1. What factors will help determine the price of a share of stock at the time of its IPO?
2. If a company needs more cash, but does not want to issue additional shares of stock, what else could it do to raise the capital?

Source: www.famousdaves.com

**Xtra!**
Today
accountingxtra.swlearning.com

---

### AUDIT LETTER

Go to the homepage for two corporations of your choice. Search for the most recent annual report for each company. Within the annual report, find the "Report of the Independent Auditor." Answer the following questions about each corporation's report.

### Instructions

1. Which financial statements did the auditors audit?
2. The consolidated financial statements are the responsibility of whom?
3. What is the auditor's responsibility related to the financial statements?
4. What company performed the audit?

---

# 12-1 Capital Stock Transactions

As a corporation grows, it may require additional capital to finance its expansion. The portion of a corporation's net income not paid to stockholders as dividends is a primary source of additional capital. Retained earnings may not, however, provide an adequate source of capital for a corporation. Both new and existing corporations may require a large increase in capital to finance rapid expansion. Thus, a corporation can acquire additional capital by selling stock to investors or borrowing money.

Articles of incorporation are usually written to permit a corporation to issue more shares of stock than it sold to initial investors. As the need arises for more capital, a corporation can issue some of the remaining authorized stock. LampLight, Inc. is authorized by its charter to issue a total of 100,000 shares of common stock and 50,000 shares of preferred stock. [*CONCEPT: Business Entity*] However, LampLight initially issued only 32,000 shares of common stock during its first year as described in Chapter 11. Thus, LampLight may sell some of the remaining shares of common or some shares of preferred stock to raise additional capital.

Once capital stock has been issued it may be reacquired by the company. Special procedures are required to account for such shares.

©GETTY IMAGES/PHOTODISC

# making ethical decisions

## Exercising Stock Options

Corporations often compensate executives with more than a salary. The compensation package often includes the right to purchase company stock at a specified price (this right is called a *stock option*). The option price is typically set higher than the current market price. If the stock price increases above the option price, the option enables the individual to purchase the stock at less than the market price. If the stock's market price never exceeds the option price, the option is worthless.

Three years ago, the board of directors of Burnett Corp. offered its new chief executive officer, Brent McGowan, an annual salary of $500,000 plus 200,000 stock options at $30. The stock was selling for $18 at the time. Brent successfully improved the corporation's profitability. When the stock reached $40 per share,

Brent exercised the stock options and purchased 200,000 shares of stock from Burnett Corp. for $6 million. Over the next year, he sold the stock on the stock exchange for an average price of $42 per share and realized a profit of $2.4 million.

The company's code of conduct states that "employees should receive compensation consistent with their contributions toward the corporation's strategic objectives."

### Instructions

Use the ethical model to analyze whether the corporation's use of stock options as executive compensation demonstrates ethical behavior.

## ISSUING PREFERRED STOCK AT PAR VALUE

**1.** Calculate the amounts to be recorded.

| No. of Shares | × | Par Value per Share | = | Total Par Value |
|---|---|---|---|---|
| 800 | × | $100.00 | = | $80,000.00 |

**2.** Write the date. **4.** Record the receipt number. **5.** Write the debit amount.

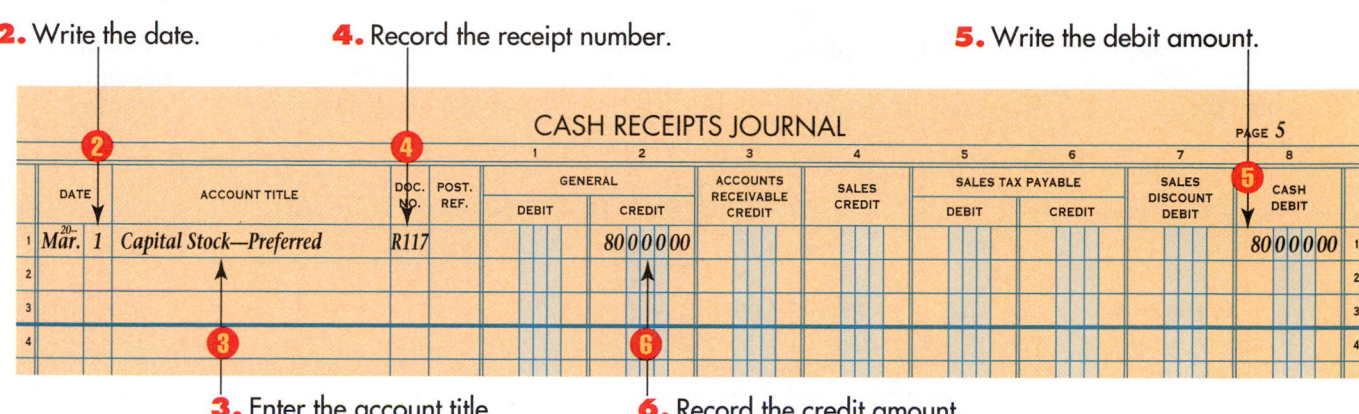

| | | | | | GENERAL | | ACCOUNTS RECEIVABLE CREDIT | SALES CREDIT | SALES TAX PAYABLE | | SALES DISCOUNT DEBIT | CASH DEBIT |
|---|---|---|---|---|---|---|---|---|---|---|---|---|
| | | | | | 1 | 2 | 3 | 4 | 5 | 6 | 7 | 8 |
| | DATE | ACCOUNT TITLE | DOC. NO. | POST. REF. | DEBIT | CREDIT | | | DEBIT | CREDIT | | |
| 1 | Mar. 1 | Capital Stock—Preferred | R117 | | | 80 000 00 | | | | | | 80 000 00 |

CASH RECEIPTS JOURNAL — PAGE 5

**3.** Enter the account title. **6.** Record the credit amount.

LampLight decided to issue preferred stock to raise additional capital. Brenda Henson paid par value, $100.00, for 800 shares of preferred stock, as shown above.

---

*March 1. Received cash from Brenda Henson for 800 shares of $100.00 par value preferred stock at $100.00 per share, $80,000.00. Receipt No. 117.*

---

Cash is debited for $80,000.00. Capital Stock—Preferred is credited for $80,000.00, the total par value of the issued preferred stock.

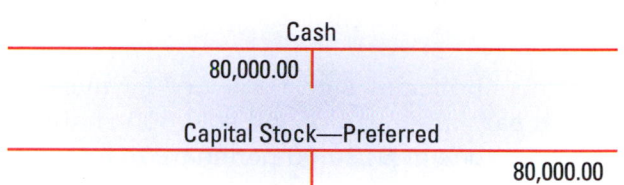

| Cash | |
|---|---|
| 80,000.00 | |

| Capital Stock—Preferred | |
|---|---|
| | 80,000.00 |

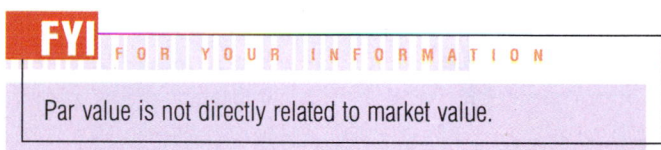

**FYI** — FOR YOUR INFORMATION

Par value is not directly related to market value.

---

## STEPS

STEPS • STEPS • STEPS • STEPS • STEPS • STEPS • STEPS • STEPS • STEPS • STEPS

### JOURNALIZE PREFERRED STOCK ISSUED AT PAR VALUE

**1** Calculate the amounts to be recorded for the sale of 800 shares of preferred stock at par.

**2** Write the date in the Date column of the cash receipts journal. Since this is the first entry on page 5 of the cash receipts journal, record the current year in the Date column.

**3** Enter the account title, *Capital Stock—Preferred,* in the Account Title column.

**4** Record the receipt number, *R117,* in the Doc. No. column.

**5** Write the debit amount, *80,000.00,* in the Cash Debit column.

**6** Record the credit amount, *80,000.00,* in the General Credit column.

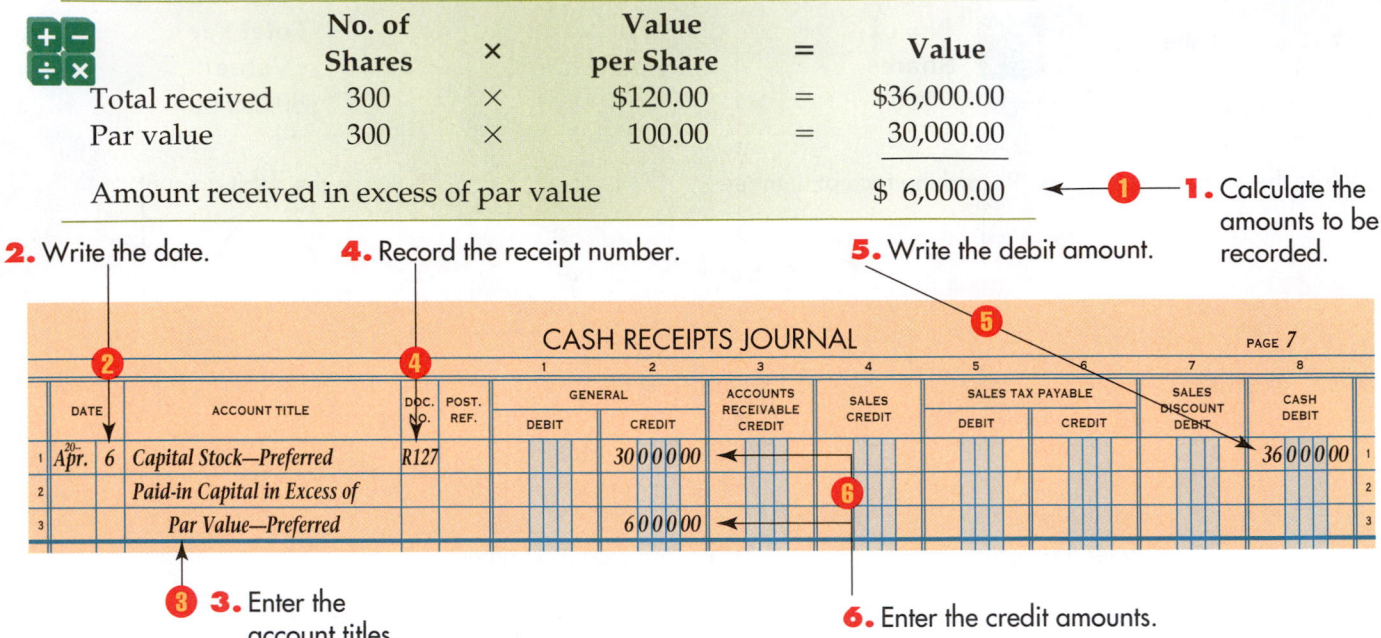

| | No. of Shares | × | Value per Share | = | Value |
|---|---|---|---|---|---|
| Total received | 300 | × | $120.00 | = | $36,000.00 |
| Par value | 300 | × | 100.00 | = | 30,000.00 |
| Amount received in excess of par value | | | | | $ 6,000.00 |

**1.** Calculate the amounts to be recorded.

**2.** Write the date.  **4.** Record the receipt number.  **5.** Write the debit amount.

**3.** Enter the account titles.

**6.** Enter the credit amounts.

Sometimes preferred stock is issued for more than its par value. LampLight sold 300 shares of preferred stock at $120.00 per share to Adam Kellogg, as shown above.

> *April 6. Received cash from Adam Kellogg for 300 shares of $100.00 par value preferred stock at $120.00 per share, $36,000.00. Receipt No. 127.*

Cash is debited for $36,000.00, the total amount received. Capital Stock—Preferred is credited for $30,000.00, the total par value of the preferred stock issued. Paid-in Capital in Excess of Par Value—Preferred is credited for $6,000.00, the amount received in excess of the par value.

Regardless of the amount received, the credit to the capital stock account always equals the par or stated value of the stock issued.

**STEPS** · STEPS · STEPS · STEPS

## JOURNALIZE PREFERRED STOCK ISSUED FOR MORE THAN PAR VALUE

**1** Calculate the amounts to be recorded for 300 shares of preferred stock sold at more than par value.

**2** Write the date in the Date column of the cash receipts journal.

**3** Enter the account titles, *Capital Stock—Preferred* and *Paid-in Capital in Excess of Par Value—Preferred*, on separate lines in the Account Title column.

**4** Record the receipt number, *R127*, in the Doc. No. column.

**5** Write the debit amount, *36,000.00*, in the Cash Debit column.

**6** Enter the appropriate credit amounts, *30,000.00* and *6,000.00*, on separate lines in the General Credit column.

**Cash**

| Apr. 6 | 36,000.00 | |
|---|---|---|

**Capital Stock—Preferred**

| | Balance | 80,000.00 |
|---|---|---|
| | Apr. 6 | 30,000.00 |
| | (New Bal. | 110,000.00) |

**Paid-in Capital in Excess of Par Value—Preferred**

| | Apr. 6 | 6,000.00 |
|---|---|---|

**FYI** FOR YOUR INFORMATION

A limited liability company (LLC) and a limited liability partnership (LLP) provide the flexibility of a partnership by allowing earnings to flow through to its partners as personal income. This feature eliminates the double-taxation penalty of a corporation.

# ISSUING PREFERRED STOCK FOR LESS THAN PAR VALUE

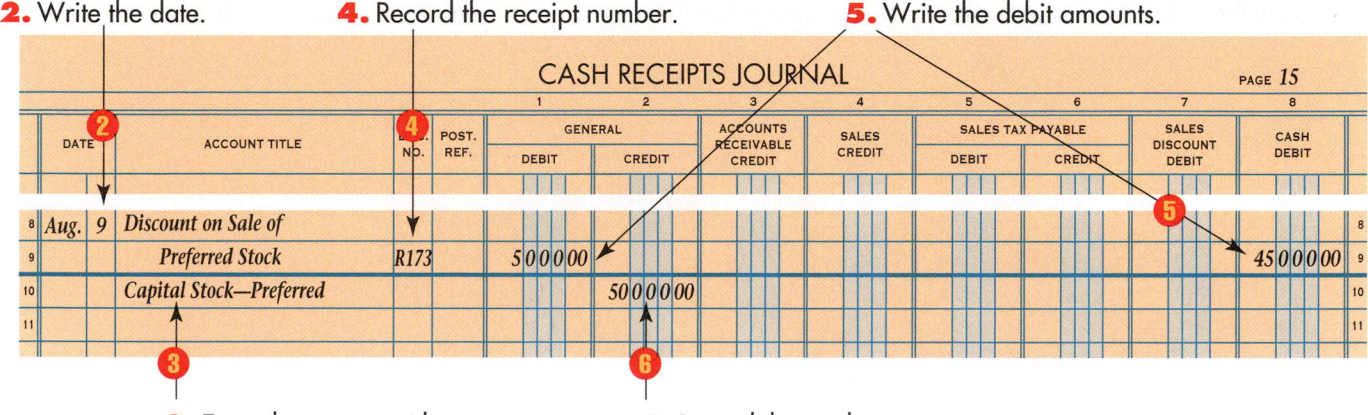

|  | No. of Shares | × | Value per Share | = | Value |
|---|---|---|---|---|---|
| Par value | 500 | × | $100.00 | = | $50,000.00 |
| Total received | 500 | × | 90.00 | = | 45,000.00 |
| Total discount |  |  |  |  | $ 5,000.00 |

**1.** Calculate the amounts to be recorded.

**2.** Write the date.      **4.** Record the receipt number.      **5.** Write the debit amounts.

### CASH RECEIPTS JOURNAL     PAGE 15

|  | DATE | ACCOUNT TITLE | DOC. NO. | POST. REF. | GENERAL DEBIT | GENERAL CREDIT | ACCOUNTS RECEIVABLE CREDIT | SALES CREDIT | SALES TAX PAYABLE DEBIT | SALES TAX PAYABLE CREDIT | SALES DISCOUNT DEBIT | CASH DEBIT |  |
|---|---|---|---|---|---|---|---|---|---|---|---|---|---|
| 8 | Aug. 9 | Discount on Sale of |  |  |  |  |  |  |  |  |  |  | 8 |
| 9 |  | Preferred Stock | R173 |  | 5 0 0 0 00 |  |  |  |  |  |  | 45 0 0 0 00 | 9 |
| 10 |  | Capital Stock—Preferred |  |  |  | 50 0 0 0 00 |  |  |  |  |  |  | 10 |
| 11 |  |  |  |  |  |  |  |  |  |  |  |  | 11 |

**3.** Enter the account titles.      **6.** Record the credit amount.

An amount less than par or stated value at which capital stock is sold is called a **discount on capital stock**. The legal treatment of discounts on capital stock varies from state to state. In some states, a stockholder may be liable for the amount of discount on par value stock if a corporation is unable to pay creditors. In other states, a stockholder is not liable for the amount of the discount.

LampLight sold 500 shares of $100.00 par value preferred stock to Hazel Deloach at a price of $90.00 per share, as shown above.

> *August 9. Received cash from Hazel Deloach for 500 shares of $100.00 par value preferred stock at $90.00 per share, $45,000.00. Receipt No. 173.*

Cash is debited for $45,000.00, the amount of cash received. Discount on Sale of Preferred Stock is debited for $5,000.00, the discount amount. Capital Stock—Preferred is credited for $50,000.00, the par value of the 500 shares of preferred stock.

| Cash | |
|---|---|
| Aug. 9 | 45,000.00 |

| Discount on Sale of Preferred Stock | |
|---|---|
| Aug. 9 | 5,000.00 |

| Capital Stock—Preferred | |
|---|---|
| Balance | 110,000.00 |
| Aug. 9 | 50,000.00 |
| (New Bal. | 160,000.00) |

**FYI** FOR YOUR INFORMATION

Discount on Sale of Preferred Stock is a contra stockholders' account; hence, it is increased with a debit.

**FYI** FOR YOUR INFORMATION

The credit to the capital stock account always equals the par or stated value of the stock issued regardless of the amount received.

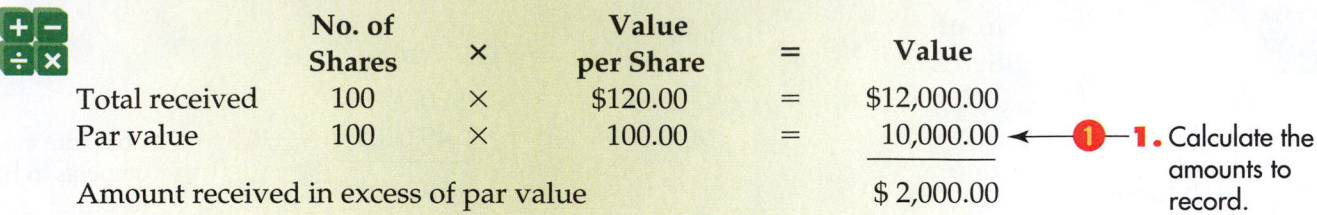

| | No. of Shares | × | Value per Share | = | Value | |
|---|---|---|---|---|---|---|
| Total received | 100 | × | $120.00 | = | $12,000.00 | |
| Par value | 100 | × | 100.00 | = | 10,000.00 | ← ❶ **1.** Calculate the amounts to record. |
| Amount received in excess of par value | | | | | $ 2,000.00 | |

**2.** Write the date.   **4.** Record the memorandum number.   **5.** Write the debit amount.

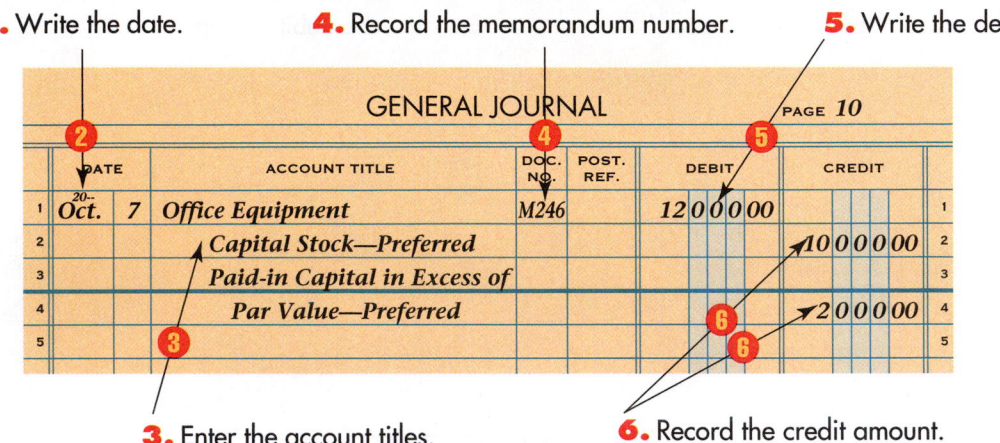

| | DATE | ACCOUNT TITLE | DOC. NO. | POST. REF. | DEBIT | CREDIT | |
|---|---|---|---|---|---|---|---|
| 1 | Oct. 7 | Office Equipment | M246 | | 12 0 0 0 00 | | 1 |
| 2 | | Capital Stock—Preferred | | | | 10 0 0 0 00 | 2 |
| 3 | | Paid-in Capital in Excess of | | | | | 3 |
| 4 | | Par Value—Preferred | | | | 2 0 0 0 00 | 4 |
| 5 | | | | | | | 5 |

GENERAL JOURNAL — PAGE 10

**3.** Enter the account titles.   **6.** Record the credit amount.

Occasionally, corporations issue capital stock in exchange for assets other than cash. When other assets are used to pay for capital stock, the investor and corporation must agree on the value of the assets and the capital stock.

LampLight issued 100 shares of preferred stock to Steven McBee in exchange for office equipment. The office equipment was accepted in full payment of the 100 shares of preferred stock. The agreed-upon total value of the equipment is $12,000.00. Therefore, the equipment fully pays for the 100 shares of preferred stock, as shown above.

*October 7. Received office equipment from Steven McBee at an agreed value of $12,000.00 for 100 shares of $100.00 par value preferred stock. Memorandum No. 246.*

Office Equipment is debited for $12,000.00. Capital Stock—Preferred is credited for $10,000.00, the total par value of the preferred stock issued.

Paid-in Capital in Excess of Par Value—Preferred is credited for $2,000.00, the amount received in excess of the par value.

| Office Equipment | |
|---|---|
| Oct. 7    12,000.00 | |

| Capital Stock—Preferred | |
|---|---|
| | Balance    160,000.00 |
| | Oct. 7    10,000.00 |
| | (New Bal.    170,000.00) |

| Paid-in Capital in Excess of Par Value—Preferred | |
|---|---|
| | Balance    6,000.00 |
| | Oct. 7    2,000.00 |
| | (New Bal.    8,000.00) |

**FYI** FOR YOUR INFORMATION

Occasionally, a firm acquires a company by issuing stock in exchange for the company's assets.

# ISSUING COMMON STOCK WITH NO PAR VALUE

| | DATE | ACCOUNT TITLE | DOC. NO. | POST. REF. | GENERAL DEBIT | GENERAL CREDIT | ACCOUNTS RECEIVABLE CREDIT | SALES CREDIT | SALES TAX PAYABLE DEBIT | SALES TAX PAYABLE CREDIT | SALES DISCOUNT DEBIT | CASH DEBIT | |
|---|---|---|---|---|---|---|---|---|---|---|---|---|---|
| 12 | July 8 | Capital Stock—Common | R148 | | | 14 000 00 | | | | | | 14 000 00 | 12 |

**CASH RECEIPTS JOURNAL** PAGE 13

Common stock often has no par value assigned to it or printed on the stock certificates. With no-par value stock, the entire amount paid by an investor is recorded in the capital stock account. Wheeler, Inc., sells no-par value common stock. The journal entry to record the transaction is shown above.

*July 8. Received cash from Elizabeth Griffin for 1,000 shares of no-par value common stock at $14.00 per share, $14,000.00. Receipt No. 148.*

Cash is debited for $14,000.00, the total amount received. Capital Stock—Common is credited for $14,000.00, the total amount received for the 1,000 shares of stock.

# ISSUING COMMON STOCK WITH A STATED VALUE

**CASH RECEIPTS JOURNAL** PAGE 19

| | DATE | ACCOUNT TITLE | DOC. NO. | POST. REF. | GENERAL DEBIT | GENERAL CREDIT | ACCOUNTS RECEIVABLE CREDIT | SALES CREDIT | SALES TAX PAYABLE DEBIT | SALES TAX PAYABLE CREDIT | SALES DISCOUNT DEBIT | CASH DEBIT | |
|---|---|---|---|---|---|---|---|---|---|---|---|---|---|
| 1 | Oct. 10 | Capital Stock—Common | R181 | | | 1 000 00 | | | | | | 1 200 00 | 1 |
| 2 | | Paid-in Capital in Excess of | | | | | | | | | | | 2 |
| 3 | | Stated Value—Common | | | | 200 00 | | | | | | | 3 |
| 4 | | | | | | | | | | | | | 4 |

Corporations may assign a value to no-par value common stock. The value is known as the stated value. A stated value to no-par value shares serves the same function as par value. Therefore, no-par value common stock with a stated value is recorded using the same procedures as par value stock. An entry for issuing common stock at stated value is shown on page 319. An entry for issuing common stock at more than stated value is shown above.

LampLight's articles of incorporation, shown on pages 315 and 316, specify that the company's common stock has a stated value of $10.00. LampLight sold 100 shares of common stock to Alice Blake for $12.00 a share, as shown above.

*October 10. Received cash from Alice Blake for 100 shares of $10.00 stated value common stock at $12.00 per share, $1,200.00. Receipt No. 181.*

Cash is debited for $1,200.00, the total amount received. Capital Stock—Common is credited for $1,000.00, the total stated value of the 100 shares. Paid-in Capital in Excess of Stated Value—Common is credited for $200.00, the amount received in excess of the stated value.

Xtra!
Study Tools
accountingxtra.swlearning.com

## term review

TERM REVIEW • TERM REVIEW

discount on capital stock

## audit your understanding

AUDIT YOUR UNDERSTANDING

1. To finance rapid expansion, how can a corporation acquire additional capital?

2. What accounts are affected, and how, when LampLight receives cash for preferred stock sold at par value?

3. What accounts are affected, and how, when LampLight receives cash for preferred stock sold for more than par value?

4. What accounts are affected, and how, when LampLight receives cash for preferred stock sold for less than par value?

5. What is the function of stated value?

## work together 12-1

WORK TOGETHER • WORK TOGETHER • WORK

### Journalizing capital stock transactions

Page 4 of a cash receipts journal and page 2 of a general journal are provided in the *Working Papers*. Your instructor will guide you through the following examples.

May 2. Received cash from Kari Kovaleski for 200 shares of $50.00 par value preferred stock at $60.00 per share, $12,000.00. Receipt No. 234.

3. Received cash from Phil Mullins for 100 shares of $50.00 par value preferred stock at $45.00 per share, $4,500.00. Receipt No. 235.

5. Received office equipment from Laura Nguyen at an agreed-upon value of $5,000.00 for 100 shares of $50.00 par value preferred stock. Memorandum No. 103.

5. Received cash from Arbus Kleinhoffer for 300 shares of $8.00 stated value common stock at $10.00 per share, $3,000.00. Receipt No. 236.

7. Received cash from Jenny Wasito for 100 shares of $8.00 stated value common stock at $8.00 per share, $800.00. Receipt No. 237.

1. Journalize each transaction completed during the current year.

## on your own 12-1

### Journalizing capital stock transactions

Page 5 of a cash receipts journal and page 3 of a general journal are provided in the *Working Papers*. Work independently to complete the following problem.

June   3.   Received cash from George Lyding for 200 shares of $80.00 par value preferred stock at $85.00 per share, $17,000.00. Receipt No. 174.

6.   Received cash from Blanca Echauri for 200 shares of $80.00 par value preferred stock at $78.00 per share, $15,600.00. Receipt No. 175.

8.   Received land from Asghar Ebadat at an agreed-upon value of $32,000.00 for 400 shares of $80.00 par value preferred stock. Memorandum No. 223.

9.   Received cash from Barbara Parisot for 100 shares of $15.00 stated value common stock at $15.00 per share, $1,500.00. Receipt No. 176.

11.   Received cash from Jin Myoung for 100 shares of $15.00 stated value common stock at $16.00 per share, $1,600.00. Receipt No. 177.

12.   Received cash from Bernadine Barthel for 200 shares of $80.00 par value preferred stock at $80.00 per share, $16,000.00. Receipt No. 178.

14.   Received office furniture from Rita Gomez at an agreed-upon value of $8,000.00 for 100 shares of $80.00 par value preferred stock. Memorandum No. 224.

1.   Journalize each transaction completed during the current year.

# Explore Accounting   EXPLORE ACCOUNTING   •   EXPLORE ACCOUNTING   •   EXPLORE ACCOUNTING

### Stock Price Fluctuation in a Market Economy

The stocks of publicly traded corporations are traded freely on domestic and international stock exchanges. These companies also publish annual reports that usually show a 5-year history of the performance of their stock. In addition, historical information about the market price of stocks in public trading can be researched using the Internet.

Individuals buy and sell stocks as investments. Institutions such as retirement plans and philanthropic organizations may invest in stocks, too. Companies may also invest in stocks to earn a return on funds that are not immediately needed for the operations of the business.

In a market economy, stock prices fluctuate constantly, based on the interaction of supply and demand for a particular stock.

### Instructions

Merito Retirement Systems wishes to invest $50,000. As comptroller, you have been asked to pick two stocks and research the performance of each stock over the past five years. Select two publicly traded stocks and research information about their selling prices during the past five years. Report the highest and lowest selling price of each stock during the past five years as well as any trends you may find in the market fluctuations.

## 12-2 Treasury Stock Transactions

### BUYING TREASURY STOCK

**1.** Write the date.     **3.** Record the check number.     **5.** Record the credit amount.

CASH PAYMENTS JOURNAL     PAGE 20

| | DATE | ACCOUNT TITLE | CK. NO. | POST. REF. | GENERAL DEBIT | GENERAL CREDIT | ACCOUNTS PAYABLE DEBIT | PURCHASES DISCOUNT CREDIT | CASH CREDIT | |
|---|---|---|---|---|---|---|---|---|---|---|
| 1 | Oct. 24 | Treasury Stock | 502 | | 6 0 0 0 00 | | | | 6 0 0 0 00 | 1 |
| 2 | | | | | | | | | | 2 |
| 3 | | | | | | | | | | 3 |
| 4 | | | | | | | | | | 4 |
| 5 | | | | | | | | | | 5 |
| 6 | | | | | | | | | | 6 |
| 7 | | | | | | | | | | 7 |

**2.** Enter the account title.     **4.** Write the debit amount.

A corporation's own stock that has been issued and reacquired is called **treasury stock**. When a corporation buys treasury stock, it reduces the number of shares outstanding. However, treasury stock is still considered to be issued stock. A corporation usually intends to use the treasury stock for a specific purpose. For example, a corporation may acquire treasury stock to be given to employees as bonus payments.

Treasury stock is not an asset of a corporation. Since treasury stock is not owned by a stockholder, the stock does not involve voting rights. Dividends are not paid on treasury stock. Once treasury stock is given or sold to a stockholder, it ceases to be treasury stock and is again capital stock outstanding. A corporation records treasury stock at the price paid regardless of the stock's par or stated value. [*CONCEPT: Historical Cost*]

*October 24. Paid cash to Francis Burns for 500 shares of $10.00 stated value common stock at $12.00 per share, $6,000.00. Check No. 502.*

Treasury Stock is debited for $6,000.00, the amount paid for the 500 shares of treasury

stock. Cash is credited for $6,000.00. The journal entry to record this transaction is shown above.

Capital stock accounts have normal credit balances. Treasury Stock is a contra capital stock account and therefore has a normal debit balance.

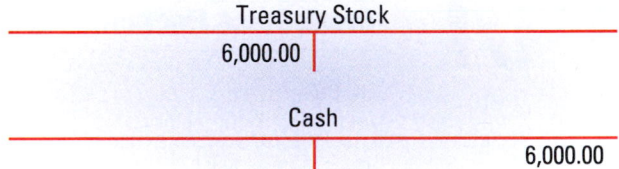

Treasury Stock

| 6,000.00 | |

Cash

| | 6,000.00 |

### STEPS • STEPS • STEPS • STEPS
**JOURNALIZE THE PURCHASE OF TREASURY STOCK**

**1** Write the date in the Date column of the cash payments journal.

**2** Enter the account title, *Treasury Stock*, in the Account Title column.

**3** Record the check number, *502*, in the Check Number column. Since only check numbers are recorded in the column, no identifying letter is necessary.

**4** Write the debit amount, *6,000.00*, in the General Debit column.

**5** Record the credit amount, *6,000.00*, in the Cash Credit column.

## SELLING TREASURY STOCK FOR ORIGINAL COST

**1.** Write the date.  **3.** Record the receipt number.  **4.** Write the debit amount.

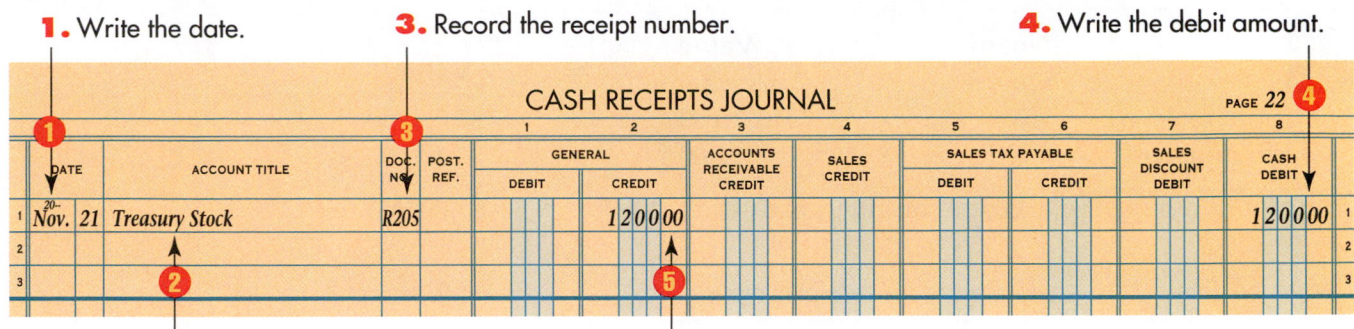

CASH RECEIPTS JOURNAL — PAGE 22

| | DATE | ACCOUNT TITLE | DOC. NO. | POST. REF. | GENERAL DEBIT | GENERAL CREDIT | ACCOUNTS RECEIVABLE CREDIT | SALES CREDIT | SALES TAX PAYABLE DEBIT | SALES TAX PAYABLE CREDIT | SALES DISCOUNT DEBIT | CASH DEBIT | |
|---|---|---|---|---|---|---|---|---|---|---|---|---|---|
| 1 | Nov. 21 | Treasury Stock | R205 | | | 1 2 0 0 00 | | | | | | 1 2 0 0 00 | 1 |
| 2 | | | | | | | | | | | | | 2 |
| 3 | | | | | | | | | | | | | 3 |

**2.** Enter the account title.  **5.** Record the credit amount.

Companies may sell treasury stock at any time. Treasury stock is generally reissued to investors who pay cash for the stock. Investors pay the current market price for the stock.

The market price of stock will be explained in Chapter 13.

The current value of stock in the marketplace may be the same as the original cost of the treasury stock. Assume LampLight sold some of its treasury stock at the $12.00 original cost, as shown above.

Cash is debited for $1,200.00. Treasury Stock is credited for $1,200.00.

| Cash | |
|---|---|
| 1,200.00 | |

| Treasury Stock | | |
|---|---|---|
| Balance | 6,000.00 | 1,200.00 |
| (New Bal. | 4,800.00) | |

---

*November 21. Received cash from Lisa Vance for 100 shares of treasury stock at $12.00 per share, $1,200.00. Treasury stock was originally bought by LampLight on October 24 at $12.00 per share. Receipt No. 205.*

---

## STEPS · STEPS · STEPS · STEPS

### JOURNALIZE THE SALE OF TREASURY STOCK FOR ORIGINAL COST

1. Write the date in the Date column of the cash receipts journal.

2. Enter the account title, *Treasury Stock*, in the Account Title column.

3. Record the receipt number identified by the letter R, *R205*, in the Doc. No. column.

4. Write the debit amount, *1,200.00*, in the Cash Debit column.

5. Record the credit amount, *1,200.00*, in the General Credit column.

**small business spotlight**

SMALL BUSINESS SPOTLIGHT

There are many challenges associated with starting a new business or growing an existing one. Over 3.5 million small business owners and aspiring entrepreneurs have looked to SCORE to help them meet these challenges. SCORE (Service Corps of Retired Executives) includes over 12,000 trained volunteer business counselors dedicated to sharing real-world business experience with their clients. SCORE business counselors provide advice in areas such as writing a business plan, managing cash flow, assessing capital needs, starting or operating a business, and buying or selling a business. With almost 400 local chapters, SCORE provides face-to-face counseling along with low-cost workshops and seminars. Program topics are often tailored to meet the specific needs of a community.

| | No. of Shares | × | Value per Share | = | Value |
|---|---|---|---|---|---|
| Total received | 200 | × | $15.00 | = | $3,000.00 |
| Original cost | 200 | × | 12.00 | = | 2,400.00 |
| Amount received in excess of original cost | | | | | $ 600.00 |

**1.** Calculate the amounts to be recorded.

**2.** Write the date.   **4.** Record the receipt number.   **5.** Write the debit amount.

### CASH RECEIPTS JOURNAL                                     PAGE 22

| | | | | | 1 | 2 | 3 | 4 | 5 | 6 | 7 | 8 |
|---|---|---|---|---|---|---|---|---|---|---|---|---|
| | DATE | ACCOUNT TITLE | DOC. NO. | POST. REF. | GENERAL DEBIT | GENERAL CREDIT | ACCOUNTS RECEIVABLE CREDIT | SALES CREDIT | SALES TAX PAYABLE DEBIT | SALES TAX PAYABLE CREDIT | SALES DISCOUNT DEBIT | CASH DEBIT |
| 8 | 25 | Treasury Stock | R216 | | | 2 4 0 0 00 | | | | | | 3 0 0 0 00 |
| 9 | | Paid-in Capital from Sale of | | | | | | | | | | |
| 10 | | Treasury Stock | | | | 6 0 0 00 | | | | | | |
| 11 | | | | | | | | | | | | |

**3.** Enter the account titles.   **6.** Record the credit amounts.

LampLight sold 200 shares of treasury stock to Mary Long for $15.00 per share, as shown above.

> **November 25. Received cash from Mary Long for 200 shares of treasury stock at $15.00 per share, $3,000.00. Treasury stock was bought on October 24 at $12.00 per share. Receipt No. 216.**

Cash is debited for $3,000.00, the total amount received from the sale of the treasury stock. Treasury Stock is credited for $2,400.00, the original cost of the 200 shares of treasury stock. Paid-in Capital from Sale of Treasury Stock is credited for $600.00, the amount received in excess of the treasury stock's original cost.

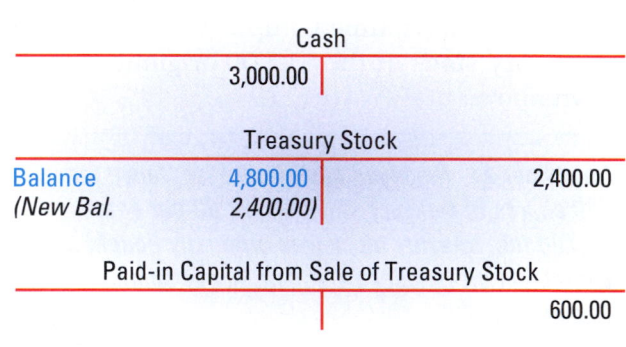

| Cash | |
|---|---|
| 3,000.00 | |

| Treasury Stock | | |
|---|---|---|
| Balance | 4,800.00 | 2,400.00 |
| (New Bal. | 2,400.00) | |

| Paid-in Capital from Sale of Treasury Stock | |
|---|---|
| | 600.00 |

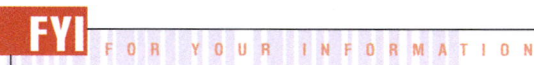

**FYI** FOR YOUR INFORMATION

A corporation may acquire treasury stock to regain control or to have additional stock to use for specific purposes such as stock dividends.

## STEPS
STEPS • STEPS • STEPS • STEPS • STEPS • STEPS • STEPS • STEPS • STEPS • STEP

### JOURNALIZE THE SALE OF TREASURY STOCK FOR MORE THAN ORIGINAL COST

**1** Calculate the amounts to be recorded for the sale of 200 shares of treasury stock at more than the original cost.

**2** Write the date in the Date column of the cash receipts journal.

**3** Enter the account titles in the Account Title column.

**4** Record the receipt number, *R216*, in the Doc. No. column.

**5** Write the debit amount in the Cash Debit column.

**6** Record the credit amounts in the General Credit column.

# SELLING TREASURY STOCK FOR LESS THAN ORIGINAL COST

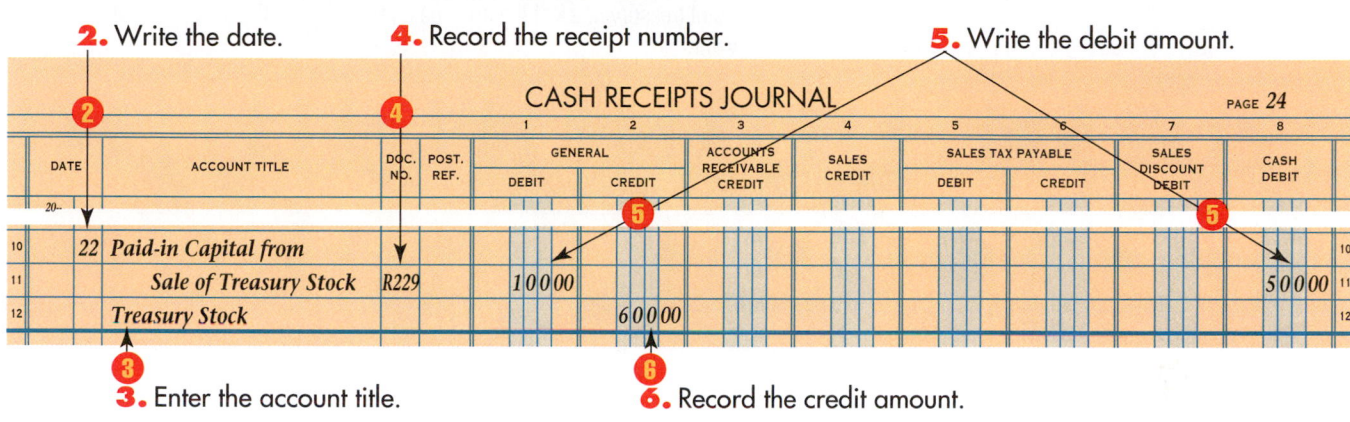

|  | No. of Shares | × | Value per Share | = | Value | |
|---|---|---|---|---|---|---|
| Original cost | 50 | × | $12.00 | = | $600.00 | **1.** Calculate the amounts to be recorded. |
| Total received | 50 | × | 10.00 | = | 500.00 | |
| Amount received less than original cost | | | | | $100.00 | |

**2.** Write the date.  **4.** Record the receipt number.  **5.** Write the debit amount.

### CASH RECEIPTS JOURNAL  PAGE 24

| | DATE | ACCOUNT TITLE | DOC. NO. | POST. REF. | GENERAL DEBIT | GENERAL CREDIT | ACCOUNTS RECEIVABLE CREDIT | SALES CREDIT | SALES TAX PAYABLE DEBIT | SALES TAX PAYABLE CREDIT | SALES DISCOUNT DEBIT | CASH DEBIT | |
|---|---|---|---|---|---|---|---|---|---|---|---|---|---|
| 10 | 22 | Paid-in Capital from | | | | | | | | | | | 10 |
| 11 | | Sale of Treasury Stock | R229 | | 100 00 | | | | | | | 500 00 | 11 |
| 12 | | Treasury Stock | | | | 600 00 | | | | | | | 12 |

**3.** Enter the account title.   **6.** Record the credit amount.

LampLight sold 50 shares of treasury stock to Frank Demetz for $10.00 per share, as shown above.

> **December 22. Received cash from Frank Demetz for 50 shares of treasury stock at $10.00 per share, $500.00. Treasury stock was originally bought October 24 at $12.00 per share. Receipt No. 229.**

Cash is debited for $500.00, the total amount of cash received. Paid-in Capital from Sale of Treasury Stock is debited for $100.00, the amount received that is less than the treasury stock's original cost. Treasury Stock is credited for $600.00, the original cost.

When treasury stock transactions occur, no entry is made in Capital Stock—Common or Capital Stock—Preferred. Treasury stock is considered to

### Cash

| | |
|---|---|
| 500.00 | |

### Paid-in Capital from Sale of Treasury Stock

| | | |
|---|---|---|
| 100.00 | Balance | 600.00 |
| | (New Bal. | 500.00) |

### Treasury Stock

| | | |
|---|---|---|
| Balance | 2,400.00 | 600.00 |
| (New Bal. | 1,800.00) | |

be issued stock. The difference between the balances of the capital stock accounts and the treasury stock account is the value of outstanding stock. After the entry on December 22 for the sale of treasury stock, the number of LampLight's outstanding shares of capital stock is calculated as follows:

|  | No. of Shares Issued | − | No. of Shares of Treasury Stock | = | No. of Shares Outstanding |
|---|---|---|---|---|---|
| Preferred | 1,700 | − | 0 | = | 1,700 |
| Common | 32,100 | − | 150 | = | 31,950 |

Xtra!
Study Tools
accountingxtra.swlearning.com

• term review

audit your understanding

## • term review

TERM REVIEW • TERM

treasury stock

## • audit your understanding

AUDIT YOUR

1. What is treasury stock?

2. What accounts are affected, and how, when treasury stock is sold for more than its original cost?

3. What accounting concept is being applied when a corporation records the purchase of treasury stock at the price paid regardless of the stock's par or stated value?

## • work together 12-2

WORK TOGETHER • WORK TOGETHER • WORK TOGETHER

### Journalizing treasury stock transactions

Page 11 of a cash receipts journal and page 8 of a cash payments journal are provided in the *Working Papers*. Your instructor will guide you through the following examples.

Mar. 9. Paid cash to Dana O'Brien for 300 shares of $20.00 stated value common stock at $22.00 per share, $6,600.00. Check No. 753.

12. Received cash from Doug Johnston for 100 shares of treasury stock at $24.00 per share, $2,400.00. Treasury stock was purchased on March 9 at $22.00 per share. Receipt No. 409.

13. Received cash from Ida Mann for 100 shares of treasury stock at $22.00 per share, $2,200.00. Treasury stock was purchased on March 9 at $22.00 per share. Receipt No. 410.

16. Received cash from Kathy Milhouse for 100 shares of treasury stock at $21.00 per share, $2,100.00. Treasury stock was purchased on March 9 at $22.00 per share. Receipt No. 411.

1. Journalize each transaction completed during the current year.

## • on your own 12-2

ON YOUR OWN • ON YOUR OWN • ON YOUR OWN • ON YOUR OWN

### Journalizing treasury stock transactions

Page 7 of a cash receipts journal and page 6 of a cash payments journal are provided in the *Working Papers*. Work independently to complete the following problem.

Aug. 22. Paid cash to Tai Arriaga for 500 shares of $15.00 stated value common stock at $15.00 per share, $7,500.00. Check No. 172.

23. Received cash from Joyce Cariel for 250 shares of treasury stock at $14.00 per share, $3,500.00. Treasury stock was purchased on August 22 at $15.00 per share. Receipt No. 85.

25. Received cash from Stan Gavin for 250 shares of treasury stock at $15.00 per share, $3,750.00. Treasury stock was purchased on August 22 at $15.00 per share. Receipt No. 86.

26. Paid cash to Cindy Hopper for 750 shares of $15.00 stated value common stock at $16.00 per share, $12,000.00. Check No. 173.

27. Received cash from Tim Coburn for 100 shares of treasury stock at $17.00 per share, $1,700.00. Treasury stock was purchased on August 26 at $16.00 per share. Receipt No. 87.

1. Journalize each transaction completed during the current year.

# 12-3 Bonds Payable Transactions

## CORPORATE BONDS PAYABLE

For a growing business, the capital needed to expand may come from three sources:

1. Using retained earnings.
2. Selling additional capital stock.
3. Borrowing the funds.

A business's management team may find that capital needed for expansion could be accumulated from retained net income during the next 5 to 10 years. However, the business may need the additional capital within the next year. A corporation's board of directors must decide whether to raise the needed capital by selling additional stock or borrowing the money.

An advantage of selling stock is that the additional capital becomes part of a corporation's permanent capital. Permanent capital does not have to be returned to stockholders as long as the business continues to operate. Another advantage is that dividends do not have to be paid to stockholders unless the earnings are sufficient to warrant such payments. A disadvantage of selling more stock to raise additional capital is that the ownership is spread over more shares and more owners.

An advantage of borrowing the additional capital is that stockholders' equity is not spread over additional shares of stock. A disadvantage

is that interest must be paid on the loan, which decreases the net income. This decrease in net income decreases the amount available for dividends. Another disadvantage of borrowing additional capital is that the amount borrowed must be repaid in the future.

Large loans are sometimes difficult to obtain for short periods. Corporations frequently borrow needed capital with the provision that the loan be repaid several years in the future. Therefore, the loan can be paid out of future earnings accumulated over several years.

Large loans may also be difficult to obtain from one bank or one individual. A printed, long-term promise to pay a specified amount on a specified date and to pay interest at stated intervals is called a **bond.** Bonds are similar to notes payable because both are written promises to pay. However, most notes payable are for one year or less, but bonds generally run for a long period of time, such as 5, 10, or 20 years. Also, bonds payable tend to be issued for larger amounts than notes payable.

All bonds representing the total amount of a loan are called a **bond issue.** A corporation usually sells an entire bond issue to a securities dealer who sells individual bonds to the public.

©GETTY IMAGES/PHOTODISC

**FYI** FOR YOUR INFORMATION

If a bond is issued for more than its face value, it is said to be sold at a "premium." Cash is debited and Bonds Payable and Premium on Bonds Payable are credited.

**1.** Record the issuance of the bonds.

| | | | | | GENERAL | | ACCOUNTS RECEIVABLE CREDIT | SALES CREDIT | SALES TAX PAYABLE | | SALES DISCOUNT DEBIT | CASH DEBIT | |
|---|---|---|---|---|---|---|---|---|---|---|---|---|---|
| | DATE | ACCOUNT TITLE | DOC. NO. | POST. REF. | DEBIT | CREDIT | | | DEBIT | CREDIT | | | |
| | | | | | 1 | 2 | 3 | 4 | 5 | 6 | 7 | 8 | |

**CASH RECEIPTS JOURNAL**   PAGE **13**

| | DATE | ACCOUNT TITLE | DOC. NO. | POST. REF. | GENERAL DEBIT | GENERAL CREDIT | ACCOUNTS RECEIVABLE CREDIT | SALES CREDIT | SALES TAX PAYABLE DEBIT | SALES TAX PAYABLE CREDIT | SALES DISCOUNT DEBIT | CASH DEBIT | |
|---|---|---|---|---|---|---|---|---|---|---|---|---|---|
| 1 | 20X0 July 1 | Bonds Payable | R246 | | | 250 000 00 | | | | | | 250 000 00 | 1 |
| 2 | | | | | | | | | | | | | 2 |

On July 1, 20X0, LampLight borrowed $250,000.00 to expand its building. LampLight issued 250, 12%, $1,000.00 par value bonds. The bonds are scheduled to mature in five years. Annual interest on the bonds is to be paid on July 1 of each year. The bond issue was sold at par value to a securities dealer. The journal entry to record the sale of the bonds is shown above.

*July 1, 20X0. Received cash for the face value of a five-year, 12%, $1,000.00 par value bond issue, $250,000.00. Receipt No. 246.*

Cash is debited for $250,000.00. Bonds Payable is credited for $250,000.00.

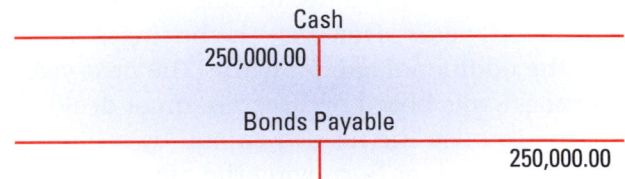

| Cash | |
|---|---|
| 250,000.00 | |

| Bonds Payable | |
|---|---|
| | 250,000.00 |

## PAYING INTEREST ON BONDS

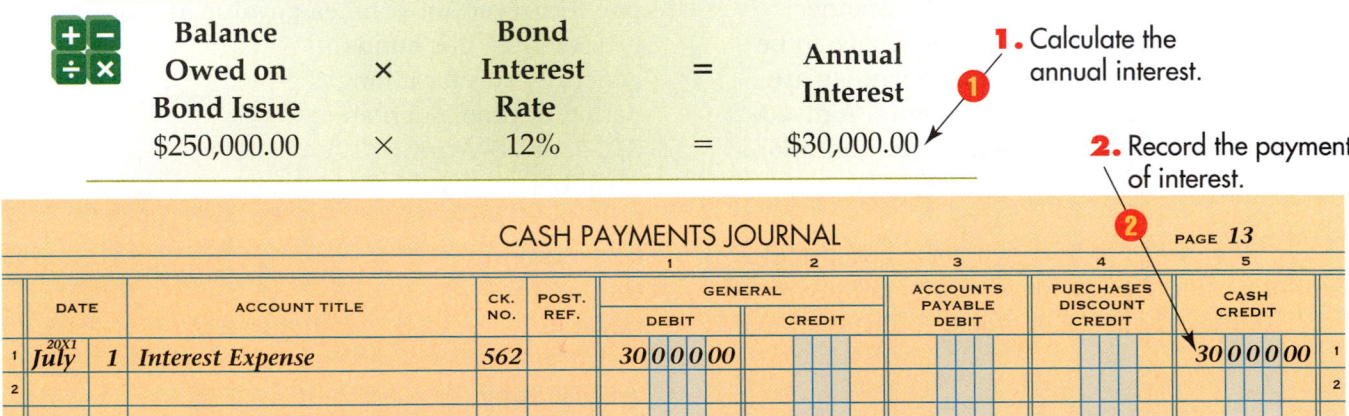

| Balance Owed on Bond Issue | × | Bond Interest Rate | = | Annual Interest |
|---|---|---|---|---|
| $250,000.00 | × | 12% | = | $30,000.00 |

**1.** Calculate the annual interest.

**2.** Record the payment of interest.

**CASH PAYMENTS JOURNAL**   PAGE **13**

| | DATE | ACCOUNT TITLE | CK. NO. | POST. REF. | GENERAL DEBIT | GENERAL CREDIT | ACCOUNTS PAYABLE DEBIT | PURCHASES DISCOUNT CREDIT | CASH CREDIT | |
|---|---|---|---|---|---|---|---|---|---|---|
| | | | | | 1 | 2 | 3 | 4 | 5 | |
| 1 | 20X1 July 1 | Interest Expense | 562 | | 30 000 00 | | | | 30 000 00 | 1 |
| 2 | | | | | | | | | | 2 |

A year's interest is paid to each bondholder on July 1 of each year until the bond's maturity date. A person or institution, usually a bank, given legal authorization to administer property for the benefit of property owners is called a **trustee**. LampLight pays the interest amount to a bond trustee who in turn handles the details of paying each individual bondholder.

*July 1, 20X1. Paid cash to bond trustee for annual interest on bond issue, $30,000.00. Check No. 562.*

Interest Expense is debited for $30,000.00. Cash is credited for $30,000.00. The journal entry to record this transaction is shown above.

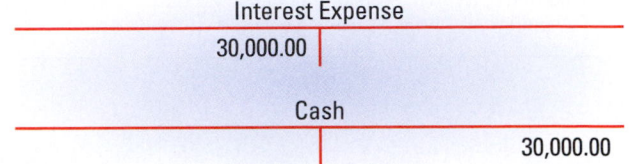

| Interest Expense | |
|---|---|
| 30,000.00 | |

| Cash | |
|---|---|
| | 30,000.00 |

Acquiring Additional Capital for a Corporation

# DEPOSITING CASH IN A BOND SINKING FUND

**1.** Record the initial payment to the bond sinking fund.

| | DATE | ACCOUNT TITLE | CK. NO. | POST. REF. | GENERAL DEBIT | GENERAL CREDIT | ACCOUNTS PAYABLE DEBIT | PURCHASES DISCOUNT CREDIT | CASH CREDIT | |
|---|---|---|---|---|---|---|---|---|---|---|
| | 20X1 | | | | | | | | | |
| 2 | 1 | Bond Sinking Fund | 563 | | 50 000 00 | | | | 50 000 00 | 2 |
| 3 | | | | | | | | | | 3 |

*CASH PAYMENTS JOURNAL* — PAGE *13*

To assure bondholders that the bond issue will be paid at maturity, LampLight annually deposits a portion of the loan value with the bond trustee. An amount set aside to pay a bond issue when due is called a **bond sinking fund**. LampLight spreads the $250,000.00 amount over the five years that the bond issue is outstanding. The bond sinking fund is increased each year by $50,000.00, one-fifth of the total principal. On the bond issue's maturity date, a total of $250,000.00 will be available in the bond sinking fund to pay the bondholders.

> *July 1, 20X1. Paid cash to bond trustee for annual deposit to bond sinking fund, $50,000.00. Check No. 563.*

Bond Sinking Fund is debited for $50,000.00. Cash is credited for $50,000.00. The entry to record the deposit for 20X1 is shown above.

# DEPOSITING CASH TO SINKING FUND AND RECORDING INCOME EARNED

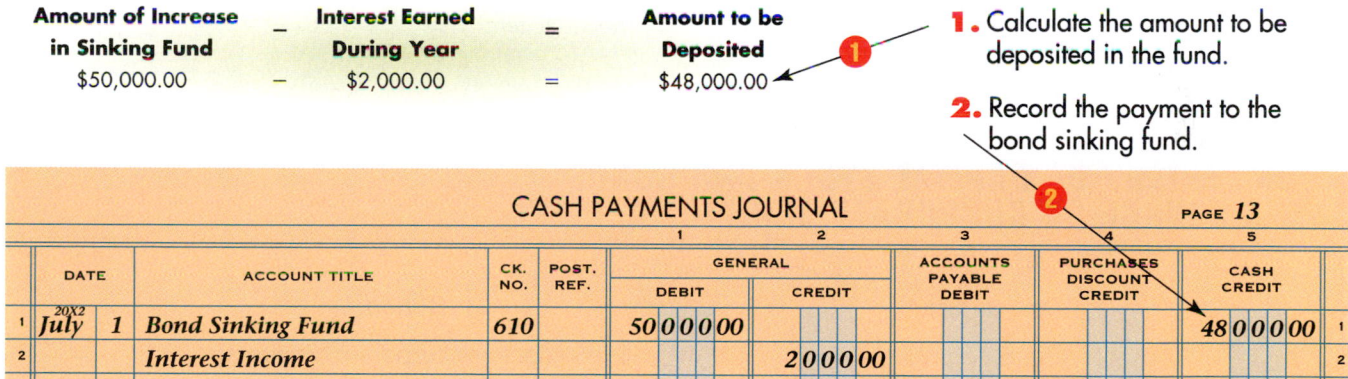

| Amount of Increase in Sinking Fund | − | Interest Earned During Year | = | Amount to be Deposited |
|---|---|---|---|---|
| $50,000.00 | − | $2,000.00 | = | $48,000.00 |

**1.** Calculate the amount to be deposited in the fund.

**2.** Record the payment to the bond sinking fund.

| | DATE | ACCOUNT TITLE | CK. NO. | POST. REF. | GENERAL DEBIT | GENERAL CREDIT | ACCOUNTS PAYABLE DEBIT | PURCHASES DISCOUNT CREDIT | CASH CREDIT | |
|---|---|---|---|---|---|---|---|---|---|---|
| | 20X2 | | | | | | | | | |
| 1 | July 1 | Bond Sinking Fund | 610 | | 50 000 00 | | | | 48 00 00 | 1 |
| 2 | | Interest Income | | | | 2 000 00 | | | | 2 |

*CASH PAYMENTS JOURNAL* — PAGE *13*

The bond trustee invests the sinking fund. The interest earned reduces the deposit that Lamp-Light must make. For example, the trustee reports to LampLight that the sinking fund investment earned $2,000.00. Thus, on July 1, 20X2, Lamp-Light pays only $48,000.00 to the trustee.

> *July 1, 20X2. Paid cash to bond trustee for annual deposit to bond sinking fund, $48,000.00, and recorded interest earned on bond sinking fund, $2,000.00. Check No. 610.*

Bond Sinking Fund is debited for $50,000.00. Cash is credited for $48,000.00, the actual amount deposited. Interest Income is credited for $2,000.00, the amount of interest earned. The journal entry to record the deposit for 20X2 is shown above.

As the bond sinking fund balance increases, the amount of interest earned in a year usually increases. Thus, the amount LampLight must deposit each year decreases.

| | DATE | | ACCOUNT TITLE | DOC. NO. | POST. REF. | DEBIT | CREDIT | |
|---|---|---|---|---|---|---|---|---|
| | GENERAL JOURNAL | | | | | | PAGE 6 | |
| 1 | July 20X4 | 1 | Bonds Payable | M600 | | 250 000 00 | | 1 |
| 2 | | | Bond Sinking Fund | | | | 250 000 00 | 2 |
| 3 | | | | | | | | 3 |

A bond sinking fund is an asset to LampLight until the trustee makes payment to the bondholders. When LampLight's bonds are due, the bond trustee uses the bond sinking fund to pay the bondholders. Paying the amounts owed to bondholders for a bond issue is called **retiring a bond issue**. The journal entry to retire the bonds is shown above.

---

*July 1, 20X4. Received notice from bond trustee that bond issue was retired using bond sinking fund, $250,000.00. Memorandum No. 600.*

---

Bonds Payable is debited for $250,000.00, the total amount of the bond issue. Bond Sinking Fund is credited for $250,000.00, the amount in the fund used to retire the bond issue. After this entry is posted, both Bonds Payable and Bond Sinking Fund will have zero balances.

All of LampLight's bond issue matures on the same date. Bonds that all mature on the same date are called **term bonds**. Sometimes portions of a bond issue mature on different dates. Portions of a bond issue that mature on different dates are called **serial bonds**. For example, a 10-year bond issue with one-tenth of the bonds maturing every year is a serial bond issue. An advantage of serial bonds is that interest does not have to be paid on the total bond issue for the total 10 years.

| Bonds Payable | | | |
|---|---|---|---|
| Retired | 250,000.00 | Balance *(New Bal. zero)* | 250,000.00 |

| Bonds Sinking Fund | | | |
|---|---|---|---|
| Balance *(New Bal. zero)* | 250,000.00 | Retired | 250,000.00 |

# COMPARISON OF CAPITAL STOCK AND BONDS AS A SOURCE OF CORPORATE CAPITAL

**Capital Stock**

1. Stockholders are corporate owners.
2. Capital Stock is a stockholders' equity account.
3. Stockholders have a secondary claim against corporate assets.
4. Dividends are paid to stockholders out of corporate net income.
5. Dividends are not fixed costs and do not have to be paid if net income is insufficient.
6. Amount received from sale of stock is relatively permanent capital; amount invested by stockholders does not have to be returned to them in foreseeable future.

**Bonds**

1. Bondholders are corporate creditors.
2. Bonds Payable is a liability account.
3. Bondholders have a primary, or first, claim against corporate assets.
4. Interest paid to bondholders is a corporate expense.
5. Interest on bonds is a fixed expense; the expense must be paid when due; payment does not depend on amount of net income.
6. Amount received from sale of bonds is not permanent; amount invested by bondholders must be returned to them on bonds' maturity date.

It can take a month or more for a company to issue bonds. The process begins when the company determines the number, par value, interest rate, and term of the bonds. The company must then arrange for a securities broker, known as an *underwriter*, obtain an audit, and receive the approval of the Securities and Exchange Commission. During this time, the market interest rate is almost certain to change from the interest rate of the bonds, known as the *stated interest rate*.

Investors will adjust the price they are willing to pay for the bond, based on the current market rate. If the market interest rate is above the stated interest rate, investors are not willing to pay full price for a bond that yields a below-market rate. Thus, the bond will be sold at a discount. However, if the market interest rate is below the stated interest rate, investors are willing to pay extra to earn an above-market rate. This bond will be sold at a premium.

Mentor Corporation is preparing to issue $2,000,000 in 7.5%, 10-year, $1,000.00 par value bonds. When the time finally arrives to issue the bonds, the market interest rate has risen to 8.0%. As a result, Mentor is able to sell the bonds for only $1,969,477.50, an amount that will enable investors to earn an 8.0% return on their investment. The interest rate earned by investors of bonds is referred to as the *effective interest rate*. Because the effective interest rate is greater than the stated interest rate, the bond is sold at a discount, as reflected in the journal entry to record the bonds.

Cash . . . . . . . . . . . 1,969,477.50
Discount on Bonds
    Payable . . . . . . . . . 30,522.50
    Bonds Payable . . . . . . . . . . . 2,000,000.00

Discount on Bonds Payable is a contra liability account. At any time, the net balance of the Discount on Bonds Payable and Bonds Payable

accounts is the book value of the bonds payable. At the end of the bond term, Mentor must pay the investors $2,000,000.00 even though the bonds were sold for less than that amount. The $2,000,000.00 credit to Bonds Payable reflects this liability.

Mentor also owes the investors a semi-annual interest payment of 7.5% on the $2,000,000.00 face value of the bonds. The amount debited to Interest Expense is calculated using the book value of the bonds multiplied by the effective interest rate. The interest payment is calculated using the face value of the bonds multiplied by the stated interest rate.

Interest Expense . . . . . . 78,779.10
    ($1,969,477.50 × 8.0% × 6/12)
    Discount on Bonds Payable . . . . . . . 3,779.10
    Cash . . . . . . . . . . . . . . . . . . . . . . 75,000.00
    ($2,000,000.00 × 7.5% × 6/12)

The difference between the two amounts, $3,779.10, is credited to Discount on Bonds Payable, reducing the balance of this account. At the final interest payment, the bonds' due date, the balance of Discount on Bonds Payable will be zero and the book value of the bonds will equal their face value.

Each year during the 5-year bond period, Mentor's interest expense will be 8.0% of the bonds' book value. Recording interest expense on bonds payable using the effective interest rate is referred to as the *effective interest rate method*.

**Instructions**

Equity Corporation is preparing to issue $3,000,000 in 8%, 10-year, $1,000.00 par value bonds. At the time of issue, the market interest rate has risen. What is the journal entry to record the bond issue if the bonds are sold for $2,843,213.00?

## terms review

bond
bond issue
trustee
bond sinking fund
retiring a bond issue
term bonds
serial bonds

## audit your understanding

1. What are two advantages of raising needed capital by selling stock?
2. What is an advantage of raising additional capital by borrowing?
3. What is a disadvantage of borrowing additional capital?
4. What accounts are affected, and how, when cash is deposited in a bond sinking fund in the second year of a bond issue?

## work together 12-3

### Journalizing bonds payable transactions

On February 1, 20X1, Cyrotech, Inc., received $300,000.00 cash for a bond issue. The bond agreement provides that a bond sinking fund is to be increased annually by $37,500.00 for the next eight years. The bond trustee has guaranteed Cyrotech an interest rate of 4% on its sinking fund investment. A cash receipts journal, cash payments journal, and general journal are provided in the *Working Papers*. Your instructor will guide you through the following examples.

Feb. 1, 20X1. Received cash for face value of an 8-year, 10%, $500.00 par value bond issue, $300,000.00. Receipt No. 135.
   1, 20X2. Paid cash to bond trustee for annual interest on bond issue, $30,000.00. Check No. 201.
   1, 20X2. Paid cash to bond trustee for first annual deposit to bond sinking fund. Check No. 202.
   1, 20X3. Paid cash to bond trustee for annual interest on bond issue, $30,000.00. Check No. 313.
   1, 20X3. Paid cash to bond trustee for annual deposit to bond sinking fund and recorded interest earned on bond sinking fund. Check No. 314. (Interest earned equals 4% of the bond sinking fund deposit made on February 1, 20X2.)
   3, 20X9. Received notice from bond trustee that bond issue was retired using bond sinking fund, $300,000.00. Memorandum 87.

1. Journalize the transactions.

## on your own 12-3

### Journalizing bonds payable transactions

On May 1, 20X1, Biotech, Inc., received $500,000.00 cash for a bond issue. The bond agreement provides that a bond sinking fund is to be increased annually by $100,000.00 for the next five years. The bond trustee has guaranteed Biotech an interest rate of 5% on its sinking fund investment. A cash receipts journal, cash payments journal, and general journal are provided in the *Working Papers*. Work independently to complete the following problem.

May 1, 20X1. Received cash for face value of a 5-year, 8%, $1,000.00 par value bond issue, $500,000.00. Receipt No. 63.
   1, 20X2. Paid cash to bond trustee for annual interest on bond issue, $40,000.00. Check No. 71.
   1, 20X2. Paid cash to bond trustee for annual deposit to bond sinking fund. Check No. 72.
   1, 20X3. Paid cash to bond trustee for annual interest on bond issue. Check No. 173.
   1, 20X3. Paid cash to bond trustee for annual deposit to bond sinking fund and recorded interest earned on bond sinking fund. Check No. 174. (Interest earned equals 5% of the bond sinking fund deposit made on May 1, 20X2.)
   2, 20X6. Received notice from bond trustee that bond issue was retired using bond sinking fund, $500,000.00. Memorandum 33.

1. Journalize the transactions.

## SUMMARY

**After completing this chapter, you can**

1. Define accounting terms related to acquiring capital for a corporation.

2. Identify accounting concepts and practices related to acquiring capital for a corporation.

3. Journalize entries for issuing additional capital stock.

4. Journalize entries for buying and selling treasury stock.

5. Journalize entries for bonds payable.

# Explore Accounting

EXPLORE ACCOUNTING • EXPLORE ACCOUNTING • EXPLORE ACCO

## Convertible Bonds

Corporations often use long-term bonds to raise the investment capital required to expand operations. A bond is a contract between the corporation and the bondholder. The corporation promises to pay the bondholder interest during the life of the bond and the bond principle at the maturity date.

A corporation can add a variety of provisions to a bond contract. One such provision is referred to as a conversion option. A bond that can be exchanged for a specified number of capital stock is called a *convertible bond*. At the bondholder's request, the bond can be traded, or converted, for a specified number of shares of the corporation.

Assume that Chris Harrison purchased a 10%, 20-year, $1,000 convertible bond from Castle Corporation. The bond is convertible to 40 shares of Castle's capital stock. Castle's stock is traded at $12 per share on the bond issuance date. Chris can elect to convert the bond any time during the life of the bond.

Chris has no incentive to convert the bond to stock until the market value of the stock climbs above the $25 conversion price ($1,000 bond/ 40 shares = $25 per share). The market price of the stock in the future will determine whether Chris elects to convert his bond.

Suppose the market price climbs to $20 per share but is not expected to increase. Chris would

not convert his bond to stock, since the converted stock would only be worth $800 ($20 × 40 shares). Thus, Chris would hold the bond to maturity and receive the $1,000 maturity value.

If the market price climbs to $30 per share, Chris can convert his bond and receive 40 shares of stock. The stock is immediately worth $1,200 ($30 × 40 shares). Chris can sell his stock, earning an instant $200 gain. However, Chris can also hold the stock in hope that the stock price will continue to rise.

Why would a corporation issue convertible bonds? When purchasing the bond, Chris knew that there was the potential to earn money in addition to the interest income if the stock rose above $25. Thus, Chris accepted a 12% interest rate on the bond instead of the 13% market rate for bonds with no conversion feature. Thus, Castle Corporation's interest expense was reduced due to the conversion feature.

**Required:**

Assume Chris converted his stock and immediately sold the stock for a $200 gain. Research how this $200 gain should be recorded in the corporation's financial statements. Do you agree with the findings of your research?

# 12-1 APPLICATION PROBLEM  PEACHTREE  QUICKBOOKS

### Journalizing capital stock transactions

PC Design, Inc., is authorized to issue 200,000 shares of $5.00 stated value common stock and 50,000 shares of 12%, $100.00 par value preferred stock. PC Design has 25,000 shares of common stock outstanding.

**Transactions:**

Feb. 8. Andre Cashman sent a check for 5,000 shares of $5.00 stated value common stock at $5.00 per share, $25,000.00. R398.

26. Jason Gutto exchanged a parcel of land at an agreed value of $30,000.00 for 300 shares of $100.00 par value preferred stock. M67.

Apr. 15. Jacquelyn Parker sent a $40,000.00 check for 400 shares of $100.00 par value preferred stock at $100.00 per share. R518.

Aug. 25. Received a $48,000.00 check from Lynn Kruschke for 500 shares of $100.00 par value preferred stock at $96.00 per share. R601.

Dec. 11. Received cash from Behrooz Behzadi for 200 shares of $100.00 par value preferred stock at $102.00 per share, $20,400.00. R698.

**Instructions:**

Journalize the transactions completed during the current year. Use page 2 of a cash receipts journal and a general journal. Source documents are abbreviated as follows: memorandum, M; receipt, R.

# 12-2 APPLICATION PROBLEM

### Journalizing treasury stock transactions

Advanced Laser, Inc., is authorized to issue 150,000 shares of $10.00 stated value common stock. Advanced Laser has 50,000 shares of stock outstanding.

**Transactions:**

Feb. 21. Paid cash to Corey Fiske for 400 shares of $10.00 stated value common stock at $10.00 per share, $4,000.00. C87.

27. Received cash from Aurelia Gillien for 125 shares of treasury stock at $10.00 per share, $1,250.00. Treasury stock was bought on February 21 at $10.00 per share. R126.

Mar. 22. Paid cash to Leona Metzger for 750 shares of $10.00 stated value common stock at $11.00 per share, $8,250.00. C138.

Apr. 15. Received cash from Efren Merrill for 275 shares of treasury stock at $12.00 per share, $3,300.00. Treasury stock was bought on February 21 at $10.00 per share. R151.

July 30. Received cash from Susan Matsuda for 300 shares of treasury stock at $10.00 per share, $3,000.00. Treasury stock was bought on March 22 at $11.00 per share. R203.

**Instructions:**

Journalize the transactions completed during the current year. Use page 2 of a cash receipts journal and page 3 of a cash payments journal. Source documents are abbreviated as follows: check, C; receipt, R.

# 12-3 APPLICATION PROBLEM

**Journalizing bonds payable transactions**

On January 1, 20X1, Security Communications, Inc., received cash, $200,000.00, for a bond issue. The bond agreement provides that a bond sinking fund is to be increased by $20,000.00 every six months for the next five years.

**Transactions:**

Jan. 1, 20X1.   Received cash for the face value of a 5-year, 9%, $1,000.00 par value bond issue, $200,000.00. R104.

July 1, 20X1.   Paid cash to bond trustee for semiannual interest on bond issue, $9,000.00. C294.

July 1, 20X1.   Paid cash to bond trustee for semiannual deposit to bond sinking fund, $20,000.00. C295.

Jan. 1, 20X2.   Paid cash to bond trustee for semiannual interest on bond issue, $9,000.00. C504.

Jan. 1, 20X2.   Paid cash to bond trustee for semiannual deposit to bond sinking fund, $19,200.00, and recorded interest earned on bond sinking fund, $800.00. C505.

Jan. 4, 20X6.   Received notice from bond trustee that bond issue was retired using bond sinking fund, $200,000.00. M290.

**Instructions:**

Journalize the transactions. Use page 1 of a cash receipts journal, page 8 of a cash payments journal, and page 1 of a general journal. Source documents are abbreviated as follows: check, C; memorandum, M; receipt, R.

# 12-4 MASTERY PROBLEM

**Journalizing stock and bond transactions**

On January 1, 20X1, Sentry VideoLink, Inc., received cash, $50,000.00, for a bond issue. The bond agreement provides that Sentry VideoLink is to increase a bond sinking fund by $5,000.00 every six months for the next five years.

**Transactions:**

Jan. 1, 20X1.   Received cash for the face value of a 5-year, 12%, $1,000.00 par value bond issue, $50,000.00. R198.

Jan. 12, 20X1.  Received cash from Stuart Peterson for 1,000 shares of $10.00 stated value common stock at $10.00 per share. R210.

Feb. 21, 20X1.  Paid cash to Ruben Mendoza for 900 shares of $10.00 stated value common stock at $12.00 per share. C97.

Feb. 28, 20X1.  Received cash from Tai Banh for 500 shares of treasury stock at $12.00 per share. Treasury stock was bought on February 21 at $12.00 per share. R215.

Mar. 13, 20X1.  Received cash from Rebecca Munson for 200 shares of $10.00 stated value common stock at $15.00 per share. R220.

Mar. 22, 20X1.  Paid cash to Dermot Concannon for 2,000 shares of $10.00 stated value common stock at $16.00 per share. C138.

Apr. 8, 20X1.   Received cash from Rachel Kaplan for 100 shares of $100.00 par value preferred stock at $101.00 per share. R226.

Apr. 15, 20X1.  Received cash from Blake Kenefick for 300 shares of treasury stock at $18.00 per share. Treasury stock was bought on February 21 at $12.00 per share. R231.

May 15, 20X1.   Received cash from Paige Anderson for 800 shares of $100.00 par value preferred stock at $97.50 per share. R232.

July 1, 20X1.   Paid cash to bond trustee for semiannual interest on bond issue, $3,000.00. C200.

July 1, 20X1.   Paid cash to bond trustee for semiannual deposit to bond sinking fund, $5,000.00. C201.

July 14, 20X1.  Received delivery equipment from Travis Kimball at an agreed-on value of $20,000.00 for 200 shares of $100.00 par value preferred stock. M148.

July 23, 20X1.   Received cash from Brad Manning for 300 shares of treasury stock at $14.00 per share. Treasury stock consisted of 100 shares bought on February 21 at $12.00 per share and 200 shares bought on March 22 at $16.00 per share. R353.

Jan. 1, 20X2.   Paid cash to bond trustee for semiannual interest on bond issue, $3,000.00. C504.

Jan. 1, 20X2.   Paid cash to bond trustee for semiannual deposit to bond sinking fund, $4,600.00, and recorded interest earned on bond sinking fund, $400.00. C505.

Jan. 1, 20X6.   Received notice from bond trustee that bond issue was retired using bond sinking fund, $50,000.00. M491.

**Instructions:**

Journalize the transactions. Use page 1 of a cash receipts journal, page 8 of a cash payments journal, and page 1 of a general journal. Source documents are abbreviated as follows: check, C; memorandum, M; receipt, R.

# 12-5 CHALLENGE PROBLEM
## Journalizing stock and bond transactions

Interspan Technologies, Inc., is authorized to issue 100,000 shares of $1.00 stated value common stock and 25,000 shares of 10%, $100.00 par value preferred stock. On January 1, 20X1, Interspan has the following outstanding stock: common stock, 40,000 shares; preferred stock, 10,000 shares. Provisions of a bond issue, January 1, 20X1, include (a) payment of interest on the bond issue on July 1 and January 1 of each year and (b) assurance by Interspan of an increase of $20,000.00 in a bond sinking fund on July 1 and January 1 of each year.

**Transactions:**

Jan. 1, 20X1.   Cash was received for the face value of a 10-year, 10%, $1,000.00 par value bond issue, $200,000.00. R51.

Feb. 5, 20X1.   Paid John Salas for 5,000 shares of $1.00 stated value common stock at $1.60 per share. C120.

Feb. 12, 20X1.   Cash was received from Michael Donato for 15,000 shares of $1.00 stated value common stock at $1.20 per share. R64.

Feb. 20, 20X1.   Carmen Romero paid cash for 500 shares of $100.00 par value preferred stock at $100.00 per share. R105.

Mar. 14, 20X1.   Office equipment was received from Elaine Zaballos at an agreed-on value of $7,000.00 for 5,000 shares of $1.00 stated value common stock. M195.

Apr. 3, 20X1.   Jennifer Chapman paid cash for 1,000 shares of treasury stock at $1.50 per share, $1,500.00. Treasury stock was bought on February 5 at $1.60 per share. R210.

May 10, 20X1.   Deana Maxson paid cash for 300 shares of $100.00 par value preferred stock at $99.00 per share. R387.

July 1, 20X1.   Paid semiannual interest to bond trustee on bonds payable. C389.

July 1, 20X1.   Paid cash to bond trustee for semiannual deposit to bond sinking fund, $20,000.00. C390.

Sept.18, 20X1.   Cash was received from Perry McCarthy for 2,500 shares of treasury stock at $2.00 per share. Treasury stock was bought on February 5 at $1.60 per share. R561.

Oct. 14, 20X1.   Raj Vaudagna paid cash for 150 shares of $100.00 par value preferred stock at $103.00 per share. R600.

Jan. 1, 20X2.   Paid cash to bond trustee for semiannual interest on bonds payable. C634.

Jan. 1, 20X2.   Paid cash to bond trustee for semiannual deposit to bond sinking fund. Interest earned on money in sinking fund since last payment on July 1, $800.00. C635.

Jan. 2, 20X6.   Received notice from bond trustee that bond issue was retired using bond sinking fund, $200,000.00. M428.

**Instructions:**

Journalize the transactions. Use page 1 of a cash receipts journal, page 2 of a cash payments journal, and page 1 of a general journal. Source documents are abbreviated as follows: check, C; memorandum, M; receipt, R.

Acquiring Additional Capital for a Corporation

### applied communication

The most important step in the employment process is the interview. During the interview, an employer will ask you a variety of questions about your abilities, qualifications, and attitudes. You must be thoroughly prepared to answer a prospective employer's questions. Two of the most frequently asked interview questions involve your qualifications for the job and your interest in working for the company.

**Required:**

1. Find a job advertisement in the newspaper or other source for a position for which you are qualified. Write several paragraphs discussing your qualifications for the job.

2. Research the company identified in the job advertisement. Write several paragraphs explaining your interest in working for the company, using specific facts about it.

### case for critical thinking

Cecil Thomas pays $12,000.00 for 2,000 shares of $5.00 stated value common stock of Datkins, Inc. A year later, Mr. Thomas sells the 2,000 shares of stock to Sally Gilliam for a total of $14,000.00. Ms. Gilliam sends a notice to Datkins so that ownership can be changed on the corporation's stock records. An accounting clerk at Datkins is not sure of the correct journal entry. What advice would you give the accounting clerk?

### SCANS workplace competency

**Thinking Skills:** Reasoning

**Concept:** Competent employees comprehend basic rules and principles and apply them in solving problems. Reasoning also includes the ability to prepare a series of conclusions, based on a set of given facts.

**Application:** You have learned a variety of accounting principles and concepts in Chapters 5-12. Using your reasoning ability, apply these new accounting principles and previously learned concepts by completing Reinforcement Activity 2, Part A.

## • auditing for errors

Gonzalez Corporation is authorized to issue 1,000,000 shares of $10.00 par value common stock and 100,000 shares of 10%, $100.00 par value preferred stock. The company has the following stock transactions:

| | |
|---|---|
| June 1 | Started the business by issuing 25,000 shares of common stock for $15 per share. |
| June 30 | Issued 3,000 shares of preferred stock for $120 per share. |
| July 7 | Bought 2,000 shares of common stock as treasury stock for $10 per share. |
| August 10 | Sold 500 shares of treasury stock for $12 per share. |
| September 30 | Issued 300 shares of preferred stock for $130 per share. |

The bookkeeper has compiled the following data related to the preferred and common stock as of September 30.

| Type of Stock | No. of Shares Issued | No. of Shares of Treasury Stock | No. of Shares Outstanding |
|---|---|---|---|
| Common | 25,500 | 2,000 | 23,500 |
| Preferred | 3,000 | 0 | 3,300 |

### Instructions:

On a separate piece of paper, redo the chart, making any necessary corrections.

## • analyzing Costco's financial statements

Corporations can issue a variety of kinds or classes of stock. Most companies issue common stock. Some companies are also authorized to issue preferred stock. Information about the par value of each kind of stock and the number of shares authorized, issued, and outstanding can be found in the equity section of a corporation's balance sheet. The following definitions will help you with this activity.

If the number of shares issues and outstanding are equal, it means that company has no treasury stock.

### Instructions:

1. Using Appendix B in this textbook, go to the balance sheet for Costco Corporation on page B-5. What kinds of stock is Costco authorized to issue?

2. What is the par value of each kind of stock?

3. How many shares of each kind of stock are authorized?

4. How many shares of preferred stock are issued as of 2003?

5. How many shares of common stock are issued as of 2003?

6. How many shares of common stock are outstanding as of 2003?

7. How many shares of treasury stock does Costco hold?

# Automated Accounting

## Understanding Graphs

### Using Graphs and Charts

Graphs and charts are pictorial representations of data that may be used to effectively communicate summary information. Graphs and charts can be produced by the computer, displayed on the monitor, and printed to a printer. Graphs and charts are used to clarify the meanings of the words and numbers that appear in the financial statements. They are commonly used to enhance presentations, track sales, monitor expenses, identify trends, and make forecasts.

Graphs and charts can be used to enhance written or oral presentations. In reports, graphs and charts add a visual break for the reader. The reader will often review the graphs and charts to get a quick summary of written material or numerical data. Speakers may use electronic presentation software or overhead transparencies to illustrate important points. Graphs and charts are often an important part of these presentations.

*Automated Accounting 8.0* and higher can generate the following types of graphs and charts:

- The Income Statement graph option will produce a bar graph of the major portions of an income statement: revenue, cost of goods sold, operating expenses, and net income.

- The Expense Distribution graph option will produce a pie chart of the expenses.

- The Top Customers option will produce a bar graph of the top five customers in the accounts receivable ledger. If there are no accounts receivable entries made in a sales journal, an "Insufficient data to graph" message will be displayed.

- The Balance Sheet graph option will produce a bar graph of assets, liabilities, and owners' equity.

- The Sales graph option will produce a line graph of the sales by

day of the month. If sales have not been recorded in the sales journal data entry window, an "Insufficient data to graph" message will be displayed.

### Creating a Graph

To prepare a graph based on financial data:

1. Choose the Graph Selection menu item from the Reports menu or click the Graphs toolbar button.

2. When the Graph Selection dialog box appears, as shown below, select an option.

3. A 3-D bar graph is shown below.

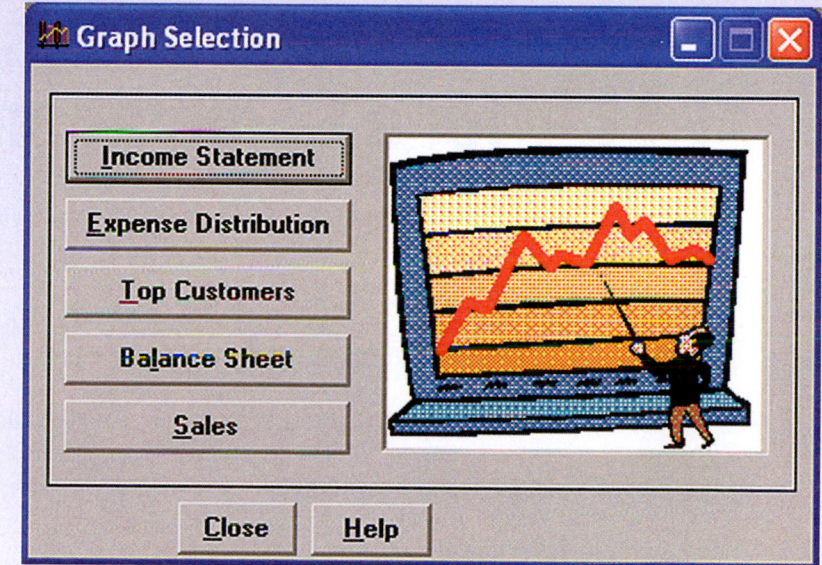

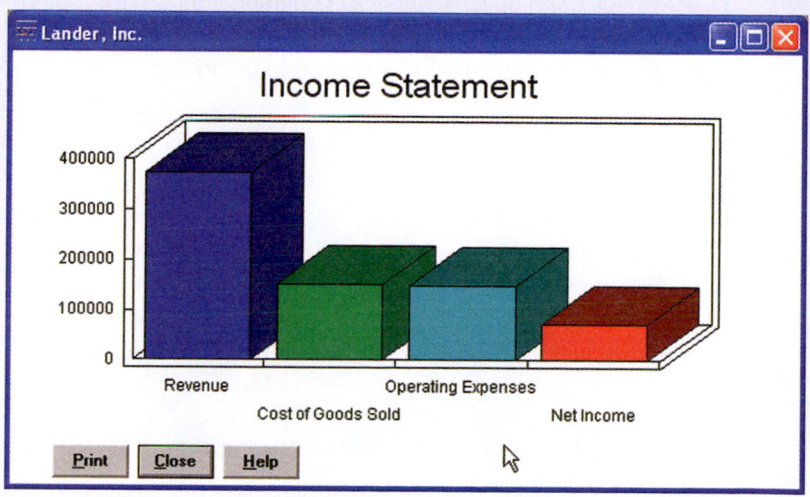

# 13 Financial Analysis and Reporting for a Corporation

*After studying Chapter 13, you will be able to:*

1. Define terms related to financial analysis and reporting for a corporation.

2. Identify concepts and practices related to financial analysis and reporting for a corporation.

3. Prepare a work sheet for a corporation.

4. Calculate federal income tax for a corporation.

5. Prepare and analyze financial statements for a corporation.

6. Prepare selected end-of-fiscal-period work for a corporation.

- amortization
- earnings per share
- equity per share
- market value

- price-earnings ratio
- rate earned on average stockholders' equity

- rate earned on average total assets

Point Your Browser
accountingxtra.swlearning.com

## • Medtronics

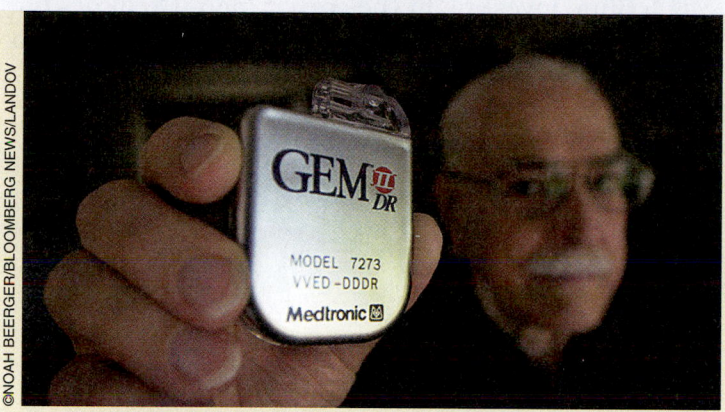

©NOAH BEERGER/BLOOMBERG NEWS/LANDOV

### MEDTRONICS: IMPROVING A LIFE EVERY SEVEN SECONDS

An opening page of the Medtronics 2003 Annual Report states, "Every 7 seconds, we help improve another life." Medtronics is a leading manufacturer of medical devices such as pacemakers, heart pumps and valves, implantable brain stimulation systems, internal insulin pumps, thoracic and lumbar spine systems, and much more.

Medtronics' mission is "to contribute to human welfare by the application of biomedical engineering in the research, design, manufacture, and sale of products that alleviate pain, restore health, and extend life."

In order to accomplish this mission, Medtronics must constantly search for new medical devices, treatments, or processes. In a business, this is commonly referred to as "Research and Development," or "R & D." Medtronics has R & D facilities throughout the world. In addition, it sometimes purchases in-process R & D when it acquires another company. All of this R & D is designed to help Medtronics remain a leader in its field.

### Critical Thinking

1. Medtronics spent $749.4 million on R & D in one year and $646.3 million the prior year. Calculate the percentage increase for R & D.
2. Pick a company outside the medical device industry. Identify the R & D in which this company would be involved.

Xtra!
Today
accountingxtra.swlearning.com

Source: www.medtronics.com

ACCOUNTING IN THE REAL WORLD • ACCOUNTING IN THE REAL WORLD • ACCOUNTING IN THE REAL WORLD

## internet activity

### COLLEGE ACCOUNTING PROGRAMS

Search the Internet for "public colleges accounting programs" in your state or a neighboring state. Search one such program and answer the following questions:

### Instructions

1. What is the name of the college or university?
2. Does this college offer a bachelor's degree (4 years) or an associate's degree (2 years)?
3. How many semester hours are required for this degree?
4. List one class that is required for this degree.

INTERNET RESEARCH ACTIVITY • INTERNET RESEARCH ACTIVITY • INTERNET RESEARCH ACTIVITY •

# 13-1 Work Sheet for a Corporation

Corporations prepare three important financial statements at the end of each fiscal period to report their financial progress and condition. [CONCEPT: Adequate Disclosure]

1. Income statement.
2. Statement of stockholders' equity.
3. Balance sheet.

Corporations normally provide an analysis of the financial statements to help interested persons understand and use the information. Information on the income statement is used to analyze component percentages and earnings per share. Information on the statement of stockholders' equity is used to analyze equity per share and determine price-earnings ratio. Balance sheet information is used to determine accounts receivable turnover ratio, the rate earned on average stockholders' equity, and the rate earned on average total assets.

A corporation's board of directors uses the information on the financial statements for making management decisions. The board of directors also uses the information to determine whether to distribute earnings to stockholders. Stockholders and other investors use the information to determine whether to begin or continue investing in the corporation. Creditors use the information to determine whether the corporation will be able to meet its credit obligations.

©GETTY IMAGES/PHOTODISC

## making ethical decisions

### Client Referrals

Mason Brick Company has asked its public accounting firm, Farris & Associates, to develop a comprehensive health and retirement program. Knowing that the firm lacks the expertise needed to perform these services, Sarah Farris, a CPA and the managing partner of Farris & Associates, refers Mason Brick Company to another CPA firm, Navarro & Simmons. In appreciation for the referral, Navarro & Simmons gives Sarah Farris an all-expense ski trip to Aspen. Neither accounting firm informs Mason Brick Company of the ski trip.

**Instructions**

Determine whether the referral was made in accordance with the AICPA *Code of Professional Conduct*.

# ORGANIZATION EXPENSE ADJUSTMENT

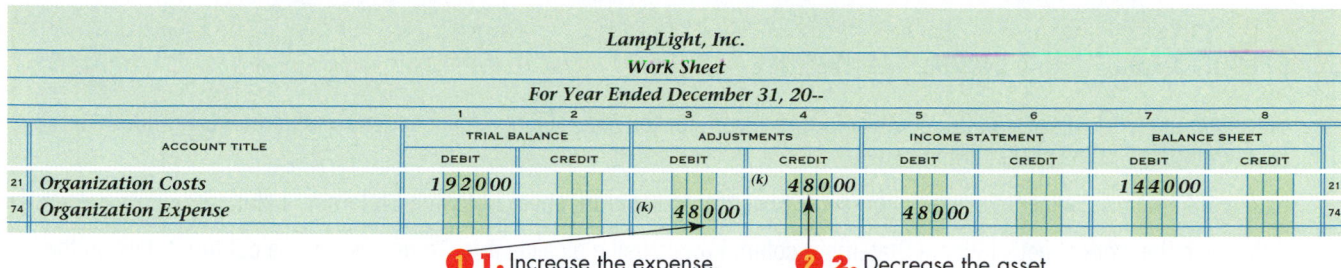

**LampLight, Inc.**
**Work Sheet**
**For Year Ended December 31, 20--**

|  | ACCOUNT TITLE | TRIAL BALANCE | | ADJUSTMENTS | | INCOME STATEMENT | | BALANCE SHEET | |  |
|---|---|---|---|---|---|---|---|---|---|---|
|  |  | DEBIT | CREDIT | DEBIT | CREDIT | DEBIT | CREDIT | DEBIT | CREDIT |  |
| 21 | Organization Costs | 1 9 2 0 00 | | | (k) 4 8 0 00 | | | 1 4 4 0 00 | | 21 |
| 74 | Organization Expense | | | (k) 4 8 0 00 | | 4 8 0 00 | | | | 74 |

**1.** Increase the expense.  **2.** Decrease the asset.

LampLight prepares a work sheet at the end of the fiscal period. Most of its adjustments are similar to those described for Zytech in Part 1. LampLight also records adjustments for organization expense and federal income tax expense.

Corporate organization costs are intangible assets. A common accounting practice is to write off intangible assets over a period of years. Recognizing a portion of an expense in each of several years is called **amortization**.

LampLight incurred total organization costs of $2,400.00. LampLight spreads the $2,400.00 expense over five years. Thus, one-fifth of this amount, $480.00, is amortized in each of the first five years. In the first year, $480.00 was amortized as an expense. An adjustment is planned on the work sheet for the second year's amortization, as shown above.

Organization Expense is debited for $480.00. Organization Costs is credited for $480.00. The new balance of Organization Costs, $1,440.00, is the amount to be amortized in the next three years.

## FYI
### FOR YOUR INFORMATION

A recent FASB rule change requires many companies to write off organization costs in the company's first fiscal year. This change will effectively eliminate the amortization of organization costs. However, amortization continues to apply to other intangible assets, such as patents and copyrights owned by a company.

# FEDERAL INCOME TAX EXPENSE ADJUSTMENT

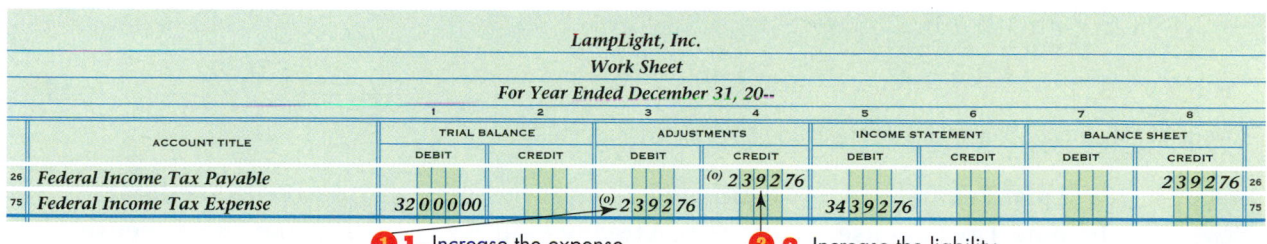

**LampLight, Inc.**
**Work Sheet**
**For Year Ended December 31, 20--**

|  | ACCOUNT TITLE | TRIAL BALANCE | | ADJUSTMENTS | | INCOME STATEMENT | | BALANCE SHEET | |  |
|---|---|---|---|---|---|---|---|---|---|---|
|  |  | DEBIT | CREDIT | DEBIT | CREDIT | DEBIT | CREDIT | DEBIT | CREDIT |  |
| 26 | Federal Income Tax Payable | | | | (o) 2 3 9 2 76 | | | | 2 3 9 2 76 | 26 |
| 75 | Federal Income Tax Expense | 32 0 0 0 00 | | (o) 2 3 9 2 76 | | 34 3 9 2 76 | | | | 75 |

**1.** Increase the expense.  **2.** Increase the liability.

At the beginning of the year, LampLight *estimated* its federal income tax for the year to be $32,000.00. LampLight paid the estimated tax to the federal government in four equal quarterly installments of $8,000.00 each. As of December

31, LampLight calculated its *actual* federal income tax to determine whether it owes additional income tax. An adjustment is planned on the work sheet for the additional amount owed, as shown above.

# CALCULATING FEDERAL INCOME TAX EXPENSE

## STEPS CALCULATING FEDERAL INCOME TAX EXPENSE

**1** Complete the work sheet's Adjustments columns except for the federal income tax expense adjustment. Do not total the Adjustments columns at this time.

**2** Extend all amounts, except Federal Income Tax Expense, to the work sheet's Income Statement columns.

**3** Determine the work sheet's Income Statement column totals using a calculator. Do not record the column totals on the work sheet. Calculate the difference between the two totals. The difference is the net income before federal income tax. LampLight's net income before federal income tax is:

| Income Statement Credit Column Total | – | Income Statement Debit Column Total before Federal Income Tax | = | Net Income before Federal Income Tax |
|---|---|---|---|---|
| $883,782.75 | – | $752,647.48 | = | $131,135.27 |

**4** Calculate the amount of federal income tax using a tax rate table furnished by the Internal Revenue Service. The Internal Revenue Service distributes corporate tax rate tables each year. LampLight's actual federal income tax is calculated as shown using the following tax rate table:

15% of net income before taxes, zero to $50,000.00
Plus 25% of net income before taxes, $50,000.00 to $75,000.00
Plus 34% of net income before taxes, $75,000.00 to $100,000.00
Plus 39% of net income before taxes, $100,000.00 to $335,000.00
Plus 34% of net income before taxes over $335,000.00

| Net Income before Taxes | × | Tax Rate | = | Federal Income Tax Amount |
|---|---|---|---|---|
| $50,000.00 | × | 15% | = | $ 7,500.00 |
| Plus 25,000.00 | × | 25% | = | 6,250.00 |
| Plus 25,000.00 | × | 34% | = | 8,500.00 |
| Plus 31,135.27 | × | 39% | = | 12,142.76 |
| $131,135.27 | | | | $34,392.76 |

**5** Calculate the amount of accrued federal income tax expense as follows:

| Total Federal Income Tax Expense | – | Estimated Federal Income Tax Already Paid | = | Accrued Federal Income Tax Expense |
|---|---|---|---|---|
| $34,392.76 | – | $32,000.00 | = | $2,392.76 |

**6** Record the federal income tax expense adjustment, as shown on page 371.

**7** Extend the new balance of Federal Income Tax Payable, *2,392.76*, to the Balance Sheet Credit column.

**8** Extend the new balance of Federal Income Tax Expense, *34,392.76*, to the Income Statement Debit column.

**9** Total the work sheet's Adjustments, Income Statement, and Balance Sheet columns as shown on pages 374–375.

Federal Income Tax Expense is debited for $2,392.76. Federal Income Tax Payable is credited for $2,392.76. The new balance of Federal Income Tax Expense, $34,392.76, is the total amount of federal income tax due based on the net income before federal income tax.

# Explore Accounting

## Contingent Liabilities

One of the duties of an accountant is to ensure that the financial statements of a company reflect a true picture of the financial position of that company. Business transactions affect the accounts of a business and are reflected in journal entries, which are posted to accounts. However, other items can affect the financial position of the company and these items are not automatically entered into the books of a business.

One such item is called a *contingent liability*. A contingent liability is a possible future obligation that arises from a current condition and is dependent upon a future event occurring. One example of a contingent liability is a pending lawsuit against a company. The possible future obligation is the chance that the company may lose the lawsuit and have to pay a penalty or fine. The current condition is the fact that the lawsuit has already been filed. The future event is the ruling of the court. Depending on the court ruling, the company may or may not have a financial obligation.

The accountant must analyze each contingent liability to determine if it must be included in the financial statements. The first step is to determine how likely it is that a loss will occur in the future. GAAP lists three possibilities: probable, possible, and remote. If it is probable that the loss will occur and if the loss can be reasonably estimated, the company must add a liability to the balance sheet in the amount of the probable loss. At the same time, a loss must be shown on the income statement.

If it is probable that the loss will occur but the loss cannot be reasonably estimated, the company does not have to add a liability to its balance sheet. However, the company must disclose the possible loss, which means that the company must tell about the lawsuit in the notes that accompany the financial statements. The same treatment is required if the chance of loss is possible.

If the chance of loss is remote, the company does not have to do anything.

### Instructions

Listed below are activities that have already occurred for which the outcome is unknown at the end of the year. For each activity, state if a liability must be added to the balance sheet, if the company must disclose the activity in the notes, or if the company can do nothing.

1. The company is involved in a lawsuit. The legal team thinks it is probable that the company will lose the suit, but it has no idea of the amount of probable loss.

2. The company has published a $1-off coupon in the local paper. The company has estimated that 35% of the coupons will be redeemed.

3. The company is involved in a second lawsuit. The legal team feels that the chance of an unfavorable verdict is remote.

**LampLight, Inc.**
**Work Sheet**
**For Year Ended December 31, 20--**

| | ACCOUNT TITLE | Trial Balance Debit | Trial Balance Credit | Adjustments Debit | Adjustments Credit | Income Statement Debit | Income Statement Credit | Balance Sheet Debit | Balance Sheet Credit |
|---|---|---|---|---|---|---|---|---|---|
| 1 | Cash | 2543640 | | | | | | 2543640 | |
| 2 | Petty Cash | 25000 | | | | | | 25000 | |
| 3 | Notes Receivable | 1000000 | | | | | | 1000000 | |
| 4 | Interest Receivable | | | (a) 100000 | | | | 100000 | |
| 5 | Accounts Receivable | 13523454 | | | | | | 13523454 | |
| 6 | Allow. for Uncoll. Accts. | | 42013 | | (b) 627750 | | | | 669763 |
| 7 | Subscriptions Receivable | | | | | | | | |
| 8 | Merchandise Inventory | 26745309 | | | (c) 869790 | | | 25875519 | |
| 9 | Supplies—Sales | 1431567 | | | (d) 586904 | | | 844663 | |
| 10 | Supplies—Administrative | 2261370 | | | (e) 1445640 | | | 815730 | |
| 11 | Prepaid Insurance | 1690000 | | | (f) 591131 | | | 1098869 | |
| 12 | Prepaid Interest | | | (g) 1047 | | | | 1047 | |
| 13 | Bond Sinking Fund | 5000000 | | | | | | 5000000 | |
| 14 | Store Equipment | 14298334 | | | | | | 14298334 | |
| 15 | Accum. Depr.—Store Equip. | | 1512300 | | (h) 1675300 | | | | 3187600 |
| 16 | Building | 16500000 | | | | | | 16500000 | |
| 17 | Accum. Depr.—Building | | 825000 | | (i) 825000 | | | | 1650000 |
| 18 | Office Equipment | 7392823 | | | | | | 7392823 | |
| 19 | Accum. Depr.—Office Equip. | | 765200 | | (j) 973413 | | | | 1738613 |
| 20 | Land | 13300000 | | | | | | 13300000 | |
| 21 | Organization Costs | 192000 | | | (k) 48000 | | | 144000 | |
| 22 | Interest Payable | | | | (l) 1500000 | | | | 1500000 |
| 23 | Accounts Payable | | 3058540 | | | | | | 3058540 |
| 24 | Employee Income Tax Pay. | | 123890 | | | | | | 123890 |
| 25 | Federal Income Tax Pay. | | | | (o) 239276 | | | | 239276 |
| 26 | Social Security Tax Payable | | 62480 | | (n) 4119 | | | | 66599 |
| 27 | Medicare Tax Payable | | 14410 | | (n) 951 | | | | 15361 |
| 28 | Salaries Payable | | | | (m) 63373 | | | | 63373 |
| 29 | Sales Tax Payable | | 215474 | | | | | | 215474 |
| 30 | Unemploy. Tax Pay.—Federal | | 8745 | | (n) 120 | | | | 8865 |
| 31 | Unemploy. Tax Pay.—State | | 59029 | | (n) 810 | | | | 59839 |
| 32 | Health Ins. Premiums Payable | | 42800 | | | | | | 42800 |
| 33 | Dividends Payable | | 2957500 | | | | | | 2957500 |
| 34 | Bonds Payable | | 25000000 | | | | | | 25000000 |
| 35 | Capital Stock—Common | | 32100000 | | | | | | 32100000 |
| 36 | Stock Subscribed—Common | | | | | | | | |

| Line | Account Title | Trial Balance Debit | Trial Balance Credit | Adjustments Debit | Adjustments Credit | Income Statement Debit | Income Statement Credit | Balance Sheet Debit | Balance Sheet Credit |
|---|---|---|---|---|---|---|---|---|---|
| 37 | Pd.in Cap. in Exc. of St. Val.—Com. | | 20000 | | | | | | 20000 |
| 38 | Capital Stock—Preferred | | 1700000 | | | | | | 1700000 |
| 39 | Stock Subscribed—Preferred | | | | | | | | |
| 40 | Pd.in Cap. in Exc. of Par Val.—Pref. | | 800000 | | | | | | 800000 |
| 41 | Disc. on Sale of Preferred Stock | 500000 | | | | | | 500000 | |
| 42 | Treasury Stock | 180000 | | | | | | 180000 | |
| 43 | Pd.in Cap. from Sale of Tr. Stock | | 50000 | | | | | | 50000 |
| 44 | Retained Earnings | | 5858835 | | | | | | 5858835 |
| 45 | Dividends—Common | 1597500 | | | | | | 1597500 | |
| 46 | Dividends—Preferred | 1360000 | | | | | | 1360000 | |
| 47 | Income Summary | | | (c) 869790 | | 869790 | | | |
| 48 | Sales | | 87295240 | | | | 87295240 | | |
| 49 | Sales Discount | 869512 | | | | 869512 | | | |
| 50 | Sales Ret. and Allow. | 290056 | | | | 290056 | | | |
| 51 | Purchases | 45539648 | | | | 45539648 | | | |
| 52 | Purchases Discount | | 671035 | | | | 671035 | | |
| 53 | Purchases Ret. and Allow. | | 267000 | | | | 267000 | | |
| 54 | Advertising Expense | 1778200 | | | | 1778200 | | | |
| 55 | Credit Card Fee Expense | 628500 | | | | 628500 | | | |
| 56 | Depr. Exp.—Store Equip. | | | (h) 1675300 | | 1675300 | | | |
| 57 | Miscellaneous Exp.—Sales | 940612 | | | | 940612 | | | |
| 58 | Salary Expense—Sales | 6322600 | | (m) 45789 | | 6368389 | | | |
| 59 | Supplies Expense—Sales | | | (a) 586904 | | 586904 | | | |
| 60 | Depr. Expense—Building | | | (g) 825000 | | 825000 | | | |
| 61 | Depr. Exp.—Office Equip. | | | (i) 973413 | | 973413 | | | |
| 62 | Insurance Expense | | | (f) 591131 | | 591131 | | | |
| 63 | Miscellaneous Exp.—Admin. | 1257068 | | | | 1257068 | | | |
| 64 | Payroll Taxes Expense | 990240 | | (n) 6000 | | 996240 | | | |
| 65 | Property Tax Expense | 670000 | | | | 670000 | | | |
| 66 | Salary Expense—Admin. | 2364333 | | (m) 17584 | | 2381917 | | | |
| 67 | Supplies Expense—Admin. | | | (e) 1445640 | | 1445640 | | | |
| 68 | Uncollectible Accounts Exp. | | | (b) 627750 | | 627750 | | | |
| 69 | Utilities Expense | 2872725 | | | | 2872725 | | | |
| 70 | Gain on Plant Assets | | | | | | | | |
| 71 | Interest Income | | 45000 | | (a) 100000 | | 145000 | | |
| 72 | Interest Expense | 1530000 | | (l) 1500000 | (g) 1047 | 3028953 | | | |
| 73 | Loss on Plant Assets | | | | | | | | |
| 74 | Organization Expense | | | (k) 48000 | | 48000 | | | |
| 75 | Federal Inc. Tax Expense | 3200000 | | (o) 239276 | | 3439276 | | | |
| 76 | | 1787944491 | 1787944491 | 9552624 | 9552624 | 78704024 | 88378275 | 106100579 | 96426328 |
| 77 | Net Inc. after Fed. Inc. Tax | | | | | 9674251 | | | 9674251 |
| 78 | | | | | | 88378275 | 88378275 | 106100579 | 106100579 |

Work Sheet for a Corporation

## • term review

amortization

TERM REVIEW

## • audit your understanding

1. What is amortization?
2. How often is estimated federal income tax paid?

AUDIT YOUR

## • work together 13-1

**Calculating federal income tax expense, recording the adjustment, and completing a work sheet**

A work sheet for Provident Electronics, Inc., for the current year is provided in the *Working Papers*. Your instructor will guide you through the following examples.

1. Calculate net income before federal income tax.

2. Calculate the amount of federal income tax using the following rates:

   15% of net income before taxes, zero to $50,000.00
   Plus 25% of net income before taxes, $50,000.00 to $75,000.00
   Plus 34% of net income before taxes, $75,000.00 to $100,000.00
   Plus 39% of net income before taxes, $100,000.00 to $335,000.00
   Plus 34% of net income before taxes over $335,000.00

3. Calculate the accrued federal income tax expense.

4. Record the adjustment on the work sheet.

5. Complete the work sheet. Save your work to complete Work Together 13-3.

WORK TOGETHER • WORK TOGETHER • WORK

## • on your own 13-1

**Calculating federal income tax expense, recording the adjustment, and completing a work sheet**

A work sheet for BRE Corporation for the current year is provided in the *Working Papers*. Work this problem independently.

1. Calculate net income before federal income tax.

2. Calculate the amount of federal income tax using the tax rates given in 4. above.

3. Calculate the accrued federal income tax expense.

4. Record the adjustment on the work sheet.

5. Complete the work sheet. Save your work to complete On Your Own 13-3.

ON YOUR OWN • ON YOUR OWN

# 13-2 Financial Statements and Analysis

## INCOME STATEMENT FOR A CORPORATION

**LampLight, Inc.**
**Income Statement**
**For Year Ended December 31, 20--**

| | | | | Percentage of Net Sales* |
|---|---|---|---|---|
| Operating Revenue: | | | | |
| Sales | | | $872,952.40 | |
| Less: Sales Discount | $ 8,695.12 | | | |
| Sales Returns and Allowances | 2,900.56 | 11,595.68 | | |
| Net Sales | | | $861,356.72 | 100.0 |
| Cost of Merchandise Sold: | | | | |
| Merchandise Inventory, Jan. 1, 20-- | | | $267,453.09 | |
| Purchases | $455,396.48 | | | |
| Less: Purchases Discount | $6,710.35 | | | |
| Purchases Returns and Allowances | 2,670.00 | 9,380.35 | | |
| Net Purchases | | | 446,016.13 | |
| Total Cost of Merchandise Available for Sale | | | $713,469.22 | |
| Less Merchandise Inventory, Dec. 31, 20-- | | | 258,755.19 | |
| Cost of Merchandise Sold | | | 454,714.03 | 52.8 |
| Gross Profit on Operations | | | $406,642.69 | 47.2 |
| Operating Expenses: | | | | |
| Selling Expenses: | | | | |
| Advertising Expense | $ 17,782.00 | | | |
| Credit Card Fee Expense | 6,285.00 | | | |
| Depreciation Expense—Store Equipment | 16,753.00 | | | |
| Miscellaneous Expense—Sales | 9,406.12 | | | |
| Salary Expense—Sales | 63,683.89 | | | |
| Supplies Expense—Sales | 5,869.04 | | | |
| Total Selling Expenses | | $119,779.05 | | 13.9 |
| Administrative Expenses: | | | | |
| Depreciation Expense—Building | $ 8,250.00 | | | |
| Depreciation Expense—Office Equipment | 9,734.13 | | | |
| Insurance Expense | 5,911.31 | | | |
| Miscellaneous Expense—Administrative | 12,570.68 | | | |
| Payroll Taxes Expense | 9,962.40 | | | |
| Property Tax Expense | 6,700.00 | | | |
| Salary Expense—Administrative | 23,819.17 | | | |
| Supplies Expense—Administrative | 14,456.40 | | | |
| Uncollectible Accounts Expense | 6,277.50 | | | |
| Utilities Expense | 28,727.25 | | | |
| Total Administrative Expenses | | 126,408.84 | | 14.7 |
| Total Operating Expenses | | | 246,187.89 | 28.6 |
| Income from Operations | | | $160,454.80 | 18.6 |
| Other Revenue: | | | | |
| Interest Income | | $ 1,450.00 | | |
| Other Expenses: | | | | |
| Interest Expense | $ 30,289.53 | | | |
| Organization Expense | 480.00 | | | |
| Total Other Expenses | | $ 30,769.53 | | |
| Net Deduction | | | 29,319.53 | 3.4 |
| Net Income before Federal Income Tax | | | $131,135.27 | 15.2 |
| Less Federal Income Tax Expense | | | 34,392.76 | 4.0 |
| Net Income after Federal Income Tax | | | $ 96,742.51 | 11.2 |

*Rounded to nearest 0.1%

LampLight uses net sales as the basis for calculating component percentages on its income statement as shown above.

## ACCEPTABLE AND ACTUAL COMPONENT PERCENTAGES

| Income Statement Items | Acceptable Component Percentages | Actual Component Percentages |
|---|---|---|
| Cost of Merchandise Sold | Not more than 55.0% | 52.8% |
| Gross Profit on Operations | Not less than 45.0% | 47.2% |
| Total Selling Expenses | Not more than 12.0% | 13.9% |
| Total Administrative Expenses | Not more than 18.0% | 14.7% |
| Total Operating Expenses | Not more than 30.0% | 28.6% |
| Income from Operations | Not less than 15.0% | 18.6% |
| Net Deduction from Other Expenses | Not more than 4.0% | 3.4% |
| Net Income before Federal Income Tax | Not less than 11.0% | 15.2% |

The percentage relationship between one financial statement item and the total that includes that item is known as a component percentage. LampLight determines acceptable component percentages for each major item of cost, expense, and income as shown above. Like Zytech in Chapter 4, LampLight does not analyze component percentages for federal income tax expense or net income after federal income tax.

For the current year, LampLight has achieved acceptable percentages for most items. However, the component percentage for total selling expenses, 13.9%, is higher than the maximum acceptable percentage, 12.0%, a negative result.

Thus, LampLight's managers further analyze the expense accounts that compose selling expenses. The managers' investigation reveals a sharp increase in the price of television advertising, one component of selling expenses. To correct this situation for the next fiscal period, Lamp-Light's managers can do the following:

1. Reduce advertising costs and continue using 12.0% as the maximum acceptable component percentage.
2. Increase the maximum acceptable component percentage to recognize the increased advertising cost.

## SHARE OF NET INCOME ASSIGNED TO PREFERRED AND COMMON STOCK

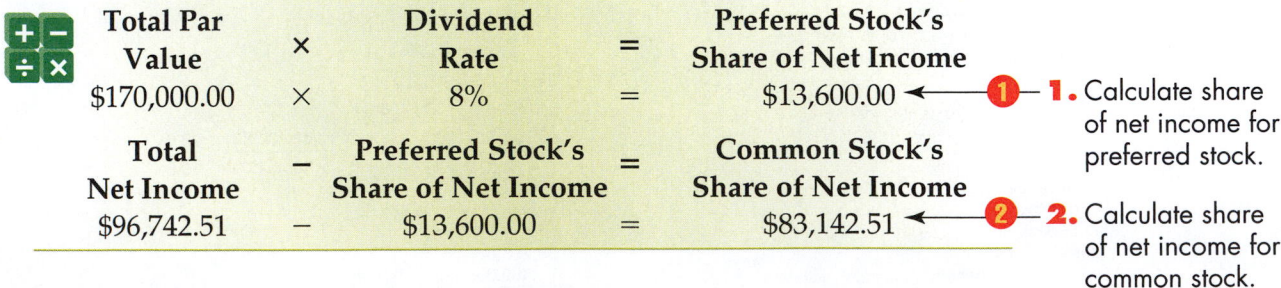

The total earnings for outstanding preferred stock equals the 8% dividend specified on the stock certificates. The total share of net income for common stock is the remainder of the net income after the preferred stock's share is deducted. These amounts are calculated as shown above.

| Share of Net Income | ÷ | Shares of Stock Outstanding | = | Earnings per Share |
|---|---|---|---|---|
| $83,142.51 | ÷ | 31,950 | = | $2.60 |

The amount of net income belonging to a single share of stock is called **earnings per share**. Earnings per share is typically calculated only on the number of common shares outstanding. For example, LampLight has 32,100 shares of common stock issued. However, 150 of these shares are treasury stock and, therefore, are not outstanding stock. LampLight has 31,950 shares of outstanding common stock (32,100 shares *less* 150 shares *equals* 31,950).

For the year ended December 31, Lamp-Light's earnings per share on common stock is calculated as shown above.

## STATEMENT OF STOCKHOLDERS' EQUITY FOR A CORPORATION

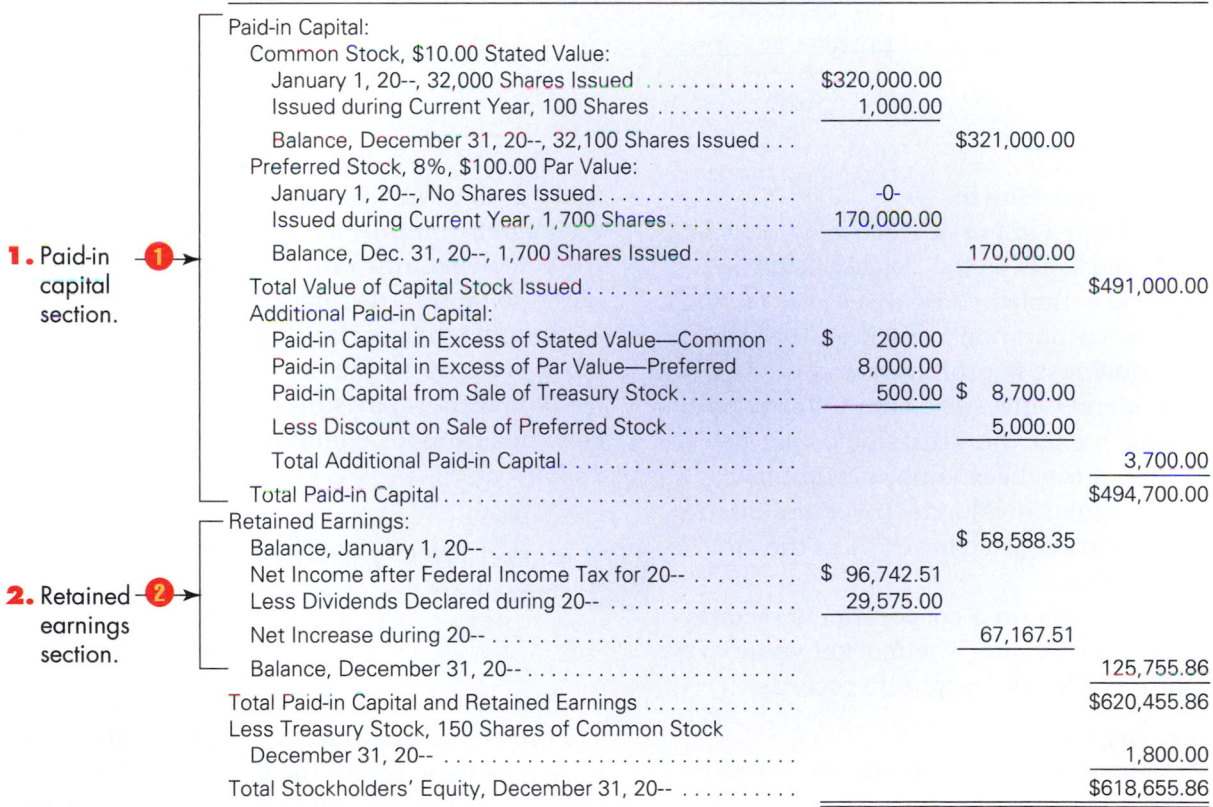

**LampLight, Inc.**
**Statement of Stockholders' Equity**
**For Year Ended December 31, 20--**

**1. Paid-in capital section.** ①

| | | | |
|---|---|---|---|
| Paid-in Capital: | | | |
| Common Stock, $10.00 Stated Value: | | | |
| January 1, 20--, 32,000 Shares Issued | $320,000.00 | | |
| Issued during Current Year, 100 Shares | 1,000.00 | | |
| Balance, December 31, 20--, 32,100 Shares Issued | | $321,000.00 | |
| Preferred Stock, 8%, $100.00 Par Value: | | | |
| January 1, 20--, No Shares Issued | -0- | | |
| Issued during Current Year, 1,700 Shares | 170,000.00 | | |
| Balance, Dec. 31, 20--, 1,700 Shares Issued | | 170,000.00 | |
| Total Value of Capital Stock Issued | | | $491,000.00 |
| Additional Paid-in Capital: | | | |
| Paid-in Capital in Excess of Stated Value—Common | $ 200.00 | | |
| Paid-in Capital in Excess of Par Value—Preferred | 8,000.00 | | |
| Paid-in Capital from Sale of Treasury Stock | 500.00 | $ 8,700.00 | |
| Less Discount on Sale of Preferred Stock | | 5,000.00 | |
| Total Additional Paid-in Capital | | | 3,700.00 |
| Total Paid-in Capital | | | $494,700.00 |

**2. Retained earnings section.** ②

| | | | |
|---|---|---|---|
| Retained Earnings: | | | |
| Balance, January 1, 20-- | | $ 58,588.35 | |
| Net Income after Federal Income Tax for 20-- | $ 96,742.51 | | |
| Less Dividends Declared during 20-- | 29,575.00 | | |
| Net Increase during 20-- | | 67,167.51 | |
| Balance, December 31, 20-- | | | 125,755.86 |
| Total Paid-in Capital and Retained Earnings | | | $620,455.86 |
| Less Treasury Stock, 150 Shares of Common Stock | | | |
| December 31, 20-- | | | 1,800.00 |
| Total Stockholders' Equity, December 31, 20-- | | | $618,655.86 |

A statement of stockholders' equity shows changes occurring in the stockholders' equity for a fiscal period. LampLight's statement of stockholders' equity has two major sections as shown above.

Some businesses prepare a statement of retained earnings instead of a statement of stockholders' equity. A statement of retained earnings includes information only about the changes in retained earnings during a fiscal period. The remainder of the information about changes in paid-in capital is placed on the corporation's balance sheet.

As of December 31, LampLight has issued $321,000.00 in common stock and $170,000.00 in preferred stock. LampLight also has $1,800.00 in treasury stock. Therefore, the total stock outstanding is $489,200.00. The total stockholders' equity, *$618,655.86*, is shown on the last line of the statement of stockholders' equity. LampLight uses information on its statement of stockholders' equity to analyze (1) equity per share, (2) market value per share, and (3) price-earnings ratio.

## Equity per Share

The amount of total stockholders' equity belonging to a single share of stock is called **equity per share**. The equity of preferred stock is equal to its total

par value, *$170,000.00*, or $100.00 per share. The remainder of the total stockholders' equity is the equity of the common stock, calculated as shown below. Common stock equity should at least equal its stated value to be acceptable. LampLight's common stock equity per share is higher than its stated value of $10.00 per share and therefore is acceptable.

©GETTY IMAGES/PHOTODISC

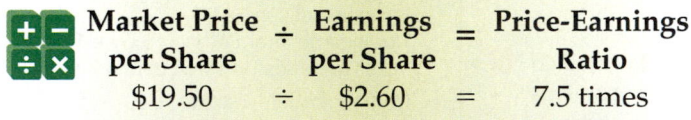

|  | Total Stockholders' Equity | ÷ | Shares of Capital Stock Outstanding | = | Equity per Share |
|---|---|---|---|---|---|
| Preferred | $170,000.00 | ÷ | 1,700 | = | $100.00 |
| Common | 448,655.86 | ÷ | 31,950 | = | 14.04 |
| Total | $618,655.86 | | | | |

## Market Value per Share

The price at which a share of stock may be sold on the stock market is called **market value**. The market value is established by investors' buying and selling the corporation's stock on the stock market. If a business is profitable and pays adequate dividends, investors often offer to pay a market price higher than the stock's par or stated value. If a business is not profitable or does not pay regular dividends, investors often offer to pay a market price lower than the stock's par or stated value.

Stock is recorded on a corporation's records at the par or stated value. The market value of stock is not recorded on corporate records.

## Price-Earnings Ratio

The relationship between the market value per share and earnings per share of a stock is called the **price-earnings ratio**. Investors usually want to buy stock in companies that are earning a reasonable amount of net income. One way

to determine whether a company is earning a reasonable amount of net income is to calculate the price-earnings ratio. The ratio is then compared to standards for similar companies.

LampLight's earnings per share on common stock is $2.60 as previously described. Using stock market reports on December 31, the price-earnings ratio for common stock is calculated as follows:

| Market Price per Share | ÷ | Earnings per Share | = | Price-Earnings Ratio |
|---|---|---|---|---|
| $19.50 | ÷ | $2.60 | = | 7.5 times |

The common stock price-earnings ratio, 7.5 times, means that the stock is selling for 7.5 times its share of the earnings. For businesses similar to LampLight, a common stock price-earnings ratio between 6.0 and 10.0 times is considered acceptable. LampLight's price-earnings ratio for common stock is acceptable.

**LampLight, Inc.**
**Balance Sheet**
**December 31, 20--**

### ASSETS

| | | | |
|---|---|---|---|
| **Current Assets:** | | | |
| Cash | | $ 25,436.40 | |
| Petty Cash | | 250.00 | |
| Notes Receivable | | 10,000.00 | |
| Interest Receivable | | 1,000.00 | |
| Accounts Receivable | $135,234.54 | | |
| Less Allowance for Uncollectible Accounts | 6,697.63 | 128,536.91 | |
| Merchandise Inventory | | 258,755.19 | |
| Supplies—Sales | | 8,446.63 | |
| Supplies—Administrative | | 8,157.30 | |
| Prepaid Insurance | | 10,988.69 | |
| Prepaid Interest | | 10.47 | |
| Total Current Assets | | | $451,581.59 |
| **Long-Term Investment:** | | | |
| Bond Sinking Fund | | | 50,000.00 |
| **Plant Assets:** | | | |
| Store Equipment | $142,983.34 | | |
| Less Accumulated Depreciation—Store Equipment | 31,876.00 | $111,107.34 | |
| Building | $165,000.00 | | |
| Less Accumulated Depreciation—Building | 16,500.00 | 148,500.00 | |
| Office Equipment | $ 73,928.23 | | |
| Less Accumulated Depreciation—Office Equipment | 17,386.13 | 56,542.10 | |
| Land | | 133,000.00 | |
| Total Plant Assets | | | 449,149.44 |
| **Intangible Assets:** | | | |
| Organization Costs | | | 1,440.00 |
| Total Assets | | | $952,171.03 |

### LIABILITIES

| | | | |
|---|---|---|---|
| **Current Liabilities:** | | | |
| Interest Payable | | $ 15,000.00 | |
| Accounts Payable | | 30,585.40 | |
| Employee Income Tax Payable | | 1,238.90 | |
| Federal Income Tax Payable | | 2,392.76 | |
| Social Security Tax Payable | | 665.99 | |
| Medicare Tax Payable | | 153.61 | |
| Salaries Payable | | 633.73 | |
| Sales Tax Payable | | 2,154.74 | |
| Unemployment Tax Payable—Federal | | 88.65 | |
| Unemployment Tax Payable—State | | 598.39 | |
| Health Insurance Premiums Payable | | 428.00 | |
| Dividends Payable | | 29,575.00 | |
| Total Current Liabilities | | | $ 83,515.17 |
| **Long-Term Liability:** | | | |
| Bonds Payable | | 250,000.00 | |
| Total Liabilities | | | $333,515.17 |

### STOCKHOLDERS' EQUITY

| | | | |
|---|---|---|---|
| Total Stockholders' Equity | | | 618,655.86 |
| Total Liabilities and Stockholders' Equity | | | $952,171.03 |

A corporate balance sheet reports assets, liabilities, and stockholders' equity on a specific date. LampLight's December 31 balance sheet is shown above. LampLight calculates three ratios based on information from the balance sheet: (1) accounts receivable turnover ratio, (2) rate earned on stockholders' equity, and (3) rate earned on total assets.

The number of times the average amount of accounts receivable is collected annually is known as the accounts receivable turnover ratio. LampLight calculates this ratio as described in the steps below.

LampLight's terms of sales are 2/10, n/30. Therefore, LampLight expects payment within 30 days. The expected accounts receivable turnover ratio is 12.2 times (365 days in a year ÷ 30 days). LampLight's average number of days for payment, 53, is higher than the expected level of 30 days. Therefore, LampLight's accounts receivable turnover ratio, 6.9 times, is unacceptable. LampLight needs to consider ways to encourage customers to pay their accounts within the credit period.

## STEPS • STEPS • STEPS • STEPS • STEPS • STEPS • STEPS • STEPS • STEPS • STEPS

### CALCULATING ACCOUNTS RECEIVABLE TURNOVER RATIO

**1** Calculate the average book value of accounts receivable. Beginning balances are obtained from the financial statements of the prior year. Ending balances are obtained from the work sheet for the current year.

| Accounts Receivable Beginning Balance | − | Allowance for Uncollectible Accounts Beginning Balance | = | Beginning Book Value |
|---|---|---|---|---|
| $124,983.89 | − | $4,362.18 | = | $120,621.71 |

| Accounts Receivable Ending Balance | − | Allowance for Uncollectible Accounts Ending Balance | = | Ending Book Value |
|---|---|---|---|---|
| $135,234.54 | − | $6,697.63 | = | $128,536.91 |

| (Beginning Book Value of Accounts Receivable | + | Ending Book Value of Accounts Receivable) | ÷ | 2 | = | Average Book Value of Accounts Receivable |
|---|---|---|---|---|---|---|
| ($120,621.71 | + | $128,536.91) | ÷ | 2 | = | $124,579.31 |

**2** Calculate the accounts receivable turnover ratio. Some businesses use separate accounts to record the amount of cash sales and net sales on account. Net sales as reported on the income statement should be used as net sales on account if the business does not record this information.

| Net Sales on Account | ÷ | Average Book Value of Accounts Receivable | = | Accounts Receivable Turnover Ratio |
|---|---|---|---|---|
| $861,356.72 | ÷ | $124,579.31 | = | 6.9 times |

**3** Calculate the average number of days for payment.

| Days in Year | ÷ | Accounts Receivable Turnover Ratio | = | Average Number of Days for Payment |
|---|---|---|---|---|
| 365 | ÷ | 6.9 | = | 53 |

## RATE EARNED ON AVERAGE STOCKHOLDERS' EQUITY

**1.** Calculate average stockholders' equity.

$$\left(\begin{array}{c} \text{January 1} \\ \text{Stockholders'} \\ \text{Equity} \\ (\$378,588.35) \end{array} \quad + \quad \begin{array}{c} \text{December 31} \\ \text{Stockholders'} \\ \text{Equity} \\ \$618,655.86) \end{array}\right) \quad \div \quad 2 \quad = \quad \begin{array}{c} \text{Average} \\ \text{Stockholders'} \\ \text{Equity} \\ \$498,622.11 \end{array}$$

| Net Income after Federal Income Tax | | Average Stockholders' Equity | | Rate Earned on Average Stockholders' Equity |
|---|---|---|---|---|
| $96,742.51 | ÷ | $498,622.11 | = | 19.4% |

**2.** Calculate the rate earned.

The relationship between net income and average stockholders' equity is called the **rate earned on average stockholders' equity**. The rate earned on average stockholders' equity for LampLight is calculated as shown above.

For each dollar that stockholders have invested, LampLight is earning $0.194 in net income. The best investment is in a corporation with the highest rate earned on average stockholders' equity. For example, Midtown, Inc., has a rate earned on average stockholders' equity of 14.2% compared to LampLight's rate of 19.4%. Based on this one analysis, an investor would choose to invest in LampLight's stock rather than Midtown's.

## RATE EARNED ON AVERAGE TOTAL ASSETS

**1.** Calculate average total assets.

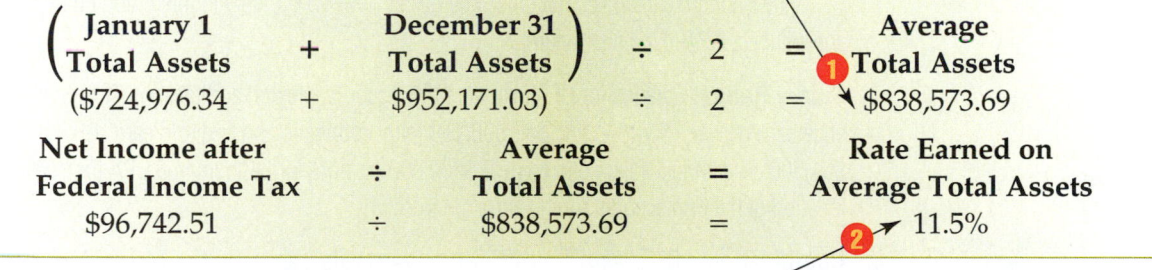

$$\left(\begin{array}{c} \text{January 1} \\ \text{Total Assets} \\ (\$724,976.34) \end{array} \quad + \quad \begin{array}{c} \text{December 31} \\ \text{Total Assets} \\ \$952,171.03) \end{array}\right) \quad \div \quad 2 \quad = \quad \begin{array}{c} \text{Average} \\ \text{Total Assets} \\ \$838,573.69 \end{array}$$

| Net Income after Federal Income Tax | | Average Total Assets | | Rate Earned on Average Total Assets |
|---|---|---|---|---|
| $96,742.51 | ÷ | $838,573.69 | = | 11.5% |

**2.** Calculate the rate earned.

The relationship between net income and average total assets is called **rate earned on average total assets**. This rate for LampLight is calculated as shown above.

For each dollar of assets that the corporation owns, the business has earnings of $0.115 after it pays federal income tax. Information published by trade organizations shows that businesses similar to LampLight tend to have a rate earned on average total assets between 10.0% and 14.0%. LampLight's rate, 11.5%, is acceptable.

Other methods to analyze corporate financial statement items are described in Chapter 17.

# careers in accounting

CAREERS IN ACCOUNTING • CAREERS IN ACCOUNTING • CAREERS IN ACCOUNTI

**Emily Gonzalez, Tax Preparer, Accounting Employee at a CPA Firm, Accounting Student, Future CPA**

COURTESY OF EMILY GONZALEZ

Emily Gonzalez's story is that of hard work and continual self-improvement. She was in New York City and just out of high school, 18 years old, without enough money for four years of college. Emily had not taken any business classes in high school, so she turned to a technical school to jump-start a career in the banking industry. To help with expenses, she started a business preparing tax returns.

After completing her program, she obtained a job in the loan department of a savings and loan company. She spent the next nine years working in customer service at a lending company and in the accounting department of an insurance company. She also completed the requirements for her insurance license.

However, Emily realized that she was lacking computer skills, so she went back to a technical college at age 28 and enrolled in a computer technology program. Before she finished the program, the school hired her as assistant controller, where she could combine her accounting experience with her new technology skills.

Then Emily decided to move back to Puerto Rico to be near her family. For the next six years, she worked in a CPA (Certified Public Accountant) firm, but realized she could not advance further in the accounting field without a degree. She moved to Florida and began working for a CPA firm, specializing in accounting for condo associations, but she did not lose sight of her dream of getting a four-year degree.

Emily is still working full time with the CPA firm, and she still has her own business preparing tax returns. However, she is also finishing a bachelor's degree in accounting. She can do this because her college classes are all online. She can stay at home with her child and be enrolled in college classes at the same time. Once she completes her degree, Emily hopes to take the CPA exam.

She's not quite there yet, but since she has achieved every goal to this point, Emily is confident that she will be a CPA in the near future.

**Salary Range:** Salaries for CPAs vary greatly. Accountants and auditors with 1 to 3 years of experience earn between $34,000 and $49,500. Senior accountants and auditors earn between $41,000 and $61,500. The annual salary can be near $200,000 or more for partners in a CPA firm. The size and location of the firm account for the variation in salary.

**Qualifications:** CPAs must pass a four-part examination, and only about 25% of those who take the examination pass every part attempted. Most states require at least a bachelor's degree to sit for the exam. Many require more education. In addition, most states require some accounting experience. Accountants and auditors must be good at working with people, as well as with business systems and computers.

**Occupational Outlook:** The job market for CPAs is expected to grow, especially for those who are familiar with the laws that have been passed as a result of recent accounting scandals.

## terms review

earnings per share

equity per share

market value

price-earnings ratio

rate earned on average
   stockholders' equity

rate earned on average total assets

## audit your understanding

1.  What does earnings per share represent?

2.  What relationship is represented by the price-earnings ratio?

3.  What amounts must be known to calculate the rate earned on average total assets?

## work together 13-2

### Analyzing Financial Statements

Financial statements for Provident Electronics, Inc., are given in the *Working Papers*. The *Working Papers* provide other selected information and forms needed to complete the problem. Your instructor will guide you through the following examples.

1.  Calculate and record on the income statement the component percentages for the indicated items. Round the percentage calculations to the nearest 0.1%.

2.  Calculate earnings per share. Round calculations to the nearest cent.

3.  Use the statement of stockholders' equity and the additional information supplied to calculate: (a) equity per share of stock and (b) the price-earnings ratio.

4.  Use the balance sheet and the additional information supplied to calculate the: (a) accounts receivable turnover ratio, (b) rate earned on average stockholders' equity, and (c) rate earned on average total assets.

## on your own 13-2

### Analyzing Financial Statements

Financial statements for BRE Corporation are given in the *Working Papers*. The *Working Papers* provide other selected information and forms needed to complete the problem. Work independently to complete the following problem.

1.  Calculate and record on the income statement the component percentages for the indicated items. Round the percentage calculations to the nearest 0.1%.

2.  Calculate earnings per share. Round calculations to the nearest cent.

3.  Use the statement of stockholders' equity and the additional information supplied to calculate: (a) equity per share of stock and (b) the price-earnings ratio.

4.  Use the balance sheet and the additional information supplied to calculate the: (a) accounts receivable turnover ratio, (b) rate earned on average stockholders' equity, and (c) rate earned on average total assets.

# 13-3 Other End-of-Fiscal-Period Work

## ADJUSTING ENTRIES

| | DATE | | ACCOUNT TITLE | DOC. NO. | POST. REF. | DEBIT | CREDIT | |
|---|---|---|---|---|---|---|---|---|
| 1 | | | **Adjusting Entries** | | | | | 1 |
| 2 | Dec.²⁰⁻⁻ | 31 | Interest Receivable | | | 1 0 0 0 00 | | 2 |
| 3 | | | Interest Income | | | | 1 0 0 0 00 | 3 |
| 4 | | 31 | Uncollectible Accounts Expense | | | 6 2 7 7 50 | | 4 |
| 5 | | | Allowance for Uncoll. Accts. | | | | 6 2 7 7 50 | 5 |
| 6 | | 31 | Income Summary | | | 8 6 9 7 90 | | 6 |
| 7 | | | Merchandise Inventory | | | | 8 6 9 7 90 | 7 |
| 8 | | 31 | Supplies Expense—Sales | | | 5 8 6 9 04 | | 8 |
| 9 | | | Supplies—Sales | | | | 5 8 6 9 04 | 9 |
| 10 | | 31 | Supplies Expense—Admin. | | | 14 4 5 6 40 | | 10 |
| 11 | | | Supplies—Admin. | | | | 14 4 5 6 40 | 11 |
| 12 | | 31 | Insurance Expense | | | 5 9 1 1 31 | | 12 |
| 13 | | | Prepaid Insurance | | | | 5 9 1 1 31 | 13 |
| 14 | | 31 | Prepaid Interest | | | 1 0 47 | | 14 |
| 15 | | | Interest Expense | | | | 1 0 47 | 15 |
| 16 | | 31 | Depreciation Exp.—Store Equip. | | | 16 7 5 3 00 | | 16 |
| 17 | | | Accum. Depr.—Store Equip. | | | | 16 7 5 3 00 | 17 |
| 18 | | 31 | Depreciation Exp.—Building | | | 8 2 5 0 00 | | 18 |
| 19 | | | Accum. Depr.—Building | | | | 8 2 5 0 00 | 19 |
| 20 | | 31 | Depreciation Exp.—Office Equip. | | | 9 7 3 4 13 | | 20 |
| 21 | | | Accum. Depr.—Office Equip. | | | | 9 7 3 4 13 | 21 |
| 22 | | 31 | Organization Expense | | | 4 8 0 00 | | 22 |
| 23 | | | Organization Costs | | | | 4 8 0 00 | 23 |
| 24 | | 31 | Interest Expense | | | 15 0 0 0 00 | | 24 |
| 25 | | | Interest Payable | | | | 15 0 0 0 00 | 25 |
| 26 | | 31 | Salary Expense—Sales | | | 4 5 7 89 | | 26 |
| 27 | | | Salary Expense—Admin. | | | 1 7 5 84 | | 27 |
| 28 | | | Salaries Payable | | | | 6 3 3 73 | 28 |
| 29 | | 31 | Payroll Taxes Expense | | | 6 0 00 | | 29 |
| 30 | | | Social Security Tax Payable | | | | 4 1 19 | 30 |
| 31 | | | Medicare Tax Payable | | | | 9 51 | 31 |
| 32 | | | Unemploy. Tax Pay.—Federal | | | | 1 20 | 32 |
| 33 | | | Unemploy. Tax Pay.—State | | | | 8 10 | 33 |
| 34 | | 31 | Federal Income Tax Expense | | | 2 3 9 2 76 | | 34 |
| 35 | | | Federal Income Tax Payable | | | | 2 3 9 2 76 | 35 |
| 36 | | | | | | | | 36 |

GENERAL JOURNAL          PAGE 13

In addition to a work sheet and financial statements, LampLight prepares adjusting entries, closing entries, a post-closing trial balance, and reversing entries. LampLight's December 31 adjusting entries are shown above.

| | DATE | | ACCOUNT TITLE | DOC. NO. | POST. REF. | DEBIT | CREDIT | |
|---|---|---|---|---|---|---|---|---|
| 1 | | | *Closing Entries* | | | | | 1 |
| 2 | 20-- Dec. | 31 | Sales | | | 872 952 40 | | 2 |
| 3 | | | Purchases Discount | | | 6 710 35 | | 3 |
| 4 | | | Purchases Returns and Allowances | | | 2 670 00 | | 4 |
| 5 | | | Interest Income | | | 1 450 00 | | 5 |
| 6 | | | Income Summary | | | | 883 782 75 | 6 |
| 7 | | 31 | Income Summary | | | 778 342 34 | | 7 |
| 8 | | | Sales Discount | | | | 8 695 12 | 8 |
| 9 | | | Sales Returns and Allowances | | | | 2 900 56 | 9 |
| 10 | | | Purchases | | | | 455 396 48 | 10 |
| 11 | | | Advertising Expense | | | | 17 782 00 | 11 |
| 12 | | | Credit Card Fee Expense | | | | 6 285 00 | 12 |
| 13 | | | Depreciation Exp.—Store Equip. | | | | 16 753 00 | 13 |
| 14 | | | Miscellaneous Exp.—Sales | | | | 9 406 12 | 14 |
| 15 | | | Salary Expense—Sales | | | | 63 683 89 | 15 |
| 16 | | | Supplies Expense—Sales | | | | 5 869 04 | 16 |
| 17 | | | Depreciation Exp.—Building | | | | 8 250 00 | 17 |
| 18 | | | Depreciation Exp.—Office Equip. | | | | 9 734 13 | 18 |
| 19 | | | Insurance Expense | | | | 5 911 31 | 19 |
| 20 | | | Miscellaneous Exp.—Admin. | | | | 12 570 68 | 20 |
| 21 | | | Payroll Taxes Expense | | | | 9 962 40 | 21 |
| 22 | | | Property Tax Expense | | | | 6 700 00 | 22 |
| 23 | | | Salary Expense—Admin. | | | | 23 819 17 | 23 |
| 24 | | | Supplies Expense—Admin. | | | | 14 456 40 | 24 |
| 25 | | | Uncollectible Accounts Expense | | | | 6 277 50 | 25 |
| 26 | | | Utilities Expense | | | | 28 727 25 | 26 |
| 27 | | | Interest Expense | | | | 30 289 53 | 27 |
| 28 | | | Organization Expense | | | | 480 00 | 28 |
| 29 | | | Federal Income Tax Expense | | | | 34 392 76 | 29 |
| 30 | | 31 | Income Summary | | | 96 742 51 | | 30 |
| 31 | | | Retained Earnings | | | | 96 742 51 | 31 |
| 32 | | 31 | Retained Earnings | | | 29 575 00 | | 32 |
| 33 | | | Dividends—Common | | | | 15 975 00 | 33 |
| 34 | | | Dividends—Preferred | | | | 13 600 00 | 34 |
| 35 | | | | | | | | 35 |

GENERAL JOURNAL — PAGE 14

LampLight records four closing entries at the end of a fiscal period.

1. Closing entry for income statement accounts with credit balances (revenue and contra cost accounts).
2. Closing entry for income statement accounts with debit balances (cost, contra revenue, and expense accounts).
3. Closing entry to record net income or net loss in the retained earnings account and close the income summary account.
4. Closing entry for the dividends accounts.

LampLight's December 31 closing entries are shown above.

**LampLight, Inc.**
**Post-Closing Trial Balance**
**December 31, 20--**

| Account Title | Debit | Credit |
|---|---:|---:|
| Cash | $ 25,436.40 | |
| Petty Cash | 250.00 | |
| Notes Receivable | 10,000.00 | |
| Interest Receivable | 1,000.00 | |
| Accounts Receivable | 135,234.54 | |
| Allowance for Uncollectible Accounts | | $ 6,697.63 |
| Subscriptions Receivable | | |
| Merchandise Inventory | 258,755.19 | |
| Supplies—Sales | 8,446.63 | |
| Supplies—Administrative | 8,157.30 | |
| Prepaid Insurance | 10,988.69 | |
| Prepaid Interest | 10.47 | |
| Bond Sinking Fund | 50,000.00 | |
| Store Equipment | 142,983.34 | |
| Accumulated Depreciation—Store Equipment | | 31,876.00 |
| Building | 165,000.00 | |
| Accumulated Depreciation—Building | | 16,500.00 |
| Office Equipment | 73,928.23 | |
| Accumulated Depreciation—Office Equipment | | 17,386.13 |
| Land | 133,000.00 | |
| Organization Costs | 1,440.00 | |
| Interest Payable | | 15,000.00 |
| Accounts Payable | | 30,585.40 |
| Employee Income Tax Payable | | 1,238.90 |
| Federal Income Tax Payable | | 2,392.76 |
| Social Security Tax Payable | | 665.99 |
| Medicare Tax Payable | | 153.61 |
| Salaries Payable | | 633.73 |
| Sales Tax Payable | | 2,154.74 |
| Unemployment Tax Payable—Federal | | 88.65 |
| Unemployment Tax Payable—State | | 598.39 |
| Health Insurance Premiums Payable | | 428.00 |
| Dividends Payable | | 29,575.00 |
| Bonds Payable | | 250,000.00 |
| Capital Stock—Common | | 321,000.00 |
| Stock Subscribed—Common | | |
| Paid-in Capital in Excess of Stated Value—Common | | 200.00 |
| Capital Stock—Preferred | | 170,000.00 |
| Stock Subscribed—Preferred | | |
| Paid-in Capital in Excess of Par Value—Preferred | | 8,000.00 |
| Discount on Sale of Preferred Stock | 5,000.00 | |
| Treasury Stock | 1,800.00 | |
| Paid-in Capital from Sale of Treasury Stock | | 500.00 |
| Retained Earnings | | 125,755.86 |
| Totals | $1,031,430.79 | $1,031,430.79 |

LampLight's December 31 post-closing trial balance is shown above.

> **REMEMBER** If the totals on the post-closing trial balance are the same, the accounting records are ready for the next fiscal period.

| | DATE | | ACCOUNT TITLE | DOC. NO. | POST. REF. | DEBIT | CREDIT | |
|---|---|---|---|---|---|---|---|---|
| 1 | | | *Reversing Entries* | | | | | 1 |
| 2 | 20-- Jan. | 1 | *Interest Income* | | | 1 0 0 0 00 | | 2 |
| 3 | | | *Interest Receivable* | | | | 1 0 0 0 00 | 3 |
| 4 | | 1 | *Interest Expense* | | | 1 0 47 | | 4 |
| 5 | | | *Prepaid Interest* | | | | 1 0 47 | 5 |
| 6 | | 1 | *Interest Payable* | | | 15 0 0 0 00 | | 6 |
| 7 | | | *Interest Expense* | | | | 15 0 0 0 00 | 7 |
| 8 | | 1 | *Salaries Payable* | | | 6 3 3 73 | | 8 |
| 9 | | | *Salary Expense—Sales* | | | | 4 5 7 89 | 9 |
| 10 | | | *Salary Expense—Administrative* | | | | 1 7 5 84 | 10 |
| 11 | | 1 | *Social Security Tax Payable* | | | 4 1 19 | | 11 |
| 12 | | | *Medicare Tax Payable* | | | 9 51 | | 12 |
| 13 | | | *Unemploy. Tax Pay.—Federal* | | | 1 20 | | 13 |
| 14 | | | *Unemploy. Tax Pay.—State* | | | 8 10 | | 14 |
| 15 | | | *Payroll Taxes Expense* | | | | 6 0 00 | 15 |
| 16 | | | | | | | | 16 |

**GENERAL JOURNAL**     PAGE **15**

If an adjusting entry creates a balance in an asset or liability account, LampLight reverses the adjusting entry. Like most corporations, however, LampLight does not reverse the adjusting entry that records federal income tax. LampLight's reversing entries recorded on January 1 are shown above.

## technology for business

TECHNOLOGY FOR BUSINESS • TECHNOLOGY FOR BUSINESS • TECHNOLOGY FOR BUSIN

### Electronic Backups

Management information systems engineers design systems to back up and archive important electronic data. A backup creates a second set of all or part of the information stored on individual computers within a local area network.

Three techniques are commonly used. First is a complete backup. All the information on the system is backed up to a storage device such as a tape or an optical disk. Complete backup requires the most time to complete, but ensures that all information is stored in another location.

The second backup method is incremental backups. Using this method, only the files that have been changed or created since the last backup are saved to the storage device. The time to complete the backup is less than the time for a total backup. However, if a system failure occurs, restoring the files will take longer. The complete backup is restored first, then each incremental backup is restored.

The most complex method of backup is known as dynamic backup. Each time a file is saved, a backup is created. Thus, if a system failure occurs, virtually no data is lost. The technology for dynamic backups is more complex and more costly than the other two methods.

Whichever method is used, backing up files is an important part of any quality management information system.

| Form **1120** | U.S. Corporation Income Tax Return | OMB No. 1545-0123 |
|---|---|---|
| Department of the Treasury Internal Revenue Service | For calendar year 20-- or tax year beginning ........., 20--, ending ........., 20 ... ▶ Instructions are separate. See page 1 for Paperwork Reduction Act Notice. | 20-- |

**A** Check if a:
(1) Consolidated return (attach Form 851) ☐
(2) Personal holding co. (attach Sch. PH) ☐
(3) Personal service corp. (as defined in Temporary Regs. sec. 1.441-4T— see instructions) ☐

Use IRS label. Otherwise, please print or type.

Name: LampLight, Inc.
Number, street, and room or suite no. (If a P.O. box, see page 6 of instructions.): 1450 Eaglewood Lane
City or town, state, and ZIP code: Nashville, TN 37207-2361

**B** Employer identification number: 74-1334457
**C** Date incorporated: 12/26/--
**D** Total assets (see Specific Instructions): $ 952,171 03

**E** Check applicable boxes: (1) Initial return ☐ (2) Final return ☐ (3) Change in address ☐

| Income | | | |
|---|---|---|---|
| 1a | Gross receipts or sales 864,257 28  b Less returns and allowances 2,900 56  c Bal ▶ | 1c | 861,356 72 |
| 2 | Cost of goods sold (Schedule A, line 8) | 2 | 454,714 03 |
| 3 | Gross profit. Subtract line 2 from line 1c | 3 | 406,642 69 |
| 4 | Dividends (Schedule C, line 19) | 4 | -0- |
| 5 | Interest | 5 | 1,450 00 |
| 6 | Gross rents | 6 | -0- |
| 7 | Gross royalties | 7 | -0- |
| 8 | Capital gain net income (attach Schedule D (Form 1120)) | 8 | -0- |
| 9 | Net gain or (loss) from Form 4797, Part II, line 20 (attach Form 4797) | 9 | -0- |
| 10 | Other income (see instructions—attach schedule) | 10 | -0- |
| 11 | **Total income.** Add lines 3 through 10 ▶ | 11 | 408,092 69 |

| Deductions (See instructions for limitations on deductions.) | | | |
|---|---|---|---|
| 12 | Compensation of officers (Schedule E, line 4) | 12 | 28,432 50 |
| 13a | Salaries and wages 59,070 56  b Less jobs credit -0-  c Balance ▶ | 13c | 59,070 56 |
| 14 | Repairs | 14 | -0- |
| 15 | Bad debts | 15 | 6,277 50 |
| 16 | Rents | 16 | -0- |
| 17 | Taxes | 17 | 16,662 40 |
| 18 | Interest | 18 | 30,289 53 |
| 19 | Charitable contributions (see instructions for 10% limitation) | 19 | -0- |
| 20 | Depreciation (attach Form 4562) 20 34,737 13 | | |
| 21 | Less depreciation claimed on Schedule A and elsewhere on return 21a -0- | 21b | 34,737 13 |
| 22 | Depletion | 22 | -0- |
| 23 | Advertising | 23 | 17,782 00 |
| 24 | Pension, profit-sharing, etc., plans | 24 | -0- |
| 25 | Employee benefit programs | 25 | -0- |
| 26 | Other deductions (attach schedule) | 26 | 83,705 80 |
| 27 | **Total deductions.** Add lines 12 through 26 ▶ | 27 | 276,957 42 |
| 28 | Taxable income before net operating loss deduction and special deductions. Subtract line 27 from line 11 | 28 | 131,135 27 |
| 29 | Less: a Net operating loss deduction (see instructions) 29a -0- | | |
| | b Special deductions (Schedule C, line 20) 29b -0- | 29c | -0- |

| Tax and Payments | | | |
|---|---|---|---|
| 30 | **Taxable income.** Subtract line 29c from line 28 | 30 | 131,135 27 |
| 31 | **Total tax** (Schedule J, line 10) | 31 | 34,392 76 |
| 32 | Payments: a 20-- overpayment credited to 20-- 32a -0- | | |
| b | 20-- estimated tax payments 32b 32,000 00 | | |
| c | Less 20-- refund applied for on Form 4466 32c ( -0- ) d Bal ▶ 32d 32,000 00 | | |
| e | Tax deposited with Form 7004 32e -0- | | |
| f | Credit from regulated investment companies (attach Form 2439) 32f -0- | | |
| g | Credit for Federal tax on fuels (attach Form 4136). See instructions 32g -0- | 32h | 32,000 00 |
| 33 | Estimated tax penalty (see instructions). Check if Form 2220 is attached ▶ ☐ | 33 | -0- |
| 34 | **Tax due.** If line 32h is smaller than the total of lines 31 and 33, enter amount owed | 34 | 2,392 76 |
| 35 | **Overpayment.** If line 32h is larger than the total of lines 31 and 33, enter amount overpaid | 35 | |
| 36 | Enter amount of line 35 you want: **Credited to 19-- estimated tax** ▶ **Refunded** ▶ | 36 | |

**Please Sign Here**
Under penalties of perjury, I declare that I have examined this return, including accompanying schedules and statements, and to the best of my knowledge and belief, it is true, correct, and complete. Declaration of preparer (other than taxpayer) is based on all information of which preparer has any knowledge.

Susan P. Boyd — Signature of officer | 3/15/-- Date | Treasurer Title

**Paid Preparer's Use Only**
Preparer's signature | Date | Check if self-employed ☐ | Preparer's social security number
Firm's name (or yours if self-employed) and address | E.I. No. ▶ | ZIP code ▶

LampLight must file a federal income tax return and pay income taxes. Page 1 of LampLight's Form 1120, U.S. Corporation Income Tax Return, is shown above.

Some amounts reported on a corporation's income statement must be modified to complete the tax return. For example, LampLight presents both payroll tax expense and property tax expense on its income statement. LampLight's managers require this information to make sound business decisions. However, the tax form requires LampLight to report only the total of all taxes.

## DISSOLVING A CORPORATION

When a corporation is dissolved, it must meet legal requirements and follow correct accounting procedures. However, corporations are rarely dissolved. When an owner (stockholder) decides not to participate in the corporation, the stockholder merely sells all shares of stock owned. The corporation is not dissolved.

The dissolution of a corporation involves many legal procedures and documents. Documents that must be filed include a notice to the state in which the business was incorporated and a notice to all creditors of the corporation. Since the dissolution of a corporation is complex, the board of directors should seek legal advice.

Once a corporation is dissolved, the liquidation process can begin. The procedure for selling noncash assets is similar to that for proprietorships and partnerships. However, since a corporation is a taxable entity, the gains and losses on the sale of noncash assets are subject to taxation. Therefore, additional tax reports for the corporation must be filed. The accounting aspects of actually liquidating a corporation are extremely complex. Therefore, obtaining professional accounting services to assist in the liquidation of a corporation is recommended.

# Explore Accounting

EXPLORE ACCOUNTING • EXPLORE ACCOUNTING • EXPLORE ACCOUNTING

### Differences Between Generally Accepted Accounting Principals (GAAP) and Tax Law: Net Income vs. Taxable Income

The net income reported by a company on its income statement is usually not the same amount reported on the company's tax return as "taxable income." The difference between net income and taxable income is caused by the rules that must be followed to calculate each amount.

Net income is calculated following accounting rules, called *Generally Accepted Accounting Principles (GAAP)*. GAAP is developed by the Financial Accounting Standards Board and is designed to give investors and others information about the financial condition of a company.

Taxable income is calculated following U.S. tax laws. Tax laws are developed by Congress, enforced by the Internal Revenue Service, and designed to collect government revenue in an equitable manner.

Sometimes the difference is permanent. For example, interest on some investments is not taxable. That means that the interest will be included in the company's net income on the income statement, but the company does not have to include the interest in taxable income for tax purposes.

Sometimes the difference is just a timing difference. For example, assume that in December 20X1, a company pays $1,000 for insurance for the next year. The company will not show the $1,000 as an income statement expense in 20X1, but it will show the expense on its 20X2 income statement. For tax purposes, the $1,000 will be a deduction against income in 20X2, not in 20X1.

**Instructions**
Use the Internet to research other differences between GAAP and tax laws. Report your findings to your class.

## • audit your understanding

1. What four closing entries are recorded at the end of the period?

2. What form is used to file the federal income tax return for a corporation?

3. How does the liquidation of a corporation differ from the liquidation of a proprietorship or partnership?

## • work together 13-3

**End-of-fiscal period work for a corporation**

Use the work sheet for Provident Electronics, Inc. from Work Together 13-1. Statement paper and pages 14, 15, and 16 of a general journal are provided in the *Working Papers*. Your instructor will guide you through the following examples.

1. Journalize the adjusting entries on page 14 of the general journal.

2. Journalize the closing entries on page 15 of the general journal.

3. Prepare a post-closing trial balance as of December 31 of the current year.

4. Journalize the reversing entries on page 16 of the general journal.

## • on your own 13-3

**End-of-fiscal period work for a corporation**

Use the work sheet for BRE Corporation from On Your Own 13-1. Statement paper and pages 8, 9, and 10 of a general journal are provided in the *Working Papers*. Your instructor will guide you through the following problem.

1. Journalize the adjusting entries on page 8 of the general journal.

2. Journalize the closing entries on page 9 of the general journal.

3. Prepare a post-closing trial balance as of December 31 of the current year.

4. Journalize the reversing entries on page 10 of the general journal.

## SUMMARY

*After completing this chapter, you can*

1. Define terms related to financial analysis and reporting for a corporation.

2. Identify concepts and practices related to financial analysis and reporting for a corporation.

3. Prepare a work sheet for a corporation.

4. Calculate federal income tax for a corporation.

5. Prepare and analyze financial statements for a corporation.

6. Prepare selected end-of-fiscal-period work for a corporation.

# Explore Accounting

EXPLORE ACCOUNTING • EXPLORE ACCOUNTING • EXPLORE ACCO

### Notes to Financial Statements

As today's business world becomes increasingly complex, investors' need for accounting information also continues to grow. Much of the information investors need goes beyond the general ledger account balances presented on financial statements. For example, the Financial Accounting Standards Board has determined that investors should have the scheduled payments on long-term debt for the next five years.

A complete set of financial statements includes four basic statements: income statement, balance sheet, statement of stockholders' equity, and statement of cash flows. The financial statements also include a variety of disclosures, called notes, that present additional information regarding amounts presented in the basic financial statements.

Each note begins with a heading that contains a number and title. The first note is typically a statement of significant account principles used to prepare the financial statements. This note would include the methods used to cost inventory, depre-

ciate assets, and other principles where management can select among acceptable alternatives.

Subsequent notes can cover a variety of topics, depending upon the individual characteristics of the company. For example, an oil company would explain how it values its crude oil reserves. Other notes might include information on inventory, fixed assets, income taxes, etc. Other significant events affecting the corporation, such as mergers, discontinued operations, and lawsuits, are also disclosed in the notes to financial statements.

**Required:**

Obtain the annual reports of three public corporations. What reference on each financial statement directs you to examine the notes to financial statements? Compare the titles of each note contained in each annual report. Which notes were presented in more than one annual report? Which notes were unique to one of the corporations?

# 13-1 APPLICATION PROBLEM

## Preparing a work sheet for a corporation

General ledger account titles and balances for Trexler, Inc., are recorded on a work sheet in the *Working Papers* accompanying this textbook.

**Instructions:**

Complete the work sheet for the current year ended December 31. Record the adjustments on the work sheet using the following information. Save your work to complete Application Problems 13-3 and 13-4.

### Adjustment Information, December 31

| | |
|---|---|
| Accrued Interest Income | $ 160.17 |
| Uncollectible Accounts Expense (estimated as 1.0% of sales on account) | |
| Sales on Account for Year | 126,405.00 |
| Merchandise Inventory | 51,450.23 |
| Sales Supplies Inventory | 1,202.70 |
| Administrative Supplies Inventory | 959.85 |
| Value of Prepaid Insurance | 1,436.58 |
| Prepaid Interest | 1.85 |
| Annual Depreciation Expense—Store Equipment | 1,294.57 |
| Annual Depreciation Expense—Building | 2,900.00 |
| Annual Depreciation Expense—Office Equipment | 3,018.64 |
| Organization Expense | 50.00 |
| Accrued Interest Expense | 4,002.57 |
| Accrued Salaries—Sales | 153.97 |
| Accrued Salaries—Administrative | 593.49 |
| Accrued Payroll Taxes—Social Security Tax | 48.59 |
| Accrued Payroll Taxes—Medicare | 11.21 |
| Accrued Payroll Taxes—Federal Unemployment Tax | 1.72 |
| Accrued Payroll Taxes—State Unemployment Tax | 11.61 |

Federal income taxes are based on the tax rate table in this chapter.

# 13-2 APPLICATION PROBLEM

## Calculating federal income taxes

During the past year, three corporations earned the following net income before federal income taxes:

| | |
|---|---|
| Corporation A | $73,932.56 |
| Corporation B | $467,032.45 |
| Corporation C | $38,296.44 |

**Instructions:**

Calculate the amount of federal income tax expense for each of the three corporations. Use the tax rate table in this chapter.

# 13-3 APPLICATION PROBLEM

### Preparing financial statements for a corporation

Use the work sheet prepared in Application Problem 13-1.

**Instructions:**

1. Prepare an income statement for the current year ended December 31.
2. Calculate and record the following component percentages: (a) cost of merchandise sold, (b) gross profit on operations, (c) total selling expenses, (d) total administrative expenses, (e) total operating expenses, (f) income from operations, (g) net addition or deduction resulting from other revenue and expenses, (h) net income before federal income tax, (i) federal income tax expense, and (j) net income after federal income tax. Round the percentage calculations to the nearest 0.1%.
3. Use the Income Statement Analysis table given in the *Working Papers.* Analyze Trexler's income statement by determining whether component percentages are within acceptable levels. If any component percentage is not within an acceptable level, suggest steps that the company should take.
4. Calculate earnings per share. Round the calculation to the nearest cent. Trexler has 10,900 shares of $10.00 stated-value common stock issued and 420 shares of $100.00 par-value preferred stock issued. Treasury stock consists of 70 shares of common stock. The dividend rate on preferred stock is 10%.
5. Prepare a statement of stockholders' equity for the current year ended December 31. Use the following additional information.

|  | January 1<br>Balance | Issued During<br>the Year | December 31<br>Balance |
|---|---|---|---|
| Common Stock: |  |  |  |
| No. of Shares | 8,000 | 2,900 | 10,900 |
| Amount | $80,000.00 | $29,000.00 | $109,000.00 |
| Preferred Stock: |  |  |  |
| No. of Shares | 150 | 270 | 420 |
| Amount | $15,000.00 | $27,000.00 | $ 42,000.00 |

Treasury stock consists of 70 shares of common stock.
The January 1 balance of Retained Earnings was $13,411.26.

6. Calculate the following items: (a) equity per share of stock and (b) price-earnings ratio. The market price of common stock on December 31 is $24.00.
7. Prepare a balance sheet for December 31 of the current year.
8. Calculate the following items:
   (a) Accounts receivable turnover ratio. Net sales on account are $126,405.00. Accounts receivable and allowance for uncollectible accounts on January 1 were $26,495.72 and $1,142.37, respectively.
   (b) Rate earned on average stockholders' equity. Total stockholders' equity on January 1 was $106,951.26.
   (c) Rate earned on average total assets. Total assets on January 1 were $233,699.75.

# 13-4 APPLICATION PROBLEM

### Completing other end-of-fiscal-period work

Use the work sheet prepared in Application Problem 13-1.

**Instructions:**

1. Journalize the adjusting entries. Use page 13 of a general journal.
2. Journalize the closing entries. Use page 14 of a general journal.
3. Journalize the reversing entries. Use page 15 of a general journal. Use January 1 of the year following the current year as the date.

### Completing end-of-fiscal-period work for a corporation

The general ledger account titles and balances for Lander, Inc., are recorded on a work sheet in the *Working Papers*.

**Instructions:**

1. Complete the work sheet for December 31 of the current year. Record the adjustments on the work sheet using the following information.

#### Adjustment Information, December 31

| | |
|---|---:|
| Accrued Interest Income | $ 277.18 |
| Uncollectible Accounts Expense (estimated as 1.0% of sales on account) | |
| Sales on Account for Year | 213,441.00 |
| Merchandise Inventory | 86,876.38 |
| Sales Supplies Inventory | 9,808.79 |
| Administrative Supplies Inventory | 3,620.75 |
| Value of Prepaid Insurance | 2,363.94 |
| Prepaid Interest | 3.12 |
| Annual Depreciation Expense—Store Equipment | 9,746.00 |
| Annual Depreciation Expense—Building | 2,400.00 |
| Annual Depreciation Expense—Office Equipment | 2,185.95 |
| Organization Expense | 75.00 |
| Accrued Interest Expense | 7,004.34 |
| Accrued Salaries—Sales | 375.65 |
| Accrued Salaries—Administrative | 1,002.13 |
| Accrued Payroll Taxes—Social Security Tax | 89.55 |
| Accrued Payroll Taxes—Medicare | 20.67 |
| Accrued Payroll Taxes—Federal Unemployment Tax | 1.27 |
| Accrued Payroll Taxes—State Unemployment Tax | 8.59 |

Federal income taxes are based on the tax rate table in this chapter.

2. Prepare an income statement. Calculate and record the following component percentages: (a) cost of merchandise sold, (b) gross profit on operations, (c) total selling expenses, (d) total administrative expenses, (e) total operating expenses, (f) income from operations, (g) net addition or deduction resulting from other revenue and expenses, (h) net income before federal income tax, (i) federal income tax expense, and (j) net income after federal income tax. Round percentage calculations to the nearest 0.1%.

3. Use the Income Statement Analysis table given in the *Working Papers*. Analyze Lander's income statement by determining whether component percentages are within acceptable levels. If any component percentage is not within an acceptable level, suggest steps that the company should take.

4. Calculate earnings per share. Round the calculation to the nearest cent. Lander has 18,400 shares of $10.00 stated-value common stock issued and 720 shares of $100.00 par-value preferred stock issued. Treasury stock consists of 90 shares of common stock. The dividend rate on preferred stock is 10%.

5. Prepare a statement of stockholders' equity for the current year ended December 31. Use the following additional information.

| | January 1<br>Balance | Issued During<br>the Year | December 31<br>Balance |
|---|---|---|---|
| Common Stock: | | | |
| No. of Shares | 18,000 | 400 | 18,400 |
| Amount | $180,000.00 | $ 4,000.00 | $184,000.00 |
| Preferred Stock: | | | |
| No. of Shares | 600 | 120 | 720 |
| Amount | $ 60,000.00 | $12,000.00 | $ 72,000.00 |

The January 1 balance of Retained Earnings was $22,645.60.

6. Calculate the following items based on information on the statement of stockholders' equity: (a) equity per share of stock and (b) price-earnings ratio. The market price of common stock on December 31 is $30.00.
7. Prepare a balance sheet for December 31 of the current year.
8. Calculate the following items based on information from the balance sheet.
   (a) Accounts receivable turnover ratio. Net sales on account were $213,441.00. Accounts receivable and allowance for doubtful accounts on January 1 were $49,435.32 and $2,146.40, respectively.
   (b) Rate earned on average stockholders' equity. Total stockholders' equity on January 1 was $290,485.60.
   (c) Rate earned on average total assets. Total assets on January 1 were $392,691.70.
9. Journalize the adjusting entries. Use page 13 of a general journal.
10. Journalize the closing entries. Use page 14 of a general journal.
11. Journalize the reversing entries. Use page 1 of a general journal. Use January 1 of the year following the current year as the date.

# 13-6 CHALLENGE PROBLEM

## Preparing a Form 1120, U.S. Corporation Income Tax Return

Goldstein, Inc., has completed its work sheet and financial statements for the fiscal year ending on December 31 of the current year. The income statement for Goldstein is in the *Working Papers*.

The following information required to prepare the tax return is obtained from company records.

Employer identification number: 65-074738
Date incorporated: January 5
Address: 7834 Industrial Road, Oxford, MS 38655-1500
Total assets: $786,986.50
Compensation of officers: $7,217.60
Estimated tax payments: $42,000.00

**Instructions:**
1. Complete the company name and address in the spaces provided on the tax form.
2. Use the information provided to complete lines D–F. Write the amount of compensation of officers on line 12. Write the estimated tax payments on line 32b.
3. Use the amounts on the income statement to complete the following lines of the tax form.

| Tax Form Line | Income Statement Account(s) |
|---|---|
| 1a | Sales less Sales Discount |
| 1b | Sales Returns and Allowances |
| 2 | Cost of Merchandise Sold |
| 5 | Interest Income |
| 13a | Salary Expense—Sales plus Salary Expense—Administrative less Compensation of officers |
| 15 | Uncollectible Accounts Expense |
| 17 | Payroll Taxes Expense plus Property Taxes |
| 18 | Interest Expense |
| 20 | The sum of the three depreciation expense accounts |
| 23 | Advertising Expense |
| 26 | All other expenses not reported on other lines |
| 31 | Federal Income Tax Expense |

4. Calculate the amounts on lines 1c, 3, 11, 13c, 21b, 27, 30, 32h, and 34 using the instructions provided on the tax form.
5. Check the accuracy of the completed tax form by comparing the amount on line 30 of the tax form to Net Income before Federal Income Tax on the income statement.
6. Write -0- on the remaining blank lines on the tax form.

# applied communication

APPLIED

The market price of a stock may change daily as its shares are traded on a stock exchange. Research and write a brief report about one of the stock exchanges. Describe such things as how a company is listed on the exchange, how shares are traded, and how an individual can find the current market price of a stock listed on the exchange.

# cases for critical thinking

CASES FOR CRITICAL THINKING

### Case 1

A corporation president suggests to the accounting department that the statement of stockholders' equity be dropped from the end-of-fiscal-period work. The president's reason is that the same information is reported on the corporation's balance sheet. The accounting department wants to continue using the statement. Which would you recommend? Why?

### Case 2

Kevin Edwards has $20,000.00 in a savings account that is earning 6% interest. He is thinking of investing the money in stock that has a stated value and a current market price of $100.00 per share. For the past three years, the stock dividends have amounted to $9.00 per share per year. Mr. Edwards asks your advice. What would you recommend? Explain your answer.

# SCANS workplace competency

SCANS WORKPLACE COMPETENCY

**Resource Competency:** Allocating Money

**Concept:** Employers need workers who can use or prepare budgets, including cost and revenue forecasts. Effective workers are able to maintain detailed records, track actual costs, calculate variances, measure budget performance, and make appropriate adjustments.

**Application:** Prepare a one-month budget projection for yourself. Identify all sources of income such as allowances, wages, monetary gifts, and other anticipated revenues. List all monthly expenses including meals, entertainment, gifts, car payments, insurance amounts, dues, savings, etc. As you track your revenues and expenses during the month, make necessary changes in order to meet your budgetary goals. At the end of the month, compare actual amounts with budgeted figures. Identify reasons for all variances.

## graphing workshop

The corporate income tax for a year divided by the net income before taxes is the *effective tax rate*. Companies track their effective tax rate over the years to determine any trends that may be occurring.

Tax data for Superior Supply Corporation for the past five years is given below.

| Year | Income Tax | Net Income before Tax |
|------|-----------|----------------------|
| 20X1 | 32,099.00 | 125,254 |
| 20X2 | 35,416.00 | 133,758 |
| 20X3 | 40,046.00 | 145,632 |
| 20X4 | 37,949.00 | 140,254 |
| 20X5 | 43,861.00 | 155,412 |

**Instructions:**

1. Calculate the effective tax rate for each year.

2. Create a line graph that will help Superior Supply Corporation determine any trends in its effective tax rate.

## analyzing Costco's financial statements

The amount of net income belonging to a single share of stock is called *earnings per share (EPS)*. EPS is shown on the income statement. In some cases, the company must calculate EPS two different ways. The formula for "basic" EPS is:

$$EPS = \text{Net Income/Number of Shares Outstanding}$$

The formula for "diluted" or "fully diluted" EPS is more complicated and can use different numbers for both the numerator and the denominator.

The formula for rate earned on average stockholders' equity is:

$$\text{Rate Earned on Average Stockholders' equity} = \text{Net Income/Average Stockholders' Equity}$$

**Instructions:**

1. Using Appendix B in this textbook, go to the income statement for Costco Corporation on page B-6. What is the basic EPS for the period ending August 2003?

2. Show the formula and amounts used to calculate the EPS for the period ending August 2003.

3. Compare the basic EPS for the three years shown on the income statement. What trend can you identify?

4. Calculate the rate earned on average stockholders' equity for the periods ending 2003 and 2002. Assume the beginning balance for the period ended 2002 was $4,882,940,000.

5. Compare the rate earned on average stockholders' equity for 2003 and 2002. What trend can you identify?

## End-of-Period Work for a Corporation

During the fiscal period, numerous transactions are analyzed, journalized, and posted. When a transaction affects more than one accounting period, an adjusting entry may be needed to match revenues and expenses with the appropriate accounting period. To complete the accounting cycle, adjusting entries are entered into the computer and verified for accuracy. The financial statements are generated, and then closing entries are generated and posted by the software.

### Trial Balance

Before adjusting entries are recorded, a trial balance is displayed and printed. The trial balance proves the equality of debits and credits in the general ledger. To display the trial balance:

1. Click the Reports toolbar button, or choose the Report Selection menu item from the Reports menu.

2. When the Report Selection dialog appears, choose the Ledger Reports option button from the Select a Report Group list.

3. Select Trial Balance from the Choose a Report to Display list.

4. Click the OK button.

   From the Trial Balance display window, the report can be printed or copied to the Clipboard in spreadsheet or word processing format.

### Adjusting Entries

The trial balance and period-end adjustment data are used as the basis for the adjusting entries. Adjusting entries are used to:

1. Transfer to expense the amount of assets consumed. For example, office supplies and prepaid insurance.

2. Update the merchandise inventory account.

3. Recognize accrued revenues and accrued expenses.

To record adjusting entries, use the following steps:

1. Click the Journal toolbar button, or choose the Journal Entries menu item from the Data menu.

2. Select the General Journal tab from the Journal Entries window, if necessary.

3. Key the adjusting entries. All adjusting entries are dated the last day of the fiscal period. *Adj. Ent.* is used as the reference for all adjusting entries.

4. Click the Post button.

### Financial Statements

The reports that summarize information from the ledgers are known as financial statements. The most common financial statements for a business organized as a corporation are the balance sheet and the income statement. *Automated Accounting 8.0* or higher can also display a retained earnings statement.

   After adjusting entries have been posted, financial statements are prepared. To display financial statements:

1. Click the Reports toolbar button, or choose the Report Selection menu item from the Reports menu. The Report Selection window displays.

2. Choose the Financial Statements option button from the Select a Report Group list.

3. Choose the financial statement report you would like to display from the Choose a Report to Display list.

4. Click the OK button.

   The up-to-date account balances stored by the software are used to calculate and display the current financial statements.

## Closing Entries

In an automated accounting system, closing entries are generated and posted by the software. The software automatically closes net income to Retained Earnings after closing the revenue and expense accounts. The dividend account is closed as well. The steps required are as follows:

1. Choose Generate Closing Journal Entries from the Options menu.

2. Click Yes to generate the closing entries.

3. The general journal will appear, containing the journal entries. Verify the accuracy of the transactions.

4. Click the Post button.

## AUTOMATING MASTERY PROBLEM 13-5

### Instructions:

1. Load *Automated Accounting 8.0* or higher software.

2. Select database AA13-5 (Advanced Course Mastery Problem 13-5) from the accounting template disk.

3. Select File from the menu bar and choose the Save As menu command. Key the path to the drive and directory that contain your data files. Save the database with a filename of XXX135 (where XXX are your initials).

4. Read the Problem Instruction screen by clicking the Browser toolbar button.

5. Refer to page 396 for data used in this problem.

6. Exit the Automated Accounting software.

# Processing and Reporting Accounting Data for a Corporation

AUTOMATED ACCOUNTING

PEACHTREE

QUICKBOOKS

This activity reinforces learning from Parts 2 through 4, Chapters 5 through 13.

## WHITEHURST, INC.

The accounting activities are for Whitehurst, Inc., a merchandising business organized as a corporation. Whitehurst sells plumbing and related products to building contractors, homeowners, and other consumers. Whitehurst's fiscal year is from January 1 through December 31.

## PART A: JOURNALIZING TRANSACTIONS

In Part A of this reinforcement activity, selected transactions for Whitehurst, Inc., completed during December of the current year, are journalized.

Whitehurst uses the chart of accounts shown on page 403. The journals used by Whitehurst are similar to those illustrated in Parts 2 through 4.

## RECORDING TRANSACTIONS

**Instructions:**

1. Journalize the following transactions completed during December of the current year. Use page 23 of a cash receipts journal, page 23 of a cash payments journal, and page 12 of a general journal. Whitehurst records prepaid interest expense initially as an expense and rent received in advance as revenue. Other prepaid and unearned items are recorded initially as assets and liabilities. Source documents are abbreviated as follows: check, C; memorandum, M; note payable, NP; note receivable, NR; receipt, R.

Dec. 1. Whitehurst's board of directors declared an annual dividend of $15,820.00. Preferred stock issued is $40,400.00 of 10%, $100.00 par-value preferred stock. Common stock issued is $11,780.00 of $10.00 stated-value common stock. Date of payment is December 30. M316.

     1. Wrote off Susan Vine's past-due account as uncollectible, $427.50. M317.

     1. Received cash for three months' rent in advance from Woodcrest, Inc., $2,400.00. R126.

     1. Discarded a store fixture: original cost, $1,050.00; total accumulated depreciation through December 31 of last year, $840.00; additional depreciation to be recorded through December 1 of the current year, $210.00. M318.

     1. Received a subscription from Delmar Adams for 30 shares of $100.00 par-value preferred stock, $3,000.00. M319.

## GENERAL LEDGER CHART OF ACCOUNTS

**Balance Sheet Accounts**

| | |
|---|---|
| **(1000)** | **ASSETS** |
| 1100 | CURRENT ASSETS |
| 1105 | Cash |
| 1110 | Petty Cash |
| 1115 | Notes Receivable |
| 1120 | Interest Receivable |
| 1125 | Accounts Receivable |
| 1130 | Allowance for Uncollectible Accounts |
| 1135 | Subscriptions Receivable |
| 1140 | Merchandise Inventory |
| 1145 | Supplies—Sales |
| 1150 | Supplies—Administrative |
| 1155 | Prepaid Insurance |
| 1160 | Prepaid Interest |
| 1200 | LONG-TERM INVESTMENT |
| 1205 | Bond Sinking Fund |
| 1300 | PLANT ASSETS |
| 1305 | Store Equipment |
| 1310 | Accumulated Depreciation—Store Equipment |
| 1315 | Building |
| 1320 | Accumulated Depreciation—Building |
| 1325 | Office Equipment |
| 1330 | Accumulated Depreciation—Office Equipment |
| 1335 | Land |
| 1400 | INTANGIBLE ASSET |
| 1405 | Organization Costs |
| **(2000)** | **LIABILITIES** |
| 2100 | CURRENT LIABILITIES |
| 2105 | Notes Payable |
| 2110 | Interest Payable |
| 2115 | Accounts Payable |
| 2120 | Employee Income Tax Payable |
| 2125 | Federal Income Tax Payable |
| 2130 | Social Security Tax Payable |
| 2133 | Medicare Tax Payable |
| 2135 | Salaries Payable |
| 2140 | Sales Tax Payable |
| 2145 | Unearned Rent |
| 2150 | Unemployment Tax Payable—Federal |
| 2155 | Unemployment Tax Payable—State |
| 2160 | Health Insurance Premiums Payable |
| 2165 | Dividends Payable |
| 2200 | LONG-TERM LIABILITY |
| 2205 | Bonds Payable |
| **(3000)** | **STOCKHOLDERS' EQUITY** |
| 3105 | Capital Stock—Common |
| 3110 | Stock Subscribed—Common |
| 3115 | Paid-in Capital in Excess of Stated Value—Common |
| 3120 | Capital Stock—Preferred |
| 3125 | Stock Subscribed—Preferred |
| 3130 | Paid-in Capital in Excess of Par Value—Preferred |
| 3135 | Treasury Stock |
| 3140 | Paid-in Capital from Sale of Treasury Stock |
| 3145 | Retained Earnings |
| 3150 | Dividends—Common |
| 3155 | Dividends—Preferred |
| 3160 | Income Summary |

**Income Statement Accounts**

| | |
|---|---|
| **(4000)** | **OPERATING REVENUE** |
| 4105 | Sales |
| 4110 | Sales Discount |
| 4115 | Sales Returns and Allowances |
| **(5000)** | **COST OF MERCHANDISE** |
| 5105 | Purchases |
| 5110 | Purchases Discount |
| 5115 | Purchases Returns and Allowances |
| **(6000)** | **OPERATING EXPENSES** |
| 6100 | Selling Expenses |
| 6105 | Advertising Expense |
| 6110 | Credit Card Fee Expense |
| 6115 | Depreciation Expense—Store Equipment |
| 6120 | Miscellaneous Expense—Sales |
| 6125 | Salary Expense—Sales |
| 6130 | Supplies Expense—Sales |
| 6200 | ADMINISTRATIVE EXPENSES |
| 6205 | Depreciation Expense—Building |
| 6210 | Depreciation Expense—Office Equipment |
| 6215 | Insurance Expense |
| 6220 | Miscellaneous Expense—Administrative |
| 6225 | Payroll Taxes Expense |
| 6230 | Property Tax Expense |
| 6235 | Salary Expense—Administrative |
| 6240 | Supplies Expense—Administrative |
| 6245 | Uncollectible Accounts Expense |
| 6250 | Utilities Expense |
| **(7000)** | **OTHER REVENUE** |
| 7105 | Gain on Plant Assets |
| 7110 | Interest Income |
| 7115 | Rent Income |
| **(8000)** | **OTHER EXPENSES** |
| 8105 | Interest Expense |
| 8110 | Loss on Plant Assets |
| 8115 | Organization Expense |
| **(9000)** | **INCOME TAX** |
| 9105 | Federal Income Tax Expense |

Dec. 2. Paid cash for office equipment, $2,650.00. C476.
4. Patrick Carson dishonored NR4, a 30-day, 10% note, maturity value due today: principal, $150.00; interest, $1.25; total, $151.25. M320.
4. Discarded an office table: original cost, $250.00; total accumulated depreciation through December 31 of last year, $150.00; additional depreciation to be recorded through December 4 of the current year, $50.00. M321.
4. Received a 60-day, 10% note from Leigh Calhoun for an extension of time on her account, $500.00. NR5.
5. Issued a 6-month, 10% note, $10,000.00. NP6.
5. Paid cash to bond trustee for annual interest on bond issue, $24,000.00. C482.
5. Paid cash to bond trustee for annual deposit to bond sinking fund, $18,400.00, and recorded interest earned on bond sinking fund, $1,600.00. C487.
6. Received cash from Leslie Johns for 700 shares of $10.00 stated-value common stock at $11.00 per share, $7,700.00. R134.
7. Received cash for the maturity value of NR1, principal, $150.00, plus interest, $2.47; total, $152.47. R136.
11. Received cash from sale of office equipment, $70.00: original cost, $700.00; total accumulated depreciation through December 31 of last year, $500.00; additional depreciation to be recorded through December 11 of the current year, $100.00. M322 and R138.
11. Paid cash to Marlin Pratt for 60 shares of $10.00 stated-value common stock at $9.00 per share, $540.00. C502.
12. Paid cash for the maturity value of NP4: principal, $300.00, plus interest, $6.00; total, $306.00. C503.
13. Received cash from Robert Shull for 200 shares of $10.00 stated-value common stock at $10.00 per share, $2,000.00. R140.
14. Received cash for the maturity value of NR2: principal, $247.50, plus interest; $4.07; total $251.57. R141.
16. Paid cash for the maturity value of NP3: principal, $1,000.00, plus interest, $16.44; total, $1,016.44. C509.
19. Received office equipment from Valerie DeLong at an agreed value of $1,000.00 for 10 shares of $100.00 par-value preferred stock. M323.
20. Received cash in full payment of Susan Vine's account, previously written off as uncollectible, $427.50. M324 and R143.
21. Paid cash, $2,000.00, plus an office microcomputer, for a new microcomputer: original cost of old microcomputer, $3,500.00; total accumulated depreciation through December 31 of last year, $2,100.00; additional depreciation to be recorded through December 21 of the current year, $700.00. M325 and C515.
27. Discounted at 12% a 60-day non-interest-bearing note, $5,000.00; proceeds, $4,900.00; interest, $100.00. NP7.
28. Received cash from James Dier for 10 shares of treasury stock at $13.00 per share, $130.00. Treasury stock was bought on December 11 at $9.00 per share. R146.
29. Received cash from sale of an old cash register used in sales, $800.00: original cost, $1,600.00; total accumulated depreciation through December 31 of last year, $896.00; additional depreciation to be recorded through December 29 of the current year, $144.00. M326 and R147.
29. Received cash from Patrick Carson for dishonored NR4: principal, $151.25, plus additional interest, $1.05; total, $152.30. R148.
29. Received cash from Delmar Adams in payment of stock subscription, $3,000.00. R149.
29. Issued Stock Certificate No. 14 to Delmar Adams for 30 shares of $100.00 par-value preferred stock, $3,000.00. M327.
30. Paid cash for annual dividend declared December 1, $15,820.00. C519.

2. Prove and rule the cash receipts and cash payments journals.

In Part B, Whitehurst's end-of-fiscal-period work is completed. This work is similar to activities described in Chapter 14. The December 31 trial balance is recorded on a work sheet in the *Working Papers* accompanying this textbook.

**Instructions:**

3. Complete the work sheet for the year ended December 31 of the current year. Record the adjustments on the work sheet using the following additional information.

Adjustment Information, December 31

| | |
|---|---:|
| Accrued interest income | $ 95.70 |
| Uncollectible accounts expense estimated as 0.1% of net sales on account. | |
| Net sales on account for year, $343,472.60. | |
| Merchandise inventory | 206,618.63 |
| Sales supplies inventory | 1,456.06 |
| Administrative supplies inventory | 730.00 |
| Value of prepaid insurance | 970.00 |
| Prepaid interest | 93.33 |
| Annual depreciation expense—store equipment | 8,300.00 |
| Annual depreciation expense—building | 1,500.00 |
| Annual depreciation expense—office equipment | 1,150.00 |
| Organization expense | 300.00 |
| Accrued interest expense | 2,025.00 |
| Accrued salaries—sales | 3,232.04 |
| Accrued salaries—administrative | 716.50 |
| Accrued payroll taxes—Social Security tax | 256.65 |
| Accrued payroll taxes—Medicare tax | 59.23 |
| Accrued payroll taxes—federal unemployment tax | 15.79 |
| Accrued payroll taxes—state unemployment tax | 106.58 |
| Rent received in advance and still unearned | 1,200.00 |

Federal income tax expense for the year is calculated at the following rates:
   15% of net income before taxes, zero to $50,000.00.
   Plus 25% of net income before taxes, $50,000.00 to $75,000.00.
   Plus 34% of net income before taxes, $75,000.00 to $100,000.00.
   Plus 39% of net income before taxes, $100,000.00 to $335,000.00.
   Plus 34% of the net income before taxes over $335,000.00.

4. Prepare an income statement. Calculate and record the following component percentages. (a) Cost of merchandise sold. (b) Gross profit on operations. (c) Total selling expenses. (d) Total administrative expenses. (e) Total operating expenses. (f) Income from operations. (g) Net addition or deduction resulting from other revenue and expenses. (h) Net income before federal income tax. (i) Federal income tax expense. (j) Net income after federal income tax. Round percentage calculations to the nearest 0.1%.

5. Analyze Whitehurst's income statement by determining if component percentages are within acceptable levels. If any component percentage is not within an acceptable level, suggest steps that the company should take. Acceptable component percentages are given in the *Working Papers*.

6. Calculate earnings per share. Round the calculation to the nearest cent. Whitehurst has 12,680 shares of $10.00 stated-value common stock issued and 444 shares of 10%, $100.00 par-value preferred stock issued. Treasury stock consists of 50 shares of common stock.

7. Prepare a statement of stockholders' equity. Use the following additional information.

|  | January 1<br>Balance | Issued During<br>the Year | December 31<br>Balance |
|---|---|---|---|
| Common stock: | | | |
| No. of shares | 11,780 | 900 | 12,680 |
| Amount | $117,800.00 | $9,000.00 | $126,800.00 |
| Preferred stock: | | | |
| No. of shares | 404 | 40 | 444 |
| Amount | $ 40,400.00 | $4,000.00 | $ 44,400.00 |

The January 1 balance of Retained Earnings was $26,759.39.

8. Calculate the following items based on information on the statement of stockholders' equity. (a) Equity per share of stock. (b) Price-earnings ratio. The market price of common stock on December 31 is $13.50.

9. Prepare a balance sheet for December 31 of the current year.

10. Calculate the following items based on information from the balance sheet. (a) Accounts receivable turnover ratio. Accounts receivable and allowance for uncollectible accounts on January 1 were $36,785.45 and $698.35, respectively. (b) Rate earned on average stockholders' equity. Total stockholders' equity on January 1 was $186,459.39. (c) Rate earned on average total assets. Total assets on January 1 were $458,204.24.

11. Use pages 13 and 14 of a general journal. Journalize the adjusting entries.

12. Use pages 14 and 15 of a general journal. Do not skip a line. Journalize the closing entries.

13. Use page 1 of a general journal. Journalize the reversing entries. Use January 1 of the year following the current year as the date.

*Activities in First Class Image Wear, Inc.:*

1. Recording transactions in special journals and a general journal.

2. Posting items to be posted individually to a general ledger and subsidiary ledgers.

3. Proving and ruling journals.

4. Posting column totals to a general ledger.

5. Preparing schedules of accounts receivable and accounts payable.

6. Preparing a trial balance on a work sheet.

7. Planning adjustments and completing a work sheet.

8. Preparing financial statements.

9. Journalizing and posting adjusting entries.

10. Journalizing and posting closing entries.

11. Preparing a post-closing trial balance.

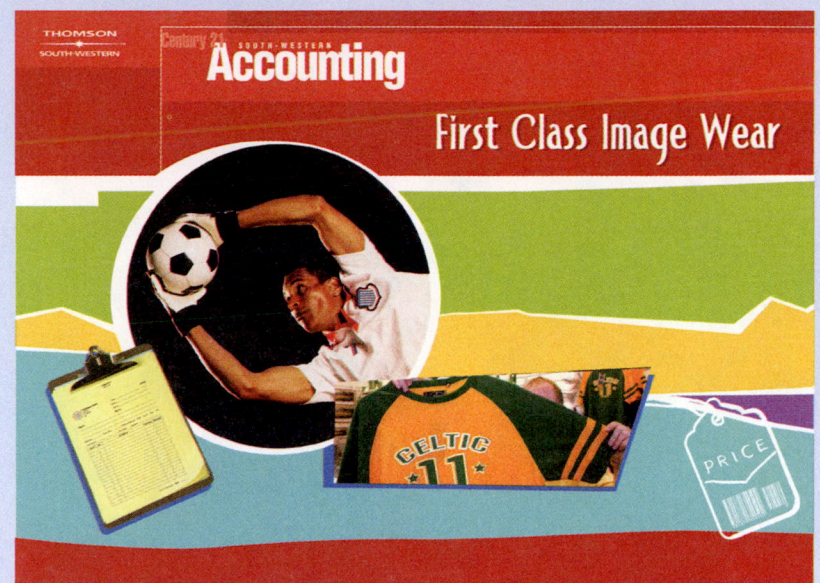

# A Business Simulation
# First Class Image Wear, Inc.

First Class Image Wear, Inc. is a merchandising business organized as a corporation. This business simulation covers the realistic transactions completed by First Class Image Wear, Inc., which sells a broad range of logo ware. The activities included in the accounting cycle for First Class Image Wear, Inc. are listed at left.

This simulation is available from the publisher in either manual or automated versions.

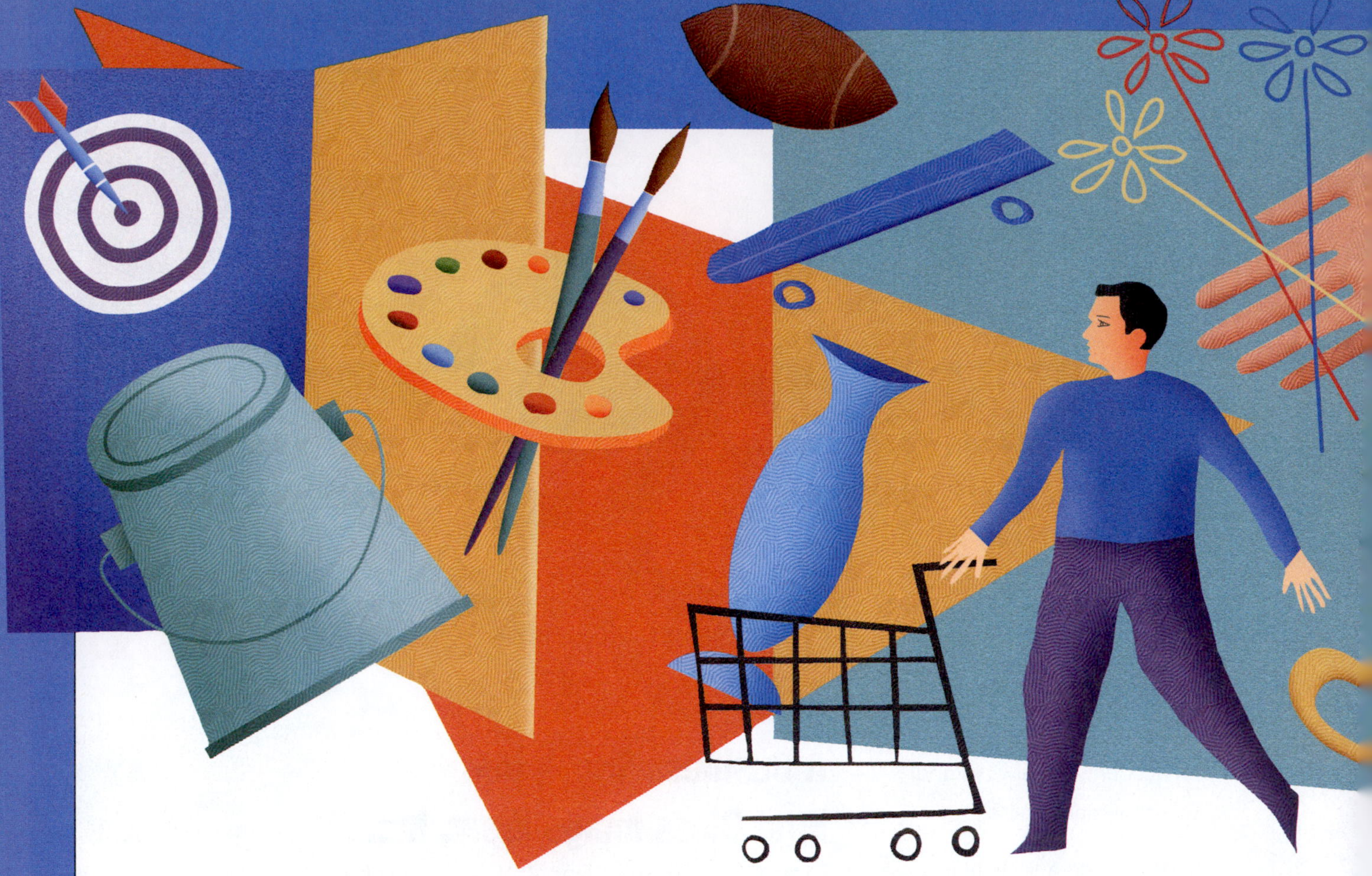

# PART 5 Management Accounting

CHAPTER

**REFLECTION, INC.
CHART OF ACCOUNTS**

**Balance Sheet Accounts**

**(1000) ASSETS**

1100   CURRENT ASSETS
1105   Cash
1110   Petty Cash
1115   Notes Receivable
1120   Interest Receivable
1125   Accounts Receivable
1130   Allowance for Uncollectible Accounts
1135   Merchandise Inventory
1140   Supplies—Sales
1145   Supplies—Administrative
1150   Prepaid Insurance

1200   PLANT ASSETS
1205   Equipment—Delivery
1210   Accumulated Depreciation—Delivery Equipment
1215   Equipment—Office
1220   Accumulated Depreciation—Office Equipment
1225   Equipment—Warehouse
1230   Accumulated Depreciation—Warehouse Equipment

1235   Building
1240   Accumulated Depreciation—Building
1245   Land

**(2000) LIABILITIES**

2100   CURRENT LIABILITIES
2105   Notes Payable
2110   Interest Payable
2115   Accounts Payable
2120   Employee Income Tax Payable
2125   Federal Income Tax Payable
2128   Social Security Tax Payable
2130   Medicare Tax Payable
2135   Sales Tax Payable
2140   Unemployment Tax Payable—Federal
2145   Unemployment Tax Payable—State
2150   Dividends Payable

2200   LONG-TERM LIABILITY
2205   Mortgage Payable

**(3000) CAPITAL**

3105   Capital Stock
3110   Retained Earnings
3115   Dividends
3120   Income Summary

**(4000) OPERATING REVENUE**

4105   Sales
4110   Sales Discount
4115   Sales Returns and Allowances

**(5000) COST OF MERCHANDISE**

5105   Purchases
5110   Purchases Discount
5115   Purchases Returns and Allowances

**(6000) OPERATING EXPENSES**

6100   SELLING EXPENSES
6105   Advertising Expense
6110   Delivery Expense
6115   Depreciation Expense—Delivery Equipment
6120   Depreciation Expense—Warehouse Equipment
6125   Miscellaneous Expense—Sales
6130   Salary Expense—Commissions
6135   Salary Expense—Regular
6140   Supplies Expense—Sales

6200   ADMINISTRATIVE EXPENSES
6205   Depreciation Expense—Office Equipment
6210   Insurance Expense
6215   Miscellaneous Expense—Administrative
6220   Payroll Taxes Expense
6225   Rent Expense
6230   Salary Expense—Administrative
6235   Supplies Expense—Administrative
6240   Uncollectible Accounts Expense
6245   Utilities Expense

**(7000) OTHER REVENUE**

7105   Gain on Plant Assets
7110   Interest Income

**(8000) OTHER EXPENSES**

8105   Interest Expense
8110   Loss on Plant Assets

**(9000) INCOME TAX**

9105   Federal Income Tax Expense

The chart of accounts for Reflection, Inc. is illustrated above for ready reference as you study Part 5 of this textbook.

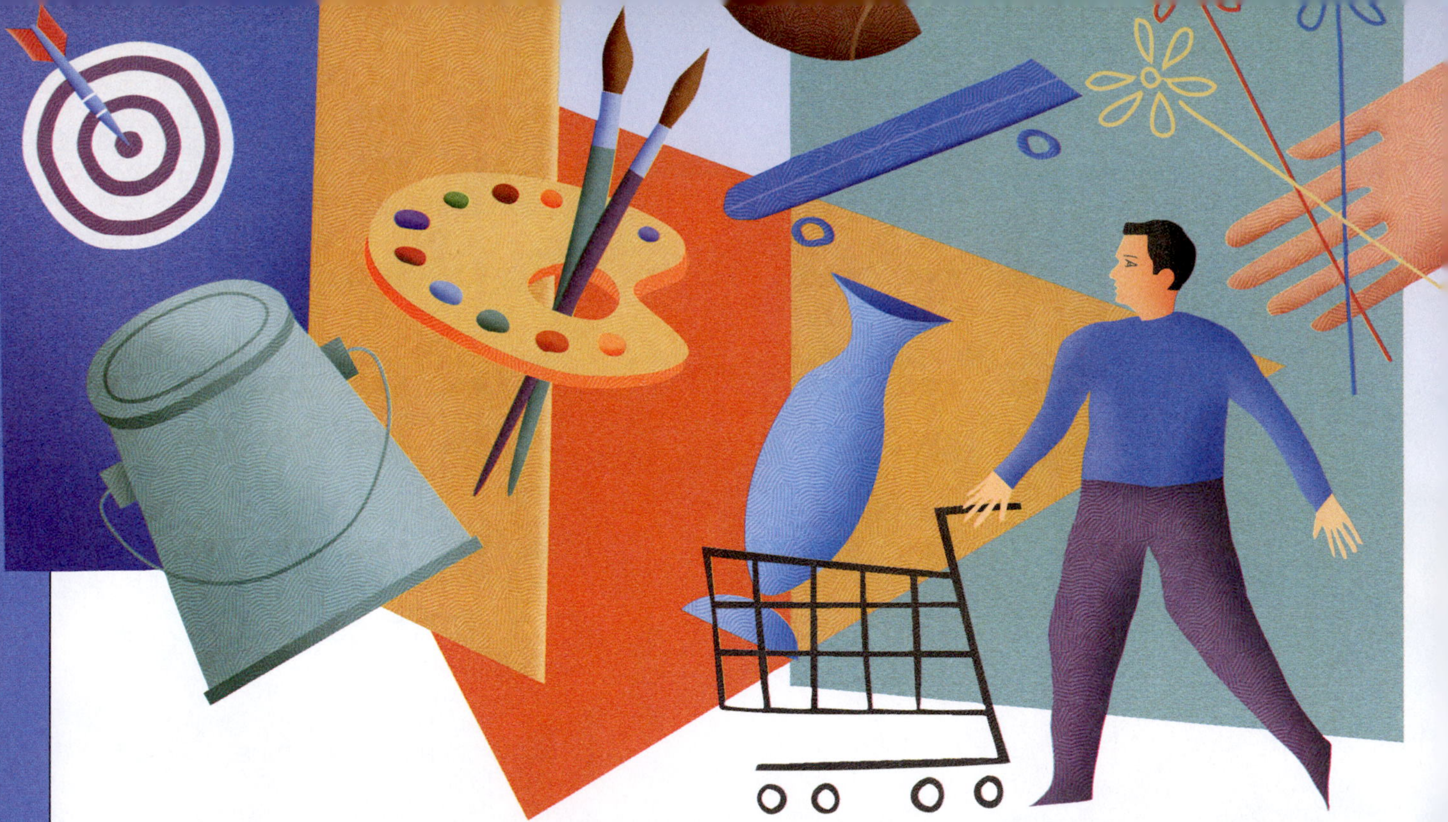

# CHAPTER 14 Budgetary Planning and Control

OBJECTIVES & TERMS

***After studying Chapter 14, you will be able to:***

1. Define accounting terms related to budgetary planning and control.
2. Identify accounting concepts and practices related to preparing and analyzing budgeted income statements and cash budgets.
3. Gather information to prepare a budget.
4. Prepare a budgeted income statement.
5. Prepare a cash budget and performance report.

- budgeting
- budget
- budget period
- comparative income statement
- sales budget schedule
- purchases budget schedule
- selling expenses budget schedule
- administrative expenses budget schedule
- other revenue and expenses budget schedule
- budgeted income statement
- cash receipts budget schedule
- cash payments budget schedule
- cash budget
- performance report

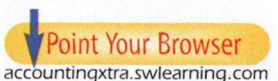

Point Your Browser
accountingxtra.swlearning.com

## • KPMG

©TONY WHITE//BLOOMBERG NEWS/LANDOV

### FORENSIC ACCOUNTING AT KPMG

With nearly 100,000 employees and $11 billion in revenue, KPMG is one of the largest accounting firms in the world. In addition to providing traditional audit and tax services, KPMG has been a leader in the area of forensic accounting—the detection, prevention, and investigation of fraud.

KPMG published its first Fraud Survey in 1994. This renowned survey profiles the impact of fraud at hundreds of medium and large organizations. Its findings are clear—the instances of fraud are increasing.

What should an organization do if it suspects fraud has occurred? Most organizations elect to conduct an investigation. Unfortunately, most organizations do not have employees with the necessary knowledge or experience. KPMG, with its wealth of forensic accounting experience, is ideally suited to perform this investigation.

Organizations often require accounting firms to submit a bid or estimate of the professional fees that will be charged to complete the investigation. To calculate an estimate, KPMG must first determine the necessary experience level and expertise of the professional staff to be assigned to the client. The hourly billing rate of each professional staff member reflects that staff's experience and expertise.

### Critical Thinking

1.  What information would KPMG require in order to calculate an estimate of the professional fees to be charged for an advisory services project?
2.  How does the level of experience and expertise affect the hourly billing rate of professional staff members?

Sources: www.us.kpmg.com/about/statistics2.asp; www.us.kpmg.com/RutUS_prod/Documents/12/FINALFraudSur.pdf

Xtra!
Today
accountingxtra.swlearning.com

## internet activity

### ORGANIZATIONAL CHARTS

Search the Internet for "organizational charts." Find the organizational charts for two organizations. Compare the charts by answering the following questions:

### Instructions

1.  What is the name of the organization?
2.  What position(s) is at the top of the chart?
3.  How many positions report directly to the top position? Name one such position.

## 14-1 Budget Planning

Business managers make a variety of business decisions each day. The quality of these decisions has a direct impact on the business's ability to improve profitability. Financial planning is one tool managers use to improve profitability. A business must earn a net income to continue in existence. [CONCEPT: Going Concern]

Planning the financial operations of a business is called **budgeting**. A written financial plan of a business for a specific period of time, expressed in dollars, is called a **budget**. [CONCEPT: Unit of Measurement] A business prepares a variety of budgets. Each budget provides managers with detailed information about a specific area of the business's operations.

A budget is a view into the future—a financial estimate of future business activities. Budget preparation begins with identifying company goals. Company goals might be to increase sales, reduce cost of merchandise sold, or increase net income. All of these goals affect budget preparation because the budget is a business's financial plan.

Two budgets commonly prepared in businesses are the budgeted income statement and the cash budget. The budgeted income statement is a projection of a business's sales, costs, expenses, and net income for a fiscal period. It is similar to a regular income statement and is sometimes known as an operating budget. The cash budget is a projection of a business's cash receipts and payments for a fiscal period. It is used to manage estimated cash shortages and overages.

©GETTY IMAGES/PHOTODISC

## making ethical decisions

### Confidentiality

Paxton Plastics manufactures molded plastic backyard play systems. Paxton is involved in several lawsuits as the result of children being injured while playing on Paxton's Slide by Slide, a double-wide sliding board. During a recent audit, Justin Portero, a CPA, learned that the company knew about structural problems with the sliding board and continued to manufacture and sell the products. Several company officers told Justin that they expect the company to lose the lawsuits but that the cost of these lawsuits will be less than the cost of recalling and replacing the sliding boards. Later that week, Justin was visiting a friend who proudly displayed his son's new Paxton's Slide by Slide.

### Instructions

Determine whether Justin, in accordance with the AICPA *Code of Professional Conduct,* can inform his friend of the problems with the play system. What recommendation would you give Justin?

## BUDGET FUNCTIONS

Budgets are projections or estimates of what will happen in the future expressed in financial terms. A carefully prepared budget reflects the best projections possible by those persons who prepare it. A completed budget shows the projected course of action for a business. A budget serves three important business functions.

1. **Planning.** In preparing a budget, managers project what will happen in the future. This view of the future helps a manager plan actions that will meet desired goals. The budgeting process forces a manager to decide which actions should be emphasized to achieve the desired goals.

2. **Operational control.** A budget projects the accomplishments of a business. It specifies the type and the amount of projected activities. By comparing actual performance with projected performance, management can judge how well a business is achieving its goals. For example, managers compare actual expenses with budgeted expenses to identify differences. By identifying actual expense items that are higher than budgeted, a business can act to reduce these amounts.

3. **Department coordination.** Profitable business growth requires all managers to be aware of the company's plans. A budget reflects these plans. Each phase of a business operation must be coordinated with all related phases. For example, to achieve projected sales, the purchasing department must know when and how much merchandise to purchase. Therefore, all management personnel must help plan and use a budget as a guide to control and coordinate sales, costs, and expenses.

## BUDGET PERIOD

The length of time covered by a budget is called the **budget period**. Usually this period is one year. Some companies also prepare a long-range budget of five years or more for special projects and plant and equipment purchases. However, the annual budget is the one used to compare current financial performance with budget plans.

An annual budget is normally prepared for a company's fiscal year. The annual budget is commonly divided into quarterly and monthly budgets. Such budget subdivisions provide frequent opportunities to evaluate how actual operations compare with budgeted operations.

A budget must be prepared in sufficient time to be communicated to the appropriate managers prior to the beginning of a budget period.

Large and complex companies start gathering budget information long before the beginning of a new budget year. Gathering information, performing analysis, making decisions, preparing the budget, and approving and communicating the budget take considerable time.

**FYI** FOR YOUR INFORMATION

Most budgets are based on forecasts of increases or decreases over previous years' performances. In zero-based budgeting, however, the data are prepared each year as though operations were being started for the first time.

Budgets cannot be exact since they show only projected sales, costs, and expenses. However, a company should project future operations as accurately as possible. A company uses many information sources.

### Company Records

The accounting and sales records of a business contain much of the information needed to prepare budgets. Accounting information about previous years' operations is used to determine trends in sales, purchases, and operating expenses. Expected price changes, sales promotion plans, and market research studies also are important in projecting activity for a budget period.

### General Economic Information

A general slowdown or speedup in the national economy may affect budget decisions. Unusually high inflation rates affect budgeted amounts. A labor strike may affect some related industries and thus affect company operations. New product development, changes in consumer buying habits, availability of merchandise, international trade, and general business conditions all must be considered when preparing budgets.

### Company Staff and Managers

Sales personnel estimate the amount of projected sales. Considering projected sales for the new budget period, other department managers project budget items for their areas of responsibility of the business.

### Good Judgment

Good judgment by the individuals preparing the budgets is essential to realistic budgets. Even after evaluating all available information, answers to many budget questions are seldom obvious. Since some information will conflict with other information, final budget decisions are based on good judgment.

©GETTY IMAGES/PHOTODISC

**REMEMBER** National magazines and newspapers are a good source of information regarding general economic conditions.

**Reflection, Inc.**
**Comparative Income Statement**
**For Years Ended December 31, 20X1 and 20X2**

| | 20X2 | 20X1 | Increase (Decrease) Amount | Increase (Decrease) Percentage* |
|---|---|---|---|---|
| Operating Revenue: | | | | |
| Net Sales | $1,880,000 | $1,700,000 | $180,000 | 10.6 |
| Cost of Merchandise Sold | 1,231,720 | 1,105,000 | 126,720 | 11.5 |
| Gross Profit on Operations | $ 648,280 | $ 595,000 | $ 53,280 | 9.0 |
| Operating Expenses: | | | | |
| Selling Expenses: | | | | |
| Advertising Expense | $ 45,120 | $ 37,800 | $ 7,320 | 19.4 |
| Delivery Expense | 150,410 | 140,640 | 9,770 | 6.9 |
| Depr. Expense—Delivery Equipment | 7,200 | 7,000 | 200 | 2.9 |
| Depr. Expense—Warehouse Equipment | 10,800 | 10,800 | 0 | 0.0 |
| Miscellaneous Expense—Sales | 11,490 | 11,960 | (470) | (3.9) |
| Salary Expense—Commissions | 75,200 | 68,000 | 7,200 | 10.6 |
| Salary Expense—Regular | 34,160 | 28,320 | 5,840 | 20.6 |
| Supplies Expense—Sales | 11,280 | 10,850 | 430 | 4.0 |
| Total Selling Expenses | $ 345,660 | $ 315,370 | $ 30,290 | 9.6 |
| Administrative Expenses: | | | | |
| Depr. Expense—Office Equipment | $ 14,400 | $ 12,000 | $ 2,400 | 20.0 |
| Insurance Expense | 4,800 | 4,500 | 300 | 6.7 |
| Miscellaneous Expense—Administrative | 38,770 | 33,640 | 5,130 | 15.2 |
| Depr. Expense—Warehouse Equipment | 19,200 | 19,200 | 0 | 0.0 |
| Payroll Taxes Expense | 22,540 | 20,590 | 1,950 | 9.5 |
| Rent Expense | 30,000 | 30,000 | 0 | 0.0 |
| Salary Expense—Administrative | 77,830 | 75,240 | 2,590 | 3.4 |
| Supplies Expense—Administrative | 13,620 | 14,600 | (980) | (6.7) |
| Uncollectible Accounts Expense | 11,280 | 10,230 | 1,050 | 10.3 |
| Utilities Expense | 10,080 | 7,320 | 2,760 | 37.7 |
| Total Administrative Expenses | $ 242,520 | $ 227,320 | $ 15,200 | 6.7 |
| Total Operating Expenses | $ 588,180 | $ 542,690 | $ 45,490 | 8.4 |
| Income from Operations | $ 60,100 | $ 52,310 | $ 7,790 | 14.9 |
| Other Expenses: | | | | |
| Interest Expense | $ 3,000 | $ 6,500 | ($ 3,500) | (53.8) |
| Net Income before Federal Income Tax | $ 57,100 | $ 45,810 | $ 11,290 | 24.6 |
| Federal Income Tax Expense | 9,280 | 6,870 | 2,410 | 35.1 |
| Net Income after Federal Income Tax | $ 47,820 | $ 38,940 | $ 8,880 | 22.8 |
| Units (sq. ft.) of Mirror Sold | 376,000 | 340,000 | 36,000 | 10.6 |

*Percentages rounded to the nearest 0.1%.

Preparation for planning a budget involves analyzing available financial information. An analysis of previous years' sales, cost, and expense amounts is an important part of budget preparation. An income statement containing sales, cost, and expense information for two or more years is called a **comparative income statement**.

Reflection, Inc., is a corporation that sells custom-cut mirrors. A comparative income statement provides the information for Reflection's analysis of previous years' sales, costs, and expenses. This statement shows trends that may be taking place in these items. The statement also highlights items that may be increasing or decreasing at a higher rate than other items on the statement. Reflection's comparative income statement is shown above.

# INTERPRETING THE COMPARATIVE INCOME STATEMENT

| Compare the percentage change in expenses or costs to the percentage change in sales. | Effect on net income |
|---|---|
| If the % increase ↑ in expenses or costs > the % increase ↑ in sales, net income ↓ decreases. | Unfavorable |
| If the % increase ↑ in expenses or costs < the % increase ↑ in sales, net income ↑ increases. | Favorable |
| If the % decrease ↓ in expenses or costs > the % decrease ↓ in sales, net income ↑ increases. | Favorable |
| If the % decrease ↓ in expenses or costs < the % decrease ↓ in sales, net income ↓ decreases. | Unfavorable |

The first column of Reflection's comparative income statement shows actual sales, costs, and expenses for 20X2, the current year. The second column shows actual amounts for 20X1, the prior year. The third column shows the amount of increase or decrease from the prior year, 20X1, to the current year, 20X2. (For example, 20X2 cost of merchandise sold, $1,231,720, *less* 20X1 cost of merchandise sold, $1,105,000, *equals* the increase, $126,720.) The fourth column shows the percentage by which the current year amount increased or decreased from the prior year amount. (For example, the cost of merchandise sold increase, $126,720, *divided* by the 20X1 amount, $1,105,000, *equals* the percentage of increase, 11.5%.) Reflection rounds percentages to the nearest 0.1%.

Managers review each increase or decrease amount on the comparative income statement. The percentage of increase or decrease indicates whether the change is favorable, unfavorable, or normal compared with net sales. If a cost or expense item increase is a higher percentage than the net sales increase, net income is unfavorably affected. However, if the net sales increase is a higher percentage than cost and expense items, net income is favorably affected. Decreases have the opposite effect. If a cost or expense item decrease is a higher percentage than the net sales decrease, net income is favorably affected. If the net sales decrease is a higher percentage than cost and expense items, net income is unfavorably affected. A summary of the effect of changes in expenses or costs on net income is shown above.

Unfavorable results require further inquiry to determine the cause. Reflection's net sales increased 10.6% over 20X1. The goal for 20X2 was to increase sales volume by 10.0%. The actual 10.6% increase resulted from an increase in units sold from 340,000 to 376,000 square feet of mirrors. The unit sales price remained at $5.00. Management attributed the increase to two factors. (1) A more intensive advertising campaign increased market share from 42.0% to 45.0%. (2) Favorable economic conditions spurred new home building and created a greater demand for mirrors.

Reflection, Inc., analyzes each cost and expense amount and percentage. For example, the cost of merchandise sold increased 11.5% over 20X1. Most of the increase resulted from the 10.6% increase in the number of units sold. In addition, the purchase price per square foot of mirrors increased during 20X2 from $3.25 per square foot to $3.30. Advertising expense increased 19.4% over 20X1. The increase is consistent with the successful effort to expand market share. Management believes that more expensive television advertising resulted in a significant increase in third and fourth quarter unit sales.

During the annual budget process, Reflection also does the following:

1. Analyzes general and industry economic conditions to determine probable changes in sales volume for the coming year.
2. Sets company goals for costs and expenses as a percentage of sales.

**REMEMBER** Comparative financial statements may be prepared for a fiscal year or a month.

## terms review

budgeting
budget
budget period
comparative income statement

## audit your understanding

1. How does the budgeting process help control expenses?
2. What is the length of time generally covered by a company's budget?
3. Will net income increase or decrease if the percentage change in expenses is less than the percentage change in net sales? Explain.

## work together 14-1

**Analyzing a comparative income statement**

The comparative income statement for San Francisco Sourdough Baking Company shows a percentage increase for net sales of 14.2%. A table is provided in the *Working Papers*. Your instructor will guide you through the following examples.

1. Indicate whether the following percentage change in cost and expense items is favorable or unfavorable:

| Cost/Expense Item | Percentage of Increase (Decrease) |
|---|---|
| Cost of Merchandise Sold | 11.0% |
| Advertising Expense | 15.1% |
| Salary Expense | 12.5% |
| Utilities Expense | (1.2%) |

## on your own 14-1

**Analyzing a comparative income statement**

The comparative income statement for Precision Racing Components, Inc., indicates a percentage increase in net sales of 8.3%. A table is provided in the *Working Papers*. Work the following problem independently.

1. Indicate whether the following percentage change in cost and expense items is favorable or unfavorable:

| Cost/Expense Item | Percentage of Increase (Decrease) |
|---|---|
| Cost of Merchandise Sold | 11.0% |
| Advertising Expense | 7.3% |
| Insurance Expense | (4.5%) |
| Rent Expense | 2.0% |

# 14-2 Budgeted Income Statement

## ANNUAL OPERATIONAL PLANS AND GOALS

**Goals for 20X3:**
1. The economy is projected to remain strong throughout 20X3. Therefore, the sales goal is to increase unit sales to 400,000 units, about a 6.4% increase. The unit sales price will be increased in the second quarter from $5.00 to $5.25 per square foot to recover merchandise cost increases in 20X2 and projected increases in the budget year.
2. Sales distribution by quarters is projected to be consistent with prior quarters.
3. The unit cost of merchandise is projected to rise from $3.30 to $3.40 in the first quarter, a 3.0% increase.
4. An automated cutting machine has been ordered. It will cost $20,000 and is projected to save approximately $10,000 per year in salary expense.
5. All employees on salary will receive a 5.0% increase in wage rate.
6. Rigid controls on all expenditures will be exercised.

After previous years' records have been analyzed, a business sets goals, develops operational plans, and prepares projection of sales, costs, and expenses for the coming year. Annual company goals establish targets that the company will work toward in the coming year. Goals help a company coordinate the efforts of all areas toward a common direction. An operational plan provides general guidelines for achieving the company's goals. Operational plans and goals generally are determined by a planning group consisting of the company's executive officers and department managers.

At Reflection, the planning group includes the president and all department managers. The planning group reviews the analysis of the previous year's comparative income statement and considers possible changes in economic conditions that may affect the company. From these discussions, the company's operational plan and goals for the coming year are determined. After reviewing company records and considering general economic conditions, Reflection's planning group develops the planning guidelines shown above.

The operational plan is converted into a more precise plan expressed in dollars by preparing a budgeted income statement. Reflection prepares separate schedules for the major parts of the bud-geted income statement. Separate schedules are prepared for sales, purchases, selling expenses, administrative expenses, and other revenue and expenses. To permit more frequent comparisons with budgeted amounts, schedules for the budget are separated into quarterly projections.

At Reflection, the accounting department is responsible for coordinating budget preparation. The sales manager is responsible for preparing the sales, purchases, and selling expenses budget schedules. The administrative manager is responsible for preparing the administrative expenses budget and the other revenue and expenses budget schedules. The accounting department then prepares the bud-geted income statement from these schedules. The completed budget, with attached schedules, is submitted to the budget committee for approval. The budget committee consists of the president and two members of Reflection's board of directors.

©GETTY IMAGES/PHOTODISC

# SALES BUDGET SCHEDULE

**1.** Enter actual and projected units.

**2.** Determine sales percentages:

| 20X2 Actual Unit Sales First Quarter | ÷ | 20X2 Actual Unit Sales | = | 20X2 Sales Percentage First Quarter |
|---|---|---|---|---|
| 91,600 | ÷ | 376,000 | = | 24.4% |

**4.** Enter unit sales prices.

**6.** Calculate total net sales.

$ 488,000
552,300
579,600
455,700
$ 2,075,600

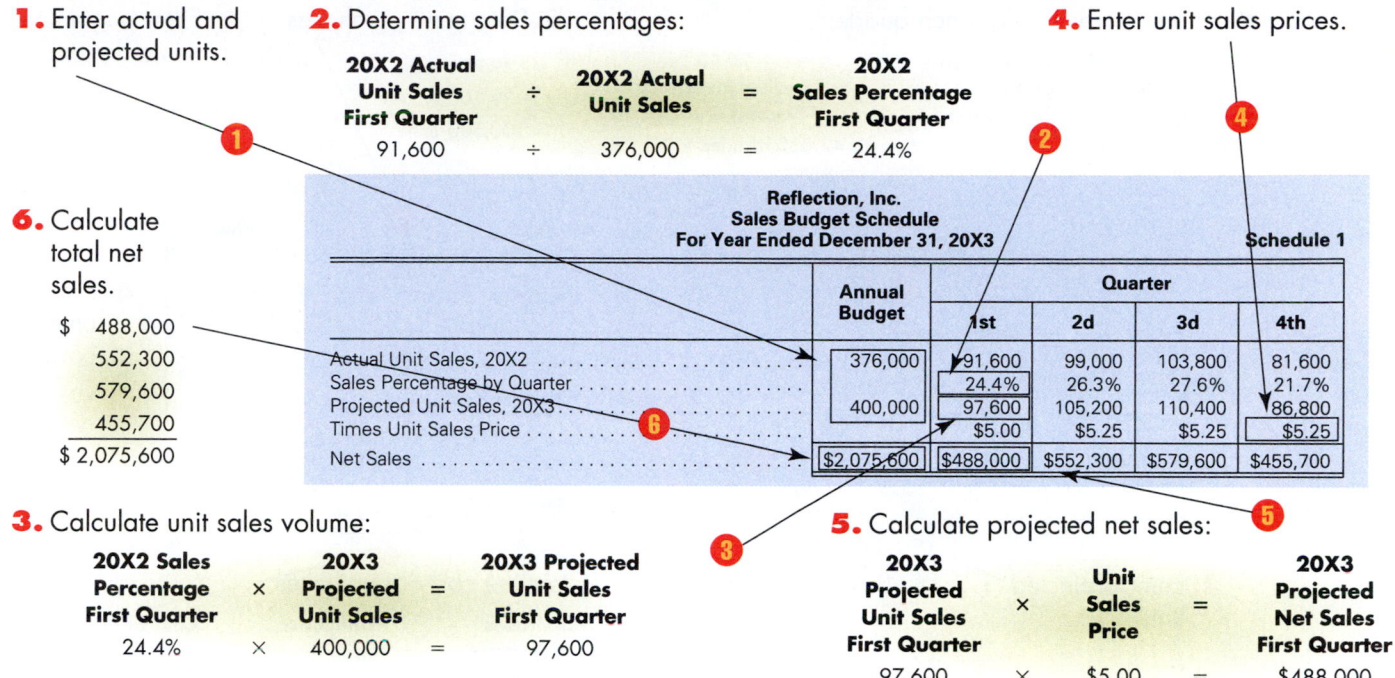

Reflection, Inc.
Sales Budget Schedule
For Year Ended December 31, 20X3

Schedule 1

|  | Annual Budget | Quarter | | | |
|---|---|---|---|---|---|
|  |  | 1st | 2d | 3d | 4th |
| Actual Unit Sales, 20X2 | 376,000 | 91,600 | 99,000 | 103,800 | 81,600 |
| Sales Percentage by Quarter |  | 24.4% | 26.3% | 27.6% | 21.7% |
| Projected Unit Sales, 20X3 | 400,000 | 97,600 | 105,200 | 110,400 | 86,800 |
| Times Unit Sales Price |  | $5.00 | $5.25 | $5.25 | $5.25 |
| Net Sales | $2,075,600 | $488,000 | $552,300 | $579,600 | $455,700 |

**3.** Calculate unit sales volume:

| 20X2 Sales Percentage First Quarter | × | 20X3 Projected Unit Sales | = | 20X3 Projected Unit Sales First Quarter |
|---|---|---|---|---|
| 24.4% | × | 400,000 | = | 97,600 |

**5.** Calculate projected net sales:

| 20X3 Projected Unit Sales First Quarter | × | Unit Sales Price | = | 20X3 Projected Net Sales First Quarter |
|---|---|---|---|---|
| 97,600 | × | $5.00 | = | $488,000 |

A statement that shows the projected net sales for a budget period is called a **sales budget schedule**. The sales budget schedule is prepared first because the other schedules are affected by the projected net sales. Projected net sales are used to estimate the amount of merchandise to purchase and the amount that may be spent for salaries, advertising, and other selling and administrative expenses.

Reflection's sales manager, with knowledge of the budget guidelines and with the assistance of sales representatives, prepares the sales budget schedule shown above. Based on the planning group's goal of a 6.4% increase in unit

sales, the budget reflects an increase from 376,000 to 400,000 units. The sales manager plans to increase the unit sales price from $5.00 to $5.25 in the second quarter. The timing of the increase was planned after reviewing competitors' selling prices and analyzing projected costs of merchandise.

Accurate projections are important for effective budgeting. However, since budgets are based on estimates, most businesses round the projected amounts to simplify the budgeting process. Reflection Inc., rounds unit projections to the nearest hundred units and dollar projections to the nearest $10.

## STEPS · STEPS · STEPS · STEPS · STEPS · STEPS · STEPS · STEPS · STEPS · STEPS
### PREPARING A SALES BUDGET SCHEDULE

**1** Enter the number of actual units, *376,000*, and projected units, *400,000*, in the Annual Budget column.

**2** Determine the sales percentages by quarter. Dividing the annual budget into quarterly segments provides more frequent opportunities to compare actual with budgeted operations.

**3** Calculate the unit sales volume for each quarter. Reflection's planning group believes that quarterly sales percentages will remain the same. Therefore, 24.4% of annual sales are expected to occur in the first quarter.

**4** Enter the unit sales prices for each quarter.

**5** Calculate projected net sales for each quarter.

**6** Calculate total net sales for 20X3.

# PURCHASES BUDGET SCHEDULE

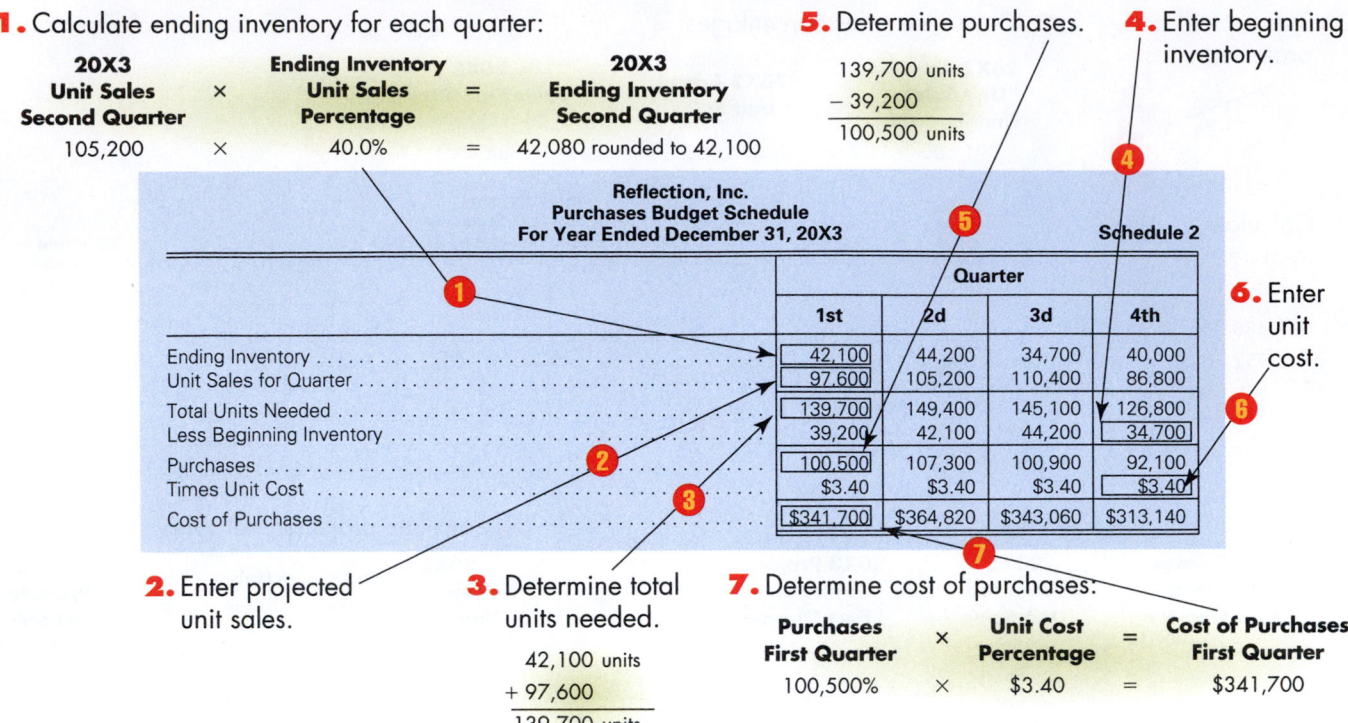

**1.** Calculate ending inventory for each quarter:

| 20X3 Unit Sales Second Quarter | × | Ending Inventory Unit Sales Percentage | = | 20X3 Ending Inventory Second Quarter |
|---|---|---|---|---|
| 105,200 | × | 40.0% | = | 42,080 rounded to 42,100 |

**5.** Determine purchases.

139,700 units
− 39,200
100,500 units

**4.** Enter beginning inventory.

**6.** Enter unit cost.

### Reflection, Inc.
### Purchases Budget Schedule
### For Year Ended December 31, 20X3

Schedule 2

| | Quarter | | | |
|---|---|---|---|---|
| | **1st** | **2d** | **3d** | **4th** |
| Ending Inventory . . . . . . . . . . . . . . . | 42,100 | 44,200 | 34,700 | 40,000 |
| Unit Sales for Quarter . . . . . . . . . . . | 97,600 | 105,200 | 110,400 | 86,800 |
| Total Units Needed . . . . . . . . . . . . . | 139,700 | 149,400 | 145,100 | 126,800 |
| Less Beginning Inventory . . . . . . . . . | 39,200 | 42,100 | 44,200 | 34,700 |
| Purchases . . . . . . . . . . . . . . . . . . . | 100,500 | 107,300 | 100,900 | 92,100 |
| Times Unit Cost . . . . . . . . . . . . . . . | $3.40 | $3.40 | $3.40 | $3.40 |
| Cost of Purchases . . . . . . . . . . . . . . | $341,700 | $364,820 | $343,060 | $313,140 |

**2.** Enter projected unit sales.

**3.** Determine total units needed.

42,100 units
+ 97,600
139,700 units

**7.** Determine cost of purchases:

| Purchases First Quarter | × | Unit Cost Percentage | = | Cost of Purchases First Quarter |
|---|---|---|---|---|
| 100,500% | × | $3.40 | = | $341,700 |

After the planning group approves the sales budget schedule, the remaining budget schedules are prepared. A statement prepared to show the projected amount of purchases that will be required during a budget period is called a **purchases budget schedule**. The following factors are considered when planning a purchases budget schedule:

1. Projected unit sales.
2. The quantity of merchandise on hand at the beginning of the budget period.
3. The quantity of merchandise needed to fill projected sales orders without having excessive inventory.
4. The price trends of merchandise to be purchased.

The sales manager prepares the purchases budget schedule shown above. The sales manager determines that the number of units in ending inventory should be about 40.0% of the number of units projected to be sold in the subsequent quarter.

## STEPS
### PREPARING A PURCHASES BUDGET SCHEDULE

STEPS • STEPS • STEPS • STEPS • STEPS • STEPS • STEPS • STEPS • STEPS • STEPS • STEPS

**1** Calculate ending inventory for each quarter. Round estimates to the nearest hundred. Use *40,000* units for the fourth quarter's ending inventory (100,000 projected to be sold in the first quarter of 20X4 × 40%).

**2** Enter projected unit sales for the quarter from the sales budget schedule.

**3** Add ending inventory units and projected sales units to determine total units needed per quarter.

**4** Enter beginning inventory, which is the same as ending inventory for the preceding quarter. Reflection's ending inventory of 39,200 units on December 31, 20X2, becomes its January 1 beginning inventory.

**5** Subtract beginning inventory from total units needed to determine total unit purchases for the quarter.

**6** Enter the unit cost for each quarter. Reflection's planning group has projected that material costs will rise from $3.30 to $3.40 per unit in the first quarter of 20X3.

**7** Multiply the unit purchases each quarter by the unit cost to determine the cost of purchases.

Budgetary Planning and Control

**Reflection, Inc.**
**Selling Expenses Budget Schedule**
**For Year Ended December 31, 20X3**                                    Schedule 3

| | Annual Budget | Quarter | | | |
|---|---|---|---|---|---|
| | | 1st | 2d | 3d | 4th |
| Advertising Expense | $ 49,820 | $11,710 | $13,260 | $ 13,910 | $10,940 |
| Delivery Expense | 160,000 | 39,040 | 42,080 | 44,160 | 34,720 |
| Depr. Expense—Delivery Equipment | 7,200 | 1,800 | 1,800 | 1,800 | 1,800 |
| Depr. Expense—Warehouse Equipment | 13,800 | 2,700 | 3,700 | 3,700 | 3,700 |
| Miscellaneous Expense—Sales | 10,380 | 2,440 | 2,760 | 2,900 | 2,280 |
| Salary Expense—Commissions | 83,020 | 19,520 | 22,090 | 23,180 | 18,230 |
| Salary Expense—Regular | 25,370 | 6,190 | 6,670 | 7,000 | 5,510 |
| Supplies Expense—Sales | 12,450 | 2,930 | 3,310 | 3,480 | 2,730 |
| Total Selling Expenses | $362,040 | $86,330 | $95,670 | $100,130 | $79,910 |

A statement prepared to show projected expenditures related directly to the selling operations is called a **selling expenses budget schedule**. The sales manager projects the information for the selling expenses budget schedule. However, other sales personnel may provide specific information. For example, the advertising manager supplies much of the advertising expense information. After selling expenses information has been projected, a selling expenses budget schedule is prepared.

Some selling expense items are relatively stable and require little budget planning. For example, depreciation expenses for delivery and warehouse equipment are reasonably stable from year to year unless new equipment is bought. On the other hand, several selling expenses increase and decrease in relation to sales increases and decreases. Reflection has a seasonal business with higher sales during the second and third quarters. The company hires more personnel and spends more for advertising and sales supplies during the heavy sales season. All of these factors are considered when a selling expenses budget schedule is made. Reflection's selling expenses budget schedule is shown above.

Reflection's sales manager uses a number of approaches to project the various selling expenses. Most selling expenses are linked closely to the amount of quarterly net sales. Reflection's management uses the following

projection guides to prepare its selling expenses budget schedule.

1. **Advertising expense.** This expense is closely related to sales and sales promotions for the year. Advertising expense for 20X2 was 2.4% ($45,120 ÷ $1,880,000) of net sales. Sales promotion emphasis will be maintained at about the same level this year. Thus, 2.4% of each quarter's projected net sales will be allocated to advertising expense. First quarter projected advertising expense is $11,710 (2.4% × $488,000 = $11,712, rounded to $11,710).

2. **Delivery expense.** This expense is closely related to the number of units sold and delivered. The previous year's delivery expense increased significantly because an external freight company was used for increased deliveries until Reflection could acquire an additional truck. Rigid cost control measures will be applied to reduce future unit delivery expenses. Delivery expense is projected to be $0.40 per unit (sq. ft.) sold times each quarter's projected unit sales. First quarter projected delivery expense is $39,040 ($0.40 × 97,600 units).

3. **Depreciation expense—delivery equipment.** No new delivery equipment will be added. Thus, depreciation expense will remain the same as for the previous year ($1,800 per quarter).

4. **Depreciation expense—warehouse equipment.** A new automated cutter will be acquired at the beginning of the second quarter, increasing quarterly depreciation expense in the second, third, and fourth quarters from $2,700 to $3,700 per quarter.

5. **Miscellaneous expense—sales.** Miscellaneous expense was 0.6% ($11,490 ÷ $1,880,000) of net sales in 20X2. Management is committed to reducing miscellaneous expense to 0.5% of net sales in 20X3. First quarter miscellaneous expense is projected as $2,440 (0.5% × $488,000).

6. **Salary expense—commissions.** Salespersons will continue to earn a 4.0% commission on net sales. First quarter commissions are projected as $19,520 (4.0% × $488,000).

7. **Salary expense—regular.** Regular salary expense is determined by salary increases and changes in activity that affect the number of people employed. The new automated cutter will reduce regular salary expense by $10,000. A 5.0% raise will be added to remaining salaries. Thus, the projected annual amount is calculated as shown below.

| Salary Expense: 20X2 Comparative Income Statement | $ 34,160 |
|---|---|
| *Less* Reduction from Automated Cutter | – 10,000 |
| Total | $ 24,160 |
| *Plus* 5.0% Rate Increase | + 1,210 |
| Projected Salary Expense—Regular | $ 25,370 |

The projected amount is allocated among the four quarters in relation to the sales percentage from the sales budget schedule. First quarter regular salaries are projected as $6,190 (24.4% × $25,370).

8. **Supplies expense—sales.** Supplies expense was 0.6% ($11,280 ÷ $1,880,000) of net sales in 20X2. The same percentage relationship is expected in 20X3. First quarter supplies expense is projected as $2,930 (0.6% × $488,000 = $2,928, rounded to $2,930).

After the quarterly amounts have been calculated and entered, the annual budget amounts are determined by totaling the quarterly amounts.

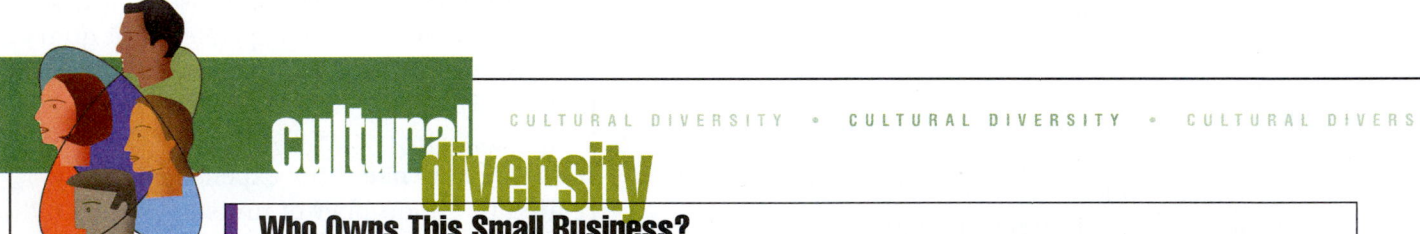

CULTURAL DIVERSITY • CULTURAL DIVERSITY • CULTURAL DIVERSITY

## cultural diversity

### Who Owns This Small Business?

In the 21st century, the answers to the question, "Who owns this small business?" is likely to be "A woman." In 1992, there were about 6 million women-owned firms. During the period of 1987 to 1992, the number of women-owned firms increased about 43 percent. The 1992 receipts of women-owned businesses were $1.574 trillion.

Women entrepreneurs start businesses at the rate of more than 4,000 per month. In 1996, women represented 36 percent of all small business owners. With the astonishing rate at which women are starting businesses, they will own a majority of all small businesses early in the 21st century.

Many of these "small businesses" employ over 100 people. Women-owned businesses are creating jobs at a faster rate than job growth in the overall economy. In fact, one out of four workers is employed in a woman-owned business.

Women-owned businesses are likely to be good community citizens. Many actively participate in their community, contribute to community projects, and provide a flexible work environment for their work force.

**Reflection, Inc.**
**Administrative Expenses Budget Schedule**
**For Year Ended December 31, 20X3**

Schedule 4

| | Annual Budget | Quarter | | | |
|---|---|---|---|---|---|
| | | 1st | 2d | 3d | 4th |
| Depr. Expense—Office Equipment ........................ | $ 14,400 | $ 3,600 | $ 3,600 | $ 3,600 | $ 3,600 |
| Insurance Expense ...................................... | 5,600 | 1,400 | 1,400 | 1,400 | 1,400 |
| Miscellaneous Expense—Administrative ................. | 36,760 | 9,190 | 9,190 | 9,190 | 9,190 |
| Payroll Taxes Expense ................................. | 22,810 | 5,540 | 5,900 | 6,070 | 5,300 |
| Rent Expense ........................................... | 30,000 | 7,500 | 7,500 | 7,500 | 7,500 |
| Salary Expense—Administrative ....................... | 81,720 | 20,430 | 20,430 | 20,430 | 20,430 |
| Supplies Expense—Administrative..................... | 14,540 | 3,420 | 3,870 | 4,060 | 3,190 |
| Uncollectible Accounts Expense ...................... | 12,450 | 2,930 | 3,310 | 3,480 | 2,730 |
| Utilities Expense ...................................... | 10,980 | 4,870 | 1,470 | 1,610 | 3,030 |
| Total Administrative Expenses....................... | $229,260 | $58,880 | $56,670 | $57,340 | $56,370 |

A statement that shows the projected expenses for all operating expenses not directly related to selling operations is called an **administrative expenses budget schedule**. The administrative manager prepares this budget schedule using information from these sources:

1. Past records.
2. Company plans.
3. Sales and selling expenses budget schedules.
4. Discussions with other managers.

After the administrative expenses have been projected, the administrative expenses budget schedule is prepared. Reflection's administrative expenses budget schedule is shown above.

Most administrative expenses are known and remain the same each period. Some administrative expenses need to be budgeted as a percentage of another amount from another budget. The following information was used to prepare the administrative expenses budget schedule.

1. **Depreciation expense—office equipment.** Recently purchased office equipment increased annual depreciation to $14,400. Annual depreciation is divided equally over the four quarters.
2. **Insurance expense.** Annual insurance is projected to increase to $5,600 primarily because of added coverage for the new automated cutting machine. An equal amount is paid each quarter.

3. **Miscellaneous expense—administrative.** Closely related to administrative salaries, miscellaneous expense was 49.8% ($38,770 ÷ $77,830) of administrative salaries in 20X2. Management is committed to reducing miscellaneous expense to 45.0% of projected administrative salaries in 20X3. First quarter miscellaneous expense is projected as $9,190 (45.0% × $20,430 = $9,194, rounded to $9,190).
4. **Payroll taxes expense.** Based on current payroll tax rates, payroll taxes expense is 12.0% of all salaries each quarter. First quarter salaries are projected as $46,140 ($19,520 + 6,190 + 20,430). Thus, payroll taxes expense is projected as $5,540 (12.0% × $46,140 = $5,537, rounded to $5,540).
5. **Rent expense.** Reflection leases the building for a known rental fee of $2,500 per month. Thus, rent expense can be projected accurately at $7,500 each quarter.
6. **Salary expense—administrative.** No new administrative personnel will be hired. Salary expense is projected as $81,720, equal to the 20X2 amount, $77,830, adjusted for a 5.0% salary rate increase. An equal amount is paid each quarter. Thus, each quarter's salary expense is projected as $20,430 ($81,720 ÷ 4).

7. **Supplies expense—administrative.** Supplies expense was 0.7% ($13,620 ÷ $1,880,000) of net sales for 20X2. The same percentage will be used in 20X3. First quarter supplies expense is projected as $3,420 (0.7% × $488,000 = $3,416, rounded to $3,420).

8. **Uncollectible accounts expense.** Closely related to net sales, uncollectible accounts expense was 0.6% ($11,280 ÷ $1,880,000) of net sales in 20X2. First quarter uncollectible accounts expense is projected as $2,930 (0.6% × $488,000 = $2,928, rounded to $2,930).

9. **Utilities expense.** Utilities expense is based on the amount of power, heat, telephone, and other utilities used in 20X2. Costs are projected to increase by 9.0%, consisting of a 5.0% projected increase in activity and a 4.0% increase in rates. Utilities expense by quarter in 20X2 is multiplied by 109% (100.0% + 9.0%) to calculate 20X3's projected utilities expense as follows:

| 20X2 Actual Utilities Expense | | × 109% = | 20X3 Projected Utilities Expense |
|---|---|---|---|
| 1st Quarter | $ 4,470 | × 109% = | $ 4,870 |
| 2d Quarter | 1,350 | × 109% = | 1,470 |
| 3d Quarter | 1,480 | × 109% = | 1,610 |
| 4th Quarter | 2,780 | × 109% = | 3,030 |
| Total | $10,080 | × 109% = | $10,980 |

## OTHER REVENUE AND EXPENSES BUDGET SCHEDULE

**Reflection, Inc.**
**Other Revenue and Expenses Budget Schedule**
**For Year Ended December 31, 20X3**

Schedule 5

| | Annual Budget | Quarter | | | |
|---|---|---|---|---|---|
| | | 1st | 2d | 3d | 4th |
| Other Expenses: | | | | | |
| Interest Expense ............................. | $2,250 | $750 | $750 | $750 | |

Budgeted revenue and expenses from activities other than normal operations are shown in a statement called **other revenue and expenses budget schedule**. Typical items in this budget are interest income, interest expense, and gains or losses on the sale of plant assets. Reflection's other revenue and expenses budget schedule is shown above. Reflection has only one other expense item and no other revenue items.

Reflection's administrative manager is responsible for projecting the information in the other revenue and expenses budget schedule. Projected interest expense, the only item in the budget, is based on the interest due on a $20,000 loan used to acquire the automated cutter. Since Reflection plans to repay the $20,000 loan at the beginning of the fourth quarter, the budget schedule shows interest expense for only three quarters.

{ **REMEMBER** Even though budgets are based on estimates, much care is taken to ensure that the estimates are as accurate as possible. }

**Reflection, Inc.**
**Budgeted Income Statement**
**For Year Ended December 31, 20X3**

| | Annual Budget | Quarter | | | |
|---|---|---|---|---|---|
| | | 1st | 2d | 3d | 4th |
| **Operating Revenue:** | | | | | |
| Net Sales (Schedule 1) | $2,075,600 | $488,000 | $552,300 | $579,600 | $455,700 |
| **Cost of Merchandise Sold:** | | | | | |
| Beginning Inventory | $ 129,360 | $129,360 | $143,140 | $150,280 | $117,980 |
| Purchases (Schedule 2) | 1,362,720 | 341,700 | 364,820 | 343,060 | 313,140 |
| Total Merchandise Available | $1,492,080 | $471,060 | $507,960 | $493,340 | $431,120 |
| Less Ending Inventory | 136,000 | 143,140 | 150,280 | 117,980 | 136,000 |
| Cost of Merchandise Sold | $1,356,080 | $327,920 | $357,680 | $375,360 | $295,120 |
| Gross Profit on Operations | $ 719,520 | $160,080 | $194,620 | $204,240 | $160,580 |
| **Operating Expenses:** | | | | | |
| Selling Expenses (Schedule 3) | $ 362,040 | $ 86,330 | $ 95,670 | $100,130 | $ 79,910 |
| Administrative Expenses (Schedule 4) | 229,260 | 58,880 | 56,670 | 57,340 | 56,370 |
| Total Operating Expenses | $ 591,300 | $145,210 | $152,340 | $157,470 | $136,280 |
| Income from Operations | $ 128,220 | $ 14,870 | $ 42,280 | $ 46,770 | $ 24,300 |
| Net Deduction (Schedule 5) | $ 2,250 | $ 750 | $ 750 | $ 750 | |
| Net Income before Federal Income Tax | $ 125,970 | $ 14,120 | $ 41,530 | $ 46,020 | $ 24,300 |
| Federal Income Tax Expense | 32,380 | 8,100 | 8,100 | 8,100 | 8,080 |
| Net Income after Federal Income Tax | $ 93,590 | $ 6,020 | $ 33,430 | $ 37,920 | $ 16,220 |

**1.** Beginning inventory:
39,200 units × $3.30 =
$129,360

**2.** Ending inventory:
42,100 units × $3.40 =
$143,140

A statement that shows a company's projected sales, costs, expenses, and net income is called a **budgeted income statement**. Since the five budget schedules contain detailed items, Reflection prepares a shortened budgeted income statement and attaches the budget schedules. Reflection's budgeted income statement is shown above.

The first quarter beginning inventory is calculated using the 20X2 unit cost, $3.30. Other inventory amounts are calculated using the unit cost for 20X3, $3.40.

Amounts from the five budget schedules allow Reflection to project net income before federal income tax. Federal income taxes are estimated using a tax rate table furnished by the Internal Revenue Service. Reflection uses the tax rate table shown below. Using these rates, Reflection calculates its federal income tax.

Quarterly income tax payments are *$8,100* ($32,380 ÷ 4 = $8,095, rounded to $8,100). Thus, Reflection's payments equal $24,300 ($8,100 × 3 quarters) through the third quarter. The fourth quarter amount equals the unpaid amount of federal income taxes, *$8,080* ($32,380 – $24,300).

15% of net income before taxes, zero to $50,000.00.
25% of net income before taxes less $5,000.00, $50,001.00 to $75,000.00.
34% of net income before taxes less $11,750.00, $75,001.00 to $100,000.00.
39% of net income before taxes less $16,750.00, $100,001.00 to $335,000.00.

| Net Income Before Federal Income Tax | × | Tax Rate | = | Federal Income Tax Expense |
|---|---|---|---|---|
| $125,970 | × | 39% less $16,750 | = | $32,378.30 rounded to $32,380 |

TERMS REVIEW • TERMS REVIEW

## terms review

sales budget schedule
purchases budget schedule
selling expenses budget schedule
administrative expenses budget
   schedule
other revenue and expenses
   budget schedule
budgeted income statement

## audit your understanding

AUDIT YOUR UNDERSTANDING

1. How do annual goals help a company?
2. What factors are considered in preparing a sales budget schedule?

## work together 14-2

WORK TOGETHER • WORK TOGETHER

**Planning for a budgeted income statement**

Actual unit sales for 20X1 were 230,000. Sterling Circuits, Inc., anticipates a 10.8% increase in unit sales for the upcoming year, 20X2. It projects that 18% of all yearly sales will occur during the first quarter. Sterling rounds unit projections to the nearest hundred units and dollar projections to the nearest $10. Your instructor will guide you through the following problem. Show your work.

1. How many units are projected to be sold during the first quarter of 20X2? If the unit sales price is $7.50, calculate the projected sales amount for the first quarter of 20X2.

2. If the desired ending inventory for the first quarter of 20X2 is 11,100 units, determine the number of units needed to meet the ending inventory and sales goals for the first quarter.

3. If the beginning inventory for the first quarter of 20X2 equals 9,400 units, how many units should be purchased to meet the inventory and sales goals for the first quarter?

4. Material costs per unit are projected to be $4.10. Compute the projected cost of purchases.

## on your own 14-2

ON YOUR OWN • ON YOUR OWN • ON YOUR OWN

**Planning for a budgeted income statement**

Actual unit sales for 20X1 were 90,000. Graphite Co. forecasts a 6.1% increase in unit sales for the upcoming year, 20X2. It projects that 20% of all yearly sales will occur during the first quarter. Graphite rounds unit projections to the nearest hundred units and dollar projections to the nearest $10. Work independently to complete the following problem. Show your work.

1. How many units are projected to be sold during the first quarter of 20X2? If the unit sales price is $16.00, calculate the projected sales amount for the first quarter of 20X2.

2. If the desired ending inventory for the first quarter of 20X2 is 4,700 units, determine the number of units needed to meet the ending inventory and sales goals for the first quarter.

3. If the beginning inventory for the first quarter of 20X2 equals 3,400 units, how many units should be purchased to meet the inventory and sales goals for the first quarter?

4. Material costs per unit are expected to be $7.80. Compute the projected cost of purchases.

# 14-3 Cash Budgets and Performance Reports

## CASH RECEIPTS BUDGET SCHEDULE

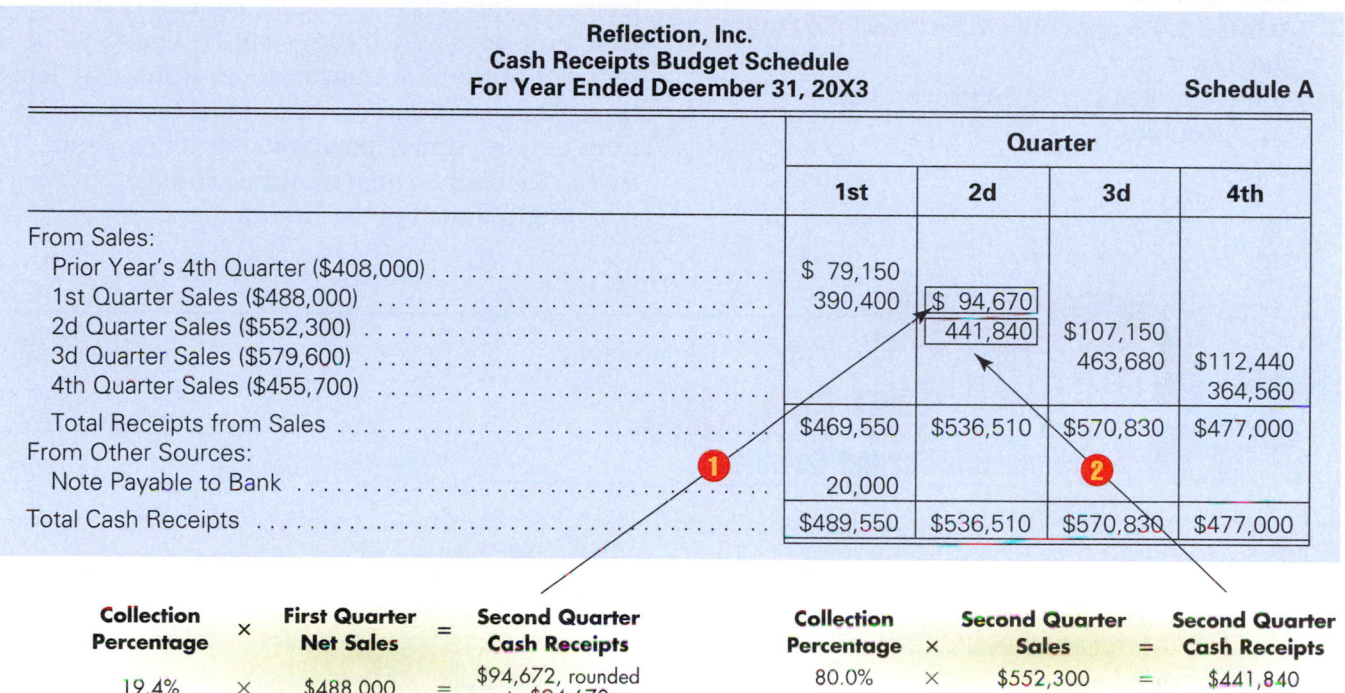

**Reflection, Inc.**
**Cash Receipts Budget Schedule**
**For Year Ended December 31, 20X3**                    **Schedule A**

| | Quarter | | | |
| --- | --- | --- | --- | --- |
| | **1st** | **2d** | **3d** | **4th** |
| From Sales: | | | | |
|   Prior Year's 4th Quarter ($408,000) | $ 79,150 | | | |
|   1st Quarter Sales ($488,000) | 390,400 | $ 94,670 | | |
|   2d Quarter Sales ($552,300) | | 441,840 | $107,150 | |
|   3d Quarter Sales ($579,600) | | | 463,680 | $112,440 |
|   4th Quarter Sales ($455,700) | | | | 364,560 |
|   Total Receipts from Sales | $469,550 | $536,510 | $570,830 | $477,000 |
| From Other Sources: | | | | |
|   Note Payable to Bank | | 20,000 | | |
| Total Cash Receipts | $489,550 | $536,510 | $570,830 | $477,000 |

| Collection Percentage | × | First Quarter Net Sales | = | Second Quarter Cash Receipts |
| --- | --- | --- | --- | --- |
| 19.4% | × | $488,000 | = | $94,672, rounded to $94,670 |

| Collection Percentage | × | Second Quarter Sales | = | Second Quarter Cash Receipts |
| --- | --- | --- | --- | --- |
| 80.0% | × | $552,300 | = | $441,840 |

Good cash management requires planning and controlling cash so that it will be available to meet obligations when they come due. Reflection prepares a cash budget to help analyze cash inflows and cash outflows. The treasurer prepares Reflection's cash budget in consultation with the budget committee. A corporation treasurer is an officer of the corporation who is usually responsible for planning the corporation's requirement for and use of cash. The treasurer analyzes

1. Projected receipts from cash sales, customers on account, and other sources.
2. Projected cash payments for ordinary expenses such as rent, payroll, and payments to vendors on account.
3. Other cash payments such as to buy plant assets or supplies.

Projected cash receipts for a budget period are reported on a statement called a **cash receipts budget schedule**. Reflection's cash receipts budget schedule is shown above. To prepare a cash receipts budget schedule, projections are composed of the following:

1. Quarterly cash sales.
2. Quarterly collections on account from customers. The amounts received from customers will not be the same as the amount of sales on account. Normally, cash is received for sales on account made during the previous one or two months. In addition, some sales returns and allowances and uncollectible accounts are likely.
3. Cash to be received quarterly from other sources.

> **REMEMBER** Many budget items are based on the budgeted estimate of sales. Therefore, the budget is only as accurate as the sales forecast.

An analysis of Reflection's sales for previous years shows the following pattern of net sales per quarter:

1. About 60.0% of all net sales are cash sales.
2. About 20.0% are sales on account collected in the same quarter. Thus, 80.0% of a quarter's net sales are collected during the same quarter.
3. About 19.4% are collected in the following quarter.
4. About 0.6% of net sales prove to be uncollectible.

Cash receipts in the first quarter include $79,150 from 20X2's fourth quarter sales on account (19.4% × $408,000 = $79,152, rounded to $79,150).

Cash sales and collections on account provide most of the cash receipts. If additional cash is needed, other sources of cash should be planned. After making a preliminary plan of projected cash receipts and cash payments, the treasurer determines that cash on hand will be reduced in the first quarter to an unusually low level. This condition could prevent the company from making timely payments for its expenditures. Therefore, the treasurer arranges to borrow $20,000 during the first quarter.

# technology for business

TECHNOLOGY FOR BUSINESS • TECHNOLOGY FOR BUSINESS • TECHNOLOGY FOR BUSI

## Numerical Format Options

Columns of data in a spreadsheet may include several different types of data. In columns E and F of the spreadsheet below, numbers are shown as currency amounts, percentage amounts, ratios, and general whole numbers.

Use of the numerical format options available on electronic spreadsheets makes the data easier to read and understand. For example, the rate earned on net sales in cells E7 and F7 are shown as percentages. In addition to numerous formatting options, the number of decimal places displayed may also be specified. Good spreadsheet design includes proper numerical formatting.

|  | A | B | C | D | E | F |
|---|---|---|---|---|---|---|
| 1 | Financial Statement Analysis | | | | | |
| 2 |  |  |  |  | Current | Prior |
| 3 |  |  |  |  | Year | Year |
| 4 | Rate Earned on Net Sales: | | | | | |
| 5 |  | Net Income after Federal Income Tax | | | $42,322 | $38,976 |
| 6 |  | Net Sales | | | 514,560 | 465,430 |
| 7 |  | Rate Earned on Net Sales | | | 8.2% | 8.4% |
| 8 | Earnings per Share: | | | | | |
| 9 |  | Net Income after Federal Income Tax | | | $42,322 | $38,976 |
| 10 |  | Shares of Stock Outstanding | | | 10,000 | 10,000 |
| 11 |  | Earnings per Share | | | $4.23 | $3.90 |
| 12 | Price-Earnings Ratio: | | | | | |
| 13 |  | Market Price per Share | | | $25.00 | $22.00 |
| 14 |  | Earnings per Share | | | $4.23 | $3.90 |
| 15 |  | Price-Earnings Ratio | | | 5.9 | 5.6 |

**Reflection, Inc.**
**Cash Payments Budget Schedule**
**For Year Ended December 31, 20X3**                                    Schedule B

| | Quarter | | | |
|---|---|---|---|---|
| | **1st** | **2d** | **3d** | **4th** |
| **For Merchandise:** | | | | |
| Prior Year's 4th Quarter Purchases ($212,500) . . . . . . . . . . . . . . . . | $ 63,750 | | | |
| 1st Quarter Purchases ($341,700) . . . . . . . . . . . . . . . . . . . . . . . . . . | 239,190 | $102,510 | | |
| 2d Quarter Purchases ($364,820) . . . . . . . . . . . . . . . . . . . . . . . . . . | | 255,370 | $109,450 | |
| 3d Quarter Purchases ($343,060) . . . . . . . . . . . . . . . . . . . . . . . . . . | | | 240,140 | $102,920 |
| 4th Quarter Purchases ($313,140) . . . . . . . . . . . . . . . . . . . . . . . . . | | | | 219,200 |
| Total Cash Payments for Purchases . . . . . . . . . . . . . . . . . . . . . | $302,940 | $357,880 | $349,590 | $322,120 |
| **For Operating Expenses:** | | | | |
| Cash Selling Expenses . . . . . . . . . . . . . . . . . . . . . . | $ 81,830 | $ 90,170 | $ 94,630 | $ 74,410 |
| Cash Administrative Expenses . . . . . . . . . . . . . . . . . . . . . . . . . . . | 52,350 | 49,760 | 50,260 | 50,040 |
| Total Cash Operating Expenses . . . . . . . . . . . . . . . . . . . . . | $134,180 | $139,930 | $144,890 | $124,450 |
| **For Other Cash Payments:** | | | | |
| Federal Income Tax Expense . . . . . . . . . . . . . . . . . . . . . . . . . . . | $ 8,100 | $ 8,100 | $ 8,100 | $ 8,080 |
| Automated Cutting Machine . . . . . . . . . . . . . . . . . . . . . . . . . . . . | 20,000 | | | |
| Cash Dividend . . . . . . . . . . . . . . . . . . . . . . . . . . | | 50,000 | | 50,000 |
| Investment . . . . . . . . . . . . . . . . . . . . . . . . . . . . . . . . . | | | | 25,000 |
| Note Payable and Interest . . . . . . . . . . . . . . . . . . . . . . . . . . . . | | | | 22,250 |
| Total Other Cash Payments . . . . . . . . . . . . . . . . . . . . . . . . | $ 28,100 | $ 58,100 | $ 8,100 | $105,330 |
| Total Cash Payments . . . . . . . . . . . . . . . . . | $465,220 | $555,910 | $502,580 | $551,900 |

Projected cash payments for a budget period are reported on a statement called a **cash payments budget schedule**. Reflection's cash payments budget schedule is shown above. To prepare the schedule, the accountant and treasurer make the following projections:

1. Quarterly cash payments for accounts payable or notes payable to vendors.
2. Quarterly cash payments for each expense item. This projection requires an analysis of the selling expenses, administrative expenses, and other revenue and expenses budget schedules.
3. Quarterly cash payments for buying equipment and other assets.
4. Quarterly cash payments for dividends.
5. Quarterly cash payments for investments.

Reflection's accountant and treasurer use the following projection guides to prepare the cash payments budget schedule.

1. **Cash payments for merchandise.** An analysis of past records for payments to vendors on account shows the following cash payment pattern:
   a. About 10.0% of all purchases are cash purchases.
   b. About 60.0% are purchases on account paid for in the quarter. Thus, 70.0% (10.0% + 60.0%) of a quarter's purchases are paid for during the same quarter.
   c. The remaining 30.0% are purchases on account paid for in the following quarter.

Cash payments are calculated using the same procedure used for cash receipts. Purchase amounts are from the purchases budget schedule. First quarter cash payments for first quarter purchases are $239,190 (70.0% × $341,700).

2. **Cash payments for operating expenses.** Cash payments for most operating expenses are made in the quarter the expense is incurred. However, the selling expenses budget schedule, shown on page 421, and the administrative expenses budget schedule, page 423, include some projected items for which cash will not be paid. For example, cash is not paid for depreciation and uncollectible accounts expenses. Therefore, these amounts are not included in the cash payments budget schedule. The first quarter's cash payments for selling expenses and for administrative expenses are calculated as follows:

| Selling Expenses | | $86,330 |
|---|---|---|
| *Less:* Depr. Exp.—Deliv. Equip. | $1,800 | |
| Depr. Exp.—Ware. Equip. | 2,700 | 4,500 |
| Cash Payment for Selling Exp. | | $81,830 |
| Administrative Expenses | | $58,880 |
| *Less:* Depr. Exp.—Office Equip. | $3,600 | |
| Uncollectible Accts. Exp. | 2,930 | 6,530 |
| Cash Payment for Admin. Exp. | | $52,350 |

3. **Other cash payments.** Reflection also plans for cash payments other than for merchandise, selling expenses, and administrative expenses. Federal income tax payments equal the quarterly federal income tax expense amounts on the budgeted income statement. Reflection also plans to buy a new automated cutting machine for $20,000 at the end of the first quarter. The company expects to pay a $50,000 cash dividend to stockholders in the second and fourth quarters. Since a large cash balance is projected for the third quarter, Reflection plans a $25,000 interest-earning investment in the fourth quarter. Also, plans call for repaying the promissory note plus interest, *$22,250*, at the beginning of the fourth quarter.

The last line of the cash payments budget schedule shows the total cash payments projected each quarter. This total indicates the minimum amount of cash that must be available each quarter.

# CASH BUDGET

**Reflection, Inc.**
**Cash Budget**
**For Year Ended December 31, 20X3**

| | Quarter | | | |
|---|---|---|---|---|
| | 1st | 2d | 3d | 4th |
| Cash Balance—Beginning . . . . . . . . . . . . . . . . . . . . . . . . . . . . | $ 21,780 | $ 46,110 | $ 26,710 | $ 94,960 |
| Cash Receipts (Schedule A) . . . . . . . . . . . . . . . . . . . . . . . | 489,550 | 536,510 | 570,830 | 477,000 |
| Cash Available . . . . . . . . . . . . . . . . . . . . . . . . | $511,330 | $582,620 | $597,540 | $571,960 |
| Less Cash Payments (Schedule B) . . . . . . . . . . . . . . . . . . . | 465,220 | 555,910 | 502,580 | 551,900 |
| Cash Balance—Ending . . . . . . . . . . . . . . . . . . . . . . . | $ 46,110 | $ 26,710 | $ 94,960 | $ 20,060 |

A statement that shows for each month or quarter a projection of a company's beginning cash balance, cash receipts, cash payments, and ending cash balance is called a **cash budget**. Reflection's cash budget, shown above, is prepared from the information in the cash receipts budget schedule and the cash payments budget schedule. The first quarter beginning cash balance is taken from the balance sheet on December 31, 20X2.

At the end of each quarter of a budget period, Reflection compares the actual cash balance with the projected cash balance shown on the cash budget. If the actual cash balance is less than the projected balance, the reasons for the decrease are determined and action is taken to correct the problem. One reason may be that some customers are not paying their accounts when they should. Another may be that expenses are exceeding budget projections. If the decrease continues, the company could have a quarter in which there is not enough cash to make all the required cash payments. If this shortage does occur, the business will have to borrow money until receipts and payments are brought into balance.

# PERFORMANCE REPORT

**Reflection, Inc.**
**Performance Report**
**For Quarter Ended March 31, 20X3**

| | Budget | Actual | Increase (Decrease) Amount | Increase (Decrease) Percentage* |
|---|---|---|---|---|
| Unit Sales (sq. ft.) | 97,600 | 98,500 | 900 | 0.9 |
| Operating Revenue: | | | | |
| Net Sales | $488,000 | $492,500 | $4,500 | 0.9 |
| Cost of Merchandise Sold | 327,920 | 330,680 | 2,760 | 0.8 |
| Gross Profit on Operations | $160,080 | $161,820 | $1,740 | 1.1 |
| Operating Expenses: | | | | |
| Selling Expenses: | | | | |
| Advertising Expense | $ 11,710 | $ 12,050 | $ 340 | 2.9 |
| Delivery Expense | 39,040 | 38,735 | (305) | (0.8) |
| Depr. Expense—Delivery Equipment | 1,800 | 1,800 | | |
| Depr. Expense—Warehouse Equipment | 2,700 | 2,700 | | |
| Miscellaneous Expense—Sales | 2,440 | 2,530 | 90 | 3.7 |
| Salary Expense—Commissions | 19,520 | 19,620 | 100 | 0.5 |
| Salary Expense—Regular | 6,190 | 6,190 | | |
| Supplies Expense—Sales | 2,930 | 2,900 | (30) | (1.0) |
| Total Selling Expenses | $ 86,330 | $ 86,525 | $ 195 | 0.2 |
| Administrative Expenses: | | | | |
| Depr. Expense—Office Equipment | $ 3,600 | $ 3,600 | | |
| Insurance Expense | 1,400 | 1,400 | | |
| Miscellaneous Expense—Administrative | 9,190 | 9,350 | $ 160 | 1.7 |
| Payroll Taxes Expense | 5,540 | 5,550 | 10 | 0.2 |
| Rent Expense | 7,500 | 7,500 | | |
| Salary Expense—Administrative | 20,430 | 20,430 | | |
| Supplies Expense—Administrative | 3,420 | 3,490 | 70 | 2.0 |
| Uncollectible Accounts Expense | 2,930 | 2,800 | (130) | (4.4) |
| Utilities Expense | 4,870 | 5,180 | 310 | 6.4 |
| Total Administrative Expenses | $ 58,880 | $ 59,300 | $ 420 | 0.7 |
| Total Operating Expenses | $145,210 | $145,825 | $ 615 | 0.4 |
| Income from Operations | 14,870 | 15,995 | $1,125 | 7.6 |
| Net Deduction | $ 750 | $ 750 | 0 | 0.0 |
| Net Income before Federal Income Tax | $ 14,120 | $ 15,245 | $1,125 | 8.0 |
| Federal Income Tax Expense | 8,100 | 8,100 | 0 | 0.0 |
| Net Income after Federal Income Tax | $ 6,020 | $ 7,145 | $1,125 | 18.7 |

*Percentages rounded to the nearest 0.1%.

At the end of each quarter, a business prepares an income statement that compares actual amounts with the budgeted income statement for the same period. This comparison shows variations between actual and projected items. A report showing a comparison of projected and actual amounts for a specific period of time is called a **performance report**.

Each quarter, Reflection prepares a quarterly performance report like the one shown on the previous page. This report is sent to the sales manager and the administrative manager. Knowing about significant differences between projected and actual income statement amounts helps the managers identify areas that need to be reviewed. By identifying large variations early, managers may be able to make changes that will correct negative effects on net income for the year. If conditions change significantly, the budget for the remainder of the year can be revised.

Preparation of a performance report is similar to preparation of a comparative income statement. However, a performance report compares actual amounts with projected amounts for the same fiscal period. A comparative income statement compares actual amounts of one fiscal period with actual amounts of a prior fiscal period.

The first amount column of the performance report shows the amounts projected for the first quarter. The second amount column shows the actual sales, costs, and expenses for the quarter. The third amount column shows how much the actual amount varies from the projected amount. For example, actual net sales, $492,500, *less* projected net sales, $488,000, *equals* the increase, $4,500. The fourth column shows the percentage, the actual amount increased or decreased from the projected amount. For example, the net sales increase, $4,500, *divided by* projected net sales, $488,000, *equals* the percentage of increase, 0.9%. Percentages are rounded to the nearest 0.1%.

An analysis is made of all significant differences to determine why the differences occurred. Normally, Reflection only considers changes of 5.0% or more to be significant. However, because the items influencing gross profit are large dollar amounts, small percentage changes affect net income significantly. Therefore, Reflection's sales manager reviews changes in net sales and cost of merchandise sold regardless of the amount of change.

Reflection's performance report indicates that three items should be reviewed:

1. Net sales.
2. Cost of merchandise sold.
3. Utilities expense.

Managers should determine what actions, if any, can correct the unfavorable situations such as the 6.4% increase in utilities expense. If the utility service cost has increased, the manager cannot change that. However, if power is being wasted, procedures may need to be changed to avoid the waste.

Managers should also determine what actions caused favorable results, such as the 0.9% increase in net sales, and encourage a continuation of those favorable actions.

©GETTY IMAGES/PHOTODISC

> **REMEMBER** Actual performance must be compared with budgeted estimates in order for a business to evaluate its budgeting procedures.

TERMS REVIEW
AUDIT YOUR
WORK TOGETHER • WORK TOGETHER • WORK TOGETHER
ON YOUR OWN • ON YOUR OWN • ON YOUR OWN

## terms review

cash receipts budget schedule
cash payments budget schedule
cash budget
performance report

## audit your understanding

1. Why is a cash budget important?
2. What information is reported in a cash budget?
3. How does a performance report differ from a comparative income statement?

## work together 14-3

### Planning for a cash budget

MicroVision's sales for previous years show that of total net sales, approximately 50% are cash sales, 30% are sales on account collected in the same quarter, 18% are sales on account collected in the next quarter, and 2% prove to be uncollectible. For the current year, net sales for the first quarter are $425,000.00 and for the second quarter, $360,500.00.

The cash payment budget schedule shows the following cash payments during the second quarter: total purchases, $289,000.00; total operating expenses, $97,840; federal income tax expense, $9,210.00; and notes payable and interest, $7,240.00. MicroVision rounds dollar projections to the nearest $10. Your instructor will guide you through the following examples.

1. Determine the total amount of cash received during the second quarter.
2. Calculate the total cash payments for the second quarter.
3. The beginning cash balance for the second quarter equals $61,560. Compute the ending cash balance for the second quarter.

## on your own 14-3

### Planning for a cash budget

MediaNet's sales for the previous years show that of total net sales, approximately 45% are cash sales, 40% are sales on account collected in the same quarter, 14% are sales on account collected in the next quarter, and 1% prove to be uncollectible. For the current year, net sales for the second quarter are $518,000.00 and for the third quarter, $670,250.00.

The cash payment budget schedule shows the following cash payments during the third quarter: total purchases, $410,000.00; total operating expenses, $101,630; federal income tax expense, $11,780.00; and cash dividend, $80,000.00. MediaNet rounds dollar projections to the nearest $10. Work the problem independently.

1. Determine the total amount of cash received during the third quarter.
2. Calculate the total cash payments for the third quarter.
3. The beginning cash balance for the third quarter equals $24,860.00. Compute the ending cash balance for the third quarter.

accountingxtra.swlearning.com

## SUMMARY

**After completing this chapter, you can**

1. Define important accounting terms related to budgetary planning and control.
2. Identify accounting concepts and practices related to preparing and analyzing budgeted income statements and cash budgets.
3. Gather information to prepare a budget.
4. Prepare a budgeted income statement.
5. Prepare a cash budget and a performance report.

# Explore Accounting

EXPLORE ACCOUNTING • EXPLORE ACCOUNTING • EXPLORE ACCO

## Spreadsheet Budgeting Tools

Budgeting has been a popular use for electronic spreadsheet programs since these software programs became readily available in the early 1980s. By entering labels for accounts and accounting periods in cells, the user can quickly tailor the structure of the budget to the nature of the business. Users create formulas to compute total revenues, expenses, and net income. Thus, with a knowledge of budgeting concepts, spreadsheet users can create a budget with a limited amount of effort.

Newer electronic spreadsheets have made budget creation even easier. These programs contain tools to assist the user in designing the budget and creating the formulas. The budget tools are especially useful for individuals with a limited knowledge of budgeting concepts. For most budgeting tools, the starting point is selecting the type and design of the budget.

**Personal or Business**
The budget tool suggests revenue and expense accounts commonly used in personal or business budgets. The user may add and delete accounts to customize the budget to the individual's needs.

**Budget or Budget vs. Actual Analysis**
The budget can be created to provide space for actual information to be entered at the end of each accounting period. The spreadsheet can be used to compute the amount or percentage difference between budget and actual amounts.

**Number of Periods**
The user identifies the starting period and the number of periods. A period can consist of a month, a quarter, or a year.

**Quarterly and Yearly Totals**
For a monthly budget, the budget tool can compute quarterly and yearly totals. With this information, the budget tool automatically creates the budget, including all labels and formulas. Format techniques, such as bolded text, numeric formats, and shaded cells, are applied to improve understanding.

**Required**
Use the budget tool of your electronic spreadsheet program to prepare a personal budget for your first year after high school.

# 14-1 APPLICATION PROBLEM

**Preparing a sales budget schedule and a purchases budget schedule**

PhotoMax, Inc., plans to prepare a sales budget schedule and a purchases budget schedule for 20X3. Management has set a sales goal of 250,000 units. After reviewing price trends, the sales manager projects that PhotoMax will need to increase its unit sales price from $12.50 to $14.00 in the first quarter.

The sales manager, after checking with the company's merchandise suppliers, projects that the cost of merchandise will increase from $7.00 to $7.50 per unit in the first quarter of 20X3.

Quarterly unit sales for 20X2 are as follows:

| 1st quarter | 58,500 units | 3d quarter | 68,900 units |
| 2d quarter | 62,700 units | 4th quarter | 43,900 units |

After considering the time required to reorder merchandise, the sales manager requests that 30.0% of the next quarter's unit sales be available in the prior quarter's ending inventory. Ending inventory for 20X2 is 27,700 units. Management projects that 65,000 units will be sold in the first quarter of 20X4.

### Instructions:

1. Prepare a sales budget schedule (Schedule 1) for the four quarters ended December 31, 20X3. PhotoMax rounds unit amounts to the nearest hundred units, dollar amounts to the nearest $10, and percentage amounts to the nearest 0.1%.
2. Prepare a purchases budget schedule (Schedule 2) for the four quarters ended December 31, 20X3.

# 14-2 APPLICATION PROBLEM

**Preparing a budgeted income statement**

The sales manager and administrative manager of Coffee Oasis have made the following projections to be used in preparing a budgeted income statement.

a. Total net sales for 20X3 are projected to be $1,400,000. In each quarter the following percentages of total net sales were made:

| 1st quarter | 20.0% | 3d quarter | 25.0% |
| 2d quarter | 25.0% | 4th quarter | 30.0% |

b. Purchases and merchandise ending inventories are projected as follows. Ending inventory for 20X2 was $88,250.

| | Purchases | Ending Inventory |
| --- | --- | --- |
| 1st quarter | $201,000 | $111,500 |
| 2d quarter | 242,500 | 110,500 |
| 3d quarter | 283,000 | 132,500 |
| 4th quarter | 246,250 | 99,250 |

c. Expenses for 20X3 are projected as follows. Except where noted, percentages are based on projected net sales. For these items, calculate each quarter's amount by multiplying the percentage times that quarter's net sales. Calculate the annual total by adding the four quarterly amounts. When a dollar amount is given, the total amount should be divided equally among the four quarters.

| Selling Expenses | | Administrative Expenses | |
|---|---|---|---|
| Advertising Expense | 1.5% | Depreciation Expense—Office Equipment | $4,800 |
| Delivery Expense | 2.7% | Insurance Expense | $6,000 |
| Depreciation Expense— | | Miscellaneous Expense— | |
| Delivery Equipment | $3,400 | Administrative | $5,600 |
| Depreciation Expense— | | Payroll Taxes Expense | 13.2% of salaries |
| Store Equipment | $4,200 | Rent Expense | $12,800 |
| Miscellaneous Expense—Sales | $15,800 | Salary Expense—Administrative | $46,000 |
| Salary Expense—Sales | 6.0% | Supplies Expense—Administrative | $4,240 |
| Supplies Expense—Sales | 2.0% | Uncollectible Accounts Expense | 0.8% |
| | | Utilities Expense | $18,400 |

Federal income taxes are calculated using the tax rate table shown in this chapter. Equal quarterly income tax payments are based on the projected annual federal income tax expense.

**Instructions:**
1. Prepare a selling expenses budget schedule (Schedule 3) for the four quarters ended December 31, 20X3. Coffee Oasis rounds all amounts to the nearest $10.
2. Prepare an administrative expenses budget schedule (Schedule 4) for the four quarters ended December 31, 20X3.
3. Prepare a budgeted income statement for the four quarters ended December 31, 20X3.

# 14-3 APPLICATION PROBLEM
### Preparing a cash budget with supporting schedules

The following table shows SeaWest Fabrication's projected net sales, purchases, and cash payments for expenses for 20X3.

| | | | Cash Payments for Expenses | |
|---|---|---|---|---|
| Quarter | Net Sales | Purchases | Selling | Administrative |
| 1st | $646,300 | $558,300 | $32,100 | $38,600 |
| 2d | 674,900 | 571,600 | 36,200 | 38,900 |
| 3d | 661,800 | 561,200 | 42,400 | 39,700 |
| 4th | 681,600 | 582,300 | 36,800 | 39,800 |

Additional information is as follows:
  a. Actual amounts for the fourth quarter of 20X2: sales, $639,200; purchases, $548,240.
  b. The balance of cash on hand on January 1, 20X3, is $35,720.
  c. In each quarter, cash sales are 10.0% and collections of accounts receivable are 50.0% of the projected net sales for the current quarter. Collections from the preceding quarter's net sales are 39.5% of that quarter. Uncollectible accounts expense is 0.5% of net sales.
  d. In each quarter, cash payments for cash purchases are 10.0% and for accounts payable 30.0% of the purchases for the current quarter. Cash payments for purchases of the preceding quarter are 60.0% of that quarter.
  e. Record only total projected cash payments for expenses as shown in the table above.
  f. In the second quarter, SeaWest will borrow $35,000 on a promissory note and will purchase equipment costing $31,600 for cash. In the third quarter dividends of $30,000 will be paid in cash. In the fourth quarter, the promissory note plus interest will be paid in cash, $37,500.
  g. Equal quarterly income tax payments are based on projected annual federal income tax expense of $7,720.

**Instructions:**
1. Prepare a cash receipts budget schedule (Schedule A) for the four quarters ended December 31, 20X3. Round all amounts to the nearest $10.
2. Prepare a cash payments budget schedule (Schedule B) for the four quarters ended December 31, 20X3.
3. Prepare a cash budget for the four quarters ended December 31, 20X3.

# 14-4 MASTERY PROBLEM

## Preparing a budgeted income statement and a cash budget with supporting budget schedules

On December 31, 20X2, the accounting records of Zylar, Inc., show the following unit sales for 20X2.

| | | | |
|---|---|---|---|
| 1st quarter | 22,000 units | 3d quarter | 34,800 units |
| 2d quarter | 34,400 units | 4th quarter | 28,800 units |

The following are additional actual amounts for the 4th quarter of 20X2.

| | |
|---|---|
| Sales (28,800 units @ $5.60) | $161,280 |
| Purchases (26,400 units @ $4.00) | 105,600 |
| Ending inventory | 12,500 units |

Management has established a unit sales goal of 130,000 units for 20X3 and 24,000 units for the first quarter of 20X4. The sales manager, after reviewing price trends and checking with the company's merchandise suppliers, projects that the unit cost of merchandise will increase from $4.00 to $4.25 in the first quarter of 20X3. Because of the increase in costs, the company will need to increase its unit sales price from $5.60 to $6.00 in the first quarter of 20X3.

After considering the time required to reorder merchandise, the sales manager requests that 40.0% of each quarter's unit sales be available in the prior quarter's ending inventory.

Expenses are projected as shown on the following page. Except where noted, percentages are based on quarterly projected net sales. For these items, calculate each quarter's amount by multiplying the percentage times that quarter's net sales. Calculate the annual total by adding the four quarterly amounts. When a dollar amount is given, the total amount should be divided equally among the four quarters.

Interest expense for each quarter is projected to be $1,250.

Federal income taxes are calculated using the tax rate table shown in this chapter. Equal quarterly income tax payments are based on the projected annual federal income tax expense.

Additional information is as follows:
a. The balance of cash on hand on January 1, 20X3, is $41,600.
b. In each quarter, cash sales are 10.0% and collections of accounts receivable are 40.0% of the projected net sales for the current quarter. Collections from the preceding quarter's net sales are 49.4% of that quarter. Uncollectible accounts expense is 0.6% of net sales.

| Selling Expenses | | Administrative Expenses | |
|---|---|---|---|
| Advertising Expense | 1.2% | Depreciation Expense—Office Equipment | $3,600 |
| Delivery Expense | 0.6% | Insurance Expense | $4,200 |
| Depreciation Expense— | | Miscellaneous Expense— | |
| Delivery Equipment | $2,400 | Administrative | $3,000 |
| Depreciation Expense— | | Payroll Taxes Expense | 12.0% of salaries |
| Store Equipment | $6,680 | Rent Expense | $9,600 |
| Miscellaneous Expense—Sales | 0.4% | Salary Expense—Administrative | $25,200 |
| Salary Expense—Sales | 5.0% | Supplies Expense—Administrative | $2,800 |
| Supplies Expense—Sales | 0.8% | Uncollectible Accounts Expense | 0.6% |
| | | Utilities Expense | 1.8% |

c. In each quarter, cash payments for cash purchases are 10.0% and for accounts payable 55.0% of the purchases for the current quarter. Cash payments for purchases of the preceding quarter are 35.0% of that quarter.
d. In the first quarter, $40,000 will be borrowed on a promissory note, and equipment costing $30,000 will be purchased for cash. In each quarter, dividends of $10,000 will be paid in cash. In the fourth quarter, the promissory note plus interest will be paid in cash, $45,000.

**Instructions:**

Prepare the following budget schedules for the year ended December 31, 20X3. Round percentage amounts to the nearest 0.1%, unit amounts to the nearest 100 units, and dollar amounts to the nearest $10.

    a. Prepare a sales budget schedule (Schedule 1).
    b. Prepare a purchases budget schedule (Schedule 2).
    c. Prepare a selling expenses budget schedule (Schedule 3).
    d. Prepare an administrative expenses budget schedule (Schedule 4).
    e. Prepare an other revenue and expenses budget schedule (Schedule 5).
    f. Prepare a budgeted income statement.
    g. Prepare a cash receipts budget schedule (Schedule A).
    h. Prepare a cash payments budget schedule (Schedule B).
    i. Prepare a cash budget.

## 14-5 CHALLENGE PROBLEM   
### Preparing a performance report

A partially completed performance report for Quasar Robotics, Inc., is in the *Working Papers.*

Quasar Robotics, Inc., has just completed its first quarter of the fiscal year ended December 31, 20X3. Management is interested in identifying significant favorable and unfavorable differences between projected and actual amounts. Quasar Robotics only considers changes of 5.0% or more to be significant. Management reviews changes in net sales and cost of merchandise regardless of the amount of change.

**Instructions:**

1. Complete the performance report by calculating the increase (decrease) from budget and percentage increase (decrease) from budget.
2. Place an asterisk (*) in the right margin by every item that is significant.

## applied communication

People often think that only accountants need to know accounting. Many students may not consider taking accounting because they have no interest in being an accountant. Whether students aspire to be doctors, teachers, lawyers, scientists, florists, or artists, they will need to use accounting to control the financial resources of their business or organization.

**Required:**

Create a presentation that could be made to your high school counselor, student body, or incoming students to persuade the audience that everyone needs accounting. Use the following guidelines.

1.  Prepare a list of skills learned in accounting that can be used in everyday life.

2.  Elaborate by writing a paragraph to discuss each skill and how advantageous it is for a person to gain the skill.

3.  Prepare graphic aids such as transparency masters that could be used to present the material.

## cases for critical thinking

### Case 1

Thomas Baker, president of Brundage Corporation, says he has observed that an increase in sales almost always results in an increase in net income. Therefore, he is considering recommending that the company set a sales goal increase of 15.0% for next year and "spare no expense" to achieve this goal. Thomas asks for your opinion regarding his recommendation. How would you respond?

### Case 2

Camille Stibbe is general manager of Alden Corporation. She suggests that the budgeted income statement and the cash budget seem to show the same information. Therefore, she recommends that one of the statements be eliminated to reduce accounting costs. What response would you make to Camille?

## SCANS workplace competency

**Interpersonal Competency:** Teaching Others

**Concept:** Employers seek employees who are willing to help others learn. Effective employees recognize training needs, assess individual performance and provide constructive feedback, and help others apply concepts and theories through coaching, mentoring, or other means.

**Application:** Prior to the chapter test, pair up with another student who is having difficulty with the accounting concepts presented in this chapter. Identify weaknesses and thoroughly explain confusing material. Use visuals and rework related chapter problems. Be positive and encouraging during your study session. Conduct a complete chapter review for the upcoming test.

## • auditing for errors

MPS Corporation manufactures and sells holiday towels. The number and unit price of the towels increase substantially during the third quarter. An accounting clerk has prepared the following sales budget for the next year. Determine if the budget has been prepared accurately.

| | Annual Budget | Quarter | | | |
|---|---|---|---|---|---|
| | | 1st | 2d | 3d | 4th |
| Actual Unit Sales, 20X2 | 62,600 | 12,400 | 12,600 | 21,400 | 16,200 |
| Sales Percentage by Quarter | | 19.8% | 20.1% | 32.4% | 25.9% |
| Projected Dollar Sales, 20X3 | 72,000 | 14,256 | 14,472 | 23,328 | 18,648 |
| Times Unit Sales Price | | 12.5 | 12.6 | 13.2 | 1.29 |
| Net Sales | $692,533 | $178,200 | $182,347 | $307,930 | $24,056 |

MPS Corporation
Sales Budget Schedule
For Year Ended December 31, 20X3

## • analyzing Costco's financial statements

From net sales to the number of warehouses, the ten-year operating and financial highlights on pages B-2–B-3 of Appendix B in this textbook provide a historical perspective to Costco's growth. This summary reports trends that are an important input in the budgeting process.

The first step of the budget process is to establish operational goals.

**Instructions:** Use the information in this report to suggest operational goals for Costco in 2004. For each item, examine the trend from 2000 to 2003 and decide what operational goal you believe Costco should attempt to achieve in 2004. Be prepared to defend your goals in class.

1. Costco will open ___ stores in 2004. (*Hint:* Calculate the percent increase in the number of warehouses each year.)

2. Costco will control expenses, reducing selling, general, and administrative expenses to ___ percent of net sales.

3. Costco will achieve a ___ percentage increase in comparable units (same store sales).

4. Costco will increase the number of business members by ____ and Gold Star members by ___. (*Hint:* Calculate the percent increase in the number of members each year.)

**Business Members:**

| | | | | |
|---|---|---|---|---|
| End of year | 4,636 | 4,476 | 4,358 | 4,170 |
| Beginning of year | 4,476 | 4,358 | 4,170 | 3,887 |
| Increase in business members | 160 | 118 | 188 | 283 |
| Percentage increase in business members | 3.6% | 2.7% | 4.5% | 7.3% |

**Gold Star Members:**

| | | | | |
|---|---|---|---|---|
| End of year | 14,984 | 14,597 | 12,737 | 10,521 |
| Beginning of year | 14,597 | 12,737 | 10,521 | 9,555 |
| Increase in Gold Star members | 387 | 1,860 | 2,216 | 966 |
| Percentage increase in Gold Star members | 2.7% | 14.6% | 21.1% | 10.1% |

## Preparing a Performance Report

A budget is a financial plan for the future. It can be used to plan revenue and expenses. A performance report is a type of financial statement that compares budgeted and actual amounts. Once budgeted data have been entered into the accounting system, a performance report can be generated.

### Entering and Changing Budget Amount Data

When the Other Activities menu item is chosen from the Data menu or the Other toolbar button is clicked, the Other Activities window containing the Budgets tab will appear. The Budgets tab allows you to enter the budgeted amounts for income statement accounts. To enter budget amounts:

1. Enter the budgeted amount for the first account (or highlight an amount you wish to change and enter a new amount).

2. Press the Tab key to move to the next account. The accounts are scrollable. When you have entered the amount for the last account visible, the accounts will scroll up so that you can enter the next budget amount.

3. When all budget amounts have been entered, click OK.

### Preparing a Performance Report

Once the budgeted amounts have been entered, a performance report may be displayed or printed. Use the following steps to display the report:

1. Click the Reports toolbar button, or choose the Reports Selection menu item from the Reports menu.

2. When the Report Selection dialog appears, choose Financial Statements from the Select a Report Group list.

3. Choose Performance Report from the Choose a Report to Display list.

4. Click OK.

The report will be displayed in the scrollable Report Viewer Window. The report may be printed and/or copied for inclusion in another application, such as a spreadsheet or word processor.

### AUTOMATING CHALLENGE PROBLEM 14-5

**Instructions:**

1. Load *Automated Accounting 8.0* or higher software.

2. Select database A14-5 (Advanced Course Challenge Problem 14-5) from the accounting template disk.

3. Select File from the menu bar and choose the Save As menu command. Key the path to the drive and directory that contain your data files. Save the database with a filename of XXX145 (where XXX are your initials).

4. Read the Problem Instruction screen by clicking the Browser tool button.

5. Refer to page 438 for data used in this problem.

6. Exit the Automated Accounting software.

# CHAPTER 15

# Management Decisions Using Cost-Volume-Profit Analysis

## OBJECTIVES & TERMS

*After studying Chapter 15, you will be able to:*

1. Define terms related to accounting information for management decisions.

2. Identify accounting concepts and practices related to preparing accounting information for management decisions.

3. Prepare an income statement reporting contribution margin.

4. Calculate the contribution margin rate.

5. Calculate the breakeven point.

6. Calculate the sales dollars and sales units required to earn a planned amount of net income.

7. Determine the effect of changes in sales volume, unit costs, and unit sales prices on net income.

8. Calculate a sales mix.

- total costs
- unit cost
- variable costs
- fixed costs
- contribution margin
- breakeven point
- sales mix

Point Your Browser
accountingxtra.swlearning.com

# • RC Cola

©RC COLA IS A TRADEMARK OF DR PEPPER/SEVEN UP, INC. © 2004 DR PEPPER/SEVEN UP, INC.

## PRODUCT INNOVATION AT RC COLA

The forerunner of RC Cola was introduced in 1905, when a young pharmacist, Claud A. Hatcher, decided to supply the family grocery store with drinks. "Chero-Cola" was part of his "Royal Crown" line of beverages. In 1928, Hatcher renamed his company the Nehi Corporation, after his successful line of fruity beverages.

In the mid-1930s, the company introduced a reformulated version of Chero-Cola under the name "Royal Crown Cola." The new cola was such a success that the company was again renamed, this time to Royal Crown Cola Co. The company was recently acquired by Cadbury Schweppes, a London-based company that owns other beverage brands, including Dr. Pepper, 7UP, Canada Dry, Mott's, Snapple, and Hawaiian Punch. Throughout its history, the company has also been an innovator. First to introduce a low-calorie, caffeine-free diet cola, and diet cherry cola, the company also introduced the all-aluminum beverage can.

Before any company introduces a new product, its managers need to understand the relationship between the expected revenues and costs. How much of the new product must be sold to make the desired profit is an important question that must be answered before the new product is introduced.

### Critical Thinking

1. Throughout its history, the Royal Crown Cola Co. was successful in introducing new products in the marketplace. Identify a company that was unsuccessful in introducing a new product.

2. Why would Cadbury Schweppes want to own so many well-known beverage brands?

Source: www.dpsu.com/rc.html; www.dpsu.com/dpsu_fact_sheets.html

Xtra!
Today
accountingxtra.swlearning.com

## INSTITUTE OF MANAGEMENT ACCOUNTANTS

Go to the homepage for the Institute of Management Accountants (IMA) (www.imanet.org). Click on the Student link.

### Instructions

1. List two resources provided for students.

2. Pick one of these two resources and examine it in more detail. List two interesting pieces of information you learned from this resource.

# 15-1 Cost Characteristics That Influence Decisions

Managers use financial statements to make good business decisions. An income statement is one source of information on which a manager can base decisions. An income statement includes information about operating revenue, cost of merchandise sold, gross profit on operations, operating expenses, and net income or net loss. By analyzing the income statement, managers can gain an understanding of the relationship among sales, costs, and expenses.

Managers can increase net income by increasing sales and/or decreasing costs and expenses. Managers, with the advice and assistance of accountants, analyze the relationships among sales, costs, and expenses to:

1. Determine the level of sales necessary to achieve planned net income.
2. Evaluate the impact of changes in sales volume, unit sales prices, and unit costs on net income.
3. Identify the strengths and weaknesses of a company.

©GETTY IMAGES/PHOTODISC

## making ethical decisions

### Due Care

Accountants will make mistakes—after all, they are human. Yet the codes of conduct for several accounting organizations require that their members exercise due care in the performance of professional services. The concept of *due care* requires accountants to strive for perfection and, as a result, earn the confidence of their clients and the financial community.

**Instructions**

Access the code of conduct for the American Institute of Certified Public Accountants and the Association of Certified Fraud Examiners. Identify adjectives the codes use to describe due care.

Management Decisions Using Cost-Volume-Profit Analysis

**Reflection, Inc.**
**Income Statement**
**For Month Ended July 31, 20--**

| | | |
|---|---|---|
| Operating Revenue: | | |
| Net Sales ........................................ | | $180,000.00 |
| Cost of Merchandise Sold ......................... | | 118,800.00 |
| Gross Profit on Operations........................ | | $ 61,200.00 |
| Operating Expenses: | | |
| Selling Expenses ............................ | $31,930.00 | |
| Administrative Expenses ..................... | 20,820.00 | |
| Total Operating Expenses ..................... | | 52,750.00 |
| Income from Operations ........................... | | $ 8,450.00 |
| Other Expenses ................................... | | 2,450.00 |
| Net Income ...................................... | | $ 6,000.00 |

## Total Costs Versus Unit Cost

All costs for a specific period of time are called **total costs**. The abbreviated income statement above shows that the total cost of the merchandise sold by Reflection, Inc. during July was $118,800.00. Total selling expenses were $31,930.00. These totals show how much money was spent for these activities during a specific period of time. [*CONCEPT: Accounting Period Cycle*]

An amount spent for one unit of a specific product or service is called a **unit cost**. Reflection sold 36,000 square feet of mirrors during July at a total cost of $118,800.00. The unit cost of each square foot of mirrors is calculated as follows:

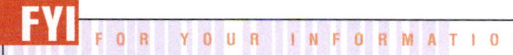

| Cost of Merchandise Sold Total Cost | ÷ | Units Sold | = | Cost of Merchandise Sold Unit Cost |
|---|---|---|---|---|
| $118,800.00 | ÷ | 36,000 | = | $3.30 |

Units may be expressed in many different terms. However, units should be expressed in terms that are meaningful to the people who are responsible for the costs. Some examples of other unit terms are gallons, liters, pounds, kilograms, inches, yards, meters, and hours. Knowing unit costs can be helpful to a manager in setting unit selling prices and in planning cost control.

**FYI** FOR YOUR INFORMATION

Spreadsheet software is often used to perform what-if analyses. Managers use what-if analyses to examine the financial results of various assumptions. For example, managers can project the net income for the next fiscal period if variable costs increase.

# VARIABLE COST CHARACTERISTICS

| | Reflection, Inc. Mirror Purchases For Period January 1–July 31, 20-- | | |
|---|---|---|---|
| **Month** | **Units Purchased** | **Unit Cost per sq. ft.** | **Total Cost** |
| January | 27,300 | $3.30 | $ 90,090.00 |
| February | 26,100 | 3.30 | 86,130.00 |
| March | 29,200 | 3.30 | 96,360.00 |
| April | 33,500 | 3.30 | 110,550.00 |
| May | 30,400 | 3.30 | 100,320.00 |
| June | 35,100 | 3.30 | 115,830.00 |
| July | 36,000 | 3.30 | 118,800.00 |

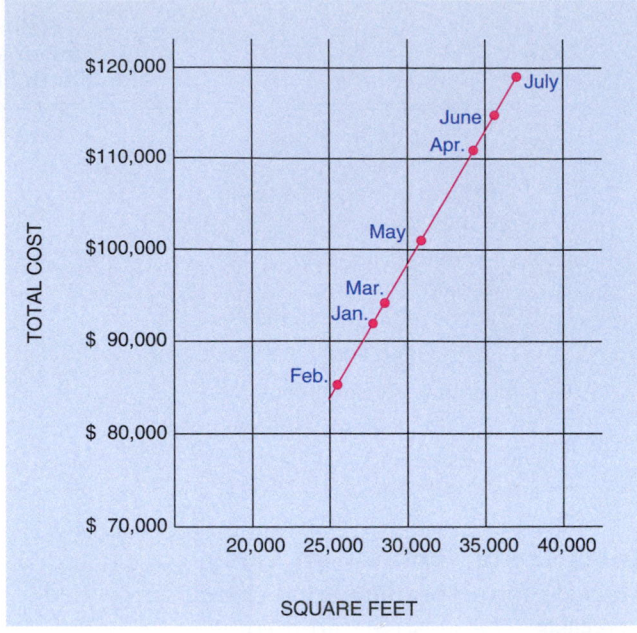

Costs may be separated into two parts: variable and fixed. Total costs that change in direct proportion to a change in the number of units are called **variable costs**. The *total* variable cost *varies* with a change in the number of units. Specifically, it increases. The *unit* variable cost *remains the same* regardless of the number of units.

For example, a business buys 1 hour of radio advertising for $150.00. Later the business buys 10 more hours of advertising for $1,500.00 (10 × $150.00 = $1,500.00). Regardless of the number of hours purchased, the unit cost of an hour of advertising is $150.00 per hour. Thus, radio advertising is a variable cost.

Reflection's mirror purchases for the months January through July are shown above. The volume of mirrors purchased ranges from a low

of 26,100 square feet in February to a high of 36,000 square feet in July. However, the price paid per square foot (unit cost) remained at $3.30 throughout the seven-month period. Therefore, these costs have the characteristics of variable costs.

Reflection's monthly costs for mirror purchases are plotted on the graph above. The line between the plotted points indicates the relationship between the number of square feet of mirrors purchased and the total cost of mirrors. The straight, upward sloped line shows that as the quantity of mirrors increases, the total cost also increases. The line is straight because Reflection's unit cost per square foot remained the same although the number of units purchased per month varied.

# FIXED COSTS

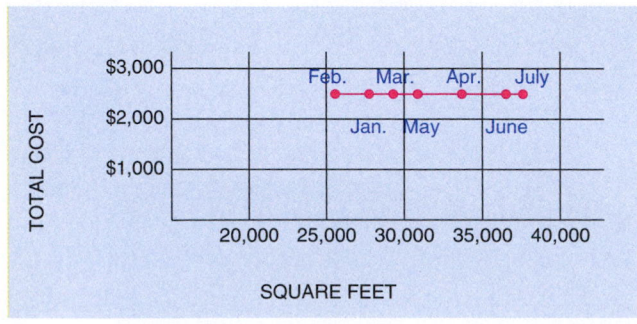

Total costs that remain constant regardless of change in business activity are called **fixed costs**. For example, Reflection's rent is $2,500.00 per month. Rent is *fixed* because the amount has been set at $2,500.00 per month regardless of how many square feet of mirrors are purchased. If each monthly rental cost is plotted on a graph and points are connected, the chart will appear as shown here. The fixed cost line is a straight line parallel to the base of the graph.

## GROSS PROFIT AND CONTRIBUTION MARGIN INCOME STATEMENTS

**Reflection, Inc.**
**Income Statement**
**For Month Ended July 31, 20--**

| | | | |
|---|---|---|---|
| Operating Revenue: | | | |
| Net Sales (36,000 sq. ft. @ $5.00) | | | $180,000.00 |
| Cost of Merchandise Sold (36,000 sq. ft. @ $3.30) | | | 118,800.00 |
| Gross Profit on Operations | | | $ 61,200.00 |
| Operating Expenses: | | | |
| Selling Expenses: | | | |
| Sales Commission (36,000 sq. ft. @ $.20) | $ 7,200.00 | | |
| Delivery Costs (36,000 sq. ft. @ $.40) | 14,400.00 | | |
| Other Variable Costs (36,000 sq. ft. @ $.15) | 5,400.00 | | |
| Other Fixed Costs | 4,930.00 | $31,930.00 | |
| Administrative Expenses: | | | |
| Rent | $ 2,500.00 | | |
| Insurance | 400.00 | | |
| Other Variable Costs (36,000 sq. ft. @ $.20) | 7,200.00 | | |
| Other Fixed Costs | 10,720.00 | 20,820.00 | |
| Total Operating Expenses | | | 52,750.00 |
| Income from Operations | | | $ 8,450.00 |
| Other Expenses | | | 2,450.00 |
| Net Income | | | $ 6,000.00 |

**Reflection, Inc.**
**Income Statement**
**For Month Ended July 31, 20--**

| | | |
|---|---|---|
| Operating Revenue: | | |
| Net Sales (36,000 sq. ft. @ $5.00) | | $180,000.00 |
| Variable Costs: | | |
| Cost of Merchandise Sold (36,000 sq. ft. @ $3.30) | $118,800.00 | |
| Sales Commission (36,000 sq. ft. @ $.20) | 7,200.00 | |
| Delivery Costs (36,000 sq. ft. @ $.40) | 14,400.00 | |
| Other Selling Costs (36,000 sq. ft. @ $.15) | 5,400.00 | |
| Other Administrative Costs (36,000 sq. ft. @ $.20) | 7,200.00 | |
| Total Variable Costs | | 153,000.00 |
| Contribution Margin | | $ 27,000.00 |
| Fixed Costs: | | |
| Rent | $ 2,500.00 | |
| Insurance | 400.00 | |
| Other Selling Costs | 4,930.00 | |
| Other Administrative Costs | 10,720.00 | |
| Other Expenses | 2,450.00 | |
| Total Fixed Costs | | 21,000.00 |
| Net Income | | $ 6,000.00 |

An income statement reports operating revenue, cost of merchandise sold, gross profit on operations, operating expenses, and net income or net loss. Gross profit is determined by subtracting cost of merchandise sold from net sales. On a typical income statement, as shown in the top portion of the illustration above, costs are shown as cost of merchandise sold, selling expenses, and administrative expenses.

Income determined by subtracting all variable costs from net sales is called **contribution margin**. Reflection's income statement shown in the bottom portion of the illustration above reports contribution margin and net income by grouping costs into two categories: variable costs and fixed costs.

## CONTRIBUTION MARGIN PER UNIT

The concept of contribution margin is important to managers because it allows them to determine the income available to cover fixed costs and provide a profit. Reflection's managers can determine from this income statement that the total contribution margin in July was $27,000.00. The contribution margin per unit is calculated as follows.

| | Total Contribution Margin | ÷ | Units Sold | = | Contribution Margin per Unit |
|---|---|---|---|---|---|
| | $27,000.00 | ÷ | 36,000 | = | $0.75 |

Thus, Reflection determined that it will earn a $0.75 contribution margin for each square foot of mirrors sold. The managers also know that the company will have $21,000.00 of fixed costs each month regardless of the number of square feet of mirrors sold. Therefore, in July Reflection earned net income of $6,000.00.

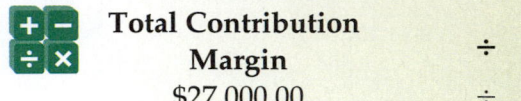

### global perspective

GLOBAL PERSPECTIVE • GLOBAL PERSPECTIVE • GLOBAL PERSPECTIVE

### International Organizations

There are many international organizations that establish trade regulations and standards to facilitate conducting business among the various countries in the world.

The United Nations plays an important role in foreign trade and has many organizations that make contributions. For example, The International Court of Justice (ICJ) decides disputes between nations, The International Monetary Fund (IMF) promotes international monetary cooperation and currency stabilization among member nations, The Universal Postal Union (UPU) promotes international cooperation in postal service, and the United Nations Children's Fund (UNICEF) provides aid to children and mothers in developing countries.

The International Chamber of Commerce (ICC) serves traders in over 100 countries. Its most important function is to issue rules on international trade practices. It is not a government agency and confines its activities to business issues rather than national policy issues.

The General Agreement on Tariffs and Trade (GATT) promotes economic growth by liberalizing world trade through requiring its member governments to reduce artificial trade restraints. There are 90 members of GATT, and the U.S. is a charter member.

The European Union (EU) is a group of 15 European democracies—Austria, Belgium, Denmark, Finland, France, Germany, Greece, the Republic of Ireland, Italy, Luxembourg, the Netherlands, Portugal, Spain, Sweden, and the United Kingdom. The EU has a short-term goal to integrate member nations' economies so members will act as a single nation for trade purposes. The EU's long-term goal is to unite member nations into a political union.

**Required**

Select one international trade organization and research the organization's creation, policies, and accomplishments.

# Explore Accounting

## Differential Costs

Teton Tours is about to depart on a one-week bus tour with an empty seat. As the tourists are loading the bus, Sandy Tanaka offers to purchase the last ticket for $600.00—well below the regular $900.00 ticket price. Should Teton Tours depart with an empty seat or accept Sandy's offer?

Managers must understand the nature or characteristics of costs to make decisions that increase income. A cost that differs between alternative actions is referred to as a *differential cost.* Only differential costs are relevant to making a decision between alternatives.

Consider the costs of the tour for each of the alternatives.

| Costs | 43 Tourists (depart with an empty seat) | 44 Tourists (accept Sandy's offer) |
|---|---|---|
| Food ($150.00 per person) | $ 6,450.00 | $ 6,600.00 |
| Hotel ($300.00 per person) | 12,900.00 | 13,200.00 |
| Admission Fees ($120.00 per person) | 5,160.00 | 5,280.00 |
| Bus Depreciation | 1,000.00 | $ 1,000.00 |
| Bus Fuel | 600.00 | 600.00 |
| Bus Driver Wages | 2,000.00 | 2,000.00 |
| Total Costs | $28,110.00 | $28,680.00 |
| Cost per Tourist | $653.72 | $651.82 |

A manager who compares the $600.00 ticket offer to the $651.82 cost per person and declines the offer is making the wrong decision. The three bus-related expenses do not change if an additional passenger joins the tour. Thus, these costs are not relevant to the decision.

The $600.00 offer should be compared only to differential costs. The food, hotel, and admission fees are $570.00 per person ($150.00 + $300.00 + $120.00 = $570.00). Thus, Teton Tours will earn an additional $30.00 ($600.00 − $570.00) by accepting Sandy's offer.

Certainly, Teton Tours cannot offer every passenger the $600.00 price and expect to earn any income. However, for this specific decision, Teton Tours earn more income by accepting a discounted ticket price than by leaving with an empty seat.

**Critical Thinking:** Recalculate the amounts shown in the table. Decide whether you agree with the decision to accept Sandy's offer.

Xtra!
Study Tools
accountingxtra.swlearning.com

## terms review

total costs
unit cost
variable costs
fixed costs
contribution margin

TERMS REVIEW

## audit your understanding

1. If total monthly fixed costs for a company were plotted on a graph for seven months, would the line drawn between the plotted points be parallel to the base or sloped? Explain why.
2. How does contribution margin differ from gross profit?

## work together 15-1

WORK TOGETHER • WORK TOGETHER • WORK TOGETHER • WORK TOGETHER • WORK

**Preparing an income statement with contribution margin**

An income statement for Wightman's Lumber is included in the *Working Papers*. Your instructor will guide you through the following examples.

1. Use the following information to prepare Wightman Lumber's January income statement reporting contribution margin. The February information will be used to complete the On Your Own below.

| | January | February |
|---|---|---|
| Net Sales | 52,000 square feet | 47,000 square feet |
| Unit Sales Price | $7.50 per square foot | $7.50 per square foot |
| Cost of Merchandise Sold | $4.60 per square foot | $4.80 per square foot |
| Selling Expenses: | | |
| Sales Commission | $.32 per square foot | $.32 per square foot |
| Delivery Cost | $.50 per square foot | $.55 per square foot |
| Other Variable Selling Expenses | $.35 per square foot | $.35 per square foot |
| Other Fixed Selling Expenses | $7,120.00 | $7,120.00 |
| Administrative Expenses: | | |
| Rent | $3,800.00 | $3,800.00 |
| Insurance | $450.00 | $450.00 |
| Other Variable Administrative Expenses | $.30 per square foot | $.33 per square foot |
| Other Fixed Administrative Expenses | $12,540.00 | $12,540.00 |

## on your own 15-1

ON YOUR OWN • ON YOUR OWN

**Preparing an income statement with contribution margin**

Use the February information from the Work Together above. An income statement for Wightman Lumber is included in the *Working Papers*. Work independently to complete this problem.

1. Prepare Wightman Lumber's February income statement reporting contribution margin.

# 15-2 Determining Breakeven

## CALCULATING THE BREAKEVEN POINT

| Contribution Margin | ÷ | Net Sales | = | Contribution Margin Rate | ❶ |
|---|---|---|---|---|---|
| $27,000.00 | ÷ | $180,000.00 | = | .15 or 15% | |

| Total Fixed Costs | ÷ | Contribution Margin Rate | = | Sales Dollar Breakeven Point | ❷ |
|---|---|---|---|---|---|
| $21,000.00 | ÷ | .15 or 15% | = | $140,000.00 | |

| Sales Dollar Breakeven Point | ÷ | Unit Sales Price | = | Unit Sales Breakeven Point | ❸ |
|---|---|---|---|---|---|
| $140,000.00 | ÷ | $5.00 | = | 28,000 units | |

If a manager is to make decisions that yield a favorable net income for a company, the manager needs two important types of information. (1) The amount of merchandise or services the company must sell to earn a favorable net income. (2) The factors that contribute most to net income.

The amount of sales at which net sales is equal to total costs is called the **breakeven point**. At the breakeven point, neither a net income nor a net loss occurs. At sales levels above the breakeven point, net income occurs. Conversely, at sales levels below the breakeven point, net loss occurs. Knowing the breakeven point allows managers to determine the amount of sales needed to start earning a profit. The breakeven point can be stated in sales dollars or unit sales as shown above.

The amounts required to calculate a breakeven point are obtained from an income statement prepared to report contribution margin, such as the income statement on page 447.

## STEPS

STEPS · STEPS · STEPS · STEPS · STEPS · STEPS · STEPS · STEPS · STEPS · STEPS

### CALCULATING A BREAKEVEN POINT

❶ Calculate the contribution margin rate by dividing the total contribution margin by net sales. The amounts are taken from historical financial statements, which are often used to project future sales and costs. Reflection uses total amounts rounded to the nearest $10 in breakeven point calculations. This rate means that for every $1.00 of revenue, $0.15 is contribution margin. The contribution rate is available to pay for fixed costs and provide net income. Variable costs change in direct proportion to changes in sales activity. Therefore, for every $1.00 of revenue, $0.85 is required for variable costs.

❷ Calculate the sales dollar breakeven point by dividing total fixed costs by the contribution margin rate. The sales dollar breakeven point is the amount of sales at which the entire contribution margin is used to pay for fixed costs. Reflection must have total sales of $140,000.00 just to recover its variable and fixed costs. More than $140,000.00 in sales must be made if the company is to earn a net income. At a sales level of exactly $140,000, total costs are $140,000 (fixed costs are $21,000 and variable costs are $119,000 [$140,000 × .85]), and Reflection achieves no net income. Any sales level less than $140,000 results in a net loss.

❸ Calculate the unit sales breakeven point by dividing the sales dollar breakeven point by the unit sales price. The unit sales breakeven point indicates the number of square feet of mirrors that Reflection must sell at $5.00 per square foot to achieve breakeven sales.

| Unit Sales Price | − | Variable Cost per Unit | = | Contribution Margin per Unit | ① |
|---|---|---|---|---|---|
| $18.00 | − | $12.00 | = | $6.00 | |
| Total Fixed Costs | ÷ | Contribution Margin per Unit | = | Unit Sales Breakeven Point | ② |
| $9,000.00 | ÷ | $6.00 | = | 1,500 units | |
| Unit Sales Breakeven Point | × | Unit Sales Price | = | Sales Dollar Breakeven Point | ③ |
| 1,500 | × | $18.00 | = | $27,000.00 | |

When a business plans to introduce a new product, management is interested in knowing how many units the company must sell to break even. Unfortunately, no financial statements exist from which sales and cost information can be obtained. Therefore, an alternative method to calculate the breakeven point using the *contribution margin per unit* rather than the *contribution margin rate* is necessary.

Reflection is considering selling desk lamps at $18.00 per unit. Management expects variable costs of $12.00 per unit with fixed costs of $9,000.00 per month. From the analysis, Reflection determines that it must sell more than 1,500 desk lamps per month before the company begins to make a net income. Thus,

management will begin selling desk lamps if it believes it can sell more than 1,500 per month.

This alternative method is also useful for calculating the breakeven point for existing products when complete financial statements are not available.

**FYI** FOR YOUR INFORMATION

The nature of some businesses requires a large investment in fixed costs. Businesses such as airlines, public utilities, and railroads have large fixed costs. These businesses may be considered riskier because much of their revenue is devoted to paying these fixed costs.

## STEPS
STEPS • STEPS • STEPS • STEPS • STEPS • STEPS • STEPS • STEPS • STEPS • STEPS

### CALCULATING A BREAKEVEN POINT FOR A NEW PRODUCT

① Calculate the contribution margin per unit by subtracting the variable cost per unit from the unit sales price. The contribution margin per unit represents the amount available per unit to cover fixed costs and earn a profit.

② Calculate the unit sales breakeven point by dividing the total fixed costs by the contribution margin per unit. The unit sales breakeven point indicates the number of units that must be sold at the projected unit sales price to cover all variable and fixed costs. If Reflection sells exactly 1,500 units, it will earn no net income, nor will it incur a net loss.

③ Calculate the sales dollar breakeven point by multiplying the unit sales breakeven point by the unit sales price. This calculation gives the revenue earned by selling 1,500 units at the projected sales price, $18.00 per unit.

©GETTY IMAGES/PHOTODISC

**Reflection, Inc.**
**Breakeven Income Statement**
**For Month Ended July 31, 20--**

| | | |
|---|---:|---:|
| Operating Revenue: | | |
| Net Sales (28,000 sq. ft. @ $5.00) .......................... | | $140,000.00 |
| Variable Costs: | | |
| Cost of Merchandise Sold (28,000 sq. ft. @ $3.30) .............. | $92,400.00 | |
| Sales Commission (28,000 sq. ft. @ $.20) ..................... | 5,600.00 | |
| Delivery Costs (28,000 sq. ft. @ $.40) ....................... | 11,200.00 | |
| Other Selling Costs (28,000 sq. ft. @ $.15) ................... | 4,200.00 | |
| Other Administrative Costs (28,000 sq. ft. @ $.20) .............. | 5,600.00 | |
| Total Variable Costs ....................... | | 119,000.00 |
| Contribution Margin ........................ | | $ 21,000.00 |
| Fixed Costs: | | |
| Rent .... | $ 2,500.00 | |
| Insurance ...... | 400.00 | |
| Other Selling Costs...... | 4,930.00 | |
| Other Administrative Costs...... | 10,720.00 | |
| Other Expenses ...... | 2,450.00 | |
| Total Fixed Costs ....................... | | 21,000.00 |
| Net Income....................... | | $ –0– |

The breakeven income statement above shows the proof for Reflection's breakeven point for mirror sales. If the breakeven point is accurate, net income is zero.

The breakeven income statement is a projection of sales and costs under specific assumptions. Reflection reports projected amounts to the nearest $10. Total sales, *$140,000.00,* is equal to the sales dollar breakeven point. Each variable cost is calculated by multiplying the unit sales breakeven point, *28,000 units,* by the unit variable cost of each cost item. The amount of each fixed cost is taken from the July income statement. The contribution margin, *$21,000.00,* is 15% of net sales, *$140,000.00.* This verifies Reflection's contribution margin rate of 15%.

CAREERS IN ACCOUNTING • CAREERS IN ACCOUNTING • CAREERS IN ACCOUNT

## careers in accounting

### Licensure Requirements for Financial Careers

Do you want to be a nurse? A hairstylist? A teacher? An accountant? These and many other careers require you to have a license. The requirements for a license vary with the career and also vary across the country.

Within the accounting and financial career areas, there are many positions that require licensure. Generally, to get a license, a person must have the right combination of education and experience and also must pass a test. Within one licensure area, the amount of education and experience required can vary from state to state. For example, the Certified Public Accountant license is granted by a governing unit within each state. Therefore, the

education and experience requirement in California may be very different from the education and experience requirements in Maine.

Someone hoping to obtain a license of any kind must be very careful to fulfill the requirements for the state in which he or she hopes to practice.

### Instructions

Pick a career within the accounting or finance field. Research the requirements for licensure for your particular state. Share your findings with your class.

TERM REVIEW
AUDIT YOUR
WORK TOGETHER • WORK TOGETHER
ON YOUR OWN • ON YOUR OWN

## • term review

breakeven point

## • audit your understanding

1.  In what two ways can the breakeven point be stated?
2.  How is the contribution margin per unit used?
3.  What is the simplest way to verify the accuracy of a breakeven calculation?

## • work together 15-2

**Calculating breakeven in sales dollars and unit sales and preparing a breakeven income statement**

An income statement for Cherie's Pizza is included in the *Working Papers*. Your instructor will guide you through the following examples.

1.  Use the following information to calculate the breakeven point in sales dollars and unit sales for *July*. The August information will be used to complete the On Your Own below.

|  | July | August |
|---|---|---|
| Net Sales | $60,000.00 | $80,000.00 |
| Unit Sales Price | $8.00 | $8.00 |
| Contribution Margin | $12,000.00 | $10,000.00 |
| Total Fixed Costs | $8,000.00 | $8,000.00 |
| Unit Variable Cost | $6.40 | $7.00 |

2.  Prepare a breakeven income statement for July of the current year. Save your work to complete Work Together 15-3.

## • on your own 15-2

**Calculating breakeven in sales dollars and unit sales and preparing a breakeven income statement**

Use the August information from the Work Together above. An income statement for Cherie's Pizza is included in the *Working Papers*. Work independently to complete this problem.

1.  Calculate the breakeven point in sales dollars and unit sales for *August*.
2.  Prepare a breakeven income statement for August of the current year. Save your work to complete On Your Own 15-3.

# 15-3 Decisions That Affect Net Income

## CALCULATING SALES TO EARN PLANNED NET INCOME

| | Total Fixed Costs | + | Planned Net Income | = | Required Contribution Margin | ❶ |
|---|---|---|---|---|---|---|
| | $21,000.00 | + | $1,500.00 | = | $22,500.00 | |
| | Required Contribution Margin | ÷ | Contribution Margin Rate | = | Sales Dollars | ❷ |
| | $22,500.00 | ÷ | .15 or 15% | = | $150,000.00 | |

Determining the breakeven point provides management with important information about the relationship of sales, variable costs, and fixed costs. Businesses do not, however, operate merely to break even. Managers need information that will assist them in achieving planned net income. The breakeven analysis can be used to calculate the dollar and unit sales needed to earn a specified amount of planned net income.

### FYI — FOR YOUR INFORMATION

Fixed costs for your school might include the depreciation on the building and the principal's salary. These costs are the same no matter how many students are enrolled.

Variable costs for your school might include the cost of computers, cafeteria lunches, and textbooks. These costs will increase or decrease depending on the number of students enrolled.

Identify other costs involved with your school. Are they fixed or variable?

## STEPS

STEPS • STEPS • STEPS • STEPS • STEPS • STEPS • STEPS • STEPS • STEPS • STEPS

### CALCULATING SALES TO EARN PLANNED NET INCOME

❶ Calculate the required contribution margin. The sum of total fixed costs and the planned net income is the contribution margin necessary both to cover fixed costs and to earn the planned amount of net income. Reflection's managers want to know the amount of total sales required to earn $1,500.00 of net income.

❷ Calculate the amount of sales dollars by dividing the required contribution margin by the contribution margin rate. Thus, Reflection must sell 30,000 square feet of mirrors ($150,000.00 total sales *divided by* the unit sales price of $5.00) to earn $1,500.00 of net income.

The required contribution margin, $22,500.00, can be divided by the contribution margin per unit, $0.75, to calculate the number of units to be sold ($22,500.00/$0.75 = 30,000).

|  | Per Unit | Number of Units | | |
|---|---|---|---|---|
|  |  | 26,000 | 28,000 | 30,000 |
| Net Sales . . . . . . . . . . . . . . . . . . | $5.00 | $130,000.00 | $140,000.00 | $150,000.00 |
| Variable Costs . . . . . . . . . . . . . . | 4.25 | 110,500.00 | 119,000.00 | 127,500.00 |
| Contribution Margin . . . . . . . . . . | $0.75 | $ 19,500.00 | $ 21,000.00 | $ 22,500.00 |
| Fixed Costs . . . . . . . . . . . . . . . . | | 21,000.00 | 21,000.00 | 21,000.00 |
| Net Income (Loss) . . . . . . . . . . . | | $ (1,500.00) | $ –0– | $ 1,500.00 |

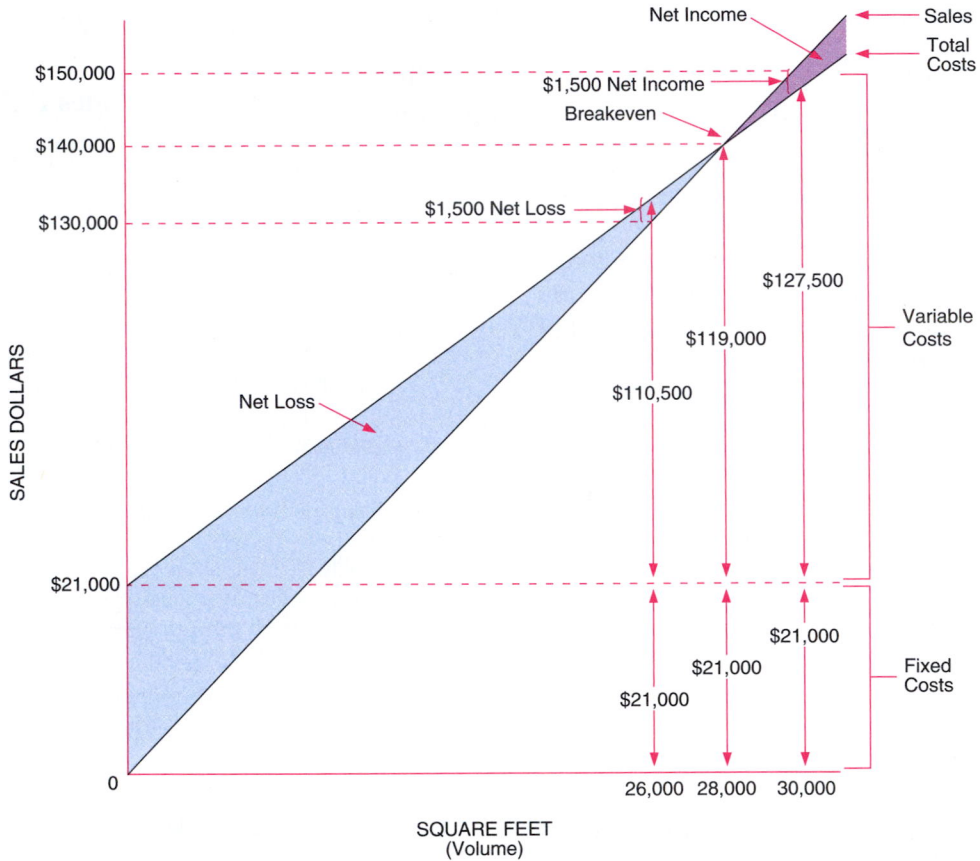

Businesses must be able to determine the change in net income that would result from changes in the relationship of sales, variable costs, and fixed costs. Reflection's managers desire answers to questions such as these: What would net income be if sales increase or decrease? Would it be profitable to change production methods? What would be the effect on net income of a decrease in unit sales price and an increase in sales volume?

Reflection has calculated its unit sales breakeven point to be 28,000 square feet. The table above shows how net income changes for a decrease or an increase of 2,000 units. For each square foot of mirrors Reflection sells, $0.75 of contribution margin is available for fixed costs and net income. At the 28,000 unit breakeven point, the $21,000.00 contribution margin pays for fixed costs, leaving no remaining amount for net income. For each square foot of mirrors above 28,000 units sold, the $0.75 per square foot contribution margin increases net income. Therefore, when 30,000 square feet of mirrors are sold, net income is expected to be $1,500.00 (2,000 square feet × $0.75 contribution margin per unit).

If only 26,000 square feet of mirrors are sold during the month, the contribution margin of $19,500.00 would not cover the fixed costs of $21,000.00. At this sales volume, a net loss of $1,500.00 would result.

The graph on the previous page shows the relationship of sales, costs, and net income as the volume changes. The sales line, beginning at zero, represents unit sales price times number of units sold. The total cost line starting at $21,000.00 (total fixed costs) represents the total fixed and variable costs for the number of units sold. No matter what the sales volume is, the fixed costs remain constant. The variable cost area represents 85% of sales regardless of volume.

At the breakeven point, the sales and total costs lines intersect, indicating that neither a net income nor a net loss will occur. If 30,000 square feet of mirrors are sold, the sales line is above the total cost line. At this sales volume, $150,000.00 of sales is higher than the sum of fixed costs ($21,000.00) and variable costs ($127,500.00), resulting in net income of $1,500.00. If sales volume is below 28,000 square feet, the total cost line is above the sales line indicating a net loss.

## EFFECT OF COST CHANGES AT AVERAGE VOLUME

| | Alternative 1 Manual Cutting | | | Alternative 2 Automated Cutting | | |
|---|---|---|---|---|---|---|
| | Per Unit | Units Sold | Total | Per Unit | Units Sold | Total |
| Net Sales . . . . . . . . . . . . . . . . . | $5.00 | 30,000 | $150,000.00 | $5.00 | 30,000 | $150,000.00 |
| Variable Costs . . . . . . . . . . . . . | 4.25 | 30,000 | 127,500.00 | 4.00 | 30,000 | 120,000.00 |
| Contribution Margin . . . . . . . . . . | $0.75 | 30,000 | $ 22,500.00 | $1.00 | 30,000 | $ 30,000.00 |
| Fixed Costs . . . . . . . . . . . . . . . | | | 21,000.00 | | | 28,500.00 |
| Net Income (Loss) . . . . . . . . . . . | | | $ 1,500.00 | | | $ 1,500.00 |

Two types of costs, variable and fixed, influence the decisions a company may make. Total variable costs increase or decrease as sales increase or decrease. Total fixed costs remain constant regardless of sales amount.

Reflection's management is concerned that the relatively low contribution margin rate makes increasing net income difficult for the company. Reflection is searching for ways to improve its percentage of net income per sales dollar. An alternate production method is being considered. The new method would automate the cutting of mirrors. A cost comparison of the two methods, Alternative 1 and Alternative 2, is shown above and is described below.

- *Alternative 1: Manual Cutting.* Variable costs per square foot of mirrors are $4.25. Reflection currently pays a crew to cut mirrors to dimensions ordered by its customers. Of the total variable costs, $0.25 per square foot represents the cost of this crew. Fixed costs are $21,000.00 per month.
- *Alternative 2: Automated Cutting.* The company buys an automated cutter and assigns the cutting crew to process orders of new product lines. The variable costs of the mirrors decrease by $0.25 per square foot to $4.00 per square foot. However, the new method requires buying the automated cutter and employing an experienced cutter at a fixed salary. Thus, fixed costs increase by $7,500.00 per month to $28,500.00.

Sales have been averaging about 30,000 square feet of mirrors per month. At a 30,000-unit sales level, net income is the same for both alternatives. With Alternative 2, the contribution margin is higher, but fixed costs also are higher. Thus, the higher fixed costs cancel the higher contribution margin.

| | Alternative 1 Manual Cutting | | | Alternative 2 Automated Cutting | | |
|---|---|---|---|---|---|---|
| | Per Unit | Units Sold | Total | Per Unit | Units Sold | Total |
| Net Sales . . . . . . . . . . . . . . . . . | $5.00 | 32,000 | $160,000.00 | $5.00 | 32,000 | $160,000.00 |
| Variable Costs . . . . . . . . . . . . . | 4.25 | 32,000 | 136,000.00 | 4.00 | 32,000 | 128,000.00 |
| Contribution Margin . . . . . . . . . . | $0.75 | 32,000 | $ 24,000.00 | $1.00 | 32,000 | $ 32,000.00 |
| Fixed Costs . . . . . . . . . . . . . . . | | | 21,000.00 | | | 28,500.00 |
| Net Income (Loss) . . . . . . . . . . . | | | $ 3,000.00 | | | $ 3,500.00 |

Reflection is planning to increase unit sales. A cost comparison with a sales volume of 32,000 units is shown above. With the increased sales volume, Alternative 2 earns a higher net income.

If Reflection expects a permanent sales increase, Alternative 2 would be more profitable than Alternative 1.

| | Alternative 1 Manual Cutting | | Alternative 2 Automated Cutting | |
|---|---|---|---|---|
| | Dollars | Percent | Dollars | Percent |
| Net Sales . . . . . . . . . . . . . . . . . | $150,000.00 | 100% | $150,000.00 | 100% |
| Variable Costs . . . . . . . . . . . . . | 127,500.00 | 85% | 120,000.00 | 80% |
| Contribution Margin . . . . . . . . . . | $ 22,500.00 | 15% | $ 30,000.00 | 20% |

**1.** Contribution margin rate, Alternative 1.

**2.** Contribution margin rate, Alternative 2.

As long as sales increase as expected, Alternative 2 will be favored. However, if sales do not increase, the results will be much different. If the number of units actually sold falls below 30,000, the results will favor Alternative 1.

What is the reason for the change in favorable alternatives? The contribution margin rate favors Alternative 2. The illustration above shows that the contribution margin rate for Alternative 1 is 15% versus 20% for Alternative 2. This means that for every $1.00 of sales from Alternative 1, $0.15 is available for fixed costs and net income. But for every $1.00 of sales from Alternative 2, $0.20 is available for fixed costs and net income.

A higher contribution margin rate is usually desirable. However, fixed costs must also be reasonable since the contribution margin must cover the fixed costs before any net income is earned. The contribution margin rate, *20%*, for the automated cutting method is more favorable. But fixed costs are $28,500.00—$7,500.00 more than fixed costs for the manual cutting method. If sales volume declines, the increased contribution margin is not enough to recover the increased fixed costs. Therefore a reduction in net income occurs.

A logical conclusion is "everything else being equal, the activity with the higher contribution margin rate is more profitable." If "everything else" is equal, selecting the more profitable choice is very simple. However, alternatives are seldom that simple because fixed costs probably differ for each alternative. Therefore, an effective business looks for the best combination of fixed and variable costs.

## EFFECT OF CHANGE IN SALES PRICE

| | Current Price | | | Price Reduction and Sales Volume Increase | | |
|---|---|---|---|---|---|---|
| | Per Unit | Units Sold | Total | Per Unit | Units Sold | Total |
| Net Sales................. | $5.00 | 30,000 | $150,000.00 | $4.75 | 36,000 | $171,000.00 |
| Variable Costs.............. | 4.25 | 30,000 | 127,500.00 | 4.25 | 36,000 | 153,000.00 |
| Contribution Margin........... | $0.75 | 30,000 | $ 22,500.00 | $0.50 | 36,000 | $ 18,000.00 |
| Fixed Costs................ | | | 21,000.00 | | | 21,000.00 |
| Net Income (Loss)........... | | | $ 1,500.00 | | | $ (3,000.00) |

Setting the sales price of a product is extremely important. If the price is set too high, potential customers will buy from another business. If the price is set too low, the company may not earn enough money to cover costs and may suffer a loss. The objective is to set sales prices that provide a reasonable amount of net income while keeping prices competitive.

Reflection earned record net income in July, selling 30,000 units. Unfortunately, Reflection's managers believe that a price reduction is necessary to sustain this sales volume. Management is considering a plan to reduce unit sales price by 5% (from $5.00 to $4.75). Management projects that the price decrease will result in a 20% increase in the average number of units sold

(from 30,000 to 36,000 units). Should Reflection implement this price reduction? The illustration above shows the effect of this price change on sales volume and net income.

Price cutting can be dangerous. In July, Reflection had a $0.75 contribution margin per square foot of mirrors sold. Average sales of 30,000 units resulted in $22,500.00 total contribution margin. A unit sales price reduction of 5% ($0.25 per unit) to $4.75 per unit reduces the contribution margin to $0.50, a 33⅓% reduction. The potential results of a price cut can be calculated. The unit sales required to maintain the net income using the new contribution margin is calculated as follows.

| Contribution Margin | ÷ | New Contribution Margin per Unit | = | Unit Sales Required to Maintain Planned Net Income |
|---|---|---|---|---|
| $22,500.00 | ÷ | $0.50 | = | 45,000 units |

A decrease in unit sales price from $5.00 to $4.75 is projected to increase average sales from 30,000 to 36,000 units. However, at $4.75, the company would have to sell a total of 45,000 units to maintain the same net income as current sales at the $5.00 price. Reducing the unit sales price by $0.25 would not be a profitable decision if the company can sell only 36,000 units.

**FYI** FOR YOUR INFORMATION

Spreadsheet software is an ideal tool to use for calculating breakeven and for analyzing the effect of price, cost, and sales mix changes. An effective spreadsheet identifies the variables used in an analysis, for example units sold, price per unit, variable costs, and fixed costs. The analysis is built by creating formulas that reference these variables. When the amounts of the variables are changed, the spreadsheet instantly recalculates the analysis and displays the results.

**VideoPort, Inc.**
**Income Statement**
**For Month Ended November 30, 20--**

| | | | |
|---|---|---|---|
| Operating Revenue: | | | |
| Net Sales | | | |
| Televisions (150 units @ $350). | | $52,500.00 | |
| VCRs (90 units @ $250). | | 22,500.00 | $75,000.00 |
| Variable Costs: | | | |
| Televisions (150 units @ $210). | | $31,500.00 | |
| VCRs (90 units @ $150). | | 13,500.00 | 45,000.00 |
| Contribution Margin. | | | $30,000.00 |
| Fixed Costs. | | | 24,000.00 |
| Net Income. | | | $ 6,000.00 |

| | Product Sales | ÷ | Net Sales | = | Sales Mix | |
|---|---|---|---|---|---|---|
| Television | $52,500.00 | ÷ | $75,000.00 | = | 70% | ❶ |
| VCR | $22,500.00 | ÷ | $75,000.00 | = | 30% | |

| Contribution Margin | ÷ | Net Sales | = | Contribution Margin Rate | |
|---|---|---|---|---|---|
| $30,000.00 | ÷ | $75,000.00 | = | .40 or 40% | ❷ |

| Total Fixed Costs | + | Planned Net Income | = | Required Contribution Margin Rate | |
|---|---|---|---|---|---|
| $24,000.00 | + | $10,000.00 | = | $34,000.00 | ❸ |

| Required Contribution Margin | ÷ | Contribution Margin Rate | = | Total Sales Dollars | |
|---|---|---|---|---|---|
| $34,000.00 | ÷ | .40 or 40% | = | $85,000.00 | ❹ |

| | Sales Mix | × | Total Sales Dollars | = | Product Sales Dollars | |
|---|---|---|---|---|---|---|
| Television | 70% | × | $85,000.00 | = | $59,500.00 | ❺ |
| VCR | 30% | × | $85,000.00 | = | $25,500.00 | |

| | Product Sales Dollars | ÷ | Unit Sales Price | = | Product Unit Sales | |
|---|---|---|---|---|---|---|
| Television | $59,500.00 | ÷ | $350.00 | = | 170 units | ❻ |
| VCR | $25,500.00 | ÷ | $250.00 | = | 102 units | |

Businesses that sell two or more products can also use breakeven point calculations to assist managers in planning. Relative distribution of sales among various products is called **sales mix**. The sales mix must be calculated to determine the breakeven point for a company that sells more than one product. VideoPort, Inc. sells televisions and videocassette recorders (VCRs). The income statement above reports VideoPort's sales and cost information for the month ended November 30.

VideoPort expects the relationship of television to VCR sales to remain relatively stable in future months. However, management has indicated its objective to improve monthly net income to $10,000.00. How many televisions and VCRs should VideoPort plan to purchase and sell?

The procedures used to calculate sales to earn a planned net income are similar to those previously described in this chapter. Six steps are used to calculate sales of more than one product to earn a planned net income.

Management Decisions Using Cost-Volume-Profit Analysis

# STEPS

## SALES MIX NEEDED TO EARN PLANNED NET INCOME

**1** Calculate the sales mix using information from the income statement. Net sales are divided by the sales amounts for each product. The total product mix must equal 100%.

**2** Calculate the contribution margin rate by dividing the contribution margin shown on the income statement by net sales.

**3** Add total fixed costs and the planned net income to determine the required contribution margin.

**4** Divide the required contribution margin by the contribution margin rate to determine the total sales dollars.

**5** Multiply the sales mix percentage by the total sales dollars to determine the sales dollars needed for each product.

**6** Divide the product sales dollars by the unit sales price to determine product unit sales. The unit sales prices are found on the income statement. The product unit sales indicate the number of units of each product that must be sold to achieve the planned net income of $10,000.00.

Managers of the television and VCR departments can now plan to accomplish these sales objectives. For example, the television department manager knows that the department must sell 20 more televisions (170 − 150 = 20) each month. Thus, the manager can plan to increase purchases and devise new sales promotion and advertising campaigns to sell the increased number of televisions.

# technology for business

TECHNOLOGY FOR BUSINESS · TECHNOLOGY FOR BUSINESS · TECHNOLOGY FOR BUSIN

## Using a Spreadsheet to Perform Breakeven Analysis

Micron, Inc., a large wholesaler, plans to introduce a new product line next year. Three lines are being considered. Micron performs extensive market research on potential new product lines. The three lines being considered have tested well.

To make the final decision among the three product lines, management has decided that the line with the lowest breakeven point will be added. The following data are available for the three product lines:

**Required**

1. Create a spreadsheet that calculates the breakeven point for the three product lines. Use descriptive column headings and row titles. [Hint: Develop the breakeven formula for the Line A. Use the Copy command to copy the formula for Lines B and C.]

2. From your analysis, which line should Micron add next year?

|  | Line A | Line B | Line C |
|---|---|---|---|
| Sales price per unit | $42.00 | $48.00 | $46.00 |
| Variable costs per unit | 18.00 | 26.00 | 14.00 |
| Fixed costs | $14,600.00 | $11,800.00 | $27,200.00 |

Xtra!
Study Tools
accountingxtra.swlearning.com

## term review

TERM REVIEW

sales mix

## audit your understanding

AUDIT YOUR

1. What two types of costs influence management's decisions?
2. To earn a planned net income, the required contribution margin must equal what two amounts?

## work together 15-3

WORK TOGETHER • WORK TOGETHER • WORK TOGETHER

**Calculating sales to earn a planned net income, calculating the effect of volume changes on net income, and calculating the effect of changes in selling price**

Use the working papers and data from Work Together 15-2. Forms for completing this Work Together are provided in the *Working Papers*. Your instructor will guide you through the following examples.

1. Assume that Cherie's Pizza wants a net income for July of $3,000. Calculate the amount of sales dollars needed to achieve this net income.
2. Determine the net income or loss if: (a) 4,000 units are sold; (b) 5,000 units are sold; (c) 6,000 units are sold.
3. Assume Cherie's Pizza normally sells 7,500 pizzas in July. If the selling price is reduced by $.50, Cherie's expects to sell 9,000 pizzas. Calculate the effect on net income of this change.

## on your own 15-3

ON YOUR OWN • ON YOUR OWN • ON YOUR OWN

**Calculating sales to earn a planned net income, calculating the effect of volume changes on net income, and calculating the effect of changes in selling price**

Use the working papers and data from On Your Own 15-2. Forms for completing this On Your Own are provided in the *Working Papers*. Work independently to complete this problem.

1. Assume Cherie's Pizza wants a net income for August of $3,000. Calculate the amount of sales dollars needed to achieve this net income.
2. Determine the net income or loss if: (a) 7,000 units are sold; (b) if 8,000 units are sold; (c) 9,000 units are sold.
3. Assume Cherie's Pizza normally sells 10,000 pizzas in August. If the selling price is increased by $.50, Cherie's expects to sell 9,500 pizzas. Calculate the effect on net income of this change.

**After completing this chapter, you can**

1. Define terms related to accounting information for management decisions.
2. Identify accounting concepts and practices related to preparing accounting information for management decisions.
3. Prepare an income statement reporting contribution margin.
4. Calculate the contribution margin rate.
5. Calculate the breakeven point.
6. Calculate the sales dollars and sales units required to earn a planned amount of net income.
7. Determine the effect of changes in sales volume, unit costs, and unit sales prices on net income.
8. Calculate a sales mix.

# Explore Accounting

EXPLORE ACCOUNTING • EXPLORE ACCOUNTING • EXPLORE ACCOU

## Mixed Costs

A cost having both fixed and variable characteristics is called a mixed cost. For example, Mason Castings uses natural gas to operate a casting furnace. Even if the company processes no castings, keeping the furnace heated incurs a cost—a fixed cost. The gas required to maintain a constant furnace temperature increases with the number of castings produced—a variable cost. Thus, natural gas expense is a mixed cost.

A statistical method used to determine the fixed and variable costs of a mixed cost is called regression analysis. Natural gas expense for the past six months can be used to estimate the fixed and variable costs.

| Units | Temperature | Expense |
|---|---|---|
| 4,653 | 28 | $5,507 |
| 4,657 | 34 | 5,869 |
| 5,423 | 43 | 6,791 |
| 6,754 | 47 | 7,697 |
| 5,876 | 58 | 7,918 |
| 6,137 | 78 | 9,249 |

Using the number of units produced and the average outdoor temperature in the multiple

regression equation allows management to estimate that the fixed cost is $1,500 and that variable costs are $60 for every degree of temperature and $.50 for every unit produced. With this information, management can accurately estimate future expenses.

**Required:**
Use the multiple regression tool of an electronic spreadsheet and the following six-month actual cost information to determine the fixed and variable amounts of labor costs. Assume that the number of units produced and the number of production days have an impact on labor costs. (Hint: Identify the cost as the dependent, y, variable and the units and days as independent, x, variables.)

| Units | Days | Cost |
|---|---|---|
| 675 | 15 | $10,025 |
| 867 | 18 | 11,801 |
| 768 | 20 | 12,304 |
| 978 | 22 | 13,728 |
| 965 | 20 | 12,895 |
| 875 | 18 | 11,825 |

# 15-1 APPLICATION PROBLEM

### Preparing an income statement reporting contribution margin

Milford Pump Company's income statement has been prepared for November of the current year.

| Milford Pump Company Income Statement For Month Ended November 30, 20-- | | | |
|---|---|---|---|
| Operating Revenue: | | | |
| Net Sales (8,700 units @ $210.00) . . . . . . . . . . . . . . . . . . | | | $1,827,000.00 |
| Cost of Merchandise Sold (8,700 units @ $145.00) . . . . . . | | | 1,261,500.00 |
| Gross Profit on Operations . . . . . . . . . . . . . . . . . . . . . . . . . | | | $ 565,500.00 |
| Operating Expenses: | | | |
| Selling Expenses: | | | |
| Sales Commission (8,700 units @ $6.00) . . . . . . . . . . . . | $52,200.00 | | |
| Delivery Costs (8,700 units @ $4.80) . . . . . . . . . . . . . . | 41,760.00 | | |
| Other Variable Costs (8,700 units @ $2.75) . . . . . . . . . | 23,925.00 | | |
| Other Fixed Costs . . . . . . . . . . . . . . . . . . . . . . . . . . . . | 76,510.00 | $194,395.00 | |
| Administrative Expenses: | | | |
| Rent . . . . . . . . . . . . . . . . . . . . . . . . . . . . . . . . . . . . . . | $15,000.00 | | |
| Insurance . . . . . . . . . . . . . . . . . . . . . . . . . . . . . . . . . . | 9,750.00 | | |
| Other Variable Costs (8,700 units @ $5.50) . . . . . . . . . | 47,850.00 | | |
| Other Fixed Costs . . . . . . . . . . . . . . . . . . . . . . . . . . . . | 45,290.00 | 117,890.00 | |
| Total Operating Expenses . . . . . . . . . . . . . . . . . . . . . . . . . . | | | 312,285.00 |
| Income from Operations . . . . . . . . . . . . . . . . . . . . . . . . . . . | | | $ 253,215.00 |
| Other Expenses. . . . . . . . . . . . . . . . . . . . . . . . . . . . . . . . . . | | | 12,000.00 |
| Net Income . . . . . . . . . . . . . . . . . . . . . . . . . . . . . . . . . . . . | | | $ 241,215.00 |

**Instructions:**
1. Prepare Milford Pump Company's November income statement reporting contribution margin.
2. Calculate the contribution margin per unit.
3. Calculate variable cost per unit. Plot variable costs and fixed costs on a graph.

# 15-2 APPLICATION PROBLEM

### Calculating contribution margin and breakeven point

Farris Electronics is considering expanding its product line to include portable radios. Management projects that radios would sell for $60.00 each. Variable costs are projected to be $25.00 with total fixed costs of $42,000.00 per month.

**Instructions:**
1. Calculate the contribution margin per unit.
2. Calculate the unit sales breakeven point.
3. Calculate the sales dollar breakeven point.
4. Farris has projected that it could sell 1,000 units per month. Should the company expand its product line to sell the portable radios? Support your answer.

# 15-3 APPLICATION PROBLEM

**Calculating plans for net income**

Dennis Williams is projecting the coming year's net income potential for Williams Paint. The paint is sold for $15.00 a gallon. Variable costs per gallon are $10.00, and annual fixed costs are $135,000.00. Complete each of the following instructions independently of the others.

**Instructions:**
1. Calculate the (a) unit sales and (b) sales dollar breakeven points.
2. If a $50,000.00 annual net income is planned, calculate the required (a) number of gallons of paint to be sold and (b) sales dollars.
3. Dennis plans to purchase a new paint mixing machine that would reduce the cost of paint by $0.50 per gallon but increase annual fixed costs by $52,000.00. Calculate the (a) unit sales and (b) sales dollar breakeven points. Should Dennis purchase the mixing machine? Explain your answer.

# 15-4 APPLICATION PROBLEM

**Calculating the effects on net income of changes in unit sales price, variable costs, fixed costs, and volume**

The following information pertains to a product sold by Gomez Company:

| | |
|---|---|
| Unit Sales Price | $12.00 |
| Unit Variable Costs | $9.60 |
| Unit Contribution Margin | $2.40 |
| Fixed Costs | $48,000.00 |

**Instructions:**
1. Determine the net income or loss
   a. if 17,000 units are sold.
   b. if 20,000 units are sold.
   c. if 23,000 units are sold.
2. Gomez Company is considering purchasing equipment that would reduce the unit variable cost to $8.50. However, fixed costs would increase to $58,000.
   a. If 20,000 units were expected to be sold, would Gomez Company's net income increase if the new equipment were purchased and used?
   b. If only 17,000 units were expected to be sold, would Gomez Company's net income increase if the new equipment were purchased and used?
3. Gomez Company believes that a 10% reduction in the unit sales price would result in a 30% increase in the number of units sold. Assume that normal sales volume before any price reduction was 20,000 units. Assume also that the equipment described in instruction 2 was not purchased, so that the fixed costs and unit variable costs were $48,000.00 and $9.60, respectively. Would the reduction in sales price increase or decrease net income?

# 15-5 APPLICATION PROBLEM

### Calculating sales mix

Schenk, Inc., sells desk lamps and desks. The following information is from the June income statement. Schenk's management is interested in knowing the number of lamps and desks it must sell to earn $10,000.00 of net income.

**Schenk, Inc.**
**Income Statement**
**For Month Ended June 30, 20--**

| | | |
|---|---:|---:|
| Net Sales: | | |
| Lamps (1,000 @ $40.00). . . . . . . . . . . . . . . . . . . . . . . . . . . . . . . . | $40,000.00 | |
| Desks (240 @ $250.00). . . . . . . . . . . . . . . . . . . . . . . . . . . . . . . | 60,000.00 | |
| Total Net Sales . . . . . . . . . . . . . . . . . . . . . . . . . . . . . . . . . . . . . | | $100,000.00 |
| Variable Costs: | | |
| Lamps (1,000 @ $30.00). . . . . . . . . . . . . . . . . . . . . . . . . . . . . . . | $30,000.00 | |
| Desks (240 @ $125.00). . . . . . . . . . . . . . . . . . . . . . . . . . . . . . | 30,000.00 | |
| Total Variable Costs . . . . . . . . . . . . . . . . . . . . . . . . . . . . . . . . | | 60,000.00 |
| Contribution Margin . . . . . . . . . . . . . . . . . . . . . . . . . . . . . . . . . . | | $ 40,000.00 |
| Fixed Costs . . . . . . . . . . . . . . . . . . . . . . . . . . . . . . . . . . . . . . . . | | 38,000.00 |
| Net Income . . . . . . . . . . . . . . . . . . . . . . . . . . . . . . . . . . . . . . . . | | $  2,000.00 |

**Instructions:**

Schenk's managers need sales information assuming that the company earns $10,000.00 of monthly net income. Calculate the following amounts to achieve the $10,000.00 planned net income.

a. Sales mix.
b. Contribution margin rate.
c. Total sales dollars.
d. Product sales dollars.
e. Product unit sales.

# 15-6 MASTERY PROBLEM

### Calculating contribution margin and breakeven point; calculating sales dollars and unit sales for planned net income

Ratliff Corporation produces lawn fertilizer spreaders. Ratliff's income statement shown on the next page has been prepared for August of the current year.

**Instructions:**

1. Prepare Ratliff's August income statement reporting contribution margin.
2. Calculate the contribution margin rate.
3. Calculate the sales dollar breakeven point.
4. Calculate the unit sales breakeven point.
5. If a $15,000.00 monthly net income is planned, calculate the required (a) sales dollars and (b) unit sales.
6. Ratliff is considering using computer-based machines to increase the productivity of the manufacturing process. The new machines would reduce variable costs by $4.20 per unit but increase monthly fixed costs by $10,000.00. Calculate the projected net income assuming that Ratliff sells 3,000 units. Should Ratliff purchase the machines? Explain your answer.

**Ratliff Corporation**
**Income Statement**
**For Month Ended August 31, 20--**

| | | |
|---|---:|---:|
| Operating Revenue: | | |
| Net Sales (3,000 units @ $25.00) | | $75,000.00 |
| Cost of Merchandise Sold (3,000 units @ $16.00) | | 48,000.00 |
| Gross Profit on Operations | | $27,000.00 |
| Operating Expenses: | | |
| Selling Expenses: | | |
| Sales Commission (3,000 units @ $0.60) | $1,800.00 | |
| Delivery Costs (3,000 units @ $0.75) | 2,250.00 | |
| Other Variable Costs (3,000 units @ $1.15) | 3,450.00 | |
| Other Fixed Costs | 3,590.00 $11,090.00 | |
| Administrative Expenses: | | |
| Rent | $1,000.00 | |
| Insurance | 600.00 | |
| Other Variable Costs (3,000 units @ $0.25) | 750.00 | |
| Other Fixed Costs | 5,610.00 7,960.00 | |
| Total Operating Expenses | | 19,050.00 |
| Income from Operations | | $ 7,950.00 |
| Other Expenses | | 800.00 |
| Net Income | | $ 7,150.00 |

# 15-7 CHALLENGE PROBLEM
### Calculating the effects on net income of changes in unit sales price, variable costs, and fixed costs

Millard, Inc., sold 68,000 computer printers last year with the following results.

**Millard, Inc.**
**Income Statement**
**For Year Ended December 31, 20--**

| | |
|---|---:|
| Net Sales (68,000 units @ $250.00) | $17,000,000.00 |
| Less Variable Costs (68,000 units @ $200.00) | 13,600,000.00 |
| Contribution Margin | $ 3,400,000.00 |
| Less Fixed Costs | 2,980,000.00 |
| Net Income | $ 420,000.00 |

Complete each of the following instructions independently of the others.

**Instructions:**
1. Millard projects that it can sell 75,000 printers next year at the current $250.00 unit sales price. However, management believes that it can increase net income by selling its printer below the unit sales price of its competitors. Millard's marketing department projects that it could sell 100,000 printers at a unit sales price of $230.00. Calculate the projected net income. Should Millard reduce the unit sales price to $230.00? Explain your answer.
2. Millard currently purchases the power cable from another manufacturer at a cost of $7.00 per unit. The company is considering producing the cable. Millard projects that it can produce the cable for $2.00 each plus annual fixed costs of $240,000.00. Calculate the projected net income assuming a sales volume of 75,000 printers. Should Millard produce the power cables? Explain your answer.

## applied communication

Charts and graphs are often used to help people understand numbers. To be helpful, charts and graphs must be clearly labeled.

**Required:**

1. Use the data from Application Problem 15-4, Instruction 1, to prepare a graph similar to the one on page 456. Label the graph clearly.

2. Prepare a brief written explanation of the graph.

## cases for critical thinking

### Case 1

George Edmonds, the new accountant for Zigler Company, has recommended the preparation of income statements reporting contribution margin rather than statements reporting gross profit. He states that the income statement with contribution margin provides better information. Kimberly Johnson, the manager, disagrees that one statement is better than the other. She says gross profit is the same as contribution margin, so it does not make any difference which statement is prepared. Which person is correct? Explain.

### Case 2

Denise Young, an accountant for Chiles Corporation, has been asked to prepare an income statement that reports contribution margin. Miss Young has asked you to prepare an analysis of three months' costs. Provide Miss Young with an analysis of these data that include the unit cost of variable costs and monthly costs of fixed costs. Explain to Miss Young how you prepared your analysis.

|  | May | June | July |
| --- | --- | --- | --- |
| Unit Sales | 400 | 500 | 600 |
| Cost of Merchandise Sold | $8,000.00 | $10,000.00 | $12,000.00 |
| Advertising Expense | 2,300.00 | 2,300.00 | 2,300.00 |
| Depreciation Expense | 1,000.00 | 1,000.00 | 1,000.00 |
| Payroll Taxes Expense | 640.00 | 800.00 | 960.00 |
| Rent Expense | 2,000.00 | 2,000.00 | 2,000.00 |
| Salary Expense | 3,200.00 | 4,000.00 | 4,800.00 |
| Supplies Expense | 1,200.00 | 1,200.00 | 1,200.00 |
| Utilities Expense | 600.00 | 750.00 | 900.00 |

## SCANS workplace competency

**Interpersonal Competency:** Serving Clients and Customers

**Concept:** Competent employees work and communicate with clients and customers to satisfy their expectations. They listen carefully to customer needs to avoid misunderstanding, remain positive when handling complaints, and are familiar with remedies to satisfy customer needs.

**Application:** Some companies promote the policy that "the customer is always right." Why do such businesses respect their clients or customers so highly? How important is good customer service? Form a task group of 3-4 students and brainstorm ideas. Discuss your group's suggestions with the class.

## • graphing workshop

Baumann Industries is considering purchasing NewMark Corporation. Baumann's board of directors has requested a breakeven analysis, based on cost data provided by NewMark's accounting department. Analyze the graph below by answering the following questions.

1. Identify each of the four lines (labeled A–D) in the graph.

2. Estimate the breakeven point in dollars and units.

3. Estimate NewMark's profit if the company can sell 9,000 units.

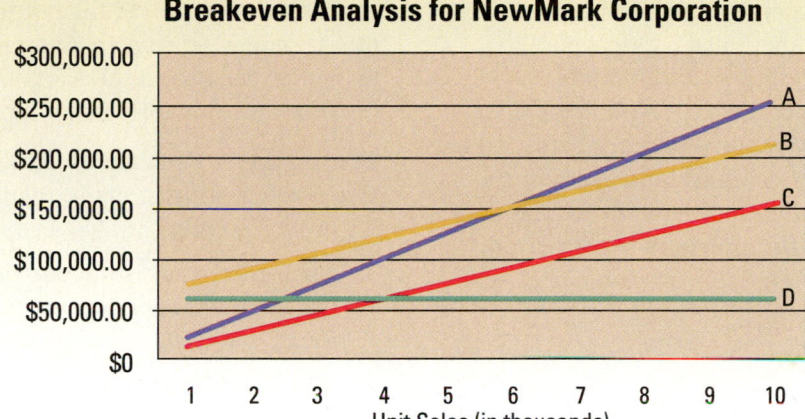

**Breakeven Analysis for NewMark Corporation**

## • analyzing Costco's financial statements

The average Costco warehouse in the United States generates an average of $112,000,000 of net sales, with 11 warehouses exceeding $200,000,000. When opening a new warehouse, Costco managers will measure the warehouse's success by how quickly its sales exceed the breakeven point.

**Instructions:**

Assume that Costco's selling, general, and administrative (SG&A) expenses are fixed costs and that merchandise costs are the only variable costs. Use this information for fiscal year 2003 to calculate a breakeven point per warehouse. Round dollar amounts to the nearest thousand dollars.

1. Calculate the average number of warehouses open during 2003 by adding the beginning- and end-of-year amounts and dividing by 2.

2. Calculate SG&A expenses per warehouse.

3. Calculate the contribution margin rate.

4. Use this information to calculate breakeven sales dollars for 2003.

# Automated Accounting

## Using Computerized Reports for Management Decisions

The accounting department of a business is responsible for generating financial reports. Managers use these reports to make informed business decisions. Individuals working as sales managers, production managers, purchasing managers, or in any other department of the business must be able to interpret accounting information to plan for and organize their business. Financial reports are also used for decision making by owners, investors, and lenders.

A computerized accounting system can provide a variety of timely reports to managers. These reports help managers compare and analyze the differences between the financial data for the current fiscal period and the previous fiscal period. Two types of financial analysis available are:

- Horizontal trend analysis
- Vertical trend analysis

Horizontal trend analysis compares the ending balance for the current fiscal period with the ending balance of the previous fiscal period for each item on the statement. The difference is reported as a percentage change. This type of analysis may be generated for both the balance sheet and the income statement.

Vertical trend analysis shows the relationship of the component parts to the total. On the income statement, total revenue (or sales) is expressed as 100%, and the other items are expressed as a percentage of total revenue. On the balance sheet, assets are expressed as a percentage of total assets, while liabilities and stockholders' equity items are expressed as a percentage of total liabilities and stockholders' equity. In *Automated Accounting 8.0* or higher, vertical analysis is included for both current and previous fiscal periods.

### Preparing a Financial Analysis Report

Use the following steps to display the horizontal and vertical trend analysis reports:

1. Click the Reports toolbar button, or choose the Reports Selection menu item from the Reports menu.

2. When the Report Selection dialog appears, choose Financial Analysis from the Select a Report Group list.

3. Choose one of the vertical or horizontal analysis reports from the Choose a Report to Display list.

4. Click OK.

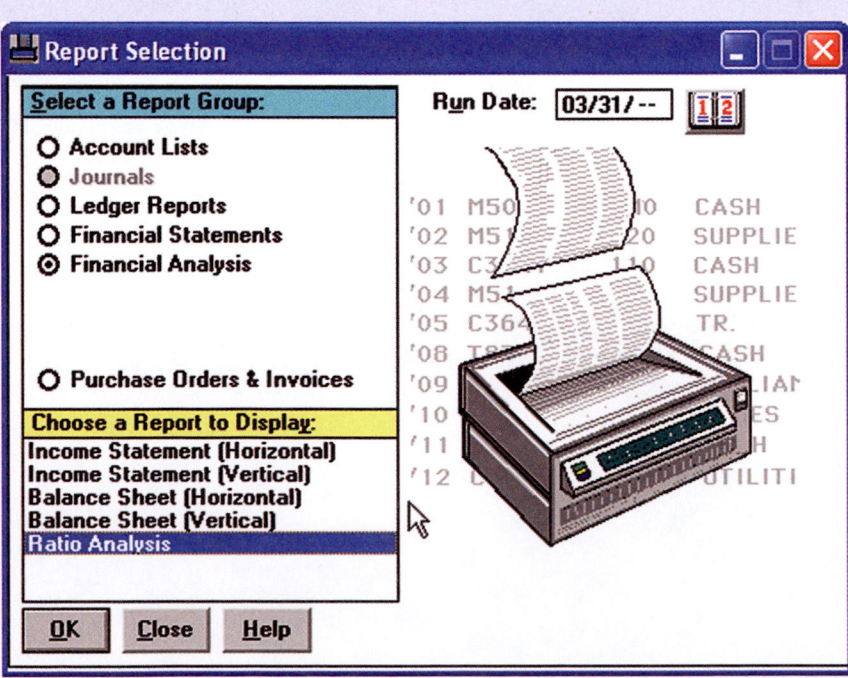

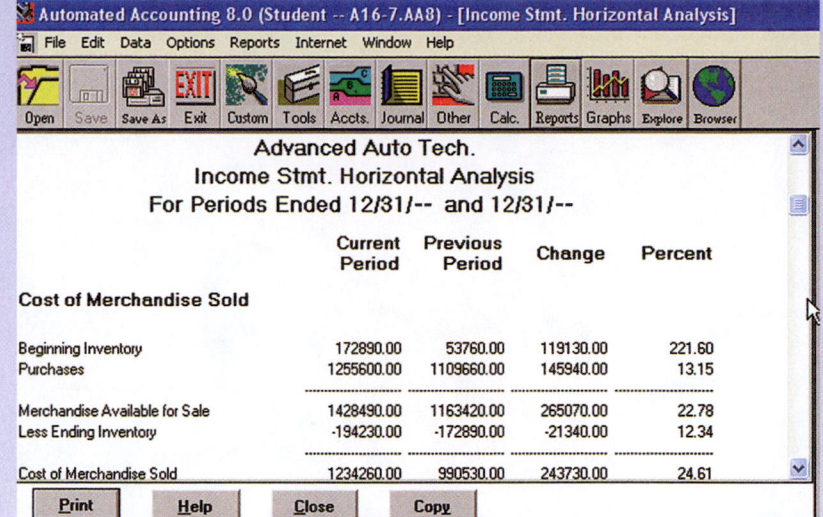

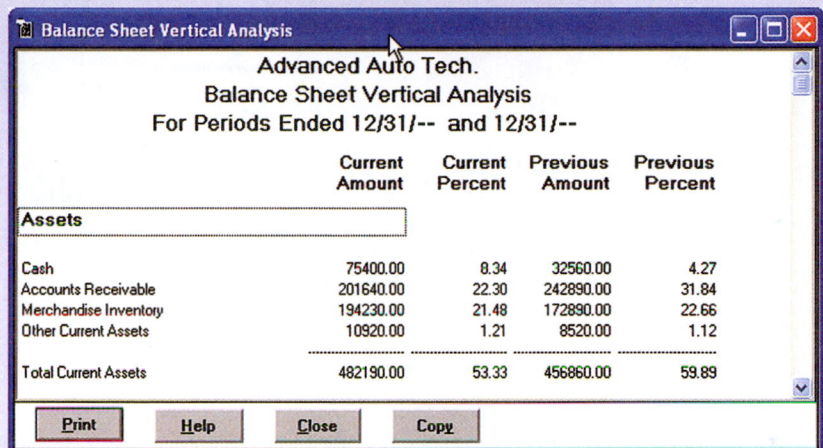

The report will be displayed in the scrollable Report Viewer Window. The report may be printed and/or copied for inclusion in another application, such as a spreadsheet or word processor.

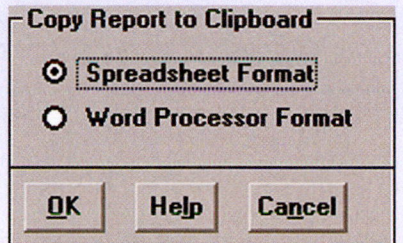

1. To print the report, click the Print button.

2. To copy the report, click the Copy button and select the format for the report. The data are copied to the Clipboard in either the spreadsheet format or the word processing format.

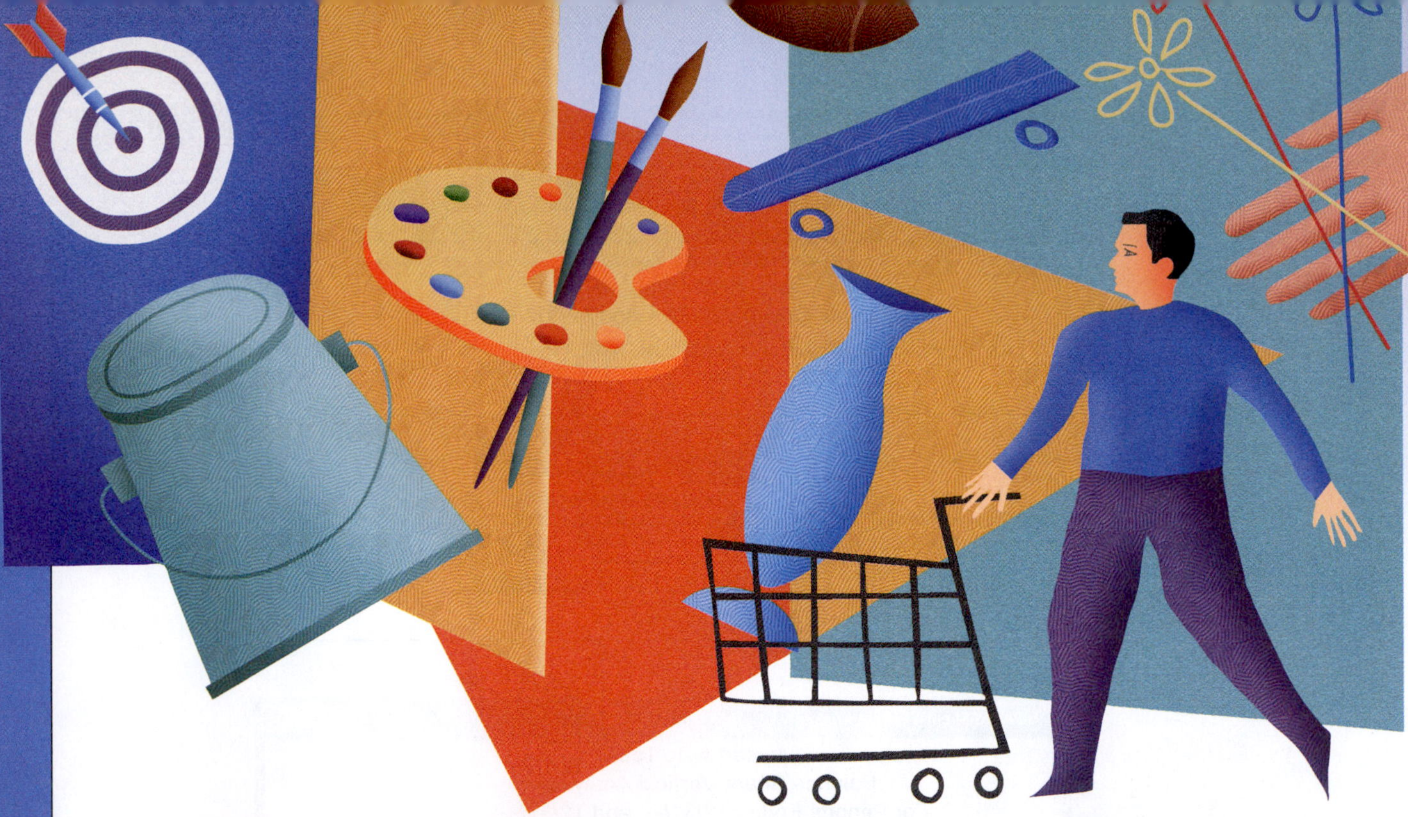

# CHAPTER 16 Management Decisions Using Present-Value Analysis

OBJECTIVES & TERMS

***After studying Chapter 16, you will be able to:***

1. Define accounting terms related to present values.
2. Identify accounting concepts and practices related to present values.
3. Calculate the future value of a single payment.
4. Calculate the present value of a future amount.
5. Make investment decisions using present values.
6. Make investment decisions using the present value of an annuity.

- time value of money
- future value
- compounding
- present value
- rate of return
- cash flows
- net cash flow
- net present value
- annuity
- present value of an annuity

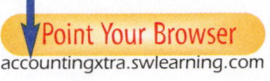

Point Your Browser
accountingxtra.swlearning.com

# • Verizon

©DANIEL ACKER/BLOOMBERG NEWS/LANDOV

## VERIZON ASKS, "CAN YOU HEAR ME NOW?"

We've all seen it—a cellular phone user pacing about, asking, "Can you hear me now?" Verizon has cleverly branded this phrase to its cellular phone business. Verizon is the largest telecommunications company, with more than 200,000 employees and $165 billion of assets.

The Verizon name is derived from two words: *veritas,* the Latin word meaning certainty and reliability, and *horizon,* signifying forward-looking and visionary. To fulfill these objectives, Verizon must continually expand and upgrade its communication systems. At the beginning of the 21st century, Verizon invested approximately $10–$12 billion per year on its communication systems. Verizon made this enormous investment on the expectation that it will generate additional revenues for years to come.

Verizon operates in an industry in which depreciation is a significant component of its operating expenses. As a result, the cash generated from fees occurs after the year that cash is paid to purchase communication equipment. When evaluating additional investments, Verizon managers must consider the timing of the investment and the related revenues.

### Critical Thinking

1. How are the costs of Verizon's communication equipment networks matched against the related revenues?
2. What does Verizon's continued investment in its communication networks indicate about today's communication technology?

accountingxtra.swlearning.com

Source: www22.verizon.com/about/

## internet activity

### BANKRUPTCY

Go to the homepage of the Legal Information Institute of the Cornell Law School (www.law.cornell.edu). Search for "bankruptcy" and look for an overview about bankruptcy laws.

### Instructions

Answer the following questions:
1. What kind of plan does bankruptcy law establish?
2. What agency supervises and litigates bankruptcy proceedings?
3. Which is the most common type of bankruptcy? What happens in this type of bankruptcy?

# 16-1 Business Decisions Using Present Values

Bank customers deposit their money in savings accounts and certificates of deposits to earn interest and increase their wealth. The expectation that invested money will increase over time is called the **time value of money**. Because of the time value of money, the promise of receiving $100.00 in three years is not worth $100.00 today. A bank customer would expect to deposit less than $100.00 today on the promise of receiving $100.00 in three years.

Like bank customers, managers must consider the time value of money when investing in plant assets. A business invests in plant assets, such as buildings, trucks, computers, and com-

puter networks to expand its operations and increase profits. When deciding whether to purchase a plant asset, managers should compare the asset's cost to the additional profits that will be earned in the future. If future profits exceed the cost, then management should purchase the asset.

When those profits are earned is an important factor in that decision. The value of a dollar earned several years from now should not be compared directly to the cost of the asset today. Managers must consider the time value of money when comparing future profits to today's costs.

## making ethical decisions

### Bribing Government Officials

Companies that operate in countries throughout the world are exposed to different cultures, social norms, and acceptable business practices. In some countries, giving bribes to government officials to gain favorable business terms is both acceptable and expected. In contrast, giving a bribe to a government official in our society is both unethical and illegal. In 1977 Congress passed the Foreign Corrupt Practices Act, which made it illegal for U.S. companies to bribe foreign government officials.

**Instructions**

Access *Everyday Values,* the code of conduct for Harley-Davidson. (To find the code, go to *www.harley-davidson.com.* Click Company, and in Corporate Governance, click the English version

under Code of Conduct. Note that Acrobat Reader is required to download and read this document.) What guidance does Harley-Davidson provide its employees in the following situations involving foreign government officials?

1. An employee, at the end of a business meeting with a government official, is considering paying for everyone's lunch.
2. To thank a mayor's staff for their help with a bike rally, an employee wants to give the mayor's staff Harley-Davidson hats or T-shirts.
3. An employee learns that a marketing company hired by Harley-Davidson has given a free motorcycle to a government official in thanks for closing a road to film a commercial.

### Future Value of $1,000.00 at 10% Interest

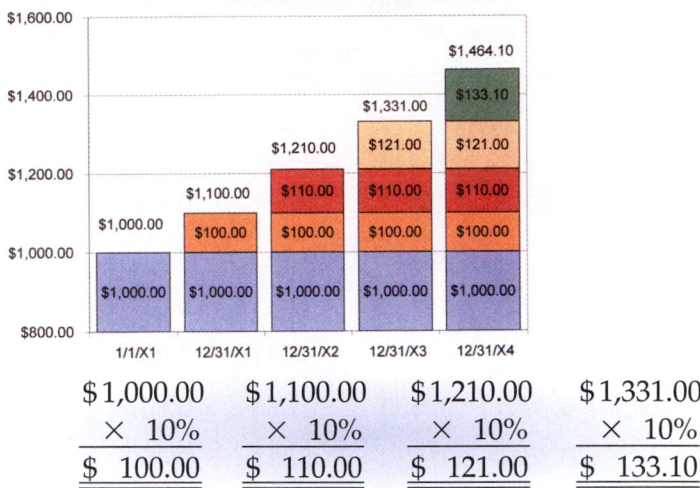

| $1,000.00 | $1,100.00 | $1,210.00 | $1,331.00 |
|---|---|---|---|
| × 10% | × 10% | × 10% | × 10% |
| $ 100.00 | $ 110.00 | $ 121.00 | $ 133.10 |

Individuals and businesses expect invested money to grow over time. The value of money invested today at some point in the future is called a **future value**. The figure above shows how the value of a $1,000.00 investment on January 1, 20X1, at 10% annual interest will grow over time. The future value of $1,000.00 invested today at 10% interest is $1,464.10 in four years.

The interest earned each year is calculated by multiplying the current investment value by the interest rate. The calculation of interest earned in the third year is shown as follows.

| Current Investment Value on 12/31/X2 | × | Interest Rate | = | Interest Earned in 20X3 |
|---|---|---|---|---|
| $1,210.00 | × | 10% | = | $121.00 |

| Current Investment Value on 12/31/X2 | + | Interest Earned in 20X3 | = | Balance on 12/31/X3 |
|---|---|---|---|---|
| $1,210.00 | + | $121.00 | = | $1,331.00 |

Each year, the interest earned increases the value of the investment. As the investment value increases, the amount of interest earned each year also increases. Interest earned in the fourth year, $133.10, is greater than the $121.00 interest earned in the third year. Earning interest on previously earned interest is called **compounding**. Compounding interest causes the annual interest earned to increase each year.

**FYI** FOR YOUR INFORMATION

A bank may advertise that its certificates of deposit earn "5% interest compounded annually." Each year the bank calculates interest earned of 5% on the outstanding account balance and adds this amount to the account. The more often (daily, monthly, or quarterly) interest is compounded, the more quickly the account balance will grow. For example, a $1,000.00 investment at 10% interest compounded semi-annually (twice each year) will grow to $1,628.90 in four years—$164.80 more than the $1,464.10 future value illustrated at the top of this page.

| **Present Value of $1** | | | | | |
|---|---|---|---|---|---|
| | Interest Rate | | | | |
| Period | 6% | 8% | 10% | 12% | 15% |
| 1 | 0.943 | 0.926 | 0.909 | 0.893 | 0.870 |
| 2 | 0.890 | 0.857 | 0.826 | 0.797 | 0.756 |
| 3 | 0.840 | 0.794 | 0.751 | 0.712 | 0.658 |
| 4 | 0.792 | 0.735 | 0.683 | 0.636 | 0.572 |
| 5 | 0.747 | 0.681 | 0.621 | 0.567 | 0.497 |
| 6 | 0.705 | 0.630 | 0.564 | 0.507 | 0.432 |
| 7 | 0.665 | 0.583 | 0.513 | 0.452 | 0.376 |
| 8 | 0.627 | 0.540 | 0.467 | 0.404 | 0.327 |
| 9 | 0.592 | 0.500 | 0.424 | 0.361 | 0.284 |
| 10 | 0.558 | 0.463 | 0.386 | 0.322 | 0.247 |

The current value of a future cash payment or receipt is called a **present value**. At 10% interest, $1,000.00 invested today will be worth $1,464.10 in four years. Therefore, $1,000.00 is the present value of $1,464.10 in four years at 10% interest.

Present value tables enable managers to calculate the present value of any future amount. The amounts in the tables are known as *present value factors.* The present value factor is determined by finding the intersection of the interest rate in the columns and the number of years in the rows. The calculation of the present value of $1,464.10 is shown below.

The present value factors in the table are rounded to three digits. Some small rounding errors may occur. Calculating the present value of $1,464.10 using a rounded present value factor results in a $0.02 rounding error. Such minor rounding errors are acceptable when managers are using present values to make business decisions.

| | |
|---|---|
| Projected Net Cash Flows | $1,464.10 |
| times Present Value Factor | × 0.683 |
| Present Value | $ 999.98 |

**FYI** FOR YOUR INFORMATION

Managers may state that a future amount has been "discounted" to the present value.

©GETTY IMAGES/PHOTODISC

| Year | Net Cash Flows | | Present Value Factor | | Present Value of Net Cash Flow |
|---|---|---|---|---|---|
| 1 | $ 500.00 | X | 0.926 | = | $ 463.00 |
| 2 | 1,500.00 | X | 0.857 | = | 1,285.50 |
| 3 | 2,000.00 | X | 0.794 | = | 1,588.00 |
| 4 | 2,000.00 | X | 0.735 | = | 1,470.00 |
| 5 | 1,500.00 | X | 0.681 | = | 1,021.50 |
| 6 | 1,000.00 | X | 0.630 | = | 630.00 |

Present Value of Net Cash Flows     $6,458.00

Investment     6,000.00

Net Present Value     $ 458.00

### Present Value of $1

| Period | Interest Rate | | | | |
|---|---|---|---|---|---|
| | 6% | 8% | 10% | 12% | 15% |
| 1 | 0.943 | 0.926 | 0.909 | 0.893 | 0.870 |
| 2 | 0.890 | 0.857 | 0.826 | 0.797 | 0.756 |
| 3 | 0.840 | 0.794 | 0.751 | 0.712 | 0.658 |
| 4 | 0.792 | 0.735 | 0.683 | 0.636 | 0.572 |
| 5 | 0.747 | 0.681 | 0.621 | 0.567 | 0.497 |
| 6 | 0.705 | 0.630 | 0.564 | 0.507 | 0.432 |
| 7 | 0.665 | 0.583 | 0.513 | 0.452 | 0.376 |
| 8 | 0.627 | 0.540 | 0.467 | 0.404 | 0.327 |
| 9 | 0.592 | 0.500 | 0.424 | 0.361 | 0.284 |
| 10 | 0.558 | 0.463 | 0.386 | 0.322 | 0.247 |

When individuals deposit money in a bank, they expect to earn interest. When businesses invest in plant assets, they expect to earn a specific amount of money beyond the cost of the asset. The relationship of money earned compared to the money invested is called the **rate of return**. Interest rates and the rate of return are stated as percentages.

As a measure of future profits, managers typically focus on the amount of cash received. The cash receipts and cash payments of a company are called **cash flows**. The difference between cash receipts and cash payments is called **net cash flow**. Managers discount future net cash flows using the desired rate of return.

Reflection, Inc. is considering purchasing a paint mixer for $6,000.00. The expected net cash flows during the mixer's six-year useful life are shown above. Management approves investments only if they earn an 8% rate of return.

Each year's cash flow is discounted using present values factors for 8%. For example, in Year 1, the first year the paint mixer is used, the net cash flow is estimated to be $500.00. The present value factor for this year is one period at 8%—0.926. The next net cash flow will be for two periods. The sum of the present values for each year is the total present value of the investment. The difference between the discounted cash flows and the investment is called the **net present value**. The net present value is the amount the business is expected to earn above its desired rate of return.

The investment in the paint mixer is expected to earn a net present value of $458.00. Reflection, Inc. should invest in the mixer because the net present value is positive. The discounted cash flows exceed the desired 8% rate of return.

©GETTY IMAGES/PHOTODISC

Xtra!
**Study Tools**
accountingxtra.swlearning.com

## terms review

TERMS REVIEW • TERMS

## audit your understanding

AUDIT YOUR UNDERSTANDING

1. Why does the amount of interest earned on an investment increase each year?
2. How is a present value factor determined?
3. How are interest rates and the rate of return stated?

## work together 16-1

### Calculating future and present values

Forms are provided in the *Working Papers*. Obtain the present value factors from the tables in the illustrations. Your instructor will guide you through the following examples.

1. Calculate the future value of a $2,000.00 investment in four years at 12% interest.
2. Calculate the present value of $25,000.00 received in four years at a 15% rate of return.
3. Lambert Company is considering the purchase of equipment costing $75,000.00 that will have a five-year useful life. Projected net cash flows from the investment are shown below. Determine the net present value of the investment, assuming a rate of return of 10%. Should the company purchase the equipment?

| Year | Cash Flows |
|------|------------|
| 1 | $ 8,000.00 |
| 2 | 25,000.00 |
| 3 | 36,000.00 |
| 4 | 22,000.00 |
| 5 | 15,000.00 |

WORK TOGETHER • WORK TOGETHER • WORK TOGETHER • WORK

## on your own 16-1

### Calculating future and present values

Forms are provided in the *Working Papers*. Obtain the present value factors from the tables in the illustrations. Work these problems independently.

1. Calculate the future value of a $25,000.00 investment in five years at 8% interest.
2. Calculate the present value of $48,000.00 received in five years at a 10% rate of return.
3. Daniel Supply Company is considering the purchase of equipment costing $150,000.00 that will have a seven-year useful life. Projected cash flows from the investment are shown below. Determine the net present value of the investment, assuming a rate of return of 8%. Should the company purchase the equipment?

| Year | Cash Flows |
|------|------------|
| 1 | $15,000.00 |
| 2 | 25,000.00 |
| 3 | 35,000.00 |
| 4 | 50,000.00 |
| 5 | 35,000.00 |
| 6 | 25,000.00 |
| 7 | 10,000.00 |

ON YOUR OWN • ON YOUR OWN • ON YOUR OWN • ON YOUR OWN

# 16-2 Present Value and Annuities

## PRESENT VALUE OF AN ANNUITY

| Year | Balance on January 1 | + | 10% Interest Earned | − | December 31 Payment | = | Balance on December 31 |
|------|---------------------|---|---------------------|---|---------------------|---|------------------------|
| 1 | $3,170.00 | + | $317.00 | − | $1,000.00 | = | $2,487.00 |
| 2 | 2,487.00 | + | 248.70 | − | 1,000.00 | = | 1,735.70 |
| 3 | 1,735.70 | + | 173.57 | − | 1,000.00 | = | 909.27 |
| 4 | 909.27 | + | 90.93 | − | 1,000.00 | = | ——* |

\* Includes a $0.20 rounding error.

Some business transactions result in equal net cash flows each year. A series of equal cash flows is called an **annuity**. An amount invested at a given interest rate that supports the payments of an annuity is called the **present value of an annuity**.

The illustration above illustrates how an initial investment of $3,170.00 earns enough interest to make a payment of $1,000.00 at the end of each of the four years. The present value of the $1,000.00, four-year 10% annuity is $3,170.00.

Each year's interest is calculated on that year's investment balance. The annual payment is then deducted to calculate the next year's beginning balance. The calculation of the amounts for the first year is shown below.

| Balance on January 1 | × | Interest Rate | = | Interest Earned |
|----------------------|---|---------------|---|-----------------|
| $3,170.00 | × | 10% | = | $317.00 |

| Balance on January 1 | + | Interest Earned | = | Pre-Payment Balance |
|----------------------|---|-----------------|---|---------------------|
| $3,170.00 | + | $317.00 | = | $3,487.00 |

| Pre-Payment Balance | − | December 31 Payment | = | Pre-Payment Balance |
|---------------------|---|---------------------|---|---------------------|
| $3,487.00 | − | $1,000.00 | = | $2,487.00 |

A present value of an annuity table contains the present value factors used to determine the net present value of an annuity. The factor is determined by the intersection of the interest rate and the number of years. The annual payment is multiplied by the present value factor to calculate the present value of the annuity.

| Present Value of an Annuity of $1 | | | | | |
|---|---|---|---|---|---|
| | Interest Rate | | | | |
| Period | 6% | 8% | 10% | 12% | 15% |
| 1 | 0.943 | 0.926 | 0.909 | 0.893 | 0.870 |
| 2 | 1.833 | 1.783 | 1.736 | 1.690 | 1.626 |
| 3 | 2.673 | 2.577 | 2.487 | 2.402 | 2.283 |
| 4 | 3.465 | 3.312 | 3.170 | 3.037 | 2.855 |
| 5 | 4.212 | 3.993 | 3.791 | 3.605 | 3.352 |
| 6 | 4.917 | 4.623 | 4.355 | 4.111 | 3.784 |
| 7 | 5.582 | 5.206 | 4.868 | 4.564 | 4.160 |
| 8 | 6.210 | 5.747 | 5.335 | 4.968 | 4.487 |
| 9 | 6.802 | 6.247 | 5.759 | 5.328 | 4.772 |
| 10 | 7.360 | 6.710 | 6.145 | 5.650 | 5.019 |

| | |
|---|---|
| Annual Payment | $ 1,000.00 |
| Present Value Factor | × 3.170 |
| Present Value of an Annuity | = $ 3,170.00 |

The calculation above shows the amount that would have to be invested today, $3,170.00 (present value of the annuity), earning 10% annual interest, with a withdrawal of $1,000.00 at the end of each year.

## technology for business

TECHNOLOGY FOR BUSINESS • TECHNOLOGY FOR BUSINESS • TECHNOLOGY FOR BUSI

### Spreadsheet Functions for Present and Future Value Analysis

A large company may have many investment decisions to make each day. There could be proposals for new equipment purchases; new factory, warehouse, or office buildings to buy, lease, or build; or new products to add. These decisions and many others can benefit from present and future value analysis. However, looking up factors on a table and performing the calculations on a calculator would not be efficient means of evaluating these business decisions.

Fortunately, modern spreadsheet software has present and future value functions. Using Excel as an example, the function for the future value of an annuity would be FV(rate, nper, pmt), where

rate is the interest rate, nper is the number of periods, and pmt is the amount of the regular payment. The present value function is similar.

In a large company, many different departments may compete for investment dollars to fund new product ideas. The accounting department may provide a spreadsheet for evaluating the different components of a proposal. Managers can use such a spreadsheet for evaluating and better defining their proposals before they are submitted to upper management, to increase the chances of approval.

| Present Value of an Annuity of $1 | | | | | |
|---|---|---|---|---|---|
| | Interest Rate | | | | |
| Period | 6% | 8% | 10% | 12% | 15% |
| 1 | 0.943 | 0.926 | 0.909 | 0.893 | 0.870 |
| 2 | 1.833 | 1.783 | 1.736 | 1.690 | 1.626 |
| 3 | 2.673 | 2.577 | 2.487 | 2.402 | 2.283 |
| 4 | 3.465 | 3.312 | 3.170 | 3.037 | 2.855 |
| 5 | 4.212 | 3.993 | 3.791 | 3.605 | 3.352 |
| 6 | 4.917 | 4.623 | 4.355 | 4.111 | 3.784 |
| 7 | 5.582 | 5.206 | 4.868 | 4.564 | 4.160 |
| 8 | 6.210 | 5.747 | 5.335 | 4.968 | 4.487 |
| 9 | 6.802 | 6.247 | 5.759 | 5.328 | 4.772 |
| 10 | 7.360 | 6.710 | 6.145 | 5.650 | 5.019 |
| 15 | 9.712 | 8.559 | 7.606 | 6.811 | 5.847 |
| 20 | 11.470 | 9.818 | 8.514 | 7.469 | 6.259 |
| 25 | 12.783 | 10.675 | 9.077 | 7.843 | 6.464 |
| 30 | 13.765 | 11.258 | 9.427 | 8.055 | 6.566 |

| | |
|---|---|
| Annual Payment | $ 50,000.00 |
| Present Value Factor | × 10.675 |
| Present Value of an Annuity | = $ 533,750.00 |

Financial advisors use the present value of an annuity to assist their clients with financial planning decisions. A common decision is to determine the amount of money individuals need to have saved before their retirement.

John and Sally Neumann expect to retire at the age of 65 and hope to live until age 90, another 25 years. They project they need $50,000.00 per year to support themselves. Assuming they can invest their money to yield an 8% rate of return, what amount do the Neumanns need to save before they retire?

The present value for an 8%, $50,000.00, 25-year annuity is $533,750.00. The present value of an annuity is calculated by multiplying the present value factor, 10.675, by the annual payment, $50,000.00. The Neumanns need to have $533,750.00 saved for their retirement.

## FYI FOR YOUR INFORMATION

The Neumanns risk running out of money if they live past 90 years of age. Insurance companies sell annuity policies to protect individuals against this risk. The annuity policy guarantees the insured will continue to receive an annual payment through lifetime. Insurance companies use the age and health of the insured to determine his or her life expectancy and, therefore, the expected life of the annuity. The present value of the annuity calculation is used to estimate the insurance company's cost of providing the annual payments.

| Present Value of an Annuity of $1 | | | | | |
|---|---|---|---|---|---|
| | Interest Rate | | | | |
| Period | 6% | 8% | 10% | 12% | 15% |
| 1 | 0.943 | 0.926 | 0.909 | 0.893 | 0.870 |
| 2 | 1.833 | 1.783 | 1.736 | 1.690 | 1.626 |
| 3 | 2.673 | 2.577 | 2.487 | 2.402 | 2.283 |
| 4 | 3.465 | 3.312 | 3.170 | 3.037 | 2.855 |
| 5 | 4.212 | 3.993 | 3.791 | 3.605 | 3.352 |
| 6 | 4.917 | 4.623 | 4.355 | 4.111 | 3.784 |
| 7 | 5.582 | 5.206 | 4.868 | 4.564 | 4.160 |
| 8 | 6.210 | 5.747 | 5.335 | 4.968 | 4.487 |
| 9 | 6.802 | 6.247 | 5.759 | 5.328 | 4.772 |
| 10 | 7.360 | 6.710 | 6.145 | 5.650 | 5.019 |
| 15 | 9.712 | 8.559 | 7.606 | 6.811 | 5.847 |
| 20 | 11.470 | 9.818 | 8.514 | 7.469 | 6.259 |
| 25 | 12.783 | 10.675 | 9.077 | 7.843 | 6.464 |
| 30 | 13.765 | 11.258 | 9.427 | 8.055 | 6.566 |

| | | |
|---|---|---|
| Annual Net Cash Flows | $ | 5,000.00 |
| Present Value Factor | × | 4.111 |
| Present Value of an Annuity | = | $ 20,555.00 |
| Investment | − | 22,000.00 |
| Net Present Value | = | $ (1,445.00) |

The concept of the present value of an annuity is also useful in making decisions about investments in plant assets. Reflection, Inc. is considering purchasing equipment for $22,000.00. The equipment will enable the company to generate net cash flows of $5,000.00 annually over the equipment's six-year useful life. Management expects assets to yield a 12% rate of return.

At a 12% rate of return, the present value of an annuity of six $5,000.00 net cash flows is $20,555.00. The net present value is a negative $1,445.00 and, therefore, the investment fails to achieve the desired 12% rate of return.

Should management purchase the equipment? It may appear logical to purchase the equipment since the net cash flows of $30,000 ($5,000.00 per year multiplied by 6 years) are greater than the cost of the equipment. However, effective managers will not purchase equipment that does not yield a positive net present value. Rather, they will continue to search for alternative uses of the $22,000.00 investment that will achieve the desired rate of return.

## terms review

TERMS REVIEW

annuity
present value of an annuity

## audit your understanding

AUDIT YOUR

1. How is the present value of an annuity calculated?
2. How can individuals use the present value of an annuity to plan for retirement?
3. How does a company determine if it should invest in plant assets?

## work together 16-2

WORK TOGETHER • WORK

**Calculating the present value of an annuity**

Forms are provided in the *Working Papers.* Your instructor will guide you through the following examples.

1. Create a schedule that shows the payment of an annuity over a four-year period. The initial investment is $8,662.76, the annual payment is $2,500.00, and the interest rate is 6%.

2. Calculate the present value of an annuity of 10 payments of $10,000.00 at an interest rate of 8%.

3. Lambert Company is considering the purchase of equipment costing $75,000.00 having a five-year useful life. Projected net cash flows from the investment are $20,000.00 annually. Determine the net present value of the investment, assuming a rate of return of 10%. Should the company purchase the equipment?

## on your own 16-2

ON YOUR OWN • ON YOUR OWN

**Calculating the present value of an annuity**

Forms are provided in the *Working Papers.* Work this problem independently.

1. Create a schedule that shows the payment of an annuity over a five-year period. The initial investment is 25,000.00, the annual payment is $6,594.94, and the interest rate is 10%.

2. Calculate the present value of an annuity of 15 payments of $5,000.00 at an interest rate of 12%.

3. Daniel Supply Company is considering the purchase of equipment costing $35,000.00 having a seven-year useful life. Projected net cash flows from the investment are $8,000.00 annually. Determine the net present value of the investment, assuming a rate of return of 8%. Should the company purchase the equipment?

## SUMMARY

**After completing this chapter, you can**

1. Define accounting terms related to present values.

2. Identify accounting concepts and practices related to present values.

3. Calculate the future value of a single payment.

4. Calculate the present value of a future amount.

5. Make investment decisions using present values.

6. Make investment decisions using the present value of an annuity.

# Explore Accounting

EXPLORE ACCOUNTING • EXPLORE ACCOUNTING • EXPLORE ACCO

## The Power of Compounding

Investing early in your life enables the power of compounding interest to increase your investment portfolio. Consider the example of two individuals: Jim Early and Sally Late. Jim began saving early in his life, investing $1,000.00 every year beginning at age 18. For many years, this was a struggle for Jim as he paid for college, started his career, established a home, and raised his children. Sally began investing rather late in her life, electing to spend all of her money until after her children were out of college. But Sally believed she could catch up and began at age 48 to invest $4,000.00 annually.

By age 58, both Jim and Sally had invested $40,000 and were beginning to think about retirement. How well will their investments support their retirement? The graph compares how their investment portfolios grew over the 40 years.

At 8% interest, Jim's portfolio has grown to $279,781 whereas Sally's portfolio is only $71,909. Why is there such a significant difference? Because of the power of compounding, money earning 8% interest will double every 9 years. That means that Jim's first $1,000.00 investment at age 18 doubled to $2,000.00 by age 27, $4,000.00 by age 36, $8,000.00 by age 45, and $16,000.00 by age 54. The original $1,000.00 will reach $32,000.00 by age 63.

**Instructions:** Using an electronic spreadsheet, create a schedule to calculate the future value of annual investments. The headings and formulas for the first two years are shown below.

|   | A | B | C | D | E | F |
|---|---|---|---|---|---|---|
| 1 | Age | Investment | Balance on January 1 | Interest Rate | Interest Earned | Balance on December 31 |
| 2 | 18 | 1000 | =+B2 | 0.08 | =+C2*D2 | =+B2+E2 |
| 3 | =+A2+1 | =+B2 | =+B3+F2 | =+D2 | =+C3*D3 | =+C3+E3 |

Copy the year 2 formulas for the remaining years. Change the age in A2, annual investment in B2, and interest rate in D2 to develop a realistic plan that will guide you toward saving $1,000,000 for your retirement.

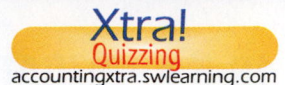
# 16-1 APPLICATION PROBLEM
## Calculating future values

John Alexander is considering putting money into the following investments:
a. A $10,000.00, five-year certificate of deposit earning 4.5% interest compounded annually
b. A $2,500.00, seven-year certificate of deposit earning 5.0% interest compounded annually

**Instructions:**
1. Determine the future value of each certificate of deposit.

# 16-2 APPLICATION PROBLEM
## Calculating present values

Logan Corporation loans money to start-up businesses that can't obtain traditional bank loans. The company loans the business money in exchange for a single future payment. Logan Company wants to make a 15% rate of return on each loan. The following future payments are expected.

| Business | Payment | Number of Years to Payment |
|---|---|---|
| April Designs | $100,000.00 | 8 |
| Putman Services | $250,000.00 | 10 |
| Zigler Books | $300,000.00 | 6 |

**Instructions:**
1. Calculate the present value of each loan.

# 16-3 APPLICATION PROBLEM
## Calculating net present value

MPS Industries is considering the purchase of equipment costing $100,000.00 having a seven-year useful life. Projected net cash flows from the investment are shown below. Determine the net present value of the investment, assuming a rate of return of 12%. Should the company purchase the equipment?

| Year | Cash Flows |
|---|---|
| 1 | $ 2,000.00 |
| 2 | 10,000.00 |
| 3 | 26,000.00 |
| 4 | 32,000.00 |
| 5 | 44,000.00 |
| 6 | 35,000.00 |
| 7 | 30,000.00 |

**Instructions:**
1. Calculate the net present value of the investment.
2. Should MPS Industries purchase the equipment? Explain your answer.

# 16-4 APPLICATION PROBLEM
## Preparing an annuity schedule

Barry Sudduth has deposited $28,367.61 in an account for his son's college education. The account yields a 5% interest rate. Barry's son is allowed to withdraw $8,000.00 at the end of each of the next four years.

**Instructions:**
1. Create a schedule that shows the payment of this annuity over a four-year period.

# 16-5 APPLICATION PROBLEM

### Calculating the present value of an annuity

Andrea Kent has won $600,000.00 in a state lottery. The state will pay her the prize in 30 annual payments of $20,000.00.

**Instructions:**

1. Assuming a 10% rate of return, calculate the present value of the prize.

# 16-6 APPLICATION PROBLEM

### Calculating the net present value using present value of an annuity

Folk Landscaping is evaluating an offer to purchase Bruce Lawn Care, its main competitor, for $250,000.00. An accountant has projected that the purchase will increase Folk's annual net cash flow by $30,000.00. Folk wants its investment to earn a 15% rate of return.

**Instructions:**

1. Calculate the net present value of the purchase, assuming the $30,000.00 net cash flow will occur for 25 years.
2. Calculate the net present value of the purchase, assuming the $30,000.00 net cash flow will occur for 30 years.
3. Should Folk Landscaping purchase Bruce Lawn Care?
4. Management has asked you to evaluate the investment for 35 and 40 years. Do you believe these calculations will change the decision?

# 16-7 MASTERY PROBLEM

### Calculating net present values

Forester Company is evaluating the purchase of equipment from two vendors. Differences in the technology and labor requirements to operate the equipment of each vendor affect the projected net cash flows. The equipment purchased from Neal Industries would cost $97,250.00 and is projected to generate total net cash flows of $168,000.00. The equipment from York Manufacturing would cost $135,200.00 and is projected to generate net cash flows totaling $235,000.00. The net cash flows for each year follow.

| Year | Neal Industries | York Manufacturing |
|------|-----------------|--------------------|
| 1 | $30,000.00 | $10,000.00 |
| 2 | 28,000.00 | 20,000.00 |
| 3 | 26,000.00 | 30,000.00 |
| 4 | 24,000.00 | 40,000.00 |
| 5 | 22,000.00 | 50,000.00 |
| 6 | 20,000.00 | 60,000.00 |
| 7 | 18,000.00 | 25,000.00 |

**Instructions:**

1. Assuming that Forester Company wants to earn a 12% rate of return, calculate the net present value of each equipment purchase.
2. Would you purchase the equipment and, if so, from which vendor?

# 16-8 CHALLENGE PROBLEM

**Calculating the future value of an annuity**

"How much do we need to invest each year to have $100,000.00 in a college fund when our child turns 18 years old?" New parents often seek similar advice from their financial advisors to establish college funds for their child. The future value of an amount invested each year at a given interest rate is known as the *future value of an annuity*. A table of future value factors is shown below.

| Future Value of an Annuity | | | | |
|---|---|---|---|---|
| | Interest Rate | | | |
| Period | 6% | 8% | 10% | 12% |
| 1 | 1.06 | 1.08 | 1.10 | 1.12 |
| 2 | 2.12 | 2.17 | 2.31 | 2.25 |
| 3 | 3.25 | 3.34 | 3.64 | 3.52 |
| 4 | 4.45 | 4.61 | 5.11 | 4.95 |
| 5 | 5.71 | 5.98 | 6.72 | 6.54 |
| 6 | 7.06 | 7.45 | 8.49 | 8.33 |
| 7 | 8.48 | 9.05 | 10.44 | 10.33 |
| 8 | 9.99 | 10.77 | 12.58 | 12.56 |
| 9 | 11.59 | 12.64 | 14.94 | 15.07 |
| 10 | 13.28 | 14.65 | 17.53 | 17.88 |
| 11 | 15.08 | 16.82 | 20.38 | 21.03 |
| 12 | 16.98 | 19.16 | 23.52 | 24.55 |
| 13 | 19.00 | 21.70 | 26.97 | 28.50 |
| 14 | 21.14 | 24.43 | 30.77 | 32.92 |
| 15 | 23.41 | 27.39 | 34.95 | 37.87 |
| 16 | 25.82 | 30.58 | 39.54 | 43.41 |
| 17 | 28.37 | 34.02 | 44.60 | 49.62 |
| 18 | 31.07 | 37.75 | 50.16 | 56.57 |
| 19 | 33.93 | 41.77 | 56.27 | 64.36 |
| 20 | 36.97 | 46.11 | 63.00 | 73.09 |

**Instructions:**

1. John and Kathy Finch want to know the expected amount of a college fund if they invest $2,500.00 each year for 18 years and earn 10% interest.
2. How will the future value of the college fund be affected if the Finches can only earn 8% interest?
3. How much will the Finches have to invest each year for 18 years (at 8% interest) if they want the fund to be $100,000.00 when their child enters college?

accountingxtra.swlearning.com

## • applied communication

As a form of advertisement, financial advisors often publish in their local newspapers short articles about financial planning issues. The articles are meant to motivate readers to manage their money better and, as a result, to hire them as their financial advisor.

**Instructions:**

You have obtained a part-time job in the office of Dumetrius Dorsey, financial planner. Using your knowledge of future and present values, write a short newspaper article designed to motivate new high school graduates to begin investing early.

## • cases for critical thinking

### Case 1

John Pedrick has just completed a meeting with the credit manager of your company. Pedrick Company is 180 days late paying its $50,000.00 outstanding account receivable. The credit manager informs you that he has negotiated a settlement with John Pedrick that provides for Pedrick Company to pay only $40,000.00 to settle the account. The payment will be received in three years. "At least I got $40,000.00 on the account," states the credit manager. Do you agree with his statement?

### Case 2

Jeanne Li was injured in a car accident caused by a negligent driver. A court settlement provides Jeanne with $10,000.00 annual payments for life to pay for her chronic medical expenses. An independent company has offered Jeanne a one-time payment of $80,000.00 in exchange for the annual payments. Jeanne has sought your advice on whether to accept this offer. What issues should Jeanne consider in making her decision?

## • SCANS workplace competency

**Thinking Skill:** Decision Making

**Concept:** Effective employees specify goals, identify constraints, suggest alternatives, consider risks, and evaluate and select the best alternative. An effective decision maker is often the highest paid individual in a company.

**Application:** If you were a loan officer at a local bank or other financial institution, how might the financial analysis presented in this chapter affect your decision making regarding a $25 million loan to a company? If you did not feel comfortable lending the entire $25 million to a business, identify several alternatives for sharing the risk or raising needed funds. Share your ideas with your classmates.

## • auditing for errors

LaBlanc, Inc., has the opportunity to purchase new equipment that will save the company $12,000.00 per year in manufacturing costs. The $62,000.00 of equipment is expected to be useful for 8 years, after which it could be sold for $2,500.00. Rosa Pedrillo, accountant, prepared the following analysis and concluded that the company should purchase the equipment.

|  | Cash Flows | Present Value Factors | Present Values |
|---|---|---|---|
| Annual savings | $12,000.00 | 5.747 | $68,964.00 |
| Salvage value | 2,500.00 | 0.540 | 1,350.00 |
| Total present value |  |  | $70,314.00 |
| Investment |  |  | 62,000.00 |
| Net present value |  |  | $ 8,314.00 |

Evaluate Rosa's analysis to determine whether it is accurate. Did Rosa make the correct decision?

## • analyzing Costco's financial statements

Numerous accounting principles require companies to discount future cash flows when estimating amounts that are reported on financial statements. For example, the present value of a $10,000 account receivable expected to be collected in two years should be reported on the balance sheet as $8,570, assuming an 8% discount rate.

Accounting principles require companies to write down the value of plant assets if the fair value of the assets is less than the recorded book value. When establishing these accounting principles, the Financial Accounting Standards Board (FASB) considered how present values should be applied to this situation. Costco presents its application of the FASB rules in the section "Impairment of Long-Lived Assets" of Note 1 on Appendix B pages B-9–B-17.

1. Does the FASB require Costco to discount future cash flows related to asset impairments? Support your answer.

2. What FASB statement provides Costco with the accounting principles required for accounting for asset impairments?

# Automated Accounting

## Using the Retirement Planner

### Planning Tools

The planning tools in *Automated Accounting* are easy-to-use applications for producing results for different types of financial investments. The calculations the software makes to produce the results are based on the present and future value concept—the time value of money.

### Retirement Plan

The Retirement Plan feature is used to perform two different calculations: (1) the annual deposit needed to provide a specific retirement income and (2) the retirement income available after making specific annual investments.

The desired calculation is chosen from the Calculate box. The item to be calculated appears grayed (or dimmed). Enter the other items, and the planner will make the calculation. For example, Martin Kingsley wants to begin saving for retirement when he is 18 years old. He wants to retire at age 65 and estimates that he will need an annual retirement income of $50,000 and assumes he will live to the age of 90. He uses an 8% annual interest rate on his investment.

When the information is entered in the appropriate fields in the Retirement Plan, the amount of the annual contribution is shown, $1,272.77. Martin Kingsley will need to make an annual investment of $1,272.77 each year from the ages of 18 to 65 in order to be able to withdraw $50,000 each year from age 65 to 90.

### The Savings Planner Report

Click the Report button to display a report of the deposits and withdrawals. A report of the findings may be displayed or printed. Click the Print button from the Retirement Plan Report window to print a copy of the report. You may also click the Copy button to copy the report in a word processing or spreadsheet format to paste the report into a document or spreadsheet for further use.

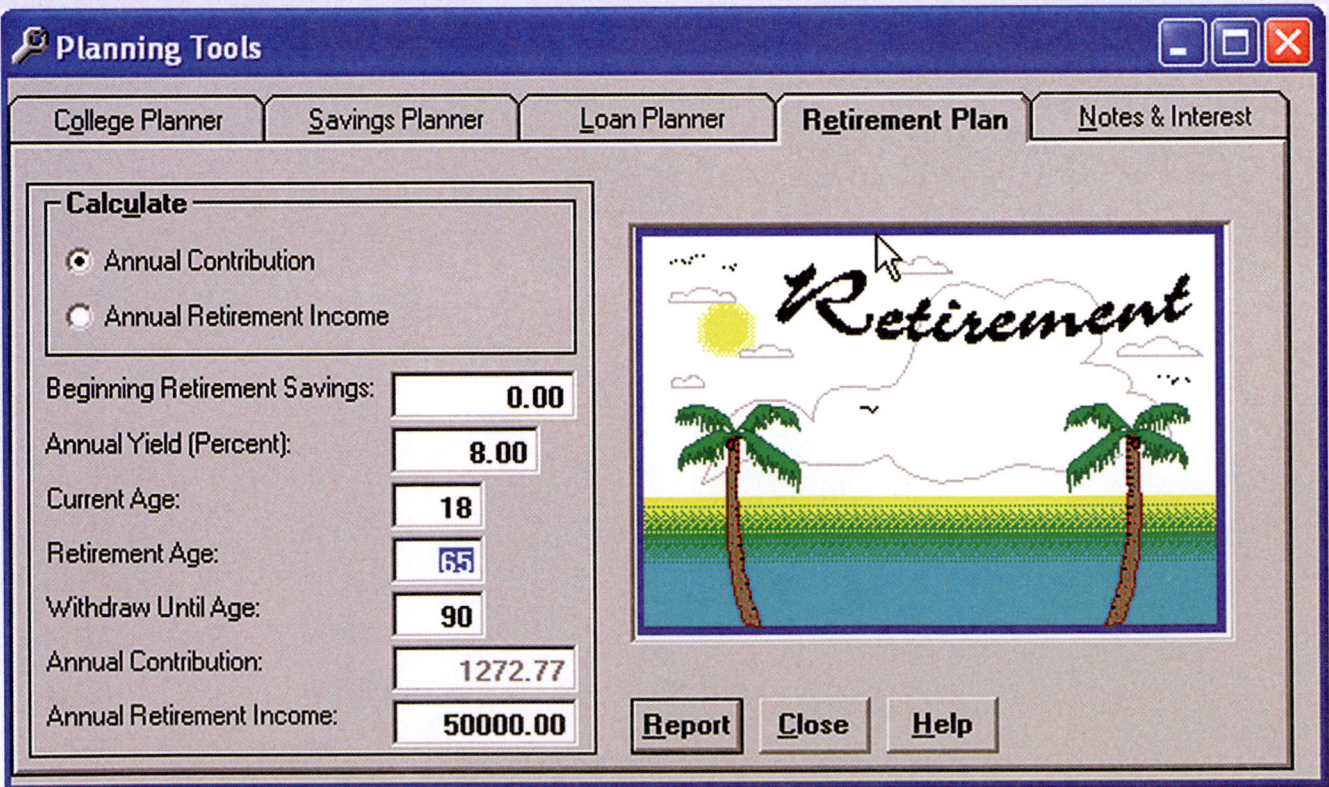

## Using the Planning Tools:
## The Retirement Plan

### Instructions:

1. Load the *Automated Accounting 8.0* or higher software.

2. Select New from the File menu.

3. Enter your name in the User Name field. Your name will then appear when you print your report.

4. Click on the Retirement Plan tab. Select Annual Contribution from the Calculate box. Enter an Annual Yield of 8%. Enter the Current Age, 18, the Retirement Age, 65, and the Withdraw Until Age, 90. Enter the desired Annual Retirement Income, $50,000.00. The Annual Contribution amount, $1,272.77, will appear in the Annual Contribution field.

5. Click on the Report command button in the Retirement Plan tab. Print the report, or copy it to the clipboard for entering into a word processor or spreadsheet application.

6. Click Close to return to the Planning Tools. Steps 4 and 5 may then be repeated for different calculation options or different data sets. Experiment with different values. Enter an amount in the Beginning Retirement Savings field to see what effect this would have on the annual contribution requirement.

7. Click Close to exit the Planning Tools. Your data is not saved when you exit the Planning Tools. Therefore, be sure to print a report, or copy the report to a word processor or spreadsheet and save it in that application.

8. Exit the Automated Accounting software.

# 17 Financial Statement Analysis

OBJECTIVES & TERMS · OBJECTIVES & TERMS · TERMS · OBJECTIVES

*After studying Chapter 17, you will be able to:*

1. Define accounting terms related to financial statement analysis.

2. Identify accounting concepts and practices related to financial statement analysis.

3. Analyze financial statements.

4. Calculate earnings performance.

5. Perform efficiency analysis.

6. Analyze the long-term financial strength of a business.

- ratio
- trend analysis
- rate earned on net sales

- working capital
- current ratio
- quick assets

- acid-test ratio
- debt ratio
- equity ratio

Point Your Browser
accountingxtra.swlearning.com

## • Yum! Brands, Inc.

©BLOOMBERG NEWS/LANDOV

### YUM! BRANDS FOCUSES ON SALES GROWTH

Yum! Brands, Inc., may be one of the most famous companies you've never heard of. The company owns some of the most respected quick-serve brands in the restaurant industry—Kentucky Fried Chicken, Pizza Hut, Taco Bell, Long John Silver's, and A&W.

Yum! managers use financial statement analysis to measure the performance of the company, each brand, and individual stores. Similar to managers of other retail businesses, Yum! managers use a measure known as *same-store sales* to evaluate sales trends at individual restaurant locations. The same-store sales measure is calculated by dividing the change in sales by the prior period's sales. Same-store sales can be calculated for a week, month, or year.

Restaurants strive to generate consistent increases in same-store sales. Popular methods of increasing sales include expanding menu options, offering value menus, providing late-night drive-up window service, and improving customer service.

To increase its same-store sales, Yum! Brands has been aggressive in opening multi-brand stores—buildings containing two brands, such as a Kentucky Fried Chicken and a Taco Bell. Families who may have difficulty agreeing where to eat enjoy the expanded menu options offered by a multi-brand store. Yum! has learned that multi-brand stores outperform single-brand stores by $300,000-$400,000 sales per year.

### Critical Thinking

1. Why can calculating the change in total sales for Yum! be a misleading measure of how customers are reacting to changes designed to increase sales?
2. What two brands would you recommend that Yum! include in its multi-brand stores? Support your answer.

Source: www.yumbrands.com/investors/annualreport/03annualreport/

**Xtra!** Today
accountingxtra.swlearning.com

### internet activity

#### NEW YORK STOCK EXCHANGE (NYSE)

Go to the homepage for the New York Stock Exchange (NYSE) (www.nyse.com). Click on "Symbol Lookup." Enter the name of a corporation to determine if its stock is traded on the NYSE and to find its trading symbol. Find the symbol for two different companies. Enter the symbol for each company into the "Quick Quote" box. Click on "Quick Quote."

#### Instructions

1. List the name and trading symbol for each company.
2. List the amount and time of the last stock trade for each company.
3. List the previous day's closing price for each company.

# 17-1 Trend Analysis and Component Percentages

Financial statements report the financial progress and condition of a business for a fiscal period. [CONCEPT: *Adequate Disclosure*]

The adequate disclosure concept states that financial statements contain the information necessary to understand a business's financial condition. Owners, managers, lenders, and investors rely on financial statements to make informed decisions. All relevant financial information must be adequately and completely disclosed on financial statements.

A business reports only the total liabilities of $200,000.00 on its balance sheet. However, the total liabilities include $75,000.00 in current liabilities and $125,000.00 in long-term liabilities. Therefore, the balance sheet does not adequately disclose the nature of the liabilities. The critical information not disclosed is that $75,000.00 is current and due within a few months.

Managers use financial information to identify areas for improving profitability. Banks and lending agencies use the information to decide whether to loan money to a business. Owners and potential owners use the information to decide whether to buy, sell, or keep their investment. Each group uses the financial information in a different way to assist with decision making.

Although financial statements provide useful information, they can be difficult to understand. For example, is a significant increase in the cost of merchandise sold an unfavorable trend? This question cannot be answered without considering information in other financial statement items, such as net sales. Financial statement analysis provides this information, since it calculates the relationships among financial statement items.

MAKING ETHICAL DECISIONS • **MAKING ETHICAL DECISIONS** • MAKING ETHICAL DECISIO

## making ethical decisions

### Could You Be a Whistle Blower?

You have just discovered that the management of your company is making improper accounting entries that substantially overstate its net income. You are concerned that if you disclose this information, the company's stock price will tumble, the company may be forced into bankruptcy, and your friends will lose their jobs. You will be branded a "whistle blower" and endure professional and personal hardships for your trouble.

The Association of Certified Fraud Examiners states that tips and complaints, rather than internal or external auditors, are the most common way that frauds are detected. Thus, it is important

that employees feel that they can communicate what they know without the fear of repercussions from their company. In an attempt to protect whistle blowers, Congress included a special whistle-blowing provision in the Sarbanes-Oxley Act of 2002 (Section 806).

#### Instructions

Write a summary of a news article that describes an individual who blew the whistle on unethical activities within a company. What sort of professional and personal hardships did he or she endure? What motivated that person to blow the whistle?

## FINANCIAL ANALYSIS OBJECTIVES

Financial analysis objectives are determined by a business's characteristics and achievements that are important to the person making the analysis. Information is analyzed to obtain more knowledge about the business's strengths and weaknesses. Common objectives for analyzing financial information are to determine (1) profitability, (2) efficiency, (3) short-term financial strength, and (4) long-term financial strength.

Financial statements, with supporting schedules, are the primary information sources to be analyzed. A statement showing two or more years' information permits a reader to compare year-to-year differences. Financial statements providing information for each of two or more fiscal periods are known as comparative financial statements. Thus, consistent preparation and reporting of financial information are essential. [*CONCEPT: Consistent Reporting*]

The consistent reporting concept states that the same accounting procedures must be followed in the same way in each accounting period. Some business decisions require a comparison of current financial statements with previous financial statements. If accounting information is recorded and reported differently each accounting period, comparisons from one accounting period to another may not be possible. For example, in one period a business reports $170,000.00 for total operating expenses and in the next period it reports $120,000 as cost of merchandise sold and $50,000 as operating expenses. A user of this information cannot adequately compare the two accounting periods. Therefore, unless a change is necessary to make information more easily understood, accounting information is reported in a consistent way for each accounting period.

## RATIO ANALYSIS

a.
| Net Sales | ÷ | Net Income | = | Stated Ratio |
|---|---|---|---|---|
| $2,000,000.00 | ÷ | $200,000.00 | = | 10 times (often stated as 10 to 1 or 10:1) |

The stated ratio means net sales is 10 times net income. Another way of stating this ratio is 10:1, or for every $10.00 of net sales, the business earns $1.00 of net income.

b.
| Net Income | ÷ | Net Sales | = | Percentage Ratio |
|---|---|---|---|---|
| $200,000.00 | ÷ | $2,000,000.00 | = | .10 or 10% |

Net income is 10% of net sales.

c.
| Net Income | ÷ | Net Sales | = | Fractional Ratio |
|---|---|---|---|---|
| $200,000.00 | ÷ | $2,000,000.00 | = | 1/10 |

Net income is one-tenth of net sales.

A comparison between two numbers showing how many times one number exceeds the other is called a **ratio**. A ratio may be expressed as a stated ratio, percentage, or fraction. For a business with net sales of $2,000,000.00 and net income of $200,000.00, the relationship may be stated as any of the ratios calculated above. All three methods of calculating and expressing ratios are correct and essentially the same. The method selected is usually determined by the statement user's preference.

**Hamilton Corporation**
**Comparative Income Statement**
**For Years Ended December 31, 20-- and 20--**

| | Current Year | Prior Year | Increase (Decrease) | |
|---|---|---|---|---|
| | | | Amount | Percentage* |
| Operating Revenue: | | | | |
| Net Sales.................... | $4,767,200 | $3,633,000 | $1,134,200 | 31.2 |
| Cost of Merchandise Sold: | | | | |
| Merchandise Inv., Jan. 1.................... | $ 423,800 | $ 232,300 | $ 191,500 | 82.4 |
| Net Purchases.................... | 2,726,900 | 2,226,900 | 500,000 | 22.5 |
| Total Cost of Mdse. Avail. for Sale .......... | $3,150,700 | $2,459,200 | $ 691,500 | 28.1 |
| Less Mdse. Inventory, Dec. 31 .......... | 547,900 | 423,800 | 124,100 | 29.3 |
| Cost of Merchandise Sold.................... | $2,602,800 | $2,035,400 | $ 567,400 | 27.9 |
| Gross Profit on Operations .................... | $2,164,400 | $1,597,600 | $ 566,800 | 35.5 |
| Operating Expenses: | | | | |
| Selling Expenses: | | | | |
| Advertising Expense .................... | $ 46,700 | $ 30,100 | $ 16,600 | 55.1 |
| Delivery Expense.................... | 74,600 | 55,200 | 19,400 | 35.1 |
| Salary Expense—Sales .................... | 912,400 | 696,800 | 215,600 | 30.9 |
| Supplies Expense .................... | 81,600 | 63,800 | 17,800 | 27.9 |
| Other Selling Expenses.................... | 102,900 | 78,700 | 24,200 | 30.7 |
| Total Selling Expenses .................... | $1,218,200 | $ 924,600 | $ 293,600 | 31.8 |
| Administrative Expenses: | | | | |
| Salary Expense—Administrative .................... | $ 290,200 | $ 229,600 | $ 60,600 | 26.4 |
| Uncollectible Accounts Expense.................... | 27,700 | 19,100 | 8,600 | 45.0 |
| Other Administrative Expenses.................... | 229,500 | 189,200 | 40,300 | 21.3 |
| Total Administrative Expenses .................... | $ 547,400 | $ 437,900 | $ 109,500 | 25.0 |
| Total Operating Expenses.................... | $1,765,600 | $1,362,500 | $ 403,100 | 29.6 |
| Income from Operations.................... | $ 398,800 | $ 235,100 | $ 163,700 | 69.6 |
| Other Expenses: | | | | |
| Interest Expense.................... | $ 62,000 | $ 52,000 | $ 10,000 | 19.2 |
| Net Income before Fed. Inc. Tax .................... | $ 336,800 | $ 183,100 | $ 153,700 | 83.9 |
| Less Federal Income Tax Exp. .................... | 114,500 | 54,700 | 59,800 | 109.3 |
| Net Income after Fed. Inc. Tax.................... | $ 222,300 | $ 128,400 | $ 93,900 | 73.1 |

*Rounded to nearest 0.1%

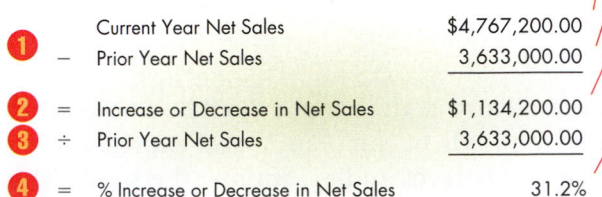

| | | | |
|---|---|---|---|
| **1** | | Current Year Net Sales | $4,767,200.00 |
| | − | Prior Year Net Sales | 3,633,000.00 |
| **2** | = | Increase or Decrease in Net Sales | $1,134,200.00 |
| **3** | ÷ | Prior Year Net Sales | 3,633,000.00 |
| **4** | = | % Increase or Decrease in Net Sales | 31.2% |

**FYI** FOR YOUR INFORMATION

The prior year is always used as the base year to calculate the percentage increase or decrease.

Trends in a business's financial condition and operating results will not be apparent from a review of a single year's financial information. Comparison of information for two or more fiscal periods is needed to determine whether a business is making satisfactory progress. A comparison of the relationship between one item on a financial statement and the same item on a previous fiscal period's financial statement is called **trend analysis**. Trend analysis is sometimes referred to as horizontal analysis. A comparative income statement with trend analysis is shown above. The calculation of the favorable trend in net sales is included in the figure.

**Hamilton Corporation**
**Comparative Statement of Stockholders' Equity**
**For Years Ended December 31, 20-- and 20--**

| | Current Year | Prior Year | Increase (Decrease) Amount | Percentage* |
|---|---|---|---|---|
| Capital Stock: | | | | |
| $10.00 Per Share | | | | |
| Balance, January 1 . . . . . . . . . . . . . . . . . . . . . . . . . . . . . | $ 500,000 | $500,000 | $ –0– | 0.0 |
| Additional Capital Stock Issued . . . . . . . . . . . . . . . . . . . | 100,000 | –0– | 100,000 | — |
| Balance, December 31 . . . . . . . . . . . . . . . . . . . . . . . . . . | $ 600,000 | $500,000 | $100,000 | 20.0 |
| Retained Earnings: | | | | |
| Balance, January 1 . . . . . . . . . . . . . . . . . . . . . . . . . . . . . | $ 349,300 | $320,900 | $ 28,400 | 8.9 |
| Net Income after Federal Income Tax . . . . . . . . . . . . . . | 222,300 | 128,400 | 93,900 | 73.1 |
| Total . . . . . . . . . . . . . . . . . . . . . . . . . . . . . . . . . . . . . . . . | $ 571,600 | $449,300 | $122,300 | 27.2 |
| Less Dividends Declared . . . . . . . . . . . . . . . . . . . . . . . . | 120,000 | 100,000 | 20,000 | 20.0 |
| Balance, December 31 . . . . . . . . . . . . . . . . . . . . . . . . . . | $ 451,600 | $349,300 | $102,300 | 29.3 |
| Total Stockholders' Equity, December 31 . . . . . . . . . . . . | $1,051,600 | $849,300 | $202,300 | 23.8 |
| Capital Stock Shares Outstanding . . . . . . . . . . . . . . . . . | 60,000 | 50,000 | 10,000 | 20.0 |

*Rounded to nearest 0.1%

The trend in stockholders' equity can be determined from information on Hamilton Company's comparative statement of stockholders' equity. Total stockholders' equity increased 23.8% from the prior year. Further review shows the increase in stockholders' equity was caused by an increase in both capital stock and net income. Management believes that the prior year's stockholders' equity was unsatisfactorily low; thus, the trend is favorable.

A percentage increase (decrease) cannot be calculated if the amount divided by is zero. Therefore, a dash (—) is recorded in the percentage column.

©GETTY IMAGES/PHOTODISC

**Hamilton Corporation**
**Comparative Balance Sheet**
**December 31, 20-- and 20--**

| | Current Year | Prior Year | Increase (Decrease) | |
|---|---|---|---|---|
| | | | Amount | Percentage* |
| **ASSETS** | | | | |
| Current Assets: | | | | |
| Cash | $ 206,100 | $ 104,300 | $101,800 | 97.6 |
| Accounts Receivable (net) | 474,000 | 569,200 | (95,200) | (16.7) |
| Merchandise Inventory | 547,900 | 423,800 | 124,100 | 29.3 |
| Other Current Assets | 26,100 | 21,300 | 4,800 | 22.5 |
| Total Current Assets | $1,254,100 | $1,118,600 | $135,500 | 12.1 |
| Total Plant Assets (net) | 813,600 | 641,100 | 172,500 | 26.9 |
| Total Assets | $2,067,700 | $1,759,700 | $308,000 | 17.5 |
| **LIABILITIES** | | | | |
| Current Liabilities: | | | | |
| Notes Payable | $ 222,200 | $ 241,600 | $ (19,400) | (8.0) |
| Interest Payable | 12,900 | 20,700 | (7,800) | (37.7) |
| Accounts Payable | 344,300 | 413,300 | (69,000) | (16.7) |
| Federal Income Tax Payable | 11,300 | 3,300 | 8,000 | 242.4 |
| Other Current Liabilities | 5,400 | 6,500 | (1,100) | (16.9) |
| Total Current Liabilities | $ 596,100 | $ 685,400 | $ (89,300) | (13.0) |
| Long-Term Liability: | | | | |
| Mortgage Payable | $ 420,000 | $ 225,000 | $195,000 | 86.7 |
| Total Liabilities | $1,016,100 | $ 910,400 | $105,700 | 11.6 |
| **STOCKHOLDERS' EQUITY** | | | | |
| Capital Stock | $ 600,000 | $ 500,000 | $100,000 | 20.0 |
| Retained Earnings | 451,600 | 349,300 | 102,300 | 29.3 |
| Total Stockholders' Equity | $1,051,600 | $ 849,300 | $202,300 | 23.8 |
| Total Liabilities and Stockholders' Equity | $2,067,700 | $1,759,700 | $308,000 | 17.5 |

*Rounded to nearest 0.1%

Changes in Hamilton's balance sheet accounts are shown above. Accounts Receivable and Plant Assets are reported at book value. Information on this statement shows that total assets increased 17.5% during the current year. This increase was caused by an 11.6% increase in total liabilities and a 23.8% increase in total stockholders' equity. This trend is considered favorable because assets are increasing and the increase came more from the significant increase in stockholders' equity than the increase in liabilities.

Comparative financial statements report a business's current and past activity. However, most financial statement readers are also interested in how well a business will do in the future. Trend analysis is one method of financial analy-sis used to help predict how well a business will perform in the future. [*CONCEPT: Adequate Disclosure*] Trend analysis is often performed using financial statements for a three-to-five-year period. Lenders and investors are very interested in how well a business will perform in the long term. Favorable trends over a period of several years often indicate that management is making good decisions.

**FYI** FOR YOUR INFORMATION

Financial statements are beneficial only to the extent that they are analyzed and used by the corporation to measure progress.

**Hamilton Corporation**
**Comparative Income Statement**
**For Years Ended December 31, 20-- and 20--**

| | Current Year | | Prior Year | |
|---|---|---|---|---|
| | Amount | Percentage* | Amount | Percentage* |
| Operating Revenue: | | | | |
| Net Sales .......................... | $4,767,200 | 100.0 | $3,633,000 | 100.0 |
| Cost of Merchandise Sold: | | | | |
| Merchandise Inv., Jan. 1 ..................... | $ 423,800 | 8.9 | $ 232,300 | 6.4 |
| Net Purchases ............................ | 2,726,900 | 57.2 | 2,226,900 | 61.3 |
| Total Cost of Mdse. Avail. for Sale............ | $3,150,700 | 66.1 | $2,459,200 | 67.7 |
| Less Mdse. Inventory, Dec. 31 ............... | 547,900 | 11.5 | 423,800 | 11.7 |
| Cost of Merchandise Sold .................... | $2,602,800 | 54.6 | $2,035,400 | 56.0 |
| Gross Profit on Operations ................... | $2,164,400 | 45.4 | $1,597,600 | 44.0 |
| Operating Expenses: | | | | |
| Selling Expenses: | | | | |
| Advertising Expense....................... | $ 46,700 | 1.0 | $ 30,100 | 0.8 |
| Delivery Expense ........................ | 74,600 | 1.6 | 55,200 | 1.5 |
| Salary Expense—Sales .................... | 912,400 | 19.1 | 696,800 | 19.2 |
| Supplies Expense ........................ | 81,600 | 1.7 | 63,800 | 1.8 |
| Other Selling Expenses ................... | 102,900 | 2.2 | 78,700 | 2.2 |
| Total Selling Expenses .................... | $1,218,200 | 25.6 | $ 924,600 | 25.5 |
| Administrative Expenses: | | | | |
| Salary Expense—Administrative ............ | $ 290,200 | 6.1 | $ 229,600 | 6.3 |
| Uncollectible Accounts Expense ............ | 27,700 | 0.6 | 19,100 | 0.5 |
| Other Administrative Expenses ............. | 229,500 | 4.8 | 189,200 | 5.2 |
| Total Administrative Expenses.............. | $ 547,400 | 11.5 | $ 437,900 | 12.1 |
| Total Operating Expenses .................. | $1,765,600 | 37.0 | $1,362,500 | 37.5 |
| Income from Operations ..................... | $ 398,800 | 8.4 | $ 235,100 | 6.5 |
| Other Expenses: | | | | |
| Interest Expense ......................... | $ 62,000 | 1.3 | $ 52,000 | 1.4 |
| Net Income before Fed. Inc. Tax............... | $ 336,800 | 7.1 | $ 183,100 | 5.0 |
| Less Federal Income Tax Exp................. | 114,500 | 2.4 | 54,700 | 1.5 |
| Net Income after Fed. Inc. Tax ............... | $ 222,300 | 4.7 | $ 128,400 | 3.5 |

*Rounded to nearest 0.1%.
Percentage totals may not equal sum of parts because of rounding.

The percentage relationship between one financial statement item and the total that includes that item is known as a component percentage. Component percentage analysis is also referred to as vertical analysis. Component percentages for items on an income statement are normally calculated as a percentage of net sales. The component percentage is shown in a separate percentage column. Hamilton's income statement with component percentages is shown above. This statement is similar to the one shown for Zytech in Chapter 4 and for LampLight in Chapter 13.

Component percentages on comparative statements show changes in a specific item from year to year. For example, Hamilton's cost of merchandise sold decreased from 56.0% to 54.6% of net sales. These percentages show a favorable trend since the cost of merchandise sold took a smaller part of each sales dollar in the current year. Similar comparisons can be made for each item on the comparative income statement. The cause of significant unfavorable changes should be investigated so that corrective action can be taken.

**Hamilton Corporation**
**Comparative Statement of Stockholders' Equity**
**For Years Ended December 31, 20-- and 20--**

| | Current Year | | Prior Year | |
|---|---|---|---|---|
| | **Amount** | **Percentage*** | **Amount** | **Percentage*** |
| Capital Stock: | | | | |
| $10.00 Per Share | | | | |
| Balance, January 1 | $ 500,000 | 47.5 | $500,000 | 58.9 |
| Additional Capital Stock Issued | 100,000 | 9.5 | 0 | 0.0 |
| Balance, December 31 | $ 600,000 | 57.1 | $500,000 | 58.9 |
| Retained Earnings: | | | | |
| Balance, January 1 | $ 349,300 | 33.2 | $320,900 | 37.8 |
| Net Income after Federal Income Tax | 222,300 | 21.1 | 128,400 | 15.1 |
| Total | $ 571,600 | 54.4 | $449,300 | 52.9 |
| Less Dividends Declared | 120,000 | 11.4 | 100,000 | 11.8 |
| Balance, December 31 | $ 451,600 | 42.9 | $349,300 | 41.1 |
| Total Stockholders' Equity, December 31 | $1,051,600 | 100.0 | $849,300 | 100.0 |
| Capital Stock Shares Outstanding | 60,000 | | 50,000 | |

*Rounded to nearest 0.1%.
Percentage totals may not equal sum of parts because of rounding.

Component percentages for items on a comparative statement of stockholders' equity are normally calculated as a percentage of total stockholders' equity. As shown above, capital stock represents 57.1% of Hamilton's stockholders' equity for the current year. The remaining 42.9% is retained earnings. Respective percentages for the prior year are 58.9% and 41.1%. Thus, little change has occurred in the component makeup of total equity. However, the percentage of dividends declared decreased slightly from 11.8% to 11.4%, an unfavorable trend for stockholders.

### Acceptable Levels of Financial Performance

For financial analysis to be useful, a company must define acceptable levels of performance for each type of analysis. For example, Wiseman Grocery considers a component percentage of 3.0% for income from operations to be very good. However, Mitchell Manufacturing Co. considers a 12.0% component percentage for income from operations the minimum acceptable result. The difference is due to the different financial characteristics of the two businesses.

The grocery company has a low investment in plant assets and sells its inventory quickly. The manufacturing company has a high investment in plant assets and holds its inventory much longer. The manufacturing company's larger investment per sales dollar means that the company must earn a higher rate on sales. Each company's management team must determine the acceptable levels of performance for each financial analysis made.

Many businesses use two major guides to determine acceptable levels of performance: (1) prior company performance and (2) comparison with published trade performance standards.

Other sources of performance guides include (1) financial and credit-reporting companies such as Dun and Bradstreet, (2) the company's planned financial objectives (budget schedules), (3) current interest rates that could be earned by investing capital elsewhere, and (4) financial information available on the Internet.

Each company's management team should determine the acceptable performance level for each financial analysis made by the company.

**Hamilton Corporation**
**Comparative Balance Sheet**
**December 31, 20-- and 20--**

| | Current Year | | Prior Year | |
|---|---|---|---|---|
| | Amount | Percentage* | Amount | Percentage* |
| **ASSETS** | | | | |
| Current Assets: | | | | |
| Cash | $ 206,100 | 10.0 | $ 104,300 | 5.9 |
| Accounts Receivable (book value) | 474,000 | 22.9 | 569,200 | 32.3 |
| Merchandise Inventory | 547,900 | 26.5 | 423,800 | 24.1 |
| Other Current Assets | 26,100 | 1.3 | 21,300 | 1.2 |
| Total Current Assets | $1,254,100 | 60.7 | $1,118,600 | 63.6 |
| Total Plant Assets (book value) | 813,600 | 39.3 | 641,100 | 36.4 |
| Total Assets | $2,067,700 | 100.0 | $1,759,700 | 100.0 |
| **LIABILITIES** | | | | |
| Current Liabilities: | | | | |
| Notes Payable | $ 222,200 | 10.7 | $ 241,600 | 13.7 |
| Interest Payable | 12,900 | 0.6 | 20,700 | 1.2 |
| Accounts Payable | 344,300 | 16.7 | 413,300 | 23.5 |
| Federal Income Tax Payable | 11,300 | 0.5 | 3,300 | 0.2 |
| Other Current Liabilities | 5,400 | 0.3 | 6,500 | 0.4 |
| Total Current Liabilities | $ 596,100 | 28.8 | $ 685,400 | 38.9 |
| Long-Term Liability: | | | | |
| Mortgage Payable | $ 420,000 | 20.3 | $ 225,000 | 12.8 |
| Total Liabilities | $1,016,100 | 49.1 | $ 910,400 | 51.7 |
| **STOCKHOLDERS' EQUITY** | | | | |
| Capital Stock | $ 600,000 | 29.0 | $ 500,000 | 28.4 |
| Retained Earnings | 451,600 | 21.8 | 349,300 | 19.8 |
| Total Stockholders' Equity | $1,051,600 | 50.9 | $ 849,300 | 48.3 |
| Total Liabilities and Stockholders' Equity | $2,067,700 | 100.0 | $1,759,700 | 100.0 |

*Rounded to nearest 0.1%.
Percentage totals may not equal sum of parts because of rounding.

Component percentages for asset amounts on a comparative balance sheet are normally calculated as a percentage of total assets. Liabilities and stockholders' equity amounts are calculated as a percentage of total liabilities and stockholders' equity. Information on Hamilton's comparative balance sheet shows that current liabilities were 28.8% of total liabilities and stockholders' equity, down from 38.9% in the prior year.

Since current liabilities were at a high percentage in the prior year, Hamilton considers the reduction from 38.9% to 28.8% as a very favor-

able change. Hamilton's investors and lenders would also be pleased with this result. Similar comparisons can be made for each item on the comparative balance sheet.

**FYI** FOR YOUR INFORMATION

An unfavorable ratio in one year may be balanced by previous actual positive results and future expected positive results. The trend in a ratio may be more important than the ratio for a particular year.

**Xtra!**
Study Tools
accountingxtra.swlearning.com

## terms review

ratio
trend analysis

## audit your understanding

1. Why do managers, banks, lending agencies, owners, and potential owners need the financial information for a business?

2. What are four common objectives for analyzing a business's financial information?

3. Which accounting concept is being applied when comparative financial statements are prepared to provide useful information for statement users?

4. What two major guides do businesses use to determine acceptable levels of performance?

## work together 17-1

**Analyzing comparative financial statements**

Baycom Corporation's comparative income statement is provided in the *Working Papers*. Your instructor will guide you through the following examples.

1. Complete the partial income statement using trend analysis. Round percentage calculations to the nearest 0.1%.

2. Complete the income statement using component percentage analysis. Round percentage calculations to the nearest 0.1%.

## on your own 17-1

**Analyzing comparative financial statements**

Baycom Corporation's comparative balance sheet is provided in the *Working Papers*. Work independently to complete the following problem.

1. Complete the comparative balance sheet using trend analysis. Round percentage calculations to the nearest 0.1%.

2. Complete the balance sheet using component percentage analysis. Round percentage calculations to the nearest 0.1%.

# 17-2 Calculating Earnings Performance and Efficiency Analysis

## EARNINGS PERFORMANCE ANALYSIS

The amount and consistency of earnings are important measures of a business's success. The earnings of a business must be satisfactory to continue operations. [CONCEPT: Going Concern] Consequently, managers, owners, and creditors are interested in an analysis of earnings perfor-

mance. Hamilton calculates five earnings performance ratios for the two most recent years. (1) Rate earned on average total assets. (2) Rate earned on average stockholders equity. (3) Rate earned on net sales. (4) Earnings per share. (5) Price-earnings ratio.

## RATE EARNED ON AVERAGE TOTAL ASSETS

**Hamilton Corporation**
**Comparative Balance Sheet**
**December 31, 20-- and 20--**

| | Current Year | | Prior Year | |
|---|---|---|---|---|
| | Amount | Percentage* | Amount | Percentage* |
| **ASSETS** | | | | |
| Current Assets: | | | | |
| Cash . . . . . . . . . . . . . . . . . . . . . . . . . . . . . | $ 206,100 | 10.0 | $ 104,300 | 5.9 |
| Accounts Receivable (book value) . . . . . . . . . . . . . . . . . . | 474,000 | 22.9 | 569,200 | 32.3 |
| Merchandise Inventory . . . . . . . . . . . . . . . . . . . | 547,900 | 26.5 | 423,800 | 24.1 |
| Other Current Assets . . . . . . . . . . . . . . . . . . . . . . . | 26,100 | 1.3 | 21,300 | 1.2 |
| Total Current Assets . . . . . . . . . . . . . . . . . . | $1,254,100 | 60.7 | $1,118,600 | 63.6 |
| Total Plant Assets (book value) . . . . . . . . . . . . . . . . . | 813,600 | 39.3 | 641,100 | 36.4 |
| Total Assets . . . . . . . . . . . . . . . . . . . . . . | $2,067,700 | 100.0 | $1,759,700 | 100.0 |

*Rounded to nearest 0.1%.

**1** ⎛ January 1
Total Assets
(1,759,700.00 ⎞ + December 31
Total Assets
$2,067,700.00) ÷ 2 = Average
Total Assets
$1,913,700.00

**2** Net Income
after Federal
Income Tax
$222,300.00 ÷ Average
Total Assets
$1,913,700.00 = Rate Earned
on Average
Total Assets
11.6%

**Hamilton Corporation**
**Comparative Income Statement**
**For Years Ended December 31, 20-- and 20--**

| | Current Year | | Prior Year | |
|---|---|---|---|---|
| | Amount | Percentage* | Amount | Percentage* |
| Other Expenses: | | | | |
| Interest Expense . . . . . . . . . . . . . . . . . . . | $ 62,000 | 1.3 | $ 52,000 | 1.4 |
| Net Income before Fed. Inc. Tax . . . . . . . . . . . . . . . . . | $ 336,800 | 7.1 | $ 183,100 | 5.0 |
| Less Federal Income Tax Exp. . . . . . . . . . . . . . . . . | 114,500 | 2.4 | 54,700 | 1.5 |
| Net Income after Fed. Inc. Tax. . . . . . . . . . . . . . . . . | $ 222,300 | 4.7 | $ 128,400 | 3.5 |

*Rounded to nearest 0.1%.

Calculating Earnings Performance and Efficiency Analysis

Lesson 17-2     **503**

# CALCULATING THE RATE EARNED ON AVERAGE TOTAL ASSETS

A business uses its assets to earn net income. If a business uses all assets as efficiently as possible, it should earn the best possible net income. The rate found by dividing net income after federal income tax by average total assets is known as the rate earned on average total assets. The rate earned on average total assets shows how well a business is using its assets to earn net income. Hamilton's rate of return on average total assets is calculated as shown on the previous page using income statement and balance sheet information.

## STEPS

### CALCULATING THE RATE OF RETURN ON AVERAGE TOTAL ASSETS

**1** Calculate average total assets. Average total assets is the average amount of assets held during a year.
   a. Add January 1 total assets and December 31 total assets. (Total assets for January 1 are the same as the total assets on the prior year's December 31 balance sheet.)
   b. Divide the total by 2.

**2** Divide net income after federal income taxes by average total assets to determine the rate earned on average total assets.

An 11.6% rate earned on average total assets means that for each $1.00 of assets, the business earned 11.6 cents. A table comparing this result to the rate for the prior year is shown below. (Some information for the prior year is taken from financial statements that are not illustrated.)

|  | Current Year | Prior Year |
|---|---|---|
| Net Income after Federal Income Tax | $ 222,300.00 | $ 128,400.00 |
| January 1 Total Assets | 1,759,700.00 | 1,437,600.00 |
| December 31 Total Assets | 2,067,700.00 | 1,759,700.00 |
| Average Total Assets | 1,913,700.00 | 1,598,650.00 |
| Rate Earned on Average Total Assets | 11.6% | 8.0% |

Hamilton compares this rate to rates of return on alternative investments. Hamilton's goal is to earn a rate of return that is at least as high as other types of investments. For example, if Hamilton can earn more by placing extra cash in government bonds, the company is not meeting its earnings goal.

Investment sources available to Hamilton are earning 10.0%. Although the prior year's investments fell below this goal, the trend in the rate earned improved significantly from 8.0% to 11.6%. Therefore, Hamilton believes that a rate earned on total assets of 11.6% is satisfactory.

©GETTY IMAGES/PHOTODISC

## FYI
FOR YOUR INFORMATION

Publications such as *Dun and Bradstreet* list various ratios for a variety of businesses.

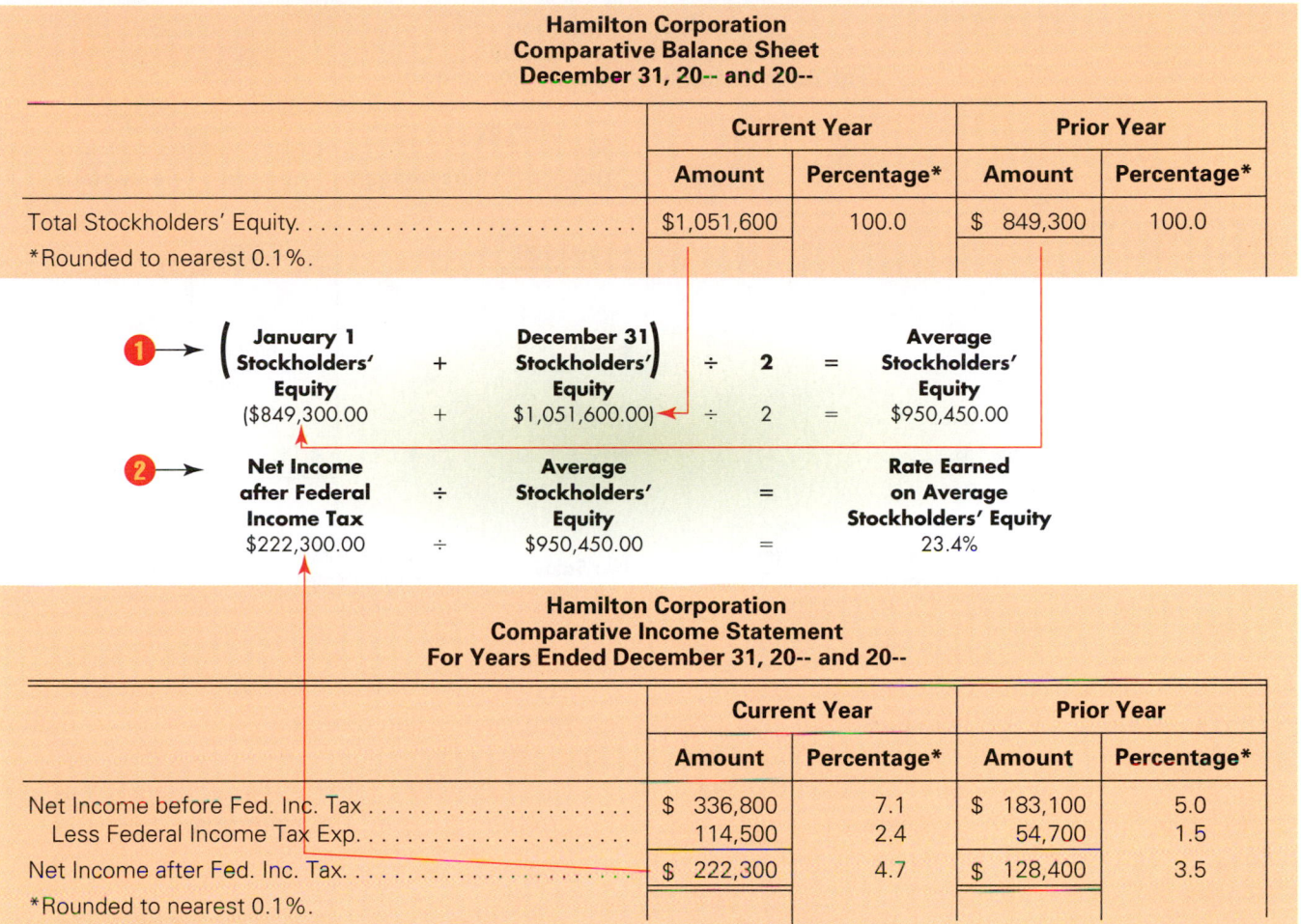

Hamilton Corporation
Comparative Balance Sheet
December 31, 20-- and 20--

| | Current Year | | Prior Year | |
|---|---|---|---|---|
| | Amount | Percentage* | Amount | Percentage* |
| Total Stockholders' Equity. . . . . . . . . . . . . . . . . . . . . . . | $1,051,600 | 100.0 | $ 849,300 | 100.0 |

*Rounded to nearest 0.1%.

1 ⟶ ( January 1 Stockholders' Equity ($849,300.00 + December 31 Stockholders' Equity $1,051,600.00) ÷ 2 = Average Stockholders' Equity $950,450.00

2 ⟶ Net Income after Federal Income Tax $222,300.00 ÷ Average Stockholders' Equity $950,450.00 = Rate Earned on Average Stockholders' Equity 23.4%

Hamilton Corporation
Comparative Income Statement
For Years Ended December 31, 20-- and 20--

| | Current Year | | Prior Year | |
|---|---|---|---|---|
| | Amount | Percentage* | Amount | Percentage* |
| Net Income before Fed. Inc. Tax . . . . . . . . . . . . . . . . . . . . | $ 336,800 | 7.1 | $ 183,100 | 5.0 |
| Less Federal Income Tax Exp. . . . . . . . . . . . . . . . . . . . | 114,500 | 2.4 | 54,700 | 1.5 |
| Net Income after Fed. Inc. Tax . . . . . . . . . . . . . . . . . . . . | $ 222,300 | 4.7 | $ 128,400 | 3.5 |

*Rounded to nearest 0.1%.

Investors compare the rate earned on stockholders' equity for several businesses to determine the best investment. Hamilton's rate earned on average stockholders' equity is calculated as shown above.

The following table compares the current year's rate to the rate for the prior year. (Some information for the prior year is taken from financial statements that are not illustrated.)

Hamilton's rate earned fell well below industry standards in the prior year. However, its rate of earnings has increased significantly from 15.4% to 23.4%. Based on the trend and a comparison with industry standards, Hamilton

achieved a satisfactory rate earned on average stockholders' equity.

**STEPS** · STEPS · STEPS · STEPS · STEP

## CALCULATING THE RATE OF RETURN ON AVERAGE STOCKHOLDERS' EQUITY

1 Calculate average stockholders' equity. (January 1 total stockholders' equity is the same as the total stockholders' equity on the prior year's December 31 balance sheet.)

2 Divide net income after federal income taxes by average total stockholders' equity to determine the rate earned on average total assets.

| | Current Year | Prior Year | Industry Standard (2 yrs.) |
|---|---|---|---|
| Net Income after Federal Income Tax | $ 222,300.00 | $128,400.00 | |
| January 1 Stockholders' Equity | 849,300.00 | 820,900.00 | |
| December 31 Stockholders' Equity | 1,051,600.00 | 849,300.00 | |
| Average Stockholders' Equity | 950,450.00 | 835,100.00 | |
| Rate Earned on Average Stockholders' Equity | 23.4% | 15.4% | 20% |

**Hamilton Corporation**
**Comparative Income Statement**
**For Years Ended December 31, 20-- and 20--**

| | Current Year | | Prior Year | |
|---|---|---|---|---|
| | **Amount** | **Percentage*** | **Amount** | **Percentage*** |
| Operating Revenue: | | | | |
|    Net Sales . . . . . . . . . . . . . . . . . . . . . . . . . . . . . . | $4,767,200 | 100.0 | $3,633,000 | 100.0 |
| | | | | |
| Other Expenses: | | | | |
|    Interest Expense . . . . . . . . . . . . . . . . . . . . . . . . | $   62,000 | 1.3 | $   52,000 | 1.4 |
| Net Income before Fed. Inc. Tax . . . . . . . . . . . . . . . . . . . . . | $ 336,800 | 7.1 | $ 183,100 | 5.0 |
|    Less Federal Income Tax Exp. . . . . . . . . . . . . . . . . . . | 114,500 | 2.4 | 54,700 | 1.5 |
| Net Income after Fed. Inc. Tax . . . . . . . . . . . . . . . . . . . . | $ 222,300 | 4.7 | $ 128,400 | 3.5 |
| *Rounded to nearest 0.1%. | | | | |

| Net Income after Federal Income Tax | ÷ | Net Sales | = | Rate Earned on Net Sales |
|---|---|---|---|---|
| **1** → $222,300.00 | ÷ | $4,767,200.00 | = | 4.7% |

A business that carefully controls costs should earn a consistent rate on net sales from year to year. The rate found by dividing net income after federal income tax by net sales is called the **rate earned on net sales**. However, if costs suddenly change, the rate earned on net sales also changes.

Hamilton's rate earned on net sales for the current year is calculated as shown above using information from the income statement.

The following table compares the current rate to the rate from the prior year.

| | Current Year | Prior Year |
|---|---|---|
| Net Income after Federal Income Tax | $  222,300.00 | $  128,400.00 |
| Net Sales | 4,767,200.00 | 3,633,000.00 |
| Rate Earned on Net Sales | 4.7% | 3.5% |

The component percentage for net income after federal income tax is the same percentage as the rate earned on net sales. In both calculations, net income is calculated as a percentage of net sales.

When determining an acceptable rate earned on net sales, Hamilton considers what is normal for similar businesses and the company's own past experience. Businesses similar to Hamilton have been earning about a 4.0% rate on net sales for the last two or three years. Based on a comparison of similar businesses, Hamilton's rate earned on net sales of 3.5% in the prior year was unsatisfactory. The trend in rate earned increased to 4.7% in the current year, a satisfactory rate. This trend should be watched closely for any future declines. When the rate earned on net sales declines, the company must increase sales or reduce costs to maintain an acceptable rate.

**Hamilton Corporation**
**Comparative Income Statement**
**For Years Ended December 31, 20-- and 20--**

| | Current Year | | Prior Year | |
|---|---|---|---|---|
| | Amount | Percentage* | Amount | Percentage* |
| Net Income before Fed. Inc. Tax . . . . . . . . . . . . . . . . . . . . | $ 336,800 | 7.1 | $ 183,100 | 5.0 |
| Less Federal Income Tax Exp. . . . . . . . . . . . . . . . . . . | 114,500 | 2.4 | 54,700 | 1.5 |
| Net Income after Fed. Inc. Tax. . . . . . . . . . . . . . . . . . . . | $ 222,300 | 4.7 | $ 128,400 | 3.5 |
| *Rounded to nearest 0.1%. | | | | |

**Hamilton Corporation**
**Comparative Balance Sheet**
**December 31, 20-- and 20--**

| | Current Year | | Prior Year | |
|---|---|---|---|---|
| | Amount | Percentage* | Amount | Percentage* |
| Total Stockholders' Equity. . . . . . . . . . . . . . . . . . . . . . . . . | $1,051,600 | 100.0 | $ 849,300 | 100.0 |
| Capital Stock Shares Outstanding . . . . . . . . . . . . . . . . . . | 60,000 | | 50,000 | |
| *Rounded to nearest 0.1%. | | | | |

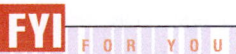

**1** → Net Income after Federal Income Tax ÷ Shares of Capital Stock Outstanding = Earnings per Share

$222,300.00 ÷ 60,000 = $3.71

The amount of net income earned on one share of common stock during a fiscal period is known as earnings per share. Stockholders and management frequently use earnings per share as a measure of success. As earnings per share increase, more people become interested in buying stock. This demand for stock causes stock prices to go up. The company then finds it easier to issue stock or borrow money.

Hamilton's earnings per share for the current year is calculated as shown above using information from the income statement and statement of stockholders' equity.

The earnings per share is calculated for the current and prior years as shown below.

| | Current Year | Prior Year |
|---|---|---|
| Net Income after Federal Income Tax | $ 222,300.00 | $128,400.00 |
| Shares of Capital Stock Outstanding | 60,000 | 50,000 |
| Earnings Per Share | $3.71 | $2.57 |

Increases in earnings per share signal stockholders that the company is continuing to increase the net income earned for each share. Hamilton knows that a positive trend is important to the company. Earnings per share increased significantly from $2.57 to $3.71, a very favorable trend.

**FYI** FOR YOUR INFORMATION

Earnings per share is one of the most widely recognized financial ratios.

| | Market Price per share | ÷ | Earnings per Share | = | Price-Earnings Ratio |
|---|---|---|---|---|---|
| | $43.50 | ÷ | $3.71 | = | 11.7 times |

Investors want to buy stock in companies that will earn a reasonable return on their investment. The relationship between the market value per share of stock and the earnings per share is known as the price-earnings ratio. As described in Chapter 13, the price-earnings ratio of a company's stock relates profitability to the amount that the investors currently pay for the stock. The price-earnings ratio is usually expressed as a stated ratio.

Hamilton's capital stock sold for $43.50 per share on December 31 of the current year. Hamilton's price-earnings ratio for the current year is calculated as shown above.

The following price-earnings ratios are calculated for the current and prior years:

| | Current Year | Prior Year |
|---|---|---|
| Market Price per Share | $43.50 | $24.50 |
| Earnings per Share | 3.71 | 2.57 |
| Price-Earnings Ratio | 11.7 times | 9.5 times |

The market price of a share of stock is determined by the amount that investors are willing to pay for it. If investors think that a company's profitability is increasing, they are usually willing to pay more for the stock. Thus, the market price of a company's stock is influenced strongly by what potential investors think the company's earnings will be in the future. Hamilton's price-earnings ratio increased from 9.5 to 11.7. This change indicates that investors considered the stock more valuable and were willing to pay more for the stock per dollar earned by the corporation in the current year. This increased demand is a favorable trend for Hamilton.

## global perspective

GLOBAL PERSPECTIVE • GLOBAL PERSPECTIVE • GLOBAL PERSPECTIVE

### International Mail

There are three categories of mail for sending documents internationally:

1. LC mail (initials for the French *lettres* and *cartes postale*—meaning "letters" and "postcards"). LC mail consists mainly of letters, letter packages, and postcards.
2. AO mail (initials for the French *Autres Objets*—meaning "other things"). AO mail usually consists of items considered printed materials, such as books, periodicals, and braille publications. This service is usually by ship and is slower than airmail.
3. CP mail (initials for the French par *Colis Postal*—meaning "by parcel post"). CP mail is the equivalent of American

parcel post. CP mail resembles fourth class domestic mail. It is the only class of mail that can be insured. This service is also usually by ship.

Special services are also offered.

#### Required

Contact the local United States Postal Service or another mail service to obtain information about:

1. Express mail.
2. International Priority Airmail.
3. Registered mail.
      Write a brief report about your findings.

## EFFICIENCY ANALYSIS

The profitability and continued growth of a business are influenced by how efficiently the business utilizes its assets. The operating cycle of a merchandising business consists of three phases. (1) Purchase merchandise. (2) Sell merchandise, frequently on account. (3) Collect the accounts receivable. Much of a business's assets are in accounts receivable and merchandise inventory. The faster a business can convert these assets to cash and begin another operating cycle, the more efficient and profitable the business will be.

## ACCOUNTS RECEIVABLE TURNOVER RATIO

### Hamilton Corporation
### Comparative Balance Sheet
### December 31, 20-- and 20--

|  | Current Year | | Prior Year | |
| --- | --- | --- | --- | --- |
|  | Amount | Percentage* | Amount | Percentage* |
| **ASSETS** | | | | |
| Current Assets: | | | | |
| Cash .................................... | $ 206,100 | 10.0 | $ 104,300 | 5.9 |
| Accounts Receivable (book value) ................ | 474,000 | 22.9 | 569,200 | 32.3 |
| Merchandise Inventory ..................... | 547,900 | 26.5 | 423,800 | 24.1 |
| *Rounded to nearest 0.1%. | | | | |

### Hamilton Corporation
### Comparative Income Statement
### For Years Ended December 31, 20-- and 20--

|  | Current Year | | Prior Year | |
| --- | --- | --- | --- | --- |
|  | Amount | Percentage* | Amount | Percentage* |
| Operating Revenue: | | | | |
| Net Sales ............................ | $4,767,200 | 100.0 | $3,633,000 | 100.0 |
| *Rounded to nearest 0.1%. | | | | |

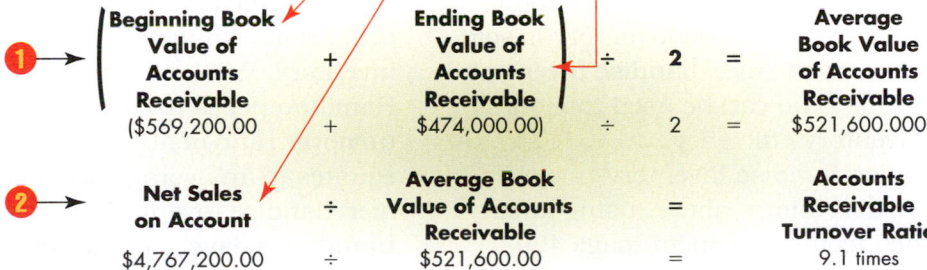

1.  (Beginning Book Value of Accounts Receivable + Ending Book Value of Accounts Receivable) ÷ 2 = Average Book Value of Accounts Receivable

    ($569,200.00 + $474,000.00) ÷ 2 = $521,600.000

2.  Net Sales on Account ÷ Average Book Value of Accounts Receivable = Accounts Receivable Turnover Ratio

    $4,767,200.00 ÷ $521,600.00 = 9.1 times

A business accepts accounts receivable to encourage sales. However, the earnings process is not complete until the business receives cash for sales on account. Thus, an efficient company closely monitors the length of time required to collect its receivables. The number of times the average amount of accounts receivable is collected annually is known as the accounts receivable turnover ratio. This ratio monitors a business's accounts receivable collection efficiency.

Hamilton's accounts receivable turnover ratio for the current year is calculated as shown above, using the information from the balance sheet and income statement.

Hamilton's turnover ratio indicates that accounts are being collected 9.1 times a year. The average number of days for customers to pay their accounts is calculated:

The accounts receivable turnover ratio for the prior year was 7.0 times. The average number of days for payment was 52 days. Hamilton's credit terms are n/30. Thus, the company's goal

| Days in Year | ÷ | Accounts Receivable Turnover Ratio | = | Average Number of Days for Payment |
|---|---|---|---|---|
| 365 | ÷ | 9.1 | = | 40 days |

is to collect accounts receivable in 30 days or less. Neither year's results meet that goal. However, the ratio improved from 7.0 to 9.1. This favorable trend means the company is becoming more efficient in its collection efforts by reducing collection of its accounts receivable from 52 to 40 days.

## MERCHANDISE INVENTORY TURNOVER RATIO

**Step 1:**

$$\left(\begin{array}{c}\text{January 1} \\ \text{Merchandise} \\ \text{Inventory}\end{array} + \begin{array}{c}\text{December 31} \\ \text{Merchandise} \\ \text{Inventory}\end{array}\right) \div 2 = \begin{array}{c}\text{Average} \\ \text{Merchandise} \\ \text{Inventory}\end{array}$$

$$(\$423,800.00 + \$547,900.00) \div 2 = \$485,850.00$$

**Step 2:**

$$\begin{array}{c}\text{Cost of} \\ \text{Merchandise} \\ \text{Sold}\end{array} \div \begin{array}{c}\text{Average} \\ \text{Merchandise} \\ \text{Inventory}\end{array} = \begin{array}{c}\text{Merchandise} \\ \text{Inventory} \\ \text{Turnover Ratio}\end{array}$$

$$\$2,602,800.00 \div \$485,850.00 = 5.4 \text{ times}$$

A company earns income when it sells merchandise. The faster it sells its merchandise inventory, the more efficient and generally more profitable the business. The number of times the average amount of merchandise inventory is sold annually is known as the merchandise inventory turnover ratio. This ratio can be used to monitor merchandise inventory efficiency.

Hamilton's merchandise inventory turnover ratio is calculated as shown above, using information from the income statement (page 499). The turnover ratio of 5.4 indicates that the inventory is being sold 5.4 times in a year. The average number of days' sales in merchandise inventory is 68 days (365 days ÷ 5.4 turnover ratio = 68 days). Last year, Hamilton had a merchandise turnover ratio of 6.2 times, resulting in an average number of days' sales in merchandise inventory of 59 days.

An optimum merchandise inventory turnover ratio is determined by two factors. (1) Amount of sales. (2) Number of days needed to replenish inventory. Previous experience indicates that Hamilton needs to maintain an inventory turnover ratio of about 6.0. This 6.0 ratio equates to an average number of days' sales in merchandise inventory of 61 days. Last year, Hamilton's days' sales in inventory was 59 days. This lower-than-desired level of inventory resulted in lost sales because some items were out of stock before new inventory arrived. However, the current year inventory level, 68 days, is satisfactory.

## term review

TERM REVIEW

rate earned on net sales

## audit your understanding

AUDIT YOUR

1. What does a rate earned on average total assets show?
2. What does a rate earned on average stockholders' equity show?
3. What does an accounts receivable turnover ratio of 9.1 indicate?

## work together 17-2

WORK TOGETHER • WORK TOGETHER

**Calculating earnings performance and efficiency analysis ratios**

Information from TeleNet Corporation's financial statements for the current year is provided in the *Working Papers.* Your instructor will guide you through the following examples.

1. Calculate the following earnings performance and efficiency ratios for the current year. Round percentage calculations to the nearest 0.1%, dollar amounts to the nearest $.01, and the price-earnings ratio to the nearest .1 (tenth).

   a. Rate earned on average total assets
   b. Rate earned on average stockholders' equity
   c. Rate earned on net sales
   d. Earnings per share
   e. Price-earnings ratio
   f. Accounts receivable turnover ratio
   g. Average number of days for accounts receivable payment
   h. Merchandise inventory turnover ratio
   i. Average number of days' sales in merchandise inventory

## on your own 17-2

ON YOUR OWN • ON YOUR OWN • ON YOUR OWN

**Calculating earnings performance and efficiency analysis ratios**

Information from Razure Adventures Company's financial statements for the current year are provided in the *Working Papers.* Work independently to complete the following problem.

1. Calculate the following earnings performance and efficiency ratios for the current year. Round percentage calculations to the nearest 0.1%, dollar amounts to the nearest $.01, and the price-earnings ratio to the nearest .1 (tenth).

   a. Rate earned on average total assets
   b. Rate earned on average stockholders' equity
   c. Rate earned on net sales
   d. Earnings per share
   e. Price-earnings ratio
   f. Accounts receivable turnover ratio
   g. Average number of days for accounts receivable payment
   h. Merchandise inventory turnover ratio
   i. Average number of days' sales in merchandise inventory

# 17-3 Calculating Financial Strength Analysis

## SHORT-TERM FINANCIAL STRENGTH ANALYSIS

A successful business needs adequate capital. A business gets capital from two sources. (1) Owners' investments and retained earnings. (2) Loans. Some capital, either owned or borrowed, is to be used for long periods of time. Some capital is borrowed for short periods of time. A business can invest capital in assets (such as equipment and buildings) for long periods of time. A business also invests in assets (such as merchandise) that will be converted back to cash in a short period of time. Short-term assets are referred to as current assets because they are consumed in a business's daily activities or exchanged for cash. Long-term assets are referred to as plant assets and are used over a long period of time.

Hamilton uses three measures to analyze short-term financial strength. (1) Working capital. (2) Current ratio. (3) Acid-test ratio.

## WORKING CAPITAL

|  | Total Current Assets | − | Total Current Liabilities | = | Working Capital |
|---|---|---|---|---|---|
| Current Year | $1,254,100.00 | − | $596,100.00 | = | $658,000.00 |
| Prior Year | $1,118,600.00 | − | $685,400.00 | = | $433,200.00 |

The amount of total current assets less total current liabilities is called **working capital**. Working capital, stated in dollars, is the amount of current assets available to the business after current liabilities are paid. It is not the amount of cash available to the business. The amount of working capital can be compared from year to year to look for a trend. However, working capital cannot be used easily to compare Hamilton with other companies in the industry.

Hamilton's working capital for December 31 of the current year and December 31 of the prior year is calculated as shown above, using information from the balance sheet (page 501).

Hamilton's working capital increased from $433,200.00 to $658,000.00, a favorable trend. A review of other financial information suggests that part of the reason for the prior year's lower working capital was the company's fast expansion. Frequently, when a business expands rapidly, it borrows money to buy more inventory and pay more employees. The rate of increased costs for merchandise and payroll may be initially greater than the rate of increase in sales and net income. In the current year, Hamilton lowered its current liabilities by issuing more capital stock and increasing long-term liabilities.

## FYI
FOR YOUR INFORMATION

The *Wall Street Journal* and many local newspapers report price-earnings ratios in their stock quotations.

## CURRENT RATIO

|  | Total Current Assets | ÷ | Total Current Liabilities | = | Current Ratio |
|---|---|---|---|---|---|
| Current Year | $1,254,100.00 | ÷ | $596,100.00 | = | 2.1 times |
| Prior Year | $1,118,600.00 | ÷ | $685,400.00 | = | 1.6 times |

A ratio that shows the numeric relationship of current assets to current liabilities is called the **current ratio**. Normally, current liabilities are expected to be paid from cash on hand plus cash soon to be received from other current assets.

The current ratio is calculated by dividing total current assets by total current liabilities. Hamilton's current ratio for the current year and the prior year are calculated as shown above, using information from the balance sheet.

The current ratio of 2.1 means that Hamilton owns $2.10 in current assets for each $1.00 needed to pay current liabilities.

Businesses similar to Hamilton try to maintain a current ratio of 2.0 times. Industry experience has shown that a business with a current ratio of less than 2.0 times has difficulty raising ready cash to pay current liabilities on time. At the same time, industry experience shows that a current ratio can be too high. If the current ratio is 3.0 times or higher, the business has more capital invested in current assets than is needed to run the business.

In the prior year, Hamilton's current ratio, 1.6, was significantly below the desired ratio. However, the current year's ratio, 2.1, is at a satisfactory level. A review of financial information suggests that part of the reason for the prior year's lower current ratio was the company's fast expansion. In the current year, Hamilton lowered its current liabilities by issuing more capital stock and increasing long-term liabilities.

## ACID-TEST RATIO

|  | Total Quick Assets (Cash + Accounts Receivable) | ÷ | Total Current Liabilities | = | Acid-Test Ratio |
|---|---|---|---|---|---|
| Current Year | ($206,100.00 + $474,000.00) | ÷ | $596,100.00 | = | 1.1 times |
| Prior Year | ($104,300.00 + $569,200.00) | ÷ | $685,400.00 | = | 1.0 times |

Those current assets that are cash or that can be quickly turned into cash are called **quick assets**. Quick assets include cash, accounts receivable, and marketable securities, but not merchandise inventory or prepaid expenses. A ratio that shows the numeric relationship of quick assets to current liabilities is called the **acid-test ratio**. This ratio shows the ability of a business to pay all current liabilities almost immediately if necessary.

Hamilton's acid-test ratio for the current year and prior year is calculated as shown above. The current year's ratio of 1.1 indicates that for each $1.00 needed to pay current liabilities, Hamilton has $1.10 available in quick assets. For companies similar to Hamilton, the desired industry standard for an acid-test ratio is between 0.9 and 1.3.

Hamilton's acid-test ratio has increased from 1.0 to 1.1, a favorable trend. Part of the cash received from the sale of capital stock and the increase in long-term liabilities was used to reduce the level of current liabilities and improve the acid-test ratio.

Businesses that are successful and are able to continue operating through both strong and weak economic periods usually have long-term financial strength. Long-term financial strength requires a balance between stockholders' capital and borrowed capital. A profitable business can be even more profitable by using borrowed capital wisely. However, borrowed capital must be repaid with interest. Continuing operation of a business with a large percentage of borrowed capital may be jeopardized if net income declines and it cannot make loan payments. Also, creditors are reluctant to loan additional money to companies with a high level of liabilities. A well-managed company monitors its long-term financial strength to ensure that a reasonable balance between stockholders' capital and borrowed capital is maintained.

Hamilton uses three measures to analyze long-term financial strength: (1) debt ratio, (2) equity ratio, and (3) equity per share.

## DEBT RATIO

| | Total Liabilities | ÷ | Total Assets | = | Debt Ratio |
|---|---|---|---|---|---|
| Current Year | $1,016,100.00 | ÷ | $2,067,700.00 | = | 49.1% |
| Prior Year | $ 910,400.00 | ÷ | $1,759,700.00 | = | 51.7% |

The ratio found by dividing total liabilities by total assets is called the **debt ratio**. This ratio shows the percentage of assets that are financed with borrowed capital (liabilities).

Hamilton's debt ratio for the current year and the prior year are calculated as shown above, using information from the balance sheet (page 501).

The current year ratio, 49.1%, indicates that for each $1.00 of assets owned by Hamilton, the company has borrowed 49.1 cents.

The average debt ratio for companies similar to Hamilton is 43.0%. Hamilton's ratios are above the industry average, an unfavorable condition. Rapid growth over the past two or three years, financed primarily through borrowed capital, has caused the unfavorable liabilities level. However, the additional capital stock that Hamilton issued this year helped lower the debt ratio from 51.7% to 49.1%. The company should consider issuing more capital stock to reduce the total liabilities to an industry average of 43.0%.

©GETTY IMAGES/PHOTODISC

# EQUITY RATIO

| | Total Stockholders' Equity | ÷ | Total Assets | = | Equity Ratio |
|---|---|---|---|---|---|
| Current Year | $1,051,600.00 | ÷ | $2,067,700.00 | = | 50.9% |
| Prior Year | $ 849,300.00 | ÷ | $1,759,700.00 | = | 48.3% |

The ratio found by dividing stockholders' equity by total assets is called the **equity ratio**. This ratio shows the percentage of assets that are provided by stockholders' equity.

Hamilton's equity ratio for the current year and the prior year are calculated as shown above, using information from the statement of stockholders' equity (page 500) and the balance sheet (page 501).

Hamilton's ratio for the current year, 50.9%, indicates that for each $1.00 of assets owned by the company, 50.9 cents' worth was acquired with stockholders' capital. The average equity ratio for companies similar to Hamilton is 57.0%. Hamilton's ratios are below the industry average, an unfavorable condition.

The debt and equity ratios show the mix of capital provided by capital borrowed and capital provided by stockholders. The sum of the two ratios equals 100%, as shown here:

| | Current Year | Prior Year |
|---|---|---|
| Debt Ratio | 49.1% | 51.7% |
| Equity Ratio | 50.9% | 48.3% |
| Totals | 100.0% | 100.0% |

The totals always equal 100% because the total liabilities and stockholders' equity represent the source of all asset ownership. Due to rapid expansion, Hamilton's prior year's equity ratio declined to an unfavorable level. In the current year, Hamilton increased the percentage of ownership provided by stockholders' equity by issuing more capital stock. Hamilton plans to continue its efforts to increase the equity ratio by reducing its liabilities and issuing additional stock.

# EQUITY PER SHARE

| | Total Stockholders' Equity | ÷ | Shares of Capital Stock Outstanding | = | Equity per Share |
|---|---|---|---|---|---|
| Current Year | $1,051,600.00 | ÷ | 60,000.00 | = | $17.53 |
| Prior Year | $ 849,300.00 | ÷ | 50,000.00 | = | $16.99 |

The amount of total stockholders' equity belonging to a single share of stock is known as equity per share. Hamilton's equity per share for the current year and the prior year are calculated as shown above, using information from the statement of stockholders' equity (page 500).

Hamilton's equity per share in the current year, $17.53, indicates that on December 31, each share of capital stock represents ownership in $17.53 of the assets.

Equity per share tells stockholders how much ownership of the company each share represents. For example, the stockholders of Hamilton know that each share represents $17.53 ownership of the total company assets. This ownership has increased from $16.99 per share in the prior year, a favorable trend.

# careers in accounting

CAREERS IN ACCOUNTING • CAREERS IN ACCOUNTING • CAREERS IN ACCOUNTI

## Tom Hughes, Forensic Accountant

COURTESY OF TOM HUGHES

Forensic accounting has gained renewed attention due to recent accounting scandals, but it has always been a part of the profession. In fact, forensic accountants were credited with putting Al Capone in prison on tax-evasion charges.

Forensic accounting is a growth area of accounting today. Forensic accountants work in most major accounting firms and are needed for developing anti-fraud programs, conducting investigations, and supporting all kinds of civil litigation. Forensic accountants work throughout the business world, in public accounting, in corporations, and in all branches of government (from the FBI and SEC to the offices of the local authorities).

Tom Hughes is a Director in the Forensic & Dispute Services practice of Deloitte & Touche LLP. Based in the Los Angeles office, Tom conducts fraud and forensic investigative services on behalf of clients throughout the entire Pacific Southwest region, with a special focus on anti-fraud consulting and fraud investigations.

He is a certified fraud examiner with more than 30 years' experience in criminal and civil investigations, both domestic and international. His expertise in fraud investigations and security comes from 27 years with the Federal Bureau of Investigation, where he served as agent-in-charge of the San Diego and Boston offices. After the FBI, Tom joined a Fortune 100 company as the Director of Corporate Security, and in May 2001 joined the ranks of Deloitte & Touche LLP. He received his B.S. in Business Administration and Accounting from Quincy University and later earned his MBA at Bradley University in Illinois.

Tom has been involved in such cases as the following:

- The defrauding of a subsidiary bank in Moscow, Russia, by its senior management, leading to an out-of-court multi-million-dollar fidelity bond insurance settlement.
- Fraud in a county government by former county executives, consultants, and other vendors, leading to the filing of civil actions against a number of individuals and companies.
- Investigating purchasing activities at one of a hotel chain's properties in Rome, Italy, that identified fictitious vendors and fraudulent bids leading to changes in procurement policies and procedures.

**Salary Range:** $30,000–$110,000 and up. Can lead to high-level careers at law firms, corporations, and government agencies such as the FBI.

**Qualifications:** B.S. in accounting, and accounting/auditing experience. A Certified Public Accountant license is almost always required. Familiarity with legal concepts and procedures is important.

**Occupational Outlook:** Forensic accounting is one of eight "careers to count on." (*U.S. News and World Report,* February 18, 2002, pp. 46–48, 50)

## terms review

working capital
current ratio
quick assets
acid-test ratio
debt ratio
equity ratio

## audit your understanding

1. What are two sources from which a business gets capital?
2. What three measures can be used to analyze short-term financial strength?
3. What is the major difference between current assets and quick assets?
4. What is the formula for the acid-test ratio?
5. Why does a well-managed company monitor its long-term financial strength?
6. What is the formula for calculating debt ratio?
7. What is the formula for calculating equity per share?

## work together 17-3

**Analyzing short-term and long-term financial strength**

Information taken from Applied Technology's comparative balance sheet is provided in the *Working Papers*. Your instructor will guide you through the following problem.

1. Calculate the following short-term financial strength analysis ratios for the current year and prior year. Round ratios to the nearest .1 (tenth). Your instructor will guide you through the examples.

   a. Working capital
   b. Current ratio
   c. Acid-test ratio
   d. Debt ratio
   e. Equity ratio
   f. Equity per share

## on your own 17-3

**Analyzing short-term and long-term financial strength**

Information taken from Online Office Supply's comparative balance sheet is provided in the *Working Papers*. Work independently to complete the following problem.

1. Calculate the following short-term financial strength analysis ratios for the current year and prior year. Round ratios to the nearest .1 (tenth). Work independently to complete the following problem.

   a. Working capital
   b. Current ratio
   c. Acid-test ratio
   d. Debt ratio
   e. Equity ratio
   f. Equity per share

SUMMARY • SUMMARY

**After completing this chapter, you can**

1. Define accounting terms related to financial statement analysis.

2. Identify accounting concepts and practices related to financial statement analysis.

3. Analyze financial statements.

4. Calculate earnings performance.

5. Perform efficiency analysis.

6. Analyze the long-term financial strength of businesses.

# Explore Accounting

EXPLORE ACCOUNTING • EXPLORE ACCOUNTING • EXPLORE ACCO

## Detailed Information on Financial Statements

Many of the financial statements used in this text report the balance of every account in the chart of accounts. These example companies have a relatively small number of accounts. Thus, every account balance can easily be reported on the financial statements.

As companies grow, it becomes impractical for them to report every account. A company with hundreds of locations, for example, is likely to have a cash account for each location. Rather than reporting each cash account balance, the company combines all cash accounts and reports a single amount on the financial statements. The same method is used to report all accounts on the financial statements. For most users of the financial statements, a single cash amount provides adequate information.

Most investors do not need to know the balance of each of the company's hundreds of cash accounts. Instead, the total cash amount is adequate for financial statement analysis. Detailed account information has rarely been available to individuals outside of the company. The cost of providing this information was not considered

worth the benefit that a few individuals might gain. However, computer technology has made the distribution of this detailed information significantly less expensive.

Accountants are starting to recognize that the detailed information can be made available at a low cost using the Internet. The traditional financial statements are likely to remain as the primary method that companies use to report their financial information. The number of users accessing the detailed information is likely to increase, however, as users become more comfortable using the Internet and learn how to evaluate detailed information to improve business decisions.

**Required:**
Examine the annual report of a corporation and identify the balance in the inventory account. Why would you expect the amount to be the total of many inventory accounts? Suggest reasons that management might need many inventory accounts. Why might you, as a potential investor, want to know the inventory balance of a particular location?

# 17-1 APPLICATION PROBLEM  QUICKBOOKS

## Analyzing comparative financial statements using trend analysis

The comparative financial statements for CyberOptic Corporation are in the *Working Papers*. The financial statements have been completed up to the trend analysis section. The following information is taken from the financial records of CyberOptic for two consecutive fiscal years ended December 31.

|  | Current Year | Prior Year |
|---|---|---|
| Accounts Receivable (book value), January 1 | $ 76,820.00 | $ 69,450.00 |
| Total Assets, January 1 | 670,670.00 | 544,200.00 |
| Total Stockholder's Equity, January 1 | 350,040.00 | 314,840.00 |
| Market Price per Share of Stock, December 31 | 23.50 | 16.50 |

**Instructions:**

1. Complete the following comparative financial statements using trend analysis. Round percentage calculations to the nearest 0.1%.
   a. Comparative income statement
   b. Comparative stockholders' equity statement
   c. Comparative balance sheet
2. Use the financial statements' trend analysis to determine whether the trend from the prior to the current year for each of the following items appears to be favorable or unfavorable. Give reasons for these trends. Save your work to complete Application Problems 17-3, 17-4, 17-5, and 17-6.
   a. Net sales
   b. Net income
   c. Total stockholders' equity
   d. Total assets

# 17-2 APPLICATION PROBLEM

## Analyzing comparative financial statements using component percentage analysis

The comparative financial statements for CyberOptic Corporation are in the *Working Papers*. The financial statements have been completed up to the comparative analysis section.

**Instructions:**

1. Complete the following comparative financial statements using component percentage analysis. Round percentage calculations to the nearest 0.1%.
   a. Comparative income statement
   b. Comparative stockholders' equity statement
   c. Comparative balance sheet
2. Use the financial statements' component percentage analysis to determine whether the current year's results for the following items, compared with those for the prior year, appear to be favorable or unfavorable. Give reasons for your responses.
   a. As a percentage of net sales:
      (1) Cost of merchandise sold
      (2) Gross profit on operations
      (3) Total operating expenses
      (4) Net income after federal income tax
   b. As a percentage of total stockholders' equity:
      (1) Retained earnings
      (2) Capital stock
   c. As a percentage of total assets or total liabilities and stockholders' equity:
      (1) Current assets
      (2) Current liabilities

# 17-3 APPLICATION PROBLEM

## Analyzing earnings performance from comparative financial statements

Use the comparative statements from Application Problem 17-1 to complete this problem.

**Instructions:**

1. Based on CyberOptic's comparative financial statements prepared in Application Problem 17-1 and the information given in the text for Application Problem 17-1, calculate the following for each year.
   a. Rate earned on average total assets
   b. Rate earned on average stockholders' equity
   c. Rate earned on net sales
   d. Earnings per share
   e. Price-earnings ratio
2. For each analysis, indicate whether a favorable or an unfavorable trend occurred from the prior to the current year. Give reasons for these trends.


# 17-4 APPLICATION PROBLEM

## Analyzing efficiency from comparative financial statements

Use the comparative statements from Application Problem 17-1 to complete this problem.

**Instructions:**

1. Based on CyberOptic's comparative financial statements prepared in Application Problem 17-1 and the information given in the text for Application Problem 17-1, calculate the following for each year. All of CyberOptic's sales are on account.
   a. Accounts receivable turnover ratio
   b. Average number of days for payment
   c. Merchandise inventory turnover ratio
   d. Average number of days' sales in merchandise inventory
2. For each analysis, indicate whether a favorable or an unfavorable trend occurred from the prior to the current year. Give reasons for these trends.


# 17-5 APPLICATION PROBLEM

## Analyzing short-term financial strength from a comparative balance sheet

Use the comparative balance sheet from Application Problem 17-1 to complete this problem.

**Instructions:**

1. Based on CyberOptic's comparative balance sheet prepared in Application Problem 17-1, calculate the following for each year.
   a. Working capital
   b. Current ratio
   c. Acid-test ratio
2. For each analysis, indicate whether a favorable or an unfavorable trend occurred from the prior to the current year. Give reasons for these trends.

# 17-6 APPLICATION PROBLEM

## Analyzing long-term financial strength from a comparative balance sheet

Use the comparative balance sheet from Application Problem 17-1 to complete this problem.

**Instructions:**

1. Based on CyberOptic's comparative balance sheet prepared in Application Problem 17-1, calculate the following for each year:
   a. Debt ratio
   b. Equity ratio
   c. Equity per share
2. For each analysis, indicate whether a favorable or an unfavorable trend occurred from the prior to the current year. Give reasons for these trends.

# 17-7 MASTERY PROBLEM    AUTOMATED ACCOUNTING

## Analyzing comparative financial statements

The comparative financial statements for Advanced Auto Technology, Inc., are in the Working Papers. The financial statements have been completed up to the financial analysis section. The following information is taken from the financial records of Advanced Auto Technology for two fiscal years ended December 31:

|  | Current Year | Prior Year |
|---|---|---|
| Accounts Receivable (book value), January 1 | $242,890.00 | $236,580.00 |
| Merchandise Inventory, January 1 | 172,890.00 | 53,760.00 |
| Total Assets, January 1 | 762,860.00 | 693,200.00 |
| Stockholders' Equity, January 1 | 373,160.00 | 306,780.00 |
| Shares of Capital Stock Outstanding, December 31 | 48,000 | 40,000 |
| Market Price per Share of Stock, December 31 | 42.50 | 30.00 |

**Instructions:**

1. Complete the following comparative financial statements using trend analysis. Round percentage calculations to the nearest 0.1%.
   a. Comparative income statement
   b. Comparative stockholders' equity statement
   c. Comparative balance sheet
2. Use the financial statements' trend analysis to determine whether the trend from the prior to the current year for each of the following items appears to be favorable or unfavorable. Give reasons for these trends.
   a. Net sales
   b. Net income
   c. Total stockholders' equity
   d. Total assets
3. Complete the comparative income statement using component percentage analysis. Round percentage calculations to the nearest 0.1%.
4. Record from the statement prepared in Instruction 3 or calculate the component percentages for each of the following. Determine whether the current year's results, compared with those for the prior year, appear to be favorable or unfavorable. Give reasons for your responses.
   a. As a percentage of net sales:
      (1) Cost of merchandise sold
      (2) Gross profit on operations
      (3) Total operating expenses
      (4) Net income after federal income tax

b. As a percentage of total stockholders' equity:
   (1) Retained earnings
   (2) Capital stock
c. As a percentage of total assets or total liabilities and stockholders' equity:
   (1) Current assets
   (2) Current liabilities
5. Based on Advanced Auto Technology's comparative financial statements, calculate the following ratios for each year.
   a. Profitability ratios:
      (1) Rate earned on average total assets
      (2) Rate earned on average stockholders' equity
      (3) Rate earned on net sales
      (4) Earnings per share
      (5) Price-earnings ratio
   b. Efficiency ratios:
      (1) Accounts receivable turnover ratio
      (2) Merchandise inventory turnover ratio
   c. Short-term financial strength ratios:
      (1) Working capital
      (2) Current ratio
      (3) Acid-test ratio
   d. Long-term financial strength ratios:
      (1) Debt ratio
      (2) Equity ratio
      (3) Equity per share
6. For each of the items in Instruction 5, indicate whether a favorable or an unfavorable trend occurred from the prior to the current year. Give reasons for these trends.

# 17-8 CHALLENGE PROBLEM

## Analyzing comparative financial statements

The comparative financial statements for CompuCircuit Corporation are in the *Working Papers*. The financial statements have been completed up to the financial analysis section. The following information is taken from the financial records of CompuCircuit for two fiscal years ended December 31:

|  | Current Year | Prior Year |
|---|---|---|
| Accounts Receivable (book value), January 1 | $105,500.00 | $ 126,400.00 |
| Total Assets, January 1 | 979,660.00 | 1,052,400.00 |
| Market Price per Share of Stock, December 31 | 7.50 | 29.50 |

**Instructions:**
1. Prepare the following comparative financial statements using trend analysis. Round percentage calculations to the nearest 0.1%.
   a. Comparative income statement
   b. Comparative stockholders' equity statement
   c. Comparative balance sheet
2. Use the financial statements' trend analysis to determine whether the trend from the prior to the current year for each of the following items appears to be favorable or unfavorable. Give reasons for these trends.
   a. Net sales
   b. Net income
   c. Total stockholders' equity
   d. Total assets
3. Complete the comparative income statement using component percentage analysis. Round percentage calculations to the nearest 0.1%.

4. Record from the statement prepared in Instruction 3 or calculate the component percentages for each of the following. Determine whether the current year's results, compared with those for the prior year, appear to be favorable or unfavorable. Give reasons for your responses.
   a. As a percentage of net sales:
      (1) Cost of merchandise sold
      (2) Gross profit on operations
      (3) Total operating expenses
      (4) Net income after federal income tax
   b. As a percentage of total stockholders' equity:
      (1) Retained earnings
      (2) Capital stock
   c. As a percentage of total assets or total liabilities and stockholders' equity:
      (1) Current assets
      (2) Current liabilities
5. Based on CompuCircuit's comparative financial statements, calculate the following ratios for each year:
   a. Profitability ratios:
      (1) Rate earned on average total assets
      (2) Rate earned on average stockholders' equity
      (3) Rate earned on net sales
      (4) Earnings per share
      (5) Price-earnings ratio
   b. Efficiency ratios:
      (1) Accounts receivable turnover ratio
      (2) Merchandise inventory turnover ratio
   c. Short-term financial strength ratios:
      (1) Working capital
      (2) Current ratio
      (3) Acid-test ratio
   d. Long-term financial strength ratios:
      (1) Debt ratio
      (2) Equity ratio
      (3) Equity per share
6. For each of the items in Instruction 5, indicate whether a favorable or an unfavorable trend occurred from the prior to the current year. Give reasons for these trends.

## applied communication

Corporate annual reports include a letter from the chief executive officer (CEO). The letter highlights achievements and positive results from the past year. If necessary, it delivers news of negative results with an explanation of the steps being taken to correct the problems.

**Required:**

Select one of the companies from the problems: CyberOptic Corporation, Advanced Auto Technology, Inc., or CompuCircuit Corporation. Assume that you are the CEO of the company. Using the information from your problem solutions, write a letter to stockholders that will appear in the company's annual report. You may add any details you would like, as long as the details are consistent with the financial analysis.

## cases for critical thinking

**Case 1**

Alpha Network Solutions has had declining net income the past four years. The company president employs you as a consultant to review the company's operations in an effort to identify the reason for the decline. As part of your analysis, you make a component percentage analysis of the company's four most recent income statements. A part of that analysis is shown below. What are the implications from the information? What are the problems or potential problems evident from this analysis? What are your suggestions to the company?

|                        | 20X4  | 20X3  | 20X2  | 20X1  |
|------------------------|-------|-------|-------|-------|
| Cost of Merchandise Sold | 62.1% | 58.4% | 55.2% | 52.5% |
| Total Selling Expenses   | 12.1% | 14.6% | 15.7% | 18.9% |

**Case 2**

Minta Perry has received year-end information, including financial statements, from her accountant. Among the information is a report that the accounts receivable turnover ratio in the prior year was 8.7 and for the current year is 6.2. Ms. Perry is overjoyed at the trend of the accounts receivable turnover ratio. Do you agree with her reaction? Explain your answer.

## SCANS workplace competency

**Interpersonal Competency:** Exercising Leadership

**Concept:** Competent leaders communicate thoughts, feelings, and ideas to justify a position. They encourage, persuade, convince, and motivate individuals or groups and responsibly challenge existing procedures, policies, or authority.

**Application:** Prepare a list of examples or cite situations in which you have displayed leadership. What do you think are the qualities of an effective leader?

## • graphing workshop

Tanisha Greggs, a stockholder in Mentar Corp., has just received a report of the company's ten-year financial performance that includes the following graph. In the report, management states that "the company has increased earnings per share for ten consecutive years." Tanisha is confused about the information presented in the graph. Help her understand the company's financial performance by answering the following questions.

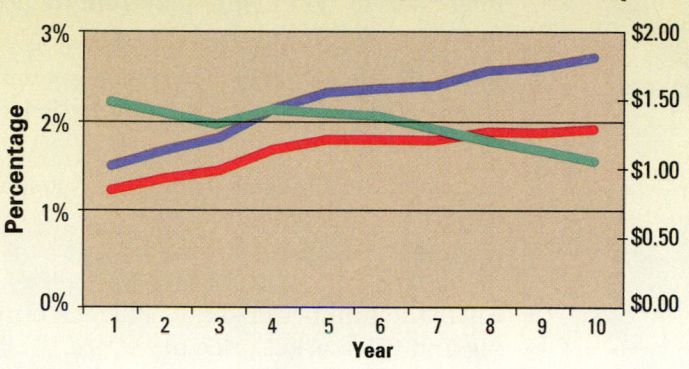

**Financial Performance Analysis for Mentar Corp.**

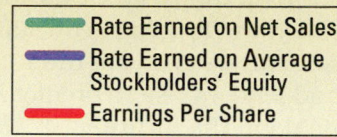

**Instructions:**

1. Has earnings per share increased each year?
2. Estimate the earnings per share for year 10.
3. Describe the trend in the rate earned on average stockholders' equity.
4. Describe the trend in the rate earned on net sales.

## • analyzing Costco's financial statements

The annual reports of publicly traded companies describe some of the financial ratios presented in this chapter. Other ratios must be calculated using the information provided in the financial statements.

Income statement amounts are the result of operations over an entire year or fiscal period. However, balance sheet amounts are the balance on a particular date. Therefore, when financial ratios use both an income statement amount and a balance sheet amount, the balance sheet amount is commonly expressed as an average of the amount at the beginning of the fiscal period and the amount at the end of the fiscal period. For example, average total assets would be the sum of total assets on January 1 plus total assets on December 31, divided by 2.

Because the balance sheet contains only two years of information, investors rely on information in multiple-year summaries to obtain the required information. Costco's ten-year operating and financial highlights (Appendix B pages B-2–B-3 in this textbook) enable readers to calculate financial ratios for several years.

**Instructions:**

Identify or calculate the following financial ratios from 2001 to 2003, using the financial statements and ten-year highlights, as appropriate.

1. Rate earned on average total assets
2. Rate earned on average stockholders' equity
3. Earnings per share
4. Price-earnings ratio (assume a market price of $46.25, $46.32, and $37.43 for 2001 to 2003, respectively)
5. Working capital
6. Current ratio
7. Debt ratio

# Automated Accounting

## Analyzing Automated Financial Statements and Ratio Analysis

One method of evaluating relationships within the financial statements is the use of ratio analysis. Ratios obtained from numbers in the financial statements may be compared to the ratios of previous years, to those of companies in similar industries, or to industry averages computed by companies such as Dow Jones or Standard & Poor's. Ratio analysis is one of the tools managers, investors, and lenders use to predict how well a business will do in the future.

Ratios used by business are commonly grouped by their objectives:

- The evaluation of short-term financial strength
- The evaluation of long-term financial strength
- Efficiency
- Earnings performance

Most of the data needed to compute the common ratios are available within the database maintained by accounting software. Additional information that the accountant may need to input to complete the analysis include the number of shares of stock outstanding and the current market price per share.

### Performing Ratio Analysis

Use the following steps to display the ratio analysis report:

1. Click the Reports toolbar button, or choose the Reports Selection menu item from the Reports menu.

2. When the Report Selection dialog appears, choose Financial Analysis from the Select a Report Group list.

3. Choose Ratio Analysis from the Choose a Report to Display list.

4. Click OK.

5. Enter the number of shares of stock outstanding and the market price per share.

6. Click OK.

The report will be displayed in the scrollable Report Viewer Window. The report may be printed and/or copied for inclusion in another application, such as a spreadsheet or word processor.

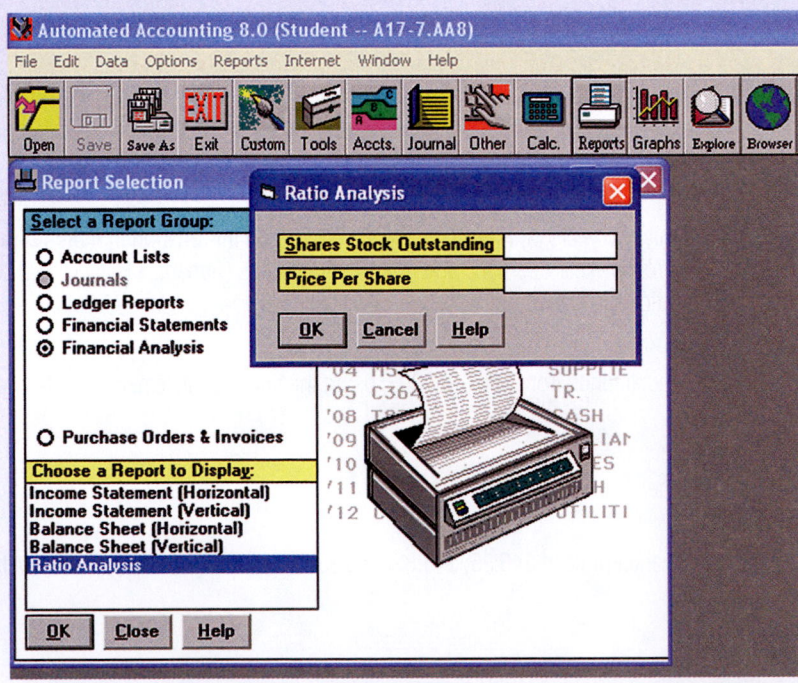

## AUTOMATING MASTERY PROBLEM 17-7

**Instructions:**

1. Load *Automated Accounting 8.0* or higher software.

2. Select database AA17-7 (Advanced Course Mastery Problem 17-7) from the accounting template disk.

3. Select File from the menu bar and choose the Save As menu command. Key the path to the drive and directory that contain your data files. Save the database with a filename of XXX177 (where XXX are your initials).

4. Read the Problem Instruction screen by clicking the Browser toolbar button.

5. Refer to page 521 for data used in this problem.

6. Exit the Automated Accounting software.

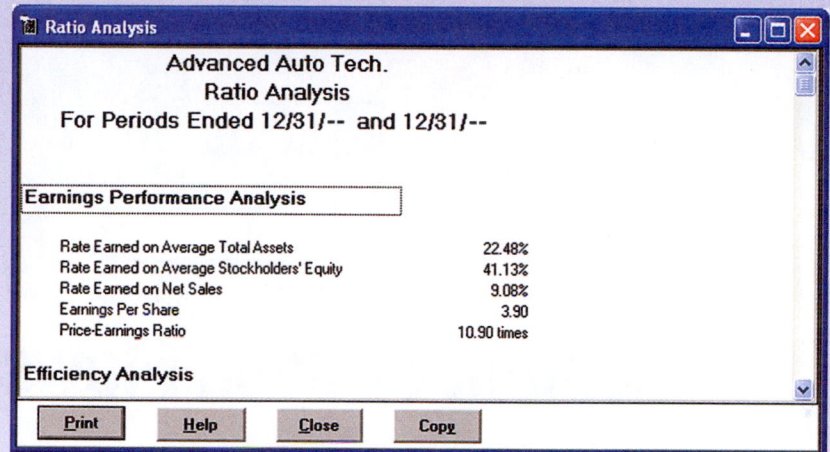

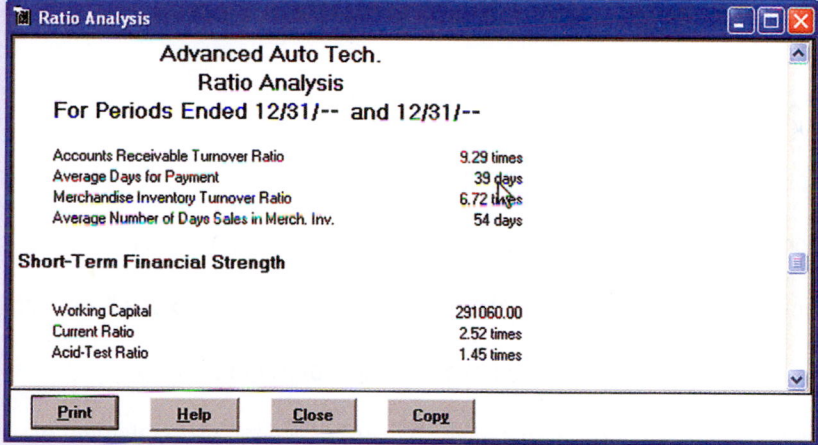

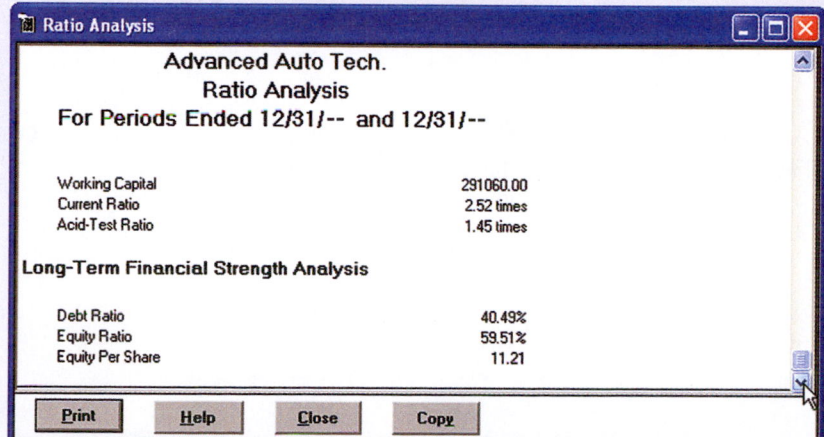

# 18 Statement of Cash Flows

**OBJECTIVES & TERMS**

**After studying Chapter 18, you will be able to:**

1. Define accounting terms related to cash flow analysis.

2. Identify accounting concepts and practices related to cash flow analysis.

3. Describe operating, investing, and financing activities and provide examples of each.

4. Prepare the operating activities section of a statement of cash flows.

5. Prepare the investing activities and financing activities sections of a statement of cash flows.

6. Prepare a statement of cash flows.

- accrual basis of accounting
- cash basis of accounting
- cash flows
- statement of cash flows
- operating activities
- investing activities
- financing activities

Point Your Browser
accountingxtra.swlearning.com

# • Hospitality Properties Trust

©GETTY IMAGES/PHOTODISC

## SPEND THE NIGHT WITH HOSPITALITY PROPERTIES TRUST

A common philosophy for business success is to delegate everything except your expertise. Hotel operators are experts at running the day-to-day operations of hotels and resorts. Building and owning hotel facilities, however, requires a different expertise. That's where Hospitality Properties Trust comes to the rescue.

Hospitality Properties Trust (HPT) leases its hotels to experienced hotel operators, including Prime Hotels and Resorts, AmeriSuites, Staybridge Suites, and several brands of Marriott. HPT owns 286 hotels with 38,577 rooms located in 38 states.

HPT is a real estate investment trust (REIT), a unique form of organization created under the tax laws of the United States. REIT tax laws require HPT to distribute most of its income to the stockholders. In exchange, the REIT is not required to pay federal income taxes.

For most corporations, earnings per share is the most recognized measure of financial performance. For a REIT, however, funds from operations (FFO) is the most important measure. HPT's board of directors uses its FFO to determine the amount of dividends to be paid. The quarterly dividend is important to HPT stockholders, who typically own the stock in order to earn HPT's regular quarterly dividend.

### Critical Thinking

1. How does a REIT differ from a typical corporation?
2. Why would the FFO of a REIT be significantly different from its earnings per share?

accountingxtra.swlearning.com

Source: www.hptreit.com

## internet activity

### SOFTWARE FOR SPECIFIC INDUSTRIES

Search the Internet for "accounting software" for a specific industry, such as agriculture, physicians, construction, lawyers, etc.

### Instructions

1. List the name of the company that sells the software.
2. List the name of the software program.

# 18-1 Understanding Cash Flow Analysis

The information presented on the income statement, balance sheet, and statement of stockholders' equity provides individuals insight into the financial condition of a business. Managers, investors, and other interested parties use this information to improve profitability, determine operating efficiency, and make informed managerial decisions. The accounting method that records revenues when they are earned and expenses when they are incurred is called the **accrual basis of accounting**. Generally accepted accounting principles (GAAP) require that most businesses use the accrual basis of accounting for their financial statements.

The accounting method that records revenues when they are received and expenses when they are paid is called the **cash basis of accounting**. Some small businesses use this method of accounting because it is easy to use and less expensive to maintain. However, cash-basis financial statements do not provide enough information about the financial condition of the business to satisfy most investors and creditors.

Accrual-based financial statements give a complete picture of the financial condition of a business. However, managers and investors may need additional information about the cash flows of a business. By analyzing cash flows, individuals can determine whether a company has enough cash to continue operating. Firms short on cash may experience problems paying expenses, purchasing new merchandise, replacing worn equipment, repaying debts, and providing owners with a return on their investment. It is critical that financial statement analysis include a study of a company's ability to produce and manage cash.

## making ethical decisions

MAKING ETHICAL DECISIONS • MAKING ETHICAL DECISIONS • MAKING ETHICAL DECISIO

### Channel Stuffing

Rivera Manufacturing's president knows that the company's income is going to fall short of published estimates by stock analysts. The company's stock will surely drop on news of the income shortfall. Two weeks before the December 31 fiscal year end, Rivera's president instructs the sales department to offer substantial discounts to customers who will place their normal first-quarter orders in December. In addition, Rivera will hold the goods in its warehouse until delivery is requested by the customers.

#### Instructions

The practice described in this case is called *channel stuffing*. Define channel stuffing and determine whether the practice is legal.

# CASH FLOW ANALYSIS

## Case Study

Two years ago, in January, Gina and Kevin Harnley formed Snow Creek Corporation for the purpose of selling ski equipment, snowboards, and related accessories. During the first year, the company produced sales of over $300,000 and earned a net income of approximately $60,000. Last year was equally impressive. Assets increased, sales exceeded $500,000, and a net income of more than $100,000 was earned. Two months into the current year, however, Snow Creek Corporation lacked the amount of cash necessary to pay its current bills. If Snow Creek was growing and profits were rising, how does one explain the company's shortage of cash and inability to pay bills?

One of the main reasons for Snow Creek's financial problems was its generous credit policy, which created a large volume of accounts receivable. Snow Creek's credit policy of "no payments for six months" definitely attracted buyers. However, problems arose when a large number of Snow Creek's customers did not make their payments on time.

Another reason for Snow Creek's difficulties was a large increase in inventory. Snow Creek required a greater level of inventory to assure that it had an adequate selection of items for a growing number of customers. It paid for the merchandise within the 30-day credit terms, but it had not yet sold much of the inventory. The company ran out of money to pay its bills. Cash was going out to purchase inventory and not enough was coming in to pay expenses.

The Harnleys, who manage the company, failed to foresee their problems because they prepared their income statements using the accrual basis of accounting. Sale amounts were recognized when snow equipment and accessories left the store, not when cash was received. Consequently, Snow Creek Corporation showed strong sales and profits. However, an analysis of the company's cash receipts and cash payments shows a different picture.

Some investors and financial analysts rely heavily on an examination of income statements and balance sheets to judge a company's performance. However, impressive profits are not always a guarantee of success in the future. For example, despite reporting a substantial net income for the year, a business may experience a cash shortage and have difficulty paying its bills. Cash flow analysis helps owners, creditors, and other interested parties:

1. Determine a company's potential to produce cash in the future.
2. Judge a company's ability to pay bills and repay debts.
3. Explain changes in the cash account balance.
4. Evaluate a company's investment and equity transactions.

**SMALL BUSINESS SPOTLIGHT**

**The U.S. Small Business Administration (SBA)** is an independent agency of the federal government. Created by an act of Congress in 1953, the SBA is dedicated to helping Americans start and operate successful small enterprises. Today, the SBA is involved in financing, training, and advocacy for small firms.

©GETTY IMAGES/PHOTODISC

**Snow Creek Corporation**
**Statement of Cash Flows**
**For Year Ended December 31, 20X2**

| | | | |
|---|---|---|---|
| Cash Flows from Operating Activities: | | | |
| Net Income | | $100,344.00 | |
| Adjustments to Net Income: | | | |
| Depreciation Expense | $ 11,605.00 | | |
| Changes in current assets and liabilities: | | | |
| Increase in accounts receivable | (110,530.00) | | |
| Decrease in supplies | 399.00 | | |
| Increase in merchandise inventory | (116,640.00) | | |
| Increase in notes payable | 38,990.00 | | |
| Increase in accounts payable | 54,924.00 | | |
| Total adjustments to net income | | ($121,252.00) | |
| Cash used for operating activities | | | ($20,908.00) |
| Cash Flows from Investing Activities: | | | |
| Addition to equipment | | ($20,680.00) | |
| Proceeds from sale of property | | 30,000.00 | |
| Cash provided by investing activities | | | $9,320.00 |
| Cash Flows from Financing Activities: | | | |
| Repayment of mortgage | | ($547.00) | |
| Proceeds from issuance of common stock | | 40,000.00 | |
| Dividend payment | | (32,000.00) | |
| Cash provided by financing activities | | | $7,453.00 |
| Net Decrease in Cash | | | ($4,135.00) |
| Cash Balance, Beginning of Period | | | 12,570.00 |
| Cash Balance, End of Period | | | $8,435.00 |

The cash receipts and cash payments of a company are called **cash flows**. A statement that summarizes cash receipts and cash payments resulting from business activities during a fiscal period is called a **statement of cash flows**. The statement, as shown above, explains the change in Cash during a fiscal period by reporting the sources (inflows or receipts) and uses (outflows or payments) of a company's cash.

By studying a company's cash flows, a manager can analyze why there were profits and yet not enough cash to pay bills. No other financial statement provides this important information.

The Harnleys made business decisions based on information reported on the income state-ment and balance sheet. They failed to realize that the revenues reported on the income statement rarely match cash receipts. If a company reports sales on account of $100,000.00, it is unlikely that the company had $100,000.00 in actual cash receipts. Not all customers pay in a timely manner.

The income statement and balance sheet are prepared using an accrual basis of accounting. The statement of cash flows is prepared using the cash basis of accounting. The cash basis of accounting recognizes revenue when cash is received and expenses when cash is paid out.

**REMEMBER** The cash inflows and outflows of a business are identified using the information presented on a company's financial statements.

## TIMING OF REVENUE RECOGNITION

|  | Accrual Basis | vs. |  | Cash Basis |
|---|---|---|---|---|
|  | Revenue recognized at the time it is *earned* |  |  | Revenue recognized at the time cash is *received* |
| Revenues | $25,000.00 |  | Revenues | $ 0.00 |
| Expenses | 0.00 |  | Expenses | 0.00 |
| Net Income | $25,000.00 |  | Net Income | $ 0.00 |

Assume that Flomax Corporation has sales on account during the year and no expenses. Under the accrual basis for accounting, revenue is recognized at the time it is earned.

**Accounts Receivable**

| 25,000.00 | |

**Sales**

| | 25,000.00 |

Assume the account receivable remains outstanding at the end of the fiscal year. Using the accrual basis of accounting, Flomax reports revenues as shown above. However, the income calculation prepared under the cash basis shows no revenue for the period, hence, no net income. Under the cash basis of accounting, revenue is not recognized until cash is received.

## TIMING OF EXPENSE RECOGNITION

|  | Accrual Basis | vs. |  | Cash Basis |
|---|---|---|---|---|
|  | Expense recognized at the time it is *incurred* |  |  | Expense recognized at the time cash is *paid* |
| Revenues | $25,000.00 |  | Revenues | $ 0.00 |
| Expenses | 3,000.00 |  | Expenses | 0.00 |
| Net Income | $22,000.00 |  | Net Income | $ 0.00 |

Similarly, the recognition of expenses does not always match the payments of cash. For example, Flomax Corporation recognizes one week of salaries earned by employees before the close of the current fiscal year. The salary expense will not be paid until the next fiscal period. Using

**Salaries Expense**

| 3,000.00 | |

**Salaries Payable**

| | 3,000.00 |

the accrual basis, Flomax recognizes the expense during the current fiscal year as shown in the T accounts.

Assume that this is Flomax Corporation's only expense of the year. Using the accrual basis of accounting, Flomax's net income is $22,000.00, as shown above. The accrual basis of accounting recognizes an expense at the time it is incurred. Using the cash basis of accounting, Flomax has no expenses to report in the current period. The cash basis recognizes an expense when cash is paid. Since no cash was received and no cash was paid, a net income of $0.00 is reported.

# CASH FLOWS FROM OPERATING ACTIVITIES

## Operating Activities

**Cash Inflows** (sources of cash)
Cash sales of merchandise
Cash sales of services
Interest income
Dividends received from the ownership of stock
  in other companies
Cash received from charge customers

**Cash Outflows** (uses of cash)
Advertising
Credit card fees
Insurance expense
Interest payments
Payroll expenses
Property tax
Utility expenses
Income tax

The statement of cash flows is divided into three sections: cash flows from *operating activities*, cash flows from *investing activities*, and cash flows from *financing activities*. The cash flows for each of these sections are calculated by analyzing the information presented on the income statement, the balance sheet, and the statement of stockholders' equity.

The cash receipts and payments necessary to operate a business on a day-to-day basis are called **operating activities**. For example, a list of common cash inflows and cash outflows from operating activities is presented here. Snow Creek Corporation uses cash to add merchandise and to pay the daily expenses required to operate the business and earn a profit.

# CASH FLOWS FROM INVESTING ACTIVITIES

## Investing Activities

**Cash Inflows** (sources of cash)
Sale of property
Sale of equipment
Sale of building
Collections of long-term loans

**Cash Outflows** (uses of cash)
Purchase of land
Purchase of equipment
Purchase of building
Purchase of patents or special licenses
Loans to other companies
Purchase of stock in other companies
Purchase of bonds in other companies

Cash receipts and cash payments involving the sale or purchase of assets used to earn revenue over a period of time are called **investing activities**. A list of common cash inflows and cash outflows involving investing activities is shown here.

Creditors, owners, and potential investors examine the investing activities to assess the future financial strength and profitability of a business. Financial analysts know that investment activities are necessary if the business is to remain profitable. If a company sells buildings and equipment to raise cash for operations, there would soon be no buildings and equipment to produce or store the goods.

**REMEMBER** Sources of cash represent cash inflows and are added on the statement of cash flows. Uses of cash represent cash outflows and are subtracted on the statement of cash flows.

## Financing Activities

**Cash Inflows** (sources of cash)
Capital stock issue
Mortgage issue
Bond issue
Long-term loans

**Cash Outflows** (uses of cash)
Purchase of treasury stock
Payment of cash dividends
Repayment of loan/note principal
Retirement of bond principal

When Gina and Kevin Harnley decided to form Snow Creek Corporation, they had to obtain the necessary funding to carry out their plan. The Harnleys decided to sell common stock to acquire the financing they needed. Cash receipts and payments involving debt or equity transactions are called **financing activities**. These activities usually involve borrowing money from creditors and repaying the principal or acquiring capital from owners and providing a return on their investment.

Financing activities are often used to ensure that an adequate balance exists in the cash account. If a firm's business activities use more cash than it receives, it must obtain additional financing.

Some financing activities reduce the cash balance. This occurs when cash is used to pay dividends, repay the principal of a loan, or purchase treasury stock. These payments of cash decrease the amount available for operating and investing activities. A list of common cash inflows and cash outflows related to financing activities is shown above.

**FYI** FOR YOUR INFORMATION

The Financial Accounting Standards Board (FASB), in *Statement No. 95,* classifies the interest paid on borrowed money as an operating activity. The reason for this classification is that the payment of interest expense on a loan is considered to have a direct impact on a firm's net income.

## technology for business

TECHNOLOGY FOR BUSINESS • TECHNOLOGY FOR BUSINESS • TECHNOLOGY FOR BUSIN

### Keeping Financial Transactions Safe

Each day, millions of financial transactions are electronically transmitted. Many of these transactions are made using the Internet. Several technologies exist to safeguard these transactions from electronic theft and fraud. Among the oldest of these technologies is encryption. Before data are transmitted, they are disguised through encryption. If the transmitted data are stolen, the thief cannot access the data. When the data reach the proper destination, the receiving party will decrypt the information. Two keys, or sets of codes, are needed. One is used to encrypt the information; the other is used to decrypt it.

A further safeguard for electronic data transmission is the use of digital certificates. These certificates are used to link the encryption key and the decryption key. Digital certificates are issued by third-party vendors. They link the encryption and decryption keys and prevent unauthorized parties from possessing the decryption key. Before digital certificates are issued, the identity of the business or individual is verified. This verification provides another level of security.

terms review
audit your understanding

## terms review

TERMS REVIEW • TERMS

accrual basis of accounting
cash basis of accounting
cash flows
statement of cash flows
operating activities
investing activities
financing activities

## audit your understanding

AUDIT YOUR UNDERSTANDING

1. Using the accrual accounting basis, when are revenues and expenses recognized?

2. Using the cash accounting basis, when are revenues and expenses recognized?

3. Identify the three categories of business activities reported on the statement of cash flows.

## work together 18-1

WORK TOGETHER • WORK TOGETHER

### Classifying cash flows

The following business transactions represent selected cash receipts (cash inflows) and cash payments (cash outflows) of Los Altos Cyclery. A blank form is provided in the *Working Papers*. Your instructor will guide you through the following problem.

1. Identify each transaction as (1) a cash inflow or cash outflow and (2) as an operating, investing, or financing activity.

   a. Receipts from the issue of capital stock.
   b. Cash purchase of office furniture.
   c. Dividend payment.
   d. Advertising expense.
   e. Receipts from the sale of merchandise.
   f. Cash received from the issue of a mortgage.
   g. Repayment of loan principal.
   h. Purchase of another company's stock.

## on your own 18-1

ON YOUR OWN • ON YOUR OWN

### Classifying cash flows

The following business transactions represent selected cash receipts (cash inflows) and cash payments (cash outflows) of Burlingame Tuxedo. A blank form is provided in the *Working Papers*. Work independently to complete this problem.

1. Identify each transaction as (1) a cash inflow or cash outflow and (2) as an operating, investing, or financing activity.

   a. Receipts from the issue of bonds.
   b. Cash purchase of office furniture.
   c. Salary expense.
   d. Receipts from tuxedo rentals.
   e. Receipts from the issue of a mortgage.
   f. Cash receipt from sale of equipment.
   g. Cash purchase of treasury stock.
   h. Payment of property taxes.

# 18-2 Preparing the Operating Activities Section of a Statement of Cash Flows

## DETERMINING CASH FLOWS FROM OPERATING ACTIVITIES

The operating activity section of the statement of cash flows reports the cash inflows and cash outflows resulting from the operation of a business. These cash flows can be indirectly determined by identifying the net income for the period and making several adjustments.

### Net Income

Net income presented on an income statement summarizes revenues and expenses generated by the operating activities of a business during the fiscal period. For this reason, net income is a good starting point for calculating the cash flows from operating activities. Since a net income eventually brings additional money into a firm, net income is viewed as a source of cash. A net loss reduces the amount of money available for expenditures and is considered to be a use of cash.

Since the income statement is prepared using the accrual basis of accounting and the statement of cash flows is prepared using the cash basis of accounting, the recognition of revenues and expenses occurs at different times. Adjustments are made to net income to recognize the timing differences.

## ADJUSTING NET INCOME FOR DEPRECIATION

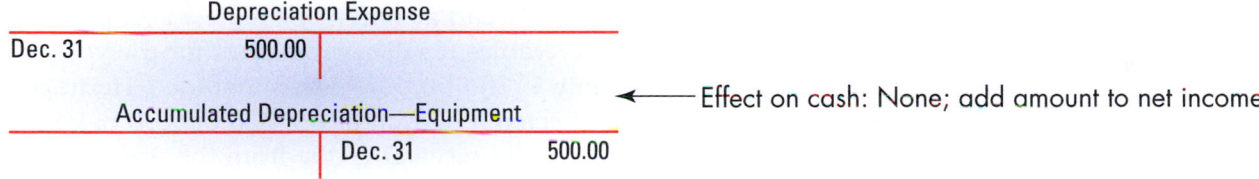

| Depreciation Expense | |
| --- | --- |
| Dec. 31  500.00 | |

| Accumulated Depreciation—Equipment | |
| --- | --- |
| | Dec. 31  500.00 |

← Effect on cash: None; add amount to net income

Depreciation expense is recognized on the income statement. However, it does not involve an outflow of cash. Since depreciation expense does not use cash, the amount is added back to the net income amount.

At the end of the fiscal year, Centaur Corporation expenses an appropriate amount of the original cost of equipment using the straight-line method of depreciation. Depreciation for the year is recorded by debiting Depreciation Expense and crediting Accumulated Depreciation—Equipment as shown above.

Notice that the credit for this transaction is Accumulated Depreciation—Equipment, not Cash. Depreciation expense does not affect the balance in the cash account. However, depreciation expense is deducted from company revenues to determine net income. Since no cash is paid out, the amount of depreciation expense reported on the income statement must be added back to net income to determine the actual cash generated from operating activities. The amount of depreciation expense added back to net income is one of the adjustments to net income to determine the actual source of cash from operations.

### FYI
FOR YOUR INFORMATION

Determine if the increase or decrease in an account represents a source of cash or a use of cash. If a change in an account represents a source of cash, it is always added on the statement of cash flows. If a change represents a use of cash, it is always subtracted.

| Cash | |
|---|---|
| Dec. 15 | 80,000.00 |

| Sales | |
|---|---|
| | Nov. 15 | 100,000.00 |

Increase in noncash current asset is a use of cash. ⟶

| Accounts Receivable | | | |
|---|---|---|---|
| Nov. 15 | 100,000.00 | Dec. 15 | 80,000.00 |
| Dec. 31 Bal. | 20,000.00 | | |

The second adjustment to net income involves changes in *noncash current assets* (current assets other than cash). Increases and decreases in noncash current assets impact cash flows and require an adjustment to net income. For example, an increase in the current asset Accounts Receivable indicates that not all of the sales on account reported for a fiscal period were collected. Consequently, an increase in accounts receivable means that cash received from sales is less than the sales amount reported on the income statement.

On November 1, Heritage Corporation began business. A T account analysis of the following transactions is shown above.

*Nov. 15. Heritage Corporation makes its only sale on account, $100,000.00.*

*Dec. 15. Heritage receives $80,000.00 as a partial payment on the account. No other collections occur during the year.*

The $20,000.00 increase in accounts receivable represents cash that has not yet been received and, therefore, must be deducted from net income to determine cash flow. This adjustment to net income informs analysts that the cash inflows from sales on account during the year were $80,000.00 ($100,000.00 − $20,000.00) and not the full $100,000.00 reported as sales on the income statement. An increase in a noncash current asset is considered to be a *use of cash*. This use of cash supports the company's daily operations by allowing the business to offer customers the option to buy now and pay later. A use of cash means a specified sum of money is no longer available for other business activities.

Noncash current assets may also decrease during a fiscal period. A decrease in a noncash current asset represents a *source of cash* and is added back to the net income amount. This concept is illustrated through the continued use of the previous example involving Heritage Corporation.

At the end of its second year in business, Heritage Corporation has a $10,000.00 balance in Accounts Receivable. From an analysis of the T account, we learn that:

1. The balance in *Accounts Receivable* at the beginning of the year was $20,000.00.
2. Sales on account of $130,000.00 were made during the year.
3. Payments on account of $140,000.00 were received.
4. The Accounts Receivable balance at the end of the year is $10,000.00.

How can a company collect $140,000.00 of receivables if sales on account for the year are only $130,000.00? In this instance, Heritage collected a portion of the $20,000.00 balance in accounts receivable due from the previous year. The balance in Accounts Receivable declined from $20,000.00 on January 1 to $10,000.00 on December 31. This decrease is added to net income to determine cash flow.

Each noncash current asset is analyzed in a similar manner to accounts receivable.

| Accounts Receivable | | | |
|---|---|---|---|
| Jan. 1 Bal. | 20,000.00 | Cash received | 140,000.00 |
| Credit sales | 130,000.00 | | |
| Dec. 31 Bal. | 10,000.00 | | |

# ANALYZING CHANGES IN CURRENT LIABILITIES

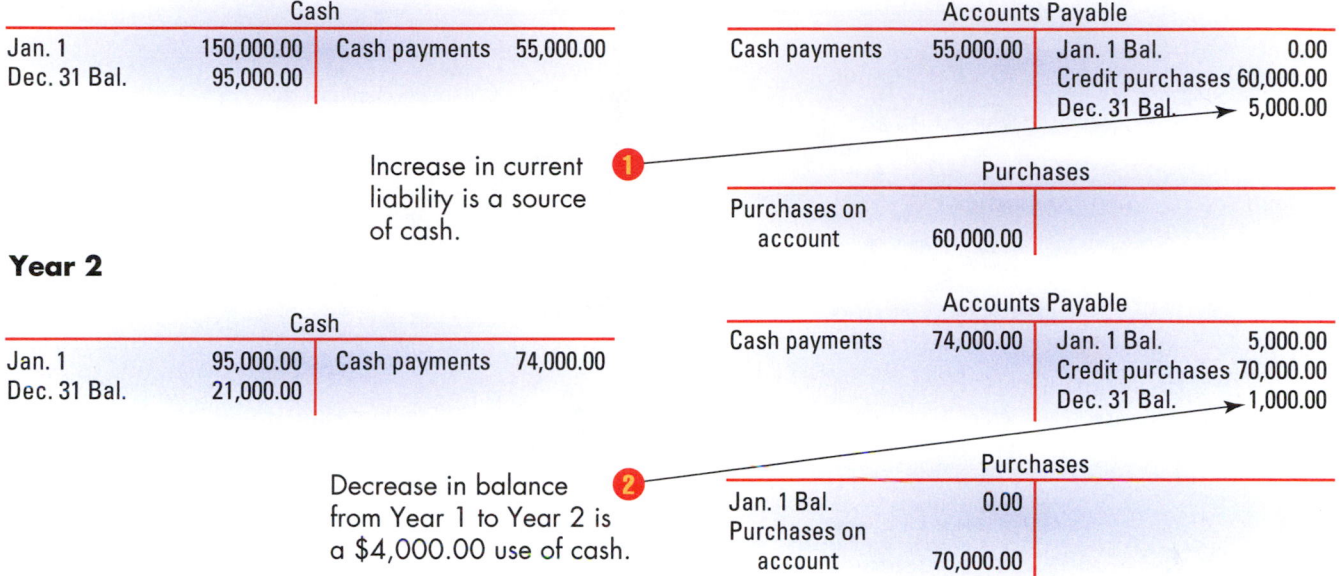

**Year 1**

| Cash | | | |
|---|---|---|---|
| Jan. 1 | 150,000.00 | Cash payments | 55,000.00 |
| Dec. 31 Bal. | 95,000.00 | | |

Increase in current liability is a source of cash. **1**

| Accounts Payable | | | |
|---|---|---|---|
| Cash payments | 55,000.00 | Jan. 1 Bal. | 0.00 |
| | | Credit purchases | 60,000.00 |
| | | Dec. 31 Bal. | 5,000.00 |

| Purchases | | | |
|---|---|---|---|
| Purchases on account | 60,000.00 | | |

**Year 2**

| Cash | | | |
|---|---|---|---|
| Jan. 1 | 95,000.00 | Cash payments | 74,000.00 |
| Dec. 31 Bal. | 21,000.00 | | |

Decrease in balance from Year 1 to Year 2 is a $4,000.00 use of cash. **2**

| Accounts Payable | | | |
|---|---|---|---|
| Cash payments | 74,000.00 | Jan. 1 Bal. | 5,000.00 |
| | | Credit purchases | 70,000.00 |
| | | Dec. 31 Bal. | 1,000.00 |

| Purchases | | | |
|---|---|---|---|
| Jan. 1 Bal. | 0.00 | | |
| Purchases on account | 70,000.00 | | |

The third adjustment to net income involves changes in current liabilities. During the operating activities of a business, increases and decreases in current liabilities occur as debts are added and paid off in the process of generating revenues. For instance, an increase in accounts payable indicates that not all of the purchases on account made during a fiscal period were paid in full. An increase in current liabilities has a positive impact on cash flows as shown for the Fairtex Corporation above.

The $5,000.00 increase in accounts payable at the end of the first year means the actual cash outflow for purchases on account was $55,000.00 and not the full $60,000.00 reported as purchases on the income statement. For this reason, net income is adjusted by adding back

$5,000.00 for the increase in a current liability. Since the company has use of the $5,000.00, the increase in a current liability represents a *source of cash.*

During the second year of operation, Fairtex Corporation was extremely aggressive in paying off its debts. In fact, the company paid off $74,000.00 of accounts payable, $4,000.00 more than the total purchases on account of $70,000.00. Why would a company pay more than it owes? In this instance, Fairtex paid a portion of the $5,000.00 accounts payable balance owed for the previous year. A decrease in a current liability represents a *use of cash* and is subtracted from the net income figure.

Each current liability is analyzed in a similar manner to accounts payable.

## SUMMARY

- Depreciation expense is *added* back to net income since it is a noncash expense
- Increases in noncash current assets (assets other than cash) and decreases in current liabilities represent *uses of cash* and are *deducted* from net income
- Decreases in noncash current assets and increases in current liabilities represent *sources of cash* and are *added* to net income

The operating activities section of the statement of cash flows shows the amount of cash actually received and paid as a result of operating a business. The adjustments to net income required to determine the cash flows from operating activities are reviewed here.

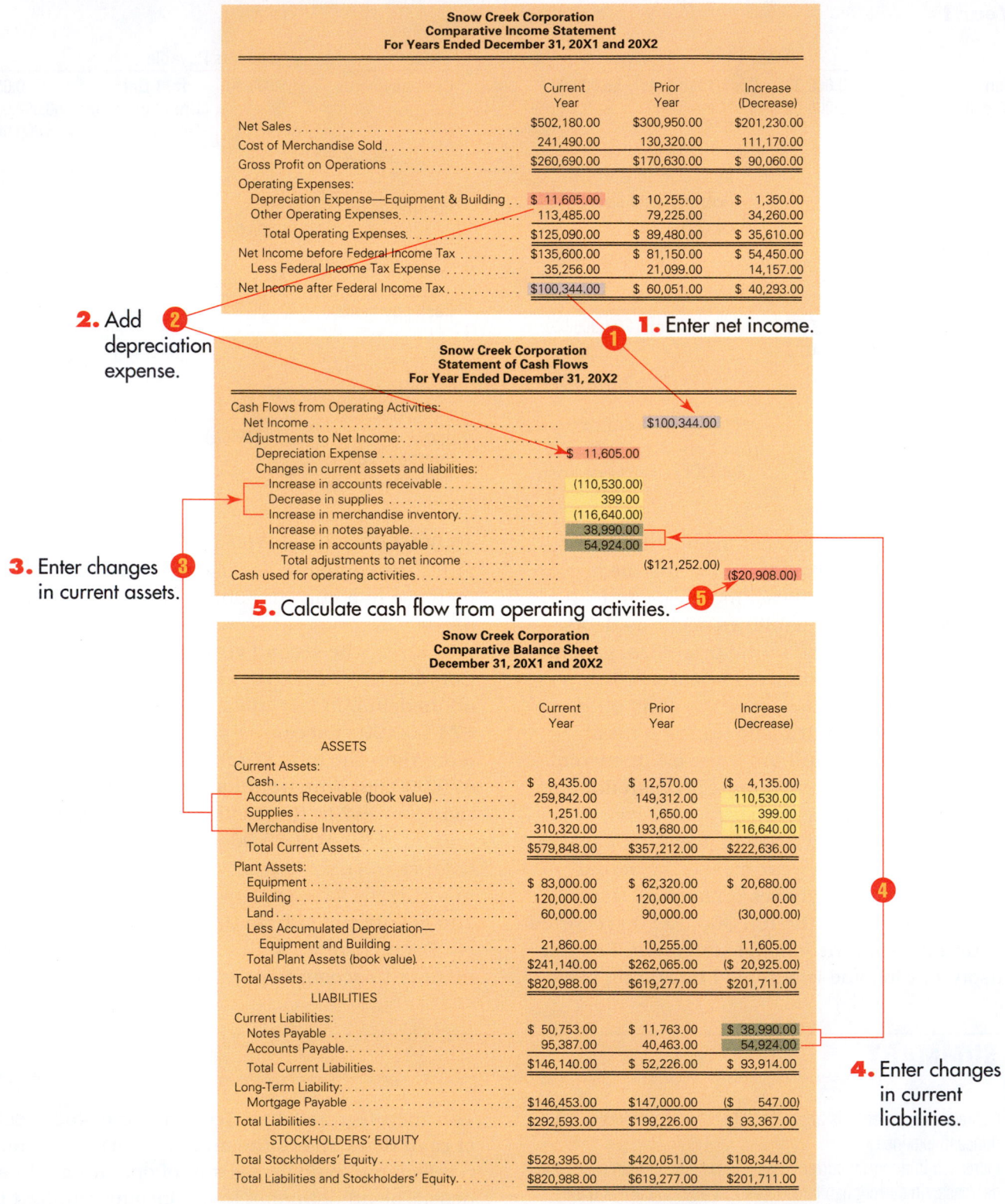

**2.** Add depreciation expense.

**1.** Enter net income.

**3.** Enter changes in current assets.

**5.** Calculate cash flow from operating activities.

**4.** Enter changes in current liabilities.

**Snow Creek Corporation**
**Comparative Income Statement**
**For Years Ended December 31, 20X1 and 20X2**

| | Current Year | Prior Year | Increase (Decrease) |
|---|---|---|---|
| Net Sales | $502,180.00 | $300,950.00 | $201,230.00 |
| Cost of Merchandise Sold | 241,490.00 | 130,320.00 | 111,170.00 |
| Gross Profit on Operations | $260,690.00 | $170,630.00 | $ 90,060.00 |
| Operating Expenses: | | | |
| Depreciation Expense—Equipment & Building | $ 11,605.00 | $ 10,255.00 | $ 1,350.00 |
| Other Operating Expenses | 113,485.00 | 79,225.00 | 34,260.00 |
| Total Operating Expenses | $125,090.00 | $ 89,480.00 | $ 35,610.00 |
| Net Income before Federal Income Tax | $135,600.00 | $ 81,150.00 | $ 54,450.00 |
| Less Federal Income Tax Expense | 35,256.00 | 21,099.00 | 14,157.00 |
| Net Income after Federal Income Tax | $100,344.00 | $ 60,051.00 | $ 40,293.00 |

**Snow Creek Corporation**
**Statement of Cash Flows**
**For Year Ended December 31, 20X2**

| | | |
|---|---|---|
| Cash Flows from Operating Activities: | | |
| Net Income | | $100,344.00 |
| Adjustments to Net Income: | | |
| Depreciation Expense | | $ 11,605.00 |
| Changes in current assets and liabilities: | | |
| Increase in accounts receivable | (110,530.00) | |
| Decrease in supplies | 399.00 | |
| Increase in merchandise inventory | (116,640.00) | |
| Increase in notes payable | 38,990.00 | |
| Increase in accounts payable | 54,924.00 | |
| Total adjustments to net income | | ($121,252.00) |
| Cash used for operating activities | | ($20,908.00) |

**Snow Creek Corporation**
**Comparative Balance Sheet**
**December 31, 20X1 and 20X2**

| | Current Year | Prior Year | Increase (Decrease) |
|---|---|---|---|
| **ASSETS** | | | |
| Current Assets: | | | |
| Cash | $ 8,435.00 | $ 12,570.00 | ($ 4,135.00) |
| Accounts Receivable (book value) | 259,842.00 | 149,312.00 | 110,530.00 |
| Supplies | 1,251.00 | 1,650.00 | 399.00 |
| Merchandise Inventory | 310,320.00 | 193,680.00 | 116,640.00 |
| Total Current Assets | $579,848.00 | $357,212.00 | $222,636.00 |
| Plant Assets: | | | |
| Equipment | $ 83,000.00 | $ 62,320.00 | $ 20,680.00 |
| Building | 120,000.00 | 120,000.00 | 0.00 |
| Land | 60,000.00 | 90,000.00 | (30,000.00) |
| Less Accumulated Depreciation— | | | |
| Equipment and Building | 21,860.00 | 10,255.00 | 11,605.00 |
| Total Plant Assets (book value) | $241,140.00 | $262,065.00 | ($ 20,925.00) |
| Total Assets | $820,988.00 | $619,277.00 | $201,711.00 |
| **LIABILITIES** | | | |
| Current Liabilities: | | | |
| Notes Payable | $ 50,753.00 | $ 11,763.00 | $ 38,990.00 |
| Accounts Payable | 95,387.00 | 40,463.00 | 54,924.00 |
| Total Current Liabilities | $146,140.00 | $ 52,226.00 | $ 93,914.00 |
| Long-Term Liability: | | | |
| Mortgage Payable | $146,453.00 | $147,000.00 | ($ 547.00) |
| Total Liabilities | $292,593.00 | $199,226.00 | $ 93,367.00 |
| **STOCKHOLDERS' EQUITY** | | | |
| Total Stockholders' Equity | $528,395.00 | $420,051.00 | $108,344.00 |
| Total Liabilities and Stockholders' Equity | $820,988.00 | $619,277.00 | $201,711.00 |

The first section of the statement of cash flows shows the cash flows from operating activities as shown above.

## REPORTING CASH FLOWS FROM OPERATING ACTIVITIES

**1**   Enter net income, *$100,344.00* as shown on Snow Creek's comparative income statement.

**2**   Add the amount of depreciation expense, *$11,605.00*, to net income.

**3**   Enter the changes in current assets as indicated in the table below.

| Change in Account | Current Year | Prior Year | Increase (Decrease) | Source or use of cash |
|---|---|---|---|---|
| Increase in Accts. Rec. | $259,842.00 | $149,312.00 | $110,530.00 | use of cash |
| Decrease in Supplies | 1,251.00 | 1,650.00 | (399.00) | source of cash |
| Increase in Mdse. Inv. | 310,320.00 | 193,680.00 | 116,640.00 | use of cash |

**4**   Enter the changes in current liabilities as indicated in the table below.

| Change in Account | Current Year | Prior Year | Increase (Decrease) | Source or use of cash |
|---|---|---|---|---|
| Increase in Notes Payable | $50,753.00 | $11,763.00 | $38,990.00 | source of cash |
| Increase in Accts. Payable | 95,387.00 | 40,463.00 | 54,924.00 | source of cash |

**5**   Determine the cash provided by operating activities (if cash increases) or the cash used by operating activities (if cash decreases). After reporting the individual adjustments to net income, the statement of cash flows shows that the actual cash requirements for Snow Creek's operating activities exceeded net income by $20,908.00. This shortfall places Snow Creek in a very serious position regarding the company's ability to meet its short-term demands for cash.

# careers in accounting

## Transferable Skills

In the process of developing specific accounting skills, you may also acquire a significant number of related skills. Many of these are listed below. These related skills are used in a variety of employment areas and are readily transferable to other occupations. Individuals who do not enter the accounting profession use many of the skills they acquired in accounting courses in whatever occupation they choose.

| | | | |
|---|---|---|---|
| analyzing | explaining | prioritizing | speaking |
| attending to details | following directions | proofreading | spelling |
| calculating | interpreting | proving | summarizing |
| clarifying | listening | reading | thinking critically |
| communicating | managing time | reasoning mathematically | verifying |
| documenting | organizing | scheduling | writing |
| evaluating | planning | solving problems | |

### Instructions

Select one of the skills listed above and describe ways in which it would be useful in an accounting career.

Xtra!
Study Tools
accountingxtra.swlearning.com

## • audit your understanding

1. Although depreciation expense is recognized on the income statement under the accrual basis of accounting, it does not involve an outflow of cash. Why?

2. What does an increase in the balance of accounts receivable indicate?

3. What does an increase in the balance of accounts payable indicate?

4. What is the starting point for calculating the cash flow from operating activities?

## • work together 18-2

**Preparing the operating activity section for a statement of cash flows**

A comparative balance sheet for Zephyr Corporation is provided in the *Working Papers*. The income statement for the current year indicates that net income was $10,160.00 and the depreciation expense was $27,300.00. Statement paper and a form for analyzing changes in accounts are also provided in the *Working Papers*. Your instructor will guide you through the following examples.

1. For each item listed on the form, record the appropriate December 31 balances for the current and prior years.

2. For each item listed on the form, classify it as a current asset or current liability.

3. Compute the amount of increase or decrease from the prior year.

4. Indicate if the increase or decrease represents a source of cash or a use of cash.

5. Prepare the operating activity section of the statement of cash flows for the current year ended December 31. Save your work to complete Work Together 18-3.

## • on your own 18-2

**Preparing the operating activity section for a statement of cash flows**

A comparative balance sheet for Cirrus Corporation is provided in the *Working Papers*. The income statement for the current year indicates that net income was $20,900.00 and the depreciation expense was $4,900.00. Statement paper and a form for analyzing changes in accounts are also provided in the *Working Papers*. Work independently to complete the following problem.

1. For each item listed on the form, record the appropriate December 31 balances for the current and prior years.

2. For each item listed on the form, classify it as a current asset or current liability.

3. Compute the amount of increase or decrease from the prior year.

4. Indicate if the increase or decrease represents a source of cash or a use of cash.

5. Prepare the operating activity section of the statement of cash flows for the current year ended December 31. Save your work to complete On Your Own 18-3.

AUDIT YOUR UNDERSTANDING

WORK TOGETHER • WORK TOGETHER

ON YOUR OWN • ON YOUR OWN • ON YOUR OWN

# 18-3 Completing the Statement of Cash Flows

## PREPARING THE INVESTING ACTIVITIES SECTION

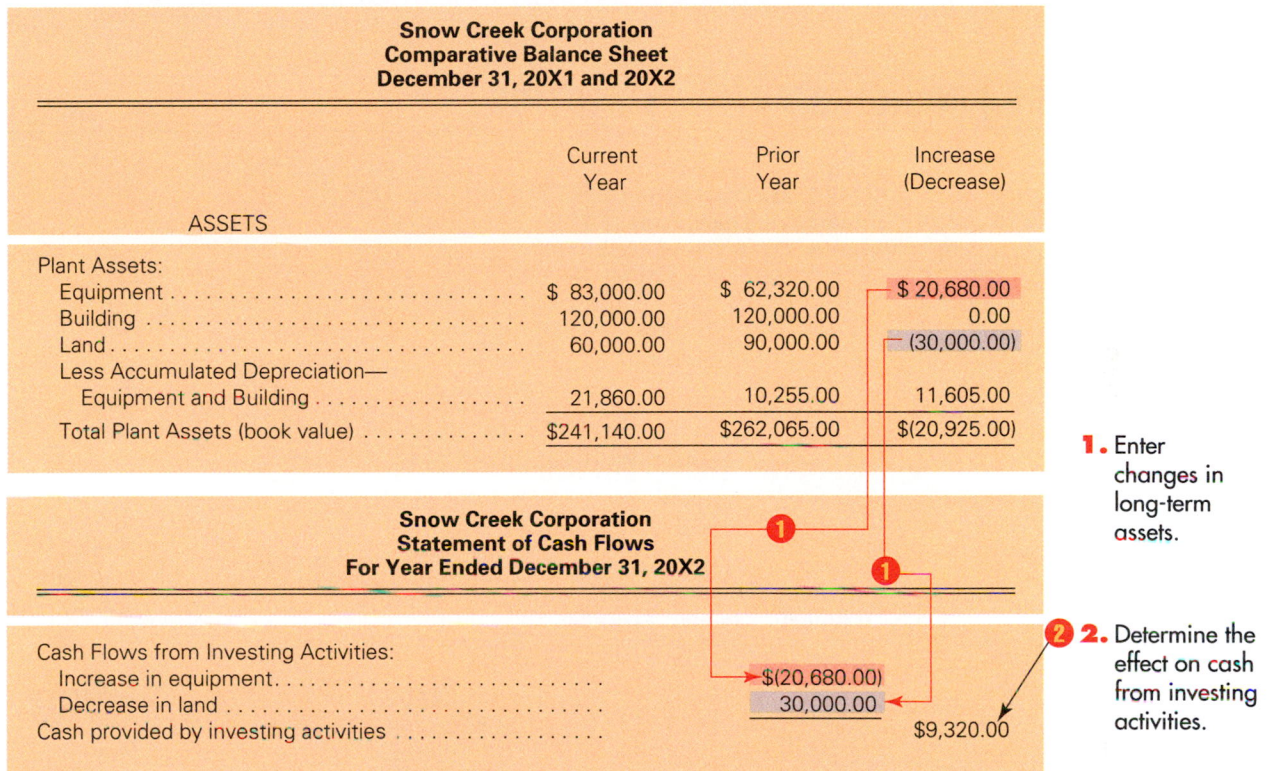

**Snow Creek Corporation**
**Comparative Balance Sheet**
**December 31, 20X1 and 20X2**

| | Current Year | Prior Year | Increase (Decrease) |
|---|---|---|---|
| **ASSETS** | | | |
| Plant Assets: | | | |
| Equipment . . . . . . . . . . . . . . . . . . . . . . . . . . . . . | $ 83,000.00 | $ 62,320.00 | $ 20,680.00 |
| Building . . . . . . . . . . . . . . . . . . . . . . . . . . . | 120,000.00 | 120,000.00 | 0.00 |
| Land . . . . . . . . . . . . . . . . . . . . . . . . . . . . . . . . | 60,000.00 | 90,000.00 | (30,000.00) |
| Less Accumulated Depreciation— | | | |
| Equipment and Building . . . . . . . . . . . . . . . . | 21,860.00 | 10,255.00 | 11,605.00 |
| Total Plant Assets (book value) . . . . . . . . . . . . | $241,140.00 | $262,065.00 | $(20,925.00) |

**1.** Enter changes in long-term assets.

**Snow Creek Corporation**
**Statement of Cash Flows**
**For Year Ended December 31, 20X2**

| | | |
|---|---|---|
| Cash Flows from Investing Activities: | | |
| Increase in equipment . . . . . . . . . . . . . . . . . . . . . . . . . . . | $(20,680.00) | |
| Decrease in land . . . . . . . . . . . . . . . . . . . . . . . . . . . . . . | 30,000.00 | |
| Cash provided by investing activities . . . . . . . . . . . . . . . . | | $9,320.00 |

**2.** Determine the effect on cash from investing activities.

Responsible investing activities are critical to the long-term success of a company. Cash flows resulting from a company's investing activities are identified by analyzing the changes in long-term assets (plant assets) presented on the comparative balance sheet. Snow Creek's investing activities section for the statement of cash flows is shown above.

# STEPS

## REPORTING CASH FLOWS FROM INVESTING ACTIVITIES

**1** Analyze changes in long-term assets. The $20,680.00 increase in equipment represents a cash outflow. The increase in a long-term asset is a use of cash. During the year, Snow Creek Corporation sold a parcel of land for $30,000, the same amount paid for the land one year earlier. The $30,000.00 decrease in the long-term asset, Land, represents a cash inflow and is a source of cash. The following table summarizes the changes.

| Change in Account | Current Year | Prior Year | Increase (Decrease) | Source or use of cash |
|---|---|---|---|---|
| Increase in Equipment | $83,000.00 | $62,320.00 | $20,680.00 | use of cash |
| Decrease in Land | 60,000.00 | 90,000.00 | ($30,000.00) | source of cash |

**2** Determine the cash provided by investing activities (if cash increases) or the cash used by investing activities (if cash decreases). Snow Creek's investing activities provided $9,320.00 in cash during the current year.

## ANALYZING CASH FLOWS FROM INVESTING ACTIVITIES

The increase in accumulated depreciation for equipment and building ($11,605.00) can be ignored. This increase matches the depreciation expense that was recorded on the income statement. The effect on cash flows was already accounted for under operating activities.

When calculating the cash flows from investing activities, it is useful to remember that:

- Increases in long-term assets generally result in cash outflows (*uses of cash*) that are subtracted on the statement of cash flows.
- Decreases in long-term assets generally result in cash inflows (*sources of cash*) that are added on the statement of cash flows.

## PREPARING THE FINANCING ACTIVITY SECTION

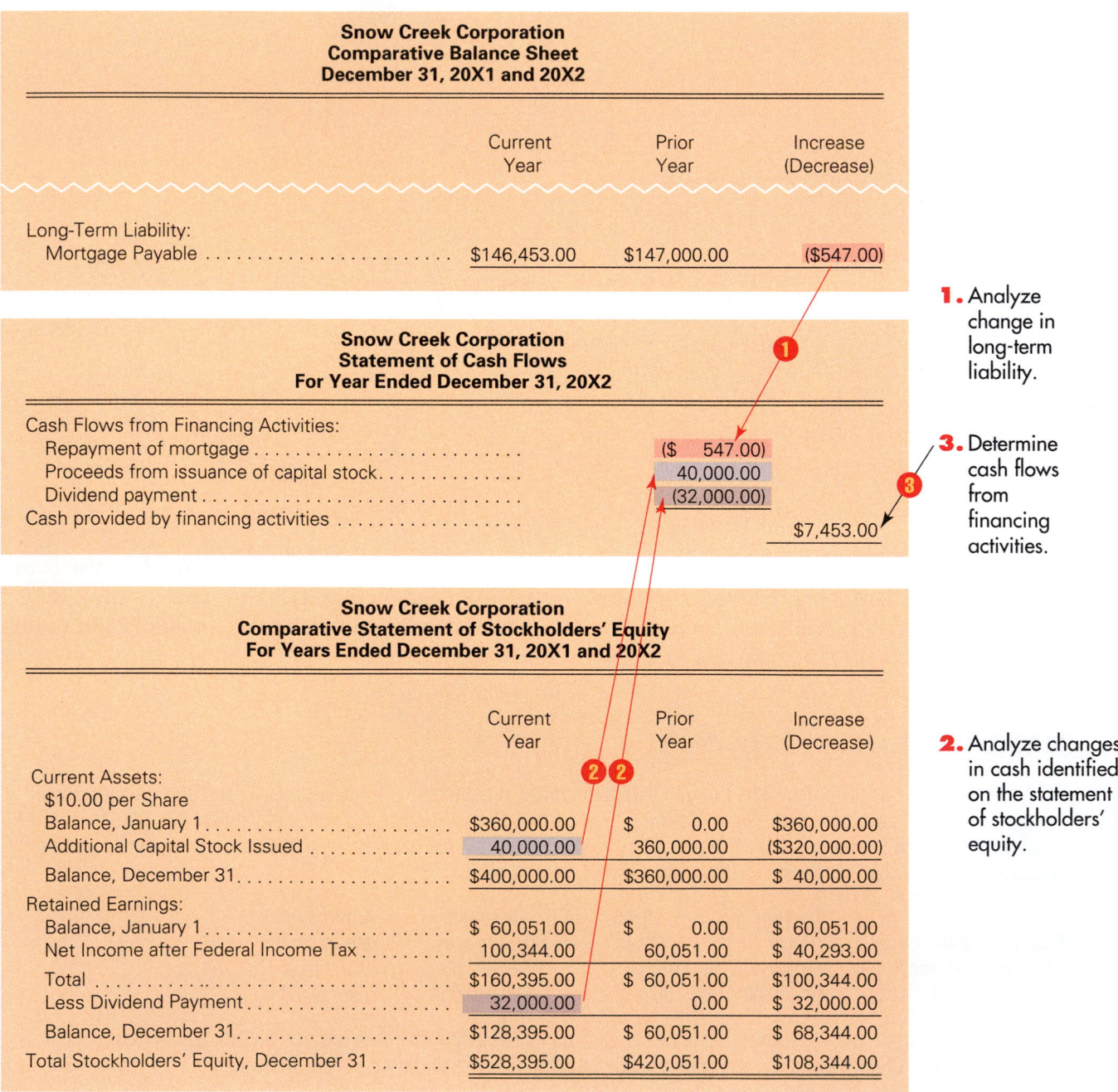

**Snow Creek Corporation**
**Comparative Balance Sheet**
**December 31, 20X1 and 20X2**

|  | Current Year | Prior Year | Increase (Decrease) |
|---|---|---|---|
| Long-Term Liability: |  |  |  |
| Mortgage Payable | $146,453.00 | $147,000.00 | ($547.00) |

**1.** Analyze change in long-term liability.

**Snow Creek Corporation**
**Statement of Cash Flows**
**For Year Ended December 31, 20X2**

| Cash Flows from Financing Activities: |  |  |
|---|---|---|
| Repayment of mortgage | ($ 547.00) |  |
| Proceeds from issuance of capital stock | 40,000.00 |  |
| Dividend payment | (32,000.00) |  |
| Cash provided by financing activities |  | $7,453.00 |

**3.** Determine cash flows from financing activities.

**Snow Creek Corporation**
**Comparative Statement of Stockholders' Equity**
**For Years Ended December 31, 20X1 and 20X2**

|  | Current Year | Prior Year | Increase (Decrease) |
|---|---|---|---|
| Current Assets: |  |  |  |
| $10.00 per Share |  |  |  |
| Balance, January 1 | $360,000.00 | $ 0.00 | $360,000.00 |
| Additional Capital Stock Issued | 40,000.00 | 360,000.00 | ($320,000.00) |
| Balance, December 31 | $400,000.00 | $360,000.00 | $ 40,000.00 |
| Retained Earnings: |  |  |  |
| Balance, January 1 | $ 60,051.00 | $ 0.00 | $ 60,051.00 |
| Net Income after Federal Income Tax | 100,344.00 | 60,051.00 | $ 40,293.00 |
| Total | $160,395.00 | $ 60,051.00 | $100,344.00 |
| Less Dividend Payment | 32,000.00 | 0.00 | $ 32,000.00 |
| Balance, December 31 | $128,395.00 | $ 60,051.00 | $ 68,344.00 |
| Total Stockholders' Equity, December 31 | $528,395.00 | $420,051.00 | $108,344.00 |

**2.** Analyze changes in cash identified on the statement of stockholders' equity.

## ANALYZING CASH FLOWS FROM FINANCING ACTIVITIES

Financing activities are often used to maintain an adequate balance in the cash account. These activities usually involve borrowing money from creditors and repaying the principal or acquiring capital from owners and providing a return on their investment. Cash flows originating from a company's financing activities are identified by examining the changes in long-term liabilities reported on the balance sheet and the changes in stockholders' equity reported on the statement of stockholders' equity. This analysis is shown on the previous page.

## STEPS
STEPS • STEPS • STEPS • STEPS • STEPS • STEPS • STEPS • STEPS • STEPS • STEPS

### REPORTING CASH FLOWS FROM FINANCING ACTIVITIES

**1** Analyze changes in long-term liabilities. The $547.00 decrease in Mortgage Payable represents a cash outflow.

**2** Analyze changes in cash identified on the statement of stockholders' equity. Snow Creek issued $40,000.00 of additional capital stock during the year. This activity resulted in a receipt of $40,000.00 from the issuance of 4,000 shares of capital stock at $10.00 per share. The sale of stock provides a source of cash. A cash dividend of $32,000.00 was paid during the year. The dividend payment represents a use of cash.

**3** Determine the cash provided by financing activities (if cash increases) or the cash used by investing activities (if cash decreases). Snow Creek's financing activities provided $7,453.00 in cash during the current year.

The statement of stockholders' equity also shows a change in Retained Earnings due to the net income of the business. Net income was the starting point for the analysis of changes in the operating activities of the business. Net income results from the operating activities of the business. Net income does not affect the financing activities of the business.

When calculating the cash flows from financing activities, it is beneficial to remember that:

- Increases in long-term liabilities and the issuance of stock generally result in cash inflows (*sources of cash*) that are added on the statement of cash flows.
- Decreases in long-term liabilities and the payment of cash dividends generally result in cash outflows (*uses of cash*) that are subtracted on the statement of cash flows.

## CALCULATE THE NET INCREASE OR DECREASE IN CASH

| | |
|---|---:|
| Cash used for operating activities (see page 540) | $(20,908.00) |
| Cash provided by investing activities (see page 543) | 9,320.00 |
| Cash provided by financing activities (see page 544) | 7,453.00 |
| Net change in cash | $ (4,135.00) |

The illustration above shows the total change in cash resulting from operating, investing, and financing activities. During the current year, Cash decreased by $4,135.00.

**REMEMBER** Financing activities involve debt or equity transactions.

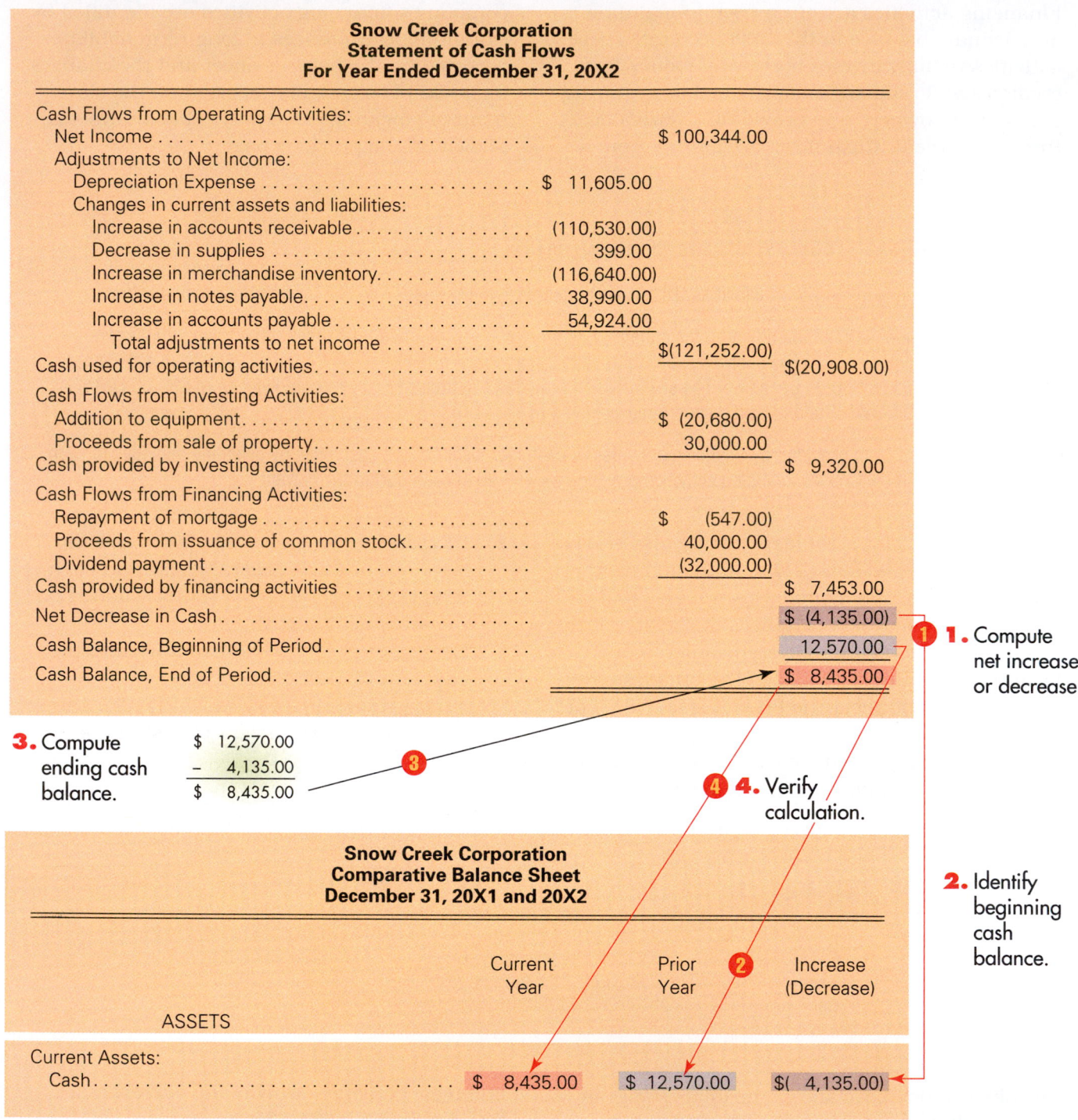

The completed statement of cash flows is shown above. The cash balances at the beginning and end of the period shown on the statement of cash flows must match the amounts shown on the comparative balance sheet.

# STEPS
## COMPLETING THE STATEMENT OF CASH FLOWS

1. Compute the net increase or decrease in Cash resulting from operating, investing, and financing activities.

2. Identify the beginning cash balance from the comparative balance sheet. The beginning cash balance for the current year is the ending cash balance from the prior year, $12,570.00.

3. Compute the ending cash balance, $8,435.00 ($12,570.00 – $4,135.00 decrease in cash).

4. Verify that the Cash Balance, End of Period matches the cash balance shown on the comparative balance sheet.

## CASH FLOW ANALYSIS SUMMARY

The intent of the statement of cash flows is to report and explain the sources and uses of a company's cash and to clarify changes in other account balances. In the case of Snow Creek Corporation, the statement of cash flows helps explain the difference between solid profits and a decrease in the cash account. Among other things, the large increases in accounts receivable and merchandise inventory (uses of cash) hampered Snow Creek's ability to pay its bills. Studying cash flows along with analyzing the income statement, statement of stockholders' equity, and the balance sheet provides a more accurate overview of a company's present and future financial condition.

©GETTY IMAGES/PHOTODISC

## audit your understanding

1. How are the cash flows resulting from a company's investing activities identified?

2. Why is an increase in accumulated depreciation on the balance sheet ignored when analyzing the cash flows from investing activities?

3. How are the cash flows originating from a company's financing activities identified?

4. How does an individual know if all cash transactions have been properly accounted for on the statement of cash flows?

AUDIT YOUR

## work together 18-3

**Preparing the investing and financing activities sections for the statement of cash flows; completing the statement of cash flows**

Use the working papers from Work Together 18-2. A comparative balance sheet and forms for analyzing changes in long-term assets, long-term liabilities, and stockholders' equity are provided in the *Working Papers*. Your instructor will guide you through the following examples.

1. Complete the changes in long-term assets and long-term liabilities form.

2. Prepare the investing activities section of the statement of cash flows.

3. Complete the changes in stockholders' equity form.

4. Prepare the financing activities section of the statement of cash flows.

5. Complete the statement of cash flows.

WORK TOGETHER • WORK TOGETHER

## on your own 18-3

**Preparing the investing and financing activities sections for the statement of cash flows; completing the statement of cash flows**

Use the working papers from On Your Own 18-2. A comparative balance sheet and forms for analyzing changes in long-term assets, long-term liabilities, and stockholders' equity are provided in the *Working Papers*. Work independently to complete the following problem.

1. Complete the changes in long-term assets and long-term liabilities form.

2. Prepare the investing activities section of the statement of cash flows.

3. Complete the changes in stockholders' equity form.

4. Prepare the financing activities section of the statement of cash flows.

5. Complete the statement of cash flows.

ON YOUR OWN • ON YOUR OWN • ON YOUR

**SUMMARY · SUMMARY · SUMMARY**

### After completing this chapter, you can

1. Define accounting terms related to cash flow analysis.

2. Identify accounting concepts and practices related to cash flow analysis.

3. Describe operating, investing, and financing activities and provide examples of each.

4. Prepare the operating activities section of a statement of cash flows.

5. Prepare the investing activities and financing activities sections of a statement of cash flows.

6. Prepare a statement of cash flows.

# Explore Accounting

EXPLORE ACCOUNTING · EXPLORE ACCOUNTING · EXPLORE ACCO

## FASB Statement No. 95

The development of generally accepted accounting principles (GAAP) is a political process. After researching an accounting issue, the Financial Accounting Standards Board (FASB) issues a proposal for a new principle in a Discussion Memorandum (DM). Interested individuals and companies submit comments about the DM to the FASB. The FASB considers their comments in producing its final statement.

A good example of this political process is FASB Statement No. 95, Statement of Cash Flows. The statement allows companies to use two methods to report cash flows from operating activities. Although the FASB recommends the direct method, most companies use the alternative indirect method. The indirect method, as illustrated in this textbook, begins with net income and makes adjustments for changes in current assets and liabilities. In contrast, the direct method reports each major class of cash receipts and cash payments, as illustrated below.

If the FASB encourages the use of the direct method, why do most companies use the indirect method? First, the indirect method was used for many years for preparing a similar statement that was required prior to FASB No. 95. Second, the

direct method requires more effort to obtain the information. Most of the information for an indirect method statement can be obtained from other financial statements. The direct method requires the company to obtain more detailed information directly from the general ledger.

**Required:**
Obtain a copy of FASB No. 95. Read the portion of the statement (paragraph 106-121) that presents the FASB's reasons for allowing companies to use either the indirect or direct methods. Do you agree with the FASB's reasons? Identify other accounting principles where two or more methods are allowed. Should alternative methods be allowed to report the same accounting information?

| Cash flows from operating activities: | |
| --- | --- |
| Cash received from customers | $670,000.00 |
| Cash paid to suppliers and employees | (540,000.00) |
| Interest paid | (34,000.00) |
| Income taxes paid | (29,000.00) |
| Net cash provided by operating activities | $ 67,000.00 |

# 18-1 APPLICATION PROBLEM
### Classifying cash flows

The following business transactions represent selected cash receipts (cash inflows) and cash payments (cash outflows) of Ridge Development Corporation.

a. dividend payment
b. payment of insurance premium
c. receipts from the signing of a note payable
d. payment of payroll taxes
e. cash purchase of computer equipment
f. sale of treasury stock
g. receipts from consulting services

**Instructions:**

Use the form provided in the *Working Papers* to identify each transaction as (1) a cash inflow or cash outflow and (2) as an operating, investing, or financing activity.

# 18-2 APPLICATION PROBLEM
### Calculating the cash flows from operating activities

The following information was taken from the financial statements of Flexcor Corporation on December 31 of the current year. The comparative income statement of Flexcor Corporation reveals the following net income and depreciation expense for the current year.

Net income          $91,460.00
Depreciation expense   12,500.00

The comparative balance sheet of Flexcor Corporation lists the following current assets and current liabilities and their ending balances for the current and prior years.

|                              | Current Year | Prior Year  |
| ---------------------------- | ------------ | ----------- |
| Accounts Receivable (book value) | $ 55,515.00 | $ 48,000.00 |
| Merchandise Inventory        | 118,316.00   | 121,000.00  |
| Supplies                     | 6,148.00     | 5,500.00    |
| Accounts Payable             | 49,762.00    | 44,000.00   |

**Instructions:**

1. In the forms provided in the *Working Papers*, record the appropriate amount for net income. Indicate if this item represents a source of cash or use of cash.
2. Record the appropriate amount for depreciation expense. Indicate if this item represents a source of cash or use of cash.
3. For each current asset and current liability, write the balances for the current year and prior year. Classify each account as a current asset or current liability. Compute the amount of increase or decrease from the prior year. Indicate if the increase or decrease represents a source of cash or a use of cash.
4. Using the information collected, prepare the cash flows from operating activities section of the statement of cash flows for the current year ending December 31. Save your work to complete Application Problem 18-3.

# 18-3 APPLICATION PROBLEM

## Calculating the cash flows from investing activities

Use the statement of cash flows started in Application Problem 18-2. The comparative balance sheet of Flexcor Corporation lists the following long-term assets and their ending balances for the current and prior years.

|  | Current Year | Prior Year |
|---|---|---|
| Office equipment | $ 22,800.00 | $ 12,500.00 |
| Office furniture | 12,210.00 | 9,000.00 |
| Land (decrease due to sale) | 100,000.00 | 140,000.00 |

**Instructions:**

1. For each account, write the balances for the current year and prior year. Compute the amount of increase or decrease from the prior year. Indicate if the increase or decrease represents a source of cash or a use of cash.
2. Using the statement of cash flows started in Application Problem 18-2, prepare the Cash Flows from Investing Activities section of the statement of cash flows. Save your work to complete Application Problem 18-4.

# 18-4 APPLICATION PROBLEM  QUICKBOOKS

## Calculating the cash flows from financing activities and completing a statement of cash flows

Use the statement of cash flows started in Application Problem 18-2. The comparative balance sheet of Flexcor Corporation lists the following long-term liability and its ending balance for the current and prior years.

|  | Current Year | Prior Year |
|---|---|---|
| Mortgage payable | $80,100.00 | $92,000.00 |

The comparative statement of stockholders' equity of Flexcor Corporation reveals the following stock and dividend information for the current year.

| | |
|---|---|
| Sale of additional common stock | 20,000.00 |
| Payment of cash dividend | 50,000.00 |

**Instructions:**

1. For the long-term liability, record the amount of increase or decrease from the prior year. Indicate if the increase or decrease represents a source of cash or a use of cash.
2. For each amount taken from the comparative statement of stockholders' equity, record the appropriate amount. Indicate if these activities represent a source of cash or use of cash.
3. Using the statement of cash flows started in Application Problem 18-2, prepare the cash flows from financing activities section of the statement of cash flows.
4. Compute the net increase or decrease resulting from operating, investing, and financing activities.
5. Record the cash balance for the beginning of the period in the form provided. Flexcor started the year with a beginning cash balance of $67,930.00.
6. Compute the cash balance for the end of the fiscal period by adding the amount of increase or decrease in cash and the beginning cash amount.
7. Complete the statement of cash flows for Flexcor Corporation by entering the net increase or decrease in cash, the beginning cash balance, and the ending cash balance.
8. Verify the accuracy of the statement of cash flows by comparing the statement's ending cash balance with the cash balance of $156,763.00 listed for the current year on Flexcor's comparative balance sheet.

## 18-5 MASTERY PROBLEM
### Preparing a statement of cash flows

Use the abbreviated comparative financial statements for West Coast Construction, Inc. in the *Working Papers.*

**Instructions:**

1. Review the comparative income statement and identify the amounts of net income (or net loss) and depreciation expense for the period. Indicate if each item represents a source of cash or use of cash.
2. Analyze the comparative balance sheet and complete the following steps:
   a. Prepare a list of current assets and current liabilities.
   b. Write the balances for the current year and prior year.
   c. Classify each account as a current asset or current liability.
   d. Compute the amount of increase or decrease from the prior year.
   e. Indicate if the increase or decrease represents a source of cash or a use of cash.
3. Analyze the comparative balance sheet and complete the following steps:
   a. Prepare a list of long-term assets.
   b. Write the balances for the current year and prior year.
   c. Compute the amount of increase or decrease from the prior year.
   d. Indicate if the increase or decrease represents a source of cash or a use of cash.
4. Reexamine the comparative balance sheet and complete the following steps:
   a. Prepare a list of long-term liabilities.
   b. Compute the amount of increase or decrease from the prior year.
   c. Indicate if the increase or decrease represents a source of cash or a use of cash.
5. Review the comparative statement of stockholders' equity and (1) identify the amounts of any additional stock issued or cash dividends paid and (2) indicate if each item represents a source of cash or use of cash.
6. Prepare the operating, investing, and financing activities sections of a statement of cash flows.
7. Enter the cash balance at the beginning of the year as shown on the comparative balance sheet.
8. Compute the cash balance for the end of the period to complete the statement of cash flows.
9. Verify the accuracy of the statement of cash flows by comparing the statement's ending cash balance with the cash balance listed for the current year on West Coast's comparative balance sheet

## 18-6 CHALLENGE PROBLEM
### Preparing a statement of cash flows

Use the abbreviated comparative financial statements for Pacific Digital Corporation in the *Working Papers.* The comparative balance sheet for Pacific Digital Corporation lists an intangible asset, Patents. The patents were granted in the first year of the business's existence. Intangible assets like Patents are written off as an expense over a period of years. Although the expense is recognized on the income statement under the accrual basis of accounting, it does not involve an outflow of cash. The cash was actually spent in an earlier period. Since the amortized patent expense shown on Pacific Digital's comparative income statement does not use cash, it is handled the same way as depreciation expense. Both patents and depreciation expense are adjustments to net income (or net loss) and presented before changes in current assets and liabilities.

**Instructions:**

Prepare a statement of cash flows for the current year for Pacific Digital Corporation.

## applied communication

You are the President of a non-profit organization that has grown quickly over the last few years. For the first time, you have had an independent accountant audit your financial records. Upon the recommendation of the accountant, your staff has begun preparing a statement of cash flows.

The organization is overseen by a volunteer board of directors. They meet monthly to review the financial stability of the organization and to assist management in developing long-range plans. At each meeting, you present the financial statements from the previous month.

**Required:**

Since most of the members of your board are not familiar with the statement of cash flows, prepare a short explanation of the purpose and use of the statement.

## case for critical thinking

Techmart Corporation is a young start-up firm that produces components for high-resolution televisions. During the last two years, sales have grown dramatically. Currently, Techmart is experiencing a cash shortage and is having difficulty purchasing manufacturing supplies and meeting its weekly payroll. Lately, the company has not been very successful in collecting its accounts receivable. The company offers its clients 90 days to pay on all receivables and does not understand why there is a shortage of cash. What suggestions can you offer the president of Techmart regarding its collection policy? Explain your recommendations. What can Techmart do during the short run to overcome its shortage of cash?

## SCANS workplace competency

**Resource Competency:** Allocating Human Resources

**Concept:** Successful supervisors can assess an employee's job knowledge and skill base, distribute work accordingly, evaluate performance, and provide feedback.

**Application:** You are the manager of a small manufacturing firm. Employees must be at their stations before the production line can start each morning. One employee, Beth Stewart, is often 10–20 minutes late to work. Consequently, production is delayed. How might you counsel this employee to eliminate her tardiness? She is a good employee who has worked for the firm for 10 years. Write out your response.

## • auditing for errors

DuWayne Streitman, a newly hired accountant, has prepared the following statement of cash flows. DuWayne has asked you to examine his statement because the ending cash balance does not equal the balance of cash. Prepare a list of any errors you identify in the statement and calculate the correct ending cash balance.

**Maher Products, Inc.**
**Statement of Cash Flows**
**December 31, 20--**

| | | | |
|---|---:|---:|---:|
| Cash Flows from Operating Activities: | | | |
| Net Income | | 92,000.00 | |
| Adjustments to Net Income: | | | |
| Depreciation Expense | 124,000.00 | | |
| Changes in current assets and liabilities: | | | |
| Decrease in accounts receivable | (2,150.00) | | |
| Increase in supplies | 4,800.00 | | |
| Decrease in merchandise inventory | (21,500.00) | | |
| Decrease in notes payable | (3,100.00) | | |
| Increase in account payable | 4,850.00 | | |
| Total adjustments to net income | | 106,900.00 | |
| Cash provided by operating activities | | | 198,900.00 |
| Cash Flows from Investing Activities: | | | |
| Addition to equipment | | (15,800.00) | |
| Repayment of mortgage | | 13,500.00 | |
| Proceeds from sale of property | | 33,600.00 | |
| Cash provided by investing activities | | | 31,300.00 |
| Cash Flows from Financing Activities: | | | |
| Proceeds from issuance of common stock | | (10,000.00) | |
| Dividend payment | | 62,000.00 | |
| Cash provided by financing activities | | | 52,000.00 |
| Net Increase in Cash | | | 282,200.00 |
| Cash Balance, Beginning of Period | | | 24,500.00 |
| Cash Balance, End of Period | | | 257,700.00 |

## • analyzing Costco's financial statements

Investors often evaluate the investing activities section of the statement of cash flows to measure the future growth of a company. A company that is investing in plant assets is more likely to generate sales growth and earn a higher level of net income.

**Instructions:**

1. Use the statement of cash flows on page B-8 of Appendix B in this textbook. Identify the cash expended on new property and equipment from 2001 to 2003.

2. Does Costco's statement of cash flows support the reported growth in the number of warehouses?

## Using the Savings Planner

### Planning Tools

Planning tools are easy-to-use applications for producing results for different types of financial investments. *Automated Accounting 8.0* and higher includes five such tools located on the different tabs included on the Planning Tools screen.

### Savings Planner

The Savings Planner is similar to the loan planner introduced in the Automated Accounting section of Chapter 11. The Savings Planner is used to perform one of three calculations:

1. The monthly contribution required to meet a target ending savings balance

2. The ending savings balance of a series of contributions

3. The number of months required to meet a specified ending savings balance

One of the calculations is chosen from the Calculate box. The item to be calculated appears grayed (or dimmed). Enter the other items and the planner will make the calculation. For example, Andrew Ruiz is saving money to pay for his living expenses at college. He places $500.00 in a money market account. He plans to add $50.00 a month. Interest is earned on the account at the rate of 6.5%. How much will Andrew have at the end of three years (36 months)? Using the Savings Planner to make the calculation, Andrew will have $2,588.92 at the end of three years, as shown here.

### The Savings Planner Report

A report of the findings may be displayed or printed. Click the Report button to display the report. Click the Print button from the Savings Plan report display to print it.

### Using Special Tools: The Savings Planner

**Instructions:**

1. Load *Automated Accounting 8.0* or higher software.

2. Select New from the File menu.

3. Click on the Tools toolbar button.

4. Click on the Savings Planner tab. Select Number of Months from the Calculate box. Enter a beginning balance of $250.00. Enter an Annual Yield of 7%. Enter a Monthly Contribution of $100.00 and an Ending Savings Balance of $2,000.00. How many months are required for the savings balance to reach $2,000.00?

5. Click on the Report command button from within the Savings Planner tab. Print the report, or copy it to the clipboard for entering into a word processor or spreadsheet application.

6. Click Close or press ESC to return to the planner. Steps 4 and 5 may then be repeated for different calculation options, or for different data sets.

7. Click Close or press ESC to exit the planner. Upon exiting a planning tool, your data will not be saved. Be sure to print a report, or copy it to a word processor or spreadsheet and save it in that application.

8. Exit the Automated Accounting software.

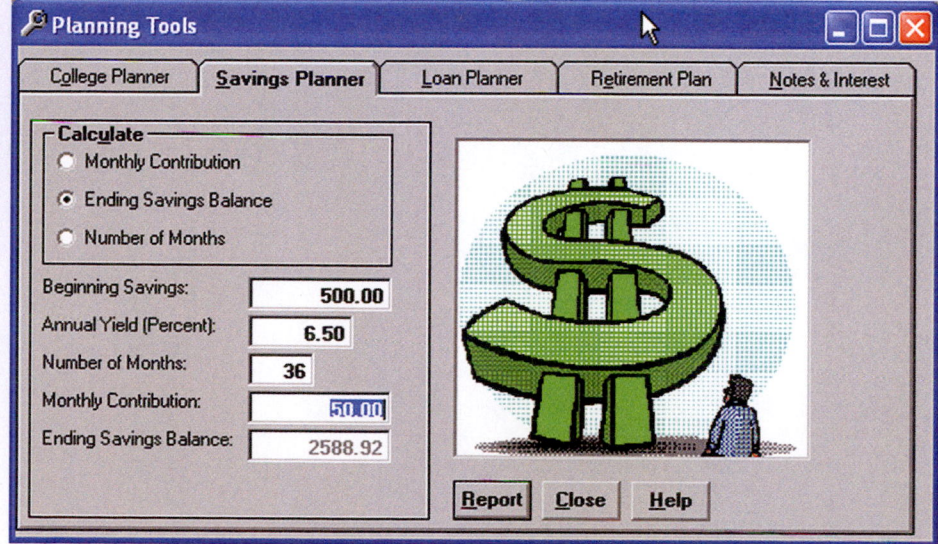

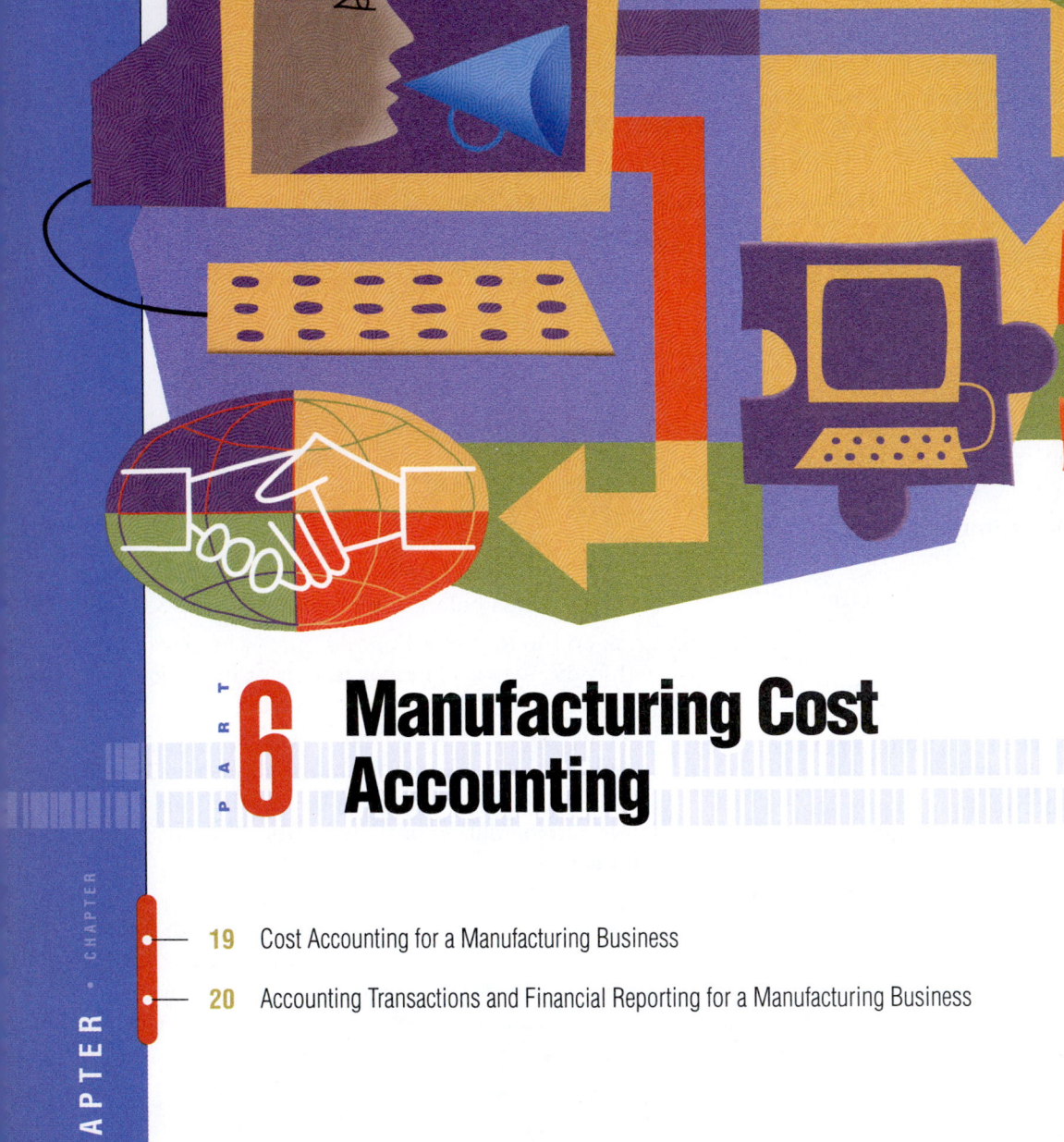

CHAPTER · CHAPTER · CHAPTER · CHAPTER

# PART 6 Manufacturing Cost Accounting

## FAXAVISION, INC.
## CHART OF ACCOUNTS

**Balance Sheet Accounts**

**(1000) ASSETS**
1100 CURRENT ASSETS
1105 Cash
1110 Petty Cash
1115 Accounts Receivable
1120 Allowance for Uncollectible Accounts
1125 Materials
1130 Work in Process
1135 Finished Goods
1140 Supplies—Factory
1145 Supplies—Sales
1150 Supplies—Administrative
1155 Prepaid Insurance
1200 PLANT ASSETS
1205 Factory Equipment
1210 Accumulated Depreciation—Factory Equipment
1215 Office Equipment
1220 Accumulated Depreciation—Office Equipment
1225 Store Equipment
1230 Accumulated Depreciation—Store Equipment
1235 Building

1240 Accumulated Depreciation—Building
1245 Land

**(2000) LIABILITIES**
2100 CURRENT LIABILITIES
2105 Accounts Payable
2110 Employee Income Tax Payable
2115 Federal Income Tax Payable
2120 Social Security Tax Payable
2123 Medicare Tax Payable
2125 Salaries Payable
2130 Unemployment Tax Payable—Federal
2135 Unemployment Tax Payable—State
2140 Dividends Payable
2200 LONG-TERM LIABILITY
2205 Mortgage Payable

**(3000) STOCKHOLDERS' EQUITY**
3105 Capital Stock
3110 Retained Earnings
3115 Dividends
3120 Income Summary

**Income Statement Accounts**

**(4000) OPERATING REVENUE**
4105 Sales

**(5000) COST OF SALES**
5105 Cost of Goods Sold

**(5500) MANUFACTURING COSTS**
5505 Factory Overhead
5510 Depreciation Expense—Factory Equipment
5515 Depreciation Expense—Building
5520 Heat, Light, and Power Expense
5525 Insurance Expense—Factory
5530 Miscellaneous Expense—Factory
5535 Payroll Taxes Expense—Factory
5540 Property Tax Expense—Factory
5545 Supplies Expense—Factory

**(6000) OPERATING EXPENSES**
6100 SELLING EXPENSES
6105 Advertising Expense
6110 Delivery Expense
6115 Depreciation Expense—Store Equipment
6120 Miscellaneous Expense—Sales
6125 Salary Expense—Sales
6130 Supplies Expense—Sales
6200 ADMINISTRATIVE EXPENSES
6205 Depreciation Expense—Office Equipment
6210 Insurance Expense—Administrative
6215 Miscellaneous Expense—Administrative
6220 Payroll Taxes Expense—Administrative
6225 Property Tax Expense—Administrative
6230 Salary Expense—Administrative
6235 Supplies Expense—Administrative
6240 Uncollectible Accounts Expense
6245 Utilities Expense—Administrative

**(7000) OTHER REVENUE**
7105 Gain on Plant Assets
7110 Miscellaneous Revenue

**(8000) OTHER EXPENSES**
8105 Interest Expense
8110 Loss on Plant Assets

**(9000) INCOME TAX**
9105 Federal Income Tax Expense

The chart of accounts for FaxaVision, Inc., is illustrated above for ready reference as you study Chapters 19 and 20 of this textbook.

# CHAPTER 19 Cost Accounting for a Manufacturing Business

**After studying Chapter 19, you will be able to:**

1. Define accounting terms related to cost accounting for a manufacturing business.

2. Identify accounting concepts and practices related to cost accounting for a manufacturing business.

3. Identify the elements of manufacturing costs: (1) direct materials, (2) direct labor, and (3) factory overhead.

4. Identify the flow of costs through the manufacturing process.

5. Prepare selected ledgers and cost sheets for a manufacturing business.

- direct materials
- direct labor
- factory overhead
- indirect materials

- indirect labor
- work in process
- finished goods
- materials ledger

- cost ledger
- finished goods ledger
- applied overhead

Point Your Browser
accountingxtra.swlearning.com

558

# • Hershey

©TIM SHAFFER/REUTERS/LANDOV

## THE WONDERFUL WORLD OF HERSHEY

Milton S. Hershey began his career as an apprentice to a candy maker in Lancaster, Pennsylvania. After a brief attempt to operate his own candy shop, he traveled to Denver, Colorado, where he learned the importance of fresh ingredients in the production of caramel. In 1886, he returned home to establish the Lancaster Caramel Company, the forerunner of today's Hershey Foods Corporation.

Mr. Hershey located his chocolate manufacturing operation in the heart of Pennsylvania's dairy country. A plentiful supply of fresh milk was a critical ingredient in the success of the company. Peanuts, cocoa, and milk are the primary raw materials in the production of Hershey products today. Equipment, labor, and packaging are just a few of the other items also included in the cost of the products.

Mr. Hershey believed that an individual is morally obligated to share the fruits of success with others. These beliefs led him to establish important components of the town that bears his name, including a bank, department store, park, churches, zoo, and a trolley system to transport workers from nearby communities. During the Great Depression, Mr. Hershey kept men at work constructing a hotel, community building, and sports arena. The Milton Hershey School continues to provide education for nearly 1,100 children whose lives have been disrupted.

### Critical Thinking

1. What are the advantages of locating a manufacturing operation near a primary source of raw materials?
2. Do you believe Mr. Hershey's support of the community affected the success of his business?

Source: www.hersheys.com/about/milton.shtml

Xtra!
Today
accountingxtra.swlearning.com

## internet activity

### MANUFACTURING INVENTORY ACCOUNTS

Manufacturing companies use different inventory accounts than merchandising businesses do.

### Instructions

Use the Internet to access the annual reports of two manufacturing companies. Using either the financial statements or the accompanying notes to the financial statements, answer the following questions for each company.

1. What three types of inventories are included in the heading "Inventories" on the balance sheet?
2. For each of the three types of inventories, calculate what percentage it is of the total inventories.

# 19-1 Elements of Manufacturing Cost

The three general types of businesses are service, merchandising, and manufacturing. Service businesses provide a needed service for their customers. Examples of service business are accounting firms, law firms, and medical practices.

Merchandising businesses sell products to customers. A merchandising business purchases products and, without changing the products' forms, sells those products to customers. Department stores and grocery stores are examples of merchandising businesses.

A manufacturing business buys materials and uses labor and machinery to change the materials into a finished product. A manufacturing business generally sells the finished product to a merchandising business, which then sells the product to customers.

FaxaVision, Inc., a facsimile manufacturing business, buys modems, print motors, cutter assemblies, document sensors, and other materials. Using labor and machinery, FaxaVision combines the materials to make facsimile machines, commonly referred to as fax machines. Merchandising businesses buy the fax machines from FaxaVision for resale to customers.

A service business needs to know the cost of providing services to be able to calculate net income. A merchandising business needs to know the cost of merchandise sold to calculate net income. For the same reason, a manufacturing company needs to know the costs required to produce finished products that it sells. To know how much finished products cost, FaxaVision keeps records of all costs involved in making the products.

## making ethical decisions

### Occupational Fraud

Despite its best efforts, a company will have employees who will demonstrate unethical behavior. In fact, many employees will steal cash, inventory, and other items of value from their employers. The use of one's employment for personal gain through the deliberate misuse of company resources is called *occupational fraud*. The Association of Certified Fraud Examiners estimates that 6% of revenues are lost to occupational fraud. Fraud reduces the wages available to pay workers and limits stockholders' return on their investment.

Auditors and managers need an understanding of the most common forms of occupational fraud. Knowing how these frauds are committed enables auditors and managers to search for signs or "red flags" of fraud. Early detection of a fraud substantially reduces the loss incurred.

#### Instructions
Access the *Report to the Nation* of the Association of Certified Fraud Examiners. Identify and explain the five most common fraudulent disbursements.

## THREE COST ELEMENTS

The manufacturing cost of any finished product includes three cost elements: (1) direct materials, (2) direct labor, and (3) factory overhead.

### Direct Materials

Materials that are of significant value in the cost of a finished product and that become an identifiable part of the product are called **direct materials**. Direct materials include all items used in the manufacturing process that have sufficient value to justify charging the cost directly to the product. [CONCEPT: Materiality] The materiality concept states that business activities creating dollar amounts large enough to affect business decisions should be recorded and reported as separate items in accounting records and financial statements. Dollar amounts that are small and not considered important in decision making may be combined with other amounts in the accounting records and financial statements. For example, modems and print motors used to manufacture fax machines are considered direct materials and accounted for separately. Connectors and gears used in the manufacture of fax machines are parts with a small enough dollar value that they are grouped together and only their total value is recorded in the accounting records.

### Direct Labor

Salaries of factory workers who make a product are called **direct labor**. Direct labor includes salaries only of persons working directly on a product. Salaries of supervisors, maintenance workers, and others whose efforts do not apply directly to the manufacture of a product are not considered to be direct labor.

### Factory Overhead

All expenses other than direct materials and direct labor that apply to making products are called **factory overhead**. Some materials used in manufacturing a product cost a very small amount for each unit produced. Materials used in the completion of a product that are of insignificant value to justify accounting for separately are called **indirect materials**. Indirect materials may include items such as glue, solder, bolts, and rivets. Materials and supplies used by the factory such as cleaning supplies and lubricants for the machinery are also classified as indirect materials.

Some factory workers devote their time to supervisory, clerical, and maintenance tasks necessary to operate the factory. Such workers include time clerks, supervisors, maintenance people, receiving clerks, and inspectors. Salaries paid to factory workers who are not actually making products are called **indirect labor**.

Other costs are also incurred in the manufacturing process. (1) Depreciation of factory buildings and equipment. (2) Repairs to factory buildings and equipment. (3) Insurance on building, equipment, and stock. (4) Taxes on property owned. (5) Heat, light, and power. All of these expenses, along with indirect materials and indirect labor, make up factory overhead.

## INVENTORIES FOR A MANUFACTURING BUSINESS

A merchandising business normally has one general ledger account for merchandise inventory. However, a manufacturing business has three inventory accounts related to the products manufactured. (1) Materials. (2) Work in Process. (3) Finished Goods. These accounts are classified as current assets of FaxaVision, Inc.

A materials inventory account shows the costs of materials on hand that have not yet been used in making a product. Products that are being manufactured but are not yet complete are called **work in process**. A work in process inventory account, therefore, shows all costs that have been spent on products that are not yet complete. Manufactured products that are fully completed are called **finished goods**. A finished goods inventory account, therefore, shows the cost of completed products still on hand and unsold.

## COST RECORDS

Manufacturing businesses keep detailed cost records for three purposes. (1) To determine accurate costs for each product made. (2) To provide specific cost information to managers who must identify high cost areas so that corrective action can be taken. (3) To provide cost summary information for journal entries.

### Subsidiary Cost Ledgers

Three subsidiary ledgers provide the detailed cost information for the three manufacturing inventory accounts.

1. **Materials Ledger.** FaxaVision uses a perpetual inventory system for direct and indirect materials. A perpetual inventory record provides detailed cost information about each type of material. A ledger containing all records of materials is called a **materials ledger.**

2. **Cost Ledger.** FaxaVision keeps a record of all charges for direct materials, direct labor, and factory overhead for each job. The record is known as a cost sheet. A cost sheet is maintained for each manufacturing job. A ledger containing all cost sheets for products in the process of being manufactured is called a **cost ledger.**

3. **Finished Goods Ledger.** The company keeps a record of each kind of finished good to provide a perpetual inventory of each product produced and its cost. A ledger containing records of all finished goods on hand is called a **finished goods ledger.** This ledger is similar to a materials ledger.

Journal entries for job costs are described in Chapter 20.

## MANUFACTURING COST FLOWS

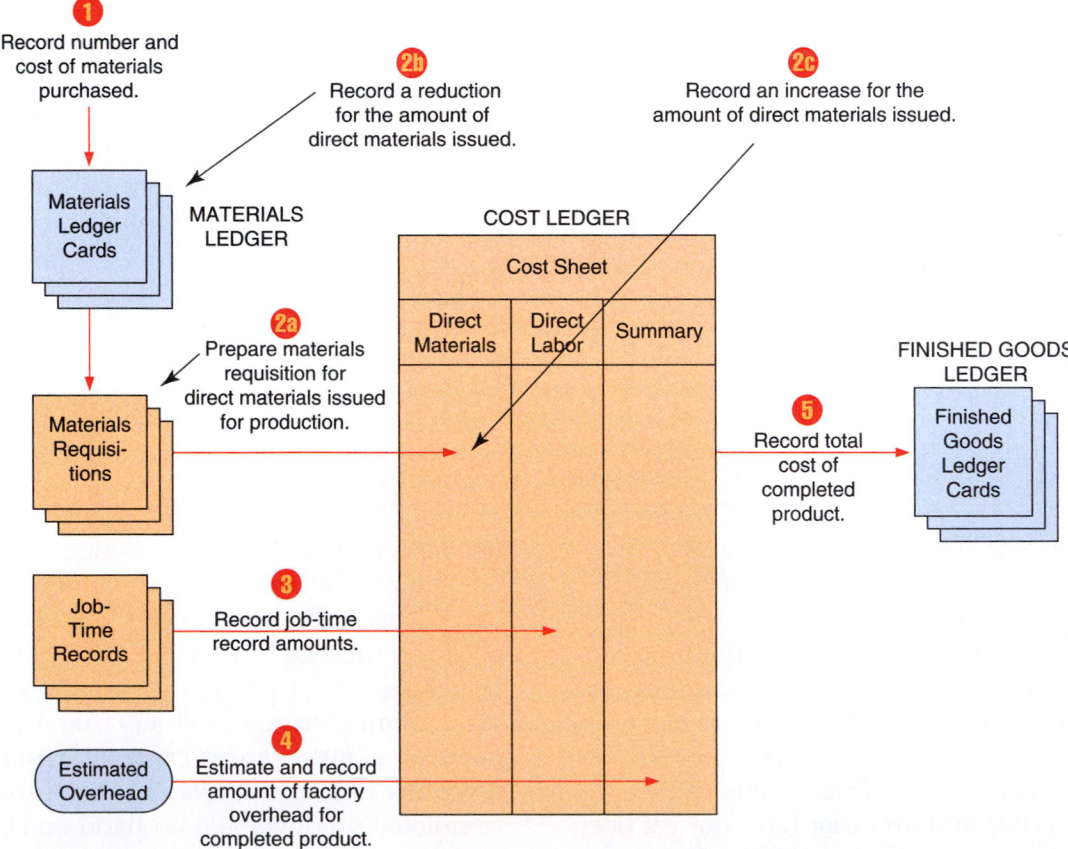

Manufacturing costs are recorded on cost forms as costs occur. The forms used and the sequence of steps followed for recording FaxaVision's manufacturing costs are shown above.

## RECORDING MANUFACTURING COSTS

**1** Record the number and cost of each kind of material purchased on materials ledger cards. This step is performed for both direct and indirect materials.

**2** Prepare a materials requisition to use when direct materials are issued for use in the factory. The amount of direct materials issued is recorded as a reduction on the materials ledger card and an increase in the Direct Materials column of the cost sheet.

**3** Prepare job-time records when direct labor is used. Time record amounts are recorded in the Direct Labor column of the cost sheet.

**4** Estimate and record the amount of factory overhead when a product is completed. The amount of factory overhead is recorded in the Summary column of the cost sheet. Estimating factory overhead is described later in this chapter.

**5** Total all costs on the cost sheet when a product is completed. Transfer the total to a finished goods ledger card.

# Explore Accounting

EXPLORE ACCOUNTING • EXPLORE ACCOUNTING • EXPLORE ACCOUNTING

## Activity-Based Costing

From the beginning of the Industrial Revolution in the mid-1800s, direct labor was a major component of manufacturing costs. Factory overhead costs, such as building depreciation, utilities, maintenance, and insurance, were costs incurred to provide workers with a safe and clean environment in which to work. As a result, it was natural for early accountants to allocate these factory overhead costs based on the direct labor (dollars or hours) incurred to manufacture a product.

Many of today's automated manufacturing processes involve little, if any, direct labor. Thus, accountants had to develop a new method for allocating factory overhead. One popular method requires accountants to identify significant activities in the manufacturing process. Allocating factory overhead based on the level of significant activities is referred to as *activity-based costing (ABC)*.

For example, the production of a pizza at a local pizza parlor involves two significant activities: assembling the ingredients and cooking the pizza. The first activity involves direct labor, but the second activity involves only cooking time in the oven. In contrast, the production of a sub sandwich involves three times as much direct labor as a pizza but no cooking in the oven. If factory overhead were applied based solely on

direct labor, the sub sandwich would improperly receive three times as much overhead cost as the pizza.

Using ABC, the accountant recognizes that a significant amount of overhead costs of the pizza parlor results from the ovens: the cost of the ovens, heating the ovens, and cooling the kitchen from the heat that escapes from the ovens. These overhead costs should be allocated to those products that require cooking. Thus, factory overhead costs related to the ovens would be applied to pizza production based on cooking time.

ABC is also used by service businesses to determine the cost of providing various services. ABC results in more accurate estimates on the cost of producing individual products and services. Managers can use this information to assist them in making better business decisions, such as the sales price of its products and the profitability of different product lines.

**Critical Thinking:** The challenge of implementing ABC is to match costs with related activities that are easy to measure. Identify the measurable activities in two different lawn maintenance services: mowing a lawn and cutting down a tree.

## terms review

TERMS REVIEW • TERMS REVIEW

direct materials
direct labor
factory overhead
indirect materials
indirect labor
work in process
finished goods
materials ledger
cost ledger
finished goods ledger

## audit your understanding

AUDIT YOUR UNDERSTANDING

1. What are the three manufacturing cost elements of a finished product?
2. What term is used to describe products that are being manufactured but are not yet complete?
3. What is the purpose of a cost sheet?

## work together 19-1

WORK TOGETHER • WORK TOGETHER

### Classifying manufacturing costs; specifying the ledger used for initial recording

An analysis sheet for Gutman's Gutters, a firm that manufactures aluminum and steel gutters, is included in the *Working Papers*. Your instructor will guide you through the following examples.

1. For each of the following costs, determine whether the cost should be classified as direct materials, direct labor, or factory overhead.
2. Specify the subsidiary ledger (materials ledger, cost ledger, finished goods ledger) in which the cost is first recorded. Save your work to complete On Your Own 19-1 below.
   a. Wages earned by an employee working on the production of gutters.
   b. Aluminum used in the production of gutters.
   c. The rent expense of the factory in which the gutters are made.
   d. A cleaning solvent used to clean production machinery.
   e. Fringe benefits received by an employee working on the production of gutters.

## on your own 19-1

ON YOUR OWN • ON YOUR OWN

### Classifying manufacturing costs; specifying the ledger used for initial recording

Use the working papers from Work Together 19-1 above. Work independently to complete the following problem.

1. For each of the following costs, determine whether the cost should be classified as direct materials, direct labor, or factory overhead.
2. Specify the subsidiary ledger (materials ledger, cost ledger, finished goods ledger) in which the cost is first recorded.
   a. Rivets used in the production of gutters.
   b. Wages earned by a maintenance employee.
   c. The property taxes of the factory.
   d. Fringe benefits of the factory supervisor.
   e. Wages earned by an employee who inspects finished gutters before they leave the factory.

# 19-2 Maintaining Manufacturing Records

## RECORDS FOR MATERIALS

**1.** Open a materials ledger card.

**2.** Record orders placed.

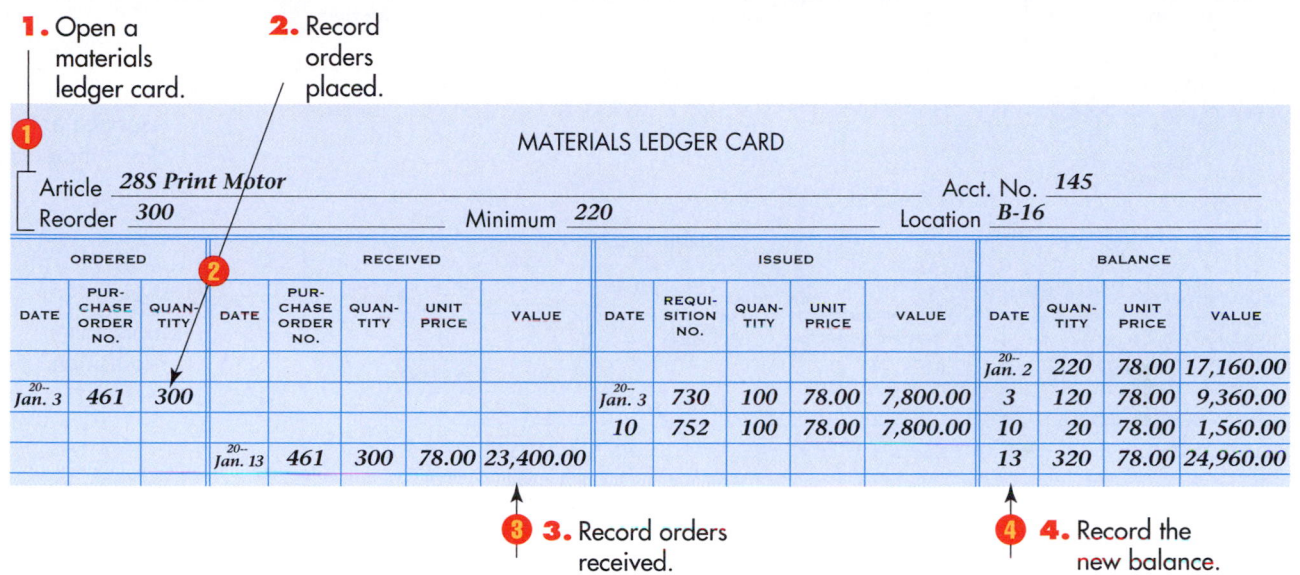

**MATERIALS LEDGER CARD**

Article _28S Print Motor_    Acct. No. _145_
Reorder _300_    Minimum _220_    Location _B-16_

| ORDERED | | | RECEIVED | | | | | ISSUED | | | | | BALANCE | | | |
|---|---|---|---|---|---|---|---|---|---|---|---|---|---|---|---|---|
| DATE | PUR-CHASE ORDER NO. | QUAN-TITY | DATE | PUR-CHASE ORDER NO. | QUAN-TITY | UNIT PRICE | VALUE | DATE | REQUI-SITION NO. | QUAN-TITY | UNIT PRICE | VALUE | DATE | QUAN-TITY | UNIT PRICE | VALUE |
| | | | | | | | | | | | | | 20--<br>Jan. 2 | 220 | 78.00 | 17,160.00 |
| 20--<br>Jan. 3 | 461 | 300 | | | | | | 20--<br>Jan. 3 | 730 | 100 | 78.00 | 7,800.00 | 3 | 120 | 78.00 | 9,360.00 |
| | | | | | | | | 10 | 752 | 100 | 78.00 | 7,800.00 | 10 | 20 | 78.00 | 1,560.00 |
| | | | 20--<br>Jan. 13 | 461 | 300 | 78.00 | 23,400.00 | | | | | | 13 | 320 | 78.00 | 24,960.00 |

**3.** Record orders received.

**4.** Record the new balance.

A manufacturing business keeps a record of materials used in the manufacturing process. The business should have on hand sufficient materials so that the manufacturing process will not be interrupted. However, too large a stock of materials requires needless investment in inventory. To provide a perpetual inventory and detailed cost information about materials, Faxa-Vision keeps a materials ledger card for each type of material. A materials ledger card is shown above.

## STEPS

### OPENING A MATERIALS LEDGER CARD AND RECORDING MATERIALS ORDERED

1. Open a materials ledger card for each type of material kept in the storeroom.
   a. Enter the name and account number of the item.
   b. Determine and record the reorder quantity and minimum quantities to be kept in stock. When the number on hand equals the minimum, the materials clerk notifies the purchasing agent to place a new order.

2. Record the date of an order, _Jan. 3_, the purchase order number, _461_, and the quantity ordered, _300_, in the Ordered columns. The data are recorded from a purchase order. The purchase order authorizes a seller to deliver goods with payment to be made later. The order was placed because the quantity on hand, 220 units, equaled the minimum level at which a new order is placed. Note that the quantity ordered equals the reorder quantity shown at the top of the ledger card.

3. When the items ordered are received, record the date, _Jan. 13_, the purchase order number, _461_, the quantity, _300_, the unit price, _78.00_, and the total value of the order, _23,400.00_, in the Received columns of the materials ledger card. The total value is the quantity, 300, multiplied by the unit price, $78.00.

4. Add the quantity and value to the previous balances and extend the amounts to the Balance columns.

Notice that the materials ledger card also shows items that have been issued. The issuing of materials will be discussed later in the chapter. The total value for all the materials ledger cards equals the balance of the materials general ledger account.

The relationship of the general ledger accounts to the forms and ledgers described in this chapter is explained in Chapter 20.

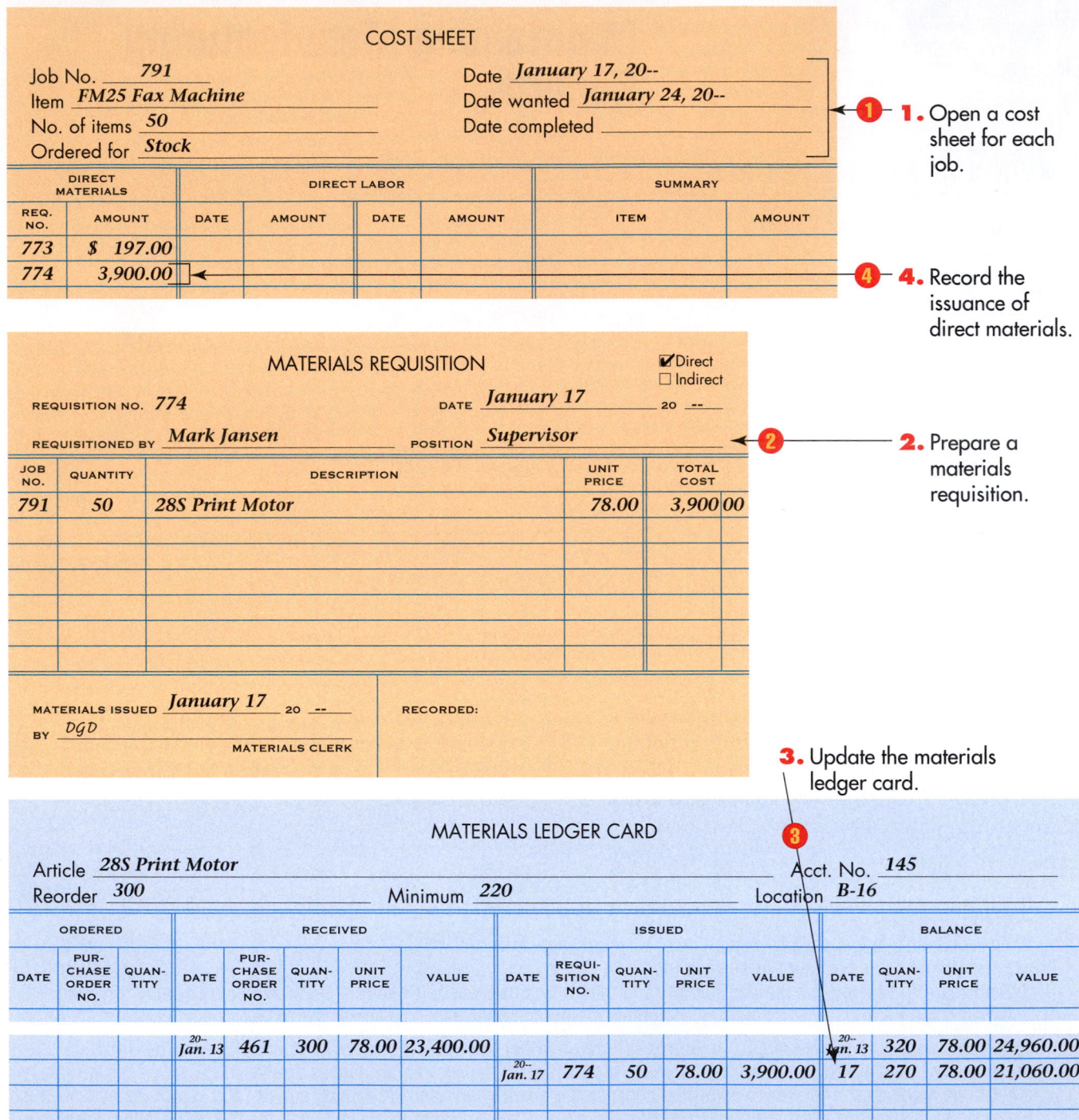

**COST SHEET**

Job No. **791**  Date **January 17, 20--**
Item **FM25 Fax Machine**  Date wanted **January 24, 20--**
No. of items **50**  Date completed _____
Ordered for **Stock**

| DIRECT MATERIALS | | DIRECT LABOR | | | | SUMMARY | |
|---|---|---|---|---|---|---|---|
| REQ. NO. | AMOUNT | DATE | AMOUNT | DATE | AMOUNT | ITEM | AMOUNT |
| 773 | $ 197.00 | | | | | | |
| 774 | 3,900.00 | | | | | | |

**1.** Open a cost sheet for each job.

**4.** Record the issuance of direct materials.

**MATERIALS REQUISITION**  ☑ Direct  ☐ Indirect

REQUISITION NO. **774**  DATE **January 17**  20 **--**
REQUISITIONED BY **Mark Jansen**  POSITION **Supervisor**

| JOB NO. | QUANTITY | DESCRIPTION | UNIT PRICE | TOTAL COST |
|---|---|---|---|---|
| 791 | 50 | 28S Print Motor | 78.00 | 3,900 00 |
| | | | | |
| | | | | |
| | | | | |
| | | | | |
| | | | | |

MATERIALS ISSUED **January 17** 20 **--**  RECORDED:
BY **DGD**
MATERIALS CLERK

**2.** Prepare a materials requisition.

**3.** Update the materials ledger card.

**MATERIALS LEDGER CARD**

Article **28S Print Motor**  Acct. No. **145**
Reorder **300**  Minimum **220**  Location **B-16**

| ORDERED | | | RECEIVED | | | | ISSUED | | | | | BALANCE | | | |
|---|---|---|---|---|---|---|---|---|---|---|---|---|---|---|---|
| DATE | PUR-CHASE ORDER NO. | QUAN-TITY | DATE | PUR-CHASE ORDER NO. | QUAN-TITY | UNIT PRICE | VALUE | DATE | REQUI-SITION NO. | QUAN-TITY | UNIT PRICE | VALUE | DATE | QUAN-TITY | UNIT PRICE | VALUE |
| | | | 20-- Jan. 13 | 461 | 300 | 78.00 | 23,400.00 | | | | | | 20-- Jan. 13 | 320 | 78.00 | 24,960.00 |
| | | | | | | | | 20-- Jan. 17 | 774 | 50 | 78.00 | 3,900.00 | 17 | 270 | 78.00 | 21,060.00 |

During the manufacturing process, all costs of making a product must be recorded. All charges for direct materials, direct labor, and factory overhead for a particular job are recorded on a cost sheet, such as the one shown above.

When direct materials are needed for a job, they are requested from the storeroom using a materials requisition form. A materials requisition form is used to authorize transfer of items from the storeroom to the factory. When materials are issued to the factory from the storeroom, the materials ledger card is updated.

## RECORDING DIRECT MATERIALS ON A COST SHEET

**1** Open a new cost sheet for each job started. When the cost accounting department receives a request from the factory department supervisor for a job number, it assigns the number and prepares a new job cost sheet. To open a new job cost sheet:

a. Enter the Job No., *791*.
b. Enter the stock number and the description of the product, *FM25 Fax Machine.*
c. Enter the number of items to be manufactured, *50.*
d. Enter the customer that ordered the item. In this case, the product will replenish FaxaVision's stock of the fax machine. Therefore, *Stock* is entered on the Ordered for line.
e. Enter the date the job number is assigned, *January 17, 20--.*
f. Enter the date the item is wanted, *January 24, 20--.*

**2** Prepare a materials requisition in triplicate. One copy of a materials requisition is kept in the factory. Two copies are sent to the materials storeroom.

a. Enter the requisition number, *774*. Requisitions are numbered in order. The next available number is assigned.
b. Enter the name of the person who is making the requisition, *Mark Jansen.*
c. Check the appropriate box to indicate whether the requisition is for direct or indirect materials. In this case, a motor is a major part of the finished product. Therefore, the Direct box is checked.
d. Enter the date of the requisition, *January 17, 20--.*
e. Enter the position of the person making the requisition, *Supervisor*. Usually, a supervisor or a manager has the authority to make the requisition.
f. Enter the job number to which the materials are being issued, *791.*
g. Enter the quantity requisitioned, *50.*
h. Enter the stock number and description, *28S Print Motor.*
i. Enter the unit price of the materials, *78.00.*
j. Enter the total cost of the materials being issued to the factory, *3,900.00*. The total cost is determined by multiplying the quantity by the unit price (50 × $78.00 = $3,900.00).
k. Record the date on which the materials are issued to the factory, *January 17, 20--.*
l. The materials clerk initials the requisition to show that the materials have been issued. One copy of the completed materials requisition is kept in the storeroom. The original requisition is sent to the cost accounting department.

**3** Update the materials ledger card. When the materials requisition is received by the cost accounting department, an entry is made in the materials ledger.

a. Enter the date the materials are issued to the factory, *January 17, 20--*, in the Date column of the Issued section of the materials ledger card.
b. Enter the requisition number, *774.*
c. Enter the quantity issued, *50.*
d. Enter the unit price, *78.00.*
e. Enter the total value of the materials issued, *3,900.00.*
f. Enter the date in the Balance Date column.
g. Enter the new quantity of the material, *270*, in the Balance Quantity column. Subtract the quantity issued from the current quantity in inventory (320 − 50 = 270) to determine the new quantity.
h. Enter the unit price, *78.00.*
i. Enter the total value of the material, *21,060.00* (270 units × $78.00 = $21,060.00).

**4** Record the issuance of direct materials on the cost sheet. When the cost accounting department receives the materials requisition, an entry is made on the cost sheet.

a. Enter the requisition number, *774*, in the Req. No. column.
b. Enter the total value of the materials issued, *3,900.00*, in the Direct Materials Amount column.

**JOB – TIME RECORD**

Employee Number ___20___  Job Number ___791___

Date ___1/17/--___

Time started ___1 p.m.___

Time finished ___5 p.m.___

Total time spent on job . . . . . . . . . . . . . . ___4.0 hrs.___

**1.** Each employee prepares a job-time record for each job worked on.

COST SHEET

Job No. ___791___          Date ___January 17, 20--___
Item ___FM25 Fax Machine___   Date wanted ___January 24, 20--___
No. of items ___50___       Date completed _____
Ordered for ___Stock___

| DIRECT MATERIALS | | DIRECT LABOR | | | SUMMARY | |
|---|---|---|---|---|---|---|
| REQ. NO. | AMOUNT | DATE | AMOUNT | DATE | AMOUNT | ITEM | AMOUNT |
| 773 | $ 197.00 | Jan. 17 | $ 556.00 | | | | |
| 774 | 3,900.00 | | | | | | |

**2.** Record the total of all the job-time records for the job.

Factory employees may work on a number of different jobs each day. Therefore, a job-time record is kept to indicate the amount of time spent on each job. At the end of each day, all job-time records are summarized. The total direct labor cost for each job is recorded on each job's cost sheet.

A job-time record for one FaxaVision employee working 4 hours on Job No. 791 is shown above. All the direct labor costs for Job No. 791 are recorded in the Direct Labor columns of the cost sheet shown above.

**STEPS** STEPS • STEPS • STEPS • STEPS • STEPS • STEPS • STEPS

## ASSIGNING DIRECT LABOR TO JOBS

Each factory employee:

**1** Prepares a job-time record for each job worked on during the day. The record includes employee number, job number, date, time started, and time finished. The employee calculates and records the total time spent on the job.

Accounting department:

**2** Totals the time on job-time records for each job and records the cost in the Direct Labor column of the cost sheet.

©GETTY IMAGES/PHOTODISC

Cost Accounting for a Manufacturing Business

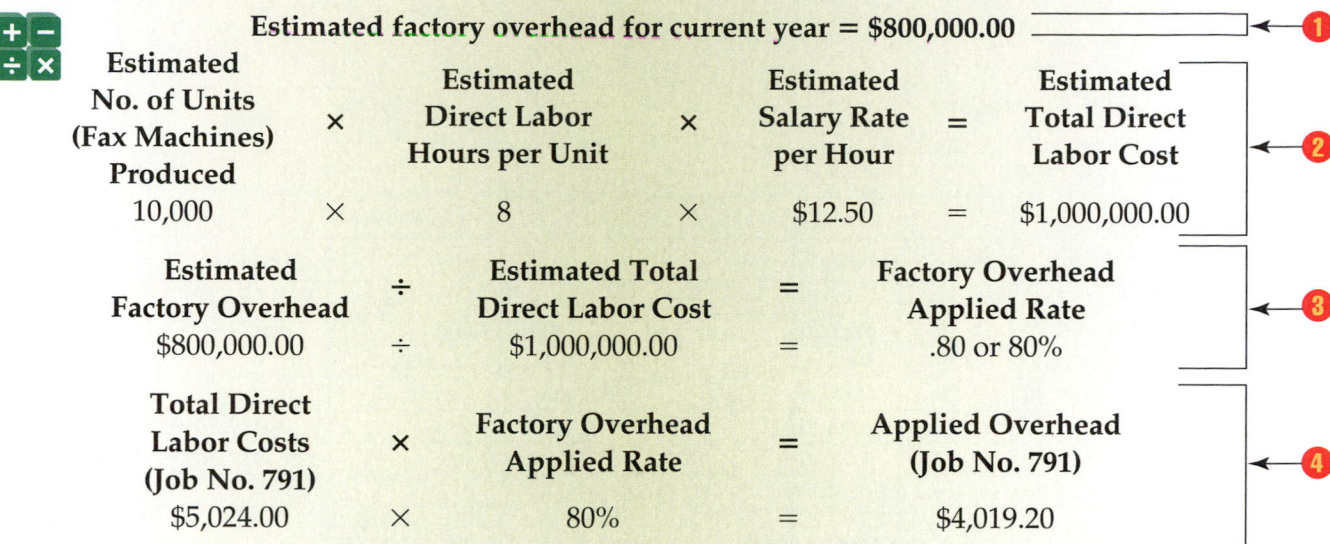

**Estimated factory overhead for current year = $800,000.00** ← 1

| Estimated No. of Units (Fax Machines) Produced | | Estimated Direct Labor Hours per Unit | | Estimated Salary Rate per Hour | | Estimated Total Direct Labor Cost | ← 2 |
|---|---|---|---|---|---|---|---|
| 10,000 | × | 8 | × | $12.50 | = | $1,000,000.00 | |

| Estimated Factory Overhead | | Estimated Total Direct Labor Cost | | Factory Overhead Applied Rate | ← 3 |
|---|---|---|---|---|---|
| $800,000.00 | ÷ | $1,000,000.00 | = | .80 or 80% | |

| Total Direct Labor Costs (Job No. 791) | | Factory Overhead Applied Rate | | Applied Overhead (Job No. 791) | ← 4 |
|---|---|---|---|---|---|
| $5,024.00 | × | 80% | = | $4,019.20 | |

Some factory overhead expenses occur regularly throughout a fiscal period, and others occur irregularly. Many factory overhead expenses are not known until the end of a fiscal period. Therefore, factory overhead expenses normally are charged to jobs by using an application rate based on a known cost such as direct labor. This method applies factory overhead expenses to all jobs and permits a company to record overhead on a cost sheet when a job is completed. The estimated amount of factory overhead recorded on cost sheets is called **applied overhead**. The applied overhead is calculated for Job No. 791 as shown above.

Applied overhead is recorded on cost sheets during the fiscal period and before all factory overhead for the current period is known. [*CONCEPT: Matching Expenses with Revenue*] Therefore, the factory overhead applied rate is calculated before the fiscal periods begins.

STEPS • STEPS • STEPS • STEPS • STEPS • STEPS • STEPS • STEPS • STEPS • STEPS • STEPS

## STEPS DETERMINING A FACTORY OVERHEAD APPLIED RATE

1. Estimate the amount of factory overhead costs for the next fiscal period. Generally, three factors are considered in estimating factory overhead. (a) Amount of factory overhead for the past several fiscal periods. (b) Number of products the factory expects to produce in the next fiscal period. (c) Expected change in unit costs of factory overhead items. FaxaVision expects to produce 10,000 fax machines during the coming year. Considering this volume, previous years' overhead, and anticipated cost increases, FaxaVision estimates factory overhead as $800,000.00.

2. Estimate the number of base units that will be used in the next fiscal period. Base units are usually cost items that can be identified easily. Direct labor cost, direct labor hours, and direct materials cost are common bases. A base unit should be selected that most closely relates to actual overhead costs. FaxaVision uses direct labor cost as a base unit because there is a close relationship between the amount of direct labor cost and factory overhead costs. FaxaVision estimates next year's direct labor cost as $1,000,000.00.

3. Calculate the factory overhead applied rate. Divide estimated factory overhead costs by the estimated base unit. FaxaVision's factory overhead applied rate is 80% of direct labor cost.

4. Calculate and record the amount of applied overhead, *4,019.20*, on the cost sheet for Job No. 791 (total direct labor for Job No. 791, $5,024.00, multiplied by the factory overhead rate, 80%).

# COMPLETING A JOB COST SHEET

**COST SHEET**

Job No. _791_
Item _FM25 Fax Machine_
No. of items _50_
Ordered for _Stock_

Date _January 17, 20--_
Date wanted _January 24, 20--_
Date completed _January 24, 20--_

| DIRECT MATERIALS | | DIRECT LABOR | | | | SUMMARY | |
|---|---|---|---|---|---|---|---|
| REQ. NO. | AMOUNT | DATE | AMOUNT | DATE | AMOUNT | ITEM | AMOUNT |
| 773 | $ 197.00 | Jan. 17 | $ 556.00 | | | Direct Materials | $ 7,769.30 |
| 774 | 3,900.00 | 18 | 966.00 | | | Direct Labor | 5,024.00 |
| 778 | 620.60 | 19 | 949.00 | | | Factory Overhead | |
| 779 | 639.80 | 20 | 992.00 | | | (80% of direct | |
| 783 | 811.00 | 23 | 1,010.00 | | | labor costs) | 4,019.20 |
| 786 | 356.50 | 24 | 551.00 | | | Total Cost | $16,812.50 |
| 787 | 1,244.40 | | $5,024.00 | | | | |
| | $7,769.30 | | | | | No. of units finished | 50 |
| | | | | | | Cost per unit | $ 336.25 |

**1.** Total direct materials.
**2.** Total direct labor.
**3.** Transfer amounts to Summary columns.
**4.** Calculate applied factory overhead.
**5.** Determine total job cost.
**6.** Determine cost per unit.

| Total Costs (Job No. 791) | ÷ | No. of Units | = | Cost per Unit |
|---|---|---|---|---|
| $16,812.50 | ÷ | 50 | = | $336.25 |

The completed cost sheet for Job No. 791 is shown above. When a job is completed, its total costs are calculated and recorded in the Summary columns of the cost sheet. Direct Materials and Direct Labor columns on the cost sheet are totaled and the totals are recorded in the Summary columns. Then factory overhead is applied to the job. A cost per unit is determined for each job.

Job No. 791 was completed on January 24. At the end of a fiscal period, cost sheets will also exist for jobs that have not been completed. The total value for all cost sheets for work still in process equals the balance of the work in process account in the general ledger. Thus, at the end of a fiscal period, cost sheets for work in process are totaled to determine ending inventory for the general ledger account Work in Process.

## STEPS COMPLETING A COST SHEET

**1** Total the Direct Materials Amount column, *$7,769.30.*

**2** Total the Direct Labor Amount column, *$5,024.00.*

**3** Transfer the direct materials and direct labor amounts to the Summary columns.

**4** Calculate and record the applied overhead, *$4,019.20,* in the Summary columns. Remember that factory overhead is applied at the rate of 80% of direct labor cost ($5,024.00 × 80% = $4,019.20).

**5** Total the three cost elements in the cost sheet's Summary columns, *$16,812.50.* This is the total cost of the job.

**6** Determine the cost per unit, *$336.25* ($16,812.50 total cost ÷ 50 units = $336.25).

## FINISHED GOODS LEDGER CARD

**1.** Complete the Manufactured/Received columns.      **2.** Enter existing inventory balance.

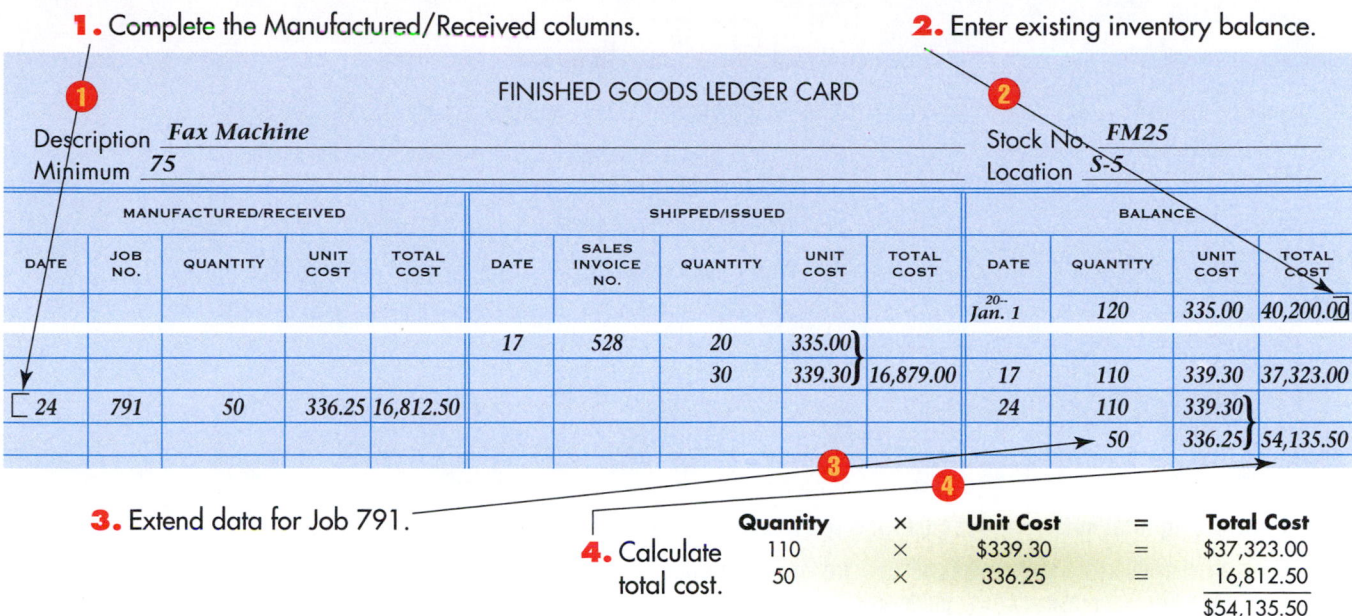

**3.** Extend data for Job 791.

**4.** Calculate total cost.

| | Quantity | × | Unit Cost | = | Total Cost |
|---|---|---|---|---|---|
| | 110 | × | $339.30 | = | $37,323.00 |
| | 50 | × | 336.25 | = | 16,812.50 |
| | | | | | $54,135.50 |

When a job is completed, the finished goods are placed in the finished goods stock area. At this time, summary information from the cost sheet is recorded on the completed product's finished goods ledger card. The entry for the completed Job No. 791 is recorded on the finished goods ledger card shown above.

The total value for all finished goods ledger cards equals the finished goods inventory account balance in the general ledger. After FaxaVision's Job No. 791 is completed and recorded, the company has 160 FM25 Fax Machines on hand at a total cost of $54,135.50. This amount will be added to the total costs of all other finished goods still on hand to determine the balance of finished goods inventory in the general ledger.

---

## STEPS

*STEPS • STEPS • STEPS • STEPS • STEPS • STEPS • STEPS • STEPS • STEPS • STEPS*

### COMPLETING A FINISHED GOODS LEDGER CARD

**1** Complete the Manufactured/Received columns of the finished goods ledger card.
a. Record the date the finished goods are transferred to the finished goods inventory, *24*.
b. Enter the Job No., *791*.
c. Enter the quantity, *50*.
d. Enter the unit cost, *336.25*.
e. Enter the total cost, *16,812.50*.

**2** Enter the existing inventory in the Balance columns.
a. Enter the date, *24*.
b. Enter the previous quantity of fax machines in inventory, *110*, and the unit cost, *339.30*. Units costs for each job may differ since the amount of direct materials and direct labor used may vary. Therefore, the unit costs for each job are kept separate.

**3** Extend the quantity, *50*, and the unit cost, *336.25*, for Job 791.

**4** Calculate the total cost of all goods in inventory, *54,135.50*. Although unit costs are kept separate, the total cost balance is combined for all units in the finished goods inventory. FaxaVision uses the first-in, first-out inventory method. Thus, the cost recorded first is the cost removed from inventory first when units are sold.

---

## • term review

applied overhead

## • audit your understanding

1. What are the four sets of columns on a materials ledger card?
2. What is the name of the form used to authorize a seller to deliver goods with payment to be made later?
3. What is the purpose of the materials requisition?
4. What is the formula for calculating the factory overhead applied rate?
5. Why are unit costs kept separate on the finished goods ledger card?

## • work together 19-2

**Determining total cost and unit cost for a job and determining total cost for a finished item**

A cost sheet and partial finished goods ledger card for Leather Originals, a manufacturer of leather furniture, are provided in the *Working Papers*. Your instructor will guide you through the following examples.

1. Complete the cost sheet for Job No. 657 by filling in the Summary columns. Factory overhead is applied based on direct labor hours. Estimated factory overhead for the period was $3,000,000. The number of estimated direct labor hours was 200,000. A total of 530 direct labor hours was used on Job No. 657.
2. Calculate a new balance for item K-39 sofa on the partial finished goods ledger card.

## • on your own 19-2

**Determining total cost and unit cost for a job and determining total cost for a finished item**

A cost sheet and partial finished goods ledger card for Leather Originals, a manufacturer of leather furniture, are provided in the *Working Papers*. Work independently to complete the following problem.

1. Complete the cost sheet for Job No. 711 by filling in the Summary columns. Factory overhead is applied based on direct labor hours. Estimated factory overhead for the period was $3,000,000. The number of estimated direct labor hours was 200,000. A total of 743 direct labor hours was used on Job No. 711.
2. Calculate a new balance for item S-68 chair on the partial finished goods ledger card.

## SUMMARY

**After completing this chapter, you can**

1. Define accounting terms related to cost accounting for a manufacturing business.

2. Identify accounting concepts and practices related to cost accounting for a manufacturing business.

3. Identify the elements of manufacturing costs: (1) direct materials, (2) direct labor, and (3) factory overhead.

4. Identify the flow of costs through the manufacturing process.

5. Prepare selected ledgers and cost sheets for a manufacturing business.

# Explore Accounting

EXPLORE ACCOUNTING • EXPLORE ACCOUNTING • EXPLORE ACCO

## Equivalent Units of Production

Two general manufacturing costing methods exist: job order costing illustrated in this chapter and process costing.

Process costing is useful when a single production process uses a continuous flow of inputs to produce the same product. To illustrate process costing, assume that Hubble Inc. began the month with 200 televisions in production. Each unit is estimated to be 20% complete as to labor. During the month, Hubble began 1,000 units and completed 800 units. At the end of the month, the 400 units in production were 70% complete. Management budgeted $40.00 of direct labor per unit. During May, the company incurred $40,000 of direct labor. If the 800 completed units are used as a measure, it would appear that the laborers have not been efficient ($40,000 ÷ 800 = $50.00 per unit).

A better number would recognize the work performed on units incomplete at the end of the

month. An estimate of the number of units that could be started and completed during a period is known as the equivalent units of production (EUP). Hubble calculates EUP as shown below.

The workers were actually more efficient than projected in the budget ($40,000 ÷ 1,040 EUP = $38.46).

**Required:**

Determine the equivalent cost per unit of labor for the following problem. Nelson Company began the month with 600 units in production, each unit 60% complete as to labor. During the current month, these units were completed. During the month, Nelson also started 2,000 units and completed 1,800 units. At the end of the month, the 200 units in production were 10% complete. Labor costs, estimated to be $9.00 per unit, were actually $20,000.

| | | | | | |
|---|---|---|---|---|---|
| Beginning Inventory | 200 units | × | 80% | = | 160 EUP |
| Started and Completed | 600 units | × | 100% | = | 600 EUP |
| Started and in Process | 400 units | × | 70% | = | 280 EUP |
| Total EUP | | | | | 1,1040 EUP |

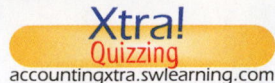
Xtra!
Quizzing
accountingxtra.swlearning.com

# 19-1 APPLICATION PROBLEM

### Classifying manufacturing costs and determining which ledger to use for initial recording

Krasnoy Tire, a maker of tires for cars, trucks, and tractors, is trying to determine how to account for various factory costs. The costs include the following:

a. Wages earned by a factory supervisor.
b. Fringe benefits of the factory supervisor.
c. The rent expense of company headquarters, which is located 10 miles from the factory.
d. Rubber used in the production of tires.
e. The property taxes of the factory.
f. Wages earned by an employee working on the production of tires.
g. Inexpensive glue used sparingly in the production of tires.
h. A cleaning solvent used to clean production machinery.
i. Wages earned by an employee who inspects finished tires before they leave the factory.
j. Wages earned by a marketing manager at company headquarters.

### Instructions:

1. For each of the costs above, determine whether the cost should be classified as direct materials, direct labor, factory overhead, or none. Hint: Only costs related to the factory or to production should be included as manufacturing costs.
2. Specify the subsidiary ledger (materials ledger, cost ledger, finished goods ledger) in which the cost is first recorded.

# 19-2 APPLICATION PROBLEM

### Completing a materials ledger card

Wilmington, Inc., manufactures heating systems. The company maintains a materials ledger for all direct materials.

### Transactions:

| Oct. | | |
|---|---|---|
| 1. | Ordered 500 T-5 thermostats. Purchase Order No. 83. | |
| 3. | Issued 110 T-5 thermostats. Materials Requisition No. 196. | |
| 4. | Issued 45 T-5 thermostats. Materials Requisition No. 200. | |
| 7. | Received 500 T-5 thermostats; unit price $39.50. Purchase Order No. 83. | |
| 12. | Issued 220 T-5 thermostats. Materials Requisition No. 207. | |
| 17. | Issued 85 T-5 thermostats. Materials Requisition No. 218. | |
| 29. | Issued 55 T-5 thermostats. Materials Requisition No. 231. | |
| 29. | Ordered 500 T-5 thermostats. Purchase Order No. 88. | |

### Instructions:

1. Prepare a materials ledger card for T-5 thermostats. The thermostat is Account No. 76. Reorder quantity is set at 500 thermostats, minimum at 175 thermostats. Inventory location is Area A18.
2. Record the beginning balance on October 1 of the current year of 175 T-5 thermostats at a unit price of $39.50.
3. Record the transactions.

## 19-3 APPLICATION PROBLEM
### Calculating factory overhead applied rate

AutoAnswer, Inc., a manufacturer of telephone answering machines, uses a factory overhead applied rate to charge overhead costs to its manufactured products.

The company manager estimates that AutoAnswer will manufacture 30,000 units next year. For this amount of production, the cost accountant estimates total factory overhead costs to be $336,000.00. Estimated direct labor cost for next year is $420,000.00.

**Instructions:**
Calculate AutoAnswer's factory overhead applied rate for next year as a percentage of direct labor cost.

## 19-4 APPLICATION PROBLEM
### Preparing a cost sheet

On July 1, Esquire Tables, Inc., began work on Job No. 309. The order is for 45 No. ET42 game tables for stock; date wanted is July 10.

**Transactions:**

| July | 1. | Direct material, $641.25. Materials Requisition No. 432. |
| | 1. | Direct labor, $465.00. Daily summary of job-time records. |
| | 2. | Direct materials, $345.00. Materials Requisition No. 438. |
| | 2. | Direct labor, $364.50. Daily summary of job-time records. |
| | 3. | Direct labor, $301.50. Daily summary of job-time records. |
| | 5. | Direct materials, $261.00. Materials Requisition No. 447. |
| | 5. | Direct labor, $285.00. Daily summary of job-time records. |
| | 8. | Direct labor, $201.00. Daily summary of job-time records. |

**Instructions:**
1. Open a cost sheet and record the transactions.
2. Complete the cost sheet, recording factory overhead at the applied rate of 75% of direct labor costs.

## 19-5 APPLICATION PROBLEM  (QUICKBOOKS)
### Recording entries in a finished goods ledger

Decatur Industries, Inc., maintains a finished goods ledger for all of its manufactured products.

**Transactions:**

| Apr. | 2. | Received from production department 210 C45 bats at a unit cost of $8.80. Job No. 315. |
| | 8. | Mike's Place, a store selling baseball equipment, cards, and memorabilia, ordered 90 C45 bats. Sales Invoice No. 511. |
| | 9. | Production department completed 140 C45 bats and sent them to finished goods inventory. The unit cost for Job No. 334 was $9.00. |
| | 14. | Sports Unlimited, a wholesale distributor of sports equipment, purchased 75 C45 bats. Sales Invoice No. 521. |
| | 16. | Job No. 339 was completed, with 100 C45 bats sent to finished goods inventory. The unit cost was $8.60. |
| | 23. | Mike's Place purchased 300 C45 bats. Sales Invoice No. 536. |
| | 27. | Sold 75 bats to The Grand Old Game, a baseball retailer. Sales Invoice No. 543. |
| | 28. | Received from production department 120 C45 bats at a unit cost of $8.85. Job No. 363. |

**Instructions:**

1. Prepare a finished goods ledger card for stock no. C45 baseball bats. Minimum quantity is set at 250 units. Inventory location is Area R-12.
2. Record the beginning balance on April 1 of the current year for 280 C45 baseball bats at a unit cost of $8.70. Decatur Industries uses the first-in, first-out method to record inventory costs.
3. Record the transactions.

## 19-6 MASTERY PROBLEM

### Preparing cost records

Gemini manufactures athletic shoes. The company records manufacturing costs by job number and uses a factory overhead applied rate to charge overhead costs to its products.

The company estimates Gemini will manufacture 50,000 shoes next year. For this amount of production, total factory overhead is estimated to be $398,800.00. Estimated direct labor costs for next year are $498,500.00.

**Instructions:**

1. Calculate Gemini's factory overhead applied rate for next year as a percentage of direct labor cost.

On May 3, Gemini began work on Job No. 283. The order is for 150 pairs of No. 52L athletic shoes for stock; date wanted May 13.

2. Open a cost sheet for Job No. 283 and record the following items.

| May | 3. | Direct materials, $862.50. Materials Requisition No. 392. |
|---|---|---|
| | 3. | Direct labor, $129.00. Daily summary of job-time records. |
| | 4. | Direct labor, $248.00. Daily summary of job-time records. |
| | 5. | Direct materials, $472.50. Materials Requisition No. 399. |
| | 5. | Direct labor, $175.00. Daily summary of job-time records. |
| | 6. | Direct labor, $192.00. Daily summary of job-time records. |
| | 7. | Direct labor, $295.00. Daily summary of job-time records. |
| | 10. | Direct materials, $360.00. Materials Requisition No. 428. |
| | 10. | Direct labor, $165.00. Daily summary of job-time records. |
| | 11. | Direct labor, $152.00. Daily summary of job-time records. |
| | 12. | Direct labor, $124.00. Daily summary of job-time records. |

3. Complete the cost sheet, recording factory overhead at the rate calculated in Instruction 1.
4. Prepare a finished goods ledger card for Stock No. 52L athletic shoes. Minimum quantity is set at 100. Inventory location is Area C-50.
5. Record on the finished goods ledger card the beginning balance on May 1. The May 1 balance of 52L athletic shoes is 140 units at a unit cost of $30.45. Gemini uses the first-in, first-out method to record inventory costs.
6. Record the following transactions on the finished goods ledger card for 52L athletic shoes.

| May | 5. | Sold 60 pairs of 52L athletic shoes. Sales Invoice No. 633. |
|---|---|---|
| | 12. | Received 150 pairs of 52L athletic shoes. Record cost from cost sheet for Job No. 283. |
| | 18. | Sold 30 pairs of 52L athletic shoes. Sales Invoice No. 652. |

# 19-7 CHALLENGE PROBLEM

## Preparing cost records

Sea Explor manufactures deep-sea diving suits. The company records manufacturing costs by job number and uses a factory overhead applied rate to charge overhead costs to its products.

Sea Explor estimates they will manufacture 10,000 diving suits next year. For this amount of production, total factory overhead is estimated to be $600,000.00. Estimated direct materials costs for next year are $80.00 for each suit manufactured. Estimated direct labor for next year is 4 labor hours for each suit at $12.50 per hour.

**Instructions:**

1. Calculate Sea Explor's factory overhead applied rate for next year for each of the following three bases. (a) Direct materials cost. (b) Direct labor cost. (c) Direct labor hours.

On May 9, Sea Explor began work on Job No. 365. The order is for 55 SE80 diving suits for stock; date wanted May 19.

2. Open a cost sheet for Job No. 365 and record the following items.

May    9.    Direct materials, $1,160.50. Materials Requisition No. 421.
         9.    Direct labor, $274.75. Daily summary of job-time records.
      10.    Direct labor, $441.00. Daily summary of job-time records.
      11.    Direct materials, $2,321.00. Materials Requisition No. 430.
      11.    Direct labor, $392.00. Daily summary of job-time records.
      12.    Direct labor, $423.00. Daily summary of job-time records.
      13.    Direct labor, $440.00. Daily summary of job-time records.
      16.    Direct materials, $1,017.50. Materials Requisition No. 438.
      16.    Direct labor, $370.00. Daily summary of job-time records.
      17.    Direct labor, $352.00. Daily summary of job-time records.
      18.    Direct labor, $181.00. Daily summary of job-time records.

3. Complete the cost sheet, recording factory overhead at the direct materials cost rate calculated in Instruction 1.
4. Prepare a finished goods ledger card for Stock No. SE80 diving suit. Minimum quantity is set at 30. Inventory location is Area J16.
5. Record on the finished goods ledger card the beginning balance on May 1. The May 1 balance of SE80 diving suits is 40 units at a unit cost of $191.50. Sea Explor uses the last-in, first-out method to record inventory costs.
6. Record the following transactions on the finished goods ledger card for SE80 diving suits.

May    11.    Sold 10 SE80 diving suits. Sales Invoice No. 450.
      18.    Received 55 SE80 diving suits. Record cost from cost sheet for Job No. 365.
      23.    Sold 30 SE80 diving suits. Sales Invoice No. 494.
      25.    Sold 25 SE80 diving suits. Sales Invoice No. 523.

## applied communication

You are appointed to participate on a time-efficiency team. The team includes factory workers, supervisors, and a representative from the accounting department. Currently the factory workers record their time on job–time sheets. They also calculate the total time worked on each job. A worker may work on three or four jobs each day. The accounting department receives about 200 job–time sheets each day. A clerk verifies the workers' calculations on the job–time records. Any changes to the total time must be initialed by a supervisor.

### Required:
The company has appointed your team to explore ways to automate the time recording process. Your job on the team is to explore bar code technology. Write a report on bar code technology. Make a recommendation to the team indicating whether bar codes could be used to replace the job–time sheets.

## cases for critical thinking

### Case 1
Century Fan Company manufactures ceiling fans. During the current year, payments were made for the following items. A new clerk classified the cost items. Are the cost items classified correctly? If not, give the correct classification and explain the reason for your corrected classification.

1. Wood to be used for fan blades. (Factory Overhead)
2. Insurance premium on the factory building. (Direct Materials)
3. Salary of factory workers assembling fans. (Factory Overhead)
4. Bolts used in assembling the fans. (Direct Materials)
5. Salary of factory supervisor. (Direct Labor)
6. Brooms used to sweep the factory floors. (Direct Materials)
7. Salary of packer who packs fan crates for shipping. (Direct Labor)
8. Paint and stain to be used on the fans. (Direct Materials)

### Case 2
Astro Company has found that total factory overhead is usually about 60% of direct labor cost. The business manufactures one product that is processed in three different manufacturing departments: A, B, and C. In Department A, much expensive machinery is used. In Department B, some machinery is used. In Department C, virtually no machinery is used, all the work being manual work. There is a great difference in the amount of time required to process various jobs in the different departments. Under these circumstances do you believe that the company should charge factory overhead to each job at the rate of 60% of direct labor? If not, what would you recommend?

## SCANS workplace competency

**Interpersonal Competency:** Negotiating

**Concept:** Companies value employees who are skillful at working toward an agreement that involves exchanging specific resources or resolving divergent interests. Such individuals set attainable goals, research the history of the conflict, present arguments objectively, reflect on what has been stated, clarify problems, resolve conflicts, adjust quickly to new ideas, propose options, and make reasonable compromises.

**Application:** Prepare a new bell schedule or annual calendar for your school. Explain and justify your position. Discuss your views with the school's administration.

## • auditing for errors

Advanced Systems is a new company that will produce a line of high-quality wood computer desks. The company's management is working on its accounting system and has prepared the following policy for classifying manufacturing costs. Determine whether any item in the policy violates generally accepted accounting principles.

| Description | Direct Materials | Direct Labor | Overhead | | |
| --- | --- | --- | --- | --- | --- |
| | | | Indirect Material | Indirect Labor | Other |
| Advertising and promotion | | | | | X |
| Delivery of finished goods to customer | | X | | | |
| Depreciation of equipment | | | | | X |
| Heat, power, and light | | | | | X |
| Inspector wages | | X | | | |
| Insurance on manufacturing building | | | | | X |
| Maintenance wages | | | | X | |
| Packing materials | | | X | | |
| Production wages | | X | | | |
| Sandpaper | X | | | | |
| Screws | | | X | | |
| Supervisor salaries | | | | X | |
| Varnish | X | | | | |
| Wood | X | | | | |

## • analyzing Costco's financial statements

Costco's selling, general, and administrative expenses (SG&A expenses) remained steady between 8.7% to 8.8% of net sales during fiscal years 1994 and 2000. For the past three years, however, these expenses have risen to between 9.2% and 9.8% of sales. Citing rising costs for healthcare, workers' compensation, and salaries, Costco's top officers state in their 2003 annual report, "These figures are unacceptable, and we are working hard to reverse this trend."

Trends in healthcare costs may prevent Costco from ever reducing SG&A expenses to 8.7% on net sales. Suppose Costco management sets a goal to reduce SG&A costs to 9.4% in 2004. Evaluate the impact this reduction would have had on the 2003 financial statements.

### Instructions:
Calculate the following items, rounding amounts to the nearest million dollars:

1. Calculate how much SG&A expenses would have been in 2003 if Costco had been able to limit these expenses to 9.4% of net sales. Round your answer to the nearest million dollars.

2. Calculate the increase in 2003 income before federal income taxes that would result from lowering SG&A expenses to 9.4% of net sales.

3. Costco's effective tax rate was 37.75% in 2003, meaning that $37.75 of taxes were paid on every $100.00 of income before federal income taxes. Calculate the increase in net income of the reduction in SG&A expenses.

4. Calculate the increase in the earnings per share. Obtain the number of common shares in the Per Share Data-Diluted section of the ten-year operating and financial highlights on pages B-2–B-3 in Appendix B of this textbook.

5. Do you agree with the statement made by Costco's top officers? How do you believe their recognition of this problem will be perceived by current and potential investors? Support your answer.

## Replacing Written Documents with Electronic Spreadsheets

The *Automated Accounting* software is not designed to provide every form and report a company may need. Reports generated in *Automated Accounting* may be copied and pasted into a spreadsheet for further use and analysis. Other forms may need to be prepared in spreadsheet software.

The electronic spreadsheet offers businesses the opportunity to increase the efficiency of employees who perform repetitive accounting tasks. Electronic spreadsheets can be designed to replace most manually prepared documents, such as a cost sheet. Formulas stored in the spreadsheet eliminate the need for the employee to make calculations and record the amount in the form. As a result, a spreadsheet form can be more efficient to complete and ensure a higher level of accuracy.

The first step in creating a form on an electronic spreadsheet is to enter the labels contained on the document. The columnar structure of the electronic spreadsheet may require the form to differ slightly from the original paper version. Making as few changes as possible in the style and layout will enable employees to quickly adapt to using a spreadsheet version of the form.

Before using the spreadsheet form, it is important to check all formulas for accuracy. Entering the data for a verified manual document should generate the same values. The spreadsheet form shown below results in the same cost per unit as the cost sheet on page 570.

### The Auditing Toolbar

Microsoft Excel contains a feature especially designed to detect errors. The auditing toolbar (View>>Toolbars>>Formula Auditing) contains a series of tools that visually track the cells used by a formula. With the cell pointer on the total of direct material in H10, selecting Trace Precedents identifies the range of cells included in the cell's sum function. Notice that the blue outline surrounding cells B10:B16 only includes the seven direct material amounts for Job No. 791. Although this job's cost per unit calculated correctly, the cost per unit of any job having more than seven requisitions, entered in cells B17:B27, would be incorrectly excluded. The auditing feature alerts the spreadsheet designer of the error so that the function at H10 can be modified to include the entire range of cells B10:B27.

## Protecting Formulas

Once the accuracy of the spreadsheet form has been verified, steps need to be taken to ensure that its accuracy is not compromised by an employee entering data where a formula is stored.

Any cell where the employee should enter data is known as an *input cell*. Changing the color of input cells (using the Font Color button on the Formatting toolbar) visually assists the employee in entering data in the correct cells. Entering a symbol, such as a question mark, in selected input cells also directs the employee's attention to these cells. In the spreadsheet below, input cells are shown in blue font with question marks.

Although the font color is helpful, cells containing formulas can be protected from being accidentally altered or erased. Protection of cells is a two-step process.

1. Change the properties of input cells to allow input (Format>>Cells>>Protection and remove the check from the Locked item). This command unlocks the input cells.

2. Turn on spreadsheet protection (Tools>> Protection>>Protect Sheet), protecting all the cells on the spreadsheet except the input cells unlocked in the previous step.

The spreadsheet form is now ready to be saved and used to create new documents. The extra time devoted to incorporating these modifications in spreadsheet forms helps ensure that accounting transactions and decisions are based on accurate data.

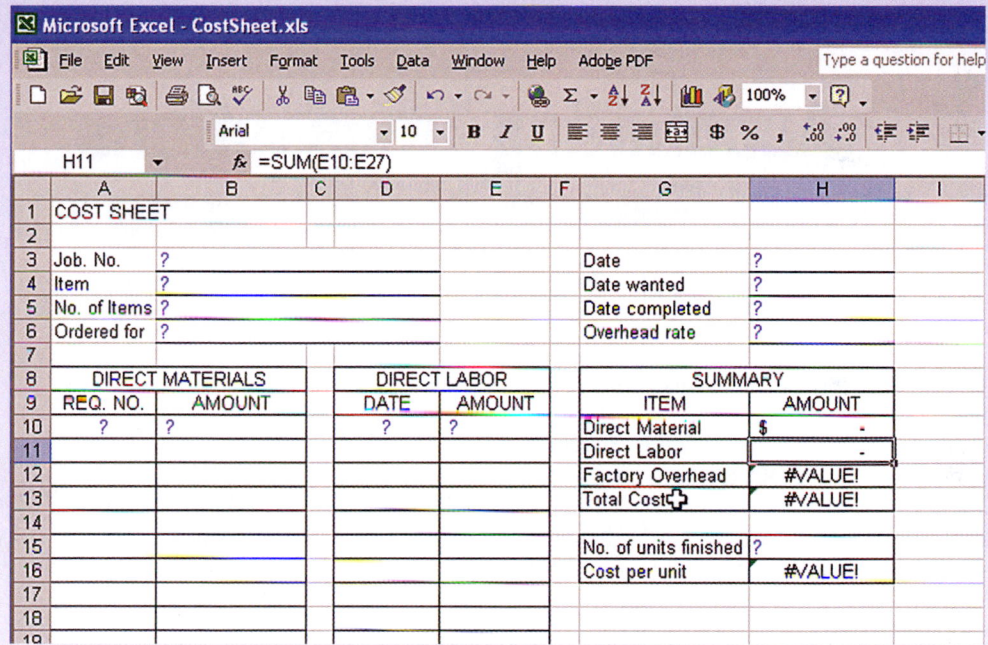

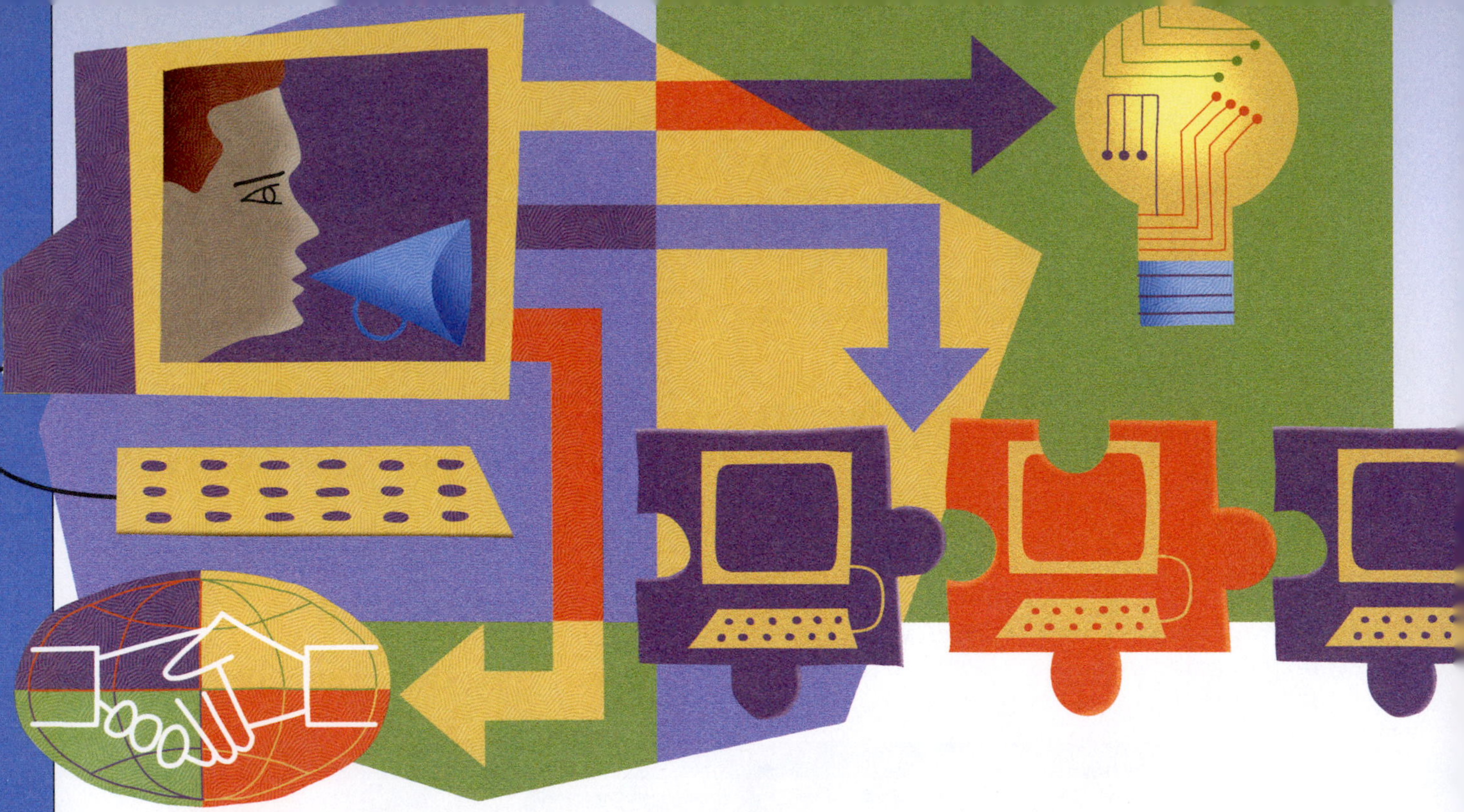

# CHAPTER 20 Accounting Transactions and Financial Reporting for a Manufacturing Business

OBJECTIVES & TERMS

***After studying Chapter 20, you will be able to:***

1. Define accounting terms related to accounting transactions and financial reporting for a manufacturing business.
2. Identify accounting concepts and practices related to accounting transactions and financial reporting for a manufacturing business.
3. Journalize transactions for a manufacturing business.
4. Prepare selected financial statements for a manufacturing business.

- underapplied overhead
- overapplied overhead
- statement of cost of goods manufactured

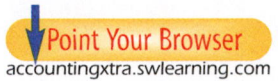

Point Your Browser
accountingxtra.swlearning.com

## • Toyota

©LUCAS SCHIFRES/LANDOV

### GAAP AT TOYOTA

Toyota, the number-two automaker, is an international company with sales and production facilities in many countries. Yet a quick review of its financial statements indicates that this Japanese company has not strayed from its Japanese roots. Its latest financial statements indicate that the company had sales exceeding 17 trillion yen, or ¥17,000,000,000,000. That's roughly $150 billion U.S. dollars.

Toyota has historically prepared two sets of financial statements: one in accordance with generally accepted accounting principles (GAAP) in Japan, the other in accordance with generally accepted accounting principles in the United States (U.S. GAAP). Beginning with its 2004 report, Toyota prepared its financial statement only in accordance with U.S. GAAP. The company believed the change would make its financial statements easier to understand and would quicken the preparation process.

The new financial statements continue to be stated in yen. However, the accounting principles used to prepare the financial statements follow U.S. GAAP.

### Critical Thinking

1. How should Toyota's financial statements, stated in yen, affect your ability to understand the reported financial information?
2. Where in the annual report do you think Toyota informs the reader of the financial statements that the statements are prepared in accordance with U.S. GAAP?

Xtra!
Today
accountingxtra.swlearning.com

Source: www.toyota.com/about/news/corporate/2004/05/11-1-finreport.html

### DIVIDENDS PAID BY CORPORATIONS

Go to the homepage for Kellogg's (www.kelloggs.com) and General Mills (www.generalmills.com). Search the site for information about dividends paid.

#### Instructions

1. List the date and the amount of the most recent dividend paid by Kellogg's.
2. List the date and the amount of the most recent dividend paid by General Mills.

# 20-1 Journalizing Manufacturing Accounting Transactions

Managing a manufacturing business requires more elaborate planning and control than managing a merchandising business. In addition to sales and administrative activities required of both types of businesses, a manufacturing business must provide the knowledge and resources needed to make the product.

Accounting for a manufacturing business is more complex than accounting for a merchandising business. To provide usable financial information for a manufacturing business, detailed cost records must be maintained throughout the manufacturing process. These detailed manufacturing cost records provide a business with information needed to price its product, analyze manufacturing costs, and make other important management decisions.

Procedures for maintaining detailed manufacturing cost records are described in Chapter 19.

In addition to detailed cost records, a manufacturing business also needs accurate financial statements. To provide financial statements, it must make journal entries to reflect cost transactions in general ledger accounts.

Manufacturing cost data are generally recorded daily to provide up-to-date cost information for managers. However, most manufacturing costs are recorded for financial reporting purposes only when up-to-date account balances are needed to prepare financial statements. These end-of-fiscal-period journal entries update the general ledger manufacturing accounts before financial statements are prepared.

MAKING ETHICAL DECISIONS · **MAKING ETHICAL DECISIONS** · MAKING ETHICAL DECISIO

## making ethical decisions

### Fair Competition

Grayson Corporation produces a line of personal care products. Last year the company invested a lot of money and effort to introduce a new shampoo. Unfortunately, the product's sales are significantly below expectations. Amy Stevens, the marketing manager, is under pressure to reverse the trend—and fast!

One of Amy's staff has suggested that they bundle the products to promote sales. In other words, the shampoo would be sold as part of a collection of products. Customers (retail stores) would have to buy the new shampoo in order to restock their shelves with the company's successful products.

**Instructions**

Access *Our Values and Policies,* the code of conduct for Procter & Gamble. What guidance does Procter & Gamble provide regarding a marketing plan such as the one described? Should Amy approve the plan? Assume that Grayson Corporation's policies are similar to Procter & Gamble's.

Source: www.pg.com/content/pdf/01_about_pg/01_about_pg_homepage/about_pg_toolbar/download_report/values_and_policies.pdf

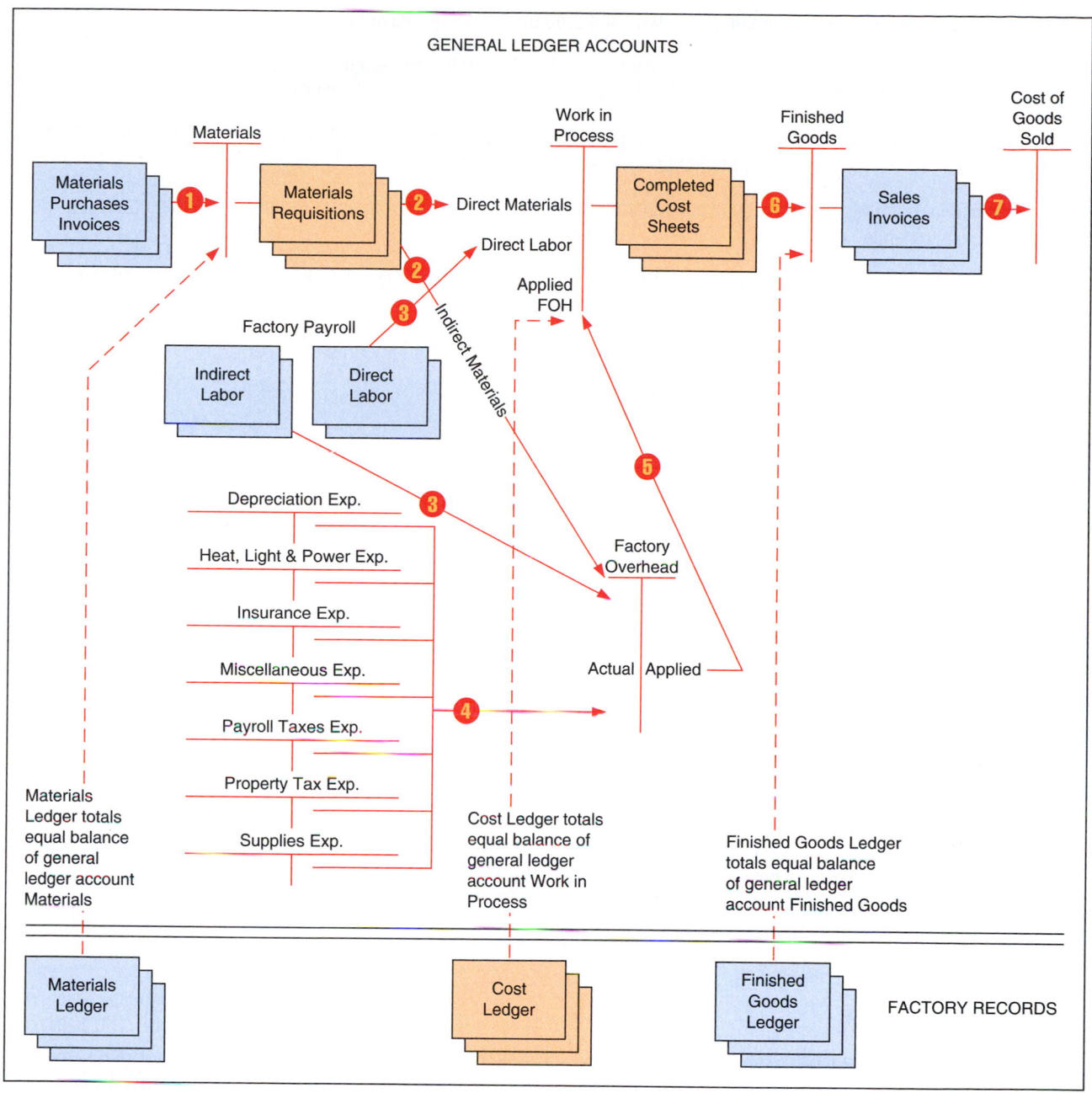

GENERAL LEDGER ACCOUNTS

All manufacturing costs flow through the manufacturing accounts. FaxaVision uses cost sheets to record direct materials, direct labor, and overhead costs of each job. This method permits the company to determine the unit costs of completed jobs. The unit costs are recorded in the company's perpetual inventory of finished goods.

Therefore, these costs are recorded through each phase of the manufacturing process. Summary journal entries update general ledger accounts for costs incurred in completing jobs, as shown above. Thus, end-of-fiscal-period inventory adjustments are not required.

## RECORDING JOURNAL ENTRIES FOR MANUFACTURING ACCOUNTS

1. Record materials purchased by debiting Materials and crediting Accounts Payable.

2. Record direct materials transferred to the factory by crediting Materials and debiting Work in Process. Record indirect materials transferred to the factory by crediting Materials and debiting Factory Overhead.

3. Record factory payroll by debiting direct labor to Work in Process, debiting indirect labor to Factory Overhead, crediting payroll liability accounts (e.g., Accounts Payable), and crediting Cash.

4. Close individual manufacturing expense accounts by debiting Factory Overhead and crediting each manufacturing expense account for its balance.

5. Record applied overhead by debiting Work in Process and crediting Factory Overhead for the total overhead amount applied during the fiscal period.

6. Record cost of products completed by crediting Work in Process and debiting Finished Goods.

7. Record cost of products sold by crediting Finished Goods and debiting Cost of Goods Sold.

## JOURNAL ENTRIES TO RECORD FACTORY PAYROLL FOR A MONTH

**3.** Credit cash for the next payroll.

**CASH PAYMENTS JOURNAL**     PAGE *2*

| | DATE | ACCOUNT TITLE | CK. NO. | POST. REF. | GENERAL DEBIT | GENERAL CREDIT | ACCOUNTS PAYABLE DEBIT | PURCHASES DISCOUNT CREDIT | CASH CREDIT | |
|---|---|---|---|---|---|---|---|---|---|---|
| 1 | Jan. 15 | Work in Process | 1194 | | 39 245 00 | | | | 41 325 38 | 1 |
| 2 | | Factory Overhead | | | 11 774 00 | | | | | 2 |
| 3 | | Employee Income Tax Payable | | | | 5 612 10 | | | | 3 |
| 4 | | Social Security Tax Payable | | | | 3 336 64 | | | | 4 |
| 5 | | Medicare Tax Payable | | | | 744 88 | | | | 5 |
| 21 | 31 | Work in Process | 1211 | | 44 255 00 | | | | 46 600 12 | 21 |
| 22 | | Factory Overhead | | | 13 276 00 | | | | | 22 |
| 23 | | Employee Income Tax Payable | | | | 6 328 40 | | | | 23 |
| 24 | | Social Security Tax Payable | | | | 3 762 53 | | | | 24 |
| 25 | | Medicare Tax Payable | | | | 839 95 | | | | 25 |

**1.** Debit the factory accounts.

**2.** Credit the three tax withholding accounts.

FaxaVision pays all factory employees twice each month. A separate payroll register is prepared for factory employees. A cash payments journal entry is prepared for each factory payroll. The journal entries for the January 15 and January 31 factory payroll for FaxaVision are shown above.

## RECORDING FACTORY PAYROLL

1. Debit Work in Process for direct labor and Factory Overhead for indirect labor.

2. Credit Employee Income Tax Payable, Social Security Tax Payable, and Medicare Tax Payable for the amounts withheld from employees.

3. Credit Cash for the net pay.

| Work in Process | |
|---|---|
| Bal. 82,579.00 | |
| 1/15 39,245.00 | |
| 1/31 44,255.00 | |

| Factory Overhead | |
|---|---|
| 1/15 11,774.00 | |
| 1/31 13,276.00 | |

| Employee Income Tax Payable | |
|---|---|
| | 1/15 5,612.10 |
| | 1/31 6,328.40 |

| Social Security Tax Payable | |
|---|---|
| | 1/15 3,336.64 |
| | 1/31 3,762.53 |

| Medicare Tax Payable | |
|---|---|
| | 1/15 744.88 |
| | 1/31 839.95 |

| Cash | |
|---|---|
| | 1/15 41,325.38 |
| | 1/31 46,600.12 |

| | DATE | | ACCOUNT CREDITED | PURCH. NO. | POST. REF. | MATERIALS DR. ACCTS. PAY. CR. | |
|---|---|---|---|---|---|---|---|
| 1 | 20-- Jan. | 4 | Oakley Electronics | 621 | | 7 0 9 7 80 | 1 |
| 24 | | 31 | Total | | | 168 6 4 2 60 | 24 |

*MATERIALS PURCHASES JOURNAL*    PAGE *1*

FaxaVision records the amount of direct and indirect materials purchased and issued in the general ledger account Materials. FaxaVision uses a perpetual inventory in the factory that permits the company to charge cost of materials to a job as materials are issued. [CONCEPT: *Matching Expenses with Revenue*]

FaxaVision uses a special materials purchases journal to record all materials purchases. Purchases are made on account; therefore, the journal has a single amount column. An entry in the materials purchases journal is shown above.

At the end of a month, the total of the materials purchases journal is posted to Materials and Accounts Payable in the general ledger.

In the materials account, the January 1 debit balance, *$121,231.20*, is the materials inventory at the beginning of the month. The January 31 debit, *$168,642.60*, is the total posted from the materials purchases journal. This represents the total cost of direct and indirect materials purchased during the month.

```
                    Materials
Jan. 1 Bal.     121,231.20 |
Jan. 31         168,642.60 |

                 Accounts Payable
                            |  Jan. 31      168,642.60
```

# RECORDING MATERIALS REQUISITIONS

| | DATE | | ACCOUNT TITLE | DOC. NO. | POST. REF. | DEBIT | CREDIT | |
|---|---|---|---|---|---|---|---|---|
| 1 | 20-- Jan. | 31 | Work in Process | M240 | | 156 4 7 7 00 | | 1 |
| 2 | | | Factory Overhead | | | 11 4 4 7 50 | | 2 |
| 3 | | | Materials | | | | 167 9 2 4 50 | 3 |

*GENERAL JOURNAL*    PAGE *1*

A materials requisition is prepared for direct materials issued for a specific job. After materials are issued, the requisition amount is recorded on a cost sheet and the requisition is filed. At the end of a month, the total value of all direct materials issued to specific jobs must be transferred from Materials to Work in Process.

A materials requisition is also prepared for indirect materials used in the factory. After the indirect materials are issued to the factory, the requisition is filed. At the end of the month, the total value of all indirect materials issued is transferred from Materials to Factory Overhead.

FaxaVision prepares a memorandum with monthly summary information of the direct materials requisitions and the indirect materials totals. The general journal entry to transfer these amounts is shown above.

## MATERIALS AND LABOR USED IN PRODUCTION

The balance in the Work in Process account, $82,579.00, is the beginning inventory of Work in Process. The other debits represent the total amounts of direct labor and direct materials used for all jobs during the month.

The debits to Factory Overhead represent the total amounts of indirect labor used and indirect materials issued during the month.

**Work in Process**

| | |
|---|---|
| Bal. | 82,579.00 |
| Jan. 15 Dir. Lab. | 39,245.00 |
| Jan. 31 Dir. Lab. | 44,255.00 |
| Jan. 31 Dir. Mat. | 156,477.00 |

**Factory Overhead**

| | |
|---|---|
| Jan. 15 Ind. Lab. | 11,774.00 |
| Jan. 31 Ind. Lab. | 13,276.00 |
| Jan. 31 Ind. Mat. | 11,447.50 |

## JOURNALIZING ACTUAL FACTORY OVERHEAD

### GENERAL JOURNAL                                     PAGE 1

| | DATE | ACCOUNT TITLE | DOC. NO. | POST. REF. | DEBIT | CREDIT | |
|---|---|---|---|---|---|---|---|
| 4 | 31 | Factory Overhead | M241 | | 30 456 00 | | 4 |
| 5 | | Depr. Exp.—Factory Equip. | | | | 2 500 00 | 5 |
| 6 | | Depr. Exp.—Building | | | | 1 300 00 | 6 |
| 7 | | Heat, Light, and Power Exp. | | | | 6 158 50 | 7 |
| 8 | | Insurance Exp.—Factory | | | | 620 00 | 8 |
| 9 | | Miscellaneous Exp.—Factory | | | | 784 40 | 9 |
| 10 | | Payroll Taxes Exp.—Factory | | | | 15 414 10 | 10 |
| 11 | | Property Tax Exp.—Factory | | | | 1 463 60 | 11 |
| 12 | | Supplies Exp.—Factory | | | | 2 215 40 | 12 |

Factory overhead includes various indirect factory expenses such as indirect labor, indirect materials, taxes, depreciation, and insurance. Actual factory overhead expenses are summarized in an account titled Factory Overhead.

Indirect labor and indirect materials are posted directly to the factory overhead account from the entries shown on pages 586 and 587. Other indirect expenses are recorded throughout the month in other manufacturing expense accounts. At the end of each month, these indirect expense account balances are transferred to the factory overhead account. The actual factory overhead can then be compared with the estimated amount of factory overhead recorded on the job cost sheets. Recall from Chapter 19 that factory overhead is estimated (applied) so that a company can record overhead on a cost sheet as soon as a job is completed.

Adjusting entries are made at the end of a fiscal period. These adjusting entries include debits to the depreciation expense, insurance expense, and supplies expense accounts. The closing entry to transfer actual overhead expenses to the factory overhead account is shown above.

After postings are completed, all actual factory overhead expense accounts are summarized in the factory overhead account.

**Factory Overhead**

| | |
|---|---|
| Jan. 15 Ind. Lab. | 11,774.00 |
| Jan. 31 Ind. Lab. | 13,276.00 |
| Jan. 31 Ind. Mat. | 11,447.50 |
| Jan. 31 Act. OH | 30,456.00 |
| (New Bal. | 66,953.50) |

# RECORDING APPLIED OVERHEAD

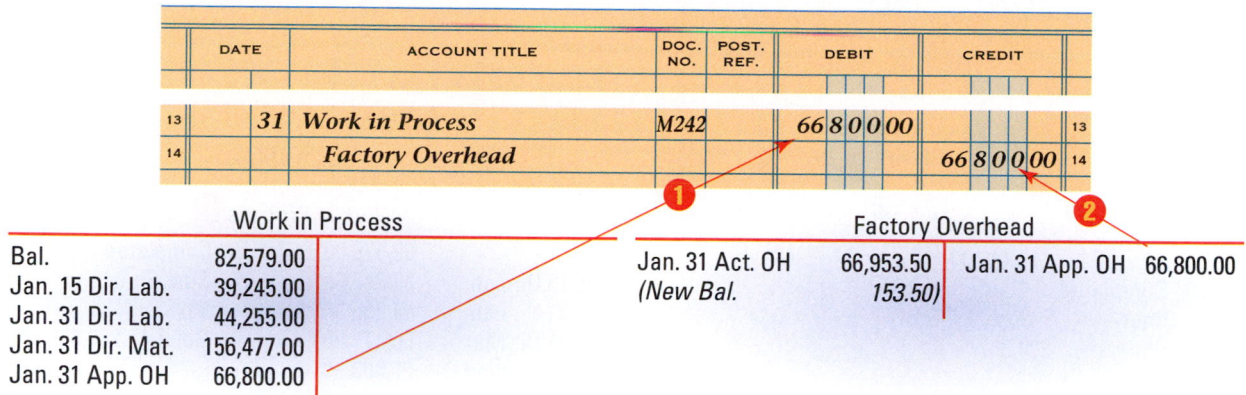

| | DATE | ACCOUNT TITLE | DOC. NO. | POST. REF. | DEBIT | CREDIT | |
|---|---|---|---|---|---|---|---|
| 13 | 31 | Work in Process | M242 | | 66 80 0 00 | | 13 |
| 14 | | Factory Overhead | | | | 66 80 0 00 | 14 |

**Work in Process**

| | |
|---|---|
| Bal. | 82,579.00 |
| Jan. 15 Dir. Lab. | 39,245.00 |
| Jan. 31 Dir. Lab. | 44,255.00 |
| Jan. 31 Dir. Mat. | 156,477.00 |
| Jan. 31 App. OH | 66,800.00 |

**Factory Overhead**

| | | | |
|---|---|---|---|
| Jan. 31 Act. OH | 66,953.50 | Jan. 31 App. OH | 66,800.00 |
| (New Bal. | 153.50) | | |

FaxaVision applies factory overhead to each job at the rate of 80% of direct labor charges. At the end of each month, FaxaVision totals the applied factory overhead recorded on all job cost sheets. Its applied factory overhead for January is $66,800.00. The journal entry to record applied factory overhead is shown above.

The factory overhead account debit, $66,953.50, is the actual factory overhead expense for the month. The credit, $66,800.00, is the applied factory overhead for the month. The account's $153.50 debit ending balance results from recording less applied factory overhead than the amount of actual factory overhead expenses.

# DISPOSING OF OVERAPPLIED AND UNDERAPPLIED FACTORY OVERHEAD BALANCES

| | DATE | ACCOUNT TITLE | DOC. NO. | POST. REF. | DEBIT | CREDIT | |
|---|---|---|---|---|---|---|---|
| 15 | 31 | Income Summary | M243 | | 1 53 50 | | 15 |
| 16 | | Factory Overhead | | | | 1 53 50 | 16 |

The rate used to calculate applied factory overhead is only an estimate. Therefore, the factory overhead account may have an ending balance. The amount by which applied factory overhead is less than actual factory overhead is called **underapplied overhead**. The debit balance, $153.50, in FaxaVision's account indicates underapplied overhead for January. The journal entry to close the factory overhead account at the end of January is shown above.

A credit balance indicates that applied factory overhead is more than actual factory overhead. The amount by which applied factory overhead is more than actual factory overhead is called **overapplied overhead**. If the factory overhead account has a credit balance, Factory Overhead is debited and Income Summary is credited for the overapplied overhead amount.

Overhead may be overapplied or underapplied for two reasons. (1) Actual expenses may be higher or lower than normal, an event that requires closer control over expenditures. (2) The factory overhead applied rate may be inaccurate. If the rate is found to be inaccurate, a revised rate is determined. The revised rate is used in the next fiscal period.

## RECORDING FINISHED GOODS TRANSACTIONS

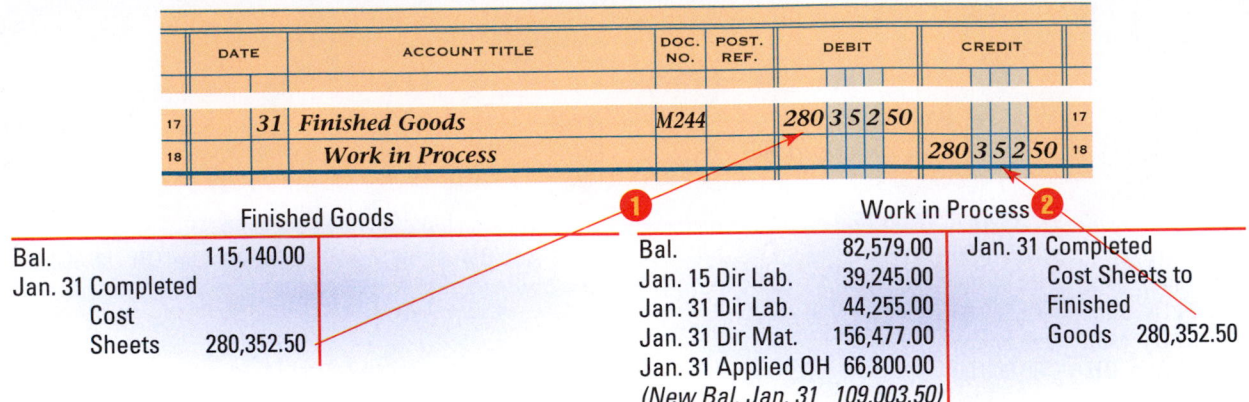

| | DATE | ACCOUNT TITLE | DOC. NO. | POST. REF. | DEBIT | CREDIT | |
|---|---|---|---|---|---|---|---|
| 17 | 31 | *Finished Goods* | M244 | | 280 352 50 | | 17 |
| 18 | | *Work in Process* | | | | 280 352 50 | 18 |

**Finished Goods**

| | |
|---|---|
| Bal. | 115,140.00 |
| Jan. 31 Completed Cost Sheets | 280,352.50 |

**Work in Process** ②

| | | |
|---|---|---|
| Bal. | 82,579.00 | Jan. 31 Completed |
| Jan. 15 Dir Lab. | 39,245.00 | Cost Sheets to |
| Jan. 31 Dir Lab. | 44,255.00 | Finished |
| Jan. 31 Dir Mat. | 156,477.00 | Goods 280,352.50 |
| Jan. 31 Applied OH | 66,800.00 | |
| *(New Bal. Jan. 31* | *109,003.50)* | |

FaxaVision totals the cost sheets for all jobs completed during the month. Its January total, $280,352.50, is the cost of work finished during the month. This amount is transferred from Work in Process to Finished Goods. The journal entry to record this transaction is shown above.

The balance in the finished goods account, $115,140.00, represents beginning inventory.

The January 31 debit to Finished Goods and credit to Work in Process, $280,352.50, represents the cost of finished goods transferred from the factory to the stockroom. The work in process account balance, $109,003.50, is the total amount of direct materials, direct labor, and applied factory overhead charged to the jobs in the ending inventory of work in process.

## RECORDING SALES AND COST OF GOODS SOLD

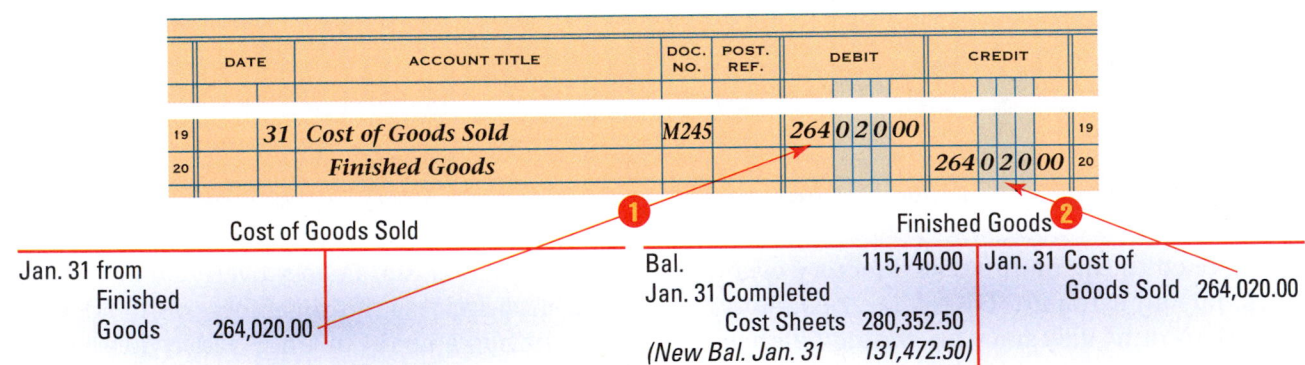

| | DATE | ACCOUNT TITLE | DOC. NO. | POST. REF. | DEBIT | CREDIT | |
|---|---|---|---|---|---|---|---|
| 19 | 31 | *Cost of Goods Sold* | M245 | | 264 020 00 | | 19 |
| 20 | | *Finished Goods* | | | | 264 020 00 | 20 |

**Cost of Goods Sold**

| | |
|---|---|
| Jan. 31 from Finished Goods | 264,020.00 |

**Finished Goods** ②

| | | |
|---|---|---|
| Bal. | 115,140.00 | Jan. 31 Cost of |
| Jan. 31 Completed | | Goods Sold 264,020.00 |
| Cost Sheets | 280,352.50 | |
| *(New Bal. Jan. 31* | *131,472.50)* | |

Since FaxaVision uses a perpetual inventory, a different procedure is used to determine and record cost of goods sold. A copy of each sales invoice is sent to the accounting department to record the sale. For each invoice, the unit cost of each product shipped and the total cost of all products shipped are calculated and recorded on the sales invoice copy.

At the end of the month, cost information on all sales invoices is totaled. The total costs recorded for FaxaVision's January sales, $264,020.00, is the cost of goods sold for the month. This number represents the total *cost* of products sold, not the revenue derived from sales (which is determined by selling price). This total cost is transferred from the inventory account Finished Goods to the cost account Cost of Goods Sold, as shown above.

The debit to Cost of Goods Sold, $264,020.00, is the cost of goods sold during the month. The credit to Finished Goods, $264,020.00, is the cost of finished goods sold during the month and removed from inventory. The finished goods account balance, $131,472.50, is the ending inventory of finished goods.

## MANUFACTURING ACCOUNTS IN THE GENERAL LEDGER

ACCOUNT *Materials* ACCOUNT NO. *1125*

| DATE | | ITEM | POST. REF. | DEBIT | CREDIT | BALANCE DEBIT | BALANCE CREDIT |
|---|---|---|---|---|---|---|---|
| 20-- Jan. | 1 | Balance | ✓ | | | 121 2 3 1 20 | |
| | 31 | | MP1 | 168 6 4 2 60 | | 289 8 7 3 80 | |
| | 31 | | G1 | | 167 9 2 4 50 | 121 9 4 9 30 | |

ACCOUNT *Work in Process* ACCOUNT NO. *1130*

| DATE | | ITEM | POST. REF. | DEBIT | CREDIT | BALANCE DEBIT | BALANCE CREDIT |
|---|---|---|---|---|---|---|---|
| 20-- Jan. | 1 | Balance | ✓ | | | 82 5 7 9 00 | |
| | 15 | | CP2 | 39 2 4 5 00 | | 121 8 2 4 00 | |
| | 31 | | CP2 | 44 2 5 5 00 | | 166 0 7 9 00 | |
| | 31 | | G1 | 156 4 7 7 00 | | 322 5 5 6 00 | |
| | 31 | | G1 | 66 8 0 0 00 | | 389 3 5 6 00 | |
| | 31 | | G1 | | 280 3 5 2 50 | 109 0 0 3 50 | |

ACCOUNT *Finished Goods* ACCOUNT NO. *1135*

| DATE | | ITEM | POST. REF. | DEBIT | CREDIT | BALANCE DEBIT | BALANCE CREDIT |
|---|---|---|---|---|---|---|---|
| 20-- Jan. | 1 | Balance | ✓ | | | 115 1 4 0 00 | |
| | 31 | | G1 | 280 3 5 2 50 | | 395 4 9 2 50 | |
| | 31 | | G1 | | 264 0 2 0 00 | 131 4 7 2 50 | |

ACCOUNT *Cost of Goods Sold* ACCOUNT NO. *5105*

| DATE | | ITEM | POST. REF. | DEBIT | CREDIT | BALANCE DEBIT | BALANCE CREDIT |
|---|---|---|---|---|---|---|---|
| 20-- Jan. | 31 | | G1 | 264 0 2 0 00 | | 264 0 2 0 00 | |

ACCOUNT *Factory Overhead* ACCOUNT NO. *5505*

| DATE | | ITEM | POST. REF. | DEBIT | CREDIT | BALANCE DEBIT | BALANCE CREDIT |
|---|---|---|---|---|---|---|---|
| 20-- Jan. | 15 | | CP2 | 11 7 7 4 00 | | 11 7 7 4 00 | |
| | 31 | | CP2 | 13 2 7 6 00 | | 25 0 5 0 00 | |
| | 31 | | G1 | 11 4 4 7 50 | | 36 4 9 7 50 | |
| | 31 | | G1 | 30 4 5 6 00 | | 66 9 5 3 50 | |
| | 31 | | G1 | | 66 8 0 0 00 | 1 5 3 50 | |
| | 31 | | G1 | | 1 5 3 50 | ——— | ——— |

The effect of posting the entries described in this chapter is shown above.

TERMS REVIEW • TERMS REVIEW • TERMS
AUDIT YOUR
WORK TOGETHER • WORK TOGETHER • WORK TOGETHER • WORK TOGETHER • WORK

## • terms review

underapplied overhead
overapplied overhead

## • audit your understanding

1. Where are direct materials, direct labor, and overhead costs for each job initially recorded?

2. After factory overhead has been applied to work in process, what does a credit balance in Factory Overhead indicate?

3. Explain the difference between actual factory overhead and applied factory overhead.

## • work together 20-1

### Preparing manufacturing journal entries

A materials purchases journal, a cash payments journal, and a general journal for Vanyo, Inc., a manufacturer of cardboard boxes, are provided in the *Working Papers*. Your instructor will guide you through the following examples.

1. Prepare journal entries for each of the following transactions or events.

   May 3. Purchased $15,400.00 of materials on account from Bushnell Corrugated.

   5. Requisitioned $2,650.00 of direct materials and $350.00 of indirect materials for the production department.

   15. Paid employees their semimonthly pay. Gross (pretax) direct labor costs were $11,200. Gross indirect labor costs were $1,600.00. Employee income tax was $1,480.00. Social security tax was 6.2% and Medicare tax was 1.45% of gross wages.

   21. Requisitioned $4,700.00 of direct materials and $2,100.00 of indirect materials for the production department.

   31. Obtained factory costs for the month: depreciation on building, $750.00; depreciation on equipment, $1,200.00; insurance, $325.00; property taxes, $545.00; utilities, $1,880.00. Assume that these expenses have already been properly accounted for and now need to be closed.

   31. Paid employees their semimonthly pay. Gross (pretax) direct labor costs were $10,150.00. Gross indirect labor costs were $1,370.00. Employee income tax was $1,220.00. Social security tax was 6.2% and Medicare tax was 1.45% of gross wages.

   31. Applied overhead at the rate of 50% of direct labor costs.

   31. Transferred cardboard boxes costing $29,920 to finished goods during the month.

   31. Sold cardboard boxes costing $24,760 during the month.

## on your own 20-1

### Preparing manufacturing journal entries

A materials purchases journal, a cash payments journal, and a general journal for Vanyo, Inc., a manufacturer of cardboard boxes, are provided in the *Working Papers*. Work independently to complete the following problem.

1.  Prepare journal entries for each of the following transactions or events.

    June  4. Purchased $8,100.00 of materials on account from Fresno, Inc.

           7. Requisitioned $3,770.00 of direct materials and $730.00 of indirect materials for the production department.

        15. Paid employees their semimonthly pay. Gross (pretax) direct labor costs were $12,590.00. Gross indirect labor costs were $1,940.00. Employee income tax was $1,780.00. Social security tax was 6.2% and Medicare tax was 1.45% of gross wages.

        15. Requisitioned $2,300.00 of direct materials and $1,530.00 of indirect materials for the production department.

        30. Obtained factory costs for the month: depreciation on building, $750.00; depreciation on equipment, $1,200.00; insurance, $325.00; property taxes, $570.00; utilities, $1,960.00. Assume that these expenses have already been properly accounted for and now need to be closed.

        30. Paid employees their semimonthly pay. Gross (pretax) direct labor costs were $10,860.00. Gross indirect labor costs were $1,785.00. Employee income tax was $1,615.00. Social security tax was 6.2% and Medicare tax was 1.45% of gross wages.

        30. Applied overhead at the rate of 50% of direct labor costs.

        30. Transferred cardboard boxes costing $35,500.00 to finished goods during the month.

        30. Sold cardboard boxes costing $32,160.00 during the month

GLOBAL PERSPECTIVE • GLOBAL PERSPECTIVE • GLOBAL PERSPECTIVE

## global perspective

### International Banking

International business transactions usually require the use of international services from a commercial bank. More than 300 U.S. banks have international banking departments to assist customers with international business.

Some specific services that are offered by commercial banks are: exchange of currency; assistance in financing exports; and collection of invoices, drafts, letters of credit, and other foreign receivables.

**Required**

Contact a local bank that has an international department. Find out the following information.

1.  With what countries does the bank have specialized relationships?

2.  Does the bank handle letters of credit? If so, what is the procedure to negotiate a letter of credit?

3.  Is financial assistance available to exporters? If so, what are the guidelines?

careers in accounting

CAREERS IN ACCOUNTING • CAREERS IN ACCOUNTING • CAREERS IN ACCOUNTI

## Rochelle Klee, Director of Accounts Payable

COURTESY OF ROCHELLE KLEE

Accounts Payable (AP) has been viewed as the department whose employees are located in the basement paying the bills. They are neither qualified nor have the authority to challenge the spending preferences of middle and executive management.

Not so these days. AP leaders and their staff play a key role in helping to contain costs and maintain strict adherence to financial controls in an age of corporate scandals. Chief Financial Officers (CFOs) are looking to their AP leaders to implement processes and systems that create efficiencies in a paper-intensive environment. AP managers also implement financial controls and reports that give accounting managers and CFOs a true picture of the costs of the company. These costs make up a large portion of the general ledger assets, expenses, and risk. CFOs need to know that their AP operations are in capable hands and attention is being paid to those details that could result in major problems if not properly managed.

Rochelle Klee is the Director of Accounts Payable for a diversified *Fortune* 100 company. Accounting was the first high school class that interested her enough to motivate her to put effort into the homework assignments and achieve an *A.* After completing nearly two years of college with an emphasis in business, her focus was not on her studies, and she left college to take a job at a company as an accounting clerk reconciling bank statements.

A formal education is only one contributing factor to success. With a basic understanding of accounting, an ability to learn from others, a willingness to work hard, and the confidence to take on new roles and responsibilities, one can achieve many things in accounting. "There was a point in time where I stated to one of my co-workers, 'I will never work in AP.' It looked like a very dull and unrewarding job to me. Less than one year later I accepted a position as the supervisor of a small AP department." With little AP experience and no supervisory experience, this new position was a challenge. After many fulfilling years, Rochelle is currently the Director of AP and thoroughly enjoys the job.

A career in Accounts Payable provides an opportunity to work with many different individuals across a company but is not without challenges. There are pressures to do more with less and the challenge of working with internal and external AP customers. Rochelle says, "When an employee asks me how to handle a situation, I first ask them what they think. Most ideas and solutions are not made by referring to the idea and solution chart for the answer, but are made by using deductive reasoning and really thinking a situation through." As much as it would seem that AP is a very basic process with a very basic set of rules, the culture and the business needs of an organization dictate the solutions that are applied.

**Salary Range:** Salaries for accounts payable managers vary with the size of the company and the city, ranging from $55,000 to over $75,000. (Source: Bureau of Labor Statistics, U.S. Department of Labor, *Occupational Outlook Handbook, 2004–05 Edition,* Bookkeeping, Accounting, and on the Internet at http://www.bls.gov/oco/ocos144.htm [visited April 04, 2005].)

**Qualifications:** High school diploma for entry-level accounts payable clerks. Accounts payable experience usually required for supervisory positions in accounts payable.

**Occupational Outlook:** Slower than average growth is predicted in accounting clerk positions as technology improves employee efficiency. Clerks in specialized areas will be in less demand than those who have a broader range of knowledge and the ability to do a wider range of accounting activities.

# 20-2 Preparing End-of-Fiscal-Period Statements

## PREPARING THE WORK SHEET

The primary purpose of cost accounting information is to help managers make better decisions. However, some of this information is also used to prepare financial statements, which may be important not only to managers inside the firm but also to investors, creditors, and others outside the organization.

Several of the procedures used to prepare a manufacturing business's work sheet and financial statements are similar to the procedures used for a merchandising business.

A work sheet is used to plan a manufacturing business's financial information for fiscal period statements just as it is for merchandising businesses. However, a manufacturing business's work sheet includes three inventory accounts and a cost of goods sold account. FaxaVision's work sheet for January is shown on pages 596 and 597.

FaxaVision's work sheet, similar to the work sheets of other manufacturing businesses using the perpetual inventory method, has several unique characteristics:

1. The entries to record direct materials, work in process, and finished goods bring manufacturing inventory accounts up to date on January 31. Thus, the balances of Materials, Work in Process, and Finished Goods are brought up to date before a work sheet is prepared.

Adjustments for these inventory accounts do not need to be planned on a work sheet.

2. The factory keeps perpetual inventory subsidiary ledgers and detailed cost records. Based on these subsidiary records, summary journal entries are made to record the flow of costs through the manufacturing process to the cost of goods sold account. Since all manufacturing costs flow toward the account Cost of Goods Sold, no other manufacturing cost accounts on the work sheet have balances. Amounts in these accounts have been transferred to either one of the inventory accounts or the cost of goods sold account. The cost of goods sold amount, *$264,020.00*, is extended to the Income Statement Debit column.

3. Income Summary has a debit balance of $153.50. This balance resulted from closing the underapplied overhead to Income Summary. The amount represents additional manufacturing costs that are not already in the inventory or cost of goods sold account. The amount is extended to the Income Statement Debit column.

Extending other accounts to the Income Statement and Balance Sheet columns and calculating net income are similar to the procedures described for corporations in Chapter 13.

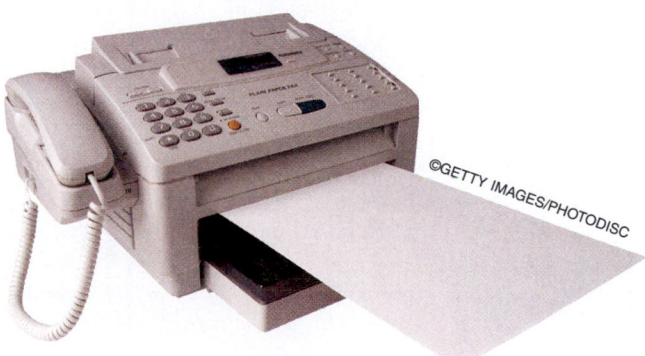

©GETTY IMAGES/PHOTODISC

**FYI** FOR YOUR INFORMATION

Robots and advanced electronic systems are used to manufacture products in many factories. The use of automated equipment to perform routine, repetitive manufacturing tasks is often referred to as "computer integrated manufacturing" (CIM).

**FaxaVision, Inc.**
**Work Sheet**
**For Month Ended January 31, 20--**

| | ACCOUNT TITLE | TRIAL BALANCE DEBIT | TRIAL BALANCE CREDIT | ADJUSTMENTS DEBIT | ADJUSTMENTS CREDIT | INCOME STATEMENT DEBIT | INCOME STATEMENT CREDIT | BALANCE SHEET DEBIT | BALANCE SHEET CREDIT | |
|---|---|---|---|---|---|---|---|---|---|---|
| 1 | Cash | 18263360 | | | | | | 18263360 | | 1 |
| 2 | Petty Cash | 30000 | | | | | | 30000 | | 2 |
| 3 | Accounts Receivable | 22420750 | | | | | | 22420750 | | 3 |
| 4 | Allow. for Uncoll. Accts. | | 454160 | | (a) 205660 | | | | 659820 | 4 |
| 5 | Materials | 12194930 | | | | | | 12194930 | | 5 |
| 6 | Work in Process | 10900350 | | | | | | 10900350 | | 6 |
| 7 | Finished Goods | 13147250 | | | | | | 13147250 | | 7 |
| 8 | Supplies—Factory | 725870 | | | | | | 725870 | | 8 |
| 9 | Supplies—Sales | 953120 | | | (b) 185020 | | | 768100 | | 9 |
| 10 | Supplies—Administrative | 242580 | | | (c) 46840 | | | 195740 | | 10 |
| 11 | Prepaid Insurance | 419860 | | | (d) 13060 | | | 406800 | | 11 |
| 12 | Factory Equipment | 18200000 | | | | | | 18200000 | | 12 |
| 13 | Accum. Depr.—Factory Equipment | | 5461000 | | | | | | 5461000 | 13 |
| 14 | Office Equipment | 2526000 | | | | | | 2526000 | | 14 |
| 15 | Accum. Depr.—Office Equipment | | 620000 | | (e) 53000 | | | | 673000 | 15 |
| 16 | Store Equipment | 2290000 | | | | | | 2290000 | | 16 |
| 17 | Accum. Depr.—Store Equipment | | 677000 | | (f) 49000 | | | | 726000 | 17 |
| 18 | Building | 39700000 | | | | | | 39700000 | | 18 |
| 19 | Accum. Depr.—Building | | 5950000 | | | | | | 5950000 | 19 |
| 20 | Land | 17700000 | | | | | | 17700000 | | 20 |
| 21 | Accounts Payable | | 18969850 | | | | | | 18969850 | 21 |
| 22 | Employee Income Tax Payable | | 1187140 | | | | | | 1187140 | 22 |
| 23 | Federal Income Tax Payable | | | | (g) 2099500 | | | | 2099500 | 23 |
| 24 | Social Security Tax Payable | | 1397906 | | | | | | 1397906 | 24 |
| 25 | Medicare Tax Payable | | 322594 | | | | | | 322594 | 25 |
| 26 | Salaries Payable | | | | | | | | | 26 |
| 27 | Unemploy. Tax Payable—Federal | | 126840 | | | | | | 126840 | 27 |
| 28 | Unemploy. Tax Payable—State | | 856170 | | | | | | 856170 | 28 |
| 29 | Dividends Payable | | | | | | | | | 29 |
| 30 | Mortgage Payable | | 10000000 | | | | | | 10000000 | 30 |
| 31 | Capital Stock | | 60000000 | | | | | | 60000000 | 31 |
| 32 | Retained Earnings | | 46963880 | | | | | | 46963880 | 32 |
| 33 | Dividends | | | | | | | | | 33 |
| 34 | Income Summary | 15350 | | | | 15350 | | | | 34 |

| | Trial Balance Debit | Trial Balance Credit | Adjustments Debit | Income Statement Debit | Income Statement Credit | Balance Sheet Debit | Balance Sheet Credit |
|---|---|---|---|---|---|---|---|
| 35 Sales | | 4114 8000 | | | 4114 8000 | | |
| 36 Cost of Goods Sold | 2640 2000 | | | 2640 2000 | | | |
| 37 Factory Overhead | | | | | | | |
| 38 Depr. Expense—Factory Equipment | | | | | | | |
| 39 Depr. Expense—Building | | | | | | | |
| 40 Heat, Light, and Power Expense | | | | | | | |
| 41 Insurance Expense—Factory | | | | | | | |
| 42 Miscellaneous Exp.—Factory | | | | | | | |
| 43 Payroll Taxes Exp.—Factory | | | | | | | |
| 44 Property Tax Exp.—Factory | | | | | | | |
| 45 Supplies Expense—Factory | | | | | | | |
| 46 Advertising Expense | 478440 | | | 478440 | | | |
| 47 Delivery Expense | 1105860 | | | 1105860 | | | |
| 48 Depr. Expense—Store Equipment | | | (f) 49000 | 49000 | | | |
| 49 Miscellaneous Expenses—Sales | 155450 | | | 155450 | | | |
| 50 Salary Expense—Sales | 2807800 | | | 2807800 | | | |
| 51 Supplies Expense—Sales | | | (b) 185020 | 185020 | | | |
| 52 Depr. Expense—Office Equipment | | | (e) 53000 | 53000 | | | |
| 53 Insurance Expense—Admin. | | | (d) 13060 | 13060 | | | |
| 54 Miscellaneous Exp.—Admin. | 218420 | | | 218420 | | | |
| 55 Payroll Taxes Exp.—Admin. | 710000 | | | 710000 | | | |
| 56 Property Tax Exp.—Admin. | 15980 | | | 15980 | | | |
| 57 Salary Expense—Admin. | 2192200 | | | 2192200 | | | |
| 58 Supplies Expense—Admin. | | | (c) 46840 | 46840 | | | |
| 59 Uncollectible Accounts Expense | | | (a) 205660 | 205660 | | | |
| 60 Utilities Expense—Admin. | 154380 | | | 154380 | | | |
| 61 Gain on Plant Assets | | | | | | | |
| 62 Miscellaneous Revenue | | | | | | | |
| 63 Interest Expense | 150000 | | | 150000 | | | |
| 64 Loss on Plant Assets | 14590 | | | 14590 | | | |
| 65 Federal Income Tax Expense | | | (g) 2099500 | 2099500 | | | |
| 66 | 1941 3 4540 | 4114 8000 | 2652080 | 3707 2550 | 4114 8000 | 1594 6 9 1 50 | 1553 9 3 7 00 |
| 67 Net Income after Fed. Inc. Tax | | | | 407 5450 | | | 407 5450 |
| 68 | | | | 4114 8000 | 4114 8000 | 1594 6 9 1 50 | 1594 6 9 1 50 |

**FaxaVision, Inc.**
**Statement of Cost of Goods Manufactured**
**For Month Ended January 31, 20--**

| | |
|---|---:|
| Direct Materials . . . . . . . . . . . . . . . . . . . . . | $156,477.00 |
| Direct Labor . . . . . . . . . . . . . . . . . . . . . . . . | 83,500.00 |
| Factory Overhead Applied . . . . . . . . . . . . . . . . . . | 66,800.00 |
| Total Cost of Work Placed in Process . . . . . . . . . . . . | $306,777.00 |
| Work in Process Inventory, Jan. 1, 20-- . . . . . . . . . . . | 82,579.00 |
| Total Cost of Work in Process During January . . . . . . . . | $389,356.00 |
| Less Work in Process Inventory, Jan. 31, 20-- . . . . . . . . | 109,003.50 |
| Cost of Goods Manufactured . . . . . . . . . . . . . . . . . | $280,352.50 |

**1.** Enter direct materials, direct labor, and factory overhead applied.

**2.** Total the cost of work placed in process.

**3.** Add beginning work in process inventory.

**4.** Subtract ending work in process inventory.

A manufacturing business prepares an income statement, a statement of stockholders' equity, and a balance sheet. These statements are similar to those previously described for other kinds of businesses. A statement showing details about the cost of finished goods is called a **statement of cost of goods manufactured**. This state-ment shows the details of the cost elements—materials, direct labor, and factory overhead—spent on the goods completed in a fiscal period. A statement of cost of goods manufactured sup-plements the income statement. FaxaVision's statement of cost of goods manufactured is shown above.

# STEPS  STEPS • STEPS • STEPS • STEPS • STEPS • STEPS • STEPS • STEPS • STEPS • STEPS • STEPS

## PREPARING A STATEMENT OF COST OF GOODS MANUFACTURED

**1** Enter direct materials, *$156,477.00*. This is the amount debited to Work in Process in the general journal, page 587. Enter direct labor, *$83,500.00*, from the cash payments journal, page 586. Enter factory overhead applied, *$66,800.00*. The amount of factory overhead is the total of the applied factory overhead recorded on cost sheets. The journal entry to record applied factory overhead was shown on page 589.

**2** Total the cost of work placed in process by adding direct materials, direct labor, and factory overhead applied.

**3** Add beginning work in process inventory, *$82,579.00*, to determine the total cost of work in process during the month.

**4** Subtract ending work in process inventory, *$109,003.50*, to determine the cost of goods manufactured during the month.

# SOURCES OF INCOME STATEMENT INFORMATION

FaxaVision's income statement for the month of January is shown on page 599. Information for FaxaVision's income statement comes from three sources:

1. Beginning and ending finished goods invento-ries, *$115,140.00* and *$131,472.50*, come from the general ledger account, page 591.

2. Cost of goods manufactured, *$280,352.50*, comes from the statement of cost of goods manufactured shown above.

3. All other amounts come from the Income Statement columns of the work sheet, pages 596–597.

Accounting Transactions and Financial Reporting for a Manufacturing Business

**FaxaVision, Inc.**
**Income Statement**
**For Month Ended January 31, 20--**

| | | | *% of Net Sales |
|---|---|---|---|
| Operating Revenue: | | | |
| Sales | | $411,480.00 | 100.0 |
| Cost of Goods Sold: | | | |
| Finished Goods Inventory, Jan. 1, 20-- | $115,140.00 | | |
| Cost of Goods Manufactured | 280,352.50 | | |
| Total Cost of Finished Goods Available for Sale | $395,492.50 | | |
| Less Finished Goods Inventory, Jan. 31, 20-- | 131,472.50 | | |
| Cost of Goods Sold | $264,020.00 | | |
| Underapplied Overhead | 153.50 | | |
| Net Cost of Goods Sold | | 264,173.50 | 64.2 |
| Gross Profit on Operations | | $147,306.50 | 35.8 |
| Operating Expenses: | | | |
| Selling Expenses: | | | |
| Advertising Expense | $ 4,784.40 | | |
| Delivery Expense | 11,058.60 | | |
| Depreciation Expense—Store Equipment | 490.00 | | |
| Miscellaneous Expense—Sales | 1,554.50 | | |
| Salary Expense—Sales | 28,078.00 | | |
| Supplies Expense—Sales | 1,850.20 | | |
| Total Selling Expenses | $ 47,815.70 | | |
| Administrative Expenses: | | | |
| Depreciation Expense—Office Equipment | $ 530.00 | | |
| Insurance Expense—Administrative | 130.60 | | |
| Miscellaneous Expense—Administrative | 2,184.20 | | |
| Payroll Taxes Expense—Administrative | 7,100.00 | | |
| Property Tax Expense—Administrative | 159.80 | | |
| Salary Expense—Administrative | 21,922.00 | | |
| Supplies Expense—Administrative | 468.40 | | |
| Uncollectible Accounts Expense | 2,056.60 | | |
| Utilities Expense—Administrative | 1,543.80 | | |
| Total Administrative Expenses | $ 36,095.40 | | |
| Total Operating Expenses | | 83,911.10 | 20.4 |
| Net Income from Operations | | $ 63,395.40 | 15.4 |
| Other Expenses: | | | |
| Interest Expense | $ 1,500.00 | | |
| Loss on Plant Assets | 145.90 | | |
| Net Deduction | | 1,645.90 | 0.4 |
| Net Income before Federal Income Tax | | $ 61,749.50 | 15.0 |
| Less Federal Income Tax Expense | | 20,995.00 | 5.1 |
| Net Income after Federal Income Tax | | $ 40,754.50 | 9.9 |

*Rounded to nearest 0.1%

This income statement differs in two ways from the income statements of merchandising businesses shown in previous chapters:

1. Cost of goods manufactured is used instead of purchases. Details of the cost of goods manufactured are given on the statement of cost of goods manufactured.

2. The amount of underapplied overhead, *$153.50*, is added to the cost of goods sold. The amount is added because applied overhead is less than the actual overhead. The

cost of goods manufactured, shown on page 598, includes the applied overhead amount rather than the actual amount. The income statement must be adjusted to reflect actual factory overhead costs. Theoretically, the underapplied or overapplied overhead should be apportioned among the work in process inventory, finished goods inventory, and cost of goods sold accounts. However, since the amount is small, it is charged entirely to cost of goods sold.

**Faxa Vision, Inc.**
**Balance Sheet**
**January 31, 20--**

### ASSETS

Current Assets:

| | | |
|---|---|---|
| Cash | | $182,633.60 |
| Petty Cash | | 300.00 |
| Accounts Receivable | $224,207.50 | |
| Less Allowance for Uncollectible Accounts | 6,598.20 | 217,609.30 |
| Materials | | 121,949.30 |
| Work in Process | | 109,003.50 |
| Finished Goods | | 131,472.50 |
| Supplies—Factory | | 7,258.70 |
| Supplies—Sales | | 7,681.00 |
| Supplies—Administrative | | 1,957.40 |
| Prepaid Insurance | | 4,068.00 |
| Total Current Assets | | $ 783,933.30 |

Plant Assets:

| | | | |
|---|---|---|---|
| Factory Equipment | $182,000.00 | | |
| Less Accumulated Depreciation—Factory Equipment | 54,610.00 | $127,390.00 | |
| Office Equipment | $ 25,260.00 | | |
| Less Accumulated Depreciation—Office Equipment | 6,730.00 | 18,530.00 | |
| Store Equipment | $ 22,900.00 | | |
| Less Accumulated Depreciation—Store Equipment | 7,260.00 | 15,640.00 | |
| Building | $397,000.00 | | |
| Less Accumulated Depreciation—Building | 59,500.00 | 337,500.00 | |
| Land | | 177,000.00 | |
| Total Plant Assets | | | 676,060.00 |
| Total Assets | | | $1,459,993.30 |

### LIABILITIES

Current Liabilities:

| | | |
|---|---|---|
| Accounts Payable | $189,698.50 | |
| Employee Income Tax Payable | 11,871.40 | |
| Federal Income Tax Payable | 20,995.00 | |
| Social Security Tax Payable | 13,979.06 | |
| Medicare Tax Payable | 3,225.94 | |
| Unemployment Tax Payable—Federal | 1,268.40 | |
| Unemployment Tax Payable—State | 8,561.70 | |
| Total Current Liabilities | | $ 249,600.00 |

Long-Term Liability:

| | | |
|---|---|---|
| Mortgage Payable | | 100,000.00 |
| Total Liabilities | | $ 349,600.00 |

### STOCKHOLDERS' EQUITY

| | | |
|---|---|---|
| Capital Stock | $600,000.00 | |
| Retained Earnings | 510,393.30 | |
| Total Stockholders' Equity | | 1,110,393.30 |
| Total Liabilities and Stockholders' Equity | | $1,459,993.30 |

The balance sheet prepared by FaxaVision on January 31, of the current year is shown above.

Except for the list of inventories, the balance sheet of a manufacturing business is similar to the balance sheet of a merchandising business. In a manufacturing business, the current assets section of the balance sheet lists three types of inventories: (1) materials, (2) work in process, and (3) finished goods.

A statement of stockholders' equity for a manufacturing business is similar to that of a merchandising business described in Chapter 13. The statement of stockholders' equity for FaxaVision is not illustrated.

## • term review

TERM REVIEW • TERM

statement of cost of goods
manufactured

## • audit your understanding

AUDIT YOUR

1.  To which work sheet column is the debit balance of Cost of Goods Sold extended?

2.  How is underapplied overhead accounted for on an income statement?

3.  In which section of the balance sheet are the three inventory accounts of a manufacturing business listed?

## • work together 20-2

WORK TOGETHER • WORK TOGETHER • WORK

### Preparing statement of cost of goods manufactured, income statement, and balance sheet

Work sheets for Bedthings, Inc., a manufacturing firm, are included in the *Working Papers*. Additional information for Bedthings for the months of March and April follow. Your instructor will guide you through the following examples.

|  | March | April |
|---|---|---|
| Cost of Direct Materials Used to Produce Finished Goods | $110,950.00 | $123,490.00 |
| Cost of Direct Labor Used to Produce Finished Goods | 82,165.00 | 88,205.00 |
| Actual Factory Overhead | 61,150.00 | 64,320.00 |
| Applied Factory Overhead | 62,310.00 | 63,730.00 |
| Beginning Finished Goods Inventory | 102,845.00 | 118,520.00 |
| Beginning Work in Process Inventory | 78,100.00 | 78,360.00 |

1.  Prepare a statement of cost of goods manufactured for March of the current year.

2.  Prepare an income statement for March of the current year.

3.  Prepare a balance sheet as of March 31 of the current year.

## • on your own 20-2

ON YOUR OWN • ON YOUR OWN

### Preparing statement of cost of goods manufactured, income statement, and balance sheet

Work sheets for Bedthings, Inc., a manufacturing firm, are included in the *Working Papers*. Use the information for April from Work Together 20-2. Work independently to complete the following problems.

1.  Prepare a statement of cost of goods manufactured for April of the current year.

2.  Prepare an income statement for April of the current year.

3.  Prepare a balance sheet as of April 30 of the current year.

## SUMMARY

*After completing this chapter, you can*

1. Define accounting terms related to accounting transactions and financial reporting for a manufacturing business.

2. Identify accounting concepts and practices related to accounting transactions and financial reporting for a manufacturing business.

3. Journalize transactions for a manufacturing business.

4. Prepare selected financial statements for a manufacturing business.

# Explore Accounting

EXPLORE ACCOUNTING • EXPLORE ACCOUNTING • EXPLORE ACCC

## ISO 9000 Certification

Downhill Cycle assembles mountain bikes from components manufactured by other companies. Rather than personally examining each supplier's manufacturing process, the managers of Downhill Cycle require its suppliers to be ISO 9000 certified. ISO 9000 certification assures customers that the company has an effective quality management system that continually evaluates and improves the production process.

The ISO certification program was developed by the International Organization of Standards (ISO), a worldwide federation of national standards organizations. ISO's role includes programs that certify the manufacturing process. To become ISO 9000 certified, a company must follow the ISO's standards for various phases of the production process, including design, development, production, inspection, and servicing. The company must maintain an information system to record its compliance with ISO standards. Finally, the company must hire an independent organization to audit its initial and continuing compliance with ISO standards. ISO 9000 certification does not assure or guarantee the production of quality products. However, ISO 9000 certification does make a positive statement about a company's commitment to quality.

Other than helping to control costs, how does ISO 9000 certification impact accounting? Accountants assist in designing and operating the information systems necessary to collect ISO 9000 compliance data. Accountants in public accounting firms are also involved in ISO 9000 certification. These firms can either assist a client to prepare for the ISO 9000 certification process or be the independent organization that audits the client and awards ISO 9000 certification.

**Required:**
Research answers to the following questions:

1. How is ISO 9000 certification similar to financial statement audits?

2. Several types of ISO certification are available. Explain the purpose of ISO 14000 standards.

3. An acronym for the International Organization of Standardization would logically be IOS. Explain why the ISO title is used for the organization and its certifications.

# 20-1 APPLICATION PROBLEM

**PEACHTREE**   **QUICKBOOKS**

## Journalizing cost accounting transactions for a manufacturing company

Perry, Inc., completed the following factory cost transactions during August of the current year:

**Transactions:**

Aug.  4.  Purchased $6,152.80 of materials from Sharon Company on account. P047.
      7.  Paid cash for machinery used for production, $3,458.00. C651.
      15. Bought supplies for use in the factory by paying $583.83 cash. C658.
      21. Had machinery repaired. Made cash payment of $1,123.00 to repairer. C667. (Miscellaneous Expense—Factory)
      24. Purchased materials on account from Hubbard Company, $3,510.72. P048. Monthly factory payroll was paid in cash, $7,599.32 (direct labor, $7,200.00, and indirect labor, $1,920.00; less deductions: employee income tax, $823.00; Social security tax, $566.87; Medicare tax, $130.81). C679.

**Instructions:**

1. Journalize the transactions. Use page 4 of a materials purchases journal and page 8 of a cash payments journal. Source documents are abbreviated as follows: check, C; purchase invoice, P.
2. Total and rule the materials purchases journal.
3. Prove and rule the cash payments journal.

# 20-2 APPLICATION PROBLEM

## Journalizing and posting entries that summarize cost records at the end of a fiscal period

The following information is taken from the records of Cramer Corporation on March 31 of the current year. The accounts and balances needed to complete this problem are provided in the *Working Papers*.

a. The total factory payroll for the month from the payroll register is $122,530.00, distributed as follows:

| | | | | |
|---|---|---|---|---|
| Work in Process | $102,570.00 | Employee Income Tax Payable | 13,478.50 |
| Factory Overhead | 19,960.00 | Social Security Tax Payable | 7,964.45 |
| Cash | 99,249.10 | Medicare Tax Payable | 1,837.95 |

b. The total of all requisitions of direct materials issued during the month is $139,419.80. The total of all requisitions of indirect materials issued during the month is $4,505.00.
c. The factory overhead to be charged to Work in Process is 68% of the direct labor cost.
d. The total of all cost sheets completed during the month is $294,313.50.
e. The total of costs recorded on all sales invoices for March is $395,800.00.

**Instructions:**

1. Journalize the factory payroll entry on page 6 of a cash payments journal. C371. Post the general debit and general credit amounts.
2. Journalize the following entries on page 3 of a general journal. Post the entries.
   a. An entry to transfer the total of all direct materials requisitions to Work in Process and indirect materials to Factory Overhead. M34.
   b. An entry to close all individual manufacturing expense accounts to Factory Overhead. M35.
   c. An entry to record applied factory overhead to Work in Process. M36.
3. Continue using page 3 of the general journal. Journalize and post the entry to close the balance of the factory overhead account to Income Summary. M37.
4. Journalize and post the entry to transfer the total of all cost sheets completed from Work in Process to Finished Goods. M38.
5. Journalize and post the entry to transfer the cost of products sold from Finished Goods to Cost of Goods Sold. M39. Save your work to complete Application Problem 20-3.

## 20-3 APPLICATION PROBLEM

**Preparing a statement of cost of goods manufactured**

Use the working papers from Application Problem 20-2 to complete this problem.

**Instructions:**

Prepare a statement of cost of goods manufactured for Cramer Corporation. The statement is for the month ended March 31 of the current year.

## 20-4 MASTERY PROBLEM

**Journalizing entries that summarize cost records at the end of a fiscal period**

The following information is taken from the records of Simmons Corporation on May 31 of the current year. The accounts and balances needed to complete this problem are provided in the *Working Papers*.

a. The total factory payroll for the month according to the payroll register is $77,430.00, distributed as follows.

| | | | |
|---|---|---|---|
| Work in Process | $58,160.00 | Employee Income Tax Payable | 8,627.50 |
| Factory Overhead | 19,270.00 | Social Security Tax Payable | 5,032.95 |
| Cash | 62,608.10 | Medicare Tax Payable | 1,161.45 |

b. The total of all requisitions of direct materials issued during the month is $64,344.00. The total of all requisitions of indirect materials issued during the month is $5,835.00.

c. The factory overhead to be charged to Work in Process is 80% of the direct labor cost.

d. The total of all cost sheets completed during the month is $166,425.00.

e. The total of costs recorded on all sales invoices for May is $258,705.00.

**Instructions:**

1. Journalize the factory payroll entry on page 10 of a cash payments journal. C711. Post the general debit and general credit amounts.
2. Journalize the following entries on page 5 of a general journal. Post the debit and credit amounts.
   a. An entry to transfer the total of all direct materials requisitions to Work in Process and indirect materials to Factory Overhead. M211.
   b. An entry to close all individual manufacturing expense accounts to Factory Overhead. M212.
   c. An entry to record applied factory overhead to Work in Process. M213.
3. Continue using page 5 of the general journal. Journalize and post the entry to close the balance of the factory overhead account to Income Summary. M214.
4. Journalize and post the entry to transfer the total of all cost sheets completed from Work in Process to Finished Goods. M215.
5. Journalize and post the entry to transfer the cost of products sold from Finished Goods to Cost of Goods Sold. M216.
6. Prepare a statement of cost of goods manufactured for the month ended May 31 of the current year.

## 20-5 CHALLENGE PROBLEM  PEACHTREE

**Journalizing entries that summarize cost records at the end of a fiscal period; preparing financial statements**

The following information is taken from the records of Cozart Company on July 31 of the current year. The accounts and balances needed to complete this problem are provided in the *Working Papers*.

Accounting Transactions and Financial Reporting for a Manufacturing Business

a. The total factory payroll for the month from the payroll register is $63,000.00, distributed as follows.

| | | | |
|---|---|---|---|
| Work in Process | $46,600.00 | Employee Income Tax Payable | 6,930.00 |
| Factory Overhead | 16,400.00 | Social Security Tax Payable | 4,095.00 |
| Cash | 51,030.00 | Medicare Tax Payable | 945.00 |

b. The total of all requisitions of direct materials issued during the month is $67,760.00. The total of all requisitions of indirect materials issued during the month is $6,990.00.

c. The factory overhead to be charged to Work in Process is 95% of the direct labor cost.

d. The total of all cost sheets completed during the month is $140,984.00.

e. The total of costs recorded on all sales invoices for July is $112,176.83.

**Instructions:**

1. Journalize the factory payroll entry on page 14 of a cash payments journal. C341. Post the general debit and general credit amounts.

2. Journalize the following entries on page 7 of a general journal. Post the entries.

   a. An entry to transfer the total of all direct materials requisitions to Work in Process and indirect materials to Factory Overhead. M698.

   b. An entry to close all individual manufacturing expense accounts to Factory Overhead. M699.

   c. An entry to record applied factory overhead to Work in Process. M700.

3. Continue using page 7 of the general journal. Journalize and post the entry to close the balance of the factory overhead account to Income Summary. M701.

4. Journalize and post the entry to transfer the total of all cost sheets completed from Work in Process to Finished Goods. M702.

5. Journalize and post the entry to transfer the cost of products sold from Finished Goods to Cost of Goods Sold. M703.

6. Prepare a statement of cost of goods manufactured for the month ended July 31 of the current year.

Cozart's general ledger accounts and their balances on July 31 of the current year are given on the work sheet in the *Working Papers*. (The Employee Income Tax Payable, Social Security Tax Payable, and Medicare Tax Payable balances differ from your ledger account balances due to additional postings completed for payroll taxes and sales and administrative salaries.)

7. Prepare an 8-column work sheet for the month ended July 31 of the current year. Record the adjustments on the work sheet using the following information.

### Adjustment Information, July 31

| | |
|---|---|
| Uncollectible Accounts Expense Estimated as 1.0% of Total Sales on Account. | |
| Sales on Account for Year | $76,275.00 |
| Sales Supplies Inventory | 1,762.50 |
| Administrative Supplies Inventory | 520.74 |
| Value of Prepaid Administrative Insurance | 1,383.30 |
| Monthly Depreciation Expense—Office Equipment | 68.51 |
| Monthly Depreciation Expense—Store Equipment | 61.88 |
| Federal Income Tax Expense Estimated for the Month | 7,807.00 |

8. Prepare an income statement for the month ended July 31 of the current year. Calculate and record the following component percentages: (a) net cost of goods sold, (b) gross profit on operations, (c) total operating expenses, (d) income from operations, (e) net addition or deduction resulting from other revenue and expenses, (f) net income before federal income tax, (g) federal income tax expense, and (h) net income after federal income tax. Round percentage calculations to the nearest 0.1%.

9. Prepare a balance sheet for July 31 of the current year. A statement of stockholders' equity is not prepared. Therefore, add the amount of net income after federal income tax to the beginning balance of Retained Earnings to obtain the ending balance.

APPLIED

## • applied communication

A new clerk has been hired at the company for which you work. You have been asked to explain the flow of materials from ordering through issuing to the factory.

**Required:**
Prepare a chart and a brief written explanation of the flow of materials.

CASE FOR CRITICAL THINKING

## • case for critical thinking

Kingston Corp., a manufacturing company, uses the perpetual inventory method for all inventory accounts. Direct materials, direct labor, and applied overhead are recorded on cost sheets similar to FaxaVision's. At the end of each month, general journal entries are made to update the general ledger manufacturing accounts. Overapplied or Underapplied Overhead is closed to Income Summary and reported on the income statement as an adjustment to the cost of goods sold.

A new accountant suggests that the company could save considerable time if a number of accounting changes are made: (1) use the periodic inventory method, (2) drop the use of applied overhead, and (3) close all manufacturing accounts to Income Summary similar to the procedure used by merchandising businesses. The accountant indicates that these new procedures would provide adequate information to prepare the income statement with a substantial time and cost saving.

Should the changes in accounting procedures be made? Will the changes provide adequate information? How will the changes affect the information now provided?

SCANS WORKPLACE COMPETENCY

## • SCANS workplace competency

**Interpersonal Competency:** Working with Cultural Diversity

**Concept:** Competent employees work well with both men and women and with people from a variety of ethnic, social, or educational backgrounds. These employees understand the cultures of others, respect the rights of others, make judgments and decisions on the basis of performance—not stereotypes—and understand the concerns of members of other ethnic and gender groups.

**Application:** Form a task group of 3-4 students, and brainstorm ideas on how your school can recognize and appreciate the diversity of cultures there. Discuss your views with the school's administration.

## graphing workshop

John and Candy Moody operate Western Ski Centers, a small retail ski store in southwest Colorado. The couple is concerned that, despite increasing sales, they appear to be making less money each year. Using an option on their accounting software, you are able to prepare the following graph of income statement data.

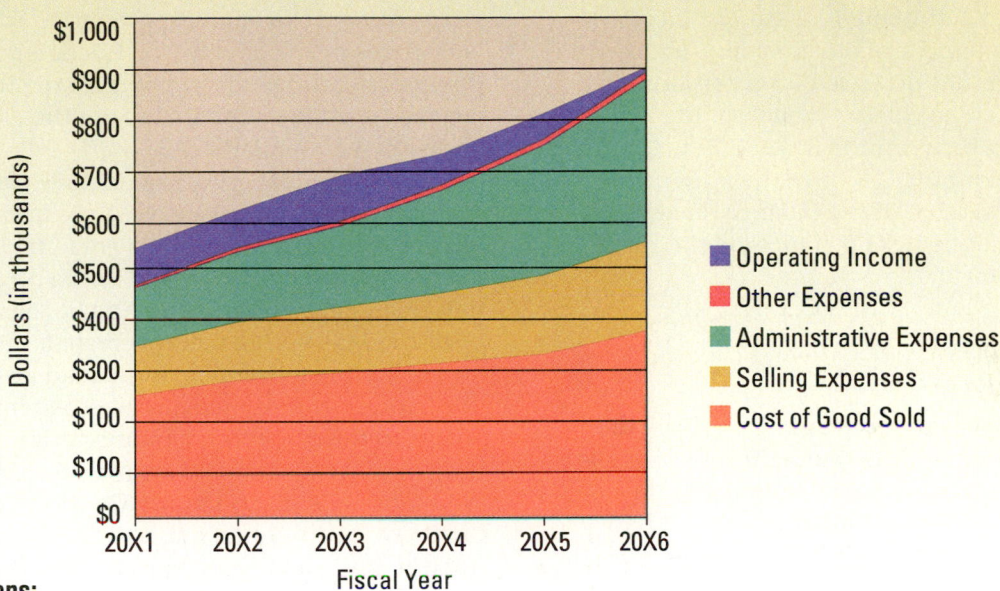

**Analysis of Income Statement**

Legend:
- Operating Income
- Other Expenses
- Administrative Expenses
- Selling Expenses
- Cost of Good Sold

**Instructions:**

1. What is represented by the top line of the graph?
2. Explain why the operating income of the business is declining.

## analyzing Costco's financial statements

Like any retail company, Costco knows that some customers will return merchandise after the sale. When a June sale is returned in July, both the sale and the sales return are recorded in the same fiscal year. A problem occurs, however, when a sale in August (Costco's fiscal year end) is returned in September. The sale is recorded in one fiscal year while the sales return is recorded in the next fiscal year.

To solve this problem, Costco estimates the amount of its current-year sales it expects to be returned in the fiscal year. This procedure attempts to make sales and sales returns in the same fiscal year.

**Instructions:**

Read the first paragraph of the Revenue Recognition section of Note 1 in Costco's financial statements in Appendix B of this textbook.

1. How does Costco estimate sales returns?
2. Identify the amount of the reserve for sales returns reported on the 2003 financial statements. How is the amount reported on the financial statements?

# Automated Accounting

## Financial Statements for a Manufacturing Business

Manufacturing businesses, as well as merchandising businesses, prepare external financial statements reporting information for all the activities of the business taken as a whole. These statements include a balance sheet, an income statement, and a statement of stockholders' equity. The statement of stockholders' equity does not differ from that prepared for a corporation operating a merchandising business, but there are differences between the balance sheet and the income statement.

The asset section of the balance sheet for a manufacturing business will include the three types of inventory:

- Materials
- Work in process
- Finished goods

The partial balance sheet below shows the inventory accounts in the currents assets section.

The liabilities and stockholders' sections of the balance sheet do not differ from the financial statements of a merchandising business. The income statement of a manufacturing company may be presented in a number of ways. Like that of a merchandising company, the statement must include cost of goods sold information. Some companies include cost of goods sold as a section of the income statement. Many large corporations prefer to use supplemental schedules prepared with a spreadsheet program to present information about the cost of goods manufactured and the cost of goods sold. By preparing supplemental schedules before preparing the income statement, accounts can include detail from the ledger accounts while still maintaining the clarity of the individual statements.

Good spreadsheet design includes formulas and clear columns and row labels. Schedules prepared on a spreadsheet will resemble manual statements and schedules. Formulas will be used for all subtotals and totals. Formulas should be manually verified when the spreadsheet is created.

Many businesses create spreadsheet templates for frequently used schedules. The template is a skeleton design with a heading, titles, and formatting in place. Formulas are placed in the subtotal and total cells. Each month, the template is opened and saved with a name to identify the report and month, such as COGS_March. The data for the current month are entered and verified. Then the report is printed.

**ABC Manufacturing**
**Partial Balance Sheet**
**Month Ended March 31, 20--**

**Assets**

Current Assets

| | |
|---|---|
| Cash | $ 182,650 |
| Accounts receivable, net | 216,600 |
| Materials | 121,950 |
| Work in process | 108,400 |
| Finished goods | 131,475 |
| Supplies | 14,740 |
| Total Current Assets | $ 775,815 |

Accounting Transactions and Financial Reporting for a Manufacturing Business

# Processing and Reporting Cost Accounting Data for a Manufacturing Business

This activity reinforces selected learning from Chapters 19 and 20. Job cost accounting processing and reporting is emphasized for a manufacturing company organized as a corporation.

## FURNITURE DECOR, INC.

Furniture Decor, Inc., is a corporation that manufactures office furniture. Furniture Decor uses a job cost accounting system to record manufacturing costs. The fiscal year is from January 1 through December 31. Monthly financial statements are prepared.

## PART A: RECORDING COST ACCOUNTING ACTIVITIES

In Part A of this reinforcement activity, Furniture Decor's daily cost accounting activities for one month will be recorded.

Furniture Decor uses the chart of accounts shown on the following page. The journals and ledgers used by Furniture Decor are similar to those illustrated in Chapters 19 and 20. The job cost sheets, selected general ledger accounts, and other accounting records or forms needed to do the cost accounting activities are provided in the *Working Papers*. Beginning balances have been recorded.

The January 31 general ledger balances are the result of posting completed during the month of January. Note that Accounts Payable has a debit balance for this reason. Also, the balances of the payroll liability accounts are the amounts posted for sales and administrative salaries for January.

## CALCULATING FACTORY OVERHEAD APPLIED RATE

**Instructions:**

1. Calculate the factory overhead applied rate based on direct labor costs. Estimated annual factory overhead costs for the current year are $306,000.00. Estimated direct labor hours to be used during the current year are 17,000 hours at an estimated rate of $15.00 per hour. Retain the calculations for use later in this reinforcement activity.

# FURNITURE DECOR, INC. CHART OF ACCOUNTS

## Balance Sheet Accounts

**(1000) ASSETS**
1100   CURRENT ASSETS
1105   Cash
1110   Petty Cash
1115   Accounts Receivable
1120   Allowance for Uncollectible Accounts
1125   Materials
1130   Work in Process
1135   Finished Goods
1140   Supplies—Factory
1145   Supplies—Sales
1150   Supplies—Administrative
1155   Prepaid Insurance
1200   PLANT ASSETS
1205   Factory Equipment
1210   Accumulated Depreciation—Factory Equipment
1215   Office Equipment
1220   Accumulated Depreciation—Office Equipment
1225   Store Equipment
1230   Accumulated Depreciation—Store Equipment
1235   Building
1240   Accumulated Depreciation—Building
1245   Land

**(2000) LIABILITIES**
2100   CURRENT LIABILITIES
2105   Accounts Payable
2110   Employee Income Tax Payable
2115   Federal Income Tax Payable
2120   Social Security Tax Payable
2123   Medicare Tax Payable
2125   Salaries Payable
2130   Unemployment Tax Payable—Federal
2135   Unemployment Tax Payable—State
2140   Dividends Payable
2200   LONG-TERM LIABILITY
2205   Mortgage Payable

**(3000) STOCKHOLDERS' EQUITY**
3105   Capital Stock
3110   Retained Earnings
3115   Dividends
3120   Income Summary

## Income Statement Accounts

**(4000) OPERATING REVENUE**
4105   Sales

**(5000) COST OF SALES**
5105   Cost of Goods Sold

**(5500) MANUFACTURING COSTS**
5505   Factory Overhead
5510   Depreciation Expense—Factory Equipment
5515   Depreciation Expense—Building
5520   Heat, Light, and Power Expense
5525   Insurance Expense—Factory
5530   Miscellaneous Expense—Factory
5535   Payroll Taxes Expense—Factory
5540   Property Tax Expense—Factory
5545   Supplies Expense—Factory

**(6000) OPERATING EXPENSES**
6100   SELLING EXPENSES
6105   Advertising Expense
6110   Delivery Expense
6115   Depreciation Expense—Store Equipment
6120   Miscellaneous Expense—Sales
6125   Salary Expense—Sales
6130   Supplies Expense—Sales
6200   ADMINISTRATIVE EXPENSES
6205   Depreciation Expense—Office Equipment
6210   Insurance Expense—Administrative
6215   Miscellaneous Expense—Administrative
6220   Payroll Taxes Expense—Administrative
6225   Property Tax Expense—Administrative
6230   Salary Expense—Administrative
6235   Supplies Expense—Administrative
6240   Uncollectible Accounts Expense
6245   Utilities Expense—Administrative

**(7000) OTHER REVENUE**
7105   Gain on Plant Assets
7110   Miscellaneous Revenue

**(8000) OTHER EXPENSES**
8105   Interest Expense
8110   Loss on Plant Assets

**(9000) INCOME TAX**
9105   Federal Income Tax Expense

**Instructions:**

2. Record the following transactions completed during January of the current year in the appropriate cost records and journals. Use page 1 of a materials purchases journal, general journal, and cash payments journal. Recording instructions are provided only for the first occurrence of each kind of transaction. Source documents are abbreviated as follows: check, C; memorandum, M; materials requisition, MR; purchase order, PO; sales invoice, S.

Jan. 3. Opened a cost sheet for Job No. 232, 250 C200 computer desks ordered for stock. Date wanted, January 12.

3. Issued direct materials to factory for Job No. 232, $5,100.00. MR750.

   Materials list: 6,000 square feet base wood @ $0.20 per square foot
   6,000 square feet laminate @ $0.60 per square feet
   187.5 pounds adhesive @ $1.60 per pound

   Record the direct materials in the materials ledger and the cost ledger.

5. Opened a cost sheet for Job No. 233, 200 P150 printer tables ordered for stock. Date wanted, January 17.

5. Issued direct materials to factory for Job No. 233, $3,400.00. MR751.

   Materials list: 4,000 square feet base wood @ $0.20 per square foot
   4,000 square feet laminate @ $0.60 per square foot
   125 pounds adhesive @ $1.60 per pound

5. Ordered 30,000 square feet base wood. PO520.

   Record the purchase order in the materials ledger.

5. Ordered 20,000 square feet laminate. PO521.

7. Ordered 1,600 casters. PO522.

7. Ordered direct materials to factory for Job No. 232, $1,250.00. MR752.

   Materials list: 1,000 casters @ $1.25 each

7. Ordered 1,000 sets hinges. PO523.

7. Recorded weekly summary of job-time records to cost ledger.

   Job No. 232    $3,300.00
   Job No. 233     1,125.00

7. Ordered 1,000 pounds adhesive. PO524.

10. Issued direct materials to factory for Job No. 233, $1,200.00. MR753.

    Materials list: 800 casters @ $1.25 each
    200 sets metal glides @ $1.00 per set

10. Ordered 300 sets of metal glides. PO525.

10. Sold 100 C200 computer desks to Office Mart. S323.

    Record only the cost in the finished goods ledger. Furniture Decor uses the first-in, first-out inventory method. Thus, the cost recorded first is the cost removed from inventory first when units are sold.

Jan. 10. Ordered 1,000 fasteners. PO526.

10. Received at materials stockroom 20,000 square feet of laminate @ $0.60 per square foot. Materials were purchased on account from Plastics Unlimited, $12,000.00. PO521.

Record all receipts of materials in the materials ledger and purchases journal.

11. Completed Job No. 232. Apply factory overhead to job. Use the rate calculated in Instruction 1. Complete the cost sheet. Interim summary of job-time records for Job No. 232, $1,387.50.

When jobs are completed in the middle of a week, Furniture Decor makes a special interim summary of job-time records for these jobs. Therefore, direct labor costs will be complete. Record the finished goods in the finished goods ledger.

12. Opened a cost sheet for Job No. 234, 120 E400 entertainment centers ordered for stock. Date wanted, January 18.

12. Issued direct materials to factory for Job No. 234, $5,100.00. MR754.

Materials list: 6,000 square feet base wood @ $0.20 per square foot
6,000 square feet laminate @ $0.60 per square foot
187.5 pounds adhesive @ $1.60 per pound

12. Received at materials stockroom 30,000 square feet of base wood @ $0.20 per square foot. Materials were purchased on account from Wood Craft, Inc., $6,000.00. PO520.

12. Received at materials stockroom 1,600 casters @ $1.25 each. Materials were purchased on account from Wheels Galore, $2,000.00. PO522.

12. Received at materials stockroom 300 sets of metal glides @ $1.00 per set. Materials were purchased on account from Simpson Company, $300.00. PO525.

14. Opened a cost sheet for Job No. 235, 150 V110 video tape cabinets for stock. Date wanted, January 27.

14. Issued direct materials to factory for Job No. 235, $2,040.00. MR755.

Materials list: 2,400 square feet base wood @ $0.20 per square foot
2,400 square feet laminate @ $0.60 per square foot
75 pounds adhesive @ $1.60 per pound

14. Recorded weekly summary of job-time records to cost ledger.

Job No. 233   $1,875.00
Job No. 234    1,800.00
Job No. 235      225.00

14. Completed Job No. 233.

17. Paid cash for semimonthly factory payroll, $11,080.80 (direct labor, $9,712.50, and indirect labor, $3,967.50, less deductions: employee income tax, $1,504.80; Social security tax, $889.20; Medicare, $205.20). C782.

Record the payroll entry in the cash payments journal. Post the general debit and general credit amounts.

17. Recorded employer factory payroll taxes, $1,942.56, for the semimonthly pay period ended January 15. Taxes owed are Social security tax, $889.20; Medicare, $205.20; federal unemployment tax, $109.44; state unemployment tax, $738.72. M308.

Record the entry in the general journal. Post the amounts.

Processing and Reporting Cost Accounting Data for a Manufacturing Business

Jan. 17. Sold 150 P150 printer tables to CompuFurnishings. S324.
   18. Issued direct materials to factory for Job No. 234, $420.00. MR756.

   Materials list: 240 sets of hinges @ $1.00 per set
                   240 fasteners @ $0.75 each

   18. Opened a cost sheet for Job No. 236, 200 B160 bookcases ordered for stock. Date wanted, January 28.
   18. Issued direct materials to factory for Job No. 236, $6,800.00. MR757.

   Materials list: 8,000 square feet base wood @ $0.20 per square foot
                   8,000 square feet laminate @ $0.60 per square foot
                   250 pounds adhesive @ $1.60 per pound

   19. Completed Job No. 234. Interim summary of job-time record for Job No. 234, $1,800.00.
   20. Sold 60 T120 TV carts to Office Mart. S325.
   21. Issued direct materials to factory for Job No. 235, $825.00. MR758.

   Materials list: 300 sets metal glides @ $1.00 per set
                   300 sets hinges @ $1.00 per set
                   300 fasteners @ $0.75 each
   21. Received at materials stockroom 1,000 pounds adhesive @ $1.60 per pound. Materials were purchased on account from Cal Adhesives, $1,600.00. P0524.
   21. Received at materials stockroom 1,000 fasteners @ $0.75 each. Materials were purchased on account from Simpson Company, $750.00. P0526.
   21. Ordered 300 sets metal glides. P0527.
   21. Posted weekly summary of job-time records to cost ledger.

   Job No. 235    $1,125.00
   Job No. 236     2,250.00

   24. Ordered 20,000 square feet laminate. P0528.
   24. Received at materials stockroom 1,000 sets of hinges @ $1.00 per set. Materials were purchased on account from Simpson Company, $1,000.00. P0523.
   25. Issued direct materials to factory for Job No. 236, $700.00. MR759.

   Materials list: 400 sets of hinges @ $1.00 per set
                   400 fasteners @ $0.75 each

   25. Opened a cost sheet for Job No. 237, 160 T120 TV carts ordered for stock. Date wanted, January 31.
   25. Issued direct materials to factory for Job No. 237, $1,904.00. MR760.

   Materials list: 2,240 square feet base wood @ $0.20 per square foot
                   2,240 square feet laminate @ $0.60 per square foot
                   70 pounds adhesive @ $1.60 per pound

   26. Sold 90 E400 entertainment centers to BizFurn. S326.
   27. Completed Job No. 235. Interim summary of job-time records for Job No. 235, $900.00.
   27. Sold 200 V110 video tape cabinets to CompuFurnishings. S327.

Jan. 28. Issued direct materials to factory for Job No. 237, $800.00. MR761.

Materials list: 640 casters @ $1.25 each

28. Opened a cost sheet for Job No. 238, 200 C200 computer desks ordered for stock. Date wanted, February 8.

28. Issued direct materials to factory for Job No. 238, $4,080.00. MR762.

Materials list: 4,800 square feet base wood @ $0.20 per square foot
4,800 square feet laminate @ $0.60 per square foot
150 pounds adhesive @ $1.60 per pound

28. Posted weekly summary of job-time records to cost ledger.

Job No. 236    $2,250.00
Job No. 237      1,440.00
Job No. 238        630.00

28. Completed Job No. 236.

28. Sold 120 B160 bookcases to Office Mart. S328.

31. Received at materials stockroom 300 metal glides @ $1.00 per set. Materials were purchased on account from Simpson Company, $300.00. P0527.

31. Received at materials stockroom indirect materials (bolts, screws, and nails). Materials were purchased on account from Grant Hardware Supplies, $1,200.00. P0519.

Record indirect materials purchases only in the materials purchases journal.

31. Posted summary of job-time records for January 31 to cost ledger.

Job No. 237    $360.00
Job No. 238      630.00

31. Sold 200 C200 computer desks to Straight Arrow, Inc. S329.

31. Completed Job No. 237.

31. Paid cash for semimonthly factory payroll, $12,988.20 (direct labor, $11,385.00, and indirect labor, $4,650.00, less deductions: employee income tax, $1,764.00; Social Security tax, $1,042.28; Medicare tax, $240.52). C856.

31. Recorded employer factory payroll taxes, $2,276.97, for the semimonthly pay period ended January 31. Taxes owed are Social Security tax, $1,042.28; Medicare tax, $240.52; federal unemployment tax, $128.28; state unemployment tax, $865.89. M345.

**Instructions:**

3. Jobs not completed on January 31 are work in process. The factory overhead for the month of January on work in process must be recorded. Apply the factory overhead rate to the direct labor costs recorded on the cost sheet for work in process. Record this amount in the Summary column with the item description *Factory Overhead for January* and the explanation of how this was calculated.

4. Total and rule the materials purchases journal. Post the total. Do not post the individual amounts. The abbreviation for the materials purchases journal is MP.

5. Prove and rule the cash payments journal. Do not post the total of the Cash Cr. column.

6. Record the following entries. Continue using page 1 of the general journal. Use January 31 as the date. Post after journalizing each entry.

   a. An entry to transfer the total of all direct materials requisitions to Work in Process and indirect materials to Factory Overhead. The total of all requisitions of direct materials issued during January is $33,619.00. The total of all requisitions of indirect materials issued is $1,181.00. M346.

   b. An entry to close all individual manufacturing expense accounts to Factory Overhead. M347.

   c. An entry to record applied factory overhead to Work in Process. (Sum of factory overhead applied to cost sheets for the month.) M348.

7. Continue using page 1 of the general journal. Journalize and post the entry to close the balance of the factory overhead account to Income Summary. M349.

8. Journalize and post the entry to transfer the total of all cost sheets completed from Work in Process to Finished Goods. M350.

9. Journalize and post the entry to transfer the cost of products sold from Finished Goods to Cost of Goods Sold. The total cost recorded on all sales invoices for January is $61,137.50. M351.

10. Prove the subsidiary ledgers as follows.

    a. Add the ending balances in the materials ledger. The ending balance of the indirect materials is $1,369.00. The total of the materials ledger must equal the ending balance of Materials in the general ledger.

    b. Add the costs recorded on all cost sheets in the cost ledger that have not been completed. This total must equal the ending balance of Work in Process in the general ledger.

    c. Add the ending balances in the finished goods ledger. This total must equal the ending balance of Finished Goods in the general ledger.

11. Prepare a statement of cost of goods manufactured for Furniture Decor, Inc. for the month ended January 31 of the current year.

In Part B of this reinforcement activity, all accounting activities have been completed up to, but not including, a trial balance for the month of January.

The January 31 balances of the general ledger accounts not provided in Part A are recorded on an 8-column work sheet in the *Working Papers.*

## Instructions:

12. Record the January 31 balances from the general ledger accounts used in Part A on the work sheet for Furniture Decor, Inc. Complete the Trial Balance columns of the work sheet.

13. Complete the work sheet for the month ended January 31 of the current year. Record the adjustments on the work sheet using the following information.

### Adjustment Information, January 31

Uncollectible accounts expense estimated as 1.0% of sales on account.
   Sales on account for month, $27,000.00.

| | |
|---|---|
| Sales supplies inventory | $1,111.35 |
| Administrative supplies inventory | 302.47 |
| Value of prepaid administrative insurance | 257.40 |
| Monthly depreciation expense—office equipment | 34.25 |
| Monthly depreciation expense—store equipment | 31.00 |
| Federal income tax expense estimated for the month | 3,682.38 |

14. Prepare an income statement for the month ended January 31 of the current year. Calculate and record the following component percentages. (a) Cost of goods sold. (b) Gross profit on operations. (c) Total operating expenses. (d) Income from operations. (e) Net addition or deduction resulting from other revenue and expenses. (f) Net income before federal income tax. (g) Federal income tax. (h) Net income after federal income tax. Round percentage calculations to the nearest 0.1%.

15. Prepare a balance sheet for January 31 of the current year. A statement of stockholders' equity is not prepared. Therefore, add the amount of net income after federal income taxes to the beginning balance of Retained Earnings to obtain the ending balance.

*Activities in Progressive Badge Company:*

1. Recording transactions in special journals and a general journal.

2. Recording items in materials ledgers, cost sheets, and finished goods ledgers.

3. Posting items to be posted individually to a general ledger and subsidiary ledgers.

4. Proving and ruling journals.

5. Recording and posting general journal entries that summarize cost records.

6. Proving the subsidiary ledgers.

7. Preparing a trial balance on a work sheet.

8. Planning adjustments and completing a work sheet.

9. Preparing financial statements.

10. Journalizing and posting adjusting entries.

11. Journalizing and posting closing entries.

12. Preparing a post-closing trial balance.

## A Business Simulation
## Progressive Badge Company

Progressive Badge Company is a manufacturing business organized as a corporation. This business simulation covers the realistic transactions completed by Progressive Badge Company, which manufactures badges for specialty retailing. The activities included in the accounting cycle for Progressive Badge Company are listed at the left.

This simulation is available from the publisher in a manual version.

# 7 Other Accounting Systems

## MALIN CARPET DESIGN
## CHART OF ACCOUNTS

### Balance Sheet Accounts

**(1000) ASSETS**

| | |
|---|---|
| 1100 | CURRENT ASSETS |
| 1105 | Cash |
| 1110 | Petty Cash |
| 1115 | Accounts Receivable |
| 1120 | Allowance for Uncollectible Accounts |
| 1125 | Supplies—Carpet |
| 1130 | Supplies—Office |
| 1135 | Prepaid Insurance |
| 1200 | Plant Assets |
| 1205 | Equipment |
| 1210 | Accumulated Depreciation—Equipment |
| 1215 | Truck |
| 1220 | Accumulated Depreciation—Truck |

**(2000) LIABILITIES**

| | |
|---|---|
| 2100 | CURRENT LIABILITIES |
| 2105 | Accounts Payable |

**(3000) OWNERS' EQUITY**

| | |
|---|---|
| 3105 | May Baker, Capital |
| 3110 | May Baker, Drawing |
| 3115 | Lindel Mattingly, Capital |
| 3120 | Lindel Mattingly, Drawing |
| 3125 | Income Summary |

**(4000) OPERATING REVENUE**

| | |
|---|---|
| 4105 | Sales |

**(5000) OPERATING EXPENSES**

| | |
|---|---|
| 5105 | Advertising Expense |
| 5110 | Depreciation Expense—Equipment |
| 5115 | Depreciation Expense—Truck |
| 5120 | Insurance Expense |
| 5125 | Miscellaneous Expense |
| 5130 | Rent Expense |
| 5135 | Supplies Expense—Carpet |
| 5140 | Supplies Expense—Office |
| 5145 | Truck Expense |
| 5150 | Uncollectible Accounts Expense |
| 5155 | Utilities Expense |

The chart of accounts for MaLin Carpet Design is illustrated above for ready reference as you study Chapters 21 and 22 of this textbook.

# 21 Organizational Structure of a Partnership

OBJECTIVES & TERMS

*After studying Chapter 21, you will be able to:*

1. Define accounting terms related to forming and expanding a partnership.

2. Identify accounting concepts and practices related to forming and expanding a partnership.

3. Journalize transactions related to forming a partnership.

4. Journalize transactions related to expanding a partnership.

- partnership agreement
- mutual agency
- goodwill

Point Your Browser
accountingxtra.swlearning.com

620

accounting in the real world

# • PricewaterhouseCoopers, LLP

## internet activity

©GETTY IMAGES

## PRICEWATERHOUSECOOPERS, LLP ASSURES CONFIDENCE IN FINANCIAL STATEMENTS

Suppose that you were shopping for a used automobile and you spotted your dream machine in the newspaper classified advertisements. The ad mentions that the vehicle is in excellent shape despite high mileage; however, the price seems a little high. Would you feel comfortable accepting the owner's word that the vehicle is in excellent condition or would you prefer an independent, third-party opinion? Most likely you would feel more confident and assured after a knowledgeable mechanic's thorough review and testing.

A major function of large accounting firms, such as PricewaterhouseCoopers, is providing assurance services. An example of assurance services is assessing the financial condition of a business and verifying the accuracy of its financial statements for clients or investors. Investors feel more confident about the financial reliability of a company after its records and operations have been reviewed by independent, knowledgeable experts.

PwC is one of the largest accounting firms in the world. It is a global enterprise employing over 122,000 individuals in offices located in 768 cities throughout 139 countries. The company is organized as a limited liability partnership with approximately 8,000 partners and generates annual revenues of over $15 billion. One of the more unusual responsibilities PwC has is its role as ballot counter for the annual Academy Awards presentation!

## Critical Thinking

1. Why is it important that accounting firms such as PwC ensure that the financial statements of companies are indeed presented fairly?
2. Review the Explore Accounting feature at the end of this chapter. List two factors that make a limited liability partnership attractive.

Source: www.pwc.com

**Xtra!**
Today
accountingxtra.swlearning.com

## FRANCHISES AVAILABLE

A franchise is a right purchased to operate a particular kind of business in a particular location. The value of a franchise is often the brand or company name that has been established. A franchise grants certain rights and also entails certain obligations to operate the business in a certain way to protect the reputation of the franchise brand.

## Instructions

Search the Internet to find franchises that are available. Investigate two franchises.

1. List the name of each franchise investigated.
2. List the amount of initial investment required for each franchise.
3. List the services or goods that the franchisee will receive for the initial investment in each franchise.

# 21-1 Forming a Partnership

A corporation is one form of business that may be owned by many persons. Large corporations may have thousands of owners. These owners are known as shareholders because they own shares of stock.

Another form of business may also have more than one owner. A business in which two or more persons combine their assets and skills is known as a partnership. Each member of a partnership is known as a partner. Partnerships generally have only a few owners (partners). Partnerships do not issue shares of stock. Each partner has an equity account. Except for recording owners' equity and income taxes, accounting procedures for a partnership are similar to those for a corporation.

Unlike a corporation, however, a partnership does not have an unlimited life. Any change in the number of partners terminates an existing partnership. When a new partner is admitted, the partners sign a new partnership agreement. The old partnership's accounting records are often continued for the new partnership. As a result, initial investment journal entries for all partners are not always needed. Journal entries are needed, however, to show clearly how the partners' equity has changed. One or both of the following journal entries may be needed:

1. To show how much the new partner invests.
2. To show how the new partner's admission affects existing partners' capital accounts.

## making ethical decisions

### Accurate Accounting Records

A company must keep an accurate and complete record of its accounting transactions. This seemingly obvious statement has, unfortunately, been forgotten at Marist Industries. Apparently the company's controller has been recording unsupported debits to Accounts Receivable and credits to Sales in order to inflate the company's sales and net income.

Nancy Nettleton, an accounting clerk, has just discovered the fraudulent accounting entries. Nancy is fearful of what might happen if she reports the transactions to the company's hotline.

Instead, she shares her discovery with friend and fellow employee Andrea Farris.

**Instructions**
Access *Setting the Standard*, the code of conduct of Lockheed Martin. What guidance does Lockheed Martin provide Nancy and Andrea? Should Andrea report the transactions even if Nancy asks her to remain silent?

PARTNERSHIP AGREEMENT

THIS CONTRACT is made and entered into this thirty-first day of December, 20--, by and between May Baker and Lindel Mattingly, of Petersburg, VA.

WITNESSETH: That the said parties have this date formed a partnership to engage in and conduct a business under the following stipulations which are a part of this contract. The partnership will begin operation January 1, 20--.

FIRST: The business shall be conducted under the name of MaLin Carpet Design, located initially at 1910 South Crater Road, Petersburg, VA 23801-2343.

SECOND: The investment of each partner is: May Baker: Equity in a business located at 1910 South Crater Road, Petersburg, VA 23801-2343, and as shown in a balance sheet to be provided by Ms. Baker on December 31, 20--. Total investment, $22,880.00. Lindel Mattingly: Cash equal to one-half of the initial investment of Ms. Baker. Total investment, $11,440.00.

THIRD: Both partners are to (a) participate in all general policy-making decisions, (b) devote full time and attention to the partnership business, and (c) engage in no other business enterprise without the written consent of the other partner. Ms. Baker is to be general manager of the business' operations.

FOURTH: Neither partner is to become a surety or bonding agent for anyone without the written consent of the other partner.

FIFTH: The partners' shares in earnings and losses of the partnership are: Ms. Baker: 5% interest on equity as of January 1 of each year; salary, $5,000.00 per year; remaining income or loss, 50%. Mr. Mattingly: 5% interest on equity as of January 1 of each year; salary, $3,000.00 per year; remaining income or loss, 50%.

SIXTH: No partner is to withdraw assets in excess of the agreed upon interest and salary without the other partner's written consent.

SEVENTH: All partnership transactions are to be recorded in accordance with standard and generally accepted accounting procedures and concepts. The partnership records are to be open at all times for inspection by either partner.

EIGHTH: In case of either partner's death or legal disability, the equity of the partners is to be determined as of the time of the death or disability of the one partner. The continuing partner is to have first option to buy the deceased/disabled partner's equity at recorded book value.

NINTH: This partnership agreement is to continue indefinitely unless (a) terminated by death of one partner, (b) terminated by either partner by giving the other partner written notice at least ninety (90) days prior to the termination date, or (c) terminated by written mutual agreement signed by both partners.

TENTH: At the termination of this partnership agreement, the partnership's assets, after all liabilities are paid, will be distributed according to the balance in partners' capital accounts.

IN WITNESS WHEREOF, the parties to this contract have set their hands and seals on the date and year written.

Signed __May Baker_____ (Seal)  Date __December 31, 20--_____

Signed __Lindel Mattingly_____ (Seal)  Date __December 31, 20--_____

A partnership is created when two or more persons agree orally or in writing to form a business using the partnership form of organization. As in other forms of business, a partnership's financial records are kept separate from those of the partners. [CONCEPT: Business Entity]

May Baker and Lindel Mattingly agree to form a partnership called MaLin Carpet Design. Prior to forming the partnership, May owned a similar business and Lindel was employed as a carpet installer.

MaLin Carpet Design provides carpet installation services to homeowners, housing developers, and businesses. The business does not sell merchandise. For this reason, it does not need general ledger accounts for merchandise inventory, purchases, purchases discount, and purchases returns and allowances. The partners, who provide all the services to customers, are not employees of the partnership. The Internal Revenue Service does not consider the money that partners receive from a partnership to be salaries. Therefore, the business does not need accounts for recording salaries and payroll taxes.

A written agreement setting forth the conditions under which a partnership is to operate is called a **partnership agreement**. A partnership's life is limited to the length of time agreed on by the partners. A partnership is terminated by the partners' mutual agreement, death of a partner, withdrawal of one partner, or admission of a new partner. In comparison, a corporation has unlimited life.

Each partner can bind a partnership to any contract. The right of all partners to contract for a partnership is called **mutual agency**. Each partner is an agent of the partnership unless restricted by agreement.

Legally, a partnership agreement may be either written or oral. However, to avoid misunderstandings, a partnership agreement should be in writing. Some but not all states require that a partnership agreement be in writing.

With an attorney's assistance, Ms. Baker and Mr. Mattingly prepare their partnership agreement, shown on the previous page. Both partners sign three copies of the partnership agreement. Each partner receives a copy for personal records, and the third copy becomes part of the partnership's records.

## PARTNERSHIP CAPITAL ACCOUNTS

The owners' equity division of a partnership's general ledger has two capital accounts for each partner.

1. An account in which to record a partner's equity includes the word *capital* in the title. The two equity accounts in MaLin's general ledger are May Baker, Capital and Lindel Mattingly, Capital.
2. An account in which the earnings taken out of the partnership during the fiscal period are recorded includes the word *drawing* in the title. Assets taken out of a business for the owner's personal use are known as withdrawals. The two accounts in MaLin's general ledger used to record withdrawals are titled May Baker, Drawing and Lindel Mattingly, Drawing.

Partners' withdrawals can be a cause of misunderstandings. For this reason, most partnership agreements include a statement controlling withdrawals. MaLin's partnership agreement has a controlling statement in item 6 of the partnership agreement.

## PARTNERS' INITIAL INVESTMENTS

Ms. Baker invests the assets of her existing business in the new partnership. According to item 2 of the partnership agreement, Ms. Baker will provide a December 31 balance sheet for her existing business.

The two partners agree on a value for all invested assets on the date the partnership begins, January 1. Ms. Baker's initial investment is $22,880.00, the agreed-upon value of her equity in her previous business. Mr. Mattingly's initial investment is cash of $11,440.00.

**FYI** FOR YOUR INFORMATION

A partnership can have an unlimited number of partners.

Organizational Structure of a Partnership

## JOURNAL ENTRIES TO RECORD PARTNERS' INITIAL INVESTMENTS

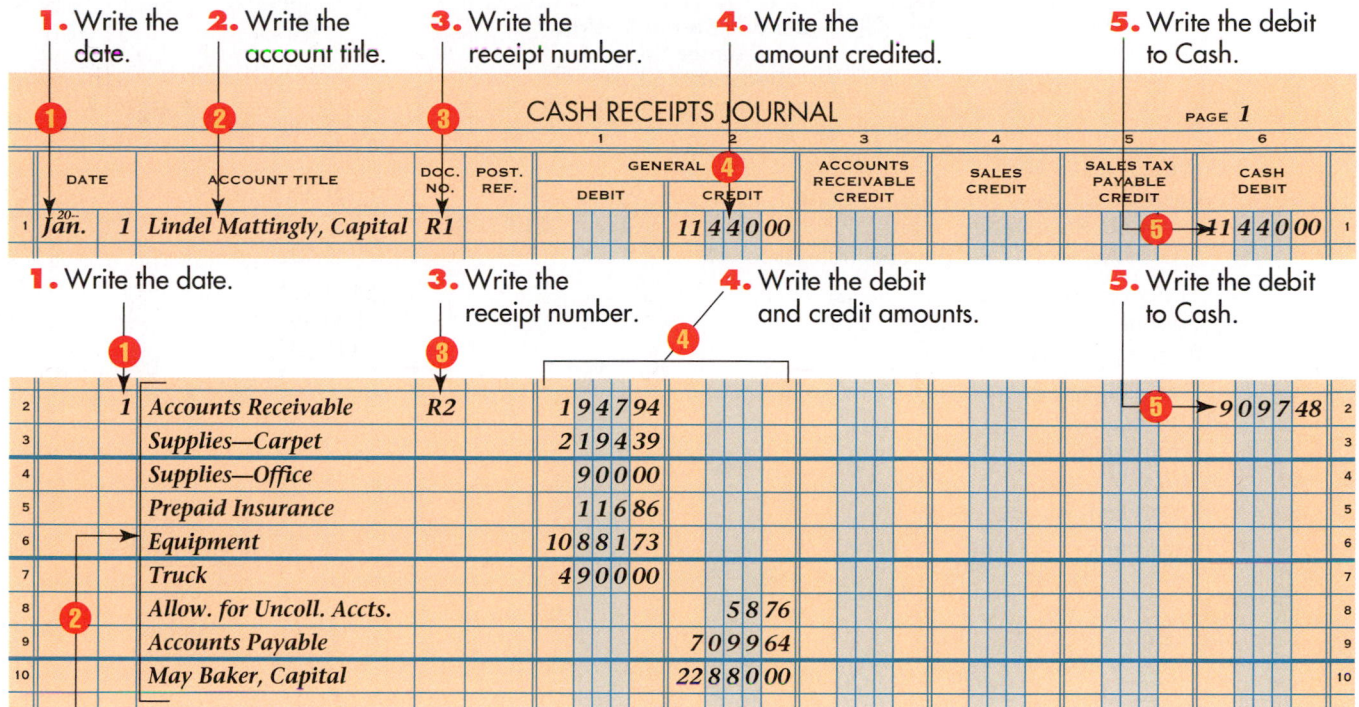

**1.** Write the date.

**2.** Write the account title.

**3.** Write the receipt number.

**4.** Write the amount credited.

**5.** Write the debit to Cash.

**1.** Write the date.

**3.** Write the receipt number.

**4.** Write the debit and credit amounts.

**5.** Write the debit to Cash.

**2.** Write the account titles debited and credited.

A separate journal entry is made for each partner's initial investment as shown above.

**January 1, 20--. Received cash from partner, Lindel Mattingly, as an initial investment, $11,440.00. Receipt No. 1.**

Cash is debited for $11,440.00. Lindel Mattingly, Capital is credited for $11,400.00.

**January 1, 20--. Accepted assets and liabilities of May Baker's existing business as an initial investment, $22,880.00. Receipt No. 2.**

All asset amounts on the balance sheet are debited. Allowance for Uncollectible Accounts and Accounts Payable are credited.

STEPS STEPS • STEPS • STEPS • STEPS • STEPS • STEPS • STEPS • STEPS • STEPS • STEPS

### JOURNALIZING RECEIPT OF PARTNERS' INITIAL INVESTMENTS

**1** Write the date, *20--, Jan 1*, in the Date column.

**2** Write the account titles in the Account Title column. For Lindel Mattingly's investment, write the account to be credited, *Lindel Mattingly, Capital.* For May Baker's investment, write the accounts to be debited, *Accounts Receivable, Supplies—Carpet, Supplies—Office, Prepaid Insurance, Equipment,* and *Truck.* Also write the accounts to be credited, *Allowance for Uncollectible Accounts, Accounts Payable,* and *May Baker, Capital.*

**3** Write the receipt numbers, *R1* and *R2*, in the Doc. No. column.

**4** Write the amounts in the General Debit and Credit columns. The only credit amount for Lindel Mattingly is *11,440.00* for the cash investment. For May Baker's investment, debit the asset accounts, *1,947.94, 2,194.39, 900.00, 116.86, 10,881.73,* and *4,900.00.* Credit the contra asset, liability, and capital accounts, *58.76, 7,099.64,* and *22,880.00.*

**5** Write the debits to Cash, *11,440.00* and *9,097.48,* in the Cash Debit column.

**Baker's Carpet Design**
**Balance Sheet**
**December 31, 20--**

### ASSETS

| | | | |
|---|---|---|---|
| **Current Assets:** | | | |
| Cash | | $ 9,097.48 | |
| Accounts Receivable | $1,947.94 | | |
| Less Allowance for Uncollectible Accounts | 58.76 | 1,889.18 | |
| Supplies—Carpet | | 2,194.39 | |
| Supplies—Office | | 900.00 | |
| Prepaid Insurance | | 116.86 | |
| Total Current Assets | | | $14,197.91 |
| **Plant Assets:** | | | |
| Equipment | | $10,881.73 | |
| Truck | | 4,900.00 | |
| Total Plant Assets | | | 15,781.73 |
| Total Assets | | | $29,979.64 |

### LIABILITIES

| | |
|---|---|
| Accounts Payable | $ 7,099.64 |

### OWNER'S EQUITY

| | |
|---|---|
| May Baker, Capital | 22,880.00 |
| Total Liabilities and Owner's Equity | $29,979.64 |

Ms. Baker's investment includes cash, other assets, and liabilities from her prior existing business. Both partners agree to any estimates shown on the balance sheet. For example, Allowance for Uncollectible Accounts is an estimate. After reviewing the accounts, Lindel and May agree that the $58.76 is a fair estimate of the amount that may become uncollectible.

A copy of the balance sheet from May Baker's previous business, shown above, is attached to a receipt to provide needed details for the journal entry. [*CONCEPT: Objective Evidence*]

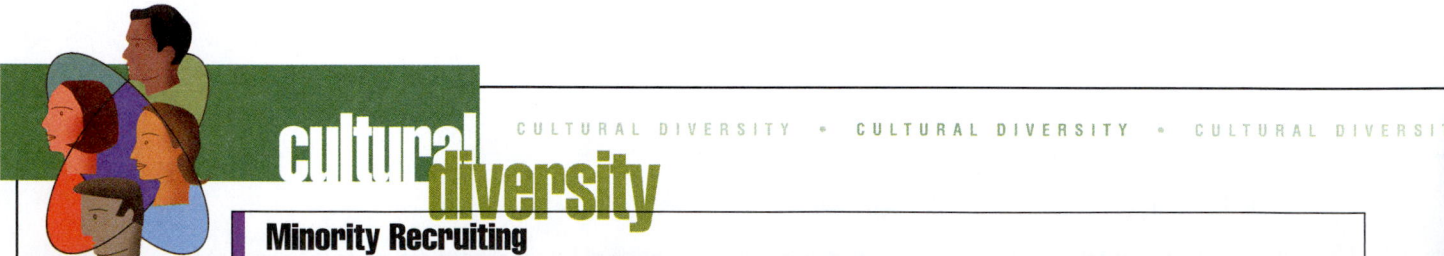

CULTURAL DIVERSITY • CULTURAL DIVERSITY • CULTURAL DIVERSIT

## cultural diversity
### Minority Recruiting

Companies today are very interested in achieving a balance in their work force. They recognize that there are advantages in a work force that has the same ethnic and cultural composition as their customers. This attitude creates opportunity for minorities.

Many cities have annual "work force diversity" job fairs in which those looking for jobs meet employers looking for employees. At these minority job fairs, a wide range of jobs may be available. Companies are especially interested in minority hiring in sales, marketing, customer service, and technical and administrative positions.

Business interest in recruiting minorities grew in the 1990s and is expected to continue to grow in the 21st century.

## terms review

partnership agreement
mutual agency

## audit your understanding

1. Why should a partnership agreement be in writing?
2. What happens to an existing partnership if a partner dies?
3. What does mutual agency mean?

## work together 21-1

### Forming a partnership

A cash receipts journal is provided in the *Working Papers*. Your instructor will guide you through the following examples.

Betty Jensen and Glen Chau agree to form a partnership on April 1 of the current year. The partnership assumes the assets and liabilities of Ms. Jensen's existing business. Mr. Chau invests cash equal to Ms. Jensen's investment. Partners share equally in all changes in equity. The March 31 balance sheet for Ms. Jensen's existing business is shown in the *Working Papers*. Source documents are abbreviated as follows: memorandum, M; receipt, R.

Apr.   1. Received cash from partner, Glen Chau, as an initial investment, $42,000.00. R1.
       1. Accepted assets and liabilities of Betty Jensen's existing business as an initial investment, $42,000.00. R2.

1. Journalize the transactions in a cash receipts journal on April 1 of the current year.

## on your own 21-1

### Forming a partnership

A cash receipts journal is provided in the *Working Papers*. Work independently to complete the following problem.

David Rice and Tanya Taylor agree to form a partnership on July 1 of the current year. The partnership assumes the assets and liabilities of Mr. Rice's existing business. Ms. Taylor invests cash equal to Mr. Rice's investment. Partners share equally in all changes in equity. The June 30 balance sheet for Mr. Rice's existing business is shown in the *Working Papers*. Source documents are abbreviated as follows: receipt, R.

July   1. Received cash from partner, Tanya Taylor, as an initial investment, $32,000.00. R1.
       1. Accepted assets and liabilities of David Rice's existing business as an initial investment, $32,000.00. R2.

1. Journalize the transactions in a cash receipts journal on July 1 of the current year.

# 21-2 Admitting Partners to Existing Partnerships

## ADMITTING A PARTNER WITH NO CHANGE IN TOTAL EQUITY

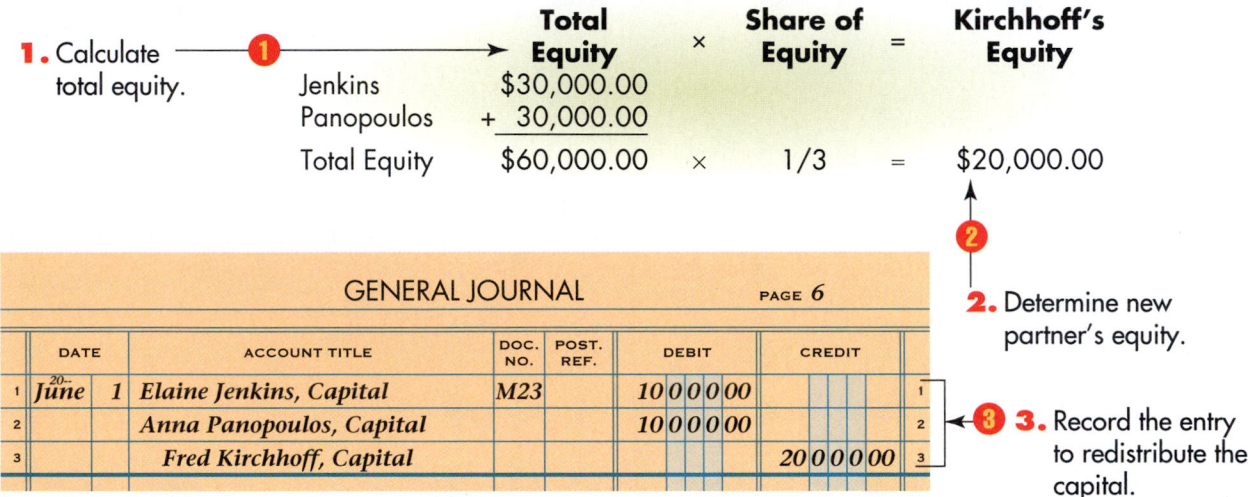

**1.** Calculate total equity.

| | Total Equity | × | Share of Equity | = | Kirchhoff's Equity |
|---|---|---|---|---|---|
| Jenkins | $30,000.00 | | | | |
| Panopoulos | + 30,000.00 | | | | |
| Total Equity | $60,000.00 | × | 1/3 | = | $20,000.00 |

**GENERAL JOURNAL**      PAGE 6

| | DATE | | ACCOUNT TITLE | DOC. NO. | POST. REF. | DEBIT | CREDIT | |
|---|---|---|---|---|---|---|---|---|
| 1 | 20-- June | 1 | Elaine Jenkins, Capital | M23 | | 10 0 0 0 00 | | 1 |
| 2 | | | Anna Panopoulos, Capital | | | 10 0 0 0 00 | | 2 |
| 3 | | | Fred Kirchhoff, Capital | | | | 20 0 0 0 00 | 3 |

**2.** Determine new partner's equity.

**3.** Record the entry to redistribute the capital.

Elaine Jenkins and Anna Panopoulos are partners in an existing business. The partners agree to admit Fred Kirchhoff as a new partner. However, the business does not need additional capital at the present time. Therefore, Elaine and Anna agree to sell part of their existing equity to Fred.

The existing partners each have $30,000.00 equity in the existing partnership. The three partners agree that Fred is to pay $20,000.00 for a one-third equity in the new partnership. Elaine and Anna receive cash from Fred for equity in the partnership. The partnership does not receive the cash from the sale of equity.

The two existing partners are each entitled to one-half of the price Fred pays for one-third of the equity of the partnership. Therefore, Fred pays $10,000.00 to both Elaine and Anna. Also, $20,000.00 of the existing equity is transferred to Fred on the partnership's records, as shown above.

The receipt of cash, a personal transaction among Elaine, Anna, and Fred, is not recorded on the partnership's records. However, the redistribution of capital is a partnership entry and is journalized.

**STEPS** • STEPS • STEPS • STEPS • STEPS • STEPS • STEPS • STEPS • STEPS • STEPS

### ADMITTING A PARTNER WITH NO CHANGE IN TOTAL EQUITY

**1** Calculate the total equity of the business, $60,000.00.

**2** Determine the new partner's equity in the partnership, $20,000.00 ($60,000.00 × 1/3).

**3** Record the entry in the general journal to transfer a portion of the existing equity to the new partner.

**REMEMBER** If partners agree to sell part of their existing equity to a new partner, the receipt of cash is a personal transaction that is not recorded on the partnership's records.

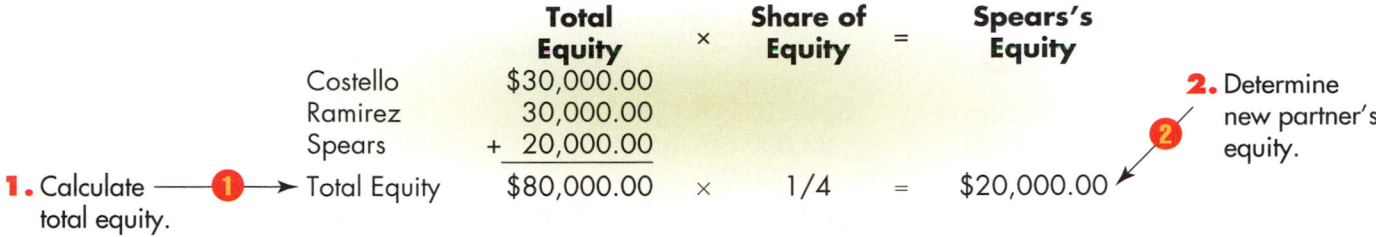

|  | Total Equity | × | Share of Equity | = | Spears's Equity |
|---|---|---|---|---|---|
| Costello | $30,000.00 | | | | |
| Ramirez | 30,000.00 | | | | |
| Spears | + 20,000.00 | | | | |

**1.** Calculate total equity. ──➀──➤ Total Equity $80,000.00 × 1/4 = $20,000.00

**2.** Determine new partner's equity. ➁

| | | | | | |

**CASH RECEIPTS JOURNAL**                                                         PAGE *13*

| | DATE | ACCOUNT TITLE | DOC. NO. | POST. REF. | GENERAL DEBIT | GENERAL CREDIT | ACCOUNTS RECEIVABLE CREDIT | SALES CREDIT | SALES TAX PAYABLE CREDIT | CASH DEBIT | |
|---|---|---|---|---|---|---|---|---|---|---|---|
| 1 | 20-- Jan. 1 | *Alan Spears, Capital* | R150 | | | 20 0 0 0 00 | | | | 20 0 0 0 00 | 1 |

**3.** Record the entry to redistribute the capital. ➂

Partnerships often seek to increase their total equity to allow the business to grow. Partnerships may seek to expand their current markets, move into new markets, or sell new types of merchandise. Additional capital gives partnerships added financial strength as the business grows.

John Costello and Juliet Ramirez are partners in an existing partnership. Each partner's equity is $30,000.00 for a total equity of $60,000.00. The existing partners agree to

admit Alan Spears as a partner with a one-fourth interest for a $20,000.00 cash investment. Alan Spears's equity is calculated as shown above. Alan's investment does not change John or Juliet's equity.

*July 1, 20--. Received cash from new partner, Alan Spears, for a one-fourth equity in the business, $20,000.00. Receipt No. 150.*

**STEPS** • STEPS • STEPS • STEPS

## ADMITTING A PARTNER WITH EQUITY EQUAL TO NEW PARTNER'S INVESTMENT

**①** Calculate the total equity of the partnership including the new partner's equity.

**②** Determine the new partner's equity.

**③** Record the entry to admit the new partner.

**FYI** FOR YOUR INFORMATION

The use of several individuals' names in the name of a business is often an indication of a partnership.

©GETTY IMAGES/PHOTODISC

**REMEMBER** The balance sheet for a partnership includes an equity account for each partner.

# ADMITTING A PARTNER WITH EQUITY GREATER THAN NEW PARTNER'S INVESTMENT

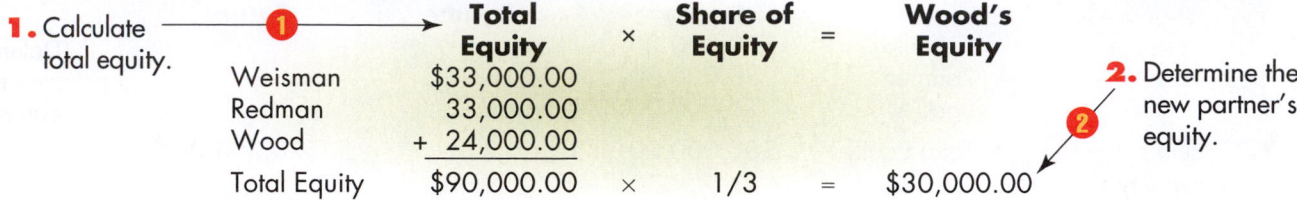

**1.** Calculate total equity. ①

| | Total Equity | × | Share of Equity | = | Wood's Equity |
|---|---|---|---|---|---|
| Weisman | $33,000.00 | | | | |
| Redman | 33,000.00 | | | | |
| Wood | + 24,000.00 | | | | |
| Total Equity | $90,000.00 | × | 1/3 | = | $30,000.00 |

**2.** Determine the new partner's equity. ②

**3.** Record the receipt of cash from the new partner.

### CASH RECEIPTS JOURNAL  PAGE 17

| | DATE | ACCOUNT TITLE | DOC. NO. | POST. REF. | GENERAL DEBIT | GENERAL CREDIT | ACCOUNTS RECEIVABLE CREDIT | SALES CREDIT | SALES TAX PAYABLE CREDIT | CASH DEBIT | |
|---|---|---|---|---|---|---|---|---|---|---|---|
| 1 | 20-- Sept. 1 | Lois Wood, Capital | R125 | | | 24 0 0 0 00 | | | | 24 0 0 0 00 | ③ 1 |

### GENERAL JOURNAL  PAGE 9

| | DATE | ACCOUNT TITLE | DOC. NO. | POST. REF. | DEBIT | CREDIT | |
|---|---|---|---|---|---|---|---|
| 1 | 20-- Sept. 1 | James Weisman, Capital | M45 | | 3 0 0 0 00 | | 1 |
| 2 | | Lisa Redman, Capital | | | 3 0 0 0 00 | | 2 |
| 3 | | Lois Wood, Capital | | | | 6 0 0 0 00 | 3 |

**4.** Record the transfer of equity to the new partner. ④

James Weisman and Lisa Redman both have equity of $33,000.00 in an existing partnership. The existing partners agree to admit Lois Wood as a partner with a one-third interest for a $24,000.00 cash investment. Lois's equity is calculated as shown above.

*September 1, 20--. Received cash from new partner, Lois Wood, for a one-third equity in the business, $24,000.00. Existing equity is redistributed as follows: from James Weisman, $3,000.00; from Lisa Redman, $3,000.00. Receipt No. 125 and Memorandum No. 45.*

Two journal entries are required to record this transaction. (1) Receipt of cash is recorded. (2) Redistribution of existing equity is recorded. These entries are shown above.

**FYI** FOR YOUR INFORMATION

One reason for admitting a new partner with greater equity than investment is when a celebrity joins the partnership, bringing name recognition and increased sales.

## STEPS  STEPS • STEPS • STEPS • STEPS • STEPS • STEPS • STEPS • STEPS • STEPS • STEPS

### ADMITTING A PARTNER WITH EQUITY GREATER THAN NEW PARTNER'S INVESTMENT

**1** Calculate the total equity, including the new partner's investment of cash.

**2** Determine the new partner's equity. In this case, the cash investment by the new partner is less than the equity that will be assigned to her.

**3** Record the receipt of cash from the new partner in the cash receipts journal.

**4** Record the transfer of equity to Lois Wood from James Weisman and Lisa Redman. After the entry, each partner's capital account has a $30,000.00 balance.

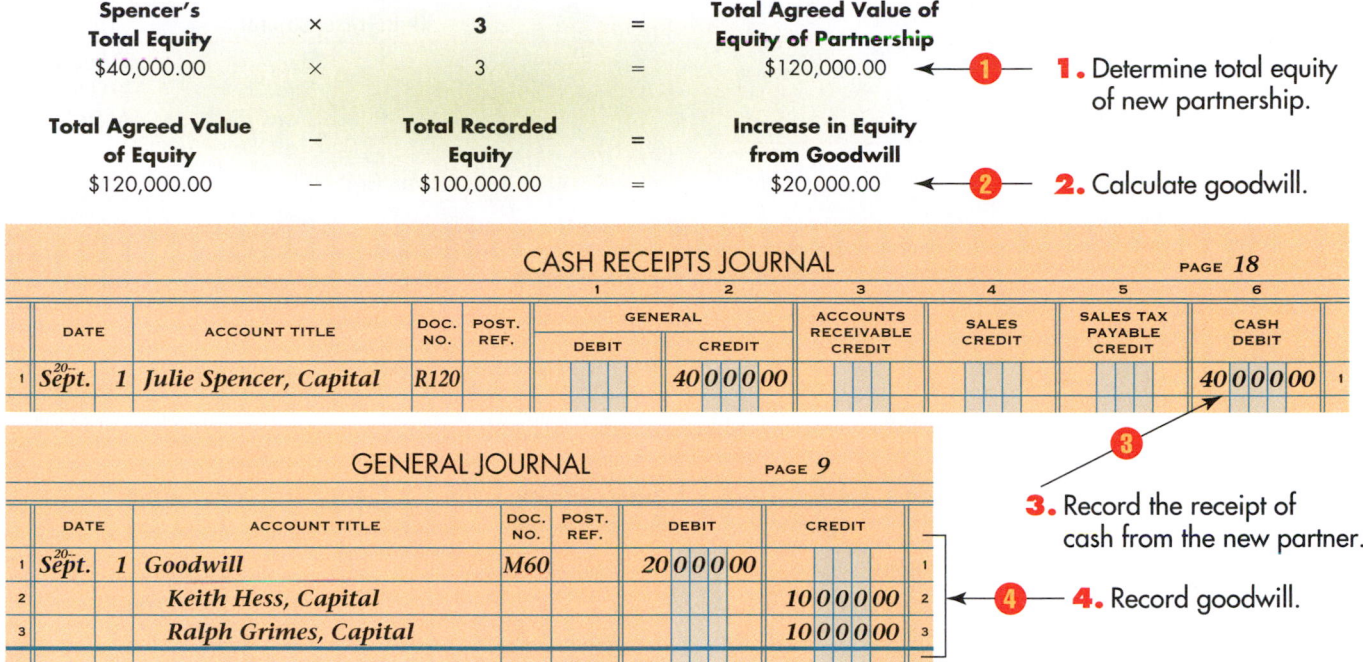

| | | | | | |
|---|---|---|---|---|---|
| Spencer's Total Equity | × | 3 | = | Total Agreed Value of Equity of Partnership | |
| $40,000.00 | × | 3 | = | $120,000.00 | ◄ ❶  **1.** Determine total equity of new partnership. |
| Total Agreed Value of Equity | − | Total Recorded Equity | = | Increase in Equity from Goodwill | |
| $120,000.00 | − | $100,000.00 | = | $20,000.00 | ◄ ❷  **2.** Calculate goodwill. |

**CASH RECEIPTS JOURNAL**                                  PAGE **18**

| | DATE | ACCOUNT TITLE | DOC. NO. | POST. REF. | GENERAL DEBIT | GENERAL CREDIT | ACCOUNTS RECEIVABLE CREDIT | SALES CREDIT | SALES TAX PAYABLE CREDIT | CASH DEBIT | |
|---|---|---|---|---|---|---|---|---|---|---|---|
| 1 | Sept. 1 | Julie Spencer, Capital | R120 | | | 40 0 0 0 00 | | | | 40 0 0 0 00 | 1 |

**3.** Record the receipt of cash from the new partner.

**GENERAL JOURNAL**                    PAGE **9**

| | DATE | ACCOUNT TITLE | DOC. NO. | POST. REF. | DEBIT | CREDIT | |
|---|---|---|---|---|---|---|---|
| 1 | Sept. 1 | Goodwill | M60 | | 20 0 0 0 00 | | 1 |
| 2 | | Keith Hess, Capital | | | | 10 0 0 0 00 | 2 |
| 3 | | Ralph Grimes, Capital | | | | 10 0 0 0 00 | 3 |

❹  **4.** Record goodwill.

Keith Hess and Ralph Grimes are partners in an existing business. Each partner's equity is $30,000.00, for a total equity of $60,000.00. The existing partners agree to admit Julie Spencer as a partner with a one-third interest for a $40,000.00 cash investment. Julie is willing to pay $40,000.00 for a one-third equity. She believes the total equity value is worth $120,000.00 after her investment.

The value of a business in excess of the total investment of owners is called **goodwill**. The partners agree that Julie's willingness to pay $40,000.00 for a one-third interest is evidence that goodwill exists. The value of goodwill is calculated as shown above.

*September 1, 20--. Received cash from new partner, Julie Spencer, for a one-third equity in the business, $40,000.00. Goodwill, $20,000.00, is distributed as follows: Keith Hess, $10,000.00; Ralph Grimes, $10,000.00. Receipt No. 120 and Memorandum No. 60.*

Two journal entries are required for this transaction. (1) Receipt of cash is recorded. (2) Distribution of goodwill is recorded. The $20,000.00 amount of equity in excess of the total recorded investment of the three partners is the value of goodwill.

**STEPS** • STEPS • STEPS • STEPS • STEPS • STEPS • STEPS • STEPS • STEPS • STEPS • STEPS • STEPS

### ADMITTING A PARTNER WHEN GOODWILL IS RECOGNIZED

❶ Determine the total equity of the new partnership by multiplying her investment, $40,000.00, by 3. The total, $120,000.00, will be the total agreed value of equity of the new partnership.

❷ Subtract the total recorded equity, $30,000.00 + $30,000.00 + $40,000.00 = $100,000.00 from the total agreed value of equity calculated in Step 1.

❸ Record the cash investment by the new partner in a cash receipts journal.

❹ Record the recognition of goodwill in the general journal.

| Cash | |
|---|---|
| Sept. 1 | 40,000.00 |

| Goodwill | |
|---|---|
| Sept. 1 | 20,000.00 |

| Keith Hess, Capital | |
|---|---|
| Bal. | 30,000.00 |
| Sept. 1 | 10,000.00 |
| (New Bal. | 40,000.00) |

| Ralph Grimes, Capital | |
|---|---|
| Bal. | 30,000.00 |
| Sept. 1 | 10,000.00 |
| (New Bal. | 40,000.00) |

| Julie Spencer, Capital | |
|---|---|
| Sept. 1 | 40,000.00 |

| | Previous Equity | + | Share of Goodwill | = | New Equity |
|---|---|---|---|---|---|
| Hess | $ 30,000.00 | + | $10,000.00 | = | $ 40,000.00 |
| Grimes | 30,000.00 | + | 10,000.00 | = | 40,000.00 |
| Spencer | + 40,000.00 | + | — | = | 40,000.00 |
| Total | $100,000.00 | + | $20,000.00 | = | $120,000.00 |

The analysis of the investment of cash by Julie Spencer and the distribution of goodwill is shown in the T accounts above. None of the goodwill is recorded in Julie Spencer's capital account. She invested $40,000.00 for a one-third share of the business. One-third of the total equity, *$120,000.00*, equals the current balance of Ms. Spencer's capital account, *$40,000.00*.

Goodwill may be recorded only at the time of a change in ownership of business. An ongoing business may be worth more than the equity value stated in the accounting records. However, goodwill may not be recorded without some evidence of its value. This evidence is provided by the willingness of an investor to pay a premium for an ownership interest in the business.

When used, the account Goodwill is located in a general ledger's Intangible Assets section. Intangible assets are nonphysical assets that have value to a business.

©GETTY IMAGES/PHOTODISC

# careers in accounting

CAREERS IN ACCOUNTING • CAREERS IN ACCOUNTING • CAREERS IN ACCOUNT

## Jennifer Albrecht Young, Group Marketing Director—North America

COURTESY OF JENNIFER ALBRECHT YOUNG

As a student at Saint Mary's College in Moraga, California, Jennifer Albrecht Young participated in an internship program affiliated with Chancellor Broadcasting in San Francisco. At the time, Jennifer was working on a Bachelor of Arts in Communications with an emphasis in Marketing. The internship provided her with the opportunity to work at a local radio station and allowed her to explore the various careers available in broadcasting. Upon graduation from Saint Mary's, she was hired full-time.

Jennifer spent the next seven years in the broadcasting industry meeting country-western celebrities, attending concerts, working media events, researching listening preferences, coordinating advertising, and selling air time. Her goal was to gain experience in a variety of job categories within the broadcast industry in order to determine her primary area of interest. After evaluating her employment experiences, Jennifer realized she had a passion and talent for marketing. At this point in her career, she decided to seek out marketing opportunities with Fortune 500 companies. Her research lead her to Robert Half International (RHI), the world's leading firm in specialized staffing and the first to match professional workers with employers in the areas of accounting, finance, and information technology.

Currently, Jennifer holds the position of Group Marketing Director—North America. Her accounting skills play a significant role in the effective performance of her department. Each week, Jennifer reviews company revenue for both North America and global operations to ensure adherence to RHI's spending parameters for advertising. During the month, she reviews and approves departmental invoices, tracks budget expenditures as they accrue, and makes the necessary adjustments to remain within budget specifications. As the group marketing director for North America, Jennifer is responsible for the on-going management and development of an annual marketing budget in excess of $40 million dollars.

**Salary Range:** $84,000–$142,000

**Qualifications:** Jennifer is strongly convinced that the best way to enter the marketing profession is through an internship program. Marketing is a broad career area that includes consumer research, brand management, public relations, advertising, pricing, promotional campaigns, product distribution, product perception, and even product development. Most entry-level positions in this field require a 4-year college degree. Jennifer believes that success in the industry is directly related to one's ability to communicate, analyze, write, and think strategically.

**Occupational Outlook:** Jennifer foresees marketing-related jobs becoming increasingly important in today's environment of evolving technologies, industry consolidations, and rapid economic growth. As consumers are bombarded with more information than they can process, marketing personnel will remain to ensure that the right people get the right information.

TERM REVIEW

AUDIT YOUR

WORK TOGETHER • WORK TOGETHER • WORK TOGETHER • WORK TOGETHER

## term review

goodwill

## audit your understanding

1. What happens to an existing partnership when a new partner is admitted?
2. When admitting a new partner, how is the new partner's equity calculated?
3. What accounts are debited and credited to record the distribution of goodwill when a new partner is admitted?

## work together 21-2

### Admitting partners to existing partnerships

Four independent situations are given below. Assume partners of the existing partnership are Maria Heath and Lisa Curtis. The new partner is Wade Torres. For each situation, prepare the appropriate journal entries to admit the new partner. Page 12 of a cash receipts journal and page 6 of a general journal are provided in the *Working Papers*. Source documents are abbreviated as follows: memorandum, M; receipt, R. Your instructor will guide you through the following examples.

1. Maria Heath and Lisa Curtis have equity of $24,000.00 each in an existing partnership. On April 1 of the current year, the two partners agree to admit Wade Torres as a third partner. Each partner agrees to sell Mr. Torres $8,000.00 of her equity and to give him a one-third share of ownership. Mr. Torres is to pay the money directly to the two original partners.

   Apr. 1. Journalized personal sale of equity to new partner, Wade Torres, $16,000.00, distributed as follows: from Maria Heath, $8,000.00; from Lisa Curtis, $8,000.00. M32.

2. Maria Heath and Lisa Curtis have equity of $80,000.00 each in the partnership. Partners share equally in all changes in equity. On April 1 of the current year, the two partners agree to admit Wade Torres as a partner with a one-third share of the total equity.

   Apr. 1. Received cash from new partner, Wade Torres, for a one-third equity in the business, $80,000.00. R101.

3. Maria Heath and Lisa Curtis have equity of $50,000.00 each in an existing partnership. The partners share equally in all changes in equity. On April 1 of the current year, the existing partners agree to admit Wade Torres with a one-third share of the total equity.

   Apr. 1. Received cash from new partner, Wade Torres, for a one-third equity in the business, $35,000. Existing equity is redistributed as follows: from Maria Heath, $5,000.00; from Lisa Curtis, $5,000.00. R125 and M31.

4. Maria Heath and Lisa Curtis have equity of $34,000.00 each in an existing business. The partners share equally in all changes in equity. On April 1 of the current year, Wade Torres is admitted as a new partner with a one-third share of the total equity.

   Apr. 1. Received cash from new partner, Wade Torres, for a one-third equity in the business, $40,000.00. Goodwill, $12,000.00, is distributed as follows: Maria Heath, $6,000.00; Lisa Curtis, $6,000.00. R89 and M22.

## on your own 21-2

### Admitting partners to existing partnerships

Four independent situations are given below. Assume that partners of the existing partnership are Kyle Bowen and Susan Wong. The new partner is Angie Mills. For each situation, prepare the appropriate journal entries to admit the new partner. Page 18 of a cash receipts journal and page 9 of a general journal are provided in the *Working Papers*. Work independently to complete the following problem.

1.  Kyle Bowen and Susan Wong have equity of $36,000.00 each in an existing partnership. On June 1 of the current year, the two partners agree to admit Angie Mills as a one-third partner. Each partner agrees to sell Ms. Mills $12,000.00 equity and to give her a one-third share of ownership. Ms. Mills is to pay the money directly to the two original partners.

    June  1.  Journalized personal sale of equity to new partner, Angie Mills, $24,000.00, distributed as follows: from Kyle Bowen, $12,000.00; from Susan Wong, $12,000.00. M36.

2.  Kyle Bowen and Susan Wong have equity of $75,000.00 each in the partnership. Partners share equally in all changes in equity. On June 1 of the current year, the two partners agree to admit Angie Mills as a partner with a one-third share of the total equity.

    June  1.  Received cash from new partner, Angie Mills, for a one-third equity in the business, $75,000.00. R142.

3.  Kyle Bowen and Susan Wong have equity of $36,000.00 each in an existing partnership. The partners share equally in all changes in equity. On June 1 of the current year, the existing partners agree to admit Angie Mills with a one-third share of the total equity.

    June  1.  Received cash from new partner, Angie Mills, for a one-third equity in the business, $30,000.00. Existing equity is redistributed as follows: from Kyle Bowen, $2,000.00; from Susan Wong, $2,000.00. R130 and M40.

4.  Kyle Bowen and Susan Wong each have $52,000.00 equity in an existing business. The partners share equally in all changes in equity. On June 1 of the current year, Angie Mills is admitted as a new partner with a one-third share of the total equity.

    June  1.  Received cash from new partner, Angie Mills, for a one-third equity in the business, $60,000.00. Goodwill, $16,000.00, is distributed as follows: Kyle Bowen, $8,000.00; Susan Wong, $8,000.00. R160 and M46.

SUMMARY · SUMMARY · SUMMARY

### After completing this chapter, you can

1. Define accounting terms related to forming and expanding a partnership.

2. Identify accounting concepts and practices related to forming and expanding a partnership.

3. Journalize transactions related to forming a partnership.

4. Journalize transactions related to expanding a partnership.

# Explore Accounting

EXPLORE ACCOUNTING · EXPLORE ACCOUNTING · EXPLORE ACCO

## Limited Liability Partnerships

The organizational structure of a corporation differs from a partnership in four ways.

1. Continuity of life. A partnership ends upon the death or withdrawal of an owner. Stockholders of a corporation buy and sell stock without affecting the life of the corporation.

2. Centralization of management. A partnership generally is managed by one or more of its partners. A corporation generally is managed by professional managers employed by the stockholders.

3. Limited liability. All partners are liable for contracts and liabilities incurred by the partnership. A corporation is treated as a separate legal entity. Thus the stockholders are not liable for the contracts or liabilities of the corporation.

4. Free transferability of interest. Generally, a partnership ends if a partner dies or withdraws. In addition, other partners must agree before a partner can sell his/her share to another person. Stockholders can buy and sell shares of a corporation without consulting other stockholders.

Because a corporation is a legal entity, a corporation must pay income taxes on its net income.

Most states allow a special kind of partnership, called a limited liability partnership and frequently referred to as an LLP. An LLP must file articles of organization with the state. The operating agreement is similar to a traditional partnership agreement. The LLP must be managed by the members or a group of managers who are elected by the members. To qualify to be taxed as a partnership, the partnership can have no more than two of the characteristics of a corporation. Most LLPs retain the two characteristics, centralization of management and limited liability.

The attractiveness of an LLP is twofold. (1) Partners can be taxed as a partnership (net income reported on individual partner's tax return). (2) Partners have limited liability for the actions of the partnership much like stockholders of a corporation. For these reasons, many partnerships have changed to an LLP.

### Required

1. Make a list of the types of businesses that would be most appropriate organized as an LLP.

2. Through additional reading about LLPs or interviewing local partners of an LLP, determine other advantages and disadvantages of an LLP.

# 21-1 APPLICATION PROBLEM

AUTOMATED ACCOUNTING    PEACHTREE    QUICKBOOKS

Xtra!
Quizzing
accountingxtra.swlearning.com

### Forming a partnership

Carmen Estrada and Paula Jeter agree to form a partnership on June 1 of the current year. The partnership assumes the assets and liabilities of Carmen's existing business. Paula invests cash equal to Carmen's investment. Partners share equally in all changes in equity. The May 31 balance sheet for Carmen's existing business is as follows.

**Carmen's Crafts**
**Balance Sheet**
**May 31, 20--**

| ASSETS | | | |
|---|---|---:|---:|
| Current Assets: | | | |
| Cash | | | $14,532.00 |
| Accounts Receivable | | $3,746.47 | |
| Less Allowance for Uncollectible Accounts | | 74.92 | 3,671.55 |
| Merchandise Inventory | | | 26,298.34 |
| Supplies | | | 670.59 |
| Total Current Assets | | | $45,172.48 |
| Plant Assets: | | | |
| Equipment | | | 9,481.12 |
| Total Assets | | | $54,653.60 |
| LIABILITIES | | | |
| Accounts Payable | | | $ 8,653.60 |
| OWNER'S EQUITY | | | |
| Carmen Estrada, Capital | | | 46,000.00 |
| Total Liabilities and Owner's Equity | | | $54,653.60 |

**Transactions:**

June   1.   Received cash from partner, Paula Jeter, as an initial investment, $46,000.00. R1.
      1.   Accepted assets and liabilities of Carmen Estrada's existing business as an initial investment, $46,000.00. R2.

**Instructions:**

Journalize the transactions using page 1 of a cash receipts journal. Source documents are abbreviated as follows: memorandum, M; receipt, R.

# 21-2 APPLICATION PROBLEM

### Admitting a partner with no change in total equity

Steven Myer and William Riggs are partners in an existing business. Each partner has equity of $30,000.00. On October 1 of the current year, the two partners agree to admit Sandra DeVito as a third partner. Each of the partners agrees to personally sell Sandra $10,000.00 of his equity and to give her a one-third share of ownership. Sandra is to pay the money directly to the two original partners.

**Transaction:**

Oct.   1.   Journalized personal sale of equity to new partner, Sandra DeVito, $20,000.00, distributed as follows: from Steven Myer, $10,000.00; from William Riggs, $10,000.00. M24.

**Instructions:**

Journalize the transaction using page 12 of a general journal.

# 21-3 APPLICATION PROBLEM

**Admitting a partner with equity equal to new partner's investment**

Susan Wang and Lelah Burch are partners in an existing business. Each partner has $60,000.00 equity in the partnership. Partners share equally in all changes in equity. On April 1 of the current year, the two partners agree to admit Daryl Wetzel as a partner with a one-third share of the total equity.

**Transaction:**

Apr.   1.   Received cash from new partner, Daryl Wetzel, for a one-third equity in the business, $60,000.00. R95.

**Instructions:**

Journalize the transaction using page 13 of a cash receipts journal.

# 21-4 APPLICATION PROBLEM

**Admitting a partner with equity greater than new partner's investment**

Stanley Neal and Helen Jobe each have equity of $40,000.00 in an existing partnership. The partners share equally in all changes in equity. On August 1 of the current year, the existing partners agree to admit Greg Talbot with a one-third share of the total equity.

**Transaction:**

Aug.   1.   Received cash from new partner, Greg Talbot, for a one-third equity in the business, $22,000.00. Existing equity is redistributed as follows: from Stanley Neal, $6,000.00; from Helen Jobe, $6,000.00. R116 and M25.

**Instructions:**

Journalize the transaction using page 14 of a cash receipts journal and page 7 of a general journal.

# 21-5 APPLICATION PROBLEM

**Admitting a partner when goodwill is recognized**

Arthur Jansky and Edward Thayer are partners, each with $27,000.00 equity in an existing business. The partners share equally in all changes in equity. On March 1 of the current year, Dean McGee is admitted as a new partner with a one-third share of the total equity.

**Transaction:**

Mar.   1.   Received cash from new partner, Dean McGee, for a one-third equity in the business, $36,000.00. Goodwill, $18,000.00, is distributed as follows: Arthur Jansky, $9,000.00; Edward Thayer, $9,000.00. R67 and M10.

**Instructions:**

Journalize the transaction using page 5 of a cash receipts journal and page 3 of a general journal.

Organizational Structure of a Partnership

### Forming and expanding a partnership

On July 1 of the current year, Roy Hatfield and Michelle Allen form a partnership. The partners share equally in all changes in equity. The partnership assumes the assets and liabilities of Roy's existing business. Michelle invests cash equal to Roy's investment. The June 30 balance sheet for Roy's existing business is as follows.

| Hatfield Financial Services Balance Sheet June 30, 20-- | | | |
|---|---|---|---|
| **ASSETS** | | | |
| Current Assets: | | | |
| Cash | | $4,291.23 | |
| Accounts Receivable | $3,303.60 | | |
| Less Allowance for Uncollectible Accounts | 35.79 | 3,267.81 | |
| Supplies | | 290.19 | |
| Total Current Assets | | | $ 7,849.23 |
| Plant Assets: | | | |
| Equipment | | | 4,378.14 |
| Total Assets | | | $12,227.37 |
| **LIABILITIES** | | | |
| Accounts Payable | | | $ 227.37 |
| **OWNER'S EQUITY** | | | |
| Roy Hatfield, Capital | | | 12,000.00 |
| Total Liabilities and Owner's Equity | | | $12,227.37 |

**Transactions:**

July 1. Received cash from partner, Michelle Allen, as an initial investment, $12,000.00. R1.

1. Accepted assets and liabilities of Roy Hatfield's existing business as an initial investment, $12,000.00. R2.

Aug. 1. Journalized personal sale of equity to new partner, Frank Boyd, $8,000.00, distributed as follows: from Michelle Allen, $4,000.00; from Roy Hatfield, $4,000.00. M8.

Oct. 1. Received cash from new partner, Danita McGrew, for a one-fourth equity in the business, $8,000.00. R80.

Oct. 20. Received cash from new partner, Donna Wells, for a one-fifth equity in the business, $7,000.00. Existing equity is redistributed as follows: from Michelle Allen, $200.00; from Roy Hatfield, $200.00; from Frank Boyd, $200.00; from Danita McGrew, $200.00. R92 and M18.

Dec. 5. Received cash from new partner, Pearl Morgan, for a one-sixth equity in the business, $8,200.00. Goodwill, $2,000.00, is distributed as follows: Roy Hatfield, $400.00; Michelle Allen, $400.00; Frank Boyd, $400.00; Danita McGrew, $400.00; Donna Wells, $400.00. R118 and M24.

**Instructions:**

Journalize the transactions using page 1 of a cash receipts journal and page 1 of a general journal.

## Forming and expanding a partnership

On May 1 of the current year, Marsha Huerta and John Ward form a partnership. The partnership assumes the assets and liabilities of the two partners' existing businesses. Partners share equally in all changes in equity. The May 1 balance sheets for the existing businesses are as follows.

**Marsha's Party Planner**
**Balance Sheet**
**May 1, 20--**

### ASSETS

| | | |
|---|---:|---:|
| Current Assets: | | |
| Cash | | $4,258.32 |
| Accounts Receivable | $2,280.56 | |
| Less Allowance for Uncollectible Accounts | 35.43 | 2,245.13 |
| Merchandise Inventory | | 6,237.29 |
| Total Current Assets | | $12,740.74 |
| Plant Assets: | | |
| Office Equipment | | 2,943.49 |
| Total Assets | | $15,684.23 |

### LIABILITIES

| | |
|---|---:|
| Accounts Payable | $ 3,684.23 |

### OWNER'S EQUITY

| | |
|---|---:|
| Marsha Huerta, Capital | 12,000.00 |
| Total Liabilities and Owner's Equity | $15,684.23 |

**Ward's Wedding Chapel**
**Balance Sheet**
**May 1, 20--**

### ASSETS

| | | |
|---|---:|---:|
| Current Assets: | | |
| Cash | $4,323.49 | |
| Supplies | 2,075.21 | |
| Merchandise Inventory | 6,342.04 | |
| Total Current Assets | | $12,740.74 |
| Plant Assets: | | |
| Office Equipment | | 2,959.88 |
| Total Assets | | $15,700.62 |

### LIABILITIES

| | |
|---|---:|
| Accounts Payable | $ 3,700.62 |

### OWNER'S EQUITY

| | |
|---|---:|
| John Ward, Capital | 12,000.00 |
| Total Liabilities and Owner's Equity | $15,700.62 |

**Transactions:**

May    1.   Accepted assets and liabilities of Marsha Huerta's existing business as an initial investment. R1.

       1.   Accepted assets and liabilities of John Ward's existing business as an initial investment. R2.

July   1.   Accepted assets of Dan Ogden's existing business as an investment of new partner for a one-third equity in the business. M80. Mr. Ogden's July 1 balance sheet is as follows.

**Dan Ogden**
**Balance Sheet**
**July 1, 20--**

ASSETS

Merchandise Inventory. . . . . . . . . . . . . . . . . . . . . . . . . . . . . $12,000.00

OWNER'S EQUITY

Dan Ogden, Capital . . . . . . . . . . . . . . . . . . . . . . . . . . . . . . $12,000.00

July   20.  Received cash from new partner, Pam Wise, for a one-fourth equity in the business, $15,000.00. R24 and M85.

Nov.   5.   Accepted assets of Rodney Stein's existing business as an investment of new partner for a one-fifth equity in the business. Goodwill, $1,000.00, is distributed as follows: Marsha Huerta, $250.00; John Ward, $250.00; Dan Ogden, $250.00; Pam Wise, $250.00. R92 and M105. Mr. Stein's November 5 balance sheet is as follows.

**Stein Supplies**
**Balance Sheet**
**November 5, 20--**

ASSETS

Cash . . . . . . . . . . . . . . . . . . . . . . . . . . . . . . . . . . . . . . . . . . $ 5,000.00
Merchandise Inventory  . . . . . . . . . . . . . . . . . . . . . . . . . .     8,000.00
Total Assets  . . . . . . . . . . . . . . . . . . . . . . . . . . . . . . . . . . . $13,000.00

OWNER'S EQUITY

Rodney Stein, Capital  . . . . . . . . . . . . . . . . . . . . . . . . . . . . $13,000.00

**Instructions:**

Journalize the transactions using page 8 of a cash receipts journal and page 4 of a general journal.

## applied communication

Partnerships have operating expenses each month. Advertising, depreciation, and rent expense are examples of those operating expenses. Controlling these expenses affects the net income of the business.

**Required:**

Identify the operating expenses for MaLin Carpet Design in this chapter. Prepare a brief report, including a pie graph, that depicts the operating expenses for the year ended December 31. Do you think MaLin is controlling its operating expenses?

## cases for critical thinking

### Case 1

Partner A contracted with a vendor to buy a computer for the partnership. Partner A did not discuss the transaction with Partner B or get Partner B's approval. Partner B refused to approve payment for the computer when it was delivered, claiming that the vendor cannot force payment because all partners did not agree to buy the computer. The vendor claims that the transaction is valid, and the partnership must pay for the computer. Is Partner B or the vendor correct? Explain.

### Case 2

Helen Cole, her husband, and her son were partners in a business. Mrs. Cole's husband died, leaving his equity in the partnership to Mrs. Cole. Mrs. Cole and her son plan to form a new partnership and continue the business. Mrs. Cole's brother owns a similar business. The brother suggests that they combine the two businesses into a corporation. What questions do you suggest Mrs. Cole answer before she decides whether to form a partnership with her son or a corporation with her son and brother?

## SCANS workplace competency

**Personal Qualities:** Integrity/Honesty

**Concept:** Employers seek individuals who display integrity and choose ethical courses of action.

**Application:** In order to be licensed as a certified public accountant, candidates must past the uniform CPA exam and the American Institute of Certified Public Accountants Professional Ethics Exam. Some states also require the passing of a state ethics exam. Contact a local CPA or use the Internet to determine your state's requirements for an ethics exam. What is the exam's content? Why is it so critical that accountants demonstrate ethical behavior? Share your findings with the class.

## • auditing for errors

Amy Cardoza, Jeff Williams, and Claire Mangoni are partners in an existing music business. Each partner's equity is $32,000, for a total equity of $96,000. The partners agree to admit Russ Hodges as a partner with a one-fourth interest for a $24,000 cash investment. The firm's bookkeeper made the following entry in the partnership's general journal, based on information recorded on R213 and M89.

| | DATE | | ACCOUNT TITLE | DOC. NO. | POST. REF. | DEBIT | CREDIT | |
|---|---|---|---|---|---|---|---|---|
| 1 | Oct. ²⁰⁻⁻ | 1 | Cash | R213 | | 24 0 0 0 00 | | 1 |
| 2 | | | Goodwill | | | 8 0 0 0 00 | | 2 |
| 3 | | | Russ Hodges, Capital | | | | 3 2 0 0 0 00 | 3 |
| 4 | | | | | | | | 4 |

GENERAL JOURNAL                                PAGE 12

**Instructions:**

1.  Do you agree with the bookkeeper's entry? Explain your answer.

2.  If you disagree, what journal entries would you make?

## • analyzing Costco's financial statements

Financial statements are interrelated and connected to one another. A change on one financial statement will have an impact on other financial statements. For example, if a corporation neglected to record a $10,000 cash payment for July rent, the cash amount reported on the balance sheet would be overstated. On the income statement, the net income would also be overstated, due to the $10,000 missing in the rent expense account. Since net income increases the retained earnings, the amount of retained earnings listed on the statements of stockholders' equity would be incorrect. And finally, since the amount of net income and year-end cash balance are reported on the statement of cash flows, that financial statement would be incorrect as well.

**Instructions:**

Refer to Costco's financial statements shown on pages B-5–B-8 in Appendix B of this textbook to answer the following questions.

1.  Determine the amount of the difference in retained earnings listed on the Consolidated Balance Sheets for August 31, 2003 and September 1, 2002. Remember, dollar amounts are reported in thousands.

2.  Locate the dollar amount calculated in question 1 on Costco's Consolidated Statements of Income for the 52 Weeks Ended August 31, 2003. What is the title for the amount?

3.  Locate the dollar amount calculated in question 1 on Costco's Consolidated Statements of Stockholders' Equity. What is the title for the amount?

4.  Locate the dollar amount calculated in question 1 on Costco's Consolidated Statements of Cash Flows for the 52 Weeks Ended August 31, 2003. What is the title for the amount?

5.  List the financial statements that would be affected by a failure to account for a $200,000 cash expenditure for advertising.

# Automated Accounting

## Setting Up Automated Accounting Systems for Partnerships

Accounting software packages can be tailored to the needs of various types of businesses. Before accounting data can be entered, information about the company must be entered. The Customize Accounting System window is used to enter company information.

### Company Info Tab

General information about a new company is specified on this tab. The company name and problem number are printed as part of the header for every report. Other information required includes business organization, features, type of business, type of income statement, and which checks will be printed from the accounting system.

### Classify Accounts Tab

For most businesses, the default account classifications will be used. However, the classification numbers can be edited if necessary.

### Required Accts. Tab

To prepare reports and perform period-ending closing tasks, certain accounts are required. Based upon the information specified on the Company Information tab, the computer will automatically search the chart of accounts to determine and list the accounts it requires. Accounts that cannot automatically be determined must be keyed.

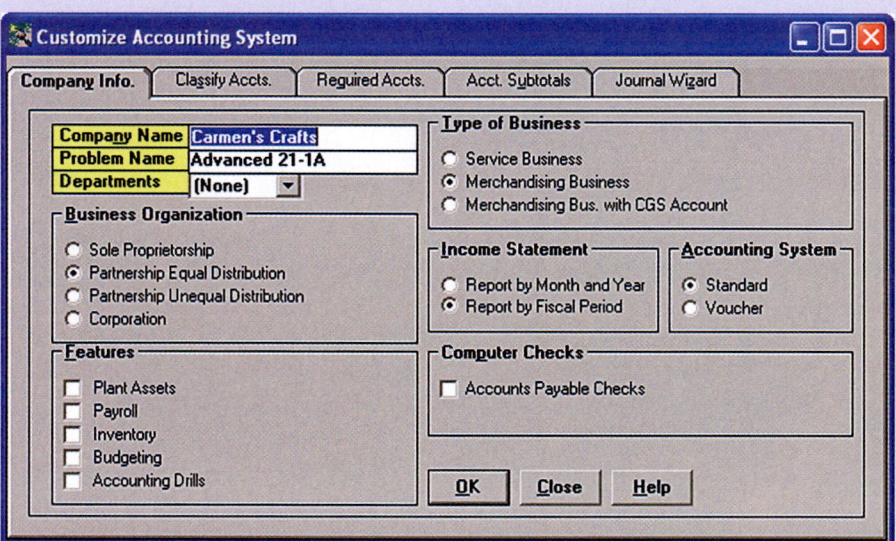

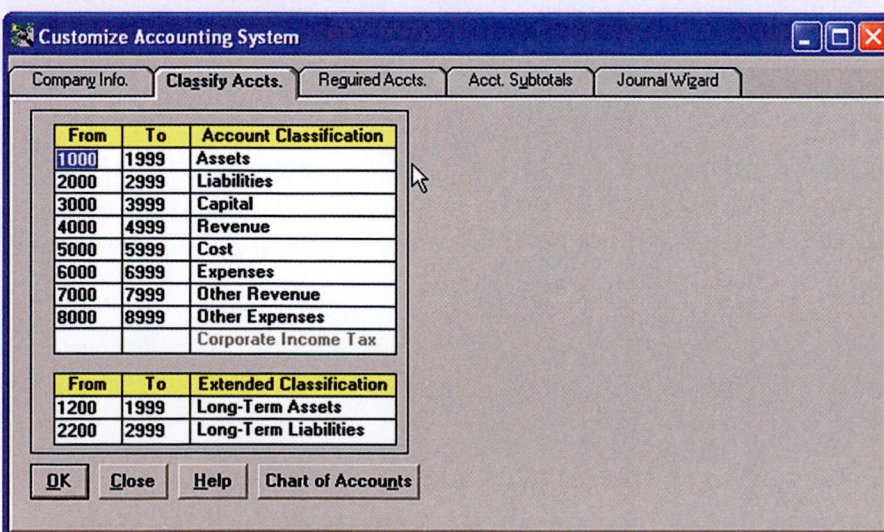

## AUTOMATING APPLICATION PROBLEM 21-1

**Instructions:**

1. Load *Automated Accounting 8.0* or higher software.

2. Select database A21-1 (Advanced Course Application Problem 21-1) from the accounting template disk.

3. Select File from the menu bar and choose the Save As menu command. Key the path to the drive and directory that contains your data files. Save the database with a filename of XXX211 (where XXX are your initials).

4. Read the Problem Instruction screen by clicking the Browser toolbar button.

5. Key the data listed in the problem.

6. Exit the Automated Accounting software.

## AUTOMATING MASTERY PROBLEM 21-6

**Instructions:**

1. Load *Automated Accounting 8.0* or higher software.

2. Select database A21-6 (Advanced Course Application Problem 21-6) from the accounting template disk.

3. Select File from the menu bar and choose the Save As menu command. Key the path to the drive and directory that contains your data files. Save the database with a filename of XXX216 (where XXX are your initials).

4. Read the Problem Instruction screen by clicking the Browser toolbar button.

5. Key the data listed in the problem.

6. Exit the Automated Accounting software.

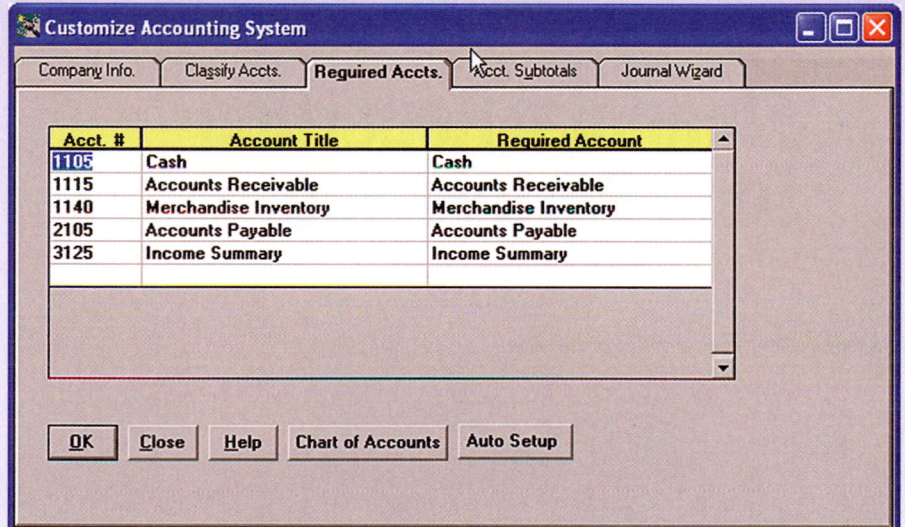

# 22 Financial Reporting for a Partnership

*After studying Chapter 22, you will be able to:*

1. Define accounting terms related to distributing earnings and completing end-of-fiscal-period work for a partnership.

2. Identify accounting concepts and practices related to distributing earnings and completing end-of-fiscal-period work for a partnership.

3. Calculate the distribution of partnership earnings.

4. Journalize entries for withdrawal of partnership earnings.

5. Complete end-of-fiscal-period work for a partnership.

6. Prepare a distribution of net income statement for a partnership.

7. Journalize entries for liquidating a partnership.

- distribution of net income statement
- deficit
- owners' equity statement
- liquidation of a partnership
- realization

Point Your Browser
accountingxtra.swlearning.com

# • Hewlett-Packard Company

©MATT STROSHANE/BLOOMBERG NEWS/LANDOV

**ACCOUNTING IN THE REAL WORLD • ACCOUNTING IN THE REAL WORLD • ACCOUNTING IN THE REAL WORLD**

## HEWLETT-PACKARD COMPANY: PARTNERING TO EXPAND GLOBAL IMPACT

In 1939, Bill Hewlett and Dave Packard formed a partnership that has evolved into one of the largest corporations in the world. The two partners began their business by developing a product known as an audio oscillator, an electronic device used by engineers to test sound equipment. In fact, one of the first companies to purchase Hewlett and Packard's audio oscillator was Walt Disney Studios, which used eight of the test instruments to create and develop a new sound system for its animated features. HP's revenues that first year totaled $5,369.

HP has grown considerably since 1939. The company recently launched 660 new products in a single year and closed that year with over 21,000 patents in force throughout the world. Today, with revenues of over $73 billion, HP is the leading consumer information technology company and sells its products in 110,000 retail outlets in more than 170 countries.

To remain competitive, the company continues to expand its operations and influence throughout the world. In 2003, HP merged with Compaq Computer Corporation. The merger allowed HP to improve cost efficiencies and offer a broad range of products and services to individual consumers, small businesses, and large corporations.

### Critical Thinking

1. How would a merger between two technology companies help improve cost efficiencies?
2. How would a merger help expand sales?

**Xtra!**
Today
accountingxtra.swlearning.com

Source: www.hp.com

---

## CPA DESIGNATION

Go to the homepage for the National Association of State Boards of Accountancy (NASBA) (www.nasba.org). This site has some information about each state's requirements for the Certified Public Accountant (CPA) designation and will link you to the State Board of Accountancy for your state.

### Instructions

1. List the age, education, and work experience requirements to be licensed as a CPA in your state.
2. List the name, address, and phone number of the State Board of Accountancy for your state.

# 22-1 Distribution and Withdrawal of Partnership Earnings

Most end-of-fiscal-period work is similar for corporations, proprietorships, and partnerships. Two major procedures are different. (1) A corporation calculates and pays income tax on its net income, but partnerships and proprietorships do not. (2) A corporation maintains separate accounts for contributed capital (Capital Stock) and earned capital (Retained Earnings). Partnerships and proprietorships combine contributed and earned capital in one account for each owner.

A corporation may distribute some, but usually not all, of its earnings to stockholders as dividends. However, partnerships, like proprietorships, distribute all earnings of the business to the owners' capital accounts. The owners may then withdraw the earnings or leave them in the business.

©GETTY IMAGES/PHOTODISC

## making ethical decisions

### Impending Merger Affects Student's Employment

Sallie Kaplan was a senior majoring in accounting at Southeastern State University when she accepted a position in the Columbus office of Jensen, Pearson & Marris, a public accounting firm. Sallie was not scheduled to begin working with the firm until after she completed her master's degree.

About the same time, John Jensen, the managing partner of the firm, agreed in principle to sell the firm to Patrel & Franklin, a large, international public accounting firm. The merger required extensive negotiations and planning. As a result, the merger was not announced to the public, existing clients, or employees (including Sallie) for over a year. Patrel & Franklin immediately announced that the Columbus office was going to be closed and its clients serviced from its New York office.

The day after the merger was announced, John offered Sallie a similar position in the New York office. For personal reasons, Sallie declined the offer. Thus, with only two months remaining before her graduation with a master's degree, Sallie again began searching for a new position in Columbus.

#### Instructions

Determine whether John Jensen's delay in telling Sallie Kaplan of the merger and office closing was ethical. Assume that the action is not illegal and does not violate any professional codes of conduct. Evaluate the impact of the decision on all the stakeholders.

# DISTRIBUTION OF PARTNERSHIP EARNINGS

All earnings of a partnership are distributed to the partners. Five methods are commonly used for calculating the distribution of partnership earnings.

1. Fixed percentage.
2. Percentage of total equity.
3. Interest on equity.
4. Salaries.
5. Combination of methods

## FIXED PERCENTAGE

| | | Total Net Income | × | Fixed Percentage | = | Share of Net Income |
|---|---|---|---|---|---|---|
| | Costa | $20,000.00 | × | 60% | = | $12,000.00 |
| | McKee | $20,000.00 | × | 40% | = | 8,000.00 |
| | Total | | | | | $20,000.00 |

The basis on which a partnership's earnings are distributed is usually stated in the partnership agreement. If a partnership agreement does not indicate how to divide the earnings, most state laws stipulate that partners share the earnings equally. For example, the earnings of two partners are shared on a fixed percentage of 50% and 50%. The law applies regardless of differences in the partners' investments, abilities, or time devoted to partnership business.

Scott Costa and Gary McKee are partners. On January 1, the partners' equities are Scott, $50,000.00 and Gary, $30,000.00. The net income for the year ended December 31 is $20,000.00. The partnership agreement states that Scott is to receive 60% and Gary is to receive 40% of the net income or net loss. The distribution of net income is calculated as shown above.

**FYI** FOR YOUR INFORMATION

Limited partnerships include owners who have limited liability and limited operating responsibilities. Limited partnerships are sometimes formed for special projects such as Broadway plays.

©GETTY IMAGES/PHOTODISC

# PERCENTAGE OF TOTAL EQUITY

|  | Partner's Equity | ÷ | Total Equity | = | Percentage of Total Equity |
|---|---|---|---|---|---|
| Costa | $50,000.00 | ÷ | $80,000.00 | = | 62.5% |
| McKee | 30,000.00 | ÷ | $80,000.00 | = | 37.5% |
| Total | $80,000.00 | | | | |

|  | Total Net Income | × | Percentage of Total Equity | = | Share of Net Income |
|---|---|---|---|---|---|
| Costa | $20,000.00 | × | 62.5% | = | $12,500.00 |
| McKee | $20,000.00 | × | 37.5% | = | 7,500.00 |
| Total | | | | | $20,000.00 |

Partners often agree to use capital account balances on the first day of a fiscal year as the basis for calculating the distribution of partnership earnings. If Scott and Gary had agreed to use this method, referred to as the *percentage of total equity method*, the percentages would be calculated as shown above.

# INTEREST ON EQUITY

|  | Partner's Equity | × | Interest Rate | = | Interest on Equity |
|---|---|---|---|---|---|
| Baker | $22,880.00 | × | 5% | = | $1,144.00 |
| Mattingly | $11,440.00 | × | 5% | = | 572.00 |

Interest on equity is often used as a method to distribute earnings when partners invest different amounts in a partnership. Partners often agree to use capital account balances on the first day of a fiscal year as the basis for this income distribution method. The partnership agreement states the interest rate.

MaLin Carpet Design's partnership agreement, Item Five, shown on page 623, stipulates that each partner is to receive 5% interest on equity. On January 1, May Baker's equity is $22,880.00 and Lindel Mattingly's equity is

$11,440.00. The interest on equity is calculated as shown above.

When the interest on equity method is used, the remaining net income or net loss is distributed using another income distribution method as described later in this chapter.

**FYI** 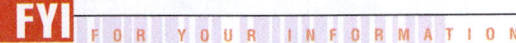 FOR YOUR INFORMATION

The rate of interest on equity is often related to the current bank prime lending rate.

## SALARIES

Salaries are often used as a method to distribute earnings when partners contribute different amounts of personal service or bring different prior experience to a partnership. The amount of salary for each partner is stated in the partnership agreement.

MaLin's partnership agreement states that salaries are to be paid as follows: May Baker, $5,000.00; Lindel Mattingly, $3,000.00. When salaries are used, the remaining net income or net loss is distributed using a combination of methods described in the following paragraphs.

## COMBINATION OF METHODS

|  | Interest on Equity | Salary | Distribution of Remaining Net Income or Net Loss |
|---|---|---|---|
| Baker | 5% | $5,000.00 | 50% |
| Mattingly | 5% | $3,000.00 | 50% |

|  | Baker | Mattingly | Distribution |
|---|---|---|---|
| Total Net Income |  |  | $37,400.00 |
| Interest on Equity | $ 1,144.00 | $ 572.00 |  |
| Salary | 5,000.00 | 3,000.00 |  |
| Total | $ 6,144.00 | $ 3,572.00 | 9,716.00 |
| Remaining Net Income |  |  | $27,684.00 |
| Distribution of Remaining Net Income | 13,842.00 | 13,842.00 |  |
| Total Distribution | $19,986.00 | $17,414.00 | $37,400.00 |

A combination of income distribution methods may be used for distributing partnership earnings. MaLin's partnership agreement states the earnings distribution as shown above. The distribution of MaLin's net income, *$37,400.00*, is calculated as shown above.

## WITHDRAWAL OF PARTNERSHIP EARNINGS

A partner often needs a portion of the annual net income before the end of a fiscal year when the actual net income is known. Thus, during a fiscal year, partners take assets out of the partnership in anticipation of the net income for the year. Assets taken out of a business for the owner's personal use are known as withdrawals. Usually the partnership agreement indicates limits on the amount of assets that may be withdrawn.

**REMEMBER** A partner may have a large capital balance yet be unable to withdraw any assets from the partnership. Cash or other assets must be available for a partner to make a withdrawal. A partner's salary is not an expense to the business.

# WITHDRAWAL OF CASH

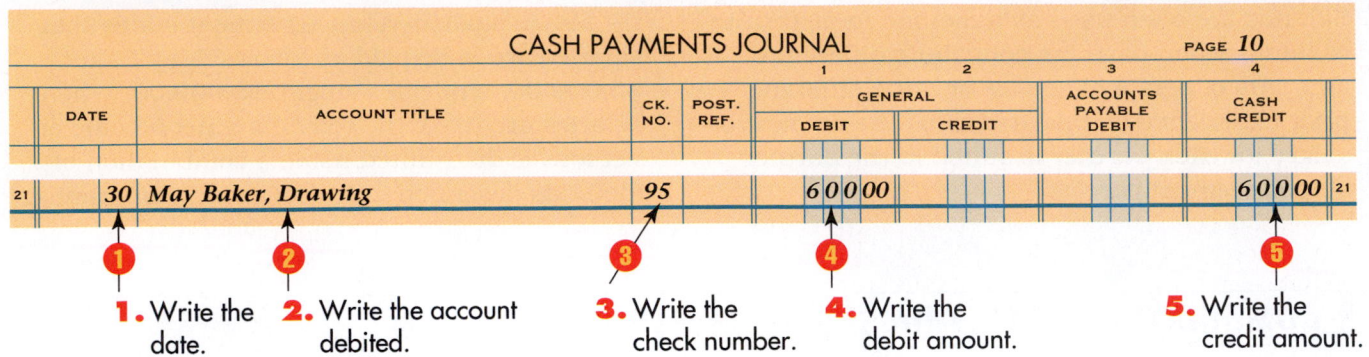

1. Write the date.
2. Write the account debited.
3. Write the check number.
4. Write the debit amount.
5. Write the credit amount.

*May 30, 20--. May Baker, partner, withdrew cash for personal use, $600.00. Check No. 95.*

May Baker, Drawing is debited for $600.00. Cash is credited for $600.00. The entry is made in the cash payments journal as shown above.

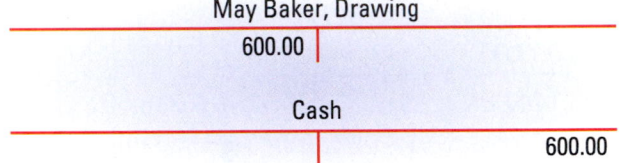

## STEPS

STEPS • STEPS • STEPS • STEPS • STEP

### PARTNER'S WITHDRAWAL OF CASH

1. Write the date, *30*, in the Date column.

2. Write the title of the account debited, *May Baker, Drawing*, in the Account Title column.

3. Write the check number, *95*, in the Ck. No. column.

4. Write the debit amount, *600.00*, in the General Debit column.

5. Write the credit amount, *600.00*, in the Cash Credit column.

# WITHDRAWAL OF ASSETS OTHER THAN CASH

1. Write the date.
2. Write the account debited.
4. Write the debit amount.

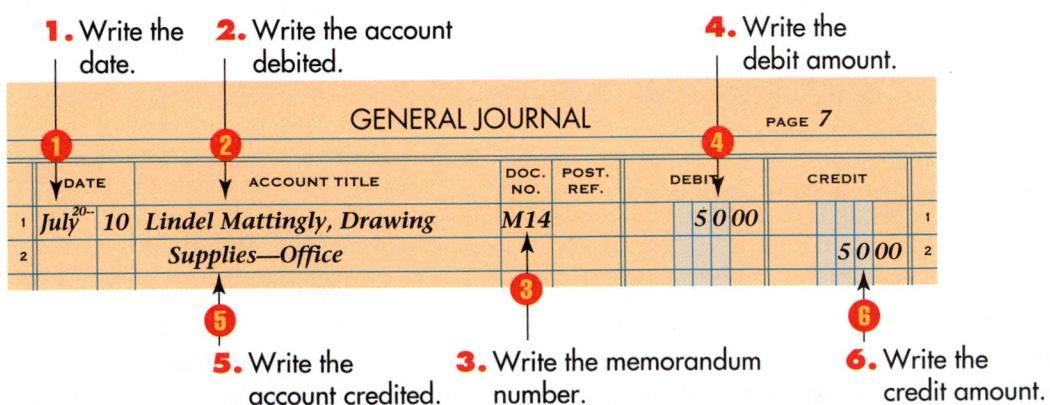

5. Write the account credited.
3. Write the memorandum number.
6. Write the credit amount.

*July 10, 20--. Lindel Mattingly, partner, withdrew office supplies for personal use, $50.00. Memorandum No. 14.*

Office supplies withdrawn for personal use are not a business expense. This transaction reduces the partnership's office supplies inven-tory and, therefore, Supplies—Office is credited. Lindel Mattingly, Drawing is debited for $50.00. Supplies—Office is credited for $50.00.

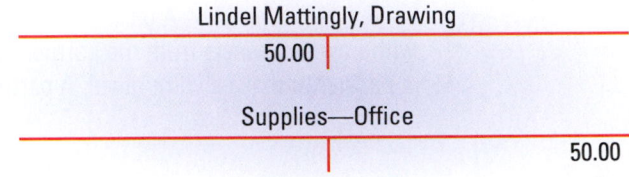

# Explore Accounting

## Accounting for Mortgage and Lease Payments

Lexington Corporation has just signed a rental agreement with Metro Financing for the use of a delivery truck. Lexington must pay $600.00 each month for five years. A provision of the lease contract allows Lexington to purchase the truck from Metro Financing for $100.00 at the end of the lease term. Lexington's bookkeeper has recorded the first lease payment using the following entry:

```
Rent Expense . . . . . . . . 600.00
   Cash  . . . . . . . . . . . . . . . . . . . . 600.00
```

Upon reviewing the monthly financial statements, Lexington's chief financial officer (CFO) recognizes that the transaction was not recorded properly. The CFO realizes that, although the form of the transaction is a lease, the substance of the transaction is a loan. GAAP provides accountants with four criteria to evaluate the substance versus the form of lease agreements. If any one of the criteria is met, the transaction is treated as a purchase. A lease with substantially the same provisions as a purchase is referred to as a *capital lease*.

The estimated cost of the asset is recorded as if the asset were purchased on account, with a bank loan or a mortgage. Lexington could have arranged a 10% bank loan to purchase the truck. Using this interest rate, the CFO estimates the value of the truck to be $28,239.22 and records the following entry:

```
Capitalize Lease
(truck) . . . . . . . . . . . . 28,239.22
   Lease Liability . . . . . . . . . . . 28,239.22
```

The lease liability is recorded as a long-term liability. Similar to any loan or mortgage payment, each payment is divided between interest and loan repayment. After calculating the monthly interest expense, the remaining portion of the payment reduces the loan principal balance. In the first month of the lease, Lexington must pay 10% interest on the recorded value of the lease liability. Thus, the following entry would be recorded:

```
Interest Expense . . . . . . . 235.33
   (28,239.22 × 10%/12)
Lease Liability  . . . . . . . . 364.67
   (600.00 − 235.33)
   Cash  . . . . . . . . . . . . . . . . . . . . . 600.00
```

Since the truck is also recorded as an asset, a separate entry would be recorded to reflect depreciation expense. Thus, the accounting entries to record a capital lease are exactly the same as if Lexington had purchased the truck with a loan from Metro Financing.

**Instructions:** Determine the transaction for recording the second month's lease payment. Note that the principal for the interest calculation is reduced by the amount of reduction in the lease liability.

## • audit your understanding

1. Where should the method of distributing partnership earnings be stated?
2. What are five common methods for distributing partnership earnings?
3. What account is debited when a partner withdraws cash for personal use?
4. What account is debited when a partner withdraws supplies for personal use?

## • work together 22-1

**Calculating partnership earnings and journalizing partnership withdrawals**

Scott Badger and Maxine Giesen are partners in a business. On December 31 of the current year, the partners' equities are Scott, $60,000.00 and Maxine, $90,000.00. The net income for the year is $60,000.00. A work sheet for calculating distribution of partners' earnings, a cash payments journal, and a general journal are provided in the *Working Papers*. Your instructor will guide you through the following examples.

1. For each of the following independent cases, calculate how the $60,000.00 net income will be distributed to the two partners.

    a. Each partner receives a fixed percentage of 50% of net income.

    b. Each partner receives a percentage of net income based on the percentage of total equity.

    c. Each partner receives 10% interest on equity. The partners share remaining net income equally.

    d. Scott receives 8% interest on equity and a salary of $18,000.00. Maxine receives 8% interest on equity and a salary of $22,500.00. The partners share remaining net income equally.

2. Record the following transactions in the appropriate journal.

    June 20, 20--.  Scott Badger, partner, withdrew cash for personal use, $750.00. Check No. 133.
    July 1, 20--.    Maxine Giesen, partner, withdrew office supplies for personal use, $45.00. Memorandum No. 23.

## on your own 22-1

**Calculating partnership earnings and journalizing partnership withdrawals**

Rose Nabors and Sam Ives are partners in a business. On December 31 of the current year, the partners' equities are Rose, $50,000 and Sam, $75,000.00. The net income for the year is $50,000.00. A work sheet for calculating distribution of partners' earnings, a cash payments journal, and a general journal are provided in the *Working Papers*. Work independently to complete the following problem.

1.  For each of the following independent cases, calculate how the $50,000.00 net income will be distributed to the two partners.

    a.  Each partner receives a fixed percentage of 50% of net income.

    b.  Each partner receives a percentage of net income based on the percentage of total equity.

    c.  Each partner receives 8% interest on equity. The partners share remaining net income equally.

    d.  Rose receives 10% interest on equity and a salary of $16,000.00. Sam receives 10% interest on equity and a salary of $14,000.00. The partners share remaining net income equally.

2.  Record the following transactions in the appropriate journal.
    Apr. 15, 20--.  Rose Nabors, partner, withdrew cash for personal use, $800.00. Check No. 126.
    Oct.  3, 20--.  Sam Ives, partner, withdrew store supplies for personal use, $120.00. Memorandum No. 18.

# business structures

BUSINESS STRUCTURES • BUSINESS STRUCTURES • BUSINESS STRUCTURES

## The FTC Franchise Rule

Successful business owners frequently seek ways to expand their businesses. One expansion technique is franchising. A franchise is a contractual arrangement in which the owner of a trademark, trade name, or copyright licenses others, under specified conditions or limitations, to use the trademark, trade name, or copyright to sell goods or services. The person or business entity granting the franchise is known as the franchisor. The person or business entity to whom the franchise is granted is known as the franchisee.

The Federal Trade Commission (FTC) Franchise Rule requires the franchisor to make a written disclosure of important information about the franchisor, the franchised business, and the franchise relationship. The disclosure should state information about the total cost, the amount of control the franchisor will have over the operations of the franchisee, the plan for termination of the franchise, and the conditions for renewal of the franchise. A franchisor must allow the potential franchisee at least 10 business days to review the disclosure document before asking the person to invest in the franchise.

Since the Franchise Rule is a trade regulation, it is enforced by the FTC. If the FTC finds that the rule has been violated, it may issue injunctions, freeze the assets of the franchisor, enact fines up to $10,000 per violation, and require that monetary compensation be given to those harmed by the actions of the franchisor.

## 22-2 End-of-Fiscal-Period Work for a Partnership

### ADJUSTMENTS ON A WORK SHEET

End-of-fiscal-period work for a partnership is similar to that for a corporation. In preparing partnership financial statements, accountants apply accounting principles in the same way during each fiscal period. [*CONCEPT: Consistent Reporting*]

All accounts in MaLin's general ledger are listed in a work sheet's Account Title column as shown on the next page. Adjustments are planned on a partnership work sheet in the same manner as on a corporate work sheet, with one exception. No adjustment for accrued federal income tax is *ever* planned on a partner-ship work sheet because partnerships do not pay federal income tax.

As described later in this chapter, partnership net income is reported to the Internal Revenue Service on the partners' personal tax returns.

Because MaLin Carpet Design does not sell merchandise, it does not need to make an adjustment for merchandise inventory. Adjustments for uncollectible accounts, supplies, insurance, and depreciation are planned on the work sheet.

### INCOME STATEMENT

**MaLin Carpet Design**
**Income Statement**
**For Year Ended December 31, 20--**

|  |  |  | % of Sales* |
|---|---|---:|---:|
| Operating Revenue: |  |  |  |
| Sales | | $72,020.27 | 100.0 |
| Operating Expenses: |  |  |  |
| Advertising Expense | $ 985.00 |  |  |
| Depreciation Expense—Equipment | 1,250.50 |  |  |
| Depreciation Expense—Truck | 918.75 |  |  |
| Insurance Expense | 503.20 |  |  |
| Miscellaneous Expense | 2,869.21 |  |  |
| Rent Expense | 8,400.00 |  |  |
| Supplies Expense—Carpet | 7,676.50 |  |  |
| Supplies Expense—Office | 1,420.00 |  |  |
| Truck Expense | 8,477.56 |  |  |
| Uncollectible Accounts Expense | 119.55 |  |  |
| Utilities Expense | 2,000.00 |  |  |
| Total Operating Expenses | | 34,620.27 | 48.1 |
| Net Income | | $37,400.00 | 51.9 |

*Rounded to the nearest 0.1%.

**MaLin Carpet Design**
**Work Sheet**
**For Year Ended December 31, 20--**

| # | ACCOUNT TITLE | TRIAL BALANCE DEBIT | TRIAL BALANCE CREDIT | ADJUSTMENTS DEBIT | ADJUSTMENTS CREDIT | INCOME STATEMENT DEBIT | INCOME STATEMENT CREDIT | BALANCE SHEET DEBIT | BALANCE SHEET CREDIT |
|---|---|---|---|---|---|---|---|---|---|
| 1 | Cash | 4280247 | | | | | | 4280247 | |
| 2 | Petty Cash | 20000 | | | | | | 20000 | |
| 3 | Accounts Receivable | 1199251 | | | | | | 1199251 | |
| 4 | Allow. for Uncollectible Accts. | | 1992 | | (a) 11955 | | | | 13947 |
| 5 | Supplies—Carpet | 930500 | | | (b) 767650 | | | 162850 | |
| 6 | Supplies—Office | 184500 | | | (c) 142000 | | | 42500 | |
| 7 | Prepaid Insurance | 134970 | | | (d) 50320 | | | 84650 | |
| 8 | Equipment | 1250497 | | | | | | 1250497 | |
| 9 | Accum. Depr.—Equipment | | | | (e) 125050 | | | | 125050 |
| 10 | Truck | 490000 | | | | | | 490000 | |
| 11 | Accum. Depr.—Truck | | | | (f) 91875 | | | | 91875 |
| 12 | Accounts Payable | | 852123 | | | | | | 852123 |
| 13 | May Baker, Capital | | 2288000 | | | | | | 2288000 |
| 14 | May Baker, Drawing | 450000 | | | | | | 450000 | |
| 15 | Lindel Mattingly, Capital | | 1144000 | | | | | | 1144000 |
| 16 | Lindel Mattingly, Drawing | 275000 | | | | | | 275000 | |
| 17 | Income Summary | | | | | | | | |
| 18 | Sales | | 7202027 | | | | 7202027 | | |
| 19 | Advertising Expense | 98500 | | | | 98500 | | | |
| 20 | Depr. Expense—Equipment | | | (e) 125050 | | 125050 | | | |
| 21 | Depr. Expense—Truck | | | (f) 91875 | | 91875 | | | |
| 22 | Insurance Expense | | | (d) 50320 | | 50320 | | | |
| 23 | Miscellaneous Expense | 286921 | | | | 286921 | | | |
| 24 | Rent Expense | 840000 | | | | 840000 | | | |
| 25 | Supplies Expense—Carpet | | | (b) 767650 | | 767650 | | | |
| 26 | Supplies Expense—Office | | | (c) 142000 | | 142000 | | | |
| 27 | Truck Expense | 847756 | | | | 847756 | | | |
| 28 | Uncollectible Accounts Expense | | | (a) 11955 | | 11955 | | | |
| 29 | Utilities Expense | 200000 | | | | 200000 | | | |
| 30 | | 11488142 | 11488142 | 1188850 | 1188850 | 3462027 | 7202027 | 8254995 | 4514995 |
| 31 | Net Income | | | | | 3740000 | | | 3740000 |
| 32 | | | | | | 7202027 | 7202027 | 8254995 | 8254995 |

## COMPONENT PERCENTAGES ON THE INCOME STATEMENT

A partnership income statement is similar to a corporation income statement with one exception. Federal income tax expense is *not* reported on a partnership income statement because a partnership does not pay federal income tax.

MaLin calculates two component percentages on its income statement as shown on page 656.

1. *Operating expenses component percentage.* MaLin expects a component percentage not more than 55.0%. Therefore, MaLin's operating expenses component percentage of 48.1% is acceptable. (Operating Expenses, \$34,620.27 ÷ Sales, \$72,020.27 = Operating Expense Component Percentage, 48.1%).
2. *Net income component percentage.* MaLin expects a component percentage not less than 45.0%. Therefore, MaLin's net income

component percentage of 51.9% is acceptable. (Net Income, \$37,400.00; Sales, \$72,020.27 = Net Income Component Percentage, 51.9%).

The net income component percentage is often high for partnerships that sell only services because they have no cost of merchandise sold. Also, the partners' salaries are not expenses of the partnership.

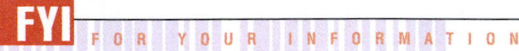

### FYI
**FOR YOUR INFORMATION**

Fields of accounting become extremely specialized as technical requirements increase. For example, some accountants specialize in accounting only for the gas and oil industry.

## DISTRIBUTION OF NET INCOME STATEMENT SHOWING A NET INCOME

**2.** Enter information for first partner.

**1.** Enter heading.

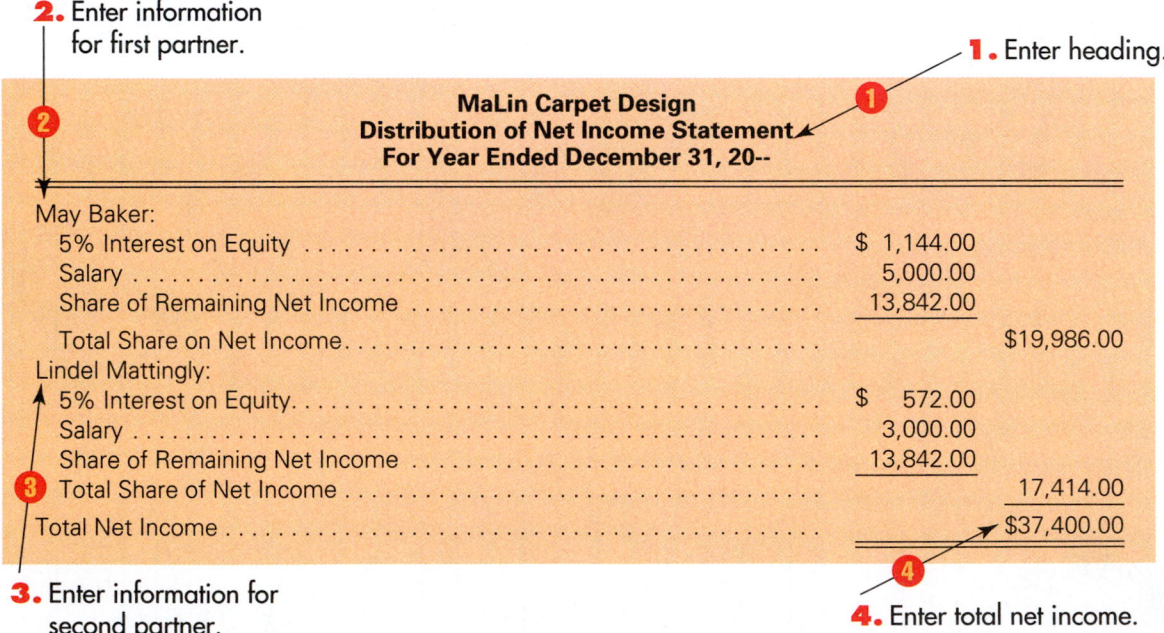

**3.** Enter information for second partner.

**4.** Enter total net income.

A partnership financial statement showing distribution of net income or net loss to partners is called a **distribution of net income statement**.

MaLin's distribution of partnership earnings for the current year was calculated as shown on

page 651. The amounts calculated are reported on the Distribution of Net Income Statement shown above.

# STEPS

## PREPARING A DISTRIBUTION OF NET INCOME STATEMENT

**1** Enter the 3-line heading, *MaLin Carpet Design, Distribution of Net Income Statement, For Year Ended December 31, 20--.*

**2** Enter the information for *May Baker.* List the distribution methods, *5% Interest on Equity, Salary,* and *Share of Remaining Net Income.* Enter the amounts of distribution for each method, *$1,144.00, $5,000.00,* and *$13,842.00,* respectively. Finally, enter the *Total Share of Net Income, $19,986.00.*

**3** Enter the information for *Lindel Mattingly.* List the distribution methods, *5% Interest on Equity, Salary,* and *Share of Remaining Net Income.* Enter the distribution amounts for each method, *$572.00, $3,000.00,* and *$13,842.00,* respectively. Finally, enter the *Total Share of Net Income, $17,414.00.*

**4** Enter *Total Net Income, $37,400.00.*

## DISTRIBUTION OF NET INCOME STATEMENT SHOWING A DEFICIT

| | Partner's Equity | × | Interest Rate | × | Time as Fraction of Year | = | Monthly Interest | |
|---|---|---|---|---|---|---|---|---|
| Ford | ($60,000.00 | × | 10%) | × | 1/12 | = | $500.00 | |
| Pope | ($54,000.00 | × | 10%) | × | 1/12 | = | 450.00 | |
| Total | | | | | | | $950.00 | |

**1.** Calculate monthly interest.

| | Total Net Income | − | Total Allowance | = | Deficit | |
|---|---|---|---|---|---|---|
| | $750.00 | − | $950.00 | = | $200.00 | |

**2.** Determine the deficit.

| | Deficit | × | Fixed Percentage | = | Partner's Share of Deficit | |
|---|---|---|---|---|---|---|
| Ford | $200.00 | × | 60% | = | $120.00 | |
| Pope | $200.00 | × | 40% | = | 80.00 | |
| Total | | | | | $200.00 | |

**3.** Calculate each partner's share of the deficit.

### Ford and Pope
### Distribution of Net Income Statement
### For Month Ended January 31, 20--

| | | |
|---|---|---|
| Jason Ford: | | |
| 10% Interest on Equity . . . . . . . . . . . . . . . . . . . . . . . . . . . . . . . . . | $500.00 | |
| Less Share of Deficit . . . . . . . . . . . . . . . . . . . . . . . . . . . . . . . . . | 120.00 | |
| Total Share of Net Income . . . . . . . . . . . . . . . . . . . . . . . . . . . . . | | $380.00 |
| Celia Pope: | | |
| 10% Interest on Equity . . . . . . . . . . . . . . . . . . . . . . . . . . . . . . . . . | $450.00 | |
| Less Share of Deficit . . . . . . . . . . . . . . . . . . . . . . . . . . . . . . . . . | 80.00 | |
| Total Share of Net Income . . . . . . . . . . . . . . . . . . . . . . . . . . . . . | | 370.00 |
| Total Net Income . . . . . . . . . . . . . . . . . . . . . . . . . . . . . . . . . . . . . | | $750.00 |

**4.** Prepare the statement.

When salaries or interest on equity are stipulated, the amounts are allowed whether sufficient net income is available. The amount by which allowances to partners exceed net income is called a **deficit**. Partners share deficits according to the partnership agreement.

On January 1, the equity of two partners is as follows: Jason Ford, $60,000.00 and Celia Pope, $54,000.00. Each partner receives a 10% annual interest on equity and shares any remaining income or deficit on a fixed percentage of 60% and 40%, respectively. For the month of January, the partnership earned a net income of $750.00. Their distribution of net income statement is shown above.

## STEPS
### PREPARING A DISTRIBUTION OF NET INCOME STATEMENT SHOWING A DEFICIT

**1** Calculate the monthly amounts due to each partner: *$500.00* for Ford and *$450.00* for Pope.

**2** Determine the deficit amount, *$200.00* ($950.00 due to both partners − $750.00 net income).

**3** Calculate each partner's share of the deficit, *120.00* for Ford and *80.00* for Pope.

**4** Prepare the distribution of net income statement showing the deficit.

## OWNERS' EQUITY STATEMENT

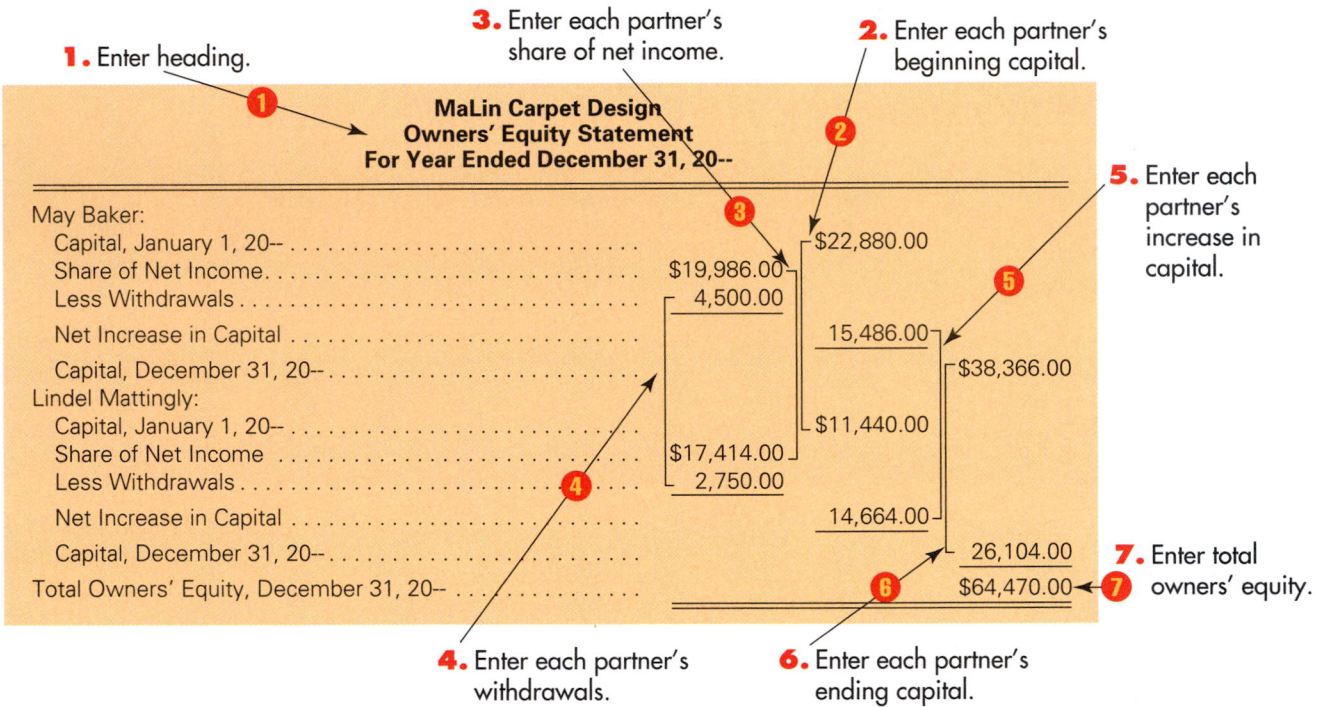

**3.** Enter each partner's share of net income.

**1.** Enter heading.

**2.** Enter each partner's beginning capital.

**5.** Enter each partner's increase in capital.

**4.** Enter each partner's withdrawals.

**6.** Enter each partner's ending capital.

**7.** Enter total owners' equity.

A corporation's equity is reported on a statement of stockholders' equity. A similar statement is prepared for a partnership. A financial statement that summarizes the changes in owners' equity during a fiscal period is called an **owners' equity statement**. The owners' equity statement shows the changes occurring in equity as shown above.

## STEPS
### PREPARING AN OWNER'S EQUITY STATEMENT

**1** Enter the 3-line heading, *MaLin Carpet Design, Owners' Equity Statement, For Year Ended December 31, 20--.*

**2** Enter each partner's capital at the beginning of the fiscal period, *$22,880.00* and *$11,440.00*. This balance is found in each partner's capital account in the general ledger.

**3** Enter each partner's total share of net income, *$19,986.00* and *$17,414.00*. These amounts are obtained from the distribution of net income statement.

**4** Enter each partner's withdrawals during the fiscal period, *$4,500.00* and *$2,750.00*. These amounts are found on the work sheet.

**5** Enter each partner's net increase in capital during the fiscal period, *$15,486.00* and *$14,664.00*.

**6** Enter each partner's capital on the last day of the fiscal period, *$38,366.00* and *$26,104.00*.

**7** Enter the partnership's total owners' equity on the last day of the fiscal period, *$64,470.00*.

Financial Reporting for a Partnership

**MaLin Carpet Design**
**Balance Sheet**
**December 31, 20--**

### ASSETS

| | | |
|---|---|---|
| Current Assets: | | |
| Cash . . . . . . . . . . . . . . . . . . . . . . . . . . . . . . . . . . . . . | | $42,802.47 |
| Petty Cash . . . . . . . . . . . . . . . . . . . . . . . . . . . . . . | | 200.00 |
| Accounts Receivable . . . . . . . . . . . . . . . . . . . . . | $11,992.51 | |
| Less Allowance for Uncollectible Accounts . . . . . . . . . | 139.47 | 11,853.04 |
| Supplies—Carpet . . . . . . . . . . . . . . . . . . . . . | | 1,628.50 |
| Supplies—Office . . . . . . . . . . . . . . . . . . . . | | 425.00 |
| Prepaid Insurance . . . . . . . . . . . . . . . . . . . . . | | 846.50 |
| Total Current Assets . . . . . . . . . . . . . . . . . . . | | $57,755.51 |
| Plant Assets: | | |
| Equipment . . . . . . . . . . . . . . . . . . . . . . . . | $12,504.97 | |
| Less Accumulated Depreciation—Equipment . . . . . . . . | 1,250.50 | $11,254.47 |
| Truck . . . . . . . . . . . . . . . . . . . . . . . . . . . . . . . . | 4,900.00 | |
| Less Accumulated Depreciation—Truck . . . . . . . . . . . | $  918.75 | 3,981.25 |
| Total Plant Assets . . . . . . . . . . . . . . . . . . . . | | 15,235.72 |
| Total Assets . . . . . . . . . . . . . . . . . . . . . . . . . . . . . | | $72,991.23 |

### LIABILITIES

| | | |
|---|---|---|
| Accounts Payable . . . . . . . . . . . . . . . . . . . . . . | | $ 8,521.23 |

### OWNERS' EQUITY

| | | |
|---|---|---|
| May Baker, Capital . . . . . . . . . . . . . . . . . . . . . . . . . . . . | $38,366.00 | |
| Lindel Mattingly, Capital . . . . . . . . . . . . . . . . . . . . | 26,104.00 | |
| Total Owners' Equity . . . . . . . . . . . . . . . . . . . . . . | | 64,470.00 |
| Total Liabilities and Owners' Equity . . . . . . . . . . . . | | $72,991.23 |

On a partnership balance sheet, each partner's ending capital is reported under the heading *Owners' Equity* as shown above.

# ADJUSTING ENTRIES

GENERAL JOURNAL                    PAGE 12

1. Adjusting entry for ❶ uncollectible accounts.

2. Adjusting entries ❷ for supplies.

3. Adjusting entry ❸ for insurance.

4. Adjusting entries ❹ for depreciation.

| | DATE | | ACCOUNT TITLE | DOC. NO. | POST. REF. | DEBIT | CREDIT | |
|---|---|---|---|---|---|---|---|---|
| 1 | | | **Adjusting Entries** | | | | | 1 |
| 2 | *Dec.*²⁰⁻⁻ | 31 | Uncollectible Accounts Expense | | | 1 1 9 55 | | 2 |
| 3 | | | Allowance for Uncoll. Accts. | | | | 1 1 9 55 | 3 |
| 4 | | 31 | Supplies Expense—Carpet | | | 7 6 7 6 50 | | 4 |
| 5 | | | Supplies—Carpet | | | | 7 6 7 6 50 | 5 |
| 6 | | 31 | Supplies Expense—Office | | | 1 4 2 0 00 | | 6 |
| 7 | | | Supplies—Office | | | | 1 4 2 0 00 | 7 |
| 8 | | 31 | Insurance Expense | | | 5 0 3 20 | | 8 |
| 9 | | | Prepaid Insurance | | | | 5 0 3 20 | 9 |
| 10 | | 31 | Depreciation Expense—Equipment | | | 1 2 5 0 50 | | 10 |
| 11 | | | Accum. Depreciation—Equipment | | | | 1 2 5 0 50 | 11 |
| 12 | | 31 | Depreciation Expense—Truck | | | 9 1 8 75 | | 12 |
| 13 | | | Accum. Depreciation—Truck | | | | 9 1 8 75 | 13 |

MaLin's adjusting entries, shown above, are made to record expenses in the fiscal period to which they apply. [*CONCEPT: Matching Expenses with Revenue*]

**1.** Close income statement accounts with credit balances.

**2.** Close income statement accounts with debit balances.

**3.** Close Income Summary.

**4.** Close partners' drawing accounts.

| | DATE | ACCOUNT TITLE | DOC. NO. | POST. REF. | DEBIT | CREDIT | |
|---|---|---|---|---|---|---|---|
| 14 | | *Closing Entries* | | | | | 14 |
| 15 | 31 | Sales | | | 72 0 20 27 | | 15 |
| 16 | | Income Summary | | | | 72 0 20 27 | 16 |
| 17 | 31 | Income Summary | | | 34 6 20 27 | | 17 |
| 18 | | Advertising Expense | | | | 9 85 00 | 18 |
| 19 | | Depreciation Exp.—Equipment | | | | 1 2 50 50 | 19 |
| 20 | | Depreciation Exp.—Truck | | | | 9 18 75 | 20 |
| 21 | | Insurance Expense | | | | 5 03 20 | 21 |
| 22 | | Miscellaneous Expense | | | | 2 8 69 21 | 22 |
| 23 | | Rent Expense | | | | 8 4 00 00 | 23 |
| 24 | | Supplies Expense—Carpet | | | | 7 6 76 50 | 24 |
| 25 | | Supplies Expense—Office | | | | 1 4 20 00 | 25 |
| 26 | | Truck Expense | | | | 8 4 77 56 | 26 |
| 27 | | Uncollectible Accts. Expense | | | | 1 19 55 | 27 |
| 28 | | Utilities Expense | | | | 2 0 00 00 | 28 |
| 29 | 31 | Income Summary | | | 37 4 00 00 | | 29 |
| 30 | | May Baker, Capital | | | | 19 9 86 00 | 30 |
| 31 | | Lindel Mattingly, Capital | | | | 17 4 14 00 | 31 |
| 32 | 31 | May Baker, Capital | | | 4 5 00 00 | | 32 |
| 33 | | May Baker, Drawing | | | | 4 5 00 00 | 33 |
| 34 | 31 | Lindel Mattingly, Capital | | | 2 7 50 00 | | 34 |
| 35 | | Lindel Mattingly, Drawing | | | | 2 7 50 00 | 35 |

GENERAL JOURNAL — PAGE 12

Closing entries for a partnership are similar to those of a corporation. The major difference is in recording distribution of earnings to the partners as shown above.

# FEDERAL INCOME TAXES OF A PARTNERSHIP

MaLin's distribution of net income statement shows salaries for each of the partners. However, the Internal Revenue Service does not consider partners to be employees of the partnership they own. The IRS classifies the partners as self-employed persons whose salaries are not an expense of the partnership. Therefore, partners' salaries are considered to be withdrawals of partnership earnings, not expenses.

A partnership does not pay income tax on its earnings. However, a partnership does submit to the IRS a partnership tax return that reports the earnings distributed to each partner. This type of return is known as an information return. In addition, partners include their respective share of the partnership net income or net loss on their personal income tax returns.

As self-employed persons, partners are entitled to old-age, survivors, disability, and hospitalization insurance benefits known collectively as social security and Medicare. Each partner personally pays a self-employment tax to qualify for social security and Medicare coverage. Therefore, the self-employment tax rate is double that of an employed individual's social security and Medicare tax rates. Thus, the same total amount of social security and Medicare taxes are paid for both self-employed persons and employees. The self-employment taxes are personal expenses of the partners, not of the partnership. Therefore, partners' self-employment social security and Medicare taxes are not recorded on partnership records. [CONCEPT: Business Entity]

The business entity concept states that financial information is recorded and reported separately from the owner's personal financial information. A business's records must not be mixed with an owner's personal records and reports. For example, a business owner may buy insurance to protect the business and insurance to protect the owner's home. Only the insurance obtained for the business is recorded in the business's financial records. The insurance purchased for the owner's personal home is recorded in the owner's personal financial records. One bank account is used for the business and another for the owner. A business exists separately from its owners.

©GETTY IMAGES/PHOTODISC

## POST-CLOSING TRIAL BALANCE

| MaLin Carpet Design<br>Post-Closing Trial Balance<br>December 31, 20-- | | |
|---|---|---|
| Account Title | Debit | Credit |
| Cash | $42,802.47 | |
| Petty Cash | 200.00 | |
| Accounts Receivable | 11,992.51 | |
| Allowance for Uncollectible Accounts | | $ 139.47 |
| Supplies—Carpet | 1,628.50 | |
| Supplies—Office | 425.00 | |
| Prepaid Insurance | 846.50 | |
| Equipment | 12,504.97 | |
| Accumulated Depreciation—Equipment | | 1,250.50 |
| Truck | 4,900.00 | |
| Accumulated Depreciation—Truck | | 918.75 |
| Accounts Payable | | 8,521.23 |
| May Baker, Capital | | 38,366.00 |
| Lindel Mattingly, Capital | | 26,104.00 |
| | $75,299.95 | $75,299.95 |

After adjusting and closing entries have been posted, MaLin prepares a post-closing trial balance as shown above. MaLin's post-closing trial balance is similar to that of a corporation with the exception of the capital accounts.

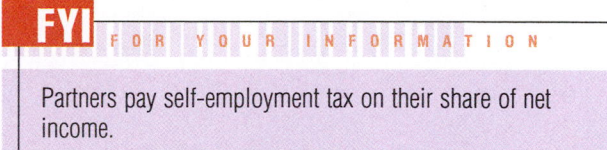

**FYI** FOR YOUR INFORMATION

Partners pay self-employment tax on their share of net income.

{ **REMEMBER** The post-closing trial balance indicates that the accounting records are ready for the next fiscal period. }

## terms review

distribution of net income
statement
deficit
owners' equity statement

TERMS REVIEW

## audit your understanding

1. Why is an adjustment for accrued federal income tax never planned on a partnership work sheet?
2. When does a deficit occur?
3. What is the purpose of the owners' equity statement?

AUDIT YOUR

## work together 22-2

WORK TOGETHER • WORK TOGETHER

### End-of-fiscal-period work for a partnership

Maria Delgado and Oren Kelso are partners in a business. Statement paper, page 15 of a general journal, and a portion of the partnership's completed work sheet for the year ended December 31 of the current year are provided in the *Working Papers*. Your instructor will guide you through the following examples.

1. Prepare an income statement. Calculate and record the component percentages for total operating expenses and net income. Round percentage calculations to the nearest 0.1%.
2. Prepare a distribution of net income statement. Each partner is to receive 8% interest on January 1 equity. Also, partners' salaries are Maria, $15,000.00 and Oren, $14,000.00. The remaining net income, net loss, or deficit is shared equally.
3. Prepare an owners' equity statement.
4. Journalize the closing entries.

## on your own 22-2

ON YOUR OWN • ON YOUR OWN

### End-of-fiscal-period work for a partnership

Jeffrey Lowe and Mona Ray are partners in a business. Statement paper, page 12 of a general journal, and a portion of the partnership's completed work sheet for the year ended December 31 of the current year are provided in the *Working Papers*. Work independently to complete the following problem.

1. Prepare an income statement. Calculate and record the component percentages for total operating expenses and net income. Round percentage calculations to the nearest 0.1%.
2. Prepare a distribution of net income statement. Each partner is to receive 8% interest on January 1 equity. Also, partners' salaries are Jeffrey, $12,000.00 and Mona, $16,000.00. The remaining net income, net loss, or deficit is shared equally.
3. Prepare an owners' equity statement.
4. Journalize the closing entries.

# 22-3 Liquidation of a Partnership

## ACCOUNT BALANCES BEFORE REALIZATION

| Cash | |
|---|---|
| 11,000.00 | |

| | Accounts Payable |
|---|---|
| | 2,500.00 |

| Supplies | |
|---|---|
| 1,000.00 | |

| | Adam Walker, Capital |
|---|---|
| | 10,000.00 |

| Truck | |
|---|---|
| 15,000.00 | |

| | Shirley Jeter, Capital |
|---|---|
| | 9,500.00 |

| | Accumulated Depreciation—Truck |
|---|---|
| | 5,000.00 |

If a partnership goes out of business, its assets are distributed to the creditors and partners. The process of paying a partnership's liabilities and distributing remaining assets to the partners is called **liquidation of a partnership**.

Cash received from the sale of assets during liquidation of a partnership is called **realization**. Typically, when a partnership is liquidated, the noncash assets are sold, and the available cash is used to pay the creditors. Any remaining cash is distributed to the partners according to each partner's total equity.

On July 31, Adam Walker and Shirley Jeter liquidated their partnership. At that time, financial statements were prepared and adjusting and closing entries were journalized and posted. After the end-of-fiscal-period work was completed, the partnership had account balances as shown above.

## GAIN ON REALIZATION

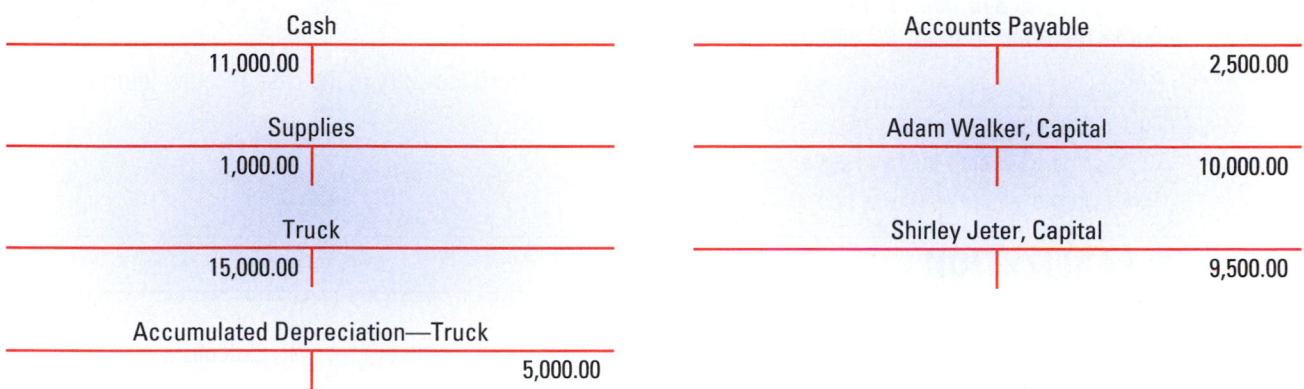

| Value of Asset Received | – | Book Value of Asset Sold | = | Gain on Realization |
|---|---|---|---|---|
| | | Cost $15,000.00 | | |
| | | Accum. Depr. 5,000.00 | | |
| Cash $12,000.00 | – | Book Value $10,000.00 | = | $2,000.00 |

1. Calculate the gain.

2. Record the entry.

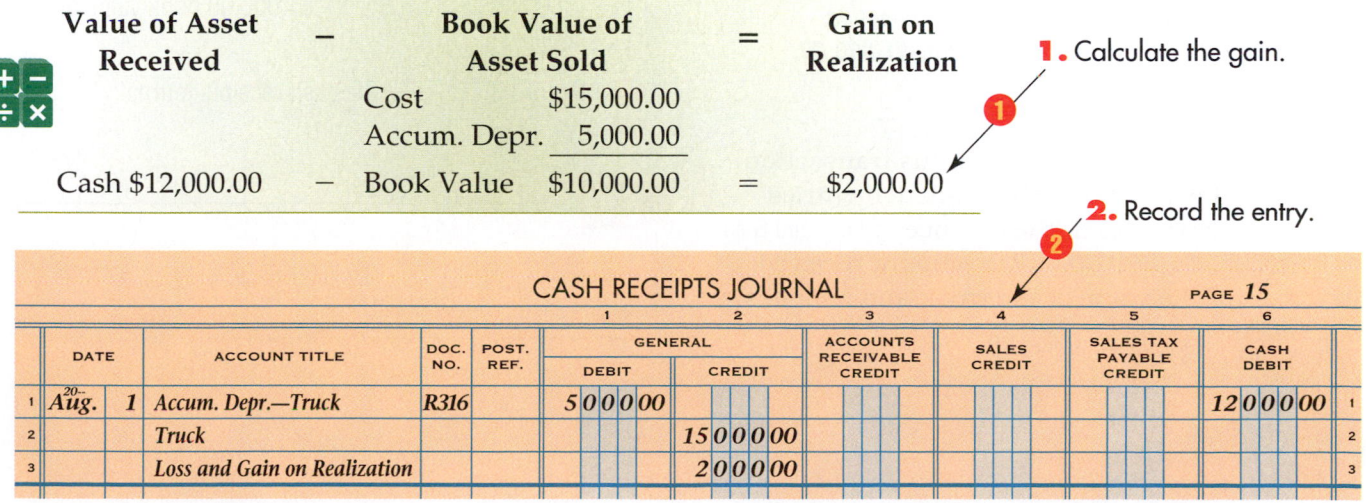

### CASH RECEIPTS JOURNAL

PAGE 15

| | | | | | 1 | 2 | 3 | 4 | 5 | 6 | |
|---|---|---|---|---|---|---|---|---|---|---|---|
| | | | | | GENERAL | | ACCOUNTS RECEIVABLE CREDIT | SALES CREDIT | SALES TAX PAYABLE CREDIT | CASH DEBIT | |
| | DATE | ACCOUNT TITLE | DOC. NO. | POST. REF. | DEBIT | CREDIT | | | | | |
| 1 | Aug. 1 | Accum. Depr.—Truck | R316 | | 5 0 0 0 00 | | | | | 12 0 0 0 00 | 1 |
| 2 | | Truck | | | | 15 0 0 0 00 | | | | | 2 |
| 3 | | Loss and Gain on Realization | | | | 2 0 0 0 00 | | | | | 3 |

## RECOGNIZING A GAIN ON REALIZATION

Noncash assets might be sold for more than the recorded book value. When this happens, the amount received in excess of the book value is recorded as a gain on realization. The gain is recorded as a credit in an account titled Loss and Gain on Realization.

> August 1, 20--. Received cash from sale of truck, $12,000.00; original cost, $15,000.00; total accumulated depreciation recorded to date, $5,000.00. Receipt No. 316.

The partnership's gain on the sale of the truck is calculated as shown on the previous page.

**STEPS** STEPS • STEPS • STEPS • STEPS
### RECOGNIZING A GAIN ON REALIZATION

1. Calculate the gain on the sale of the asset, *$2,000.00* ($12,000.00 cash received − $10,000.00 book value of asset).

2. Record the entry in the cash receipts journal.

## LOSS ON REALIZATION

1. Calculate the loss.

| | Value of Asset Received | − | Book Value of Asset Sold | = | Loss on Realization |
|---|---|---|---|---|---|
| | Cash $800.00 | − | Supplies $1,000.00 | = | $(200.00) |

2. Record the entry.

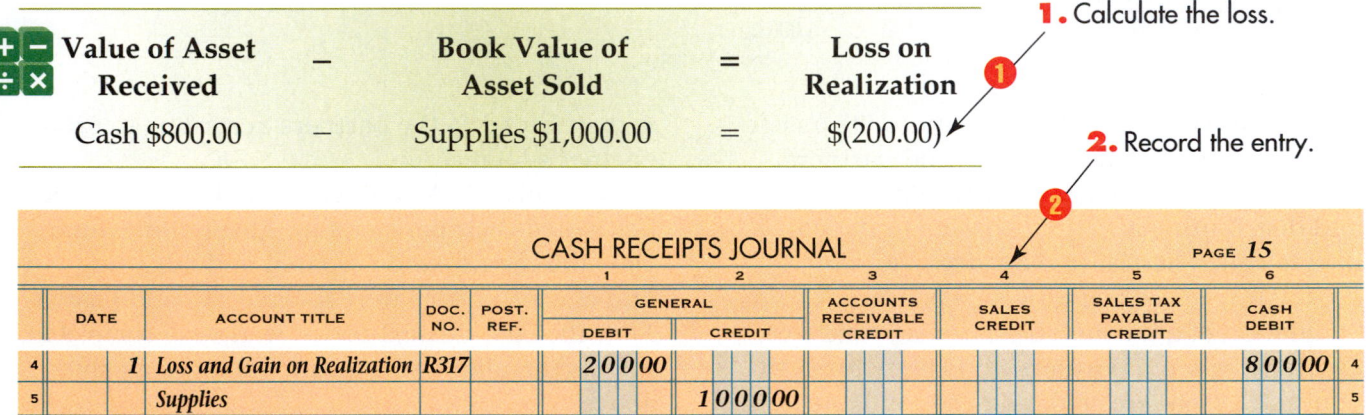

| | DATE | ACCOUNT TITLE | DOC. NO. | POST. REF. | GENERAL DEBIT | GENERAL CREDIT | ACCOUNTS RECEIVABLE CREDIT | SALES CREDIT | SALES TAX PAYABLE CREDIT | CASH DEBIT | |
|---|---|---|---|---|---|---|---|---|---|---|---|
| 4 | 1 | Loss and Gain on Realization | R317 | | 2 0 0 00 | | | | | 8 0 0 00 | 4 |
| 5 | | Supplies | | | | 1 0 0 0 00 | | | | | 5 |

**CASH RECEIPTS JOURNAL**     PAGE *15*

Sometimes during liquidation, the sale of an asset brings in less cash than the recorded book value.

> August 1. Received cash from sale of supplies, $800.00; balance of supplies account, $1,000.00. Receipt No. 317.

The journal entry to record this transaction is shown above. After both liquidation entries have been journalized, the balance of Loss and Gain on Realization, *$1,800.00,* is the amount received in excess of the value of the truck and supplies combined.

**STEPS** STEPS • STEPS • STEPS • STEPS
### RECOGNIZING A LOSS ON REALIZATION

1. Calculate the loss on the sale of the asset, *$200.00* ($800.00 cash received − $1,000.00 book value of supplies).

2. Record the entry in the cash receipts journal.

**FYI** FOR YOUR INFORMATION

A partnership usually tries to sell the business before it begins the process of liquidation.

# LIQUIDATING LIABILITIES

| DATE | | ACCOUNT TITLE | CK. NO. | POST. REF. | GENERAL | | ACCOUNTS PAYABLE DEBIT | CASH CREDIT |
|---|---|---|---|---|---|---|---|---|
| | | | | | DEBIT | CREDIT | | |
| Aug. | 4 | Accounts Payable | 422 | | 2 5 0 0 00 | | | 2 5 0 0 00 |

CASH PAYMENTS JOURNAL — PAGE 15

The partnership's available cash is used to pay creditors. The entry is recorded in the cash payments journal as shown above.

> **August 4, 20--. Paid cash to all creditors for the amounts owed, $2,500.00. Check No. 422.**

# ACCOUNT BALANCES AFTER LIQUIDATION OF NONCASH ASSETS AND PAYMENT OF LIABILITIES

| Cash | | | | Shirley Jeter, Capital | |
|---|---|---|---|---|---|
| Bal. | 21,300.00 | | | Bal. | 9,500.00 |

| Adam Walker, Capital | | | | Loss and Gain on Realization | |
|---|---|---|---|---|---|
| | Bal. | 10,000.00 | | Bal. | 1,800.00 |

When this transaction has been journalized and posted, the partnership has only four general ledger accounts with balances as shown above.

## technology for business

### Spreadsheet Activity—Distribution of Partnership Earnings

All Season Golf Center is an indoor golf facility with six computerized golf simulators. The partnership is owned by Arthur Wilson and Pamela Kim. According to the partnership agreement, Arthur receives 8% interest on equity and a salary of $22,000.00. Pamela receives 8% interest on equity and a salary of $18,000.00. The remainder of net income is divided equally. For the current year, net income for All Season Golf Center is $52,000.00.

**Required**

1. Create a distribution of partnership earnings spreadsheet. Use the calculation on page 651 as a model. Write formulas to calculate interest on equity, salary, division of remaining income, and the total distribution. Save the spreadsheet. Print a copy of the distribution of partnership earnings.

2. Use the spreadsheet to calculate the distribution of partnership earnings for the next year assuming net income is $66,000.00.

| | Balance of Loss and Gain on Realization | × | Fixed Percentage | = | Share of the Balance of Loss and Gain on Realization | |
|---|---|---|---|---|---|---|
| Walker | $1,800.00 | × | 60% | = | $1,080.00 | |
| Jeter | $1,800.00 | × | 40% | = | 720.00 | |
| Total | | | | | $1,800.00 | |

**1.** Calculate each partner's share of gain or loss.

**GENERAL JOURNAL**                    PAGE 8

**2.** Record entry to distribute gain or loss.

| | DATE | | ACCOUNT TITLE | DOC. NO. | POST. REF. | DEBIT | CREDIT | |
|---|---|---|---|---|---|---|---|---|
| 1 | 20-- Aug. | 6 | Loss and Gain on Realization | M412 | | 1 8 0 0 00 | | 1 |
| 2 | | | Adam Walker, Capital | | | | 1 0 8 0 00 | 2 |
| 3 | | | Shirley Jeter, Capital | | | | 7 2 0 00 | 3 |

When all creditors have been paid, the balance of Loss and Gain on Realization is distributed to the partners. A credit balance indicates a gain on realization. A debit balance indicates a loss. The distribution is based on the method of distributing net income or net loss as stated in the partnership agreement. The percentages for the Walker and Jeter partnership are Adam, 60%, and Shirley, 40%. The distribution of the balance of Loss and Gain on Realization is calculated as shown above.

*August 6, 20--. Recorded distribution of gain on realization: to Adam Walker, $1,080.00; to Shirley Jeter, $720.00. Memorandum No. 412.*

If a loss on realization is distributed to the partners, Loss and Gain on Realization is credited to close the account. Each partner's capital account is debited for the partner's share of the loss on realization.

# DISTRIBUTING REMAINING CASH TO PARTNERS

**CASH PAYMENTS JOURNAL**                    PAGE 15

| | DATE | | ACCOUNT TITLE | CK. NO. | POST. REF. | GENERAL DEBIT | GENERAL CREDIT | ACCOUNTS PAYABLE DEBIT | CASH CREDIT | |
|---|---|---|---|---|---|---|---|---|---|---|
| 2 | | 6 | Adam Walker, Capital | 423 | | 11 0 8 0 00 | | | 11 0 8 0 00 | 2 |
| 3 | | 6 | Shirley Jeter, Capital | 424 | | 10 2 2 0 00 | | | 10 2 2 0 00 | 3 |

Any remaining cash is distributed to the partners. The cash is distributed according to each partner's capital account balance regardless of the method used to distribute net income or net loss.

After this journal entry is journalized, as shown above, and posted, all of the partnership's general ledger accounts will have zero balances. The partnership is liquidated.

*August 6. Recorded final distribution of remaining cash to partners: to Adam Walker, $11,080.00; to Shirley Jeter, $10,220.00. Check Nos. 423 and 424.*

TERMS REVIEW

## terms review

liquidation of a partnership
realization

## audit your understanding

1. What is meant by the term "realization"?
2. What accounts are debited when distributing remaining cash to partners during liquidation?

AUDIT YOUR

## work together 22-3

WORK TOGETHER  •  WORK TOGETHER

**Liquidation of a partnership**

Jason Edson and Peggy Karam agreed to liquidate their partnership on April 30 of the current year. On that date, after financial statements were prepared and closing entries were posted, the general ledger accounts had the balances shown in the *Working Papers*.

A cash receipts journal, page 6, a cash payments journal, page 8, and a general journal, page 4, are provided in the *Working Papers*. Your instructor will guide you through the following examples.

May   1. Received cash from sale of office equipment, $6,000.00. R86.
       1. Received cash from sale of supplies, $950.00. R87.
       3. Received cash from sale of truck, $7,500.00. R88.
       5. Paid cash to all creditors for amounts owed. C116.
       6. Distributed loss or gain to Jason Edson, 60%; to Peggy Karam, 40%. M21.
       6. Distributed remaining cash to partners. C117 and C118.

1. Journalize the transactions.

## on your own 22-3

ON YOUR OWN  •  ON YOUR OWN  •  ON YOUR OWN

**Liquidation of a partnership**

Denise Oxley and Charles Tatum agreed to liquidate their partnership on May 31 of the current year. On that date, after financial statements were prepared and closing entries were posted, the general ledger accounts had the balances shown in the *Working Papers*.

A cash receipts journal, page 8, a cash payments journal, page 10, and a general journal, page 5, are provided in the *Working Papers*. Work independently to complete the following problem.

June   1. Received cash from sale of office equipment, $6,200.00. R96.
       1. Received cash from sale of supplies. $900.00. R97.
       3. Received cash from sale of truck, $9,000.00. R98.
       5. Paid cash to all creditors for amounts owed. C125.
       6. Distributed loss or gain to Denise Oxley, 60%; to Charles Tatum, 40%. M29.
       6. Distributed remaining cash to partners. C126 and C127.

1. Journalize the transactions.

SUMMARY · SUMMARY · SUMMARY

**After completing this chapter, you can**

1. Define accounting terms related to distributing earnings and completing end-of-fiscal-period work for a partnership.
2. Identify accounting concepts and practices related to distributing earnings and completing end-of-fiscal-period work for a partnership.
3. Calculate the distribution of partnership earnings.
4. Journalize entries for withdrawal of partnership earnings.
5. Complete end-of-fiscal-period work for a partnership.
6. Prepare a distribution of net income statement for a partnership.
7. Journalize entries for liquidating a partnership.

# Explore Accounting

EXPLORE ACCOUNTING • EXPLORE ACCOUNTING • EXPLORE ACCO

## Determining Value of Partnership

When a partnership decides to add another partner or an existing partner wants to withdraw, the value of a partnership must be determined. The book value of a partnership is not necessarily an equitable value to the new or existing partners. Therefore, before admitting a new partner or retiring one, a current equitable value should be determined for the partnership. Three common methods used to value a partnership are (1) comparable sales, (2) appraisal, and (3) income capitalization.

*Comparable sales method.* This method attempts to compare other comparable businesses that have been sold recently with the partnership business being valued. Factors to be considered in selecting comparable businesses are type, size, and location of the business. If a comparable business recently sold for $500,000.00, this provides a sound basis for valuing the partnership at $500,000.00 regardless of the book value of the partnership.

*Appraisal method.* This method estimates the current fair market value of each of the assets and liabilities. A professional appraiser would be employed to determine the value of the assets and liabilities of the business.

*Income capitalization method.* This method places most emphasis on the expected future earnings capacity of the business. The buyer of a business or share of a partnership probably is making the investment for the anticipated future earnings of the business. This method places a value on the business based on those expected future earnings.

**Required:**

Assume that you are a doctor. You have been offered a one-quarter interest in a growing medical practice located in a fast-growth area. Which method of valuing the existing partnership would you prefer? Explain the reason for your choice.

# 22-1 APPLICATION PROBLEM

### Calculating partnership earnings

Jill Fargo and Sheila Kain are partners in a business called Fargo and Kain. On December 31 of the current year, the partners' equities are Jill, $80,000.00 and Sheila, $120,000.00. The net income for the year is $80,000.00.

**Instructions:**

For each of the following independent cases, calculate how the $80,000.00 net income will be distributed to the two partners.
1. Each partner receives a fixed percentage of 50% of net income.
2. Each partner receives a percentage of net income based on the percentage of total equity.
3. Each partner receives 12% interest on equity. The partners share remaining net income, net loss, or deficit equally.
4. Jill receives a salary of $24,000.00; Sheila receives a salary of $30,000.00. The partners share remaining net income, net loss, or deficit on a fixed percentage of Jill, 40% and Sheila, 60%.
5. Jill is to receive 10% interest on equity and a salary of $24,000.00. Sheila is to receive 8% interest on equity and a salary of $30,000.00. The partners share remaining net income, net loss, or deficit equally.
6. Jill is to receive 15% interest on equity and a salary of $30,000.00. Sheila is to receive 15% interest on equity and a salary of $36,000.00. The partners share remaining net income, net loss, or deficit equally.

# 22-2 APPLICATION PROBLEM

### Journalizing partners' withdrawals

Janet Agnew and Buford Franco are partners in a business. Each partner withdraws assets during May of the current year.

**Transactions:**

June   5.   Janet Agnew, partner, withdrew office supplies for personal use, $400.00. M46.
      26.   Buford Franco, partner, withdrew cash for personal use, $600.00. C284.

**Instructions:**

Journalize the transactions using page 12 of a cash payments journal and page 6 of a general journal.

# 22-3 APPLICATION PROBLEM

### Completing end-of-fiscal-period work for a partnership

Susan Poole and Ann Dodd are partners in a business called Plantasia. The partnership's work sheet for the year ended December 31 of the current year is provided in the *Working Papers*.

**Instructions:**

1. Prepare an income statement. Calculate and record the component percentages for total operating expenses and net income. Round percentage calculations to the nearest 0.1%.
2. Prepare a distribution of net income statement. The partners share in net income, net loss, or deficit according to each partner's percentage of total equity. The January 1 equity is Susan, $23,400.00 and Ann, $12,600.00. Round percentage calculations to the nearest 0.1%.
3. Prepare an owners' equity statement.
4. Prepare a balance sheet.
5. Journalize the adjusting entries using page 12 of a general journal.
6. Journalize the closing entries on the same general journal page.

# 22-4 APPLICATION PROBLEM

### Liquidating a partnership

Donald Winn and Judy Reed agreed to liquidate their partnership on June 30 of the current year. On that date, after financial statements were prepared and closing entries were posted, the general ledger accounts had the following balances.

| | |
|---|---:|
| Cash | $ 5,000.00 |
| Supplies | 500.00 |
| Office Equipment | 10,000.00 |
| Accumulated Depreciation—Office Equipment | 5,500.00 |
| Truck | 17,000.00 |
| Accumulated Depreciation—Truck | 12,200.00 |
| Accounts Payable | 500.00 |
| Donald Winn, Capital | 7,300.00 |
| Judy Reed, Capital | 7,000.00 |

The following transactions occurred during July of the current year.

**Transactions:**

| July | 1. | Received cash from sale of office equipment, $4,000.00. R114. |
|---|---|---|
| | 1. | Received cash from sale of supplies, $200.00. R115. |
| | 3. | Received cash from sale of truck, $5,000.00. R116. |
| | 5. | Paid cash to all creditors for amounts owed. C156. |
| | 6. | Distributed balance of Loss and Gain on Realization to Donald Winn, 65%; to Judy Reed, 35%. M34. |
| | 6. | Distributed remaining cash to partners. C157 and C158. |

**Instructions:**

Journalize the transactions. Use page 13 of a cash receipts journal, page 13 of a cash payments journal, and page 7 of a general journal.

# 22-5 MASTERY PROBLEM

### Completing end-of-fiscal-period work for a partnership

Sarah Saxon and Jane Rolf are partners in a business called J & S Service. The partnership's work sheet for the year ended December 31 of the current year is provided in the *Working Papers*.

**Instructions:**

1. Prepare an income statement. Calculate and record the component percentage for total operating expenses and net income. Round percentage computations to the nearest 0.1%.
2. Prepare a distribution of net income statement. Each partner is to receive 10% interest on January 1 equity. The January 1 equity is Sarah, $15,000.00 and Jane, $12,000.00. Also, partners' salaries are Sarah, $10,000.00 and Jane, $15,000.00. The partners share remaining net income, net loss, or deficit equally.
3. Prepare an owners' equity statement.
4. Prepare a balance sheet.
5. Journalize the adjusting entries using page 12 of a general journal.
6. Journalize the closing entries on the same general journal page.

### Completing end-of-fiscal-period work for a partnership

Theresa Doran and Roy Eden are partners in a business called D & E Sales. The partnership's work sheet for the year ended December 31 of the current year is provided in the *Working Papers*.

**Instructions:**

1. Prepare an income statement. Calculate and record the component percentages for cost of merchandise sold, gross profit on operations, total operating expenses, and net income or net loss. Round percentage calculations to the nearest 0.1%. If there is a net loss, use a minus sign with the component percentage.

2. Prepare a distribution of net income statement. Each partner is to receive 10% interest on January 1 equity. The January 1 equity is Theresa, $24,250.00 and Roy, $21,500.00. Also, partners' salaries are Theresa, $12,000.00 and Roy, $10,000.00. The remaining net income, net loss, or deficit is shared as follows: Theresa, 55%; Roy, 45%.

3. Prepare an owners' equity statement.

4. Prepare a balance sheet.

Xtra!
Enrichment
accountingxtra.swlearning.com

## applied communication

APPLIED COMMUNICATION

Brian Hughes and Wendy Perez formed a partnership five years ago. The partnership has been very successful and is growing rapidly. The partners are evaluating future actions for the next five years. They are projecting continued growth of their business. Brian and Wendy are trying to decide whether they should incorporate their business.

**Required:**

Write a short report explaining the advantages and disadvantages of a partnership versus a corporation that Brian and Wendy can use in making their decision.

## cases for critical thinking

CASES FOR CRITICAL THINKING

### Case 1

Lola Stroud invests $30,000.00 in a partnership. Her partner, Juan Santo, invests $50,000.00. Miss Stroud has 10 years' experience in a similar business; Mr. Santo has no experience. Miss Stroud is to spend about 20 hours a week working for the partnership. Mr. Santo is to work full-time. Which method of distributing partnership earnings would you suggest for this partnership? Explain your answer.

### Case 2

The P & A partnership does not prepare a distribution of net income statement or an owners' equity statement at the end of a fiscal period. Instead, the information is all reported in detail on the partnership's balance sheet. Is this an acceptable practice? Explain your answer.

## SCANS workplace competency

SCANS WORKPLACE COMPETENCY

**Technology Competency:** Selecting Technology

**Concept:** Competent employees judge which set of procedures, tools, machines, computers, and software will produce the desired results. Capable employees evaluate a situation and select the appropriate technology.

**Application:** You are a partner in a small service business. Evaluate several accounting software programs and recommend one that best fits your company's needs in preparing financial statements similar to the ones presented in this chapter. Consider the type of computers your firm owns, memory capabilities, cost, ease of use, support services, and other potential uses. Justify your answer with an oral presentation that incorporates the use of technology.

## graphing workshop

The partnership of Nguyen, Mendoza, Carlton, and Anderson has agreed to use the capital account balances shown in the graph as the basis for calculating the distribution of partnership earnings.

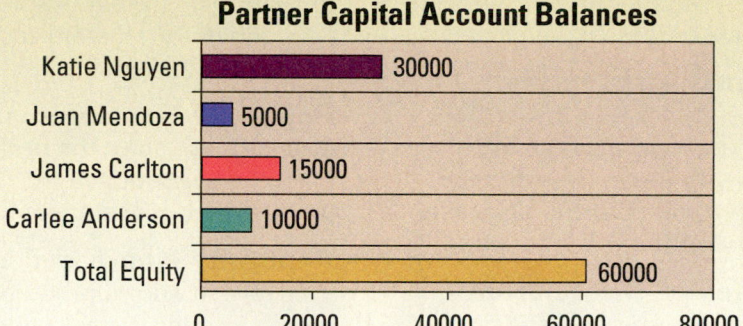

**Partner Capital Account Balances**

| | |
|---|---|
| Katie Nguyen | 30000 |
| Juan Mendoza | 5000 |
| James Carlton | 15000 |
| Carlee Anderson | 10000 |
| Total Equity | 60000 |

**Instructions:**

1. Using the *percentage of total equity method,* calculate the percentages for each partner that will be used to distribute partnership earnings. Round to the nearest tenth of a percent.

2. Determine each partner's share of $40,000 net income.

3. Determine each partner's share of a $30,000 net loss.

## analyzing Costco's financial statements

An American corporation must pay federal income tax based on the amount of its net income. The amount of income tax varies from year to year, based on earnings, corporate tax brackets, tax legislation, and changing tax regulations. For Costco, the amount of federal income tax paid during 2001 through 2003 represents a substantial expense. The effective tax rate for a corporation can be calculated by dividing the "provision for income taxes" amount by the "income before income taxes" amount. An awareness of the effective tax rate can help a corporation create a strategic plan for future earnings.

**Instructions:**

Refer to Costco's Consolidated Statements of Income on page B-6 of Appendix B in this textbook, and complete the following items.

1. List the "provision for income taxes" amounts for the 52 weeks ended August 31, 2003, September 1, 2002, and September 2, 2001.

2. Calculate the effective tax rates for the 52 weeks ended August 31, 2003, September 1, 2002, and September 2, 2001. Round calculations to the nearest .01%.

3. Determine how much Costco would have paid in federal income taxes in 2003 had the company used the 2001 effective tax rate. What was the amount of tax savings for 2003?

4. Determine the amount of federal income tax paid for every $100 of profit earned before taxes during the 52 weeks ended August 31, 2003.

## Generating Financial Reports for a Partnership

Financial statements for partnerships are similar to the statements prepared for other types of business organizations. The primary difference is the distribution of net income or loss to the partners.

### Partnership with Equal Distribution

When the Company Info. tab of the Customize Accounting System window specifies the business organization as Partnership Equal Distribution, *Automated Accounting 8.0* will perform all closing entries needed at the end of the fiscal period.

### Partnership with Unequal Distribution

When the Company Info. tab specifies the business organization as Partnership Unequal Distribution, *Automated Accounting 8.0* will close revenue and expense accounts. However, journal entries must be entered to distribute the income or loss to the partners' accounts. The journal entries required to complete the closing process are:

1. Closing the amount in Income Summary to the partners' capital accounts.

2. Closing the partners' drawing accounts to their capital accounts.

### Income Statement

The software will display net income or loss in two formats. The format is specified in the Company Info. tab of the Customize Accounting System window.

### Report by Fiscal Period

This format shows the profitability of the business from the beginning of the fiscal year until the time when the income statement is displayed.

### Report by Month and Year

This format shows profitability for the current month and for the year to date.

### AUTOMATING MASTERY PROBLEM 22-5

### Instructions:

1. Load *Automated Accounting 8.0* or higher software.

2. Select database A22-5 (Advanced Course Mastery Problem 22-5) from the accounting template disk.

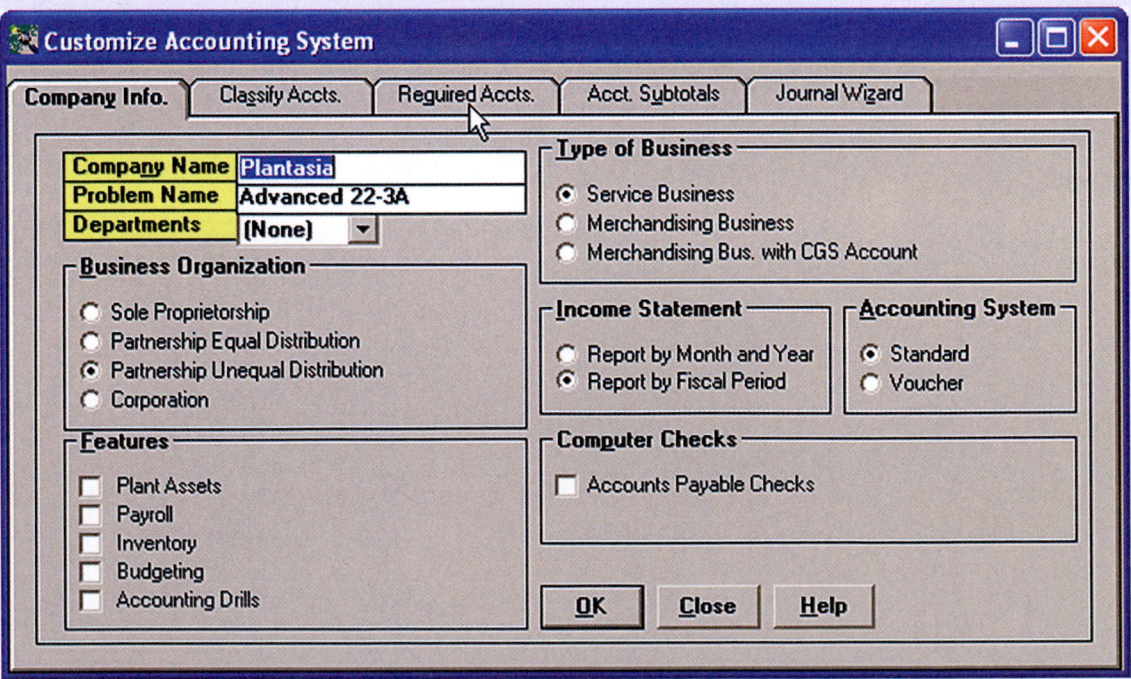

3. Select File from the menu bar and choose the Save As menu command. Key the path to the drive and directory that contains your data files. Save the database with a filename of XXX225 (where XXX are your initials).

4. Read the Problem Instruction screen by clicking the Browser toolbar button.

5. Refer to page 672 for data used in this problem.

6. Exit the Automated Accounting software.

## AUTOMATING CHALLENGE PROBLEM 22-6

### Instructions:

1. Load *Automated Accounting 8.0* or higher software.

2. Select database A22-6 (Advanced Course Mastery Problem 22-6) from the accounting template disk.

3. Select File from the menu bar and choose the Save As menu command. Key the path to the drive and directory that contains your data files. Save the database with a filename of XXX226 (where XXX are your initials).

4. Read the Problem Instruction screen by clicking the Browser toolbar button.

5. Refer to page 673 for data used in this problem.

6. Exit the Automated Accounting software.

# 23 Budgeting and Accounting for a Not-for-Profit Organization

*After studying Chapter 23, you will be able to:*

1. Define accounting terms related to budgeting and accounting for a not-for-profit governmental organization.

2. Identify accounting concepts and practices related to budgeting and accounting for a not-for-profit governmental organization.

3. Describe the process used to develop an operating budget.

4. Journalize budget transactions for a not-for-profit organization.

5. Journalize revenues for a not-for-profit organization.

6. Journalize expenditures, encumbrances, and other transactions for a not-for-profit organization.

- not-for-profit organization
- fund
- expenditure
- operating budget
- appropriations
- tax levy
- encumbrance
- general fixed assets
- certificate of deposit

Point Your Browser
accountingxtra.swlearning.com

678

# accounting in the real world

## • The United States Postal Service

TYLER MALLORY/EPA/LANDOV

### THE UNITED STATES POSTAL SERVICE ADAPTS TO A CHANGING BUSINESS ENVIRONMENT

The concept of a postal service for the United Colonies was initially approved by the members of the second Continental Congress at their July, 1775 assembly in Philadelphia. Do you know whom they appointed as the first Postmaster General? If you replied Benjamin Franklin, you are correct. Today, that agency has evolved into the United States Postal Service (USPS), whose mission is to provide every individual in America with convenient, affordable, efficient, and universal mail service regardless of geographic location.

Although the United States Postal Service is a non-profit governmental agency, it operates much like a profit-oriented corporation. For example, USPS has a board of governors that sets overall agency policy, employs a Postmaster General who functions as a CEO, publishes an annual report that lists financial information, and has even sponsored a professional bicycle racing team. Like other business entities, USPS is very concerned about its overall profitability. After reporting several losses for the years immediately after 2000, the agency responded by restructuring its operations and using technological advancements to improve postal efficiencies. Consequently, in 2003, USPS reported a net income of $3.9 billion.

### Critical Thinking

1. In 2003, the postal system grew by 1.9 million delivery points. First-class mail volume, however, declined by over 3 billion pieces. What factors might contribute to the increasing number of delivery points and the decreasing amount of mail volume?
2. How might the mission of the USPS and its non-profit status affect profitability?

Xtra!
Today
accountingxtra.swlearning.com

Source: www.usps.com

## internet activity

### CMA DESIGNATION

Go to the homepage of the Institute of Management Accountants (IMA) (www.imanet.org). In order to have the Chartered Management Accountant (CMA) designation, a person must belong to the IMA. Search the site to find the following information.

### Instructions

1. List the seven criteria necessary in order to become a CMA.
2. Find the IMA chapter nearest to you. List the city and state in which that chapter is located.

ACCOUNTING IN THE REAL WORLD • ACCOUNTING IN THE REAL WORLD • ACCOUNTING IN THE REAL WORLD •

INTERNET RESEARCH ACTIVITY • INTERNET RESEARCH ACTIVITY • INTERNET RESEARCH ACTIVITY •

**679**

# 23-1 Not-for-Profit Organizations

All businesses, whether organized as proprietorships, partnerships, or corporations, have a common objective—to earn a profit. Some organizations are formed for purposes other than earning a profit. An organization providing goods or services with neither a conscious motive nor expectation of earning a profit is called a **not-for-profit organization**. Not-for-profit organizations are also referred to as nonprofit organizations.

Both businesses and not-for-profit organizations provide goods and/or services. Business owners generally invest in a business for the purpose of earning a profit. Not-for-profit organizations, however, are formed to provide needed goods or services to a group of individuals without regard to earning a profit. The primary purpose of the organization is to make available the needed goods or services that may not be available otherwise.

## FYI
### FOR YOUR INFORMATION

GASB has proposed a new statement. If this new statement is adopted, governmental entities would be required to prepare financial statements from an entity-wide perspective and a fund perspective. Governmental entities would be required to place a value on all infrastructure assets, such as roads and curbs, and to set up depreciation schedules for these assets.

©GETTY IMAGES/PHOTODISC

## making ethical decisions

### Evaluating Auditor Independence

Martin Samuels has such a successful business that he is considering selling stock on one of the national stock exchanges. In order to sell the stock, the government requires that the business obtain an audit. Naturally, Martin turns to his brother Frank, a partner in an accounting firm, and asks that his firm perform the audit.

**Instructions**

Refer to the Code of Professional Conduct of the American Institute of Certified Public Accountants. Read Rule 101 related to independence. Can Frank's accounting firm perform the audit?

## Types of Not-for-Profit Organizations

Not-for-profit organizations may differ as to the types of goods or services they provide, their sources of revenues, or the procedures they use to select their leaders or managers. Major types of not-for-profit organizations are as follows.

1. Governmental, such as federal, state, county, city, town, and village.
2. Educational, such as elementary, secondary, and post-secondary schools.
3. Health, such as hospitals and nursing homes.
4. Charitable, such as United Way, United Fund, and American Red Cross.
5. Foundational, including trusts and corporations organized for charitable and educational purposes, such as the Carnegie Foundation and the Ford Foundation.
6. Religious, such as churches and other religious organizations.

Since not-for-profit organizations have a common objective, they share many of the same needs for financial information. Thus, the accounting system and many of the financial reports are similar for all not-for-profit organizations. However, because of differences in goods or services provided, sources of revenues, or methods of leadership selection, their accounting procedures and reports are modified for the specific type of organization.

## Purpose of Governmental Organizations

All individuals are affected by or are members of one or more governmental organizations. Also, more individuals are employed by governmental organizations than any other type of not-for-profit organization. Therefore, Chapters 23 and 24 emphasize accounting for local governmental organizations.

A governmental organization's purpose is normally to provide needed goods or services that would be impossible for individuals to provide for themselves. For example, the federal government provides national defense for all citizens of the nation. Individual states and cities would find it difficult and very inefficient to provide for their own defense from foreign pressures. Similarly, cities provide police and fire protection that would be very expensive and inefficient for individuals to provide for themselves.

©GETTY IMAGES/PHOTODISC

A governmental organization has four major characteristics that affect the accounting system.

1. *No profit motive exists.* A business's success can be measured by whether or not it earns a profit. A business that is inefficient, or not competitive, will not earn a profit. Without profits, a business will soon be unable to continue operations. However, since a governmental organization does not intend to earn a profit, success is much more difficult to measure. As long as money is available, a governmental organization can continue to operate regardless of its efficiency or inefficiency.

2. *Leadership is subject to frequent change.* Policy-making bodies of governmental organizations are generally elected by popular vote of the group's members. Thus, the leadership depends on the political process and may change frequently. Therefore, policies and long-range goals may change when the leadership changes. These frequent changes make effective long-range planning difficult.

3. *Users of services do not necessarily pay for the services.* Revenues for governmental organizations are provided primarily by taxation on property, retail sales, or income. Organization members who have the greatest amount of property or income provide the greatest amount of revenues. However, the goods or services are normally provided to all members of the organization based on need. The amount that individuals pay is not directly related to the benefits they receive. Therefore, individuals have decreased incentive for ensuring that services are administered efficiently.

4. *Conflicting pressures for differing objectives exist.* No direct relationship exists between who pays for and who receives the services provided by a governmental organization. Therefore, individuals generally support the organizational objective most advantageous

to themselves. For example, some citizens of a city may place the construction of a city library high on their list of priorities. Others, who seldom use a library, may place this project low on their list of priorities. Consequently, services provided by a governmental organization are usually determined through negotiation and compromise among the different interest groups. This procedure does not necessarily provide for the best services or the most efficiency.

The characteristics of governmental organizations have affected the development of governmental accounting systems. Therefore, numerous financial and legal regulations for determining the source and amount of revenues and for planning and executing expenditures of funds are required.

## Characteristics of Governmental Accounting Systems

Six accounting practices are similar for business and governmental organizations.

1. The accounting equation (assets equal liabilities plus equities) is applied.
2. An appropriate chart of accounts is prepared.
3. Transactions are analyzed into debit and credit elements.
4. Transactions are journalized and posted to ledgers.
5. Financial statements are prepared for each fiscal period.
6. Most of the same accounting concepts are applied.

The characteristics of governmental organizations and the conditions in which they operate create information and control requirements that differ from those of businesses. Because of these differences, governmental accounting and financial reporting differ in several ways from business accounting and financial reporting.

| Eastfield General Fund | |
|---|---|
| **ASSETS** | |
| Cash. . . . . . . . . . . . . . . . . . | $350,000.00 |
| Taxes Receivable . . . . . . . . . | 50,000.00 |
| Total Assets . . . . . . . . . . . . . | $400,000.00 |
| **LIABILITIES AND FUND EQUITY** | |
| Liabilities: | |
| Accounts Payable . . . . . . . . | $ 60,000.00 |
| Fund Equity: | |
| Fund Balance . . . . . . . . . . | 340,000.00 |
| Total Liabilities and | |
| Fund Equity. . . . . . . . . . . . | $400,000.00 |

| Eastfield Library Fund | |
|---|---|
| **ASSETS** | |
| Cash. . . . . . . . . . . . . . . . . . | $70,000.00 |
| **LIABILITIES AND FUND EQUITY** | |
| Liabilities: | |
| Accounts Payable . . . . . . . . | $ 5,000.00 |
| Fund Equity: | |
| Fund Balance . . . . . . . . . . . | 65,000.00 |
| Total Liabilities and | |
| Fund Equity. . . . . . . . . . . . | $70,000.00 |

The accounting system for a business includes a single accounting entity. That is, all accounts used to record accounting transactions for the entire business are part of a single set of accounts. Within this set of accounts, assets must equal liabilities plus equities. A governmental accounting entity with a set of accounts in which assets always equal liabilities plus equities is called a **fund**. A governmental unit, such as a city, may have several different funds.

A fund accounting system emphasizes strong controls on the use of funds. The amount in a fund can be spent only for the specified purpose of the fund. Different funds may be created for different purposes. For example, the town of Eastfield has two funds: (1) a general fund and (2) a library fund. Balance sheets for the two funds are shown above.

The town of Eastfield has total assets of $470,000.00 (general fund, $400,00.00, *plus* library fund, $70,000.00). However, the assets are accounted for separately. Assets in the library fund may be used only for library purposes. General fund assets may be used for other authorized town expenditures. Each fund is kept as a separate set of accounts.

The fund equity, similar to owners' equity for a business, is the net amount of assets available for use. For example, Eastfield's library fund equity is $65,000.00 (assets, $70,000.00, *less* liabilities, $5,000.00). If $6,000.00 cash is spent for library salaries, total assets available for

spending would be reduced to $64,000.00 ($70,000.00 *less* $6,000.00). The fund equity account, Fund Balance, would be reduced to $59,000.00 (assets, $64,000.00, *less* liabilities, $5,000.00). After this transaction, the fund remains in balance. The governmental accounting equation, assets equal liabilities plus fund equity, is in balance.

Types of funds vary with the type of not-for-profit organization and the types of goods or services provided. A unique set of funds normally is used for each type of organization—federal government, state and local governments, hospitals, schools, etc.

## Modified Accrual Accounting

Most businesses use accrual accounting so that revenue and expenses incurred during a fiscal period determine the resulting net income for the period. [CONCEPT: *Matching Expenses with Revenue*] In governmental accounting, modified accrual accounting is used. In modified accrual accounting, revenues are recorded in the accounting period in which they become measurable and available. For example, property taxes become measurable and available as soon as the amount is determined and tax statements are sent to property owners. However, sales taxes cannot be determined until sales are made. Thus, sales tax revenue is recognized when the taxes are received from merchants.

## DIFFERENCE BETWEEN EXPENSES AND EXPENDITURES

Cash disbursements and liabilities incurred for the cost of goods delivered or services rendered are called **expenditures**. In modified accrual accounting, expenditures are generally recognized when a liability is incurred. Therefore, governmental organizations record expenditures rather than expenses. An important distinction is made between expenditures and expenses. Businesses emphasize matching expenses with revenue in each fiscal period. However, governmental accounting emphasizes determining and controlling revenues and expenditures during a fiscal period. For example, if a business buys a truck, Plant Asset or Truck is debited and Cash or Notes Payable is credited. No expense is incurred until the truck is used. If a governmental organization buys a truck, Expenditure is debited and Cash or Notes Payable is credited. The amount of money spent or liability incurred is recorded, not the expense. Thus, expenditures are decreases in net financial resources. Emphasis is placed on control of the net financial resources, not on matching expenses with revenue. Thus, modified accrual accounting is used for measuring financial position and operating results of governmental organizations.

## FINANCIAL REPORTING EMPHASIS

Both business and governmental organizations prepare financial statements at the end of a fiscal period. [CONCEPT: Accounting Period Cycle] However, because the organizations have different objectives, their charts of accounts and statements differ. The chart of accounts for Sparta appears on the next page.

The two most common financial statements prepared by businesses are an income statement and a balance sheet. The two most common financial statements prepared by governmental organizations are a statement of revenues, expenditures, and changes in fund balance and a balance sheet (described in Chapter 24).

Businesses prepare income statements to report the amount of net income earned during a fiscal period. Earning a net income is not an objective of governmental organizations. However, identifying and controlling the sources of revenues and the expenditure of funds are emphasized as part of the control process. Therefore, a statement of revenues, expenditures, and changes in fund balance is prepared.

A business' balance sheet reports the assets, liabilities, and owners' equity of the business at the end of a fiscal period. A governmental organization's balance sheet also reports the current assets and liabilities of the organization at the end of a fiscal period. However, no specific ownership of a governmental organization exists. Therefore, assets less liabilities is reported as fund equity.

## BUDGETING

Both businesses and governmental organizations prepare budgets. The primary purpose of all budgets is planning and control. For businesses, planning is required to prepare the budget. During the fiscal period, budgeted amounts are compared with actual amounts to provide information to management about the effectiveness of cost control. Planning is also required to prepare a budget for a governmental organization. However, an approved governmental budget becomes (1) a legal authorization to spend and (2) a legal limit on the amount that can be spent.

## TOWN OF SPARTA GENERAL FUND CHART OF ACCOUNTS

**Balance Sheet Accounts**

**(1000) ASSETS**
1010 Cash
1020 Taxes Receivable—Current
1030 Allowance for Uncollectible Taxes—Current
1040 Taxes Receivable—Delinquent
1050 Allowance for Uncollectible Taxes—Delinquent
1060 Interest Receivable
1070 Allowance for Uncollectible Interest
1080 Inventory of Supplies
1090 Investments—Short Term

**(2000) LIABILITIES**
2010 Accounts Payable
2020 Notes Payable

**(3000) FUND EQUITY**
3010 Unreserved Fund Balance
3020 Reserve for Encumbrances—Current Year
3030 Reserve for Encumbrances—Prior Year
3040 Reserve for Inventory of Supplies

**Revenue and Expenditure Accounts**

**(4000) REVENUES**
4010 Property Tax Revenue
4020 Interest Revenue
4030 Other Revenue

**(5000) EXPENDITURES**
5100 GENERAL GOVERNMENT
5110 Expenditure—Personnel, General Government
5120 Expenditure—Supplies, General Government
5130 Expenditure—Other Charges, General Government
5140 Expenditure—Capital Outlays, General Government

5200 PUBLIC SAFETY
5210 Expenditure—Personnel, Public Safety
5220 Expenditure—Supplies, Public Safety
5230 Expenditure—Other Charges, Public Safety
5240 Expenditure—Capital Outlays, Public Safety

5300 PUBLIC WORKS
5310 Expenditure—Personnel, Public Works

5320 Expenditure—Supplies, Public Works
5330 Expenditure—Other Charges, Public Works
5340 Expenditure—Capital Outlays, Public Works

5400 RECREATION
5410 Expenditure—Personnel, Recreation
5420 Expenditure—Supplies, Recreation
5430 Expenditure—Other Charges, Recreation
5440 Expenditure—Capital Outlays, Recreation

**Budgetary Accounts**

**(6000) BUDGETARY**
6010 Estimated Revenues
6020 Appropriations
6030 Budgetary Fund Balance

6100 GENERAL GOVERNMENT
6110 Encumbrance—Personnel, General Government
6120 Encumbrance—Supplies, General Government
6130 Encumbrance—Other Charges, General Government
6140 Encumbrance—Capital Outlays, General Government

6200 PUBLIC SAFETY
6210 Encumbrance—Personnel, Public Safety
6220 Encumbrance—Supplies, Public Safety
6230 Encumbrance—Other Charges, Public Safety
6240 Encumbrance—Capital Outlays, Public Safety

6300 PUBLIC WORKS
6310 Encumbrance—Personnel, Public Works
6320 Encumbrance—Supplies, Public Works
6330 Encumbrance—Other Charges, Public Works
6340 Encumbrance—Capital Outlays, Public Works

6400 RECREATION
6410 Encumbrance—Personnel, Recreation
6420 Encumbrance—Supplies, Recreation
6430 Encumbrance—Other Charges, Recreation
6440 Encumbrance—Capital Outlays, Recreation

The chart of accounts for Sparta is illustrated above for ready reference as you study Chapters 23 and 24 of this textbook.

©GETTY IMAGES/PHOTODISC

**REMEMBER** Governmental organizations record expenditures rather than expenses.

**Town of Sparta**
**Annual Operating Budget—General Fund**
**For Year Ended December 31, 20--**

### ESTIMATED REVENUES

| | | |
|---|---:|---:|
| Property Tax | $1,594,000.00 | |
| Interest | 10,000.00 | |
| Other | 2,500.00 | |
| Total Estimated Revenues | | $1,606,500.00 |

### ESTIMATED EXPENDITURES AND BUDGETARY FUND BALANCE

| | | |
|---|---:|---:|
| General Government: | | |
| Personnel | $ 263,280.00 | |
| Supplies | 12,150.00 | |
| Other Charges | 113,400.00 | |
| Capital Outlays | 16,220.00 | |
| Total General Government | | $ 405,050.00 |
| Public Safety: | | |
| Personnel | $ 589,200.00 | |
| Supplies | 20,000.00 | |
| Other Charges | 153,150.00 | |
| Capital Outlays | 90,300.00 | |
| Total Public Safety | | 852,650.00 |
| Public Works: | | |
| Personnel | $ 113,400.00 | |
| Supplies | 5,600.00 | |
| Other Charges | 47,500.00 | |
| Capital Outlays | 51,500.00 | |
| Total Public Works | | 218,000.00 |
| Recreation: | | |
| Personnel | $ 58,260.00 | |
| Supplies | 1,970.00 | |
| Other Charges | 25,250.00 | |
| Capital Outlays | 11,620.00 | |
| Total Recreation | | 97,100.00 |
| Total Estimated Expenditures | | $1,572,800.00 |
| Budgetary Fund Balance | | 33,700.00 |
| Total Estimated Expenditures and Budgetary Fund Balance | | $1,606,500.00 |

A plan of current expenditures and the proposed means of financing those expenditures is called an **operating budget**. A governmental fund's annual operating budget authorizes and provides the basis for control of financial operations during a fiscal year. Since each governmental fund is a separate accounting entity, an operating budget is normally prepared to show the estimated revenues, estimated expenditures, and budgetary fund balance for each fund. The operating budget shown above was prepared for the general fund of the town of Sparta.

Sparta organizes revenue accounts by source of revenue. Expenditure accounts are organized by department and type of expenditure. Some organizations maintain subsidiary accounts for each of the general ledger accounts to provide more detail about the sources of revenues and types of expenditures. Because of its small size, Sparta maintains only the general ledger accounts listed in its chart of accounts on the previous page.

Some basic procedures are followed to prepare an annual governmental operating budget.

1.  Departments of the governmental organization submit budget requests to the chief executive of the organization. Requests are based on an analysis of expenditures for the previous year and expected changes in expenditures for the coming year.
2.  The chief executive reviews budget requests with department heads. When budget requests are acceptable to the chief executive, departmental requests are consolidated into a single budget request for the organization. The chief executive then submits the operating budget to the legislative body. The legislative body is a group of persons normally elected by the citizens/members of the organization and granted authority to make laws for the organization.
3.  The legislative body approves the operating budget. The approved operating budget becomes an authorization to spend the amounts listed in the budget. Before the operating budget can be approved, revenues plus the available amount of fund equity must be at least as great as the expenditures. If the expenditures are more than the total of expected revenues and available fund equity, the expected sources of revenue must be increased or expenditures decreased.

Sparta is a small town with a town manager and five town council members. The council members are elected to their positions. One member of the council serves as mayor. The council serves as the legislative body for Sparta. The council appoints the town manager who works full time as chief executive of the town. Sparta has three department heads: public safety director, public works director, and recreation director. Because Sparta is small and most of its revenues come from property taxes, the accounting system contains only one fund—a general fund.

At the request of the town manager, Sparta's three department heads analyze the current year's expenditures and expected changes, and then prepare budget requests for the next year. The town manager reviews the budget requests and prepares a single operating budget for Sparta's general fund for next year. The operating budget is submitted to the town council.

The town council represents the interests of all the town's citizens. Thus, the council should evaluate the operating budget from at least four perspectives. (1) Are adequate services being provided? (2) Are the services desired by a majority of citizens? (3) Are the amounts requested essential to provide the desired level of services? (4) Does the city have the financial capacity to support the budget?

The approved operating budget determines the amount of revenues needed for the year. The town's tax rate necessary to provide the needed funds for the approved operating budget is then determined.

After completing its review, the Sparta council formally approves next year's governmental operating budget. The approved governmental operating budget becomes authorization for the town manager and department heads to make expenditures as specified in the budget.

Approval of an annual governmental operating budget by the proper authorities provides legal authorization to make expenditures in accordance with the approved budget. Authorizations to make expenditures for specified purposes are called **appropriations**. Sparta's approved operating budget has appropriations that authorize expenditures up to the amounts stated in the budget. The tax rate is then set at a rate that will raise at least enough revenue to cover the appropriations.

Many governmental organizations have restrictions as to the amount that taxes can be increased. Public hearings may be required before taxes can be increased. A formal vote in an election may also be required. If a proposed operating budget exceeds the amount of taxes and other estimated revenue, the budget may need to be reduced to the level of available revenues.

| | DATE | | ACCOUNT TITLE | DOC. NO. | POST. REF. | GENERAL | | CASH | | |
|---|---|---|---|---|---|---|---|---|---|---|
| | | | | | | DEBIT 1 | CREDIT 2 | DEBIT 3 | CREDIT 4 | |
| 1 | Jan. 20-- | 2 | Estimated Revenues | M35 | | 1606 500 00 | | | | 1 |
| 2 | | | Appropriations | | | | 1572 800 00 | | | 2 |
| 3 | | | Budgetary Fund Balance | | | | 33 700 00 | | | 3 |

JOURNAL — PAGE 1

As an additional control measure, Sparta journalizes its approved operating budget as shown above. Budgetary accounts are for control purposes and are closed at the end of a fiscal period.

Governmental organizations, like businesses, record accounting transactions initially in a journal. Source documents are the basis for the journal entries. Governmental organizations may use a multi-column journal, a general journal, or special journals adapted to the organization's needs. Sparta uses a multi-column journal.

---

**January 2. Recorded Sparta's approved operating budget: estimated revenues, $1,606,500.00; appropriations, $1,572,800.00; budgetary fund balance, $33,700.00. Memorandum No. 35.**

---

Estimated Revenues is increased by a debit for the amount of budgeted revenues, *$1,606,500.00.* Estimated Revenues has a normal debit balance, opposite the normal credit balance of an actual revenue account. Appropriations is increased by a credit for the amount of Sparta's budgeted expenditures, *$1,572,800.00.* Appropriations has a normal credit balance, opposite the normal debit balance of the actual expenditure accounts. Budgetary Fund Balance is increased by a credit, *$33,700.00* (estimated revenues, $1,606,500.00, *less* appropriations, $1,572,800.00).

A separate revenue account will be credited as revenues are earned. Balances of the two accounts, Estimated Revenues and Revenues, can be reviewed to compare the amount of actual revenues earned and the amount of revenues estimated to be earned. If actual revenues are not as great as expected, expenditures may need to

be reduced to avoid exceeding available funds. Recording the estimated revenues in the budgetary account Estimated Revenues provides this planning and control information.

| Estimated Revenues | |
|---|---|
| Jan. 2    1,606,500.00 | |

| Appropriations | |
|---|---|
| | Jan. 2    1,572,800.00 |

| Budgetary Fund Balance | |
|---|---|
| | Jan. 2    33,700.00 |

Separate expenditure accounts will be debited as actual expenditures are made. Ensuring that expenditures do not exceed the appropriations (budgeted expenditures) is essential for governmental organizations. Periodically, the appropriations account balance can be compared with the total of expenditure account balances to avoid overspending appropriations. Appropriations less total expenditures is the amount still available for spending. Recording appropriations in the budgetary account Appropriations provides this additional control information. Each department also keeps records of its appropriated and expended amounts to ensure that no department exceeds its appropriation amounts.

If appropriations exceed estimated revenues, Budgetary Fund Balance is debited to make the total debits equal the total credits. However, most governmental organizations normally set their revenue sources slightly above appropriations to avoid exceeding appropriations.

## terms review

not-for-profit organization
fund
expenditure
operating budget
appropriations

TERMS REVIEW • TERMS REVIEW

## audit your understanding

1. What four characteristics affect the accounting system for a governmental organization?
2. List the accounting practices that are similar for businesses and governmental organizations.
3. What is a fund?
4. What is the purpose of a governmental operating budget?
5. What accounts are debited and credited to journalize a governmental organization's approved operating budget?

AUDIT YOUR UNDERSTANDING

## work together 23-1

**Journalizing governmental operating budgets**

The town of Powell approved its annual general fund operating budgets effective January 1 of the current year. Your instructor will guide you through the following example.

1. Journalize the entry to record the following operating budget for the town of Powell.

| Estimated Revenues | Appropriations | Budgetary Fund Balance |
|---|---|---|
| $843,000.00 | $836,800.00 | $6,200.00 |

WORK TOGETHER • WORK

## on your own 23-1

**Journalizing governmental operating budgets**

The town of Worthington approved its annual general fund operating budgets effective January 1 of the current year. Work independently to complete the following problem.

1. Journalize the entry to record the following operating budget for the town of Worthington.

| Estimated Revenues | Appropriations | Budgetary Fund Balance |
|---|---|---|
| $2,461,000.00 | $2,423,000.00 | $38,000.00 |

ON YOUR OWN • ON YOUR OWN

# 23-2 Journalizing Revenues

## JOURNALIZING CURRENT PROPERTY TAX REVENUES

**1.** Total taxes levied.

| | | | | | GENERAL | | CASH | | |
|---|---|---|---|---|---|---|---|---|---|
| | | | | | 1 | 2 | 3 | 4 | |
| | DATE | ACCOUNT TITLE | DOC. NO. | POST. REF. | DEBIT | CREDIT | DEBIT | CREDIT | |
| 4 | 2 | Taxes Receivable—Current | M36 | | 1610 00 0 00 | | | | 4 |
| 5 | | Allowance for Uncollectible Taxes—Current | | | | 16 00 0 00 | | | 5 |
| 6 | | Property Tax Revenue | | | | 1594 00 0 00 | | | 6 |

JOURNAL PAGE *1*

**2.** Estimated losses for taxes not collected.

**3.** Revenue recognized from tax levy.

Governmental fund revenues are recorded in the accounting period in which the revenues become measurable and available.

When property tax rates have been set and tax amounts calculated, taxes are levied on all taxable property. Authorized action taken by a governmental organization to collect taxes by legal authority is called a **tax levy**. Levied property taxes are considered measurable and available because they become a legal obligation of property owners. Therefore, when the levy is made, a journal entry is made to record property tax revenue as shown above. Although tax levies are legal obligations of property owners, some property owners do not pay their taxes. Legal action may eventually be taken against these property owners in an effort to collect the taxes. Even

with these actions, a government generally does not collect all the taxes levied. On January 2, Sparta authorized its tax levy and sent out property tax statements to property owners. Sparta estimated that $16,000.00 of property taxes will not be collected.

*January 2. Recorded property tax levy: taxes receivable—current, $1,610,000.00; allowance for uncollectible taxes—current, $16,000.00; property tax revenue, $1,594,000.00. Memorandum No. 36.*

| Taxes Receivable—Current | |
|---|---|
| Jan. 2    1,610,000.00 | |

| Allowance for Uncollectible Taxes—Current | |
|---|---|
| | Jan. 2    16,000.00 |

| Property Tax Revenue | |
|---|---|
| | Jan. 2    1,594,000.00 |

## STEPS  STEPS • STEPS • STEPS • STEPS
### JOURNALIZING CURRENT PROPERTY TAX REVENUE

**1** Debit *Taxes Receivable—Current* for the total amount of tax levied, *$1,610,000.00*. This amount is the total of the tax statements sent to taxpayers.

**2** Credit the contra asset account, *Allowance for Uncollectible Taxes—Current*, for the amount of estimated loss, *$16,000.00*.

**3** Credit the revenue account, *Property Tax Revenue*, for the amount of revenue recognized, *$1,594,000.00*. This amount is the total tax levy, $1,610,000.00, *less* the allowance for current uncollectible taxes, $16,000.00.

## COLLECTION OF CURRENT PROPERTY TAXES

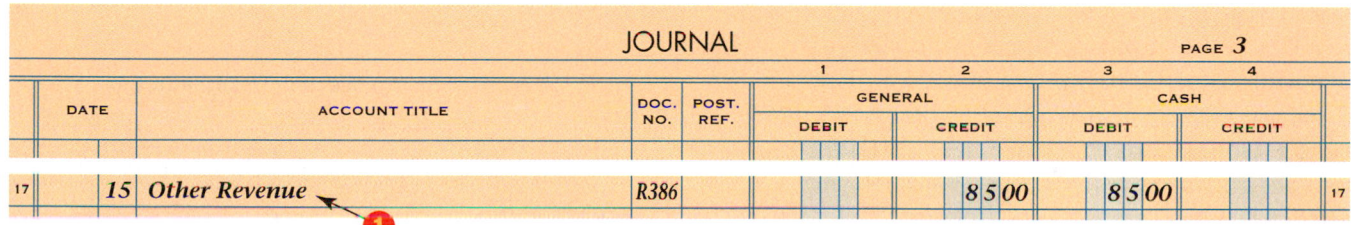

| | DATE | ACCOUNT TITLE | DOC. NO. | POST. REF. | GENERAL DEBIT | GENERAL CREDIT | CASH DEBIT | CASH CREDIT | |
|---|---|---|---|---|---|---|---|---|---|
| 12 | 10 | Taxes Receivable—Current | R371 | | | 194 000 00 | 194 000 00 | | 12 |

Cash received for property taxes reduces the taxes receivable account as shown above.

---

*January 10. Received cash for current taxes receivable, $194,000.00. Receipt No. 371.*

---

Cash is increased by a debit for the amount of cash received, *$194,000.00.* Taxes Receivable—

Current is decreased by a credit for the same amount, *$194,000.00.*

| Cash | |
|---|---|
| Jan. 10    194,000.00 | |

| Taxes Receivable—Current | |
|---|---|
| Bal.    1,610,000.00 | Jan. 10    194,000.00 |

## OTHER REVENUE

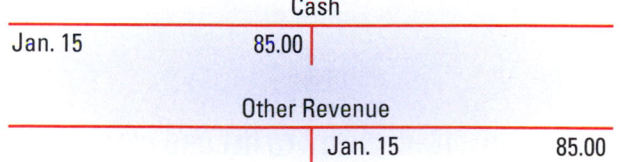

| | DATE | ACCOUNT TITLE | DOC. NO. | POST. REF. | GENERAL DEBIT | GENERAL CREDIT | CASH DEBIT | CASH CREDIT | |
|---|---|---|---|---|---|---|---|---|---|
| 17 | 15 | Other Revenue | R386 | | | 85 00 | 85 00 | | 17 |

**1.** Revenue that is not measurable until received.

Some revenues, such as fines, inspection charges, parking meter receipts, and penalties, are normally not known and, thus, are not measurable until cash is received. A journal entry to record such revenues, therefore, is generally made only when cash is received as shown above.

---

*January 15. Received cash from traffic fines, $85.00. Receipt No. 386.*

---

Cash is increased by a debit for the amount of cash received, *$85.00.* Other Revenue is increased by a credit for the same amount, *$85.00.*

| Cash | |
|---|---|
| Jan. 15    85.00 | |

| Other Revenue | |
|---|---|
| | Jan. 15    85.00 |

**FYI** FOR YOUR INFORMATION

In some states, the operating budget is not officially approved until it is reviewed by tax committees at the county and state level.

**1.** Entry to record delinquent property taxes.

| | DATE | | ACCOUNT TITLE | DOC. NO. | POST. REF. | GENERAL DEBIT | GENERAL CREDIT | CASH DEBIT | CASH CREDIT | |
|---|---|---|---|---|---|---|---|---|---|---|
| 1 | Mar. | 1 | *Taxes Receivable—Delinquent* | M65 | | 64 2 0 0 00 | | | | 1 |
| 2 | | | *Allowance for Uncollectible Taxes—Current* | | | 16 0 0 0 00 | | | | 2 |
| 3 | | | *Taxes Receivable—Current* | | | | 64 2 0 0 00 | | | 3 |
| 4 | | | *Allowance for Uncollectible Taxes—Delinquent* | | | | 16 0 0 0 00 | | | 4 |
| 20 | | 20 | *Taxes Receivable—Delinquent* | R420 | | | 12 0 0 0 00 | 12 0 0 0 00 | | 20 |

JOURNAL — PAGE 21

**2.** Entry to record collection of delinquent property taxes.

Tax payments specify the date that property taxes are due and payable. Taxes not paid by the specified date are reclassified as delinquent. Sparta's property taxes are due on February 28. On March 1, taxes not paid are considered delinquent. On that date, a journal entry is made to transfer uncollected taxes from current to delinquent status as shown above.

Taxes that Sparta expects to collect are accounted for by using two accounts, Taxes Receivable—Current and Allowance for Uncollectible Taxes—Current. Delinquent taxes are accounted for using two accounts, Taxes Receivable—Delinquent and Allowance for Uncollectible Taxes—Delinquent. A journal entry transfers the balances of the two current accounts to the two delinquent accounts.

*March 1. Recorded reclassification of current taxes receivable to delinquent status, $64,200.00, and the accompanying allowance for uncollectible accounts, $16,000.00. Memorandum No. 65.*

**Taxes Receivable—Delinquent**

| Mar. 1 | 64,200.00 | |
|---|---|---|

**Allowance for Uncollectible Taxes—Current**

| Mar. 1 | 16,000.00 | Bal. | 16,000.00 |
|---|---|---|---|

**Taxes Receivable—Current**

| Bal. | 64,200.00 | Mar. 1 | 64,200.00 |
|---|---|---|---|

**Allowance for Uncollectible Taxes—Delinquent**

| | Mar. 1 | 16,000.00 |
|---|---|---|

## STEPS

JOURNALIZING ENTRY TO RECORD DELINQUENT PROPERTY TAXES

**1** Debit *Taxes Receivable—Delinquent* for the amount of current taxes becoming delinquent, *$64,200.00*. Debit the contra asset account, *Allowance for Uncollectible Taxes—Current*, for the balance in that account, *$16,000.00*.

**2** Credit *Taxes Receivable—Current* for the amount of current taxes becoming delinquent, *$64,200.00*. Credit *Allowance for Uncollectible Taxes—Delinquent* for the amount of allowance on the delinquent taxes, *$16,000.00*.

### Collection of Delinquent Property Taxes

Although some taxes become delinquent, Sparta continues efforts to collect these taxes. Cash received for delinquent taxes reduces Taxes Receivable—Delinquent as shown above.

*March 20. Received cash for delinquent taxes receivable, $12,000.00. Receipt No. 420.*

Cash is increased by a debit for the amount received, *$12,000.00*. Taxes Receivable—Delinquent is decreased by a credit for the same amount, *$12,000.00*.

# careers in accounting

## Suresh Bhat, Financial Specialist

COURTESY OF SURESH BHAT

As a freshman at Oak Grove High School in San Jose, California, Suresh Bhat enrolled in classes that would ultimately prepare him for a career in medicine. His initial career plans were going well until he signed up for a business elective his junior year. That one class, accounting, changed everything. Suddenly, he was exposed to a curriculum that was both new and intellectually challenging. Throughout the year, he became aware of the many career opportunities within the field of business. His first year of accounting was such a success that he decided to enroll in advanced accounting for his senior year. After participating in two years of high school accounting, Suresh realized that his passion resided in the business arena and not in medicine.

Suresh pursued an undergraduate degree at the University of California, Berkeley. He graduated in 1990 with a Bachelor of Science in Business Administration. He obtained his certified public accountant (CPA) license in 1993 and later returned to UC Berkeley to acquire a Master's in Business Administration (MBA).

His first employment experience was with Deloitte & Touche, one of the world's largest and most prestigious accounting firms. Early in his accounting career, Suresh realized that the financial aspects of running a company appealed to him more than the accounting side of business. Finance personnel concentrate on money. Their responsibilities include finding funds to operate and expand a business and, in some instances, securing capital to acquire another company. They also manage cash resources on hand and help businesses plan for their financial futures.

After obtaining his CPA license, Suresh left Deloitte & Touche and accepted an employment offer from Bank of America. Here, he used his accounting background to evaluate the money requirements of businesses to fund growth, secure inventory, purchase new technologies, remodel facilities, and operate overseas.

Presently, Suresh is a vice-president of finance for Charles Schwab. This firm helps individuals and companies invest their money in stocks, bonds, and mutual funds. Suresh's duties at Charles Schwab include capital planning, budgeting, forecasting, strategic planning, risk analysis, and mergers and acquisitions. It is a demanding job but an exciting one that requires both accounting and finance skills.

**Salary Range:** $100,000–$200,000 + 20–40% bonus

**Qualifications:** To start your entry-level career in the financial services industry, Suresh recommends an undergraduate degree in business, strong people skills, and a talent for creative problem solving. Suresh believes that students seeking more information about careers in finance should secure an e-mail mentor.

**Occupational Outlook:** The future holds many possibilities for Suresh. Eventually, he sees himself as a managing partner at an accounting firm, a company treasurer, or perhaps a chief financial officer (CFO) for a major corporation. With his background in accounting and finance, all of these career options are available to Suresh.

## term review

tax levy

## audit your understanding

1. When is a journal entry made to record property tax revenue?
2. What accounts are affected, and how, when a taxpayer pays current property taxes?
3. What accounts are affected, and how, when a taxpayer pays property taxes two months after the due date?

## work together 23-2

**Journalizing governmental revenue transactions**

Groveport's town council recently approved the town's general fund operating budget for the current year. Use page 1 of the journal provided in the *Working Papers*. Your instructor will guide you through the following examples.

Jan. 1. Recorded property tax levy: taxes receivable—current, $2,400,000.00; allowance for uncollectible taxes—current, $24,000.00; property tax revenue, $2,376,000.00. M34.
  14. Received cash from traffic fines, $1,354.00. R84. (Other Revenue)
Feb. 11. Received cash for current taxes receivable, $973,000.00. R113.
Mar. 1. Recorded reclassification of current taxes receivable to delinquent status, $96,200.00, and the accompanying allowance for uncollectible accounts, $24,000.00. M68.
  12. Received cash for delinquent taxes receivable, $30,300.00. R157.

1. Journalize the selected transactions.

## on your own 23-2

**Journalizing governmental revenue transactions**

Centuria's town council recently approved the town's general fund operating budget for the current year. Use page 1 of the journal provided in the *Working Papers*. Work independently to complete the following problem.

Jan. 1. Recorded property tax levy: taxes receivable—current, $1,200,000.00; allowance for uncollectible taxes—current, $12,000.00; property tax revenue, $1,188,000.00. M163.
  20. Received cash from parking meter receipts, $894.00. R541. (Other Revenue)
Feb. 11. Received cash for current taxes receivable, $485,200.00. R596.
Mar. 1. Recorded reclassification of current taxes receivable to delinquent status, $48,100.00, and the accompanying allowance for uncollectible accounts, $12,000.00. M225.
  15. Received cash for delinquent taxes receivable, $15,150.00. R628.

1. Journalize the selected transactions.

# 23-3 Journalizing Expenditures, Encumbrances, and Other Transactions

## JOURNALIZING EXPENDITURES

| | | | | | GENERAL | | CASH | |
|---|---|---|---|---|---|---|---|---|
| DATE | ACCOUNT TITLE | DOC. NO. | POST. REF. | | 1 | 2 | 3 | 4 |
| | | | | | DEBIT | CREDIT | DEBIT | CREDIT |
| Jan. 10 | Expenditure—Other Charges, Public Safety | C355 | | | 290 00 | | | 290 00 |

JOURNAL                                                                   PAGE 3

A primary objective of governmental accounting is to control the financial resources. Governmental accounting focuses on measuring changes in financial resources rather than determining net income. Therefore, in governmental accounting, expenditures rather than expenses are recorded. The use of two special accounting procedures enhances the control of expenditures.

1. Expenditures are classified into categories to assign specific responsibility for the expenditure and to analyze the purpose of the expenditure. For example, Expenditure—Personnel, Public Safety is one of Sparta's expenditure accounts. Personnel indicates the type of expenditure (salaries for personnel). Public Safety indicates the department for which the personnel expenditures were made.

2. Budgetary accounts are used to record estimated amounts of expenditures to protect against overspending the budgeted amounts. To accomplish this control procedure, encumbrance accounts are used. A commitment to pay for goods or services that have been ordered but not yet provided is called an **encumbrance**. When an order that will require a future expenditure is placed, a budgetary encumbrance account is debited for the estimated amount. This entry reduces the fund balance and ensures that commitments and expenditures will not be greater than funds available.

Exact amounts of some expenditures are known as soon as the obligation is determined. For example, the amount and due date of payment for utility costs is known when the utility statement is received. The entry to record the expenditure is shown above.

### January 10. Paid cash for electrical service in public safety department, $290.00. Check No. 355.

Expenditure—Other Charges, Public Safety is increased by a debit for the cost of the electrical service, $290.00. Cash is decreased by a credit for the same amount, $290.00.

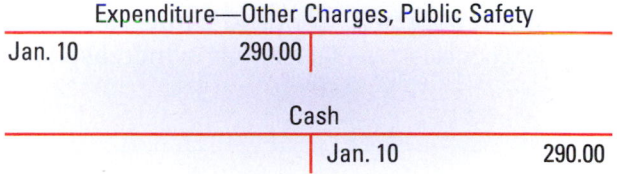

The major control of expenditures is achieved by holding department heads accountable for expenditures in their department. Classification of expenditures is used to analyze major types of expenditures within each department. For Sparta, each department's expenditures are recorded in one of four classifications: personnel, supplies, other charges, or capital outlays. The other charges classification is used for all expenditures except salaries and related personnel expenditures, supplies expenditures, and capital outlays. Capital outlays is used for expenditures that will benefit future years.

| | | | | | GENERAL | | CASH | | |
|---|---|---|---|---|---|---|---|---|---|
| DATE | | ACCOUNT TITLE | DOC. NO. | POST. REF. | DEBIT | CREDIT | DEBIT | CREDIT | |
| 12 | 12 | *Encumbrance—Supplies, Public Works* | M40 | | 3 8 0 00 | | | | 12 |
| 13 | | *Reserve for Encumbrances—Current Year* | | | | 3 8 0 00 | | | 13 |

JOURNAL — PAGE 3

To avoid spending more resources than are available, encumbrance accounts are used. When goods or services are ordered that will be provided at a later date, an obligation for a future expenditure is made. Resources have not yet been used, but there is a promise to give up those resources when ordered goods or services are delivered. Encumbering resources is a way of setting aside the amount estimated to be needed to pay for the ordered goods or services. When the goods or services are delivered, the estimated amount is removed from the encumbrance account and the exact amount of the expenditure is journalized in an expenditure account.

**January 12. Encumbered estimated amount for supplies in public works department, $380.00. Memorandum No. 40.**

The budgetary account Encumbrance—Supplies, Public Works is increased by a debit for the amount of the order, $380.00. The fund equity account Reserve for Encumbrances—Current Year is increased by a credit for the amount of the supplies order, $380.00 as shown above. This account serves as an offsetting account for the encumbrance account and shows that this amount of the fund equity is reserved for an encumbrance.

| Encumbrance—Supplies, Public Works | |
|---|---|
| Jan. 12      380.00 | |

| Reserve for Encumbrance—Current Year | |
|---|---|
| | Jan. 12      380.00 |

Expenditures plus encumbrances for a specific account equal the total commitment that has been made against the appropriated amount for that account. The appropriated amount less the encumbrances and expenditures equals the amount that can still be spent. For example, Sparta appropriated $5,600.00 for supplies for the public works department. If expenditures are $900.00 and encumbrances are $380.00, then $4,320.00 is still available for public works supplies expenditures.

| Appropriated for Supplies | − | Expenditures | − | Encumbrances | = | Amount Still Available |
|---|---|---|---|---|---|---|
| $5,600.00 | − | $900.00 | − | $380.00 | = | $4,320.00 |

**1.** Entry to cancel encumbrance.

| | DATE | ACCOUNT TITLE | DOC. NO. | POST. REF. | GENERAL DEBIT | GENERAL CREDIT | CASH DEBIT | CASH CREDIT | |
|---|---|---|---|---|---|---|---|---|---|
| 10 | 25 | Reserve for Encumbrances—Current Year | M46 | | 380 00 | | | | 10 |
| 11 | | Encumbrance—Supplies, Public Works | | | | 380 00 | | | 11 |
| 12 | 25 | Expenditure—Supplies, Public Works | C362 | | 375 00 | | | 375 00 | 12 |

JOURNAL     PAGE 6

**2.** Entry to record expenditure.

When goods or services that have been encumbered are received, two entries must be made.

1. The encumbrance entry is reversed to remove the estimated amount from the encumbrance and reserve for encumbrance accounts.
2. The expenditure is recorded.

These entries are illustrated above.

> January 25. Paid cash for public works department supplies, $375.00, encumbered January 12 per Memorandum No. 40. Memorandum No. 46 and Check No. 362.

**Effect of first entry**

Reserve for Encumbrances—Current Year

| | |
|---|---|
| Jan. 25    380.00 | Jan. 12    380.00 |
| | (New Bal. zero) |

Encumbrance—Supplies, Public Works

| | |
|---|---|
| Jan. 12    380.00 | Jan. 25    380.00 |
| (New Bal. zero) | |

**Effect of second entry**

Expenditure—Supplies, Public Works

| | |
|---|---|
| Jan. 25    375.00 | |

Cash

| | |
|---|---|
| | Jan. 25    375.00 |

## STEPS

STEPS • STEPS • STEPS • STEPS

### JOURNALIZING EXPENDITURES FOR AMOUNT ENCUMBERED

**1** Debit *Reserve for Encumbrances—Current Year* and credit *Encumbrance—Supplies, Public Works* for *380.00*. The entry cancels the encumbrance entry by removing the estimated amount from the encumbrance and reserve for encumbrance accounts. The encumbrance is no longer needed since it is no longer outstanding. The encumbrance was for an estimated amount, *$380.00*. When the supplies were delivered, the actual cost was $375.00. The actual amount of an expenditure sometimes differs from the amount estimated when an order is placed.

**2** Debit *Expenditure—Supplies, Public Works* and credit *Cash* for the actual cost of supplies, *$375.00*.

©GETTY IMAGES/PHOTODISC

## JOURNALIZING EXPENDITURES BENEFITING FUTURE PERIODS

| | DATE | ACCOUNT TITLE | DOC. NO. | POST. REF. | GENERAL DEBIT | GENERAL CREDIT | CASH DEBIT | CASH CREDIT | |
|---|---|---|---|---|---|---|---|---|---|
| | | | | | 1 | 2 | 3 | 4 | |
| 17 | 10 | Expenditure—Capital Outlays, Gen. Gov't. | C400 | | 9 0 0 00 | | | 9 0 0 00 | 17 |

JOURNAL     PAGE 21

Governmental organizations are formed to provide services that their members need, not to earn a profit. A business records the cost of property, such as a computer, as an asset. The business then depreciates the asset over its useful life. The depreciation expense is matched with revenue earned in each fiscal period. Since governmental organizations do not earn net income, they have no need for expense information. However, controlling the expenditure of funds is important. When money is spent for capital outlays, the amount is recorded as an expenditure in the period spent even though the item may benefit several accounting periods.

On March 10, Sparta's general government department bought a new computer.

*March 10. Paid cash for a computer for general government department, $900.00. Check No. 400.*

Expenditure—Capital Outlays, General Government is increased by a debit for the cost of the computer, $900.00. Cash is decreased by a credit for the same amount, $900.00. The journal entry is shown above.

Governmental properties that benefit future periods are called **general fixed assets**. Most governmental organizations keep a record of general fixed assets. This record helps to safeguard the government's ownership of the property. Sparta keeps a card file with information about each general fixed asset.

## JOURNALIZING THE ISSUANCE OF LIABILITIES

| | DATE | ACCOUNT TITLE | DOC. NO. | POST. REF. | GENERAL DEBIT | GENERAL CREDIT | CASH DEBIT | CASH CREDIT | |
|---|---|---|---|---|---|---|---|---|---|
| | | | | | 1 | 2 | 3 | 4 | |
| 15 | 4 | Notes Payable | NP26 | | | 100 0 0 0 00 | 100 0 0 0 00 | | 15 |

JOURNAL     PAGE 1

Governmental organizations may need to borrow cash for short periods until tax money is received. At other times, these organizations have cash to invest for short periods until the cash is needed to pay expenditures. Sparta sends tax statements to property owners on January 1 each year. Taxes can be paid anytime from January 1 through February 28. Consequently, the town may need to borrow cash until taxes are received.

*January 4. Issued a 1-month, 9% note, $100,000.00. Note Payable No. 26.*

Cash is increased by a debit for the amount received, $100,000.00. Notes Payable is increased by a credit for the same amount, $100,000.00. The journal entry to record this transaction is shown above.

## JOURNALIZING THE PAYMENT OF LIABILITIES

| | DATE | ACCOUNT TITLE | DOC. NO. | POST. REF. | GENERAL DEBIT | GENERAL CREDIT | CASH DEBIT | CASH CREDIT | |
|---|---|---|---|---|---|---|---|---|---|
| | | | | | **1** | **2** | **3** | **4** | |
| 22 | 4 | Notes Payable | C370 | | 100 000 00 | | | 100 750 00 | 22 |
| 23 | | Expenditure—Other Charges, Gen. Gov't. | | | 7 50 00 | | | | 23 |
| 24 | | | | | | | | | 24 |

*(JOURNAL, PAGE 8)*

When Sparta's note payable is due on February 4, the amount of the note plus interest expense is paid to the bank.

*February 4. Paid cash for the maturity value of NP26: principal, $100,000.00, plus interest, $750.00; total, $100,750.00. Check No. 370.*

Notes Payable is decreased by a debit, $100,000.00. Expenditure—Other Charges, General Government is increased by a debit for the amount of interest expense, $750.00. Cash is decreased by a credit for the total amount paid, $100,750.00. The journal entry is shown above.

## INVESTING IN SHORT-TERM INVESTMENTS

| | DATE | ACCOUNT TITLE | DOC. NO. | POST. REF. | GENERAL DEBIT | GENERAL CREDIT | CASH DEBIT | CASH CREDIT | |
|---|---|---|---|---|---|---|---|---|---|
| | | | | | **1** | **2** | **3** | **4** | |
| 19 | 1 | Investments—Short Term | C385 | | 300 000 00 | | | 300 000 00 | 19 |
| 20 | | | | | | | | | 20 |

*(JOURNAL, PAGE 21)*

Most of Sparta's property taxes, the major portion of the town's revenue, are collected by March 1 each year. Cash that will not be needed for several months is placed in short-term investments. Interest on these investments provides additional revenue.

*March 1. Paid cash for a 4-month, 8% certificate of deposit, $300,000.00. Check No. 385.*

A document issued by a bank as evidence of money invested with the bank is called a **certificate of deposit**. The time and interest rate to be paid are included on the certificate.

Investments—Short Term is increased by a debit for the amount of the certificate, $300,000.00. Cash is decreased by a credit for the same amount, $300,000.00. The journal entry is shown above.

> **REMEMBER** The interest rate of a certificate of deposit usually increases as the time period increases. Interest rates of certificates are frequently tied to the prime rate.

| | | DATE | ACCOUNT TITLE | DOC. NO. | POST. REF. | GENERAL | | CASH | |
|---|---|---|---|---|---|---|---|---|---|
| | | | | | | DEBIT | CREDIT | DEBIT | CREDIT |
| 22 | 1 | | Investments—Short Term | R572 | | | 300 00 0 00 | 308 00 0 00 | | 22 |
| 23 | | | Interest Revenue | | | | 8 00 0 00 | | | 23 |

*JOURNAL*      PAGE *51*

When the certificate of deposit is due on July 1, cash is received for the original cost of the investment plus interest revenue earned.

> **July 1. Received cash for the maturity value of certificate of deposit due today: principal, $300,000.00, plus interest, $8,000.00; total, $308,000.00. Receipt No. 572.**

Cash is increased by a debit for the amount of cash received, $308,000.00. Investments—Short Term is decreased by a credit for the certificate of deposit's original cost, $300,000.00. Interest Revenue is increased by a credit for the amount of interest earned, $8,000.00. The journal entry is shown above.

GLOBAL PERSPECTIVE • GLOBAL PERSPECTIVE • GLOBAL PERSPECTIVE

## global perspective

### International Travel

International travel usually requires a passport. A passport is a formal document that allows exit from and reentry into a country. It proves citizenship and provides identity for the traveler.

First-time passport applicants must complete an application, which may be obtained from a United States Postal Service office. The application must be submitted with the following:

1. Proof of U.S. citizenship (usually a certified birth certificate).
2. Proof of identity (typically a document such as a driver's license).
3. Two identical 2" x 2" photographs (These photos must meet certain criteria. Many local photo studios advertise passport photo service.)
4. Fee. (The applicable fee when this textbook was written was $65.)

This information must be sent to a designated postal service office; a clerk of a federal or state court of records or a judge or clerk of a probate court who accepts applications; a U.S. consular official; or an agent at a passport agency in Boston, Chicago, Honolulu, Houston, Los Angeles, Miami, New Orleans, New York, Philadelphia, San Francisco, Seattle, Stamford, or Washington, D.C.

**Required**

Complete the following information that will be transferable to a passport application.

NAME: first, middle, and last name
ADDRESS: street, city, state, zip, country
PLACE OF BIRTH: city, state, country
DATE OF BIRTH: month, day, year
PERSONAL: Social Security number, height, color of hair, color of eyes
PHONE NUMBER: area code and home phone
FAMILY: father's name, birthplace, birth date, U.S. citizen (yes or no), mother's name, birthplace, birth date, U.S. citizen (yes or no)

TERMS REVIEW
AUDIT YOUR
WORK TOGETHER • WORK TOGETHER • WORK TOGETHER
ON YOUR OWN • ON YOUR OWN • ON YOUR OWN

## terms review

encumbrance
general fixed assets
certificate of deposit

## audit your understanding

1. What is an encumbrance?
2. What two entries are required when goods or services that have been encumbered are received?
3. Why does a governmental organization not record depreciation expense?
4. What is a certificate of deposit?

## work together 23-3

**Journalizing governmental encumbrances, expenditures, and other transactions**

The town of River Falls uses a general fund for all financial transactions. Expenditures are recorded by type of expenditure and by department. The four categories of expenditures are personnel, supplies, other charges, and capital outlays. Departments are General Government, Public Safety, Public Works, and Recreation.

Page 1 of a journal is provided in the *Working Papers*. Source documents are abbreviated as follows: memorandum, M; check, C; notes payable, NP. Your instructor will guide you through the following examples.

Jan. 11. Paid cash for electrical service in public works department, $238.00. C482.
16. Encumbered estimated amount for supplies in public safety department, $155.00. M111.
19. Issued a one-month, 12% note, $200,000.00. NP15.
27. Paid cash for public safety department supplies, $151.00, encumbered January 16 per M111. M125 and C497.
Feb. 6. Paid cash for printer for general government department, $395.00. C520. (Capital Outlays)
19. Paid cash for the maturity value of NP15: principal, $200,00.00, plus interest, $2,000.00; total $202,000.00. C538.
Mar. 16. Paid cash for a 3-month, 10% certificate of deposit, $150,000.00. C567.
June 16. Received cash for the maturity value of certificate of deposit due today; principal, $150,000.00, plus interest, $3,750.00; total, $153,750.00. R312.

1. Journalize the transactions completed during the current year.

## on your own 23-3

**Journalizing governmental encumbrances, expenditures, and other transactions**

The town of Annandale uses a general fund for all financial transactions. Expenditures are recorded by type of expenditure and by department. The four categories of expenditures are personnel, supplies, other charges, and capital outlays. Departments are General Government, Public Safety, Public Works, and Recreation.

Page 1 of a journal is provided in the *Working Papers*. Source documents are abbreviated as follows: memorandum, M; check, C; notes payable, NP. Work independently to complete the following problem.

Jan. 12. Paid cash for consultant's services in recreation department, $500.00. C267. (Personnel)
17. Encumbered estimated amount for supplies in public works department, $215.00. M88.
20. Issued a one-month, 10% note, $50,000.00. NP10.
28. Paid cash for public works department supplies, $211.00, encumbered January 17 per M88. M95 and C282.
Feb. 7. Paid cash for desk for public safety department, $375.00. C294. (Capital Outlays)
20. Paid cash for the maturity value of NP10: principal, $50,00.00, plus interest, $416.67; total $50,416.67. C322.
Mar. 17. Paid cash for a 3-month, 12% certificate of deposit, $75,000.00. C351.
June 17. Received cash for the maturity value of certificate of deposit due today; principal, $75,000.00, plus interest, $2,250.00; total, $77,250.00. R101.

1. Journalize the transactions completed during the current year.

## SUMMARY

*After completing this chapter, you can*

1. Define accounting terms related to budgeting and accounting for a not-for-profit governmental organization.

2. Identify accounting concepts and practices related to budgeting and accounting for a not-for-profit governmental organization.

3. Describe the process used to develop an operating budget.

4. Journalize budget transactions for a not-for-profit organization.

5. Journalize revenues for a not-for-profit organization.

6. Journalize expenditures, encumbrances, and other transactions for a not-for-profit organization.

# Explore Accounting

EXPLORE ACCOUNTING • EXPLORE ACCOUNTING • EXPLORE ACCOU

## Accounting in Not-for-Profit Organizations

When asked to think about accounting careers available in the not-for-profit sector, most people think about city, county, and state positions. Most often, these positions involve completing the accounting and reporting tasks required by these governmental agencies. However, there are other accounting-related careers in the not-for-profit sector that offer the opportunity for exciting and challenging positions. These opportunities include working for the Federal Bureau of Investigation (FBI), the Internal Revenue Service (IRS), and/or insurance companies in an area called "forensic accounting."

Forensic accounting is the investigation of accounting records and reports when fraud and/or embezzlement is suspected. Forensic accountants may help investigate crimes such as extortion, fraud, and embezzlement.

FBI agents may use interview and research techniques to investigate crimes. Requirements for employment as an FBI agent working in the accounting field include a four-year accounting degree from an accredited school and at least one year of experience in accounting or auditing. In addition, an agent must be a citizen of the U.S. between the ages of 23 and 35 and in good physical condition.

The IRS also employs accountants in various areas. Internal revenue agents are accountants who, by looking at the accounting records and tax returns of a business, determine if the business owes taxes and, if so, how much.

The IRS also employs internal auditors who examine the procedures and operations used with the IRS itself. A third position within the IRS is that of special agent. Special agents investigate tax fraud cases. Requirements for employment within the IRS vary, but most do include a four-year degree with some experience in the accounting field.

Insurance companies also hire accountants to assist in investigating cases involving suspected insurance fraud.

**Required:**
Contact the director of the FBI or a local IRS recruitment office to request more detailed information on job opportunities, requirements, and application procedures. Report your findings in written form.

# 23-1 APPLICATION PROBLEM
### Journalizing governmental operating budgets

Three towns, Appleton, Milltown, and Wilson, approved their annual general fund operating budgets effective January 1 of the current year. The available information about the budgets is as follows.

| | Estimated Revenues | Budgetary Appropriations | Fund Balance |
|---|---|---|---|
| Appleton | $2,050,000.00 | $2,009,000.00 | $41,000.00 |
| Milltown | 794,500.00 | 789,200.00 | 5,300.00 |
| Wilson | 1,754,000.00 | 1,722,500.00 | 31,500.00 |

**Instructions:**
Journalize the entry to record the operating budgets for each of the three towns for the current year. Use page 1 of a journal.

# 23-2 APPLICATION PROBLEM
### Journalizing governmental revenue transactions

Dalton's town council recently approved the town's general fund operating budget for the current year.

**Transactions:**

Jan. 1. Recorded property tax levy: taxes receivable—current, $1,100,000.00; allowance for uncollectible taxes—current, $11,000.00; property tax revenue, $1,089,000.00. M88.
8. Received cash for current taxes receivable, $97,600.00. R134.
14. Received cash from traffic fines, $56.00. R147. (Other Revenue)
Feb. 11. Received cash for current taxes receivable, $172,350.00. R194.
16. Received cash from parking meter receipts, $274.50. R212. (Other Revenue)
Mar. 1. Recorded reclassification of current taxes receivable to delinquent status, $56,800.00, and the accompanying allowance for uncollectible accounts, $11,000.00. M107.
12. Received cash for delinquent taxes receivable, $10,700.00. R259.

**Instructions:**
Journalize the transactions for the current year. Use page 1 of a journal.

# 23-3 APPLICATION PROBLEM   `PEACHTREE`  `QUICKBOOKS`
### Journalizing governmental encumbrances, expenditures, and other transactions

The town of Templeton uses a general fund for all financial transactions. Expenditures are recorded by type of expenditure and by department. The four categories of expenditures are personnel, supplies, other charges, and capital outlays. Departments are: General Government, Public Safety, Public Works, and Recreation.

**Transactions:**

Jan. 11. Paid cash for supplies in public works department, $205.00. C244.
15. Encumbered estimated amount for supplies in public safety department, $235.00. M33.
Jan. 16. Issued a one-month, 10% note, $150,000.00. NP6.
28. Paid cash for public safety department supplies, $232.00, encumbered January 15 per M33. M40 and C258.
Feb. 5. Paid cash for calculator for general government department, $255.00. C267. (Capital Outlays)
16. Paid cash for the maturity value of NP6: principal, $150,000.00, plus interest, $1,250.00; total, $151,250.00. C279.
28. Encumbered estimated amount for supplies in public works department, $276.00. M49.

| Mar. | 15. | Paid cash for a 3-month, 8% certificate of deposit, $200,000.00. C296. |
|---|---|---|
| | 18. | Paid cash for public works department supplies, $278.00, encumbered February 28 per M49. M58 and C315. |
| | 21. | Paid cash for consultant's services in recreation department, $360.00. C322. (Personnel) |
| June | 15. | Received cash for the maturity value of certificate of deposit due today: principal, $200,000.00, plus interest, $4,000.00; total, $204,000.00. R184. |

**Instructions:**
Journalize the transactions for the current year. Use page 1 of a journal.

# 23-4 MASTERY PROBLEM  PEACHTREE  QUICKBOOKS

## Journalizing governmental transactions

The town of Ingalls uses a general fund for all financial transactions. Expenditures are recorded by type of expenditure and by department. The four categories of expenditures are personnel, supplies, other charges, and capital outlays. Departments are: General Government, Public Safety, Public Works, and Recreation.

**Transactions:**

| Jan. | 2. | Recorded current year's approved operating budget: estimated revenues, $1,270,000.00; appropriations, $1,224,000.00; budgetary fund balance, $46,000.00. M42. |
|---|---|---|
| | 2. | Recorded current year's property tax levy: taxes receivable—current, $1,220,000.00; allowance for uncollectible taxes—current, $12,200.00; property tax revenue, $1,207,800.00. M43. |
| | 9. | Received cash for current taxes receivable, $57,300.00. R105. |
| | 11. | Paid cash for gas utility service in general government department, $234.00. C168. |
| | 12. | Issued a 2-month, 9% note, $200,000.00. NP7. |
| | 16. | Encumbered estimated amount for supplies in public works department, $165.00. M54. |
| | 20. | Received cash from traffic fines, $225.00. R111. (Other Revenue) |
| | 30. | Paid cash for lawn mower for public works department, $450.00. (Capital Outlays) C182. |
| Feb. | 6. | Paid cash for public works department supplies, $170.00, encumbered January 16 per M54. M58 and C190. |
| | 24. | Encumbered estimated amount for supplies in recreation department, $133.00. M69. |
| Mar. | 1. | Recorded reclassification of current taxes receivable to delinquent status, $51,400.00, and the accompanying allowance for uncollectible accounts, $12,200.00. M76. |
| | 12. | Paid cash for the maturity value of NP7: principal, $200,000.00, plus interest, $3,000.00; total, $203,000.00. C222. |
| | 20. | Paid cash for a 3-month, 8% certificate of deposit, $400,000.00. C234. |
| | 22. | Paid cash for recreation department supplies, $131.00, encumbered February 24 per M69. M88 and C241. |
| Apr. | 10. | Received cash for delinquent taxes receivable, $21,000.00. R355. |
| | 25. | Paid cash for consultant's services in recreation department, $500.00. C266. (Personnel) |
| June | 20. | Received cash for the maturity value of certificate of deposit due today: principal, $400,000.00, plus interest, $8,000.00; total, $408,000.00. R497. |

**Instructions:**
Journalize the transactions for the current year. Use page 1 of a journal.

# 23-5 CHALLENGE PROBLEM

## Journalizing governmental transactions

The town of Mabank uses a general fund for all financial transactions. Expenditures are recorded by type of expenditure and by department. The four categories of expenditures are personnel, supplies, other charges, and capital outlays. Departments are General Government, Public Safety, Public Works, and Recreation.

**Transactions:**

Jan. 2. Recorded current year's approved operating budget: estimated revenues, $1,528,000.00; appropriations, $1,542,100.00; budgetary fund balance, $14,100.00. M88.

(Note: Most towns prohibit deficit spending. In this case, a town would be prohibited from having a debit balance in the budgetary fund balance account. However, if sufficient fund equity is available at the beginning of a year, a town council may choose to appropriate more than the estimated revenues. The available fund equity would then be used for the amount that expenditures exceed revenues for the current period.)

2. Recorded current year's property tax levy: total amount of tax statements sent, $1,452,000.00; uncollectible taxes estimated at 1% of total tax levy. M89.

9. Received cash for current taxes receivable, $64,700.00. R111.

17. Paid cash for electric utility service in public works department, $286.00. C131.

20. Issued a 2-month, 12% note, $175,000.00. NP14.

25. Encumbered estimated amount for supplies in public safety department, $170.00. M102.

Feb. 3. Received cash from parking meter receipts, $1,158.00. R152.

10. Paid cash for public safety department supplies, $162.00, encumbered January 25 per M102. M130 and C188.

21. Paid cash for swing set for recreation department, $575.00. C199. (Capital Outlays)

Mar. 1. Recorded reclassification of current taxes receivable to delinquent status, $158,100.00, and the accompanying allowance for uncollectible accounts. M154.

Mar. 15. Paid cash for a 4-month, 9% certificate of deposit, $500,000.00. C220.

20. Paid cash for the maturity value of NP14: principal, $175,000.00, plus interest. C230.

21. Received cash for delinquent taxes receivable, $22,500.00. R206.

Apr. 4. Encumbered estimated amount for printer in general government department, $880.00. M178. (Capital Outlays)

16. Paid cash for general government department printer, $898.00, encumbered April 4 per M178. M190 and C267.

July 15. Received cash for the maturity value of certificate of deposit due today, $500,000.00, plus interest. R289.

**Instructions:**

Journalize the transactions for the current year. Use page 1 of a journal.

## applied communication

When property taxes become delinquent, the city for which you work issues a Notice of Delinquency to the property owner. The notice is a form letter that includes:

- The address of the property
- The census tract number
- The name and address of the property owner
- The total tax due
- The amount of the tax that is delinquent

**Required:**

You have been asked to create a new form for the Notice of Delinquency. The form should be created to allow data to be merged into the form. Use the mail merge or similar feature of your word processor to create a suitable form letter.

## cases for critical thinking

### Case 1

The town of Oneida has three funds in its accounting system: general, library, and recreation. Oneida's new town manager, Donna Ward, has questioned the necessity of having three separate governmental funds. Ms. Ward suggests combining all the funds into a single general fund. What do you recommend? Explain your answer.

### Case 2

Edwin Mansky, a new accounting clerk with the town of Thornton, has been struggling with accounting entries involving encumbrances. He suggests that no entries be made until goods or services are received. When goods are received, an expenditure would be recorded. Encumbrances would not be necessary and the final results would be the same. What is your response to Mr. Mansky's suggestion? Explain your answer.

## SCANS workplace competency

**Technology Competency:** Applying Technology to Task

**Concept:** Technology-oriented employees use computers, software, and other related equipment to complete desired tasks.

**Application:** With your instructor's permission, contact a variety of local businesses, retailers, financial institutions, not-for-profit organizations, service providers, and educational institutions. Ask them to provide examples of how technology is used within their organizations to operate their businesses. Technology includes software, the Internet, e-mail, automated equipment, cellular phones, wireless systems, servers, data processing, networks, sensors, scanners, inventory tags, electronic registers, and fax machines. Present your findings to the class, using some form of technology.

## • auditing for errors

An office clerk for the Town of Yorkville prepared the chart below, which lists all the account titles from the town's chart of accounts. For each account, a "+" (for an increase) or "−" (for a decrease) was recorded in the appropriate debit and credit column to show the impact of a debit or credit to each account's balance. The last column indicates the normal balance for each account. The intent of creating the chart is to provide an easy reference tool to help new accounting clerks accurately record journal entries and calculate general ledger balances.

**Instructions:**

Review the office clerk's chart below. Make a new chart so that the reference tool is accurate.

| Account Title | Debit | Credit | Normal Balance |
|---|:---:|:---:|:---:|
| Cash | + | − | Dr. |
| Taxes Receivable—Current | − | + | Dr. |
| All. for Uncoll. Taxes—Current | + | − | Dr. |
| Taxes Receivable—Delinquent | − | + | Dr. |
| All. for Uncoll. Taxes—Delinquent | + | − | Dr. |
| Inventory of Supplies | − | + | Dr. |
| Accounts Payable | − | + | Cr. |
| Unreserved Fund Balance | − | + | Cr. |
| Reserve for Encumbrances—Current Year | + | − | Cr. |
| Reserve for Encumbrances—Prior Year | + | − | Cr. |
| Reserve for Inventory of Supplies | + | − | Dr. |
| Property Tax Revenue | − | + | Cr. |
| Other Revenue | − | + | Cr. |
| Expenditure—Personnel, General Government | + | − | Dr. |
| Expenditure—Supplies, General Government | + | − | Dr. |
| Expenditure—Other Charges, General Government | + | − | Dr. |
| Estimated Revenues | − | + | Cr. |
| Appropriations | − | + | Cr. |
| Budgetary Fund Balance | − | + | Cr. |
| Encumbrance—Personnel, General Government | + | − | Dr. |
| Encumbrance—Supplies, General Government | + | − | Cr. |
| Encumbrance—Other Charges, General Government | − | + | Cr. |

## • analyzing Costco's financial statements

Costco expects payment for merchandise at the time of sale. The company accepts cash, checks, debit cards, and credit cards. The company does not set up individual Costco accounts so that customers may buy now and pay Costco later. Therefore, the consolidated balance sheets do not show accounts receivable.

**Instructions:**

Using Appendix B in this textbook, refer to Costco's Notes to Consolidated Financial Statements to answer the following questions.

1. What is the content of net receivables?

2. What are the amounts for allowance for doubtful accounts on August 31, 2003 and September 1, 2002?

3. Do you think the allowance for doubtful accounts would increase or decrease if Costco granted credit to its customers?

## Using Automated Reports for Analyzing Budget to Actual Business Activity

Businesses develop budgets as part of their planning processes. Budgets define in number terms the plans and expectations for the coming year. Budgets may be prepared by one or more managers or owners of the business. However, some businesses include all levels of management in their budgeting process. By including more people in the process, businesses expect greater success in meeting the goals established in the budgets.

The most common type of budget shows expected revenues and expenses for the coming year. Other types of budgets assist in planning for capital expenditures and cash management.

### Entering Budget Data

*Automated Accounting 8.0* and higher allows yearly budget amounts to be entered for all revenue and expense accounts. The data are entered using the Budgets tab of the Other Activities window. The complete list of revenue and expense accounts appears in the window as shown in the first illustration. Amounts are keyed for each account. The amounts should be the total planned revenue or expenditure for the year. (Note that accounts may not be added from this screen.)

Budgeted amounts can be changed as often as necessary. However, the amounts are generally updated only once a year. In many companies, budgets are prepared in November and December of the current year. The new budget amounts can then be entered into the software at the first of the year.

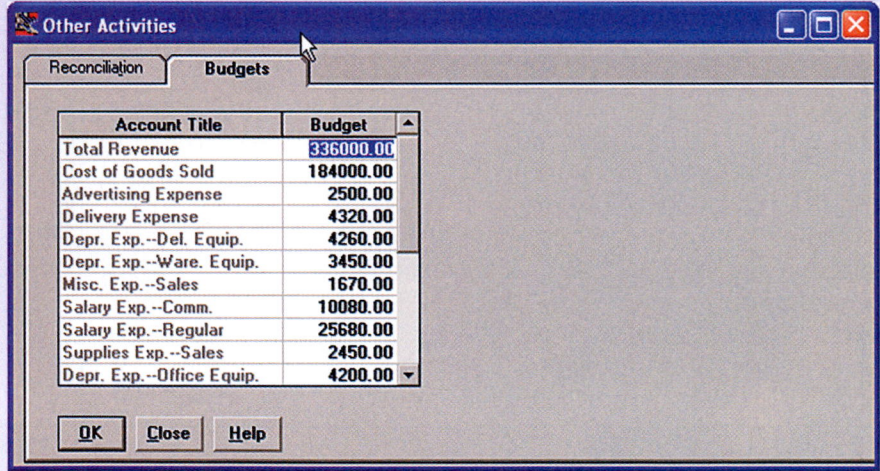

## Using Budgets to Prepare Performance Reports

Before budgets can be used, two steps must be taken:

1. The Budgeting feature must be active. To activate this feature, click the check box beside Budgeting. This option is one of the features available in the Company Info. tab of the Customize Accounting System window as shown here.

2. Budget amounts must be entered for all revenue and expense accounts as described below.

When these steps have been taken, performance reports can be displayed as shown here. The performance report compares the budgeted amount to the actual amount for each revenue and expense. The report has four columns:

1. Budget. Shows the budgeted amount for the appropriate period.

2. Actual. Shows the amount reported for the revenue or expense on the income statement.

3. Diff. from Budget. Shows the difference between the budgeted amount and the actual amount

4. %. Displays the difference from budget expressed as a percentage.

The performance report is accessed through the Report Selection window. The report may be displayed or printed in the same manner as other financial reports.

## Evaluating Performance Reports

Managers and business owners use performance reports to spot trends and to identify potential problem areas. If revenues are falling below budget, action can be taken to increase sales. If an expense category substantially exceeds budget, action may be needed to control the expenditure.

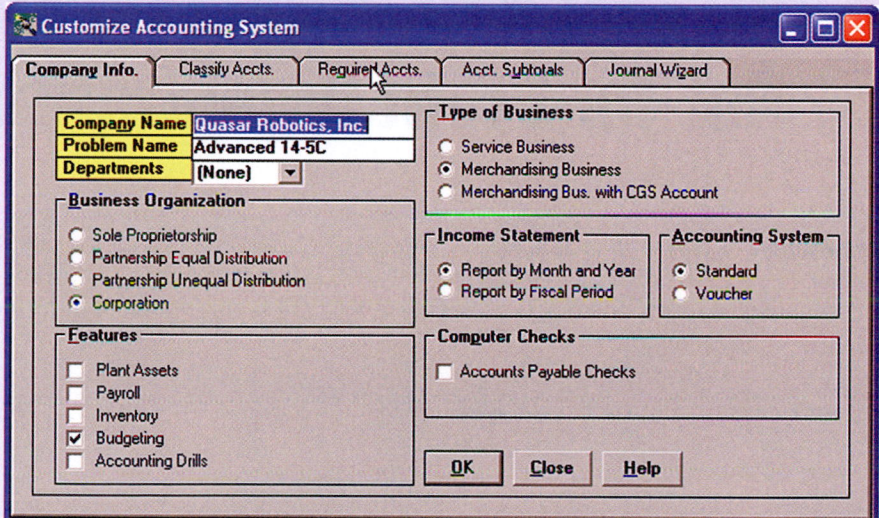

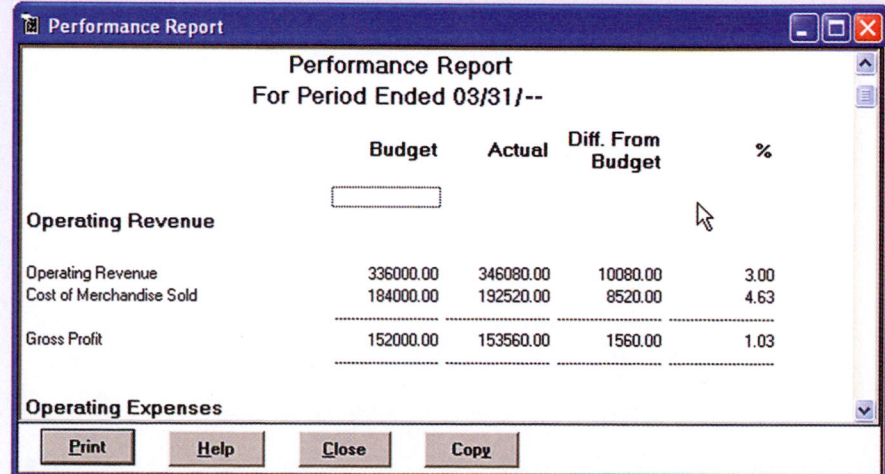

# 24 Financial Reporting for a Not-for-Profit Organization

*After studying Chapter 24, you will be able to:*

1. Identify accounting concepts and practices related to financial reporting for a not-for-profit governmental organization.

2. Prepare a worksheet for a governmental organization.

3. Prepare financial statements for a governmental organization.

4. Record adjusting and closing entries for a governmental organization.

Point Your Browser
accountingxtra.swlearning.com

# • San Jose

GETTY IMAGES

## THE CITY OF SAN JOSE RESPONDS TO AN ECONOMIC DOWNTURN

San Jose was founded in 1777 and served as the first civilian settlement in California. Today, with a population of over 925,000, San Jose qualifies as the 11th largest city in the United States. It is recognized as the capital of Silicon Valley and is home for some of the most technologically oriented businesses in the world.

The city's total budget is normally in excess of $2 billion and is broken down into three main categories: general funds, special purpose funds, and capital funds. General funds are used to pay for expenses needed to operate the city. These might include maintaining police and fire services, libraries, public works, parks, recreation, cultural activities, and transportation. Special purpose funds are used for operations that receive special monies restricted for specific purposes, such as airports, water treatment, housing, waste management, storm sewers, or convention centers. Capital funds are used to improve the city's infrastructure, including road improvements, new police and fire stations, parks, community facilities, water pollution controls, library buildings, and additional street lights.

The economic downturn that began in 2001 had a significant impact on San Jose's operating budget. Sales tax receipts, the city's largest source of revenue for the general fund, declined considerably during the early 2000s. San Jose's proposed budget for the 2004–2005 operating year showed a $70 million funding gap for the general fund. Due to the shortage of revenues, the city was forced to make difficult decisions regarding its expenditures.

### Critical Thinking

1.  If you were a city manager or a city council member, what suggestions might you recommend to increase revenues in order to reduce the gap?
2.  If you were a city manager or a city council member, what suggestions might you recommend to decrease expenditures in order to reduce the gap? Remember, if you are a city council member you need to keep in mind the best interests of your district's constituents. Election is just around the corner.

Source: www.sanjoseca.gov

Xtra!
Today
accountingxtra.swlearning.com

## ONLINE COLLEGE ACCOUNTING CLASSES

Online learning can be very convenient for a person who cannot travel to a campus at set times to take a course or program of study. However, online learning still requires a commitment of time. An online course may take the same commitment of time as a conventional course, or even more.

### Instructions

Search the Internet for "online accounting courses." Find two online accounting courses and answer the following questions about each course.

1.  What are the names of the schools offering the online accounting courses?
2.  How would you find out more information about the courses and the schools?

# 24-1 Preparing a Work Sheet for a Governmental Organization

Both businesses and not-for-profit organizations prepare financial statements periodically to report the results of financial activities. [CONCEPT: Accounting Period Cycle] However, financial information needed for not-for-profit organizations differs from that needed for businesses. A business measures performance primarily through determining the amount of net income. Thus, the accounting records are designed to emphasize the measurement of net income. In addition, the purpose of the income statement is to report the net income of the business. However, a not-for-profit organization's performance is measured primarily by the services provided and the efficiency with which resources are

used. A not-for-profit organization does not prepare an income statement. Instead, it prepares a statement of revenues, expenditures, and changes in fund balance. A not-for-profit organization's financial statements are designed to provide information for the following purposes.

1. To make decisions about the use of resources.
2. To assess services provided and the ability to provide those services.
3. To assess management's financial accountability and performance.
4. To determine the assets, liabilities, and fund equity of the organization.

## making ethical decisions

### Your Personal Code of Conduct

Throughout this textbook you have evaluated a variety of ethical issues, researched the code of conduct of several professional organizations, and sought guidance in the code of conduct of real businesses. By completing these activities, you have learned one valuable lesson—ethical behavior is simply good business. Establishing and following a code of conduct provides direction for the business and its employees, ensuring that decisions are in the best long-term interest of the business and its stakeholders.

Do you have a code of conduct for your life? As an employee, colleague, business manager, or accountant, if you have a personal

code of conduct you will be able to make both personal and business decisions that benefit your career and every stakeholder who is affected by your decisions in the long-term.

### Instructions

Write a personal code of conduct. Begin by identifying six to ten major topics. Then write a single sentence that summarizes your beliefs for each major topic. Finish your code of conduct by adding additional information that will guide you in the future.

# RECORDING A TRIAL BALANCE ON A WORK SHEET

## Town of Sparta General Fund
### Work Sheet
### For Year Ended December 31, 20--

| | ACCOUNT TITLE | TRIAL BALANCE DEBIT | TRIAL BALANCE CREDIT |
|---|---|---|---|
| 1 | Cash | 78 3 6 0 00 | |
| 2 | Taxes Receivable—Current | | |
| 3 | Allow. for Uncoll. Taxes—Cur. | | |
| 4 | Taxes Receivable—Delinquent | 15 6 4 0 00 | |
| 5 | Allow. for Uncoll. Taxes—Delin. | | 8 7 5 0 00 |
| 6 | Interest Receivable | | |
| 7 | Allow. for Uncoll. Interest | | |
| 8 | Inventory of Supplies | | |
| 9 | Investments—Short Term | | |
| 10 | Accounts Payable | | 36 1 2 5 00 |
| 11 | Notes Payable | | |
| 12 | Unreserved Fund Balance | | 11 7 0 5 00 |
| 13 | Res. for Encum.—Current Year | | 1 6 4 0 00 |
| 14 | Res. for Encum.—Prior Year | | |
| 15 | Reserve for Inv. of Supplies | | |
| 16 | Property Tax Revenue | | 1594 0 0 0 00 |
| 17 | Interest Revenue | | 8 7 8 5 00 |
| 18 | Other Revenue | | 2 6 2 5 00 |
| 19 | Expend.—Personnel, Gen. Gov't. | 263 1 7 5 00 | |
| 20 | Expend.—Supplies, Gen. Gov't. | 11 9 4 0 00 | |
| 21 | Expend.—Other Chgs., Gen. Gov't. | 112 3 8 0 00 | |
| 22 | Expend.—Cap. Outlays, Gen. Gov't. | 16 0 0 0 00 | |
| 23 | Expend.—Personnel, Public Safety | 588 6 5 0 00 | |
| 24 | Expend.—Supplies, Public Safety | 19 7 9 0 00 | |
| 25 | Expend.—Other Chgs., Pub. Safety | 152 6 3 5 00 | |
| 26 | Expend.—Cap. Outlays, Pub. Safety | 89 3 5 0 00 | |
| 27 | Expend.—Personnel, Public Works | 113 3 0 0 00 | |
| 28 | Expend.—Supplies, Public Works | 5 5 4 0 00 | |
| 29 | Expend.—Other Chgs., Pub. Works | 47 3 4 0 00 | |
| 30 | Expend.—Cap. Outlays, Pub. Works | 51 1 7 5 00 | |
| 31 | Expend.—Personnel, Recreation | 58 1 1 0 00 | |
| 32 | Expend.—Supplies, Recreation | 1 9 6 0 00 | |
| 33 | Expend.—Other Chgs., Recreation | 25 1 0 5 00 | |
| 34 | Expend.—Cap. Outlays, Recreation | 11 5 4 0 00 | |
| 35 | Estimated Revenues | 1606 5 0 0 00 | |
| 36 | Appropriations | | 1572 8 0 0 00 |
| 37 | Budgetary Fund Balance | | 33 7 0 0 00 |
| 38 | Encum.—Supplies, Public Safety | 1 6 4 0 00 | |
| 39 | | 3270 1 3 0 00 | 3270 1 3 0 00 |
| 40 | Excess of Revenues Over Expend. | | |
| 41 | | | |

**1.** List all General Ledger accounts—except Encumbrances.

**2.** List encumbrance account with a balance.

**3.** Calculate totals.

The town of Sparta uses an eight-column work sheet similar to the one used by LampLight, Inc., in Part 4. However, the work sheets differ in one set of columns. Sparta's work sheet has Revenues/Expenditures Debit and Credit columns. LampLight's work sheet has Income Statement Debit and Credit columns.

A trial balance is entered in the Trial Balance columns as the first step in preparing a work sheet. All general ledger accounts except encumbrances are listed in the Account Title column in the same order as they appear in the general ledger, as shown here. Only encumbrance accounts with balances are listed. The Trial Balance columns are totaled to prove the equality of debits and credits.

## STEPS
STEPS • STEPS • STEPS • STEPS • STEP

### RECORDING A TRIAL BALANCE ON A WORK SHEET

**1** List all general ledger accounts except encumbrances in the Account Title column in the same order as they appear in the general ledger.

**2** List only those encumbrance accounts with a balance in the Account Title column.

**3** Total the trial balance columns. Compare totals to verify that the totals are equal.

## FYI
FOR YOUR INFORMATION

Governments often issue bonds to pay for large projects, such as building schools and highways. Investors are not required to pay federal income tax on the interest income on these bonds.

Preparing a Work Sheet for a Governmental Organization

**Town of Sparta General Fund**

**Work Sheet**

**For Year Ended December 31, 20--**

| | ACCOUNT TITLE | TRIAL BALANCE | | ADJUSTMENTS | | REVENUES/EXPENDITURES | | BALANCE SHEET | | |
|---|---|---|---|---|---|---|---|---|---|---|
| | | 1 DEBIT | 2 CREDIT | 3 DEBIT | 4 CREDIT | 5 DEBIT | 6 CREDIT | 7 DEBIT | 8 CREDIT | |
| 6 | Interest Receivable | | | | | | | | | 6 |
| 7 | Allow. for Uncoll. Interest | | | | | | | | | 7 |
| 8 | Inventory of Supplies | | | (a)2 8 2 0 00 | | | | | | 8 |
| 9 | Investments—Short Term | | | | | | | | | 9 |
| 10 | Accounts Payable | | 36 1 2 5 00 | | | | | | | 10 |
| 11 | Notes Payable | | | | | | | | | 11 |
| 12 | Unreserved Fund Balance | | 11 7 0 5 00 | | | | | | | 12 |
| 13 | Res. for Encum.—Current Year | | 1 6 4 0 00 | | | | | | | 13 |
| 14 | Res. for Encum.—Prior Year | | | | | | | | | 14 |
| 15 | Reserve for Inv. of Supplies | | | | (a)2 8 2 0 00 | | | | | 15 |
| 16 | Property Tax Revenue | | 1594 0 0 0 00 | | | | | | | 16 |
| 17 | Interest Revenue | | 8 7 8 5 00 | | | | | | | 17 |

Some general ledger accounts for governmental funds need to be brought up to date before financial statements are prepared. However, since governmental funds report expenditures and not expenses, no adjustments are needed for expense accounts. The actual amounts that have been spent and recorded as expenditures are the amounts reported.

Since governmental funds recognize revenues when the revenues become measurable and available, an adjustment may be needed to record some revenues.

Adjustments are planned on a work sheet. Sparta makes adjustments to three accounts: (1) Inventory of Supplies. (2) Interest Revenue. (3) Reserve for Encumbrances—Current Year.

### Inventory of Supplies Adjustment

When supplies are bought, an expenditure account is debited. Some supplies may be unused at the end of a fiscal period. These unused supplies should be reported as an asset. [CONCEPT: Adequate Disclosure] Thus, an adjustment is made at the end of a fiscal period to record the remaining amount of supplies inventory as an asset, as shown above. Expenditure accounts debited when supplies were bought are

not adjusted. When an expenditure is made during a fiscal period, the expenditure is reported regardless of the purpose.

The total account balances of a governmental fund represent the equity of that fund. Thus, assets *less* liabilities *equals* total fund equity, which, unless reserved for a specified purpose, should represent resources that are available for appropriations and spending. The inventory of supplies, however, will be used by the organization. Therefore, this asset is not available for spending. To show that this asset, Inventory of Supplies, is not available for other uses, an equal amount of fund equity is reserved. Thus, the amount is credited to a restricted fund equity account titled Reserve for Inventory of Supplies.

Inventory of Supplies, an asset account, is increased by a debit for the amount of supplies on hand, *$2,820.00*. Reserve for Inventory of Supplies is increased by a credit for the same amount, *$2,820.00*.

| Inventory of Supplies | |
|---|---|
| Adj. *(a)* 2,820.00 | |

| Reserve for Inventory of Supplies | |
|---|---|
| | Adj. *(a)* 2,820.00 |

**Town of Sparta General Fund**

**Work Sheet**

**For Year Ended December 31, 20--**

| | ACCOUNT TITLE | TRIAL BALANCE | | ADJUSTMENTS | | REVENUES/EXPENDITURES | | BALANCE SHEET | | |
|---|---|---|---|---|---|---|---|---|---|---|
| | | DEBIT | CREDIT | DEBIT | CREDIT | DEBIT | CREDIT | DEBIT | CREDIT | |
| 6 | Interest Receivable | | | (b) 2 565 00 | | | | | | 6 |
| 7 | Allow. for Uncoll. Interest | | | | (b) 513 00 | | | | | 7 |
| 8 | Inventory of Supplies | | | (a) 2 820 00 | | | | | | 8 |
| 9 | Investments—Short Term | | | | | | | | | 9 |
| 10 | Accounts Payable | | 36 125 00 | | | | | | | 10 |
| 11 | Notes Payable | | | | | | | | | 11 |
| 12 | Unreserved Fund Balance | | 11 705 00 | | | | | | | 12 |
| 13 | Res. for Encum.—Current Year | | 1 640 00 | (c) 1 640 00 | | | | | | 13 |
| 14 | Res. for Encum.—Prior Year | | | | (c) 1 640 00 | | | | | 14 |
| 15 | Reserve for Inv. of Supplies | | | | (a) 2 820 00 | | | | | 15 |
| 16 | Property Tax Revenue | | 1 594 000 00 | | | | | | | 16 |
| 17 | Interest Revenue | | 8 785 00 | | (b) 2 052 00 | | | | | 17 |
| 38 | Encum.—Supplies, Public Safety | 1 640 00 | | | | | | | | 38 |
| 39 | | 3 270 130 00 | 3 270 130 00 | 7 025 00 | 7 025 00 | | | | | 39 |

Interest is assessed on all delinquent taxes. Interest on delinquent taxes becomes measurable and available when it is assessed. Thus, to bring the accounts up to date and record revenue earned but not collected at the end of the year, an adjustment is made, as shown above.

Sparta's interest earned but not yet collected on December 31 is $2,565.00. Experience has shown that approximately 20% of this amount, $513.00 ($2,565.00 × 20%), will not be collected. Thus, the amount expected to be collected, $2,052.00 ($2,565.00 − $513.00), is recorded as revenue.

**Interest Receivable**

| | |
|---|---|
| Adj. (b) 2,565.00 | |

**Allowance for Uncollectible Interest**

| | |
|---|---|
| | Adj. (b) 513.00 |

**Interest Revenue**

| | |
|---|---|
| | Adj. (b) 2,052.00 |

At the end of a fiscal year, a governmental organization may have outstanding encumbrances—orders that have not yet been delivered. When goods are delivered that were encumbered against the preceding year's appropriations, the amount should not be recorded as an expenditure of the current period. Therefore, at the end of a fiscal period, the balance of Reserve for Encumbrances—Current Year, the amount of encumbrances outstanding, should be reclassified to prior year status. Then, when the prior year's orders arrive, they can be debited to Reserve for Encumbrances—Prior Year, rather than current year's expenditures. This procedure prevents charging expenditures of one year to another year's appropriations.

**Reserve for Encumbrances—Current Year**

| | |
|---|---|
| Adj. (c) 1,640.00 | Bal. 1,640.00 |
| | (New Bal. zero) |

**Reserve for Encumbrances—Prior Year**

| | |
|---|---|
| | Adj. (c) 1,640.00 |

**Town of Sparta General Fund**

**Work Sheet**

**For Year Ended December 31, 20--**

| | TRIAL BALANCE | | ADJUSTMENTS | | REVENUES/EXPENDITURES | | BALANCE SHEET | |
| ACCOUNT TITLE | DEBIT | CREDIT | DEBIT | CREDIT | DEBIT | CREDIT | DEBIT | CREDIT |
|---|---|---|---|---|---|---|---|---|
| 1 Cash | 78,360.00 | | | | | | 78,360.00 | |
| 2 Taxes Receivable—Current | | | | | | | | |
| 3 Allow. for Uncoll. Taxes—Cur. | | | | | | | | |
| 4 Taxes Receivable—Delinquent | 15,640.00 | | | | | | 15,640.00 | |
| 5 Allow. for Uncoll. Taxes—Delin. | | 8,750.00 | | | | | | 8,750.00 |
| 6 Interest Receivable | | | (b)2,565.00 | | | | 2,565.00 | |
| 7 Allow. for Uncoll. Interest | | | | (b)513.00 | | | | 513.00 |
| 8 Inventory of Supplies | | | (a)2,820.00 | | | | 2,820.00 | |
| 9 Investments—Short Term | | | | | | | | |
| 10 Accounts Payable | | 36,125.00 | | | | | | 36,125.00 |
| 11 Notes Payable | | | | | | | | |
| 12 Unreserved Fund Balance | | 11,705.00 | | | | | | 11,705.00 |
| 13 Res. for Encum.—Current Year | | 1,640.00 | (c)1,640.00 | | | | | |
| 14 Res. for Encum.—Prior Year | | | | (c)1,640.00 | | 1,640.00 | | |
| 15 Reserve for Inv. of Supplies | | | | (a)2,820.00 | | | | 2,820.00 |
| 16 Property Tax Revenue | | 1,594,000.00 | | | | 1,594,000.00 | | |
| 17 Interest Revenue | | 8,785.00 | | (b)2,052.00 | | 10,837.00 | | |
| 18 Other Revenue | | 2,625.00 | | | | 2,625.00 | | |
| 19 Expend.—Personnel, Gen. Gov't. | 263,175.00 | | | | 263,175.00 | | | |
| 20 Expend.—Supplies, Gen. Gov't. | 11,940.00 | | | | 11,940.00 | | | |
| 21 Expend.—Other Chgs., Gen. Gov't. | 112,380.00 | | | | 112,380.00 | | | |
| 22 Expend.—Cap. Outlays, Gen. Gov't. | 16,000.00 | | | | 16,000.00 | | | |
| 23 Expend.—Personnel, Public Safety | 588,650.00 | | | | 588,650.00 [403,495.00 / 588,650.00] | | | |
| 24 Expend.—Supplies, Public Safety | 19,790.00 | | | | 19,790.00 | | | |
| 25 Expend.—Other Chgs., Pub. Safety | 152,635.00 | | | | 152,635.00 | | | |
| 26 Expend.—Cap. Outlays, Pub. Safety | 89,350.00 | | | | 89,350.00 | | | |
| 27 Expend.—Personnel, Public Works | 113,300.00 | | | | 113,300.00 [850,425.00 / 113,300.00] | | | |
| 28 Expend.—Supplies, Public Works | 5,540.00 | | | | 5,540.00 | | | |
| 29 Expend.—Other Chgs., Pub. Works | 47,340.00 | | | | 47,340.00 | | | |
| 30 Expend.—Cap. Outlays, Pub. Works | 51,175.00 | | | | 51,175.00 | | | |
| 31 Expend.—Personnel, Recreation | 58,110.00 | | | | 58,110.00 [217,355.00 / 58,110.00] | | | |
| 32 Expend.—Supplies, Recreation | 1,960.00 | | | | 1,960.00 | | | |
| 33 Expend.—Other Chgs., Recreation | 25,105.00 | | | | 25,105.00 | | | |
| 34 Expend.—Cap. Outlays, Recreation | 11,540.00 | | | | 11,540.00 | | | |
| 35 Estimated Revenues | 1,606,500.00 | | | | [96,715.00 / 1,606,500.00] | | | |
| 36 Appropriations | | 1,572,800.00 | | | | 1,572,800.00 | | |
| 37 Budgetary Fund Balance | | 33,700.00 | | | | 33,700.00 | | |
| 38 Encum.—Supplies, Public Safety | 1,640.00 | | | | 1,640.00 | | | |
| 39 | 3,270,130.00 | 3,270,130.00 | 7,025.00 | 7,025.00 | 3,176,130.00 | 3,215,602.00 | 993,850.00 | 599,130.00 |
| 40 Excess of Revenues Over Expend. | | | | | 39,472.00 | | | 39,472.00 |
| 41 | | | | | 3,215,602.00 | 3,215,602.00 | 993,850.00 | 993,850.00 |

All asset, liability and fund equity account balances except Reserve for Encumbrances—Prior Year are extended to the Balance Sheet columns on the work sheet.

Financial Reporting for a Not-for-Profit Organization

The reserve for encumbrances accounts are listed as balance sheet accounts in the chart of accounts. During a fiscal period, the current year reserve for encumbrances account is used as a balancing account for the encumbrance accounts. Fund equity is not actually reduced when encumbrances are recorded. Therefore, the current year's reserve for encumbrances account is considered to be a budgetary account until accounts are closed at the end of a fiscal period. Therefore, the balance of Reserve for Encumbrances—Prior Year is extended to the Revenues/Expenditures columns of the work sheet, as shown on the previous page.

The balances of all temporary accounts are also extended to the work sheet's Revenues/Expenditures columns. Temporary accounts are closed at the end of each fiscal period. Temporary accounts include all revenue, expenditure, and budgetary accounts.

## CALCULATING THE EXCESS OF REVENUES OVER EXPENDITURES

|  |  |  |
|---|---|---|
|  | Revenues/Expenditures Credit column total (line 39) | $ 3,215,602.00 |
| *Less* | Revenues/Expenditures Debit column total (line 39) | 3,176,130.00 |
| *Equals* | Excess of revenues over expenditures | $ 39,472.00 |

The Revenues/Expenditures and Balance Sheet columns are totaled. Totals are written as shown on line 39 of the work sheet shown on the previous page. The difference between the Revenues/Expenditures Credit column total and the Debit column total is the excess of revenues over expenditures. If the Debit column total is larger, the difference is the excess of expenditures over revenues. Sparta's excess of revenues over expenditures is calculated as shown above.

## COMPLETING THE WORK SHEET

The excess of revenues over expenditures, $39,472.00, is written under the work sheet's Revenues/Expenditures Debit column total on line 40 to make the two Revenues/Expenditures columns balance. The words *Excess of Revenues Over Expend.* are written in the Account Title column on the same line.

Sparta's excess of revenues over expenditures, $39,472.00, is also written under the Balance Sheet Credit column total on line 40 to make the two Balance Sheet columns balance.

When there is an excess of expenditures over revenues, the excess amount is written on a work sheet in the Revenues/Expenditures Credit and Balance Sheet Debit columns.

After the excess of revenues over expenditures is recorded on the work sheet, the last four columns are totaled again and ruled. Both pairs of Sparta's totals are the same. When the totals of each pair of columns are the same, the work sheet is assumed to be correct.

After the work sheet is completed, expenditures in the Revenues/Expenditures Debit column are totaled for each department. These totals are used in the preparation of financial statements. Departmental totals are written in small numbers below the amount of the last listed expenditure for the department. For General Government, lines 19 through 22, the total, $403,495.00, is written below line 22. For Public Safety, lines 23 through 26, the total, $850,425.00, is written below line 26. For Public Works, lines 27 through 30, the total, $217,355.00, is written below line 30. For Recreation, lines 31 through 34, the total, $96,715.00, is written below line 34.

## audit your understanding

1. What columns on a governmental organization's work sheet replace the Income Statement columns on a business's work sheet?
2. What accounts are affected, and how, when an interest revenue adjustment is recorded for a governmental organization?
3. To which column of a work sheet is the balance of Reserve for Encumbrances—Prior Year extended?
4. How is the excess of revenues over expenditures calculated on the work sheet?

## work together 24-1

**Preparing a work sheet for a governmental organization**

The town of Anoka uses a general fund. The trial balance for December 31 of the current year is recorded on a work sheet in the *Working Papers*. Your instructor will guide you through the following examples.

1. Analyze the following adjustment information and record the adjustments on the work sheet.

   | | |
   |---|---|
   | Supplies Inventory | $2,925.00 |
   | Interest Revenue Due but not Collected | 2,490.00 |

   An estimated 20% of the interest revenue due will not be collected.
   The reserve for encumbrances for the current year is reclassified to prior year status.

2. Complete the work sheet. Save your work to complete Work Together 24-2 and 24-3.

## on your own 24-1

**Preparing a work sheet for a governmental organization**

The town of Annandale uses a general fund. The trial balance for December 31 of the current year is recorded on a work sheet in the *Working Papers*. Work independently to complete the following problem.

1. Analyze the following adjustment information and record the adjustments on the work sheet.

   | | |
   |---|---|
   | Supplies Inventory | $1,870.00 |
   | Interest Revenue Due but not Collected | 2,180.00 |

   An estimated 20% of the interest revenue due will not be collected.
   The reserve for encumbrances for the current year is reclassified to prior year status.

2. Complete the work sheet. Save your work to complete On Your Own 24-2 and 24-3.

# 24-2 Preparing Financial Statements for a Governmental Organization

## STATEMENT OF REVENUES, EXPENDITURES, AND CHANGES IN FUND BALANCE—BUDGET AND ACTUAL

**2.** List expenditures.  **1.** List revenues.

**Town of Sparta General Fund**
**Statement of Revenues, Expenditures, and Changes in Fund Balance—Budget and Actual**
**For Year Ended December 31, 20--**

| | Budget | Actual | Variance—Favorable (Unfavorable) |
|---|---|---|---|
| Revenues: | | | |
| Property Tax Revenue | $1,594,000.00 | $1,594,000.00 | — |
| Interest Revenue | 10,000.00 | 10,837.00 | $ 837.00 |
| Other Revenue | 2,500.00 | 2,625.00 | 125.00 |
| Total Revenues | $1,606,500.00 | $1,607,462.00 | $ 962.00 |
| Expenditures: | | | |
| General Government | $ 405,050.00 | $ 403,495.00 | $ 1,555.00 |
| Public Safety | 852,650.00 | 850,425.00 | 2,225.00 |
| Public Works | 218,000.00 | 217,355.00 | 645.00 |
| Recreation | 97,100.00 | 96,715.00 | 385.00 |
| Total Expenditures | $1,572,800.00 | $1,567,990.00 | $ 4,810.00 |
| Excess of Revenues Over Expenditures | $ 33,700.00 | $ 39,472.00 | $ 5,772.00 |
| Less Outstanding Encumbrances, Dec. 31, 20– | — | 1,640.00 | (1,640.00) |
| Increase in Unreserved Fund Balance for Year | $ 33,700.00 | $ 37,832.00 | $ 4,132.00 |
| Unreserved Fund Balance, Jan. 1, 20– | 11,705.00 | 11,705.00 | — |
| Unreserved Fund Balance, Dec. 31, 20– | $ 45,405.00 | $ 49,537.00 | $ 4,132.00 |

**3.** Calculate excess of revenue over expenditures.

**5.** Determine change in unreserved fund balance.

**4.** Record outstanding encumbrances.

**7.** Calculate ending fund balance.

**6.** Record beginning fund balance.

Financial statements are prepared for each governmental fund. [*CONCEPT: Adequate Disclosure*] Sparta prepares two financial statements for its general fund. (1) Statement of revenues, expenditures, and changes in fund balance—budget and actual. (2) Balance sheet.

A statement of revenues, expenditures, and changes in fund balance—budget and actual reports the amount of revenues earned and expenditures made for a fiscal period. The changes in the unreserved fund balance from the beginning to the end of the fiscal period are also reported. In addition, actual revenues, expenditures, and unreserved fund balance are compared with budgeted amounts for a fiscal period. [*CONCEPT: Accounting Period Cycle*]

Sparta's general fund statement of revenues, expenditures, and changes in fund balance—budget and actual for the fiscal year ended December 31 is shown above.

Information used to prepare the Budget column is obtained from the annual operating budget shown in Chapter 23, page 686. Information needed to prepare the Actual column is obtained from the work sheet's Revenues/Expenditures columns. The beginning fund balance that is used in both the Budget and Actual columns is obtained from the prior year's balance sheet.

## STEPS

### PREPARING THE STATEMENT OF REVENUES, EXPENDITURES, AND CHANGES IN FUND BALANCE— BUDGET AND ACTUAL

**1** List revenues by source. Sparta has three sources of revenues: property taxes, interest, and other. The total of all three sources of revenues is also shown.

**2** List expenditures as totals for each department. Departments are responsible for controlling expenditures through budgeting and appropriations of specific amounts for each department. Thus, to aid the control process, amounts actually spent are reported for each responsible department. The total expenditures for the whole fund are also shown on the statement.

**3** Calculate the excess of revenues over expenditures. If expenditures exceed revenues, the difference is labeled "excess of expenditures over revenues."

**4** Record any outstanding encumbrances for the current year. Outstanding encumbrances are not deducted in figuring excess of revenues over expenditures. However, funds will be required in the future when the goods for which the encumbrances were made are delivered. Therefore, current year's encumbrances should be reported as a reduction in the current year's excess of revenues rather than in the next year when goods are paid for. Because no amount is budgeted for the encumbrances, the amount shown in the budget column is zero.

**5** Deduct outstanding encumbrances from excess of revenues over expenditures to determine the change in the unreserved fund balance for the year. The remaining excess of revenues over expenditures is an increase in the unreserved fund balance for the current year.

**6** Record the beginning unreserved fund balance. This January 1 balance is obtained from the prior year's balance sheet.

**7** Calculate the ending unreserved fund balance. The increase in the unreserved fund balance for the year plus the beginning unreserved fund balance equals the ending unreserved fund balance.

Each amount recorded in the Variance column is the difference between the budget and actual amounts for the item. For example, the variance for other revenue is $125.00 (actual, $2,625.00, *less* budget, $2,500.00). Variances are considered favorable if actual results are better than the amount budgeted for that item. When actual revenues are more than budgeted revenues, variances are favorable. When actual revenues are less than budgeted revenues, variances are unfavorable. When actual expenditures are less than budgeted expenditures, variances are favorable. When actual expenditures are more than budgeted expenditures, variances are unfavorable. A reserve for encumbrances variance has the same effect as an expenditure variance. Because encumbrances are not budgeted, any variance will be unfavorable since an actual encumbrance will cause an increase. Unfavorable variances are indicated by placing the amounts in parentheses.

### FYI
FOR YOUR INFORMATION

Governmental financial statements are often published in local newspapers.

**REMEMBER** Parentheses are placed around unfavorable variances to show negative results.

# careers in accounting

CAREERS IN ACCOUNTING • CAREERS IN ACCOUNTING • CAREERS IN ACCOUNT

## Jerry Bienias, Vice President of Finance and Technical Operations

COURTESY OF JERRY BIENIAS

Do you have to be an expert in plastics in order to be successful as the Vice President of Finance and Technical Operations at a plastic molding company? Not according to Jerry Bienias, the person in that position. With over 20 years of experience, Jerry feels that "business is business, no matter what industry you are in."

Jerry's education includes a B.S. degree in Finance. He is also a Certified Management Accountant (CMA). He began his career holding numerous accounting positions at one company, including inventory accountant, cost accountant, cost analyst, and cost accounting supervisor. These positions gave him a great opportunity to not only expand his managerial and cost accounting skills but also offered the opportunity to develop his business skills. By working on many project teams looking at expanding into new markets, implementing new business systems, and analyzing business processes to reduce costs and remain competitive, he learned important lessons about business in general.

Jerry summarizes the importance of a broad background when he says, "In all cases, a strong grasp of how to identify and understand the costs in a business and then use that information to make informed business decisions is critical to success."

They are continually facing challenges at Donnelly Custom Manufacturing in Alexandria, Minnesota. Jerry says,"We are now faced with trying to reconfigure our businesses to compete in a world market where some companies pay employees 25 cents per hour—with no health benefits." These challenges may seem insurmountable, but Jerry believes that "a strong understanding of managerial and cost accounting principles and a willingness to expand beyond just accounting into the overall discipline of business can present a person with a challenging and rewarding career that can last a lifetime."

**Salary Range:** Salaries for financial managers vary with the size of the company and the industry, ranging from $75,000 to over $200,000.

**Qualifications:** Minimum educational level is a bachelor's degree in finance, accounting, economics, or business administration. A professional certification is also helpful. Interpersonal skills, especially working as part of a team, are important. Broad business knowledge, clear communications, creative thinking, and problem solving are also required skills.

**Occupational Outlook:** This occupational area moves with the economy. When the economy expands, newly created companies as well as established companies that are expanding will be looking for financial managers. Economic downturns will decrease the need for financial managers.

**Town of Sparta General Fund**
**Balance Sheet**
**December 31, 20--**

### ASSETS

| | | |
|---|---|---|
| Cash................................................. | | $78,360.00 |
| Taxes Receivable—Delinquent ............................ | $15,640.00 | |
| Less Allowance for Uncollectible Taxes—Delinquent ............... | 8,750.00 | 6,890.00 |
| Interest Receivable ................................. | $ 2,565.00 | |
| Less Allowance for Uncollectible Interest ...................... | 513.00 | 2,052.00 |
| Inventory of Supplies ................................. | | 2,820.00 |
| Total Assets ...................................... | | $90,122.00 |

### LIABILITIES AND FUND EQUITY

| | | |
|---|---|---|
| Liabilities: | | |
| Accounts Payable................................... | | $36,125.00 |
| Fund Equity: | | |
| Unreserved Fund Balance ............................ | $49,537.00 | |
| Reserve for Encumbrances—Prior Year..................... | 1,640.00 | |
| Reserve for Inventory of Supplies ....................... | 2,820.00 | |
| Total Fund Equity .................................. | | 53,997.00 |
| Total Liabilities and Fund Equity........................ | | $90,122.00 |

A governmental fund balance sheet reports information about assets, liabilities, and fund equity for a specific date, usually the last day of a fiscal period. [CONCEPT: Adequate Disclosure] Assets and liabilities on a governmental fund balance sheet have characteristics similar to those on a corporation's balance sheet. However, a governmental fund does not have specific owners. Therefore, a governmental fund has no owners' equity section. Instead, the difference between assets and liabilities is reported as fund equity. Thus, unless restricted, fund equity represents the amount that is available for expenditures or encumbrances.

On December 31, Sparta's fund equity, consisting of three fund equity account balances, is $53,997.00. The Unreserved Fund Balance, *$49,537.00*, represents equity in the fund that has no restrictions (Total fund equity, $53,997.00, less Reserve for Encumbrances—Prior Year, $1,640.00, and less Reserve for Inventory of Supplies, $2,820.00). With proper authorization, Sparta may appropriate this amount for expenditures.

The other two fund equity account balances are reserved for specific purposes. The Reserve for Encumbrances—Prior Year, *$1,640.00*, is an amount of equity set aside for an encumbrance outstanding on December 31 of the prior year. When the goods arrive and are paid for in the current year for an order that was encumbered in a prior year, Reserve for Encumbrances—Prior Year is debited rather than Expenditures. Payment of the prior year's order closes the reserve for encumbrances account. The entry also avoids recording an expenditure in the current year for goods ordered in a prior year.

The Reserve for Inventory of Supplies, *$2,820.00*, represents the equity in inventory of supplies. Although supplies are assets, they are available for use, not spending. Therefore, part of the fund equity is reserved for the amount of supplies on hand. This reserve avoids appropriating the amount of equity that is represented by the asset supplies.

On a governmental fund balance sheet, total assets must equal total liabilities and fund equity. Sparta's balance sheet has total assets of $90,122.00. The total liabilities and fund equity is the same amount. The balance sheet is in balance and assumed to be correct.

## • audit your understanding

1. What are the three columns found on a statement of revenues, expenditures, and changes in fund balance—budget and actual?

2. Where is the information obtained to prepare the Actual column of the statement of revenues, expenditures, and changes in fund balance—budget and actual?

3. When actual expenditures are less than budgeted expenditures, is the variance favorable or unfavorable?

4. What must total assets equal on a governmental fund balance sheet?

## • work together 24-2

**Preparing financial statements for a governmental organization**

Use the working papers from Work Together 24-1. The town of Anoka's general fund operating budget for the current year is given in the *Working Papers*. Your instructor will guide you through the following examples.

1. Prepare a statement of revenues, expenditures, and changes in fund balance—budget and actual for the year ended December 31 of the current year.

2. Prepare a balance sheet for December 31 of the current year.

## • on your own 24-2

**Preparing financial statements for a governmental organization**

Use the working papers from On Your Own 24-1. The town of Annandale's general fund operating budget for the current year is given in the *Working Papers*. Work independently to complete the following problem.

1. Prepare a statement of revenues, expenditures, and changes in fund balance—budget and actual for the year ended December 31 of the current year.

2. Prepare a balance sheet for December 31 of the current year.

# 24-3 Recording Adjusting and Closing Entries for a Governmental Organization

## ADJUSTING AND CLOSING ENTRIES

| | DATE | | ACCOUNT TITLE | DOC. NO. | POST. REF. | GENERAL DEBIT | GENERAL CREDIT | CASH DEBIT | CASH CREDIT | |
|---|---|---|---|---|---|---|---|---|---|---|
| | | | **Adjusting Entries** | | | | | | | 1 |
| 2 | Dec. | 31 | Inventory of Supplies | | | 2 8 2 0 00 | | | | 2 |
| 3 | | | Reserve for Inventory of Supplies | | | | 2 8 2 0 00 | | | 3 |
| 4 | | 31 | Interest Receivable | | | 2 5 6 5 00 | | | | 4 |
| 5 | | | Allowance for Uncollectible Interest | | | | 5 1 3 00 | | | 5 |
| 6 | | | Interest Revenue | | | | 2 0 5 2 00 | | | 6 |
| 7 | | 31 | Reserve for Encumbrances—Current Year | | | 1 6 4 0 00 | | | | 7 |
| 8 | | | Reserve for Encumbrances—Prior Year | | | | 1 6 4 0 00 | | | 8 |
| 9 | | | **Closing Entries** | | | | | | | 9 |
| 10 | | 31 | Property Tax Revenue | | | 1594 0 0 0 00 | | | | 10 |
| 11 | | | Interest Revenue | | | 1 0 8 3 7 00 | | | | 11 |
| 12 | | | Other Revenue | | | 2 6 2 5 00 | | | | 12 |
| 13 | | | Unreserved Fund Balance | | | | 1607 4 6 2 00 | | | 13 |
| 14 | | 31 | Unreserved Fund Balance | | | 1567 9 9 0 00 | | | | 14 |
| 15 | | | Expenditure—Personnel, General Government | | | | 263 1 7 5 00 | | | 15 |
| 16 | | | Expenditure—Supplies, General Government | | | | 1 1 9 4 0 00 | | | 16 |
| 17 | | | Expenditure—Other Charges, General Government | | | | 112 3 8 0 00 | | | 17 |
| 18 | | | Expenditure—Capital Outlays, General Government | | | | 1 6 0 0 0 00 | | | 18 |
| 19 | | | Expenditure—Personnel, Public Safety | | | | 588 6 5 0 00 | | | 19 |
| 20 | | | Expenditure—Supplies, Public Safety | | | | 1 9 7 9 0 00 | | | 20 |
| 21 | | | Expenditure—Other Charges, Public Safety | | | | 152 6 3 5 00 | | | 21 |
| 22 | | | Expenditure—Capital Outlays, Public Safety | | | | 8 9 3 5 0 00 | | | 22 |
| 23 | | | Expenditure—Personnel, Public Works | | | | 113 3 0 0 00 | | | 23 |
| 24 | | | Expenditure—Supplies, Public Works | | | | 5 5 4 0 00 | | | 24 |
| 25 | | | Expenditure—Other Charges, Public Works | | | | 4 7 3 4 0 00 | | | 25 |
| 26 | | | Expenditure—Capital Outlays, Public Works | | | | 51 1 7 5 00 | | | 26 |
| 27 | | | Expenditure—Personnel, Recreation | | | | 58 1 1 0 00 | | | 27 |
| 28 | | | Expenditure—Supplies, Recreation | | | | 1 9 6 0 00 | | | 28 |
| 29 | | | Expenditure—Other Charges, Recreation | | | | 25 1 0 5 00 | | | 29 |
| 30 | | | Expenditure—Capital Outlays, Recreation | | | | 11 5 4 0 00 | | | 30 |
| 31 | | | Appropriations | | | 1572 8 0 0 00 | | | | 31 |
| 32 | | 31 | Budgetary Fund Balance | | | 33 7 0 0 00 | | | | 32 |
| 33 | | | Estimated Revenues | | | | 1606 5 0 0 00 | | | 33 |
| 34 | | | Unreserved Fund Balance | | | 1 6 4 0 00 | | | | 34 |
| 35 | | 31 | Encumbrance—Supplies, Public Safety | | | | 1 6 4 0 00 | | | 35 |

JOURNAL — PAGE 48

Sparta's adjusting entries are recorded on December 31, as shown above. Information needed for Sparta's adjusting entries is obtained from the work sheet's Adjustment columns.

**REMEMBER** Governmental budgetary accounts are temporary accounts that are extended to the work sheet Revenue/Expenditures columns and closed at the end of the fiscal year.

Sparta's closing entries are also recorded on December 31, as shown on the previous page. Information needed for the closing entries is obtained from the work sheet's Revenues/Expenditures columns. The following four entries are made:

1. Close all revenue accounts to the unreserved fund balance account.
2. Close all expenditure accounts to the unreserved fund balance account.
3. Close the budgetary accounts. At the beginning of the fiscal year, estimated revenues and appropriations were recorded based on the approved operating budget. At the end of the fiscal year, these budgetary accounts are closed. This entry is the opposite of the original entry to record the operating budget.
4. Close the outstanding encumbrance accounts to the unreserved fund balance account. This entry reduces the unreserved fund balance account by the amount of the outstanding encumbrance for supplies, public safety, $1,640.00.

The balance of Reserve for Encumbrances—Prior Year, $1,640.00, has been a budgetary account balance. Thus, the account balance is listed in the work sheet's Revenues/Expenditures Credit column. However, after the outstanding encumbrance account is closed to Unreserved Fund Balance, Reserve for Encumbrances—Prior Year is considered a fund equity account. The account, therefore, is not closed. This account balance now is the amount of total fund equity that is reserved for outstanding encumbrances.

After posting the closing entries, all temporary accounts have zero balances and are prepared for a new fiscal period. The difference between revenues and expenditures has been transferred to the unreserved fund balance account. Fund equity amounts that are not available for appropriations are recorded in reserve accounts.

# PREPARING A POST-CLOSING TRIAL BALANCE FOR A GOVERNMENTAL ORGANIZATION

| Town of Sparta General Fund Post-Closing Trial Balance December 31, 20-- | | |
|---|---|---|
| Cash | $78,360.00 | |
| Taxes Receivable—Delinquent | 15,640.00 | |
| Allowance for Uncollectible Taxes—Delinquent | | $ 8,750.00 |
| Interest Receivable | 2,565.00 | |
| Allowance for Uncollectible Interest | | 513.00 |
| Inventory of Supplies | 2,820.00 | |
| Accounts Payable | | 36,125.00 |
| Reserve for Encumbrances—Prior Year | | 1,640.00 |
| Reserve for Inventory of Supplies | | 2,820.00 |
| Unreserved Fund Balance | | 49,537.00 |
| Totals | $99,385.00 | $99,385.00 |

After all end-of-fiscal-period activities are complete, a post-closing trial balance is prepared to prove the equality of debits and credits in the account balances, as shown above. Because the debit and credit balance totals equal, the general ledger accounts are ready for the new fiscal period. [CONCEPT: Accounting Period Cycle]

## • audit your understanding

1. What are the sources of information for a governmental organization's adjusting entries?

2. Into what account are revenue and expenditure accounts closed?

3. What accounts are debited and credited to close the budgetary accounts?

4. Which of the following accounts will appear on a post-closing trial balance?

   Appropriations
   Reserve for Encumbrances—Prior Year
   Property Tax Revenue
   Taxes Receivable—Delinquent
   Budgetary Fund Balance
   Unreserved Fund Balance

## • work together 24-3

**Journalizing adjusting and closing entries for a governmental organization**

Use the working papers from Work Together 24-1. Page 40 of a journal form is provided in the *Working Papers*. Your instructor will guide you through the following examples.

1. Journalize the adjusting entries.

2. Journalize the closing entries.

## • on your own 24-3

**Journalizing adjusting and closing entries for a governmental organization**

Use the working papers from On Your Own 24-1. Page 52 of a journal form is provided in the *Working Papers*. Work independently to complete the following problem.

1. Journalize the adjusting entries.

2. Journalize the closing entries.

**SUMMARY**

*After completing this chapter, you can*

1. Identify accounting concepts and practices related to financial reporting for a not-for-profit governmental organization.

2. Prepare a worksheet for a governmental organization.

3. Prepare financial statements for a governmental organization.

4. Record adjusting and closing entries for a governmental organization.

# Explore Accounting

EXPLORE ACCOUNTING • EXPLORE ACCOUNTING • EXPLORE ACCO

## Governmental Accounting Standards Board

Governmental accounting is governed by the Governmental Accounting Standards Board (GASB). GASB was organized in 1984 to establish standards of financial accounting and reporting for governmental entities. These standards cover the preparation of external financial reports.

GASB's mission is "to establish and improve standards of state and local governmental accounting and financial reporting that will: (1) Result in useful information for users of financial reports and (2) Guide and educate the public, including issuers, auditors, and users of those financial reports."

When developing a new standard, GASB follows a process that permits input from individuals and groups. A task force studies a topic, seeks advice of experts, and may write a Discussion Memorandum. This Discussion Memorandum defines the problem, discusses the issue, and presents alternative solutions and the arguments and implications of each alternative solution.

A public hearing is then held to allow interested individuals or groups to give input relative to the issue and to suggest alternative solutions. Written input is also accepted. Board members study the comments made during the open hearing period and discuss the issue until they have reached a conclusion.

An Exposure Draft is written and voted on by the Board. If a majority of the seven-member board approves the Exposure Draft, it is issued. Generally, a period of 60 days or more is allowed for written comments on the draft. After this public comment period is over, the Board will again study the comments received and issue a final Statement.

This Statement, when issued, will explain the new statement, its effective date, background information, and the basis for the Board's decision.

The seven members of the Board are selected from government, public accounting, and accounting education associations. Each member serves on a part-time basis.

**Required:**
Using your local library or the Internet, find the most recent Statement of Standard that has been issued by GASB. Report your findings in written form. Include the name and the effective date of the new Standard.

# 24-1 APPLICATION PROBLEM

### Preparing a work sheet for a governmental organization

The town of Winona uses a general fund. The trial balance for December 31 of the current year is recorded on a work sheet in the *Working Papers*. The following adjustment information is available.

#### Adjustment Information, December 31

| | |
|---|---|
| Supplies Inventory | $3,534.00 |
| Interest Revenue Due but not Collected | 2,900.00 |

An estimated 20% of the interest revenue due will not be collected.
The reserve for encumbrances for the current year is reclassified to prior year status.

**Instructions:**

1. Analyze the adjustment information and record the adjustments on the work sheet.
2. Complete the work sheet. Save your work to complete Application Problems 24-2 and 24-3.


# 24-2 APPLICATION PROBLEM

### Preparing financial statements for a governmental organization

Use the work sheet prepared in Application Problem 24-1 to complete this problem.

The town of Winona's general fund operating budget for the current year is shown on page 729.

**Instructions:**

1. Prepare a statement of revenues, expenditures, and changes in fund balance—budget and actual for the year ended December 31 of the current year. The unreserved fund balance on January 1 was $41,244.00.
2. Prepare a balance sheet for December 31 of the current year.


# 24-3 APPLICATION PROBLEM      PEACHTREE

### Journalizing adjusting and closing entries for a governmental organization

Use the work sheet prepared in Application Problem 24-1 to complete this problem.

**Instructions:**

1. Use page 23 of a journal. Journalize the adjusting entries.
2. Continue using page 23 of a journal. Journalize the closing entries.

**Town of Winona**
**Annual Operating Budget—General Fund**
**For Year Ended December 31, 20--**

### ESTIMATED REVENUES

| | | |
|---|---:|---:|
| Property Tax | $1,459,000.00 | |
| Interest | 8,950.00 | |
| Other | 9,000.00 | |
| Total Estimated Revenues | | $1,476,950.00 |

### ESTIMATED EXPENDITURES AND BUDGETARY FUND BALANCE

| | | |
|---|---:|---:|
| General Government: | | |
|    Personnel | $ 250,250.00 | |
|    Supplies | 13,230.00 | |
|    Other Charges | 124,740.00 | |
|    Capital Outlays | 14,600.00 | |
|    Total General Government | | $ 402,820.00 |
| Public Safety: | | |
|    Personnel | $ 414,740.00 | |
|    Supplies | 22,000.00 | |
|    Other Charges | 168,460.00 | |
|    Capital Outlays | 81,270.00 | |
|    Total Public Safety | | 686,470.00 |
| Public Works: | | |
|    Personnel | $ 157,730.00 | |
|    Supplies | 6,160.00 | |
|    Other Charges | 52,250.00 | |
|    Capital Outlays | 46,350.00 | |
|    Total Public Works | | 262,490.00 |
| Recreation: | | |
|    Personnel | $ 55,350.00 | |
|    Supplies | 22,170.00 | |
|    Other Charges | 27,780.00 | |
|    Capital Outlays | 10,460.00 | |
|    Total Recreation | | 115,760.00 |
| Total Estimated Expenditures | | $1,467,540.00 |
| Budgetary Fund Balance | | 9,410.00 |
| Total Estimated Expenditures and Budgetary Fund Balance | | $1,476,950.00 |

## 24-4 MASTERY PROBLEM  `PEACHTREE`  `QUICKBOOKS`

### Completing the end-of-fiscal-period work for a governmental organization

The town of Duluth uses a general fund. The trial balance for December 31 of the current year is recorded on a work sheet in the *Working Papers*. The following adjustment information is available.

### Adjustment Information, December 31

| | |
|---|---|
| Supplies Inventory | $2,900.00 |
| Interest Revenue Due but not Collected | 2,350.00 |

An estimated 20% of the interest revenue due will not be collected.
The reserve for encumbrances for the current year is reclassified to prior year status.

**Instructions:**

1. Analyze the adjustment information and record the adjustments on the work sheet.
2. Complete the work sheet.

Duluth's general fund operating budget for the current fiscal year is as follows.

**Town of Duluth**
**Annual Operating Budget—General Fund**
**For Year Ended December 31, 20--**

ESTIMATED REVENUES

| | | |
|---|---:|---:|
| Property Tax | $1,265,000.00 | |
| Interest | 7,250.00 | |
| Other | 7,750.00 | |
| Total Estimated Revenues | | $1,280,000.00 |

ESTIMATED EXPENDITURES AND BUDGETARY FUND BALANCE

| | | |
|---|---:|---:|
| General Government: | | |
| Personnel | $ 211,750.00 | |
| Supplies | 11,360.00 | |
| Other Charges | 106,700.00 | |
| Capital Outlays | 12,390.00 | |
| Total General Government | | $ 342,200.00 |
| Public Safety: | | |
| Personnel | $ 397,590.00 | |
| Supplies | 18,900.00 | |
| Other Charges | 144,290.00 | |
| Capital Outlays | 72,320.00 | |
| Total Public Safety | | 633,100.00 |
| Public Works: | | |
| Personnel | $ 92,270.00 | |
| Supplies | 5,280.00 | |
| Other Charges | 44,770.00 | |
| Capital Outlays | 39,680.00 | |
| Total Public Works | | 182,000.00 |
| Recreation: | | |
| Personnel | $ 48,220.00 | |
| Supplies | 1,880.00 | |
| Other Charges | 23,690.00 | |
| Capital Outlays | 8,910.00 | |
| Total Recreation | | 82,700.00 |
| Total Estimated Expenditures | | $1,240,000.00 |
| Budgetary Fund Balance | | 40,000.00 |
| Total Estimated Expenditures and Budgetary Fund Balance | | $1,280,000.00 |

3. Prepare a statement of revenues, expenditures, and changes in fund balance—budget and actual for the year ended December 31 of the current year. The unreserved fund balance on January 1 was $35,550.00.
4. Prepare a balance sheet for December 31 of the current year.
5. Use page 42 of a journal. Journalize the adjusting entries.
6. Continue using page 42 of the journal. Journalize the closing entries.

The town of Plymouth uses a general fund. The trial balance for December 31 of the current year is recorded on a work sheet in the *Working Papers*. The following adjustment information is available.

**Adjustment Information, December 31**

| | |
|---|---|
| Supplies Inventory | $3,382.00 |
| Interest Revenue Due but not Collected | 6,080.00 |

An estimated 20% of the interest revenue due will not be collected.

The reserve for encumbrances for the current year is reclassified to prior year status.

Plymouth's general fund operating budget for the current fiscal year is shown as follows.

### Town of Plymouth
### Annual Operating Budget—General Fund
### For Year Ended December 31, 20--

#### ESTIMATED REVENUES AND BUDGETARY FUND BALANCE

| | | |
|---|---:|---:|
| Property Tax | $1,455,900.00 | |
| Interest | 13,360.00 | |
| Other | 16,580.00 | |
| Total Estimated Revenues | | $1,485,840.00 |
| Budgetary Fund Balance | | 25,320.00 |
| Estimated Revenues and Budgetary Fund Balance | | $1,511,160.00 |

#### ESTIMATED EXPENDITURES

| | | |
|---|---:|---:|
| General Government: | | |
| Personnel | $ 260,480.00 | |
| Supplies | 14,280.00 | |
| Other Charges | 130,240.00 | |
| Capital Outlays | 15,130.00 | |
| Total General Government | | $ 420,130.00 |
| Public Safety: | | |
| Personnel | $ 484,610.00 | |
| Supplies | 23,080.00 | |
| Other Charges | 176,920.00 | |
| Capital Outlays | 84,920.00 | |
| Total Public Safety | | 769,530.00 |
| Public Works: | | |
| Personnel | $ 113,300.00 | |
| Supplies | 6,660.00 | |
| Other Charges | 53,120.00 | |
| Capital Outlays | 48,875.00 | |
| Total Public Works | | 221,955.00 |
| Recreation: | | |
| Personnel | $ 56,855.00 | |
| Supplies | 2,790.00 | |
| Other Charges | 28,925.00 | |
| Capital Outlays | 10,975.00 | |
| Total Recreation | | 99,545.00 |
| Total Estimated Expenditures | | $1,511,160.00 |

Plymouth's town council permits departmental managers to exceed budgeted amounts for supplies, other charges, and capital outlays. However, total amounts expended for these three types of expenditure must be within the total budget amounts for these three items within each department.

Plymouth is prohibited from deficit spending. However, if sufficient funds are on hand at the beginning of a year, the town council may choose to appropriate more than the estimated revenues. Sufficient funds are on hand when the beginning fund balance plus estimated revenues equals or exceeds appropriations.

**Instructions:**

1. Analyze the adjustment information and record the adjustments on the work sheet.
2. Complete the work sheet.
3. Prepare a statement of revenues, expenditures, and changes in fund balance—budget and actual for the year ended December 31 of the current year. The unreserved fund balance on January 1 was $63,450.00.
4. Prepare a balance sheet for December 31 of the current year.
5. Use page 40 of a journal. Journalize the adjusting entries.
6. Continue using page 40 of the journal. Journalize the closing entries.

## applied communication

applied communication

In this course, you have learned a wide variety of facts and concepts about accounting and the business world. Regardless of your future educational and career goals, this knowledge will provide you with a sound foundation to become a productive member of society.

**Instructions:**

Prepare an essay to discuss how your knowledge of accounting will be useful to you in the future. How will accounting help you to complete your education, obtain a job, start a business, make personal investment decisions, and be succcessful in other facets of your life?

## cases for critical thinking

cases for critical thinking

### Case 1

The town of Spearman's statement of revenue, expenditures, and changes in fund balance—budget and actual lists expenditures by type. Expenditures listed are personnel, supplies, other charges, and capital outlays. Charles Lambert, a new accountant, suggested that expenditures be reported on this statement by departmental organization. Do you agree with Mr. Lambert? Explain your response.

### Case 2

Vicki Bonilla, a new accounting clerk for the town of Evergreen, recorded the closing entries for the current year. Miss Bonilla questions the necessity of making a closing entry for encumbrance accounts with balances. She suggests not closing the encumbrances. Then when items are received for which the encumbrances were recorded, make the regular journal entries. That is, (1) reverse the encumbrance entry and (2) debit Expenditures and credit Cash. Do you agree with Miss Bonilla? Explain your response.

## SCANS workplace competency

SCANS workplace competency

**Personal Qualities:** Self-Management

**Concept:** Successful employees are able to assess their own knowledge, skill, and abilities accurately, set well-defined and realistic personal goals, monitor progress toward goal attainment, motivate themselves, exhibit self-control, respond to feedback non-defensively, and initiate action.

**Application:** Write down three realistic goals that you can achieve in one month. Remember, a long-term goal is attained by accomplishing many short-term goals. Your goals may be related to academics, attendance, tardiness, athletics, nutrition, exercise, homework, relationships, activities, college research, employment, or behavior. Make these goals challenging yet obtainable. Review your progress after two weeks and make needed adjustments. Prepare two copies of your goals; give one to your instructor and post the other in a location where you can review your goals every day.

APPLIED COMMUNICATION

CASES FOR CRITICAL THINKING

SCANS WORKPLACE COMPETENCY

## graphing workshop

The town of Riverdale prepared a graph charting the budgeted and actual expenditures for each of its four departments.

**Instructions:**

Analyze the graph to answer the following questions.

1. Which departments showed favorable variances regarding their expenditures?
2. Which departments showed unfavorable variances regarding their expenditures?
3. Which department had the largest budget for expenditures? Approximately how much?

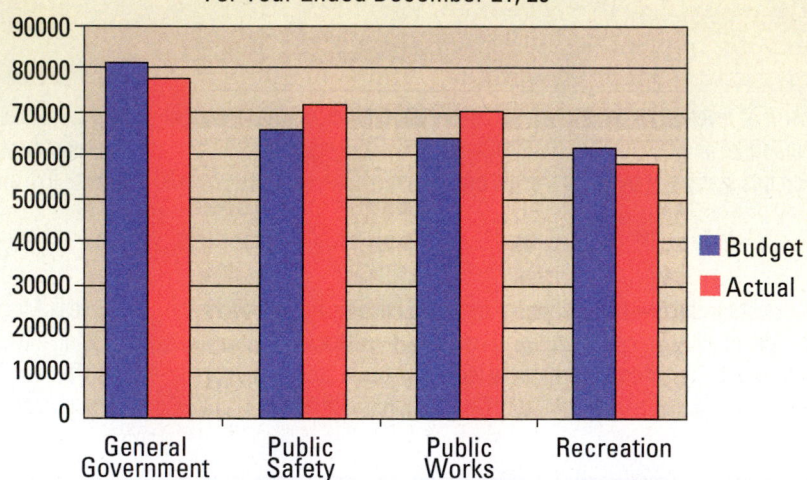

**Town of Riverdale**
**Statement of Expenditures**
For Year Ended December 21, 20--

## analyzing Costco's financial statements

Every publicly traded company is required to have an annual audit of its financial statements. Independent auditors—accountants from outside the company—examine how a company records transactions and prepares its financial statements. Auditors examine the records that support the financial records of a business to ensure that generally accepted accounting principles are followed. Based on their audit, the auditors issue an opinion that states whether the financial statements "present fairly, in all material respects, the consolidated financial position" of the company. The auditors' opinion gives external users confidence in the financial statement information. With this confidence, individuals and other companies are more likely to enter into business transactions.

**Instructions:**

Using Appendix B in this textbook, refer to the Independent Auditors' Report on page B-4 to answer the following questions.

1. List the four financial statements that were verified by independent auditors.
2. Identify the two fiscal periods reviewed by independent auditors.
3. State why the auditors' opinion does not cover all of the fiscal periods presented on the financial statements.
4. State whether the independent auditors are required by auditing standards to obtain "total and complete" assurance that the financial statements are free of material misstatement. Explain.
5. Determine if the independent auditors examine every business transaction conducted by Costco. Explain.
6. Name the public accounting firm and which office was responsible for the audit of Costco's financial statements in 2003.

## Using the Journal Wizard to Customize the Appearance of Journals

Throughout this text, the column headings in the journals have varied depending on the needs of the business. For example, departmentalized businesses have columns in the purchases journal for purchases made by each department.

### Customizing Journals

*Automated Accounting 8.0* and higher includes a utility that allows the user to define the amount columns to be included in the various journals. This utility is the Journal Wizard. A wizard is simply a step-by-step guide created by the programmer to help the user easily modify some aspect of the software or to easily complete a complex task.

The Journal Wizard is a tab located on the Customize Accounting System window. Before it can be used, a company must be set up. Modifications to journals should be made before any data are entered into the journals.

The control buttons for the wizard are located at the bottom of the Journal Wizard tab at the left. The buttons direct the user through the process. The user can move to the next screen, back a screen, finish the process, close the wizard without completing the task, or get help.

For each screen of the wizard, the user must carefully read the screen and make the appropriate choice. The screens contained in the wizard are described in the following paragraphs.

### Select Journal

Only one journal at a time may be modified. If General Journal is selected, the next two screens do not appear.

### Establish Offsetting Account

In most cases, the default account that appears with this screen will be the correct choice. However, the user may modify the account, the column type, and the column heading.

### General Debit and Credit

This screen allows the user to include a General Debit and General Credit column in the journal. The default choice of the software is generally correct.

### Special Journal Columns

This screen is used to identify all special columns in the journal. The user enters the account title, the header, and checks whether the account will be debited or credited. The header may have two lines. Each line is limited to 7 to 9 characters depending upon the font and the letters used.

After all items have been specified, click the Finish button. The Journal Wizard will complete the process. The modified journal will be available each time the company and problem are used. This journal is associated with the open company and problem. No other companies or problems are affected.

### USING THE JOURNAL WIZARD

(Note: This template does not use data from a problem in the text.)

### Instructions:

1. Load *Automated Accounting 8.0* or higher software.

2. Select database ARA-2 from the accounting template disk.

3. Select File from the menu bar and choose the Save As menu command. Key the path to the drive and directory that contains your data files. Save the database with a filename of XXX241 (where XXX are your initials).

4. Access Problem Instructions by clicking the Browser tool bar button.

5. Click the Custom tool and change the Company Info. to two departments.

6. Change the chart of accounts so that there are two purchase accounts: Purchases—Dept. 1 and Purchases—Dept. 2.

7. Use the Journal Wizard to change the purchases journal. Replace the Purch. Debit column with a Debit column for each of the two new purchases accounts.

8. Create a purchase on account transaction for each department and enter each in the purchases journal to test whether the journal has been changed properly.

9. Repeat the process for the sales journal and the cash receipts journal if time permits. Note that you will first need to change the chart of accounts so that there is a Sales account for each department. Note: To be a complete departmentalized accounting system, it would also be necessary to departmentalize the purchases and sales discount and returns and allowances account. However the purpose of this problem is to experiment with the Journal Wizard.

10. Exit the Automated Accounting software.

# Accounting Concepts

Accountants follow concepts commonly accepted by the profession as guides for reporting and interpreting accounting information. The accounting procedures described in this textbook are based on the application of accepted concepts. Eleven commonly accepted concepts are described in this appendix and referenced throughout the textbook.

## ACCOUNTING CONCEPTS

### Accounting Period Cycle

*Changes in financial information are reported for a specific period of time in the form of financial statements.*

Financial statements summarize the financial information that a business records. The time period for which financial statements are prepared depends on the needs of the business. An accounting period may be one month, three months, six months, or one year. For tax purposes, every business prepares financial statements at the end of each year.

### Adequate Disclosure

*Financial statements contain all information necessary to understand a business' financial condition.*

Owners, managers, lenders, and investors rely on financial statements to make informed decisions. All relevant financial information must be adequately and completely disclosed on financial statements.

A business reports only the total liabilities of $200,000.00 on its balance sheet. However, the total liabilities include $75,000.00 in current liabilities and $125,000.00 in long-term liabilities. Therefore, the balance sheet does not adequately disclose the nature of the liabilities. The critical information not disclosed is that $75,000.00 is current and due within a few months.

### Business Entity

*Financial information is recorded and reported separately from the owner's personal financial information.*

A business's records must not be mixed with an owner's personal records and reports. For example, a business owner may buy insurance to protect the business and insurance to protect the owner's home. Only the insurance obtained for the business is recorded in the business' financial records. The insurance purchased for the owner's personal home is recorded in the owner's personal financial records. One bank account is used for the business and another for the owner. A business exists separately from its owners.

### Consistent Reporting

*The same accounting procedures must be followed in the same way in each accounting period.*

Business decisions are based on the financial information reported on financial statements. Some decisions require a comparison of current financial statements with previous financial statements. If accounting information is recorded and reported differently each accounting period, comparisons from one accounting period to another may not be possible. For example, in one period a business reports $170,000.00 for total operating expenses and in the next period it reports $120,000 as cost of merchandise sold and $50,000 as operating expenses. A user of this information cannot adequately compare the two accounting periods. Therefore, unless a change is necessary to make information more easily understood, accounting information is reported in a consistent way for each accounting period.

## Going Concern

*Financial statements are prepared with the expectation that a business will remain in operation indefinitely.*

New businesses are started with the expectation that they will be successful. Accounting records and financial statements are designed as though businesses will continue indefinitely. A business bought store equipment for $30,000.00. The store equipment is expected to last 10 years. Yearly depreciation, therefore, is recorded and reported based on the expected life of the equipment. After six years of the expected 10-year life, the equipment's book value (cost less accumulated depreciation) is $13,200.00. If the business ended operations and the equipment had to be sold, the amount received may be less than the $13,200.00. However, accounting records are maintained with the expectation that the business will remain in operation indefinitely and that the cost will be allocated over the useful life of the equipment. The equipment value, therefore, remains $13,200.00 on the records regardless of what the equipment may be worth when sold.

## Historical Cost

*The actual amount paid for merchandise or other items bought is recorded.*

The actual amount paid for an item in a business transaction may be different from the value. For example, OfficeMart purchased a delivery truck valued at $20,000.00 and advertised at a sale price of $18,000.00. OfficeMart negotiated to purchase the delivery truck for $17,000.00 The amount recorded in accounting records for the delivery truck is the historical cost, $17,000.00—the actual amount paid.

Six months later, OfficeMart sells the delivery truck to Flowers by Giverney for $15,000.00. For Flowers by Giverney, the historical cost of the delivery truck is $15,000.00.

## Matching Expenses with Revenue

*The revenue from business activities and the expenses associated with earning that revenue are recorded in the same accounting period.*

Business activities for an accounting period are summarized in financial statements. To adequately report how a business performed during an accounting period, all revenue earned as a result of business operations must be reported. Likewise, all expenses incurred in producing the revenue during the same accounting period must be reported. Matching expenses with revenue gives a true picture of business operations for an accounting period.

For example, a business had sales of $100,000.00 in December. Expenses before adjustment were $80,000.00. Adjustments for items such as uncollectible accounts expense, supplies expense, and depreciation expense totaled $5,000.00. Therefore, total expenses for December should be reported as $85,000.00. The matching of expenses with revenues results in an accurate report of net income of $15,000.00. By including all expenses, readers of the financial statements have a more complete picture of the financial condition of the business.

## Materiality

*Business activities creating dollar amounts large enough to affect business decisions should be recorded and reported as separate items in accounting items in accounting records and financial statements.*

Business transactions are recorded in accounting records and reported in financial statements in dollar amounts. How the amounts are recorded and reported depends on the amount involved and the relative importance of the item in making business decisions. Dollar amounts that are large will generally be considered in making decisions about future operations. A separate accounting record is kept for items with dollar amounts large enough to be considered in making decisions about future operations. Dollar amounts that are small and not considered important in decision making may be combined with other amounts in the accounting records and financial statements.

For example, modems and print motors used to manufacture fax machines are considered direct materials and accounted for separately. Connectors and gears used in the manufacture of fax machines are parts with a small enough dollar value that they are grouped together and their total value is recorded in the accounting records as indirect material.

## Objective Evidence

*A source document is prepared for each transaction.*

The source document is the original business paper indicating that the transaction did occur and that the amounts recorded in the accounting records are accurate and true. For example, a check is the original business paper for cash payments. The original business paper for purchases on account is the purchase invoice. When accounting information reported on the financial statements needs to be verified, an accountant will first check the accounting record. If the details of an entry need further checking, an accountant will then check the business papers as objective evidence that the transaction did occur.

## Realization of Revenue

*Revenue is recorded at the time goods or services are sold.*

A business may sell either goods or services. Cash may be received at the time of sale or an agreement may be made to receive payment at a later date. Regardless of when cash is actually received, the sale amount is recorded in the accounting records at the time of sale. For example, a business sells office furniture for $2,000.00. The business agrees to an initial payment of $400.00 with the remaining balance to be divided in four monthly payments of $400.00 each. The full $2,000.00 of revenue is recorded at the time of sale even though $1,600.00 will be paid later.

## Unit Of Measurement

*Business transactions are reported in numbers that have common values—that is, using a common unit of measurement.*

All transactions are recorded in accounting records in terms of money. Useful nonfinancial information may also be recorded to describe the nature of a business transaction. If part of the information in the accounting records is financial and part is nonfinancial, the financial statements will not be clear. For example, if Zytech states its sales in number of units sold (nonfinancial) and its expenses in dollars (financial), net profit cannot be calculated. Instead, total expenses (financial) subtracted from money taken in through sales (financial) equals profit.

# *Annual Report 2003*

YEAR ENDED AUGUST 31, 2003

2003

# TEN YEAR OPERATING AND FINANCIAL HIGHLIGHTS
## (dollars in millions, except per share data)

| WAREHOUSES IN OPERATIONS | 2003 | | 2002 | | 2001 | | 2000 | |
|---|---|---|---|---|---|---|---|---|
| Beginning of year | 374 | | 345 | | 313 | | 292 | |
| Openings | 29 | | 35 | | 39 | | 25 | |
| Closings | (6) | | (6) | | (7) | | (4) | |
| End of year | 397 | | 374 | | 345 | | 313 | |
| **OPERATING RESULTS** | | | | | | | | |
| Revenue | | | | | | | | |
| Net Sales | $41,693 | 100.0% | $37,993 | 100.0% | $34,137 | 100.0% | $31,621 | 100.0% |
| Membership fees and other | 853 | 2.0 | 769 | 2.0 | 660 | 1.9 | 543 | 1.7 |
| Total revenue | 42,546 | 102.0 | 38,762 | 102.0 | 34,797 | 101.9 | 32,164 | 101.7 |
| Operating expenses | | | | | | | | |
| Merchandise costs | 37,235 | 89.3 | 33,983 | 89.4 | 30,598 | 89.6 | 28,322 | 89.6 |
| Selling, general and administrative expenses | 4,097 | 9.8 | 3,576 | 9.4 | 3,129 | 9.2 | 2,756 | 8.7 |
| Preopening expenses | 37 | 0.1 | 51 | 0.1 | 60 | 0.2 | 42 | 0.1 |
| Provision for impaired assets and closing costs | 20 | 0.0 | 21 | 0.1 | 18 | — | 7 | — |
| Operating expenses | 41,389 | 99.2 | 37,631 | 99.0 | 33,805 | 99.0 | 31,127 | 98.4 |
| Operating income | 1,157 | 2.8 | 1,131 | 3.0 | 992 | 2.9 | 1,037 | 3.3 |
| Other income (expenses) | | | | | | | | |
| Interest expense | (37) | (0.1) | (29) | (0.1) | (32) | (0.1) | (39) | (0.1) |
| Interest income and other | 38 | 0.1 | 36 | 0.1 | 43 | 0.1 | 54 | 0.2 |
| Provision for merger and restructuring expenses | — | | — | | — | | — | |
| Income from continuing operations before income taxes and cumulative effect of accounting change | 1,158 | 2.8 | 1,138 | 3.0 | 1,003 | 2.9 | 1,052 | 3.3 |
| Provision for income taxes | 437 | 1.1 | 438 | 1.2 | 401 | 1.1 | 421 | 1.3 |
| Income from continuing operations before cumulative effect of accounting change | 721 | 1.7 | 700 | 1.8 | 602 | 1.8 | 631 | 2.0 |
| Cumulative effect of accounting change, net of tax | — | | — | | — | | — | |
| Income from continuing operations | 721 | 1.7 | 700 | 1.8 | 602 | 1.8 | 631 | 2.0 |
| Discontinued operations: | | | | | | | | |
| Income (loss), net of tax | — | — | — | — | — | — | — | — |
| Loss on disposal | — | — | — | — | — | — | — | — |
| Net income (loss) | $ 721 | 1.7% | $ 700 | 1.8% | $ 602 | 1.8% | $ 631 | 2.0% |
| **Per Share Data—Diluted** | | | | | | | | |
| Income from continuing operations before cumulative effect of accounting change | $ 1.53 | | $ 1.48 | | $ 1.29 | | $ 1.35 | |
| Cumulative effect of accounting change, net of tax | — | | — | | — | | — | |
| Income from continuing operations | 1.53 | | 1.48 | | 1.29 | | 1.35 | |
| Discontinued operations: | | | | | | | | |
| Income (loss), net of tax | — | | — | | — | | — | |
| Loss on disposal | — | | — | | — | | — | |
| Net income (loss) | $ 1.53 | | $ 1.48 | | $ 1.29 | | $ 1.35 | |
| Shares used in calculation (000's) | 479,326 | | 479,262 | | 475,827 | | 475,737 | |
| **Balance Sheet Data** | | | | | | | | |
| Working capital (deficit) | $ 700 | | $ 181 | | $ (230) | | $ 66 | |
| Property and equipment, net | 6,960 | | 6,524 | | 5,827 | | 4,834 | |
| Total assets | 13,192 | | 11,620 | | 10,090 | | 8,634 | |
| Short-term debt | 47 | | 104 | | 195 | | 10 | |
| Long-term debt and capital lease obligations | 1,290 | | 1,211 | | 859 | | 790 | |
| Stockholders' equity | 6,555 | | 5,694 | | 4,883 | | 4,240 | |
| **SALES INCREASE (DECREASE) FROM PRIOR YEAR** | | | | | | | | |
| Total | 10% | | 11% | | 8% | | 17% | |
| Comparable units | 5% | | 6% | | 4% | | 11% | |
| **MEMBERS AT YEAR END (000'S)** | | | | | | | | |
| Business (primary cardholders) | 4,636 | | 4,476 | | 4,358 | | 4,170 | |
| Gold Star | 14,984 | | 14,597 | | 12,737 | | 10,521 | |

| | 1999 | | 1998 | | 1997 | | 1996 | | 1995 | | 1994 | |
|---|---|---|---|---|---|---|---|---|---|---|---|---|
| | 278 | | 261 | | 252 | | 240 | | 221 | | 200 | |
| | 21 | | 18 | | 17 | | 20 | | 24 | | 29 | |
| | (7) | | (1) | | (8) | | (8) | | (5) | | (8) | |
| | 292 | | 278 | | 261 | | 252 | | 240 | | 221 | |
| | | | | | | | | | | | | |
| | $26,976 | 100.0% | $23,830 | 100.0% | $21,484 | 100.0% | $19,214 | 100.0% | $17,906 | 100.0% | $16,161 | 100.0% |
| | 480 | 1.8 | 440 | 1.8 | 390 | 1.8 | 352 | 1.8 | 341 | 1.9 | 320 | 2.0 |
| | 27,456 | 101.8 | 24,270 | 101.8 | 21,874 | 101.8 | 19,566 | 101.8 | 18,247 | 101.9 | 16,481 | 102.0 |
| | | | | | | | | | | | | |
| | 24,170 | 89.6 | 21,380 | 89.7 | 19,314 | 89.9 | 17,345 | 90.3 | 16,226 | 90.6 | 14,663 | 90.7 |
| | 2,338 | 8.7 | 2,070 | 8.7 | 1,877 | 8.7 | 1,691 | 8.8 | 1,556 | 8.7 | 1,426 | 8.8 |
| | 31 | 0.1 | 27 | 0.1 | 27 | 0.1 | 29 | 0.1 | 25 | 0.1 | 25 | 0.2 |
| | 57 | 0.2 | 6 | — | 75 | 0.4 | 10 | — | 7 | — | 7 | — |
| | 26,596 | 98.6 | 23,483 | 98.5 | 21,293 | 99.1 | 19,075 | 99.2 | 17,814 | 99.5 | 16,121 | 99.8 |
| | 860 | 3.2 | 787 | 3.3 | 581 | 2.7 | 491 | 2.6 | 433 | 2.4 | 360 | 2.2 |
| | | | | | | | | | | | | |
| | (45) | (0.2) | (48) | (0.2) | (76) | (0.4) | (78) | (0.4) | (68) | (0.4) | (50) | (0.3) |
| | 44 | 0.2 | 27 | 0.1 | 15 | 0.1 | 11 | — | 3 | — | 14 | 0.1 |
| | — | — | — | — | — | — | — | — | — | — | (120) | (0.7) |
| | 859 | 3.2 | 766 | 3.2 | 520 | 2.4 | 424 | 2.2 | 368 | 2.0 | 204 | 1.3 |
| | 344 | 1.3 | 306 | 1.3 | 208 | 0.9 | 175 | 0.9 | 151 | 0.8 | 93 | 0.6 |
| | 515 | 1.9 | 460 | 1.9 | 312 | 1.5 | 249 | 1.3 | 217 | 1.2 | 111 | 0.7 |
| | (118) | (0.4) | — | — | — | — | — | — | — | — | — | — |
| | 397 | 1.5 | 460 | 1.9 | 312 | 1.5 | 249 | 1.3 | 217 | 1.2 | 111 | 0.7 |
| | — | — | — | — | — | — | — | — | — | — | (41) | (0.3) |
| | — | — | — | — | — | — | — | — | (83) | (0.5) | (182) | (1.1) |
| | $ 397 | 1.5% | $ 460 | 1.9% | $ 312 | 1.5% | $ 249 | 1.3% | $ 134 | 0.7% | $ (112) | (0.7%) |
| | | | | | | | | | | | | |
| | $ 1.11 | | $ 1.01 | | $ 0.73 | | $ 0.61 | | $ 0.53 | | $ 0.25 | |
| | (0.25) | | — | | — | | — | | — | | — | |
| | 0.86 | | 1.01 | | 0.73 | | 0.61 | | 0.53 | | 0.25 | |
| | — | | — | | — | | — | | — | | (0.09) | |
| | — | | — | | — | | — | | (0.19) | | (0.42) | |
| | $ 0.86 | | $ 1.01 | | $ 0.73 | | $ 0.61 | | $ 0.34 | | $ (0.26) | |
| | 471,120 | | 463,371 | | 449,336 | | 435,781 | | 447,219 | | 438,664 | |
| | | | | | | | | | | | | |
| | $ 450 | | $ 431 | | $ 146 | | $ 57 | | $ 9 | | $ (113) | |
| | 3,907 | | 3,395 | | 3,155 | | 2,888 | | 2,535 | | 2,146 | |
| | 7,505 | | 6,260 | | 5,476 | | 4,912 | | 4,437 | | 4,236 | |
| | — | | — | | 25 | | 60 | | 76 | | 149 | |
| | 919 | | 930 | | 917 | | 1,229 | | 1,095 | | 795 | |
| | 3,532 | | 2,966 | | 2468 | | 1,778 | | 1,531 | | 1,685 | |
| | | | | | | | | | | | | |
| | 13% | | 11% | | 12% | | 7% | | 11% | | 7% | |
| | 10% | | 8% | | 9% | | 5% | | 2% | | (3%) | |
| | 3,887 | | 3,676 | | 3,537 | | 3,435 | | 3,318 | | 3,228 | |
| | 9,555 | | 8,654 | | 7,845 | | 7,076 | | 6,683 | | 6,088 | |

# INDEPENDENT AUDITORS' REPORT

To the Board of Directors and Shareholders:

We have audited the accompanying consolidated balance sheets of Costco Wholesale Corporation and subsidiaries as of August 31, 2003 and September 1, 2002 and the related consolidated statements of income, stockholders' equity and cash flows for the 52 weeks then ended. These consolidated financial statements are the responsibility of the Company's management. Our responsibility is to express an opinion on these consolidated financial statements based on our audits. The accompanying consolidated financial statements of Costco Wholesale Corporation and subsidiaries as of September 2, 2001 were audited by other auditors who have ceased operations. Those auditors expressed an unqualified opinion on those consolidated financial statements in their report dated October 8, 2001.

We conducted our audits in accordance with auditing standards generally accepted in the United States of America. Those standards require that we plan and perform the audit to obtain reasonable assurance about whether the consolidated financial statements are free of material misstatement. An audit includes examining, on a test basis, evidence supporting the amounts and disclosures in the consolidated financial statements. An audit also includes assessing the accounting principles used and significant estimates made by management, as well as evaluating the overall consolidated financial statement presentation. We believe that our audits provide a reasonable basis for our opinion.

In our opinion, the consolidated financial statements referred to above present fairly, in all material respects, the consolidated financial position of Costco Wholesale Corporation and subsidiaries as of August 31, 2003 and September 1, 2002, and the results of their operations and their cash flows for the 52 weeks then ended in conformity with accounting principles generally accepted in the United States of America.

As discussed in Note 1 to the consolidated financial statements, the Company changed its method of accounting for stock-based compensation effective September 3, 2002.

*KPMG LLP*

Seattle, Washington
October 6, 2003

# COSTCO WHOLESALE CORPORATION
## CONSOLIDATED BALANCE SHEETS
### (dollars in thousands except par value)

| | August 31, 2003 | September 1, 2002 |
|---|---|---|
| **ASSETS** | | |
| **CURRENT ASSETS** | | |
| Cash and cash equivalents | $ 1,545,439 | $ 805,518 |
| Receivables, net | 556,090 | 474,861 |
| Merchandise inventories | 3,339,428 | 3,127,221 |
| Other current assets | 270,581 | 222,939 |
| Total current assets | 5,711,538 | 4,630,539 |
| **PROPERTY AND EQUIPMENT** | | |
| Land | 2,173,685 | 2,017,184 |
| Buildings, leaseholds and land improvements | 4,831,236 | 4,367,395 |
| Equipment and fixtures | 1,846,324 | 1,733,979 |
| Construction in progress | 154,181 | 198,744 |
| | 9,005,426 | 8,317,302 |
| Less accumulated depreciation and amortization | (2,045,418) | (1,793,683) |
| Net property and equipment | 6,960,008 | 6,523,619 |
| **OTHER ASSETS** | 520,142 | 466,105 |
| | $13,191,688 | $11,620,263 |
| **LIABILITIES AND STOCKHOLDERS' EQUITY** | | |
| **CURRENT LIABILITIES** | | |
| Short-term borrowings | $ 47,421 | $ 103,774 |
| Accounts payable | 3,131,320 | 2,884,269 |
| Accrued salaries and benefits | 734,261 | 589,927 |
| Accrued sales and other taxes | 207,392 | 163,273 |
| Deferred membership income | 401,357 | 360,515 |
| Other current liabilities | 489,356 | 347,975 |
| Total current liabilities | 5,011,107 | 4,449,733 |
| **LONG-TERM DEBT** | 1,289,649 | 1,210,638 |
| **DEFERRED INCOME TAXES AND OTHER LIABILITIES** | 209,835 | 145,925 |
| Total liabilities | 6,510,591 | 5,806,296 |
| **COMMITMENTS AND CONTINGENCIES** | | |
| **MINORITY INTEREST** | 126,117 | 119,730 |
| **STOCKHOLDERS' EQUITY** | | |
| Preferred stock $.005 par value; 100,000,000 shares authorized; no shares issued and outstanding | — | — |
| Common stock $.005 par value; 900,000,000 shares authorized; 457,479,000 and 455,325,000 shares issued and outstanding | 2,287 | 2,277 |
| Additional paid-in capital | 1,280,942 | 1,220,954 |
| Other accumulated comprehensive loss | (77,980) | (157,725) |
| Retained earnings | 5,349,731 | 4,628,731 |
| Total stockholders' equity | 6,554,980 | 5,694,237 |
| | $13,191,688 | $11,620,263 |

The accompanying notes are an integral part of these consolidated financial statements.

## COSTCO WHOLESALE CORPORATION

## CONSOLIDATED STATEMENTS OF INCOME
### (dollars in thousands, except per share data)

| | 52 Weeks Ended August 31, 2003 | 52 Weeks Ended September 1, 2002 | 52 Weeks Ended September 2, 2001 |
|---|---|---|---|
| **REVENUE** | | | |
| Net sales | $41,692,699 | $37,993,093 | $34,137,021 |
| Membership fees and other | 852,853 | 769,406 | 660,016 |
| Total revenue | 42,545,552 | 38,762,499 | 34,797,037 |
| **OPERATING EXPENSES** | | | |
| Merchandise costs | 37,235,383 | 33,983,121 | 30,598,140 |
| Selling, general and administrative | 4,097,398 | 3,575,536 | 3,129,059 |
| Preopening expenses | 36,643 | 51,257 | 59,571 |
| Provision for impaired assets and closing costs | 19,500 | 21,050 | 18,000 |
| Operating income | 1,156,628 | 1,131,535 | 992,267 |
| **OTHER INCOME (EXPENSE)** | | | |
| Interest expense | (36,920) | (29,096) | (32,024) |
| Interest income and other | 38,525 | 35,745 | 43,238 |
| **INCOME BEFORE INCOME TAXES** | 1,158,233 | 1,138,184 | 1,003,481 |
| Provision for income taxes | 437,233 | 438,201 | 401,392 |
| **NET INCOME** | $ 721,000 | $ 699,983 | $ 602,089 |
| **NET INCOME PER COMMON SHARE:** | | | |
| Basic | $ 1.58 | $ 1.54 | $ 1.34 |
| Diluted | $ 1.53 | $ 1.48 | $ 1.29 |
| Shares used in calculation (000's) | | | |
| Basic | 456,335 | 453,650 | 449,631 |
| Diluted | 479,326 | 479,262 | 475,827 |

The accompanying notes are an integral part of these consolidated financial statements.

# COSTCO WHOLESALE CORPORATION
## CONSOLIDATED STATEMENTS OF STOCKHOLDERS' EQUITY
### For the 52 weeks ended August 31, 2003, the 52 weeks ended September 1, 2002 and the 52 weeks ended September 2, 2001
### (in thousands)

| | Common Stock | | Additional Paid-In Capital | Other Accumulated Comprehensive Income/(Loss) | Retained Earnings | Total |
| --- | --- | --- | --- | --- | --- | --- |
| | Shares | Amount | | | | |
| BALANCE AT SEPTEMBER 3, 2000 . . . . . | 447,297 | $2,236 | $1,028,414 | $(117,029) | $3,326,659 | $4,240,280 |
| Comprehensive Income | | | | | | |
| Net Income . . . . . . . . . . . . . . . . . . . . . . . | — | — | — | — | 602,089 | 602,089 |
| Other accumulated comprehensive loss | | | | | | |
| Foreign currency translation | | | | | | |
| adjustment . . . . . . . . . . . . . . . . . . . . . . | — | — | — | (56,581) | — | (56,581) |
| Total comprehensive income . . . . . . . . | — | — | — | (56,581) | 602,089 | 545,508 |
| Stock options exercised including income tax | | | | | | |
| benefits and other . . . . . . . . . . . . . . . . . . . | 4,457 | 23 | 97,129 | — | — | 97,152 |
| BALANCE AT SEPTEMBER 2, 2001 . . . . . | 451,754 | 2,259 | 1,125,543 | (173,610) | 3,928,748 | 4,882,940 |
| Comprehensive Income | | | | | | |
| Net Income . . . . . . . . . . . . . . . . . . . . . . . | — | — | — | — | 699,983 | 699,983 |
| Other accumulated comprehensive income | | | | | | |
| Foreign currency translation | | | | | | |
| adjustment . . . . . . . . . . . . . . . . . . . . . . | — | — | — | 15,885 | — | 15,885 |
| Total comprehensive income . . . . . . . . | — | — | — | 15,885 | 699,983 | 715,868 |
| Stock options exercised including income tax | | | | | | |
| benefits and other . . . . . . . . . . . . . . . . . . . | 3,571 | 18 | 95,402 | — | — | 95,420 |
| Conversion of convertible debentures . . . . . . | — | — | 9 | — | — | 9 |
| BALANCE AT SEPTEMBER 1, 2002 . . . . . | 455,325 | 2,277 | 1,220,954 | (157,725) | 4,628,731 | 5,694,237 |
| Comprehensive Income | | | | | | |
| Net Income . . . . . . . . . . . . . . . . . . . . . . . | — | — | — | — | 721,000 | 721,000 |
| Other accumulated comprehensive income | | | | | | |
| Foreign currency translation | | | | | | |
| adjustment . . . . . . . . . . . . . . . . . . . . . . | — | — | — | 79,745 | — | 79,745 |
| Total comprehensive income . . . . . . . . | — | — | — | 79,745 | 721,000 | 800,745 |
| Stock options exercised including income tax | | | | | | |
| benefits and other . . . . . . . . . . . . . . . . . . . | 2,154 | 10 | 47,919 | — | — | 47,929 |
| Stock-based compensation . . . . . . . . . . . . . . | — | — | 12,069 | — | — | 12,069 |
| BALANCE AT AUGUST 31, 2003 . . . . . . . | 457,479 | $2,287 | $1,280,942 | $ (77,980) | $5,349,731 | $6,554,980 |

The accompanying notes are an integral part of these consolidated financial statements.

# COSTCO WHOLESALE CORPORATION

## CONSOLIDATED STATEMENTS OF CASH FLOWS

### (dollars in thousands)

| | 52 Weeks Ended August 31, 2003 | 52 Weeks Ended September 1, 2002 | 52 Weeks Ended September 2, 2001 |
|---|---|---|---|
| **CASH FLOWS FROM OPERATING ACTIVITIES** | | | |
| Net income | $ 721,000 | $ 699,983 | $ 602,089 |
| Adjustments to reconcile net income to net cash provided by operating activities: | | | |
| Depreciation and amortization | 391,302 | 341,781 | 301,297 |
| Accretion of discount on zero coupon notes | 17,852 | 17,233 | 16,654 |
| Stock-based compensation | 12,069 | — | — |
| Undistributed equity earnings in affiliates | (21,612) | (21,485) | (17,719) |
| Net loss/(gain) on sale of property and equipment and other | 4,907 | 4,001 | (15,934) |
| Provision for impaired assets | 4,697 | — | 15,231 |
| Change in deferred income taxes | 68,693 | 12,179 | 40,797 |
| Tax benefit from exercise of stock options | 12,348 | 27,171 | 32,552 |
| Change in receivables, other current assets, deferred income, accrued and other current liabilities | 232,167 | 129,883 | (6,159) |
| Increase in merchandise inventories | (162,759) | (380,158) | (271,355) |
| Increase in accounts payable | 226,544 | 187,655 | 335,110 |
| Total adjustments | 786,208 | 318,260 | 430,474 |
| Net cash provided by operating activities | 1,507,208 | 1,018,243 | 1,032,563 |
| **CASH FLOWS FROM INVESTING ACTIVITIES** | | | |
| Additions to property and equipment | (810,665) | (1,038,605) | (1,447,549) |
| Proceeds from the sale of property and equipment | 51,829 | 32,849 | 110,002 |
| Investment in unconsolidated joint venture | — | (1,000) | (28,500) |
| Decrease in short-term investments | — | 4,928 | 41,599 |
| Increase in other assets and other, net | (31,752) | (31,987) | (15,395) |
| Net cash used in investing activities | (790,588) | (1,033,815) | (1,339,843) |
| **CASH FLOWS FROM FINANCING ACTIVITIES** | | | |
| (Repayments)/proceeds from short-term borrowings, net | (58,144) | (99,175) | 185,942 |
| Net proceeds from issuance of long-term debt | 59,424 | 300,000 | 81,951 |
| Repayments of long-term debt | (11,823) | (18,540) | (159,328) |
| Changes in bank checks outstanding | (31,639) | (35,136) | 216,661 |
| Proceeds from minority interests | 6,087 | 3,908 | 7,119 |
| Exercise of stock options | 34,667 | 66,771 | 62,000 |
| Net cash (used in)/provided by financing activities | (1,428) | 217,828 | 394,345 |
| **EFFECT OF EXCHANGE RATE CHANGES ON CASH** | 24,729 | 677 | (8,985) |
| Increase in cash and cash equivalents | 739,921 | 202,933 | 78,080 |
| **CASH AND CASH EQUIVALENTS BEGINNING OF YEAR** | 805,518 | 602,585 | 524,505 |
| **CASH AND CASH EQUIVALENTS END OF YEAR** | $1,545,439 | $ 805,518 | $ 602,585 |
| **SUPPLEMENTAL DISCLOSURE OF CASH FLOW INFORMATION:** | | | |
| Cash paid during the year for: | | | |
| Interest (excludes amounts capitalized) | $ 20,861 | $ 9,511 | $ 14,761 |
| Income taxes | $ 320,546 | $ 351,003 | $ 363,649 |

The accompanying notes are an integral part of these consolidated financial statements.

## COSTCO WHOLESALE CORPORATION

## NOTES TO CONSOLIDATED FINANCIAL STATEMENTS
### (dollars in thousands, except per share data)

### Note 1—Summary of Significant Accounting Policies

*Basis of Presentation*

The consolidated financial statements include the accounts of Costco Wholesale Corporation, a Washington corporation, and its subsidiaries ("Costco" or the "Company"). All material inter-company transactions between the Company and its subsidiaries have been eliminated in consolidation. Costco primarily operates membership warehouses under the Costco Wholesale name.

Costco operates membership warehouses that offer low prices on a limited selection of nationally branded and selected private label products in a wide range of merchandise categories in no-frills, self-service warehouse facilities. At August 31, 2003, Costco operated 418 warehouse clubs: 309 in the United States; 61 in Canada; 15 in the United Kingdom; five in Korea; three in Taiwan; four in Japan; and 21 warehouses in Mexico with a joint venture partner.

The Company's investment in the Costco Mexico joint venture and in other unconsolidated joint ventures that are less than majority owned are accounted for under the equity method. The investment in Costco Mexico is included in other assets and was $167,293 at August 31, 2003 and $157,312 at September 1, 2002. The equity in earnings of Costco Mexico is included in interest income and other and for fiscal 2003, 2002 and 2001, was $21,400, $21,028 and $17,378, respectively. The amount of retained earnings that represents undistributed earnings of Costco Mexico was $86,074 and $64,674 at August 31, 2003 and September 1, 2002, respectively.

*Fiscal Years*

The Company reports on a 52/53-week fiscal year basis, which ends on the Sunday nearest August 31st. Fiscal years 2003, 2002 and 2001, were 52-week years.

*Cash Equivalents*

The Company considers all highly liquid investments with a maturity of three months or less at the date of purchase and proceeds due from credit and debit card transactions with settlement terms of less than five days to be cash equivalents. Of the total cash and cash equivalents of $1,545,439 at August 31, 2003 and $805,518 at September 1, 2002, credit and debit card receivables were $412,861 and $351,788, respectively.

*Receivables, net*

Receivables consist primarily of vendor rebates and promotional allowances, receivables from government tax authorities and other miscellaneous amounts due to the Company, and are net of allowance for doubtful accounts of $1,529 at August 31, 2003 and $2,224 at September 1, 2002. Management determines the allowance for doubtful accounts based on known troubled accounts and historical experience applied to an aging of accounts.

*Vendor Rebates and Allowances*

Periodic payments from vendors in the form of buy downs, volume or other purchase discounts that are evidenced by signed agreements are reflected in the carrying value of the inventory when earned and as a component of cost of sales as the merchandise is sold. Other consideration received from vendors is generally recorded as a reduction of merchandise costs upon completion of contractual milestones, terms of the related agreement, or by other systematic and rational approach.

## NOTES TO CONSOLIDATED FINANCIAL STATEMENTS
**(dollars in thousands, except per share data) (Continued)**

### Note 1—Summary of Significant Accounting Policies (Continued)

*Merchandise Inventories*

Merchandise inventories are valued at the lower of cost or market as determined primarily by the retail inventory method, and are stated using the last-in, first-out (LIFO) method for substantially all U.S. merchandise inventories. Merchandise inventories for all foreign operations are primarily valued by the retail method of accounting, and are stated using the first-in, first-out (FIFO) method. The Company believes the LIFO method more fairly presents the results of operations by more closely matching current costs with current revenues. The Company records an adjustment each quarter for the expected annual effect of inflation and these estimates are adjusted to actual results determined at year-end. The Company considers in its calculation of the LIFO cost the estimated net realizable value of inventory in those inventory pools where deflation exists and records a write down of inventory where estimated net realizable value is less than LIFO inventory. The LIFO inventory adjustment for the fourth quarter of fiscal 2003 increased gross margin by approximately $14,650 as compared to $21,000 in the fourth quarter of fiscal 2002. If all merchandise inventories had been valued using the first-in, first-out (FIFO) method, inventories would have been lower by $19,500 at August 31, 2003 and higher by $150 at September 1, 2002.

| | August 31, 2003 | September 1, 2002 |
|---|---|---|
| Merchandise inventories consist of: | | |
| United States (primarily LIFO) | $2,668,342 | $2,552,820 |
| Foreign (FIFO) | 671,086 | 574,401 |
| Total | $3,339,428 | $3,127,221 |

The Company provides for estimated inventory losses between physical inventory counts on the basis of a standard percentage of sales. This provision is adjusted periodically to reflect the actual shrinkage results of the physical inventory counts, which generally occur in the second and fourth quarters of the Company's fiscal year.

*Property and Equipment*

Property and equipment are stated at cost. Depreciation and amortization expenses are computed using the straight-line method for financial reporting purposes. Buildings are generally depreciated over twenty-five to thirty-five years; equipment and fixtures are depreciated over three to ten years; and leasehold improvements are amortized over the initial term of the lease.

Interest costs incurred on property and equipment during the construction period are capitalized. The amount of interest costs capitalized was $3,272 in fiscal 2003, $13,480 in fiscal 2002, and $19,157 in fiscal 2001.

*Impairment of Long-Lived Assets*

The Company periodically evaluates the realizability of long-lived assets for impairment when events or changes in circumstances occur, which may indicate the carrying amount of the asset may not be recoverable. The Company evaluates the carrying value of the asset by comparing the estimated future undiscounted cash flows generated from the use of the asset and its eventual disposition with the asset's reported net book value. In accordance with Statement of Financial Accounting Standards (SFAS) No. 144, the Company recorded a pre-tax, non-cash charge of $4,697 in fiscal 2003 and $0 and $15,231 in fiscal 2002 and 2001, respectively, reflecting its estimate of impairment relating to scheduled warehouse closings. The charge reflects the difference between the carrying value and fair value, which was based on estimated market valuations for those assets whose carrying value is not currently anticipated to be recoverable through future cash flows.

## Note 1—Summary of Significant Accounting Policies (Continued)

*Goodwill*

Goodwill, net of accumulated amortization, resulting from certain business combinations is included in other assets, and totaled $46,549 at August 31, 2003 and $43,920 at September 1, 2002. On September 3, 2001, the Company adopted SFAS No. 142, "Accounting for Goodwill and Other Intangibles," which specifies that goodwill and some intangible assets will no longer be amortized, but instead will be subject to periodic impairment testing. Accordingly, the Company reviews previously reported goodwill for impairment on an annual basis, or more frequently if circumstances dictate. In fiscal 2001 goodwill was amortized on a straight-line basis over lives ranging from two to forty years and was periodically evaluated for impairment as circumstances dictated. The effects on net income and net income per share data would not be significant if the Company had followed the provisions of SFAS No. 142 in the year ended September 2, 2001.

*Accounts Payable*

The Company's banking system provides for the daily replenishment of major bank accounts as checks are presented. Accordingly, included in accounts payable at August 31, 2003 and September 1, 2002 are $216,980 and $235,458 respectively, representing the excess of outstanding checks over cash on deposit at the banks on which the checks were drawn.

*Insurance/Self Insurance Liabilities*

The Company uses a combination of insurance and self-insurance mechanisms to provide for the potential liabilities for workers' compensation, general liability, property insurance, director and officers' liability, vehicle liability and employee health care benefits. Liabilities associated with the risks that are retained by the Company are estimated, in part, by considering historical claims experience and outside expertise, demographic factors, severity factors and other actuarial assumptions. The estimated accruals for these liabilities could be significantly affected if future occurrences and claims differ from these assumptions and historical trends.

*Derivatives*

The Company has limited involvement with derivative financial instruments and uses them only to manage well-defined interest rate and foreign exchange risks. Forward foreign exchange contracts are used to hedge the impact of fluctuations of foreign exchange on inventory purchases. The only significant derivative instruments the Company holds are interest rate swaps, which the Company uses to manage the interest rate risk associated with its borrowings and to manage the Company's mix of fixed and variable-rate debt. As of August 31, 2003, the Company had "fixed-to-floating" interest rate swaps with an aggregate notional amount of $600,000 and an aggregate fair value of $34,204, which is recorded in other assets. These swaps were entered into effective November 13, 2001, and March 25, 2002, and are designated and qualify as fair value hedges of the Company's $300,000 7⅛% Senior Notes and the Company's $300,000 5½% Senior Notes, respectively. As the terms of the swaps match those of the underlying hedged debt, the changes in the fair value of these swaps are offset by corresponding changes in the fair value recorded on the hedged debt, and result in no net earnings impact.

*Foreign Currency Translations*

The functional currencies of the Company's international subsidiaries are the local currency of the country in which the subsidiary is located. Assets and liabilities recorded in foreign currencies, as well as the Company's investment in the Costco Mexico joint venture, are translated at the exchange rate on the balance sheet date. Translation adjustments resulting from this process are charged or credited to other comprehensive income (loss). Revenue and expenses of the Company's consolidated foreign operations are translated at average rates of exchange prevailing during the year. Gains and losses on foreign currency transactions are included in expenses and were not significant in either fiscal 2003 or 2002.

## NOTES TO CONSOLIDATED FINANCIAL STATEMENTS
(dollars in thousands, except per share data) (Continued)

### Note 1—Summary of Significant Accounting Policies (Continued)

*Revenue Recognition*

The Company recognizes sales, net of estimated returns, at the time the member takes possession of merchandise or receives services. When the Company collects payment from customers prior to the transfer of ownership of merchandise or the performance of services, the amount received is recorded as deferred revenue. The Company provides for estimated sales returns based on historical returns levels. The reserve for sales returns (sales returns net of cost of goods sold) was $4,869 and $3,507 at August 31, 2003 and September 1, 2002, respectively.

Membership fee revenue represents annual membership fees paid by substantially all of the Company's members. The Company accounts for membership fee revenue on a "deferred basis," whereby membership fee revenue is recognized ratably over the one-year life of the membership. The Company's Executive members qualify for a 2% reward (which can be redeemed at Costco warehouses), up to a maximum of $500 per year, on all qualified purchases made at Costco. The Company accounts for this 2% reward as a reduction in sales, with the related liability being classified within other current liabilities. The sales reduction and corresponding liability are computed after giving effect to the estimated impact of non-redemptions based on historical data. The reduction in sales for the fiscal years ended August 31, 2003, September 1, 2002 and September 2, 2001, and the related liability as of those dates were as follows:

| | Fiscal Year Ended | | |
| --- | --- | --- | --- |
| | August 31, 2003 | September 1, 2002 | September 2, 2001 |
| Two-percent reward sales reduction . . . . . . . . . . . . . . . . . . . . . . | $169,612 | $143,637 | $84,243 |
| Two-percent unredeemed reward liability . . . . . . . . . . . . . . . . . | $114,681 | $ 94,448 | $57,840 |

*Merchandise Costs*

Merchandise costs consist of the purchase price of inventory sold, inbound shipping charges and all costs related to our depot operations, including freight from depots to selling warehouses. Merchandise costs also include salaries, benefits, depreciation on production equipment, and other related expenses incurred in certain fresh foods and ancillary departments.

*Selling, General and Administrative Expenses*

Selling, general and administrative expenses consist primarily of salaries, benefits and workers' compensation costs for warehouse employees, other than fresh foods and certain ancillary businesses, as well as all regional and home office employees, including buying personnel. Selling, general and administrative expenses also include utilities, bank charges and substantially all building and equipment depreciation, as well as other operating costs incurred to support warehouse operations.

*Marketing and Promotional Expenses*

Costco's policy is generally to limit marketing and promotional expenses to new warehouse openings, occasional direct mail marketing to prospective new members and annual direct mail marketing programs to existing members promoting selected merchandise. Marketing and promotional costs are expensed as incurred.

*Preopening Expenses*

Preopening expenses related to new warehouses, major remodels/expansions, regional offices and other startup operations are expensed as incurred.

## Note 1—Summary of Significant Accounting Policies (Continued)

*Stock-Based Compensation*

The Company adopted the fair value based method of recording stock options consistent with SFAS No. 123 "Accounting for Stock-Based Compensation," for all employee stock options granted subsequent to fiscal year end 2002. Specifically, the Company adopted SFAS No. 123 using the "prospective method" with guidance provided from SFAS No. 148 "Accounting for Stock-Based Compensation—Transition and Disclosure." All employee stock option grants made in fiscal 2003 and in future years will be expensed over the stock option vesting period based on the fair value at the date the options are granted. Prior to fiscal 2003 the Company applied Accounting Principles Board Opinion (APB) No. 25 and related interpretations in accounting for stock options. Because the Company granted stock options to employees at exercise prices equal to fair market value on the date of grant, accordingly, no compensation cost was recognized for option grants.

Had compensation costs for the Company's stock-based compensation plans been determined based on the fair value at the grant dates for awards made prior to fiscal 2003, under those plans and consistent with SFAS No. 123, the Company's net income and net income per share would have been reduced to the pro forma amounts indicated below:

| | Fiscal Year Ended | | |
| --- | --- | --- | --- |
| | August 31, 2003 | September 1, 2002 | September 2, 2001 |
| Net income, as reported | $721,000 | $699,983 | $602,089 |
| Add: Stock-based employee compensation expense included in reported net income, net of related tax effects | 7,513 | — | — |
| Deduct: Total stock-based employee compensation expense determined under fair value based methods for all awards, net of related tax effects | (70,257) | (75,743) | (65,077) |
| Pro-forma net income | $658,256 | $624,240 | $537,012 |
| Earnings per share: | | | |
| Basic—as reported | $ 1.58 | $ 1.54 | $ 1.34 |
| Basic—pro-forma | $ 1.44 | $ 1.38 | $ 1.19 |
| Diluted—as reported | $ 1.53 | $ 1.48 | $ 1.29 |
| Diluted—pro-forma | $ 1.40 | $ 1.32 | $ 1.15 |

*Fair Value of Financial Instruments*

The carrying value of the Company's financial instruments, including cash and cash equivalents, short-term investments and receivables approximate fair value due to their short-term nature or variable interest rates. The fair value of fixed rate debt at August 31, 2003 and September 1, 2002 was $1,415,252 and $1,382,569, respectively.

*Reorganization of Canadian Administrative Operations*

On January 17, 2001, the Company announced plans to reorganize and consolidate the administration of its operations in Canada. Total costs related to the reorganization were $26,765 pre-tax, of which $7,765 pre-tax ($4,775 after-tax, or $.01 per diluted share) was expensed in fiscal 2002 and $19,000 pre-tax ($11,400 after-tax, or $.02 per diluted share) was expensed in fiscal 2001 and reported as part of the provision for impaired assets and closing costs. These costs consisted primarily of employee severance, implementation and consolidation of support systems and employee relocation. The reorganization was completed in the first quarter of fiscal 2002.

## NOTES TO CONSOLIDATED FINANCIAL STATEMENTS
### (dollars in thousands, except per share data) (Continued)

### Note 1—Summary of Significant Accounting Policies (Continued)

*Closing Costs*

Warehouse closing costs incurred relate principally to the Company's efforts to relocate certain warehouses that were not otherwise impaired to larger and better-located facilities. The provision for fiscal 2003 included charges of $11,836 for warehouse closing expenses and $2,967 for losses on the sale of real property. The fiscal 2002 provision included charges of $13,683 for warehouse closing expenses and $7,765 for Canadian administrative reorganization, which were offset by $398 of net gains on the sale of real property. As of August 31, 2003, the Company's reserve for warehouse closing costs was $8,609, of which $7,833 related to lease obligations. This compares to a reserve for warehouse closing costs of $11,845 at September 1, 2002, of which $10,395 related to lease obligations.

*Interest Income and Other*

Interest income and other includes:

|  | Fiscal Year Ended | | |
|---|---|---|---|
|  | August 31, 2003 | September 1, 2002 | September 2, 2001 |
| Interest income | $21,200 | $16,005 | $25,908 |
| Minority interest/earnings of affiliates and other | 17,325 | 19,740 | 17,330 |
| Total | $38,525 | $35,745 | $43,238 |

*Income Taxes*

The Company accounts for income taxes under the provisions of SFAS No. 109, "Accounting for Income Taxes." That standard requires companies to account for deferred income taxes using the asset and liability method.

Under the asset and liability method of SFAS No. 109, deferred tax assets and liabilities are recognized for the future tax consequences attributed to differences between the financial statement carrying amounts of existing assets and liabilities and their respective tax bases and tax credits and loss carry-forwards. Deferred tax assets and liabilities are measured using enacted tax rates expected to apply to taxable income in the years in which those temporary differences and carry-forwards are expected to be recovered or settled. The effect on deferred tax assets and liabilities of a change in tax rates is recognized in income in the period that includes the enactment date. A valuation allowance is established when necessary to reduce deferred tax assets to amounts expected to be realized.

## Note 1—Summary of Significant Accounting Policies (Continued)

*Net Income Per Common and Common Equivalent Share*

The following data show the amounts used in computing earnings per share and the effect on income and the weighted average number of shares of dilutive potential common stock.

| | 52 Weeks Ended August 31, 2003 | 52 Weeks Ended September 1, 2002 | 52 Weeks Ended September 2, 2001 |
|---|---|---|---|
| Net income available to common stockholders used in basic EPS | $721,000 | $699,983 | $602,089 |
| Interest on convertible bonds, net of tax | 11,109 | 10,602 | 9,992 |
| Net income available to common stockholders after assumed conversions of dilutive securities | $732,109 | $710,585 | $612,081 |
| Weighted average number of common shares used in basic EPS (000's) | 456,335 | 453,650 | 449,631 |
| Stock options (000's) | 3,646 | 6,267 | 6,851 |
| Conversion of convertible bonds (000's) | 19,345 | 19,345 | 19,345 |
| Weighted number of common shares and dilutive potential common stock used in diluted EPS (000's) | 479,326 | 479,262 | 475,827 |

The diluted share base calculation for fiscal years ended August 31, 2003, September 1, 2002 and September 2, 2001, excludes 33,362,000, 6,908,000 and 7,108,000 stock options outstanding, respectively. These options are excluded due to their anti-dilutive effect.

On November 30, 2001, the Company's Board of Directors approved a stock repurchase program authorizing the repurchase of up to $500,000 of Costco Common Stock through November 30, 2004. Under the program, the Company can repurchase shares at any time in the open market or in private transactions as market conditions warrant. The repurchased shares would constitute authorized, but non-issued shares and would be used for general corporate purposes, including stock option grants under stock option programs. To date, no shares have been repurchased under this program.

*Recent Accounting Pronouncements*

In June 2001, the Financial Accounting Standards Board (FASB) issued SFAS No. 143, "Accounting for Asset Retirement Obligations," which provides the accounting requirements for retirement obligations associated with tangible long-lived assets. SFAS No. 143 requires entities to record the fair value of a liability for an asset retirement obligation in the period in which it is incurred. SFAS No. 143 was effective for the Company's 2003 fiscal year. The adoption of SFAS No. 143 did not have a material impact on the Company's consolidated results of operations, financial position or cash flows.

In August 2001, the FASB issued SFAS No. 144, "Accounting for the Impairment or Disposal of Long-Lived Assets," effective for the Company's 2003 fiscal year. This Statement supersedes FASB Statement No. 121, "Accounting for the Impairment of Long-Lived Assets and for Long-Lived Assets to Be Disposed Of," and other related accounting guidance. The adoption of SFAS No. 144 did not have a material impact on the Company's consolidated results of operations, financial position, or cash flows.

In June 2002, the FASB issued SFAS No. 146, "Accounting for Costs Associated with Exit or Disposal Activities." This statement addresses financial accounting and reporting for costs associated with exit or disposal activities and nullifies Emerging Issues Task Force (EITF) Issue No. 94-3, "Liability Recognition for Certain Employee Termination Benefits and Other Costs to Exit an Activity (including Certain Costs Incurred in a Restructuring)." This statement requires that a liability for a cost associated with an exit or disposal activity should be recognized at fair value when the liability is incurred. SFAS No. 146 was effective for the Company's

**NOTES TO CONSOLIDATED FINANCIAL STATEMENTS**
**(dollars in thousands, except per share data) (Continued)**

**Note 1—Summary of Significant Accounting Policies (Continued)**

2003 fiscal year. The adoption of SFAS No. 146 did not have a material impact on the Company's consolidated results of operations, financial position or cash flows, other than to impact the timing of charges related to future warehouse relocations.

In December 2002, the FASB issued SFAS No. 148, "Accounting for Stock-Based Compensation—Transition and Disclosure," which provides guidance for transition to the fair value based method of accounting for stock-based employee compensation and the required financial statement disclosure. Effective September 3, 2002 the Company adopted the fair value based method of accounting for stock-based compensation. See Note (1) and Note (5) of the Company's consolidated financial statements.

In November 2002, the FASB issued FASB Interpretation No. 45, "Guarantor's Accounting and Disclosure Requirements for Guarantees, Including Indirect Guarantees of Indebtedness of Others." This standard established financial statement disclosure requirements for companies that enter into or modify certain types of guarantees subsequent to December 31, 2002. Beginning in calendar 2003, the standard requires that companies record the fair value of certain types of guarantees as a liability in the financial statements. The adoption of this interpretation did not have a material impact on the Company's consolidated results of operations, financial position or cash flows.

In January 2003, the FASB issued FASB Interpretation No. 46 "Consolidation of Variable Interest Entities." In general, a variable interest entity is a corporation, partnership, trust, or any other legal structure used for business purposes that either does not have equity investors with voting rights or has equity investors that do not provide sufficient financial resources for the entity to support its activities. Interpretation No. 46 requires a variable interest entity to be consolidated by a company if that company is subject to a majority of the risk of loss from the variable interest entity's activities or entitled to receive a majority of the entity's residual returns or both. The consolidation requirements of Interpretation No. 46 apply immediately to variable interest entities created after January 31, 2003. The consolidation requirements apply to older entities in the first fiscal year or interim period beginning after June 15, 2003. Certain of the disclosure requirements apply in all financial statements issued after January 31, 2003, regardless of when the variable interest entity was established. The adoption of the Interpretation did not have a material impact on the Company's consolidated results of operation, financial position or cash flows.

In November 2002, the EITF reached a consensus on EITF 00-21, "Revenue Arrangements with Multiple Deliverables," with respect to determining when and how to allocate revenue from sales with multiple deliverables. The EITF 00-21 consensus provides a framework for determining when and how to allocate revenue from sales with multiple deliverables based on a determination of whether the multiple deliverables qualify to be accounted for as separate units of accounting. The consensus is effective prospectively for arrangements entered into in fiscal periods beginning after June 15, 2003. The adoption of this consensus did not have a material impact on the Company's consolidated results of operations, financial position or cash flows.

In November 2002, the EITF reached consensus on certain issues discussed in EITF 02-16, "Accounting by a Customer (Including a Reseller) for Certain Consideration Received from a Vendor," with respect to determining how a reseller should characterize consideration received from a vendor and when to recognize and how to measure that consideration in its income statement. Requirements for recognizing volume-based rebates are effective for arrangements entered into or modified after November 21, 2002 and resellers with other supplier payments should generally apply the new rules prospectively for agreements entered into or modified after December 31, 2002. The adoption of this consensus did not have a material impact on the Company's consolidated results of operations, financial position or cash flows in fiscal 2003 and is not expected to have a significant impact in the future on an annual basis. However, the Company does expect the adoption of this consensus to impact interim quarterly financial information, commencing with the first quarter of fiscal 2004, as the applica-

## Note 1—Summary of Significant Accounting Policies (Continued)

tion of the consensus will result in a change in the timing for the recognition of some vendor allowances for certain agreements entered into subsequent to December 31, 2002.

### Use of Estimates

The preparation of financial statements in conformity with accounting principles generally accepted in the United States requires management to make estimates and assumptions that affect the reported amounts of assets and liabilities at the date of the financial statements and the reported amounts of revenues and expenses during the reporting period. Actual results could differ from those estimates.

## Note 2—Comprehensive Income

Comprehensive income is net income, plus certain other items that are recorded directly to stockholders' equity. Comprehensive income was $800,745 for fiscal 2003 and $715,868 for fiscal 2002. Foreign currency translation adjustments are the predominant components applied to net income to calculate the Company's comprehensive income.

## Note 3—Debt

### Bank Lines of Credit and Commercial Paper Programs

The Company has in place a $500,000 commercial paper program supported by a $300,000 bank credit facility with a group of 10 banks, of which $150,000 expires on November 9, 2004 and $150,000 expires on November 15, 2005. At August 31, 2003, no amounts were outstanding under the commercial paper program and no amounts were outstanding under the credit facility.

In addition, a wholly owned Canadian subsidiary has a $144,000 commercial paper program supported by a $43,000 bank credit facility with a Canadian bank, which expires in March 2004. At August 31, 2003, no amounts were outstanding under the Canadian commercial paper program or the bank credit facility.

The Company has agreed to limit the combined amount outstanding under the U.S. and Canadian commercial paper programs to the $343,000 combined amounts of the respective supporting bank credit facilities.

The Company's wholly-owned Japanese subsidiary has a short-term ¥3 billion ($25,782) bank line of credit, which expires in November 2004. At August 31, 2003, no amounts were outstanding under the line of credit.

The Company's UK subsidiary has a £60 million ($94,842) bank revolving credit facility and a £20 million ($31,614) bank overdraft facility, both expiring in February 2007. At August 31, 2003, $47,421 was outstanding under the revolving credit facility with an applicable interest rate of 4.413% and no amounts were outstanding under the bank overdraft facility.

### Letters of Credit

The Company has letter of credit facilities (for commercial and standby letters of credit), totaling approximately $369,000. The outstanding commitments under these facilities at August 31, 2003 totaled approximately $125,000, including approximately $44,000 in standby letters of credit.

# Using a Calculator and Computer Keypad

## KINDS OF CALCULATORS

Many different models of calculators, both desktop and handheld, are available. All calculators have their own features and particular placement of operating keys. Therefore, it is necessary to refer to the operator's manual for specific instructions and locations of the operating keys for the calculator being used. A typical keyboard of a desktop calculator is shown in the illustration.

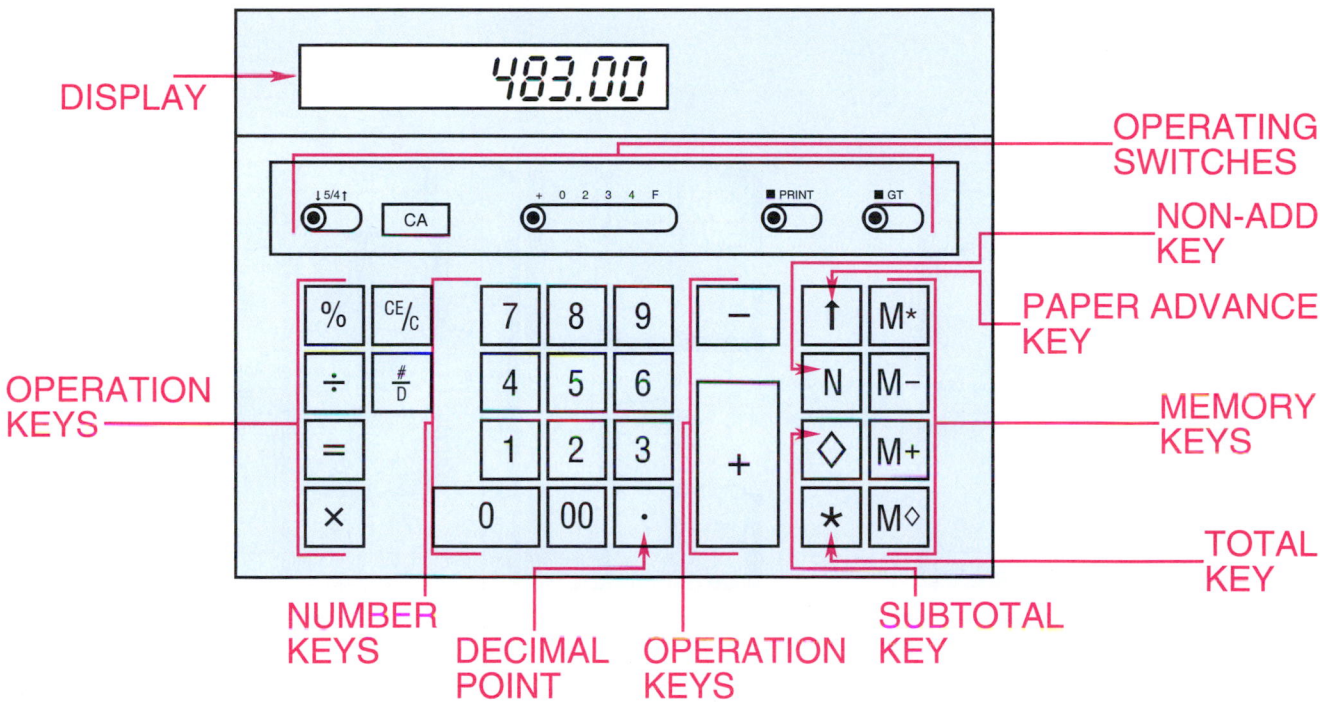

DISPLAY

OPERATING SWITCHES

NON-ADD KEY

PAPER ADVANCE KEY

OPERATION KEYS

MEMORY KEYS

TOTAL KEY

NUMBER KEYS

DECIMAL POINT

OPERATION KEYS

SUBTOTAL KEY

## DESKTOP CALCULATOR SETTINGS

Several operating switches on a desktop calculator must be engaged before the calculator will produce the desired results.

The *decimal selector* sets the appropriate decimal places necessary for the numbers that will be entered. For example, if the decimal selector is set at 2, both the numbers entered and the answer will have two decimal places. If the decimal selector is set at F, the calculator automatically sets the decimal places. The F setting allows the answer to be unrounded and carried out to the maximum number of decimal places possible.

The *decimal rounding selector* rounds the answers. The down arrow position will drop any digits beyond the last digit desired. The up arrow position will drop any digits beyond the last digit desired and round the last digit up. In the 5/4 position, the calculator rounds the last desired digit up only when the following digit is 5 or greater. If the following digit is less than 5, the last desired digit remains unchanged.

The *GT* or *grand total switch* in the on position accumulates totals.

## KINDS OF COMPUTER KEYBOARDS

The computer has a keypad on the right side of the keyboard, called the *numeric keypad*. Even though several styles of keyboards are found, there are two basic layouts for the numeric keypad. The standard layout and enhanced layout are shown in the illustration. On the standard keyboard, the directional arrow keys are found on the number keys. To use the numbers, press the key called *Num Lock*. (This key is found above the "7" key.) When the Num Lock is turned on, numbers are entered when the keys on the keypad are pressed. When the Num Lock is off, the arrow, Home, Page Up, Page Down, End, Insert, and Delete keys can be used.

The enhanced keyboards have the arrow keys and the other directional keys mentioned above to the left of the numeric keypad. When using the keypad on an enhanced keyboard, Num Lock can remain on.

The asterisk (*) performs a different function on the computer than the calculator. The asterisk on the calculator is used for the total while the computer uses it for multiplication.

Another difference is the division key. The computer key is the forward slash key (/). The calculator key uses the division key (÷).

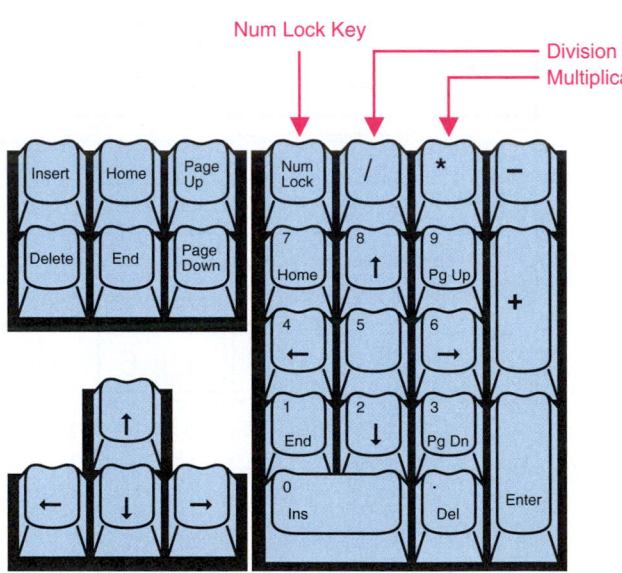

Num Lock Key

Division Key
Multiplication Key

Standard
Keyboard Layout

Enhanced
Keyboard Layout

## TEN-KEY TOUCH SYSTEM

Striking the numbers 0 to 9 on a calculator or numeric keypad without looking at the keyboard is called the *touch system*. Using the touch system develops both speed and accuracy.

The 4, 5, and 6 keys are called the *home row*. If the right hand is used for the keyboard, the index finger is placed on the 4 key, the middle finger on the 5 key, and the ring finger on the 6 key. If the left hand is used, the ring finger is

placed on the 4 key, the middle finger on the 5 key, and the index finger on the 6 key.

Place the fingers on the home row keys. Curve the fingers and keep the wrist straight. These keys may feel slightly concaved or the 5 key may have a raised dot. The differences in the home row allow the operator to recognize the home row by touch rather than by sight.

Maintain the position of the fingers on the home row. The finger used to strike the 4 key will also strike the 7 key and the 1 key. Stretch the finger up to reach the 7 key; then stretch the finger down to reach the 1 key. Visualize the position of these keys.

Again, place the fingers on the home row. Stretch the finger that strikes the 5 key up to reach the 8 key, then down to reach the 2 key. Likewise, stretch the finger that strikes the 6 key up to strike the 9 key and down to strike the 3 key. This same finger will stretch down again to hit the decimal point.

If the right hand is used, the thumb will be used to strike the 0 and 00 keys and the little finger to strike the addition key. If the left hand is used, the little finger will be used to strike the 0 and 00 keys and the thumb to strike the addition key.

## HANDHELD CALCULATORS

Handheld calculators are slightly different from desktop calculators, not only in their size and features but also in their operation. Refer to the operator's manual for specific instructions for the calculator being used.

On a handheld calculator, the numeric keys are usually very close together. In addition, the keys do not respond to touch as easily as on a desktop calculator. Therefore, the touch system is usually not used on a handheld calculator.

## PERFORMING MATHEMATICAL OPERATIONS ON DESKTOP CALCULATORS

Mathematical operations can be performed on a calculator both quickly and efficiently. The basic operations of addition, subtraction, multiplication, and division are used frequently on a calculator.

### Addition

Each number to be added is called an *addend*. The answer to an addition problem is called the *sum*.

Addition is performed by entering an addend and striking the addition key (+). All numbers are entered on a calculator in the exact order they are given. To enter the number 4,455.65, strike the 4, 4, 5, 5, decimal, 6, and 5 keys in that order, and then strike the addition key. Commas are not entered. Continue in this manner until all addends have been entered. To obtain the sum, strike the total key on the calculator.

### Subtraction

The top number or first number of a subtraction problem is called the *minuend*. The number to be subtracted from the minuend is called the *subtrahend*. The answer to a subtraction problem is called the *difference*.

Subtraction is performed by first entering the minuend and striking the addition key (+). The subtrahend is then entered, followed by the minus key (−), followed by the total key.

### Multiplication

The number to be multiplied is called the *multiplicand*. The number of times the multiplicand will be multiplied is called the *multiplier*. The answer to a multiplication problem is called the *product*.

Multiplication is performed by entering the multiplicand and striking the multiplication key (×). The multiplier is then entered, followed by the equals key (=). The calculator will automatically multiply and give the product.

### Division

The number to be divided is called the *dividend*. The number the dividend will be divided by is called the *divisor*. The answer to a division problem is called the *quotient*.

Division is performed by entering the dividend and striking the division key (÷). The divisor is then entered, followed by the equals key (=). The calculator will automatically divide and give the quotient.

### Correcting Errors

If an error is made while using a calculator, several methods of correction may be used. If an incorrect number has been entered and the addition key or equals key has not yet been struck, strike the clear entry (CE) key one time.

This key will clear only the last number that was entered. However, if the clear entry key is depressed more than one time, the entire problem will be cleared on some calculators. If an incorrect number has been entered and the addition key has been struck, strike the minus key one time only. This will automatically subtract the last number added, thus removing it from the total.

## PERFORMING MATHEMATICAL OPERATIONS ON COMPUTERS AND HANDHELD CALCULATORS

On a computer keypad or a handheld calculator, addition is performed in much the same way as on a desktop calculator. However, after the + key is depressed, the display usually shows the accumulated total. Therefore, the total key is not found. Some computer programs will not calculate the total until Enter is pressed.

Subtraction is performed differently on many computer keypads and handheld calculators. The minuend is usually entered, followed by the minus (−) key. Then the subtrahend is entered. Pressing either the + key or the = key will display the difference. Some computer programs will not calculate the difference until Enter is pressed.

Multiplication and division are performed the same way on a computer keypad and handheld calculator as on a desktop calculator. Keep in mind that computers use the * for multiplication and / for division.

## SAFETY CONCERNS

Whenever electrical equipment such as a calculator or computer is being operated in a classroom or office, several safety rules apply. These rules protect the operator of the equipment, other persons in the environment, and the equipment itself.

1. Do not unplug equipment by pulling on the electrical cord. Instead, grasp the plug at the outlet and remove it.
2. Do not stretch electrical cords across an aisle where someone might trip over them.
3. Avoid food and beverages near the equipment where a spill might result in an electrical short.
4. Do not attempt to remove the cover of a calculator, computer, or keyboard for any reason while the power is turned on.
5. Do not attempt to repair equipment while it is plugged in.
6. Always turn the power off or unplug equipment when finished using it.

## CALCULATION DRILLS

### Instructions for Desktop Calculators
Complete each drill using the touch method. Set the decimal selector at the setting indicated in each drill. Compare the answer on the calculator to the answer in the book. If the two are the same, progress to the next problem. It is not necessary to enter 00 in the cents column if the decimal selector is set at 0-F. However, digits other than zeros in the cents column must be entered preceded by a decimal point.

### Instructions for Computer Keypads
Complete each drill using the touch method. There is no decimal selector on computer keypads. Set the number of decimal places as directed in the instructions for the computer program. In spreadsheets, for example, use the formatting options to set the number of decimal places. When the drill indicates "F" for floating, leave the computer application in its default format. Compare the answer on the computer

monitor to the answer in the book. If the two are the same, progress to the next problem. It is not necessary to enter 00 in the cents column. However, digits other than zeros in the cents column must be entered preceded by a decimal point.

## DRILL C-1  Performing addition using the home row keys
### Decimal Selector—2

| | | | | |
|---|---|---|---|---|
| 4.00 | 44.00 | 444.00 | 4,444.00 | 44,444.00 |
| 5.00 | 55.00 | 555.00 | 5,555.00 | 55,555.00 |
| 6.00 | 66.00 | 666.00 | 6,666.00 | 66,666.00 |
| 5.00 | 45.00 | 455.00 | 4,455.00 | 44,556.00 |
| 4.00 | 46.00 | 466.00 | 4,466.00 | 44,565.00 |
| 5.00 | 54.00 | 544.00 | 5,544.00 | 55,446.00 |
| 6.00 | 56.00 | 566.00 | 5,566.00 | 55,664.00 |
| 5.00 | 65.00 | 655.00 | 6,655.00 | 66,554.00 |
| 4.00 | 64.00 | 644.00 | 6,644.00 | 66,555.00 |
| 5.00 | 66.00 | 654.00 | 6,545.00 | 65,465.00 |
| 49.00 | 561.00 | 5,649.00 | 56,540.00 | 565,470.00 |

## DRILL C-2  Performing addition using the 0, 1, 4, and 7 keys
### Decimal Selector—2

| | | | | |
|---|---|---|---|---|
| 4.00 | 11.00 | 444.00 | 4,440.00 | 44,000.00 |
| 7.00 | 44.00 | 777.00 | 7,770.00 | 77,000.00 |
| 4.00 | 74.00 | 111.00 | 1,110.00 | 11,000.00 |
| 1.00 | 71.00 | 741.00 | 4,400.00 | 41,000.00 |
| 4.00 | 70.00 | 740.00 | 1,100.00 | 71,000.00 |
| 7.00 | 10.00 | 101.00 | 4,007.00 | 10,000.00 |
| 4.00 | 14.00 | 140.00 | 7,001.00 | 10,100.00 |
| 1.00 | 17.00 | 701.00 | 1,007.00 | 40,100.00 |
| 4.00 | 40.00 | 700.00 | 1,004.00 | 70,100.00 |
| 7.00 | 77.00 | 407.00 | 7,700.00 | 74,100.00 |
| 43.00 | 428.00 | 4,862.00 | 39,539.00 | 448,400.00 |

## DRILL C-3  Performing addition using the 2, 5, and 8 keys
### Decimal Selector—2

| | | | | |
|---|---|---|---|---|
| 5.00 | 58.00 | 588.00 | 8,888.00 | 88,855.00 |
| 8.00 | 52.00 | 522.00 | 5,555.00 | 88,822.00 |
| 5.00 | 85.00 | 888.00 | 2,222.00 | 88,852.00 |
| 2.00 | 52.00 | 222.00 | 8,525.00 | 88,222.00 |
| 5.00 | 25.00 | 258.00 | 2,585.00 | 85,258.00 |
| 8.00 | 58.00 | 852.00 | 8,258.00 | 22,255.00 |
| 5.00 | 82.00 | 225.00 | 8,585.00 | 22,288.00 |
| 2.00 | 28.00 | 885.00 | 5,258.00 | 22,258.00 |
| 5.00 | 88.00 | 882.00 | 2,852.00 | 22,888.00 |
| 8.00 | 22.00 | 228.00 | 2,288.00 | 25,852.00 |
| 53.00 | 550.00 | 5,550.00 | 55,016.00 | 555,550.00 |

## DRILL C-4 Performing addition using the 3, 6, 9, and decimal point keys
### Decimal Selector—2

| | | | | |
|---|---|---|---|---|
| 6.00 | 66.66 | 666.66 | 6,666.99 | 66,699.33 |
| 9.00 | 99.99 | 999.99 | 9,999.66 | 99,966.66 |
| 6.00 | 33.33 | 333.33 | 3,333.99 | 33,366.33 |
| 3.00 | 33.66 | 666.99 | 3,366.99 | 36,963.36 |
| 6.36 | 33.99 | 999.66 | 6,699.33 | 69,636.36 |
| 3.36 | 99.66 | 333.66 | 9,966.33 | 33,333.66 |
| 9.36 | 99.33 | 696.36 | 9,636.69 | 66,666.99 |
| 9.63 | 33.36 | 369.63 | 3,696.36 | 99,999.33 |
| 6.33 | 33.69 | 336.69 | 6,963.99 | 96,369.63 |
| 9.93 | 69.63 | 963.36 | 6,699.33 | 36,963.36 |
| 68.97 | 603.30 | 6,366.33 | 67,029.66 | 639,965.01 |

## DRILL C-5 Performing subtraction using all number keys
### Decimal Selector—F

| | | | | |
|---|---|---|---|---|
| 456.73 | 789.01 | 741.00 | 852.55 | 987.98 |
| −123.21 | −456.00 | −258.10 | −369.88 | −102.55 |
| 333.52 | 333.01 | 482.90 | 482.67 | 885.43 |

## DRILL C-6 Performing multiplication using all number keys
### Decimal Selector—F

| | | | | |
|---|---|---|---|---|
| 654.05 | 975.01 | 487.10 | 123.56 | 803.75 |
| × 12.66 | × 27.19 | × 30.21 | × 50.09 | × 1.45 |
| 8,280.273 | 26,510.5219 | 14,715.291 | 6,189.1204 | 1,165.4375 |

## DRILL C-7 Performing division using all number keys
### Decimal Selector—F

| | | | | |
|---|---|---|---|---|
| 900.56 | ÷ | 450.28 | = | 2. |
| 500.25 | ÷ | 100.05 | = | 5. |
| 135.66 | ÷ | 6.65 | = | 20.4 |
| 269.155 | ÷ | 105.55 | = | 2.550023685* |
| 985.66 | ÷ | 22.66 | = | 43.49779346* |

*Number of decimal places may vary, due to machine capacity.

# Recycling Problems

## RECYCLING PROBLEM 1-1

### Journalizing departmental purchases and cash payments

ShowRoom Floors has two departments: Carpeting and Linoleum. All of the vendors from which merchandise is purchased on account offer terms of 2/10, n/30. Source documents are abbreviated as follows: check, C; debit memorandum, DM; purchase invoice, P.

**Transactions:**

| | | |
|---|---|---|
| Nov. | 1. | Paid cash for administrative supplies, $62.50. C301. |
| | 2. | Paid cash for rent, $1,000.00. C302. |
| | 4. | Paid cash on account to Lyndale Linoleum, $2,763.60, covering P176 for linoleum for $2,820.00, less discount, $56.40. C303. |
| | 5. | Purchased carpeting on account from King Carpets, $3,740.00. P178. |
| | 7. | Paid cash on account to Floors and More, $1,651.30, covering P177 for linoleum for $1,685.00, less discount, $33.70. C304. |
| | 8. | Returned carpeting to King Carpets, $186.00, from P178. DM19. |
| | 10. | Purchased linoleum on account from Mercury Floors, $2,680.00. P179. |
| | 12. | Paid cash on account to King Carpets, $3,482.92, covering P178 for carpeting for $3,740.00, less DM19 for $186.00, and less discount, $71.08. C305. |
| | 14. | Purchased carpeting on account from Carpet Distributors, $2,670.00. P180. |
| | 14. | Paid cash for advertising, $82.50. C306. |
| | 15. | Returned linoleum to Floors and More, $212.40, from P177. DM20. |
| | 15. | Returned carpeting to Carpet Distributors, $450.00, from P180. DM21. |
| | 17. | Paid cash on account to Mercury Floors, $2,626.40, covering P179 for linoleum for $2,680.00, less discount, $53.60. C307. |
| | 18. | Purchased linoleum on account from Mercury Floors, $1,360.00. P181. |
| | 19. | Paid cash for administrative supplies, $62.75. C308. |
| | 21. | Paid cash on account to Carpet Distributors, $2,175.60, covering P180 for carpeting for $2,670.00, less DM21 for $450.00, and less discount, $44.40. C309. |
| | 24. | Purchased carpeting on account from King Carpets, $1,925.00. P182. |
| | 25. | Paid cash on account to Mercury Floors, $1,332.80, covering P181 for linoleum for $1,360.00, less discount, $27.20. C310. |
| | 28. | Purchased linoleum on account from Lyndale Linoleum, $4,340.00. P183. |
| | 30. | Paid cash to replenish the petty cash fund, $214.00: administrative supplies, $65.50; advertising, $87.30; miscellaneous, $61.20. C311. |

**Instructions:**

1. Journalize the transactions completed during November of the current year. Page 11 of a purchases journal, page 8 of a general journal, and page 21 of a cash payments journal are provided in the *Recycling Problem Working Papers*.
2. Prove and rule the special journals.

**Journalizing department sales, sales returns and allowances, and cash receipts**

Phoenix Computing, Inc., has two departments: Hardware and Software.

### Instructions:

1. Journalize the transactions completed during April of the current year. Calculate and record sales tax on all sales and sales returns and allowances as described in this chapter. Page 4 of a sales journal and a general journal and page 7 of a cash receipts journal are provided in the *Recycling Problem Working Papers*. Phoenix Computing offers its customers terms of 2/10, n/30. The sales tax rate is 5%. Source documents are abbreviated as follows: credit memorandum, CM; receipt, R; sales invoice, S; terminal summary, TS.

### Transactions:

Apr.
1. Sold hardware on account to Davis Design Co., $1,640.00, plus sales tax. S119.
2. Recorded cash and credit card sales: hardware, $3,170.00; software, $2,690.00; plus sales tax. TS22.
5. Received cash on account from Western Co., for software purchased on S116 for $176.40, less discount. R72.
5. Granted credit to Odum Personnel Agency for software returned, $30.00, plus sales tax, from S118. CM21.
8. Sold software on account to Geig Enterprises, $680.00, plus sales tax. S120.
8. Received cash on account from O'Leary Management Co., for hardware purchased on S117 for $892.50, less discount. R73.
9. Received cash on account from Odum Personnel Agency for software purchased on S118 for $176.40, less CM21 for $31.50, less discount. R74.
9. Recorded cash and credit card sales: hardware, $5,780.00; software, $4,620.00; plus sales tax. TS23.
11. Received cash on account from Davis Design Co. for hardware purchased on S119 for $1,722.00, less discount. R75.
13. Sold software on account to Newman Data Co., $75.00, plus sales tax. S121.
15. Sold hardware on account to O'Leary Management Co., $480.00, plus sales tax. S122.
16. Recorded cash and credit card sales: hardware, $6,210.00; software, $5,030.00; plus sales tax. TS24.
18. Received cash on account from Geig Enterprises, for software purchased on S120 for $714.00, less discount. R76.
19. Granted credit to Newman Data Co. for software returned, $18.00, plus sales tax, from S121. CM22.
22. Sold hardware on account to Melrose Schools, $1,640.00; no sales tax. S123.
23. Received cash on account from Newman Data Co. for software purchased on S121 for $78.75, less CM22 ($18.00 plus sales tax), less discount. R77.
23. Recorded cash and credit card sales: hardware, $6,630.00; software, $4,720.00; plus sales tax. TS25.
25. Received cash on account from O'Leary Management Co. for hardware purchased on S122 for $504.00, less discount. R78.
27. Sold software on account to Odum Personnel Agency, $100.00; plus sales tax. S124.
30. Recorded cash and credit card sales: hardware, $3,890.00; software, $3,930.00; plus sales tax. TS26.

2. Prove and rule the sales journal.
3. Prove and rule the cash receipts journal.

**Completing payroll records, journalizing payment of a payroll, and journalizing payroll taxes**

Sheridan Shoes has two departments: Men's Shoes and Women's Shoes. A biweekly payroll system of 26 pay periods per year is used. Salesclerks and employees in the accounting department are paid on an hourly basis and receive 1½ times the regular hourly rate for all hours worked over 80 each pay period. Departmental supervisors are paid a biweekly salary and receive monthly commissions of 1% of net sales. Commissions are paid in the first pay period of the following month.

**Instructions:**

1. In the *Recycling Problem Working Papers*, prepare the commissions record for each departmental supervisor for the month ended January 31 of the current year. Use the basic payroll information provided in the problem table. The following additional information is needed to complete the commission records.
   a. Men's Shoes department: sales on account, $5,143.77; cash and credit card sales, $9,656.04; sales discount, $115.17; sales returns and allowances, $389.94.
   b. Women's Shoes department: sales on account, $6,712.50; cash and credit card sales, $9,320.40; sales discount, $124.30; sales returns and allowances, $517.60.

| Employee | | Position | Dept. | Marital Status | Allow. | Total Hours | Regular Pay | Overtime Pay |
|---|---|---|---|---|---|---|---|---|
| No. | Name | | | | | | | |
| 1 | Aldrich, Joan J. | Salesclerk | W | M | 2 | 83 | $520.00 | $29.25 |
| 2 | Bryant, Mark K. | Supervisor | M | S | 1 | — | 525.00 | — |
| 3 | Colfax, Mary D. | Clerk | A | S | 2 | 82 | 520.00 | 19.50 |
| 4 | Emerson, Theodore A. | Salesclerk | M | M | 3 | 80 | 525.00 | — |
| 5 | James, Kelly A. | Salesclerk | W | M | 2 | 84 | 600.00 | 45.00 |
| 6 | Newton, Loretta M. | Supervisor | W | M | 4 | — | 610.00 | — |
| 7 | Penn, Joseph P. | Clerk | A | M | 3 | 82 | 648.00 | 24.30 |
| 8 | Russell, Eileen R. | Salesclerk | M | S | 1 | 84 | 440.00 | 33.00 |
| 9 | Thomas, Emily R. | Salesclerk | M | S | 1 | 83 | 456.00 | 25.65 |
| 10 | Washburn, Mark S. | Salesclerk | W | S | 2 | 83 | 448.00 | 25.20 |

Departments: Men's Shoes, M; Women's Shoes, W; Administrative, A

2. Prepare Sheridan Shoes' payroll register for the biweekly pay period ended February 13 and paid February 20 of the current year. The following additional data are needed to complete the payroll register.
   a. A deduction for federal tax is to be made from each employee's total earnings. Use the appropriate income tax withholding tables shown in Chapter 3.
   b. A deduction of 4.5% for state income tax is to be made from each employee's total earnings.
   c. A deduction of 6.2% for social security tax and 1.45% for Medicare tax is to be made from each employee's total earnings.
   d. All employees have dental insurance, $9.10, and health insurance, $13.40, deducted from their pay each biweekly pay period. Write the letter *D* in front of the dental insurance deduction and the letter *H* in front of the health insurance deduction.
3. Complete Joan Aldrich's employee earnings record for the third pay period ended February 13 of the current year. The following data about Joan Aldrich are needed to complete the record.
   a. Hourly rate, $6.50.
   b. Social security number, 514-30-2258.
4. Journalize the February 20 payroll payment, using page 4 of a cash payments journal. The source document is Check No. 125.
5. Use a grid similar to the one in Chapter 3 to calculate departmental payroll taxes. Employer tax rates are social security, 6.2%; Medicare, 1.45%; federal unemployment, 0.8%; and state unemployment, 5.4%.
6. Journalize the employer payroll taxes using page 4 of a general journal. Use February 20 of the current year as the date. The source document is Memorandum No. 10.

# RECYCLING PROBLEM 4-1

**Completing end-of-fiscal-period work for a merchandising business using departmental margins**

Lawn Care is a merchandising business that specializes in lawn mowers and mower parts. The trial balance on December 31 of the current year is provided in the Trial Balance columns of the work sheet in the *Recycling Problem Working Papers*.

**Instructions:**

1. Complete the 12-column work sheet for the year ended December 31 of the current year. The following adjusting information is available. Extend amounts to the proper debit and credit columns for Departmental Margin Statement—Mowers, Departmental Margin Statement—Parts, Income Statement, and Balance Sheet. Accounts on trial balance lines 55–63 are classified as indirect expenses.

### Adjustment Information, December 31

Uncollectible accounts expense—mowers estimated as 1.0% of sales on account.

| | |
|---|---|
| Sales on account for year | $78,000.00 |
| Merchandise Inventory—Mowers | $74,220.30 |
| Merchandise Inventory—Parts | 54,853.00 |
| Supplies Used—Administrative | 1,609.00 |
| Supplies Used—Mowers | 2,413.00 |
| Supplies Used—Parts | 4,023.00 |
| Insurance Expired | 5,550.00 |
| Depreciation Expense—Office Equipment | 359.00 |
| Depreciation Expense—Store Equipment, Mowers | 896.00 |
| Depreciation Expense—Store Equipment, Parts | 582.00 |
| Federal Income Tax Expense for the Year | 6,566.64 |

2. Prepare a departmental margin statement for each department. Calculate and record the component percentages for each item on the statements. Round percentage calculations to the nearest 0.1%.
3. Prepare an income statement. Calculate and record the component percentages for each item on the statements. Round percentage calculations to the nearest 0.1%.

# RECYCLING PROBLEM 5-1

**Journalizing transactions in a voucher system**

Walston Company uses a voucher system, including a voucher register and a check register, similar to those described in Chapter 5.

**Transactions:**

May  1.  Purchased merchandise on account from Moraska Company, $790.00. V30.
     2.  Bought sales supplies on account from Waldoch Supplies, $159.78. V31.
     4.  Bought store equipment on account from Murphy Equipment, $1,449.77. V32.
     8.  Purchased merchandise on account from Westhaven Company, $1,278.00. V33.
     8.  Paid cash to Moraska Company, $774.20, covering V30 for $790.00, less 2% discount, $15.80. C19.
    10.  Made a deposit in the checking account, $2,957.50.
    14.  Received invoice for delivery service from Davis Delivery, $29.50. V34.
    14.  Paid cash to Davis Delivery, $29.50, covering V34. C20.
    14.  Issued DM5 to Westhaven Company for return of merchandise purchased, $170.00. Cancel V33. V35.
    15.  Paid cash to Westhaven Company, $1,085.84, covering V35 for $1,108.00, less 2% discount, $22.16. C21.

16. Recorded voucher for semimonthly payroll for period ended May 15, $1,396.47 (total payroll: sales, $1,116.00; administrative, $744.00; less deductions: employee income tax payable—federal, $280.50; employee income tax payable—state, $34.23; social security tax payable, $120.90; Medicare tax payable, $27.90). V36.
16. Paid cash for semimonthly payroll, $1,396.47, covering V36. C22.
22. Paid cash to Waldoch Supplies, $159.78, covering V31. C23.
25. Bought office equipment on account from Yurik Company, $1,979.99. V37.
29. Made a deposit in the checking account, $1,279.51.
30. Purchased merchandise on account from Moraska Company, $1,875.95. V38.

**Instructions:**
1. Page 7 of a check register is provided in the *Recycling Problem Working Papers*. Record the bank balance brought forward on May 1 of the current year, $6,597.66.
2. Journalize the transactions completed during May of the current year. Use page 8 of a voucher register and page 7 of a check register. When a voucher is paid or canceled, make appropriate notations in the voucher register. Source documents are abbreviated as follows: check, C; debit memorandum, DM; voucher, V.
3. Prove and rule both the voucher register and the check register.

## RECYCLING PROBLEM 6-1

**Determining cost of merchandise inventory; estimating cost of merchandise using estimating methods; calculating merchandise inventory turnover ratio and average number of days' sales in merchandise inventory**

On December 31 of the current year, Rackley, Inc., took a periodic inventory. Selected information about the inventory is provided in the *Recycling Problem Working Papers*.

**Instructions:**
1. Calculate the total inventory costs using the fifo, lifo, and weighted-average inventory costing methods, using the form provided in the *Recycling Problems Working Papers*.
2. Rackley uses the weighted-average costing method to determine the cost of inventory. Use the market price to determine the cost of inventory using the lower of cost or market method. Total the Lower of Cost or Market column.
3. Calculate the corporation's estimated ending inventory using the gross profit method of estimating inventory. The gross profit percentage is 40%. The following information is obtained from the corporation's records on December 31 of the current year:

| Item | Cost | Retail |
|------|------|--------|
| Beginning merchandise inventory | $ 400.00 | $ 670.00 |
| Net purchases to date | 3,000.00 | 5,080.00 |
| Net sales to date | — | 4,600.00 |

4. Calculate the corporation's estimated ending inventory using the retail method of estimating inventory. Round the percentage to the nearest 0.1%.
5. Use the information and the estimated inventory calculated in Instruction 4. Calculate the corporation's merchandise inventory turnover ratio. Round the ratio to the nearest 0.1%.
6. Calculate the corporation's average number of days' sales in merchandise inventory. Round the amount to the nearest day.

## RECYCLING PROBLEM 7-1

**Estimating and journalizing uncollectible accounts using a percentage of net sales—allowance method; calculating and journalizing the adjusting entry for uncollectible accounts expense**

Motion, Inc., uses the allowance method of recording uncollectible accounts expense.

**Transactions:**

Jan.    18.   Wrote off Judith Tessman's past-due account as uncollectible, $43.96. M25.

Mar.    4.    Wrote off James York's past-due account as uncollectible, $80.85. M34.

Mar.    28.   Received cash in full payment of Judith Tessman's account, previously written off as uncollectible, $43.96. M45 and R83.

June    20.   Wrote off Beverly Axel's past-due account as uncollectible, $17.16. M63.

Oct.    7.    Wrote off Tanya Wadsworth's past-due account as uncollectible, $108.15. M79.

Dec.    11.   Received cash in full payment of James York's account, previously written off as uncollectible, $80.85. M87 and R97.

**Instructions:**

1. Journalize the transactions completed during the current year. Page 1 of a general journal and page 1 of a cash receipts journal are provided in the *Recycling Problem Working Papers*.

2. Journalize the adjusting entry for uncollectible accounts expense on December 31 of the current year. Motion, Inc., has the following account balances on December 31 before adjusting entries are recorded.

| | |
|---|---|
| Accounts Receivable | $ 19,768.25 |
| Sales | 104,463.79 |
| Sales Discount | 1,573.58 |
| Sales Returns and Allowances | 901.42 |

Motion, Inc., estimates that the amount of uncollectible accounts expense is equal to 0.5% of net sales.

3. If all the entries recorded in the general journal and cash receipts journal were posted, including the adjusting entry, what would be the new balance of Allowance for Uncollectible Accounts? The January 1 balance of Allowance for Uncollectible Accounts, before the transactions for the year were recorded, was $1,434.61.

## RECYCLING PROBLEM 8-1

**Journalizing transactions for plant assets**

Ludden, Inc., uses the straight-line method of calculating depreciation expense. Ludden uses one plant asset account, Office Equipment.

**Transactions:**

Jan. 5, 20X1.     Paid cash for chair, $200.00: estimated salvage value, none; estimated useful life, 2 years; Serial No., none. C30.

Mar. 3, 20X1.     Paid cash for desk, $650.00: estimated salvage value, $150.00; estimated useful life, 4 years; Serial No., D125. C45.

Jan. 5, 20X2.     Paid cash for file cabinet, $300.00: estimated salvage value, $75.00; estimated useful life, 5 years; Serial No., F325. C115.

July 3, 20X2.     Paid cash for table, $270.00: estimated salvage value, $20.00; estimated useful life, 10 years; Serial No., none. C170.

Jan. 3, 20X3.     Discarded chair bought in 20X1. M50.

Mar. 5, 20X3.     Received cash for sale of desk, Serial No., D125, $300.00. M55 and R50.

June 29, 20X3.    Paid cash, $200.00, plus old file cabinet, Serial No. F325, for new file cabinet: estimated salvage value of new cabinet, $80.00; estimated useful life of new cabinet, 5 years; Serial No. of new cabinet, F915. M70 and C200.

July 1, 20X3.     Paid cash for typewriter, $1,000.00: estimated salvage value, $200.00; estimated useful life, 5 years; Serial No., A6501M341. C230.

**Instructions:**

Journalize the transactions. Journalize an entry for additional depreciation expense if needed. Page 1 of a general journal, page 5 of a cash receipts journal, and page 5 of a cash payments journal are provided in the *Recycling Problem Working Papers*.

## RECYCLING PROBLEM 8-2

**Calculating depreciation expense**

On January 5 of the current year, Burdick, Inc., paid cash for a new company car, $15,000.00: estimated salvage value, $1,500.00; estimated useful life, 5 years. Forms used to prepare the depreciation tables are provided in the *Recycling Problem Working Papers*.

**Instructions:**
1. Prepare a depreciation table, similar to one in Chapter 8, showing depreciation expense calculated using the straight-line, declining-balance, and sum-of-the-years'-digits methods.
2. Assume that Burdick's car has an estimated useful life of 100,000 miles. Also assume that the car is driven the following number of miles: 1st year, 27,000; 2d year, 23,000; 3d year, 15,000; 4th year, 20,000; 5th year, 15,000. Prepare a depreciation table, similar to one in Chapter 8, using the production-unit method of calculating depreciation expense.

## RECYCLING PROBLEM 8-3

**Calculating and journalizing property tax**

Amluxson, Inc., has real property with an assessed value of $400,000.00. The tax rate in the city where the property is located is 5% of assessed value. Property tax is paid in two installments.

**Instructions:**
1. Calculate Amluxson's total annual property tax for the current year.
2. Journalize the payment of the first installment of property tax on May 1. Page 9 of a cash payments journal is provided in the *Recycling Problem Working Papers*. Check No. 142.

## RECYCLING PROBLEM 9-1

**Journalizing adjusting and reversing entries for prepaid expenses initially recorded as expenses and for accrued expenses**

Sutton, Inc., completed the following transactions during the current year. Sutton initially records prepaid expenses as expenses. Source documents are abbreviated as follows: check, C; note payable, NP.

**Transactions:**

Aug.  1.  Issued a 1-month, 10% note, $700.00. NP1.
Sept.  1.  Paid cash for the maturity value of NP1: principal, $700.00, plus interest, $5.83; total, $705.83. C95.
Sept.  1.  Issued a 150-day, 10% note, $1,300.00. NP2.
Oct.  1.  Issued a 120-day, 12% note, $1,500.00. NP3.
Dec.  1.  Discounted at 12% a 60-day non-interest-bearing note, $800.00; proceeds, $784.00, interest, $16.00. NP4.

**Instructions:**

1. Calculate the maturity dates for Notes Payable Nos. 2, 3, and 4.
2. Journalize the transactions. Page 15 of a cash receipts journal and page 17 of a cash payments journal are provided in the *Recycling Problem Working Papers*.
3. Sutton, Inc., has the following general ledger balances on December 31 of the current year before adjusting entries are recorded.

| | |
|---|---|
| Supplies Expense—Administrative | $600.00 |
| Supplies Expense—Sales | 900.00 |
| Insurance Expense | 800.00 |

Using the following adjustment information, journalize the adjusting entries for prepaid and accrued expenses on December 31. Use page 13 of a general journal.

**Adjustment Information, December 31**

| | |
|---|---|
| Administrative Supplies Inventory | $300.00 |
| Sales Supplies Inventory | 350.00 |
| Value of Prepaid Insurance | 400.00 |
| Remaining Prepaid Interest | 8.00 |
| Accrued Interest on Notes Payable | 89.19 |
| Accrued Salaries—Administrative | 250.00 |
| Accrued Salaries—Sales | 215.00 |
| Accrued Payroll Taxes—Social Security Tax | 30.23 |
| Accrued Payroll Taxes—Medicare Tax | 6.97 |
| Accrued Payroll Taxes—Federal Unemployment Tax | 3.72 |
| Accrued Payroll Taxes—State Unemployment Tax | 25.11 |
| Accrued Federal Income Tax | 400.00 |

4. Journalize the reversing entries on January 1 of the next year. Use page 1 of a general journal.

## RECYCLING PROBLEM 10-1

**Journalizing notes receivable, unearned revenue, and accrued revenue initially recorded as revenue transactions**

Marastreet, Inc., completed the following transactions during the current year. Marastreet initially records unearned items as revenue.

**Transactions:**

July  1. Received a 60-day, 10% note from Juan Beldoza for an extension of time on his account, $200.00. NR20.

July  5. Received a 2-month, 12% note from David Symanski for an extension of time on his account, $400.00. NR21.

Aug.  30. Juan Beldoza dishonored NR20, a 60-day, 10% note, maturity value due today: principal, $200.00; interest $3.33; total, $203.33. M39.

Sept.  5. Received cash for the maturity value of NR21: principal, $400.00, plus interest, $8.00; total, $408.00. R70.

Nov.  1. Received cash for three months' rent in advance from Clarkson, Inc., $1,800.00. R75.

Nov.  29. Received cash from Juan Beldoza for dishonored NR20: maturity value, $203.33, plus additional interest, $5.14; total, $208.47. R90.

**Instructions:**

1. Journalize the transactions. Page 7 of a general journal and page 17 of a cash receipts journal are provided in the *Recycling Problem Working Papers*. Source documents are abbreviated as follows: memorandum, M; note receivable, NR; receipt, R.
2. Continue using page 7 of the general journal. Journalize the adjusting entries using the following information.

**Adjustment Information, December 31**

| | |
|---|---|
| Accrued Interest on Notes Receivable | $ 17.57 |
| Rent Received in Advance and Still Unearned | 600.00 |

3. Journalize the reversing entries on January 1 of the next year. Use page 8 of a general journal.

## RECYCLING PROBLEM 11-1

**Journalizing transactions for starting a corporation, paying dividends, and preparing a balance sheet**

Hillcrest, Inc., received its charter on July 1 of the current year. The corporation is authorized to issue 500,000 shares of $1.00 stated-value common stock and 1,000 shares of 8%, $50.00 par-value preferred stock.

**Transactions:**

July  5. Received cash from five incorporators for 300,000 shares of $1.00 stated-value common stock, $300,000.00. R1-5.

July  8. Paid cash to George Quitman as reimbursement for organization costs, $4,000.00. C1.

July  12. Received a subscription from Angela Smith for 50,000 shares of $1.00 stated-value common stock, $50,000.00. M1.

July  25. Received a subscription from Dayne Wilson for 5,000 shares of $1.00 stated-value common stock, $5,000.00. M2.

Aug.  10. Received cash from Dayne Wilson in payment of stock subscription, $5,000.00. R6.

Aug.  10. Issued Stock Certificate No. 6 to Dayne Wilson for 5,000 shares of $1.00 stated-value common stock, $5,000.00. M3.

Oct.  1. Received cash from Angela Smith in partial payment of stock subscription, $25,000.00. R7.

Oct.  15. Received a subscription from Lance Mosier for 30,000 shares of $1.00 stated-value common stock, $30,000.00. M4.

Nov.  1. Received cash from Angela Smith in final payment of stock subscription, $25,000.00. R8.

Nov.  1. Issued Stock Certificate No. 7 to Angela Smith for 50,000 shares of $1.00 stated-value common stock, $50,000.00. M5.

**Instructions:**

1. Journalize the transactions. Page 1 of a cash receipts journal, a cash payments journal, and a general journal are provided in the *Recycling Problem Working Papers.*
2. Prepare a balance sheet for Hillcrest, Inc., as of November 2 of the current year.
3. Journalize the following transactions completed during the following two years to record the declaration and payment of the dividends. Continue using page 1 of the general journal and the cash payments journal.

Nov.  24. Hillcrest's board of directors declared an annual dividend of $50,000.00. Preferred stock issued is $250,000.00 of 8%, $50.00 par-value preferred stock. Common stock issued is $400,000.00 of $1.00 stated-value common stock. Date of payment is January 15. M106.

Jan.  15. Paid cash for annual dividend declared November 24, $50,000.00. C257.

## RECYCLING PROBLEM 12-1

**Journalizing stocks and bonds transactions**

Fleming, Inc., is authorized to issue 200,000 shares of $20.00 stated-value common stock and 50,000 shares of 12%, $200.00 par-value preferred stock.

**Transactions:**

Jan. 1, 20X1.   Received cash for the face value of a 5-year, 10%, $1,000.00 par-value bond issue, $100,000.00. R104.

Jan. 8, 20X1.   Received cash from Mary Brooker for 800 shares of $20.00 stated-value common stock at $20.00 per share, $16,000.00. R110.

Feb. 15, 20X1. Paid cash to Alfred Clark for 800 shares of $20.00 stated-value common stock at $21.00 per share, $16,800.00. C124.

Feb. 27, 20X1. Received cash from Connie Boyle for 300 shares of $200.00 par-value preferred stock at $198.00 per share, $59,400.00. R127.

Mar. 13, 20X1. Received cash from Edward Timmell for 100 shares of $20.00 stated-value common stock at $21.00 per share, $2,100.00. R143.

Mar. 22, 20X1. Received cash from Carol Petre for 200 shares of treasury stock at $21.00 per share, $4,200.00. Treasury stock was bought on February 15 at $21.00 per share. R149.

Apr. 15, 20X1. Received cash from Dennis Cochran for 100 shares of treasury stock at $22.00 per share, $2,200.00. Treasury stock was bought on February 15 at $21.00 per share. R155.

Apr. 21, 20X1. Received cash from David Vassel for 300 shares of $200.00 par-value preferred stock at $202.00 per share, $60,600.00. R156.

July 1, 20X1.   Paid cash to bond trustee for semiannual interest on bond issue, $5,000.00. C308.

July 1, 20X1.   Paid cash to bond trustee for semiannual deposit to bond sinking fund, $10,000.00. C309.

July 12, 20X1. Received store equipment from Jake Smith at an agreed value of $50,000.00 for 250 shares of $200.00 par-value preferred stock. M361.

July 30, 20X1. Received cash from Lester Branch for 100 shares of treasury stock at $20.50 per share, $2,050.00. Treasury stock was bought on February 15 at $21.00 per share. R215.

Jan. 1, 20X2.   Paid cash to bond trustee for semiannual interest on bond issue, $5,000.00. C519.

Jan. 1, 20X2.   Paid cash to bond trustee for semiannual deposit to bond sinking fund, $9,700.00, and recorded interest earned on bond sinking fund, $300.00. C520.

Jan. 5, 20X6.   Received notice from bond trustee that bond issue was retired using bond sinking fund, $100,000.00. M491.

**Instructions:**

Journalize the following transactions. Page 1 of a cash receipts journal, page 2 of a cash payments journal, and page 7 of a general journal are provided in the *Recycling Problem Working Papers*.

## RECYCLING PROBLEM 13-1

**End-of-fiscal-period work for a corporation**

The trial balance of Nichol, Inc., on December 31 of the current year is provided in the Trial Balance columns of the work sheet in the *Recycling Problem Working Papers*. Statement paper is also provided in the *Recycling Problem Working Papers*.

**Instructions:**

1. Complete the work sheet. Use the following information to prepare the adjustments.

## Adjustment Information, December 31

| | |
|---|---:|
| Accrued Interest Income | $ 122.33 |
| Uncollectible accounts expense estimated as 1.0% of sales on account. | |
| Sales on account for year, | $277,474.00 |
| Merchandise Inventory | 110,939.29 |
| Sales Supplies Inventory | 4,951.42 |
| Administrative Supplies Inventory | 6,106.97 |
| Value of Prepaid Insurance | 3,153.46 |
| Prepaid Interest | 4.06 |
| Annual Depreciation Expense—Store Equipment | 8,126.28 |
| Annual Depreciation Expense—Office Equipment | 10,615.31 |
| Organization Expense | 100.00 |
| Accrued Interest Expense | 9,005.64 |
| Accrued Salaries—Sales | 488.36 |
| Accrued Salaries—Administrative | 1,302.77 |
| Accrued Payroll Taxes—Social Security Tax | 116.42 |
| Accrued Payroll Taxes—Medicare Tax | 26.87 |
| Accrued Payroll Taxes—Federal Unemployment Tax | 1.69 |
| Accrued Payroll Taxes—State Unemployment Tax | 11.39 |

Use the tax rates listed on page 372 in Chapter 13 to calculate the federal income tax for the year.

2. Prepare an income statement. Calculate and record the following component percentages. (a) Cost of merchandise sold. (b) Gross profit on operations. (c) Total selling expenses. (d) Total administrative expenses. (e) Total operating expenses. (f) Income from operations. (g) Net addition or deduction resulting from other revenue and expenses. (h) Net income before federal income tax. (i) Federal income tax expense. (j) Net income after federal income tax. Round percentage calculations to the nearest 0.1%.

3. Analyze Nichol's income statement by determining if component percentages are within acceptable levels. If any component percentage is not within an acceptable level, suggest steps that the company should take. Nichol considers the following component percentages acceptable.

| | |
|---|---|
| Cost of merchandise sold | Not more than 43.0% |
| Gross profit on operations | Not less than 57.0% |
| Total selling expenses | Not more than 13.06% |
| Total administrative expenses | Not more than 18.0% |
| Total operating expenses | Not more than 31.0% |
| Income from operations | Not less than 26.0% |
| Net deduction from other revenue and expenses | Not more than 8.0% |
| Net income before federal income tax | Not less than 18.0% |

4. Calculate earnings per share. Nichol's has 24,000 shares of $5.00 stated-value common stock issued and 940 shares of $100.00 par-value preferred stock issued. Treasury stock consists of 160 shares of common stock. The dividend rate on preferred stock is 10.0%.

5. Prepare a statement of stockholders' equity for the year ended December 31 of the current year. Use the following additional information.

| | January 1 Balance | Issued During the Year | December 31 Balance |
|---|---|---|---|
| Common stock: | | | |
| No. of shares | 20,000 | 4,000 | 24,000 |
| Amount | $100,000.00 | $20,000.00 | $120,000.00 |
| Preferred stock: | | | |
| No. of shares | 900 | 40 | 940 |
| Amount | $90,000.00 | $4,000.00 | $94,000.00 |

The January 1 balance of Retained Earnings was $29,439.29.

6. Calculate the following items based on information from the statement of stockholders' equity. (a) Equity per share of stock. (b) Price-earnings ratio. The market price of common stock on December 31 is $24.25.

7. Prepare a balance sheet for December 31 of the current year.
8. Calculate the following items based on information from the balance sheet. Net sales on account are $277,474.00. (a) Accounts receivable turnover ratio. Accounts receivable and allowance for uncollectible accounts on January 1 were $64,984.46 and $2,482.57, respectively. (b) Rate earned on average stockholders' equity. Total stockholders' equity on January 1 was $216,559.29. (c) Rate earned on average total assets. Total assets on January 1 were $421,689.57.
9. Journalize the adjusting entries. Use page 13 of a general journal.
10. Journalize the closing entries. Use page 14 of a general journal.
11. Journalize the reversing entries. Use page 15 of a general journal. Use January 1 of the following year as the date.

## RECYCLING PROBLEM 14-1

**Preparing a budgeted income statement and a cash budget with supporting budget schedules**

On December 31, 20X2, the accounting records of Reilly Corporation show the following unit sales for 20X2.

| | | | |
|---|---|---|---|
| 1st quarter | 20,600 units | 3d quarter | 22,800 units |
| 2d quarter | 21,500 units | 4th quarter | 35,100 units |

The following are additional actual amounts for the 4th quarter of 20X2.

| | |
|---|---|
| Sales (35,100 units @ $5.00) | $175,500 |
| Purchases (29,400 units @ $2.60) | 76,440 |
| Ending inventory | 11,500 units |

Management has established a unit sales goal of 120,000 units for 20X3 and 25,000 units for the first quarter of 20X4. The sales manager, after reviewing price trends and checking with the company's merchandise suppliers, projects the unit cost of merchandise will increase from $2.60 to $2.80 in the first quarter of 20X3. Because of the increase in costs, the company will need to increase its unit sales price from $5.00 to $5.20 in the first quarter of 20X3. After considering the time required to reorder merchandise, the sales manager requests that 50.0% of each quarter's unit sales be available in the prior quarter's ending inventory. Expenses are projected as follows. Except where noted, percentages are based on quarterly projected net sales. For these items, calculate each quarter's amount by multiplying the percentage times that quarter's net sales. Calculate the annual total by adding the four quarterly amounts. When a dollar amount is given, the total amount should be divided equally among the four quarters.

### Selling Expenses
| | |
|---|---|
| Advertising Expense | 1.2% |
| Delivery Expense | 0.7% |
| Depreciation Expense—Delivery Equipment | $4,200 |
| Depreciation Expense—Store Equipment | $1,800 |
| Miscellaneous Expense—Sales | 0.2% |
| Salary Expense—Sales | 5.4% |
| Supplies Expense—Sales | 0.8% |

### Administrative Expenses
| | |
|---|---|
| Depreciation Expense—Office Equipment | $1,440 |
| Insurance Expense | $3,640 |
| Miscellaneous Expense—Administrative | $2,400 |
| Payroll Taxes Expense | 12.0% of salaries |
| Rent Expense | $6,640 |
| Salary Expense—Administrative | $26,000 |
| Supplies Expense—Administrative | $1,800 |
| Uncollectible Accounts Expense | 0.5% |
| Utilities Expense | 1.5% |

Interest expense for each quarter is projected to be $450.

Federal income taxes are calculated using the tax rates listed on page 372 in Chapter 13. Equal quarterly income tax payments are based on the projected annual federal income tax expense.

Additional information is listed as follows.
a. The balance of cash on hand on January 1, 20X3 is $22,540.
b. In each quarter, cash sales are 20.0% and collections of accounts receivable are 25.0% of the projected net sales for the current quarter. Collections from the preceding quarter's net sales are 54.5% of that quarter. Uncollectible accounts expense is 0.5% of net sales.
c. In each quarter, cash payments for cash purchases are 10.0% and for accounts payable 50.0% of the purchases for the current quarter. Cash payments for purchases of the preceding quarter are 40.0% of that quarter.
d. In the first quarter, $12,000 will be borrowed on a promissory note, and equipment costing $17,500 will be purchased for cash. In each quarter, dividends of $15,000 will be paid in cash. In the fourth quarter, the promissory note plus interest will be paid in cash, $13,800.

**Instructions:**

Prepare the following budget schedules for the year ended December 31, 20X3. Use the forms provided in the *Recycling Problem Working Papers*. Round percentage amounts to the nearest 0.1%, unit amounts to the nearest 100 units, and dollar amounts to the nearest $10.
1. Prepare a sales budget schedule (Schedule 1).
2. Prepare a purchases budget schedule (Schedule 2).
3. Prepare a selling expenses budget schedule (Schedule 3).
4. Prepare an administrative expenses budget schedule (Schedule 4).
5. Prepare another revenue and expenses budget schedule (Schedule 5).
6. Prepare a budgeted income statement.
7. Prepare a cash receipts budget schedule (Schedule A).
8. Prepare a cash payments budget schedule (Schedule B).
9. Prepare a cash budget.

## RECYCLING PROBLEM 15-1

**Calculating contribution margin and breakeven point; calculating sales dollars and unit sales for planned net income**

NewWave Cycle, Inc., manufactures and sells racing bicycles. The company's income statement for January of the current year appears in the *Recycling Problem Working Papers*.

**Instructions:**
1. Prepare NewWave Cycle's January income statement reporting contribution margin using the form provided in the *Recycling Problems Working Papers*.
2. Calculate the contribution margin rate.
3. Calculate the sales dollar breakeven point.
4. Calculate the unit sales breakeven point.
5. If an $18,000.00 monthly net income is planned, calculate the required (a) sales dollars and (b) number of cycles to be sold.
6. NewWave Cycle currently produces one of the components of its cycles. However, the company can also purchase the component from another company, reducing fixed costs by $5,000.00 per month, but increasing variable costs by $25.00 per cycle. Calculate the projected net income assuming NewWave Cycle sells 180 cycles per month. Should NewWave Cycle purchase the component from another company? Explain your answer.

**Calculating net present values**

ReTrax Company is evaluating the purchase of equipment from two vendors. Differences in the technology and labor requirements to operate the equipment of each vendor affect the projected net cash flows. The equipment purchased from Lione Industries would cost $115,000.00 and is projected to generate total net cash flows of $177,000.00. The equipment from Timco Manufacturing would cost $135,200.00 and is projected to generate net cash flows totaling $251,000.00. The net cash flows for each year follow.

| Year | Lione Industries | Timco Manufacturing |
|------|------------------|---------------------|
| 1 | $32,000.00 | $15,000.00 |
| 2 | 29,000.00 | 24,000.00 |
| 3 | 31,000.00 | 35,000.00 |
| 4 | 27,000.00 | 42,000.00 |
| 5 | 24,000.00 | 48,000.00 |
| 6 | 19,000.00 | 58,000.00 |
| 7 | 15,000.00 | 29,000.00 |

**Instructions:**
1. Assuming that ReTrax Company wants to earn a 15% rate of return, calculate the net present value of each equipment purchase.
2. Would you purchase the equipment and, if so, from which vendor?

**Preparing and analyzing comparative financial statements**

Information taken from the financial records of Reardon Corporation for two fiscal years ended December 31 are provided in the *Recycling Problem Working Papers*.

The following additional information is known:

| | | |
|---|---|---|
| Dividends Declared | $25,000.00 | $25,000.00 |
| Shares of Capital Stock Outstanding | 3,000 | 3,000 |
| Accounts Receivable (Book Value), January 1 | 62,430.00 | 59,480.00 |
| Merchandise Inventory, January 1 | $229,690.00 | $120,830.00 |
| Total Assets, January 1 | 493,180.00 | 421,200.00 |
| Capital Stock, January 1 | 300,000.00 | 300,000.00 |
| Retained Earnings, January 1 | 49,860.00 | 43,220.00 |
| Market Price per Share of Stock, December 31 | 112.50 | 123.00 |

**Instructions:**
1. Prepare the following comparative financial statements using trend analysis. Use the forms provided in the *Recycling Problem Working Papers*. Round percentage calculations to the nearest 0.1%.
   a. Comparative income statement
   b. Comparative stockholders' equity statement
   c. Comparative balance sheet
2. Use the financial statements' trend analysis to determine if the trend from the prior to current year for each of the following items appears to be favorable or unfavorable. Give reasons for these trends.
   a. Net sales
   b. Net income
   c. Total stockholders' equity
   d. Total assets
3. Prepare a comparative income statement using component percentage analysis. Round percentage calculations to the nearest 0.1%.

4. Record from the statement prepared in Instruction 3 or calculate the component percentages for each of the following. Determine if the current year's results, compared with the prior year, appear to be favorable or unfavorable. Give reasons for your responses.
   a. As a percentage of net sales:
      1. Cost of merchandise sold
      2. Gross profit on operations
      3. Total operating expenses
      4. Net income after federal income tax
   b. As a percentage of total stockholders' equity:
      1. Retained earnings
      2. Capital stock
   c. As a percentage of total assets or total liabilities and stockholders' equity:
      1. Current assets
      2. Current liabilities
5. Based on Reardon's comparative financial statements, calculate the following ratios for each year.
   a. Profitability ratios:
      1. Rate earned on average total assets
      2. Rate earned on average stockholders' equity
      3. Rate earned on net sales
      4. Earnings per share
      5. Price-earnings ratio
   b. Efficiency ratios:
      1. Accounts receivable turnover ratio
      2. Merchandise inventory turnover
   c. Short-term financial strength ratios:
      1. Working capital
      2. Current ratio
      3. Acid-test ratio
   d. Long-term financial strength ratios:
      1. Debt ratio
      2. Equity ratio
      3. Equity per share
6. For each of the items in Instruction 5, indicate if there appears to be a favorable or an unfavorable trend from the prior to current year. Give reasons for these trends.

## RECYCLING PROBLEM 18-1

**Preparing a statement of cash flows**

An analysis of the annual income statement and comparative balance sheet of Cascade Trucking Supply, Inc., reveals the following net income, depreciation expense, amortization costs, and changes in current assets and current liabilities:

| | |
|---|---|
| Net Income | $122,370.00 |
| Amortized Organization Costs | 10,000.00 |
| Depreciation Expense | 51,500.00 |
| Increase in Notes Receivable | 5,100.00 |
| Decrease in Accounts Receivable | 35,600.00 |
| Increase in Supplies | 3,300.00 |
| Increase in Merchandise Inventory | 68,200.00 |
| Decrease in Notes Payable | 8,700.00 |
| Increase in Accounts Payable | 14,000.00 |
| Decrease in Salaries Payable | 1,200.00 |

## Instructions:

1. Prepare the cash flows from operating activities section of the statement of cash flows for the current year ending December 31. Use the form provided in the *Recycling Problem Working Papers*.

   An analysis of the current comparative balance sheet of Cascade Trucking Supply, Inc., shows the following changes in long-term assets:

   | | | | |
   |---|---|---|---|
   | Increase in Office Equipment | $30,200.00 | Increase in Building | $154,000.00 |
   | Increase in Office Furniture | 12,340.00 | Decrease in Land Due to Sale | 75,000.00 |

2. Prepare the cash flows from investing activities section.

   An examination of the comparative balance sheet and statement of stockholders' equity of Cascade Trucking Supply, Inc., reveals the following changes in long-term liabilities and stockholders' equity:

   | | |
   |---|---|
   | Increase in Mortgage Payable | $40,000.00 |
   | Sale of Common Stock | 20,000.00 |
   | Payment of Cash Dividend | 25,500.00 |

3. Prepare the cash flows from financing activities section.
4. Compute the net increase or decrease in cash resulting from the operating, investing, and financing activities of the business.
5. Enter a beginning cash balance of $98,700.00 on the statement of cash flows.
6. Complete the statement of cash flows for Cascade Trucking Supply, Inc., by computing the ending cash balance for the fiscal year ending December 31.
7. Verify the accuracy of the statement of cash flows by comparing its ending cash balance with the cash balance of $158,630.00 listed for the current year on Cascade Trucking Supply's comparative balance sheet.

## RECYCLING PROBLEM 19-1

### Preparing cost records

Air Wave, Inc., manufactures CB (citizen band) radios. The company records manufacturing costs by job number and uses a factory overhead applied rate to charge overhead costs to its products. The company estimates it will manufacture 5,000 radios next year. For this amount of production, total factory overhead is estimated to be $198,000.00. Estimated direct labor costs for next year are $220,000.00. On November 6, Air Wave began work on Job No. 753. The order is for 30 No. LR75 CB radios for stock, date wanted November 21.

### Transactions:

| | | |
|---|---|---|
| Nov. | 6. | Direct materials, $762.00. Materials Requisition No. 524. |
| | 6. | Direct labor, $120.00. Daily summary of job-time records. |
| | 7. | Direct labor, $180.00. Daily summary of job-time records. |
| | 8. | Direct materials, $230.00. Materials Requisition No. 535. |
| | 8. | Direct labor, $136.00. Daily summary of job-time records. |
| | 9. | Direct labor, $126.00. Daily summary of job-time records. |
| | 10. | Direct materials, $185.00. Materials Requisition No. 542. |
| | 10. | Direct labor, $210.00. Daily summary of job-time records. |
| | 13. | Direct materials, $156.00. Materials Requisition No. 548. |
| | 13. | Direct labor, $198.00. Daily summary of job-time records. |
| | 14. | Direct materials, $112.00. Materials Requisition No. 556. |
| | 14. | Direct labor, $186.00. Daily summary of job-time records. |
| | 15. | Direct materials, $145.00. Materials Requisition No. 563. |
| | 15. | Direct labor, $112.00. Daily summary of job-time records. |
| | 16. | Direct labor, $52.00. Daily summary of job-time records. |

**Instructions:**

1. Calculate Air Wave's factory overhead applied rate for next year as a percentage of direct labor cost.
2. Open a cost sheet for job No. 753 and record the transactions. Use the job cost sheet provided in the *Recycling Problem Working Papers*.
3. Complete the cost sheet, recording factory overhead at the rate calculated in Instruction 1.
4. Prepare a finished goods ledger card for Stock No. LR75 CB radio. Minimum quantity is set at 10. Inventory location is Area B-11.
5. Record on the finished goods ledger card the beginning balance on November 1. The November 1 balance of LR75 CB radios is 20 units at a unit cost of $133.50. Air Wave uses the first-in, first-out method to record inventory costs.
6. Record the following transactions on the finished goods ledger card for LR75 CB radios.

Nov.  10.  Sold 8 LR75 CB radios. Sales Invoice No. 743.
16.  Received 30 LR75 CB radios. Record cost from cost sheet for Job No. 753.
21.  Sold 20 LR75 CB radios. Sales Invoice No. 757.

## RECYCLING PROBLEM 20-1

**Journalizing entries that summarize cost records at the end of a fiscal period; preparing statement of cost of goods manufactured**

The following information is taken from the records of Bartley Company on January 31 of the current year.

a. The various general ledger accounts used in recording actual factory overhead expenses during the month have the following balances on January 31.

| | | |
|---|---|---|
| 5510 | Depreciation Expense—Factory Equipment | $ 2,885.12 |
| 5515 | Depreciation Expense—Building | 1,411.20 |
| 5520 | Heat, Light, and Power Expense | 4,527.60 |
| 5525 | Insurance Expense—Factory | 752.64 |
| 5530 | Miscellaneous Expense—Factory | 6,890.24 |
| 5535 | Payroll Taxes Expense—Factory | 21,868.00 |
| 5540 | Property Tax Expense—Factory | 3,044.16 |
| 5545 | Supplies Expense—Factory | 9,031.68 |

b. Inventory accounts have the following balances on January 1.

| | |
|---|---|
| Account No. 1125 Materials | $272,244.00 |
| Account No. 1130 Work in Process | 95,961.60 |
| Account No. 1135 Finished Goods | 71,442.00 |

c. The following accounts are needed for completing the posting. No beginning balances are needed.

| | | | | |
|---|---|---|---|---|
| 2110 | Employee Income Tax Payable | | 3120 | Income Summary |
| 2120 | Social Security Tax Payable | | 5105 | Cost of Goods Sold |
| 2125 | Medicare Tax Payable | | 5505 | Factory Overhead |

d. The total factory payroll for the month according to the payroll register is $154,000.00, distributed as follows.

| | | | | |
|---|---|---|---|---|
| Work in Process | $114,520.00 | | Employee Income Tax Payable | $16,940.00 |
| Factory Overhead | 39,480.00 | | Social Security Tax Payable | 10,010.00 |
| Cash | 124,740.00 | | Medicare Tax Payable | 2,310.00 |

e. The total of all requisitions of direct materials issued during the month is $126,115.00. The total of all requisitions of indirect materials issued during the month is $10,085.00.

f. The factory overhead to be charged to Work in Process is 87% of the direct labor cost.

g. The total of all cost sheets completed during the month is $314,440.00.

h. The total of costs recorded on all sales invoices for January is $327,026.00.

**Instructions:**
1. Open ledger accounts and record balances for information items in (a), (b), and (c). Use the accounts provided in the *Recycling Problem Working Papers*.
2. Journalize the factory payroll entry on page 2 of a cash payments journal. C1012. Post the general debit and general credit amounts.
3. Journalize the following entries on page 1 of a general journal. Post the entries.
   a. An entry to transfer the total of all direct materials requisitions to Work in Process and indirect materials to Factory Overhead. M844.
   b. An entry to close all individual manufacturing expense accounts to Factory Overhead. M845.
   c. An entry to record applied factory overhead to Work in Process. M846.
4. Continue using page 1 of the general journal. Journalize and post the entry to close the balance of the factory overhead account to Income Summary. M847.
5. Journalize and post the entry to transfer the total of all cost sheets completed from Work in Process to Finished Goods. M848.
6. Journalize and post the entry to transfer the cost of products sold from Finished Goods to Cost of Goods Sold. M849.
7. Prepare for Bartley Company a statement of cost of goods manufactured for the month ended January 31 of the current year.

## RECYCLING PROBLEM 21-1

### Forming and expanding a partnership

On January 1 of the current year, Richard Meyer and Susan Rusk form a partnership. The partnership accepts the assets and liabilities of Mr. Meyer's existing business. Miss Rusk invests cash equal to Mr. Meyers' investment. The partners share equally in all changes in equity. The January 1 balance sheet for Mr. Meyer's existing business is provided in the *Recycling Problem Working Papers*.

**Transactions:**

Jan.   1.   Received cash from partner, Susan Rusk, as an initial investment, $6,000.00. R1.
          1.   Accepted assets and liabilities of Richard Meyer's existing business as an initial investment, $6,000.00. R2.

Mar.  1.   Journalized personal sale of equity to new partner, Luke Chin, $4,000.00, distributed as follows: from Richard Meyer, $2,000.00; from Susan Rusk, $2,000.00. M18.

Aug.  1.   Received cash from new partner, Penney Cory, for a one-fourth equity in the business, $4,000.00. R92.

Sept. 2.   Received cash from new partner, Chad Breslau, for a one-fifth equity in the business, $3,600.00. Existing equity is redistributed as follows: from Richard Meyer, $80.00; from Susan Rusk, $80.00; from Luke Chin, $80.00; from Penney Cory, $80.00. R121 and M32.

Nov.  1.   Received cash from new partner, Sharon Logan, for a one-sixth equity in the business, $4,200.00. Goodwill, $1,400.00, is distributed as follows: Richard Meyer, $280.00; Susan Rusk, $280.00; Luke Chin, $280.00; Penney Cory, $280.00; Chad Breslau, $280.00. R181 and M42.

**Instructions:**

Journalize the transactions. Page 1 of a cash receipts journal and page 1 of a general journal are provided in the *Recycling Problem Working Papers*. Source documents are abbreviated as follows: memorandum, M; receipt, R.

## Completing end-of-fiscal-period work for a partnership

James Dyson and Gerald Nickle are partners in a partnership called Fast Service Plumbing. The partnership's work sheet for the year ended December 31 of the current year is provided in the *Recycling Problem Working Papers*. Statement paper is also provided in the *Recycling Problem Working Papers*.

**Instructions:**

1. Prepare an income statement. Calculate and record the component percentages for total operating expenses and for net income. Round percentage calculations to the nearest 0.1%.
2. Prepare a distribution of net income statement. Each partner is to receive 8% interest on January 1 equity. The January 1 equity is: Mr. Dyson, $22,000.00; Mr. Nickle, $20,000.00. Also, the partners' salaries are: Mr. Dyson, $10,000.00; Mr. Nickle, $8,000.00. The partners share remaining net income, net loss, or deficit equally.
3. Prepare an owners' equity statement.
4. Prepare a balance sheet.
5. Journalize the adjusting entries. Use page 12 of a general journal.
6. Continue using page 12 of the general journal. Journalize the closing entries.

## Journalizing governmental transactions

The town of Osage uses a general fund for all financial transactions. Expenditures are recorded by type of expenditure and by department. The four categories of expenditures are: personnel, supplies, other charges, and capital outlays. Departments are: General Government, Public Safety, Public Works, and Recreation.

**Transactions:**

Jan.  2. Recorded current year's approved operating budget: estimated revenues, $1,148,500.00; appropriations, $1,113,000.00; budgetary fund balance, $35,500.00. M35.

2. Recorded current year's property tax levy: taxes receivable—current, $1,033,000.00; allowance for uncollectible taxes—current, $15,500.00; property tax revenue, $1,017,500.00. M36.

9. Paid cash for gas utility service in recreation department, $182.00. C134.

15. Issued a 1-month, 9% note, $100,000.00. NP7.

16. Received cash for current taxes receivable, $61,200.00. R85.

19. Encumbered estimated amount for supplies in general government department, $120.00. M52.

31. Received cash from traffic fines, $490.00. R100. (Other Revenue)

Feb.  3. Paid cash for general government department supplies, $117.00, encumbered January 19 per M52. M61 and C155.

15. Paid cash for the maturity value of NP7: principal, $100,000.00, plus interest, $750.00; total, $100,750.00. C189.

22. Paid cash for library books for recreation department, $450.00. C192. (Capital Outlays)

Mar.  1. Recorded reclassification of current taxes receivable to delinquent status, $72,000.00, and the accompanying allowance for uncollectible accounts, $15,500.00. M73.

15. Paid cash for a 4-month, 8% certificate of deposit, $300,000.00. C209.

Apr.  5. Encumbered estimated amount for supplies in public safety department, $250.00. M94.

18. Received cash for delinquent taxes receivable, $34,500.00. R255.

26. Paid cash for public safety department supplies, $254.00, encumbered April 5 per M94. M102 and C244.

May  8. Paid cash for consultant's services in general government department, $500.00. C265. (Personnel)

July 15. Received cash for the maturity value of certificate of deposit due today: principal, $300,000.00, plus interest, $8,000.00; total $308,000.00. R314.

**Instructions:**

Journalize the transactions completed during the current year. Page 1 of a journal is provided in the *Recycling Problem Working Papers.*

## RECYCLING PROBLEM 24-1

### Completing end-of-fiscal-period work for a governmental organization

The town of Weston uses a general fund. The trial balance on December 31 of the current year is provided in the Trial Balance columns of the work sheet in the *Recycling Problem Working Papers.* Statement paper is also provided in the *Recycling Problem Working Papers.*

**Instructions:**

1.  Analyze the following adjustment information and record the adjustments on the work sheet.

#### Adjustment Information, December 31

| | |
|---|---|
| Supplies inventory | $3,380.00 |
| Interest revenue due but not collected | 3,650.00 |

An estimated 20% of the interest revenue due will not be collected.
The reserve for encumbrances for the current year is reclassified to prior year status.

2.  Complete the work sheet.

    Weston's general fund operating budget for the current fiscal year is provided in the *Recycling Problem Working Papers.*

3.  Prepare a statement of revenues, expenditures, and changes in fund balance—budget and actual for the year ended December 31 of the current year. The unreserved fund balance on January 1 was $47,610.00.

4.  Prepare a balance sheet for December 31 of the current year.

5.  Journalize the adjusting and closing entries. Use page 48 of a journal.

# Answers to Audit Your Understanding

## Chapter 1, Page 11

1. Assets = Liabilities + Owner's Equity.
2. An asset account has a normal debit balance; a revenue account has a normal credit balance.
3. (1) A separate numeric listing is provided for each ledger division. (2) A predesigned arrangement of numbers is provided within each ledger division. (3) Account number digits are spaced to allow the addition of new accounts.

## Chapter 1, Page 17

1. Purchases—Video is debited; Accounts Payable is credited.
2. Accounts Payable is debited; Purchases Returns and Allowances—Video is credited.

## Chapter 1, Page 24

1. Accounts Payable is debited; Cash and Purchases Discount—Video are credited.
2. In the General Debit and Credit columns of the cash payments journal.
3. To assure that all expenses are recorded during the fiscal period in which they occurred.

## Chapter 2, Page 43

1. A tax-exempt customer is not required to pay sales tax. Examples include federal, state, and local government agencies; nonprofit educational institutions; and certain religious and charitable organizations.
2. A credit memorandum is issued by a vendor to show the amount deducted from the customer's account for returns and allowances.

## Chapter 2, Page 50

1. A 2% sales discount may be deducted if sales on account are paid within 10 days of the invoice date. All sales on account must be paid within 30 days of the invoice date.
2. Both cash sales and credit card sales result in an immediate increase in the bank account balance.

## Chapter 3, Page 68

1. Federal income tax, social security tax, and Medicare tax.
2. By consulting withholding tax tables provided by the Internal Revenue Service.
3. Total Earnings − Total Deductions = Net Pay.
4. Total earnings for the pay period.

## Chapter 3, Page 76

1. Cash.
2. a. Employer social security tax.
   b. Employer Medicare tax.
   c. Federal unemployment tax.
   d. State unemployment tax.

## Chapter 4, Page 91

1. a. Each manager is assigned responsibility for those revenues, costs, and expenses for which the manager can make decisions and affect the outcome.
   b. The revenues, costs, and expenses must be readily identifiable with the manager's unit.
2. Revenue, cost of merchandise sold, and direct expenses.
3. The amount of the invoice that applies to each department should be recorded separately.

## Chapter 4, Page 97

1. Interim departmental statement of gross profit, departmental statement of gross profit, estimated merchandise inventory sheet.
2. Periodic inventory and perpetual inventory.
3. Operating Revenue, Cost of Merchandise Sold, and Gross Profit on Operations.

## Chapter 4, Page 110

1. Schedule of accounts receivable and schedule of accounts payable.
2. To bring certain general ledger accounts up to date.

3. Asset, liability, and stockholders' equity accounts.

## Chapter 4, Page 117

1. Totals are obtained from the departmental margin statements.
2. By dividing the amount on each line by the amount of departmental net sales.
3. (1) Current period's departmental margin component percentage compared with the company-assigned departmental margin goal and (2) current period's departmental margin component percentage compared with previous periods' departmental margin component percentages.
4. Account titles and balances are obtained from the Income Statement columns of the work sheet.

## Chapter 4, Page 124

1. To update general ledger accounts at the end of a fiscal period.
2. All temporary accounts or all income statement accounts and the dividends account.
3. To prove that debits equal credits in the general ledger after closing entries have been prepared.
4. a. Prepare schedules of accounts receivable and accounts payable.
   b. Prepare a trial balance on the work sheet and complete the work sheet.
   c. Prepare financial statements.
   d. Journalize and post adjusting and closing entries.
   e. Prepare a post-closing trial balance.

## Chapter 5, Page 149

1. Vouchers Payable.
2. To serve as an additional control: all vouchers can be accounted for.
3. Purchases journal.

## Chapter 5, Page 153

1. Cash payments journal.
2. According to the name of the vendor.
3. Vouchers Payable.

## Chapter 5, Page 159

1. Vouchers Payable is debited; Purchases Returns and Allowances is credited.

2. Remove the voucher from the unpaid voucher file and write Canceled across Section 5.
3. A payroll register.

## Chapter 6, Page 175

1. a. Cost of beginning merchandise inventory.
   b. Cost of the net purchases added to the inventory during the fiscal period.
2. Understated.
3. a. By physically counting the items.
   b. By keeping a continuous record showing the number purchased and sold for each item.

## Chapter 6, Page 181

1. A method that best matches the revenue and costs for that business during the fiscal period.
2. The last-in, first-out (lifo) method.
3. The first-in, first-out (fifo) method.
4. a. The cost of the inventory using the fifo, lifo, or weighted-average method.
   b. The current market price of the inventory.

## Chapter 6, Page 186

1. That a continuing relationship exists between gross profit and net sales.
2. Separate records of both cost and retail prices for net purchases, net sales, and beginning merchandise inventory.
3. That the business sold the average merchandise inventory five times during the current year.
4. Days in year (365) divided by merchandise inventory turnover ratio equals average number of days' sales in merchandise inventory.

## Chapter 7, Page 203

1. When a customer's account is believed to be uncollectible, it should be written off because it is no longer an asset of the business.
2. Uncollectible Accounts Expense is debited; Accounts Receivable is credited. The customer's account in the accounts receivable ledger is also credited.
3. To provide a complete history of a customer's credit activities.

## Chapter 7, Page 210

1.  a.  Percentage of sales method.
    b.  Percentage of accounts receivable method.
2.  Net sales times the percentage expected to be uncollectible equals the estimated uncollectible accounts expense.
3.  a.  Compute an estimate for each age group.
    b.  Compute the total estimate.
    c.  Subtract the current balance of Allowance for Uncollectible Accounts.
    d.  Compute the addition to the allowance account.

## Chapter 7, Page 213

1.  Net sales on account divided by average book value of accounts receivable equals accounts receivable turnover ratio.
2.  Customers are taking about 60 days to pay their accounts. The business needs to encourage more prompt payment in order to reduce the number of days to receive payment to 30 days.
3.  Business can be lost as some customers may buy from competitors with less restrictive credit terms.

## Chapter 8, Page 228

1.  a.  General information completed when the asset is bought.
    b.  Disposal section completed when the asset is discarded, sold, or traded.
    c.  Section to record annual depreciation expense.
2.  The entry does not involve the purchase of merchandise.
3.  Property Tax Expense is debited; Cash is credited.

## Chapter 8, Page 234

1.  Over the useful life of the plant asset.
2.  Matching Expenses with Revenue.
3.  Because of its permanent nature, depreciation is not recorded for land.
4.  Original cost, estimated salvage value, and estimated useful life.
5.  A calendar month.

## Chapter 8, Page 241

1.  The date, type, and amount of disposal.
2.  Depreciation Expense will be debited; Accumulated Depreciation will be credited to bring the accounts up to date before disposal.
3.  Cash received minus the book value of the asset sold.
4.  Cash plus the book value of the store equipment traded equals the book value of the new store equipment.

## Chapter 8, Page 248

1.  Declining balance.
2.  The amount of use the asset receives.
3.  Tons of mineral mined times the depletion rate equals the annual depletion expense. The depletion rate is calculated by dividing the estimated total value of the mineral resource by the estimated number of tons of the mineral to be recovered.

## Chapter 9, Page 265

1.  Principal times interest rate times fraction of a year equals the interest to be paid on a note.
2.  As an annual rate.
3.  Principal and interest expense.

## Chapter 9, Page 271

1.  Matching Expenses with Revenue.
2.  To record the amount of supplies used during the period as an expense.
3.  If an adjusting entry creates a balance in an asset or a liability account, the adjusting entry is reversed.

## Chapter 9, Page 279

1.  a.  Accrued interest expense.
    b.  Accrued salary expense.
    c.  Accrued employer payroll taxes expense.
    d.  Accrued federal income tax.
2.  Interest Expense is debited; Interest Payable is credited.
3.  Salaries Payable, Employee Income Tax Payable, Social Security Tax Payable, and Medicare Tax Payable are debited; Salary Expense (for each department) is credited.

## Chapter 10, Page 296

1. To provide an extension of time to pay on account.
2. Accounts Receivable is debited; Notes Receivable and Interest Income are credited.
3. The additional interest is charged from maturity date to payment date.

## Chapter 10, Page 302

1. Cash is debited; Rent Income is credited.
2. If the adjusting entry creates a balance in an asset or liability account.
3. Unearned Rent is debited; Rent Income is credited.
4. Interest Receivable is debited; Interest Income is credited.
5. Interest Income is debited; Interest Receivable is credited.

## Chapter 11, Page 322

1. Determine corporate policies and select corporate officers to supervise the day-to-day management of the corporation.
2. a. The right to vote at stockholders' meetings.
   b. The right to share in the corporation's earnings.
   c. The right to share in the distribution of a corporation's assets if a corporation ceases operations and sells its assets.
3. Common stock and preferred stock.
4. A single summary general ledger capital account is used for each kind of stock issued.
5. Cash is debited; Capital Stock—Common is credited.
6. a. An incorporation fee paid to the state when the articles of incorporation are submitted.
   b. Attorney fees for legal services during the process of incorporation.
   c. Other incidental expenses incurred prior to receiving a charter.

## Chapter 11, Page 327

1. Stock Subscribed is debited; Capital Stock is credited. (The kind of stock issued will be included in the account title.)
2. Under the heading Intangible Assets, as the last subdivision of the Assets section.

## Chapter 11, Page 332

1. The board of directors.
2. The corporation is obligated to pay the dividend.
3. a. To avoid a large number of entries in the corporation's cash payments journal.
   b. To reserve cash specifically for paying dividends.

## Chapter 12, Page 348

1. Selling stock to investors and borrowing money.
2. Cash is debited; Capital Stock—Preferred is credited.
3. Cash is debited; Capital Stock—Preferred and Paid-in Capital in Excess of Par Value—Preferred are credited.
4. Cash and Discount on Sale of Preferred Stock are debited; Capital Stock—Preferred is credited.
5. May be assigned to no-par value stock and it serves the same function as par value.

## Chapter 12, Page 354

1. Stock that has been issued and reacquired by a corporation.
2. Cash is debited; Treasury Stock and Paid-in Capital from Sale of Treasury Stock are credited.
3. Historical Cost.

## Chapter 12, Page 360

1. a. Additional capital becomes part of a corporation's permanent capital.
   b. Dividends do not have to be paid unless earnings are sufficient.
2. Stockholders' equity is not spread over additional shares of stock.
3. Interest must be paid on the loan, which decreases net income.
4. Bond Sinking Fund is debited; Cash and Interest Income are credited.

## Chapter 13, Page 376

1. Recognizing a portion of an intangible expense over a period of years.
2. Quarterly.

## Chapter 13, Page 385

1. The amount of net income belonging to a single share of stock.

2. The relationship between the market value per share and earnings per share.
3. Total assets at the beginning and end of the fiscal period and net income after federal income tax.

## Chapter 13, Page 392

1. a. Closing entry for income statement accounts with credit balances.
   b. Closing entry for income statement accounts with debit balances.
   c. Closing entry to record net income or net loss in the retained earnings account and close the income summary account.
   d. Closing entry for the dividends account.
2. Form 1120.
3. The gains and losses on the sale of non-cash assets are subject to taxation. Thus, additional tax reports for the corporation must be filed.

## Chapter 14, Page 417

1. A business can control expenses by comparing actual expenses with projected expenses. The comparison identifies differences where costs are higher than projected. The business can then take action to correct the differences.
2. One year.
3. Net income will increase. If net sales increase at a higher percentage than cost and expense items, net income will be favorably affected.

## Chapter 14, Page 426

1. Establish targets to work toward in the coming year; help coordinate the efforts of all areas toward a common direction.
2. Previous net sales and the trend in net sales for a period of several years, general economic conditions, consumer buying trends, competition, new products on the market, and such activities as planned special sales.

## Chapter 14, Page 433

1. Good cash management requires the planning and controlling of cash so that cash will be available to meet obligations when due.
2. Projected beginning cash balance, cash receipts, cash payments, and ending cash balance.

3. A performance report compares actual amounts with projected amounts for the same fiscal period. A comparative income statement compares actual amounts of one fiscal period with actual amounts of a prior fiscal period.

## Chapter 15, Page 450

1. The line would be straight, parallel to the base. The line is straight because fixed costs are exactly the same for each month.
2. Gross profit is determined by subtracting only the cost of merchandise sold from net sales. Contribution margin is determined by subtracting all variable costs from net sales.

## Chapter 15, Page 454

1. In sales dollars or unit sales.
2. As an alternative method to calculate the breakeven point when no financial statements exist.
3. Prepare an income statement using the breakeven point numbers. If the breakeven point is accurate, net income will be zero.

## Chapter 15, Page 462

1. Fixed costs and variable costs.
2. Total fixed costs plus planned net income.

## Chapter 16, Page 478

1. Compounding interest causes the annual interest earned to increase each year.
2. The present value factor is determined by finding the intersection of the interest rate in the columns and the number of years in the rows in a present value table.
3. As percentages.

## Chapter 16, Page 483

1. The annual payment is multiplied by the present value factor to calculate the present value of the annuity.
2. They can determine the amount of money they need to have saved before their retirement.
3. Effective managers will not purchase equipment that does not yield a positive net present value. Rather, they will search for alternative uses of an investment that will achieve the desired rate of return.

## Chapter 17, Page 502

1. To assist in decision making. For managers: to identify areas for improving profitability. For lenders: to decide whether to loan money to a business. For owners and potential owners: to decide whether to buy, sell, or keep their investment.
2. Determine (a) profitability, (b) efficiency, (c) short-term financial strength, and (d) long-term financial strength.
3. Adequate disclosure.
4. Prior company performance and comparison with published trade performance standards.

## Chapter 17, Page 511

1. How well a business is using its assets to earn net income.
2. How much net income stockholders' investment is earning.
3. Accounts are being collected 9.1 times a year.

## Chapter 17, Page 517

1. a. Owners' investments and retained earnings.
   b. Loans.
2. a. Working capital.
   b. Current ratio.
   c. Acid-test ratio.
3. Quick assets include all current assets except merchandise inventory and prepaid expenses.
4. Total quick assets divided by total current liabilities equals the acid-test ratio.
5. The debt ratio, equity ratio, and equity per share.
6. Total liabilities divided by total assets equals the debt ratio.
7. Total stockholders' equity divided by shares of capital stock outstanding equals equity per share.

## Chapter 18, Page 536

1. The accrual basis of accounting recognizes revenue when it is earned and expenses when they are incurred.
2. The cash basis of accounting recognizes revenue when cash is received and expenses when cash is paid out.
3. a. Operating activities.
   b. Investing activities.
   c. Financing activities.

## Chapter 18, Page 542

1. The actual cash outflow occurred in a prior fiscal period when the asset was bought.
2. A company made more credit sales than it collected during the year.
3. A company owes more to its vendors at the end of the year than at the beginning of the year.
4. Net income (net loss).

## Chapter 18, Page 548

1. By analyzing the changes in long-term assets (plant assets) on the comparative balance sheet.
2. The increase in accumulated depreciation matches the depreciation expense that was recorded on the income statement. The effect on cash flows due to depreciation expense was already accounted for under operating activities.
3. By examining the changes in long-term liabilities on the balance sheet and reviewing the statement of stockholders' equity.
4. If the Cash Balance, End of Period shown on the statement of cash flows equals the current year's cash balance reported on the comparative balance sheet.

## Chapter 19, Page 564

1. a. Direct materials.
   b. Direct labor.
   c. Factory overhead.
2. Work in process.
3. To keep a record of all charges for direct materials, direct labor, and factory overhead for each specific job.

## Chapter 19, Page 572

1. Ordered, received, issued, and balance.
2. Purchase order.
3. To authorize transfer of items from the storeroom to the factory.
4. Estimated factory overhead divided by estimated direct labor cost equals factory overhead applied rate.
5. Because the unit costs of each job frequently are different.

## Chapter 20, Page 592

1. On cost sheets.
2. Overapplied overhead.

3. Applied factory overhead is only an estimate used to assign factory overhead to jobs. The amount of actual factory overhead is determined at the end of the period; it consists of the actual costs for indirect labor, indirect materials, and other factory expenses.

## Chapter 20, Page 601

1. Income Statement Debit column.
2. Underapplied overhead is added to the cost of goods sold.
3. Current Assets.

## Chapter 21, Page 627

1. To avoid misunderstandings. Some states require that partnership agreements be in writing.
2. The existing partnership is terminated.
3. The right of all partners to contract for a partnership.

## Chapter 21, Page 634

1. The existing partnership is terminated.
2. Total equity (including investment by new partner) multiplied by new partner's share of equity equals the new partner's equity.
3. Goodwill is debited; existing partners' capital accounts are credited.

## Chapter 22, Page 654

1. In the partnership agreement.
2. a. Fixed percentage.
   b. Percentage of total equity.
   c. Interest on equity.
   d. Salaries.
   e. Combination of methods.
3. The partner's drawing account.
4. The partner's drawing account.

## Chapter 22, Page 664

1. Because a partnership does not pay federal income tax.
2. When the allowances to partners exceed net income.
3. To summarize the changes in owners' equity during the fiscal period.

## Chapter 22, Page 669

1. Cash received from the sale of assets during liquidation of a partnership.
2. The partners' capital accounts.

## Chapter 23, Page 689

1. a. No profit motive exists.
   b. Leadership is subject to frequent change.
   c. Users of services do not necessarily pay for the services.
   d. Conflicting pressures for differing objectives exist.
2. a. The accounting equation is applied.
   b. An appropriate chart of accounts is prepared.
   c. Transactions are analyzed into debit and credit elements.
   d. Transactions are journalized and posted to ledgers.
   e. Financial statements are prepared for each fiscal period.
   f. Most of the same accounting concepts are applied.
3. A governmental accounting entity with a set of accounts in which assets always equal liabilities plus equities.
4. To authorize and provide the basis for control of financial operations during a fiscal year.
5. Estimated Revenues is debited; Appropriations and Budgetary Fund Balance are credited.

## Chapter 23, Page 694

1. When property taxes are levied.
2. Cash is debited; Taxes Receivable—Current is credited.
3. Cash is debited; Taxes Receivable—Delinquent is credited.

## Chapter 23, Page 701

1. A commitment to pay for goods or services that have been ordered but not yet provided.
2. a. The encumbrance entry is reversed to remove the estimated amount from the encumbrance and reserve for encumbrance accounts.
   b. The expenditure is recorded.
3. Because the organization does not earn a net income and therefore has no need for expense information.
4. A document issued by a bank as evidence of money invested with the bank.

## Chapter 24, Page 718

1. Revenues/Expenditures.
2. Interest Receivable is debited; Allowance for Uncollectible Interest and Interest Revenue are credited.

3. Revenues/Expenditures Credit column.
4. Revenues/Expenditures Credit column total less Revenues/Expenditures Debit column total equals excess of revenues over expenditures.

## Chapter 24, Page 723

1. a. Revenues.
   b. Expenditures.
   c. Changes in unreserved fund balance.
2. The work sheet.
3. Favorable.

4. Total assets must equal total liabilities and fund equity.

## Chapter 24, Page 726

1. Work sheet's Adjustments columns.
2. Unreserved Fund Balance.
3. Appropriations and Budgetary Fund Balance are debited; Estimated Revenues is credited.
4. Reserve for Encumbrances—Prior Year; Taxes Receivable—Delinquent; Unreserved Fund Balance.

# GLOSSARY

## A

**Acid-test ratio.** A ratio that shows the numeric relationship of quick assets to current liabilities. (p. 513)

**Account.** A record summarizing all the information pertaining to a single item in the accounting equation. (p. 9)

**Accounting cycle.** The series of accounting activities included in recording financial information for a fiscal period. (p. 123)

**Accounting equation.** An equation showing the relationship among assets, liabilities, and owner's equity. (p. 7)

**Accounts receivable turnover ratio.** The number of times the average amount of accounts receivable is collected during a specified period. (p. 211)

**Accrual basis of accounting.** The accounting method that records revenues when they are earned and expenses when they are incurred. (p. 530)

**Accrued expenses.** Expenses incurred in one fiscal period but not paid until a later fiscal period. (p. 272)

**Accrued revenue.** Revenue earned in one fiscal period but not received until a later fiscal period. (p. 299)

**Adjusting entries.** Journal entries recorded to update general ledger accounts at the end of a fiscal period. (p. 118)

**Administrative expenses budget schedule.** A statement that shows the projected expenses for all operating expenses not directly related to selling operations. (p. 423)

**Aging accounts receivable.** Analyzing accounts receivable according to when they are due. (p. 206)

**Allowance method of recording losses from uncollectible accounts.** Crediting the estimated value of uncollectible accounts to a contra account. (p. 204)

**Amortization.** Recognizing a portion of an expense in each of several years. (p. 371)

**Annuity.** A series of equal cash flows. (p. 479)

**Applied overhead.** The estimated amount of factory overhead recorded on cost sheets. (p. 569)

**Appropriations.** Authorizations to make expenditures for specified purposes. (p. 687)

**Articles of incorporation.** A written application requesting permission to form a corporation. (p. 315)

**Assessed value.** The value of an asset determined by tax authorities for the purpose of calculating taxes. (p. 227)

**Asset.** Anything of value that is owned. (p. 7)

**Automatic check deposit.** Depositing payroll checks directly to an employee's checking or savings account in a specified bank. (p. 70)

**Average number of days' sales in merchandise inventory.** The period of time needed to sell an average amount of merchandise inventory. (p. 184)

## B

**Balance sheet.** A financial statement that reports assets, liabilities, and owners' equity on a specific date. (p. 116)

**Board of directors.** A group of persons elected by the stockholders to manage a corporation. (p. 315)

**Bond.** A printed, long-term promise to pay a specified amount on a specified date and to pay interest at stated intervals. (p. 355)

**Bond issue.** All bonds representing the total amount of a loan. (p. 355)

**Bond sinking fund.** An amount set aside to pay a bond issue when due. (p. 357)

**Book value of a plant asset.** The original cost of a plant asset minus accumulated depreciation. (p. 231)

**Book value of accounts receivable.** The difference between the balance of Accounts Receivable and its contra account, Allowance for Uncollectible Accounts. (p. 211)

**Breakeven point.** The amount of sales at which net sales is equal to total costs. (p. 451)

**Budget.** A written financial plan of a business for a specific period of time, expressed in dollars. (p. 412)

**Budget period.** The length of time covered by a budget. (p. 413)

**Budgeted income statement.** A statement that shows a company's projected sales, costs, expenses, and net income. (p. 425)

**Budgeting.** Planning the financial operations of a business. (p. 412)

## C

**Capital stock.** Total shares of ownership in a corporation. (p. 115)

**Cash basis.** The accounting method that records revenues when they are received and expenses when they are paid. (p. 530)

**Cash budget.** A statement that shows for each month or quarter a projection of a company's beginning cash balance, cash receipts, cash payments, and ending cash balance. (p. 430)

**Cash discount.** A deduction that a vendor allows on the invoice amount to encourage prompt payment. (p. 18)

**Cash flows.** The cash receipts and cash payments of a company. (pp. 477, 532)

**Cash payments budget schedule.** A statement that reports projected cash payments for a budget period. (p. 429)

**Cash receipts budget schedule.** A statement that reports projected cash receipts for a budget period. (p. 427)

**Certificate of deposit.** A document issued by a bank as evidence of money invested with the bank. (p. 699)

**Charter.** The approved articles of incorporation. (p. 315)

**Check register.** A journal used in a voucher system to record cash payments. (p. 151)

**Closing entries.** Journal entries used to prepare temporary accounts for a new fiscal period. (p. 119)

**Common stock.** Stock that does not give stockholders any special preferences. (p. 316)

**Comparative income statement.** An income statement containing sales, cost, and expense information for two or more years. (p. 415)

**Component percentage.** The percentage relationship between one financial statement item and the total that includes that item. (p. 95)

**Compounding.** Earning interest on previously earned interest. (p. 475)

**Consignee.** The person or business that receives goods on consignment. (p. 172)

**Consignment.** Goods that are given to a business to sell but for which title remains with the vendor. (p. 172)

**Consignor.** The person or business that gives goods on consignment. (p. 172)

**Contra account.** An account that reduces a related account on a financial statement. (p. 16)

**Contribution margin.** Income determined by subtracting all variable costs from net sales. (p. 447)

**Controlling account.** An account in a general ledger that summarizes all accounts in a subsidiary ledger. (p. 10)

**Corporation.** An organization with the legal rights of a person and that may be owned by many persons. (p. 314)

**Cost ledger.** A ledger containing all cost sheets for products in the process of being manufactured. (p. 562)

**Credit memorandum.** The source document prepared by the vendor showing the amount deducted for returns and allowances. (p. 40)

**Current ratio.** A ratio that shows the numeric relationship of current assets to current liabilities. (p. 513)

## D

**Date of a note.** The day a note is issued. (p. 261)

**Date of declaration.** The date on which a board of directors votes to distribute a dividend. (p. 328)

**Date of payment.** The date on which dividends are actually to be paid to stockholders. (p. 328)

**Date of record.** The date that determines which stockholders are to receive dividends. (p. 328)

**Debit memorandum.** A form prepared by the customer showing the price deduction for purchase returns and allowances. (p. 16)

**Debt ratio.** The ratio found by dividing total liabilities by total assets. (p. 514)

**Declaring a dividend.** Action by a board of directors to distribute corporate earnings to stockholder. (p. 328)

**Declining-balance method of depreciation.** Multiplying the book value at the end of each fiscal period by a constant depreciation rate. (p. 242)

**Deficit.** The amount by which allowances to partners exceed net income. (p. 659)

**Departmental accounting system.** An accounting system showing accounting information for two or more departments. (p. 12)

**Departmental margin.** The revenue earned by a department less its cost of merchandise sold and less its direct expenses. (p. 89)

**Departmental margin statement.** A statement that reports departmental margin for a specific department. (p. 89)

**Departmental statement of gross profit.** A statement showing gross profit for each department. (p. 93)

**Depletion.** The decrease in the value of a plant asset because of the removal of a natural resource. (p. 247)

**Depreciation expense.** The portion of a plant asset's cost that is transferred to an expense account in each fiscal period during a plant asset's useful life. (p. 106)

**Direct expense.** An operating expense identifiable with and chargeable to the operation of a specific department. (p. 89)

**Direct labor.** Salaries of factory workers who make a product. (p. 561)

**Direct materials.** Materials that are of significant value in the cost of a finished product and that become an identifiable part of the product. (p. 561)

**Direct write-off method of recording losses from uncollectible accounts.** Recording uncollectible accounts expense only when an amount is actually known to be uncollectible. (p. 201)

**Discount on capital stock.** An amount less than par or stated value at which capital stock is sold. (p. 345)

**Dishonored note.** A note that is not paid when due. (p. 293)

**Distribution of net income statement.** A partnership financial statement showing distribution of net income or net loss to partners. (p. 658)

**Dividends.** Earnings distributed to stockholders. (p. 115)

**Double-entry accounting.** The recording of debit and credit parts of a transaction. (p. 8)

## E

**Earnings per share.** The amount of net income belonging to a single share of stock. (p. 379)

**Electronic funds transfer (EFT).** A computerized cash payments system that transfers funds without the use of checks, currency, or other paper documents. (p. 70)

**Employee earnings record.** A business form used to record details affecting payments made to an employee. (p. 67)

**Encumbrance.** A commitment to pay for goods or services that have been ordered but not yet provided. (p. 695)

**Equities.** Financial rights to the assets of a business. (p. 7)

**Equity per share.** The amount of total stockholders' equity belonging to a single share of stock. (p. 379)

**Equity ratio.** The ratio found by dividing stockholders' equity by total assets. (p. 515)

**Expenditures.** Cash disbursements and liabilities incurred for the cost of goods delivered or services rendered. (p. 684)

## F

**Factory overhead.** All expenses other than direct materials and direct labor that apply to making products. (p. 561)

**File maintenance.** The procedure for arranging accounts in a general ledger, assigning account numbers, and keeping records current. (p. 10)

**Financing activities.** Cash receipts and payments involving debt or equity transactions. (p. 535)

**Finished goods.** Manufactured products that are fully completed. (p. 561)

**Finished goods ledger.** A ledger containing records of all finished goods on hand. (p. 562)

**First-in, first-out inventory costing method.** Using the price of merchandise purchased first to calculate the cost of merchandise sold first. (p. 176)

**Fiscal period.** The length of time for which a business summarizes and reports financial information. (p. 88)

**Fixed costs.** Total costs that remain constant regardless of change in business activity. (p. 446)

**Fund.** A governmental accounting entity with a set of accounts in which assets always equal liabilities plus equities. (p. 683)

**Future value.** The value of money invested today at some point in the future. (p. 475)

## G

**General fixed assets.** Governmental properties that benefit future periods. (p. 698)

**General ledger.** A ledger that contains all accounts needed to prepare financial statements. (p. 10)

**Goodwill.** The value of a business in excess of the total investment of owners. (p. 631)

**Gross profit.** The amount of revenue from sales less the cost of goods sold. (p. 93)

**Gross profit method of estimating an inventory.** Estimating inventory by using the previous year's percentage of gross profit on operations. (p. 93)

**I**

**Income statement.** A financial statement showing the revenue and expenses for a fiscal period. (p. 114)

**Indirect expense.** An operating expense chargeable to overall business operations and not identifiable with a specific department. (p. 89)

**Indirect labor.** Salaries paid to factory workers who are not actually making products. (p. 561)

**Indirect materials.** Materials used in the completion of a product that are of insignificant value to justify accounting for separately. (p. 561)

**Intangible assets.** Assets of a non-physical nature that have value for a business. (p. 326)

**Interest.** An amount paid for the use of money for a period of time. (p. 261)

**Interest expense.** The interest accrued on money borrowed. (p. 263)

**Interest rate of a note.** The percentage of the principal that is paid for use of the money. (p. 261)

**Inventory record.** A form used during a periodic inventory to record information about each item of merchandise on hand. (p. 174)

**Investing activities.** Cash receipts and cash payments involving the sale or purchase of assets used to earn revenue over a period of time. (p. 534)

**J**

**Journal.** A form for recording transactions in chronological order. (p. 8)

**L**

**Last-in, first-out inventory costing method.** Using the price of merchandise purchased last to calculate the cost of merchandise sold first. (p. 177)

**Ledger.** A group of accounts. (p. 10)

**Liability.** An amount owed by a business. (p. 7)

**Liquidation of a partnership.** The process of paying a partnership's liabilities and distributing remaining assets to the partners. (p. 665)

**Lower of cost or market inventory costing method.** Using the lower of cost or market price to calculate the cost of ending merchandise inventory. (p. 180)

**M**

**Market value.** The price at which a share of stock may be sold on the stock market. (p. 380)

**Materials ledger.** A ledger containing all records of materials. (p. 562)

**Maturity date of a note.** The date a note is due. (p. 261)

**Maturity value.** The amount that is due on the maturity date of a note. (p. 263)

**Merchandise inventory turnover ratio.** The number of times the average amount of merchandise inventory is sold during a specific period of time. (p. 184)

**Merchandising business.** A business that purchases and sells goods. (p. 12)

**Modified Accelerated Cost Recovery System (MACRS).** A depreciation method required by the Internal Revenue Service to be used for income tax calculation purposes for most plant assets placed in service after 1986. (p. 246)

**Mutual agency.** The right of all partners to contract for a partnership. (p. 624)

**N**

**Net cash flow.** The difference between cash receipts and cash payments. (p. 477)

**Net present value.** The difference between the discounted cash flows and the investment. (p. 477)

**No-par-value stock.** A share of stock that has no authorized value printed on the stock certificate. (p. 317)

**Not-for-profit organization.** An organization providing goods or services with neither a conscious motive nor expectation of earning a profit. (p. 680)

**Notes payable.** Promissory notes signed by a business and given to a creditor. (p. 261)

**Notes receivable.** Promissory notes that a business accepts from customers. (p. 291)

**O**

**Operating activities.** The cash receipts and payments necessary to operate a business on a day-to-day basis. (p. 534)

**Operating budget.** A plan of current expenditures and the proposed means of financing those expenditures. (p. 686)

**Organization costs.** Fees and other expenses of organizing a corporation. (p. 320)

**Other revenue and expenses budget schedule.** A statement showing budgeted revenue and expenses from activities other than normal operations. (p. 424)

**Overapplied overhead.** The amount by which applied factory overhead is more than actual factory overhead. (p. 589)

**Owner's equity.** The amount remaining after the value of all liabilities is subtracted from the value of all assets. (p. 7)

**Owners' equity statement.** A financial statement that summarizes the changes in owners' equity during a fiscal period. (p. 660)

**P**

**Par value.** A value assigned to a share of stock and printed on the stock certificate. (p. 317)

**Par-value stock.** A share of stock that has an authorized value printed on the stock certificate. (p. 317)

**Partnership agreement.** A written agreement setting forth the conditions under which a partnership is to operate. (p. 624)

**Pay period.** The period covered by a salary payment. (p. 60)

**Payroll.** The total amount earned by all employees for a pay period. (p. 60)

**Payroll register.** A business form used to record payroll information. (p. 64)

**Payroll taxes.** Taxes based on the payroll of a business. (p. 60)

**Performance report.** A report showing a comparison of projected and actual amounts for a specific period of time. (p. 432)

**Periodic inventory.** A merchandise inventory determined by counting, weighing, or measuring items of merchandise on hand. (p. 93)

**Perpetual inventory.** A merchandise inventory determined by keeping a continuous record of increases, decreases, and balance on hand. (p. 93)

**Personal property.** All property not classified as real property. (p. 227)

**Petty cash.** An amount of cash kept on hand and used for making small payments. (p. 22)

**Plant asset record.** An accounting form on which a business records information about each plant asset. (p. 225)

**Plant assets.** Assets that will be used for a number of years in the operation of a business. (p. 106)

**Point-of-sale (POS) terminal.** A computer used to collect, store, and report all the information of a sales transaction. (p. 47)

**Post-closing trial balance.** A trial balance prepared after the closing entries are posted. (p. 122)

**Posting.** Transferring transaction information from a journal entry to a ledger account. (p. 14)

**Preferred stock.** Stock that gives stockholders preference in earnings and other rights. (p. 316)

**Prepaid expenses.** Expenses paid in one fiscal period but not reported as expenses until a later fiscal period. (p. 266)

**Present value.** The current value of a future cash payment or receipt. (p. 476)

**Present value of an annuity.** An amount invested at a given interest rate that supports the payments of an annuity. (p. 479)

**Price-earnings ratio.** The relationship between the market value per share and earnings per share of a stock. (p. 380)

**Principal of a note.** The original amount of a note. (p. 261)

**Production-unit method of depreciation.** Calculating estimated annual depreciation expense based on the amount of production expected from a plant asset. (p. 245)

**Promissory note.** A written and signed promise to pay a sum of money at a specified time. (p. 261)

**Purchase order.** A completed form authorizing a seller to deliver goods with payment to be made later. (p. 173)

**Purchases budget schedule.** A statement prepared to show the projected amount of purchases that will be required during a budget period. (p. 420)

**Purchases discount.** A cash discount on purchases taken by a customer. (p. 18)

### Q

**Quick assets.** Those current assets that are cash or that can be quickly turned into cash. (p. 513)

### R

**Rate earned on average stockholders' equity.** The relationship between net income and average stockholders' equity. (p. 383)

**Rate earned on average total assets.** The relationship between net income and average total assets. (p. 383)

**Rate earned on net sales.** The rate found by dividing net income after federal income tax by net sales. (p. 506)

**Rate of return.** The relationship of money earned compared to the money invested. (p. 477)

**Ratio.** A comparison between two numbers showing how many times one number exceeds the other. (p. 495)

**Real property.** Land and anything attached to it. (p. 227)

**Realization.** Cash received from the sale of assets during liquidation of a partnership. (p. 665)

**Responsibility accounting.** Assigning control of business revenues, costs, and expenses as a responsibility of a specific manager. (p. 89)

**Responsibility statements.** Financial statements reporting revenue, costs, and direct expenses under a specific department's control. (p. 111)

**Retail method of estimating inventory.** Estimating inventory by using a percentage based on both cost and retail prices. (p. 183)

**Retained earnings.** An amount earned by a corporation and not yet distributed to stockholders. (p. 115)

**Retiring a bond issue.** Paying the amounts owed to bondholders for a bond issue. (p. 358)

**Reversing entry.** An entry made at the beginning of one fiscal period to reverse an adjusting entry made in the previous fiscal period. (p. 269)

### S

**Salary.** The money paid for employee services. (p. 60)

**Sales budget schedule.** A statement that shows the projected net sales for a budget period. (p. 419)

**Sales discount.** A cash discount on sales. (p. 44)

**Sales mix.** Relative distribution of sales among various products. (p. 460)

**Schedule of accounts payable.** A list of vendor accounts, account balances, and total amount due all vendors. (p. 99)

**Schedule of accounts receivable.** A list of customer accounts, account balances, and total amount due from all customers. (p. 99)

**Selling expenses budget schedule.** A statement prepared to show projected expenditures related directly to the selling operations. (p. 421)

**Serial bonds.** Portions of a bond issue that mature on different dates. (p. 358)

**Source documents.** Original business papers from which information about business transactions is obtained. (p. 7)

**Special journal.** A journal used to record only one kind of transaction. (p. 8)

**Stated-value stock.** No-par-value stock that is assigned a value by the corporation. (p. 317)

**Statement of cash flows.** A statement that summarizes cash receipts and cash payments resulting from business activities during a fiscal period. (p. 532)

**Statement of cost of goods manufactured.** A statement showing details about the cost of finished goods. (p. 598)

**Statement of stockholders' equity.** A financial statement that shows changes in a corporation's ownership for a fiscal period. (p. 115)

**Stock certificate.** Written evidence of the number of shares that each stockholder owns in a corporation. (p. 317)

**Stock ledger.** A file of stock records for all merchandise on hand. (p. 173)

**Stock record.** A form used to show the type of merchandise, quantity received, quantity sold, and balance on hand. (p. 173)

**Stockholders' equity.** The owner's equity in a corporation. (p. 7)

**Straight-line method of depreciation.** Charging an equal amount of depreciation expense for a plant asset in each year of useful life. (p. 230)

**Subscribing for capital stock.** Entering into an agreement with a corporation to buy capital stock and pay at a later date. (p. 324)

**Subsidiary ledger.** A ledger that is summarized in a single general ledger account. (p. 10)

**Sum-of-the-years'-digits method of depreciation.** Using fractions based on the number of years of a plant asset's useful life to calculate depreciation. (p. 243)

### T

**Tax base.** The maximum amount of earnings on which a tax is calculated. (p. 61)

**Tax levy.** Authorized action taken by a governmental organization to collect taxes by legal authority. (p. 690)

**Term bonds.** Bonds that all mature on the same date. (p. 358)

**Terminal summary.** The report that summarizes the cash and credit card sales of a point-of-sale terminal. (p. 47)

**Time value of money.** The expectation that invested money will increase over time. (p. 474)

**Total costs.** All costs for a specific period of time. (p. 445)

**Treasury stock.** A corporation's own stock that has been issued and reacquired. (p. 350)

**Trend analysis.** A comparison of the relationship between one item on a financial statement and the same item on a previous fiscal period's financial statement. (p. 496)

**Trial balance.** A proof of the equality of debits and credits in a general ledger. (p. 100)

**Trustee.** A person or institution, usually a bank, given legal authorization to administer property for the benefit of property owners. (p. 356)

 **U**

**Uncollectible accounts.** Accounts receivable that cannot be collected. (p. 200)

**Underapplied overhead.** The amount by which applied factory overhead is less than actual factory overhead. (p. 589)

**Unearned revenue.** Revenue received in one fiscal period but not earned until the next fiscal period. (p. 297)

**Unit cost.** An amount spent for one unit of a specific product or service. (p. 445)

 **V**

**Variable costs.** Total costs that change in direct proportion to a change in the number of units. (p. 446)

**Voucher.** A business form used to show an authorized person's approval for a cash payment. (p. 144)

**Voucher check.** A check with space for writing details about a cash payment. (p. 150)

**Voucher register.** A journal used to record vouchers. (p. 144)

**Voucher system.** A set of procedures for controlling cash payments by preparing and approving vouchers before payments are made. (p. 144)

 **W**

**Weighted-average inventory costing method.** Using the average cost of beginning inventory plus merchandise purchased during a fiscal period to calculate the cost of merchandise sold. (p. 178)

**Withholding allowance.** A deduction from total earnings for each person legally supported by a taxpayer. (p. 61)

**Work in process.** Products that are being manufactured but are not yet complete. (p. 561)

**Work sheet.** A columnar accounting form used to summarize the general ledger information needed to prepare financial statements. (p. 100)

**Working capital.** The amount of total current assets less total current liabilities. (p. 512)

**Writing off an account.** Canceling the balance of a customer account because the customer is not expected to pay. (p. 200)

# INDEX